HANDBOOK OF
Child and
Adolescent
Psychiatry

Joseph D. Noshpitz / Editor-in-Chief

VOLUME SEVEN

Advances and New Directions

PAUL L. ADAMS AND EFRAIN BLEIBERG

EDITORS

John Wiley & Sons, Inc.
New York • Chichester • Weinheim • Brisbane • Singapore • Toronto

ISBN 0-471-55079-5 (vol. 1)
     0-471-55075-2 (vol. 2)
     0-471-55076-0 (vol. 3)
     0-471-55078-7 (vol. 4)
     0-471-19330-5 (vol. 5)
     0-471-19331-3 (vol. 6)
     0-471-19332-1 (vol. 7)
     0-471-19329-1 (vols. 5, 6, 7)
     0-471-19328-3 (7 vol. set)

Printed in the United State of America

10 9 8 7 6 5 4 3 2 1

In Memoriam

Joseph D. Noshpitz, M.D.
1922–1997

DEDICATION

This set of volumes grows out of an attitude that reflects the field itself. To put it succinctly, the basic theme of child and adolescent psychiatry is hope. Albeit formally a medical discipline, child and adolescent psychiatry is a field of growth, of unfolding, of progressive advance; like childhood itself, it is a realm of building toward a future and finding ways to better the outcome for the young. But within the field, an even greater theme inspires an even more dominant regard. For, beyond treating children, child and adolescent psychiatry is ultimately about rearing children. This is literally the first time in human history that we are on the verge of knowing *how* to rear a child. While people have reared children since we were arboreal, they did it by instinct, or by cultural practice, or in keeping with grandma's injunctions, or by reenacting the memories, conscious and unconscious, of their own childhood experiences. They did what they did for many reasons, but never because they really knew what their actions portended, what caused what, what was a precondition for what, or what meant what.

At this moment in history, however, things are different. The efforts of researchers, neuroscientists, child developmental specialists—in short, of the host of those who seek to understand, treat, and educate children and to work with parents—are beginning to converge and to produce a body of knowledge that tells us what children are, what they need, what hurts them, and what helps them. Hard science has begun to study the fetus, rating scales and in-depth therapeutic techniques have emerged for the mother with the infant in her arms, increasing precision is being achieved in assessing temperament, in measuring mother/infant fit, and in detecting the forerunners of personality organization. Adolescence and the intricacies of pubertal transformation are being explored as never before. Indeed, a quiet revolution is coming into being: the gradual dissemination of knowledge about child rearing that, within a few generations, could well alter the quality of the human beings who fall under its aegis.

If children—all children—could be reared in a fashion that gave them a healthier organization of conscience, that preserved the buds of cognitive growth and helped these to flower (instead of pinching them off as so many current practices do), that could recognize from the outset any special needs a child might have in respect to impulse control or emotional stability—and could step in from the earliest moments in development with the appropriate tactics and strategies, anodynes and remedies, techniques of healing and practices of enabling to allow the youngster to better manage his or her inner life and interpersonal transactions—consider what fruit this would bear.

Today this is far more than a dream, far more than a wistful yearning for a better day to come. The beginnings are already accomplished, much of the initial work has been done, the directions of future research are becoming ever more evident. The heretofore cryptic equations of development are beginning to be found and some of their solutions to be discerned, the once-mystical runes are being read—and are here inscribed in page after page of research report and clinical observation.

Some of the initial changes are already well under way. As with all science first a process of de-mystification must occur. Bit by bit, we have had to unlearn a host of formulaic mythologies about children and about parenting that have been part of Western civilization for centuries.

We have indeed begun to do so. We have been able to admit to the realities of child abuse, first to the violence directed toward children and then to their sexual exploitation. And we have had to admit to children's sexuality. Simply to allow those things to appear in print, to become part of common parlance, has taken immense cultural energy, the overcoming of tremendous defensiveness; after all, such things had been known but not spoken of for generations. Right now the sanctity, the hallowed quality of family life, is the focus of enormous cultural upheaval. There is much to suggest that the nuclear family set in the bosom of a body of extended kin relationships that had for so long served as the basic site for human child rearing is no longer the most likely context within which future generations of our children will grow. The quest is on for new social arrangements, and it is within this milieu that the impact of scientific knowledge, the huge and ever-increasing array of insights into the nature of childhood, the chemistry of human relationships, the psychodynamics of parent-child interplay—in short, within the area of development that this work so carefully details—that we find the wellsprings of hope. As nursery schools, kindergartens, grade schools, and high schools become more sophisticated, as the psychiatric diagnostic manuals become more specific and more differentiated, as doctors become better trained and better prepared to address human issues with dynamic understanding, as what children need in order to grow well becomes ever more part of everyday cultural practice, the realization of this hope will slowly and quietly steal across the face of our civilization, and we will produce children who will be emotionally sounder, cognitively stronger, and mentally healthier than their parents. These volumes are dedicated to advancing this goal.

Joseph D. Noshpitz, M.D.
Editor-in-Chief

PREFACE

Some 16 years ago the first two volumes of the *Basic Handbook of Child Psychiatry* were published, to be followed shortly by volumes III and IV, and then, in 1985, by the fifth volume. More than a decade has passed since that volume was released, during which time the field of child psychiatry has advanced at a remarkable pace. Indeed, it has even changed its name to be more inclusive of the teenage years. New advances in neuroscience, in genetics, in psychoanalytic theory, in psychopharmacology, in animal studies—new findings in a host of areas have poured out during these years. It is therefore necessary to revise the handbook, to reorganize it, to update many of the clinical accounts, and to bring it to the level where the active practitioner can use its encyclopedic format to explore the enormous variety of clinical possibilities he or she may encounter.

The focus of this work is on development. It is no exaggeration to look on child development as the basic science of child and adolescent psychiatry. Development is so vital a concern that in this revision, we have abandoned the classical way of presenting the material. Rather than following tradition, wherein development, diagnosis and assessment, syndromes, treatment, and so on are discussed for a variety of related topics, in these volumes the bulk of the material is presented developmentally. Thus, volumes I, II, and III focus on development and syndromes of infancy and preschool, of grade school, and of adolescence, respectively. Within each of these larger sections, the material on development comes first, followed by chapters on syndromes, conceptualized as disturbances of development. While syndromes are described in depth, they are discussed only within the framework of the developmental level under study. Volume IV, entitled "Varieties of Development," explores a host of ecological niches within which children are reared.

Volume V includes an unusually rich banquet of studies on the assessment and evaluation of children, adolescents, and their families. Volume VI reports on the basic science issues of the field and the current status of the various treatment techniques. Volume VII contains sections on consultation/liaison, emergencies in child and adolescent psychiatry, the prehistory of child and adolescent psychiatry, current cultural issues that impinge on young people, forensic issues involving children and youth, and professional challenges facing the child and adolescent psychiatrist.

The intention of the work is to be as comprehensive and as readable as possible. In an encyclopedic work of this sort, concerns always arise as to how much space to allot to each topic and to which topics should be covered. To deal with such questions, a number of readers reviewed each submission. One editor had primary responsibility for each section; a coeditor also reviewed submissions. Then the editor of another section reviewed the submissions, exchanging his or her chapters with the first colleague so that someone outside the section read each chapter. In addition, one editor reviewed all submissions with an eye to contradictions or excessive overlap. Finally, the editor-in-chief reviewed and commented on a large proportion of the materials submitted. In short, while the submission process was not juried, a number of readers reviewed each chapter. Each author was confronted with the in cumulative critiques and asked to make appropriate changes. Most did so cheerfully, although not always with alacrity.

The writing and review process lasted from about 1990 to 1996. For much of this time, a host of authors were busy writing, revising, and polishing their work. The editors worked unstintingly, suffering all the ups and downs that accompany large projects: many meetings, huge expenses, moments of despair, episodes of elation, professional growth on the part of practically all the participants (a couple of authors who never came through with their material may be presumed to have shrunk), profound disappointments and thrilling breakthroughs, lost causes that were snatched from the jaws of defeat and borne aloft to victory, and, ultimately, the final feeling that we did it!

I speak for all the editors when I say that it was our purpose and it is our earnest wish that these volumes make for better understanding of young people, greater access to knowledge about children and adolescents, a richer sense of what this field of human endeavor entails, and a better outcome for the growth, development, mental health, and happiness of all the young in our land and of those who would help them.

Joseph D. Noshpitz, M.D.
Editor-in-Chief

CONTENTS

Contents

SECTION III / Prevention and Risk Factors

SECTION IV / Consultation and Child and Adolescent Psychiatry

SECTION V / Emergency Assessment and Intervention

Contents

SECTION VI / Forensic Child and Adolescent Psychiatry

SECTION VII / Professional Issues in Child and Adolescent Psychiatry

CONTRIBUTORS

PAUL L. ADAMS, M.A., M.D.
Professor of Child Psychiatry, University of Tennessee, School of Medicine, Memphis, Tennessee; Faculty Coordinator, The Kentucky Psychoanalytic Institute, Louisville, Kentucky.

NORMAN ALESSI, M.D.
Associate Professor, Department of Psychiatry, University of Michigan Hospital, Ann Arbor, Michigan.

DARRYL ANDERSON, Ph.D., M.D.
General Practitioner, Private Practice, Irvine, Kentucky.

ALAN APTER, M.D.
Chairman, Department of Psychiatry, Sackler School of Medicine, University of Tel Aviv, Tel Aviv, Israel; Director, Division of Child and Adolescent Psychiatry, Geha Psychiatric Hospital, Petah Tikva, Israel.

MARILYN BENOIT, M.D.
Associate Professor of Psychiatry and Behavioral Sciences and Pediatrics, The George Washington University Medical Center, Washington, D.C.; Medical Executive Director, Devereaux Children's Center, Washington, D.C.

EUGENE V. BERESIN, M.D.
Director of Child and Adolescent Psychiatry, Residency Training, Massachusetts General Hospital, Boston, Massachusetts and McLean Hospital, Belmont, Massachusetts; Assistant Professor of Psychiatry, Harvard Medical School, Boston, Massachusetts.

CURTIS R. BERGSTRAND, Ph.D.
Professor and Chair, Department of Sociology, Bellarmine College, Louisville, Kentucky.

IRVING H. BERKOVITZ, M.D.
Clinical Professor in Psychiatry, Unviersity of California at Los Angeles School of Medicine, Los Angeles, California; Private Practice, Los Angeles, California.

WILLIAM BERNET, M.D.
Associate Professor of Psychiatry, Vanderbilt University School of Medicine; Director, Vanderbilt Forensic Psychiatry; Medical Director, The Psychiatric Hospital at Vanderbilt, Nashville, Tennessee.

LARRY K. BROWN, M.D.
Director, Consultation-Liaison Services, Department of Child and Family Psychiatry, Rhode Island Hospital; Associate Professor, Department of Psychiatry and Human Behavior, Brown University School of Medicine, Providence, Rhode Island.

MARY LYNN DELL, M.D., M.T.S., Th.M.
Director, Inpatient Services, Child Guidance Center of Children's Hospital of Philadelphia; Assistant Professor of Psychiatry, University of Pennsylvania, Philadelphia, Pennsylvania.

SPENCER ETH, M.D.
Vice-Chair and Clinical Director, Department of Psychiatry, Saint Vincents Hospital and Medical Center; Professor of Psychiatry, New York Medical College, New York, New York.

DANIEL R. FISHER, M.D.
Attending Psychiatrist, Centennial Peaks Hospital, Louisville, Colorado.

LOIS FLAHERTY, M.D.
Private Practice, Bluebell, Pennsylvania.

SARAH ROBINSON FLICK, M.D.
Assistant Professor of Psychiatry and Behavioral Sciences, Baylor College of Medicine, Houston, Texas.

IVAN FRAS, M.D., F.A.C.P.
Private Practice, Psychiatry and Child Psychiatry, Binghamton, New York; Diplomate, American Board of Psychiatry and Neurology.

GREGORY K. FRITZ, M.D.
Director of Child and Family Psychiatry and Division of Child and Adolescent Psychiatry, Rhode Island Hospital; Professor of Psychiatry, Brown University School of Medicine, Providence, Rhode Island.

DONALD S. GAIR, M.D.
Professor of Psychiatry and Chairman, Department of Child Psychiatry and Child Development, Boston University School of Medicine, Boston, Massachusetts.

MOHAMMAD GHAZIUDDIN, M.D.
Assistant Professor, Department of Child and Adolescent Psychiatry, University of Michigan Medical Center, Ann Arbor, Michigan.

DANIEL T. GOYETTE
Public Defender, Executive Director, Jefferson District Public Defender Corporation, Louisville, Kentucky.

GAIL RITCHIE HENSON, Ph.D.
Professor and Chairperson, Department of Communications, Bellarmine College, Louisville, Kentucky.

DAVID B. HERZOG, M.D.
Professor of Psychiatry, Harvard Medical School, Boston, Massachusetts.

JERRY HESTON, M.D.
Associate Professor of Child and Adolescent Psychiatry, University of Tennessee, Memphis, Tennessee.

CHARLES E. HOLZER, III, Ph.D.
Professor, Department of Psychiatry and Behavioral Sciences, University of Texas Medical Branch, Galveston, Texas.

Contributors

CHRISTOPHER PAUL HOLZER

DAVID G. INWOOD, M.D.
Director, Outpatient Child and Adolescent Psychiatry Services, Downstate Mental Hygiene Associates; Clinical Assistant Professor of Psychiatry, State University of New York, Brooklyn, New York.

STEVEN L. JAFFE, M.D.
Professor of Psychiatry, Emory University School of Medicine; Clinical Professor of Psychiatry, Morehouse School of Medicine; Medical Director, Child and Adolescent Services, Charter Peachford Hospital, Atlanta, Georgia.

MICHAEL S. JELLINEK, M.D.
Professor of Psychiatry and of Pediatrics, Harvard Medical School, Boston, Massachusetts.

SANDRA KAPLAN, M.D.
Associate Professor of Clinical Psychiatry, Cornell University Medical College, New York, New York; Associate Chairperson, Department of Psychiatry for Child and Adolescent Psychiatry, North Shore University Hospital, Manhasset, New York.

CHARLES KEITH, M.D.
Professor, Department of Psychiatry, Division of Child and Adolescent Psychiatry, Duke University Medical Center, Durham, North Carolina.

ERNEST A. KENDRICK, M.D.
Clinical Assistant Professor of Psychiatry, Baylor College of Medicine; Vice-President, Quest Healthcare, P.A., Centers for Behavior and Pain Medicine, Houston, Texas.

LAUREL J. KISER, PH.D.
Professor with tenure, Department of Psychiatry, Division of Child and Adolescent Psychiatry, University of Tennessee, Memphis, Tennessee.

HAROLD S. KOPLEWICZ, M.D.
Professor of Clinical Psychiatry; Vice-Chair, Department of Psychiatry; Director, Child and Adolescent Psychiatry; Director, NYU Child Study Center, New York University Medical Center, New York, New York.

JOHN F. McDERMOTT, JR., M.D.
Professor Emeritus, University of Hawaii School of Medicine, Honolulu, Hawaii.

JUDITH R. MILNER, M.D., M.ED.
Private Practice, Snohomish, Washington.

KLAUS MINDE, M.D., F.R.C.P.(C.)
Head, Division of Child Psychiatry, Professor of Psychiatry and Pediatrics, McGill University; Director, Department of Psychiatry, Montreal Children's Hospital, Montreal, Quebec, Canada.

REGINA MINDE, PH.D.
Montreal, Quebec, Canada.

MARSHA H. NELSON, M.A.S.W.
Vice-President, Clinical Policy, Value Behavioral Health, Falls Church, Virginia.

JOSEPH D. NOSHPITZ, M.D.
Dr. Noshpitz passed away in April of 1997. At that time, he was Clinical Professor of Psychiatry and Behavioral Science at George Washington University and had a private practice in Washington, D.C.

HARRIS B. PECK, M.D.
Professor Emeritus, Albert Einstein College of Medicine, Bronx, New York; Member of Executive Committee, Psychiatrists for Social Responsibility, New York; Director of Center for Psychosocial Issues in the Nuclear Age.

DANIEL PILOWSKY, M.D.
Assistant Professor, Division of Child Psychiatry, Johns Hopkins Medical School, Bethesda, Maryland.

ELIZABETH PINNER, M.A.
Department of Child Psychiatry, Columbia University, New York State Psychiatric Institute, New York, New York.

DAVID B. PRUITT, M.D.
Professor and Director, Division of Child and Adolescent Psychiatry, University of Tennessee, Memphis, Tennessee.

ALVIN A ROSENFELD, M.D.
Private and Consulting Practice in New York, New York and Greenwich, Connecticut; Co-Chair, Committee on Adoption and Foster Care, American Academy of Child and Adolescent Psychiatry.

PEDRO RUIZ, M.D.
Professor and Vice-Chair, Department of Psychiatry and Behavioral Sciences, University of Texas Medical School at Houston, Houston, Texas.

DIANE H. SCHETKY, M.D.
Private Practice of Forensic Psychiatry, Rockport, Maine; Associate Clinical Professor of Psychiatry, University of Vermont College of Medicine at Maine Medical Center, Portland, Maine.

NANCY A. SCHREPF, PSY.D.
Clinical Psychologist, Luther Luckett Correctional Complex, LaGrange, Kentucky.

PETER SCHULER
Public Defender, Jefferson District Public Defender Corporation, Louisville, Kentucky.

IAN A. SHAFFER, M.D.
Executive Vice-President and Chief Medical Officer, Value Behavioral Health, Falls Church, Virginia.

BRYNA SIEGEL, PH.D.
Director, Pervasive Developmental Disorders Clinic; Associate Adjunct Professor, Child and Adolescent Psychiatry, University of California, San Francisco, California.

MORTON M. SILVERMAN, M.D.
Associate Professor of Psychiatry; Director, Student Counseling and Resource Service; Associate Dean of Students, The University of Chicago, Chicago, Illinois.

JOSEPH I. SISON, M.D.
Child, Adolescent, and Adult Psychiatry, Clinical Facility, University of California at Davis Medical Center; Private Practice, Sacramento, California.

EDWARD SPERLING, M.D.
Clinical Professor of Psychiatry, Albert Einstein College of Medicine, Bronx, New York.

NADA L. STOTLAND, M.D.
Chair, Department of Psychiatry and Substance Abuse Services, Illinois Masonic Medical Center, Chicago, Illinois.

JEFFREY W. SWANSON, PH.D.
Assistant Professor of Psychiatry and Behavioral Sciences, Duke University Medical Center, Durham, North Carolina.

SHERRY L. THAGGARD, M.D.
Clinical Assistant Professor, University of Alabama School of Medicine, Huntsville, Alabama.

CHRISTOPHER R. THOMAS, M.D.
Associate Professor of Psychiatry and Behavioral Sciences, Division of Child and Adolescent Psychiatry, University of Texas Medical Branch, Galveston, Texas.

V. SUSAN VILLANI, M.D.
Staff Child Psychiatrist, Sheppard Pratt Health System, Baltimore, Maryland.

WILLIAM J. WINSLADE, PH.D., J.D.
James Wade Rockwell Professor of Philosophy in Medicine, Institute for the Medical Humanities, University of Texas Medical Branch at Galveston, Galveston, Texas.

SECTION I

A Brief History of Child Mental Health in the United States: The Precursors of Child and Adolescent Psychiatry

Joseph D. Noshpitz

The Cultural Context

Child and adolescent psychiatry is essentially a 20th-century phenomenon. It emerged, however, as the outcome of forces and tensions that were set in train during the preceding century and that found their final expression in the establishment of this discipline in our own times. In presenting some of these precursors, it seems appropriate to begin with a survey of the major sociocultural factors that prevailed in the 19th century and to offer a picture of how children were regarded and how their needs were addressed then. It is my view that only within a context of the history of childhood itself can the mental health issues of children be given adequate meaning. Hence this chapter dwells initially on the story of children, adolescents, and their families during the 19th and early 20th centuries and then moves on to an account of the discipline of child and adolescent psychiatry.

It is evident that we are embarking on a voyage with many ports of call. It is also obvious that we shall have to make choices about what is to be reviewed and what omitted. Let us begin with some of the larger forces at work in both creating and shaping the field. Consider gender. It is no exaggeration to say that the initiation of much of the significant work to help children was achieved by the concerted effort of able and determined women. The examples are everywhere. In early 20th-century psychoanalysis, for example, the basic principles and methods of the field were defined by Sigmund Freud and his largely male circle of followers. The application of this discipline to children, however, was originally accomplished by Hermione Hug Hellmuth and later Anna Freud. In the course of establishing the basic tenets of child analysis, Miss Freud formed a Kinder seminar, which had several notable female members. An alternative school of child analysis was created by another extraordinary woman, Melanie Klein.

Another example is the establishment of the juvenile court. The great energizers and "heavy lifters" in Chicago who promoted the initial legislation that brought the first court into being were a group of unusual women, among them Jane Addams, Julia Lathrop, and Ethel Dummer. Ultimately it was through their concerns and efforts that the first true child psychiatrist was engaged, William R. Healy.

In short, gender is a significant presence on the scene throughout. It is perhaps most marked when we consider in broad outline the nature of the human impulses that worked toward the establishment of services for children. Generally speaking, there were two persistent qualities: the compassionate mind-set that reached out to relieve suffering, compensate for deprivation, and help those wounded in body and spirit; and the defensive outlook that saw in the dangerous classes (in street youths in particular) a brooding threat of riot, miscreance, and disorder, and that sought to use law, method, theory, professionalism, and social action to prevent such social eruption. In a sense, these are again female and male principles—not exclusively, but nonetheless suggestively—working together and sometimes interchangeably to inspire programmatic action and to create social forms (Platt, 1977).

Yet another realm of investigation is ethnicity. For the most part, only a few aspects of this realm of discourse are included in this chapter although in its own way it is as vital as any area we speak of. Thus, the lifestyle of the family in the settled East was a very different thing from the adaptations of the family on the frontier. The way of life of the rural American was a far cry from that of the city dweller. Each immigrant group had its own way of rearing its children, as, indeed, did the slaves and freedmen who played so signal a role during this tempestuous time. Native Americans were raising children as well, as were Mexican Americans and the members of religious groups as varied as Latter-Day Saints and Orthodox Jews. Because of the richness and variety of these many patterns of child rearing, we have had to omit discussion of most and to confine ourselves largely to relating the city/farm contrasts that seemed to play a particularly significant role in the course of the relevant transitions.

Aside from ethnicity, the roles of religion, geographic locus, technological change, and others are addressed briefly in our attempts to highlight the pivotal issues.

THE BEGINNINGS

The precursors to child and adolescent psychiatry as we know it today were essentially 19th-century emergents. In particular, during that period a series of transformations took place that totally changed the way children and adolescents were regarded by the American culture and that created the matrix within which the new discipline could develop. At the outset of the 1800s, the country was a mere 24 years old, Thomas Jefferson had just been elected president, there were 16 states in the Union, and the Industrial Revolution was getting under way but had not yet impinged upon the life of the average citizen. It was a century of radical transformations interrupted by many alarms and crises. In 1803 the Louisiana Purchase added immeasurably to the sweep of the country and enlarged the sense of national selfhood to a heady degree. In the wake of this acquisition, as treaties were concluded with the Native Americans and lands were opened up, a steady stream of Americans moved westward after 1820 and began to settle these new territories. Numerous technical advances enhanced this movement: The first commercial steamboat plied the Mississippi in 1811 and 1812; the Erie Canal opened in 1826 and allowed a direct route to the Great Lakes and the adjacent territories; railroads were being constructed by the 1840s and transcontinental rail traffic established itself by the 1880s and 1890s. In 1847 the Latter-Day Saints—Mormons—settled in Utah. The California Gold Rush, which began in 1849 (following the discovery of open lodes of gold the year before) was not perhaps a population shift of demographic proportions but was extraordinarily evocative to the nation's imagination, as were the great migrations to Oregon that occurred around the same time. In the late 1860s ranching spread over the plains and gave the United States its cowboy hero, whose glory still glows brightly. Probably the last great frontier was opened by the Homestead Act of 1862, which made cheap land available for anyone who was willing to get there, stake a claim, and work the soil.

As for crises, there were plenty. The War of 1812, the Mexican War, the Civil War, the Indian Wars (actually a series of major skirmishes between the U.S. Army and various Native American groups), and the Spanish American War erupted at various points throughout the 1800s, and each lent its own morbid color to citizens' everyday lives. The business cycle established itself, and many swoops and dives, expansions and depressions, impinged on individual patterns of earning and on each householder's sense of economic security.

These radical demographic changes were occurring internally to alter the complexion of the existing population, but they are only part of the story. Along with all these, a tidal wave of new immigrants poured into the country and sought haven in the newly emerging cities. Soon their presence would play a powerful role in the new syntheses that would emerge.

CALVINISM VS. ROMANTICISM

Let us now turn to those historical themes that bear on children. Two major attitudes were prevalent throughout the century—Calvinism and Romanticism, (Contratto, 1984). From a values standpoint, the earlier decades of the 19th century were dominated by a Calvinist view of childhood. Children were essentially greedy, dirty, and unruly; to tame them and bring them to proper behavior, it was necessary to curb their impulses and correct their behavior with whatever level of punishment and restriction was required. The woodshed was a normal part of family discipline—painful, no doubt, but necessary. In school the same approach prevailed, and the three Rs were "taught to the tune of the hickory stick."

This outlook pervaded the content of education as well. In 1800 anyone going further than the elementary skills of reading, writing, and ciphering was exposed to heavy inculcations of Caesar, Virgil, Ovid, Euripides, Plato, Homer, and others, all in the original tongue. Mastery of such knowledge and the ability to interlace one's conversation with appropriate Latin and Greek quotations were a sign of learning and gentility. However, despite the aristocratic pretensions associated with such attainment, in the bustling democracy of 19th-century America this view of the proper nature of education came under attack.

By the end of the century, the Calvinist fervor had dimmed (although it never disappeared), and an alternative outlook was in ascendance. Let us examine how this occurred in greater detail. The Puritans, who gave American values their original color, had held to a belief in predestination, infant damnation, and the total depravity of man. In short order, however, a host of new ideas came into direct conflict with these views. The very nature of the American Revolution, for example, made for a trend toward secularization. Ideas such as progress, the freedom of the individual for self-determination, and the dignity and respect merited by each person were part of that revolutionary movement. In addition, the advance of rationalism and technology gave more and more grounds for making attainment in this world central to living rather than striving for humility and self-abnegation in preparation for the next.

One of the great by-products of 18th-century Enlightenment had been a "critical examination of previously accepted doctrines and institutions from the point of view of rationalism" (Morris, 1976, p. 434). This, in concert with the Industrial Revolution, had, in the 19th century, produced a radical departure from the religious hegemony of prior eras. With the great leaps forward of current technology, the ground was prepared for new ideas about humankind. Perhaps no intellectual advance of the time was more influential (and controversial) than the writings of Charles Darwin. When he published his work on the origin of the species and the descent of man in 1859, his ideas were immediately taken up and used in the service of an extraordinary variety of doctrines. For example, Herbert Spencer in England and William Graham Sumner in the United States elaborated a theory called Social Darwinism. According to this view, government should keep out of the way of business and commerce. That realm was where the fit—namely the talented, the energetic, the venturesome, and the intelligent—would survive and improve the species, whereas the lazy, the intemperate, the diseased, the retarded, and the inadequate would fall by the wayside and die out.

A second derivative was eugenics, a doctrine that sought to improve the race by better breeding. This meant that people with desirable traits must be identified and encouraged to reproduce; at the same time, the undesirables must be sought out and ways found to keep them from breeding. It was viewed as counterproductive to apply medical skills to perpetuate the life of the feebleminded, the vulnerable and the diseased, and thus allow their lines to continue. The recommendations arising from this view included sterilization, marriage restriction, and prolonged institutionalization of "unfit" segments of society.

This thinking played into the concept of class as well. There were the genetically superior, who were evidently the best people, and there were the more or less defective, who were readily identified as, first of all, poor, and then as ethnically or racially different. It is obvious that much of this ran counter to many basic American values—that all men are created equal, that everyone could rise in society, and the like.

Such hereditarian thinking took form during the epoch between 1870 and 1905, a time when a great mass of immigrants was traversing the oceans to enter the country. Citizens became concerned about paupers, epileptics, delinquents, the retarded—and foreigners.

By the end of the 19th century one or another variety of Darwinism was a major force. Perhaps no claim was more ardently asserted, however, than the alleged "proof" this doctrine offered for the inferiority of women. It was posited that women were less evolved than men; in particular, they were more emotional than men (self-evidently a lower stage of evolution) and possessed a lesser intellect. Among other things, this argument was used against women's suffrage.

However, aside from such eccentric byroads, these points of view were acting to erode or at least to diminish the role of religion in the national awareness and to make for an ever more secular society. Even before the Industrial Revolution had begun to impinge on daily life, these stirrings had begun to make themselves felt. Within the framework of existing religious practices, various compromises had emerged, some of which were more or less radical. Thus, during the 18th century, deism flourished and fostered a temporal ethic to replace the traditional focus on divinity. Unitarianism became an important presence on the national scene, and the Transcendentalists (Henry David Thoreau, Ralph Waldo Emerson, and others of like mind) offered a more spiritual and romantic theology (man is good at the core and, through constant reform, seeks always to better his world). For the bulk of the population, however, such radical departures were not easily arrived at, and more conservative views prevailed. Thus, while most continued to believe that people were inherently sinful, they could accept the view that God is benevolent and that salvation could be achieved through conversion or a leap of faith. Heaven, hell, miracles, and revelation continued to be key words.

External factors played their role as well. Although many English settlers came to colonial America, no bishop had been sent by the Church of England to officiate over the church establishment there. Nor did the Loyalist leanings of many of its practicing members foster adherence to its tenets among newly arrived immigrants. That, coupled with the spirit of freedom and the emphasis on individual expression in all things nurtured by the revolutionary zeal of the new republic, led to a breakdown in many accepted religious practices and, in time, to the formation of numerous Protestant sects.

During the first half of the 18th century there had been a huge renewal of religious faith. So widespread and so intense was this movement as to be dubbed the Great Awakening. It introduced a note of revivalism into the way many Americans worshipped and began to give religious practices in the colonies their own indigenous form. A Second Great Awakening arose early in the 19th century. It reached its apogee in the 1820s, when the idea of doing good works was added to the striving for salvation. This coupled duty and devotion to the need for social reform. Ultimately, this notion of dedicating one's life to the improvement of others, to working with the poor and helping the downtrodden, would become one of the great dynamic forces that poured its energy into a variety of crucial efforts to better the lives of children. Among others, it played a major role in directing the efforts of Jane Addams and Charles Loring Brace.

As mentioned earlier, it is important to note that much of this passion for reform was instigated and maintained by women. Thus during the 1830s and 1840s, more than 400 chapters of the American Female Moral Reform Society spread from New England to the mid-Atlantic states. At the end of the century, the National Congress of Mothers was established and attracted a huge following. Such causes as female suffrage and temperance attracted enormous numbers of adherents and ultimately achieved critical changes in law. The transformation of the role and valuation of children in American life took place within this matrix.

More specifically, as time passed, the Calvinist outlook toward children came to be largely replaced by an alternative perspective, one more in keeping with the thinking of Jean-Jacques Rousseau. According to this French master, children were essentially good; if they behaved badly, it is all too likely that they were spoiled by the failure of adults to rear them properly. Children needed love and understanding, they had to be guided rather than forced, they needed a good example rather than stern correction, and they were supposed to be happy rather than productive.

Each of these two value sets had profound implications, both economically and behaviorally. Thus, the Calvinist view implied that children should be taught early to work, to be frugal, to be seen and not heard, and to be humble and obedient. Rousseau, on the other hand, emphasized children's need for self-expression, for a proper education, for an enjoyable childhood. These attitudes underlay many of the great debates of the 19th century about compulsory education, child labor, and child protection. Indeed, these views worked themselves into the very core of family life.

THE TRANSFORMATION FROM PATERNALISM TO THE PRIMACY OF MOTHER LOVE

According to the Calvinist doctrine, the child was assumed to need firm paternal guidance. Father's principles might be administered by mother, but it was father who set the tone and enforced the standards. The child was declared to have rampant impulses that, if not curbed, would lead to rebellion and antisocial behavior. The early 19th century retained the former doctrine that the purity of patriarchal values, paternal firmness and masculine sternness, were necessary both to set a child on the straight and narrow path and to keep him or her there until internalization of parental (that is to say paternal) values took over.

By the end of the century, however, this outlook had undergone a radical change. By the early 20th century, the image of father as model and enforcer had given way to the pervasive influence of the dominance of mother love.

THE INDUSTRIAL REVOLUTION: THE ROLE OF WORK

Another benchmark of changing attitudes and values was the Industrial Revolution. In particular, there was a great transformation in the nature of work. On the farm, and for the small family business, the children had worked side by side with father, while mother stayed at home and, with her cooking and caregiving, made it possible for the work of earning to be done.

With the advance of the Industrial Revolution, manufacturing and corporate office life began to absorb more and more of the working population. As a result, father would be away from home much of the time, and mother would be the primary caregiver and child manager. Father's role became secondary and supportive ("Wait till your father comes home!"), and the mother/child interaction moved to the fore as the central site for child-rearing efforts. Let us look at that transition in more detail.

During the 19th century, the United States was being transformed from a country of farms and small rural villages to a country of cities. The beginnings of the American Revolution had more or less coincided with the Industrial Revolution, and things were changing rapidly. The railroad and telegraph replaced the stage coach and the Pony Express, and there were profound alterations in both the size and the composition of the population—where it came from, where it lived, the way it earned its bread, and the level of its wealth.

The pace of innovation can be perceived with particular clarity if we consider what was happening in medicine during this era. In describing this, Abt-Garrison remarks that

... it is only necessary to mention Laennec's stethoscope (1819), thoracentesis, perfected by Trousseau (1843), ... (and others), ... ether anesthesia (1846–47), Helmholtz's ophthalmoscope (1851), Manuel Garcia's laryngoscope (1855), ... the hypodermic syringe of C. G. Pravas (1851–53), ... Koch's tubercle bacillus (1881) and tuberculin (1890), Ehrlich's diazo-reaction for acetone (1882), diphtheria antitoxin (Roux and von Behring [1890–93]), the Roentgen rays (1893), H. Quincke's lumbar puncture (1895) and Gaertner's tonometer (1899). (1965, p. 113)

CHANGE IN THE NATURE OF WORK

Thus, in 1800, the country was still largely agrarian with most people living on farms and in and around the numerous small towns and villages. But the industrial transformation was soon under way. There was a growing national and world population to feed, clothe, house, and entertain, and changes came quickly. As noted, the rapid industrialization had brought about a profound alteration in the way people lived; in particular, it had changed where and how they worked. This in turn led to the emergence of a new family ethos.

One of the first industries to appear was the textile mill, where cloth was made on large mechanical looms. The mill had many effects on the family. To begin with, the man who worked in a factory had to leave home in order to go to his place of employment; since mother stayed home with the children, the quality of family life was inevitably transformed. For another, spinning yarn at home (once a mainstay of the female domain) no longer made sense; better-quality cloth could be bought cheaply at the general store. Third, a man earning a salary could perhaps save some money and either rise within the context of the larger industrial complex within which he labored or, eventually, go into business for himself. More than that, with industry came commerce, and with these came banking, investment, financing, stock brokering, and a host of supportive services. All these required special staffing, and training and numerous ancillary personnel to support such an effort. In short, an emerging middle class appeared, thrived, and began to develop a whole new way of life.

The appearance of a new, monied, city-dwelling populace altered many things; in particular, it changed the role of women. For her part, the farm woman who had had so much to do when she was producing food, cloth, soap, and a variety of other family necessities now had more time to spend raising her children.

IMMIGRATION AND ITS IMPLICATIONS

Thus far the rise in population has been described in terms of the flight from the farms to the cities. But another aspect of this swelling of the numbers of city dwellers needs mention, the influx of new immigrants into the United States. Between 1821 and 1932, 34,244,000 new arrivals came to American shores. It was as if a whole European country had moved across the Atlantic to resettle itself in the New World. Thomas writes (1968, p. 296) that "... the average rate of growth of population in each decade of the nineteenth century was twenty-nine percent in the United States."

These are astronomical figures, and they account in part for some of the quality of American life during that epoch. In the earlier part of the 19th century, most immigrants had come from northern and western Europe; as the century closed, those flooding in were from the southern and eastern parts of that continent. By and large, those who came were fleeing the ravages of hunger or political persecution. For example, in Ireland, the potato crop had failed in 1845, and a terrible famine ensued. To make matters worse, the great landholders had responded by violently evicting thousands of starving peasants from their homes. Thus at one stroke a whole population was suddenly deprived of both food and shelter. Faced with such tribulations, the beckoning of the New World was irresistible, and a torrent of Irish immigrants poured into the port cities of the United States. For the most part they were uneducated farmers, and they took the most menial jobs available. Characteristically, their sons became laborers and their daughters servants. By and large they were looked down on and treated as stupid, oafish drinkers and brawlers. Their image was not helped by the fact that in the big cities, many of the dangerous gangs that roamed the streets were comprised of the first-generation offspring of this group.

Meanwhile, in the rural areas of southwest Germany, a severe political crisis had erupted in 1848 (it kept the country in ferment until 1854) and led to the widespread flight of many thousands of people. A good many of them were skilled craftsmen. When they arrived in the United States, many were able to achieve a fairly rapid integration into their new country. But many others underwent vicissitudes not unlike those of the Irish.

The concern for and the effort to relieve the plight of these immigrants were among the major driving forces that kindled the ardor of reform in so many of the new middle class. In particular, the felt need to help the children of these destitute new arrivals played a major role in marshaling the energies of a vast corpus of right-minded people, consisting largely of those who were reaping the benefits of national growth and seeking to live out their ideals. In particular, they comprised the group called the Child Savers.

DEMOGRAPHICS: THE FALL IN BIRTH RATE

Meanwhile, other major transformations were taking place in the larger body of Americans, changes of a more subtle but nonetheless powerful character that swept silently through the lives of American families. Perhaps most important was the fall in birth rate. In 1800 the average national birth rate was 50 per 1,000. By 1900 this had fallen to a mere 18.5 per 1,000. Or, whereas an average white woman in 1800 was fated to bear 7.04 children, by 1900 this figure had fallen to 3.56. Since there was no national program for birth control, and neither pill nor diaphragm was available, we might wonder: How was this achieved? Miriam Lewin (1984) suggests that this became possible through a process she calls "psychic birth control."

To explain this it is important to return again to the theme of changes in the role of women during the 19th century. Early in the 1800s, one important image of womanhood had been the pioneer woman. It was she who faced adversity unflinchingly, participated in the long treks out west to claim land and build a new country, bore children under the most adverse conditions, loaded her husband's gun when he fought off hostile Indians, and produced and nurtured a large family. As the century advanced, however, instead of underlining her robustness and her ability to tolerate adversity, the culture took up what Barbara Harris (1984) named "the cult of true womanhood." According to this doctrine, women were religious, asexual, home-loving, and submissive. Intellectually, they were regarded as inferior to men; hence they could not play an equal role in public affairs. Accordingly, women belonged in the home, and men in the marketplace and government. This doctrine defined women as emotional, delicate, weak, and less substantial than men but, at the same time, morally superior. Thus women were considered to be lacking in sexual interest and incapable of sexual pleasure. They were forced to tolerate the animalistic propensities of men but did not share them. Indeed, medical opinion of the day asserted that women should not move during sexual intercourse lest they render their husbands impotent. Passivity and limitation were the rule. Hence, birth control became a matter of continence and withdrawal (psychic birth control).

These principles governed the experience of "good" women. "Bad" women were something else; sacred and profane love were well understood within such a context. Men controlled themselves within marriage and sought the company of prostitutes or servants for their less inhibited experiences. And the birth rate fell. This resulted in an even more subtle change in family dynamics. With fewer births, there were longer intervals between pregnancies, and mothers had more time to get to know each child and to struggle with the individual problems of rearing that youngster. This too served to shift the responsibility for the moral development of the child from the father to the mother.

Another significant factor was the tendency of many women, especially those who had some higher education, never to marry. Indeed, Lewin (1984) notes that "Between 1865 and 1874 the proportion of ever-married women dropped to the lowest point it has ever reached in the United States" (p. 64). By the end of the 19th century, this cohort of women who had either small families or no families played a considerable role in bringing about many of the social changes affecting children. They were self-conscious bearers of morality, and they took on the burdens of social reform as their proper mission.

Another of the silent transformations of the time was the break between generations that the enormous changes tended to bring about. When parents were farmers and the children city dwellers and/or factory workers, the disparity between generations was radical. Similarly, when parents were immigrants and children were Americanized, rather characteristic stresses were generated in the intergenerational dialogue (W. E. Moore, 1968). To say the least, the tendency of children to break with parental traditions was enhanced markedly by this sequence. Much of the American interest in the new, the innovative, and the inventive may have been conditioned by this element in the national mix.

TRANSFORMATION OF THE ATTITUDE TOWARD CHILDREN

The economics of childhood have become an area of considerable interest (Zelizer, 1985). It was especially noteworthy that at the beginning of the 19th century, when the population was largely rural and the chief source of income was agriculture, each new child could be considered an economic asset. From a very early age, children could contribute in substantial ways to the life and work of the farm. Feeding chickens and collecting eggs, helping with food preparation (to feed a sizable family plus some hired help), setting the table, participating in the many home industries such as spinning and soap making were all well within the compass of preschoolers. Needless to say, for older children, more complex and burdensome employment was always awaiting assignment. Since the birth rate was high, tending to the younger sibs was one of many important chores. The actual dollars and cents have been worked out, and it is evident that, generally speaking, under those conditions, a child was a financial asset.

As the century wore on and the Industrial Revolution gained momentum, the center of population moved toward the cities, the focus of earning centered in the offices and factories, and the ability of children to earn money fell off sharply. Instead of an economic asset, city children became a genuine financial liability; they cost money to raise, feed, clothe, and educate, but they returned nothing tangible by way of a work product until they were largely grown. Economically, they were worthless, particularly among the middle-class sector of the population, where even such jobs as bootblack and street errand runner were not encouraged for children.

On the other hand, the need for training for the new occupations in the service sector often mandated prolonged periods of schooling: This cost money to begin with and put off earning capacity until even later.

In brief, as the century progressed, the economically remunerative farm child became an economically worthless, even expensive presence in middle-class city life. To be sure, this change did not take place all at once. It began with the more affluent sector of the population and only gradually spread to embrace everyone. Throughout the 19th century, for working-class people, children still retained a meaningful economic value. At relatively young ages, youngsters could be put to work in factories and at some of the simpler service tasks. Indeed, in some factories the workbenches were peopled largely by children. Many poorer families needed both the earnings of the older children and the household help of the younger ones merely to survive.

Gradually, however, childhood in general came to be regarded as precious. The economically worthless middle-class child became sentimentalized and, in many ways, romanticized. A new public emphasis emerged that led to profound cultural and legal changes. The juvenile court appeared, child welfare became a cause célèbre, adoption practices were revised, and legislation was passed to protect children from the abuse and economic exploitation typical of the time.

Part of the romantic outlook of the day included a wish to preserve and prolong childhood innocence; an essential moralism (bad behavior was always punished by later failures of health, e.g., a shortened life span, insanity, etc.); a preference for farm experience, small-town life, and country ways as simple, wholesome, and healthy; and a condemnation of city life and city ways (with much inveighing against rich food, devotion to fashion, balls, etc.) as sources of physical debility and moral decay.

POST–CIVIL WAR GUILT

It is not altogether clear what made for this striking cultural shift in the way children were regarded. The change in patterns of work and earning is, of course, one factor. Another possibility is the effect of the Civil War. It might well be that a nation that had disrupted so many of its families and killed so many of its sons, its fathers, and its brothers would bear a tremendous burden of national guilt. However justified the expenditure of lives might have seemed at the time, once society began the work of picking up the pieces, there might well have been an outpouring of efforts to undo what had been done (in some displaced, symbolic way) as well as one was able and to make life a little better after the spiritual havoc that had been wreaked on so many.

In any case, the attitude toward children underwent a profound transformation.

BIRTH RATES: SURVIVAL AND ATTACHMENT

Another view is that with new health technology (e.g., vaccination, certification of milk, etc.), the greater survival of babies allowed for the establishment of deeper emotional bonds toward one's children. When infant mortality was high, in sheer self-defense, parents did not allow themselves to become too committed to a new arrival, lest they lose the child and have then to go through the pangs of intense mourning. With a safer outlook for survival, the natural tendency toward attachment and idealization of the infant could be allowed full expression.

From a late 20th-century standpoint, it is not easy to understand that prior to the 19th century, the death of a young child was a minor event, likely to give rise to either indifference or resignation. Typically the parents did not even attend the funeral, nor did they wear mourning garb, arm bands, or other symbols of sorrow. In the United States, grief tended to be restrained. When one infant was lost, another child was soon produced; the new one often was given the name of the sib that had been lost.

In the course of the 19th century, however, for the middle-class family, the death of a child became the most intolerable of losses. If anything, there was a magnification of mourning (Douglas, 1977) that might well involve an entire neighborhood. Indeed, the whole culture participated, and there was an outpouring of literature in the form of poems, pamphlets, and wise counsel advising how to express grief and manage loss.

By the late 19th century, lower-class families had adopted the middle-class patterns of parenting and responded to the loss of a child in similar fashion. In the United States, ". . . the romantic cult of the dead child was . . . transformed into a public campaign for the preservation of child life . . ." (Douglas, 1977, p. 27).

THE UNWANTED INFANT: BABY FARMING

Paradoxically, with the large families so characteristic of the early part of the century, it was inevitable that there would also be many unwanted children. For people living in poverty in particu-

lar, the advent of a new baby might be something less than an unalloyed blessing. All too often some means was sought for disposing of such newcomers, often in infancy, but occasionally in the case of older children as well. In 1870 it was hard to dispose of an unwanted child. Where the child was an infant, the usual recourse was a "baby farmer," so called, who made a profession of getting rid of such undesirables—for a fee. During the 19th century, many older children were placed in foster care—and accepted by foster parents to add to the family's workforce. By and large, adoptive practices too were dominated by the quest for child labor. It was not until the end of that century that the desire to adopt came to be motivated by wanting a baby to love. Then the earlier practice of paying people to take children gave way to paying—and handsomely—in order to *get* a child.

For the older child, a tradition of exchanging care for labor had been established in colonial times and was expressed in the widespread social practice of apprenticeship. Ostensibly designed to teach a trade, for many poor children it was the only way to obtain a home. According to custom, the child would stay with his master until age 18 and would then be sent forth as a journeyman to fend for himself; at that point he would be given a little money, perhaps some cattle, a set of clothes, and a new Bible.

Such care sufficed for the early part of the century. Once the sentimental revolution had taken place, however, these earlier arrangements were no longer tolerable. Younger children could not be given over to baby farmers to board or older children handed over to employers as workers. This was incompatible with the new outlook. Editorials began to appear challenging the practice of baby farming. Indeed, now only acceptance into a home for loving care was considered appropriate.

THE ISSUE OF PAID PARENTING

Where no other resources were available for a child in need, various forms of institutional care were available in a variety of settings. As the 19th century began, these were chiefly in the form of almshouses for the poor and asylums for the orphan. By the end of the century, the emphasis had shifted to foster homes as the optimum site for child placement. This succeeded because people were eager to get good servants and dependable workers. Accordingly, girls were easily placed with people who wanted help around the house; at the same time, however, there was always a need for sturdy boys who were not afraid to work. In response to the newly emerging attitudes, agencies began to offer both: an opportunity for the youngster to contribute and do his or her share of the world's work and the promise of a loving home along with a place in the family. To aid in this process, as the cities grew, one of the side products of their growth was an ever-larger concentration of the poor and the bereft. In the face of this mounting problem, a series of volunteer groups began to work assiduously to place children in good homes. The first was established in 1883 in Illinois; it was known as the Illinois Children's Home and Aid Society. Soon similar Children's Aid Societies were founded in many other states.

By the 1860s, however, a cohort of youngsters had emerged for whom the stated arrangements had failed and who had to be kept in institutions. Either there was something about these children that made it impossible to place them, or, once placed, they were returned soon. The common issue was that they could not or would not work to earn their keep; as a result, the foster parents had no further use for them. A new idea was then introduced, namely: to pay boarding homes to take them in. As the concept of child labor was becoming ever more dubious, paid parenting became a more common solution. The goal was to keep children in school and to shield them from exploitation.

Inevitably, those who sought to have children accepted as an act of humane charity protested this practice; it was, they asserted, another version of baby farming. Those involved in placement sought to blunt this objection by focusing on the intangible components of boarding care, namely: the interest and affection the boarding parents invested in the youngsters thus taken in. Nonetheless, for many, any form of paid parenting was morally suspect.

ADOPTION

Early in the 20th century, there was an ever-increasing trend toward adoption for the love of children. By the later 1920s, the emphasis had shifted from finding homes for babies, to finding enough babies for the many claimant homes. During the latter decades of the 19th century, the average adoptive parent had been a member of the working class; by the 1920s, however, wealthy, prosperous, often prominent people predominated. The demand for infants was especially intense; however, if babies were unavailable, those easiest to place were children under 3. Agencies were amazed to find that they could not meet the demand. In particular, the most commonly expressed yearning of prospective adoptive parents was to have a golden-haired, blue-eyed little girl. It seemed as if people wished for a kind of idealized doll that could be adorned endlessly. (Jewish homes, however, continued to prefer boys.) In short, by this time, the sentimental value of the child overrode all other considerations. Now new warnings had to be issued: Instead of concern with exploitation and profiteering at the expense of a child, prospective adoptive parents were cautioned against expecting a child to be a trouble-free toy, a fulfiller of thwarted hopes, a replacement for something missing in one's life, or a means for realizing an ambition.

Responsible social agencies were setting standards for adoptive homes and screening applicants carefully. Nonetheless, the majority of adoptions were arranged informally, sometimes through newspaper ads in the personal or miscellaneous columns, sometimes through well-meaning intermediaries, and, all too often, through bootleg profiteers. A "black market" in babies grew up, and business boomed. Where a woman could be found who was carrying a pregnancy she did not want, it became everyday practice to pay her medical expenses—and perhaps offer her a bonus—in return for her baby. By the mid-20th century, some babies sold for as much as $10,000. The ever-falling birth rate began to affect the availability of infants for adoption. Soon the ratio of those wanting infants to the number offered was said to be 10 to 1. Along with this, the demand for older children dwindled to vanishing. Once the economic incentive for taking in children was removed, there remained only the emotional imperative—and that in turn translated into infants.

Agencies began to ask for adoption fees. Once the sacredness of the child became fully accepted, the provision of compensation for boarding homes for infants and foster care for older children became a conflicted and ambiguous issue. Much compromise, denial, and occasional assumption of extreme positions ensued. On the one hand, one hears such foster caregivers accused of purely mercenary motives; on the other, one hears of them going to court to battle with biologic parents, because the foster parents have reared and have come to love this child and now seek the assignment of permanent parental rights.

Child-Rearing Instruction

As a result of these extraordinary 19th-century transitions (country to city, working child to sentimentalized child, paternal to maternal dominance of child management, predominantly working-class values to the authority of the middle-class outlook, agricultural society to industrial economy), the previously accepted modes for rearing children had to be adapted to wholly new conditions. In the nature of things, a profound uncertainty began to be felt. People nationwide could no longer rely on principles derived from their rural backgrounds or ethnic lifestyles and were very eager for advice on how best to raise and educate their young in the new setting. In an attempt to respond to this clamorous need, a host of voices was raised in a great counterpoint of instruction. Many wives and mothers felt called on to communicate the values and methods that emerged from their personal experience. Their efforts ran parallel with a host of idealistic men of the cloth who published everything from manuals to parables.

Pediatricians also began to influence this tumultuous arena. Such books began to appear as Sachs's 1895 *Treatise on the Nervous Diseases of Children*. Perhaps the best-known and most influential work of its time was Luther Emmet Holt's *The Care and Feeding of Children*. First published in 1894, it went through many editions. In the worldview of the pediatric practitioners of that day, much that influenced nervous behavior in children was a function of physiologic ailments caused by incorrect feeding or improperly prepared milk. (Hence the inclusion of feeding in the manual of child rearing.)

The Role of Education

Prior to the 19th century, there had been limited free public education in America. There had not been a great deal of pressure from the populace to require that this be offered. One need not be literate to work on the farm; there were no technical manuals included in the sale of livestock; and much of what went into craft work was taught by apprenticeship rather than through formal course work or by perusing self-help books. To be sure, it was important to be able to read the Bible. In addition, the founders of American civilization were well aware that true democracy could come about only through the efforts of an informed electorate. But no requirement for informing the children of the nation was built into the Constitution, and, to this day, the matter of education is still considered a state responsibility rather than a national concern (although, admittedly, this is beginning to change).

The Calvinist Puritans who founded Massachusetts established it as a religious commonwealth. In order to ensure the transmission of the true faith to its children, in 1642 the General Court of Massachusetts required by law that all children should be employed and be able to read the Bible and the laws of the community. Five years later the court ordered every town of 50 families "to employ a teacher of reading and writing whose fees should be paid either by the parents or by the town community."

Within a few years, Connecticut and New Hampshire had both followed suit. By and large, for many years, schools retained a strong religious cast (the widely used *New England Primer* was full of little religious homilies). With the passage of time, however, the secularization of American life transformed this early school system (designed only for Puritans) into the beginnings of free public education for all children. This process was facilitated by the introduction of the Monotorial system. Created by John Lancaster in England in 1798, this was a plan to lower the costs of schooling and to make it more available to the poor. It involved using older students as monitors to tutor younger ones—thus, one teacher could minister to hundreds of pupils. The monitors were given cut and dried formulae that they then applied to their charges. This quick fix caught on instantly, and the idea spread like wildfire; indeed, the existing religious schools in England quickly adopted the same system. More than that, the idea leapt the Atlantic, and in 1806 the Free School Society of New York introduced such a program into the United States.

Albeit cheap, the Lancastrian plan ended up with a relatively weak educational impact, and, by 1850, its popularity had waned. The public recognized that to get a good education, well-trained teachers were needed, not well-intentioned students using a mechanical formula.

Another borrowing from England was the Sunday school. Its chief popularizer was one Robert Raikes of Gloucester, an English manufacturer. In order to help the poor to a better life, in 1780 he opened a Sunday school for children and adults. Again it was taken up readily by a willing public, a Sunday School Society was formed, and, by 1786, it took root in America. Soon it became a significant element in the rearing of most American children.

Yet another English educational idea that was transferred to the colonies was the notion of industrial training. As early as 1641, the Scottish Parliament had encouraged the establishment of textile schools in the countryside. In the colony of Virginia, the 1646 legislature provided for settings where poor children should learn carding, knitting, and spinning in public flax houses. Humanitarian and idealistic philanthropies kept various versions of such manual learning alive as a way of improving the status of the poor. The advent of the Industrial Revolution added the powerful incentive of a need for trained technical workers to operate the equipment of the new factories and offices, and, over time, manual training (later to be known as vocational training) persisted as a theme in American life.

But England was not the only source of educational departures. The first kindergarten was opened in Prussia in 1873, the brainchild of Friedrich Froebel, a German educator with a mystical bent. "It was to be, as the name implies, a garden in which children grew up as trees and flowers grow" (Mulhern, 1946, p. 379). Mrs. Carl Schultz, a German political refugee fleeing the 1848 revolution, opened the first kindergarten on American shores in Watertown, Wisconsin, in 1855. (A few years before that, the Prussian government had closed the original classes because they were suspected of socialist leanings.) Five years after Mrs. Schultz had initiated this pattern of education, Elizabeth P. Peabody had opened the first English-language kindergarten in the country. (The original Watertown setting had utilized German.) Public kindergartens were initiated in St. Louis in 1873. The movement spread rapidly, and, by 1900, there were nearly 500 such settings the country over.

EDUCATION AND THE CITIES

As the Industrial Revolution advanced, however, as the demographic importance of cities grew ever more dominant, and as the nature of work was transformed, the demand for a well-educated, adaptable workforce grew apace. The country needed a literate, sophisticated corps of versatile employees. In the course of this evolution, education became ever more critical. Pragmatically, it was an essential requirement for one to progress through the new socioeconomic contexts being established; on a more personal level, it gave the individual a sense of integration into the ongoing cultural process and progress of the era.

Platt (1977) makes the point that the earlier educational efforts of the 19th century (from 1820 to 1840) were dominated by men, whereas the subsequent reforms (such as the juvenile court) involving moral salvation were created and fostered by women. It was certainly true that during much of the 19th century, winter school was taught by men and attended largely by girls and the older boys (from 10 to 12 on up). In the eastern part of the United States, women could exchange child-rearing advice and offer one another mutual support in numerous maternal associations. These groups defined their responsibilities as attending to children up to age 10. After that the men took over. However, the full incorporation of a boy into adult life usually awaited puberty, at 15 or 16. Father might then offer a boy full pay for a day's work or hire him out to a neighbor.

Children began to work early. In homes where learning was more highly esteemed, a boy might be placed in an environment that would foster his education. More commonly, however, he would be given a post as a "boy of all work," that is to say, he would be sent out to work essentially as a servant. Boys were thus positioned sometime between 7 and 14. At 14, apprenticeship might be introduced into a boy's life. When this operated as it should, it was the sure road to learning a craft or a trade.

THE ACADEMY

A distinctive form of education that had flourished from the late 18th century on was the academy. For a time there were many of these; they consisted of private educational settings geared to the rhythm of farm life. Youngsters might attend them for brief intervals, usually when the call for labor in the fields was at a minimum. Often attendance was transient and unstable; one went for a while, took what courses one could, and moved on, only to return after some extended interval.

Young people of all ages were in class at once, depending on the vagaries of individual proclivity, family values, circumstance, and season. Some of the academies were better established than others (e.g., Exeter); many were ephemeral arrangements, as seasonal and as transient as their clientele. By and large, these were not expensive settings, although they might be well beyond the means of many small farmers and laborers.

PUBLIC SCHOOL

At the same time, many communities had public arrangements for more regular schooling, although this too was only sporadically attended by youngsters of a wide variety of ages. Girls tended to begin school earlier and to stop earlier than boys, usually at 15 or 16. Poor boys who had no apprenticeship might stay on longer.

Nor, for many children, was home any more stable a setting. As noted, many young boys left home during their grade-school years to work as servants. Albeit away for much of the time, during their tenure of service they might return home for longer or shorter intervals, before leaving home finally for their "start in life." Such a final departure might come as early as 14, although it was usually later. It seems safe to say that at this moment in history, protracted dependency at home was of much briefer duration than in the late 20th century.

Prior to 1840, there was relatively little emphasis on rising in the world and attaining success. Parents expected much hierarchical deference. Schoolmasters were in a less fortunate position. They had no principal, bureaucracy, or school system to back up their authority; maintaining order in their heterogeneous class could be quite a challenge. This situation was not helped by the fact that some of their students might be older than they were. The schoolmasters often were community outsiders who boarded with the parents of their students. Given their lack of hierarchical authority, they enforced discipline by being punitive, distant, and stiff.

Some of the schoolmaster's most powerful weapons were physical punishment, humiliation, or both. A student could be required to squat with his back to the wall, to stoop for hours, to bend over the master's footstool in order to be whipped, or to shave with a wooden razor.

To be sure, students had their means for striking back. Student mutinies and disruptions occurred, and "breaking out," "carrying out," "turning out," or "barring out" the teacher were ritual practices that usually involved the informed teacher allowing himself to be carried out and tormented until he gave in and granted some demanded holiday. Sometimes, however, it became more serious, especially when a group of older adolescents wanted to rid themselves of a particular teacher. Some masters would head off this kind of trouble by thrashing the ringleader before the whole thing began. All in all, Horace Mann, one of the great educators of that day, regarded this set of practices as an enormous evil.

COLLEGE

In the early 1800s, higher education usually meant attending college. One of the major reasons for going to college was to enter the ministry. With the growth of the cities, however, many students with other interests and from a variety of backgrounds began to attend. The authorities who ran the college modeled themselves exclusively according to the patriarchal stance and insisted on order to the point of obsessionality. College staff were, in a sense, *in loco parentis;* however, they felt they had to be much stricter than parents were. Accordingly, there were many rules. Indeed, the quality of discipline was remarkably petty, with strict enforcement of insignificant regulations and much overbearing officiousness on the part of staff. For their part, the students reacted by forming their own groups. Often these would take form as literary societies that offered privacy, conviviality, and intellectual stimulation. Thus, a lively extracurricular life flourished alongside the stuffy agenda of formal studies.

In a more directly rebellious fashion, students would engage in remarkable pranks: ringing the chapel bell at night, leaving dead ducks in the chapel, or having wild snowball fights that broke windows. Beyond that, at times there were riots and rebellions. (There is even an account of the murder of a college president by a student.) (Kett, 1977, p. 53). Much fighting occurred between rival factions of students.

Social freedom could be gained by boarding in town and by unchaperoned dating. However, as the century advanced and colleges tended to become universities, there was a considerable evolution of student styles as well. H. L. Horowitz (1987) suggests that as the 19th century came to an end, 3 different kinds of student subcultures had emerged. One group she calls the "college men." Chiefly the sons of well-to-do parents, these were essentially an anti-intellectual coterie who frowned on studiousness, derided the "grinds," and promoted an extracurriculum of their own devising. They fostered "style," leadership and competitiveness, and tried in many ways to undercut the teaching and values of the faculty. Their epitome was achieved in the character of fraternity life in the late 19th and early 20th centuries.

A second group were largely from poorer backgrounds. These students usually were looked at with contempt by the "college men" and excluded by the fraternities; Horowitz calls these the "outsiders." They were young men who saw in college a way to better themselves; often they were headed for teaching careers or for the ministry; they took the college curriculum very seriously; and they sought to gain or to retain the good opinion of their teachers. As education became ever more tightly linked to career advancement, this group became more and more prominent.

A third type of student was also present, termed by Horowitz "the rebels." These were true intellectuals, concerned with the political and ideological issues of their times and often involved in cultural, esthetic, or organizational movements. These young people tried to link their academic lives with the major currents of the day; they were the political activists, and they might stage protests against the teaching of a particular professor or the affiliations of the college itself with some cause they considered dubious.

Generally speaking, the young people who went to school or to academies and on to college had to have some resources in their lives that bore them up, paid their expenses, and allowed them to pursue whatever level of academic achievement they attained. But as we have noted, there was much poverty in the land and large populations of children without any resources. For such youngsters the issue was not education; instead it involved such basics as nourishment, lodging, medical care, safety, and the like. In short, for them the primary concern was survival.

Child Welfare Institutions

Concern for the plight of children in distress always had been a factor on the American scene, although it had taken different forms at different epochs. Among the notable landmarks was the es-

tablishment of the first orphanage on the continent in New Orleans, in 1729. Some say that a great smallpox epidemic had swept the community that year and left a host of orphans in its wake. The sisters at the Ursuline convent felt called upon to care for these unfortunates and created the orphanage to do so. Others would have it that the orphans then in need of care were the products of a series of Indian massacres. Sixty-one years later, in 1790, the first public orphanage was organized in Charlestown, South Carolina.

The beginnings of institutional care for persons with retardation has a curious history (Rosen, Clark, Kivitz, 1976; Tyor and Bell, 1984). Initially, little or no distinction was drawn between the retarded and the insane. When parents could no longer care for the afflicted persons at home, they usually were confined in almshouses or in jails. Gradually, a series of studies (chiefly in France) began to distinguish persons with mentally retardation as a separate group. Indeed, a series of educational techniques were suggested that were felt to offer hope to this group. J. Itard, for example, was able to attain a measure of change in the Wild Boy of Aveyron. P. Pinel was publishing case studies and describing techniques for the re-education of the severely retarded. Various enterprising American specialists learned of these approaches and were eager to try them.

In 1829 the New England Asylum for the Blind opened its doors for the care and rehabilitation of the visually impaired. It was shortly renamed the Perkins Institute and achieved particular fame when Samuel Gridley Howe became its director in 1831. He was a man of unusual gifts; among other things, he successfully treated Laura Bridgeman, a blind deaf-mute who entered the setting in 1839. This impressive feat attracted national attention. On the basis of such accomplishments and in response to his appeal, in May 1848 the Massachusetts legislature created the Experimental School for Teaching and Training Idiotic Children, appropriating $2,500 annually for a three-year test period. The Experimental School was to be located at the Perkins Institute, and Howe was appointed its director.

The earliest school for mentally retarded people was established by Dr. Hervey B. Wilbur. Dr. Wilbur, also of Massachusetts, had heard of Edouard Seguin's work in France and had sent abroad for his book, entitled *Traitment moral, hygiène et éducation des idiots et des autres enfants*. He studied it carefully, and then began to apply it to a group of private patients. He opened a school in his home 3 months before the Experimental School at Perkins and provided private care for many years.

In spite of their numbers and their profound disabilities, retarded individuals were in many ways less of a social problem than delinquent youths. It was self-evident that putting young miscreants into almshouses or jails was counterproductive. For one thing, they were missing out on the education and the training that would offer whatever hope they might have for rehabilitation; for another, they were exposed for long idle hours to seasoned criminals who gave them a different kind of education. The New York House of Refuge was an initial effort to come to grips with the needs of troubled delinquents who were seen as requiring protection and order in their lives rather than retaliation and extraction of the price they must pay society for their misdeeds. The later-established reform school was what its name implied, a recognition that youths who went wrong were misguided and needed reform rather than punishment.

CHILD PROTECTION

There was another side to this as well. A deeply buried strain in our culture regards children as individuals to be seen and not heard, would not spare the rod lest the child be spoiled, and turns away from much evidence of abuse and misuse of children and adolescents as merely incidental to what child rearing requires. A famous example is the 1874 case where 9-year-old Mary Ellen was being abused mercilessly by her foster parents in a New York City tenement. The neighbors were horrified but helpless as the terrible mistreatment went on; according to the law, parents could do what they liked with their children, and the state had no right to intervene. Etta Wheeler, a church worker, went to visit a dying friend whose last wish was that Wheeler help this tormented child. Wheeler called the matter to the attention of Henry Bargh, who was head of the Society for the Prevention of Cruelty to Animals. He brought charges and pressed the case on the grounds that a child merited at least the same justice as any common cur. The judge concurred, issued a writ of habeus corpus, had the child removed from the foster home, and gave her into the custody of a setting for disturbed adolescents.

The following year, 1875, saw the founding of the New York Society for the Prevention of Cruelty to Children. Other such organizations arose in many nearby municipalities, often combining the functions of responding to cruelty toward both children and animals. (Where they did not combine functions, there were always more humane societies protecting animals than there were for children.) Finally, governmental agencies began to take over some of these functions and the Protective Services were born.

In 1876 the New York Society for the Prevention of Cruelty to Children promoted an act in the state legislature "to prevent and punish wrongs to children." By and large, these early organizations were concerned with child rescue; they sought to prosecute parents rather than to help improve family life. Later on, however, the preventive goal emerged with considerable force.

In writing about the child and the law, Rosenheim (1976) suggests that 2 approaches to child protection emerged at the time. One was deviancy control and the other, structural reform. Structural reform in the United States involved the intertwining of compulsory education and child labor laws as mutually enhancing protective support for children. In England, things had evolved differently, with child labor laws being directed toward individual industries (e.g., chimney sweeping, mining, work in mills, etc.) as journalistic exposés thrust the specific evils of each into public awareness. In the United States, the goal was to secure blanket prohibition of child labor and to insist that children spend the working day in school.

In terms of reform, the first group of children to be addressed were those who were blind, deaf, or retarded, and whose problems might respond to specialized educational techniques. Later more effort was funneled into working with delinquents and homeless neglected children who might need rescue. Volunteers often were concerned with the parallel tasks of both salvation and reeducation. With the passage of time, however, the role of incensed community observers or the efforts of specialized philanthropic groups gradually gave way to the functioning of governmental bureaucracies. Bit by bit, a host of more or less well-trained professionals edged out the community volunteers, and the Child Savers were replaced by specialized therapists of various kinds. Thus the emphasis shifted to child protection, where the presumably passive child needs a guardian of some kind to see that adequate care is given and to ward off evil influences or mistreatment.

Children in the City

During the late 19th and early 20th centuries, the streets were the natural and universal playground for children, both rich and poor. The poor children also found work in the streets: They sold papers, peddled goods, ran errands, bootblacked, or sold ice. Some scavenged, gathering salable trash for vending. Some begged.

In the 1890s deaths among preschool children were about 40% of all deaths. By the 1920s, this had fallen to 21.7%. Inoculations, vaccination, and quarantine had begun the process of controlling the major communicable diseases, although younger children were still susceptible. But a new source of danger had emerged. By 1910 accidents had become the leading cause of death of children 5 to 14 years of age. Railroads, streetcars, and soon automobiles became the new killers of the young. By 1920 accidents had become the fourth leading cause of death for the 0- to -5 age group, moving up to second place in 1940. By 1914, 60% of New York City's traffic victims were under 15, with the mortality rate particularly heavy between ages 5 and 10.

In the first decade of the 20th century, whenever a horse or a trolley killed a child, a street mob would assemble and often attempt forthwith to execute the driver. For their part, however, in this unsupervised arena of the street, the children often teased drivers and motormen and otherwise tempted fate and engaged in riotous behavior. Many laws were passed in an attempt to control street behavior, and many children were arrested for such practices as endangering property, obstructing the sidewalk, assault, loitering, and disturbing the peace. Left to their own devices, the streets would hum with children's activity; once a policeman appeared, everything would stop.

From the 1880s on, the appearance of children on the city streets had been recognized as an expression of urban poverty. Many regarded this as evidence of child neglect, an element that contributed to a later life of crime. One attempt to deal with this was the establishment of the Playground Association of America in 1906. Thousands of public playgrounds were built all over the country to the considerable enrichment of children's lives; in terms of crime prevention, however, it is difficult to assess their effectiveness.

SAFETY CAMPAIGNS

Eventually, in 1913, streetcar companies began a series of safety campaigns. These spread, and "Safety First!" became a movement of sorts within the major cities. Everything from rewriting nursery rhymes, to contests, to safety lectures, to "Safety Sundays," to organized group mourning around a "Child Memorial" in New York's Central Park were invoked. Insurance companies and automobile manufacturers contributed actively to these causes. In 1920 the radio personality "Uncle Robert" began a popular series of broadcasts on child safety.

There was an ever-deepening sense of moral offensiveness to the killing of children. To the former personal grief and outrage were now added collective mourning and memorialization.

During the 19th century, death, disease, and even war were regarded as acts of God, perhaps punishment for sins. But, with the advance of knowledge and technical mastery of the environment, human control became ever more important. Someone was to blame: the driver, the trolley company, the industrialist, the employer, or perhaps the heedless mother. Someone could be confronted and made to pay.

The emphasis on protecting children has several roots. For one thing, the killing of a child was regarded as almost sacrilegious. This resonated with and was amplified by the constant emphasis on safety. In order to avoid painful and expensive damage suits, the various corporate entities associated with transportation had waged these campaigns with fervor. Another significant element was the widespread availability of automobiles. As the auto reached new neighborhoods, middle-class as well as lower-class children began to be killed and injured in the streets. The construction of playgrounds, the development of playrooms in homes, the emergence of safety patrols at school crossings, the various safety campaigns, and the changes in public behavior as a result of mass education all played a role in reducing the incidence of these tragic events.

INSURING CHILDREN

Among other innovations that came with the late 19th century was the notion of insuring children, so that parents could be compensated if their offspring were killed. In relatively short order, however, this began to be viewed as morally offensive.

Insurance for children was launched in the 1870s, primarily in the form of burial insurance. Prior to that, fraternal societies and mutual aid groups among immigrants provided, among other things, for burial needs. Unfortunately, their financial practices were unregulated and often uncertain. Then, in 1875, Prudential Life Insurance began offering coverage for children less than 10 years of age. The average face value for such a policy was about $100, with agents calling at the home weekly to collect the 5 or 10 cent premiums. By 1895 Prudential had received $33 million in premiums, employed some 10,000 agents, and insured over 1 million children. (This practice had started much earlier in England; by the same date, some 4 million children were covered there.)

However, many people looked askance at this form of merchandising and considered it against the public interest. Occasionally attempts were made to define child insurance as illegal; Colorado passed such an ordinance in 1893. Those who stood in such opposition felt that they were taking part in a moral crusade.

The Child Savers in particular were opposed to any materialistic orientation toward childhood. Among their stated goals was a determination to protect the sanctity of childhood as well as the lives of individual children. They found the commercialization of children's death to be particularly repugnant; it was by its very nature a profanation of childhood. More than that, they feared that by making a child's death profitable, certain parents might make such an outcome more likely. The Child Savers regarded the poor in general, and immigrant families in particular, as prone to brutality and drunkenness, and thus likely to be tempted by this source of money. The insurance companies riposted by fighting the devil with fire—by stressing the priceless emotional value of a child rather than touting its cash value. In fact, repeated investigations found no cases of child abuse prompted by a plan to collect insurance money. So far as could be determined, children were insured for love and not for money.

It came down to a judgment call: do poor people love and value their children as much as do middle-class people? Those who favored insurance saw in it the desire for a decent burial and a proper mourning and memorialization of the child, rather than looking to the child's death as a source for ready cash.

For their part, the courts supported the insurance programs, holding that a family had a pecuniary interest in the life of a child; had he or she lived, the child eventually would have earned money to help support the family.

It is not unlikely that the flowering of such insurance at this time was a result of the middle-class values reaching down into and becoming part of the working-class ethos. The sentimentalization of the sacred child demanded a new level of mourning, which the insurance would now allow.

It is interesting that at the same time that the insurance business got under way, mortality rates for children began to fall. Among other influences, insurance companies were active in disseminating information about hygiene and child care.

LEGAL AWARDS FOR THE DEATH OF A CHILD

At the end of the 19th century, if a child was killed in an accident, the court would award a wrongful death claim according to the following formula: how much would the child have earned minus how much would the child have cost. Most awards ranged from $2,000 to $5,000, and most were paid to poor families, who, in fact, depended to a significant degree on the child's earnings. As major transportation modalities expanded, there was a marked increase in the number of deaths and claims. As the transition in outlook advanced from economic worth to sentimental pricelessness, a new set of formulae came into being. With more and more middle-class families involved, the traditional equation ran full tilt into the new regard for the sacred and invaluable character of the child/parent relationship. Some now came to regard the former nominal award as immoral, and here and there judges began to set aside such awards as lacking in human feeling. Just as accident cases began to flood the courts, various comments began to be heard about the importance of parental feelings. By 1916 court decisions had begun to address parental anguish and suffering or to give weight to the loss of the comfort and society of the child. Despite fierce opposition, rewards began to increase. This opened the door to a highly controversial set of arrangements, and debate continues on the morality of assigning pecuniary awards to compensate for grief and loss.

Child Labor

From the time of the first colonies, American children had always worked. By ages 6 to 8 they became "little adults," either contributing to the household or holding an apprenticeship and thus unburdening the household. With the advance of the Industrial Revolution, nimble little fingers were distinctly welcome in the new factories. The 1900 census reported 1 child (defined as ages 10 to 15) in 6 to be gainfully employed. This in fact excluded many workers under 10 as well as those "helping out" the family on farms or in shops. By 1930 this figure had decreased sixfold (in absolute numbers, from 186,358 to less than 30,000 children so employed).

From the outset, many voices had been raised to oppose this pattern of child labor. Many or more endorsed it. As the century advanced and attitudes toward children shifted, the battle became more intense. Altogether the struggle lasted some 50 years, from the 1870s until the 1930s. It was the subject of abrasive public contention, with sharply edged views expressed on both sides. For those against child labor, the image of a child working in a mine or factory was a violation of almost religious character. It was a moral outrage that deprived a child of that unique and precious heritage, a happy childhood, that is the right of every growing human being. Whereas those who spoke for child labor viewed this opposition as a denial of a child's right to earn for the family, to grow in character, to learn at an early age to take pride in productivity, and to bear responsibility. "The price of a useful, wage-earning child was directly counterpoised to the moral value of an economically useless but emotionally priceless child" (Zelizer, 1985, p. 57).

It seems likely that in the late 19th century, for the poor family, child labor was critical to survival. In general, a child and not a wife was the usual secondary wage earner, and a third of the income of many families derived from children's wages. Between 1870 and 1900 there was an increase of over 1 million child laborers. A third of those engaged by the southern textile mills were between 10 and 13, or younger. From the family's point of view, the child's earnings were the equivalent of health insurance, often the only buffer against the primary wage earner's illness or disability. Nonetheless, by 1900 child labor began to be defined as exploitation and was considered a major social problem.

During much of the 19th century, the working child was taken so much for granted that not until 1870 did the Census Bureau begin to record children who worked as a separate category. Indeed, up to that time, most of the concern about children had been directed not to those who worked by rather at the ones who did not, namely young street urchins in the big cities. As the century wore on, however, all this changed, and more and more voices began to be heard decrying the employment of children. Soon this took the form of organized social and political action.

The first local Child Labor Committee was formed in 1901 and a National Child Labor Committee in 1904. Within the decade, 25 state and local committees of this kind existed. Many exposés were published to highlight the abuse and mistreatment of children in the workplace.

Among the many reasons advanced to explain the shift in values were:

1. The success of the Industrial Revolution and the great 1930 Depression.
2. The rapid multiplication of factories and work sites between 1870 and 1930. Augmented incomes and an increased standard of living allowed people to get by without needing the income from their children. Compulsory education laws strengthened this trend.
3. The great influx of new immigrants provided an alternative source of cheap labor.
4. The new technology tended to eliminate the kinds of work that children could do. In particular, such devices as the pneumatic tube, the telephone, and the cash register reduced the utility of runners, messengers, and transporters of small burdens.

It is hard to assess the validity of any of these explanations; all may have contributed in some measure to the change. In any case, in response to the conflicting voices, society found a characteristic compromise. It passed laws forbidding child labor and then failed to enforce them. By 1899, 28 states had some legal protection for children, but the laws were, by and large, easily evaded and ineffective. Thus, children could not work—unless they could get a poverty permit that declared their work to be necessary. In point of fact, a state that regulated child labor was at an economic disadvantage when compared to states that did not (a factor that did not encourage enforcement).

The first attempt at passing a national law was in 1906, when Indiana's Senator Albert J. Beveridge offered such legislation, only to have it roundly defeated. Over the next decade, continued effort of this kind eventually wore away the resistance, and, by 1916, the law was on the books. But not for long; within 2 years the Supreme Court had declared it unconstitutional. A similar sequence was played out in 1919, with a similar outcome in 1922.

In the face of these reverses, a constitutional amendment was proposed and passed by Congress in 1924. A huge national debate ensued, an 34 states rejected the amendment. In 1933 a new effort was initiated and again defeated. Only after the Great Depression had been raging for nearly 10 years was it possible, in 1938, to pass the Fair Labor Standards Act with a section that explicitly banned child labor.

THE NATURE OF THE OPPOSITION

Why was the opposition to such a proposal so strong? To begin with, there were economic reasons. In 1920 over 1 million children (ages 10 to 15) were still at work, particularly on the farms and in the southern mills. Accordingly, the National Association of Manufacturers and the American Farm Bureau Federation were among the principal opponents of the proposed amendments. Quite apart from these powerful groups, a significant sector of the population was concerned about states' rights and viewed the proposal as a federal intrusion on local autonomy.

A deeper issue also troubled the voters: a profound cultural uncertainty about children. Those who endorsed child labor contrasted it to child idleness. Editorial writers inveighed to the effect that "If a child is not trained to useful work before the age of 18, we shall have a nation of paupers and thieves."

Aside from the polemics, in a very real sense, limiting child labor threatened the economic status of many a lower-class family. Many immigrant families in particular took the notion of their children working for granted; how else did one maintain a family? Many parents passionately insisted on their right to have their children work. Thoughtful people saw this attempt to regulate child labor as an effort at governmental intrusion into family life. Children were not so much the issue; it was the sanctity of the family, indeed, the very freedom of a family for self-determination that was at stake.

On the other side of the debate, child labor was regarded as a wicked commercialization of "child life." The first chairman of the National Child Labor Committee declared that "Childhood shall be sacred" (Adler, 1924). Driven by greed, employers were said to seek to turn children into profits. No one, it was argued, should say that it is good for children to work unless he puts his own children into the mill. The parents of working children were accused of extortion and exploitation. It was criminal to expect children to pay for their own upkeep—or for their families to make money out of their labors. This was something that only uncivilized foreign immigrants would do. In effect, a new equation was offered, namely: "If children were useful and produced money, they were not properly loved" (Kett, 1977, p. 72). In short, children should be objects of sentiment only.

The issue did indeed drive people to study more closely just what it is exactly that children need. Voices were raised recognizing the difficulties inherent in each of the extreme positions and asking instead: What level of work is good for children and what level is exploitative and immoral?

The earlier attempts at legislative regulation were not so much concerned with the age of the involved child worker as with the number of hours worked and whether provision had been made to allow time for adequate schooling. One of the great points of contention arose toward the end of the century when attempts were made to set age limits. Gradually the legal age for working was raised from 10, to 12, to 14.

The nature of work was also a battleground, with a special focus on mill, mine, and factory work. Farmwork, on the other hand, was endorsed by all as good for both children and families. Accordingly, it was regularly excluded from proposed legislative efforts to regulate child labor. However, even here there were some serious challenges. During the 1920s, investigators disclosed that on many farms, children as young as 6 were bearing heavy burdens of toil and drudgery and that many were being kept out of school (in defiance of law) to work at their assigned tasks. More than that, some of these children were being sent to work at adjacent farms in order to bring home wages.

Street work (shining shoes, delivering papers, running messages, etc.) also was considered acceptable, until people began to look closely at just what these children were exposed to and introduced various limitations and qualifications—for example, selling papers was bad, but delivering papers was good; acting as a day messenger was good, but doing this at night was bad. These various street occupations were, by and large, the realm of the boys; the home—where the girls worked—was generally considered a proper workplace. Still, when mother was doing factory piecework at home, this concept also was challenged.

One rather peculiar controversy concerned children employed as actors and entertainers. From 1876 onward this issue raged as part of the battle over child labor. Paradoxically, the actors' work was to portray the purely emotional—in contrast to the economically useful—youngster. Thus, children portrayed by these young actors usually were the sacred or the sentimental ones, loved for themselves alone.

As noted, not until 1938 did a law get on the books that was not rejected by the courts. The Fair Labor Standards Act exempted newsboys, actors, and children employed by their own parents (usually in agriculture). In a sense, this defined certain kinds of work as being educational or character-building activities and not really a form of wage earning. Thus was the sentimental child preserved.

In the wake of this development, the allowance system for children gradually came into being. This was established first in middle-class homes and later taken up by working-class families. Now that children had stopped being wage earners, parents began to fund them on a regular basis. Moreover, an ever-expanding array of items was being offered to beguile children into spending. Candy, ice cream, chewing gum, nickel movies, all were available if one had the money. Despite this, allowance money usually was thought of in educational terms, as a training in consumerism.

The New York Children's Aid Society: Child Placement on the Grand Scale

Quite a different set of parameters were invoked to create a social support system for the impoverished child. As mentioned, early in the century almshouses and orphanages took in many waifs—who, in turn, often had to work hard in order to maintain the establishment. Even then, however, at 14 or 15, most youngsters were placed in foster homes as workers. The most famous placement

arrangement was that accomplished by the Reverend Charles Loring Brace and the New York Children's Aid Society; it became a model for similar agencies the country over. Those in charge would collect urchins from the city streets, some with no family and others whose family could not give care to the child but would still have to give permission. Generally poor families that put their children into the hands of the society signed over custody as well. Once all was in order, the children would be loaded aboard a train and head out for the farms of the north-central states. At each small town along the way, they would stop off, and the children would be offered as candidates for work on the farms. Unlike apprenticeship, there was no written contract: It was a simple exchange of work for keep, with the expressed hope that the youngsters would become part of the families that had accepted them. This will be explored in greater detail next.

CHARLES LORING BRACE

It is worth looking at the issues and theories that influenced the Reverend Brace and drove him to undertake the projects for which he is remembered. He represents a transitional figure in the transformation of values from the paternalistic to the maternal outlooks. In considering the role of youth in society, he saw the alienated sector of young people as a distinct and present danger against which society had to take measures in order to protect itself. This would certainly fit the description of a paternalistic defensive strategy. More than that, his solution to the problem—putting children to work cultivating the soil—fits that model as well. However, it is evident from his writing that he hoped too that each child who was taken in would find a place in the hearts and the home of the accepting family. This smacks more of the maternal outlook.

After his program had continued for 25 years, Brace wrote a summary description of his work:

The "dangerous classes" of New York are mainly American born, but the children of Irish and German immigrants. . . . They are far more brutal than the peasantry from whom they descend, and they are much banded together in associations, such as "Dead Rabbit," "Plugugly," and various target companies. . . . They are ready for any offense or crime, however degraded or bloody. New York has never experienced the full effect of the nurture of these youthful ruffians as she will one day. . . . (Brace, 1880/1967, p. 27)

Brace goes on to estimate that out of the million or so inhabitants of New York, the number of homeless and vagrant youths varied between 20,000 and 30,000 (i.e., 2 to 3%).

Among the causes of crime, he cited ignorance (as measured by illiteracy), orphan status, emigration, and want of a trade (lack of training). He bemoaned, among other things "the increasing aversion of American children, whether poor or rich, to learn anything thoroughly," and he found the solution of all these problems to be "the steady demand for juvenile labor in the country districts, and the substantial rewards which await industry there" (p. 38). Curiously enough, he did not give much weight to genetics. He quoted Darwinian doctrine but felt that the tendencies toward criminality and debasement tended to cancel themselves out. They had poor survival value and would self-destruct, whereas the healthier genetic traits would survive. Moreover, the character of American life, its hopefulness, freedom, and ambition, were constant forces making for better adjustment. Even the mobility of American life, otherwise so destructive, was here converted into an asset. "The fact that tenants must forever be 'moving' in New York is a preventive of some of the worst evils among the lower poor. The mill of American life which grinds up so many delicate and fragile things, has its uses, when it is turned on the vicious fragments of the lower strata of society. . . . There is little inherited criminality and pauperism" (Brace, 1880/1967, p. 47).

Crowding, on the other hand, was, in Brace's view, far more significant as a vector pressing the young toward a life of crime. Thus, he quotes an 1865 report that gave the Fourth Ward of New York City "the fearful rate of 290,000 to the square mile." (At that time the most squalid areas of London had 75,816 persons to the square mile.) Since half of the population of New York lived in tenements (where 14 people sometimes crowded into one room), the problem was widespread.

Overcrowding was seen as particularly detrimental to the proper development of the girl child, who "passes almost unconsciously the line of purity at an early age," while the boys "become, as by a law of nature, petty thieves, pickpockets, street rovers, beggars and burglars" (Brace, 1880/1967, p. 55).

For Brace, the cure for all these social maladies was self-evident: "The best of all Asylums for the outcast child, is the *farmer's home.*"

In order to get the children into these homes, a number of rural areas would be designated, and circulars and advance notices sent out to the local newspapers and weeklies. In effect, the message would be: Boys and girls looking for homes and ready to work. Would anyone want to add someone like that to their family? Characteristically, a flood of responses would pour in. Initially, Brace and his group would try to answer each one individually, but that proved impracticable. An alternative method developed: They would write to a given farming community telling of their mission and announcing the time of their arrival. A company of boys was organized, cleaned, clothed, and dispatched by train to the target station. There a dense crowd would have gathered awaiting the new arrivals. The children were put up for the night among the various families present. The following day, at a public meeting in church or the town hall, a committee of leading citizens would be formed, and the representative of the New York Children's Aid Society would tell about the mission and recount some of the children's background. People then would be invited to apply for individual youngsters. All sorts of people would come forward, childless couples seeking to adopt, compassionate families touched by the sight of homeless youths, and farmers needing extra hands to work their land. There would be some haggling and discussion within the committee, and, at length, all the children would be assigned.

On follow-up, Brace estimated that some 2% of the younger children and 4% of those over 15 failed to work out. Over time, the children were scattered all over the East and Midwest; among others, Pennsylvania, Ohio, Indiana, and Illinois are mentioned as sites of placement. By 1880 Brace estimated that some 20,000 to 24,000 children had thus been given homes.

Adolescence in the Nineteenth Century

In demarcating the experience of adolescents during the 19th and early 20th centuries, several critical transitional epochs acted to shape the prospects and lifestyle of youths of that time. According to Kett (1977), the first of these began during the interval between 1780 and 1840, when:

1. Powerful forces uprooted youth from the farming environment that had been the characteristic center of population for 18th-century America.
2. There was an ensuing repositioning of youths in the big cities that were springing up all over the country.
3. Much of the lure that drew these newcomers were the new educational, occupational, and economic opportunities offered within the hectic metropolitan environments.
4. At the same time great dangers awaited youths arising from the increasing disorderliness, violence, and entrapments that these settings thrust upon the unwary or the ill-prepared.

A second great transition transpired between 1880 and 1900. This was the beginning of a radical differentiation of economic opportunities between the better-prepared middle-class youth and the often newly arrived lower-class young.

As the 19th century drew to a close, a third transition took place between 1890 and 1920. As the city populations grew, and more and more troubled youths became manifest presences, a host of reformers, psychologists, educators, counselors, and youth workers began to shape the concept of adolescence. The earlier notion, that these young troublemakers were rash, heedless, thoughtless, and impulsive, gave way to a new image. They were now regarded as victims, vulnerable, passive, and awkward, as much sinned against as sinning. One of the milestones in this new definition of youth was the 1904 publication of *Adolescence* by G. Stanley Hall. Hall saw the teen years as a unique stage in the life cycle, different from the prior period of childhood and not yet coextensive with the forthcoming era of adulthood. This adolescent phase was marked by a special kind of aesthetic sensibility and inner turmoil, and, in turn, needed separate understanding and address. Hall's work had a powerful influence in fostering and legitimizing the establishment of separate institutions that segregated teenagers from contact with troubled adults. Overall, the concept of adolescence that emerged was conditioned by the social forces of the era and reflected the demographic and industrial conditions of the late 19th and early 20th centuries. Let us look at these in greater detail.

DEMOGRAPHICS OF ADOLESCENCE

In the early 19th century, the life span was much briefer than today. It did not permit many children to know their parents as adults. In fact, only about 20% of parents survived to see their children's majority, and there were many orphans. In the early decades of the century, such parentless youngsters typically were taken in by some surviving relative. One result of this demographic reality was a constant eddying of population in search of cheaper housing and better jobs.

In the early 1800s, infancy was a time of female dominance. Most families lived on farms, and the child was cared for by mother, older sister, or some female relative who had come to live with the family. Shortly after children began to walk, however, they were assigned chores, and soon they were required to engage in serious and productive farm labor. When children attained school age, there would be farm work full time during the summer and schooling during the winter.

Biologic differences between early 19th-century and later 20th-century youths were present as well. Around 1800, puberty came later than it does at present; for boys it was usually at about 16, and for girls a year earlier. Males did not attain their final height until about 25.

EARLY 19TH-CENTURY EVANGELICAL MOVEMENT: THE SECOND GREAT AWAKENING

A significant evangelical youth movement took place during this same early 19th century period. Between 1790 and 1840 there arose what came to be called the Second Great Awakening. It included commitment to ideology, scorn for worldly goods, willingness to sacrifice for a cause, and involvement in moral movements with political overtones (such as temperance and abolition). Such a development might well have been an initial reaction to the inroads of the Industrial Revolution. In effect, as it was viewed at the time, the power of secular man, the inventor of tools and the manipulator of nature, was being matched against that of the divine Creator. Those who held more traditional religious views lashed back at the new wave of rational empiricism. A massive outpouring of religious enthusiasm swept one section of the nation after another, and there was a great deal of religious activism. Many people underwent religious conversion, and many turned to missionary work. Christian motherhood became an important idea, and, within that context, a great deal was published about child rearing. (For example, the dates at which relevant magazines came into being give some hint of the associated ferment. In particular, *Mother's Magazine* was founded in 1832, *Parent's Magazine* in 1840, and *Mother's Assistant* in 1841.) Mothers' groups met to discuss how to apply evangelical principles to child rearing. Indeed, "family ideology in the 19th century was distinctive not just for its fervor but for the preeminent position it gave to motherhood" (Kett, 1977, p. 79). This reached its apogee when the National Congress of Mothers was established in 1897. Two thousand people attended the opening meeting where President Theodore Roosevelt gave an address. By 1920 it had 190,000 members in 36 states.

Religious conversion was a common means of firming up identity. If a youth spoke before the congregation, it meant entry into adulthood. After 1840, however, the focus on conversion as such dwindled, and interest shifted to direct social and political activism. This was not a surprising development in a country riven by disputes about slavery and building up toward the Civil War.

SOCIAL STRUCTURES FOR YOUTHS DURING THE NINETEENTH CENTURY

It is noteworthy that in 1800, the median age of the population was 16 (Kett, 1977, p. 36). With so many young about and with such uncertain family ties, it is not surprising that a great many social organizations appeared geared to the needs of this population. In particular, a host of diverse associations for youths came into being, including various church groups and town-organized voluntary military companies that served at once as militia, social clubs, and welcoming institutions. Many lower-class youths belonged to such bodies, and the meetings were colored by a good deal of drinking and fighting. Younger children were not supposed to belong, but the lower age limits were seldom enforced, and many members were 13 or 14 years old.

However, the variety of opportunities to join and mingle with peers was much more extensive. There were sites of social exchange calculated to attract the more intellectual youngsters; they had a self-instructional character and often called themselves lyceums. Then there were temperance societies, debating groups, and mechanics' associations; there were apprentice associations and, of rather special importance, volunteer fire companies. In the cities where many of these youths migrated, there were literary clubs for boys and girls and such arrangements as the Young Men's Christian Association (YMCA; another import from England).

Volunteer Fire Companies: Volunteer fire departments exemplified youth culture of positive character. Regular fire companies had an associated group of "volunteer aides" with their own rules and organization; these were populated chiefly by youths under 18. In general, fire departments were social fraternities as well as civic agencies. On the way to a fire, the youngest boys often rioted or fought with members of other companies—essentially gang fights—each seeking to be the group that would collect the insurance bonus for fighting the fire.

By the mid 1800s the demand arose for strictly professional firefighters; once this became the rule, the boys were the first to go.

Entertainment: The new urban population demanded entertainment, which led to the formation of both professional and amateur theatrical companies. Many young people between 13 and 25 became involved.

Young ladies could date at about 16. There was in particular much socializing among cousins. (Families were very large and in some towns everyone was related at some level.) There were many "bees": logging bees, quilting bees, and apple bees, which usually ended in supper and dancing.

For added entertainment, there was much roving about. The buggy was important, and the hayride. Certain practices ritualized at school created a great deal of excitement and activity. Mock commencements would be staged by freshmen; unpopular teachers who refused to grant desired holidays would be "turned out." In western states there might be "shooting up the town" on holidays. Dances, parties, and sleigh rides were always popular.

Street life was a critical part of the cities' milieu. In addition to their other involvements with their society, street gangs were particularly active on election day as errand-bearers, runners, and strong-arm squads. A sort of street culture developed with its own rules and values: There was an admiration for physical prowess, a high valuation was set on peer loyalty, and an intense antipathy felt and expressed toward the young of other social or ethnic groups. (This sort of outlook was to be found among the college students as well.) As a true middle class emerged, this value cluster became identified as the lower-class style.

ECONOMIC GROWTH: WHAT IT MEANT
TO MOVE TO THE CITY

The opening of the 19th century was dominated by the war with England. As the century advanced and the cities grew, the maritime ports in particular felt the enormous impact of expanded trade; they became more and more wealthy, and they experienced an insatiable need for all kinds of tradesmen, support staff, operating personnel, and technicians for the now rapidly growing industries. Opportunities for advancement were both rich and numerous, and word of great successes got back to the countryside.

On the farms of the United States, the young saw only drudgery and a poor future; the image of the city was one filled with glitter and possibility; and they migrated to the cities by the thousands. Kett (1977) observes that the Calvinist notion of being "called" changed its meaning in the first half of the 19th century, acquiring connotations of occupational mobility. For young men thus uprooted, many books were published as guides to behavior—and sold extraordinarily well. Youth came to be defined as that group of young people between 15 and 25 who had left home for the city on a "returnless voyage." Nor was this state of mind confined by gender; girls were as likely to leave home for the city as were young men, and often did so at an earlier age (15 to 19). These young women became schoolteachers, worked in stores, or got jobs as factory girls.

Obviously no single fate awaited these youngsters. By and large, however, moving to the city was not simply a plunge into the unknown. Many young people stayed with relatives, friends of the family, or in boarding houses run by former members of their towns. For those who truly had no contacts, settings such as the YMCA gave them an initial connectedness in the new milieu. Once employed, a goodly percentage of these ex-ruralites entered the middle class by finding opportunities in crafts, municipal jobs, industry, commerce, transportation, or the professions. The late migrators (who made their journey to the city after turning 30) were more likely to be professionals who were transferring the site of their activity to a wider stage. As transportation was difficult, after someone had left home for a "start in life," visiting was rare. Because these young urban dwellers could no longer depend upon the advice and mentoring of their families, conduct manuals came into vogue.

BOOKS OF ADVICE FOR ADOLESCENTS

Those who wrote advice for youths did not counsel return to the farm or early marriage. Instead they spoke for conserving youthful energy. One needed to possess a strenuous will and to replace tentativeness with a sturdy decisive approach. "Internal, invincible determination" was the key. This grew readily from the message of revivalism; radical individualism was the underlying threat that bound these approaches together. The point was to carry the young past the gap between the traditional values of their rearing and the new conditions they faced. Values such as humility gave way to ambition and assertiveness as the means by which to make one's way. On the other hand, youths were advised to forgo self-indulgence in order to further their commitment to achievement.

MORAL EDUCATION

Prior to 1840, education had been largely sporadic, casual, and sometimes chaotic. Now, however, a more planned academic environment emerged. In part, this was occasioned by the need of industry and commerce for businesslike efficiency. The new school settings became ever more regulated; this affected the younger cohort of children (7 to 13) more immediately and directly. England had faced this issue; there moral supervision and earnest solicitude were invoked in order to make schools into nurseries of Christian character. The crux of the educational effort was to get children to internalize moral restraints as a way of building character. This led to the principle of controlling a child's total environment. As part of this effort, the family milieu was critical, and parents were encouraged to induce children to read moral tales that would illustrate the good and bad choices one might make.

In the United States, moral tales were embodied in Sunday school novels. The family came to be regarded as a rearing force, with the noted shift from male dominance of households to the role of women as the primary custodians of children's moral development.

In many ways, this was a reaction to the impact of the city environment. The notion of Christian nurture represented an effort by the family to define an inner island of security and tranquility and then to protect it from the storm outside. Within the city, once family members stepped across the threshold of home, they faced abrasive individualism, relentless competitiveness, wild business fluctuations, problematic immigrants, and chaotic streets. Given all that, the challenge was to create a domestic environment that would guarantee the moral development of the child. Even colleges began to shift responsibility for behavioral control to the parents by sending home regular report cards. In the homes, the sense of child as father to the man became an article of faith.

SUNDAY SCHOOL

As noted, Sunday school first emerged in England and came to the United States in 1786. This form of education was conducted both by lay people and by clergy; originally the classes were mostly for the poor. In the 1820s there was an effort to convert children en masse and involved not only street waifs but children in general. With this, the role of the clergy expanded, and the focus shifted from the poor (who often did not relish this instruction as highly as one would have wished) to the middle-class children (who would, after all, be the future parishioners). The goal of Sunday school was the gradual conversion of the child under the impact of Christian nurture. The controlled environment of the right-thinking family would be the agency of moral growth. This fit in well with the needs of the times. After 1840, Sunday school teaching emphasized the value of business efficiency. There was no room left for sowing wild oats or for introspective brooding about the self. The cardinal virtues now were steadiness, a good name, good moral standing, and at least an outward appearance of respectability.

Educating the Masses

Meanwhile, the problem of educating the large number of children and youths was a pressing concern everywhere. Among the authorities who now emerged were Horace Mann, Henry Barnard, and Calvin Stowe. Using Prussian and Swiss models, they began to demonstrate how the creation of a total environment within a boarding school setting could further learning. Bancroft's North Hill School in Northampton, Massachusetts, became a model for boarding schools such as Groton.

These reformers wanted school to be a protective place that would both guard children from city iniquities and educate them. The school year was advanced from weeks, to months, to most of the year. Nonattendance was defined as deviant; after 1850, as public schools picked up this philosophy, compulsory education laws were enacted and, in a few areas, school absence was declared to be illegal. Initially, however, in most areas these laws were seldom, or only slackly, enforced. Thus, by 1860, Massachusetts was responding to chronic truants by incarcerating them in reform schools.

Graded school texts were introduced. Female teachers were to be present in winter as well as summer. Better training for teachers became accepted practice. Schools began to be classified by age and attainment.

There had been early attempts to start children in school at 4 or 5, but medical opinion soon put a stop to that. In 1832 Amariah Brigham published *Remarks on the Influence of Mental Cultivation upon Health*. In it he defined precocity as pathological; too much education too early would surely lead to insanity.

The notion took root that female teachers were more appropriate for younger children, while the male teachers would address themselves to the older high school students. Educational reformers wanted all children to attend public schools, and they sought to elevate the moral tone of such settings in order to bring in the middle class. As for lower-class students, education for them was regarded as a cheap form of policing.

Thus, the new ideology was the cultivation of character by family and school. Unfortunately, this did not work out very well for the older boys; unless college bound, they tended to drop out before finishing their high school training. The schools responded by pushing learning into the youngsters through the earlier grades as rapidly as possible, so that by 14, if they did drop out, they would at least have the rudiments and perhaps a little more. For these "large boys," a similar dropout rate was noted in the Sunday schools.

DELINQUENCY: THE HOUSE OF REFUGE AND THE REFORM SCHOOL

By the mid-1700s, the long-established practice of apprenticeship was already falling off. The new immigrants and the practice of slavery took up the positions formerly filled by untutored and unskilled youths. At the same time, a host of dependent children emerged who required public care.

This led to the spread of workhouses and almshouses; within the precincts of these settings, paupers, the insane, and the aged all shared common space with institutionalized children.

Prisons were opened. In New York, the first prison was opened in 1796. This in turn was followed by the establishment of asylums. By 1816 New York State had built one at the New York Hospital.

Since most of the settings where children were kept, including the prisons, were evidently corruptive of children, Houses of Refuge were developed in the mid-1820s, the first being the New York House of Refuge, which opened in 1825. The children they harbored were for the most part status offenders. It was soon evident, however, that they were not achieving their objectives, and soon they were supplanted by agencies with a very different philosophy. The Houses of Refuge had been designed to provide placement and care for the abandoned street waifs who survived by pilfering and a catch-as-catch-can existence. By the mid-1850s, immigrant children were almost three-quarters of the residents of the New York House of Refuge, two-thirds of the Philadelphia House, and more than one-half of the Cincinnati House. The quality of care was terrible, and in relatively short order, the Houses of Refuge were replaced by reformatories and industrial schools.

As cities grew, a more obdurate and hardened youth offender became common; mere refuge was no longer the issue, and the perceived need was to bring about reform. Hence, in the 1840s and 1850s, a different set of agencies were established to accomplish such reform. The first was the Massachusetts State Reform School for Boys founded in Westborough in 1847. Seven years later, in Lancaster, Massachusetts, the first reform school for girls came into being. This girls' school was modeled after the recently created European models in Germany and France. In Germany, Johann H. Wichern had founded the Rauhe House. Wichern felt that street children needed a homelike atmosphere to compensate for what had been lacking in their formative years. Therefore, albeit a congregate setting, a house mother was provided (and, perhaps, a house father) to give the youngsters care. Unfortunately, in the United States, cities were growing so rapidly that from the time the reform schools opened, they were inundated with difficult children and teenagers. These agencies became dumping grounds for the most troublesome youths, and in short order they became brutalized and regimented. The language that defined them was lofty and spoke of nurture and reform; in fact, what ensued was the creation of crowded prisons for the young.

THE ROLE OF WORK: APPRENTICESHIP AND TRAINING

As mentioned, early in the 19th century, the chief form of work for a young man was agriculture and crafts. Manufacturing was just beginning, and that in only a few industries. For the beginner who wanted to learn a craft, an apprenticeship was the primary site for training. The apprenticeship system involved a journeyman establishing his own shop and engaging his own apprentices to help him do job work. Sometimes the journeyman might work within the confines of an existing factory and train his apprentices there.

By 1870 and thereafter, however, high-speed industry was developing. The large factories worked in quite a different way and effectively put an end to the apprenticeship system. These new industries divided the tasks of production into single units for which they hired poorly paid youths rather than more expensive journeymen; these young employees would achieve their maximum income by age 25, and their earnings would trend downward from there.

Within other parts of the economy, service jobs were in ever-growing demand. There was a need for secretaries, salespeople, bookkeepers, bankers, accountants, clerks, telegraphers, and others with similar skills. These positions, however, were attained largely by middle-class youths—youngsters who had continued in school until age 16 instead of dropping out at 14, as their poorer cousins did. Immigrants eagerly snapped up many of the menial and poorer paid factory jobs.

Changes in Education

Thus, by the latter decades of the 19th century, the extent of one's education was beginning to have a powerful impact on one's economic prospects. The high school, college, and professional school system replaced apprenticeship training as the royal road to success; the diploma became the new ticket of entry. Professional schools expanded as never before: students thronged into law, medicine, dentistry, veterinary science, and pharmacy.

The number of professional schools established between 1876 and 1900 was double that which came into being from 1851 to 1875. By 1900 engineering was becoming a profession. The only schooling to fall off in numbers was the training in theology. At the start of the 19th century, a clerical career had been one of the leading, if not the leading, profession. Now, in the face of the secular revolution of the times, the count of applicants for divinity training fell off sharply.

THE HIGH SCHOOL

At first the high schools were the principal route to professional schools. By 1850 these high schools had departed far from the older academies, whose subject matter was tied to the workplace. High schools had a systematic, formally set curriculum. Hence, attending and completing high school meant a considerably greater delay for entry into the workforce. Among other things, this transformation meant a shift in the character of a cultural ideal. Thus, early in the century, for most young people, shop training and learning through doing were the models for perfecting one's skills and achieving respect. As the century advanced, it was book learning, the mastery of formal courses of study and the acquisition of degrees, that attained preeminence.

TRANSFORMATION OF MEDICAL TRAINING

This transformation was true for medicine as well. In the 1820s and 1830s, there was a proliferation of medical schools. A would-be physician would attend a session at such a school, or perhaps work for a time as apprentice to a physician, and then, having mastered the rudiments, would go out and practice for a while for on-the-job learning. Soon he would return to take another course at the medical school, at which point the M.D. degree would be awarded. As the decades went on, this became more and more formalized, but it was not until the 1890s that a consecutive 4-year course was required in order to get the degree and the right to practice.

The two themes, learning through doing vs. formal academic training, continued to play a role in American life, values, and educational practices thereafter. These resonated in many ways with other cultural issues: town vs. gown, men of action vs. absentminded professors, those with horse sense vs. effete intellectuals, blue collar vs. white collar, intellectual hauteur vs. yeoman pride, and

so on. In a more removed but perhaps no less vital a fashion, it may well have continued to express the gender theme, namely: Men teach by doing, women by instructing. A man may throw a child into the water to have him learn to swim; a woman is likely to support the child's midriff while telling him to paddle and kick.

Demographics: Age of Population

Along with the tremendous fall in birth rate, an accompanying demographic change of the time was a shift in the average age of the population, from a plurality of people 20 to 29 years of age to a population whose bulk was 30 to 39 years old. Indeed, between 1840 and 1900 the percentage of the population aged 45 to 64 nearly doubled. For youths, this had several implications. For one thing, more and more young people would go through adolescence with their parents alive and available. However, it also meant that when they went out into the job market, there were more and more people in the way of rapid advancement; they had to wait longer and compete harder in order to get ahead. Another factor that acted to truncate hope and close off possibilities was the closing of the American frontier. Since the country was founded, there had always been an open door in the West, beckoning the disaffected young person with limitless land and unfettered freedom. This had been part of the national psyche. In the post–Civil War years, that too gradually disappeared. All these, coupled with the ever-increasing demand for longer courses of study, led to a feeling of narrowing of opportunity for the late 19th-century young man or woman. Some of the values that emerged at the time (as expressed in the books of advice and manuals of instruction to youths) included ascetic self-discipline, the importance for prolonging the period of preparation for adulthood, the necessity of husbanding one's vital energy during one's early years, and an esteem for physical strength.

Perhaps as one of the aftershocks of the Civil War, physical culture was esteemed as essential to character building. Strength was considered of primary survival value for youths who wanted to get ahead. Physical fitness became almost an obsession. Country life and a farm background were idealized as sources both of moral innocence and sturdy body building—and hence for the development of a strong character. During the last 2 decades of the century, manual training offered as part of schooling was considered to be a way of inculcating city children with country virtues; this became something of a movement during those years.

The Direct Precursors of Child and Adolescent Psychiatry

We turn now to those events that more immediately gave rise to the emergence of child and adolescent psychiatry as a separate discipline. Here we must follow three somewhat distinct lines of historical development. They arose in different times and places but came eventually to intersect—and at their juncture, the new discipline came into being. The first such line is embodied in the cluster of professional disciplines that concerned themselves with child mental health. This involves the story of psychiatry itself as it took organizational form on the American scene. It is, briefly, the account of the emergence of the American Psychiatric Association and the subsequent extension of the ideas of psychiatrists to embrace the needs of children. It touches as well on the fields of pediatrics, psychology, and social work.

The second is the work of the Child Savers and tells how the abolitionist and reform movements of the mid-19th century produced the extraordinary people and events that brought the first juvenile court and then the first child psychiatric clinic into being. The third is the account of the mental hygiene movement. It begins with the life story of an extraordinary man whose mental illness begot a passion for preventing such suffering in others and whose life course brought mental hygiene out of the realm of the theoretical and the desirable and into the province of practice and method.

The First Line of Development: The Emerging Disciplines

Early English law recognized two categories of mental disturbance, idiots, whose defect was present from birth on and would persist throughout the lifetime, and lunatics, whose disturbances had

their onset later in life and promised some possibility of recovery.

As the communal character of feudal society gave way to the wage system, it forced families to differentiate out of the community matrix and to rely on their own resources. The Elizabethan Poor Laws of 1601 defined the family as the primary caretaker of its members; when the family could not care for its own, the community would then step in. The Puritans saw humans as in need of "stern molding of social standards in order to produce a good society" (Blum et al., 1981). This in turn required that family, church, and community work together and cooperate in the raising of children. In time, law also came to play a part in this undertaking, especially for difficult or unusual cases.

The general expectation was that it was the family's responsibility to teach the child to read, write, and acquire a trade. According to statute, disobedient, idle, or stubborn children could be harshly punished—by death; in fact, however, there is no record of such a punishment ever being meted out. The usual recourse was for such a troublesome child to be boarded out, or indentured as an apprentice for some extended period. Under the law, there came into being a roughly developmental approach to the responsibility of children. Below age 7, no criminal responsibility could be assigned. From 7 to 14 a child could be evaluated by a jury for his or her ability to tell right from wrong—and could even be sentenced to death. Above 14, adult law applied.

The usual punishments of the time were stocks, pillories, or some other form of corporal punishment or the practice of indenturing children. Certain deviants could be sent to one of the few workhouses or almshouses in existence.

FOUNDING OF THE AMERICAN PSYCHIATRIC ASSOCIATION

Thirteen psychiatrists established the organization that eventually would give rise to the American Psychiatric Association (Bernstein 1994). Some rather unexpected opinions emerge from their expressed views. For example, in 1832, Dr. A. Brigham published a work entitled: *Remarks on the Influence of Mental Cultivation and Mental Excitement upon Health.* In the introduction to the third (1845) edition, he says: "The object of this work is to awaken public attention to the importance of making some modification in the method of educating children, which prevails in the present day. It is intended to show the necessity of giving more attention to the health and growth of the body, and less to the cultivations of the mind, especially in early life, than is now given."

He goes on to demonstrate by numerous case examples that the Industrial Revolution had given rise to the idea that knowledge is power. Unfortunately, as he saw it, this had been overdone; when parents believed that knowledge alone is power, they would accordingly try to stuff the heads of their children with excessive learning. He pleaded:

I beseech parents, therefore, to pause before they attempt to make prodigies of their own children. Though they may not destroy them by the measures they adopt to effect this purpose, yet they will surely enfeeble their bodies, and greatly dispose them to nervous affections. Early mental excitement will serve only to bring forth beautiful but premature flowers, which are destined soon to wither away without producing fruit. (quoted in Deutsch, 1944, p. 327)

It is worth noting that Brigham was the founder and first editor of the *American Journal of Insanity* in 1844. His book was considered the first book on child guidance; it was also the most popular American work on mind-body relationships (later to be called psychosomatic medicine and, still later, holistic medicine) in the first half of the 19th century.

The founding of the American Psychiatric Association came about in this way (Overholser, 1944). Among the many changes brought about by the Industrial Revolution was an increasing awareness of the mental health problems in society. It was commonly believed that many of these problems were due to the mounting complexity of both city life and professional career requirements. Dorothea Dix had led a movement to make the public and professionals more conscious of what was going on in the many care settings for the mentally ill. She had begun her work in 1841, made her first great report to the Massachusetts legislature in 1843, and initiated a process of exposés and increasing public awareness that went on until 1861. At the time, there were relatively few psychiatric hospitals; most of the insane were kept in almshouses, poorhouses, or prisons under squalid and dehumanizing conditions. One consequence of Dix's work was the establishment of more mental hospitals. Another, however, was a general impression that mental illness was spreading rapidly.

It is hard to say what impact this had on psychiatrists who worked in mental institutions. In October 1844 a group of 13 physicians met at the Jones Hotel in Philadelphia and formed as Association of Medical Superintendents of American Institutions for the Insane—4 years before the American Medical Association was founded.

It is noteworthy that as this association of state hospital superintendents began to achieve a certain recognition and to establish itself as a significant presence, it became the target of a focused attack from the neurological profession. Since the association had been established as a highly exclusive club, with membership limited to hospital superintendents, neurologists were excluded. In response, the superintendents opened up their ranks to all institutional psychiatrists and, in 1892, changed the name of their organization to the American Medico-Psychological Association. Needless to say, with this restriction removed, their numbers augmented rapidly. At the outset, however, few of the members had any interest in disturbed children, and work in that realm awaited the opening of the 20th century. Meanwhile, many other forces were operating that helped pave the way for the appearance of child psychiatry.

ADOLF MEYER

As the 19th century drew to a close, the major centers for training and research in medicine in general, and for psychiatry in particular, were still in Europe. It is therefore not surprising that one of the great bridging figures between child and adult psychiatry was a European. Adolf Meyer was a Swiss national, and his work was of incalculable influence on the progress of American psychiatry (Shaw, 1983). Indeed, up to World War II, his methods and values were the dominant force in shaping the direction and style of the discipline in the United States.

Adolf Meyer was one of the many immigrants to the United States during the 19th century. And, like so many of that group, he made enormous contributions to the country he had chosen. Born in Niederwenungen, Switzerland, on September 13, 1866, he went to medical school in Zurich and graduated in 1892. In the course of his studies, he traveled about Europe and wrote his doctoral thesis on the reptilian brain. He sought an academic appointment but was unsuccessful, whereupon he left Europe to come to the United States.

In his adopted homeland he taught neurology at the University of Chicago. He became friends with John Dewey, came under the influence of William James, and associated with the Hull House group. Three years after he began his work, he was offered a post as neuropathologist at the Eastern Hospital for the Insane at Kankakee, Illinois. Shortly after he had left Europe, his mother had gone into a 3-year-long deep depression. His concern for his mother had much to do with kindling his interest in psychiatry and in studying the ways in which a concatenation of life events brought mental illness into being. Another factor that influenced his thinking was the lack of any meaningful connection between what he saw in the brain anatomy of the state hospital inmates and what he observed in their behavior and in the nature of their illnesses.

Meyer was living and working at a time when the theories of transmission of mental illness and of brain degeneration were in the ascendent. However, his own observations drove him to study the life experiences of his patients. This led to ever more emphasis on early experience; soon he was inquiring into his patients' childhood and looking for connections between early occurrences and later symptoms.

Later, Meyer became a professor of psychiatry at Cornell University and began to publish a series of papers that would set American psychiatry on a new path. He had observed characteristic behavioral patterns that arose when people of different constitutional styles encountered stressful life experiences. He called these "reaction patterns," and maintained a profound belief that it was precisely such "reactions" that dominated both normal behavior and psychopathology. In particular, such response patterns began in childhood; over time, diverse patterns of reaction elaborated from the initial core formations, and these, then, would persist the lifetime through. This idea lent coherence to the study of human behavior, placed its roots in childhood, and offered a site for both intervention (make people aware of the patterns and work on changing them) and prevention (address the way these patterns formed in childhood and seek modes of child rearing that would lessen the likelihood of developing adverse or symptomatic reactions).

This idea had a profound effect on diagnosis as well. The different psychiatric syndromes were not diseases or degenerations; instead they represented specific reaction patterns. These reactions had become habitual, and the habits thus established constituted the illness. The habits could deteriorate, in which case such progressive conditions as dementia praecox could appear. Thus, such trends as suspiciousness, hypochondriasis, complaining, or withdrawal into passivity were habitual reaction patterns that could become exaggerated to the point of illness.

When Sigmund Freud, Carl Jung, and Alfred Adler visited the United States in 1909, Meyer presented a paper that congratulated them on unraveling some of the symbolic meanings of dementia praecox but that also challenged Jung's "toxic" theory as too organic. Meyer would here seem to betray a strong antiorganic bias. However, Lauretta Bender later reported that Meyer once told her: "If I tell them [the students] there is an organic contribution, they will give up any hope of treating schizophrenia" (Shaw, 1983, p. 9).

In fact, Meyer always insisted on a balanced view of human behavior. Somatic, psychological, and social data all had to be weighed and incorporated into the picture of the disorder. It was this eclectic approach that his students disseminated and that became the hallmark of American psychiatric thinking. Meyer's conceptual framework was called psychobiology; it sought to integrate mind and body, past and present, behavior and personality, as well as biography and psychopathology. It led to an emphasis on development, on the assumption that each disturbance had a unique pattern with a coherent origin and discernible progression.

As early as 1895, Meyer was lecturing on the importance of early childhood experience and talking about how environmental factors could affect the child even in the preschool years (Shaw, 1983). Ultimately his work created the climate within which psychoanalysis took root and flowered so abundantly during subsequent decades.

Another major dimension of Meyerian thought was the role of adaptation. Pathology consisted of "adaptations that are not working well" (quoted in Shaw, 1983, p. 14). Thus, mental disorders were a set of unfortunate habits that had developed as maladaptive reactions to stress. The quality and nature of ongoing interactions gave psychopathology its overt character. Hence, important were not only development and habitual response patterns but the nature of environmental stress as well. Context was critical, so that in studying a child, one had simultaneously to work with home and family life.

Therapy, then, consisted in large part of reconstruction, of getting the patient to become aware of habitual patterns of reaction and interaction, so that an attempt could be made to modify these patterns. Where environmental change was feasible, that was included as well.

Several elements were not embraced by this approach. Thus, no stages of development were described, the notion of unconscious factors in mental life were not accepted—Meyer told Lauretta Bender: "I don't believe in psychoanalysis; it's based on the unconscious, and I don't have one" (quoted in Shaw, 1983, p. 14)—and transference was not referred to. Nonetheless, Meyer welcomed the contribution of psychoanalysis and was a charter member of the American Psychoanalytic Association when it was organized.

In 1904, in keeping with Meyer's views on the importance of family and community, his wife, Mary Potter Brooks, began making visits to the homes of her husband's hospitalized patients. She obtained background and developmental histories as well as a picture of what the environment would be like when the patient returned home. Eventually her contribution was considered indispensable, and she has been called the first psychiatric social worker.

Meyer was active in many spheres of American life; he was central in bringing psychiatry into the framework of American medicine. He was an active and creative figure in the mental hygiene movement, brought the psychiatry ward into the sphere of medical training, had psychology made part of the medical curriculum, and recommended board certification for psychiatrists. In essence, he legitimated psychiatry as a true medical discipline to which all medical students should be exposed.

At the time, the number of mentally ill in the country was estimated at 17,457 (about 1 for every 1,000 in the population). Of these, some 2,561 were in institutions; the rest resided in their homes, in prisons, or in poorhouses. About 20 institutions existed in the then 21 states (plus the District of Columbia). For the most part these settings were not large; the most populous, in Worcester, Massachusetts, housed 255 patients. Diagnostically the major emphasis fell on phrenology and brain disease. Theories of etiology tended to highlight masturbation, smoking, and alcohol. Moral treatment excited a certain interest but was not much practiced. But even at this early time there were voices speaking to an intuitive but nonetheless sensitive and accurate recognition of the origins of mental illness.

By the end of the 19th century, social work was a well-established profession, psychology had achieved increasing definition as a scientific discipline, and adult psychiatry was attaining more recognition within the province of medicine.

PSYCHOLOGY

During the latter part of the 19th century, psychology was maturing as a discipline. In particular, psychologists began to devote themselves to the study and management of mentally retarded individuals. An initial wave of optimism had been generated by the work of Philippe Pinel; as this had subsided, it was replaced by a relatively despairing pessimism. At that juncture, many physicians withdrew from the field, and the psychologists became the chief professionals to concern themselves with this population. In 1896 Lightner Witmer proposed the opening of "a psychological clinic supplemented by a training school in the nature of a hospital school for the treatment of all classes of children suffering from retardation or physical defects interfering with school progress." The clinic actually opened the following year 1897, and Witmer designated what he did there as "clinical psychology" (T. V. Moore, 1944).

In France, the advancing work on establishing a system for free public education had run full tilt into the fact that not all students were able to make equal use of schooling. Some way had to be found to distinguish on a fair and objective basis those students who should continue in public school from those who needed a different form of training. A commission had been established to study "Measures to Be Taken Showing the Benefits of Instruction for Defective Children." One member of the commission, Alfred Binet, was a well-known psychologist. Accordingly he was asked to come up with some means for making the necessary determinations. He associated himself with a psychiatrist, Theodore Simon, and, by 1905, they had devised a series of tasks to measure a quantitative number of abilities. The collective score was then regarded as a precise measure of intelligence (Binet & Simon, 1905).

This instrument was in many ways imperfect; nonetheless, it was the first standard psychological test and stands as a great milestone in behavioral science. It came quickly to the attention of American scholars. In New Jersey, a new Department of Research had been established at the Vineland State Training School (a state school for retarded people). Its first director was a psychologist named Earnest Goddard. In 1908 he visited Europe and encountered the Binet-Simon test. It struck him as a rather unlikely sort of attempt, but he took it home and tried it out on a number of his cases. *Mirabile dictu,* it worked, consistently and objectively. He was impressed and, forthwith, shared his new knowledge with his American colleagues. It was taken up eagerly, and a whole new dimension of evaluative competence was added to the armamentarium of mental health practitioners.

In 1908, when William Healy, the founder of the first child psychiatric clinic, traveled about the country looking for advice about his proposed new program, the only places he found anything approaching "a well-rounded study of a young human individual were Witmer's clinic in Philadelphia and Goddard's and Johnston's work at Vineland" (Wagner, 1984).

The second psychological clinic at a university was established by Carl Emil Seashore in 1910; by 1914 there were 19 such clinics in universities and medical schools across the United States. Twenty years later there were 755.

ADVANCES IN PEDIATRICS

At the time, pediatrics was a relatively new medical specialty. It had its beginnings in Europe in the 18th century and only gradually took hold in the United States. Certainly its greatest early figure was Abraham Jacobi (Abt-Garrison, 1965). He was born in 1830 and grew up to practice pediatrics in Westphalia. In the course of growing up, he was imprisoned for 2 years for lèse-majesté. In 1853 he escaped and fled to America. Four years after his arrival, he was lecturing in pediatrics at the College of Physicians and Surgeons of New York. In 1860 he was appointed to the first special chair of diseases of children in that college. He remained there for 4 years; in 1865 he moved to a similar clinical chair at the University of New York. Subsequently he became clinical professor of pediatrics at the Medical Department of Columbia College, a post he held for the next 9 years. Overall, he taught pediatrics in New York City for 42 years—and was almost the only such teacher of his epoch. He is credited with being the first practitioner in the United States ever to do bedside teaching; eventually this practice was taken up by practitioners of internal medicine. He gained immense respect for his capacity as a physician/teacher and did much to launch pediatrics as a medical specialty. Yet, he was never given an academic appointment.

The first academic professor of pediatric medicine was Thomas Morgan Rotch. A true pioneer and one of the leading advocates for the use of pure milk for infants, he was appointed to the Harvard Medical School faculty in 1874.

By the mid-1800s, most large cities already had a children's hospital. The idea had been initiated by Dr. Charles West in England. His hospital, located in Great Ormund Street, London, opened its doors in February 1852. During the next 10 years it treated over 200,000 outpatients and over 10,000 inpatients. The first American hospital setting designed exclusively for children was the Children's Hospital of Philadelphia, which was established in 1855. The role of milk in spreading such diseases as tuberculosis had been recognized, and a safe milk campaign was launched. This led to the establishment of milk stations and depots where poor mothers could get pasteurized milk free or at cost. Within the professional realm, in 1881 Dr. Abraham Jacobi organized the Pediatric Section of the American Medical Society. Six years later, in 1887, the American Pediatric Society was formed.

The Progressives (a political group we would today call the liberals) established the preservation of child life as a national priority; they measured success by the fall in the infant/child mortality rates. In the 1890s, a school health movement joined the child welfare campaign, and school doctors and nurses were appointed. In 1908 the first public bureau to deal exclusively with child health was formed in New York City. Baby health stations run by public health nurses spread rapidly. Finally, in 1912, the Children's Bureau "officially certified the conservation of child life as a national concern." By 1921 the Sheppard-Towner Bill passed Congress by large majorities. It provided for grants-in-aid to the states to promote infant and maternal health and welfare. In 1929 it was allowed to expire because of opposition by the American Medical Association!

The Second Line of Development: The Role of the Abolitionists

As the new, idealistic and democratic country had taken form, the recognition that some of its members were enslaved and lacked all freedom provided a jarring contrast. Here, within the very echo of the ringing declarations of freedom, were human beings who could be bought and sold as chattel and who could never become free unless their masters chose to manumit them. It was a fearful reminder of the precariousness and tenuousness of freedom, and, for some, it created a moral discord they could not fail to heed. A culture of abolitionism arose, taking form for some as a variety of political assertion, and for others, as a site for values to be translated into direct action. This meant participation in the Underground Railroad, a covert and illegal operation that spirited runaway slaves from site to site on their way to Canada, where slavery was illegal. The tension between the concepts of freedom and slavery was one of the major dynamics of the Civil War. It also stirred up a certain humanitarian fervor that later translated into a concern with another group of victims, the children of the poor. These advocates, whose fiery need to save children was a vital force, made a major assault on entrenched practices for the management of children in trouble.

One of the consequences of this turmoil was the emergence of a unique set of perspectives that produced ever wider cultural ripples throughout the country, representing a true ascendancy of the Rousseau ideal. Collectively they were the property of the Child Savers (Platt, 1977). These were for the most part members of a sizable sector of middle-class women who flourished toward the end of the 19th century. Generally speaking, they had leisure, education, money, and, often enough, considerable (albeit indirect) political and financial influence. They had small or no families, they had adequate household help, and they had husbands (or friends who had husbands) in industry, law, and government. By and large, they were people who combined goodwill, compassion, and hard common sense, and who worked to better conditions in their society. For some, it was a respectable hobby; but for others, it became a consuming commitment.

One area that engaged them with particular intensity was their desire to better the lives of the many distressed and delinquent children who roamed the streets of the big cities and who were in frequent contact with the legal system. The Child Savers operated on the premise that it was simply wrong to treat children badly and that maltreatment could not help but have an effect on how misused children would grow up. The Child Savers thought delinquency could be understood by assuming that if children were treated badly when they were very young, they would react badly when they got older. Hence, the thing to do

was to find what was wrong with the way children had been reared, to treat them better, and thus to set things right.

Many elements to be found in the transformations within religion and law as well as in the arena of politics contributed to this thinking. They arose from the American preoccupation with freedom, from the evolution of American religious thought, from the work of the abolitionists prior to the Civil War, and, in particular, from the plight of the "huddled masses striving to be free" who now filled so many transitional areas in American cities. These were the new immigrants, at sea in a tumultuous new country, crowded into city slums, deprived of the most elementary amenities, and exploited by everyone (landlords, employers, sometimes the police, and all too often, the bullies within their own communities). So unfortunate was the plight of some of these people that the mere awareness of so much suffering affected the sensibilities of a middle class freed from the burdens of immediate survival, still akindle with abolitionist fervor, and all too aware of the differences between the state of the haves and the have-nots.

THE CHILD SAVERS

Because of the intensity of their convictions about the issue of freedom for all, it was in the nature of things that the abolitionists, who chose the freeing of the slaves as their primary cause, were drawn into active involvement in public affairs. Once the Civil War had been fought and the slaves freed, some abolitionists gave up all further political activity. A sizable percentage, however, cast about in their communities for other sites and other causes to which they could dedicate their energies.

More than that, the children of these activists had been raised in homes where they had become imbued with the parental libertarian fire. These young people now sought in their turn for new frontiers for their efforts. This contributed in large part to the emergence of both a coterie of people who took on the mission of rescuing children in need as well as to the social philosophy of Progressivism. Toward the end of the 19th century, this Progressive movement played an active role in national affairs. Eventually, during the early 20th century, it found concrete political expression in the form of the Progressive Party.

Much of the thinking of this group took its model from the new developments in medicine.

In the wake of Louis Pasteur's germ theory of disease, the ensuing progress in preventive medicine created tremendous optimism. All that had to be done was to locate the single cause of a disease—or a social ill—and could be eliminated.

Parallel with that, it was a time of social reform. The emergence of the Progressive movement was in part a reaction to the growth of large industries and the curtailments of political and economic freedom for which they were blamed. The opposition to this status quo came not from the largely uneducated immigrant poor on the bottom of the economic ladder but from members of the middle class, merchants, small manufacturers, and business and professional people. Academics, lawyers, farmers, and clergy joined their efforts as well. One of the emphases on which they insisted was that everyone was to be regarded as an individual and not as a cog in a vast machine. There was a sense of national guilt for permitting the rise of privilege for the few and a state of continuing misery for the many. There was also a clearly perceived sense of future threat from the masses, which was regularly expressed in the writings of those involved.

Muckrakers were busy uncovering evils and injustices.

There were movements for abolishing the slums, for decent housing for the poor, against the evils of child labor and unsanitary factory conditions, for improved wages and hours for working people, against political corruption in municipal government, for better protection of infant and maternal health, for the fuller utilization of known public health principles to build a sturdier and happier nation. . . . It was in this favored climate that the mental hygiene movement was founded. (Deutsch, 1944, p. 355)

Ida Tarbell wrote about the sins of Standard Oil, Upton Sinclair about slaughterhouses and meat packing, and Lincoln Stephens about local politics.

On a more theoretical level, John Dewey spoke for pragmatism and offered a critique of the entrenched conservative ideology. Many communities revised their charters and political systems; labor practices were revamped, and such innovative practices as the 8-hour day, the minimum wage, and paid vacations were introduced. Housing and penal codes were adopted. The Wisconsin Idea sponsored by Governor Robert LaFollette led to state regulation of railroad rates, direct primaries, a pure-food law, a corrupt practices act, and the like.

Federal laws followed suit, including The Sherman Anti-Trust Act, meat inspection, pure food and drug laws, workman's compensation, The Clayton Anti-Trust Act, the Federal Reserve Act. Even the Constitution was changed with amendments to provide for federal income tax, the direct election of senators, and the initial steps toward the enfranchisement of women. This great rolling wave of reform did not stop until America's entry into World War I in 1917.

In Chicago the spirit of activism in the service of achieving social change found particularly powerful expression. The Chicago Women's Club was founded in 1876 and was one of the most vocal and effective agencies pressing for prison reform, child welfare, and for the establishment of a juvenile court.

MISSION HOUSES/JANE ADDAMS

Thus, toward the end of the 19th century, the concept of child rescue had become an important theme in American life. It was expressed with particular vitality in the work of Jane Addams (Whitman, 1985). This altogether remarkable woman (who eventually earned a Nobel Peace Prize) was the eighth of 9 children. She was born in 1860 in Cedarville, Illinois. Her father, a member of the Illinois state legislature, was a Quaker, a friend of Abraham Lincoln, and an ardent abolitionist. When she was 2, her mother died, but a stepmother (who entered the family when Jane was 5) actively furthered Jane's career aspirations. Miss Addams has been described as an "ugly pigeon-toed child with a deformed spine that prevented her from bearing children" (Platt, 1977, p. 93). At 17, she entered the Rockford Female Seminary, where she became a popular student leader. Strong efforts were made to persuade her to become a missionary, but these she stoutly resisted; her dream was to study medicine and to "live with the poor." When she graduated at 21, she accordingly entered the Women's Medical College of Pennsylvania, but she soon recognized that this was not for her. That feeling, plus poor health, caused her to withdraw, and, in 1883, she decided to join her stepmother on a trip to England, where she could continue her education. After they made their journey, Jane returned to the United States where she lived with her family, took a number of courses, and worked in the black community. She was eager to do something for the unfortunates in society; indeed, when she returned to Europe for another visit in 1887, she became depressed at some of the abysmal slum conditions she encountered there. However, she also had occasion to visit a new development in London, a settlement house called Toynbee Hall that had been established 4 years earlier by a group of idealistic young men. This new social entity seized on her imagination; it offered a concrete way of bringing aid and succor where it was most needed. She resolved to return to the United States, take a house in a poor neighborhood, and put her ideas to the test. She discussed these plans with a former classmate and a close friend, Ellen Gates Starr, who was at the time an art teacher. Addams's idea evoked an enthusiastic response from Starr, and the two women set about putting their plan into action.

They scoured Chicago and found a faded mansion called Hull House, which stood in the midst of the 19th Ward, a Chicago slum populated almost entirely by immigrants. On September 18, 1889, Addams and Starr opened their doors and invited anyone in the neighborhood to come in and partake of what they had to offer. They began meeting needs of the people in their community in a host of ways. Soon they were running ". . . children's clubs, a nursery, an art gallery, a circulating library, and courses in language, history, music, painting, dancing, and mathematics . . . Dozens of clubs were organized to aid working women, an employment bureau was established, and a lunchroom and a nursery for children of working mothers were opened" (Morris et al., 1979, p. 9). They also got word out to the larger community that they were interested in volunteers who might like to come and join in the work.

Within a few years, Hull House was a busy place. Each week the staff and volunteers provided some service or other to at least 2,000 men, women, and children. In addition to the educational, social, and health care dimensions of what they were doing, Hull House contained an art gallery, a little theater group, and a music school.

At the outset, finances were simple; Addams put up whatever financial support was necessary from her own pocket. But the combination of an expanding program coupled with an economic depression drove her to contact philanthropists in the community. At the same time, she and her group became actively involved with political issues. They helped pass an Illinois factory inspection act and were important in the establishment of the first juvenile court. The nature of Addams's interests is perhaps best captured in the titles of the books she would write: *Democracy and Social Ethics* in 1902, *The Spirit of Youth and the City Streets* in 1909, and (in a work on prostitution) *A New Conscience and an Ancient Evil* in 1912. She summed up some of her experiences in *Twenty Years at Hull House* in 1910. She was the first woman to be granted an honorary degree at Yale University.

THE IMPLICATIONS OF HULL HOUSE

As a project, Hull House was a crystal dropped into a supersaturated solution. America was well past the travail of the Civil War, and the huge expansion of industry and finance that had come in the wake of that war was absorbing the energies of the country and creating both myths and millionaires. New ideas were running riot, fortunes were made and lost every day, and, despite a wildly oscillating business cycle, opportunities beckoned everywhere. From all over the world, immigrants were pouring in endless shiploads into the newly invigorated United States. The result was enormous concentrations of capital surrounded by equally sizable masses of needy immigrant workers. Often they were exploited, uneducated or undereducated, essentially lost in a new land and with nowhere to go for sustenance or redress in the face of adversity except to strangers. Americans at that time were compassionate, as they recognized that everyone in the country was descended from immigrants, the fervent abolitionist zeal had not yet spent itself, the reverberations of the Second Great Awakening were still echoing, and the model of Hull House was a rousing stimulus for the training and preparation of a great many committed individuals determined to help those in need. Everyone from John Dewey, the philosopher, to Julia Lathrop, the first head of the Children's Bureau, spent time there; it was a crucible for the formation of the ideas, the ideals, and the practices that have dominated child care to this day. Among other things, it continued to further the concept that public action by the citizenry in helping one another was the key to positive social change. It was a major site for the exploration of one of the dominant schools of thought of the day, the Progressives.

The climate created in Chicago by the work of Jane Addams and the presence of Hull House set the stage for another great leap forward, the establishment of the first juvenile court in that city in 1899.

The Juvenile Court

Many of those associated with Hull House were interested in children's welfare. The many immigrants in the teeming, unhealthy slums of the big city had enormous impact on those idealistic young Americans, an impact augmented by the dreadful life stories of the impoverished youngsters who roamed these neighborhoods, often in flight from despairing and abusive parents, often in quest of their own nurturance and survival, and often in trouble with the law. Child rescue became an enduring cause, and, in particular, the efforts to save children who seemed to be heading for destructive criminal careers evoked intense and passionate responses. The Hull House practitioners were peculiarly American in their approach. They never developed a formal body of theory about how to understand the terrible social conditions surrounding them; initially there was no single canon of political doctrine, moral precept, or ethical formulation associated with their work. But they designed and put in practice a great many practical techniques for helping.

Two women in particular, Lucy Fowler and Julia Lathrop, were concerned with the many youngsters who were hauled before the bar of justice and treated like adult criminals. Lathrop spent 20 years as a full-time resident at Hull House and became an ardent crusader for the rights of the poor, especially the young, the ill, and the mentally disturbed. It was plain to these women that when such young people got in trouble, they needed a very different sort of management from that which was usually meted out to them. They needed a measure of understanding, a decent environment, an appropriate education—in short, a societal response that was just not available in ordinary jurisprudence. A Chicago Juvenile Protective Association had been formed to seek to ameliorate the plight of such children; now, with Lathrop and Fowler's energies added, this group went to work to develop the sort of agency they believed was necessary.

THE CHICAGO WOMEN'S CLUB AND THE JUVENILE PROTECTIVE ASSOCIATION

Among other supporters of Hull House was an organization founded in 1876 called the Chicago Women's Club. In 1883, this association of doughty, altruistic, tough-minded Progressives was already working on the issues of children and the law. Among other things, members had arranged for matrons to help care for child prisoners, supported compulsory education, saw to it that youngsters embroiled with the law continued to get their schooling, and, in particular, lobbied actively and pressed vigorously for the passage of a juvenile court bill. In 1899 their efforts bore fruit. The bill creating the first such court was passed, and, the following year, the court began to function. It had a separate judge and a separate jail for children, and it had its own probation department. It became the model for similar arrangements all over the United States.

A board of directors managed the affairs of the Chicago Juvenile Protective Association. Once the juvenile court had opened its doors, board members would meet at Hull House and review the cases coming before the court. It was soon evident that even if they had the best of intentions, the judges had no understanding of the children they were judging: what caused them to get in trouble in the first place and what was needed to help get them out of it. Indeed, the knowledge base for the understanding of delinquency simply did not exist. Aside from some unproven theories (some of them pessimistically biological, others precious or sanctimonious), no firm grasp on the nature of the problem was available. The judges could send youngsters to various (for the most part unsatisfactory) institutions, to foster care, or back to their own homes. There was, however, little rhyme or reason to why a particular option was selected. Clearly, more had to be known about how to prescribe and implement an optimal course of action.

The board members of the Chicago Juvenile Protective Association cast about for experts in the field, and many turned to a local neurologist who had taken an interest in delinquency. His name was William R. Healy, and he was fated to play a central role in the development and child and adolescent psychiatry.

William R. Healy, M.D.

Born in England on January 20, 1869, William R. Healy grew up in a family dominated by a strict fundamentalist father and a warm, supportive mother. The youngest of 4 children, he was brought to the United States (courtesy of his mother's uncle) shortly before his 10th birthday and reared in a poor part of Chicago. Young William had to quit school when he was 12 in order to "help out" with his earnings. Indeed, at some periods during his childhood he was hungry. Nonetheless, he continued to pursue his education, largely on his own, and showed so much promise that he attracted the support of an influential mentor. With this backing, he was able to enter Harvard as a special student and, ultimately, to attend Rush Medical School. He was awarded his M.D. degree in 1900.

From early on, he was drawn to the problems posed by mental disorders and completed a year of postgraduate work at a state mental hospital. Back in Chicago, after several years of general practice he was able to go to Europe to study neurology. In time he completed this training, returned to Chicago, and settled into private practice as a neurologist. His interest in mental problems continued, however, and on one occasion he observed publicly that a number of youths classified as delinquent were in fact victims of such untreated medical problems as epilepsy. This later gave a lecture on delinquency at the University of Chicago school of social work (or, as it was known at that time, the School of Civics and Philanthropy) on "Physical and Psychical Factors Underlying Dependency and Delinquency." This offering was so successful that he was asked to teach a course on delinquency at the school. Many of those who attended the course were associated with Hull House. Association members believed that proper education and appropriate changes in the environment could alter the lives of young malefactors in a positive way. However, no one knew exactly what factors caused youngsters to follow a delinquent path or what specific interventions were needed to alter their lives for the better.

A number of board members met with Healy and asked him to consider the problem and offer them his recommendations. In April 1908, submitted a proposal for a 5-year study to be conducted by an experienced medical professional familiar with psychological thinking. The goal would be to determine the cause(s) of delinquency, to work up a diagnostic classification, and to study various interventions and their outcomes. The outline included several additional suggestions, namely: that 500 juvenile court cases be studied (preferably by the same observer), that the literature of the field be surveyed (including the use of appropriate statistical methods), and that a visit be paid to the several agencies around the country currently at work dealing with this population.

The board accepted these recommendations and promptly put them into action. The staff at Hull House carried out the literature review; their findings showed that popular belief focused on Lombroso's hereditary criminal types. As for statistical data, no valid studies of delinquency were then available. And when visits to current settings were undertaken, only 2 clinics were found that did anything remotely scientific and substantial for children: Lightner Witmer's psycho-educational clinic in Pittsburgh, Pennsylvania, and Henry Goddard's setting in Vineland, New Jersey. The matter of selecting a researcher to carry out the study was a complex and crucial issue that was assigned to Ethel Dummer.

Among the members of the Juvenile Protective Association board, Mrs. Ethel Dummer was a veritable powerhouse of energy and ideas. She was a remarkable woman, a philanthropist who had already given considerable funding to the support of mental health and who seemed to infuse energy, enthusiasm, and substance into whatever project she undertook. Early in 1909, she contacted 12 outstanding psychiatrists, pediatricians, and psychologists, described Dr. Healy's plan, and asked for recommendations. Two names came up, Dr. Harry Linenthal as first choice, and Dr. Healy himself as second. Dr. Linenthal did not take the position; it was then offered to Healy, and in March 1909, he accepted.

THE JUVENILE PSYCHOPATHIC INSTITUTE

Healy thereupon organized the Juvenile Psychopathic Institute (at the time, the term *psychopathic* spoke for prevention, research, and active treatment). The institute was the site of his study; the actual data collection was done at a clinic he organized in association with the juvenile court. At the time that he opened his clinic in April 1909, it had 3 employees: himself as director, Grace Fernald, a psychologist associated with the clinic, and a secretary. The clinic was situated in the detention area of the same building that lodged the juvenile court, a slum building just across from Hull House. Mrs. Dummer put up $5,000 a year for the 5-year project. Since psychiatric social work did not exist as a recognized discipline the court's probation officers—mostly women—carried out the casework. They visited homes and schools, collected background and family data to round out the clinical picture, and worked with the families. Soon the emphasis fell on bringing together the different disciplines and integrating the findings of the several specialists.

Healy himself conducted most of the evaluative work. He was deeply interested in psychological testing methods that had recently been developed. He and Fernald consulted with Professor James Rolland Angell, who was chairman of the Department of Psychology at the University of Chicago, and pooled their skills to develop a number of psychological tests. Once their evaluation was completed, careful follow-up studies took place.

At the outset, Healy sat with the judges as the juvenile court held session. However, he felt that without a thorough study, he had little to offer about what was wrong with a child or how he or she should be managed. Accordingly, he gave up that practice and declared that he would render recommendations only after the total evaluation had been completed. Thus, he combined careful research with active clinical service.

Early in his work, Healy had been invited to lecture at Harvard; when he appeared there, he created something of a sensation. Among those who attended his lecture was Augusta Bronner, an outstanding psychology student. She was so inspired by his ideas that she was moved to join his staff in 1913. Years later, after his wife had died, Healy married Augusta Bronner.

In the study, in addition to the physical examination, Healy would have several interviews with the youth alone and would conduct additional sessions with the parents. The examination followed the case study model that had been proposed by Dr. Adolph Meyer of Johns Hopkins. The psychologist presented a variety of tests, and the probation officer supplied an account of the boy's previous offenses, his schooling, and his home life. Ultimately, a detailed survey of the youngster's life emerged.

Healy formulated a case study technique (based on the team approach) that was enormously impressive to the practitioners of the time. Thus, in a variety of ways, much of what he did set a model for courts and clinics across the country.

Paradoxically, as the reputation of his work waxed, his own satisfaction with his efforts waned. His clinic was considered an ever more exemplary model for courts and communities everywhere to emulate. For example, in 1910, Healy published an article entitled "A System for Recording Data Concerning Criminals" in the *Journal of the American Institute of Criminal Law and Criminology*. Numerous judges read his report and went to Chicago to visit the Juvenile Psychopathic Institute. In particular, Judge Harvey H. Baker, a juvenile judge in Boston, visited in 1912 and again in 1913. Impressed by what he encountered, Judge Baker determined that Boston needed a comparable institute. Unfortunately, the judge died in 1915, but the Judge Baker Foundation, established in his name, gave concrete form to his ideas, and 2 years later Healy and psychologist Augusta Bronner moved to Boston to head the foundation.

Healy did not make this change easily. However, at least two factors in his work in Chicago troubled him. For one thing, his clinic provided only a diagnostic service. Beyond choice of placement, little could be done to help the many troubled youngsters. Healy wanted to engage in more direct treatment, but the nature and pressures of his situation made that impossible.

The other major difficulty was financial. Mrs. Dummer had put up the money for the first 5 years of the study; funds ran out in 1914. The county then picked up the burden of financing the clinic, and immediately tried to cut off funding for the psychologist. With the help of the Hull House group, this disaster was averted, but it put Healy on notice that his situation had changed. When he was offered the opportunity to set up a similar arrangement in Boston, he negotiated a $14,000 yearly income for the clinic, which would include salaries for himself, a psychologist, a social worker, and office staff. He further stipulated a 10-year guarantee of support and the promise that he would have more of an opportunity to deal with therapeutic issues. His terms were met, and, in 1917, the transfer effected. Dr. Bronner accompanied Healy and his wife to Boston.

IMPLICATIONS OF HEALY'S STUDY

In order to carry out the terms of his mission, Healy conducted an intensive examination of a large number of cases. In case after case he concluded that there was no single generic cause for delinquency. Instead, each child had to be studied as a separate individual, and in each instance, a unique constellation determined the nature of the disturbed behavior. Some factors tended to repeat a good deal, such as mental defect (the current language for retardation), bad home conditions, and physical disability of some kind. No one factor, however, was either necessary or sufficient to initiate a delinquent pattern. Rather than naming some discernible sociocultural factor (such as immigrant status, big-city slum life, crowding, poor parenting, etc.) as the sole or primary cause of delinquency, Healy emphasized that each individual case had to be studied for its own inner structure. Schlossman (1983) points out that Healy may well have disappointed the group of social activists who engaged him. The Progressives of that day saw the causes of delinquency as social and environmental. Accordingly, they had designed the juvenile court like an educational model. In their view, delinquency, was caused by ignorance and inadequate socialization; it should be correctable by loving remonstrance and reeducation. Treatment would come down to the probation officer working with the family and child in the home in order to achieve better home conditions and moral uplift. Had Healy named some aberration in the social fabric as the culprit, his sponsors would have attacked the problem vigorously; however, Healy concluded that this view was at once simplistic, inaccurate, and insufficient. Without denying the importance of the environment and its influences, he nonetheless shifted the focus for the application of efforts from concern with the child's environment to concentration on the inner workings of the child's mind. He described a complex web of causation producing some variety of mental disturbance in the child and turned to formulating a diagnosis and prescribing appropriate treatment. In short, he found a clinical rather than a social solution to the problem of delinquency.

THE JUDGE BAKER FOUNDATION

The clinic established by the Judge Baker Foundation was a far cry from the bare-bones, slum-based setting in Chicago. The new clinic occupied 5 rooms in a downtown office building and was well equipped and pleasantly designed. Once the work got under way, the clinic grew rapidly; by 1930, it was using 17 rooms in that building.

When it opened, the clinic was one of only 11 guidance clinics in the country and the only one in Boston. Both Healy and Bronner were active in public education. There was much exchange with other child professionals; Healy conducted a class for teachers at Boston University School of Education, and Bronner spent a third of her time in the community speaking before various groups and clubs.

Meanwhile the clinic concept had caught on, and here and there, one juvenile court after another would emulate Healy and set up its own service.

THE ADVENT OF THE TEAM APPROACH

To be sure, all this was not happening in a vacuum. A parallel development was taking place within mental health. At the Boston Psychopathic Hospital, a creative and forward-looking psychiatrist, Dr. Elmer Earnest Southard, was inspiring a group of students (among them Karl Menninger) to consider prevention and early intervention on an outpatient basis; in effect, this offered an alternative approach to the musty state hospital practice that dominated psychiatry of that time. Southard was at once a pathologist, psychiatrist, logician, philosopher, and chess master. Commenting on these aspects of Southard's life, Healy was later to add: "But withal, it was not these evidences of great mental stature that made Southard seem so admirable to those who knew him. Rather it was the quality of his human relationships . . . generosity . . . friendship . . . a certain springiness of the fiber of his personality, arousing the best . . . that the other fellow had to offer . . ." (Healy, 1929).

Working in tandem with Mary Jarrett, one of the founders of psychiatric social work (the other—as noted earlier—was said to have been Adolph Meyer's wife), Southard had created his own concept of the "team approach," where different disciplines pooled their efforts to present a many-sided view of the patient. This resonated powerfully with Healy's outlook; when Healy followed Southard's model and incorporated psychiatrist, psychologist, and social worker into a coherent functional unit, the child guidance team was born. At the Judge Baker Foundation, the three disciplines formed a core group that would combine its efforts in systematic fashion to diagnose and treat troubled children. For the next 50 years, this "team approach" would be the dominant model for the way child psychiatric work was carried out.

THE INDIVIDUAL DELINQUENT

In 1915 Healy published the formal report of the study that he had been originally invited to undertake. Entitled *The Individual Delinquent*, this work set the tone for the approach to troubled children that would define child and adolescent psychiatry thereafter. As noted, Healy abandoned the notion of any single cause or fixed cluster of causes for delinquency. There were always multiple causes, and the constellation was unique for each individual child. This embrace of the complexity and variety of etiologic factors at once dispelled some long-cherished myths (that people were born criminals beyond redemption) and indicated a method and approach that would include the full array of possible contributing factors: genetics, family history, family structure, individual developmental history, early traumatic events, overall health, neurological status, the role of substance abuse, subcultural involvements, intellectual vagaries, school difficulties, and other unique individual factors. To this day, Healy's book remains a classic in the field.

As the array of schools, social agencies, and child mental health professionals involved in any given case increased in number and variety, the procedures for allowing them all to hear one another's findings and for integrating their efforts became more formal. The clinical case conference gradually elaborated. Healy had the clinical-pathological conferences at the Harvard Medical School to use as a model; as it developed, the case conference became a primary site for clinical decision making, for staff evaluation, and for student and staff training. Soon social work, psychology, and, in time, child psychiatry trainees came to the clinic as part of their preparation. This early model of a multistaff clinical case conference would become a core part of child guidance work and training.

The Third Line of Development: Clifford Beers and Mental Hygiene

Having thus rendered some account of the emergence of the clinic idea, let us shift to the third great axis along which child and adolescent psychiatry developed and study the emergence of the concept of mental hygiene.

EARLY VIEWS OF THE ETIOLOGY OF DELINQUENCY AND MENTAL ILLNESS

Historically, physicians had noted the effects of the passions on mental health since the latter part of the eighteenth century. But the term *mental hygiene* is said to have appeared initially as the title of a book by Dr. William Sweetser, first published in 1843. Dr. Sweetser was professor of the theory and practice of physic at the University of Virginia; the full title of his book was *Mental Hygiene. An Examination of the Intellect and Passions, Designed to Illustrate Their Influence on Health and the Duration of Life*. Among his other observations, Dr. Sweetser noted that "Those of the medical profession . . . concentrating their attention on the physical, are too prone to neglect the mental causes of disease. . . . The true origin of [some patients'] malady is some inward rooted sorrow, which moral balm alone can reach" (quoted in Deutsch, 1944, p. 325).

Another work in this area was that of Cook (1859) who was concerned with the prevention of mental illness. In his article on mental hygiene in the *American Journal of Insanity*, he noted that most cases of mental illness had their beginnings in early childhood. Hence, the main responsibility for establishing mental health fell to the parents. He noted how many American fathers were strangers to their children and how so many parents say one thing and do another, "spreading out into an unconscious social hypocrisy which pervades many homes" (quoted in Deutsch, 1944, p. 277).

In 1863, Isaac Ray also published a work entitled *Mental Hygiene*. His notion of etiology, however, emphasized geography and climate as begetters of mental illness. In general, a good deal was made of mental hygiene during the 1800s, but more as a sense of lofty images advanced by thoughtful and serious people, than a practical doctrine. These authors expressed both the hope and the wish to promote mental health and prevent mental illness, but, in their day, there was no discipline or methodology available to implement their views. Nor, for the most part, did the public either understand or support their perspective. A major confrontation of some kind was needed before this approach could be translated into realistic practice. The key events may well have been those circumstances attending America's participation in World War I.

Bromberg (1982) commented: "It is not too much to say that the mental hygiene movement did not become a meaningful social movement until 'shell shock' was recognized as a meaningful social issue among returning soldiers."

During the latter half of the 19th century, it was usual to consider severe poverty (pauperism), severe mental retardation, and the grosser forms of insanity as a single cluster of related difficulties. In

41

1860 Augustin Morel, a French psychiatrist, had promulgated the degeneracy theory of causation. This amounted to saying that there was a hereditary weakness passed on from generation to generation that caused insanity. Moreover, associated physical stigmata characterized the unfortunate bearers of this taint.

Ceasare Lombroso, professor of legal medicine at the University of Turin, brought the methods of physical anthropology to the study of criminals (Wolfgang, 1968). He was the first to use the term *the born criminal,* a designation suggested to him by his younger colleague, Enrico Ferri. Lombroso emphasized the concept of atavism. Inborn delinquency was not, in his view, natural to contemporary humankind. Hence criminal tendencies represented a biological throwback to some earlier stage of evolution (as seen in primitive races). The atavistic criminal could be distinguished by characteristic stigmata. In his book, *L'Ouomo Delinquente (Criminal Man)* (1876), Lombroso described the body and facies of the born criminal.

Criminals more often than noncriminals had traits that resembled savages or animals. The criminal tended to have a primitive brain, an unusual cephalic index (either large like the mongoloids or small like the negroids), long arms, prehensile feet, a scanty beard but hairy body, large incisors, flattened nose, furtive eyes and an angular skull . . . thieves were characterized by small, restless eyes, thick eyebrows, a crooked nose, thin beard, and narrow receding forehead. Sex criminals had bright eyes, a cracked voice, blond hair, and a delicate face. Murderers had cold, glassy eyes, a hooked aquiline nose (like a bird of prey), large cheeks and jaws, long ears, dark hair, and canine teeth . . . the born criminal was a distinct anthropological type of mankind, closely related to other types of human defectives (quoted in Haller, 1984, p. 15).

Marc Nordau, a Hungarian psychiatrist, popularized Morel's degeneracy theory in the 1890s, and in the same year, Havelock Ellis published *The Criminal,* introducing European criminal anthropology to the United States. In the popular press, terms began to appear such as *morbid heredity, hereditary degeneration, atavism,* and *arrested development* that expressed this point of view. To some, this sequestration of criminality and delinquency to a part of humankind different from the rest was a comforting doctrine and, accordingly, gained a considerable following. In particular, it allowed some part of the emerging middle class to identify itself as distinct from the immigrant/lower-class population that was so evidently tainted by these genetic deficiencies.

This outlook achieved enormous reinforcement from a number of case reports that arose on the American scene. Two that gained particular notoriety were the accounts of the Jukes and the Kallikaks.

A New York city merchant named Richard R. Dugdale loved to study social problems and was active in a number of societies concerned with such matters. In 1874 he was on an inspection trip for the Prison Association of New York, and, in one rural jail, he found six members of a single family in jail at the same time. Fascinated by the implications of this, he proceeded to track down as many members of this family as he could. He found a common ancestor in the form of a colonial frontiersman who had had two sons. These sons married into a family of six sisters, whom Dugdale called the Jukes. By interviewing older members of this community and tracking through poorhouse lists, court records, and prison files, he assembled data on 709 members of the Jukes clan with an account of many of their activities. These included: 18 brothel keepers, 128 prostitutes, 200+ on the dole, and 76 convicted of crimes. Dugdale estimated that the family cost the public well over $1 million. This case was so detailed and so convincing that it became a basic document in all future studies of heredity. While Dugdale himself recognized the importance of environmental factors, the Jukes were presented as a major argument for the hereditarians' position. If the original breeding could have been curtailed, a huge sum would have been saved.

Many thoughtful people challenged this assessment of the situation. The individuals in this unfortunate family had been brought up under very deleterious circumstances; why should not their bad environment have as much of an influence on their behavior as the alleged heredity? Other instances, however, served in turn to rebut this objection.

In 1897 Deborah Kallikak (a pseudonym comprised of the Greek words for "good" and "bad"), then 8 years old, was brought to Vineland for care. When her family connections were explored, it turned out that Deborah's great-great-great grandfather had been Martin Kallikak, a militiaman in the Revolutionary Army. At a tavern, he met a retarded girl who presently bore him a bastard son. The son (later known as Old Horror) was given his father's name and sired a family whom later generations would consider degenerates. The descendants were carefully traced, and everywhere the picture was one of licentious behavior, poverty, and mental retardation. All told, Old Horror gave rise to 480 offspring; by actual count, 143 were retarded, 46 normal, and the remainder uncertain. Within this population of descendants, there were 26 children born out of wedlock, 33 guilty of sexual offenses (chiefly prostitution), 24 alcoholics, 3 epileptics, 3 criminals, and 82 who died as infants.

More significant still, however, Martin Kallikak later married a Quaker girl, and their progeny included numerous doctors, lawyers, judges, and teachers—all in all, honorable and productive citizens. Both families shared the same name but were apparently unaware of their connection.

Goddard assembled these data and, in 1912, published a book entitled *The Kallikak Family*. This study was said to demonstrate that degeneracy and feeblemindedness were hereditary and were basic to much of society's crime and poverty. Had the original mother of this miserable tribe been sterilized, lamented Goddard, how much societal pain, grief, and expense would have been prevented.

Within the social framework, the 3 sites where children with genetic disorders were likely to be encountered were among the retarded, the delinquent, and the homeless. Institutions for the retarded had begun in 1831, when Elias Howe had established the Perkins School. Somewhat paradoxically, this was the leading edge of a great wave of hope that had spread from France. There Edouard Seguin, a prominent psychiatrist, began to treat an idiot boy in Paris and published his results in 1839. Based on his work with severely retarded children, he had formulated a plausible and optimistic treatment approach. Among others, it influenced Maria Montessori, who herself would be a prominent leader in creating remedial environments for backward children. In 1842 Seguin was appointed to a school for idiots at Bicetre in Paris and began to apply his method. However, he got caught up in the then-tumultuous French political life, things went badly for his group, and, in 1848, he emigrated to the United States. The approach he had developed promised to set aright all that had gone awry in the production of a retarded person; and, in his new country, it generated a huge outpouring of euphoric commitment to the implementation of its techniques. Alas for wishful idealism: Seguin's method ultimately proved a resounding failure, and, by the end of the century, the gloomy genetic outlook prevailed. The Jukes and the Kallikaks were the models for hereditary disturbances, and this

thinking embraced both the delinquent and the street child. Like Lombroso's criminal type (with perhaps a dash of Calvinist predestination), these youngsters were regarded as fated to fall prey to their unfortunate heredity.

Of all those who saw heredity at work in shaping the human condition, the staff in charge of institutions for the feebleminded were perhaps the most convinced. What gave this position a special edge was the widely accepted view that mental deficiency was in fact dangerous. Mental retardation was thought to have a close relationship to delinquency. Indeed, it was easy to move from the universe of intellectual backwardness to the realm of morality and to assume that similar forces were at work. Just as one person could suffer from a failure to develop intellectually, another could be lacking in adequate development of morality. Accordingly, even where cognitive competence was preserved, the notion of moral imbecility was invoked to explain the behavior of the incorrigible youths. Institutions were opened to house the unfortunates whose behavior attested to their deficiencies and whose progeny threatened to continue the troublesome patterns. Ultimately, many asylums were built to house the incurables, protect them from public mistreatment, and protect the public from the ill effects of their behavior.

Although probably the predominant view, this hereditarian outlook was by no means the only stance held by professionals. Psychiatrists and neurologists had pinpointed a number of alternative sources of mental illness; they specified certain kinds of childhood behavior or aberrations in the way children were reared, and they published papers or books about their findings. Thus they felt that masturbation was an important cause of insanity and described a category of illness that they designated as "masturbatory insanity." As noted earlier, they regarded overly intensive education as another source of severe emotional difficulty; it made for "precocity," which was posited to be a grave factor among the forces making for mental illness.

In order to follow the strands of the mental hygiene theme, however, we must shift our attention to a very different area. A young Connecticut businessman named Clifford Beers had become depressed and, in 1900, had made a suicide attempt. He was admitted to a mental hospital and began a treatment career that lasted 3 years and that led him to seek care in three different hospitals. In the course of these institutionalizations, he encountered many gross brutalities and humiliations inflicted on his own person, and he was spectator to similar treatment visited on a host of others. He tried to do something about this via letters and wrote to the President of the United States, to the governor of Connecticut, and to many other officials, all of whom were equally unresponsive. In time, Beers's depression gave way to a period of elation, and he developed a grandiose plan for the worldwide reform of asylum abuses. Indeed, to gather data for his project, he would get the attendants to throw him into the violent wards where he could document the worst horrors. He took copious notes of what he was learning and filled up the available writing paper at such a rate that he had to have rolls of wrapping paper brought to his room.

Finally his condition improved, and in 1903 he emerged as recovered, but with his resolution to bring about reform undimmed. He threw himself into this effort and became so excited by his project that he returned to the hospital voluntarily for a brief fourth stay before rejoining his community. Once returned home, he went back to his former business, but his heart was not in it. He decided to devote himself to hospital reform full time and felt that the best way to do this was to write a book about his experiences. In this he was much influenced by the story of Harriet Beecher Stowe's *Uncle Tom's Cabin.* When that work had appeared, it had had an enormous impact on the antislavery movement. He resolved to write an account of his own experience as the most effective vehicle for his message. He reviewed his copious notes, reworked them, wrote his manuscript, and sent copies of the document to many eminent psychiatrists as well as to several literary figures. In the book, he proposed the organization of a national committee both to comfort the afflicted and their families and to seek to prevent mental illness. Among others who reviewed this work, Dr. Adolph Meyer corresponded with him and suggested the name Mental Hygiene as the title of the committee. Beers accepted the suggestion forthwith.

When it appeared, the book was an instant success. It did indeed emulate *Uncle Tom's Cabin* in that it had a powerful widespread influence. Heartened by this reception and guided by some of those he consulted, in May 1908 Beers organized an initial effort in his own state and called it the Connecticut Society of Mental Hygiene. This too was so successful that in February of the following year, in New York City, he established the National Committee for Mental Hygiene with 12 charter members. Besides Beers himself, the committee included such notables as Julia Lathrop and Adolph Meyer.

THE NATIONAL COMMITTEE ON MENTAL HYGIENE

Initially, however, the new body had trouble getting started. As they conceptualized their mission, the members felt an urgent need to establish a mental health database by making large population surveys. Funds were short, however, and there was no easy way to proceed. At the outset, the Rockerfeller Foundation had paid the staff salaries and funded some of the initial survey work. After World War I, however, the Rockerfeller Foundation withdrew its support. It was interested primarily in medical research, and it felt that the emphasis of the committee's work tended to minimize biology. In 1912 Henry Phipps, a railroad magnate turned philanthropist, gave the committee a $50,000 bequest. That year the committee engaged Dr. Thomas W. Salmon of the United States Public Health Service to conduct a series of mental health studies, and by 1915 he was the committee's first medical director at a salary of $7,000 per year. His task was to go forward with the mental health studies, and his efforts were so fruitful that when the United States entered World War I, the task of organizing a psychiatric branch for the Army Medical Corps was put into the hands of the National Committee for Mental Hygiene. Dr. Salmon was appointed chief of psychiatry for the American Expeditionary Force.

The war catalyzed many developments in mental health, in particular, the importance of life history and of environmental factors in establishing and maintaining mental health. Social workers became the professional aspect of this new kind of understanding, and they were turned to more and more as mental hygiene developed.

THE EMERGENCE OF PSYCHIATRIC SOCIAL WORK

It should be noted that in 1922, the collaboration of Mary C. Jarrett with Dr. Elmer Southard at Boston Psychopathic Hospital had produced a jointly written book, *The Kingdom of Evils,* where the description of psychiatric social work was first delineated. However, it should also be noted that Dr. W. Malamud (1944), in speaking of Adolf Meyer's work, comments: "the importance of understanding mental diseases as reactions to life situations ... [made it] necessary to have information concerning his family history, his social setting, and his own life history. This necessitated a host of co-workers ... in this way psychiatric social work came into being. ..."

The work of the committee was by no means without internal problems. In particular, from the outset, there were difficulties between Beers and Adolf Meyer. Meyer felt that Beers should take direction from a physician and that the new body should be led by a psychiatrist; Beers, however, felt it should be run by a layman. More than that, in the beginning, Meyer had opposed forming a national organization; indeed, it was in response to his urging that Beers had first formed the Connecticut Association. But in this, Meyer finally gave way and allowed Beers's full project to be realized. Beers was intent on accomplishing a series of state and local surveys on the mental health status of the nation. His feeling was that just as the Flexner Report had transformed medical education, so a revelation of the true extent of mental illness would stir citizens to effective action. To accomplish such data collection was expensive, however, and Beers had early wanted to approach Phipps for help with the funding. As it happened, Phipps had recently contributed the money to establish the Phipps Clinic at Johns Hopkins where Meyer was located, and this placed Meyer in an awkward position. If he joined Beers's effort, in effect he would be competing with himself. As a result of all these factors, the tension between Meyer and Beers mounted, and, in 1910, Meyer withdrew from the committee. Within a year, Phipps had provided the funding for the surveys and promised more such bequests in the future.

In 1921 the National Committee on Mental Hygiene got Commonwealth Fund support to create a Division on the Prevention of Delinquency. It was this division that then funded the Child Guidance Clinics and launched child psychiatry as a discipline. It is noteworthy that just as that effort was getting under way, in 1922, Dr. Thomas Salmon left his post to become a professor at Columbia University, and was replaced by Frankwood E. Williams as medical director of the committee. Ironically, in 1939, Beers was readmitted to the Butler Mental Hospital in Providence, Rhode Island and remained there until his death in 1943 at age 67.

Meanwhile, the products of 19th-century capitalism were bearing fruit and beginning to play a role in child mental health. As huge amounts of capital accumulated in private hands, these sums came to be disbursed via both individual philanthropies and foundations. We have already seen the role of such donors as Mrs. Dummer on the formation of Healy's clinic. Subsequently, the Rockerfeller Foundation and Commonwealth Fund came into being and materially influenced the course of mental health research and services. In particular the Commonwealth Fund became interested in child welfare and delinquency, and sought advice on how best to invest its money in order to achieve a useful outcome.

In 1920, it turned to the then head of the Department of Child Welfare at the New York School of Social Work, Henry Thurston, and asked him to come up with some recommendations. He, in turn, invited a number of interested professionals to act as an advisory committee and to come together for a weekend during April 1921 at Lakewood, New Jersey. Among those who convened were Healy and Bronner of the Judge Baker Foundation, Salmon of the National Committee for Mental Hygiene, and Dr. Bernard Glueck of the Department of Mental Hygiene of the New York School of Social Work. There were also representatives of social work, psychology, education, and the juvenile court. Over a 3-day weekend, they came up with 12 recommendations. The board of the Commonwealth Fund decided to invest in 2 of them. One was the establishment of a clinic and training center at the New York School of Social Work for the evaluation and treatment of children and for the training of a variety of mental health personnel to staff the newly forming clinics. The other was a variation of one of the Advisory Committee's recommendations to enlarge and expand the work of the Judge Baker Foundation clinic. Instead, the board chose to have the National Committee of Mental Hygiene act as organizer and coordinator of a series of demonstration child guidance clinics that would be established all over the country.

The National Committee of Mental Hygiene set up a Division on the Prevention of Delinquency to handle this program. Since the clinics were to be associated with the juvenile courts, the initial step was to write to 225 such Courts describing the program and inviting their participation. About 15% (35 courts) responded, of whom less than half (13) accepted the invitation.

THE DEMONSTRATION CLINICS

With these acceptances in hand, it was decided to begin opening a series of clinics, with the first one destined for St. Louis, Missouri. Accordingly, in April 1922, the St. Louis Demonstration Juvenile Court Clinic was launched. The psychiatrist who directed the clinic was I. J. Heldt, M.D., and the staff included a psychologist and a psychiatric social worker. In anticipation of its advent, the community had identified a group of seriously disturbed youngsters whose problems had long been recognized; as soon as the clinic opened its doors, it was flooded with this troubled population, confronted with a public expectation for rapid change, and, in short order, overwhelmed. The Commonwealth Fund had offered to support the clinic for its first 6 months. By December of 1922, 2 bond issues to further fund the clinic had failed, and it presently drifted, dwindled, and died.

A second demonstration clinic in Norfolk, Virginia, was also directed by Dr. Heldt. This time it was more adequately staffed; it also had more cases referred from the community than from the court. Nonetheless, after the first months of Commonwealth funding, when the question arose of further supporting the clinic, the city refused to finance the undertaking, and that clinic too fell by the wayside.

The Dallas clinic was next. Profiting from previous experience, this time financing was sought from private rather than public sources, with eventual reliance on the Community Chest. It was different as well in that Dr. Lawson Lowery was the psychiatrist-director; soon he would play the same role in the formation of 2 additional demonstration clinics. Yet a third innovation was a change in name; for the first time, the Dallas clinic called itself a Child Guidance Clinic and thus led the way to an ever-increasing drift from the original tie to the Juvenile Court. Thereafter, child guidance clinics would be community-based operations, each with its own individual regional character and each responding to the unique needs of its local population. (Some practitioners who were there at the time have remarked privately to the author that many people did not like bringing their children to a psychiatric clinic. Hence the change in name had huge public relations significance.)

Minneapolis-St. Paul, Los Angeles, Cleveland, and Philadelphia also had each demonstration clinics. Each found its necessary community recognition, and each became a permanent service within the area where it had been initiated. Fred H. Allen was director of the Philadelphia Clinic, Lawson Lowery of the Minneapolis-St. Paul and Cleveland settings, and R. P. Truitt of the Los Angeles Child Guidance Service.

The Philadelphia Clinic, established in March 1925, was the last of the demonstrations sponsored by the Commonwealth Fund. Altogether 5 of the 7 tries had resulted in a well-founded, permanent service supported by the local community. More important still, however, was the fact that during the 5 years of the Commonwealth project, nearly 100 clinics were established in other communities all over the United States. In effect, child guidance had taken root, not in its original form as an arm of the juvenile court, but in a new, self-defined fashion, to help agencies and families with the everyday problems of troubled and errant children. These clinics focused on education, prevention, and consultation, and work with delinquents was either turned away from or treated as a peripheral part of the task, rather than as its core. Besides their direct influences, the very presence of the clinic and its activities served to spread the values and the concepts of child guidance and mental hygiene throughout the surrounding communities. It seems fair to say that the clinics played a significant role in psychologizing the United States (Smith, 1934).

More than that, these clinics became the site for the emergence of the discipline of child and adolescent psychiatry. In each clinic the psychiatrist was the captain of a team and was referred to as a child psychiatrist. Child psychiatry was defined as that which such a clinic director did, and, before many years had passed, this coterie of professionals had emerged as a unique group with its own set of competencies and its own transmissible values. The emphasis on development as a basic science underlying its operation, the attainment of a body of highly specialized skills at interviewing and understanding children, the mastery of team organization and leadership, the formulation of a new set of diagnostic entities and a new style of diagnostic thinking along with a singular set of assessment tactics, the creation of a novel array of therapeutic interventions, and a genuine redefinition of mental illness in terms of its origins and earliest manifestations were among the rich products of child guidance work. They were the competencies and the everyday work of the child psychiatrist. The wish to understand children in order to better their lives was transmuted from good intention, noble concept, and abstract yearning to a realized behavior in the everyday operations of this group of professionals.

It was, then, this confluence of advances in psychiatry, psychology, and social work, fused with the awesome humanitarianism of Jane Addams and her Hull House group and urged on by the driving energy of Beers and the mental hygiene movement, that together brought into being both the child guidance clinic and the discipline we to-day know as child and adolescent psychiatry. All these in turn had emerged from the matrix of the 19th-century transitions and events that created a climate where children could be valued, the needs of youths could be recognized, and the larger culture had both the wealth and the leisure to devote itself to the betterment of the lives of the young.

REFERENCES

Abt-Garrison, (1965). *History of pediatrics, with new chapters by Arthur F. Abt, M.D.* Philadelphia: W. B. Saunders.

Adler, F. (1924, April 24). The nation and child labor. *New York Times*, p. 6.

Aries, P. (1962). *Centuries of childhood: A social history of family life.* New York: Knopf.

Bernstein, D. M. (1994, January). The thirteen founders. *American Journal of Psychiatry 151* (1), 19.

Binet, A., & Simon, T. (1905). Application des methodes nouvelles au diagnostic du niveau intellectuel chez les enfants normaux et anormaux d'hospice et d'ecole primaire. *L'Annee Psychologique, 11,* 245–366.

Blum, J. M., Morgan, E. S., Rose, W. L., Schlesinger, A. M., Jr., Stampp, K. M., & Woodward, C. V. (1981). *The national experience: A history of the United States* (5th ed.). New York: Harcourt Brace Jovanovich.

Brace, C. L. (1880/1967). *The dangerous classes of New York, and twenty years work among them* (3d ed.). Montclair, NJ: Patterson Smith.

Brigham A. (1832). *Remarks on the influence of mental cultivation and mental excitement upon health.*

Bromberg, W. (1982). *Psychiatry between the wars, 1918–1945: A recollection.* Westport, CT: Greenwood Press.

Contratto, S. (1984). Mother: Social sculptor and trustee of the faith. In M. Lewin (Ed.), *In the shadow of the past: Psychology portrays the sexes: A social and intellectual history* (pp. 226–255). New York: Columbia University Press.

Cook, G. (1859). Mental hygiene. *American Journal of Insanity, 15,* 272–282, 353–365.

Deutsch, A. (1944). The history of mental hygiene. In J. K. Hall, G. Z. Zilboorg, & H. A. Bunker (Eds.), *One hundred years of American psychiatry* (pp. 325–365): New York: Columbia University Press.

Douglas, A. (1977). *The feminization of American culture.* New York: Avon Books.

Hall, G. S. (1904). *Adolescence.*

Haller, M. H. (1984). *Eugenics: Hereditarian attitudes in American thought.* New Brunswick, NJ: Rutgers University Press.

Harris, B. J. (1984). The power of the past: History and the psychology of women. In M. Lewin (Ed.), *In the shadow of the past: Psychology portrays the sexes: A social and intellectual history* (pp. 1–25). New York: Columbia University Press.

Healy, W. (1915). *The individual delinquent: A text-book of diagnosis and prognosis for all concerned in understanding offenders.* Boston: Little, Brown and Co.

Healy, W. (1929). Elmer Earnest Southard: An appreciation. *Journal of Juvenile Research, 13* (3).

Holt, L. E. (1894). *The care and feeding of children.*

Horowitz, H. L. (1987). *Campus life: Undergraduate cultures from the end of the eighteenth century to the present.* New York: Knopf.

Kett, J. F. (1977). *Rites of passage: Adolescence in America 1790 to the present.* New York: Basic Books.

Levy, D. (1968). Child psychiatry. In D. L. Sills (Ed.), *International encyclopedia of the social sciences,* vol. 12 (pp. 613–622). New York: Macmillan and Free Press.

Lewin, M. (Ed.). (1984). *In the shadow of the past: Psychology portrays the sexes: A social and intellectual history.* New York: Columbia University Press.

Lombroso, C. (1876). *L'Ouomo delinquente in rapporto all'-antropologia, alla giurisprudenza ed alla discipline carcerarie,* 5th ed. (3 vols.). Turin (Italy): Bocca.

Malamud, W. (1944). The history of psychiatric therapies. In J. K. Hall, G. Z. Zilboorg, & H. A. Bunker (Eds.), *One hundred years of American psychiatry* (pp. 273–323). New York: Columbia University Press.

Moore, T. V. (1944). A century of psychology in its relationship to American psychiatry. In J. K. Hall, G. Z. Zilboorg, & H. A. Bunker (Eds.), *One hundred years of American psychiatry* (pp. 443–477). New York: Columbia University Press.

Moore, W. E. (1968). Industrialization: Social aspects. In D. L. Sills, *International encyclopedia of the social sciences* (pp. 263–270). New York: Macmillan and Free Press.

Morris, W. (Ed.). (1976). *The American heritage dictionary of the English language.* Boston: Houghton Mifflin Co.

Mulhern, J. (1946). *A history of education.* New York: Ronald Press.

Overholser, W. (1944). The founding and the founders of the association. In J. K. Hall, G. Z. Zilboorg, & H. A. Bunker (Eds.), *One hundred years of American psychiatry* (pp. 45–72). New York: Columbia University Press.

Platt, A. M. (1977). *The child Savers: The invention of delinquency,* 2nd ed. Chicago: University of Chicago Press.

Quinn, K. (1992, November 20). "Myths, blind alleys"

characterize children's movement, says Quinn. *Psychiatric News,* p. 2.

Ray, I. (1863). *Mental hygiene.* Boston: Ticknor & Fields.

Rosen, M., Clark, G. R., & Kivitz, M. S. (Eds.). (1976). *A history of mental retardation: Collected papers* (Vols. 1–2). Baltimore, MD: University Park Press.

Rosenheim, M. K. (1976). The child and the law. In E. H. Grotberg (Ed.), *200 years of children* (pp. 423–386). Washington, DC: U.S. Office of Health, Education, and Welfare, Office of Human Development, Office of Child Development.

Sachs, B. (1895). *Treatise on the nervous diseases of children.* New York: William Wood & Co.

Schlossman, S. L. (1983). Juvenile justice: History and philosophy. In S. H. Kadish, (Editor-in-Chief), *Encyclopedia of crime and justice* (Vol. 3). New York: Free Press.

Shaw, J. A. (1983). *Adolf Meyer and the emerging concepts of mental health.* Paper presented at the annual meeting of the American Academy of Child and Adolescent Psychiatry, San Francisco, CA.

Smith, G. (1934). *Child guidance clinics, a quarter century of development.* New York: Commonwealth Fund.

Sweetser, W. (1843). *Mental hygiene.* New York: J. and H. G. Langley.

Thomas, B. (1968). Migration II: Economic Aspects. In D. L. Sills (Ed.), *International encyclopedia of the social sciences* (Vol. 10). New York: Macmillan and Free Press.

Tyor, P. L., & Bell, L. V. (1984). *Caring for the retarded in America: A history.* Westport, CT: Greenwood Press.

Whitman, A. (Ed.). (1985). *American reformers: An H. W. Wilson biographical dictionary.* New York: H. W. Wilson and Co.

Wolfgang, M. E. (1968). Ceasare Lombroso. In D. L. Sills (Ed.), *International encyclopedia of the social sciences* (Vol. 9, pp. 471–473). New York: Macmillan and Free Press.

Zelizer, V. A. (1985). *Pricing the priceless child: The changing social value of children.* New York: Basic Books.

SECTION II
The Impact of Sociocultural Events

PART I
The Sexual Revolution
Paul L. Adams

Editor's Note

This section on sociocultural events concerning young people is the natural site for displaying the biopsychosocial paradigm for psychiatric discourse. There is no better way to begin this section than with "The Sexual Revolution." Are not increased candor, openness, and directness concerning our sexual imagery, desire, and behavior surely of importance in the lives of children and adolescents? Hence the sexual revolution is our take-off topic.

Introduction

It is not easy to be crisp and succinct about the sexual revolution, yet it is not necessary to be definitive or long-winded. It is imperative to acknowledge and to summarize. But, of course, undertaking such a task is a bit dangerous since the topic is often hot, sometimes taboo, but seldom dispassionate.

Here I aim to "sketch in" some of the imperatives for sexual freedom and some of the blocks or impedances put in place to inhibit it—for adults as well as for adolescents and children. This chapter begins by defining the term "sexual revolution" and naming some of its forerunners in sexology, psychoanalysis, anthropology, social science, and creative literature. Since women have been illustrious in changing sexual mores during the past five or six decades, some historical background material on females and their sexuality is presented.

Next, some other general features of the sexual revolution are described: its adult emphasis, minimizing children as sexual; its stress on recreative, not procreative, sexual acts; its enlargement of sexual horizons to include heterosexual, homosexual, and bisexual endeavors; its refusal to observe rigid type-casting of sexual orientation; its espousal of sex education and permitted masturbation for young people; its risk of touting carnality (sexual immorality); and its advocacy of more natural ease (less "compulsivity") in sexual interactions. What is presented to children and adolescents is not an unmixed blessing, to be sure.

Following a fuller characterization of sexual revolution, this part considers homosexuality—along with its counterpoint, heterosexuality, and its middle ground admixture, bisexuality—as developmental issues. The greater acceptance of some of the homosexualities is, for many, a case in point that the sexual revolution occurred, only to be shot down in a counterrevolutionary backlash related to AIDS. Concepts of core gender identity, sex role differentiation, sexual orientation and preference are covered with respect to development of children and adolescents centering around homosexuality (and, to a lesser extent, bisexuality).

Then this chapter deals with six of the barriers to sexual freedom in our contemporary life: the family, sexually transmitted diseases, antihomosexual bias, morality both religious and secular, adolescent peer influences, and shortage of money. The chapter concludes by taking stock of sexual freedom in the contemporary world, considering briefly questions of promiscuity, virginity, easy divorce, hate crimes, births out of wedlock, shifting conceptions of gender, and—close to psychiatry—myths of a latency period for children and a universal Oedipus complex.

Definition

The sexual revolution as described here denotes a partly fulfilled, loosely organized movement or project in the 20th century, aimed at activating radical sociocultural changes. If realized, that endeavor will move society toward permitting sexual behavior and tolerating sexual diversity. Accompanying this is a trend toward "outing"—greater honesty or candor about one's sexual behavior. The current transformation of American sexual mores began in the 1950s and probably continues to the present, with a peak occurring in the late 1960s and 1970s. It is a revolution primarily in personal sexual behavior, although it is accompanied by cognitive, fantasy, attitudinal, and emotional changes that take the revolution far beyond the individual and well into the sociocultural realm. The coming out of a homosexual or bisexual congressman or the publicizing of senators' womanizing pales beside the changes in popular culture—the explicit sex (and violence) shown in the movies, the nontraditional sexuality talked about so often on television talk shows, the fact of coeducational dormitories as a norm on college campuses, the flourishing of gay and lesbian support groups among high school students, open discussion of condom use on daily television, and the raging debates about abortion. Ours is a time of personal sexual expressions that may have occurred always, but up until recently they remained closeted. The recent sociocultural changes involving public talk and institutionalized expressions of sexual freedom have made for telling marks on social history.

Throughout Western history, the acceptance of sexual freedom would appear to have alternated cyclically with its suppression. The cycles occur slowly, however, and many who are caught up in the enthusiasm of sexual liberation do not recall the era of Puritanism that preceded their time of liberation, nor do they consider that repression may soon reappear. Past epochs of antisexual attitudes have waxed mostly during times when sexually transmitted diseases have been greatly feared, perhaps foretelling for us today a new epoch of AIDS-related antisexuality. Yet, in time, no doubt, another new generation probably will usher in a period of greater sexual permissiveness, claim afresh that it has invented or discovered totally original and different modes of sexuality, and assert smugly that it has attained unprecedented heights of sexual satisfaction.

Forerunners to Sexual Freedom

Wilhem Reich (1927/1961, 1931/1969) coupled his plea for the sexual liberation of young people with a call for socialism. Other, less radical psychiatrists and psychoanalysts (some before and some after Reich), even when calling for sexual liberation, did not include the young and did not see the struggle for sexual freedom in a larger sociocultural context. Neither were they prone to provide many particulars of their envisaged sexual revolution—or sexual reform through education and enlightenment.

Sigmund Freud and Havelock Ellis are examples of sexology's conservatives who often dubbed themselves "nonpolitical." Reich, however, originally proposed that orgasm was an integral part of a life of health, vitality, and freedom from neurosis, and that if the revolution was to last, sexuality had to be a part of a larger sociocultural revolution. Thus sexuality became political and stood in a complementary relation with political revolution.

While Freud stayed relatively conservative in his views about sexual behavior, condoning mainly the sexuality endorsed by his Roman Catholic papal contemporaries, Wilhelm Reich was the first to regard child and adolescent masturbation, heterosexual experimentation, contraception, and nonprocreative sexuality in a positive light. Reich was, nonetheless, almost as androcentric and antifeminist as Freud. Indeed, most apostles of sexual freedom have been adults, and men, and for them, the sexual freedom of women and children has not been a top priority.

Anthropologists contributed to our understanding of sexuality in a broadened cultural context and demonstrated that not all sociocultural constructions of sexuality are negating (often called "sex negative"). Margaret Mead (1928, 1935, 1949) and Bronislaw Malinowski (1927/1969) showed that in Samoa and the Trobriand Islands, young people can be sexually active with healthy consequences (a thing I heard Anna Freud attest to in 1966, to the consternation of some of her associates at the Hampstead Child Therapy Clinic). The psychoanalytic anthropologist Geza Roheim concurred as early as the 1920s, and the psychoanalytic anthropologist George Devereux (1951, 90–107) wrote admiringly of the Mohave approach to sexual enlightenment and practice:

The latency period is absent among the Mohave, probably because of the tolerant attitude of the adults toward infantile sexuality. Sexual education consisted in the inculcation of sexual *ethics,* rather than of sexual *morality,* and in the teaching of sexual rites and observances, and of sexual techniques. The latter type of instruction was accidental and amounted to a tacit noninterference with opportunities to observe parental intercourse.

Such observations made witnessing the primal scene less of a trauma. Reich had always said such witnessing was, in the West, a function of housing—thus giving a sociopolitical twist to a "psychic trauma."

Alfred Kinsey and Wardell Pomeroy, biologists and sexologists, were the first to research the sexuality of a sample of American men (1948). Adopting the occupational styles of census enumerators and ecologists, those investigators surveyed, tallied, and reported on what their research subjects did (or claimed they did) to reach orgasm—and with what frequency. Although often passed over, the Kinsey group saw that men were on a heterosexual-homosexual continuum, not in one or the other dichotomous category. At that time, numerous critics remarked that the Kinsey report acted as if sexuality occurred without any socioemotional context. Unabashed by criticism, in 1953 the Kinsey group published a parallel survey of a group of women.

To be sure, scientific researchers were only one source of the ideas that gave impetus to the sexual revolution; intellectuals and artists played a major role as well. From the 1930s on the works of D. H. Lawrence, Mabel Dodge Lujan, Anais Nin, Henry Miller, and others opened the way for later sexual liberationists to travel. In 1954 the social philosopher and intellectual critic Herbert Marcuse published his view that Freudians tended to bank too much on the "overly administered reality principle." For his part, Marcuse suggested more liberation of Eros. By 1959 another sexual revolutionary, Norman O. Brown, invoked the name of Freud in the book *Life Against Death: The Psychoanalytical Meaning of History,* in which he called for a resurrection of the body and for adults to return to the polymorphic perversity of childhood.

Also, throughout the 1950s and on into the subsequent decades, the Grove Press in New York became a major cultural influence by publishing a large catalog of classics in erotica, pornography, and obscenity; this had a powerful influence on popular culture. One particularly important book was *Eros Denied* by Wayland Young (Briton Lord Kennet), published in 1964, a paean to sexuality that castigated sex-negative culture.

Scientific work itself continued with great popularization and public discussion. William Masters, a male gynecologist, and Virginia Johnson, a female social scientist, followed Kinsey and associates with a monumental contribution to sexology, *Human Sexual Response* (1966). This was soon elaborated with clinical applications by *Human Sexual Inadequacy* (1970). Masters and Johnson broke many icons, particularly about human female sexuality, and the reverberations still are being felt around the world.

From the 1950s on, American life and manners experienced an information explosion about female sexuality. From the 1960s until the present, women have been in the vanguard of the sexual revolution. For good or ill, women continue to be the main adult players in this continuing social process. This is not meant to diminish the largely male beatnik efflorescence, nor the wave of male homosexual blue movies, nor the great increase in obscenity and pornography in popular books, magazines, and films that arose after the 1950s; but women and the women's movement carried a special torch throughout this era. Women generally do see sexuality in its broader contexts of personal lives and cultural existence, and that seems to be a distinctive feature of the feminine or feminist sexual legacy to the present generation of both males and females. Women who are feminists stress the needs and prowess of the female, her frequent favoring of loving, holding, and bonding (in contrast to the male's reputed going for the gold of performance and orgasm), and sometimes contend that only another woman can do the caring and relationship-building that women crave as a part of a gratifying sexual and spiritual life. This chapter assumes that women are both the experts and the vanguard of a sexual revolution that sees sexuality differently—including their partners' sexuality—within a sociocultural and interpersonal context, that is, viewing sexuality as immersed in prosocial values.

Brief Historical Note on Views of Female Sexuality

Although scientists and young male microscopists had long known about the morphology and movements of human spermatozoa, there was a long scientific lag in isolating, visualizing, and probing the human ovum. That feat was accomplished only in the 1920s. Before then, only the large chicken egg had served as the animal model or analog for anatomical and most embryological study; for early human development, very early abortuses had had to suffice. Today technology has made it possible to fertilize human eggs in vivo and in vitro and to store eggs for future use.

Men may still control some of the manipulations of fertilized eggs, since males rate highly their roles as sperm donors and sometimes litigate fiercely for their rights over their sperm, but women have taken greater charge of owning and controlling their own eggs, whether graced by fertilization or not. Perhaps an unbiased naturalist would observe that both sperm and egg are equally important, but eggs, in the normal course of events are, in truth, fewer and dearer than spermatozoa.

Men have propounded many kinds of sex ideologies that are consistent with keeping males more powerful. The myth of the vaginal orgasm was a fine example of a distorted male perspective. If a man could have a "peak experience" while enjoying the moist mucosal surrounding when penis was in vagina, it may be an understandable male error that he proceeded to preach that that very insertion was exactly what a woman wanted too. Thus it was believed that a nonneurotic woman had both vaginal and clitoridal orgasms but *preferred* the former; it was believed that there was a G-spot, variably located on the introitus, and that when this spot was pressed it operated through an innervation independent of the tug on the periclitoridal tissues. Many males believed that simultaneous female and male orgasm was an easily attainable ideal. Of course, homosexual males (or females) might have taught heterosexual men the sanity of taking turns and the practical wisdom of petting and clitoridal stimulation right up to one or two female orgasms prior to intromission. But heterosexual men seldom sought advisors in those homosexual ranks. It was as if males were motivated forever to neglect the clitoris. Envy? Heterophobia? Or simple narcissism that inhibits empathy?

The clitoris is the principal focus of the recent escalation in our knowledge of female sexuality— and of much sexuality that conjoins females and males. The clitoris is *the* organ of sexual pleasure and orgasm when lubricated, and it accounts for the polyorgasmic capabilities of the human female, giving her a virtuosity and abandon that males, equipped less effectively, can only observe and enjoy but not imitate or adopt (Masters, Johnson, & Kolodny, 1995). The clitoris, compared to an unshielded penis in vagina, has no immediately evident function for biological adaptation of the species—unless exuberant sexuality for sheer pleasure is regarded as significant for reproductive and biological evolution. The male American way of summarizing the issue is that greater sexual pleasure of the female, conjoined to male ejaculation, is what gives evolutionary utility to a clitoris.

The clitoris is not, as small boys often think, an inferior analog or substitute for the penis. Indeed it is, as an organ of pleasure, far superior to the penis, and in the eyes of many, the clitoris is more esthetically pleasing. Unlike the penis, the clitoris does not do any double service as a urinary and/or ejaculatory conduit but is a more highly specialized and evolved organ that seems to be there exclusively for hedonistic uses by its owner and her partners. It might not be stretching the truth too much to say that the sexual revolution has been waged and won with the clitoris and its admirers' good press.

Other Features of the Sexual Revolution

The sexual revolution has emphasized adult more than child or adolescent sexuality. Within adult ranks, the revolution seems to have had more adult male than female proponents who speak out. The enduring texts of sexual freedom seem to some to reside in *Playboy*, *Penthouse*, and *Esquire*, magazines with largely male audiences, but perhaps one could say more judiciously that they are more importantly located in the male-dominated Supreme Court decisions of *Roe v. Wade* and the redeeming value of Joyce's *Ulysses*, or the repeated upholdings of the Bill of Rights. Still, women have taken charge of what men began—whether calmly and politely or shrilly and raucously—and have tried to eradicate the double standard that men earlier imposed for their male advantage.

The focus of the sexual revolution has been on recreative more than procreative sexuality. The revolution's domain of freedom has broadened to include more than heterosexuality "with penis in vagina." And it has embraced many devices to prevent pregnancy and childbirth. Some have contended that without the contraceptive technology of the latter half of the 20th century, our present era of sexuality as a recreational endeavor would not have been possible. That might be so. The sexual revolution has embraced each and every advance and experiment in contraception, from the condom, to the pill, to intrauterine devices. Similarly, the sexual revolutionary's support is always for abortion according to the woman's wants (free choice, abortion on demand). Such an ideology would be inconceivable were we not in an age of advanced contraception.

Sexual freedom that does not exploit has been espoused for children and for adult homosexual, bisexual, and heterosexual persons. Even some erosion of the boundaries around each of that typecast threesome (homo-, bi-, and heterosexual) has been advocated by sexual revolutionists. Adults who lived through the sexual revolution do not ardently advocate heterosexism or homophobia-homoparanoia, but instead adopt a kinder and gentler stance for a more fluid and versatile sexual career following only one's adult tastes and preferences. Sometimes children's sexual freedom is endorsed as well, but commonly there is restraint about spelling out the reaches of that freedom. Consequently, the typical example given of children's sexual freedom by many adult spokespersons is sexual information and enlightenment. Give knowledge to the children, but give fun to adults, some have said.

"Sex education" in home and school has complemented and been strengthened by the sexual revolution. Since the 1940s and 1950s, progressive school districts have taught children and adolescents about sexuality. The evidence is not in to answer the question whether sex education has enhanced sexual freedom of the young, but it may have encouraged experimentation; certainly that has been true of some drug education programs that hoped to warn youths against drug experimentation. Today masturbation, at least, is seldom condemned by educated and honest parents and teachers—an attainment to which psychoanalysts and psychiatrists have contributed mightily. The post-Freudian psychoanalytic literature, coeval with the sexual revolution, has done much to detoxify and demystify the meaning and sequelae of frequent masturbation both by the young and other age groups.

Overall, the sexual revolution has extolled eroticism and carnality in contemporary society. It has advanced what some have termed "the spirit of Satyricon," condoning promiscuous polymorphous sexual pleasure, or, in its more old-fashioned formulation, "sexual immorality." Although a general proscription of adult-with-child sexuality has persisted among them, a few sexual revolutionaries have tried to equate pedophilia with sexual freedom for children. An association to promote "man-boy love" has formed and grown since the 1960s, wrapping itself in sexual freedom's banner. Likewise, a pro-incest lobby worked hard to conceal itself within a movement for sexual liberation, but to date, the sexual revolutionary mainstream has opposed pedophilia and incest and regarded such practices as only an exploitation and betrayal of children. When one of the participants in sexuality is a child or adolescent, many clinicians use the rule of thumb that an age difference of more than 5 years always entails exploitation. Age boundaries seem to be stronger than gender boundaries when those caught up in the sexual revolution consider adults' sexual rights and responsibilities.

In general, compulsive or obsessive sexuality has not been condoned by sexual revolutionaries, and the attitude that one should have no need to be overly strenuous or insistent about sexuality has caught hold, more widely than deeply. Considerable revulsion is shown from time to time against that compulsive fusion of power and lust, husband rape of wife, and against rape in general. Other forms of compulsive, not natural and easy, sexuality have been opposed by sexologists in the counseling or therapy fields; among them are such forms as compulsive ejaculation in the male or compulsive orgasm-seeking in both male and female. Sexual revolutionaries have endorsed, in their stead, acceptance of nonorgastic intimacy and Taoist and tantric copulation, for example.

Homosexuality as a Developmental Issue

The sexual revolution has produced some unanticipated by-products. It has produced both lessened rigidity about sex-role behavior and at the same time adhered to more rigid stereotypes about sexual orientation and certain sexuality preferences. In an earlier era, even if predominantly heterosexual in longing and behavior, everyone was regarded as having some homosexual proclivities. In that bygone era, both Sigmund Freud and Harry Stack Sullivan postulated a "normal homosexual phase" in late latency. In fact, Sullivan did not regard homosexuality as rigidly stage-bound behavior. Freud declined to support a contemporary gay liberation movement, precisely on the grounds that by declaring homosexuality to be too special and separate from the norm, it dehumanized and clouded the homosexuality of all persons. When a homosexual orientation becomes enshrined as a separate subculture or way of life, even if esteem and political power accrue to the self-identified gay or lesbian group, the remainder of the population is made out to have no homosexual interests or acts. In the long run, anti-homosexual bias may not decrease when being gay is affirmed as a special way of life. That can have dangerous consequences.

Neither Freud nor Sullivan made much of the specialness of homosexual acts and desires. Only thoroughgoing Philistines, to their way of thinking, made a great to-do about such isosexual choices. In the 1940s, homosexual adults, such as the poet Robert Duncan, proclaimed their lack of specialness, their feeling of solidarity with all struggling humanity. Paul Goodman, the anarchist poet and essayist, celebrated himself as a more fully rounded sexual being when he affirmed his "queerness" along with his other sexual tendencies. André Gide (1924/1950), in writing *Corydon*, had made a plea for the universality, not the particularity, of homosexual behavior integrated into a life with heterosexual interests and activities. Indeed, most urbane heterosexual adult males of Duncan's (if not Gide's) generation recalled without scorn the facts of their sexual experimentation with homosexual partners during childhood and adolescence if not later—or their adult dreams of outright or quasi-homosexual encounters. Diversity was not an outrage for them.

Today, however, again and again, the case is made for homosexuality as a special endowment, for homosexuality as being manifested in earlier and earlier childhood, for homosexuality as an immutable marker of one's core human identity, and for homosexuality as a monolithic "way of life." Naturally, too, in a biologizing era such as the present one, a "biological substrate" is sought avidly (Pool, 1993) and almost prayerfully. Thus homosexuality is said to be inborn to persons with special brain size and hemispheric configuration, or with an intersex (i.e., intermediate between male and female) count of cells in the preoptic nuclei of known homosexual persons, usually males. Twin studies and family studies provide only circumstantial evidence that homosexuality "runs in families," but the results of such family researches are declared as if they give proof positive that homoerotic and homosexual acts of adults flow undoubtedly from one's genetic makeup. For many of the reasons cited, homosexuality is now an important developmental issue in the aftermath of (and possibly backlash from) the sexual revolution.

CORE GENDER IDENTITY

Core gender identity—knowing and cathecting one's gender—is not often up in the air for any child. The gender of ascription, however, is most influential in gender assignment; and that ascription is made ultimately by oneself. Characteristically the ascription mirrors the attitudes and values of one's mothering person, even in cases of ambiguous genitalia, androgen-insensitive testes or such other anomalies. There is no real evidence that persons who later become predominantly homosexual have any consistent variation in early core gender identity. That identity is usually genetically congruent—matching what one's genetic as well as genital makeup is—and it is no different for homosexual or bisexual individuals whether in childhood or later. Most homosexual men regard themselves as men and most lesbian women view themselves as women.

Core gender identity, referring to a fundamental ingredient of selfhood, is established usually by 30 months of age, paralleling in time and import the establishment of the child's *body image* or *schema* and the *nuclear self-concept* (either "I am a good egg" or "I am of little value"). My clinical experience has shown that children who manifest homosexual behavior differ hardly at all in their core gender identity from children who have only heterosexual or no sexual experience. When they do state that they want to be of a different gender, it is most often a protest against real or imagined mistreatment that they perceive as being based on their ascribed (and profoundly accepted) gender.

Another assertion that I would make from personal experience is this: Transsexuals, who certainly do have a core gender identity disturbance, are not the same as homosexual or bisexual children and adolescents. The views of Zucker and Green (1991), for example, who deal with clinical populations, not children drawn widely from sampling the general community, tend to blur these distinctions and claim that effeminate or girlish "sissy boys" evidence some form of gender identity disorder (GID) of childhood and become "at risk" for homosexuality, less so for transsexualism, in adulthood. It is as if all cross-gender stereotype-busting heralds homosexuality *or* transsexualism. Homophobic and misogynist males whom I have encountered in my clinical work often despise homosexual males, largely on the grounds that they are perceived as too much like women, instead of seeing adult homosexual males as persons who have developed greater androgyny—granted, a development seldom made in young child subjects of clinical research.

Zuger (1988) argued that children who want to be of other than their assigned gender should be regarded as homosexual children. I personally like the more judicious statements of Coates, Friedman, and Wolfe (1991):

This position is a mistake on empirical and conceptual grounds. Evidence from the most extensive prospective study of boys with GID to date has not demonstrated that homosexuality is the inevitable outcome of childhood GID (Green, 1987). In our view, gender identity differentiation, erotic development, and erotic object crystallization reciprocally influence each other at multiple levels of organization. We believe that conceptually to conflate gender identity, erotic development, and erotic object orientation, at this point in our understanding of these issues will obscure the development of a differentiated conceptualization of this disorder and interfere with scientific progress in this area of research. (p. 517)

Masculinity in girls (tomboyishness) and femininity in boys (sissiness) show no strong predictive value for subsequent homosexuality or bisexuality in the great majority of youths known to me. Such sex-role differentiation as boyish or girlish behavior does not consolidate securely until between about 48 and 60 months of age, the kindergarten epoch. In an earlier era, theoretical commitments led many in child psychiatry to assert that very early onset of stereotyped gender behavior occurred in toddlers and preschool children. But subsequent research has demonstrated that boys and girls equally like phallic and "inner-space" toys until late preschool or kindergarten age, and "cognitive differences in coding and memory are not observed, but differences in field independence, characteristic of males in adolescence and adulthood, favor females in the preschool years" (Birns, 1977). Those investigators who combine curiosity with a developmental perspective are the persons now doing enhanced scientific research.

Because learning societal preferences concerning gender roles is dependent on cognitive level, brighter children are both easier to enculturate and easier to make skeptical regarding the traditional gender schema. Gifted children may learn both to conform and to be inwardly rejecting of the societal values and prescriptions about sex-role behavior. Kohlberg (1968) demonstrated this when he reported that

the bright boys are preferentially oriented to the adult male at age four, at a time when the average boys are preferentially oriented to the adult female. As they grow older, the bright boys seem to shift to a preferential orientation to females, and then from seven to ten, to shift once more to a neutral orientation.... From age five to seven the average boys begin to become more female oriented, as the bright boys had done two years earlier. (p. 150)

Sex-role differentiation is plausibly regarded as largely a function of societal definition, stereotyping, and sociocultural construction, played out against the component temperament of each child. To use a male example, a mild and agreeable boy may be more easily typecast as a sissy than a rough-and-tumble little fighter; both boys, however, may develop bisexual or homosexual identities at a later stage in life. Although some 85% of adult homosexual males recall some gender nonconformity (such as cross-dressing) during childhood, 15% do not, and it is a telling datum that 55% of heterosexual men also recall childhood gender nonconformity (Small, 1993). Sex-role behavior in childhood or later really does not tell us very specifically about later sexual orientation.

SEXUAL ORIENTATION OR SEXUAL PREFERENCE?

Sexual orientation is a rubric that should be reserved for individuals who have become sexually active and not be applied to novices in the realm of sexuality. The term is better saved for a more experienced person than for a child or even a young adolescent. Much juvenile sexual experience is so facultative, accidental, and like a "convenience sampling" that it does not warrant too much closure in making predictions. If a child has and enjoys homosexual contacts with a peer, there is greater likelihood that such an encounter will recur later; but opposite-sex encounters, by accident or design, are not precluded for such a homosexually experienced child, particularly if imaginative, gifted, or just bright. Adolescents do engage in a wider range of genital contacts, but even their experimentation with heterosexuality and homosexuality does not cast a rigid die. It seems likely (Weinberg, Williams, & Pryor, 1994) that persons not so specially gifted will, during their adolescence, most often follow a homosexual first experience with a homosexual adult orientation and a heterosexual first experience with a heterosexual adult orientation. The bisexual adult orientation more frequently results from a heterosexual first experience—to which a later "add on" of homosexual eroticism has occurred. Only adults can know and claim their genuine sexual orientation (gay, straight, or in between).

Formerly, habitually choosing same-sex partners by a grown woman or man was called their "homosexual sexual preference." Nowadays, however, "preference" is said to have overly cognitive and overly willful connotations; a segment of the gay community proclaims that gay persons are born, not made; thus, today the "politically correct" term is "orientation," not "preference." It may be that an iron-clad sexual orientation to homosexuality (or heterosexuality) is merely an unexamined sexual preference. Possibly, seeing one's preferences as being driven genetically from birth onward and as being beyond one's control is just an occult, blind zone in an otherwise-examined life.

Many who do examine their sexual careers using introspection discover that they have a marked bipotentiality for both homosexual and heterosexual acts. They report that their bisexuality was not some childish or teenage confusion or reluctance to come out as fully gay or fully straight. Instead, they see their sexual bipotentiality when it is bisexually expressed as but another of the existential dilemmas that accompany being human. Perhaps—and this is my conjecture—our genetic makeup is for bisexuality and for neither exclusive homosexuality nor exclusive heterosexuality. Assuredly, Weinberg, Williams, and Pryor (1994) came to the same conclusion following an empirical study of a large group of bisexual females, males, and transsexuals in San Francisco:

All individuals seem to have the potential to be sexually attracted to both sexes. This potential may remain throughout a person's life and may be activated at any time. . . .

Bisexuality occurs when people adopt an open gender schema, a mode of thinking and perception opposed to traditional views of gender. Central to this is the understanding that gender and sexual preference are independent. . . . When people learn that gender and sexual preference do not necessarily go together, they are more likely to entertain having sex with both men and women. (pp. 296–297)

Surely, self-acceptance may be a more laborious, larger, and more complex challenge than making the facile speculation that one has an innate, biological substrate that presumably restricts one to being either gay or straight, but not in between. The sexual revolution has made us examine and reexamine such issues.

Conditions Impeding Sexual Freedom

Many sociocultural conditions flow together to limit unfettered sexuality despite sexual revolution. Six brakes on sexual freedom persisting today deserve consideration: the family, sexually transmitted diseases, antihomosexual bias, religious and secular morality, adolescent peer pressure, and lack of money. These circumstances, singly or together, may be part of a puritanical surge or may be only countervailing trends to balance out the biosocial imperative to engage in unfettered sexuality.

THE FAMILY

The family's function as a regulator and channeler of human lust and sexuality has long been remarked by social scientists. The family that maintains and actualizes a taboo against incest is controlling sexuality in what most think a wholesome way; the family that enacts a long-term commitment between the adult partners is controlling adultery and infidelity in a way that many see as salutary; the family that is headed by two consenting adults who are sexually pleasing to one another, and sexually active, is a family that enhances its own stability through providing richness of sexual opportunity that can hardly be matched anywhere except in a family. So by offering grand opportunity to adults within some protective limits, the family puts at least a mild brake on the Satyricon spirit of its members. The monogamous American family provides few sexual opportunities for children and adolescents, who are encouraged either to look outside of the family or to remain chaste and sexually inactive as long as their minority status lasts.

SEXUALLY TRANSMITTED DISEASES

First, herpes and later AIDS have joined a long list of scourges that are transmitted in the body fluids (including mucus, blood, and semen) of human beings. As has always occurred with sexually transmitted diseases, human immunodeficiency virus (HIV) infection has tended to curb promiscuity or, more charitably, nonmonogamous sexuality. Since bisexual people are less monogamous than either heterosexual or homosexual persons, during an AIDS scourge they have become for many the particular target of hatred. Since it is incurable, AIDS has engendered "safe sex," that is, a barrier-laden sexuality, designed to protect partners from rash exchanges of bodily fluids during sexual interaction. This, in turn, lends an air of caution to all casual sexual encounters, whether homosexual or heterosexual, and, in effect, makes them not casual, not spontaneous. Sexual planning or restraint in almost any form seems antithetical to the eudemonical spirit of our narcissistic era. Still, when love is threatened and rational considerations are entertained, sexual promiscuity is curbed. For self-destructive or self-defeating personalities, in contrast, the same threat can spur ever greater sexual excesses.

ANTIHOMOSEXUAL BIAS

Antihomosexual bias is prevalent as a brake on the sexual freedom of young people. In early childhood, adults endeavor to curb and proscribe any homosexual or androgynous behavior in boys or (to a lesser extent) in girls. Even more decisively, adults try to eradicate any actual genital contact made by young children, especially with same-sex partners. Misogyny, heterosexism, and childism are all conjoined as attitudes and institutions in antihomosexual bias and antisexual revolution attitudes and deeds.

RELIGIOUS AND SECULAR MORALITY

Religious and secular morality are other nearly perennial curbs on sexual expression, serving always to lead the person inclined to be sexually active not to let go in nymphomania or satyriasis but instead to ponder, reflect, question, and seek insight. The pressure of morality is toward self-restraint instead of action. Just say no. Religious (but also secular humanistic) moralists often condone and encourage some candor (a bit) about sexual matters, but they always preach against "too open" licentious sexuality or talk. In other words, even when they seek to overthrow intense Puritanism, moralists advocate moral and ethical contemplation as always indispensable, and sometimes preferable, to action. They advocate responsibility even as they claim that human happiness puts sexuality high on its list of contributors and must be honored. It is safe to say that being ethically alert and responsible always curbs promiscuity.

ADOLESCENT PEER PRESSURE

Several observers, including some psychiatrists, have commented upon the streak of antipromiscuity found in many adolescent subcultures. The peer subculture of adolescents is not monolithic in promoting "being sexually active" but may take a stance against promiscuity. Few adolescents see their loss of virginity as soon as the thought occurs to them as a compulsory rite of passage from childhood to adulthood. Adolescent peer pressures are not always conducive to orgies.

LACK OF MONEY

Lack of economic opportunity—of money—remains as a formidable impediment to sexual freedom, especially of the young. If impoverished young parents long unrequitedly for a night in a motel, the situation is more hopeless still for the poor adolescents who are not married. The Janus Report (1993) opined: "The major constraint on the expression of a free-wheeling sexual life-style is a lack of money. . . . [Indeed, s]ocial restrictions on the expression of sexuality have been minimized. At the same time, an emphasis on the old values or the importance of marriage, of married love, and even of fidelity have been maintained for all age groups" (p. 349).

Current Status of Sexual Freedom

The present state of American attitudes and practices regarding sexuality cannot be assessed readily. Still, some changed conditions are notable and warrant a brief summary here.

While there is a great interest in sexuality and in sexual freedom, these remain embroiled topics, taboo topics, both for research and for public education. In particular, any sexuality research done with children as subjects is strictly forbidden. Any researcher or teacher who deals openly with childhood sexuality is, at best, regarded as a probable subversive and, at worst, as a probable pedophiliac voyeur. Research about genitality is more suspect than research about "psychosexual" matters with children.

On the matter of youthful promiscuity, considerable opposition, caution, and restraint seem to reign, but there are also some countervailing pressures to condone such youthful activity. Carl G. Jung contended that adolescent promiscuity carried a preventive weight because it minimized the chances of irrupted promiscuity in later life when enduring relationships with a spouse and offspring could be jeopardized by midlife flings. Jung's viewpoint appears to have withstood the test of time and to have been validated, at least for clinicians. With adolescents and young adults we call it experimentation and think it possibly wholesome, while with the middle-aged we call it foolish, immoral promiscuity.

The cult of virginity today has weakened, probably with no chance of reestablishment in the foreseeable future. The double standard, requiring chastity of young women and almost mandating sexual experience for the male, appears to be a relic of the past. Today young people usually see the cult of virginity as a foolish yoke, especially for self-respecting young females. *The Janus Report on Sexual Behavior* (1993) revealed that 2 to 3% of young people ages 18 to 26 years (and even 3% of males 51 to 64) reported that they had their "first full sexual relations before achieving ten years of age. Eighteen percent of young male adults (18–26) had their first intercourse between 11 and 14 years of age; 70% reported 15–18 years as their age of losing virginity" (p. 36).

These days fewer young women in the West are forced to enter into marriage with intact hymens or with a "spotless sexual past"; simultaneously, fewer young women are driven into prostitution as a way of livelihood and life. Especially in Europe's Roman Catholic countries, prostitution always has been a "shadow institution," a darkened mirror, of premarital chastity and virginity. Parceling women out into either madonnas or whores, and believing that some bad women may be needed in order to protect the good ones, is antiquated. How can young people's play with one another's body orifices and appendages be taken as so deadly serious when it can occur so easily and comfortably among androgynous youths? The derogatory attitudes toward females that were packaged together with such chivalry concerning female chastity (and acceptance of male hegemony) in the cult of virginity are also weak relics of a bygone era.

No-fault divorce has flourished contemporaneously with the sexual revolution, and free divorce is extolled by many sexual revolutionists, as a part of their eudemonical outlook. Easy divorce is seen as a blessing by adults who want out of a marriage, but it can be said with certainty that it has not brought an improved family life for children and adolescents. Today, 50% of marriages end in divorce. Divorce and remarriage are the rule for many adults, as if to fulfill Margaret Mead's prophecy that 3 marriages are needed in life's different epochs: the young one for sex, a later one for children, and the third for companionship. Many Americans do not stop with 3 and do not attain their desired goal in any.

In a time that displays little civility, there appears to be a growing sensibility against hate crimes such as "gay bashing." That may be a sequel of tolerance generated in the sexual revolution. Many communities have seen a growth in progress to guarantee "fairness" in housing, employment, and insurance for persons who live in a homosexual lifestyle. An "out" homosexual minority, perhaps of fewer than 10% of the entire U.S. population, seems to more and more people to be no gigantic threat and to be undeserving of the vicious discrimination still waged against it in both attitudes and institutions. Nevertheless, antihomosexual bias remains entrenched in American sociocultural life and is a dark force arrayed against sexual freedom.

Births out of wedlock are not officially condoned in the United States, but their incidence is rapidly increasing among women of all classes. These births, too, are an index of the sexual revolution. Between 1980 and 1989, according to the National Center for Health Statistics, births to unmarried women almost doubled, increasing from 668,000 to 1,200,000. By 1990 some 40,000 young women under 20 years of age were leaving school annually because of pregnancy. If unaided, these young women and their offspring constitute great psychosocial liabilities for the United States.

It is evident that many American women are having babies and rearing them without men. By 1990 some 17% of families were mother-only, and a fourth of our families were mother-only by 1995. When women do live with men, women are taking control of the bedroom, dictating to men about their safe-sex requirements, making their own choices about contraception or abortion, and stating unabashedly what they like sexually. Thousands of women today are choosing premarital sex, extramarital affairs, open marriages, and non-marriage or marriage without children. Women control both procreational and recreational sexuality; after all, they do give birth to babies and may run greater risks in an AIDS epoch. Myths about husband power, male power, or father power sound ever feebler and more contrived.

Still, some increase in androgyny (blending masculine and feminine attitudes and behaviors) has occurred among males and females. More than ever before, fathers are being less traditionally masculine and are participating as family members, including giving more care to children. Women, on the other hand, are also undertaking less traditionally feminine things and, whether by preference or necessity, are entering the marketplace, mostly in low-paying jobs but fighting for pay equity with males.

One new trend that may reflect some androgynous effects of the sexual revolution is the increase in father-only households with children. From 1970 to 1989 the number of children in father-only households grew from 500,000 to nearly 1.5 million. And while in 1970 only 32,000 American children lived with never-married dads, by 1990, 448,000 children lived in almost 197,000 father-only households. Surely some portion of those men are homosexual fathers, but their exact number has only been estimated.

Despite sexual revolution, for some child analysts and psychiatrists the myth of childhood latency persists—that there is a time following resolution of the Oedipus complex when the child spurns all genitality and becomes a good student, scout, and rule-server consolidating identification with the same-sex parent. In truth, some children during the elementary school years do show a relative latency or quiescence, but a seasoned worldwide perspective would have to hold that latency is far from the universal developmental stage that some might have expected. Presumably, such an elementary school youngster is waiting for the hormonal rush of puberty to restore some awareness both of others as sexual beings and of his or her own genitals as demanding gratification through orgasm. The myth of latency holds on even when preteens are sexually active and young women become pregnant before they have ever had any experience of menarcheal menstruation. The myth holds out despite our knowledge that young children from birth onward seem to be in a state of readiness for sexual arousal: Newborn

girls manifest vaginal lubrication cyclically and neonatal boys show penile tumescence cyclically (Masters, Johnson, & Kolodny, 1995).

For psychiatrists, any summary on the sexual revolution must include a word about the Oedipus complex, once considered to be central to neuroses and universal in human psychosexual development. The Oedipus-complex myth's staying power is phenomenal. It persists even when millions of children are growing up in homes without any adult male present on any meaningful basis and leading lives psychically blighted far more by a shortage of economic resources than of adult males. The blight of preoedipal and nonoedipal traumata in many such children has received close attention from many psychoanalytic writers, but people with classical training still look for oedipal constellations, still look for triangulation where there is only a tense dyad. Some diehards persist in viewing the father, even when nonexistent, as the central figure in the child's emotional world.

Conclusion

Psychiatrists, particularly psychoanalysts, have trumpeted some of the attainments of the sexual revolution, but its impact on the personal lives of these psychiatrists probably has not been formidable. One explanation of their blasé attitude may be that the sexual revolution brought little new to psychiatrists regarding nonmonogamous relations. Some psychiatrists appear to contend that since Krafft-Ebing and Freud, there was nothing new under the sun regarding human sexuality. Another group of psychiatrists may know from personal experience that affordable promiscuity, bisexuality, and other polymorphous expressions of lust antedated the sexual revolution, if the latter is dated as post-1960. Psychiatrists as a group tend to keep their personal lives discreetly closeted; the sexual revolution has permitted them to be more openly antipuritanical, however. Yet, after the sexual revolution, their sexuality with patients often came to be highlighted in public discussion. Singling out psychiatrists seemed unjustified to me, since according to my own personal knowledge, more pediatricians and internists have sex with patients (or mothers of patients) than do psychiatrists. Other physicians have not made big headlines, however, because their patients do not seem so dependent and vulnerable or because the American Medical Association has publicized mainly psychiatric corruption in these matters.

Psychiatric diagnosis, as embodied in diagnostic manuals and official nomenclature, surely is no harbinger of childhood sexual freedom. Mention there (as in the fourth edition of the *Diagnostic and Statistical Manual of Mental Disorders*) of the sexuality of children is rare; when it is mentioned, it is regarded as a diagnostic criterion for conduct disorder. This is in keeping with the spirit of Krafft-Ebing, who saw many forms of healthy (adult) sexuality as criteria of degeneracy and constitutional psychopathic inferiority. The sexual revolution has not succeeded yet in depathologizing the sex play of children.

Before another century has elapsed, childhood sexuality, too, may be depathologized. The child may enjoy rights to private masturbation and consensual sexual play with the genitals of agemates both female and male. Childhood eroticism may increase, since when adults are sexually preoccupied, children are likely to be similarly disposed and even to be more prone to be sexually abused by adults.

Perhaps when sexual freedom has shown its benefits for all ages, the compulsive tone of tension and guilt that permeates sexuality today will no longer pervade anyone's sexuality. In the future, I hope that sexual freedom for children will be a positive program that stands independent from adult sexual immoralities, allowing freedom for the young while unalterably opposing adults' sexual exploitation of children.

REFERENCES

Birns, B. (1977). The emergence and socialization of sex differences in the earliest years. In S. Chess & A. Thomas (Eds.), *Annual progress in child psychiatry and child development*. New York: Brunner/Mazel.

Brown, N. (1959). *Life against death: The psychoanalytical meaning of history*. Middletown, CT: Wesleyan University Press.

Coates, S., Friedman, R. C., & Wolfe, S. (1991). The etiology of boyhood gender identity disorder: A model for integrating temperament, development, and psychodynamics. *Psychoanalytic Dialogues, 1*(4), 481–523.

Devereux, G. (1951). The primal scene and juvenile heterosexuality in Mohave society. In G. B. Wilber & W. Muensterberger (Eds.), *Psychoanalysis and culture*. New York: International Universities Press.

Gide, A. (1950). *Corydon*. (With comment on second dialogue by Frank Beach; Trans. H. Gibb). New York: Farrar, Straus & Company. (Originally published 1924.)

Green, R. (1987). *The "sissy boy" syndrome and the development of homosexuality*. New Haven, CT: Yale University Press.

Janus, S., & Janus, C. (1993). *The Janus Report on sexual behavior*. New York: John Wiley & Sons.

Kinsey, A., & Pomeroy, W. (1948). *Sexual behavior in the human male*. Philadelphia: W. B. Saunders.

Kinsey, A., & Pomeroy, W. (1953). *Sexual behavior in the human female*. Philadelphia: W. B. Saunders.

Kohlberg, L. (1968). A cognitive-developmental analysis of the children's sex-role concept and attitudes. In E. Maccoby (Ed.), *The development of sex differences*. Stanford, CT: Stanford University Press.

Malinowski, B. (1969). *Sex and repression in savage society*. Cleveland: World Publishing Company. (Originally published 1927.)

Marcuse, H. (1955). *Eros and civilization*. Boston: Beacon Press.

Masters, W., & Johnson, V. (1966). *Human sexual response*. Boston: Little, Brown.

Masters, W., & Johnson, V. (1970). *Human sexual inadequacy*. Boston: Little, Brown.

Masters, W., Johnson, V., & Kolodny, R. (1995). *Human sexuality* (5th ed.). New York: HarperCollins.

Mead, M. (1928). *Coming of age in Samoa: A psychological study of primitive youth for Western civilisation*. (Foreword by F. Boas.)

Mead, M. (1935). Sex and temperament in three primitive societies. New York: William Morrow.

Mead, M. (1949). *Male and female: A study of the sexes in a changing world*. New York: William Morrow.

Pool, R. (1993). Evidence for homosexuality gene. *Science, 261*, 291–292.

Reich, W. (1942). The function of the orgasm. New York: Noonday Press. (Originally published 1927.)

Reich, W. (1945/1969). *The sexual revolution* (4th ed.). New York: Farrar, Straus & Giroux. (Originally published in German in 1931.)

Small, M. F. (1993, March). The gay debate: Is homosexuality a matter of choice or chance? *American Health*, 70–76.

Weinberg, M., Williams, C., & Pryor, D. (1994). *Dual attraction: Understanding bisexuality*. New York: Oxford University Press.

Young, W. (1964). *Eros denied*. New York: Grove Press.

Zuger, B. (1988). Is early effeminate behavior in boys early homosexuality? *Comprehensive Psychiatry, 29*, 509–519.

PART II
Families and Young People

1 / The Changing American Family

Curtis R. Bergstrand

Over the past two decades, discussions of the family in the popular media usually have been accompanied by a mood of crisis. The family, it is frequently claimed, is going through an unprecedented collapse in its ability to meet human needs. Increases in divorce rates, family violence, dual-earner families, single-parent homes, and voluntarily childless couples all are interpreted as symptomatic of the decline in the family as an institution.

A sociologist often views such symptoms quite differently from the general public or even from those in other disciplines within the social sciences. To the sociologist, the family is an institution that reflects the cultural values of the society in which it exists and, to borrow the metaphor of a "system," is intricately interdependent with all other institutions and the changes through which they are going. Just as a physician does not view a single organ in isolation from other organs in the body system, a sociologist interprets family change in relation to changes occurring in all other social institutions.

It is also assumed in sociology that a fundamental prerequisite to all human relationships is that participants in social interaction share certain rules, guidelines, or definitions of the situation that make their actions meaningful, predictable, and productive. An extreme example of the absence of such norms is the chaos that occurs when someone yells "fire" in a theater. What makes a situation such as this so frightening, and potentially destructive, is that competition and conflict in human interaction is not governed by clearly defined norms of deference, role obligations, and social rituals. Without a blueprint for interaction accepted by all parties, potentially constructive

conflict is reduced to random destruction.

It is the theme of this chapter that the family in the United States is indeed in crisis, but not for the reasons usually identified. Many of the supposed symptoms of family decline just mentioned are viewed here as attempts to construct alternative institutional forms of family life to replace the obsolete model that is currently idealized in our culture—the isolated nuclear breadwinner/homemaker family and the roles associated with it. This family form, which we can call the Leave-it-to-Beaver ideal, is functional in the early stages of industrialization, particularly in capitalistic economies. It is characterized by a rigid division of labor and a corresponding isolation of life experiences by both age and sex in the household. A "cult of privacy" (Zinn & Eitzen, 1990) arises that lends itself easily to geographic mobility by severing ties to extended kin and community. Recent demographic and economic changes associated with our emergence into a postindustrial economy, however, have made this family form woefully inadequate to meet human needs.

To continue to cling conceptually to a dysfunctional family form that statistically accounts for less than 10% of actual families (Zinn & Eitzen, 1990) leaves us in the chaotic position of having no clear definitions of the situation, no patterned rituals of interaction, that are appropriate for the majority of households in the United States. In the Leave-it-to-Beaver script a part has not even been written for the stepparent, for multiple parenting following serial marriages, or for men and women sharing domestic and career responsibilities in a dual-career marriage. It is no wonder that, regardless how hard we try, the quality of our relationships seems to be deteriorating. Politically, morally, and legally we have refused to recognize as legitimate alternatives to this ideal such as single-parent families, homosexual couples, communal families, and other alternatives.

Finally, it will be argued in this chapter that in spite of the crisis mentality accompanying analyses of the family today, these changes have been more evolutionary than revolutionary. Most if not all of the "crises" experienced by the contemporary American family began over 100 years ago and reflect an accumulation of forces that simply have come to fruition and note in the last couple of decades. The illusion that contemporary families somehow deviate from historical patterns is fostered by comparing them to the relatively stable nuclear families of the 1950s—the decade most of us who reflect upon and write about the family today remember nostalgically as the "ideal" expression of family structure and interaction. If anything, however, the 1950s was an aberrant decade in the evolution of the family in 20th-century America and has yet to be explained satisfactorily (Skolnick & Skolnick, 1983).

Variety in Today's Family Forms

If there is a single trait that could be said to uniquely characterize today's family, it would be the variety of forms it is taking. Although the 2-parent breadwinner/homemaker family remains the cultural ideal, it constitutes less than 10% of families in the United States. Twenty percent of families are headed by only 1 parent, and 64% of all women with children under 18 work outside the home (Zinn & Eitzen, 1990). Voluntary singlehood and delayed marriages are becoming more commonplace. In the early 1980s, 12% of women and 17% of men in the 30- to 34-year age category had never married, twice what it was in 1970 ("Past-30 Group," 1984). Live-in relationships also have increased dramatically. In 1988, 2.6 million households were headed by unmarried couples, up 1.6 million from 1980 (Zinn & Eitzen, 1990).

Those who do get married are marrying later and having fewer children. In 1960 the median age at marriage was 20.3 years for women and 22.8 for men. By 1988 those figures had changed to 23.6 and 25.9 respectively (Zinn & Eitzen, 1990). Fertility rates have been declining steadily in American history, reaching an all-time low in the early 1990s. In 1960 the average family size was 3.67 members. By 1988 it had dropped to 3.17, the smallest ever. Between 5 and 7% of couples today are voluntarily childless—an attitude unheard of a generation ago (Blake, 1982; Jones, Tepperman, and Wilson, 1995).

But this cross-sectional look at the variety of forms the American family is taking is not the only way we can view change. Due to dramatic increases in life expectancy over the last century, individuals typically live through and therefore experience more family forms than previous generations. For example, a typical American female today may have been raised in a traditional breadwinner/homemaker family during early childhood, live in a single-parent family when her parents divorce, live alone in her early 20s, live with a boyfriend for several years, marry and have children in a dual-earner commuter marriage in her 30s, take care of a multigenerational household of her own children and aging parents in her 40s, divorce and remarry into a blended family in her 40s or 50s, become widowed and live alone again in her 60s, and perhaps share an apartment or condominium with other social security recipients in her 70s and 80s. The traditional breadwinner/homemaker family as a modal family form, then, is rapidly losing ground not only in statistical incidence but as a lived experience by most people in our society.

A discussion of variety in family life today would not be complete without mention of the increased ethnic diversity brought about by a flood of recent immigrants to our society. The declining overall birthrate in the United States is a reflection of the birthrates of the white majority. The Hispanic population, which includes Mexican, Puerto Rican, and Cuban nationals as well as natives of Central and South America, is growing at 5 times the rate of overall population growth in the United States. In 1988 Hispanics constituted 8.1% of the U.S. population; in some areas, such as southern California, they comprise 25% of the citizenry. It is projected that by the year 2020 they will be the largest minority in the United States (Zinn & Eitzen, 1990). Asians, including Chinese, Filipinos, Japanese, Vietnamese, Koreans, Asian Indians, Laotians, Thais, and Indonesians, comprised about 2.1% of the population in 1985 (Zinn & Eitzen, 1990).

It is not clear yet what lasting contributions these "new immigrants" will make to family diversity in our society. Both groups are very family oriented and have strong ties to kinship support networks. Beyond that, they differ dramatically in their socioeconomic and family characteristics. Hispanics tend to have high fertility rates and high separation and divorce rates, and to be overrepresented among those in poverty. Asians, sometimes referred to as the "model minority," have incomes higher than the average American, have low fertility and divorce rates, and are higher than the average in the United States on American College Test (A.C.T.) scores and other measures of educational attainment (Zinn & Eitzen, 1990).

Private and Public Spheres: The Dual-Earner Family

A major structural change occurring in the American family is the increase in the number of dual-earner and dual-career families. In 1940, 10% of mothers with children under 18 worked. By 1987 that figure had jumped to 64%. The proportion of women in the workforce has been increasing steadily for a century but began to reach a critical mass in the 1970s. By 1980 the number of married women who worked outnumbered those who assumed the traditional housewife role for the first time in the twentieth century (Levitan, Belous, & Gallo, 1988). How working women were viewed by society was also changing. Before World War II mainly lower-class women worked, and working was viewed as a stigma. By the 1960s college-educated women were seeking employment, which gave the working woman a new respectability (Skolnick & Skolnick, 1983; Jones, Tepperman, and Wilson, 1995).

Numerous factors have contributed to this increase in women in the workplace and the changing attitudes toward female employment by society, including:

- Increased divorce rates necessitating that women become self-supporting
- Advances in technology that have made homemaking less time-consuming, more expensive, and less challenging
- Increased educational levels of women that are not utilized in the homemaker role
- Longer life spans and the consequent lengthening of the "empty nest" period making women feel increasingly useless in the homemaker role
- The women's movement, which raised the consciousness of women about their right to self-fulfillment in the public sphere

- Increasing availability of child care, which has enabled women with young children to leave the home more easily
- Advances in birth control technology, particularly the birth control pill, which freed women from unwanted pregnancies

The most pervasive social change bringing about an increase in female employment, however, was the "deindustrialization" of the American economy, which began in the late 1950s. Referred to variously as a postindustrial, service, or information society, its primary characteristic is a shift from heavy industry to "service" or "information processing" as the largest source of employment for American workers.

This has had a profound effect on our society in two ways. First, it increased the unemployment rates of males employed in blue-collar positions and opened up a vast number of nonunionized, service-sector positions traditionally held by women. Second, the lower wages and fringe benefits of service sector jobs has resulted in the "shrinking middle-class" phenomenon and the necessity of dual-earner households to make ends meet. Research consistently has shown that the primary motive for women working is to supplement the family income (Hiller & Philliber, 1980; Landry & Jendrik, 1978):

Making a living has become a family enterprise, since it now requires two incomes for most families to get by when a decade or so ago one income would suffice for a middle-class lifestyle. . . . This shift toward dual-income families is important in at least three ways. First, there is the necessity of two incomes to maintain an adequate lifestyle, which limits the choice for those women who would rather stay at home to raise their children. Second, women's work tends to be poorly paid (approximately 70 cents for every dollar a man makes). Women workers are, for the most part, second class citizens in the occupational world, and this form of patriarchy has implications for marriage dynamics. . . . Third, although dual-earning families bring in more family income, the amount left after expenses is lowered considerably by the additional costs of such items as transportation, clothing, and child care. (Zinn & Eitzen, 1990, 151)

How has this increase in wives' employment affected families? Overall, men seem to approve of their wives working outside of the home (Ross et al., 1983). It is generally not true that husbands are threatened by their wives making more money than they do. On the contrary, often they welcome the extra income. Men and women, however, do not appear to share equally in the burdens of a two-career family.

Research supports the conclusion that housework is very sex-segregated in the United States. Husbands were found to spend about one-third as much time on housework as their wives, whether their wives worked or not. Husbands do not share equally in housework even when they are unemployed and the wife works full time. Husbands tend to do more housework the better educated they are, the younger they are, and if there is a child in the household under age 2. There appears to be little difference by social class or ethnicity in this household division of labor (Berk, 1988; Hartmann, 1981; Miller & Garison, 1982; Pleck, 1977; Vanek, 1983).

Although husbands generally approve of their wives' working, dissatisfaction tends to occur if they perceive their wives as having less time for companionship, communication, and affection (Spitz & South, 1985; White, 1983), or if difficulties arise in the coordination of family roles—especially child care (Zinn & Eitzen, 1990). Unemployed husbands actually may resent the successes of their wives because it increases their own sense of inadequacy (Keith & Schafer, 1980).

The success of dual-earner families also seems to be related to their socioeconomic status. The higher the couple's educational level and socioeconomic status, the greater the acceptance of the wife's working (Piotrkowski, Rapoport, & Rapoport, 1987). Lower- and working-class women are more likely to see their rightful place as in the traditional role of mother and homemaker (Blumstein & Shwartz, 1983; Oakley, 1974).

Kanter (1984) points out that the shift worked by the husband or wife can be an indicator of the kind of problems that will arise in a 2-earner family. The night shift for either or both of the spouses frequently results in friction between the marital partners. The afternoon shift for the husband can lead to difficulties in fulfilling the father role.

Very little research has been done on the specific effects of two-earner families on children, and the findings we do have are contradictory. On the one hand, children of 2-career families have been found to hold less stereotyped gender role images and to be more responsible and self-reliant. On the other hand, they are more likely to engage prematurely in sex and drug use (Broderick, 1988) and to spend less time with their parents in leisure activities than children from single-earner families (Levitan et al., 1988).

In terms of overall marital satisfaction, research to date shows no differences exist between dual- and single-earner families (Piotrkowski et al., 1987, p. 257; Jones, Tepperman, and Wilson, 1995). A strong correlation does exist, however, between working wives and divorce, especially for women in their 30s and 40s at the top of the career ladder in terms of power, prestige, and income. These women are 4 times more likely to divorce than other women and less likely to remarry (Booth, Brinkerhoff, & White, 1984). This fact can be partially explained by the greater financial independence and freedom of choice afforded to successful women. They are not dependent on a marriage for financial security and do not have to make choices based on this criterion. On the other hand, they have a much smaller pool of eligible males to choose from than other women. Since men tend to "marry down" (to be attracted to women who are younger and less successful than themselves), these successful women have a difficult time finding men similar to them in age and socioeconomic standing.

What effect does working outside the home have on women themselves? Our society seems to hold 2 contrasting images of the working woman, both of which have had some support in the research literature. One image is of the housewife and mother who is able to complete her identity through employment outside the home. Working wives have been found to be more self-reliant, to have greater self-esteem and sense of well-being, to have more interpersonal power and political involvement, to have more power within the family, and to have greater physical health and lowered anxiety (Hershey & Werner, 1975).

This image of the working wife is consistent with the idea that the multiple roles one must play to be a mother, housewife, and employee essentially complement or buffer each other rather than conflict. The concept of "psychological buffering" (Zinn & Eitzen, 1990) assumes that multiple roles can lead to greater happiness because disappointments in one sphere of life can be offset by successes in another. For example, problems with one's children or marriage can be "buffered" by successes in one's occupational role.

In contrast to this image is that of the harried "supermom" whose conflicting role obligations eventually lead to burnout and emotional breakdown. Piotrkowski and Crits-Christoph (1981) report that, rather than work and home life serving as buffers for each other, stress and tension in women's work lives frequently spill over into their home lives. The higher the prestige of the woman's job, the more likely this spillover is to occur.

Numerous other studies have supported the role conflict and burnout view of the working mother. Stains and Pleck (1983) found that husbands responded to overwork by neglecting their families, while wives responded by trying to be "supermoms" and absorbing the stresses caused by conflicting role obligations. Balancing these roles is rarely successful, however, and conflicts between career and the care of children leave women fatigued, emotionally depleted, and guilty. The more hours a woman works, the greater the tendency toward depression if there are children at home (Cleary & Mechanic, 1983; Schumm and Bugaighis, 1986).

Women generally sacrifice more to make two-earner families work (Skinner, 1984). To cope with the physical and emotional overload of multiple role conflicts, women often sacrifice their careers, or they may enlist family members to help with chores and schedule activities more efficiently, or they simply may give priority to their children over a clean house (Zinn & Eitzen, 1990).

The truth probably lies somewhere between these extreme images of the burned-out supermom and the fulfilled career woman. What does seem to be clear is that whether a woman experiences stress or fulfillment in employment outside the home depends to a great extent on how supportive her husband is of her working. Without his support she is likely to experience stress and depression (Keith & Schaefer, 1980, 1983).

The social and economic conditions necessitating two-earner families today are unlikely to change within the next few decades. The transition to a service economy and competition from other industrializing countries in the world marketplace are likely to keep wages depressed and the American standard of living relatively low. On the positive side for families, there is likely to be an increase in types of fringe benefits, flextime, contract work, and other alternative work arrangements that benefit families.

In a recent case study of a Fortune 500 corporation which had won praise for its "family friendly" policies, Hochschild (1997) found that a surprisingly low 5% of its employees with families chose to take advantage of these benefits which would allow them to spend more quality time at home. In-depth interviews with these subjects revealed that they did not perceive their home life as being as satisfying as their work life. At work they had a supportive and satisfying social life and efforts for the company were reinforced with immediate and tangible rewards. Neither of these benefits was experienced in the subjects' home lives, so they preferred to spend increasing amounts of time at work away from their spouses and children. Hochschild's research will need to be replicated to determine how widespread this attitude actually is and how it is affecting home life, but it raises some concerns about the commitment of adults to families and children in today's world.

The literature reviewed in this chapter on the effects of working wives on family instability were inconclusive. What seems more clear is that, despite personal satisfactions that women may get from working, they tend to experience task and emotional overload at home because both men and women continue to cling to the ideal of the "breadwinner/homemaker" family wherein the master status of women is that of homemaker and mother. To the extent that children are negatively affected, it appears to be in the decreased amount of time parents have to supervise and interact with them.

There is no reason to believe that a family system in which both husband and wife contribute to the family livelihood by working outside the home is necessarily harmful in itself. The family as a self-supporting "production unit" has been the dominant family form throughout human history (Zinn & Eitzen, 1990). There are two major differences, however, between today's dual-earner families and the preindustrial farm family and cottage industry family unit of the past.

First, the typical dual-earner family today does not work together as a unit and share the experience of each other's work worlds. As family members spend less time with each other and more time in diverse work settings, communication often becomes difficult and differences in values and life goals can threaten the marital relationship. The service economy has opened up new jobs not only for women but for adolescents. Between 1947 and 1980 the number of teenagers who are in school and working increased by 65% for boys and 240% for girls (Zinn & Eitzen, 1990). Unlike the family work units of the past, however, where sons and daughters worked side by side with their parents with the common goal of increasing the family income, today's teenager works away from home in jobs no one else wants almost entirely for discretionary income (Zinn &

Eitzen, 1990). This fragmentation of life experiences, combined with the pervasive ideology that says that the man's rightful place in the home is as breadwinner, creates tension and dissension within today's family.

Second, the geographical mobility of today's family has privatized and isolated it from support systems of kin and community. In the absence of such support systems, it is not surprising that both parents, but especially the mother, experiences role overload in trying to meet all the family's needs (Jones, Tepperman, and Wilson, 1995).

Divorce

Because divorce rates are one of the most visible indicators of family instability, they have become a source of great concern among contemporary observers of the family. Five out of 10 first marriages and 6 out of 10 second marriages will end in divorce in the United States, the highest rates of all industrialized countries in the world. (See Table 1.1.) Historically, divorce rates have been rising steadily since at least 1860, when the effects of urbanization and industrialization began to set in. They have had a tendency to rise more rapidly after major wars, especially World War II, and to slow down during economic recessions. An unusually rapid rise in the rates occurred from 1960 to 1976 due to a number of factors unique to that historical period—the Vietnam War, the feminist movement, the liberalization of divorce laws, and the "baby boom" generation reaching its peak divorce-prone years (Broderick, 1988).

Divorce rates also show substantial differences by race. As Table 1.2 shows, blacks have the highest rates followed by Hispanics and then whites. Although we do not know exactly why these differences exist, rates of divorce appear to reflect the proportion of each of these groups that is in poverty.

The Feminization of Poverty

Men and women are not equally affected by divorce. From a financial standpoint, women are far more disadvantaged than men by the divorce process and its aftermath. One study in Los Angeles

TABLE 1.1

Divorce Rates (Per 1,000 Persons) for the Major Industrial Democracies: 1990

Country	1990
United States	4.7
England	2.9
Canada	2.9
Sweden	2.3
West Germany	1.9
France	1.9
Japan	1.3
Italy	.5

Source: Demographic Yearbook. United Nations. 1992.
Note. From *What's Happening to the American Family?* (p. 26) by S. A. Levitan, R. S. Belous, & F. Gallo, 1988, Baltimore, MD: Johns Hopkins University Press; Reprinted with permission.

TABLE 1.2

Divorced Persons Per 1,000 Married Persons with Spouse Present, by Race/Ethnicity

	Race/Ethnicity		
Year	White	Black	Hispanic
1960	33	62	(N/A)
1970	44	83	61
1980	92	203	98
1986	124	248	139

Note. U.S. Bureau of the Census, "Marital Status and Living Arrangements," Current Population Reports. Series P–20, No. 418 (December 1987), p. 7.

County found that within a year after divorce, the wives' income dropped 73% while the husband's increased 42% (Weitzman, 1985). There are several reasons for this financial discrepancy.

First, gender-neutral rules that accompanied "no-fault" divorce laws were intended to treat men and women equally. Instead, they have deprived divorced women, especially older homemakers and young mothers, of equitable economic settlements (Weitzman, 1985; Jones, Tepperman, and Wilson, 1995).

Second, women are much more likely to be awarded custody of the children after a divorce, but only 48% of women due child support in 1985 actually received all they were supposed to, 26% received a partial amount, and 26% received none ("Average Child Support," 1987, p. 15).

Finally, the responsibilities of child care place limitations on the career options of women, particularly in a society such as ours where the private sector is comparatively unsympathetic to the needs of families. The result of this financial hardship upon women has been that women and their dependent children have become the fastest growing demographic groups in poverty in the U.S., a phenomenon that has come to be known as the "feminization of poverty." (Duncan et al., 1984; Jencks, 1982; Jones, Tepperman, & Wilson, 1995).

Effects of Divorce Upon Children

What about the effects of divorce upon children? Actually we know very little about its long-term effects, and most research has been limited to white, middle-class children. There is some evidence that age, social class position, and gender of children have some bearing on how they will be affected by divorce.

The younger the child at the time of the divorce, the greater the likelihood of adjustment problems later, especially when adolescence is reached. Older children tend to act out as a response to divorce, while younger ones are more likely to withdraw and experience problems of abandonment and guilt (Elias, 1983).

The lower the child's socioeconomic status, the greater the adjustment problems after divorce seem to be. Much of this probably has to do with the greater financial stresses placed on this stratum by divorce (Kinard & Reinherz, 1984).

A substantial body of research has accumulated that suggests that boys are affected more negatively by divorce than girls. They display more acting-out and aggressive behavior, decreased school performance, greater alcohol and drug use, and generally take twice as long to adjust to divorce as do girls (Franke, 1983). The reasons for this are not well understood, but one possible explanation is that boys are more likely than girls to live with their opposite-sex parent, thereby being deprived of a consistent male role model (Kinard & Reinherz, 1984). Another possible explanation is that parents tend to fight more in front of boys and to stay together longer in a conflictual

marriage when there are male children, thereby exposing them to more marital discord (Franke, 1983). To complicate this issue even further, some research suggests that the effect of divorce on girls is just as great as it is on boys but that the effects are delayed or more latent. It has been found, for example, that girls from broken homes are more likely than boys to have unstable marriages later (Glenn & Cramer, 1985; Jones, Tepperman, & Wilson, 1995).

What can we conclude about the effects of divorce on family members and the future of marital stability in our society? It is unlikely that divorce per se and the loss of one parent as a primary caregiver is necessarily harmful to children. The loss of a parent is certainly not new to the American family, since a century ago a child was as likely to experience the loss of a parent through death as one is today through divorce (Zinn & Eitzen, 1990). There is also no evidence that multiple parenting through remarriage and stepfamilies today is necessarily harmful, since multiple parenting in various forms has been practiced successfully throughout human history. We also know that the negative effects of divorce can be offset by a warm, loving relationship with one parent, a relative, or some other adult.

Divorce is not so much the problem as the sequence of events that frequently follow it—parental conflict, geographic mobility, and declining income. As we shall see, divorce rates are unlikely to decline in the future. What our society lacks is institutionalized ways of helping families cope with transitions in family living, transitions that will become more and more a part of our lives in the future. When there are no institutionalized ways of dealing with change, there is a tendency to resort to conflict, and the greatest harm to children appears to be parental conflict, whether it occurs within intact homes or in postdivorce families.

Our society has not constructed an adequate definition, for example, of the role of a stepparent. Our conception of the "ideal" family as the single-earner, two-parent nuclear unit has almost disappeared statistically, yet we have few if any alternative conceptualizations of legitimate family life. Our system of social welfare, which is supposed to ease the burdens of family transitions, provides inadequate financial support for families and even encourages further family breakup.

While the institution of the family will experience periodic and short-term fluctuations in divorce rates in the next century, the overall trend is likely to be for rates to remain as high as they are now or even go up. The reason is the underlying sociological forces affecting the family that are unlikely to reverse in the foreseeable future (Jones, Tepperman, & Wilson, 1995).

The first of these forces are the multiple effects of "modernization"—the Industrial Revolution, urbanization, and capitalist economic development—upon the conception of the self. The effects of these profound social changes are relatively constant in all modern contemporary societies. They tend to have an impact on the family as an institution in the following ways.

"Individualism" at the expense of familism increases as educational levels increase and social mobility weakens ties to traditional institutions. Pressures become greater to make family structures conform to individual needs, resulting in experiments in a variety of family forms and even voluntary singlehood.

The family has been transformed from a "production unit" that meets a variety of survival needs to a "consumer unit" that specializes in the emotional nurturance and self-actualization of its members. Romantic love becomes the primary basis for choosing a spouse, and expectations for "happiness" within the family rise dramatically.

A related phenomenon is what Skolnick and Skolnick (1983) call *psychological gentrification.* Partly stimulated by the new service economy but encouraged by the educational benefits for GIs following World War II, the postwar era witnessed a virtual explosion in the number of people going to college. Its effect was to create a population more sophisticated, cosmopolitan, and introspective than at any previous time in our history. Both men and women had come to expect more from themselves and their relationships, and this new psychological sophistication was reflected in the proliferation of self-help books in the marketplace.

Another factor affecting the family is the *demographic revolution.* Between 1920 and 1986 the life expectancy of men increased by 17 years and of women, 23 years. Whereas in 1920 men and women could expect to live to be 54 and 55 respectively, in 1986 they could expect to live to be 71 and 78 (Zinn & Eitzen, 1990). The result of the vastly increased life span has been to shrink the parental phase of the life course and add several new phases to the stages of married life. A typical couple getting married today can expect to live together for 50 years, the last 25 of which will be without children in the household. The new com-

plexity in relationships necessitates that couples look more carefully at the personal and sexual fulfillment of their marriage and at the possibility of careers for women during and following the childbearing years.

A final demographic factor affecting families is the emergence of the "baby boom" generation following World War II. Population "booms" have predictable effects on the generation experiencing them, and this most recent example has been no exception. They typically experience high levels of stress due to intense competition in all arenas of life and a shortage of social services because of the vast numbers who need them. The "midlife crisis" became a reality in this generation of baby boomers as careers became bottlenecked by too many people seeking too few promotional opportunities. As expected, this generation has unusually high rates of suicide, mental illness, crime, and family disorganization (Zinn & Eitzen, 1990).

Single Parenthood

One of the obvious consequences of rising divorce rates is an increase in single-parent households. As shown in Table 1.3, the proportion of families with only one parent present has risen substantially since 1960, but the rates have risen particularly fast for selected minorities. Ninety percent of all single-parent homes are headed by females. Five million mothers and 700,000 fathers in the workforce are single parents (Axel, 1985).

Research concerning the effects of single-parent homes on children has largely concluded that it has a negative impact. Children from such homes appear to have higher rates of emotional disorders, greater drug use, and poorer school performance. The greater the number of children in a single-parent family, the greater the stress on the parent, and the more likely the parent is to use restrictive parenting practices, which increase the hostility between parent and child. If a single mother goes to work for the first time after a divorce, it is likely to increase the sense of loss and deprivation in the children (Zinn & Eitzen, 1990).

Nine-tenths of all single-parent families are headed by a female, but there is some evidence that the greater number of problems these children experience is not due to the absence of the father. Instead it may be the emotional and task overload experienced by these parents and their

TABLE 1.3
*Percentage of Single-Parent Families
by Ethnic Group*

	1960	1980	1988	1994
White	7	15	19	19
Hispanic	N.A.	21	30	29
Black	22	46	54	59

Source: U.S. Dept. of Commerce, Bur. of the Census, Current Populations Reports, Series P–20, Household and Family Characteristics, various years. Washington, D.C.: U.S. Gov't Printing Office.

inability to manage their lives (Herzog & Sudia, 1973; Weiss, 1979; Jones, Tepperman, & Wilson, 1995).

The decreased income of the single parent, particularly females, as discussed earlier in this chapter, has its own negative effect on the well-being of the children (Weitzman, 1985). Some research suggests that this is the only important difference between one- and two-parent homes (Mueller & Cooper, 1986; Shaw, 1982). It also has been found that single-parent families change residences up to 3 times more frequently than other families, a factor that may also have a bearing on the adjustment of children ("Children from One-Parent Families," 1980).

Remarriage

The lack of institutionalized alternatives to the nuclear family ideal is painfully evident in the dismal success rates of second marriages. These marriages are even more likely to fail than first marriages; many attribute this failure to conflicts among stepchildren and stepparents (Cherlin, 1978; Lamanna & Reidman, 1981).

Remarriage rates also reflect some gender biases that are endemic to our society. Five-sixths of all divorced men as compared to three-fourths of all divorced women eventually remarry. This fact partially reflects that men have a shorter life expectancy, leaving women a smaller pool of eligible men to choose from. But it also suggests that ageism in our society may affect men and women differently. The older a woman is at the time of divorce, the fewer chances she has to remarry. This is not the case, however, for men (Bumpass, Rind-

fuss, & Janosik, 1978). Aging for men tends to increase their attractiveness as their prestige, power, and wealth increases. As the educational level and socioeconomic position of women increase, however, the chances of their remarrying after divorce diminishes (Zinn & Eitzen, 1990).

Family Violence

Family violence, including spouse abuse, child abuse, sibling abuse, and parent abuse, runs a close second to rising divorce rates in the public mind as an indicator of family decline. The incidence, severity, and historical trends of violence in families is much more difficult to determine than are rates of divorce, since this behavior is almost always hidden and frequently unreported to the police. Some estimates of contemporary family violence in the United States are as follows:

- From a sample of 3,520 couples representative of the general population in 1985, 4.4% of wives reported one or more physical attacks of severe violence by their spouse over the past year and 11.3% reported acts of minor violence (Straus & Gelles, 1985).
- A psychologist specializing in helping abuse victims has estimated that 50% of all women will be battering victims at some point in their lives (Walker, 1979).
- The FBI estimates that wife beating, which occurs every 18 seconds, is the most frequently occurring crime in the country (Bukovinski, 1982; Shapiro, 1977).
- Sixteen percent of college students reported their parents had been physically violent toward one another within the past year (Straus, 1974).
- In 3% of divorce actions, husbands mentioned the wife's physical abuse as a reason for seeking a divorce; 37% of wives in divorce actions mentioned their husband's physical abuse as a reason (Steinmetz, 1977).
- Seven percent of the respondents to a newspaper survey reported experiencing marital rape. In another study, 12% of the married women in a San Francisco study reported being the victim of some form of forced sex in marriage (Frieze, 1983).
- Two-thirds of parents had used some form of violence toward their children; 97% of parents of 3-year-olds used violence while only 33% of parents of 15- to 17-year-olds did so (Gelles & Strauss, 1988).
- The rate of severe violence—kicking, biting, punching, hitting or trying to hit with an object,

beating, threatening with or using a gun or knife—was estimated at 10.7% of families (Gelles & Strauss, 1988).

- By the time women in the United States reach age 18, 1 out of every 4 has been the victim of sexual molestation. Thirty-eight percent of these molestations are incestuous, or 1 out of every 10 women (Forward & Buck, 1978; Jones, Tepperman, and Wilson, 1995).
- It is estimated that for every reported case of incest, 20 go unreported (Geiser, 1979).
- It is estimated that 1 out of every 10 elderly persons living with a family member has been abused in some manner and that anywhere from 700,000 to 1.1 million are victims of abuse (Pillemer & Finkelhor, 1986).

Many sociologists have observed that intimate groups have a high potential for violence, since the very characteristic that holds them together—intimate knowledge of each other—also makes them extremely vulnerable to the misuse of power within the group. Knowing just how to "push another's buttons" during conflicts can easily lead to uncontrolled violence. Although the family probably has always been vulnerable to this kind of internal conflict, certain social structural and ideological characteristics of our society have provided opportunities for this violence to be more easily manifested.

First, the family in any culture is a microcosm of the larger society and its value system. That the American family is violent should not be surprising, since our culture has always manifested and glorified violence. It has been a dominant theme in literature and folklore (Lynn, 1979), the media, and popular music (Corey, 1983). By the time children are 14 years old, they have witnessed 11,000 television murders. There are an average of 13.3 violent acts per prime-time television hour ("TV's Worst Offenders," 1985). The overwhelming proportion of American parents consider it part of their role to train sons to be tough. The Violence Commission survey reveals that 70% of respondents believed that it is good for boys to have a few fistfights (Gelles & Straus, 1988). Within the family, 90% of all parents condone using physical violence to discipline their children (Steinmetz & Straus, 1973). Clearly, physical aggression against other family members is considered "normal violence" in the American family (Jones, Tepperman, and Wilson, 1995).

The second of these characteristics is the extreme privacy that has become associated with the modern industrial family. Most families throughout human history have been strongly controlled by kinship groups and community. Only with the geographical mobility and ethos of individualism of the modern industrial family have ties to kin and community broken down. This breakdown, however, has created a family setting in which abuse, violence, and exploitation can occur virtually unchecked by those outside the nuclear family unit.

Conclusion and Clinical Implications

The theme of this chapter has been that the family in America is indeed experiencing a crisis of transition—a transition that has its sources in the institutional, demographic, and cultural evolution of our society. While painful for the individuals caught in this crisis, the transition itself is inevitable, irreversible, and, perhaps in many ways, desirable. The tragedy is not that change is occurring, since change has become routine and expected in modern complex societies; the tragedy lies in our failure to adapt to it as quickly as possible so that human suffering is held to a minimum.

To adapt constructively to these changes, we must reconceptualize and legitimate new structures, roles, and rules of family life. Our current idealized scripts for loving, communicating, problem solving, and parenting are simply inadequate for the majority of today's families. Second, we must help build meaningful support systems for families involving kinship groups, neighborhoods, communities, self-help groups, and formal government agencies.

The clinician in his or her practice can assume a leadership role in constructing, along with clients themselves, these new blueprints for family life. At a minimum, the clinician could be helpful in the following ways:

- Be nonjudgmental about "alternative" lifestyles of clients such as divorce, single parenting, gay relationships, and others.
- Keep up with the literature on nontraditional families and the unique problems they face.
- Include all blended family members in group therapy, and place responsibility for the welfare of the children and peacemaking within the family on the adults' shoulders.
- Take a leadership role in helping families establish agreed-upon rules of authority and interaction between biological and stepparents and siblings.

- Help single mothers learn to set limits with their children, and help the children to accept new relationships with men.
- Encourage equalitarian relationships among couples and help them to formulate and identify, when

appropriate, with roles other than those associated with the "breadwinner/homemaker" family.
- Assist families whenever possible in networking and establishing support systems in their communities.

REFERENCES

Average child support pay drops by 12.4% from 1983. (1987, August 23). *New York Times*, p. 15.

Axel, H. (1985). *Corporations and families: Changing practices and perspectives*. New York: The Conference Board.

Berk, S. F. (1988). Women's unpaid labor: Home and community. In A. H. Stromberg & S. Harkess (Eds.), *Women working* (pp. 287–302). Mountain View, CA: Mayfield.

Blake, J. (1982). Demographic revolution and family evolution: Some implications for American women. In P. W. Berman & E. R. Rainey (Eds.), *Women: A developmental perspective* (pp. 299–312). NIH Publication No. 82–2298. Washington, DC:

Blumstein, P., & Swartz, P. (1983). *American couples: Money, work, sex*. New York: William Morrow.

Booth, A., Brinkerhoff, D., & White, L. (1984). The impact of parental divorce on courtship. *Journal of Marriage and the Family, 46*, 85–94.

Broderick, C. B. (1988). *Marriage and the family*. Englewood Cliffs, NJ: Prentice-Hall.

Bukovinski, J. (1982, March 9). A wife is abused every 18 seconds, FBI says. *Rocky Mountain News*, 38, 42.

Bumpass, L. L., Rindfuss, R. R., & Janosik, R. B. (1978). Age and marital status at first birth and the pace of subsequent fertility. *Demography, 15*, 75–86.

Cherlin, A. J. (1978). Remarriage as an incomplete institution. *American Journal of Sociology, 84*, 634–651.

Children from one-parent families. (1980). *American Educator, 4* (Winter), 12–13.

Cleary, P., & Mechanic, D. (1983). Sex differences in psychological distress among married people. *Journal of Health and Social Behavior, 24*, 111–121.

Corey, J. (1983, July 31). The networks shrug off violence. *New York Times*.

Doudan, C., & McBride, F. (1981). Where are the men for the women at the top? In P. J. Stein (Ed.), *Single life* (pp. 21–33). New York: St. Martin's Press.

Duncan, G. J. (1984). *Years of poverty, years of plenty*. Ann Arbor: Survey Research Center, Institute for Social Research, University of Michigan.

Elias, M. (1983, June 15). Tots take the worst blows in divorce. *USA Today*, 3D.

Forward, S., & Buck, C. (1978). *Betrayal of innocence: Incest and its devastation*. Los Angeles: J. P. Tarcher.

Franke, L. B. (1983, July 3). The Sons of Divorce. *Denver Post Contemporary*, 30–31.

Frieze, I. H. (1983). Investigating the causes and consequences of marital rape. *Signs, 8* (Spring), 532–553.

Geiser, R. L. (1979). *Hidden victims: The sexual abuse of children*. Boston: Beacon Press.

Gelles, R. J., & Strauss, M. A. (1988). Determinants of violence in the family. In W. R. Burr (Eds.), *Contem-*

porary theories about the family (Vol. 1, pp. 549–581). New York: Free Press.

Glenn, N. D., & Kramer, K. (1985). The psychological well-being of adult children of divorce. *Journal of Marriage and the Family, 47*, 905–912.

Hartmann, H. I. (1981). The family as the locus of gender, class, and political struggle: The example of housework. *Signs, 6* (3), 366–394.

Hershey, L., & Werner, E. (1975). Dominance in marital decision-making in women's liberation and women's non-liberation families. *Family Process, 14*, 223–232.

Herzog, E., & Sudia, C. (1973). Children in fatherless families. In B. M. Caldwell & N. H. Riccuiti (Eds.), *Review of child development research* (Vol. 3, pp. 141–232). Chicago: University of Chicago Press.

Hiller, D. B. & Philliber, W. W. (1980). Necessity, compatibility and status attainment as factors in labor force participation of married women. *Journal of Marriage and the Family, 42*, 347–365.

Jencks, C. (1982). Divorced mothers, unite! *Psychology Today, 16* (November), 73–75.

Jones, C., Tepperman, L., and Wilson, S. (1995). *The Futures of the Family*. Englewood Cliffs, NJ.: Prentice-Hall, Inc.

Kanter, R. M. (1984). Jobs and families: Impact of working roles on family life. In P. Voydanoff (Ed.), *Work and family* (pp. 111–118). Palo Alto, CA: Mayfield.

Keith, P., & Schafer, R. (1980). Role strain and depression in two-job families. *Family Relations, 29*, 483–494.

Keith, P., & Schafer, R. (1983). Employment Characteristics of Both Spouses and Depression in Two-parent Families, *Journal of Marriage and the Family, 45*: 877–884.

Kinard, E. M., & Reinherz, H. (1984). Marital disruption: Effects on behavioral and emotional functioning in children. *Journal of Family Issues, 5* (March), 90–115.

Lamanna, M. A., & Reidman, A. (1981). *Marriages and families: Making choices throughout the life cycle*. Belmont, CA: Wadsworth.

Landry, B., & Jendrik, M. P. (1978). The employment of wives in middle-class Black families. *Journal of Marriage and the Family, 40*, 787–797.

Levitan, S. A., Belous, R. S., & Gallo, F. (1988). *What's happening to the American family?* (rev. ed.). Baltimore: Johns Hopkins University Press.

Lynn, K. (1979). Violence in American literature and folklore. In H. D. Graham & T. R. Gurr (Eds.), *Violence in America* (pp. 133–143). Beverly Hills, CA: Sage Publications.

Mueller, D. P., & Cooper, P. W. (1986). Children of

single-parent families: How they fare as young adults. *Family Relations, 35,* 169–176.

Miller, J., & Garison, H. H. (1982). Sex roles: The division of labor at home and in the workplace. *Annual Review of Sociology, 8,* 237–262.

Oakley, A. (1974). *The sociology of housework.* New York: Pantheon.

Past-30 group of unmarrieds found in big rise by census. (1984, May 21). *New York Times,* p. 9.

Pillemer, K. A., & Finkelhor, D. (1986, November). *The prevalence of elder abuse.* Paper presented at the annual meetings of the Gerontological Society of America, Chicago, IL.

Piotrkowski, C., & Crits-Christoph, P. (1981). Women's jobs and family adjustment. *Journal of Family Issues, 2,* 126–147.

Piotrkowski, C., Rapoport, R., & Rapoport, R. (1987). Families and work. In M. B. Sussman & S. Steinmetz (Eds.), *Handbook of marriage and the family* (pp. 251–283). New York: Plenum Press.

Pleck, J. H. (1977). The work-family role system. *Social Problems, 24,* 417–427.

Preston, S. H. (1984). Children and the elderly: Divergent paths for America's dependents. *Demography, 21,* 435–457.

Ross, C. E., Mirowsky, J., and Huber, J. (1983). Dividing Work, Shaping Work, and In-Between: Marriage Patterns and Depression. *American Sociological Review, 48:* 809–823.

Schumm, W. R., & Bugaighis, M. A. (1986). Marital quality over the marital career: Alternative explanations. *Journal of Marriage and the Family, 48,* 165–168.

Shaw, L. B. (1982). High school completion for young women. *Journal of Family Issues, 3,* 147–163.

Shapiro, L. (1977). Violence: The most obscene fantasy. *Mother Jones, 2,* 11–12.

Skinner, D. A. (1984). Dual-Career Family Stress and Coping. In P. Voydanoff (ed.), *Work and Family.* Palo Alto, CA: Mayfield, pp. 261–271.

Skolnick, A., & Skolnick, J. (1983). *Family in transition.* Boston: Little, Brown.

Spitz, G. D. & South, S. J. (1985). Women's employment, time expenditure, and divorce. *Journal of Family Issues, 6,* 307–329.

Stains, G. L., & Pleck, J. L. (1983). *The impact of work schedule on family life.* Ann Arbor: University of Michigan Press.

Steinmetz, S. K. (1977). Wifebeating, husbandbeating—A comparison of the use of violence between spouses to resolve marital conflicts. In M. Roy (Ed.), *Battered women* (pp. 63–71). New York: Van Nostrand Reinhold.

Steinmetz, S. K., & Straus, M. (1973). The family as a cradle of violence. *Society, 10,* 50–56.

Straus, M. (1974). Leveling, civility, and violence in the family. *Journal of Marriage and the Family, 36,* 13–27.

Straus, M., & Gelles, R. J. (1985, November). *Societal change and change in family violence from 1975 to 1985 as revealed by two national surveys.* Paper presented at the meetings of the American Society of Criminology.

TV's worst offenders. (1985, November 15). *U.S.A. Today,* p. D1.

U.S. Bureau of the Census. (1989). *Households, families, marital status, and living arrangements: March 1988. Current Population Reports.* Series P-20, No. 432 (September). Washington, DC: U.S. Government Printing Office.

White, L. K. (1983). Determinants of spousal interactions: Marital structure or marital structure or marital happiness. *Journal of Marriage and the Family, 45,* 511–520.

Vanek, J. (1983). Household work, wage work, and sexual equality. In A. Skolnick & J. Skolnick (Eds.), *Family in transition* (4th ed., pp. 176–189). Boston: Little, Brown.

Walker, L. (1979). *The battered woman.* New York: Harper & Row.

Weiss, R. S. (1979). *Going it alone: The family life and social situation of the single parent.* New York: Basic Books.

Weitzman, L. (1985). *The divorce revolution: The unexpected social and economic consequences for women and children in America.* New York: Free Press.

Zinn, M. B., & Eitzen, D. S. (1990). *Diversity in families.* New York: Harper & Row.

2 / Mother-Only, Father-Only Families

Judith R. Milner and Paul L. Adams

Definition and Prevalence

Over the past few decades there have been vast increases in the number of single-parent families. In fact, the United States now leads the world in the incidence of divorce and single-parent families. Some pertinent statistics were reported by Wetzel in the *Monthly Labor Review* (1990). Between 1970 and 1989 the number of households maintained by men more than doubled, to 2.8 million, and those maintained by women soared 98%, to 10.9 million. In 1989, 16.5% of all family households were maintained by women, compared with 9.2% in 1950. In addition, 1.9 million mother-child subfamilies lived in someone else's household, usually the home of the maternal grandparents.

Origins of single-parent families also have changed. In 1950 an important contributor to the number of female-headed households was widowhood—approximately 30% of the total. By 1989 the percentage of family households maintained by widows had shrunk to 7% of the total, while the proportion maintained by divorced, separated, or never-married women had risen from about 70% in 1950 to 93%. Also, families maintained by never-married women increased 10 fold over the past 2 decades, rising from 248,000 in 1970 to 2.7 million in 1988.

Children of single parents, especially single mothers, are much more likely than children in intact marriages to be living in poverty. In 1988 the poverty rate for female-headed households was 44.7%. This means that in 1988, 20% of all children—1 in 5—was living in poverty. The socioeconomic gap between children and adults is broadening, particularly for children under 6 years of age. In 1994 the poverty rate for children under 6 was 24.5% (U.S. Bureau of the Census, 1996). Although most poor children are white, blacks and Hispanics are disproportionately represented, with 51% of black children and 44% of Hispanic children living in poverty, compared to 14% of white children (Allen, 1994). Children who grow up in poor families are more likely to experience homelessness, to have poor educational attainment, and to have increased involvement with the criminal justice system, unsuccessful work histories, and severely limited socioeconomic potential. These youths often are born out of wedlock, to teenage mothers who have not finished high school.

Against this bleak statistical backdrop, let us look more closely at the quality of these children's experience. What is life like for children in single-parent families, whether mother-headed or father-headed?

Types of Mother-Only Families

Mother-only families are two-generation households in which a child (or children) live solely with one parent, the mother. While other caregivers—notably the maternal grandmother—may cohabit with mother and children and function as the mother's auxiliaries, no adult-male partner cohabits with the mother and forms a conjugal pair or subsystem with her. The household compositions of mother-only families are surprisingly diverse; Kellam, Ensminger, and Turner (1977) found over 34 household types for African American children living with a parental setup of mother only, out of a total of 84 family forms. Some of the family compositions found in a Chicago impoverished area called Woodlawn were mother-aunt, mother-grandmother, mother and woman boarder, and so on.

Mother-only families emerge, as depicted in Table 2.1, along seven main pathways. The first four produce children born out of wedlock, along with those whose parents divorced, those with a father who absconded, and those whose father died. In these first four types, the father's apartness has an aura of finality; in the remaining three subtypes the father's remoteness may or may not be so fixed and the mother-only family may cease if father returns from an overseas job, prison, prisoner-of-war camp, or prolonged hospitalization. Even a hasty inspection of the table suggests that the breakdown of intact families is

TABLE 2.1

Types of Mother-Only Families

Mother never married
Mother and father divorced
Mother deserted by father
Mother widowed

Father working away
Father incarcerated
Father hospitalized   .

---

multidetermined, that numerous socioeconomic forces in contemporary society serve to erode two-parent family life, and that some types of mother-only families are numerous while others are relatively rare.

Since the cast of characters in young children's lives carries a lot of weight in the children's self-esteem and attachments, psychiatrists long have comprehended that the details of one's primary family composition are very telling. A firstborn son feels very different from a middle daughter or a youngest daughter, and so on. Similarly, in the mother-only family the precise cause of the father's absence or nonexistence is an important datum for psychiatric work, because it molds the child's perceptual and apperceptive world and affects his or her self-concept. In consequence, children who are told that they are bastards, no matter how beloved, may find some stigma attached to themselves or, more appropriately for respectability, to the mother and father. Children whose father died sober in an automobile accident and who left some money for survivors (as in life insurance and social security payments to survivors of insured workers) are more advantaged than children born out of wedlock to an impoverished teenage mother. Children whose father's work abroad coincided with a trial of separation between the parents have higher respectability than children whose father is away in prison for sexually abusing a child. Children whose father is ill and undergoing prolonged hospitalization are less stigmatized than children whose father deserted with his whereabouts unknown.

Attitudes toward the absent father by child and mother do not always match. A male child may, in safeguarding his own selfhood, feel partial to a father whom the mother loathes. Under such circumstances, the child usually keeps his own opinion quiet, respecting the mother's wishes not to hear a discordant message from her offspring.

Sometimes the mother can pull herself together sufficiently to say that the child has a right to his or her own feelings and attachments—and to mean it. That is a heroic stance for any bereft mother but some can pull it off, thinking of the child's welfare. Such a mother is empathetically trying to assume the child's role in her imagination, so that she can serve him or her with a wholesome compassion. We do know that mother-son relationship tends to be more problematic in mother-only families than mother-daughter relationships.

Epidemiological Considerations

Poverty and its correlates are commonplace in mother-only families of all races. In recent years some government press releases and briefings have claimed that divorce causes poverty; however, a more judicious statement would be that, for many children in the United States, the sudden loss of a relatively advantaged breadwinner creates or equals poverty. We can understand that wealthy women—widows, never-married mothers, or divorcees—heading mother-only families do not know poverty. Poverty comes not from fatherlessness but from inadequate economic resources. It may look as if divorce causes poverty, because two-thirds or more of a family's income depart when a father departs, whether through divorce, death, desertion, or otherwise. If money for mother's and child(ren)'s survival continues even though the father leaves, however, the remaining family is not thrown into poverty overnight but has a fighting chance at survival and at meeting the needs of young children.

Every second American marriage (50%) ends in divorce, and in most cases children remain with mothers for caregiving. Among Americans generally, 1 in every 6 children is born out of wedlock, but among African Americans, over 1 in 2 babies now born are in that cohort. Today widowing by death of father is an uncommon cause of a mother-only family, even though most psychodynamic writers continue to emphasize father's death as a cause of a mother-only family. A 30-year lag time in psychodynamic theorizing is more than a generation, and psychodynamic views on father absence need to be updated. Most children in mother-only families are either born out of wedlock or survivors of parental divorce. One-fifth to one-fourth of children in the United States today live with their mother only.

Structural Subsystems in Mother-Only Families

Unless there are two parents, a child's family lacks a conjugal subsystem as a consistent and regular feature of its structure. Sometimes mothers who head families with children may set up a new conjugal subsystem that is not enmeshed in the whole life of the family; but, by definition, if an adult male is regularly present, under whatever circumstances, the family cannot be considered a mother-only family. If a transient, part-time conjugal subsystem emerges—on the side, Back Street style, under cover and after dark—the children still live in a mother-only family, regardless of how much occasional companionship and carnal pleasure their mother receives. So do the children whose mothers have a series of paramours who are present during the day. Such arrangements reflect those in hunting-and-gathering economies (before agriculture, when fathers came home to stay) and are not intrinsic to the stable life of the family as we have come to know it among peasants and industrial wage workers worldwide.

Yet the mother-only family does constitute a viable system, containing (1) a bigenerational subsystem, (2) a parenting or caregiving subsystem and, when there is more than 1 child, (3) a sibling subsystem. Those structural features suffice to make it a family that could subserve society's needs and children's needs were it not hampered by economic, social, or mental pathology.

In every family, the boundaries that exist between the two generations set up a bigenerational subsystem. There are boundaries on sexual activities, on the giving and receiving of security, and perhaps on hierarchy and status. These boundaries are based on differences in role and age. In mother-only families, hierarchical distinctions may be reduced. The mother does not proclaim the Fourth Commandment, "Honor thy father and thy mother," quite so strongly to her children with whom she is sharing an existence that often requires a lot of mutual respect if they are all to survive. Of course, there is much variety in parental discipline styles, and some mothers who are

the sole parent may become stridently authoritarian, at least for a time.

The parenting subsystem is distinctive in the mother-only family. The mother may become overloaded by chores and responsibilities, having no male partner with whom she can even commiserate and recreate. Therefore, she may find it hard to provide the security and succor that children must have. On the other hand, many mothers are able to parent better without a man; they find relief in not having to "check it out" with a mate each time a decision involving the children arises. For their part, the children may prefer having a single adult to turn to for guidance and counsel.

If there are two or more children, a sibling subsystem is present; often it is strengthened when there is only a mother present. The siblings stick together, learn to share and take turns in household chores and responsibilities, and might develop a power center that will dilute the mother's absolutism if she has a tendency in that direction. The siblings are resources both to the single mother and to one another.

Major Conflicts or Tensions in Mother-Only Families

Any dynamic formulation of the mother-only family has to recognize several issues, in particular: the family's principal sources of friction and conflict, its needs and values, its functional and defensive styles, and the community and societal milieu in which it operates. Ambivalence and conflict are abundant in mother-only families, but not necessarily more than in two-parent families.

Idealization and derogation—by turns—of the absent parent may be an important dynamism. Both children and mother may spend considerable energy comparing and contrasting what was but has been lost. However, if predivorce conflict between father and current members of the household was at a high pitch, there may be sighs of relief all around. Only the bruised survivors of an angry divorce know fully how blissful divorce can be. But even so, the children may long for the absent father, because their mindset seems to be that two parents are just right, and at times they cling to a real or imagined relationship to each parent, even though the parents may have come to despise each other.

The mother's depression, task inundation, emotional overloading, and general insecurity may be a source of stress and strain within mother-only families. In one possible scenario, the mother feels guilty for her loneliness and rates herself as inadequate to meet all the things that her children need done. Mothers of sons, in particular, may worry how they can be good examples of masculinity or how they, being female, would ever be able to curb and discipline an unruly boy. In actuality, often they have had plentiful experience being the most significant parent, and even chief cop and disciplinarian, before the marriage breakup; but they falter and waver when they realize that Father, often an *eminence grise,* will not be checking in at night. Realistic or not, doubts and tensions arise in the solo mother.

The major source of difficulty for a solo mother's family lies not in fantasy or inner conflict but in the realm of economic reality. Economic want—the specters of real hunger, homelessness, and being ill-clad—haunts most mother-only families of both divorced and never-wed types. Survival itself is not guaranteed in the United States, and poverty can alter the ambiance of an entire family. We shall return to economic deprivation when we consider the neighborhood, community, and society.

Shame in being different, in being a minority (for only 1 in 4 children lives with mother only), in being "illegitimate" or deserted or having a father in prison also can be painful for members of a mother-only family. Even neighbors and schoolteachers can be heard to say, "What can you expect? The kid comes from a broken family. The kid has no father."

In addition to conflicts and ambivalences that are specific to the mother-only condition, the family's members partake of all other forms of human deviance. Childism, covering all antichild attitudes and practices, truly the universal oppression, also can be a blight in the mother-only family; so can sexism and racism and all the developmental crises that befall any family with growing, individuating children. Neuroses, reactive disorders, mood disorders, conduct disorders, and all the severe psychopathologic states can be visited on mother-only families. Nor are such families spared the many human problems with sexual desire and anger, with loving and working, living and dying.

Needs and Values Pervading Mother-Only Families

Certain beliefs and values seem to be more characteristic of the mother-only family than of other families. Four such attitudinal properties will be sketched.

NEGATIVE SELF-EVALUATIONS

Negative self-evaluations are rampant in many mother-only families. Just as anti-Semitism or sexism can become incorporated as Jewish or female self-hatred, society's devaluation of the mother-only family seeps into the family members themselves. Often they regard themselves as lacking or being incomplete. Through rationalization and other distortions, it becomes all too easy to blame all adversities and disappointments on the fact of fatherlessness. Work with mother-only families has led us to quip that there is no father so revered as an absent one, above all a dead one. Our terminology for the mother-only family does not compliment its members: a broken family, an eroded family, a partial family, a fatherless family. But when fathers are present, they seldom do every wondrous thing that may be imputed to them by members of a mother-only household.

DETERMINATION TO SURVIVE

Countervailing their overvaluation of a man's presence is a determination to make do, to survive. In the process, the family members develop an *esprit de corps* that is expressed in the notion "We have to be in this all together." Everyone seems to know an integrated group effort is indispensable. A comrades-in-battle spirit takes over in many mother-only families, providing values that aid the members' coping and give meaning to their struggle to make do.

OUTER-DIRECTED BELIEF SYSTEM

The children in these families have an outer-directed belief system. Repeatedly, studies of deprived children, especially those in mother-only homes, demonstrate an external locus of control. Sometimes this is only a vague fatalism that the luck of the draw gives them little grounds for optimism, but at other times it is a starkly projective ("paranoid") attitude that the world is like a threatening jungle. Probably such paranoid insight can be highly adaptive and useful for poor people, and it may rank higher morally than the strictly ethical self-blaming and depressive orientation that is so much promulgated in psychotherapy with middle-class persons. If depressive insight leads us to do something about ourselves, then paranoid insight may facilitate our changing our human institutions. A combination of ethical and utopical values could be highly useful in the ghetto.

LONG-TERM EFFECTS

Living amid decaying buildings, cities, and economic institutions, the urban underclass finds existence to be "a life full of holes." Is such a life, according to the Moghrebi saying, better than no life at all? With easiest access to the underground economy or to lowest-paid service jobs carrying no fringe benefits or protections, members of the underclass often may turn to illicit work or a rickety welfare system to aid their survival. Going it alone is not easy for a woman with children in North America. An atmosphere of making do with flimsy string, instead of the required rope, pervades the household. As a corollary, the children, not surprisingly, may grow up with a gambling, catch-as-catch-can, main-chance ethos that shocks and perplexes the respectable and affluent classes.

Coping Styles and Cost-to-Hazard, Cost-to-Benefit Ratios

Viewing the coping styles of mother-only families as compromise formations is fairly sound. Dialectics of militancy vs. giving up, dangers vs. securities, imperious needs vs. outer and inner inhibitions, risks vs. benefits, all prevail in mother-only families. Chief among the deficits, as stated earlier, are the lack of a conjugal parenting pair and the lack of a man's income. The dangers are primarily economic, but also may include academic or school problems and problems in sex-role differentiation. The risks of mental disorders are concentrated in the overlapping anxiety-mood-disruptive behavior–antisocial–alcoholism–drug abuse categories, disorders that show a high incidence of familial aggregation. A vicious circle ensues; as the family's poverty increases, so does the mother's psychopathology; and as mother's mental adjustment declines, so does the children's. Psychiatrists currently biologize familial aggregations of mental disorders; in another climate, such intrafamilial prevalence might be thought to be socially derived since poverty or speaking Spanish or eating pork also runs in families but is not gene-produced.

Certain elaborated traits are reinforced in mother-only households. Hutchinson and Spangler-Hirsch (1988–1989) have found that children from single-parent families are good decision makers and that they have unique strengths and maturities that children in nuclear families do not. Also, in the single-parent family there seems to exist a respect for the diversity that exists among families and persons and respect for individuality that allows 1 child to eat hot dogs for breakfast while another eats a dry cereal or bread coated with peanut butter. If it works and does not harm, it seems valid to diversify. Also, "adhocracy" seems to reign in many mother-only households, connoting both an underorganization and a lack in rigid planning, but also inducing a flexibility that allows for effective coping with uncertainty and novelty—a vital ingredient of creativity.

Mother-only families arrange somehow to achieve advantages in their disadvantage. Examples would be the child who, by some role reversal, learns to give some needed care and support to a depressed, overworked mother; a child who assumes earlier responsibility and autonomy, who feels like a valued person not shut out from the adult world of work and competence; a child who is creatively streetwise and plucky and will not be abused or exploited by any strange adult; a child who doubts and questions the regimentation of the public school and will not cooperate if his or her imagination is not condoned and enhanced; a child who will not perpetuate patriarchal values in his or her own family when grown and giving care to children; a child whose gender identity may be intact but who has skills and interests that are androgynous, combining what may be stereotypically defined and assigned to both genders.

Psychiatry and Fatherless Children

Psychiatric opinion and clinical research with mother-only families have not been articulated well to date. Few empirical studies have been done. Assumptions, rhetoric, and overgeneralizing from personal or vivid single-case studies have been the rule. Psychiatrists, in short, have tended to idealize the father's place in the child's emotional world, to suspect dire pathology whenever a lone mother is attempting to save a child's life and to rear that child as a worthwhile, fully human person. More than that, psychiatrists often idealize the father's place in the child's emotional world. Many psychiatric concepts—Oedipus, Elektra, Phaedra, and Cinderella complexes, for instance—impugn the motives of children; but the usual psychiatric verdict of evil intent is leveled against mothers. Mothers have not received favorable press from psychiatrists in general; they have been labeled neurotigenic and schizophrenogenic, overprotective, pampering, coddling, rejecting, neurotic, narcissistic, and, woe to them, just plain anxious in their dealings with men and children.

A few solid findings have emerged, mainly from social scientists and not from the efforts of psychiatrists. As a group, children from mother-only families are poor; the concomitants and sequelae of their poverty can be, and probably ought to be, dissected out from their nonfathered condition. Unless this is done, then multiple pathologies attendant on poverty will be attributed to the fatherless condition, which distorts the truth of the mother-only family's existence.

Other psychiatric conclusions can be made. First, as a group, mother-only children experience a relative shortage of both economic and interpersonal security. In fact, they lack both fathering and mothering; mothers work disproportionately more often when they head up households with children. Such mothers cannot find the extra energy for caregiving that a nonworking mother whose husband is employed may provide to her children. What children need from a parent are infusions of security and special care or protection, but they are indiscriminate about the gender of the parent. From a child's standpoint, two or more devoted parents would always be better than one, regardless of gender. What a child sorely craves, and needs, is the total fund of derived security from empathetic and loving parenting persons.

There is another sane and sound psychiatric conclusion about a child in a mother-only family. Core gender identity is formed by 30 months of age, at a maturational level that finds even children in two-parent families heavily enmeshed with their mothers. That means that mothers stand by in watchful waiting, scarcely ever doing much guiding, as the child confirms her or his gender identity and interrelated body image and self-concept. As principal caregivers to young children, mothers shepherd both boys and girls during their identity formation; even in two-parent families, fathers often are not heavily involved with their offspring.

As a group, children from mother-only families tend to have higher verbal skills than children from two-parent families. In boys, verbal skills are higher than mathematical skills, but the math skills are also adequate; girls show lower math scores than boys but higher verbal ones. Formerly it was said that boys from fatherless families showed "the feminine pattern of high-verbal low-math (Vm)," but closer inspection of the data has revealed that the boys are also solid in math; they are, however, particularly gifted in verbal skills relative to boys from 2-parent families.

Since children from mother-only families are at risk for poverty, they tend to display the mental disorders that attend impoverishment, particularly the mood disorders, disruptive behavior disorders (including conduct and antisocial disorders), substance use disorders, and anxiety disorders. Reducing the risk for those disorders by making special provisions against their falling into poverty would be excellent preventive medicine. All families need more than their own moxie and inner resources if they are to be effective in the 1990s. Mother-only families only highlight the needs for social programs and policies that will benefit and not erode families with children.

Mother-Only Families in Neighborhood and Society

The two-parent family extends out into the macrocosm of the larger social surround; the mother-only family is driven, sometimes in desperation, to do the same. Most industrialized nations provide family allowances from the government based on the number of children in a family, but not the United States. In this country children comprise the majority of the nation's poverty group, an achievement unparalleled in all the industrialized countries of the world, in the eastern and western blocs both. Since 1980 the percentage rate of increase of impoverishment among women and children has been so enormous that by the year 2000, if the current trend is not interrupted, virtually all of the U.S. poor will be women or children. Mother-only families take a foremost place in all of those statistics. Children in such families are among the most imperiled portion of our population.

Even a two-parent family needs outside resources to sustain its viability. Since the majority of mothers go out to work today, day care for children is required; economic assistance becomes necessary when economic depressions or recessions occur or when parents are let go from jobs that will never be reopened to them. They need help when economic institutions falter and fail for families—closing the smokestack industries and lowering the parents' wages by ushering them into "service jobs" that are not unionized and that provide inadequate pay for a family to live well. The situation is graver still for mother-only families. Such families must obtain more money at once, after job loss. But obtaining welfare, food stamps, subsidized housing, and Supplemental Security Income (SSI) is becoming increasingly arduous. The federal funds formerly given to human services now are diverted to paying the national debt, and states must match the reduced federal funds that are available, which states often find a heavy burden. Consequently, the numbers of poor now exceed 30 million, and more mother-only families swell the ranks of homeless Americans.

Mother-only families suffer the scourges of urban poverty and of inner-city dwelling. They preach a brand of paranoia, of necessity, because they generally are powerless to protect their children from crimes. Occasionally mothers are led to overcontrol and enmeshment, to a vigilance that trusts nobody but implores the children not to go outside for play and to double-lock and triple-lock their doors and windows. When their own dependency needs are not met, children do not grow up to be dependable and easy adults.

Their neighborhoods are prime examples of urban decay and abandonment. Rare gentrification programs oust the poor from the neighborhood, hence "urban renewals" and return of the belt-tightening affluent from the suburbs to the city give very little benefit to impoverished mother-only families. Institutionally as well, the urban neighborhood is blighted. Shops, churches, banks, recreational facilities, movie theaters are absent. There is no supportive network in the community for inner-city mother-only families, and they participate precious little in communal affairs.

Mothers who head families with children become experts in managing scarcity; they are better at making do than most people with Ph.D. degrees in economics. They combine an array of welfare supports with loans from relatives and friends, taking in boarders, doing moonlighting and cottage industry work, rare payments from the child's father or regular allowances from a boyfriend—and by dint of heroic efforts, they paste together a budget that is seldom written down anywhere but that enables survival of the mother and her family. Small bits from multiple sources additively empower their family's survival. It would be foolish to extol their accomplishments without decrying their plight, but such mothers show an amazing capability for getting blood from turnips.

Like all families of the working and lower classes, mother-only families are endangered and at risk today. Their ability to survive, needing such a lot but receiving so little, is heartwarming. In the future, it seems likely that the United States will join other advanced nations in doing better with regard to families containing young children.

Changing Roles of Fathers— Single and Otherwise

Although certainly not as prevalent as mother-only families, father-only families are on the increase and merit address. Like mother-only families, father-only families can occur through mother's death or illness, by desertion or default, by adoption, and by court-ordered decisions involving custody battles or cases of abuse or neglect. The most common etiological factor is the current emphasis on the best interests of the child rather than the tender years presumption. In approximately 10% of custody cases now, fathers are awarded custody. Yet even then, when fathers do gain custody and visitation privileges, many renege within 2 or more years, relegating the responsibility for primary caregiving elsewhere.

Other societal changes also have contributed to increasing the opportunities for father's involvement in caregiving activities, even in the intact family. Over half of the mothers of young children work outside the home. As more women work and in fact break into administrative positions and male-dominated fields, many men are now unemployed. Some of these men will remain so because of the structure of the economy, the decline of the smokestack industries, and the fact that automation and robotics have made many workers obsolete and redundant. When fathers are not able to be breadwinners, family life changes and the father's role in the family is altered. Even if his wife works, he must seek food stamps, unemployment insurance payments, and any and every form of income supplementation for the family. The unemployed father soon discovers that when he is not earning, even with a working wife, the family's income is reduced to approximately one-third of its former level.

Nevertheless, unemployed fathers are available to their children more than they ever were when regularly and gainfully employed. That is not an unmixed blessing for the children, but it does permit fathers to undertake the essentials of child care, housekeeping, and home economics. They can test out their prior contentions that cleaning toilets or changing diapers, when done with love, can be highly ennobling work. Unemployed fathers, therefore, may retreat into active participation in the family-for-children. When they do, these more androgynous child-caring men become much more salient in the lives of children and make fathers' place much more significant and often much more positive and constructive. This, however, is not necessarily the case. Unemployed fathers also may be more prone to depression, alcohol and drug abuse, angry outbursts, and impatience. Unfortunately, unemployed fathers do not always view child care as a new and welcomed opportunity to spend more quality time with children.

Karl Marx was the type of father who welcomed such opportunities over a century ago. He hated working for wages and spent hours in libraries but was rarely gainfully employed. Marx had a lot of time to spend with his children; he was an active, loving, dynamic father who played with the children, respected their wants and wishes, recited Shakespeare to them, told them highly imaginative and original stories, tried to meet their emotional needs, and was never violent or brainwashing in his dealings with them. He was a delightful unemployed father but a bad provider. Against the grain of the 19th century, Marx spent a lot of time, as an unemployed person, in the company of his wife and children. His respect for women and children was so enormous, perhaps as a result of his work schedule, that he must have seemed almost unmanly to his neighbors.

Today, following in the footsteps of Karl Marx, many working-class and middle-class fathers have learned that child care—intimate daily interaction with children—is too vital and too much fun ever to be left to women exclusively. This trend will strengthen the father's position in the family. Another trend, tending to call men out of the shadows and into participation in the family with children, is militant feminism. This trend is more positive than widespread male unemployment. Feminism is a bright spot in our contemporary national life, both in politics and in making society more fit for children. After all, a sexist society can make life miserable for women, but a society so unhappy for women is one that also is likely to be unfit for children—and for men too. Feminist young mothers insist, sometimes abrasively and sometimes matter-of-factly, that the children's fathers take a much more visible and dynamic part in the life of the children. That aids the trend to have fathers participate more and to become more vital in children's lives. Since children need all the parenting they can derive from any source, it is bound to be beneficial for children.

When young male parents do become immersed in attending prenatal classes, helping the mother-to-be in her adaptations to pregnancy, assisting at the time of the labor and delivery and helping out in the postpartum period, then feeding, picking up, and caring for the baby, and joining with the mother in a 5- or 6-year period of servitude to the needs of the child—each child—they become involved and committed fathers.

These true male parents put to shame the stereotyped views of psychiatrists and other mental health workers; the parents on the front line in reality display a broad pluralism, diversity, eclecticism, and heterogeneity that boggle the rigid expectations and hopes of psychiatrists and other theorizers. Male and female parents may alternate in being Mr. Mom and Ms. Mom, then spelling each other as major breadwinner and careerist; the father may take the maternity leave, or both parents may go onto a part-time schedule. In Sweden, since 1974, the Parental Insurance System has offered to Swedish fathers and mothers 9 months of paid leave (at 90% of their previous salary). The plan has a legally enforceable guarantee of reemployment at the same salary level. Alas, our government is proud to be alone among the industrialized nations of the world in *not* supplying young families with any form of economic assistance. Such a position is detrimental to the well-being of children.

Although, since the time of the Industrial Revolution, the father has been largely work-oriented and uninvolved in child rearing, currently there are countervailing trends against excluding fathers. Only unemployment and the women's movement have been referred to here. Regarding the involvement of fathers in children's daily lives, we are in a fluid situation at the present time. When they are present, fathers can participate a great deal in families; however, usually they are not that active because there are few societal inducements to involve them in the intimate daily lives of women and children. Consequently, middle-class suburban fathers today may spend no more than a few minutes daily with their infant offspring.

Children who have been privileged to have had highly involved fathers will see them as extremely important figures. Those who have not known such a father will not understand why all the fuss is made about a father. In all likelihood, the gaps between the two groups will widen.

Father-Only Families— What Do We Know about Them?

Certainly there is even less empirical research looking at the functioning of the father-only family than at the mother-only family. Some of what we do know has been reviewed by Levy (1985), Kelly (1987), and Bronstein and Cowan (1988). We can make some generalizations here. Single-parent fathers tend to be, for the most part, fathers who have been divorced or separated from their wives and awarded custody by the court. These single fathers as a group tend to have better education, higher-paying jobs, and to be better off financially than single mothers as a group. These fathers tend to be assertive, self-confident, and emotionally, socially, and financially stable. They report the

first year of single parenting as the most difficult. They tend to do better with it if they have had previous experience with rearing, nurturing, and disciplining their children, if they are knowledgeable about child development, and if they come from homes in which their own fathers were involved in child-rearing activities.

Although single fathers may be confident in their own child-rearing abilities and viewed as being so by their children, the community may not view them as competent. Some reports indicate that the single father is viewed with suspicion and often not accepted by neighbors, child care personnel, or teachers. Because of this, often he is not included in parent meetings, seminars, and other parent training groups that could improve his skills as a parent, thus making his success more difficult to achieve.

Overall, children in father-only families show no gross differences from children in mother-only families in the areas of self-esteem, anxiety, sex-role typing, maturity, independence, psychosomatic and behavior problems, and social competence. Most studies seem to show that given equal parenting capabilities, children tend to fare better with the same-sex parent. All things not being equal, children probably are better off with the psychologically healthier parent, since children's difficulty in adjusting to parental separation seems to be related to the degree of psychopathology in the caregiving parent. When divorce is involved, the more pre- and post-divorce conflict there is between the divorcing parents, the more detrimental it is for the children in all areas of adjustment.

In conclusion, even though more and better research is needed in this area, we are dealing with two very different groups of people when we speak of single mothers and single fathers. Single fathers tend to have above-average incomes and educational attainments. Certainly single mothers could do with some of these benefits. Children raised in father-only families have fewer difficulties heaped upon them than children raised in mother-only families; ill effects in mother-only families have often been attributed to fatherlessness per se. Economic security seems to help. Medicaid is a help, but it only goes so far, and over time it is becoming more restrictive. Many mother-only families await governmental intervention to assure their well-being before it is too late.

REFERENCES

Allen, C. E. (1994). "Families in Poverty." *Nursing Clinics of North America, 29* (3), 377–393.

Bronstein, P., & Cowan, C. P. (1988). *Fatherhood today: Men's changing role in the family.* New York: Wiley-Interscience.

Hutchinson, R. L., & Spangler-Hirsch, S. L. (1988–1989). Children of divorce: Developmental and clinical issues. *Journal of Divorce, 12* (2–3), 5–24.

Kellam, S. G., Ensminger, M. E., & Turner, R. J. (1977). Family structure and mental health of children. *Archives of General Psychiatry, 34,* 1012–1022.

Kelly, J. B. (1987). *Longer-term adjustment in children of divorce: Converging findings and implications for practice.* Paper presented at the annual meeting of the American Psychological Association, New York.

Levy, A. M. (1985). Father custody. In D. H. Schetky & E. P. Benedek (Eds.), *Emerging issues in child psychiatry and the law.* New York: Brunner/Mazel.

Segal, E. A. (1991). The juvenilization of poverty in the 1980s. *Social Work, 36* (5), 454–457.

U.S. Bureau of the Census. (1996, February). *Current population reports, Series P23–191.* Washington, DC: U.S. Government Printing Office.

Wetzel, J. R. (1990, March). American families: 75 years of change. *Monthly Labor Review,* 4–13.

3 / Feminism and the Rearing of Children

Nancy A. Schrepf

It has long been known that the well-being of all young people is directly related to the emotional health of their primary caregiver, the formation of their own unique biological character, and the degree and type of stimulation available to them in the home and community environment. The relative happiness of a mother with her roles in adult life has been found to be correlated with the subsequent provision of "good-enough" child-rearing practices to offspring. Because of this essential fact, a discussion of the historical and present-day philosophies of the feminist movement will be presented in order to make sense out of what women expect of themselves today as well as the place they have been given in the social order.

The theme of this chapter is not expressly devoted to feminism, however. It is more particularly related to the conjoint effects of the feminist movement on the rearing of women's offspring. A discussion of the historical underpinnings of feminism is helpful in deciphering current trends in family and childrearing philosophy and practice. Additionally, other considerations related to secondary consequences of the women's movement are discussed, including the rise of the dual-earner and dual-career families, psychological effects of the multiplicity of roles women assume in this complex society, economic considerations affecting women and children as a result of an overwhelming divorce rate, the current state of children, and clinical considerations in the treatment of families that are at risk from the demands and stresses of the modern world.

The Feminist Movement: A Turbulent History

Confusion exists regarding an operational definition of feminism. In the earliest stages of the feminist movement, women who associated themselves with this ideology had political battles to fight as well as the responsibility of describing to the world the state of ignorance and servility to which women were condemned by social custom and training.

The feminism of the 1960s and 1970s, on the other hand, was as much intellectual and emotional as it was political. It was a new way of conceptualizing one-half the human experience. Touching the minds and hearts of every American man, woman, and child, women's oppression was viewed as a condition so pervasive and insidious that it equaled the experiences of other disadvantaged minority groups.

In the late 1970s and early 1980s, however, the feminist movement suffered from the political backlash of the New Right (Faludi, 1991; Lipset, 1982). Identifying the feminist cause as the enemy of women, this powerful fundamentalist crusade spurred an attack against women's equality to the extent that women themselves were recruited to attack each other. This movement against feminism was not developed because of women's achievement of equality but instead by the increasing probability that they may win it. The conservative New Right used a strategy designed to divide women's allegiances; single women were pitted against married women, employed women against homemakers, older against younger, class versus class, and childless females against virtuous mothers.

In 1997 it appeared as if the issues facing women took a back burner to the more publicized foci of childhood abuse, homelessness, and unemployment. Somehow, conceptualizing a direct connection between the practical gains of the feminist movement and its direct impact on the manner in which mothers raise their children has been forgotten or whitewashed in favor of more pressing concrete day-to-day issues. Finding a solution to these complex social problems is critical, and yet they overlap the feminist issue in that to dissipate all societal ills, a basic and simple philosophy of respect for human beings does need to develop in our present culture.

THE FIRST WAVE

In the early years of preindustrial America, religious upheavals produced not only the growth of the Protestant movement but also a move away from the homebound "family" economy to a new world of trade and commerce. At the same time, a transformation in the structure of the family began, and the emergence of the Victorian ideology of family life was born (Ryan, 1981; Smelser & Halpern, 1978). Social reform movements developed out of these economic, religious, and structural changes, including the first wave of feminism, the antislavery movements, and the concept of utopian societies. The burgeoning women's movement made its statement by focusing on women's suffrage and aiding in the liberation of southern slaves.

In colonial times, women participated with their men in securing, producing, and marketing goods and services, most frequently from a home base. In addition to holding joint responsibility for providing for the economic well-being of the fam-

ily, the female in the household was responsible for the education, health, and housekeeping services to family members. In the 19th century, unmarried women with a feminist leaning generally chose a life of celibacy and spinsterhood in exchange for a life outside the home (Skolnick, 1991).

As men moved into the sphere of the community, some of the other preindustrial responsibilities of the family shifted to the newly developed formal institutions, such as the church, hospitals, and schools. Care and socialization of children, services for the mentally and physically ill, and religious education moved out of the purview of the woman and into the hands of the larger society. Economic and political shifts began to occur, and the concept of the "family breadwinner" developed (Holder & Anderson, 1989). Similar to Pleck's (1977) definition of "master status," men were socialized as the workers outside the home and domestic responsibilities became women's main roles.

The events that shaped the feminist movement of the 1960s and 1970s had its roots in the culture of the 1950s (Friedan, 1963). During this period, the world of work and the world of the family were clearly divided into two separate spheres, each successfully independent of the other (Hareven, 1987; Holder & Anderson, 1989). Gender-based divisions of labor were seen as the "ideal" roles for men and women, and various theories were developed in order to offer credence to this point of view (Parsons & Bales, 1955). During the 1950s, women were increasingly socialized to manage the home, care for the young, and, in general, perform the more nurturing parental and spousal activities. Men, on the other hand, directed their attention and energy to participation in the community at large—not only to earn an income to support their family but also to influence the governing of the social group to which they belonged. This legacy of separate spheres has kept the division of labor between the sexes both strongly separated and unevenly rewarded.

For middle-class families, the focus of the nuclear unit was redirected toward the children; it was more private and segregated from both extended family members and the community at large, and it served as a haven from the slings and arrows of an increasingly alien world. The noted economist John Kenneth Galbraith suggested that in large part, middle-class women's roles changed in postindustrial America due to the need for people who both serve and manage consumption. He hypothesized that women were elected to replace the old servant class, and menial labor was redefined as a way to express love (Andre, 1981).

The plight of minority and working-class women, however, was different than that of the middle and professional classes. While families with economic means kept their women at home, rural and immigrant women were being recruited into the New England textile mills. In the southern states, black women, including one-fourth of all married and two-thirds of all widowed blacks, were working outside the family (Blau & Ferber, 1986).

THE SECOND WAVE

The second wave of feminism did not occur in this country until approximately a century after the first. Of all of the social movements of the 1960s, the second wave of the feminist movement had one of the biggest influences on both public and private life. The feminist movement of the 1960s and 1970s was a much more complicated phenomenon than the first wave. Despite the public portrayal of a smiling, complacent middle-class homemaker and mother, the reality of the housewife's day-to-day existence in many cases suggested a life filled with frustration, boredom, and dissatisfaction (Skolnick, 1991).

The second wave of feminism resulted in a challenge to this way of life. The narrow and rigid role of "homemaker as ideal" was challenged in a dramatic way by the new liberal nature of thought, as were cultural conceptualizations of the meaning of home and family, masculinity, femininity, work, and sexuality. More and more women were beginning to view previous stereotypical patterns of behavior that had been governed by traditional sex roles as unfair and arbitrary.

In spite of the increasing challenges for women born out of the feminist philosophy—advanced education, rising divorce rates, more involvement in the workforce, and liberation of sexual norms—an intellectual understanding of the emotional and intellectual aspects of the movement followed, albeit more slowly than the behavioral changes (McLaughlin et al., 1988). The earlier impression that all feminists were man-hating, childless fanatics eventually was transformed by mainstream culture, which watered down the extremist position nurtured by politicians, the media, and advertising.

THE THIRD WAVE

A review of history suggests that social changes as well as the movements that propel them give rise to backlash responses targeted at reversing their effects (Faludi, 1991; Skolnick, 1991). Regardless of poor public press, some unfortunate tactics by movement leaders, and a rhetoric that received a great deal of criticism from most Americans, nothing could have forestalled the blossoming of the antifeminist backlash. The new consensus, cited by one feminist critic, proposed that "the family is our last refuge, our last defense against predatory selfishness, loneliness and rootlessness, the idea that there could be a desirable alternative to the family is no longer taken seriously" (Willis, 1981, p. 187).

The second wave of feminism was perceived as a failure from both the supporters and opponents of the Equal Rights Amendment (ERA). The women's movement also was charged with neglecting the needs of ethnic and minority women and the working and poor classes, placing too much emphasis and financial resources into fighting for the ERA, not addressing itself to the needs of full-time mothers and housewives, and emphasizing equality at the expense of women's special needs such as children, child support, and maternity leave.

Changes in the family structure were in large part a result of a movement that challenged the deeply rooted feelings and anxieties of American culture. Because of these challenges and previous hostility toward and fear of revolution in the family structure, the antifeminist backlash response was directed not only toward the concept of feminism itself but to the same changes that led to feminism in the first place. The liberation of women and the concomitant achievements that resulted posed realistic threats to the self-interest and identity of many Americans. A seemingly benign proposal advocated by the National Organization for Women (NOW) put forth a declaration of a true partnership between men and women—an equitable sharing of responsibilities of home and children—which was made out as a challenge to the social order (Hole & Levine, 1971).

The backlash movement of the 1980s was similar to the sequence of events that happened in the previous chapters of the women's movement. The socioeconomic and cultural changes altered the lives of all American women significantly, particularly those representative of the middle class. Traditional women who saw their role as homemaker threatened by a shift toward feminist arguments allied themselves with conservative clergymen and business interests to oppose the changes and demands of the women's movement (Skolnick, 1991). The antifeminists began to blame feminism for all social problems related to the deterioration of the family—from the overwhelming divorce rate, to the alleged emasculation of men—when in fact these trends had begun well before the rise of "women's liberation" (Cherlin, 1981). Women had changed, in some cases the law had changed, but formal equalities granted by the legal system did not alter the painful realities that most women faced in everyday life. Barriers on both the home front and the workplace were stronger and more complex than they initially seemed. Women as well as the system of the family had reformed, but other institutions and men had not fully accepted or adapted to these alterations.

In analyzing the contraindications of the traditionalism and self-sufficiency that characterized the family system of the 1950s, it appeared that the 1960s' response to the prevailing values was made in the form of a countercultural challenge as well as rampant demographic population movement. At that time, the stress and anxiety of the change process was dramatic, perplexing, and widespread. The response to what many people considered to be frightening social trends resulted in a much more conservative backlash movement. In the later part of the 1970s, public opinion about the family was governed by nostalgia and mourning about cultural narcissism and decay (Lasch, 1979). In an attempt to soften the discord of the rapid shifts appearing in almost every aspect of life in the late 1970s, adult men and women grasped onto their previous traditions and turned to what they considered to be "better times" for comfort. Economic and political despair settled over the country as the character of the American people was placed on trial.

Swinging back toward historical traditions, materialism, and the merits of the nuclear family structure, the postcounterculture years were more settled yet oppressive for the middle class. Some authors' view of the "affluent worker" caught up in the values of the "Me Decade" was not as stereotypical of the culture-at-large as most Americans were given to believe, however (Carroll, 1990; Lasch, 1976, 1979; Wolfe, 1976/1982). Economic unrest, unemployment, inequality, and overt class divergence were penetrating families

that earlier had been blessed with adequate living standards (Wolfe, 1976/1982). For those families that remained a part of the middle or professional classes, family life also was becoming more characterized by isolation with a focus on more intense and intimate interpersonal relationships between family members—an intensity and intimacy that may have contributed to an increase in the dysfunctionality of the family system.

Revisionist views of feminism were at work. From politics, advertising, television, and the cinema to authors of the 1980s, and 1990s scholars, and even the mental health profession, attempts were made to crush what seemed to be the strides and accomplishments of the second wave of feminism. According to Faludi (1991), a backlash against the women's movement is successful only to the extent that it does not seem to be political, that it is not even a battle at all. In what she described as the "Backlash Brain Trust," information against feminist values began to be internalized by women in their minds—the result being a form of backlash against themselves.

The media presented the works of a selected few second-wave feminist authors as recantations of feminism itself. A case in point was Betty Friedan's second book, *The Second Stage* (1981), which appeared to renounce the previous principles and strategies that Friedan had offered movement participants success a decade earlier. Challenging the previous platform, Friedan stated that feminists had not only ignored women who assumed more traditional roles but had used political tactics that were too masculine and aggressive. The same regressionist views have been espoused in 1997. In an article in the *Detroit News*, Marney Rich Keenman interviewed journalist Iris Krasnow who was formerly employed by United Press International in Washington, D.C. After self-reported soul-searching regarding her multiple roles as career woman and mother, Krasnow came to the revelation that "feminism in the 1990s is as much, if not more, about the nursery as it is the news room" (Keenman, 1997, p. 2). Many mothers without financial means and a thriving career may not be at liberty to make a choice between work and full-time mothering, however.

Shouts from backlash contributors cried that the feminist movement finally had realized its errors; it had seen the light and would now move toward a more realistic position for women—back to their rightful place in the home. Similar to the

19th-century concept of separate spheres, Friedan called for women to promote their issues and interests from their domestic domain. She suggested that "women will rediscover the family circle as the base of their identity and human control" (Friedan, 1981, p. 64). In Faludi's (1991) opinion, one of the reasons second-wave scholars and authors wrote such criticisms of the previous movement was because of personal spite and competition for a revered place in the feminist order.

For the most part, however, the problem of building a new framework for the feminist movement was forsaken in the 1980s and 1990s. According to Fuchs (1988) the only women to have benefitted from the women's movement are white, middle-class, unmarried, well-educated, and childless. What he implies, then, is that the women's movement has given women license to delay childbearing for the sakes of their careers.

Additionally at this point, "relational" scholars focused their efforts on specifying "women's special natures"; in essence, reifying their differences from men, particularly their nurturing and caring qualities. The proponents of women's differences found themselves to be the new center of media attention receiving critical acclaim for what may have been a veiled and simplistic refurbishing of old Victorian thought. Not only did persons sensitive to women's issues use and interpret the words of relational feminists; so too did politicians, corporate executives, and religious leaders of the fundamentalist Right movement whose agendas were to define women not only as different but as unequal.

The Current State of the Feminist Movement

The current state of the feminist movement is decidedly unclear. Entering the 1990s, some representatives of the media as well as advertisers and politicians were heralding this decade as the "Decade of Women." There is little certainty regarding the specifics of this declaration and, to date, there is no concrete evidence to support it. Klein (1996) succinctly summarized the current climate for feminist thought. She stated that in this age of political correctness, mainstream theorists as well as popular media shy away from overt attacks on feminism and have instead relegated its discussion to the status of a "crazy aunt in the attic" of philosophical and public discourse.

Feminist women ask, "When will it finally be time for us to reach an equality with men that is not superficially decreed by law alone?" They question whether the traditional woman will continue to be idealized, supported, and nurtured as the accepted role for the adult female. If the answer to this question is affirmative, working women will continue to suffer untold oppression at the hands of bureaucracies administered by men. Also they will be forced to believe that they are simply weaker emotionally and less intelligent when they take a position of challenging their circumstances. Faludi (1991) reported the words of Ruth Mandel, director of the Center for the American Woman and Politics: "No, this isn't the year for women—it wasn't the year in 1986 or 1988, and it won't be in '90 or '92" (p. 460).

The major question being asked by every woman and man with a feminist consciousness centers around the energy, or its lack, that a majority of women feel because of the overload and complexity of their lives; generally, how does this multiplicity of women's roles relate to their relationships with loved ones and, most particularly, their children? Is the current state of women's equal rights an issue at all or are women, for the most part, so involved in the tireless day-to-day activities of their existences that concentrating on whether they have an ideology to propel them is hardly a conscious thought?

Although this chapter reflects a liberal feminist position, most likely no ideological discussion can paint an accurate portrait of the conceptual framework devised by the "woman on the street" in her thinking about issues related to her personhood and the rearing of her children. Many women are not consciously aware that oppression exists in their lives; nor do they ruminate excessively about the consequences of their condition. Scholars, researchers, the media, and politicians apparently are more aware of the secondary effects of the inconsistencies in feminist philosophy than are those who suffer the adversities of it—most importantly, the typical American woman and her offspring. In order to develop a clearer understanding of the experiences of women in this decade, let us look to the current state of the various roles that they assume as workers, breadwinners, mothers, and wives.

Effects of the Feminist Movement on Women's Lives

THE TRADITIONAL FAMILY

> I myself have never been able to find out precisely what feminism is. I only know that people call me a feminist whenever I express sentiments that differentiate me from a doormat.
>
> —WEST, 1913

The traditional family system with father in the workforce and mother at home continues to remain a prevalent style even though many women have moved outside the singular sphere of the household to the world of work. According to research on gender roles, the social status of the housewife often is determined by the husband's career. However, even when the husband holds high-ranking status by virtue of his profession, the role of homemaker usually is devalued. Generally, no economic value has been placed on the many important duties that women perform. In her 1986 study of women's personal and financial experience entitled *A Lesser Life: The Myth of Women's Liberation in America,* Sylvia Hewlett estimated that it takes approximately 60 hours per week to provide physical and emotional support for a family of four. If women and children had value in the traditional family system, women's work of rearing children would be seen as much more important. With a minimum of exceptions, more than 99% of all people who list their occupation as that of homemaker are women. Usually they do not earn a wage and have little discretionary income of their own. Even in the best of marriages which can be defined by limited marital strife, adequate financial means, and relatively emotionally stable offspring—homemakers' lives give evidence that the traditional pattern is difficult to sustain. These women who report adequate role contentment have paid a considerable price in restriction of self-development (Levinson, 1997).

While this may be true in the case of the financially stable, two parent, heterosexual, white families, little research has been done to find out how the traditional women's views were represented when other races, classes, sexual orientations, and ethnicities are taken into account (Okin, 1997). According to this author, most African-American and working-class parents are rather unlikely to view homemaking and mothering oppressive. As mothers who have no option but to work long hours—both at home and at work—they may see the situation granted to white, professional class, traditional women as an unattainable ideal.

Without financial means, women are unable to support themselves and their children independently, and many remain in inadequate or abusive marriages because of this. With the growing opinion that women's workforce options are dramatically improved as well as the passing of no-fault divorce laws, traditional females may not gain the income needed after finding themselves and their children alone without the financial support of their husbands. Becoming a single parent abandoned to raise young offspring alone or divorcing at midlife with older children to support has forced poverty onto many women and those in their care. Other than successful skills as a mother and domestic, homemakers frequently are left with limited training in other forms of employment, no job history, and poor self-esteem. Even in traditional family structures, who have the support of relatives or who utilize unregulated day care services, may not be able to keep up with the demands as more and more women enter the work force (Jones, Tepperman, Wilson, 1995).

The general focus of the home in the traditional family is child-centered, although the impact on children of having full-time maternal care is not yet clear (Hoffman, 1979; Lamb, 1984). What is considered to be the major factor in any child's adjustment is congruence between what the mother wants to do and what she is doing. For example, more psychological distress is found in mothers who want to work and cannot; and conversely, in those who would like to be full-time homemakers but must work (Skolnick, 1991).

Additionally, it is thought that the advent of midlife is more difficult for the traditional woman to negotiate than for the career female. With children being raised and leaving home, the couple may need to renegotiate the parameters of their relationship. When couples disagree at this stage of their marriage about the wife's employment outside the home, it has been found that more wives want to be employed than their husbands want them to be, and that disagreement can result in marital unhappiness. Spouses who have managed to obtain non–child-centered interests are usually less vulnerable to marital strife because the focus of the relationship is not directed solely on "the couple."

With the divorce rate at approximately 50%, traditional women and their children are more at risk for losing needed income and future earning potential. Men leave marriages with their status and earning abilities intact. Research studies have found a direct relationship between an ex-wife's economic recovery following a divorce and her employment status while married. Women who were employed during marriage were likely to receive 80% of their average family income when studied 4 years postdivorce. Alternatively, women who had not been employed before divorce were only receiving 50% of that average 4 years after the marital dissolution had occurred. If a financial dilemma is present in a newly constituted single-parent family, it directly affects a mother's ability to maintain the child-centered household that is the earmark of the traditional family. When women are forced to move into the workplace without the added support of a partner to take up some of the child care duties, youngsters often are left to fend for themselves, leaving them with the arduous task of self-parenting without the requisite knowledge and judgment to perform this skill in an adequate manner.

WOMEN'S ENTRY INTO THE WORKFORCE

Dual-Earner Couples: The traditional nuclear family with a father employed outside the home, a homemaking mother, and children in school is evident in only 7% of nuclear family systems. While this is only a small percentage of families, the "mother myth" continues to influence how the role of mothering is viewed when women move into the workplace. According to Russo (1979), the "myth" suggests that a "good" mother must be physically present to attend to her infants' every need. When the child becomes school age, the mother may be free to pursue other activities as long as they do not interfere with the young person's after-school arrangements. These conditions of the motherhood myth remain despite compelling evidence to support the idea that constant availability is not a necessity.

Children are not harmed solely by women moving outside the sphere of the home environment. Their self-esteem, intelligence, self-concept, school functioning, and ability to form relationships with others is not impaired because of maternal employment (Braverman, 1989).

Most working women are married and live with their husbands and children. Whether their socioeconomic status is blue or white collar, most modern family systems need additional income regardless of race. Although this family form is considered typical by modern standards, neither social policy nor social attitudes are in synchrony with the need for this way of structuring the nuclear unit (Hoffman, 1989). Because of this fact, much research has been done in order to decry the negative aspects of the two-earner family (Barnett, Biener, & Baruch, 1987). In reviewing the literature on stress and its relationship to gender, these authors hypothesized that the focus on the negative stress factors found in working women was likely due to the assumption that they already have two primary roles: those of wife and mother.

In spite of this complexity of roles, there is increasing evidence that employed females who also serve their families report greater psychological and physical well-being than those women who remain at home on a full-time basis, provided that sole economic support of the family is not an overriding issue for these women (Barnett et al., 1987; Baruch, Barnett, & Rivers, 1983; Merikangas, Prusoff, Kupfer, & Frank, 1985). These findings may be representative of the expansion hypothesis of human energy, which states that individuals who succumb to multiple responsibilities receive a wide variety of rewards from each role, including increased self-esteem, financial gain, and more avenues for positive feedback (Holder & Anderson, 1989). Traditionally, men have benefited from multiple roles; now women are beginning to receive similar satisfactions.

In addition to increased self-esteem and sense of personal accomplishment, working wives are more self-reliant and less needful of affection and social involvement than women in traditional housewife roles (Burke & Weir, 1976; Hershey & Warner, 1975). Even in jobs that provide limited pay, women report benefits; most frequently cited are improved social contacts and an increased satisfaction with life. Along with accumulating personal gains, there appears to be no difference in marital satisfaction between employed and unemployed wives. However, marital dissatisfaction increased with decline in socioeconomic status or when the husband was unemployed. Also, men were more likely to abuse their wives if their job status was inferior to that of either their spouses or their fathers-in-law.

Tasks in dual-earner families are essentially divided along gender lines, with men performing yard duties and women assigned to housework and child rearing. As income, occupation, and prestige increased for females, men share more in domestic functions; generally, they are no longer in a bartering position for unpaid domestic services.

Even though women can benefit from the psychological buffering of a divergence of roles, contrasting evidence indicated that the resultant role strain for women who are employed full time and have the additional responsibilities of young children can be very great. Women typically sacrifice more than men do. They tend to cope with the multiplicity of roles by prioritizing responsibilities; children often emerge as their first priority followed by attention to career and household duties. Conflicts between career and family can leave women feeling guilty, fatigued, and emotionally depleted. The more hours they work, the more they tend to be depressed if small children are left in the care of others. These women reported more physical distress than women with small children who work on a part-time basis (Arber, Gilbert, & Dale, 1985; Cleary & Mechanic, 1983).

Overall, women's boundary between home and work appears to be more permeable than it is for men. Raised on the psychological theories of the 1950s, most females of childbearing age have heard repeatedly that if they enter the workforce, their children will suffer. Since working women retain primary child care responsibilities, they often report increased role conflict and worry about balancing the duties of home and work. More often it is the woman who cancels work obligations to remain at home with an ailing child. Women also reported more preoccupation with domestic matters during work hours and spent more time in telephone consultation with offspring than men do (Sekaran, 1986). Families with powerful social networks that can respond in times of need have more protection from the impact of these day-to-day emergencies.

Problems do not diminish for the mother of school-age children. For the older child with no stay-at-home parent, the length of the school day is too short and community after-school and weekend programs are too few to alleviate the associated parental stress. In 1986 an estimated 5 to 10 million children fell into the category of "latchkey children," a term that refers to school-age young people who remain at home alone after school without parental supervision. While there is insufficient research to determine specific negative results of the impact on children of less parental supervision, parents whose children are seen in clinical settings frequently report this issue as con-

tributing to stress in the parent-child relationship. Occasionally women take job positions that are lower in pay and less rewarding emotionally and intellectually in order to combine the tasks of work and home more effectively.

Maternal employment alone reveals little about the well-being of children. A working mother's attitude, the amount of emotional and practical support she receives, and the quality of child care available to her play a critical role in her morale and subsequent functioning in the family. Bronfenbrunner and Crouter (1982) suggested that children whose mothers work were no more likely to suffer from developmental or behavioral problems than those who do not. No direct effects on children raised in dual-earner families have been found, but both positive and negative consequences have been hypothesized. Children of working parents hold less stereotypical gender-related images and frequently are more responsible and self-reliant. On the negative side, unsupervised offspring are more likely to engage prematurely in sex, criminal activity, and drug use.

Some recommendations that often lead to contentment in dual-earner families have been hypothesized by researchers. Dual-earner couples are more content if both partners are involved in similar occupations. Working couples find the relationship more satisfying if the wife has remained in the same job during the course of the marriage, she is gratified by her work, and her husband allows her to discuss problems with the job at her own discretion. Additionally, family contentment is increased when the wife sees her husband as supportive in child-rearing and household work, and the husband is able to assess accurately his spouse's fluctuating level of stress. Parents of older youngsters are generally more satisfied than those with younger offspring; those who share jointly in child care duties report less marital strife. Finally, even in the 1990s, couples that agree that the husband's career is more important than his wife's report more satisfaction than those that feel their occupations are of equal worth.

Dual-Career Couples: A difference should be noted between dual-earner and dual-career couples. Although much has been written about the dual-career family system, only 14% of dual-earner marital relationships fall into this category. The major discrepancy between the dual-career and the dual-earner couples is that while the dual-earner female establishes the child and home responsibilities as top priorities, career men and women, who are philosophically egalitarian, are not as willing to compromise issues related to their respective careers. It has been reported that childless professional couples have a better opportunity to balance the demands of career and relationship responsibilities than those with offspring.

A dual-career couple theoretically has formed an equal union in which both heads of a household develop an uninterrupted career—instead of a job—and simultaneously create a family life. The pressures for women involved in this marital arrangement can be even greater than those in either the dual-earner or traditional family systems. While unrealistic, the goal of what has been described as the "supermom" syndrome remains the standard from which many career women evaluate their expectations. Even though many professional women precariously balance their roles as experts in their fields as well as competent mothers and wives, there is only minimal evidence to suggest that most dual-career marriages are an equal partnership, despite the fact that couples believe they want them to be.

Statistical trends have indicated that this group may increase in number as women advance professionally. Couples like these are following uncharted waters and have few role models to propel them. Negotiations between partners can be difficult, as is evidenced by the fact that the divorce rate for women educated 5 or more years post–high school is higher than for any other group except those without high school diplomas (Houseknecht, Vaughn, & Macke, 1984).

The benefits for dual-career families include a substantial financial income, which aids not only in the quality of material life but in the ability to hire support services for housekeeping and child care. Professional colleagiality can improve marital satisfaction, and research supports the idea that partners in the marriage are more self-sufficient and self-reliant than their counterparts in dual-earner relationships (Burke & Weir, 1976). It has also been found that children of professional mothers are more independent and highly motivated than others (Hoffman, 1979).

Despite the obvious satisfactions, the dual-career couple faces the innumerable hazards of demanding professions. The possibilities of occupational relocation, long working hours, and extensive commitments can lead to incompatible choice-making and major compromises if the couple intends to remain married. Steil (1984) suggested that women more often either deny promotion of their own career or move because of the husband's obligations when conflicts in career interests arise.

Professional women cannot compete with men in terms of salary and prestige in the workplace. Hewlett (1986) believes that the wage gaps between men and women can be explained by brief interruptions in women's careers because of childbearing and rearing responsibilities. Jones, Tepperman, & Wilson (1995) revealed that childbearing at any age is associated with a reduction in labor force activity and earning power. Other authors state that even when women start with the same education and entry-level salaries as their male counterparts, 10 or more years into their professional careers they will have lower rank and salaries. As a general rule, women even in the dual-career families provide most of the child care and homemaking services.

Even if it were possible, simply changing these inequalities would not assure a woman's rise up the career ladder. The fact that most men are used to dealing with the opposite sex primarily as people to meet their needs for nurturance or sexual gratification may impair their ability to perceive women's capacities accurately (Holder & Anderson, 1989). Male supervisors generally see women as less committed to their professions than men because of their overriding allegiance to their children, and men tend to view women who exhibit traditionally "male" personality characteristics such as assertiveness and expression of anger as suspicious or "odd."

The Current State of American Children

Let us move from a discussion of the strengths and weaknesses of particular family systems to the effects of structural and societal problems on the current state of America's children. Despite the backlash movement of the 1960s and 1970s, mainstream American attitudes toward women's roles, the family, and childhood have been transformed in many ways (Hoschild, 1997; Jones, Tepperman, & Wilson, 1995; Skolnick, 1991). Although changes have not been quite as pervasive as some authors have suggested, most wives and mothers have not returned home from the workforce to their previous roles as full-time caregivers and domestics, children remain unsupervised in many aspects of their lives, and the divorce rate has leveled off but has not decreased sufficiently in many years—positive and negative trends that support the strides and complications that the liberal political movements have made.

DIVORCE AND CHILDREN

Divorce is simply one consequence of the complexity of factors that comprise our high-stress, high-risk society. Increasing divorce rates are not directly the result of newfound feminist leanings among modern women and men. Although professional women are four times more likely to divorce than traditional women, the impact for the full-time homemaker and her offspring can be much more devastating in terms of its financial and psychological effects.

Research on the effects of divorce on family members has been mixed (Skolnick, 1991; Jones, Tepperman, & Wilson, 1995). Wallerstein and Blakesless (1989) suggested that we know surprisingly little regarding the long-term consequences of marital dissolution. According to Hewlett (1986), in 1940 there was 1 divorce for every 6 marriages, while in 1990, there was 1 for every 2 marriages. Today, demographers predict that 2 out of every 3 first marriages will end in divorce. Jones, et al., 1995 and Skolnick (1991) and other authors indicate that we need to accept the fact that the institution of marriage is here to stay along with divorce, working mothers, and single-parent families. Although marriage will still be a viable social grouping, future indicators suggest that the structure of this configuration will be markedly altered by the year 2000. (Jones, etal. 1995).

The impact of divorce on children is harsher in the United States than for other countries. Researchers now consider divorce to be only one component of the long deterioration process in a failed marriage. It is difficult to separate the effects of divorce from other factors, such as conflict between parents before and after separating, economic loss as a result of divorce, loss of family home, and the possibility that children will lose friends or be forced to change schools. In a longitudinal study of 131 white, middle-class children of divorce, Wallerstein and Blakesless (1989) found that 50% of the subjects studied experienced a wide variety of psychiatric symptoms upon reaching adulthood; they were typically more worried, self-depreciating, angry, and lower-achieving than men and women from intact homes.

According to Elias (1983) and Adams, Milner, and Schrepf (1984), the age of the child at the time of marital dissolution often is related to specific behavioral problems. Younger children of divorcing couples frequently exhibit adjustment problems later in childhood, particularly during adolescence. Behavioral symptoms typically vary according to age; young children tend to withdraw, while older children frequently act out aggressively. The most common age group affected by marital dissolution are those children under age 7. Adjustment issues for these youngsters include fear of abandonment and guilt regarding the marital breakup. Authors such as Francke (1983) also have identified a gender difference in adjustment of male and female offspring following divorce. Boys rather than girls appear to display a more difficult adjustment, which is manifested by aggressive behavior, a greater need for attention, lower school achievement, and a higher rate of drug and alcohol abuse. Studies indicate that boys usually take twice as long as girls to adjust to divorce and are more likely to exhibit behavioral problems during adolescence.

While not many studies have compared divorced families to problematic intact families, there is increasing evidence that parental conflict—shouting, hitting, and/or cold hostility—is a key factor in eroding a child's psychological well-being (Adams et al., 1984; Skolnick, 1991). Furstenberg and Cherlin (1991) found that the main issue for children of divorce was the quality of their continuing relationship with the parents, particularly the mother.

Some authors believe that there should be less focus on the form the family takes and more emphasis on supporting the well-being of children in all families. According to Adams, et al., (1984) and Skolnick (1991), the United States has been less careful than other countries to ensure that children are provided for in the period following the marital breakup. There is a need for policy changes in the economic arrangements following divorce that would greatly reduce the stress and disruption children experience. Bohannan (1985) reported the need for cultural models of successful divorce and postdivorce families in order to offer parents and their children better choices in problem resolution.

A GROWING UNDERCLASS — POVERTY AND ITS EFFECTS

One of the most insidious consequences of divorce for women and children is the economic fallout that accompanies it. Historically, women and their young could rely on marriage to provide a financially secure way of life. Without considering the emotional component of modern marriages, traditional unions provided a practical division of labor for the family unit. Times have changed, however. While marriage has provided job security for women in the past, traditional women of the 1990s cannot rely on it for lifetime job security (Hewlett, 1986; Jones, et al., 1995).

In 1983 children from single-parent households constituted approximately one-quarter of the entire population of children; they represented one-half of all poor children. Nine out of 10 children reside with their mothers following divorce, and without child support, the single-parent's income may be depressed as much as 70%. Reporting a 1982 Census Bureau survey, Hewlett (1986) revealed that 41% of custodial mothers are not awarded child support from the courts, and of the 5 million single mothers who are legally awarded support payments, only one-third collect the full amount on a consistent basis. Generally speaking, 60% of divorced fathers contribute nothing to the financial security of their children. Research studies have indicated, however, that the majority of fathers can afford to comply with court orders and are able to live adequately even if they did pay for support of their children.

Problems are even graver for African American children. In the 1970s and 1980s, there appeared to be a crisis in black families, as evidenced by the decline in marriage rates and a dramatic increase in female-headed households (Skolnick, 1991). Many of the most disturbing changes associated with the poverty underclass have been associated with economic changes that have occurred in recent years. For example, unskilled, fairly well-paying inner-city jobs have declined in number or moved as industries have relocated to outlying regions. Additionally, higher unemployment rates have led to more persistent and concentrated poverty in the inner city. Along with this, a set of mutually reinforcing problems has developed that affect the lives of children raised in low-income areas—increased familial discord, homelessness, an increase in welfare dependence, higher crime rates, drug and alcohol dependence, and other hazards associated with an insecure economic and emotional life.

EFFECTS OF CHANGING FAMILY PATTERNS

Every generation makes speakable their concerns regarding the welfare of children. Today the majority of American people believe that the quality of children's lives has declined since their own childhood. Melman, Lazarus, and Rivlin (1990) and Jones, et al., 1995 stated that with the heightened increase in divorce rate and the vast rise not only in domestic violence but single-parent families and childhood group care, coupled with decreased sibling size and working mothers, children's familial circumstances have changed markedly from that of their parents.

Some positive outcomes can be gleaned from recent trends in nuclear family organization. The average American child's physical health has improved dramatically since the 1960s in spite of America's comparatively high mortality rate. Decrease in family size allows children to experience greater financial resources even though the median family income has decreased in recent years. Additionally, the educational level for adults has increased remarkably since the 1950s, particularly among black women.

More negative trends have developed in the last few years, most related to troubling social behavior exhibited by young people such as delinquency, gang membership, drug use, and early sexual activity. According to researchers such as Uhlenberg and Eggebeen (1986), teenage suicide, a behavior considered an indicator of the emotional well-being among American youths, has more than doubled in the 20-year period between 1960 and 1980. Changes in family patterns have been blamed for these increases, among other culprits.

Many of the difficulties facing children have been linked primarily to economic factors. When financial concerns affect families and communities, violence is more predominant. Generally, violence is perpetuated by the culture in which it survives. The right of citizens to purchase handguns and the Supreme Court's decision to allow teachers to use corporal punishment in the schools are only two ways that violence is promoted in American society.

In the smaller sphere of the family unit, the way in which the nuclear family is organized also can lead to violence. According to Zinn and Eitzen

(1990), what was ideally a small group of people founded on loving relationships frequently can become a unit focused on power struggles between family members when any form of stress develops. Even with feminist strides being made, male dominance in families has been perpetuated not only by the legal system in our own country but also by religious and educational institutions. When the inequality in the family hierarchy is pervasive and mismanaged—power is unequally distributed between partners—abuse of all parties, including children, can occur.

Because the family organization is responsible for many different aspects of people's lives,—moral, religious and political education, family emotional and financial well-being—power struggles can develop, particularly in traditional families. The inherently private nature of the family unit has been an additional characteristic that enhances the possibility of familial violence. Negative consequences of privacy have focused primarily on insulation of family members from society-at-large, which unfortunately leaves childhood victims of abuse from seeking any outside assistance.

SPOUSE ABUSE IN THE AGE OF FEMINISM

Spouse abuse, which is on the rise, most often refers to physical abuse of a marriage partner but also can include forms of sexual, verbal, and emotional abuse. Children in spouse-abusing homes receive the residual effects of this trauma not only by witnessing the subjugation and brutalizing of a primary role model but also by experiencing the secondary effects of this long-term disruption in the home (Eth & Pynoos, 1985; Herman, 1992; Jones, et al., 1995).

Incidence rates of spouse abuse have been difficult to attain because of unreliable reporting, particularly among the middle and upper classes. Gelles and Straus (1988) also indicated that minority and poor families were overrepresented in most samples because data on these groups were more easily attainable. A 1985 study by Straus and Gelles selected a sample of 3,520 general population couples. At least 11.3% of wives reported minor to severe acts of violence during a 1-year period of research. In clinical populations, the incidence rates appeared to be between 25 and 50% of all couples, and occurred in at least a minor form on sporadic occasions throughout the marriage.

In spite of the difficulties in reporting spouse abuse, researchers and clinicians believe that it is a fairly common practice. Although wife abuse is represented in all socioeconomic strata, it tends to be found more often in families that are experiencing some kind of economic hardship.

Family conditions that trigger spouse abuse include: a family history of violence, unwelcomed pregnancy, couples prone to verbal aggression, men who are less successful or less intelligent than their spouses and/or their fathers-in-law, men who suffer from job failure, male sexual dysfunction or excessive jealousy, and, in many cases, the use of alcohol or drugs by the husband prior to the occurrence of the abuse (Edelson, Eiskovits, & Guttman, 1985; Gelles, 1977).

While wife abuse is known to be a complex phenomenon, few answers can provide assistance to women and children in families like these. Additional factors contributing to a spouse-abusing environment revolve around a societal climate that supports violence generally. Also, a culture that keeps women in a secondary status and accepts the use of physical violence to control women continues to support the notion of "family as battleground"—an arrangement that encourages inequality, disharmony, and terror in the isolated milieu of the nuclear unit.

CHILD ABUSE AND NEGLECT AS A RESULT OF MODERN FAMILY PERILS

> With the exception of the police and the military, the family is perhaps the most violent social group, and the home the most violent social setting in our society.
> —GELLES AND STRAUS, 1979 P. 130

Child abuse and neglect go hand-in-hand with poverty, dysfunctional family systems, disrespect of women and children, and conservative political beliefs. Any act by a parent, whether overt or covert, that places a child at risk is considered to be a form of child abuse—an act potentially harmful to the child. The best estimate currently available on violence toward children has been found in a national study by Gelles and Straus conducted in 1985. According to these authors, two-thirds of parents have used some form of violence toward their offspring sometime during their upbringing. Second, 10.7% of parents used severe violence, which includes beating, hitting or threatening with an object including a knife or gun, kicking, and so on. These rates were considered to be only a rough estimate of the childhood abuse that occurs, as general population samples are reluctant to be truthful about behaviors against children that are socially and legally unacceptable.

Reasons for these alarming rates of childhood abuse are again complex and varied, and include personal, social, and cultural factors. Unlike popular myth, most child-abusing parents are not necessarily mentally ill or characteriologically impaired. Individual personality traits, such as an inability to control aggressive feelings, an inability to cope adequately with stress, an overabundance of life failures, poor ego strength, and a role model of abuse during the parents' own childhood, may contribute to the perpetration of abuse. Failure to learn parenting skills, loss of a parent, separation from the mother, or rearing in a disruptive home are additional precursors to becoming abusing parents themselves. Chronic alcohol or drug consumption is a common trait among perpetrators and is also associated with other factors that produce strain and disruption in stable family patterns: greater unemployment, poor health, isolation, low self-esteem, and preoccupation with individual problems at the expense of others. As is true with wife abuse, reported childhood abuse and neglect is more likely to occur in families of lower socioeconomic status and families with increased stress stemming from a variety of sources.

Unemployment is another condition associated with physical harm to children. It may lead to poverty—the most grievous form of violence against children—and low self-esteem related to job loss, which is often seen as a symbol of failure in a "success-oriented" society. Concomitantly, depression or other psychiatric symptoms can occur secondary to loss of job and income. Unemployed persons are also homebound, increasing their time spent with children.

Race also is found to be a significant variable related to child abuse. Nonwhite ethnic groups have been found to be disproportionately poor and unemployed, and are generally victims of ongoing discrimination. There are also cultural differences in parenting styles, particularly with reference to the disciplining of children. Some studies (Alvy, Harrison, Rosen, & Fuentes, 1982) have indicated that black parents use more authoritarian methods of child rearing, including the use of physical punishment such as spanking, possibly suggesting that black children have a greater chance of being victims of child abuse than other ethnic groups.

According to Breines and Gordon (1983), men are much more inclined than women to be the assailants in all forms of family violence except child abuse, where women are the perpetrators as frequently as men. Women are almost always the parent interacting most often with children and are more likely than men to be in stressful economic circumstances. If the mother is the single parent, she feels more responsibility and guilt than the father for the failures of her offspring. Williams (1980) suggests that there is an increased rate of child abuse among women because they are placed in a role—that of mother—that can be uncomfortable or unnatural to all womenkind. For those women who do not find child care their most fulfilling or rewarding activity, or who are forced into the role of mother because of inadequate contraceptive methods, beliefs opposing abortion, or who are placed in marginal economic situations, child abuse and neglect exist at an alarmingly higher rate.

Incest is a special case of child abuse related to sexual behavior. In the 1950s, incidence rates estimated that approximately 1 in 16 girls were victims of sexual trauma in the home (Geiser, 1979). By the time a woman in the United States reached the age of 18, she had a 1 in 4 chance of being sexually abused; for males, the rate was found to be approximately 1 in 50. More recent studies (Courtois, 1988; Lew, 1990) have suggested higher rates for both males and females, particularly among mental health and prison populations.

All of these forms of familial violence dramatically affect the lives of children. The more conservative the governmental structure of society, the less likely the chance of developing strong economic and personal support systems for disadvantaged and high-risk families. Additionally, conservative trends in thinking frequently minimize the issues surrounding women's inequality, limit regard for women's work, and denegrate the importance of their role as primary caregivers to children.

Clinical Considerations in Dealing with Abused Children

Psychological outcomes of societal and familial violence have been discussed throughout this chapter. While the effects of particular forms of abuse vary in terms of degree and chronicity, it is clear that children are at grave peril within our modern culture. While every abused child cannot be lumped into a single clinical category, a general symptom picture has been discussed in the literature that relates to the long-term effects of living in a dysfunctional environment.

According to Herman (1992), chronic childhood abuse is most evident in the family environments of pervasive terror that have been described in this chapter. In family systems like these, ordinary caregiving relations have become profoundly distorted. Even though this nuclear unit is destructive to the adults in the family, children who live in this fearful climate of domination often are attracted and attached to those who most grievously abuse and neglect them.

In addition to living under constant threat to self or other beloved family members or pets, children in abusive households reported an overwhelming sense of helplessness and hopelessness. Parental power is often arbitrary and absolute. Survivors indicate that often the most frightening aspect of abuse is the unpredictable nature of the violence. Predictability of the abusing parents is generally slightly less stressful compared to the caregiver who provides inconsistent messages and/or abuse to the child.

The clinician must deal with any young person's response to the stress of childhood trauma on an individual basis; however, a symptom picture closely associated with the diagnosis of posttraumatic stress disorder most succinctly presents the key effects of living in a dysfunctional family environment. Children's early responses to psychic trauma generally involve negative effects on cognitive functioning (including memory, school performance, and learning), affect, relationships with others, vegetative function, level of aggressivity, acting-out potential, and formulation of later psychiatric syndromes. The child's developmental level at the time of the abuse is also significant and can shape the youngster's subsequent reactions for the rest of his or her life.

Intervening in the lives of children whose families may experience serious dysfunction is much more difficult because the young person most often must remain in the symptom-producing home, continually reexperiencing the helplessness and agony of being raised by incapable people. Some kind of association with the parents is generally useful in helping to ease the child's burden; education in appropriate child care strategies can assist parents if they are motivated to alter abusive patterns. Treatment of adults as well as children in these kinds of families is a desired goal that requires a long-term commitment to psychotherapy by all family members involved.

Chronic abuse causes serious psychological damage to people entrapped in an environment where they cannot escape. Even healthy individuals who are exposed to long-term abuse and neglect are no longer ordinary or healthy following their escape. Practitioners as well as the public at large tend to blame the victims of abuse for their victimization. However, the search for characteristics of the victim that contributed to his or her own abuse is futile and interferes with the psychological understanding and diagnosis of the patient who comes for treatment.

Conclusion

In tying together the concepts that are the focus of this chapter, it appears as if the feminist movement has not addressed directly the way in which women feel about their role as parent and nurturer to children. In theory, feminism espouses equality, pride, and independence for women from a time-honored history of male domination. Even if these values could be applied, they are not correlated to the disintegration of the family system or the decline in emotional well-being of children, as many conservative thinkers would have us believe. How the individual woman who holds either a traditional or feminist ideology applies her belief system to actual day-to-day living remains unclear. Most women today cannot "do it all." Weary of multiple roles and battles for equity in the marriage and workplace gives cause to wonder how much energy is left for mothering, personal growth, maintenance of primary relationships, and issues of job and life satisfaction.

A covert trend might also be undermining familial happiness. A startling study of corporate women (Hochschild, 1997) described one company who developed a management orientation which promoted family friendly strategies to entice career women to work there. The research findings suggested that extended benefits such as on-site day care services, and family leave, were utilized by only 5% of the female executives. Additionally, the management paradigm attempted also to replicate a working environment which mimicked the behavior of women's personal relationships—informality, positive reinforcement, and a consistent reward system—which ultimately served to make the workplace more compelling than their home lives in terms of familiarity, respect, and lack of significant day-to-day conflict. A frightening generalization might be gleaned from this outcome. When women find more personal rewards and satisfaction from the workplace than they do from their home lives, children suffer.

What does appear to correlate better with "good-enough" parenting ability and maternal satisfaction is a woman's happiness and contentment with her lot in life. If a woman remains in a traditional role, does this provide her with enough meaning and achievement so that she considers her life to be successful? If she is a professional or employed woman, is she able to juggle a variety of roles, maintain her dignity in all areas of her life, and still establish a priority for her offspring? No research supports the notion that if a woman theoretically supports and applies a feminist ideology to her life, she will be a better mother. There is some mounting evidence for the notion that the level of a woman's emotional and spiritual contentment is directly correlated to all aspects of her life, particularly in the handling of relationships with cherished loved ones.

REFERENCES

Adams, P., Milner, J., & Schrepf, N. (1984). *Fatherless children.* New York: John Wiley & Sons.

Alvy, K., Harrison, D., Rosen, L., & Fuentes, E. (1982). *Black parenting: An empirical study with implications for parent trainers and therapists.* Studio City, CA: Center for Improvement of Child Caring.

Andre, R. (1981). *Homemakers: The forgotten workers.* Chicago: The University of Chicago Press.

Arber, S., Gilbert, G. N., & Dale, A. (1985). Paid employment and women's health: A benefit or a source of role strain? *Sociology of Health and Illness, 7* (3).

Barnett, R., Biener, L., & Baruch, G. (1987). *Gender and stress.* New York: Free Press.

Baruch, G., Barnett, R., & Rivers, C. (1983). *Lifeprints: New patterns of love and work for today's women.* New York: New American Library.

Blau, P., & Ferber, M. (1986). *The economics of women, men, and work.* Englewood Cliffs, NJ: Prentice-Hall.

Blumstein, P., & Schwartz, P. (1983). *American couples: Money, work, sex.* New York: William Morrow.

Bohannan, P. (1985). *All the happy families: Exploring the varieties of family life.* New York: McGraw-Hill.

Braverman, L. (1989). Beyond the myth of motherhood. In M. McGoldrick, C. Anderson, & F. Walsh, (Eds.), *Women in families: A framework for family therapy.* New York: W. W. Norton.

Breines, W., & Gordon, L. (1983, Spring). The new scholarship on family violence. *Signs, 8,* 490–531.

Bronfenbrunner, U., & Crouter, A. (1982). Work and family through time and space. In S. Kamerman & C. Hayes (Eds.), *Families that work: Children in a changing world.* Washington, DC: National Academy Press.

Burke, R., & Weir, J. (1976). Relationship of wives' employment status to husband, wife and pair satisfaction. *Journal of Marriage and the Family, 38,* 279–287.

Carroll, P. (1990). *Keeping time: Memory, nostalgia, and the art of history.* Athens: University of Georgia Press.

Cherlin, A. (1981). *Marriage, divorce, remarriage.* Cambridge University Press.

Cleary, P., & Mechanic, D. (1983, June). Sex differences in psychological distress among married people. *Journal of Health and Social Behavior, 24,* 111–121.

Courtois, C. (1988). *Healing the incest wound: Adult Survivors in Therapy.* New York: W. W. Norton.

Edelson, J., Eiskovits, Z., & Guttman, E. (1983, June). Men who batter women. *Journal of Family Issues, 6,* 229–247.

Elias, M. (1983, June 15). Tots take the worst blows in divorce. *USA Today,* p. 3D.

Eth, S., & Pynoos, R. (1985). Developmental perspective on psychic trauma in childhood. In C. Figley (Ed.), *Trauma and its wake* (Vol. 1). New York: Brunner/Mazel.

Faludi, S. (1991). *Backlash: The undeclared war against American women.* New York: Crown Publishers.

Francke, L. (1983, July 3). The sons of divorce. *Denver Post Contemporary,* pp. 30–31.

Friedan, B. (1963). *The feminine mystique.* New York: Dell Books.

Friedan, B. (1981). *The second stage.* New York: Dell Books.

Fuchs, V. (1988). *How we live: An economic perspective on American's from birth to death.* Cambridge, MA: Harvard University Press.

Furstenberg, F., & Cherlin, A. (1991). *Divided families: What happens to children when parents part.* Cambridge, MA: Harvard University Press.

Geiser, R. (1979). *Hidden victims: The sexual abuse of children.* Boston: Beacon Press.

Gelles, R. (1977). No place to go: The social dynamics of marital violence. In M. Roy (Ed.), *Battered women.* New York: Van Nostrand.

Gelles, R., & Straus, M. (1979). Determinants of violence in the family. In W. Burr et al. (Eds.), *Contemporary values about the family* (Vol. 1). New York: Free Press.

Gelles, R., & Straus, M. (1988). *Intimate violence.* New York: Simon & Schuster.

Hareven, T. (1987). Historical analysis of the family. In M. Sussman & G. Steinmetz (Eds.), *Handbook of marriage and the family.* New York: Plenum Press

Herman, J. (1992). *Trauma and recovery*. New York: Basic Books.

Hershey, L., & Werner, E. (1975). Dominance in marital decision-making in women's liberation and women's non-liberation families. *Family Process, 14*, 223–232.

Hewlett, S. (1986). *A lesser life: The myth of women's liberation in America*. New York: Warner Books.

Hewlett, S. (1991). *When the bough breaks: The cost of neglecting our children*. New York: Basic Books.

Hochschild, A. (1997). *Timebind: When work becomes home and home becomes work*. New York: Henry Holt & Co.

Hoffman, L. (1979). Maternal employment: 1979. *American Psychologist, 34*, 859–865.

Hoffman, L. (1989). Effects of maternal employment in the two-parent family. *American Psychologist, 44* (22).

Holder, D., & Anderson, C. (1989). Women, work, and the family. In M. McGoldrick, C. Anderson, & F. Walsh (Eds.), *Women in families: A framework for family therapy*. New York: W. W. Norton.

Hole, J., & Levine, E. (1971). *Rebirth of feminism*. New York: Quadrangle Books.

Houseknecht, S., Vaughn, S., & Macke, A. (1984, February). Marital disruption among professional women: The timing of career and family events. *Social Problems, 31*, 273–284.

Jones, C., Tepperman, L., & Wilson, S. (1995). *The futures of the family*. Englewood Cliffs, N.J.: Prentice-Hall, Inc.

Keenman, M. (May 9, 1997). *The Detroit News*, p. 2.

Keith, P., & Schaffer, R. (1983). Role strain and depression in two-job families. *Family Relations, 29*, 483–494.

Klein, E. (1996). *Feminism under fire*. Amherst, NY: Prometheus Books.

Lamb, R. (1984). Fathers, mothers and children in the 1980s: Family influences on child development. In K. Borman et al. (Eds.), *Women in the workplace: Effects on families*. Ablex Publications.

Landry, B., & Jendrick, N. (1978). The employment of wives in middle class Black families. *Journal of Marriage and the Family, 40*, 787–797.

Lasch, C. (1976, September 30). The narcissist society. *New York Review of Books*, 5–8, 10–13.

Lasch, C. (1979). *The culture of narcissism*. New York: Norton.

Levinson, D. (1997). *The seasons of a woman's life*. New York: Ballantine Books.

Lew, M. (1990). *Victims no longer*. New York: Harper & Row.

Lipset, S. (1982). Failures of extremism. *Transactional Society, 20* (1), 48–58.

McLaughlin, S., Melber, B., Billy, J., Zimmerle, D., Winges, L., & Johnson, T. (1988). *The changing lives of American women*. Chapel Hill: University of North Carolina Press.

Mellman, M., Lazarus, E., & Rivlin, A. (1990). Family time, family values. In D. Blackenhorn, S. Bayme, & J. B. Elhstain (Eds.), *Rebuilding the nest: A new commitment to the American family*. Milwaukee, WI: Family Service America.

Merikangas, K., Prusoff, B., Kupfer, D., & Frank, E.

(1985). Marital adjustment in major depression. *Journal of Affective Disorders, 9*, 5–11.

Okin, Susan. (1997). Families and Feminist Theory: Reevaluating an overemphasis on differences. *APA Newsletters* Vol. 96 (1), pp. 1–5.

Parsons, T., & Bales, R. (1955). *Family socialization and interaction process*. New York: Free Press.

Piotrkowski, C., & Christoph, P. (1981). Women's jobs and family adjustment. *Journal of Family Issues, 2*, 126–147.

Pleck, J. (1977, April). The work-family role. *Social Problems, 24*, 417–427.

Russo, N. (1979). Overview: Sex roles, fertility, and the motherhood mandate. *Psychology of Women Quarterly, 4*, 7–15.

Ryan, M. (1981). *Cradle of the middle class: The family in Oneida County, New York, 1790–1865*. New York: Cambridge University Press.

Sekaran, U. (1986). *Dual-career families: Contemporary organizational and counseling issues*. San Francisco: Jossey-Bass.

Skolnick, A. (1991). *Embattled paradise: The American family in an age of uncertainty*. New York: Basic Books.

Smelser, N., & Halpern, S. (1978). The historical triangulation of family, economy, and education. *American Journal of Sociology, 84*.

Stains, G., & Pleck, J. (1983). *The impact of work schedule in family life*. Ann Arbor: University of Michigan.

Steil, J. (1984). Marital relationships and mental health: The psychic costs of inequality. In J. Freeman (Ed.), *Women: A feminist perspective*. Palo Alto, CA: Mayfield.

Straus, M., & Gelles, R. (1985, November). *Societal change and change in family violence from 1975 to 1985 as revealed by two national surveys*. Paper presented at the meeting of the American Society of Criminology.

Uhlenberg, P., & Eggebeen, D. (1986). The declining well-being of American adolescents. *The Public Interest, 82*, 25–38.

Ulbrich, P., & Huber, J. (1981, August). Observing parental violence: Distribution and effects. *Journal of Marriage and the Family, 43*, 623–631.

Wallerstein, J., & Blakesless, S. (1989). *Second chances: Men, women and children a decade after divorce*. New York: Ticknor & Fields.

West, R. (1913). The clarion. In C. Kramarae & P. Treichler (Eds.), *A feminist dictionary*. London: Pandora Press.

Williams, G. (1980). Toward the eradication of child abuse and neglect at home. In G. Williams & J. Money (Eds.), *Traumatic abuse and the neglect of children at home*. Baltimore: Johns Hopkins University Press.

Willis, E. (1981). *Beginning to see the light*. New York: Knopf.

Wolfe, T. (1982). The me decade and the third great awakening. In *Tom Wolfe: The purple decades* (pp. 265–293). New York: Berkeley Books. (Originally published 1976.)

Zinn, M., & Eitzen, D. (1990). *Diversity in families*, 2nd ed. New York: Harper & Row.

PART III

Out-of-Home Child Care and Child and Adolescent Development

4 / Foster Care

Alvin Rosenfeld and Daniel Pilowsky

Although child and adolescent psychiatrists have a deep, abiding interest in children's well-being, foster care has been primarily the domain of social workers and social welfare agencies. When disturbed children or adolescents are discussed at psychiatric conferences, the fact that they are in foster care may be mentioned as part of their life experience, but it usually is spoken of as incidental. However, we think that in the lives of foster children and their families, being in care is a central, shaping experience.

Foster care can be very helpful, even though it subjects children to considerable emotional distress, including a painful separation from their families. Despite the profound psychological impact out-of-home care has on children, only a small percentage of child psychiatrists work as part of multidisciplinary teams that help foster children. In part that may be because the child psychiatrist who chooses this work will be immersed in collaborative, often difficult, poorly remunerated work that usually is under a social worker's administrative leadership and is not part of the medical or mental health systems.

"Foster care" is both a generic and a specific term. Used generically, it refers to children living in several different types of out-of-home placement, such as foster boarding homes, group homes, residential treatment centers, and the like. Used specifically, "foster care" refers to children living with families headed by adults who are not their parents but who receive public and/or phil-

The authors would like to thank José Alfaro of the New York Children's Aid Society for his constructive criticisms and suggestions.

anthropic support to care for them. This chapter discusses family foster care only, whether the parents are unrelated or members of the child's extended family (kinship foster care).

By the end of 1992, approximately 442,000 American children were in out-of-home placement, a population 60% larger than the 276,000 children in care in 1985 (American Public Welfare Association, 1993a, b). Children in foster homes usually come from seriously troubled families, many of which have had difficulty giving the minimal food, shelter, and sustenance that a child needs to grow physically and emotionally (Rosenfeld, Pilowsky, et al., 1997). Most of these children have been abused, neglected, or have suffered severe emotional deprivations (Rosenfeld, Altman, Alfaro, & Pilowsky, 1994). Foster children often were born with biological difficulties, such as the fetal alcohol syndrome or intrauterine exposure to cocaine or heroin. Many have pediatric and dental problems. A disproportionate number suffer from developmental disabilities.

Foster children often have biological parents who are troubled. Some suffer from mental illness or have been incarcerated; many are serious abusers of alcohol or drugs; some are homeless. Recently, a growing number suffer from AIDS. "Child welfare can play an ameliorative role [in these situations], but it cannot solve basic problems such as drug addiction, housing shortages, and unemployment" (Alfaro et al., 1987). Children enter foster care with scars from having lived through highly traumatic experiences. They become part of foster families that are expected to live with them relatively comfortably. Given these children's past experiences and disturbing behavior, that can be quite a challenge.

Although foster care tries to help, it causes children unavoidable pain by making them endure separation from their biological parents. Even a culturally and racially sensitive agency can not always find foster homes in the child's neighborhood. So some children may be placed far from their extended families and communities. Selective factors determine which children are removed. A national study (Lindsey, 1991) found that parents' inadequate income, not how severely the child had been abused, best predicted whether a child is placed in foster care rather than supportive services being provided to the biological family.

History

EARLY HISTORY

The origins of foster care reach back to the first human beings who had to decide what to do with orphans or with children whose parents were unable or unwilling to care for them. In some cultures, orphaned children were adopted; in others, unwanted children were sold into slavery or killed through drowning or exposure. In fact, some interpret the biblical story of Abraham's trip to sacrifice his beloved Isaac, and the Lord's staying his hand and accepting a scapegoat in the child's place, as being the first injunction against the then prevalent practices of killing or sacrificing children.

As Boswell (1988) pointed out, the word "foster" comes from a Norse root that means "food" and "support." It refers to a form of support that allowed a family to care for a child who had no legal standing with that family as heir or slave. Even in antiquity, "foster care was probably practiced on a limited basis . . . 'Under ancient Jewish laws and customs, children lacking parental care became members of the household of other relatives, if such there were, who reared them for adult life.' The early church boarded destitute children with 'worthy widows'" (Kadushin, 1974).

In the early Middle Ages, Visigoth law made provisions for parents to entrust their child's rearing to someone else for a modest fee. By the time the child was 10, he or she was expected to repay his or her upkeep. Usually a couple fostered out only some of its offspring. In a situation reminis-

cent of today, some biological parents in Visigoth communities visited the children they had fostered out; others never saw them again. But in contrast to abandoned children, the foster child's legal relationship to the biological parents was retained so the child could not be sold into slavery and ultimately shared in the parents' estate.

THE AMERICAN EXPERIENCE

The Visigoth type of fostering-out was not a system for the poor. In contrast, the American foster care system grew out of the English practice of indenture and developed for children who were orphaned, destitute, or abandoned (Kadushin, 1973). In an era when the family farm, flock, or business was partially powered by children's work, indentured children contributed needed labor in exchange for food, shelter, and training for an adult occupation. In an age of subsistence agriculture, this could equal the difference between life and death. But indenture was often cruel to the child and, in some ways, resembled slavery. After slavery was abolished, the practices of indenture and of returning indentured runaways became particularly hard to justify.

A new method was pioneered in the mid-1850s. Charles L. Brace, a young Protestant minister affiliated with New York City's Children's Aid Society, advocated "free foster homes." He wanted to get children out of almshouses and orphanages, and to give them a chance to become productive citizens. Believing that there were many empty places at the table in mid-Western farm families, he organized trainloads of children and sent them West, where farm families, short of labor, took them in. It was hoped that this new start would ultimately help them develop into independent, free adults. These children were far from their biological families and from what Brace believed was the evil effect of cities.

This approach was later called "exclusive," because it excluded the biological parents. It raised objections from both parents who were separated from their children and from religious groups that felt that their denomination's children were being stolen and reared in another faith. In addition, the Children's Aid Society had little supervisory control over children placed 1,000 or more miles away from New York City. Reports began to filter back East that families who took in these foster children sometimes severely maltreated them. Although Brace disputed allegations, his purported research was severely flawed (Kadushin, 1974).

The 1909 White House Conference on Care of Dependent children advocated *local* foster homes and was the model for more recent forms of fostering, which have been termed "inclusive" because the child is placed close to the biological family and is expected to stay involved with family members; the biological parents' rights as well as the rights and obligations of the foster parents have been more clearly defined (Stein, 1987).

During the upheavals of World War II, Anna Freud, Cyril Burt, and others observed that children taken from their parents' London homes and placed in homes in the countryside during the air battle over England fared worse and had more psychiatric symptoms than children left with their parents despite bombings and dangers. Around the same time, Spitz described the terrible ravages of "hospitalism"; Bowlby reported that many children who later became delinquent had suffered a separation from their primary parent very early in their lives. Years later, Bronfenbrenner and others asserted that every child's most fundamental need was a dedicated, constant parent who was passionately committed to him or her.

In the 1970s, Goldstein and his colleagues Anna Freud and Solnit (1973, 1979) published two highly influential books that asserted forcefully that a child's relationship to the *psychological* parent is more important than blood ties. Furthermore, they felt that the parent-child relationship had to be permanent and exclusive to count as psychological parenting. Data showed that contrary to Goldstein et al.'s permanency principle, for many children, foster care was not a short-term solution to a parent's temporary incapacity: A significant percentage of children were in foster care for over 2 years; many had multiple placements. Goldstein et al. maintained that multiple placements and foster homes that lasted for years without a firm commitment to continuity deprived children of their fundamental need for emotional constancy.

In the 1960s, some experts felt that because some states were heavily dependent on Aid for Families with Dependent Children and/or Foster Care monies after 1961 or 1962, they had no real incentive to move children out of foster care (Stein, 1987). A number of studies in the 1970s, which collectively came to be known as "permanency-planning projects," showed that goal-oriented written case plans and assertive case work, combined with intensive services to a child's birth parents could facilitate family reunification and permanent planning for children (Stein, 1987).

While experts disagree over whether or not permanency planning advocates overstated their claims, the contention that good practice could dramatically reduce the foster care population influence child welfare practice. Foster care began to be portrayed "as something that had to be 'prevented' at all costs like a disease or a social problem" (Alfaro, personal communication). In 1980 the federal government passed Public Law 96–272, the Adoption Assistance and Child Welfare Act, which

was designed to end the drift of children in foster care; encourage planning for permanency for each child within a hierarchy of desirable options, ranging from returning the child to his or her biological parents, through adoption, to long-term foster care; provide for oversight to move cases through the child welfare system; and develop preventative services to avert the family breakdown that removal of children from the home entails. (Fein, 1991)

Child welfare agencies were pressured to decide, often within 18 to 24 months, whether the child could be returned to his or her parents or be freed for adoption.

Legislators hoped that fewer children would enter, and remain in, care; government policy encouraged localities to get children out of the system and to keep them out. Fiscal concerns pushed in the same direction. By 1984 permanency planning seemed to have delivered on its promise; the foster care population had declined dramatically. Major child welfare agencies were anticipating that soon they would be closing their foster care departments. But after 1985, with little warning, the number of children in care grew dramatically. No doubt, the appearance of crack cocaine as a street drug accounted for a good part of the increase. But the dramatic increase in the number of child abuse and neglect cases also was involved, as was the increasing number of single-parent families, often headed by teenagers. Some groups, such as the New York City Mayor's Task Force on Child Abuse and Neglect, presented data that showed that permanency planning and preventive service advocates had oversold what they could do. But whatever the cause, the numbers were striking. In New York City, while only 16,787 children were in care at the end of fiscal year 1985, in June 1991, 49,814 children were in placement.

That left the system with great problems. The policy change that PL 96–272 brought about had disassembled an existing system; many foster homes had closed. Women who had been foster parents found gainful employment in the general workforce. When the demand for foster homes increased suddenly and dramatically, most states and cities could not find them easily. According to anecdotal reports, the quality of new homes they did find did not compare favorably with what had been before. And more were needed. When the courts ruled in the New York "Eugene F." class action suit that if a child's relatives fostered the child they were to receive the same financial benefits as unrelated families, many children were placed in kinship homes. By 1991, over 40% of foster homes in New York City were kinship foster homes (Child Welfare League of America [hereafter CWLA], 1994).

Working in Foster Care

A child and adolescent psychiatrist working with foster families and a foster care agency will get involved with a complex system that has many components. Frequently the law and courts are involved. Ultimately any clinical assessment of a foster child will require that the psychiatrist understand the child, the foster parents, the natural parents, and the context of the agency.

LEGAL FRAMEWORK

The legal framework that governs child welfare policy at the federal level consists principally of two titles of the Social Security Act (PL 96–272), Title IV-B and Title IV-E. Amended in 1993 (Omnibus Budget Reconciliation Act [OBRA] of 1993), this law is also known as PL 103–66.

Title IV-B provides federal funding to states for child welfare services and requires that children in out-of-home care receive some minimal protective measures. It gives states significant flexibility to develop services and programs as they see fit. OBRA 1993 added funding for family preservation and support services.

Title IV-E provides federal funding to states for taking care of foster children and for other related costs such as administration, training, and services for children in state care. Title IV-E funding is an open-ended entitlement. It pays states for each child placed away from home as long as certain conditions are met and the child's birth family is eligible for Aid to Families with Dependent Children. (For details, see CWLA, 1994, pp. 25–27.)

Approximately 47% of children in out-of-home care were eligible for Title IV-E funding in 1991 (CWLA, 1994). Children placed in kinship care may be eligible for Title IV-E funding (CWLA, 1994).

Title IV-E expects states to make "reasonable efforts" to keep families together and mandates that children who have to be removed be placed in the "least restrictive" setting available. What efforts are "reasonable" and what needs to be done to guarantee family preservation while at the same time protecting a child from abuse remains an ongoing debate. Some argue that more needs to be done to "empower" biological families; others argue that "reasonable efforts have become extraordinary efforts to keep families together at all costs" (*Washington Social Legislation Bulletin*, 1996).

THE FOSTER CARE CHILD

What is it like to become a foster child? Today most children in foster care, other than newborns, have been placed suddenly, for their protection, after their parents have been reported for severely abusing or neglecting them (Rosenfeld et al., 1994). Frequently the children cannot be prepared in advance and are confused and traumatized in the earliest hours of separation (Folman, 1996, personal communication). The child placed in a nonkinship foster home suddenly is living with strangers, a new family he or she is supposed to accept comfortably. Since foster homes in the child's neighborhood may not have openings, the child may also find himself or herself in a new neighborhood and school, away from friends and a familiar environment.

This would stress any child. But many children who enter foster care have been deprived and abused before they were placed, which makes tolerating such extreme stress even harder for them. So when children first are placed, many become anxious, frightened, and confused. Some regress, usually only temporarily, for instance becoming enuretic. Others, often those with preexisting psychiatric and emotional problems, cannot adjust and may need to be moved to another placement.

Children placed in foster homes often miss their parent or parents, even those who have abused and neglected them. The children worry that they will not see their biological parents or return to them. "Parentified" children who have helped care for their parents and siblings may become very upset because placement interferes with their doing the job they have devoted themselves to; they may feel that in adjusting to a foster home they are abrogating their responsibilities to parents and siblings. The following clinical vignette illustrates such a situation.

Case Example: A 15-year-old boy was placed in a kinship foster home with an adult sister and her husband. On several occasions the boy ran away from the kinship foster home overnight to join his mother, an alcoholic who was living in a dilapidated building and drinking heavily. When the child was told that running away jeopardized his placement, he replied, "I go over to visit my mother because I want to convince her to go to an [alcohol rehabilitation] program, but she doesn't listen." To this boy, his responsibility to parent his own mother outweighed any obligation he had to his personal future.

Other than newborns in foster care, whose emotional situation resembles that of adopted newborns, foster children often are despondent and suffer from low self-esteem. Many consider themselves "throwaway" or "bad" kids who have no value to anyone. This self-image is intensified if they have been placed with a foster family while one or more of their siblings remain with the biological parents. Some see themselves as bad because their parents have told them repeatedly that they are no good or have caused all the family's problems. To explain to themselves why they have been derogated, maltreated, and/or abandoned, many foster children idealize their abusive parents and argue that they themselves were not worthy of their good parents' love. While this psychological mechanism seems twisted on the surface, it defends the children psychologically against total despair. The ones who use this defensive maneuver feel more in control of their situation and retain the hope that if they only try harder to be "good," their parents will love them. If they concluded that their parents were "bad," their situation would be hopeless (Rosenfeld & Wasserman, 1990). To paraphrase Winnicott, better a sinner in a house ruled by the Lord than a saint in a house ruled by Satan.

No matter what children's specific experiences have been, relationships to the parents are central to their identity and emotional well-being; disturbing these relationships can be excruciating (Bowlby, 1958). Because foster children are separated from their biological parents, often against their will, many times they feel angry, deprived, and long to be reunited with their parents. Therefore, addressing the vicissitudes of attachment

and separation is crucial if a placement is to succeed. Many localities have respected this need by trying to keep sibling groups together and advocating for kinship foster care as the preferable option. Whether these approaches help children do better in the long run remains unproven and even questionable.

In our clinical experience, the intense initial discomfort many children feel when they first enter foster care diminishes after a few weeks. Yet some experience an intense loyalty conflict; if they like the foster parents, they feel they are betraying their natural parents. Natural parents who disparage the foster parents intensify a child's conflict. Clinical experience suggests that the more severely the child had been deprived while in the biological parents' care and the more intense the denied anger is, the more rigidly the child idealizes the natural parents. The child may feel that compared to these truly caring biological parents created out of wishful thinking, distortion, and deep need, the foster parents are insensitive and deficient. To keep loyalty to the natural parents intact, the child may need to keep distant from, or be oppositional toward, the foster parents. This can make them less than endearing. The less nurturance the child has received, the more frantically he or she may push to reunite with the biological family. If adoption is planned and imminent but the child has not agreed emotionally, he or she may act out to disrupt the plan.

THE FOSTER PARENTS

Every foster family has its own reasons for fostering children. Some parents are altruistic and want to help needy children. Some need financial compensation. Others see fostering as a solution to the "empty-nest syndrome," or wish to rescue children from "bad parents," or want to adopt a child. This last reason often motivates people who want to foster newborns. After all, many foster children eventually are freed for adoption, and most are adopted by their foster parents.

As Fein (1991) pointed out, fostering has survived because low-paid women's labor has been plentiful. As more women enter the work force full time, fewer will become foster parents. One study found that in 1991, the number of qualified foster parents available nationally was 30% lower than it had been in 1984. At a time when fewer foster families are available and many more are needed, careful screening is important so that as many people as possible who are suitable, or who have constructive motivations for becoming foster parents, are given that opportunity. Foster families can be very sensitive to and supportive of children's needs, indifferent to children, or, unfortunately, abusive. While a foster home that provides a caring environment may help children heal the scars of abuse, a neglectful or abusive one can only deepen the despair and hopelessness that the children experienced prior to placement, because it confirms to the children that their situation is hopeless. Psychiatrists may play a significant role in improving the screening and assessment of foster parent applicants so these unfortunate children are not retraumatized. But the United States desperately needs to raise the quality of our foster homes, a problem this country has not yet addressed.

While we hope changes come to pass, many homes that now take in foster children may not optimize a child's potential for growth. It would be nice if our national priorities valued and rewarded foster parenthood so that more children could be in foster homes that are closer to optimal.

Foster parenthood has within it several contradictions:

First, most foster parents are told that they are temporary caregivers who need to be sensitive to the child's background and to work to maintain the child's relationship with the biological parents. Yet in caring for a foster child, people who are deeply nurturing, the ones who can be truly emotionally helpful, become attached to the child. That attachment can make it emotionally difficult for foster parents to cooperate with the plan to return the child to the natural parent, particularly one who has been abusive. Some foster parents will try to undermine the child's relationship with the biological parent and hope the placement will become long term.

Since social workers do most of the clinical work with foster parents, they need to form a therapeutic alliance with them. If clear plans have been drawn up for the child, the foster parents need to be told exactly what they are. The foster parents' feelings need to be explored. A psychiatrist consulting about a child needs to ask the social worker about the foster parents' attitude toward the particular child and his or her placement.

Second, foster parents live with ambiguous roles. They are referred to as "parents" but cannot make decisions that parents routinely make, such as those regarding the foster child's education, religion, and medical care. This becomes even more complicated in kinship homes where the foster child and foster parent are blood relatives yet have to work with an agency that carries considerable legal responsibility.

Third, the severe maltreatment many older foster children have suffered has disturbed them deeply; others are psychiatrically ill. State agencies often want to make believe that all foster children need is a good home. Almost everyone in the field agrees that this assumption is erroneous. In fact, foster children in California constitute 4% of the Medicaid population but use 40–50% of the mental health dollars for children (Halfon, Berkowitz, Klee, 1992). Many foster parents are insufficiently trained to deal with unsettling emotional difficulties that foster children bring to their homes—for instance, a sexually abused child who is behaving provocatively or the highly disturbing feelings that ensued in foster parents when their foster son finally trusted them enough to confide that his biological mother had slammed his penis with a 2-by-4. Some foster homes are expected to be therapeutic institutions; yet foster parents often are unable or cannot fairly be expected to fulfill such a role. The cynical feel that foster care is society's attempt to deal with deeply disturbed children as inexpensively as possible; some municipal officials argue that calling many foster children emotionally disturbed is insulting and untrue. But we believe that the evidence that these children have major mental health needs is irrefutable (Rosenfeld, et al, 1997). Therapeutic or specialized foster homes, which have 1 or 2 children and a more highly skilled foster family, often are considered a solution to this dilemma (Reddy and Pfeiffer, 1997; Rosenfeld, Altman, & Kaufman, 1997).

THE NATURAL PARENTS

Many parents whose children enter foster care are addicted to substances, come from chaotic circumstances, and live disordered lives. Some may be incarcerated or hospitalized. Some biological parents are relieved to be freed of a burden in their already overburdened lives. Many others feel ashamed of their failure; some of them project their disappointment and consider themselves innocent victims. They are enraged at the agency that they feel has victimized them, angry that a social worker has treated them as "bad" and taken their child away. Some may make serious physical threats against these workers.

The foster care agency tries to arrange visitation shortly after the child is placed. Some parents visit regularly, if they are able to. From the moment the child enters care; they call lawyers and other agencies to press for their child's immediate return. Others completely abandon the child. The majority are inconsistent and erratic. Some parents promise that they will visit and then do not show up. The child is crestfallen. In many agency settings, parents are expected to visit their child twice a month, initially supervised by an agency worker at the agency's office. Later visits may be unsupervised. When things go well and a return to the biological parents' care is considered likely, parents can take the child out for a day or for a weekend visit as the time for return draws nearer.

Consistent visitation is the single most powerful predictor that the child ultimately will return to the biological parents' care (Lawder, Poulin, & Andrew, 1986). Therefore, when parents visit their children inconsistently, the agency worker needs to explore why this is happening. Failure to visit may relate to a parents' ambivalence toward the child, to practical difficulties such as transportation and getting someone to care for other children, or to addiction or mental illness.

Foster care agencies are obligated to arrange a program to rehabilitate the natural parents. The child's return to their care is contingent upon the parents' compliance. Parents may be expected to attend a drug rehabilitation program, complete a parent education program, enter individual psychotherapy, join a program to treat sexual offenders, secure a clean and safe apartment, and the like. The unfortunate, empirical reality in many cases is that once the child is removed, the biological parents end up receiving fewer services than they had before, which makes it even harder for them to get the child back.

Often rehabilitative programs are discussed with the natural parents without addressing their feelings of profound shame, anger, and despair. Some parents deny that the abuse or neglect was severe or even that it occurred. Others readily admit to it and may feel deeply ashamed of what they had done. Almost all feel humiliated. Others, usually antisocial parents, comply superficially with the rehabilitation program. Rather than changing their ways, they try to ingratiate themselves with the agency. Many abusive parents use projection and projective identification extensively in relating to their child. This is usually a poor prognostic sign.

THE SOCIAL SERVICE AGENCY

The various aspects of foster care usually are managed through a local, public service or not-for-profit child welfare agency. It finds, trains, and pays the foster parents, monitors the care the child receives, and arranges social services for both the child and the natural parents. Under twin pressures of expanded need and restricted funding, agencies are currently being "deprofessionalized": Fewer master's degree–level social workers are doing child welfare work.

Nationally, 46% of foster children are white, 37.1% are black, and 10.2% are Hispanic (American Public Welfare Association, 1991). However, in some localities, such as New York City, children in foster care are primarily African American and Hispanic. Because African American and Hispanic *children* are over-represented, members of those communities argue that "their" children would be better served by local, community-based agencies and a minority staff, which they maintain is intrinsically more sensitive to their unique cultures, needs, and the special strengths of the culturally divergent family. They argue that white workers all too often focus on the family's weakness and turmoil.

Representatives of the culturally divergent communities often feel that "Eurocentric" prejudice, not just countertransference feelings toward abusive parents, interferes with the agency's making serious efforts to engage the natural parents so that their child can be returned to their care. Others argue that idealism or "guilt" of white, middle-class workers often makes them more sympathetic and less punitive to chaotic, destructive parents. Saying that members of this or that group are superior seems prejudicial just in and of itself. But empirical data are not yet available that could help administrators select only *individuals* who can work most successfully with disadvantaged, nonmajority families.

Some children in foster homes see the agency as an evil force that separated them from their natural parents. They mingle a perception of the agency's enormous power over their future with their own fantasies and projections about "bogeymen" and "witches." Reality-based explanations sometimes help such children deal with such feelings but, given the power of these inner demons, they usually have minimal effect. The competing pressures on workers are so intense, and the problems of the poor can be so intransigent, that many workers burn out or simply leave the field.

Although optimally a child would have 1 social worker who knows him or her, the family, and the situation throughout the time the child is in care, worker turnover often is rapid. At times, annual turnover in N.Y.C. Child Protective Service was 80%. So children who have suffered a break in parental relationships often do not find object constancy in their worker either.

Every psychiatric consultant needs to know about child development and the emotional reactions that characterize ages and stages. But one working with foster care agencies also needs to understand the laws and regulations that govern foster care; these vary from locality to locality. For instance, every state has its own rules that govern the process of terminating parental rights. So a discussion of them is beyond the scope of this chapter. But when professionals ask the state to terminate parental rights, they cannot simply write that a natural child cannot return to her mother's care because the mother is mentally ill, for example. Since the agency is mandated to make diligent efforts to rehabilitate the natural parents, the family's official record including psychiatric reports must document in a legally appropriate fashion that the agency has made diligent efforts to engage and rehabilitate the parent. Furthermore, in the case of a psychiatrically impaired parent, the psychiatrist must specify how the mother's mental condition impairs her ability to care for her child, using examples of actual incidents as illustrations. Prognosis, so difficult in our field, is important. How long does the psychiatrist expect it will take the parent to rehabilitate himself or herself?

As mentioned, some parents may threaten, intimidate, and frighten the case workers. The agency needs to have security arrangements that allow workers to feel safe even when telling irate parents that they cannot have their child back, certainly not today. And workers often find it hard to clarify their obligation to the child. Many see their role as saving abused children. Others are more thorough in their efforts to engage biological parents, to be sensitive to their needs, and to work with their strengths. They are mindful of the interrelationships in families and may seek out people in the extended family—or even a minister the family trusts—who may be important family resources for the foster child. Others have unrealistic notions; they believe that every parent loves his or her child and that, with enough support, each biological parent will become a nurturing individual. Often the seasoned child and ado-

lescent psychiatrist or other senior mental health professional is the one who has to remind everyone of reality (Rosenfeld & Newberger, 1977). In the cases where a worker's hopes and rose-colored glasses overlook a parent's gross, and potentially violent, inadequacy, children may be severely reabused or even killed when they return home.

But even under more adequate circumstances, all workers, whatever their personality, need to face the reality that they will be returning children to homes they consider less than optimal for a child's physical and emotional growth. And despite their best efforts, no one knows how to rehabilitate some parents. That is reality, not professional incompetence. Yet even when it is crystal clear that a child and parent cannot be reunited, both need help to deal with their grief, profound disappointment and sense of inadequacy, and, in some cases, relief.

The foster care system is beset with contradictions and unhappiness. Who wants to tell a mother that she cannot have her child back or to tell a child who desperately wants to go back home that this will not happen? The system is underfunded, often overly bureaucratic, and consequently insensitive. With the obstacles facing foster care workers, child and adolescent psychiatrists working in this system, families, and children, what is remarkable is that sometimes the system works relatively well, although hardly ever optimally.

Treatment Issues

Children in foster care may present a wide variety of psychiatric disorders; only a few remarks about their treatment will be made here. Numerous articles provide far more detailed discussions (Fine, 1993; Fraiberg, 1962; Gallagher et al, 1995; Pilowsky, 1992; Pilowsky & Kates, 1996; Rosenfeld & Wasserman, 1990; Steinhauer, 1991).

Naturally the treatment issues will depend on the child's age, developmental stage, clinical condition, and life experiences. In assessing and treating foster children, the professional needs to consider the child, biological and foster parents, and the agency. The psychiatrist needs to be aware that foster children tend to regress during their first few weeks in placement. An increasing number of foster children are born addicted to cocaine or heroin, exposed to alcohol and drugs in utero, and/or are HIV positive; organic damage is always a possibility; this can make a careful pediatric, neurologic, and neuropsychological evaluation important. Infants who have serious medical illnesses or who may be HIV positive often need to be considered for special foster homes.

Children in foster care find the uncertainty of their situation painful. Often they benefit from an ongoing explanation of possible plans for their future, without giving them a false reassurance.

Follow-up Studies

We will mention only a few pertinent studies. In a prospective study, Fanshel and Shinn (1978) followed up 742 0- to 12-year-old New York City children placed in family foster care in 1966. Five years later, 36.4% were still in care, 56.1% were discharged, 4.6% were placed in mental institutions or special residential facilities, and 2.9% were placed in adoptive homes. As expected, 86% of the children whose parents visited consistently eventually were discharged from foster care.

But contrary to the widespread belief that foster care harms children, these researchers concluded that "continued tenure in foster care is not demonstrably deleterious with respect to IQ change, school performance, or the measures of emotional adjustment we employed" (Fanshel & Shinn, 1978, p. 491). Overall, regardless of whether children remained in foster care, 25 to 33% were considered emotionally impaired. The absence of a comparison group drawn from low-income children in the general population limits the generalizations one can make from these figures. However, the authors point out that investigations other researchers had done with children of similar background revealed a similar frequency of emotional disorders. Furthermore, compared to Fanshel's study population, children currently coming into care are far more likely to have been abused and neglected; in our experience, a higher percentage seem to be emotionally disturbed.

Although foster care often is accused of causing children's emotional difficulties, Fanshel is not alone in finding that children in foster care did better than children returned home. As Fein (1991) pointed out, "Many studies demonstrated equal or better developmental outcomes for children in foster care than for those who returned

home (Fanshel & Shinn, 1978; Wald, Carlsmith, & Leiderman, 1988). The measures included personal adjustment, self-esteem, physical care, school achievement, and IQ" (p. 579). Outcomes such as these have led critics of foster care, such as Wald, to soften their public stance. Widom (1991) found that for children placed outside the home because of early childhood abuse and neglect, placement alone did not appear to increase the risk of criminal behavior. Abuse and neglect were the relevant variables.

But foster children have reasons to be troubled. Many enter care with psychopathology. Ingalls, Hatch, and Merservey's (1984) study of New York State children in foster care reported that 40% were categorized as having symptoms such as thought disorder, paranoia, suicide attempts, eating disorders, self-abuse, and attention deficit disorder. We suspect that the percentage would be higher today. [Addendum B]

A major retrospective study (Festinger, 1983) surveyed young adults who were discharged from foster care (including family foster care and group care) on or after the age of maturity. The researchers studied their social, occupational, and emotional adjustment when they had become adults using a set of questions that other researchers surveying adults in the general American population had used previously. Surprisingly, they found only a few consistent differences between the former foster care children and adults from the general population: Those who had been in foster care were less likely to be married and were more likely to have lower educational achievement. Regarding educational achievement, socioeconomic status is a confounding variable. Contrary to predictions by clinicians, these researchers found no striking differences between the 2 groups in their assessment of former foster children's self-image and their sense of self worth. However, these conclusions may not hold for children coming into foster care today who, by all accounts, are far more disturbed and disturbing.

Family Preservation

The term "family preservation" refers to a variety of child welfare programs aimed at strengthening the family so that children of troubled families can remain at home, thus preventing out-of-home placement. These programs usually are targeted toward families where child abuse, neglect, and seriously disturbed relationships have been reported. Family preservation programs may provide a wide array of services, including housing assistance, securing the services of a homemaker, nursery care, and respite care as well as traditional social, psychological, and psychiatric services. The hope is that these programs will play a significant role in preventing out-of-home placement. It remains to be seen whether promising early reports weather the test of time.

However, even with the most skilled and sensitive interventions, not all families can be preserved; some researchers feel that proponents of these programs have overstated the success the programs can have. Whatever the facts turn out to be, chaotic, disorganized, abusive families likely will continue to live in our communities. Family foster care, other forms of out-of-home placement, and adoption will remain significant options, particularly for abused and neglected children who cannot safely return to their biological parents' homes. What family preservation programs may achieve (and this remains to be proven conclusively) is a decrease in the explosive growth of the foster care population. But ultimately, preventing the breakdown of so many poor families may require that a wide array of services, such as special services targeted to single, teenage mothers; health care for all children and their families; affordable or free day care for all children of working mothers; low income housing; and fewer drugs on the streets be universally available. Society at large will have to decide whether it will provide all of these services. Welfare reform in 1996 suggests that the federal government will likely provide fewer, not more, services to indigent welfare mothers and to children in need.

Recent Issues in Foster Care

In the past 2 decades, foster care has changed in some important ways. First, the number of children whose parents are addicted to drugs has increased dramatically. One or both of the child's parents and sometimes even the child are HIV positive.

Second, foster care policy now places children in kinship foster care whenever possible. Although responsible professionals have widely divergent views on whether this policy makes good sense (Rosenfeld et al, 1997), it has become official policy in many jurisdictions. The number of children in kinship care has increased dramatically. For example, in New York City it rose from 1,000 in 1986 to 24,000 in 1992 (CWLA, 1994). This increase has challenged traditional approaches to permanency planning. Kinship foster parents are often reluctant to adopt the children they care for. They do not wish to offend the children's biological parents, who usually are their sons and daughters, by terminating their parental rights and adopting their foster children, yet they want to continue to foster their kin (CWLA, 1994). A new legal status, "kinship guardianship," which is a permanent guardianship by relatives without formal adoption, has been proposed to deal with this dilemma. Whether such proposals will become practice is unclear.

Third, increasing numbers of teenagers have entered the foster care system. Many of them will not be adopted; nor will they return to the care of their biological parents. Planning for their future as adults who can take care of themselves ("independent living") is a challenge to the foster care system and, ultimately to society.

COMMUNITY-BASED FOSTER CARE

The new approach of community-based foster care currently is being piloted in Los Angeles, with other localities expected to adopt it soon. In this approach, children are placed, whenever possible, in the same neighborhood where they lived before entering care. Attempts to involve the biological parents are made as soon as possible. Foster care agencies are expected to have small, decentralized neighborhood units, not the single, citywide central offices that characterize many agencies in large cities. The newly created neighborhood units are expected to become intensely involved with the local schools, churches, and community organizations. Although this system theoretically is appealing, it is premature to judge whether it will have a positive impact on foster children's lives. It is another in a long chain of panaceas. To date, none has stood the test of time.

MANAGED CARE

Medicaid recipients, including foster children, are or soon will be enrolled in managed care organizations. While some propose that managed care provides new opportunities to provide cost-effective quality care, others predict that abused and neglected children simply will get fewer services (Flint, Yudkowsky, & Tang, 1995; Hughes, Newacheck, Stoddard, & Halfon, 1995). Managed care has advocated shorter psychiatric hospitalizations for children. Thus, prematurely discharged or barely stabilized foster children may be returned to a foster care system that is unprepared to meet their needs.

If managed care companies are to serve foster children well, they will need to provide high levels of pediatric neurological, psychiatric, and remedial services. These are expensive. In view of the extensive services these children need, managed care companies may simply conclude that they cannot serve this population profitably (Rosenfeld, 1995).

WELFARE REFORM

Welfare reform legislation approved in 1996 is expected to ultimately have a profound impact on foster care. As more families become economically unable to care for their children and use up their lifetime benefits, more children may enter the already overburdened foster care system. Poverty, which the 1909 White House Conference decided was not a reason for children to enter foster care, may again become one.

Title IV-E funds are available to states for each foster child whose birth family is eligible for Aid to Families with Dependent Children (AFDC). As welfare reform is implemented, many families automatically will become ineligible for AFDC benefits after 2 years. If their children are placed

in foster care after the family became AFDC ineligible, they may not be eligible for Title IV-E funding. Thus, foster care funding may be negatively impacted while the number of children entering care increases. This situation may represent the greatest challenge foster care has faced in recent years. Ultimately, the fate of foster children and their families will depend on society's willingness to pay for the numerous therapeutic and remedial services that these damaged children and their families require.

Conclusion

The foster care system was developed for predominantly healthy children whose parents were temporarily or permanently unable to rear them. Of late it has become home to an increasing number of psychiatrically ill and emotionally troubled youngsters. For some children, it has become a mental hospital without walls. Yet children in the system receive far too few mental health services, both because states makes too few funds available and because the foster care system has been unattractive for highly skilled individuals to work in. Yet these children represent a great reservoir of unmet needs (Rosenfeld, Pilowsky, et al., 1997). We hope that someday society realizes that if we do not heal these children's wounds when they are young and open to intervention, we will pay a far higher price when they get older and take their frustration out on society at large (Rosenfeld & Wasserman, 1990).

REFERENCES

Alfaro, J., et al. (1987, July). Confusion and contradiction in child welfare: The ignored impact of faulty policies. New York: Mayor's Task Force on Child Abuse and Neglect.

American Public Welfare Association. (1991). *Characteristics of children in substitute and adoptive care: A statistical analysis of the VCIS National Child Welfare Data*. Washington, DC: Author.

American Public Welfare Association. (1993a). *VCIS Research notes: U.S. child substitute care flow data for FY 92 and current trends in the state child substitute care populations*. Washington, DC: Author.

American Public Welfare Association. (1993b). *Voluntary Cooperative Information System: Characteristics of children in substitute and adoptive care, based*

on FY 82 through FY 89 data. Washington, DC: Author.

Boswell, J. (1988). *The kindness of strangers*. New York: Pantheon Books.

Bowlby, J. (1958). Psychoanalysis and child care. In J. D. Sutherland (Ed.), *Psychoanalysis and contemporary thought* (pp. 33–57). London: Hogarth Press.

Child Welfare League of America. (1994). *Kinship Care: A natural bridge*. Washington, DC: Author.

Fanshel, D., & Shinn, E. B. (1978). *Children in foster care*. New York: Columbia University Press.

Fein, E. (1991). Issues in foster family care: Where do we stand? *American Journal of Orthopsychiatry, 61*, 578–583.

Festinger, T. (1983). *No one ever asked us . . . A post-*

script to foster care. New York: Columbia University Press.

Fine, P. (1993). *A Developmental Network Approach to Therapeutic Foster Care.* Washington, DC: Child Welfare League of America.

Flint, S. S., Yudkowsky, B. K., & Tang, S. S. (1995). Children and Medicaid entitlement: What have we got to lose. *Pediatrics, 96,* 967.

Fraiberg, S. (1962). A therapeutic approach to reactive ego disturbances in children in placement. *American Journal of Orthopsychiatry, 32,* 18–32.

Gallagher, M. M., Leavitt, K. S., Kimmel, H. P. (1995). "Mental health treatment of cumulatively/repetitively traumatized children." *Smith College Studies in Social Work* 65: 205–237.

Goldstein, J., Freud, A., & Solnit, A. (1973). *Beyond the best interest of the child.* New York: Free Press.

Goldstein, J., Freud, A., & Solnit, A. (1979). *Before the best interest of the child.* New York: Free Press.

Halfon, N., Berkowitz, G., Klee, L. (1992). Mental health utilization by children in foster care in California, *Pediatrics* 89:1238–1244.

Hughes, D., Newacheck, P., Stoddard, J. J., & Halfon, N. (1995). Medicaid managed care: Can it work for children? *Pediatrics, 95,* 591–594.

Ingalls, R., Hatch, R., & Merservey, (1984). *Characteristics of children in out-of-home care.* Albany, NY: New York State Council on Children and Families.

Kadushin, A. (1974). *Child welfare services* (2nd ed.). New York: Macmillan.

Katz, P. (1968). Dynamics and treatment of foster children. *Canadian Psychiatric Association Journal, 13,* 295–299.

Lawder, E. A., Poulin, J. E., & Andrew, R. G. (1986). A study of 185 foster children 5 years after placement. *Child Welfare, 65,* 241–251.

Lindsey, D. (1991). Factors affecting the foster care placement decision. *American Orthopsychiatric Association Journal, 61,* 272–281.

Pilowsky, D. (1992). Short-term psychotherapy with children in foster care. In J. O'Brien, D. Pilowsky, & O. Lewis (Eds.), *Psychotherapies with children: Adapting the psychodynamic approach.* Washington, DC: American Psychiatric Press. pp. 291–311.

Pilowsky, D. J., & Kates, W. G. (1996). Foster children in acute crisis: Assessing critical aspects of attachment. *Journal of the American Academy of Child and Adolescent Psychiatry, 35,* 1095–1097.

Reddy, L. A., Pfeiffer, S. I. (1997). Effectiveness of Treatment Foster Care with Children and Adolescents: A Review of outcome studies. *JAACAP, 36:* 581–588.

Rosenfeld, A. A. (1995). Child adolescent mental disorders research. *Archives of General Psychiatry, 52,* 729–731.

Rosenfeld, A. A., Altman, R., Alfaro, J., & Pilowsky, D. J. (1994). Foster care, child abuse and neglect, and termination of parental rights. *Child and Adolescent Psychiatric Clinics of North America, 3,* 877–893.

Rosenfeld, A. A., Altman, R., & Kaufman, I. (1997). Foster care. In Schreter, R. K., Sharfstein, S. S., & C. A. Shreter, *Managing care, not dollars: The continuum of mental health services,* Washington, DC: American Psychiatric Press. Pp. 125–138.

Rosenfeld, A. A., & Newberger, E. H. (1977). Compassion versus control: Conceptual and practical pitfalls in the broadened definition of child abuse. *Journal of the American Medical Association, 237,* 2086–2088.

Rosenfeld, A. A., Pilowsky, D. J., Fine, P., Thorpe, M., Fein, E., Simms, M. D., Halfon, N., Irwin, M., Alfaro, J., Saletsky, R., Nickman, S. (1997). Foster Care: An update. *Journal of the American Academy of Child and Adolescent Psychiatry, 36:* 448–457.

Rosenfeld, A. A., & Wasserman, S. (1990). *Healing the heart: A therapeutic approach to disturbed children in group care.* Washington, DC: Child Welfare League of America.

Stein, T. J. (1987). Foster care for children. In A. Minahan (Editor-in-Chief), *Encyclopedia of Social Work* (18th ed.). Silver Spring, MD: National Association of Social Workers.

Steinhauer, P. D. (1991). *The Least Detrimental Alternative.* Toronto: University of Toronto Press.

Tatara, T., & Pettiford, E. K. (1983, 1985). *Characteristics of children in substitute and adoptive care.* Washington, DC: Voluntary Cooperative Information System, American Public Welfare Association.

Wald, M. S., Carlsmith, J. M., Leiderman, P. H. (1988). *Protecting Abused and Neglected Children,* Stanford, Ca; Stanford U Press.

Washington Social Legislation Bulletin, 34, 181, November 25, 1996.

Widom, C. S. (1991). The role of placement experiences in mediating the criminal consequences of early childhood victimization. *Journal of the American Orthopsychiatric Association, 61,* 195–209.

5 / Clinical Implications of Early Day Care

Bryna Siegel and Alvin A Rosenfeld

The Sociology of Day Care

American families and society have changed dramatically in the last 40 years, altering the way parents live and raise their children. Yet the United States has not developed a comprehensive plan for supporting family life. Social scientists are certain that in addition to endowment, early experiences influence the child's view of the world, of individuality, of loyalty to the family and to the larger social group. If children are our future, one aspect of a national plan for family life would be to provide experiences that optimize a child's ability to be a productive adult. Since so many young children are in day care, it seems that society as a whole would take a deep interest in this early experience. Yet we have no organized policy assuring that children in day care receive a high quality of services. Furthermore, far too little funding has been allocated to help us understand day care's effects, both positive and negative.

Other countries use day care to achieve national goals. For example, Sweden supports both extensive parental leave and day care. While that country's system is sensitive to the needs of both infants and new parents it breeds dependence on its form of social democracy and, for better or worse, serves to perpetuate the system. The Chinese government advocates strong central leadership. So it encourages one-child families as well as group day care. This implies a future society with no brothers, sisters, uncles, or cousins—a system that encourages replacing filial loyalties with loyalty to the cohort in which children have been raised.

A BRIEF HISTORY OF U.S. DAY CARE

Other than in the Head Start program, in which the United States has not had an approach to day care that uses it to achieve pro-social goals in the broadest sense. The quality of American day care receives little regulation. The National Day Care Study (Stallings, 1978) and National Day Care Home Study (Devine-Hawkins, 1981) formed the basis for draft regulations known as FIDCR (Fed-

eral Interagency Day Care Requirements), which would have mandated basic aspects of day care quality. FIDCR promulgated center-based infant day care with one to three staff: child ratios for children younger than 2 and group sizes of six or fewer; and 1 to 4 ratios for 2- to 4-year-olds, with group sizes of 12 or fewer. Quality family day care was defined as no more than five children to one caregiver, with no more than two children under two years old. Center day care workers were to have a two-year associate's-level child development credential. After Ronald Reagan was elected president, FIDCR was never enacted; in 1991 only three states had laws for day care centers as stringent as FIDCR, and only 10 used FIDCR for family day care.

A weaker mandate, Public Law 98–473 (the Model Child Care Standards Act) was subsequently passed. It placed more emphasis on training in child abuse recognition than on child development. Thus, it did little to assure that children in day care would receive care designed to promote their cognitive and emotional development. While sensational stories about child abuse in day care centers fill the newspapers and terrify parents, in actuality, child abuse still is several times more likely to occur in the child's own home than in day care.

The need for quality day care is obvious. The percentage of American women in the workforce has grown almost tenfold since World War II. In 1990, 75% of all American mothers worked (projections from Zigler & Hall, 1988). About an equal proportion of mothers of infants, toddlers, preschoolers, and school-age children were working. Economic, societal, and familial factors are contributing to the increasing use of day care; each may have direct or indirect impact on the developmental status of children receiving day care.

MATERNAL EMPLOYMENT

The trend toward higher levels of maternal employment can be observed across the board in high, medium, and low socioeconomic groups. Some women have entered the labor force or are participating in it more fully as a result of the women's movement. However, two-thirds of women work because they have to: They are single, divorced, widowed, or have husbands who earn less than $15,000 a year (Birns & Zimmerman, 1987). No studies have specifically addressed child outcomes in children of mothers who "have to" work versus those who "want to" work. What research has shown is that mothers more satisfied with their roles (either as worker or mother) are more positive about parenting than those in unsatisfactory roles (i.e., staying at home when the preference would be to work or vice versa; Cf. Hock, 1976).

Studies of the effects of day care generally note that upper-income families have the greatest access to nonfamilial in-home care and that family day care is generally the least costly form of day care and therefore is most used by lower income families. No specific studies have really explored possible interactions among socioeconomic status, type of day care, and child outcome, or how contact between day care and home during the day may mediate the effects of day care;—for example, on-site corporate day care where there may be parental visits during the day, or in-home care where one-to-one contact between parent and caregiver may be higher. In many 2-parent families, both parents have to work to support a lifestyle that a single income once could support. While it is clear that parents spend less time with children when they work outside the home, it remains unclear how time with children *is* allocated, i.e., feeding, driving, and parents completing work assignments at home versus time spent in "quality" activities such as reading, listening to reports of the child's day, going to enrichment activities together, etc. There has been little specific investigation of how overall number of hours of parental contact relate to child outcomes.

Social Support

On an interpersonal level, extra-familial contacts become a salient source of family socialization. In the past, many parents lived close to extended family and participated in informal networks with friends who already were parents. New parents had easy access to instruction, feedback, or reinforcement for quality parenting. That is no longer the case. Today's parents are more likely to learn about early parenting from the mass media, from childbirth educators, and from day care providers who may have distinct philosophies about child rearing that may conflict with the parents' own cultural and ethical values. First-time mothers and fathers may engage in more trial-and-error parenting, which probably adds stress to the marital relationship as well as to the parent-child relationship.

Societal Attitudes

The women's movement has promoted societal attitudes that have changed the status of working women. The movement has focused attention on female workers as being more self-satisfied and more likely to experience higher self-esteem than women who are "just" mothers. The "bring-home-the-bacon" wife-mother-worker is idealized in the media in everything from perfume commercials, to stories about newswomen who purportedly nurse their newborns in their dressing rooms.

These appealing, heroic images do not accurately reflect the reality that many mothers experience. Less often on public display are similar, realistic images of women who cope marginally with the stress and strain of trying to manage too many demanding roles. Working mothers and fathers may be exhausted when they return from work, and often are too drained to "parent" in the ways they have idealized. Recent research has suggested that parents may try to escape this conundrum by making the workplace the refuge that home life traditionally offered, while home life becomes more like work (Hochschild, 1997). So they may feel inadequate as parents, particularly when they compare themselves to the idealized parenting sometimes portrayed by the media. The quality of the time that day care children do spend with parents has been postulated to account for the "effects of day care" at least as much as the quality of the day care itself. There is concern that the quality of parenting for children with extensive hours in day care may be developmentally less optimal than when there is 1 full-time parent at home or when fewer hours of day care are used. No specific research addresses effects of day care according to patterns of use; for example, whether 6 hours per day, 5 days per week, has any different effect than 10 hours per day 3 days per week, and so on. As we discuss later, studies have addressed only total numbers of hours in care per week.

Demographic, Economic, Societal, and Familial Trends Related to Day Care Use

DEFINITION OF DAY CARE

The phrase "family day care" refers to situations in which a single primary caregiver, with or without helpers, takes care of children in her (almost always the caregiver is female) own home. This type of care is the most prevalent in the United States today, serving 56% of children. "In-home care," where children remain in their own home but receive care from someone other than a parent, is used by 26% of families. "Day care centers" serve only 18% of children.

With so many children being cared for during the day by people who are not their parents, it seems important to understand the effects this care has on children's development. But what questions are most relevant to whether day care is constructive for children? Is it whether day care increases the chance that psychopathology will develop in some individuals (in the sense of increasing the likelihood of having a *Diagnostistic and Statistical Manual* diagnosis in adulthood)? Or does day care create more subtle changes in personality because it may increase the risk of having an insecure attachment to the mother in infancy? Or is day care more likely to produce individuals with a different orientation toward relationships with other individuals, groups, and society? Cross-cultural work (e.g., Bettelheim, 1969) on children raised in Israeli *kibbutzim* has suggested that early group rearing may leave a distinctive impression on adult personality: strong group altruism, but possibly less drive to obtain and sustain dyadic relationships. It has been difficult to ascertain from current research whether any psychological effects of day care on the developing child result from day care—or are they effects of specific acculturation goals, or of nonparental care, or of repeated parental separation, or of being cared for by a parent who already has a full-time (nonparenting) job to do each day in addition to caring for the child who receives day care?

Much research on day care has focused on immediately measurable outcomes as the salient indicator of any undesirable psychological effects that day care may contribute. There may also be an implicit suggestion that what differences that may be revealed by short term outcome research may tend to wash out with maturation. Methodological concerns about measurement sensitivity (e.g., what aspects of attachment may *not* be measured by a laboratory measure of attachment such as the Strange Situation? [Belsky & Braungart, 1991]), sleeper effects (e.g., later parenting skills of children raised in day care), and the appropriate units of analysis (e.g., intrapsychic functioning vs. social interaction vs. societal altruism) have not always been well addressed in research to date.

So far no longitudinal research has been carried out following children 10, 15, or 20 years after infant day care. Even if such studies were conducted, they would be subject to cohort effects because the personal, family, and social ecology of an infant placed in day care has changed so much in the last 20 years. For now, any long-term effects of day care can be only the subject of speculation based on knowledge of short-term outcomes.

QUALITY OF DAY CARE

Some studies focus on the psychological development of children in day care while regarding the day care itself more or less as a "black box." Other studies characterize samples according to numbers of hours per week the child spends in day care, the type of day care used, and sometimes community- versus university-based care (with the assumption that university-based care is higher quality). Studies such as the National Day Care Studies cited earlier have aimed at characterizing the quality of day care and have tended to focus on variables with implications for policy such as staff ratio, group size, and credentialing of staff. A study sponsored by the National Institute of Child Health and Development (NICHD) included measures of cognitive and social stimulation provided by caregivers in order to better define day care quality (Belsky, 1997).

One study (Goossens & Ijzendoorn, 1990) examined quality of attachment to caregivers in day care and found that those children with secure attachments to caregivers had more "sensitive" interactions with them in a free-play session, suggesting that quality of interaction is important, even if studies do not always take it into account or measure it in detailed ways. Provence (1989) examined day care from a more purely mother-infant psychodynamic point of view. What she felt made for high-quality day care was when caregivers facilitate "good" separations from parents and then provide "good-enough" care compared to the parents' care. Another desirable component of "quality" care is continuity between home and day care. This may be problematic, for Zigler and Turner (1982) have noted that parents spend only an average of 7.2 minutes per day in their child's day care setting.

Day Care's Impact on Social and Emotional Development

ATTACHMENT STUDIES

Historically, research from a psychoanalytic and sociobiological perspective suggests that infants and young children needed a single person to whom they have an intense, ongoing mothering relationship. The reasoning was that if prolonged separation from the mother can cause depression and detachment (c.f. Bowlby, 1969; Freud & Burlingham, 1944), then perhaps the cumulative effect of many daily separations would have the same effect. For this reason a number of studies in the last 20 years have tried to ascertain whether day care experiences contribute to an infant's or toddler's insecure attachment to the mother. The countervailing theory, which holds that children in day care are mentally well, has come from cross-cultural work and from studies such as one by Shaeffer and Emerson (1964), which demonstrated that children can maintain several secure attachments simultaneously. Most recently, the NICHD multi-site study of day care has seemed to support this conclusion as well, suggesting that significantly more variance in a child's social and emotional development could be explained by home factors rather than day care factors.

The most comprehensive empirical answer on day care's effect on attachment comes from meta-analytic studies, one made by Belsky and Rovine (1988), which aggregated the results from children in Strange Situations (c.f. Ainsworth, Blehar, Waters, & Wall, 1978) done with 491 infants and toddlers in 6 studies. The second was a meta anal-ysis of 897 subjects across 13 studies (Lamb, Sternberg, & Prodpromidis, 1992). The Strange Situation measures attachment by classifying babies as secure or insecure based on exploration, separation, and reunion behavior in several standard episodes involving a caregiver and a stranger/examiner. The studies included children from different socioeconomic groups who were enrolled in center, family, and in-home day care. Significantly higher rates of insecure attachment to mothers were found in children receiving more than 20 hours per week of day care (43%) compared to those receiving less than 20 hours per week (26%), which is not significantly different from the base rate in a non–day care population. Therefore, day care can be seen as a risk factor for precipitating an insecure attachment, but the fact that 57% of children in day care remained securely attached to mothers makes clear that there is not a direct causal link between the two. Similarly, the Lamb, Sternberg & Prodromidis study found that while there was the most secure attachment among non-day children insecure attachment was related to a complex of factors—not just 20 or more hours per week, but also to whether early care care had been full or part-time, and whether care was provided by a relative or professional caregiver. They also found more insecure attachment among those whose care was initiated between 7 and 12 months of age (a time related to the onset of stranger anxiety), further bolstering the likelihood that individual differences in attachment 'vulnerability' may be activated by certain types of day care practices, though not solely causative of insecure attachment.

Some investigators (e.g., Clarke-Stewart, 1989) have asked whether attachment, as measured by the Strange Situation, is "psychologically equivalent" for day care children who are more accustomed to separation from parents and whether avoidance in those children is really a reflection of increased independence from adults rather than insecurity. This question was answered in a study by Belsky and Braungart (1991), who compared 2 samples of insecurely attached infants with more vs. less than 20 hours per week of day care. Those infants in day care more than 20 hours fussed more, cried more, and played less during Strange Situations. These findings also support the idea that day care may be a "risk factor" for the insecurely attached infant and that, in these more vulnerable children, extra amounts of day care may correlate with a gradient of maladaptation.

AGGRESSION AND NONCOMPLIANCE

The correlates of insecure attachment and avoidance of adults that have received the most attention in day care children are reduced levels of compliance and aggressiveness (Rubenstein, Howes, & Boyle, 1981; Schwarz, Krolick, & Strickland, 1973). Noncompliance and aggressiveness appear to be heavily mediated by day care quality indicators such as staff ratio and group size. Little evidence has been gathered to tell us whether children who display higher rates of these negative behaviors in day care do so in other settings, or whether these traits persist at higher rates after they outgrow day care. A meta-analytic study of 11 research reports, (Mattlock & Green, 1990) examining social and emotional development of day care children found that positive effects of day care included better group adjustment according to teachers, as well as broader sex role concepts. However, nine of 11 studies cited increased aggression to peers and non-compliance to adults. As in the larger meta-analyses of attachment, quality of day care, parent stress, (as well as SES) were mediators.

Although an increase in negative behaviors in children in day care has been reported by several investigators, there does seem to be relative protection for nondisadvantaged children who receive high-quality care, such as from an excellent university-based day care center. Field (1991, 1994) studied children who received infant day care at the University of Miami's Mailman Center; the children were followed for as long as through the sixth grade. These children showed no sociometric deficits and, in fact, were rated more popular, attractive, and affectionate by peers or teachers. Similarly, in earlier work, Clarke-Stewart and Fein (1983) found that children in day care with trained caregivers and small group size showed more cooperativeness and greater assertiveness with peers. These results are intriguing, because they suggest that those who are given the opportunity to do best in day care may have more adaptive and positive skills for group functioning. In one study, more temperamentally vulnerable children showed reduction in aggression and noncompliance and increased sociability (Volling & Feagans, 1995), suggesting that higher quality day care may introduce behavioral improvements if it provides more authoritative child-rearing practices than may be available in the child's own home.

Using the Findings of Day Care Research Clinically

Child psychiatry is interested in preventing untoward experiences and in promoting children's general welfare. That alone would make day care a concern for child psychiatrists. But the issue becomes more personal since so many child psychiatrists have their children cared for by a nonparent at least part time. The results of studies on day care also may have other practical applications for child psychiatry practice. Because federal standards are lacking, mental health professionals can provide an important service if they help parents understand the characteristics of good-quality day care. Areas for clinical consultation and treatment planning involving day care may include:

1. Making decisions about supplemental care for infants and toddlers with mentally impaired mothers
2. Using day care as respite and role-modeling for parents who are at risk to abuse or neglect their children
3. Helping parents deal with their children's adjustment reactions to day care
4. Planning for the interaction between individual differences such as temperament, and selection of day care for a particularly "difficult" or immature child
5. Selecting day care for a child given a known *Diagnostic and Statistical Manual* diagnosis
6. Consulting with day care programs about fostering quality caregiver-child interaction, or handling behavior problems that frequently arise in day care, such as aggressiveness

Many parents can get help finding quality day care from local child care coordinating councils. Such agencies coordinate local referral for placement of licensed family and group day care, but are typically less helpful for parents seeking private in-home or family day care. Most family day care is not licensed, since a number of providers work solely on word of mouth referral. Because of the lack of regulatory control, the fact that a family day care provider lacks a license says little or nothing about the quality of care offered. Another increasingly available day care option for school-aged children is after-school care at the child's elementary school. Most day care needs to be obtained on a "caveat emptor" basis by parents who obtain some consumer education on the topic from local child care agencies or other child experts. Few formal resources exist for obtaining suitable day care for children already considered at-risk.

DAY CARE FOR THE CHILD FROM A DISADVANTAGED FAMILY

Day care research has shown that very good quality day care is better for the cognitive development of children of lower socioeconomic status than staying at home (Burchinal, Lee, & Ramey, 1989; Spitz, 1992). Disadvantaged infants and toddlers learn more, and speak sooner and better when in very good quality care than do their peers who are not in day care. However, some studies suggest that these benefits may wash out by kindergarten or first grade. Yet good day care programs also may promote better parenting skills, child involvement, and esteem of the parenting role. No studies have examined specifically whether day care has beneficial effects on children whose primary caregivers have major psychiatric disorders. But the research on socioeconomically disadvantaged children would support the contention that day care would likely be a helpful intervention for such mothers.

INDIVIDUAL DIFFERENCES IN ADJUSTMENT TO DAY CARE

Individual differences that may be relevant to day care adjustment include: difficulty of the infant in being handled, soothed, and fed by multiple caregivers; rhythmicity of the infant's state organization; temperament; or security of attachment at the time of day care entry. Developmental stage and its interactions with these individual differences may partly define "risk" inherent in day care entry for certain more vulnerable children. For example, it would be useful clinically to know whether very early day care experiences may incrementally predispose separation-sensitive, insecurely attached children to future disorders. Does entry into care at certain critical developmental stages compound risk for such children? Are children who show insecure attachment while in day care (such as at the onset of stranger anxiety) more day care-quality sensitive? Are the children more likely to benefit from day care with a single or primary caregiver, or react more negatively to frequent changes in care arrangements? These considerations should be part of a day care-quality assessment procedure that clinicians consider when faced with an insecurely attached child who will be receiving day care.

DEVELOPMENTAL STAGE AND INITIATION OF DAY CARE

Many mothers make plans to return to work even before becoming pregnant. Many others make such plans shortly thereafter. Employers and economic exigencies impose constraints that tend to reinforce these plans and prevent new mothers who find they would like more time at home with their children, or decide after the child is born that they would prefer to work fewer hours, from doing so. These nonpsychological factors leave the new or expectant parent with little latitude in deciding about day care placement based on her own changing psychology as a parent or on the infant's characteristics as they become known. There may be risk to the child's day care adjustment when the mother's own feelings of readiness to leave the baby or the infant's unique temperament gets too little credence in the return-to-work decision. It is possible that a mother with a preset time to return to work might act differently toward an infant right from the beginning than would a mother who does not anticipate that frequent, extended separations would begin so soon.

Since research suggests that infants with less than 20 hours per week of nonparental care are at less risk to develop insecure attachments, partial work returns (i.e., less than 20 hours per week) may be a useful intervention for babies that may seem at risk to develop insecure attachments because of less than optimal parent-infant "fit." Similarly, the literature suggests that there may be particularly beneficial effects of care with a relative in the first several months. And if aspects of attachment theory are right, a mother who is encouraged to suppress, to some extent, her strongest maternal feelings may be depriving her infant of the passion that the child needs in the first year or two of life. Encouraging paternal leave time to keep down the numbers of hours in day care would be another intervention.

The child's developmental stage may offer the clinician some clues as to making a fit between a particular child and the type of day care to be selected: In-home care or family day care may be most beneficial to infants because of a more simple, home-like environment. The earlier in the first year, the more important may be likely to be true. The home environment is less complex than a center, health risks are low, and the baby can begin to adopt a routine. The child has one caregiver who can learn his or her rhythms as the infant learns to recognize people and objects as permanent.

By the time the child is mobile, or at about 1 year, family day care may become a relatively better alternative, even for the family that can afford individualized in-home care. At this stage, the child learns primarily by manipulating everyday objects in the environment, rather than through play with formal curriculum materials. In family day care, there is exposure to a familylike grouping of peers but, more important, there is a homelike rather than group-based environment, still with one significant caregiver. As long as the child is preverbal, one individual caregiver arguably makes the most sense, because that person can learn to respond consistently to an individual child's idiosyncratic signals.

By the time the child is verbal and can express him- or herself reliably, even under stress (2½ to 3 years old), a day care center or preschool may offer relatively more benefits. A preschool tends to offer a wide variety of age-appropriate play materials and a diverse group of peers to facilitate friendship formation. It also offers more opportunities for constant physical motion and exploration.

Long-Term Effects of Day Care: Implications for Future Research

It is possible that American children raised with substantial amounts of nonparental care will be different with respect to how they interact with their contemporaries, though not necessarily psychologically better or worse off. Since day care

as a social and economic institution has been accepted as part of contemporary America, the mental health professional should attempt to understand its possible effects on personality development and to find ways of enhancing its quality both as a quality setting for typically-developing children and as a clinical, protective resource for vulnerable children.

Conclusions

Child development experts and mental health professionals working with families who use day care should provide recommendations for such use based on the family's functioning, an appraisal of the parent-child relationship, and the individual characteristics of the child. A combined understanding of research on day care, child development, and risks to development is needed to help families use day care in a way most suitable for an individual child and for the parent-child dyad. In a visit to a day care center or a family day care home, it is possible to see children with warm, loving relationships to caregivers that give an observer little reason to suspect that the adult is not actually the parent. On the other end of the continuum, day care environments exist where it is possible to get the impression that the children perceive adults as a depersonalized "they." These children see adults as useful in fulfilling instrumental requests but are not related to as separate individuals. Children need one-to-one relationships if they are to grow with good one-to-one interpersonal skills. As we learn more about relevant caregiver training and individual differences in response to day care as a treatment and put more private and public monies into day care, the concerns about psychological risks of day care should lessen.

REFERENCES

Ainsworth, M. D. S., Blehar, M. C., Waters, E., & Wall, S. (1978). *Patterns of attachment.* Hillsdale, NJ: Lawrence Erlbaum.

Barglow, P., Vaughn, B., & Molitor, N. (1987). Effects of maternal absence due to employment on the quality of mother-infant attachment in a low-risk sample, 58, 945–954.

Belsky, J., & Braungart, J. M. (1991). Are insecure-

avoidant infants with extensive day-care experience less stressed by and more independent in the Strange Situation? *Child Development, 62,* 567–571.

Belsky, J., & Rovine, M. J. (1988). Non-maternal care in the first year of life, and the security of parent-infant attachment. *Child Development, 59,* 157–167.

Bettelheim, B. (1969). *The children of the dream.* Toronto: Macmillan.

Birns, B., & Zimmerman, L. (1987). On infant day care. *American Journal of Orthopsychiatry, 57* (1), 138–140.

Bowlby, J. (1969). *Attachment and loss: Vol. 1: Attachment.* New York: Basic Books.

Burchinal, M., Lee, M., & Ramey, C. (1989). Type of day care and preschool intellectual development in disadvantaged children. *60,* 128–137.

Clarke-Stewart, K. A. (1989). Infant day care: Maligned or malignant? *American Psychologist, 44* (2), 266–273, 1989.

Clarke-Stewart, K. A. and Fein, G. G. Early childhood programs. In M. M. Haith & J. J. Campos (Eds) *Handbook of Child Psychology* (4th ed): Vol 2. 'Infancy & developmental psychobiology (pgs 917–1000) NY: Wiley, 1983.

Devine-Hawkins, P. (1981). *Family day care in the U.S.* U.S. Department of Health and Human Services Pub. No. (OHDS) 80–30287.

Field, T. (1991). Quality infant day-care and grade school behavior and performance. *Child Development, 62,* 863–870.

Field, T. Infant day care facilitates later social behavior & school performance. In H. Goelman & E. Jacobs (Eds). *Children's Play in Child Care Settings,* SUNY Press, Albany, NY, 1994.

Freud, A., & Burlingham, D. (1944). *Infants without families.* New York: International Universities Press.

Hochschild, A. *The Time Bind: When Work Becomes Home and Home Becomes Work,* Henry Holt & Co., (1997).

Hock, E. (1976). *Alternative approaches to child-rearing and their effects of the mother-child relationship. Final report.* Office of Child Development, U.S. Department of Health, Education, and Welfare.

Lamb, M. E., Sternberg, K. J., Prodromidis, M. Nonmaternal care & the security of infant-mother attachment: A reanalysis of the data. *Infant Behavioral &*

Development, 15, 71–83 (1992).

Matlock, J. R., & Green, V. P. The effects of day care on the social & emotional development of infants, toddlers & preschoolers. *Early Child Development & Care,* 64, 55–59, 1990.

Provence, S. (1989). Resolved: Day care is the best care for children under five of working Americans. *Journal of the American Academy of Child and Adolescent Psychiatry, 28* (1), 131–133.

Rubenstein, J., Howes, C., & Boyle, P. (1981). A two-year follow-up of infants in community-based day care. *Journal of Child Psychology and Child Psychiatry, 8,* 1–11.

Schwarz, J. C., Krolick, G., & Strickland, R. G. (1973). Effects of early day care experience on adjustment to a new environment. *American Journal of Orthopsychiatry, 43,* 340–348.

Shaefer, H. R., & Emerson, P. E. The development of social attachments in infancy. *Monographs of the Society for Research in Child Development,* 29, 3, 1–77, 1964.

Spitz, H. H. Does the Carolina Abcedarian Early Intervention Project prevent sociocultural mental retardation? *Intelligence,* 16, 2, 225–237, 1992.

Stallings, J., et al. (1978). *National day care study. Report for administration for children, youth and families.* U.S. Department of Health, Education, and Welfare.

Volling, B. L., & Feagans, L. V. Infant day care and children's social competence. *Infant Behavior & Development,* 18, 2, 177–188, 1995.

Zigler, E., & Hall, N. W. (1988). Day care and its effects on children: An overview for pediatric health professionals. *Journal of Developmental and Behavioral Pediatrics, 9* (1), 38–46.

Zigler, E., & Turner, P. (1982). Parents and day care workers: A failed partnership? In E. Zigler & E. Gordon (Eds.). *Day care: Scientific and social policy issues.* Boston: Auburn House.

6 / Children and Adolescents in Institutions

Laurel J. Kiser

Institution 1. The act of instituting. 2. a. An important custom, relationship, or behavioral pattern in a culture or society. b. Informal. A lasting feature: FIXTURE. 3. a. An established organization or foundation, esp. one dedicated to public service. b. The building or buildings housing such an organization. 4. A place of confinement, as a mental asylum.
— *Webster's Second New International Dictionary*

A fact of life for American children and adolescents is their participation in some form of insti-

tutional care. Although our culture views the nuclear family as the basic institution for child rearing, much of this responsibility currently is delegated to other institutions. Thus it is necessary for the child and adolescent psychiatrist and, indeed, for any professional involved in understanding and treating children and adolescents to investigate the significance, structures, functions, and orientations of institutions. An in-depth look at institutions involving children and adolescents includes developmental considerations and risk factors, effectiveness and long-term outcomes, economic considerations, and medicolegal aspects.

Institutional care for children and adolescents is multifaceted. Early social work analysts described 3 functions for institutions: relief, rehabilitation, and reconstruction (Fein & Clarke-Stewart, 1973). The functions of institutional care for children and adolescents range from imparting knowledge and enculturation, such as schools and camps, to providing care in lieu of family structures, such as day care, group homes, and foster care arrangements, to taking care of ill or disruptive children, such as hospitals, residential treatment centers, and prisons/correctional facilities. For sick, abandoned, or unwanted children, the institution replaces the notions "home and family."

The Family as Institution

The family is the primary institution in American culture designated the responsibility for child care (National Commission on Children, 1991). "Family, however defined by society, is generally perceived as the fundamental unit responsible for and capable of providing a child on a continuing basis with an environment which serves his numerous physical and mental needs during immaturity" (Goldstein, Freud, & Solnit, 1979, p. 13). In order to understand the role of other institutions in the lives of children and adolescents, it is important to review the critical functions of the primary institution, the family.

The family serves 4 primary purposes. The first is to provide for the child during the period of immaturity and dependency. This includes providing basic survival needs, such as food, shelter, and protection from dangers as well as affection and security, stimulation and regulation. From an ethological point of view, the basis of the family is rooted in survival of individuals and their offspring. Both parenting behavior and attachment behavior are preprogrammed to a certain extent to ensure survival of the species (Bowlby, 1988). Although the details of these patterns of behavior are learned through enculturation, they are basically instinctual, activated by specific circumstances, and accompanied by strong emotional responses.

The second purpose served by the family is the creation of an identification and sense of belonging. "Noting the role of 'meaning regulation,' . . . the family provides a model for answering the basic existential question, 'Who are you?' for its members" (Wolin & Bennett, 1984, p. 403). The creation of an emotional sense of "home," of knowing that one belongs, translates into a sense of trust and security. This sense of identification and belonging is created and reinforced by repeated patterns of interaction, continuity in relationships, and family rituals. "Ritual life in families is important because it reinforces the family identity and gives all members a shared and necessary sense of belonging" (Wolin & Bennett, 1984, p. 402).

Third, the family provides the mechanisms necessary for the child's socialization or "adaptation to community standards." The family functions to assure stability and continuity of individual members as well as of the individual members to society. David Reiss (1989) views "family process as a primary mechanism of maintaining continuity of social forms" (p. 200). Family interactions and rituals not only provide a sense of identity to family members but also "convey the commonality of the family with the culture" (Wolin & Bennett, 1984, p. 404).

The fourth purpose of family life is perpetuation of the family and the practice of parenthood (Bowlby, 1988). Children learn about being part of a family by experiencing family life. They learn how to parent by being parented. In forming an identification with their parents, by internalizing those relationships, children learn to relate to others, including their own children. Patterns of family interaction cycle from one generation to the next. Healthy family functioning and parenting styles are passed along as well as unhealthy, abusive ones. Data on family characteristics of children in institutions indicate that many are born to parents who were also institutionalized as children (Sholevar, 1980).

The essential role of the family to the well-being and healthy development of children was ratified by the United Nations Convention on the Rights of the Child (UN General Assembly, 1989) in its call for protection of a child's right to a *family environment*. The provisions of this convention demonstrate the value of "ensuring the presence of the elements of family environment, even when a child does not live with his or her family of origin" (Melton, 1996, p. 1237).

Developmental Considerations

Because institutional care for children occurs across a variety of ages and for various lengths of time, it is crucial to understand the developmental accomplishments that can be affected significantly by institutionalization. Doing so necessitates consideration of the age and developmental stage of the child or adolescent at the time of institutionalization.

René Spitz was one of the pioneers in the study of the effects of institutionalization on children. His observations of infants separated from their mothers and cared for by a surrogate in a penal institute laid the groundwork for attachment theory as well as documenting the reactions of children to institutional care. Clinically, the infants, during their 3 months' separation, became less interested in their surroundings, did not eat well and gain weight, and began self-stimulating, stereotypic movements (Bowlby, 1982).

Attachment, separation, and relationship formation are basic developmental issues that can be tellingly affected by institutional care (Bowlby, 1965; Stern, 1985). In fact, children and adolescents in institutions commonly have a disturbed ability to form relationships and to demonstrate affection (Sholevar, 1980). A brief review here of the developmental processes involved in attachment and relationship formation helps to highlight the importance of these issues.

During the first 6 months of life, the infant forms an attachment to his or her primary caregiver(s). The constant presence of this companion during the first couple of years of life cements this attachment relationship. As the child approaches preschool age, between 4 and 5 years, the ability to represent this relationship internally has developed, allowing greater toleration of absences from attachment figures. Finally, by about 8 to 9 years of age, the child is able to sustain longer periods of separation because of the stability of the working model or internal representation of these critical attachment relationships. As the child matures over time, he or she creates a "psychological parent," formed through daily interactions, shared experiences, and rituals (Goldstein et al., 1979). This working model of the attachment relationship is generalized to other relationships, including those with peers. Thus separation from primary caregivers by means of institutionalization will have various effects on the course of relationship development, depending on the age of child and the length of separation.

In addition to attachment and relationship development, other developmental milestones must be considered when designing institutions for children and adolescents and in making decisions about whether to use institutional care with a child or adolescent. Developmental theories, such as those of Erikson, Freud, or Piaget, postulate stages of growth and maturation for social, psychological, and cognitive development. These theories, along with clinical data about human growth and development starting with infancy, indicate specific developmental needs and tasks associated with different ages. Table 6.1 presents the critical developmental needs that should be addressed in all institutional settings.

Institutions for Enculturation

Many institutions are established for the purpose of providing education and recreation for normal, healthy, and beloved children. These institutions augment and supplement the 4 primary functions of the family. Institutions in this group include, but are not limited to, day care settings, schools (public, private, and boarding), and camps.

It is important to stress that the institutions discussed in this section do not and cannot substitute for the functions provided by the family. In fact,

TABLE 6.1

Developmental Considerations

Age (years)	Developmental Goals	
0–3	Consistent caregiver	Play
	Satisfaction of basic needs	Communication
	Stimulation and regulation	Nurturance
3–6	Physical skill development	Independence
	Social interaction	Role models
	Structure and limits	Nurturance
	Learning experiences	Play
6–12	Cooperative interaction	Role models
	Structure and limits	Socialization
	Learning experiences	
13–18	Goals and expectations	Intimacy
	Positive peer group	Privacy
	Structure and limits	Individuality
	Sense of community	Responsibility

parental involvement in selecting, monitoring, and participating with the institution providing care for their child is critical for assuring quality of care and for attaining the goals established by the institution.

DAY CARE

Changes in our social and economic environment often are reflected in the types of institutions that are established to care for our children. Nowhere is this more evident than in the expanding utilization and need for day care. During the 1970s and 1980s, an increasing number of women joined the workforce, creating an enormous demand for nonparental child care for infants, toddlers, children, and adolescents. Over half of the infants in the United States are cared for by nonparental caregivers while their mothers and fathers are earning a living (Clarke-Stewart, 1989). This percentage grows as children get older. What types of institutions are designed to provide care for our children while we work, and what is the effect of day care on a child's overall development?

A variety of day care models are available, including day care centers, child development centers, nursery schools and group day care homes, and agencies providing extended care (before- and after-school care). Models of day care differ on the quality of care provided and the emphasis of the program. These differences are amplified by the variety of individual programs established. Aspects of day care that can differ dramatically between centers include physical location and materials, staff ratios and levels of training, curriculum offerings, emphasis on socialization, and structure and control (Clarke-Stewart, 1991; Fein & Clarke-Stewart, 1973). States and a variety of organizations set standards for day care centers and attempt to regulate the quality of care provided in homes.

Of the different aspects of day care, 4 variables seem "most, clearly, consistently, and independently related to children's behavior and development . . . the physical environment, the caregiver's behavior, the curriculum, and the number of children" (Clarke-Stewart, 1991, p. 33). None of these characteristics is easily described as in a linear relationship with the children's behavior or development. For example, more space is not necessarily better space or more conducive to a positive day care experience. Furthermore, ecological studies have noted that limiting the number of toys available to preschoolers increases the amount of sociodramatic play observed (Kounin & Gump, 1974). On each of these 4 variables, quality is most important. The significant dimensions represented include the organization of the space and quality of the materials; the affective quality of the interactions between the caregiver and the children; the caregiver's understanding of child development; the mix among educational, intellectual experiences and socialization; the developmental adjustment of staff-child ratios; and the appropriate balance between peer activities and adult-child interactions.

Early research on child care indicated that children who attend day care settings for part or all of the day show advanced skill development in a variety of areas. They appear to be more advanced cognitively and socially (as evidenced by higher scores on IQ tests, advanced language skills, increased feelings of self-confidence, advanced knowledge of social rules, greater degrees of social competence, and more independence than children who do not attend day care). However, the gains do not appear to be permanent; longitudinal research has demonstrated an equalizing effect as all children begin formal schooling. Evidence also suggests that placement of a child in a day care setting alters the day-to-day interactions between the parents and the child at home (Edwards, Logue, Loehr, & Roth, 1987). Current research is demonstrating differential effects of day care depending on the quality of care provided and individual aspects of the child, such as attachment security (Egelund & Hiester, 1995).

As the number of women with school-age children who enter the workplace continues to grow, so do the number of children requiring extended care. In fact, it is estimated that between 4 to 7 million school-age children are left on their own either before or after school (Zigler & Finn-Stevenson, 1996). Studies into the effectiveness of after-school care, especially with low-income populations, suggest that participation in formal after-school programs produces benefits over parental care, informal adult supervision, and self-care, including better academic achievement and social/emotional adjustment (Posner & Vandell, 1994; Zigler & Finn-Stevenson, 1996).

The ever-increasing need for day care and the high cost of quality day care create a major problem for urban policy makers and for society. The fact that local, state, and federal governments and also employers leave the funding of day care primarily to parents makes the experience of quality day care a privilege only some children experience (Zigler & Finn-Stevenson, 1996).

SCHOOLS

The primary mission of schools is to educate the population. With the explosion of knowledge and technology in the 20th century, the curriculum requirements of schooling have increased proportionately. In addition, the multiplicity of student needs has significantly changed. Many students view elementary and secondary education as preparatory for postgraduate education; others view it as preparation for vocational programs; while others view it as providing basic life skills. Each of these tracks requires a different curriculum.

As institutions for learning, how are American schools meeting these challenges? Some indicators point to problems. For instance, achievement scores and college-entrance exam scores for high school students have been declining since the 1960s. Over 15% of the nation's 17-year-olds are unable to read, a number that increases to almost 40% for minority youth (Gross & Gross, 1985). Expectations for achievement as measured by homework assignments, grading standards, graduation requirements, and the like are not adequate and do not compare favorably with standards used by other industrialized nations (Gross & Gross, 1985; Kantrowitz & Wingert, 1991).

Moreover, the missions of schools in American culture are multifaceted and extend well beyond the imparting or gaining of knowledge. Four primary goals of schooling include vocational, intellectual, social, and personal (Goodlad, 1984). Schools are established to function as vehicles for political, social, and economic change and thus are in a position to influence social, emotional, and moral development. Again, it is important to note that the institutions discussed in this section are only supplemental to the family. Families need to be involved significantly in the process of schooling, functioning as partners.

Given the functions for which schools are designed, the characteristics of schools as institutions for learning have some interesting characteristics worthy of study (Goodlad, 1984; Linney & Seidman, 1989). Ecological psychology (Barker, 1968) draws attention to the interactions between behavior and environmental characteristics. Patterns of behavior are fairly predictable given specific environmental characteristics, including space and furnishings, a specific time span, a defined population, and patterns of behavior appropriate to that setting. According to this model, schools, as institutions, are powerful determinants of the behavior elicited from their students.

Thus, the structure of the learning experience and the classroom set the stage. For the most part, classroom learning activities are standardized, highly structured, individual activities. The most common communications in classrooms are downward from teacher to student (about 70%) (Goodlad, 1984; Linney & Seidman, 1989). Goodlad's (1984) study of school characteristics documented less than 5% of classroom time spent in question-and-answer dialogues and less than 1% spent on questions involving reasoning skills. Work assignments and learning activities are teacher-directed with little input from students. Especially in the upper grade levels, teacher behavior in the classroom includes little corrective behavior and little positive reinforcement (Goodlad, 1984).

These interactional patterns may serve a regulatory function, but they create little opportunity for problem-solving, creativity, small-group activity, and cooperative peer exchanges. Moreover, teacher-directed learning and seatwork seem to be conversely related to student participation and on-task behavior. Finally, theories of learning clearly demonstrate the importance of feedback and immediate, positive reinforcement to the learning process. However, studies of school environments and teacher behaviors in the classroom do not demonstrate application of theory to practice.

The structure of the classroom, teacher behavior, and educational atmosphere currently offered translate into an environment that does not favor learning. In fact, students, when responding to questions about what they like best about school, list "friends" first and "teachers" and "classes" toward the bottom of the list (Goodlad, 1984). Studies of schooling and classroom environments describe the atmosphere in most schools as "passive," "regimented," "routinized," "flat," "sterile," and "affectively neutral" (Goodlad, 1984; Gross & Gross, 1985). Goodlad (1984) concludes:

Four elements of classroom life in the schools of our sample come through loud and clear from our data. First, the vehicle for teaching and learning is the total group. Second, the teacher is the strategic, pivotal figure in this group. Third, the norms governing the group derive primarily from what is required to maintain the teacher's strategic role. Fourth, the emotional tone is neither harsh and punitive nor warm and joyful; it might be described most accurately as flat. (p. 108)

Crowded school conditions provide another example of the school environment and its effects on student achievement and well-being. Barker and Gump (1964) demonstrated a significant relationship between school size and student participation; larger schools with greater competition for roles and participation are more likely to foster student apathy and alienation. Trends in American education have favored development of larger and larger schools and increased classroom size without a corresponding expansion of the number of activities or roles available for student participation (Linney & Seidman, 1989).

When we recognize these social regularities inherent in American schools, it is not surprising that many schools have a difficult time meeting their goals and objectives. Indeed, currently much is being written about the failure of our public education system. Problems abound, such as inadequate funding, inequities in funding between school systems, inadequate reimbursement for educators, inability to provide a safe and secure learning environment, and substandard academic curriculums. Under these conditions, approximately 40% of school-age children and adolescents are at risk for school failure or dropout (National Commission on Children, 1991). What then are the necessary ingredients for successful schooling?

An effective school is characterized by (a) strong leadership, that is a principal who is an active and energetic force in the school; (b) an atmosphere that is orderly and not oppressive; (c) teachers who participate in decision making; (d) a principal and teachers who have high expectations that children will learn; (e) a curricular emphasis on academics; and (f) frequent monitoring of students' performance. (Linney & Seidman, 1989, p. 337)

Solutions to these problems are not easily obtained. The National Commission on Children recommends the following series of reforms:

a rigorous and challenging academic curriculum; measures to recruit and retain skilled teachers; measures to improve the effectiveness of principals; school-based management; greater accountability by all parties responsible for the quality of education; improvements in the school environment; equitable financing across all school districts. (1991, p. 26)

Institutions for Dependent Children

A second set of institutions in the United States were established for the purpose of providing a home for unwanted and neglected children. The majority of children and adolescents placed in these institutions are there because their parents cannot provide for them or are unable to care for them. Institutions in this category must act as replacements for the functions of the family. These institutions range from those that most closely resemble the home environment to those that house many children and adolescents in a group setting. They include foster homes, group homes, and residential placements.

Institutional care for children and adolescents out of their homes did not exist in the United States until after the American Revolution (Weithorn, 1988). Children and adolescents, if in need of care or ill, were cared for by the community, family members, or neighbors. Orphanages, established during the 1700s, represent the first institutional settings. In modern times, institutional care for children and adolescents is provided under the auspices of three separate systems: welfare, juvenile justice, and mental health.

Dramatic increases in the number of children requiring out-of-home placements have occurred during the late 1980s, in contrast to the declines seen in the 1970s and early 1980s (National Commission on Children, 1991). In 1989 statistics showed nearly 5% of children and adolescents being cared for by substitute caregivers; of these 2% were cared for by relatives, 2% were cared for by adoptive parents, and 1% were in foster-care situations (Fine, 1991). Recent estimates project that between 500,000 and 840,000 children will be in foster care by 1995 (National Commission on Children, 1991; Kiesler, 1991). The reason for the increase is based partly on the increasing number of families living below the poverty level, the disintegration of the family, and the increasing reports of abuse and neglect.

In part, however, the increases in children removed from their homes is policy-driven:

Federal funding for preventive efforts to keep families together is fixed each year under the provisions of Title IV-B of the Child Welfare and Adoption Assistance Act and has barely grown in the past decade, while funding for out-of-home care is supported by Title IV-E, an open-ended entitlement that grows automatically according to need. This encourages states to place chil-

BOX 6.1

Bright Spots:

Networking Through Special Foster Care Programs

The basic premise of networking in the therapeutic foster care placements described is that
the foster family becomes an extension of the biological or nuclear family, and this family network is again broadened to include the social
services caseworker and other mental health
professionals. This extended "family" system
then attempts to address the needs and problems
of the child and nuclear family. The main goal of
this type of intervention is to support the continued development of relationships between a
child and the significant adults in this child's life,
regardless of their ability to provide adequate
parenting. The principles upon which these programs are established derive from family network concepts.

In order to make these placements work,
"cases [are] evaluated, diagnosed, and carefully
matched with foster homes; the agency support[s] the basic premises of the program; the
foster-care team carrie[s] a small case load; foster
parents function as therapists in a process of corrective socialization; the integrity of foster homes
[is] respected; regular group meetings [are] held
with foster parents for training, case planning,
and support; surrogate extended family like relationships between the child's foster and biological families [are] encouraged; and adequate professional backup [is] provided or located as
required" (Fine & Carnevale, 1984, pp. 82–83).

---

dren in out-of-home care rather than to help troubled
families overcome their problems and maintain custody
of their children. (National Commission on Children,
1991, p. 31)

Reversal of these policies is in the best interests
of children and families.

Some salient facts known about out-of-home
placements include: The typical child was 11 to
12 years of age, white, and placed in care for 17
months. That child is also more likely than normal
to be suffering from emotional, medical, or developmental delays (Fine, 1991; Hoagwood & Rupp,
1994). Most children and adolescents removed
from their parents' custody are placed temporarily
in a series of settings with little longevity or stability to their placements. The result of this transitory process includes the formation of a number
of very tenuous and ambivalent relationships both
with caregivers and with peers (Bush, 1980). The
most effective care is provided to younger children in stable placements that most closely mirror
the "normal family" setting, and the positive ef-

fects decrease as the children become older when
placed and the size of the institution increases
(Bush, 1980; Fine, 1991; Goldstein et al., 1979).
Regardless of the type of institution, children and
adolescents in out-of-home placements frequently need help with issues of separation, loss,
identity, continuity, and crisis (Grigsby, 1996).

FOSTER CARE

The foster care movement is a response to the
problem of placing dependent children outside of
the home. For fostered children, the home of a
family member other than the parents is the first
option explored. If no such placement is available,
licensed foster care homes are explored. A typical
foster care family will include several foster care
children, often unrelated to each other. Many
times parents who provide foster care receive
minimal training, limited information regarding
the foster child placed in their home, and insufficient financial assistance.

The parent-child relationship in foster homes
is often tenuous and demanding. Due to the temporary nature of foster placements, neither the
child nor the parents have any sense of security
surrounding their developing relationship. Frequently, this is complicated by the ongoing and often dysfunctional interactions between the child
and his or her biological parent(s) (Fuller, 1981).
In addition, the child placed in a foster family often tries to reestablish the dynamics and interactions of the biological family in the new placement
(Fine, 1991).

A variety of special foster care programs have
been initiated to improve the foster care arrangement, especially for children and adolescents with
special needs (Grigsby, 1996). Therapeutic foster
homes are established to care for children and adolescents with psychiatric needs, abuse histories,
or other illness. Often these programs are affiliated with mental health agencies that provide
training for the foster parents, ongoing therapeutic services for the child and family, and support
services.

GROUP HOMES AND RESIDENTIAL
GROUP CARE

Establishment of the group home was a movement away from institutionalization and toward a
more family-oriented facility for children and adolescents. "A group home is a small living unit, generally a house, . . . for 6 to 12 children, located in

a neighborhood, . . . staffed 24 hours a day by employees known traditionally as houseparents . . ." (Taylor, 1980, p. 259). Group homes are different from other forms of care for dependent children because of "their small size, their reliance on other community resources such as public schools, and the lack of restraints on the movement of residents within the community" (Grigsby, 1996, p. 910).

As such, group homes typically are more appropriate for older children and adolescents who no longer require or can no longer tolerate the emotionality, security, and nurturance of family life. Often group home residents are transitioning from therapeutic or correctional settings because they no longer require the restrictiveness of the more intensive placement. The mix of residents and the group dynamics established are crucial to the group home environment.

One of the primary goals of the group home setting is to provide an orderly living environment where daily living skills and events are practiced with regularity. The introduction of routines and rituals into the lives of many of these children provides the structure and stability necessary for successful functioning. One of the most difficult problems encountered by group homes is the recruitment and retention of qualified and caring house parents who can create and maintain such an environment (Grigsby, 1996).

Residential group care is perhaps the prototype of institutional care for children and adolescents. These facilities house large numbers of residents in a dormitorylike setting. Bush (1980), in an interesting study of the attitudes of children and adolescents about various out-of-home placements, provided data indicating overwhelming evidence that children do not find large institutions supportive placements. "The children who were living in institutions . . . felt less comfortable, loved, looked after, trusted, cared about, and wanted than children in any other form of surrogate care . . ." (p. 244).

Bush's (1980) study raised additional concerns in terms of the goodness of fit between dependent children and institutional care, namely the stigma attached to and the power of the peer culture in many of these institutions. By being placed in an institutional setting that uses behavior modification techniques and other therapeutic techniques for managing behavior, children become labeled as disturbed by association. In addition, these techniques often are ineffective due to the overwhelming power of the peer culture.

INSTITUTIONS FOR ILL CHILDREN

The third form of institutional care for children and adolescents provides care for the ill or disruptive. Residents in these institutions include those who are physically and/or mentally ill and those with behavioral disorders or who are delinquent. These institutions must provide replacements for the functions of the family and many times also must provide some corrective function. They include hospitals, residential treatment centers, and correctional facilities.

The Pediatric Hospital: For many children and adolescents, brief and/or extended hospital stays cannot be avoided. Although there has been a movement toward providing medical care on an outpatient basis, in some cases this is not possible. Over 3 million children and adolescents are treated in pediatric hospitals each year (Sack & Woodcock, 1984), primarily in the 130 children's hospitals across the country (Greene, 1989).

Children and adolescents requiring hospital care experience many traumatic psychological and environmental changes. Caring for the physical and psychological needs of hospitalized children and adolescents is critical. Although there is little evidence that a single hospitalization causes any lasting effects, due to developmental and personality characteristics, each child and adolescent reacts differently to illness and hospitalization. Disruption of a child's normal environment and routine, pain and suffering, anxiety and questions about illness and death all make a hospital stay traumatic for most youngsters. The ability of a child and the parents to cope with such severe stresses becomes an important indicator of the overall hospital experience.

Due to the stresses involved, in addition to providing the necessary medical care, the pediatric hospital ward must be designed as a reasonable system in which a child can live. Important aspects of this include:

1. Unlimited visiting hours and opportunities for parents to live in when appropriate.
2. Well-organized recreational and play programs.
3. Educational facilities and programs.
4. In-service training programs for staff that emphasize special emotional needs of children, such as their different sense of time and their ways of expressing fear and anxiety. (Sack & Woodcock, 1984, p. 109)

Also important are programs that introduce and familiarize staff with parent-child coping styles and interactional patterns as well as with the corresponding techniques for modifying parental coping styles to maximize the child's ability to cope functionally with the stress (Melamed, 1991). Additional programs for providing an understanding and preparation for procedures are recommended (Mrazek, 1996).

Cost-containment forces are increasingly pressing for children to be treated in lower-cost community hospitals versus pediatric hospitals (Greene, 1989). Although this movement may save money, it fails to heed the experiences of children placed in medical settings that are not sensitive to their developmental needs.

The Psychiatric Hospital: Psychiatric hospitalization of children and adolescents began in the 1920s but became widely offered only in the 1970s. Admissions to psychiatric inpatient facilities increased eightfold between the 1920s and the 1970s, continued to increase dramatically through the 1980s, and have begun to decrease in the 1990s. The rapid increases in utilization of psychiatric inpatient care for children and adolescents was accompanied by a shift in provider from the public sector to the private, for-profit corporation (Kiesler, 1991). However, more recent trends (the introduction of managed care with stringent medical necessity criteria, the increased recognition and expansion in availability of community- and home-based alternatives, and changes in insurance benefits) have slowed the utilization of inpatient care dramatically during the early 1990s.

Psychiatric hospitalization for children and adolescents includes a variety of services. Short-term, crisis intervention stays are for youths exhibiting symptoms that place themselves in immediate danger. Intermediate-term facilities provide inpatient services for those children and adolescents unable to return home or to less restrictive care following a brief hospitalization. Psychiatric hospitalization for children and adolescents provides 2 unique advantages for staff and providers, at least, over alternative modalities: (1) a consistent, therapeutic milieu 24 hours a day and (2) the opportunity to provide a multimodal treatment approach under a single, coordinated theoretical orientation and within a relatively closed system (Petti, 1980).

Traditionally, therapeutic services delivered in inpatient psychiatric units included milieu therapies, behavior therapies, individual and group psychotherapies, psychopharmacology, parental involvement, and education provided by a multidisciplinary team of psychiatrists, pediatricians, psychologists, social workers, nurses, occupational and recreational therapists, and special educators.

The basic premise of psychiatric hospital care for children and adolescents is the requirement for a certain level of restrictiveness in order to provide safety and security for the patient. Psychiatric inpatient units differ, however, on the level of restrictiveness offered. Factors that indicate the level of restrictiveness on a unit are security of the facility (locked or unlocked); use of seclusion and restraints; restriction of access to parents, family members, and peers; and ability to leave the unit for visits to home and community. The level of restrictiveness maintained often is based on philosophy, theoretical orientation of the unit, or staff training and comfort levels. Medico-legal issues also are considered. Many times these variables are paramount, with patient therapeutic needs left out of the equation.

The level of restrictiveness of many inpatient units may be an indication of the type of patients treated. The most common diagnostic group found in child psychiatric inpatient units is behavior or conduct disorders (Kiesler, 1991; Pfeiffer, 1989; Wizner, 1991a). In fact, the percentage of adolescents admitted to inpatient care within this diagnostic group ranges from 30 to 70%, although there are no systematic outcome studies or research-based admission criteria (Lock & Strauss, 1994). Additionally, children most likely hospitalized for the treatment of psychiatric disorders are depressed, poor, male, and black (Kiesler, 1991). These cases are remarkably similar to juvenile status offenders, many of whom were treated in the juvenile justice system prior to the 1960s (Weithorn, 1988).

Rapid growth in inpatient psychiatric hospitalization would be justified if accompanied by empirical evidence of clinical effectiveness. However, the scientific community has not been able to provide such empirical justification. Pfeiffer (1989) reviewed 32 studies of outcome and follow-up of children and adolescents treated in psychiatric inpatient units between 1975 and 1987. Although many of these studies reported generally positive outcomes, conceptual and methodological problems rendered their conclusions difficult to accept.

"In many instances, hospital care itself provides little therapeutic intervention; however, it removes the child from the community, reducing stress on parents, schools, etc., and provides chemical and physical restraints for the child's difficult behavior" (Berlin, 1978, p. 1044). Problems with hospital care for children and adolescents

BOX 6.2

Bright Spots:

The Day Hospital–Inn Model

The day hospital–inn model is especially appropriate for dealing with the mental health needs of seriously disturbed adolescents. A day hospital program in conjunction with residential facilities allows for the provision of therapeutic services and rehabilitation. For adolescents who require more structure than can be provided by outpatient services yet who do not require the restrictiveness of inpatient services; the combination of clinical services and residential placement adds versatility. "Patients can be transferred between the inpatient unit and the day hospital as necessary, and they can move from sleeping at the inn to sleeping at home as their particular situations dictate" (Dickey, Berren, Santiago, & Breslau, 1990, p. 420).

(noted in 1969 by the Joint Commission on the Mental Health of Children and again in 1979 by the Children's Defense Fund [Wizner, 1991a]) include shortages of medical and professional staff, limited resources for educational and recreational activities, and inadequate facilities.

The majority opinion among policy makers is that further decreases in psychiatric hospitalization of children and adolescents are necessary (Eamon, 1994; Kiesler, 1991; Weithorn, 1988). Along with these decreases is a more subtle mandate for modifications in the type of care delivered. Current medical necessity criteria for admission and continued stays in inpatient care favor the use of this level of care for crisis intervention and severely limit the ability to begin or carry out active treatment in this setting. Inpatient units now have to respond by designing treatment settings, policies and procedures, and staffing patterns that are responsive to the delivery of care to a more acutely disturbed population for brief, often 2- to 3-day, stays.

Residential Treatment Centers: Residential treatment centers represent an important component of institutional care for children and adolescents in the United States. In 1988, 440 such centers reported to the National Institute of Mental Health (Sunshine, Witkin, Atay, & Mandersheid, 1991). Patient characteristics reported indicate that the majority (94%) of those treated in residential treatment centers were children and adolescents (under 18 years of age), 70% were male, and approximately 62% were white. Over half of

the patients treated were diagnosed with a mental disorder as their primary disability. In 1988, 70% of all patients receiving residential treatment care from any mental health organization were children and youths.

Services provided in hospital and residential settings for children and adolescents often are similar (Harper & Geraty, 1985; Lewis & Summerville, 1991; Marsden, McDermott, & Miner, 1970; Woolston, 1991). Since the length of stay for children and adolescents in residential settings is prolonged and the frequency of severe learning disabilities is high within this population, the provision of quality special educational services takes on a remarkable significance.

The results of treatment within residential settings are not well researched, although some studies and some clinicians report improvement in general functioning and in symptom reduction. However, the improvements noted within the residential treatment setting often were temporary and did not generalize to improved functioning outside the therapeutic milieu (Lewis & Summerville, 1991).

Correctional Facilities: Finally, children and adolescents also are detained in residential facilities for correctional purposes. The standard for detention is typically a fluctuating, sometimes uneven balance between protecting the needs of the community and serving the best interests of the child. However, the legal standards of conduct upheld by the Juvenile Justice System include behaviors that would not be considered crimes if committed by adults and reflect mainly developmental and moral considerations. Proscribed behaviors include truancy, sexual promiscuity, running away, and disobedience toward parents. Furthermore, placement decisions often are based on the availability of a particular slot rather than on the needs of the child and family.

Statistics from the U.S. Department of Justice indicate that approximately 65,000 adolescents resided in correctional facilities in 1991. This population consisted of mostly males (82%) between the ages of 14 and 17 years (79%). Minorities represent a significant proportion of those confined (63%). Some disturbing trends are evident in recent statistics suggesting that more juveniles are being confined for crimes against persons and for drug-related offenses (Parent et al., 1994).

Four approaches to handling juvenile delinquents exist: punishment, incapacitation, rehabilitation, and reintegration (Hobbs, 1975). Rehabilitation programs advocate a treatment approach

BOX 6.3

Bright Spots:

Providing Mental Health Services

to Adjudicated Youth

In Michigan, adolescents residing in the two state training schools receive a variety of services provided by the Hawthorn Center Clinic Adjudicated Youth, sponsored and coordinated by the Michigan Department of Mental Health. Provision of these services represents a cooperative effort between the Department of Social Services, who maintains jurisdiction over the training schools, and the Department of Mental Health. Staff from the Hawthorn Center serve both as consultants to the two schools, as well as provide direct clinical services. Direct mental health services rendered include psychoeducational groups for specialty groups, such as victims or perpetrators of sexual abuse; assessment, diagnosis, and treatment of psychiatric disorders; neuropsychological testing and vocational counseling; transition and aftercare services. ("A Mental Health Program," 1990)

for the offender, and the reintegration model adds an emphasis on returning the offender to an environment that has been altered to be more conducive to successful functioning outside of the justice system.

Historically, the placement of juveniles in correctional facilities has been problematic. Correctional placements and training schools, in reality, have focused on punishment and incapacitation. They are typically crowded, inadequate, inaccessible, and underfunded. "In the absence of specialized personal care and treatment, an atmosphere of hostility, insensitivity, and futility often permeates days marked by idle time, needless regimentation and impersonality, and continual degradation" (Hobbs, 1975, p. 154). Substantial and widespread problems in juvenile detention facilities include crowded living conditions, inadequate health care, problems with escapes and injuries, and suicidal behavior. "On an annualized basis, more than 11,000 juveniles engage in more than 17,000 incidents of suicidal behavior in juvenile facilities" (Parent et al., 1994, p. 10).

Research has not demonstrated the effectiveness of incarceration for ameliorating juvenile delinquency, either in reducing recidivism or lessening symptoms (Lewis, Yeager, Lovely, Stein, & Cobham-Portorreal, 1994; Wizner, 1991b). A variety of community options seems better suited for

serving the needs of children and adolescents in need of corrections. These programs include halfway houses, community day treatment programs, probationary supervision programs, and the like. The Willie M. Program in North Carolina provides an excellent model for treating adjudicated youth in the least restrictive environment (Keith, 1988).

Children's Rights

The issue of institutional care for children and adolescents is complicated by the dependent status of minors and the lack of legal protection afforded them. Many times decisions about child placements are based on social policy, theoretical considerations, and economics, not on the best interests of the child. Legal protection for minors in placement decisions is minimal (Wizner, 1991a). For instance, in many states the decision to place a child in an inpatient treatment facility is left strictly to the parents and the admitting physician. Not taken into account are the parent-child conflicts of interest or the admitting physician's possible conflicts of interest, and the minor is left with little recourse once the doors lock behind him or her. Without legal protection, children can do little to protect themselves from the negative effects of institutionalization.

Thus in protecting the rights of children and adolescents, issues of stigma, expectancy effect, and self-fulfilling prophecy need to be considered. What are the messages delivered to our children and adolescents in the various forms of institutional care that they receive? American society places a great deal of emphasis on normalcy—with stigma attached to dependent status and to physical and mental illness. Children and adolescents raised in residential, institutional settings grow up with the message that they are unwanted, expensive to society, and not worth much. Children and adolescents requiring psychiatric institutionalization must deal with messages from peers, family, teachers, and the medical profession regarding their lack of emotional stability.

Another significant concern related to out-of-home placements for children and adolescents is the tendency for parents and children to become dependent on the institution. "If the environment of the institution is particularly structured, sheltered, or regimented, then adjustment to this environment can result in a loss of skills or a reluctance to cope with the out-of-institution environment" (Hobbs, 1975, p. 135). Because many residential placements function simply as replacements for the family without emphasizing changing the family environment or the community supports available, the family and the children quickly become accustomed to being taken care of, acting functional only when cared for, and start to rely on the institution. This problem is labeled by various names—"hospital-dependent" or the "adoption process"—and has serious ramifications for the entire provider system.

Public Policy

Public policy plays a major role in determining the types of institutional care available to children and adolescents, the amount of funding allocated to specific programs, and "admission criteria" necessary for entry into the out-of-home service delivery system. Specific policy issues have been raised, of necessity, throughout this chapter.

One of the most important policy issues is the arbitrary divisions made between welfare, education, health juvenile justice, and mental health. Consequential concerns are raised by the lack of coordination (especially in funding) between the federal services (Inouye, 1988). Parents, children, and professionals have difficulty navigating all of the different systems in order to develop treatment plans that satisfy the needs of the child. This problem is magnified by the requirement in many states that custody of a minor child with serious emotional disturbances be surrendered in order to receive funding for intensive services (Cohen, Harris, Gottlieb, & Best, 1991).

Historical overviews of institutional care for children and adolescents track the utilization of the variety of institutional settings. Large fluctuations in admission rates can be traced to correspond to shifts in public policy mandates. For example, deinstitutionalization policies have been adopted by each of the provider systems at various times in the past. These policy mandates have resulted in shifting of children and adolescents between the provider systems rather than absolutely decreasing the numbers of children and adolescents receiving care in institutions (Weithorn, 1988; Woolston, 1991). The cycling of admission rates among the three service providers

has been termed "transinstitutionalization" (Weithorn, 1988).

Economics

Economic considerations frequently influence the decisions made regarding institutional care provided for children and adolescents. Poverty and inability to provide financially for children is one of the main causes for the breakdown of families. Quality day care and schooling are dependent on sufficient funding. Placement decisions for dependent and ill children often are driven by financial considerations rather than the interests of the child.

The costs of institutional care for children and youths, whether it be education, dependent care, health care, or corrections programs, are staggering. For illustration, the cost of treatment in residential treatment centers rose from $978 million in 1986 to $1.305 billion in 1988 (Sunshine et al., 1991), and psychiatric care for children and adolescents in general hospitals alone (at a cost of approximately $700 per day) is $1.65 billion annually (Kiesler & Simpkins, 1991). Current daily charges range from $700 to $1,500.

Inpatient psychiatric treatment of adolescents provides perhaps the most striking example of utilization driven by economic policy. The insurance industry, in addressing concerns regarding coverage for mental illness, designed policies that favor the use of in-hospital services. Thus the lucrative nature of inpatient psychiatric care for children and adolescents led to large-scale overutilization of the modality and the proliferation of for-profit, institutional programs. This traditional emphasis on costly institutionalization has been maintained at the expense of viable alternatives, such as community-based programs, family preservation programs, case management, and coordination services (Inouye, 1988). Recent changes in benefit structures limiting inpatient benefits have resulted in decreases in both admissions and length of stay (Patrick, Padgett, Burns, Schlesinger, & Cohen, 1993). Policy redesign must include safeguards designed to prevent clinical decision making from being overly influenced by marketplace considerations (Craig, 1988).

The application of clinical economics in the planning of service delivery should help alleviate some of these problems. Two methods of analysis provide indications of the value of a treatment procedure, taking into account both outcomes and costs. Cost-effectiveness analysis and cost/ benefit analysis can be used to make the important decisions regarding the alternative uses of limited resources (Eisenberg, 1989).

Concluding Remarks

This survey of institutional care for children and adolescents examined the functions for which institutions are utilized in American culture and the success of these institutions in meeting their objectives. Upon reading through this chapter, the author is struck by the fundamental problems facing institutional care for our children and adolescents: (1) the crumbling structure of the American family, ravaged by divorce and economic pressures; (2) the failure of institutional care to replace the functions of the family and meet objectives; and (3) the role of economics in institutional policy and placement decisions.

Certainly there are bright spots—quality institutions that provide child-centered treatment. However, bright spots are not enough. The fact remains that although many remedies for the problems noted were proposed in the 1960 and 1970s and practiced before the American Revolution, they have not been adopted. The use of a systems/ecological approach that favors preservation of the family and coordinated efforts among families, schools, communities, and health care providers to support community-based care is not a new idea (Bowlby, 1965; Hobbs, 1975; Goldstein et al., 1979). Ensuring that the child maintains ties to the family and community broadcasts the crucial message that children are wanted (Adams, 1991). In 1970 the Canadian Commission on Emotional and Learning Disorders in Children summarized: "Responsibility for the children in any community should rest permanently with the parents, the local school system, and the community agencies, and no aspect of that responsibility should be handed over to a residential unit or treatment center except as part of a community-based treatment plan" (cited in Hobbs, 1975, p. 139).

REFERENCES

Adams, P. L. (1991). *The impact of no policy*. Paper presented at the American Academy of Child and Adolescent Psychiatry Conference, San Francisco, CA.

Barker, R. G. (1968). Ecological psychology: Concepts and methods for studying the environment of human behavior. Stanford, CA: Stanford University Press.

Barker, R. G., & Gump, P. V. (1964). Big school, small school. Stanford, CA: Stanford University Press.

Berlin, I. N. (1978). Developmental issues in the psychiatric hospitalization of children. *American Journal of Psychiatry, 135* (9), 1044–1048.

Bowlby, J. (1965). Child care and the growth of love. Baltimore, MD: Penguin Books.

Bowlby, J. (1982). *Attachment.* New York: Basic Books.

Bowlby, J. (1988). *A secure base.* New York: Basic Books.

Bush, M. (1980). Institutions for dependent and neglected children: Therapeutic option of choice or last resort? *American Journal of Orthopsychiatry, 50* (2), 239–255.

Clarke-Stewart, K. A. (1989). Infant day care, maligned or malignant? *American Psychologist, 44* (2), 266–273.

Clarke-Stewart, K. A. (1991). Making sense of research on childcare: Consequences for children's development. *Montessori Life, 3* (4), 32–38.

Cohen, R., Harris, R., Gottlieb, S., & Best, A. M. (1991). States' use of transfer of custody as a requirement for providing services to emotionally disturbed children. *Hospital and Community Psychiatry, 42* (5), 526–530.

Craig, T. J. (1988). Economics and inpatient care. *Psychiatric Annals, 18* (2), 75–79.

Dickey, B., Berren, M., Santiago, J., & Breslau, J. A. (1990). Patterns of service use and costs in model day hospital-inn programs in Boston and Tucson. *Hospital and Community Psychiatry, 41* (4), 419–424.

Eamon, M. K. (1994). Institutionalizing children and adolescents in private psychiatric hospitals. *Social Work, 39* (5), 588–594.

Edwards, C. P., Logue, M. E., Loehr, S. R., & Roth, S. B. (1987). The effects of day care participation on parent-infant interaction at home. *American Journal of Orthopsychiatry, 57* (1), 116–119.

Egeland, B., & Hiester, M. (1995). The long-term consequences of infant day-care and mother-infant attachment. *Child Development, 66* (2), 474–485.

Eisenberg, J. M. (1989). Clinical economics, A guide to the economic analysis of clinical practices. *Journal of the American Medical Association, 262* (20), 2879–2886.

Erikson, E. H. (1963). *Childhood and society.* New York: W. W. Norton.

Fein, G. G., & Clarke-Stewart, A. (1973). *Day care in context.* New York: John Wiley & Sons.

Fine, P. (1991). *Psychiatric work with children and adolescents in foster home care: A perspective on training.* Unpublished manuscript.

Fine, P., & Carnevale, P. (1984). Network Aspects of treatment for incestuously abused children. In I. R. Stuart & J. G. Greer (Eds.), *Victims of sexual aggression: Treatment of men, women, and children* (pp. 75–90). New York: Van Nostrand Reinhold.

Freud, S. (1936). *The ego and mechanisms of defense.* New York: International Universities Press.

Fuller, R. L. (1981). Adoption, foster care, and other living arrangements. In R. C. Simons & H. Pardes (Eds.), *Understanding human behavior in health and illness,* 2nd ed. (pp. 266–271). Baltimore, MD: Williams & Wilkins.

Goldstein, J., Freud, A., & Solnit, A. J. (1979). *Beyond the best interests of the child.* New York: Free Press.

Goodlad, J. L. (1984). *A place called school.* New York: McGraw-Hill.

Greene, J. (1989, March 31). Children's hospitals. *Modern Healthcare,* 18–23.

Grigsby, R. K. (1996). Consultation with youth shelters, group homes, foster care homes, and Big Brothers/Big Sisters programs. In M. Lewis (Ed.), *Child and adolescent psychiatry: A comprehensive textbook,* 2nd ed., (pp. 909–914). Baltimore, MD: Williams & Wilkins.

Gross, B., & Gross, R. (1985). *The great school debate.* New York: Simon & Schuster.

Harper, G., & Geraty, R. (1985). Hospital and residential treatment. In A. Michels & J. Cavenor (Eds.), *Psychiatry* (Vol. 2, pp. 477–497). New York: Lippincott.

Hoagwood, K., & Rupp, A. (1994). Mental health service needs, use, and costs for children and adolescents with mental disorders and their families: Preliminary evidence. In R. W. Manderscheid & M. A. Sonnenschein (Eds.), *Mental health, United States, 1994* (pp. 52–61). Washington, DC: U.S. Department of Health and Human Services.

Hobbs, N. (1975). *The futures of children.* San Francisco: Jossey-Bass.

Inouye, D. K. (1988). Children's mental health issues. *American Psychologist, 43* (10), 813–816.

Kantrowitz, B., & Wingert, P. (1991, December 2). The best schools in the world. *Newsweek,* 51–52.

Keith, C. R. (1988). Community treatment of violent youth: Seven years of experience with a class action suit. *Journal of the American Academy of Child and Adolescent Psychiatry, 27* (5), 600–604.

Kiesler, C. A. (1991). *The psychiatric inpatient care of children: The failure of public policy.* The Julian and Jessie Harrison Distinguished Visiting Professor Lecture in Mental Health, University of Tennessee, Memphis.

Kiesler, C. A., & Simpkins, C. (1991). Changes in psychiatric inpatient treatment of children and youth in general hospitals: 1980–1985. *Hospital and Community Psychiatry, 42* (6), 601–604.

Kounin, J. S., & Gump, P. V. (1974). Signal systems and the task-related behavior of preschool children. *Journal of Educational Psychology, 66* (4), 554–562.

Lewis, M., & Summerville, J. W. (1991). Residential treatment. In M. Lewis (Ed.), *Child and adolescent psychiatry: A comprehensive textbook* (pp. 895–902). Baltimore, MD: Williams & Wilkins.

Lewis, D. O., Yeager, C. A., Lovely, R., Stein, A., & Cobham-Portorreal, C. S. (1994). A clinical follow-up of delinquent males: Ignored vulnerabilities, unmet needs, and the perpetuation of violence. *Journal of the American Academy of Child and Adolescent Psychiatry, 33* (4), 518–528.

Linney, J. A., & Seidman, E. (1989). The future of schooling. *American Psychologist, 44* (2), 336–340.

Lock, J., & Strauss, G. D. (1994). Psychiatric hospitalization of adolescents for conduct disorder. *Hospital and Community Psychiatry, 45* (9), 925–928.

Marsden, G., McDermott, J., & Miner, D. (1970). Residential treatment of children: A survey of institutional characteristics. *Journal of the American Academy of Child Psychiatry, 9,* 332–346.

Melamed, B. (1991). Putting the cart before the horse: Anxiety and coping in hospitalized children. *Science Agenda, 5* (1), 10–12.

Melton, G. (1996). The child's right to a family environment. *American Psychologist, 51* (12), 1234–1238.

A mental health program for juvenile offenders in state training schools. (1990). *Hospital and Community Psychiatry, 41* (10), 1127–1128.

Mrazek, D. A. (1996). Chronic pediatric illness and multiple hospitalizations. In M. Lewis (Ed.), *Child and adolescent psychiatry: A comprehensive textbook,* 2nd ed., (pp. 1058–1066). Baltimore, MD: Williams & Wilkins.

National Commission on Children. (1991). *Beyond rhetoric: A new American agenda for children and families.* Executive Summary. Washington, DC, Government Printing Office.

Parent, D. G., Leiter, V., Kennedy, S., Livens, L., Wentworth, D., & Wilcox, S. (1994). Conditions of confinement: Juvenile detention and corrections facilities. Washington, D.C. U.S. Department of Justice.

Patrick, C., Padgett, D. K., Burns, B. J., Schlesinger, H. J., & Cohen, J. (1993). Use of inpatient services by a national population: Do benefits make a difference? *Journal of the American Academy of Child and Adolescent Psychiatry, 32* (1), 144–152.

Peters, T., & Austin, N. (1985). *A passion for excellence.* New York: Random House.

Petti, T. A. (1980). Residential and inpatient treatment. In G. P. Sholevar, R. M. Benson, & B. J. Blinder (Eds.), *Emotional disorders in children and adolescents* (pp. 209–228). New York: Spectrum Publications.

Pfeiffer, S. I. (1989). Follow-up of children and adolescents treated in psychiatric facilities: A methodology review. *The Psychiatric Hospital, 20* (1), 15–20.

Piaget, J. (1962). *Play, dreams, and imitation in childhood.* New York: W. W. Norton.

Posner, J. K., & Vandell, D. L. (1994). Low-income children's after-school care: Are there beneficial effects of after-school programs? *Child Development, 65* (2), 440–456.

Reiss, D. (1989). The represented and practicing family: Contrasting visions of family continuity. In A. J. Sameroff & R. N. Emde (Eds.), *Relationship disturbances in early childhood* (pp. 191–220). New York: Basic Books.

Sack, W. H., & Woodcock, H. M. (1984). Child psychiatry consultation in a pediatric ward. In N. R. Bernstein & J. N. Sussex (Eds.), *Handbook of psychiatric consultation with children and youth.* New York: Spectrum Publications.

Sholevar, G. P. (1980). Families of institutionalized children. In G. P. Sholevar, R. M. Benson, & B. J. Blinder (Eds.), *Emotional disorders in children and adolescents* (pp. 181–190). New York: Spectrum Publications.

Stern, D. (1985). *The interpersonal world of the infant: A view from psychoanalysis and developmental psychology.* New York: Basic Books.

Sunshine, J. H., Witkin, M. J., Atay, J. E., & Mandersheid, R. W. (1991). *Residential treatment centers and other organized mental health care for children and youth: United States, 1988.* National Institute of Mental Health Statistical Note No. 198. Dept. of Health and Human Services Public Health Service, Alcohol, Drug Abuse, and Mental Health Administration.

Taylor, J. L. (1980). Community-based group homes. In G. P. Sholevar, R. M. Benson, & B. J. Blinder (Eds.), *Emotional disorders in children and adolescents medical and psychological approaches to treatment* (pp. 259–268). Jamaica, NY: Spectrum Publications.

Weithorn, L. (1988). Mental hospitalization of troublesome youth: An analysis of skyrocketing admission rates. *Stanford Law Review, 40* (3), 773–838.

Wizner, S. (1991a). Legal considerations in the psychiatric hospitalization of children and adolescents. In M. Lewis (Ed.), *Child and adolescent psychiatry: A comprehensive textbook* (pp. 1118–1123). Baltimore, MD: Williams & Wilkins.

Wizner, S. (1991b). The mental health professional in the juvenile justice system. In M. Lewis (Ed.), *Child and adolescent psychiatry: A comprehensive textbook* (pp. 1123–1126). Baltimore, MD: Williams & Wilkins.

Wolin, S. J., & Bennett, L. A. (1984). Family rituals. *Family Process, 23,* 401–420.

Woolston, J. L. (1991). Psychiatric inpatient services for children. In M. Lewis (Ed.), *Child and adolescent psychiatry: A comprehensive textbook* (pp. 890–894). Baltimore, MD: Williams & Wilkins.

Zigler, E. F., & Finn-Stevenson, M. (1996). National policies for children, adolescents, and families. In M. Lewis (Ed.), *Child and adolescent psychiatry: A comprehensive textbook,* 2nd ed. (pp. 1186–1195). Baltimore, MD: Williams & Wilkins.

PART IV
The Conduct-Disordered Delinquent and Society
Charles Keith

Both primitive and industrialized societies control violence and unruliness in youths and young adults through various combinations of religious, punitive, and educative efforts. Except during periods of generalized societal breakdown, societies are by and large successful at containing delinquent, rule-breaking behavior within tolerable limits. Upsurges of violence result in societal backlash and intensified attempts at resuming social control.

For example, there is evidence that youthful violence and drunkenness were rampant in the United States in the 1830s and 1840s; these lawless behaviors spawned temperance societies and religious zealousness dedicated to controlling them. Although epidemiological data are lacking, anecdotal evidence suggests that this violence leveled off and stabilized by the late 1800s (Wilson, 1983) in spite of the upsurge of immigration and the upheavals of industrialization and urbanization.

Increasing sensitivity to the needs of youths and continuing concern with delinquency were an important feature of the social revolution of the 1890s and early 1900s in the United States. Child labor laws were enacted. Tax-supported public education was expanded. Juvenile courts were established, and the first scientific psychological journal devoted to adolescents was inaugurated.

In the early 1900s feminist reformers Jane Addams, Julia Lathrop, and Elizabeth Drummer approached neurologist William Healy, M.D., with the request that he establish a research center devoted to the prevention of delinquency. The Juvenile Psychopathic Institute was born, as was modern child psychiatry. Healy's treatise, *The Individual Delinquent* (1915) presented in-depth case studies of families and the social milieus of delinquents that have a distinctly modern ring. His treatment recommendations may sound naive by today's standards, as they involve attempts at correcting the ills in the youths' social milieus along with a heavy dose of moralizing. However, when we think of the admonitions a modern judge might enunciate while ordering a youth to undergo mental health interventions, parole, or incarceration, then we can appreciate that treatment views have not changed that much in more than 75 years. The hope and excitement engendered by Healy's findings led to the founding of child guidance clinics in the 1920s; these clinics were chartered with a clear mandate to prevent delinquency utilizing the scientific findings of the day.

What has changed since the 1920s? Clearly, we have a much more sophisticated knowledge of the epidemiology of violence and delinquency in youths and increased appreciation of the psychodynamic and familial interactions that are such powerful determinants of delinquency. There is a beginning appreciation of the genetic and biological correlates of violence in youths. The challenge for the clinician and researcher is to place these emerging findings in the context of society's multifaceted efforts to contain and modify antisocial behavior and to maintain the equilibrium between rule-abiding and rule-breaking forces so crucial to societal stability. The central thesis of this chapter is that our stable society has been, and is, successful at maintaining a workable equilibrium between law-breaking and law-abiding tendencies within our youths. This perhaps controversial thesis is backed up by the fact that there is no hard scientific evidence that rule-breaking and lawlessness among youths have increased significantly over the past 30 years. Wilson (1983) believes there was probably an actual increase in delinquency and crime rates in the 1960s and early 1970s in the United States. These rates appear to be stabilizing again. This may be hard to believe when we are bombarded with accounts of urban drug warfare and what appear to be annual increases in crime rates announced by law agencies and the media.

Yet, the media now report that there are decreases in violent youthful crime in the United States in the mid 1990s. It should be noted that the overall murder rate in the U.S. was 9.4/ 100,000 population in 1971 & 8.9/100,000 population in 1994. Murder is the most accurate measure of severe violence as it is least affected by changes in laws and community legal standards. Have murders committed by youth under 18 also declined? In 1993, there were 2,930 murders committed by youth under 18. In 1994 this number declined to 2,838.

Violence rates in youths under 18 have fallen less rapidly during the recent overall decline in violence because of the vulnerability of lower SES African-American males. For instance, in 1994, white males under 18 committed 1,194 murders where as African-American males committed 1,842. Adjusting for population, African-American youths are seven times more likely to commit murder than their white counterparts. (U.S. Department of Justice, Federal Bureau of Investigation. Crime in the United States 1994 in Washington D.C., USG P.G. 1995 p 226). This striking disparity is calling forth community action as epitomized by the Million Man March in Washington DC (1996) and many local action groups to "save our youth." (We should remind ourselves that 99.9+% of African-American males do not commit murder.)

Victimization rates and self-reports of criminal activities in youth have declined since the 1980s (Source Book of Criminal Justice Statistics, Hindelang Criminal Justice Research Center, Albany N.Y. 1996). Thus there is hard evidence that our society is containing violence in its youth and young adults.

The overall historical perspective is that our society is maintaining a viable, workable equilibrium between violence and law-breaking and law-abiding behavior of its youths. This positive perspective runs counter to commonly held views concerning delinquency, such as "nothing works" or "we are losing control of our youths."

Definitional Issues

Before describing our current understanding of "delinquents" and their relationship with society,

it is important to address some oft-confused terminology. The terms "delinquent" and the diagnosis of "conduct disorder" from the third edition of the *Diagnostic and Statistical Manual of Mental Disorders (DSM-III)* often are used synonymously and interchangeably. However, it is important to keep in mind that the term "delinquent" is primarily a legal concept designating a youth brought before a court and convicted of a crime. Ninety percent of these youths are charged with nonpersonally violent crimes; the majority will not be charged again with a crime. An unknown percentage will continue delinquent behavior, since 90% of crimes go undetected. A vast number of youths move through our court system and are given the label "delinquent." By the age of 20, over 25% of all male youths have a nontraffic–related court record in the United States. Several industrialized Western nations have similar percentages of youths involved with the courts. Many of these youths do not have a psychiatric disturbance. A youth can become legally delinquent through a piece of momentary bad luck, by not having the financial means to hire good legal representation, or by having impulsively committed a crime while angry or intoxicated. Out of this large group of legally defined delinquents, only about 20% will become recidivistic, more violence-prone offenders (Wolfgang, 1978).

The term "conduct disorder" as defined by *DSM-III-R* attempts to describe patterns of disruptive behaviors ranging from mild to more severe and violent that persist over time. Studies that involve incarcerated delinquents and/or recidivistic chronic offenders have demonstrated a virtual 100% overlap between the legal concept of delinquency and the diagnosis of severe conduct disorder (Meyers & Kemph, 1990). Diagnosis of mild conduct disorder involving lying, running away, and truancy overlaps with the erstwhile legal category of "status offender." The term "status offender" has designated youths who were disobedient and could not be maintained in the family or in schools but who had not committed a legal crime. Our legal system has undergone a major shift in recent years by discarding the "status offender" category due to court rulings declaring that it is unconstitutional to place youths under legal restrictions or detention unless they have broken a law.

A Composite Portrait of the Conduct-disordered Delinquent

Recent reviews (Keith, 1987; Lewis, 1991a,b) have detailed current neuropsychiatric findings concerning the conduct-disordered delinquent. Rather than repeat these details, I will present the composite picture that has emerged over recent decades. This portrait of the delinquent has considerable consistency regardless of the investigators' points of view.

The modal conduct-disordered delinquent is a male (85 to 90%) in chronological middle adolescence. Disadvantaged, minority youths are overrepresented in this population, often due to inadequate legal representation, lack of resources for placement in the mental health system, and the cumulative risk factors of poverty and racism. Those who have had behavioral problems since early childhood with dysfunctional parents who punish inconsistently or are abusive (Lahey et al., 1988; Pfeffer, Zuckerman, Plutchik, & Mizruchi, 1987) tend to become the more severe, violent adolescent delinquent. (See Widom 1989a, b for a cautionary note concerning violence-begets-violence theories.) If attention deficit disorder, lower IQ, true learning disability, and school truancy are present, the prognosis becomes poorer. Substance abuse is frequently comorbid and quite interactive with delinquent behavioral patterns in approximately 50% of adolescent conduct-disordered youths. These early-onset delinquents are more likely to engage in violent crimes than adolescent-onset delinquents and are more likely to persist in violent criminal activity uninterruptedly into adulthood. They also may have a neurobiological vulnerability, such as hypo- or hyperarousal of the central and autonomic nervous system, as evidenced by altered evoked cortical and galvanic skin responses or deficient behavioral inhibition systems (Moffitt & Mednick, 1988; Raine & Venables, 1988; Raine, Venables, & Williams, 1990; Walker et al., 1991).

Lowered levels of dopamine-beta-hydroxylase often are found in conduct-disordered youths as compared with non–conduct-disordered controls (Bowden, Deutsch, & Swanson, 1988; Rogeness et al., 1988). An increasingly robust finding in recent years has been lowered levels of the serotonin metabolite 5-hydroxyindoleacetic acid (5-HIAA) in the spinal fluid of violent, suicidal adolescents and adults. A recent study demonstrated lowered levels of spinal fluid 5-HIAA in behavior-disordered children and early adolescents who had not committed the violent acts reported in the studies of later adolescents and young adults just mentioned (Kruesi et al., 1990).

Whether these neurobiological and neurotransmitter vulnerabilities are genetic trait markers, a result of early environmental influences, or a combination thereof is still not known.

In contrast to early-onset conduct-disordered youths, pubertal-onset delinquents tend to have less dysfunctional parents and less history of physical and sexual abuse and academic problems; they have a better prognosis, since a majority will spontaneously reduce and/or cease criminality as they progress through adolescence into young adulthood.

The emergence of other syndromes, such as schizophrenia, paranoia, major depression, attention deficit disorder, and various seizure disorders, either in childhood or adolescence, usually fuels and exacerbates disordered impulsive behavior (Biederman, Newcorn, & Sprich, 1991; Faraone, Biederman, Keenan, & Tsuang, 1991; Mannuzza et al., 1991; Moffitt, 1990). The more repetitive and violent the delinquent acts, the more likely there will be comorbidity.

To flesh out the picture, I will now redescribe this modal delinquent from a developmental point of view.

The early-onset delinquent is born into a dysfunctional parental caregiving system, often consisting of a poverty-stressed single mother who has been verbally and physically abused by the father, who often does not assume a significant role as a caregiver. Abuse can begin before birth in the scenario of fetal abuse via maternal substance abuse or physical violence against the uterus containing the fetus (Condon, 1986; McFarlane, 1989). Thus, the mother of the delinquent-to-be often is ill equipped to provide a satisfactory holding environment for the infant. Excessive states of infantile unpleasure (Parens, 1979) lead to early tantrums or actual attempts to strike the mother by 12 months of age (Fraiberg, 1982; Galenson, 1983).

By the second year of life, when internalization of behavioral controls becomes a crucial developmental task, future problems are settling into place. Running, darting, biting, and continuing tantrums repeatedly interfere with focused attention, beginning sublimation, and the early use of words, which in normal development replaces impulsive behavior to communicate needs. Thus, the future delinquent's lower verbal IQ and attentional difficulties may well be based in these first and second years of life in addition to whatever central nervous system vulnerability brought into the world.

By age 3, when children are learning to mold to group demands in day center, nursery, or family care, these predelinquent children already are being singled out by caregivers as "hard to manage" and having difficulty abiding by rules (Campbell, 1989). The solidification of identifications with prosocial authority figures and respect for female caregivers, important tasks of the oedipal phase, are damaged as these children continue to struggle with rather than submit to and identify with authority. Thus, by age 5, these predelinquent children are ill equipped to enter the formal classroom, where sufficient behavioral controls and sublimation abilities are mandatory.

It is now known that persistent behavioral problems by age 6 combined with inconsistent, dysfunctional parental care are highly predictive of conduct disturbance and sociopathy at age 20 (Farrington, 1989; Kelso & Stewart, 1986; Loeber, 1987, 1991; Offord & Fleming, 1991; Capaldi, & Bank,; Tolan, 1987). As these children enter latency, they are increasingly out of step with normal elementary school-age children, who have pleasure in abiding by the rules of parents and educational authorities. The usual sublimations of latency—collecting, hobbies, and passionate interests such as learning about baseball players or dinosaurs—often are absent in predelinquent children. Participation in latency-age, competitive peer activities is problematic as hostile, aggressive outbursts override the rules of the games and peer pressures. Sociogram studies regularly show that the elementary school-age predelinquent is unpopular with and rejected by peers (Coie et al., 1989). Referral to the mental health system increases dramatically through the elementary school years as does placement of these children in special educational programs, such as self-contained classrooms. Some predelinquent children, through further development and interventions by parents, schools, and the mental health system, learn to control their behavior and move out of the ranks of the predelinquent. Other children enter this predelinquent group, although the yearly incidence is unknown. It is now known from several epidemiological studies that at any one point in time, the prevalence of conduct disorder in elementary school-age children is in the 5 to 7% range (Costello, 1989). There remains a core group of children whose individual misbehaviors and problematic parent-child interactional patterns remain essentially unchanged through the latency years. These children and parents often become locked into downward-spiraling, negative interactional behaviors with the various change forces e.g. schools & social services in our society and thereby have less and less chance to move out of the predelinquent category.

By the late latency years, ages 10 to 12, the courts become increasingly involved and are asked to take over parental roles through limit setting and ordering the provision of educational and psychiatric services. Substance abuse, including early smoking, increases at ages 10 to 12, as do school truancy and mounting academic difficulties, such as repeated grade failures (Larson, 1988; Moffitt & Silva, 1988; Zagar, Arbit, Hughes, Busell, & Bush, 1989). Further exclusion from normal peer group activities increases the conduct-disordered youth's sense of alienation from society and its pressures toward prosocial activities. More ominous behaviors now appear with increased frequency—stealing from family members, shoplifting, fire-setting (Gaynor, 1991), cruelty to animals, and violent physical and sexual attacks on others. This group of persistently conduct-disordered youths are in grave danger as they enter puberty, with its upsurge of aggressive and sexual drives (Kavoussi, Kaplan, & Becker, 1988) and demands for separation and independence from parental authorities. Substance abuse, particularly alcohol usage, by severely conduct-disordered adolescents reaches high proportions (Collins, 1989; Goldstein, 1989; Greenbaum, Prange, Friedman, & Silver, 1991; Irwin, Schuckit, & Smith, 1990; Milin, Halikas, Meller, & Morse, 1991). It has been estimated that half or more of the destructive, interpersonally violent crimes committed by delinquent adolescents occur when they are intoxicated (Bush, Zagar, Hughes, Arbit, & Russell, 1990).

Whatever controls the parent had are shaken by the conduct-disordered early adolescent's increased physical size and freedom to roam the streets. Courts, educators, and clinicians are at this point searching and groping for resources and facilities to provide controls and safety for these youths and the community. The impulsive and annoying behaviors of the prepubertal years become fraught with real danger and the resulting imposition of serious societal sanctions. The fisticuffs of an 8-year-old can now become a serious physical assault inflicting injury or death and leading to lifelong legal sanctions that can further damage or virtually end the delinquent adolescent's chance eventually to assume prosocial identity roles of adulthood. Hence society's efforts to control and modify delinquent behavior are directed not only to changing current psychopathology but also to preventing future developmental damage.

Those whose onset of delinquency occurs in early adolescence usually have fewer risk factors in their background and, hence, have mastered the prepubertal developmental stages with better sublimation skills and academic strengths, more normal peer relationships, and more evidence of functional, internalized moral values proscribing destructive acting out. Hence, these late-onset delinquent youths tend to do better in treatment programs, respond more often to court sanctions with behavioral improvement, and have a better chance to move into an adulthood free of antisocial behavior.

Masculine pronouns have been used in this chapter since conduct-disordered delinquency is primarily a male issue and the vast majority of research and clinical literature describes male subjects. Females are predisposed to adolescent aggressive, law-breaking behavior by the same parental and developmental vulnerabilities as described for males (Benedek, 1979; Erskine, 1984). Offord, Allen, and Abrams (1978) have suggested that female delinquents may be more vulnerable than males to parental relationship disruptions.

Girls' conduct disorder symptoms tend to cluster in the mild to moderate range of the *DSM-III-R* criteria: stealing, truancy, lying, and the like. Lewis, et al. (1991) found in a follow-up study of delinquent girls that they were less prone than their male counterparts to violent behaviors in adulthood. However, they were at high risk for becoming victims of violence and had severe difficulty caring for their infants.

The search for biologic vulnerabilities in female delinquency has centered around the study of crime rates during phases of the menstrual cycle. Crime rates may be somewhat elevated during the premenstrual and menstrual phases (Widom & Ames, 1988), but studies on the topic have had methodological problems and have provided few, if any, leads for more specific research concerning individual vulnerability. Aggressive, violent youth have been divided into two broad somewhat overlapping groups i.e., the first is the affective, impulsive type characterized by youth who can become easily aroused and agitated by internal and exter-

nal stimuli resulting in emotional aggressive outbursts towards authorities, peers and family. The second general group includes the more controlled, predatory youth who tend to commit instrumental acts of violence e.g., planned robberies involving stranger victims. The majority of violent youth in outpatient and inpatient mental health services are of the former type and hence more amenable to the supportive, psychotherapeutic and psychopharmacologic interventions described in this chapter. The controlled predatory youth appears more responsive to behavioral programs including the punishment brought about by incarceration. (Vitiellio, B. & Staff, D. M. 1997)

The Interaction of Society with Delinquents

A core of primarily early-onset delinquents with their multiple risk factors and frequent negative interactions with society remain relatively unaffected by society's usual modes of changing delinquents into law-abiding youth. Fortunately, these are the minority of delinquents. The majority have fewer risk factors and a tendency to late-onset conduct disorder, which render them more susceptible to influence by prosocial societal interventions. Hence these later delinquents frequently move out of the conduct-disordered delinquency role. Society's prosocial change forces are legion; often they either go unnoticed or are sometimes viewed as ineffective or trivial by clinicians and social critics. However, just as cumulative risk factors increase entrance into delinquency, so do cumulative prosocial forces result in a constant egress from delinquency, thus maintaining the vital equilibrium between law-breaking and law-abiding necessary for social stability (Farrington, Gallagher, Morley, St. Ledger, & West, 1988).

Many social egress forces are continually pushing and pulling the delinquent and his family into more normative, prosocial behaviors. The following five will be discussed below.

a) schools
b) the legal system
c) decrease in substance use and abuse
d) early out-of-home care
e) prevention programs

f) care systems for chronically mentally ill aggressive youth
g) other social forces

SCHOOLS

We have already mentioned the obvious pressures toward conformity applied continuously by schools and adult authority figures, normal peer-group pressures in school settings and in the background, the community support and moral values underpinning the school structure.

LEGAL SYSTEM

Even more obvious are the pressures, sanctions, and punishments promulgated by the legal system. Many youths cease delinquent behavior out of fear of legal punishment. The large majority of delinquent youths appear in court only once. Wilson (1983) points out that laws against crime provide additional insurance for law-abiding youths so that they do not slip up and become legal delinquents. Laws also stop some delinquency-prone youths because of the fear of punishment—laws make them think twice before engaging in delinquency, thus reducing either the violence or rate of any consequence criminality. And finally, the same laws may have little or no impact on a core of "hardened" delinquents. Thus, the ultimate purpose of laws as well as prevention and treatment efforts is not to end delinquent criminal acts but to contain the incidence and prevalence within tolerable societal bounds.

Somewhat less obvious are broad social forces that impact on the risk factors leading to delinquency. Only a few will be described; the list could be extended into dozens or more.

There has been a general decrease in substance abuse among youth during the late 1980s and early 1990s, due in part to our society's negative reaction to illegal drugs and alcohol. There has been an explosion of drug prevention programs, liquor and cigarette advertising has been curtailed, adolescent Alcoholic Anonymous groups are increasingly available, the legal drinking age has been raised, legal sanctions against drunken driving have increased, and so on. Any one of these developments may seem only distantly related to delinquency, and it is difficult if not impossible to demonstrate conclusively that any one of these developments has substantially decreased substance abuse. However, all of these developments are certainly important factors in the recent decrease in substance use among youths. Considering that substance abuse and intoxication are major components and "releasers" of delinquent, violent acts, then a general reduction of youthful substance abuse will most likely reduce the incidence and prevalence of delinquent acts in some youths. As noted earlier, a core of youths will remain relatively impervious to society's efforts to curb substance abuse and hence will continue to become intoxicated and violent. Some social commentators tend to look at these youths and say that substance abuse preventive efforts do not work; they overlook those youths for whom the efforts are working, since they are improving and moving out of our purview.

Our society is moving, whether we like it or not, toward nonparental and out-of-home care of children ages 6 weeks to 3 years. Sixty-seventy percent of all toddlers are now cared for during most of their waking hours by someone other than the biological parents. Tax-supported public education has extended its programs downward to ages 2 and 3 and may very well assume ultimate responsibility of our chaotic, early child-care system in the foreseeable future. If delinquent patterns are settling into place by ages 1 to 2, as proposed earlier in this chapter, there will be the opportunity for much earlier identification and intervention into predelinquent behavioral patterns than occurs presently. Balancing the potentially positive outcomes of early intervention are concerns about the developmental impact of peer aggression in day care, particularly in the large number of programs that are poorly managed (Bagley, 1989).

Skeptics state that we have tried to prevent delinquency for more than 75 years in our society and nothing works. However, closer observation shows that a systematic and intensive prevention program targeted toward demonstrable, causative factors has never been attempted. Prevention of delinquency does not mean its elimination. Rather it denotes the containment of delinquency within tolerable bounds and perhaps its reduction. For instance, if someday it could be demonstrated that the prevalence rate of conduct-disordered youths was reduced from its current 5 to 7% to 3 to 4%, this would surely be considered a major victory.

Does our society still support significant delinquency prevention programs? The answer is yes as evidenced by the recent funding by the National Institute of Mental Health of a major, multicenter study involving various treatment interventions with 6- to 7-year-old aggressive children who will be followed over 12 years to see if adolescent delinquency is reduced as compared with nonintervention control groups (Coie et al., 1991). In this study, the interventions, based on social-cognition theory, consist of parent therapy programs, intensive teacher training, a social skill training program for the children and academic tutoring. These interventions will take place over 2 years for each behaviorally disturbed child and family, then will be reintroduced as boosters during the later elementary school years. Parental cooperation and active involvement in the treatment interventions will be key components of the project. Follow-up studies in adolescence will then determine whether the interventions have been successful in reducing delinquency rates as compared with nontreatment control groups. This is the largest research program in terms of dollars ever funded by the National Institute of Mental Health, which attests to society's continuing concern with delinquency prevention.

This research project, depending as it does on parental cooperation, will necessarily be dealing with the medium to mild range of conduct disturbances rather than with more severely disturbed children who have experienced markedly inadequate or absent parenting. Although the final results may demonstrate otherwise, it can reasonably be predicted that this intensive, ongoing treatment effort will demonstrate positive results. Preliminary results indicate a significant reduction of aggressive behavior in the treatment youth as compared with the controls (Bierman, K. L., et al., 1996). A somewhat similar but smaller prospective study involving multimodal treatment of conduct-disordered, at-risk elementary school-age boys showed that adolescent delinquency was significantly reduced as compared with a minimal treatment control group (Satterfield, Satterfield, & Schell, 1987). It also may be surmised that the researchers will suggest that their treatment efforts should have started at ages 1 to 3 rather than ages 6 to 7, as was concluded from the initial Headstart experience. It would certainly be informative if piggyback research proposals could be implemented to study the treatment failures with in-depth neuropsychiatric evaluations.

Another prosocial societal force is the current movement of our society toward provision of community care for the chronically mentally ill. How is this connected with delinquency? A substantial subset of early-onset delinquents can be viewed as chronically mentally ill. In these individuals, it is abundantly clear that, by adolescence, their development has been severely damaged and in some areas is irremediable. Family and parental supports often are inadequate or never were present; thus the community was required to provide basic care. Comorbidity in this group of youths is extensive, as noted earlier. Many of these youths fulfill criteria of chronic mental illness, since they require long-term supportive community care with the clinical goal of stabilization rather than remediation and cure. Clinical experience demonstrates that when these youths can be provided sufficient, ongoing basic care, protection, and adequate treatment of their comorbid illnesses, their delinquency rates decline or can even cease. Antisocial impulsive behaviors often recur when their basic care is threatened, as when they lose a group home placement or when medication regimes break down. These issues can be illustrated through a brief description of our society's most extensive tax-supported community care program for violent, conduct-disordered youth—the Willie M. Program in North Carolina.

In 1979 a class action suit was brought against the State of North Carolina alleging that violent delinquent youths were not provided adequate mental health and educational resources. The state acquiesced to the allegations and inaugurated a comprehensive spectrum of community-based treatment services for violent youths of any age through 18 (Keith, 1988). An active oversight panel under the direction of the court has closely monitored the state's compliance over the years. Since the program's inception, over 3,000 youths have been designated class members through documented evidence of their persistent violence against people. The average age of entry is 14 to 15, although a few children enter as early as ages 3 to 6. At any one time, only 1 to 2% of the youths are in hospitals or other institutions. The philosophy of the program is to maintain Willie M. youth in the community through supportive care including intensive case manager services, apartment living arrangements, foster care, and so on. Although a parent or a legal guardian must approve of the youths' entry into the program, most youths are essentially referred by community agencies that have experienced lengthy frustrations at trying to set up treatment programs through meager, fragmented community services. Once admitted to the program, a youth is assigned a case manager whose responsibility is to guarantee that reasonable living arrangements and treatment services are arranged according to the youth's needs. If these services are not available, the class action suit specifically dictates that appropriate services must be created. A youth cannot be rejected from the program even if he breaks laws, runs away, or becomes assaultive. Parents are no longer legal guardians in approximately 40% of the Willie M. youth; in the vast majority of the remainder, the parenting, family structure is inadequate to non-existent. Functioning fathers are present in only 5 to 10% of the cases. Comorbidity is high as many of these youths suffer from organicity, severe long-standing learning problems, chronic depression, borderline syndromes, and, at times, schizophrenia. In some Willie M. programs, as many as 50% of the youths are on psychotropic medication regimens. Again and again, it is the clinical experience of those working in the program that provision of adequate care and structure for these anxious, distressed, out-of-control youths leads to a calming and significant reduction in irritability and aggressive behavior. Some youths need 2 to 3 years of care before they can become settled long enough to use and internalize the program's structure, which then results in a decrease of acting out.

The State of North Carolina spends approximately $24,000 per year for each Willie M. youth, a fact that results in a great deal of media and political criticism. Many if not most mental health professionals, including child psychiatrists, have criticized the program, particularly its philosophy of treating youths in the least restrictive environment. However, critics often forget that most of these youths are at high risk for repeated hospitalizations or institutionalization, which can quickly cost much more than $24,000 a year. Also, critics overlook the fact that the majority of these youths are chronically mentally ill and require long-term, supportive community care. (Hence, follow-up studies are by and large irrelevant since chronically mentally ill persons often deteriorate on leaving supportive community programs.) Child psychiatry as well as much of society has yet to come to grips with the fact that proper supportive care of chronically mentally ill persons in the community is expensive, although for the most part it is much more humane and less expensive than long-term institutionalization. The Willie M. Program in North Carolina is a flagship setting the standards for tax-supported care of violent and aggressive mentally ill youths.

Other social forces that reduce delinquency include religious conversions and the quasi-religious experiences of those deeply involved in Alcoholics Anonymous, which bring to an end many youths' conduct-disordered behavior. The provision and availability of employment for youths can tip the balance from stealing money to working for pay. Citizens' groups organized to patrol neighborhoods and set up programs to keep youths occupied and off the streets can have a major impact on those delinquents in the immediate geographical area. The presence of sufficient numbers of foot-patrolling police officers has long been viewed as having positive impact on a neighborhood's confidence that delinquency can be controlled and the streets made safer. The removal of temptation through adequate fencing, lighting, and locking can reduce delinquency rates.

All of the major sociological theories concerning the origins of delinquency and crime also can be cited as commonsense explanations of community and economic factors that are part of the vast web of social forces creating, fostering and controlling crime (Sutherland & Cressey, 1966).

Psychiatric Principles in the Management and Treatment of Conduct-Disordered Juvenile Delinquents

As with any other syndrome in our field, rational treatment can be based only on a properly conducted diagnostic evaluation. However, perhaps more than with any other syndrome, the diagnostic evaluation of the conduct-disordered youth always is closely intertwined with the surrounding community, which plays a primary role in supporting and sanctioning any subsequent treatment endeavors. Although differing views and conflicts inevitably arise between the clinical perspective and the courts, schools, social services, and other agencies responsible for aspects of the conduct-disordered youth's life, the clinician must maintain respect for the fundamental roles these community agencies will play in providing the necessary foundation for whatever treatment emerges from the diagnostic evaluation.

THE DIAGNOSTIC EVALUATION PROCESS

Diagnostic Interviews with the Delinquent: The conduct disorder diagnosis describes a series of externalizing behaviors only, with no descriptors concerning internal feeling states or how the patient experiences the world (Lewis, 1991a). Paradoxically, this listing of conduct-disordered behaviors is powerfully predictive of future disordered behavior. Yet at the same time, the conduct-disordered diagnosis is one of the most superficially descriptive of our *DSM* categories. Thus, the critical task of the diagnostic process with the delinquent is to "flesh out" particular behaviors and place them into context with what is going through the youth's mind—that is, identifying feeling states and thought processes that result in specific aggressive behaviors. For instance, was a physical assault the result of self-punitive, depressive thought patterns; acting on paranoid fears or hallucinatory commands; desperate attempts to get money to buy street drugs for an escalating drug dependency; an attempt to get jailed or hospitalized to escape an intolerable family milieu? This fleshing-out process is easy to push aside, since no other syndrome in our diagnostic nomenclature is so vulnerable to stereotypical labeling, for example, viewing the conduct disordered youth prior to interviewing as unmotivated, nonreflective, having no insight or capacity to change, and being essentially a "bad" youth rather than a psychiatrically ill patient. These stereotyping tendencies are accentuated by society's ever-present need to punish and the community's anger at being hurt and attacked by the youth. Our society waxes and wanes in its urge to punish delinquents. For instance, currently the pendulum is swinging toward increased punishment as more adolescents are transferred to adult courts for trial and sentencing for serious crimes (Barnum, 1987; Debate Forum, 1989).

Diagnosticians can become so focused on the rule-breaking behaviors that they overlook assessing the delinquent's personality strengths. Clinicians must try to determine in which areas in the delinquent's life guilt and more adaptive defenses provide a check on his aggressive behaviors. Can the youth interact and play consistently by rules in certain areas? Are there activities and interests arising from sublimations that remain intact in spite of aggressive outbursts in other areas of his life? What healthy relationships can the adolescent sustain and protect from his hostile urges? Assessing and documenting the strengths and capacities for alliance building is the cornerstone of the diagnostic evaluation, as the clinician builds a treatment program upon the youth's strengths, not on the acting-out behaviors.

It should be remembered that antisocial acts are sporadic, often interspersed by weeks or months of generally prosocial behavior. What forces within the youth and within his environment maintain these controls? What concatenation of events both within and outside the delinquent serve as triggers and releasers of aggressive or antisocial behaviors? Focusing on the proximal forces and events immediately preceding destructive behavior can provide a key ingredient for building a treatment program designed to prevent destructive behavior as quickly as possible.

The Diagnostic Evaluation of the Parent(s): The modal profiles of the delinquent described earlier emphasize the major role played by parental psychopathology. Here again, the danger arises of the clinician stereotypically labeling parents as inadequate rather than viewing them as concerned, conflicted persons who often are trying their best in spite of limitations from their individual backgrounds and their own personal psychopathology. Most parents of delinquent youths also are caring as best they can for their other children, most of whom are not conduct disordered. Studies have shown that children raised in large families, particularly when there are 5 or more children, are at increased risk for conduct-disordered behavior. Although economic and other factors are involved in this heightened risk, common sense suggests that parents' capacities often are stretched to the breaking point trying to supply the needs of their children. However, in the eyes of the vulnerable, conduct-disordered child, the parents often appear inadequate, ungiving, and unloving.

What conditions both within the parents and within their milieu permit more appropriate, consistent parenting with the child? Does a parent have emotional disturbances that must be treated at the same time as the youth's? If 2 functioning parents are still fulfilling parental roles with the behavior-disordered youth, then how do these parental interactions either foster or interfere with their discipline and care?

Further Assessment of Interacting Comorbid Conditions within the Delinquent Youth and the Parent(s)

Some of the following conditions are sometimes hard to elicit on initial history-taking with the parents and the delinquent youth. Often only accumulated observations and therapeutic "listening" to parents' and youths' emotional and cognitive styles can provide clues concerning affective disturbances, substance abuse and/or sexual and physical abuse, attentional problems, episodic disordered behavior, organic brain damage, test results.

AFFECTIVE DISTURBANCES

Are there mood swings? Do irritable states periodically emerge? Is there increased motoric movements or the need to be "on the run"? Occasionally, clear-cut maniclike symptoms can alternate with depression (Ney, Colbert, Newman, & Young, 1986), but more often the clinician is looking for the expression of affective pressures in motoric and behavioral patterns. Is there evidence of self-mutilation, which is common among conduct-disordered youth (Chowanec, Josephson, Coleman, & Davis, 1991)? How do the youth and parents manage anxiety? A stereotypic view exists that conduct-disturbed youth never experience inner discomfort, including anxiety. Nothing could be further from the truth. Furthermore, anxiety and/or externally perceived fears are common proximal causes of aggressive outbursts.

ABUSE

Is there direct or indirect evidence of substance abuse and/or sexual and physical abuse in the past and currently? Abuse pathologies occur more frequently with delinquency than perhaps with any other condition in childhood or adolescence.

ATTENTIONAL PROBLEMS

Are there attentional problems within the youth and/or his parents? Sometimes observers' concerns about openly delinquent, aggressive behavior divert the diagnostic focus away from subtle attentional problems that can arise either from high levels of poorly mastered anxiety and/or from neuropsychological control imbalances.

PATTERN OF DISORDERED BEHAVIOR

Is the disordered behavior episodic and hard to predict? This pattern might be suggestive of abnormal central nervous system limbic discharge activity. Are there signs and symptoms of psychological organicity—evidence of higher cortical

level dysfunction? Over the decades, investigators have agreed that conduct-disordered youth as a group have a high prevalence of organicity, which calls for thorough educational and psychological testing.

ORGANIC BRAIN DAMAGE

Is there evidence of organic brain damage as evidenced by soft and/or hard signs noted in the neurological examination, electroencephalogram abnormalities, and the like? Some investigators believe signs of organic brain damage are quite frequent within the severely disturbed delinquent population (Lewis, 1984) whereas others find only a mild increase of prevalence over nondelinquent populations (Benedek & Cornell, 1989; McManus, Brickman, Alessi, & Grapentine, 1985). Is there evidence of a schizophrenic reaction, periodic psychotic episodes, or paranoid reactions? All of these can be the proximal triggers of delinquent violence. Sensitive clinical interviewing and projective psychological testing can pick up more subtle manifestations of these conditions. It must be emphasized that these comorbid conditions must be investigated just as thoroughly within the parents and the family background as within the delinquent youth himself.

TESTING

Clinical, neuropsychological, and educational testing are vital components of the diagnostic process. Projective tests can further elucidate the perceived familial dynamics into psychic forces and attributional biases leading to aggressive behavior. They also can give important clues to testing comorbid conditions, such as depression or schizophrenic thought patterns. Neuropsychological testing can provide information concerning the visual and auditory-motor integrative problems that result in the learning disabilities so common in youths with conduct disorders. Educational testing elucidates achievement levels and learning patterns so important in planning the educational component of the ensuing treatment program.

Assessment of the Delinquent Youth's and Parents' Relationship with the Community

Any treatment program that results from the diagnostic evaluation involving a delinquent youth and his family will necessarily involve a close alliance with the community. Thus, involvement of the school and legal systems, social services, and other supportive community services is a crucial task for the diagnostician.

THE SCHOOL SYSTEM

How well a school provides an ongoing holding environment for youths with a conduct disorder often holds the key whether a treatment program will succeed or fail. Educational systems and their schools often can tolerate many kinds of childhood psychopathologies except conduct-disordered behaviors, which frequently result in ejection of the delinquent youth from the school setting. Rule-breaking behaviors and the resulting group contagion effects are usually viewed as antagonistic and destructive to the school's primary goals of group learning and enforcement of group rules.

The passage of Public Law 94-142 (1975) granted disabled youths their rights to an education. School systems, through whatever means available, are responsible for remediation of any emotional or physical disabilities that impeded the youths' classroom learning. Interestingly, the one exception granted to education was in the area of conduct disorder problems. Currently, testimony in Congress by American Psychiatric Association officials and others may bring about an emendation to PL 94-142 so that conduct disorder–type disturbances are no longer excluded from coverage. However, since the passage of the original bill, most school systems have dramatically increased their assumption of responsibility for providing school programs for children with all types of psychopathology, including conduct disturbances. In-school suspension programs and self-contained classrooms are the most common educational modalities utilized by schools to retain, cope with, and it is hoped, modify conduct-disordered delinquent behavior within the school setting. At times these programs are viewed as dumping grounds for unruly youths, where at best containment is accomplished and at worst group dynamics accelerate disordered behavior. However, many of these programs are run by sensitive educators who are providing thoughtful educational treatment for these youths and who can be crucial purveyors of valuable clinical information to the diagnostician.

THE LEGAL SYSTEM

Many delinquent youths are heading toward, on the verge of, or already in the legal system at the time of the diagnostic evaluation. Knowledge of the current legal climate surrounding the delinquent youth, specifics about the youth's antisocial behavior, and the spelling out the multiple legal options facing the court are often at the core of diagnostic and treatment planning.

SOCIAL SERVICES

A significant proportion of seriously delinquent youths are involved with social service agencies through court-ordered treatment programs involving the agency, involvement with sexual and physical abuse protection services, or because parental rights have been removed, making the community social service agency the legal guardian. Thus, a diagnostic evaluation often involves obtaining information from and gaining cooperation with agency workers. At times, social service agencies have case managers available through special programs to participate in diagnostic evaluations and the treatment programs that might ensue.

OTHER SUPPORTIVE COMMUNITY SERVICES

Families with delinquent youths often have been involved with community agencies such as Alcoholics Anonymous, shelters for abused families, and previous mental health treatment programs of various sorts. How well or how poorly the family and the delinquent have used these services provides crucial diagnostic information concerning how to set up future treatment programs.

Treatment

The following principles of treatment flow naturally from the diagnostic evaluation just outlined.

PROVISION OF BASIC CARE AND ADEQUATE EXTERNAL CONTROLS

First and foremost must be the provision of basic care and adequate external controls for the protection of the delinquent youth as well as the community (Clarke, 1985). Treatment can succeed only when community forces participate in and support the treatment program. Treatment cannot proceed when there is an aura of ongoing dangerousness or when treating personnel are fearful of criticism or liability from the court or the press. Thus, clinicians often must consider whether treatment should take place under a court order to provide the necessary external controls and community sanction. This question frequently arises when parental support and limit-setting abilities are insufficient in relation to the youth's delinquent behavior. Sometimes a youth can remain within the family setting through the use of a case manager, in-home support services, or weekend respite care. If the youth must be out of the home for a time, then resources must be available within the community mental health, legal, or social service system to provide basic care. At times, the community's ability to detain the youth occasionally for brief periods proves invaluable in managing crises and providing a cooling-off period for the youth and his caregivers. The needs of the delinquent youth and his family must be matched as much as possible with the community's ability to provide basic supportive care. Unless this basic care is mandated by law, such as in the North Carolina Willie M. Program, often community agencies have insufficient services available or are unable to integrate these services well enough with other aspects of the treatment program; the resulting frequent disruptions and breakdown of care may cause bursts of delinquent behavior and pressures for institutionalization. This fundamental aspect of the treatment program—the provision and maintenance of basic care for the seriously delinquent conduct-disordered youth when there are insufficient parental support and controls—is most difficult and frustrating for clinicians. In practical terms, it involves establishing a community team of caregivers. Any team of this type can function over time only with a respected team leader. While team leadership can be written into a court order, this is no guarantee that a leader with sufficient skills and confidence will emerge to carry out this most difficult task.

Only when these basic care issues have been addressed satisfactorily can the clinician move on to further specific treatment recommendations with a reasonable prospect for success.

PSYCHOLOGICAL THERAPIES

Parent Therapy: The clinician establishes a parental alliance while fostering the parents' capacity to observe and think about discipline and child care issues rather than acting angrily in response to their child's unruly behavior. As with all process-oriented treatment, the clinician must begin where the parents are and move forward at their pace. Often the parents have experienced years of helplessness and/or rage regarding their child or adolescent's conduct-disordered behavior. Of course, at times, this parent therapy will involve work with other than biological parents, such as foster parents or whoever in the community has assumed the primary parental role. When a social service case worker is the only person at a particular time fulfilling that role, then, of course, this modality shifts to a consultation model.

Family Therapy: If the family system is sufficiently intact, including 1 or more parents or involved caregivers, then family therapy, usually involving the presence of the delinquent youth in the sessions, is a powerful treatment modality (Curry, Weincrot, & Koehler, 1984; Wells, 1988).

In family therapy, both parental caregivers and the delinquent youth (and perhaps the siblings) can grapple with and learn about their interactive and self-defeating struggles. Increased consistency of discipline, firmer controls, and increased use of words rather than action can lead to dramatic reductions of delinquent activity. Both parent therapy and family therapy often are the primary modes of intervention with predelinquent latency-age youth when family controls are still sufficiently intact.

Individual Psychotherapy: Some workers have stated that individual psychotherapy is ineffective in the treatment of delinquent youths, citing the results of the Cambridge-Summerville Youth Study carried out during the 1930s and 1940s (Puig-Antich, 1982). However, close examination of that study reveals that regularly scheduled psychotherapy as usually practiced in offices and clinics was not carried out. The delinquent youths actually were seen once a month in supportive casework. Clinical experience indicates that many conduct-disordered youths can use a psychotherapeutic relationship productively to increase their mastery over aggressive impulses through learning to verbalize rather than act out conflicts (Keith, 1984; Marohn, 1982; Marshall, 1979). As already noted, psychotherapy can be effective only when a youth's basic care needs are attended to and there are sufficient external controls in his environment while he is undergoing psychotherapy. For instance, a tightly structured, well-supervised parole plan may be a necessary precondition before psychotherapy can be effective. Some delinquent youths with higher-level ego structures and evidence of neurotic conflicts can use insight-oriented psychotherapy. Others with less well-structured ego functioning will be able to utilize supportive, defense-building psychotherapy.

Cognitive-Behavioral Therapy: This highly structured, task-oriented psychotherapy can supply necessary psychological structure and clarity of thinking, which often are poorly developed in delinquents (Arbuthnot & Gordon, 1986). Forms of this therapy are probably the most common modalities used in inpatient and training school settings (Varley, 1984).

Group Therapy: Currently, most group therapies conducted with delinquent youths use a cognitive-behavioral orientation. However, almost all the other schools of group therapy, including psychodynamic group approaches, have been utilized with delinquent youths. If properly conducted in controlled settings, consistently positive outcomes have been demonstrated (Lavin, Trabka, & Kahn, 1984).

COMMUNITY TREATMENT RESOURCES

The Legal System: The importance of the support and sanctioning of treatment by the courts has been described already. Court-mandated treatment as part of a community probation plan can provide sufficient backbone to the treatment process to spell the difference between success or failure. The fear of punishment or actual punishment as represented by locking up a youth in a detention home for a brief period or actual commitment to a training school has been shown to reduce subsequent delinquent activity (Murray & Cox, 1979). This runs counter to a common notion that sentencing a youth to training school only produces increased criminality. In fact, placing an out-of-control, frightened youth in a humane, well-run training school can provide relief of anxiety and a sense of security, and result in a dramatic reduction of aggressive behavior.

Schools: Many community schools supply a range of educational and supportive counseling services for delinquent youths, including self-contained classrooms, remedial educational programs, group counseling, vocational rehabilitation services, and multiple opportunities to interact with normal peer groups. Of course, individual schools and school systems vary widely in their ability to supply these services (Rutter et al., 1979). The fact remains that the vast majority of predelinquent and delinquent youths are in public school settings and that most of society's efforts and attempts to control, change, and educate delinquents occur in the public schools (Hawkins, VonCleve, & Catalano, 1991).

Social Services: In many instances, social workers and social service agencies become the arms of the court carrying out court-ordered treatment efforts in the community. Frequently these social workers provide liaison among the court counselors, judges, schools, and mental health facilities. For the many delinquent youths who have been removed from their parental homes and placed under legal guardianship of social services, the role of the social worker clearly becomes that of in loco parentis.

Other Helping Agencies: The availability of helping agencies and individuals varies widely from community to community but can include churches, the Salvation Army, Big Brother–Big Sister programs, YMCAs or YWCAs, support programs for battered women (Wolfe, Jaffe, Wilson, & Zak, 1985), and individual citizen volunteers who become involved and interested in a particular delinquent. Often clinicians are out of touch with these community resources, and thus at times they do not consider utilizing these potential change forces when setting up treatment programs for delinquents.

PSYCHOPHARMACOLOGICAL THERAPY

In recent years the psychopharmacological treatment of aggressive behavior has achieved a more solidly accepted position within the clinical arena (Campbell, Cohen, & Small, 1982; Leventhal, 1984; Stewart, Myers, Burket, & Lyles, 1990).

A basic principle of the psychopharmacological treatment of conduct-disordered, aggressive behavior is to treat the comorbid syndromes that appear to have the most likelihood of being the proximal triggers of aggressive delinquent behavior. If delinquent behavior occurs within the context of attentional difficulties, then stimulants would most likely be considered. If delinquent behaviors occur as possible corollaries of shifting, episodic, irritable moods, then a trial of lithium often is considered to treat a cyclic affective disturbance. Phenothiazines may be utilized when there is evidence of a psychotic or schizophrenic process. Carbamazepine often is considered for episodic, violent episodes that seem unpredictable from personality or environmental cues. Antidepressants are utilized when various signs and symptoms of depressiveness or depression are present. Beta blockers, such as propranolol, are considered when aggressive behaviors occur in the context of anxiety and tension. With the increasing evidence that the severity of aggressive delinquent behavior may be indirectly corollated with spinal fluid levels of 5-HIAA, an increasing usage of serotonin uptake blockers, such as fluoxetine and sertraline as front-line drugs, can be predicted (Birmaher et al., 1990; Brown et al., 1988).

Sometimes there are only hints or suggestions of comorbid conditions. Often there are no apparent clues as to comorbid conditions and the clinician faces the decision whether to prescribe medication for what appears to be "pure" conduct-disordered, delinquent behavior. Some say this is carrying empiricism to unjustified extremes. Yet many clinicians have had the experience of empirically prescribing trials of the medications just listed. Suddenly a particular medication, or combination of two or more, "clicks" and the formerly out-of-control youth settles down as inner tension decreases. This can be a vital turning point for particular youths who up to that time had not been able to use community treatment resources because of their persistent agitation and periodic aggressive outbursts.

Conclusion

This chapter has focused on the interaction of the conduct-disordered delinquent with society. The development, management, and treatment of this delinquency can be understood most productively within the context of our society's belief systems and its organizational structures—courts and schools that deal with rule-breaking, violent behaviors of youths. When the clinician can ally with society's prosocial change forces, then the opportunity for positive treatment outcome is enhanced for youths suffering from the oft-persistent and difficult syndrome of conduct-disordered delinquency.

REFERENCES

Arbuthnot, J., & Gordon, D. A. (1986). Behavioral and cognitive effects of a moral reasoning development intervention for high-risk behavior-disordered adolescents. *Journal of Consulting and Clinical Psychology, 54* (2), 208–216.

Bagley, C. (1989). Aggression and anxiety in day care graduates. *Psychological Reports, 64,* 250.

Barnum, R. (1987). Child psychiatry and the law, clinical evaluation of juvenile delinquents facing transfer to adult court. *Journal of the American Academy of Child and Adolescent Psychiatry, 26* (6), 922–925.

Benedek, E. (1979). Female delinquency: Fantasies, facts and future. In S. C. Feinstein & P. L. Giovacchini (Eds.), *Adolescent psychiatry* (Vol. 7, pp. 524–437). Chicago: University of Chicago Press.

Benedek, E., & Cornell, D. (Eds.). (1989). *Juvenile homicide.* Washington, DC: American Psychiatric Press.

Biederman, J., Newcorn, J., & Sprich, S. (1991). Comorbidity of attention deficit hyperactivity disorder with conduct, depressive, anxiety, and other disorders. *American Journal of Psychiatry, 148,* 564–577.

Bierman, K. L., Coie, J. D., K. A. Dodge, M. T., Greenberg, J. E. Lochman, R. J. McMahon, Social Skill Training in the FAST Track Program in R. Peters & R. J. McMahon (Eds.) Prevention and Early Intervention: Childhood Disorders; Substance Use & Delinquency. Newburg Park, CA: Gage 1996)

Birmaher, B., Stanley, M., Greenhill, L., Twomey, J. Gavrilescu, A., & Rabinovich, H. (1990). Platelet imipramine binding in children and adolescents with impulsive behavior. *Journal of the American Academy of Child and Adolescent Psychiatry, 29* (6), 914–918.

Bowden, C. L., Deutsch, C. K., & Swanson, J. M. (1988). Plasma dopamine-B-hydroxylase and platelet monoamine oxidase in attention deficit disorder and conduct disorder. *Journal of the American Academy of Child and Adolescent Psychiatry, 27* (2), 171–174.

Brown, C. S., Kent, T. A., Bryant, S. G., Gevedon, R. M., Campbell, J. L., Felthous, A. R., Barratt, E. S., & Rose, R. M. (1988). Blood platelet uptake of serotonin in episodic aggression. *Psychiatry Research, 27,* 5–12.

Bush, K. G., Zagar, R., Hughes, J. R., Arbit, J., & Russell, R. E. (1990). Adolescents who kill. *Journal of Clinical Psychology, 46* (4), 472–485.

Campbell, M., Cohen, I. L., & Small, A. M. (1982). Drugs in aggressive behavior. *Journal of the American Academy of Child Psychiatry, 21,* 107–117.

Campbell, S. B., & Ewing, L. J. (1990). Follow-up of hard-to-manage preschoolers: Adjustment at age 9 and predictors of continuing symptoms. *Journal of Child Psychology and Psychiatry, 31* (6), 871–889.

Chowanec, G. D., Josephson, A. M., Coleman, C., & Davis, H. (1991). *Journal of the American Child and Adolescent Psychiatry, 30* (2), 202–207.

Clarke, R. V. G. (1985). Jack Tizard Memorial lecture: Delinquency, environment and intervention. *Journal of Child Psychology and Psychiatry, 26* (4), 505–523.

Coie, J., Lochman, J. E., & Terry, R. (1990, January). *Childhood peer rejection and aggression as predictors of multiple forms of disorder in early adolescence.* Paper presented at annual meeting of Society for Research in Child and Adolescent Psychopathology, Miami, FL.

Coie, J. D., Bierman, K., Dodge, M., Greenberg, J., Lochman, J., McMahon, R., Conduct Problems Prevention Research Group. A Developmental and Clinical Model for the Prevention of Conduct Disorders: The FAST Track Program. Development and Psychopathology, 4 509–527 1992.

Collins, J. J. (1989). Alcohol and interpersonal violence. In N. A. Weiner & M. E. Wolfgang (Eds.), *Pathways to criminal violence* (pp. 49–67). Newbury Park, CA: Sage Publications.

Condon, J. T. (1986). The spectrum of fetal abuse in pregnant women. *Nervous and Mental Disease, 174* (9), 509–516.

Costello, E. J. (1989). Developments in child psychiatric epidemiology. *Journal of the American Academy of Child and Adolescent Psychiatry, 28* (6), 836–841.

Curry, J. F., Weincrot, S. I., & Koehler, F. (1984). Family therapy with aggressive and delinquent adolescents. In C. R. Keith (Ed.), *The aggressive adolescent* (pp. 209–239). New York: Free Press.

Erskine, C. (1984). Female delinquency, feminism and psychoanalysis. In C. R. Keith (Ed.), *The aggressive adolescent* (pp. 403–451). New York: Free Press.

Faraone, S. V., Biederman, J., Keenan, K., & Tsuang, M. T. (1991). Separation of DSM-III attention deficit disorder and conduct disorder: Evidence from a family-genetic study of American child psychiatric patients. *Psychological Medicine* 21: 109–21, Feb 1991.

Farrington, D. P. (1989). Early predictors of adolescent aggression and adult violence. *Violence and Victims, 4* (2), 79–100.

Farrington, D. P., Gallagher, B., Morley, L., St. Ledger, R. J., & West, D. J. (1988). Are there any successful men from criminogenic backgrounds? *Psychiatry, 51* (1), 116–130.

Fraiberg, S. (1982). Pathologic defenses in infancy. *Psychoanalytic Quarterly, 51,* 612–635.

Galenson, E. (1983). *A pain-pleasure behavioral complex in mothers and infants.* Paper presented at the Vulnerable Child Discussion Group, American Psychoanalytic Association, New York.

Gaynor, J. (1991). Firesetting. In M. Lewis (Ed.), *Child and adolescent psychiatry: A comprehensive textbook* (pp. 591–603). Baltimore, MD: Williams & Wilkins.

Goldstein, P. J. (1989). In N. A. Weiner and M. E. Wolfgang (Eds.), *Pathways to criminal violence* (pp. 16–48). Newbury Park, CA: Sage Publications.

Greenbaum, P. E., Prange, M. E., Friedman, R. M., & Silver, S. E. (1991). Substance abuse prevalence and comorbidity with other psychiatric disorders among adolescents with severe emotional disturbances. *Journal of the American Academy of Child and Adolescent Psychiatry, 30* (4), 575–583.

Hawkins, D. J., VonCleve, E., & Catalano, R. (1991). Reducing early childhood aggression: Results of a primary prevention program. *Journal of the American Academy of Child and Adolescent Psychiatry, 30* (2), 208–217.

Healy, W. (1915). *The individual delinquent.* Boston: Little, Brown & Co.

Irwin, M., Schuckit, M., & Smith, T. L. (1990). Clinical importance of age at onset in type 1 and type 2 primary alcoholics. *Archives of General Psychiatry, 47,* 320–324.

Kavoussi, R. J., Kaplan, M., & Becker, J. V. (1988). Psychiatric diagnoses in adolescent sex offenders. *Journal of the American Academy of Child and Adolescent Psychiatry, 27* (2), 241–243.

Keith, C. R. (1984). Individual psychotherapy and psychoanalysis with the aggressive adolescent: A historical review. In C. R. Keith (Ed.), *The aggressive adolescent* (pp. 191–208). New York: Free Press.

Keith, C. R. (1987). Violent youth. In J. D. Noshpitz (Ed.), *Basic handbook of child psychiatry* (pp. 111–122). New York: Basic Books.

Keith, C. R. (1988). Community treatment of violent youth: Seven years of experience with a class action suit. *Journal of the American Academy of Child and Adolescent Psychiatry, 27* (5), 600–604.

Kelso, J., & Stewart, M. A. (1986). Factors which predict the persistence of aggressive conduct disorder. *Journal of Child Psychology and Psychiatry, 27* (1), 77–86.

Kruesi, M. J. P., Rapoport, J. L., Hamburger, S., Hibbs, E., Potter, W. Z., Lenane, M., & Brown, G. L. (1990). Cerebrospinal fluid monoamine metabolites, aggression, and impulsivity in disruptive behavior disorders of children and adolescents. *Archives of General Psychiatry, 47,* 419–425.

Lahey, B. B., Piacentini, J. C., McBurnett, K., Stone, P., Hartdagen, S., & Hynd, G. (1988). Psychopathology in the parents of children with conduct disorder and hyperactivity. *Journal of the American Academy of Child and Adolescent Psychiatry, 27* (2), 163–170.

Larson, K. A. (1988). A research review and alternative hypothesis explaining the link between learning disability and delinquency. *Journal of Learning Disabilities, 21* (6), 357–363.

Lavin, G. K., Trabka, S., & Kahn, E. M. (1984). Group therapy with aggressive and delinquent adolescents. In C. R. Keith (Ed.), *The aggressive adolescent* (pp. 240–267). New York: Free Press.

Leventhal, B. L. (1984). The neuropharmacology of violent and aggressive behavior in children and adolescents. In C. R. Keith (Ed.), *The aggressive adolescent* (pp. 299–358). New York: Free Press.

Lewis, D. O. (1991a). Conduct disorder. In M. Lewis (Ed.), *Child and adolescent psychiatry: A comprehensive textbook* (pp. 561–571). Baltimore: Williams & Wilkins.

Lewis, D. O. (1991b). The development of the symptom of violence. In M. Lewis (Ed.), *Child and adolescent psychiatry: A comprehensive textbook* (pp. 331–340). Baltimore: Williams & Wilkins.

Lewis, D. O. (Ed.). (1981). *Vulnerabilities to delinquency*. New York: SP Medical and Scientific Books.

Loeber, R. (1987). The prevalence, correlates, and continuity of serious conduct problems in elementary school children. *Criminology, 25* (3), 615–642.

Loeber, R. (1991). Antisocial behavior: More enduring than changeable? *Journal of the American Academy of Child and Adolescent Psychiatry, 30* (3), 393–397.

Mannuzza, S., Klein, R. G., Konig, P. H., Giampino, T. L., et al. (1991). Criminality and childhood hyperactivity. *Archives of General Psychiatry, 48,* 667–668.

Marohn, R. C. (1982). Adolescent violence: Causes and treatment. *Journal of the American Academy of Child Psychiatry, 21* (4), 354–360.

Marshall, R. J. (1979). Antisocial youth. In J. D. Noshpitz (Ed.), *Basic handbook of child psychiatry* (Vol. 3, pp. 536–554). New York: Basic Books.

McFarlane, J. (1989). Battering during pregnancy: Tip of an iceberg revealed. *Women and Health, 15* (1), 69–84.

McManus, M., Brickman, A., Alessi, N., & Grapentine, W. L. (1985). Neurological dysfunction in serious delinquents. *Journal of the American Academy of Child Psychiatry, 24* (4), 481–486.

Meyers, W. C., & Kemph, J. P. (1990). DSM-III-R classification of murderous youth: Help or hindrance? *Journal of Clinical Psychiatry, 51* (6), 239–242.

Milin, R., Halikas, J. A., Meller, J. E., & Morse, C. (1991). Psychopathology among substance-abusing juvenile offenders. *Journal of the American Academy of Child and Adolescent Psychiatry, 30* (4), 569–574.

Moffitt, T. E. (1990). Juvenile delinquency and attention deficit disorder: Boys' developmental trajectories from age 3 to age 15. *Child Development, 61,* 893–910.

Moffitt, T. E., & Mednick, S. A. (Eds.). (1988). *Biological contributions to crime causation*. Dordrecht: Martinus Nijhoff Publishers.

Moffitt, T. E., & Silva, P. A. (1988). Neuropsychological deficit and self-reported delinquency in an unselected birth cohort. *Journal of the American Academy of Child and Adolescent Psychiatry, 27* (2), 233–240.

Murray, C. A., & Cox, L. A. (1979). *Beyond probation.* Beverly Hills, CA: Sage Publications.

Ney, P., Colbert, P., Newman, B., & Young, J. (1986). Aggressive behavior and learning difficulties as symptoms of depression in children. *Child Psychiatry and Human Development, 17,* (1), 3–14.

Offord, D. R., Allen, N., & Abrams, N. (1978). Parental psychiatric illness, broken homes and delinquency. *Journal of the American Academy of Child Psychiatry, 17,* 224–238.

Offord, D. R., & Fleming, J. E. (1991). Epidemiology. In M. Lewis (Ed.), *Child and adolescent psychiatry:*

A comprehensive textbook (pp. 1156–1168). Baltimore, MD: Williams & Wilkins.

Parens, H. (1979). *The development of aggression in early childhood.* New York: Jason Aronson.

Patterson, G. R., Capaldi, D., & Bank, L. (1991). An early starter model for predicting delinquency. In D. Pepler, Rubin, K. H., Bank, L. Hillsdale, (Eds.), *The development and treatment of childhood aggression,* L. E. Earlbaum, Hillsdale, N.J.

Pfeffer, C. R., Zuckerman, S., Plutchik, R., & Mizruchi, M. S. (1987). Assaultive behavior in normal school children. *Child Psychiatry and Human Development, 17* (3), 166–176.

Puig-Antich, J. (1982). Major depression and conduct disorder in prepuberty. *Journal of the American Academy of Child Psychiatry, 21,* 118–128.

Raine, A., & Venables, P. H. (1988). Enhanced P3 evoked potentials and longer P3 recovery times in psychopaths. *Psychophysiology, 25* (1), 30–38.

Raine, A., Venables, P. H., & Williams, M. (1990). Relationships between central and autonomic measures of arousal at age 15 years and criminality at age 24 years. *Archives of General Psychiatry, 47,* 1003–1007.

Rogeness, G. A., Maas, J. W., Javors, M. A., Macedo, C. A., Harris, W. R., & Hoppe, S. K. (1988). Diagnoses, catecholamine metabolism, and plasma dopamine-B-hydrozylase. *Journal of the American Academy of Child and Adolescent Psychiatry, 27* (1), 121–125.

Rutter, M., Maughan, B., Mortimore, P., Ouston, J. et al. (1979). *Fifteen thousand hours.* Cambridge, MA: Harvard University Press.

Satterfield, J. H., Satterfield, B. T., & Schell, A. M. (1987). Therapeutic interventions to prevent delinquency in hyperactive boys. *Journal of the American Academy of Child and Adolescent Psychiatry, 26* (1), 56–64.

Stewart, J., Myers, W. C., Burket, R. C., & Lyles, W. B. (1990). A review of the pharmacotherapy of aggression in children and adolescents. *Journal of the American Academy of Child and Adolescent Psychiatry, 29* (2), 269–277.

Sutherland, E. H., & Cressey, D. R. (1966). Principles of criminology, 7th ed. rev. Philadelphia: J. B. Lippincott.

Terr, L. C. (Ed.). (1989). Debate forum. *Journal of the American Academy of Child and Adolescent Psychiatry, 28* (3), 450–454.

Tolan, P. H. (1987). Implications of age of onset for delinquency risk. *Journal of Abnormal Child Psychology, 15* (1), 47–65.

Varley, W. H. (1984). Behavior modification approaches to the aggressive adolescent. In C. R. Keith (Ed.), *The aggressive adolescent* (pp. 268–298). New York: Free Press.

Vitiello, B., Stoff, D. M. (March 1997). "Subtypes of Aggression and their Relevance to Child Psychiatry," *Journal of the American Academy of Child and Adolescent Psychiatry,* 36:3, 307–315.

Walker, J. L., Lahey, B. B., Russo, M. F., Frick, P. J., Christ, M. A., McBurnett, K., Loeber, R., Stouthamer-Loeber, M., Green, S. M. (1991). Anxiety, inhibition, and conduct disorder in children: I. Relations to social impairment. *Journal of the American*

Academy of Child and Adolescent Psychiatry, 30 (2), 187–191.

Wells, K. (1988). Family therapy. In J. L. Matson (Ed.), *Handbook of treatment approaches in childhood psychopathology* (pp. 45–61). New York: Plenum Press.

Widom, C. S. (1989). The cycle of violence. *Science, 24,* 160–166.

Widom, C. S. (1989). The Intergenerational Transmission of Violence PP 137–201. *Pathways to criminal violence,* Ed. N. Weiner & M. E. Wolfgang. Newbury Park, CA: Sage Publications.

Widom, C. S., & Ames, A. (1988). Biology and female crime. In T. E. Moffitt & S. A. Mednick (Eds.), *Biological contributions to crime causation* (pp. 308–331). Dordrecht: Martinus Nijhoff Publishers.

Wilson, C. P. (Ed.). (1983). *Fear of being fat: The treatment of anorexia nervosa and bulimia.* New York: Jason Aronson.

Wolfe, D. A., Jaffe, P., Wilson, S. K., & Zak, L. (1985). Children of battered women: The relation of child behavior to family violence and maternal stress. *Journal of Consulting and Clinical Psychology, 53* (5), 657–665.

Wolfgang, M. E. (1978). Real and perceived changes of crime and punishment. *Daedalus, 108* 143–157.

Zagar, R., Arbit, J., Hughes, J. R., Busell, R. E., & Bush, K. Developmental and Disruptive Behavior Disorders among Delinquents. (1989). *Journal of the American Academy of Child and Adolescent Psychiatry, 28* (2), 437–440.

PART V

Religion, Parenting, and the Mental Health of Children and Adolescents

Jeffrey W. Swanson

Children live in two worlds—the one defined by their immediate experience and outlook shared with peers, the other dominated by parental superpowers who may (or may not) meet their needs and who personify their aspirations and fears. But in addition, insofar as children tend to acquire their parents' moral sensibilities, membership in religious communities, and beliefs in unseen entities with extraordinary powers, they confront a third order of being—one that offers a revealing window on personal development. The shape of the gods and demons of childhood may reflect a young person's most profound views of an emerging self, as he or she confronts a symbolic world delineated by adults. Such views illuminate the contours of a child's emotional and psychological vulnerabilities and personal trajectory. Moreover, the most deliberate actions of parents toward their progeny often are motivated by traditional ideologies involving notions of ultimate reality and the peculiar demands of faith. Such parental demands and ideologies may impinge powerfully—in complex ways—on children's developmental pathways, conditioning the range of their choices and chances for leading healthy, productive lives.

This chapter generally examines ways in which religion and religious parenting may affect the mental health of children and adolescents. The overall point to be made is that religious beliefs, practices, language, symbols, and associations often form an important part of the cultural and developmental context in which psychiatric illnesses can occur and that religious perspectives often determine the social and personal meanings of such illnesses, significantly shaping their clinical presentation and course. Unfortunately, global statements about such matters (although perhaps irresistible) may prove quite hazardous to the truth in particular instances. On this point, Guy Swanson

in a preface to *The Birth of the Gods* (1964) aptly invoked Evans-Pritchard (1954): "... generalizations about 'religion' are discreditable. They are always too ambitious and take account of only a few of the facts." (p. 6). Nevertheless, Swanson added, "... generalizations can provide fruitful direction for descriptive research, just as careful and detailed depictions of social life stimulate generalizations" (p. viii). The observations to follow are offered in that spirit.

While a number of volumes deal with religious parenting and children's mental health, they often take the form of sectarian tracts or else (if scholarly) tend to be long on conceptual insights—illustrated by selected case anecdotes—but short on scientific rigor. A number of fairly well-developed areas of scholarship (theories of moral development, e.g.) do overlap with the topic at hand, and quite a few studies have yielded information that is useful at least for thinking about religion and mental health in childhood, albeit within a specific cultural setting. However, I am aware of no large-scale epidemiologic studies that have directly and comprehensively assessed the effects, over time, of religious parenting and youthful religiosity on mental disorder among children in any culture.

Much of the available literature on religion and mental health and illness is focused on adults and contains only derivative, peripheral, or retrospective implications for youths. Specific issues that have been addressed include, for example:

1. Whether adults with selected mental illnesses and personality disorders are likely to have had a particular sort of religious experience as children
2. How religious beliefs can foster and/or justify various kinds of child abuse and neglect, with negative consequences for social-psychological development and adult mental health
3. How certain problems in social-psychological

development may be expressed in religious concepts or beliefs

4. How religious ideologies can induce morbid guilt, anxiety, and obsessions
5. How involvement in religious groups can promote healthy living and lower mortality
6. How extremist religious movements ("cults") tend to employ techniques of coercive persuasion and exploit family ideology to recruit psychologically vulnerable youths
7. How ecstatic religious experiences and spirit possession may (or may not) be distinguished from psychotic states, and how psychotic delusions may appropriate religious ideas and imagery
8. How religion may be used in healthy vs. maladaptive ways to cope with stress and to meet developmental challenges
9. How adults should (or should not) inculcate religion in children
10. How psychiatrists in general should approach religion in their patients

A list of related research areas and approaches (with a few selected references of varying scholarly and scientific merit) might include the following:

- The sociobiological functions of religion (Bromley, 1991; Wenegrat, 1990)
- The stage-developing of moral values (Armsby, 1971; Coles, 1986; Damon, 1988; Kagan & Lamb, 1987; Kohlberg, 1984; Loomba, 1967; Pattison, 1969)
- Philosophy, methods, and effects of religious education (Guerra, Benson, & Donahue, 1989; Holley, 1978; Hull, 1982; Isert, 1969; Odermann, 1990; Thompson, 1988)
- The psychological benefits and pitfalls of religious upbringing (Barr, 1978; Chesen, 1972; Hanna, Myer, & Ottens, 1994; Lee, 1985; Richards, 1991; Sharp, 1986; Sloat, 1992; Stewart, 1967)
- Child and adolescent religiosity, family dynamics, and psychopathology (Adams, 1972, 1973; Bender, 1969, 1974; Francis, Pearson, & Kay, 1983; Lukianowicz, 1969)
- Adults' narrative reconstruction and psychological integration of youthful religiosity and conversion experiences (Swanson, 1995; Ullman, 1989);
- Adult psychopathology and religious background in childhood or adolescence (Tennant, Bebbington, & Hurry, 1982; Vergote, 1988)
- The role of pastoral care in the mental health of families and children (Faddis, 1960; Lum, 1971)
- Religion, social support, and psychological well-being (Capps, 1985; Donahue & Benson, 1995; Ellison, 1991)
- Patients' vs. psychiatrists' religion, psychotherapy for overtly religious patients, and the psychoana-

lytic foundations of religion, including transference and countertransference (Chance, 1988; Jones, 1991; Lovinger, 1985; McDargh, 1986; Peteet, 1985; Spero, 1985)
- Occurrence and sequelae of childhood sexual, physical, and psychological abuse perpetrated in a religious context or justified by religious ideology (Bottoms, Shaver, Goodman, & Qin, 1995; Capps, 1992; Greven, 1991; Manlow, 1995; Straus, 1995)

My aim in this chapter is not to provide a comprehensive summary or catalog of existing knowledge in these areas. (A useful review of the literature in a number of these areas may be found in Benson, Masters, and Larson [1997].) Rather, I set forth the following modest goals: (1) to sensitize mental health professionals regarding the potential significance of religious phenomena to the understanding of psychiatric illness and well-being in children and adolescents; (2) to offer a general conceptual framework—a way to think about religion and mental health in the context of parent-child relationships and the development of life stories; and (3) to suggest some questions about child rearing and religion that may need to be addressed by mental health practitioners and researchers who are concerned with children.

Approaches to Religion

How do we think about religion and religiosity in general? Among empirically measured psychological formulations, perhaps the most influential has been Gordon Allport's distinction between *extrinsic* (i.e., religion as a comforting and useful social convention) and *intrinsic* (i.e., religion as a meaningful, mature, motivating view of the world and matters of ultimate concern) (Allport, 1950). Allport's Religious Orientation Scale has been criticized on empirical and conceptual grounds. For example, his original view of intrinsic/extrinsic as mutually exclusive polar opposites could not account for data showing that these orientations often occur together in the same people. And Batson noted that Allport's typology excluded certain attributes that may attend mature religious faith, such as cognitive complexity, tentative belief, and doubt—what Batson called the "quest" orientation. (See Batson, 1976; Batson & Raynor-Price, 1983; Donahue, 1985; Ventis, 1995.)

Among sociological characterizations of religion, two general approaches have predominated.

One sort of description has emphasized the *substance* of religious beliefs and experiences, for example, the transcendent or supernatural aura of religious phenomena that evoke powerful but conflicting emotions such as awe and fear, love and resistance, guilt and forgiveness. The other approach has emphasized the *function* of religion, for example, the sociocultural purposes and psychological needs that religion fulfills in the lives of individuals and communities. The kinds of symbols that religious communities construct and sustain are needed, as Wuthnow (1988) has observed, "to integrate a person's biography, to provide answers to questions about meaning and purpose in life, and to interpret experiences of great anguish or great ecstasy that fall at the margins of everyday life."

Both approaches have limitations. On the one hand, as Wuthnow (1988) noted, "[s]ubstantive definitions run into difficulty because many non-Western religions do not include conceptions of the supernatural; and even in Western tradition, certain definitions of God have become difficult to associate with simple distinctions between the natural and supernatural." On the other hand, purely functional approaches often fail to discriminate between belief systems traditionally recognized as religious and strong ideological persuasions or social movements that may affect people in the same way or meet similar needs in their lives.

In any event, from a mental health point of view, it seems important to recognize that religious belief systems typically include two kinds of components: the internal, private, experiential features of religion; and the external, public, cultural, and social-structural features of religion. As Lovinger (1985) and others have noted, psychotherapists working with overtly religious patients must try to interpret the former features within the context of the latter—to understand individual religious experience and symbolic imagery not only in terms of personal psychological conflicts, needs, and defenses but also against the social landscape of the religious group, religious culture, or subculture. Ideally, therapists and patients discover jointly what is "healthy" vs. "unhealthy" religion in a patient's experience. Such a discovery involves more than, for example, telling the difference between pathological delusions and legitimate shared religious beliefs. Indeed, some "legitimate" religious doctrines may be more harmful to certain individuals—especially when reinforced by a whole community—than privately held false beliefs.

A functional approach to religion is perhaps most appropriate in the work of mental health professionals—but this functional approach must not prejudge or debunk the significance of transcendent reality as a substantive feature of patients' experience and devotion. From this point of view, several questions may be addressed:

1. How (and under what conditions) might religion cause or compound mental disorder?
2. How might religion prevent psychological distress and promote well-being?
3. How might religion help those who suffer from mental illness?

Thus, such an approach seeks to identify the potential role of religion in the etiology and experience of illness, in the promotion of health, and in the treatment and care of persons who become ill. It goes beyond the either/or of whether religion is good or bad, to the complex assessment of *how* the pathological or destructive potential of religion is distinguished from the healthy and constructive uses of religious symbols and religious sources of support for given individuals. The way in which such distinctions are made sets the tone of encounter between mental health professionals and religious people.

The Significance of Religion and Mental Illness in Popular Culture vs. Psychiatry

In Western thought and culture, mental illness and religious piety have shown a peculiar affinity. Indeed, often they have been understood as two sides of the same coin. Both may involve moral careers, dramatic personal transformations, the alteration or heightening of subjectivity, and the passions. Both are bound up with value judgments applied to the human self. Both produce a suspension or transcendence of the assumed order of things in everyday life, and both have been noted to express the meaning of an alternative personal experience in the language of myth and ritual. In an important sense, the publicly inaccessible world—of an inner or radically *Other* kind—is what finally matters to religious devotees and is what troubles people with mental illness.

And yet mental illness and religion carry strongly conflicting moral charges in popular culture (which tends to be friendly toward religion). Ordinary talk about these phenomena evokes strong feelings about what is good and bad, setting religion and mental problems at odds. Religious people attach meaning to suffering in their world, while those with mental illness suffer the loss of meaning in theirs. Mental illness produces fear, while religion offers comfort to many. Mental illness leads to confusion and loss of control, while religion promises understanding and mastery. Mental illness leads to isolation, despair, and death, while religion is supposed to provide hope and life in the community. Mental illness may involve insidious self-deception, while religion claims ultimate truth. Mental illness may be manifest as grandiose self-indulgence at the expense of others' well-being and safety, while religion associates itself with altruism and acts of goodwill. Plato's *Phaedrus* notwithstanding, mental illness has been seen more often as the work of the devil than as a gift from the gods.

However, beginning with Sigmund Freud, psychiatry has held, for the most part, a demystified and pathologized view of religion, one sharply at odds with religion's general esteem in popular culture. As summarized recently by Jones (1991), Freud developed at least 2 accounts of the origins and psychological foundations of religious devotion, neither of which was flattering to believers. In *Totem and Taboo* (1913/1952) he proposed that religion arose out of primal guilt over the unconscious oedipal wishes of sons to kill their fathers—a myth with historical origins in primitive times, Freud argued. Guilt then was assuaged through idealization of the dead patriarch and by obsessional repetition of rituals of devotion. This amounted to a diagnosis of religion as collective neurosis. In *Future of an Illusion* (1927/1964), Freud offered a somewhat more sociological explanation: Religion existed because it fulfilled certain infantile needs for a developing humanity—needs for consolation and security and for the taming of asocial instincts. As Jones (1991) rendered it, Freud was suggesting that ". . . through fantasy, religion reduces the terror of an uncaring nature by personalizing the natural order, removes the fear of death by providing an illusion of immortality, and reconciles us to the social necessity of self-denial by promising to reward us for it in the hereafter" (p. 2).

Contemporary psychoanalysts have recognized the limitations of these reductionistic Freudian formulations. As summarized by Meissner (1984):

The two primary criticisms that have been leveled against Freud's view of religion are that he based it on the notion of the internalization and reexternalization exclusively of a paternal imago—derived from the vicissitudes of the father-son Oedipal relationship, with its inherent conflict and ambivalence—and that he provided an account of religious experience that looks in a rather limited and prejudicial fashion at the more infantile dimensions and derivatives of religious experience. (p. 137)

Post-Freudians such as Meissner (1984) and Jones (1991) tend to be more accepting of religion as a potentially healthy, mature feature of the experience of human beings in their "relatedness" to one another and to the world around them. Jones, a professor of religion and a clinical psychologist, has expanded the notions of transference and countertransference into a general interpretation of religious experience that leaves plenty of room for New Age theological speculation: "If there is no escaping dependency on a self-object milieu, there is nothing childish about acknowledging connection to a self-sustaining universal matrix" (p. 135).

Meissner, a Catholic psychoanalyst, has proposed his own developmental schema that accounts for a range of religious experience in terms of the qualities of reciprocal human relationships that begin early in childhood and are carried into maturity. Just as human relationships can be either supportive or destructive for individuals, so religious experiences and beliefs can either be ego-adaptive or psychopathogenic. Whereas Freud identified the idea of God with the projection of an idealized patriarch, Meissner highlighted the importance of a nurturing mother on a child's early imaginings about God:

. . . the child's early experiences of "mirroring" in interaction with the mother provide the basis for important elements in the structuring of his concept of God. In his experiences of the mother as a loving and caring presence, in nursing, and in the mother's participation in the act of mirroring by which the child finds himself narcissistically embraced, admired, recognized, and cherished, he finds a symbiotic union with the mother that can serve as the basis for an evolving sense of trust, acceptance, and security. . . . The rudiments of the mirroring phase . . . may be distilled into the person's experience of his relationship with God. If the mirroring has been defective, he may enter further stages of life with a basic sense of being cut off or lost . . . (1984, pp. 138–139).

Sixty years after Freud identified religion with infantile dependency and predicted that humanity eventually would grow out of it, rational science no longer poses as the panacea to the human condition—and religion is still very much with us. Meissner allows for the rare possibility that mature adults can achieve a genuine "integration of faith experience." Of those few, Meissner rhapsodized: "The love of God in these souls seems wholly unselfconscious, stripped of the residues of infantile narcissism, and yet capable of integration into a life of activity, responsibility, and generative fulfillment. They often seem capable of profoundly meaningful object relations that are characterized by selfless love and acceptance of others" (1984, p. 157).

Clearly, however, post-Freudian psychoanalytic commentary on religion cannot be characterized generally as pro-religious. Two thematic ideas about religion—both found in Freud's (1927/ 1964) writing—still retain significance for many psychotherapists: the image of religion-as-child-likeness and the metaphor of religion-as-narcotic. Pathology-centered critiques persist, such as a study by Antoine Vergote (1988), entitled *Guilt and Desire: Religious Attitudes and Their Pathological Derivatives.* Under this rubric, Vergote examined unhealthy spiritual affinities ranging from religious hallucinations, visions and demonism, to morbid anxiety and guilt, to obsessional neurosis and what he calls the "tactical displacement of neurosis onto religion."

Religion as Childlike Dependency

Some therapists view extreme religious devotion in adult patients as a form of infantile narcissism and parent-separation anxiety they never outgrew, often signifying a generalized developmental impasse and often resulting from traumatic early events. According to Wenegrat (1990), for example, when the attachment needs of young children are not met, their longings for affection and approval may be carried over into adulthood and displaced onto a religious belief system—a phenomenon with sociobiological significance:

Infants spend much of their time and energy maintaining proximity to caretakers. For constitutional or developmental reasons, certain adults, too, are easily provoked into proximity-maintaining behaviors modeled on those of the infant. . . . [T]hese individuals, because of the way they cling to potential caretakers, often appear dependent.

Like dependent persons, religious persons tend to be obedient, conforming, and anxious to obtain external approval. . . . [R]eligious beliefs promise to serve attachment needs, whenever these needs are salient in adult life. . . . [P]rayers and rituals depict God as an attachment figure. Those who believe in such a god imagine that they are never far from a caretaking figure. The Twenty-third Psalm, for instance, depicts God fulfilling the watchful, protective, and nurturant functions of the ideal mother. (pp. 31–32)

When such dependent religious persons become parents themselves, some therapists note that they tend to "smother" their own offspring with demands for affection and conformity to an idealized image of themselves—again, often expressed in the idiom of religious piety and legitimized as "God's will" or the teaching of the Bible or the church. A case cited by Sloat (1992), a Christian psychotherapist, involved a patient's mother who fulfilled her own narcissistic attachment needs through the device of a coerced "family altar" of Bible-reading and prayer (a common practice in many evangelical Christian homes). During this time, Mother was at the center of attention and in control of her children. She manipulated family interaction along the lines of a psychological subtext underlying a supposedly spiritual exercise. The children scarcely dared to interrupt her lengthy testimonies and prayers (in which they appeared as spiritual caricatures of themselves), for Mother's authority became fused with God's. Their own expressions had to meet the demands of her script, while their other needs and wishes were ignored. "In using spiritual concepts for her own protection," Sloat observed, "Mother made herself a god of sorts, demanding total loyalty to her wishes and requiring her children to sacrifice themselves on the altar of her personal needs" (p. 88).

While such cases do occur, and Sloat's insights may be useful in selected therapeutic situations, clearly they do not amount to a general psychological critique of religious belief in persons who presumably do not suffer from mental health problems. Unfortunately, many psychiatrists and other therapists tend to focus exclusively on the defensive, narcissistic, or infantile features of individual religious belief, since such aspects often are bound up in the pathology of religious people who come to their attention. This tends to produce an attitude on the part of some mental health professionals toward religion in general that is often unbalanced and patronizing.

Such attitudes are common as well in the framing of traditional theory and research in the sociology of religion, especially regarding the functions of religion among the poor, oppressed, and ill-educated. A recent example is found in a sociological study by Ellison (1991), who examined the cognitive and affective functions of religious beliefs for individuals under varying conditions of social life. Using data from a large survey, he developed statistical models showing that individuals with strong religious beliefs have "higher levels of life satisfaction, greater personal happiness, and fewer negative psychosocial consequences of traumatic life events" (p. 80). But he also found a negative interaction effect between formal education and "existential religious certainty" in the statistical prediction of psychological well-being. That is to say, the salubrious effect of religious belief on mental health turned out to be strongest among those who lacked formal education (i.e., those most like children, in the view of academics), and the effect weakened as educational level increased. As Ellison put it, "Personal religious faith and/or practice may compensate for the lack of more sophisticated cognitive resources" (p. 83).

Religion as Narcotic

Evoking Freud's (and also Karl Marx's) other metaphor for religion, some mental health professionals tend to view their patients' religious experience as a sort of psychoactive substance: While religion has euphoric potential, it is acquired at a price and can be dangerous—particularly when used by those (notably children) vulnerable to its toxic side effects and addictive qualities. Interestingly, such views are held by a few therapists who are themselves committed to religion as well as by some who are personally inimical to it. Consider two books, by Chesen (1972) and Sloat (1992), entitled respectively *Religion May Be Hazardous to Your Health* and *The Dangers of Growing Up in a Christian Home*. The former psychotherapist is a self-proclaimed nonreligious Jew, the latter a committed evangelical Protestant. Each attributed his present insights to the overcoming of certain pathogenic effects of a strict religious upbringing.

Chesen likened Hebrew school to sitting on a bench beneath a skyscraper, peering up and counting its windows backward, right to left, for seven years. In his opinion, this was religious education "administered by people who had an incredible lack of insight with children." The net result, in his words: "I can still read Hebrew, but still do not understand a word of it" (p. 135). Although Chesen as an adult claimed to enjoy Jewish holidays and to feel a "sense of Jewish identity that goes with [his] background," the best he could do for a personal credo was "gravitate toward belief in some kind of nebulous creational force." He could not honestly imagine a God who listened to him or an afterlife that awaited him. "On the other hand," Chesen added, almost wistfully evoking the lost innocence of childhood, "I tend to envy those who do have such genuine beliefs" (pp. 135–136).

Writing in the 1970s, psychiatrist Chesen postured as a Ralph Nader of religion, offering his book as a consumer warning to those in the market for some persuasion of divinity. Chesen conceded (a bit grudgingly) that these products have their uses and can even work as a "therapeutic adjunct" (p. 110). Religious proscriptions become a "prophylaxis against suicide." (p. 111). Prayer is better than worry. Anticipating a pleasant afterlife is perhaps more healthy-minded than the existential funk of death anxiety, for people who cannot accept their own mortality. Belief in some concept of God enhances mental stability in many people, and religious affiliation offers a "portable cultural milieu" (p. 103).

Nevertheless, Chesen argued that religion could act like a poison, causing or compounding several kinds of mental health problems: emotional instability, psychotic reactions, maladaptive coping with life situations, impeded cognitive and social development in children. Chesen suggested that a strict religious upbringing can interfere with the emergence of "flexible thinking processes" and tends to produce adults (excluding himself, one presumes) whose thinking is "rigid, confined and stereotyped" (p. 8). Patterns of thought deeply rooted during youth can later place people in "irreversible, unresolvable dilemmas, leading to permanent unhappiness," (p. 74) he added, offering the predictable example of strict Catholics and birth control.

Chesen contrasted the natural sensitivity, pliability, simplicity, uniqueness, and delicate growth processes of a maturing child with the rigidity of organized religion foisted upon him or her—an "archaic and complex system of ideas and attitudes." His own childhood perceptions of Judaism seem particularly apropos to this characterization.

Adults whose thinking patterns become ossified by such intense and prolonged religious indoctrination are more prone to emotional instability, Chesen argued. In particular, he implicated religion for the punitive consciences that many people carry around, which render them incapable of "conscious recognition of [their] normal drives" and "therefore unable to deal with them in times of stress" (p. 34). This statement turns out mostly to be about sex and aggression.

Finally, Chesen maintained that intense religious happenings and exposure to cryptic sacred texts can precipitate (or aggravate) psychotic reactions in vulnerable individuals. Religious events and material are thus ill advised for people with a "tenuous grasp on reality." (p. 42). In Chesen's view, it is hardly an accident that delusional systems tend to be built around conventional religious beliefs and that "Biblical material often provides the theme and variations that are the content of a psychotic episode" (p. 47).

By comparison, Sloat (1992) wrote in detail about the bitter medicine of his own Christian upbringing, but in the end he took a more positive stance toward religious commitment (of the correct kind, that is). One especially poignant passage sets the tone of his early memories:

Hellfire was a fearful reality that was graphically portrayed on a regular basis in my home church. . . . The rich man. His parched tongue. The wide gulf between him and Abraham's bosom. The flames burning his body. The endless agony, worsened knowing it will never cease. The utter misery and fear of it all. As the minister became emotional, his voice would rise in increasing crescendo, bordering on becoming hoarse, and then fall to a quiet, soft pleading. He spent twenty-five minutes frightening everyone, and only five minutes showing the way out. (pp. 114–115)

Boone (1989), in her critical essay on the discourse of fundamentalism, offered several other examples of the kind of fear-mongering sermon to which Sloat referred. In one such text, printed in the fundamentalist publication *Sword of the Lord,* the Reverend Curtis Hutson evoked the image of a psychiatric ward in his description of Hell. Pondering the mental constitution of the people God would send there, Hutson suggested the rather bizarre notion that God somehow would have to reconstitute the souls of reprobates to make it possible for them to suffer eternal torment—a capacity notably absent in the "mortal body." In another of Boone's examples, taken from a 1981 issue of *The Sword of the Lord,* preacher J. C. Ryle aimed his message specifically at children:

In Hell there is no laughter and smiling. There is nothing but "wailing and gnashing of teeth." In Hell there is no happiness. Those who go there cry night and day without stopping. . . . I am afraid that many children are going to Hell. I see many boys and girls who know they are sinners but have never asked Jesus to save them. Where will they go if they die. There is only one other place to which they can go. They must go to Hell. (p. 101)

Boone suggested that such sermons amount to "mental child abuse."

Sloat (1992) cited other distortions of Christianity that can be psychologically damaging to children, such as the "dangerous self-righteousness" of many evangelical Christian parents. He attributed this to the parents' own moral upbringing organized around the avoidance of a "master list of sins." Sloat attempted to disabuse such parents of their warped concepts of Christian humility and self-abnegation, on which he blamed their unaccepting attitudes and failure to praise their children. Models of rigid patriarchal authority—attributed by them to God-inspired Scripture—may lead parents to fail to consider their children's feelings and to nurture their individual expressions. Many Christian parents are thus hypocritical, in Sloat's view. To compensate for their own feelings of failure and unresolved conflict with a raging superego, they demand perfection and scrupulosity in their children, using God and the Bible to legitimate their claims. They rigidly bifurcate the world into black and white and overprotect their children from any influences they see as profane.

Margaret Sharp (1986), another Christian psychologist (who is also a Methodist pastor), corroborated Sloat and Boone: "It is an unfortunate fact that there is a certain kind of rigid, religious upbringing, less common now perhaps than formerly but still sometimes found, which tends to repress not only the intellectual exploration of faith but also tends to inhibit those very emotions which, if repressed, are the most damaging" (p. 30).

Beyond the Secularization Hypothesis

Most of the aforementioned commentators on the role of religion in mental health, whether pro or con, go to some length to examine features of mental health but fall short of providing sophisticated interpretations of religion. According to Larson, Pattison, Blazer, Omran, and Kaplan (1986), this imbalance is symptomatic of the undeveloped state of research on religious phenomena in psychiatry. Larson et al. conducted a systematic content analysis of religious variables in research articles published in four major psychiatric journals in the 1970s and early 1980s. By comparison to scholarship in sociology and psychology of religion, these authors concluded that psychiatric research on religion "lacks conceptual and methodological sophistication" (p. 329).

The currency of the "secularization hypothesis" among psychiatrists illustrates the point that Larson et al. made. This hypothesis is the notion that the evolution of modern, rational society has led inevitably to the decline of religion and will bring about its eventual demise (which is the view that Freud held, of course). Up until the 1970s, most secular students of religion tended to accept this hypothesis without question. Today the whole issue has been reframed by new research concerning the way religion itself evolves in response to its social surround: As Robert Wuthnow (1988) put it, "Modern religion is resilient yet subject to cultural influences; it does not simply survive or decline, but adapts to its environment in complex ways" (p. 475).

In fact, contemporary scholars of religion now tend to approach their subject matter in a way that psychotherapists might find particularly useful. Rather than either stereotyping or ignoring religion, therapists in this vein would accord religious beliefs and practices the same investigative attention they have given to other symbolic dimensions of their patients' lives. They would set out with the recognition that religious symbols and activities are of profound significance to many people in modern and postmodern society—in ways of which they may or may not be aware—and that the meaning of symbols and symbolic action is not static but fluid. Religious meanings are not so much given in the traditional texts in which sacred symbols are embedded but in living "texts of identity"—new narratives produced in the nexus of shared religious understandings and the unique life stories of individuals. A fine example of how a psychologist has probed the contextual meaning of religion in several contemporary life stories of adults is John Kotre's (1984) *Outliving the Self: Generativity and Interpretation of Lives.*

Many mental health professionals and researchers proceed as if the secularization hypothesis were an undisputed intellectual view and as if this somehow implied, further, that all religion may be treated as an illusion or a lingering sign of infantile dependency. For example, Stanford psychiatrist Brant Wenegrat (1990) began his book on "the sociobiology and psychology of religion," by defining his topic as "any and all beliefs in imaginary beings with supernatural powers." He elaborated: "I have *assumed* that religious beliefs are factually erroneous—that is, that religious beliefs are cultural inventions. . . . [S]elective retention theories require that these beliefs subserve, or promise to subserve, innately probable strategies of either the faithful or their masters. Otherwise they would more or less quickly be changed or discarded" (p. 29).

Whatever the scientific merit of this approach, it is important for mental health professionals at least to recognize that such attitudes and values are likely to conflict with those of many (if not most) people who seek their clinical attention. While psychiatrists are nailing the coffin on mind-body dualism, many of their patients (and those who care for them) in the surrounding pluralism of cultures continue to think of the mental and physical (not to mention the spiritual) as distinct realms of being. Thus, afflictions of mind and body persist in different categories with variant social meanings. The moral connotations of mental illness are not necessarily diminished merely because psychiatrists or mental health client advocates attack such stigmatizing views as fossils of medieval culture. Rather, many parents and their offspring continue to view psychiatric illness in deep-seated moral terms—as bad, a threat to personhood and personal integrity, of a different order from physical illness. Many who themselves suffer from psychiatric disorders view their own afflictions as a sickness of spirit as well as mind.

The Life-Story Approach to Religion and Mental Health and Illness

Figure V.1 outlines a conceptual approach to human development based on the idea of life storytelling. Movement from left to right across this model represents narrative development of a "plotline," as the narrator's character faces challenges, pursues goals, overcomes obstacles—all the while reinterpreting, reinventing, and retell-

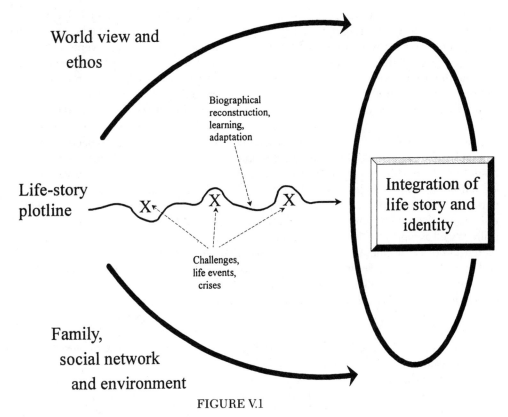

FIGURE V.1

Life-Story Approach to Personal Development

ing the story to himself or herself and others. Maturation of character (middle vector) is accompanied by a widening of the scope of worldview and ethos (above) and is supported by a deepening and broadening of social network (below).

Psychologists who take a life-story approach to human development and therapy (e.g., Cohler, 1988; Kotre, 1984; Rosenwald & Ochberg, 1992) tend mostly to focus on adults, since adults are more sophisticated storytellers with more "material" to offer. However, children tell life stories too—and the epics that adults eventually spin out usually are revised versions of stories begun in childhood.

Several features of a story make it an apt metaphor—and an effective vehicle—for the interpretation of a human life. Stories have beginnings and endings. They are carried along by the intrigue of plots, subplots, and intertwining themes that may symbolically connect diverse episodes and events. Stories take place against a social and cultural landscape. They develop characters whose actions, attributes, and fate may teach moral and practical lessons. Stories are legacies passed from one generation to another. Perhaps most important, stories are told or written from distinctive

points of view, by authors and narrators, to various audiences—interlocutors whose voices are heard explicitly or implicitly throughout a text.

The story (or multiple stories) of one's life thus are constantly being revised and retold in the light of new experiences and encounters. Unexpected challenges, events, and crises generate twists of plot and discontinuities in life narratives. But seeing one's life as a story to be told, with some meaning to be discovered, may enable a person eventually to integrate difficult experiences of loss and apparent failure. Adaptation takes place as a person learns from his or her accrued experiences in responding to such challenges, in ways that restore balance, harmony, direction, and forward movement to a life story. Biographical reconstruction is the process of revising and retelling a life story from the point of view of the present moment, thus integrating, reshaping, or even forgetting life-historical events according to the demands of the story's own *telos*, which seeks coherence, meaning, integrity, and aesthetic sensibility (Cohler, 1988; Kotre, 1984; MacAdams, 1985). Life-as-story implies an interpretation of experience in which the person exists simultaneously as narrator, internal audience, and primary

161

character. Possibilities always exist for a different telling and a different hearing of the story. Things may turn out another way in the end—and also, things may *begin* differently this time.

From the point of view of life-story psychology, the therapist's role is like that of an experienced ghostwriter who collaborates with a client to produce a penetrating and authentic autobiography, one that reads well and rings true. Life problems are approached as textual problems; the restoration of mental health thus equals restoration of a life narrative. Working together over an extended period of time, therapist and client record reminiscences, select and organize material chronologically as well as topically, identify plot and themes, sketch and revise outlines of sections and chapters and episodes, describe settings and background, develop characters and fill in a narrative line with interesting details that raise and answer key questions, resolving conflicts while maintaining dramatic tension.

Religion potentially affects life-story development in positive as well as negative ways, beginning early in childhood. Religious beliefs and values influence children, in the first place, because they affect parenting. In the hands of parents, strong religious convictions provide a script for child rearing that is often a mixed blessing for children. While religiously committed parenting may meet children's basic psychosocial needs, it may restrict their possibilities for living out a story that is their own.

For instance, parents and religious groups that believe that children are gifts from God with eternal souls (but sinful natures) may love and protect them—but may also be motivated to induce bornagain experiences in their children and to inculcate them with rigid doctrines and overly strict moral codes. From early childhood onward, children immersed in a religious environment may have to follow a nearly invariant script that lays out the template and significance of their existence. When they are later exposed to the larger social and cultural pluralism within which their enclave exists, they may experience distress and confusion. In such cases, psychological symptoms may remain covert.

Kurokawa (1969) illustrated such phenomena in a study of acculturation and mental health among 460 Mennonite children who were being brought up in religious communities more or less closed off from the surrounding Canadian society. Kurokawa found that few of these children manifested overt signs of maladjustment and noted that the Mennonites' highly structured, authoritarian social system prevented children from acting out painful feelings in antisocial ways. However, this researcher did find covert symptoms of psychological disturbance in many of these children who outwardly appeared to be well adjusted. Such symptoms included diverse somatic complaints (headaches, stomach upset, shortness of breath), habit disturbances (e.g., nail biting, rocking, twitching), and depressive and anxiety symptoms (e.g., fear, worry, nightmares, sleep problems). In Kurokawa's interpretation: "The success in the socializing function of the [Mennonite] family is primarily due to the sacred quality attributed to the family. It is the authority of God which figures powerfully, and parents are only intermediaries who have been given the authority by God and Jesus to command men in Their name. Strict obedience to parents is a teaching profoundly stressed . . ." (pp. 700–702).

Primary relations with parents, siblings, peers, and a widening social network form the basis—the floor—that sustains the whole process of human development. The key problems for psychological development in childhood and adolescence (and also the tools for their resolution) come from within the network of primary social relationships—from parents, to begin with. These are the main characters in life stories. Significantly, such relationships also provide the matrix of individual religious understandings and practice.

For adolescents and young adults who feel isolated and lonely, and are in fact cut off from their families and other social networks, joining a marginal religious group headed by a charismatic patriarchal figure sometimes offers a substitute "loving family." For example, in their classic study of converts to a religious cult, Lofland and Stark (1965) noted poignantly that most converts were so alienated that "they could, for the most part, simply fall out of relatively conventional society unnoticed" (p. 873).

However, religious conversion can have the opposite meaning as well. Conversion can be a "way of maintaining relations with parents from whom the young adult is unable to separate" (Wenegrat 1990, p. 38). Wenegrat cited a study by Roberts (1965) that examined a small sample of students at an evangelical Christian college who had experienced a sudden conversion to the faith of their parents. Roberts found that these sudden "converts" displayed significantly more neurotic characteristics on psychological tests compared to the remainder of his sample. Roberts concluded that these sudden conversions signified capitulations to parents and were "regressive solutions to adolescent emancipation problems" (Wenegrat, 1990, p. 39; see also Richards, 1991).

Roberts's findings could be interpreted somewhat differently, however. It is not uncommon for some children growing up in a fundamentalist Christian environment to have multiple experiences of "conversion" to their parents' faith, just to make sure they are "saved." In such cases, culturally constructed ideas about the sinful nature of the self and the literal existence of Hell beyond the grave play on the characteristic insecurities of children. An example is seen in the following testimony, which I originally quoted in my study of identity and ideology among evangelical missionaries in Ecuador (Swanson, 1995):

I am a preacher's kid. . . . Let me start with when I accepted Jesus as my Savior. I was five years old, and the Holy Spirit convicted me of sin. I knew, even as a five-year-old, that I did things that were wrong. I can remember the actual feeling that I had, that Sunday morning in church, that I did things that were wrong and that I needed a savior. I needed Jesus to take away my sin. My feeling of sin was mainly from fighting with my brother, who was one year younger. I also knew, because I'd had training in my home, that Jesus had come to take away my feeling of guilt. So that day I just asked him to forgive my sins. That was the point when I became a Christian. But then as a seven-year-old, I heard an evangelist preach on hell, and I got worried. I knew that I still did things that were wrong. And so, after the service that night, I called my dad into my room and I told him that I was concerned. I knew Jesus had forgiven me of my sins, but I still did things that were wrong. I felt like I needed him to pray for me. And so he did. . . . I remember that he prayed for me, that the feeling of guilt would just be lifted from me. And I remember actually feeling that sin was lifted from me. (p. 39)

Consider also the following case from the same study: "All the time I was growing up, I never did really feel that I was saved. I went forward at least a dozen times, in different churches, to accept the Lord. But I never felt saved." (p. 51).

This statement takes on deeper meaning, perhaps, in light of other information that emerges in the life story:

As a kid in school, I had an enormous hang-up. I never knew how to read, so I hated school with a passion . . .

and in Sunday school, when they'd say, "Let's go around in a circle and each read a verse of this Bible chapter"— I'd leave before it came my turn to read. . . . Then I went to Japan, in the service. There was an old missionary there, about sixty-five years old, and he finally led me to the Lord—or led me to the assurance of my salvation. There was [also] a Christian G.I. who took me under his wing. He said, "You've got to learn how to read." He would read one page in this book, *Romans Verse by Verse*, in about two minutes. And I would read the next page in about a half hour. I hated it, but I knew that there was only one way to be a servant of the Lord, and that was to study the Bible. So I had to learn to read, at that age. It was very, very difficult. But I did it. And I did go to Bible school and I graduated, and became a missionary. (p. 51)

On the face of it, this testimony is about a child who felt ashamed and isolated because of a learning problem. But on a deeper level, it is about a religious subcultural group in which Bible-reading signifies the membership and identity of the saved—so that a child's inability to apprehend the word of God through his own eyes may be experienced as a damning moral defect. Thus, in this story, the "assurance of salvation" emerges in conjunction with the overcoming of illiteracy, which had loomed as an impasse in the moral career.

Downton (1979), in his study of the "sacred journeys" of young converts to Divine Light Mission, claimed he could easily tell which of his subjects had experienced religion-induced emotional trauma in childhood. They seemed overtly to be seeking relief from an overwhelming sense of fault and sin. But sometimes religious behavior expresses veiled hostility toward parents, according to Wenegrat (1990). He cited cases such as Jewish youths becoming fundamentalist Christians, or (alternatively) becoming more orthodox or pious than their parents—thus "honor[ing] their parents' religion, but in a fashion that emphasizes their parents' shortcomings" (p. 36).

Other examples from my research (Swanson, 1995) are found in the narratives of evangelical missionaries who, as children, experienced various kinds of estrangement—sometimes including psychological abandonment by their parents—but then went on to enter the missionary vocation.

My parents were missionaries. I was seven years old when they decided to go back to the mission field, and I was left in a mission home. I was one of twenty-seven kids living under one roof, and we had three adults to take care of us. From the time I was seven years old until I graduated from high school, I saw my parents just a couple of times, for six months each. I was essentially on my own.

The fact that today I am a missionary at all is still a mystery to a lot of my teachers, and to the people who were involved in my upbringing. . . . It was a very traumatic, difficult time. I resented it. I rebelled. I was an extrovert, but I felt very insecure and inferior. . . . I went around scaring people off, instead of winning friendships. I think that's a syndrome that's very common among missionary kids who are raised away from their parents, because the people who raise them really don't have the ability to love them as we love our own children. Consequently, we are rejected, in that kind of a setting.

Somewhere along the line—though it's not something I take credit for—I turned my life over to God, and God decided to use something that was a diamond in the rough. It was the result of when I finally called out to God. . . . Through accepting myself, I began to accept my parents. And I think the basis of acceptance is forgiveness. If I do think they did it wrong, it's forgiven, and it's forgotten that they did it wrong. Now, of course, I couldn't do that with my own son—leave him in a children's home. Nevertheless . . . now that I have buried my dad, I think more highly of him than I have ever thought of him before. (p. 57)

Religion cannot be viewed as something that is suddenly acquired or disposed of—put on, taken off, or altered like a suit of clothes. Rather, it must be interpreted in the context of a person's entire life story. Religious ideas and symbolic images often are bound up at the core of a person's overarching worldview, which includes a sense of place and time and subsumes the key motives and values that plot the course of psychosocial maturation from infancy onward.

In Figure V.1, the central question for the effect of worldview on the eventual integration of life story and identity lies in whether *Weltanschauung* tends to expand or restrict the range of development. In principle, a health-promoting worldview accommodates diverse, dissonant, and problematic experience by expanding a person's adaptive repertoire of cognitive interpretations and active responses to the challenges, threats, and crises that inevitably attend development in a pluralistic social environment. A health-inhibiting worldview, by contrast, narrows the range of such responses and thus constricts the environment and the experiential scope within which development can occur. Religious ideologies—transcendent belief systems grounded in particular social structures—are among the most powerful determinants of worldview elasticity.

The Social Context of Moral Development in Children

These ideas are borne out in studies of how children typically learn to distinguish "right" from "wrong" and acquire the ability to make moral choices in particular situations. As Damon (1988) observed: "Like adults, children have an elaborate social life from which troubling moral problems frequently arise. . . . Simply by virtue of their participation in essential social relationships, children encounter the classic moral issues facing humans everywhere: issues of fairness, honesty, responsibility, kindness, and obedience. . . . Broad variations in social experience can lead to broad differences in children's moral orientation" (p. 117).

Damon cited evidence that conventional sex-role expectations and experiences in Western societies tend to incline girls more toward a "morality of caring" and boys more toward a "morality of rules and justice." But he argued that such expectations can be interrogated and broadened, so that "boys and girls alike can learn to use both the morality of caring and the morality of justice with equal facility" (p. 118). Along similar lines, Edwards (1987) notes:

Children do not simply "receive" knowledge of standards, nor do they autonomously "construct" it without cultural assistance. Rather they "reconstruct" culturally appropriate moral meaning systems. That is, with increasing age and experience, children apply progressively more complex and mobile logical schemas to cultural distinctions and categories; they transform what they are told and what they experience into their own self-organized realities. These realities are idiosyncratic to each individual child and yet bear witness to extensive cross-cultural commonalities in early moral reasoning. . . . (p. 149)

Schweder, Mahapatra, and Miller (1987) reviewed 3 alternative theories of moral development in children that have important implications for approaches to the study of religion and parenting. Earlier cognitive-developmental theories (e.g., that of Kohlberg) argued that moral development in children was linked to a universal sequence of stages of cognitive maturation and interpersonal experiences with rules and conventional obligations. Social interaction theories (e.g., that of Turiel) suggested, on the contrary, that even very young children can distinguish between moral obligations and conventional obligations.

The two are not connected developmentally but arise from different kinds of social experiences. One kind of experience bears an obvious and intrinsic connection to justice, rights, harm, the welfare of others, and the like; the other kind does not.

A third theoretical alternative denies the assertion that children universally distinguish between conventional and moral obligations, suggesting instead that this happens only "in those cultures like our own where the social order has been separated ideologically from the natural moral order" (Schweder et al., 1987, p. 3). This third position carries the relativistic implication that the culturally constructed nature of distinctions between different kinds of obligations renders them culturally specific. Especially in contemporary pluralistic cultures that are based on notions of the autonomy of the self and an ethic of personal choice, the detachment of the affairs of ordinary social life from shared notions of a natural moral order results in existential uncertainty and a sense of anomie. Peter Berger (1969) and other sociologists have argued that such contingencies of modernity perpetuate a demand for religious ideologies and institutions that mediate between the two—that seem to provide a plausible, transcendent rationale not only for rules of conduct in everyday life but for the very act of living a life that ends in death. In a commodified social world where religion becomes a consumer choice, one of the most important "markets" for religion consists of parents who are worried about their children's moral development within a relativistic environment.

Edwards (1987) likewise critiqued universalist-cognitive-developmental theories of the acquisition of moral values by means of a comparative ethnographic study of children's "moral encounters" in different cultures. Edwards demonstrated that cultures vary considerably in the "organization of social encounters surrounding rules and their transgression" (p. 148). While not denying that children are "active moral reasoners," he argued that "adults and other socializing agents always scaffold moral development for children by emphasizing those dimensions of moral situations that are important. (p. 123). One of the important functions of religious ideology, of course, is to "hide the scaffolding" of moral commitments—to conceal the culturally constructed nature of moral rules and standards as well as conventions by imbuing them with transcendence.

Some of these points were illustrated in a research report by Kahana (1970), who studied ideas about dreams among 24 Hasidic boys ages 4 to 16 years. Kahana noted that this ultra-orthodox Jewish group viewed dreams as "messages sent by God and as serving definite ends assigned by Providence" (p. 4). He became interested in how the beliefs of this highly structured, bounded, religious community might influence the course of cognitive development, which is hypothesized by some to follow a universal sequence of stages. Kahana's findings suggested that in young children, Hasidic religious teachings tended to accelerate the acquisition of ideas about nonmaterial reality and dreams in particular. Interestingly, however, he noted a pattern of "cognitive regression" among his preadolescent and adolescent subjects, who also displayed considerable uncertainty and confusion regarding the origin and location of dreams. Kahana offered the following interpretation:

The Hasidic culture puts a premium on learning. But as children get older and temptations of the secular world become more threatening, there is an increasing discouragement of questioning and of independent thinking. A fearful attitude may develop in the growing child regarding all questions which do not have a ready answer. . . . Since the upsurge of libidinal drives has no behavioral outlet among Hasidic children, anxieties and conflicts may have to be resolved by intrapsychic means. It is possible that the apparent behavioral adjustment of the Hasidic adolescent is accomplished at the price of cognitive regression which serves to reduce anxiety. (p. 8)

In assessing the impact of religious teaching on a child's development and well-being, it is important to note that such understandings interact with other processes—some perhaps universal, others culturally specific. Not infrequently, psychological problems occur in children whose cultural groups face conflict and rapid transition. Gluckman (1966) offered some interesting illustrations of such interaction in a study of Maori children in New Zealand. In one vignette, Christian missionaries were trying to eradicate traditional Maori beliefs among impressionable adolescents they hoped to win as converts. One strategy in their efforts to undermine the Maori faith was to demonstrate that Maoris could, in fact, transgress their own moral rules with impunity. Hence, they encouraged local adolescent girls to defy the Maori taboo that prohibits menstruating females from sitting on toilet seats. A number of girls bravely did so. Then one of them became ill with an acute viral infection. "Within a few hours," Gluckman noted, "some dozen transgressors were all exhibiting various manifestations of anxiety. The common feature to all cases was hyperventilation" (p. 327).

Religion as Meaning and Belonging

Viewed broadly, religious issues tend to retain significance even to people who claim not to be "religious" in ordinary terms. Insofar as religion may be equated with basic worldview, it becomes salient to virtually every therapeutic encounter, according to Peck (1978):

[Psychotherapists routinely think] . . . that if patients don't consider themselves religious by virtue of their belief in God or their church membership, they are lacking in religion and the matter therefore needs no further scrutiny. But the fact of the matter is that everyone has an explicit or implicit set of ideas as to the essential nature of the world. Do patients envision the universe as basically chaotic and without meaning so that it is only sensible for them to grab whatever little pleasure they can whenever it is available? Do they see the world as a dog-eat-dog place where ruthlessness is essential for their survival? Or do they see it as a nurturing sort of place in which something good will always turn up and in which they need not fret much about the future? Or a place that owes them a living no matter how they conduct their lives? Or a universe of rigid law in which they will be struck down and cast away if they step even slightly out of line? Et cetera. There are all manner of different world views that people have. Sooner or later in the course of psychotherapy most therapists will come to recognize how a patient views the world, but if the therapist is specifically on the lookout for it, he or she will come to this recognition sooner rather than later. And it is essential that therapists arrive at this knowledge, for the world view of patients is always an essential part of their problems, and a correction in their world view is necessary for their cure. So I say to those I supervise: "Find out your patients' religions even if they say they don't have any." (p. 186)

Peck thus suggested that religion-as-worldview is neither intrinsically "bad" nor "good" for people; it can be either, or both; but it is always very significant to their values and thus very important for psychotherapists to assess.

On the positive side, religious traditions and texts can provide a coherent "script" that motivates life-story development—along with membership in a community whose shared experience, outlook, and interpretation of history maintains the plausibility of such a script. Religious participation thus links individual experience to larger stories and myths and gives people a sense of their communal past. Particularly in Western culture, religion holds up the idea of an individual moral self who sets out on a journey through life (e.g., *The Pilgrim's Progress*). Progress in the journey is measured by accomplishments in the world, by lessons learned, by wisdom accrued. By the logic of religious theodicy, suffering along the way can be seen as a redemptive tempering of the self. Finally, religion offers a way to interpret experiences of failure, personal disorganization, disorientation, and discontinuity in development; in particular, the religious idea of conversion—the spiritual transformation of a self—provides an imagery and a template for starting over and reinterpreting a disappointing past in terms of a new spiritual identity (Swanson, 1995; Ullman, 1989).

On the negative side, religious ideologies sometimes breed "greedy institutions" (Coser & Coser, 1979) that swallow up their members' individuality, creativity, and personal resources to serve the needs of charismatic leaders or powerful elites. The scripts of identity to which the adherents of some religions must conform are so rigid and unresponsive to contemporary human experience and existential dilemmas that they tend to quash authentic personal development and adaptive coping. The excessive legalism and self-abasement demanded by some religious systems—whereby even the minutiae of daily life and thought must bear the weight of judgment by moral absolutes—can create in some vulnerable souls (including children and adolescents) a paralyzing sense of guilt and self-absorbed vigilance. As mentioned previously (Sloat, 1992), poorly adapted parents sometimes use religious motives and exigencies in bad faith—that is, to justify the subjugation of their children to the service of their own emotional needs and dependencies. Finally, persons prone to ecstatic states of consciousness, delusions, and hallucinations may find affinities with religious imagery and ideas such as spirit possession as well as religious worldviews that posit ordinary human action as the opaque arena of cosmic moral warfare (Spanos, 1989). Such ideologies—whether maintained in isolation or held up by a surrounding religious group with strong external boundaries—may have a deleterious effect on the well-being, adaptive functioning, and coherence of identity in persons vulnerable to psychotic illness.

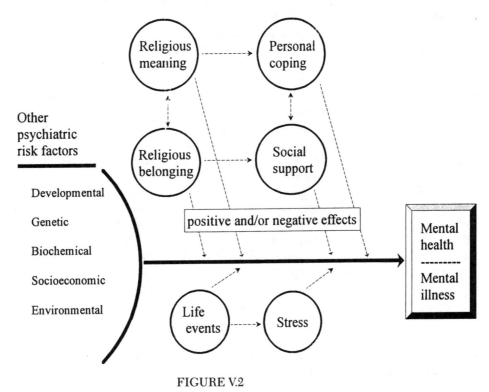

FIGURE V.2

Conceptual Model of Religion's Contribution to Mental Health/Mental Illness

Figure V.2 presents a conceptual summary of some of the ways in which religious participation and interpretation can affect mental health and illness. As shown, religion is not a primary determinant of mental health but acts rather as a mediating variable between a set of prior risk factors and the resulting psychiatric condition of an individual.

On the one hand (for example), a person's biochemical makeup, early developmental impoverishment, and/or socioeconomic marginality may predispose that individual to psychiatric disorder. Stressful life events threaten to precipitate disorder in a person already at risk. In that case, religion may have the potential to prevent mental illness in at least two ways: first, by offering a coherent interpretation of life experience that includes misfortune, suffering, and death—thus rendering such experience meaningful and more tolerable (Cook & Wimberley, 1983; McGrath, 1987); second, by providing a community of supportive others—religious cobelievers who are motivated to offer both emotional and instrumental assistance to a person in need.

On the other hand, certain kinds of religious interpretations and affiliations may actually compound psychopathology in vulnerable individuals.

Obvious (but perhaps not very common) examples include people with severe personality disorders, psychotic illnesses, or manic conditions who get involved with religious groups whose belief systems may accommodate, reinforce, and perpetuate psychiatric symptoms under such rubrics as demonic possession, being filled with the Holy Spirit, prophesying and speaking in tongues, and exercising charismatic spiritual authority. Also, religious attributions of blame, failure, unworthiness, sinfulness, and so on may be destructive to the well-being of a person with a fragile sense of self, rendering such a person less able to cope with distressing life events. Negative attributions may have an especially ill effect when they carry the weight of a religious community from whom the person then feels cut off and isolated.

Conclusion

Religious ideas, symbols, and communities continue to exert a significant influence in the lives of (perhaps most) children and parents in the world—those who are healthy but especially those who are ill. Thus the field of child and adolescent psychiatry, as a humanistic healing art as well as a biomedical science, must, at some point, concern itself with religion.

Mental health professionals who are most effective in treating psychiatric disorders in children and adolescents realize that the features of a person's inner world—including religious beliefs especially—are no less clinically significant than other "observable" aspects of mental illness. Such therapists do not prejudge what is "pathological religion" and what is "healthy religion" in patients who approach them; rather, they may discover and distinguish helpful vs. harmful features of religious worldviews and associations by mutual interpretation (and sometimes by fostering reinterpretation) of an individual's unique life story. In

practical terms, this means that religious meanings, commitments, and affiliations ideally should be inquired about in the diagnostic evaluation process and also incorporated into psychotherapy and other treatment approaches.

In order to accomplish this, psychiatrists ideally must learn as much as they can about the symbolic worlds their patients inhabit—to "stand in" and consider things religious from their patients' point of view. Second, however, they must attempt reflectively to "stand out," over against their encounters with overtly religious patients, and to view such encounters with a "third eye" trained back on their own worldview and religious (or antireligious) posture, bearing in mind how such a posture may affect the formation and continuance of genuine therapeutic relationships.

REFERENCES

Adams, P. L. (1972). Family characteristics of obsessive children. *American Journal of Psychiatry, 128,* 1414–1417.

Adams, P. L. (1973). *Obsessive children: A sociopsychiatric study.* New York: Brunner/Mazel.

Allport, G. (1950). *The individual and his religion: A psychological interpretation.* New York: MacMillan.

Armsby, R. E. (1971). A reexamination of the development of moral judgments in children. *Child Development, 42,* 1241–1248.

Barr, R. R. (1978). How not to raise our children: Theology and insecurity in childhood. *Religious Education, 73,* 707–713.

Batson, C. (1976). Religion as prosocial: Agent or double agent? *Journal for the Scientific Study of Religion, 21,* 119–122.

Batson, C. and Raynor-Price, L. (1983). Religious orientation and complexity of thought about existential concerns. *Journal for the Scientific Study of Religion, 22,* 38–50.

Bender, L. (1969). A longitudinal study of schizophrenic children with autism. *Hospital & Community Psychiatry, 20,* 230–237.

Bender, L. (1974). The family patterns of 100 schizophrenic children observed at Bellevue, 1935–1952. *Journal of Autism & Childhood Schizophrenia, 4,* 279–292.

Benson, P. L., Masters, K., & Larson, D. (1997). Religious influences on child and adolescent development. In J. D. Noshpitz, (Ed.), *Handbook of child and adolescent psychiatry* (Vol. 4, pp. 206–219). New York: John Wiley & Sons.

Berger, P. L. (1969). *The sacred canopy: Elements of a sociological theory of religion.* Garden City, NY: Doubleday.

Boone, K. C. (1989). *The Bible tells them so: The discourse of Protestant fundamentalism.* Albany: State University of New York.

Bottoms, B. L., Shaver, P. R., Goodman, G. S., & Qin, J. (1995). In the name of God: A profile of religion-related child abuse. *Journal of Social Issues, 51* (2), 85–112.

Bromley, D. G. (Ed.). (1991). *Religion and the social order: New developments in theory and research.* Greenwich, CT: JAI Press.

Capps, D. (1985). Religion and psychological well-being. In P. E. Hammond (Ed.), *The sacred in a secular age: Toward revision in the scientific study of religion.* Berkeley: University of California Press, pp 237–256.

Capps, D. (1992). Religion and child abuse: Perfect together. *Journal for the Scientific Study of Religion, 31,* 1–14.

Cavalletti, S. (1983). *The religious potential of the child: The description of an experience with children from ages three to six,* trans P. M. Coulter & J. M. Coulter. New York: Paulist Press.

Chance, S. (1988). God, patients, and psychiatrists. *Psychiatric Annals, 18,* 432–435.

Chesen, E. S. (1972). *Religion may be hazardous to your health.* New York: Wyden.

Cohler, B. J. (1988). The human studies and the life history. *Social Science Review, 62,* 552–576.

Coles, R. (1986). *The moral life of children.* Boston: Atlantic Monthly Press.

Coles, R. (1990). *The spiritual life of children.* Boston: Houghton Mifflin.

Cook, J. A., & Wimberley, D. W. (1983). If I should die before I wake: Religious commitment and adjustment to the death of a child. *Journal for the Scientific Study of Religion, 22,* 222–238.

Coser, R. L., & Coser, L. A. (1979). Jonestown as perverse utopia. *Dissent, 26,* 158–163.

Damon, W. (1988). *The moral child: Nurturing children's natural moral growth.* New York: Free Press.

Donahue, M. J. (1985). Intrinsic and extrinsic religiousness: Review and meta-analysis. *Journal of Personality and Social Psychology, 48,* 400–419.

Donahue, M. J., & Benson, P. L. (1995). Religion and the well-being of adolescents. *Journal of Social Issues, 51* (2), 145–161.

Downton, J. V. (1979). *Sacred journeys: The conversion of young Americans to Divine Light Mission.* New York: Columbia University Press.

Edwards, C. P. (1987). Culture and the construction of moral values: A comparative ethnography of moral encounters in two cultural settings. In J. Kagan & S. Lamb (Eds.), *The emergence of morality in young children* (pp. 123–149). Chicago: University of Chicago Press.

Ellison, C. G. (1991). Religious involvement and subjective well-being. *Journal of Health and Social Behavior, 32,* 80–99.

Evans-Pritchard, E. E. (1954). Religion. In E. E. Evans-Pritchard et al. (Eds.), *The institutions of primitive society* (p. 6). Glencoe, IL: Free Press.

Faddis, J. (1969). Ministering to children. *Pastoral Psychology, 20,* 44–49.

Francis, L. J., Pearson, P. R., & Kay, W. K. (1983). Neuroticism and religiosity among English schoolchildren. *Journal of Social Psychology, 121,* 149–150.

Freud, S. (1952). *Totem and taboo.* New York: W. W. Norton. Originally published 1913.

Freud, S. (1964). *The future of an illusion.* New York: Doubleday. Originally published 1927.

Gluckman, L. K. (1966). Aspects of the background of Maori children. *British Journal of Medical Psychology, 39,* 319–327.

Greven, P. (1991). Spare the child: The religious roots of punishment and the psychological impact of physical abuse. New York: Vintage Books.

Guerra, M., Benson, P., & Donahue, M. (1989). *The heart of the matter: Effects of catholic high schools on student values, beliefs, and behaviors.* Washington, DC: Catholic Educational Association.

Hanna, F. J., Myer, R. A., & Ottens, A. J. (1994). The effects of early religious training: Implications for counseling and development. *Counseling and Values, 39* (1), 32–41.

Holley, R. (1978). *Religious education and religious understanding: An introduction to the philosophy of religious education.* London: Routledge & Kegan Paul.

Hull, J. (Ed.). (1982). *New directions in religious education.* Basingstoke, England: The Falmer House.

Isert, L. (1969). Religious education in the light of current psychological concepts of development. *Catholic Educational Review, 66,* 656–663.

Jones, J. W. (1991). *Contemporary psychoanalysis and religion: Transference and transcendence.* New Haven, CT: Yale University Press.

Kagan, J., & Lamb, S. (Eds.). (1987). *The emergence of morality in young children.* Chicago: University of Chicago Press.

Kahana, B. (1970). Stages of the dream concept among Hasidic children. *Journal of Genetic Psychology, 116,* 3–9.

Kohlberg, L. (1984). *The psychology of moral development: The nature and validity of moral stages.* San Francisco: Harper & Row.

Kotre, J. (1984). *Outliving the self: Generativity and the interpretation of lives.* Baltimore, MD: Johns Hopkins University Press.

Kurokawa, M. (1969). Acculturation and mental health of Mennonite children. *Child Development, 40,* 689–705.

Larson, D. B., Pattison, E. M., Blazer, D. G., Omran, A., & Kaplan, B. H. (1986). Systematic analysis of research on religious variables in four major psychiatric journals, 1978–1982. *American Journal of Psychiatry, 143,* 329–334.

Lee, C. (1985). The good-enough family. *Journal of Psychology & Theology, 3,* 182–189.

Lofland, J., & Stark, R. (1965). Becoming a world saver. A theory of conversion to a deviant perspective. *American Sociological Review, 30,* 862–875.

Loomba, R. M. (1967). Moral and religious development in childhood and youth. *Psychologia: An international Journal of Psychology in the Orient, 10,* 25–32.

Lovinger, R. J. (1985). Religious imagery in the psychotherapy of a borderline patient. In M. H. Spero (Ed.), *Psychotherapy of the religious patient.* Springfield, IL: Charles C Thomas, pp. 181–207.

Ludwig, D. J., Weber, T., & Iben, D. (1974). Letters to God: A study of children's religious concepts. *Journal of Psychology & Theology, 2,* 31–35.

Lukianowicz, N. (1969). Hallucinations in nonpsychotic children. *Psychiatria Clinica, 2,* 321–337.

Lum, D. (1971). New challenges in mental health of children: For church and community. *Pastoral Psychology, 22,* 14–22.

MacAdams, D. (1985). *Power, intimacy, and the life story.* Chicago: Dorsey Press.

Manlow, J. L. (1995). *Faith born of seduction: Sexual trauma, body image, and religion.* New York: New York University Press.

McDargh, J. (1986). God, mother and me: An object relational perspective on religious material. *Pastoral Psychology, 34,* 251–263.

McGrath, E. A. (1987). *Supportive or non-supportive religious beliefs of children with life-threatening diseases.* Unpublished doctoral dissertation, New York University, New York.

Meissner, W. W. (1984). *Psychoanalysis and religious experience.* New Haven, CT: Yale University Press.

Odermann, V. J. (1990). Coming down to earth: A narrative methodology for promoting human growth and development. *Studies in Formative Spirituality, 11,* 47–56.

Pattison, E. M. (1969). The development of moral values in children. *Pastoral Psychology, 20,* 14–30.

Peck, M. S. (1978). *The road less traveled.* New York: Simon & Schuster.

Peteet, J. R. (1985). Clinical intersections between the religion of the psychiatrist and his patients. In M. H. Spero (Ed.), *Psychotherapy of the religious patient.* Springfield, IL: Charles C Thomas., pp. 63–84.

Ratcliff, D. (1985). The development of children's religious concepts: Research review. *Journal of Psychology & Christianity, 4,* 35–43.

Richards, P. S. (1991). Religious devoutness in college students: Relations with emotional adjustment and psychological separation from parents. *Journal of Counseling Psychology, 38* (2), 189–196.

Roberts, F. J. (1965). Some psychological factors in religious conversion. *British Journal of Social and Clinical Psychology, 4,* 185.

Rosenwald, G. C., & Ochberg, R. L. (Eds.). (1992). *Sto-*

ried lives: The cultural politics of self-understanding. New Haven, CT: Yale University Press.

Schweder, R., Mahapatra, M., & Miller, J. (1987). Culture and moral development. In J. Kagan & S. Lamb (Eds.), The emergence of morality in young children. Chicago: University of Chicago Press, pp. 1–83.

Sharp, M. (1986). What do we really want for our children? A psychologist's view of christian upbringing. London: Epworth Press.

Sloat, D. E. (1992). The dangers of growing up in a Christian home. New York: Thomas Nelson.

Spanos, N. (1989). Hypnosis, demon possession, and multiple personality: Strategic enactments and disavowals of responsibilities for actions. In C. A. Ward (Ed.), Altered states of consciousness and mental health: A cross-cultural perspective (pp. 96–124). Newbury Park, CA: Sage Publications.

Spero, M. H. (Ed.). (1985). Psychotherapy of the religious patient. Springfield, IL: Charles C Thomas.

Stewart, C. W. (1967). Adolescent religion: A developmental study of the religion of youth. New York: Abingdon Press.

Straus, M. (1995). Beating the devil out of them: Corporal punishment in American families. New York: Lexington Books.

Swanson, J. (1995). Echoes of the call: Identity and ideology among American missionaries in Ecuador. New York: Oxford University Press.

Swanson, G. (1965). The birth of the gods. Ann Arbor: University of Michigan Press, p. viii.

Tennant, C., Bebbington, P., & Hurry, J. (1982). Social experiences in childhood and adult psychiatric morbidity: A multiple regression analysis. Psychological Medicine, 12, 321–327.

Ullman, C. (1989). The transformed self: The psychology of religious conversion. New York: Plenum Press.

Ventis, W. L. (1995). The relationship between religion and mental health. Journal of Social Issues, 51 (2), 33–49.

Vergote, A. (1988). Guilt and desire: Religious attitudes and their pathological derivatives. (M. H. Wood, Trans.). New Haven, CT: Yale University Press.

Wenegrat, B. (1990). The divine archetype: The sociobiology and psychology of religion. Lexington, MA: Lexington Books.

Williams, R. (1971). A theory of God-concept readiness: From the Piagetian theories of child artificialism and the origin of religious feeling in children. Religious Education, 66, 62–66.

Wuthnow, R. J. (1988). Sociology of religion. In N. Smelser (Ed.), Handbook of sociology (pp. 473–509). Newbury Park, CA: Sage Publications, p. 474.

PART VI
AIDS in Children and Adolescents
Edward Sperling

Among all the illnesses and infections that can cause serious morbidity and mortality in children, childhood AIDS stands apart. Other illnesses, such as childhood cancers, are generally confined to the child patient, but because pediatric AIDS is almost always transmitted from an HIV-positive mother to the child, AIDS in children is a family disease. The development of AIDS in a young child is frequently the first sign to the mother or to both parents that they are HIV positive. Children with AIDS, therefore, are dying children of dying parents.

In addition, these children and families must cope with an unparalleled combination of psychosocial difficulties:

- The fact that AIDS is a preventable disease results in intense feelings of guilt and anger in addition to the sadness and despair that accompany other fatal illnesses.
- There is an overrepresentation of intravenous drug users and prostitutes among HIV-positive parents.
- Parents tend to be poor and to belong to minority groups.
- People who are HIV positive present a risk to the rest of the population and are both feared and shunned.
- AIDS is a chronic illness, with the stresses that attend the care of chronically ill patients.

Furthermore, during the first decade after which AIDS was first described in children (Oleske et al., 1983; Rubinstein et al., 1983), AIDS has spread from a few large urban centers to become a worldwide pandemic. By January 1995 a cumulative total of 1,025,073 AIDS cases (out of an estimated 6 million cases) had been re-

The author wishes to express his gratitude for the invaluable help of the following people in writing the section on a model day care center for children with AIDS: Carolyn Lelyveld, Director; Naomi Buchanan, M.S.W., Assistant Director; Henry Adam, M.D., Medical Director; and Allison Bell, Ph.D., staff psychologist.

ported to the World Health Organization (WHO), representing a 20% increase over the previous year. About 18 million adults and 1.5 million children are estimated to have been infected with the HIV virus since the beginning of the epidemic. Sexual transmission accounts for over three-quarters of the adult cases. Eighty percent of cases are diagnosed in Latin America, Asia, and Africa (Groopman et al., 1996).

Definition and Epidemiology of AIDS in Children and Adolescents

The presenting signs and symptoms of HIV are often nonspecific, and a high index of suspicion is needed for early identification and diagnosis. The diagnosis is made on the basis of clinical findings known to be associated with AIDS in children in addition to a positive serology. The most common conditions associated with pediatric AIDS are failure to thrive, pneumocystis, carenii pneumonia, lymphocytic interstitial pneumonia, recurrent bacterial infections, and candida esophagitis. It should be kept in mind that HIV antibodies during the first 15 months of life may represent maternal antibodies passively transferred to the fetus in utero.

Epidemiology of AIDS in Children in the United States

Through December 1995, 6,948 children in the United States under 13 years of age had been reported to the Centers for Disease Control to have AIDS (Centers for Disease Control and Preven-

tion, 1996). Over 95% of these children acquired the virus "vertically," that is, in utero or during childbirth from an HIV-positive mother. The remaining 4 to 5% of HIV-positive children acquire the disease through contact with contaminated fluids (e.g., blood transfusions), sexual abuse at the hands of an HIV-positive person, or through unknown routes. Simply sharing a household with HIV-positive family members, while using the same dishes and toothbrushes, has not resulted in transmission. Several family studies have verified this, although there have been a few exceptional reports of single cases transmitted "horizontally" through the family. In one such instance the transmission seems to have occurred through two brothers sharing a razor blade for shaving (Centers for Disease Control, 1994). Because the overwhelming number of children acquire the virus from their mothers, their racial/ethnic and geographical distribution parallels that of women with AIDS: 57% of (prenatally) acquired AIDS among African American children and 26% in Hispanic children. These incidence rates among African American and Hispanic children are respectively 21 and 13 times the incidence in Caucasian children. Of the mothers, 42% were reported to be intravenous drug abusers, and 32% were sexual partners of infected men, of whom 56% abused intravenous drugs.

An uncommon route of infection is through breast milk in nursing children. When breast milk substitutes are readily available, women infected with HIV are discouraged from breast feeding. In developing countries, however, when breast feeding is associated with improved child survival and safe and effective alternatives are lacking, the World Health Organization continues to consider that the benefits of breast feeding to outweigh the risks for most HIV-infected mothers.

Although transmission of HIV virus through sexual abuse of children in uncommon, this route should be considered in appropriate circumstances.

Epidemiology of AIDS
in Adolescents

While the number of adolescents harboring the HIV virus is large and increasing, the number of cases of AIDS reported by the Centers for Dis-

ease Control in this age group is relatively low; for example, by December 1995 there were 2,354 cases reported in adolescents ages 13 to 19. These figures mask the extent of the epidemic in adolescents, because adolescents who acquire the virus begin to show signs of clinical illness only after the latency period that precedes the outbreak of AIDS. The incubation period, seldom less than 2 years, is estimated to have a mean of 8 years. Thus the age group of early adulthood—ages 19 to 29 —reveals the extent of HIV in adolescents. By 1989 some 24,000 cases of AIDS were diagnosed in this group of young adults. By the use of back-calculation, it is estimated that from 1981 through 1987, approximately 17,000 persons ages 13 to 19 were infected by HIV, indicating a large reservoir of virus in this age group (Centers for Disease Control and Prevention, 1996; Goldsmith, 1993). At that time, hemophilia or coagulation disorder and blood transfusions accounted for over 50% in younger adolescents and for 25% of cases in older adolescents. Since 1985 blood and plasma products have become relatively safe so that a growing majority of adolescent HIV spread is through high-risk heterosexual and homosexual contact, through intravenous drug abuse, or both. Disadvantaged populations, including minority groups, runaway adolescents, and Job Corps applicants, evidence disproportionately high HIV prevalence rates (Conway et al., 1993).

Clinical Course of the Illness
in Children

As mentioned earlier, the diagnosis of AIDS in infants and children is made by a combination of clinical findings and seropositivity. If the serological status of the mother is unknown, there is nothing in the course of the pregnancy or the neonatal period that would lead one to suspect that the infant is seropositive. Newborns who are HIV positive cannot be distinguished from normals, despite the fact that many of them have acquired the virus as early as the 8th to 15th week of gestation. There have been reports of a characteristic HIV-positive embryopathy, which includes microcephaly, prominent boxlike forehead, hypertelorism, slanted eyes, with flattened nasal bridge, and patulous lips. This is a disputed finding, and even if these features are present, they develop only after

6 months and are of no help in diagnosing AIDS in early infancy. The serological tests for HIV antibodies that are used in making the diagnosis in adults, namely the ELISSA and the Inkblot tests, are not helpful during the first 15 months of life. They can establish only that these antibodies are present in the infant but cannot distinguish between maternal antibodies and those produced by the infant itself in response to the virus. If the mother is seropositive, her antibodies will be transmitted to the fetus, and these may persist for 15 months and occasionally longer. The "gold standard" for making an early diagnosis would be to isolate the virus from the infant's body. While there are experimental methods for isolating the virus, or serial fragments, these are still in the laboratory stage and not yet useful for clinical practice (Rogers, Ou, Kilbourne, & Schochetman, 1991). Similarly, it is possible to distinguish between maternal antibodies and those produced by an infant of 6 months and older, but these methods also are not yet available for clinical use.

Another confounding factor in making the diagnosis in infancy is that most children born of HIV-positive mothers do not themselves develop AIDS. It is estimated that 15 to 40% of children of HIV-positive mothers go on to develop the disease. The reason why this particular fraction of children develops AIDS while the majority do not is unknown. No correlation has been found between the mother's state of health, immune status, use of drugs, or any other parameter in the fetus or in its delivery that has shed any light on this issue, although there has been an intriguing difference between the transmission rate in the European Collaborative Group Study in which 16.4% of infants born to HIV-infected mothers developed AIDS (Newell et al., 1996) and other studies, which yielded rates from 25 to 40%. Mothers in the collaborative study who were all HIV positive had a 2.8% incidence of AIDS, whereas another comparative group had an 18% incidence of maternal AIDS. Increased illness in children was correlated with vaginal delivery (as contrasted with cesarean section) and with a low CD4 cell count in the mothers. Mothers have given birth to twins of whom only 1 went on to develop AIDS, and mothers have had children who have not developed AIDS subsequent to bearing children who did develop the illness. An infant who is discovered to be HIV positive therefore raises many uncertainties about diagnosis and prognosis, which add a special stress to the parent, the family, and medical caregivers.

The clinical course of AIDS in children differs significantly from the course of AIDS in adults. In children the latency period is of the order of several months, as compared to the 8 to 15 years of latency observed in adults. Children do not manifest the mononucleosislike onset of AIDS seen in adults. Lymphocytic interstitial pneumonitis, rare in adults, occurs in nearly half the cases in children. Pneumocystis carinii pneumonia is one of the most common opportunistic infections in children, whereas Kaposi's sarcoma, a common malignancy in adults with AIDS, is exceedingly rare in children.

In children common clinical features include failure to thrive, malaise, fever, lymphadenopathy, parotitis, hepatosplenomegaly, respiratory tract infections, chronic persistent or recurrent diarrhea, and persistent oral candidiasis. The central nervous system often is involved—in 40 to 90% of cases (Belman, 1992)—and may produce devastating neurological dysfunction.

AIDS in perinatally infected children appears to occur in a bimodal fashion: Children who become symptomatic before 1 year of age develop opportunistic infections (median age 5 to 7 months) and have HIV-related encephalopathy, which usually manifests itself at 9 to 15 months. This pattern of disease presentation is associated with rapid progression and early mortality. Members of a second group, who do not develop these early symptoms but instead later develop lymphocytic interstitial pneumonitis or recurrent bacterial infections, are likely to survive beyond 5 years of age. Although the disease eventually appears to progress in most children within 5 years, in some cases perinatally infected children have remained symptom-free for up to 10 years. (The author observed one such child who died at the age of 14.)

Infection Through Transfusion

In 1985 HIV antibody testing was initiated for blood donation to blood banks, and new HIV infection from this source has been reduced dramatically. In 1990 the risk from transfusions from 1 unit of blood was estimated as ranging from 1 in 36,000 to 1 in 153,000. The risk is not zero because of donation made in the so-called window period—the time between when a person becomes infected with HIV and when he or she begins to produce antibodies to the virus. This

period is usually about 3 months but may last as long as 6 months. Viral inactivation procedures for blood, as contrasted to plasma products, have not yet been realized. It is therefore important for physicians to explain the reasons for and the risks and benefits of transfusion and alternative treatments for their patients.

Hemophilia, Blood Products, and HIV

The history of hemophilia and HIV is a dramatic and poignant one (Mason & Olson, 1990). Hemophilia occurs almost exclusively in males. There are approximately 20,000 hemophiliacs in the United States, 13,000 of whom have the more serious A form. Prior to 1965, the treatment of choice was the infusion of fresh or frozen plasma to provide the needed clotting factors, particularly factor VIII. This treatment was very inefficient and had to be supplemented by supportive measures to ameliorate the arthritis secondary to bleeding into the large joints. By age 12 most children experienced crippling arthritis, and surviving adults were typically wheelchair bound. The median age of death for hemophiliacs in 1968 was 19.6 years. With the development of pooled factor concentrate in the late 1960s, the outlook for these patients changed dramatically for the better. Patients lived longer (median age of death in 1974 was 30.7 years), felt more comfortable, and led more active, independent lives. In the late 1970s, however, the nation's blood supply began to be contaminated with HIV, and cases of AIDS began to rise in the hemophiliac population in the early 1980s. Considering that a severe hemophiliac treated regularly by pooled factor was exposed to blood products from 800,000 to 1 million donors per year, it is not surprising that at present virtually all adult type A hemophiliacs are HIV positive. In 1985 it became possible to deactivate the HIV element in the blood factor supply so that spread by this route was eliminated. Currently there is a pool of children over age 12 who harbor HIV and who are developing and will continue to develop full-blown AIDS after the latency period. This adolescent population now accounts for some 20% of all reported AIDS in the adolescent age group. The unique combination of AIDS with

the preexisting chronic illness of hemophilia will be taken up later in this chapter.

Central Nervous System and HIV

Of critical importance to the clinical course of pediatric AIDS is the involvement of the central nervous system. The most extensive studies of such children have been reported by Belman (1992) and her collaborators, in which 61 out of 68 children with symptomatic HIV illness manifested central nervous system dysfunction. This extensive longitudinal study (4 years of observation at time of publication) revealed several subtypes of clinical course, ranging from a "rapidly progressive" course in which months of initial development were followed by rapid deterioration, a "subacute progressive" course in which the same sequence of development and deterioration progressed at a slower pace—for example, several years rather than several months, a "plateau" course in which the children reached a certain level of development and maintained that level over a period of months to years, and a "static" course in which the children progressed but at a slower than normal pace, accompanied by cognitive deficits, plus or minus neurological impairment. Some 25% of the children followed this static course, while the majority manifested a combination of subacute and plateau variations. The most frequent manifestations of central nervous system involvement included acquired microcephaly, cognitive impairment, and bilateral pyramidal tract signs.

Animal studies and human fetal examination have found HIV in brain tissues during fetal development. The AIDS virus is neurotrophic and causes an HIV encephalitis. Cortical atrophy and calcification in the basal ganglia have been found in radiographic studies. The brain also may be affected by opportunistic infection and cerebrovascular complication, resulting in ischemic infarctions or cerebral hemorrhages. It is possible that the high percentage of central nervous system involvement (90%) reported by Belman may be related to the fact that these children were inner-city children, many of whom were exposed to drugs, such as crack cocaine, during fetal development and were subjected to generally poor nutritional and medical care both before and after birth. Some smaller and more cross-sectional studies suggest a lower incidence, but it is too early to generalize from this beginning research literature.

Overall Clinical Considerations

Despite the unique psychosocial constellation that pediatric AIDS presents, it can be regarded as one form among others of a chronic illness of childhood with a fatal outcome (Edelson, 1991). It shares these features with malignant neoplasms of childhood with cystic fibrosis, degenerative diseases of the central nervous system (e.g., Tay-Sachs disease), and muscular dystrophy. As a chronic illness, it presents severe challenges to the patient, family, health care network, and society at large. At present the outcome of pediatric AIDS is fatal, but until recently, this was also true of childhood leukemia; before the advent of antileukemic chemotheraphy, the median survival from time of diagnosis was 2 months; today the outlook is for long-term disease-free intervals or even cure. The striking characteristics of AIDS as an illness in childhood is that it is an infectious illness most often acquired in fetal life or at birth with a course characterized by retarded development, neurological involvement, a downhill course with acute and plateau phases, opportunistic infections (especially pneumocystis carinii pneumonia and candidiasis), and an unusual pulmonary inflammation—lymphocytic interstitial pneumonitis.

Pediatric AIDS as a Chronic Illness

Children with chronic illnesses of various sorts share important needs that call for a noncategorical approach to the patient and family. Many facets of care need to be attended to, including frequent visits to doctors, transportation to and from the health care facility, dealing with the stigma of handicap, arranging for the finances of care, dealing with social agencies, coping with chronic and repeated episodes of illness and disability, and dealing with the fatigue and despair of such complex and daunting care. The need for a primary physician to coordinate this care, working with a

group of professionals, is paramount but is often lacking. Day care and school arrangements have to fit into the overall plan for the child.

A Model Day Care Center for Children with AIDS

In June 1986 the Bronx Municipal Hospital Center opened a day care center for children infected with HIV. Funded by a grant from the City Council of New York, the AIDS Day Care Center opened on a specially renovated hospital ward with the goal of providing a quality educational and group experience for 25 children ages 6 months to 7 years. In addition, the center would offer respite and support for families and other caregivers of these children and provide a program for the hospital's "boarder" children—HIV-positive children who are abandoned by their families and are living on the pediatric service. At that time, no other day care program would knowingly accept an HIV-positive child. The staff consisted of an educational director, 7 teachers, a full-time nurse, a social worker, and an office associate. There also was a part-time pediatric medical director, 2 bus drivers, transportation aides, and dietary and housekeeping aides. Psychiatric consultation was provided by the author. The center was open 5 days per week, 52 weeks per year, from 9:00 A.M. to 3:30 P.M. There were 3 classes, one for infants up to age 3 and two others for the older children. Families were offered a weekly group and a weekly parents' breakfast, and the center's kitchen was always open to them. The psychiatric consultant met weekly with the entire staff.

The children in the center were almost all from minority backgrounds, reflecting the epidemiology of this illness in this area. The casual observer would be struck with the normality of the scene. The children were able to relate and were active. The infants were given more individual care, while the older children were involved in group play and other activities. Some children showed signs of the earlier-described AIDS fetopathy, but what was more striking were swollen cervical lymph nodes and swollen parotid glands. There were a few runny noses and husky voices. One little girl was weak, preferred to rest most of the day, and looked depressed. What was most sur-

175

prising was the discrepancy between the appearance and developmental level of the children and their age. Typically a child who appeared to be 4 years old was in reality 6, so that the group as a whole appeared and behaved at a level considerably below their chronological ages. There were occasional episodes of oppositional and aggressive behavior, but this was true for only a few children and did not seem out of keeping with the group's generally disturbed backgrounds and development as a whole. More noteworthy were lags in language, speech articulation, level of symbolic play, and fine motor development.

SICKNESS AND DYING

Since all the children in the center were suffering from active HIV infection, there were special concerns around the optimal health care of each child, spread of secondary infections, and the children's reactions to their own and to each other's illnesses and dying. All children entering the center were carefully screened for immunizations and for other illnesses, such as hepatitis and parasites. Each child was regularly examined by the on-site nurse and pediatrician. At the first sign of intercurrent infection, the child could be placed in an isolation room and appropriate examination, treatment, hospitalization, or referral could be made. Each child had a chart with daily progress notes recorded by the nurse and/or pediatrician. During a 1-year period, 16 out of 24 children were hospitalized for an average stay of 6 days. There were no epidemic outbreaks of illnesses and no problem of serious secondary infections.

Four children died during a 1-year period. After the first death, staff members suffered from a feeling of futility about their work. This was reversed when the mother of that child returned to the center to express her feelings of grief and connectedness to the staff. At the subsequent deaths, staff members were invited and actively participated in the children's funerals. One of the mothers died of AIDS, and staff members decided to tell the children at a special meeting that one of their classmates was not in the center because her mother had died. The children had a chance to express their sadness and worries. They were assured that their friend was all right, and they eagerly lined up at the speaker phone to talk to that child, who was at home. Parents were told about the death and how it was handled with the children at the next regular parents' meeting. One mother turned away, thus expressing that she would not have wanted her child to know, which began a series of discussions about how staff members could not let people disappear without explanations and comments. Later, when this same mother's child died, she returned to the center to be there when the children were told. She wanted to be where her child had been in life, and she wanted the children to see that she was all right.

Communication and confidentiality in the center were vital issues. The center was called simply the Day Care Center. Children were picked up and delivered home by minivans with signs bearing that name. Parents became adept at concealing from their neighbors or from curious passersby how they could afford such day care and why it was not available to everyone. The occasional family whose members were known by their community to harbor the HIV virus faced harassment and threats, such as threatening notes left on their apartment doors. It was staff policy not to tell the children the name of their illness or why they were selected to be at the center. The waiting room, however, had many articles and printed information about AIDS for parents and others to peruse. The oldest child in the center, a 9-year-old girl, figured out her diagnosis from TV references to the illness. She handled this information confidentially with the staff and her family.

DISCLOSURE ISSUES

When dealing with AIDS, the issues of disclosure to children and adolescents are so complex and emotionally loaded that there is no precedent to follow. Each child and family must be appraised individually. The model of pediatric oncology, in which considerable research indicates the benefit of disclosure of life-threatening illness in many cases, is not easily translated to AIDS. Here family and cultural issues, the question of burdening the child with secret information, the uncovering of other secrets such as the child's paternity, in addition to the unique constellation of psychosocial issues listed earlier call for especially careful consideration before information is disclosed (Bonuck et al., 1993; Lipson et al., 1994).

STAFF ISSUES

The center staff members rigorously adhered to infection control guidelines set by the Centers for Disease Control. They were comfortable with interacting closely with the children and did not seem to be afraid of contracting the virus. A number of staff members had backgrounds of service, such as serving in the Peace Corps, teaching disabled children, or were from deeply religious backgrounds. They described, sometimes with amusement, how they had to be careful about telling people what sort of work they did: At a cocktail party people might shy away from you if they learned you were working with children with AIDS. Despite their idealism and pride in helping such desperate families, job burnout was one of the first topics to come up in staff meetings with the consulting psychiatrist. Comparisons were discussed with working on a renal dialysis unit for children, a burn unit, and other such stressful work settings. Staff members received a good deal of emotional support from each other and from their director (Miller & Gillies, 1996; Miller, Turner, & Moses, 1990).

The consulting psychiatrist met with staff members weekly, with the subject of each meeting being left up to them. In addition to suggestions about how to deal with burnout, staff members were interested in learning about child development—normal and abnormal, how to deal with the parental pathology, the anatomy of the central nervous system, how the children's symptoms were explained by their brain damage or family background, and how to manage difficult behavior problems as they arose in the classroom. Sensitive issues of interstaff feelings were not emphasized. There were some complaints about work issues, such as the need for more time off and vacations.

AIDS IN ADOLESCENTS

At present the principal routes of infection in adolescents are through unprotected sex and by intravenous drug abusers sharing needles. These two groups overlap, as drug abusers engage in unprotected sex with others who may or may not be drug abusers. While together these 2 groups account for the majority of HIV-positive adolescents, no comparative statistics about their relative frequency are available. Unsafe sex may be homosexual or heterosexual; in either case, anal intercourse appears to provide a greater risk than vaginal or oral contact. Anal intercourse is not rare among heterosexuals, as some female adolescents see this as a way of avoiding pregnancy and/or maintaining virginity. An increased risk factor of young gay males is that their initial partners often are considerably older than they and therefore are more likely to be HIV positive. Adolescent females appear to be the most rapidly growing seg-

ment of HIV-positive youths, receiving the virus from unsafe sex with HIV-positive males. Members of minority and low economic groups are disproportionately represented among adolescents with AIDS.

The number of reported cases of AIDS in adolescents—less than 1% of all AIDS cases—gives a falsely reassuring picture of the extent and potential of the HIV epidemic in this age group.

Considering the latency period of this illness, by extrapolating backward it is estimated that the number of HIV-positive adolescents is in the tens of thousands. Considering that half of high school students of both sexes have had sexual intercourse before graduation and that teenagers have the highest rate of sexually transmitted diseases of any age group, the teenage population appears poised for a rapidly escalating rise in HIV infection. From 1991 to 1993 the number of 13- to 21-year-olds in the United States who were HIV positive had risen by 77%. Extensive blood screening by the U.S. Job Corps, a federally funded residential program for high school dropouts or graduates 16 to 21 years of age who require additional education or training to hold meaningful employment, revealed an HIV-positive rate 4 times the rate in this age group than in the general population (Conway et al., 1993). Among the students 16 and 17 years of age, seroprevalence was higher in females (2.3 per 1,000) than in males (1.5 per 1,000), although for the entire group the rates were slightly higher for males.

Furthermore, this survey showed the wide and growing penetration of HIV into rural areas. As usual, minority groups were hardest hit. Among black and Hispanic adolescents, nearly 1 in 80 (1 in 40 in the Northeast) 21-year-olds were HIV positive, a remarkably high rate for a group that does not represent adolescents at highest risk, such as runaways, crack cocaine users, and active intravenous drug abusers.

Adolescents' immune systems are well developed, so that the symptoms and signs of AIDS in adolescents are generally the same as in adults. Adolescents, however, present psychological issues characteristic of their stage of development. They are dependent on adults for emotional and financial support. They need reliable caregivers whom they can emulate and from whom they can differentiate. This requires the ability to test their own ideas and to take some risks, but in a framework of safety and caregiving. But just those adolescents most at risk for AIDS frequently have little or no support, or even the opposite—neglectful and abusive parents who are negative role models, who have rejected their children sometimes because they are gay or because of other parental psychopathology. The parents themselves have to deal with prejudice, poverty, and the consequences of drug abuse and other illegal behavior.

Adolescents also are just learning to deal with their powerfully emerging sexuality, and they rely on their peers and adult culture to develop their mores. Popular media such as television and rap music make it clear that breaking the rules can titillate the public and make media stars of the perpetrators. Digging into the sexual histories of our political leaders does not supply our youths with edifying models.

Adolescents also tend to not plan for the long term and to see themselves as invulnerable. By now most of them know the essential facts about the transmission of HIV (Brown & Fritz, 1988; DiClemente, 1993), but only a small minority regularly use condoms or feel that they themselves are personally at risk for AIDS. Government officials, school boards, and the clergy lend support to this denial by offering simplistic advice, such as to "just say no," rather than offering comprehensive sexual and behavioral education, providing condoms free of charge, and experimenting with the exchange of clean needles for contaminated ones (Gellin & Rogers, 1992). Homeless youths frequently have no community caregiving services and must rely on "survival sex" to support themselves on the street. Many of these adolescents have become so alienated that they have little patience with efforts to protect them and may even welcome becoming HIV positive so that they do not have to worry about their status; they also may have little or no concern about placing their sexual partners at risk—they may even welcome it as an expression of their rage.

Psychiatric Issues in HIV-Positive Children, Adolescents, and Their Families

Since AIDS in children is essentially a family illness, a broad-based team approach is necessary. The pediatrician usually makes the diagnosis in the child, with the parents then becoming involved. The initial reaction in the family can be expected to be tumultuous—a varying mixture of shock, disbelief, denial, anger, anxiety, and depression. Ideally the pediatrician should be part of a team including nurses, aides, and mental health workers familiar with the course of this disease. A child psychiatric consultant can help to assess the ongoing development of the child, the stability of the family, the stress on the caregiving staff, and related social issues concerning confidentiality and high-risk behavior. The consultant should be familiar with community laws and resources dealing with this illness and also should be skilled in dealing with chronic illness (Meyers & Weitzman, 1991), with grieving, and with dealing with catastrophic reactions. The child psychiatrist can integrate the medical, neurological, behavioral, developmental, and caregiving issues, thereby helping the primary caregivers to arrive at coherent planning for the child and family. A nonjudgmental therapeutic attitude is essential (Spiegel & Meyers, 1991). The consultant can help to explicate the difference between developmental gaps, traumatic reactions, and defensive behaviors. Therapeutic communication employing play and other age-appropriate techniques can be fostered and interpreted by the consultant.

As noted, adolescents with AIDS fall into 2 main groups: those infected through blood products and those infected through high-risk behavior. These groups have different characteristics. Hemophiliacs are generally male, are not predominantly of minority background, are used to dealing with a chronic illness, and have a network of professionals whom they know well and on whom they can rely (Mason & Olson, 1990). They do not share the stigma of being associated with homosexual activities or of abusing drugs, and do not want to be associated with these groups. Feeling victimized, they may tend to deny the implications of their HIV status and may place their sexual partners at risk. The child psychiatrist can only hope to be effective as part of the caregiving network of this somewhat closed society of patients and professionals.

High-risk adolescents may react to the diagnosis of AIDS in many ways: Denial, anger, and omnipotence are not uncommon (Miller et al., 1990). This is a group that has not been systematically studied, and our information is anecdotal. Some youngsters will seek "revenge" by indulging in unbridled sexual and/or needle-sharing activities.

Others may deny their HIV status and carry on with their lives as usual. Many of these youngsters do not trust the adult establishment and can best be reached through peer group work wherever they congregate, whether at schools, in community programs for adolescents, on the streets, or even in their "shooting galleries."

Parents of HIV-positive children have to face the most daunting issues of illness and death. In addition to the risk factors listed earlier, if the parents are HIV positive, they have to face their own premature death and the death of their infected children. Infected parents will not live to see their healthy children grow into maturity, and they must plan for the future of their orphans (Michaels & Levine, 1992). It is estimated that by the year 2000, there will be at least 80,000 AIDS orphans in the 5 most affected states: New York, California, Florida, Texas, and New Jersey. The magnitude of these problems requires a broad national effort. The AIDS Day Care Center described earlier offers one such model of care and points out the various kinds of support—medical, social, financial, and psychological—that these families need.

Prevention and Social Policy

Despite the fact that a tremendous amount of information has been gathered in the past decade about the structure and behavior of the HIV virus, the goal of an effective vaccine remains elusive. A major obstacle in achieving this goal is this virus's rapid rate of mutation. We therefore cannot rely on a "magic bullet" to end this crisis. Since the routes of transmission are controllable, prevention becomes of paramount importance. Although seemingly within our grasp, the prevention of spread faces significant obstacles:

- Educational efforts have been marginally successful in changing unsafe behaviors in adolescents (DiClemente, 1993; Gellin & Rogers, 1992).
- Since AIDS is concentrated in geographical "hot spots" and in minority and socially ostracized groups, many people do not regard AIDS as a problem in their community or in their lives.
- Homophobic attitudes have blocked epidemiological research so that we do not have such basic facts as the prevalence of homosexuality in our adolescent or adult populations. Estimates vary from 1 to 10%.

- Certain people believe that sex education and making condoms and clean needles more available means that society is condoning teenage sexual intercourse and intravenous drug abuse.
- Similar attitudes have restricted comprehensive sex education in schools.
- The approach to substance abuse on the national level has concentrated on punishment rather than treatment, so that there are far fewer openings in drug rehabilitation programs than those who apply for such treatment.
- The public receives inadequate and contradictory messages about AIDS from the federal government. In 1987 the U.S. Congress imposed international travel restrictions for those with "dangerously contagious diseases" and added adult HIV infection to this list. In this connection, Surgeon General C. Everett Koop in 1986 stated clearly that "shaking hands, social kissing, coughing or sneezing will not transmit the AIDS virus. Nor has AIDS been contracted from swimming pools or bathing in hot tubs, or from eating in restaurants. . . . AIDS is not contracted from sharing bed linen, towels, cups, straws, dishes or any other eating utensils. You cannot get AIDS from toilets, doorknobs, telephones, office machinery, or household furniture." This level of clarity in defining "casual contact" is important in reducing unfounded fears and discrimination against AIDS patients.

It is clear that AIDS presents a severe challenge to our social values. A national policy of education, health care for catastrophic illness, increased treatment for substance abuse, working within the community of children and adolescents—in schools, clubs, religious organizations, on the streets—is urgently necessary. There are heartening research findings. A recent report from the National Institute of Allergy and Infectious Diseases has demonstrated that transmission of HIV from mother to infants can be reduced by two-thirds by treating HIV-positive pregnant women with zidovudin (AZT) (Cotton, 1994). The use of combined protease inhibitors holds out the promise that AIDS may be arrested in its relentless course and may be treatable much like other chronic illnesses (Deeks et al., 1997; Krasinski et al., 1994). There are even preliminary signs that college-age students are changing their attitudes toward AIDS patients, recognizing that all of society is affected rather than just a handful of minority stigmatized groups (Van de Ven, 1996). As caregiving clinicians, we must educate ourselves about these issues, have the courage to deal with victims of this disease, and advocate for enlightened social policy.

REFERENCES

Belman, A. L. (1992). Acquired immunodeficiency syndrome and the childs central nervous system. *Pediatric Clinics of North America, 39* (4), 691–714.

Bonuck, K. A., et al. (1993). AIDS and families: Cultural, psychosocial, and functional impacts. *Social Work in Health Care, 18* (2), 175–189.

Brown, L. K., & Fritz, G. K. (1988). Children's knowledge and attitudes about AIDS. *Journal of the American Academy of Child and Adolescent Psychiatry, 27* (4), 504–508.

Centers for Disease Control. (1994). HIV transmission between two adolescent brothers with hemophilia. *Journal of the American Medical Association, 271* (4), 262–264.

Centers for Disease Control and Prevention. (1996). AIDS cases by sex, age at diagnosis. *AIDS, 10* (12), 1452–1453.

Conway, G. A., et al. (1993). Trends in HIV prevalence among disadvantaged youth. *Journal of the American Medical Association, 269* (22), 2887–2889.

Cotton, P. (1994). Medical news and perspectives: Trial halted after drug cuts maternal HIV transmission rate by two thirds. *Journal of the American Medical Association, 271* (11), 807.

Deeks, S. G., et al. (1997). HIV-1 Protease inhibitors (Review). *Journal of the American Medical Association, 277* (2), 145–153.

DiClemente, R. J. (1993). Preventing HIV/AIDS among adolescents. *Journal of the American Medical Association, 270* (6), 760–776.

Edelson, P. J. (1991). Preface. In P. J. Edelson (Ed.), *Pediatric Clinics of North America, 38* (1), xi–xii.

Gellin, B. G., & Rogers, D. E. (1992). Technical successes and social failures: Approaching the second decade of the Aids epidemic. In V. T. De Vita, Jr., S. Hellman, & S. A. Rosenberg (Eds.), *AIDS: Etiology, diagnosis, treatment, and prevention* (3rd ed., pp. 497–502). Philadelphia: J. B. Lippincott.

Goldsmith, M. F. (1993). "Invisible" epidemic now becomes visible as HIV/AIDS pandemic reaches adolescents. *Journal of the American Medical Association, 270* (1), 16–19.

Groopman, J. E., et al. (1996). A year in review. *AIDS, 10* (Suppl.).

Koop, C. E. (1986). *Surgeon General's report on acquired immune deficiency syndrome.* Washington, DC: U.S. Government Printing Office.

Krasinski, K., et al. (1994). Antiretroviral therapy for children. *Acta Pediatrica (Suppl.), 400,* 63–69.

Lipson, M., et al. (1994). Disclosure of diagnosis to children with human immunodeficiency virus or acquired immunodeficiency syndrome. *Journal of Developmental and Behavioral Pediatrics, 15* (3), S61–65.

Mason, P. J., & Olson, R. A. (1990). Psychosocial aspects of AIDS and HIV infection in pediatric hemophilia patients. In J. M. Siebert & R. A. Olson (Eds.), *Children, adolescents, & AIDS* (pp. 61–91). Lincoln: University of Nebraska Press.

Meyers, A., & Weitzman, M. (1991). Pediatric HIV disease: The newest chronic illness of childhood. *Pediatric Clinics of North America, 38* (1), 169–194.

Michaels, D., & Levine, C. (1992). Estimates of the number of motherless youth orphaned by AIDS in the United States. *Journal of the American Medical Association, 268* (24), 3456–3461.

Miller, D., & Gillies, P. (1996). Is there life after work? Experiences of HIV and oncology health staff. *AIDS Care, 8* (2), 167–182.

Miller, H. G., Turner, C. F., & Moses, L. E. (1990). *AIDS, The second decade.* Washington, DC: National Academy Press.

Newell, M., et al. (1996). Verical transmission of HIV-1: Maternal immune status and obstetric factors. *AIDS, 10* (14), 1675–1681.

Oleske, J., Minnefore, A., Cooper, R., et al. (1983). Immune deficiency syndrome in children. *Journal of the American Medical Association, 249,* 2345–2349.

Rogers, M. F., Ou, C., Kilbourne, B., & Schochetman, G. (1991). Advances and problems in the diagnosis of HIV infection in infants. In P. A. Pizzo & C. M. Wilfert (Eds.), *Pediatric AIDS: The challenge of HIV infection in infants, children, and adolescents* (pp. 159–174) Baltimore, MD: Williams & Wilkins.

Rubinstein, A., Sicklick, M., Gupta, A., et al. (1983). Acquired immunodeficiency with reversed T4/T8 ratios in infants born to promiscuous drug-addicted mothers. *Journal of the American Medical Association, 249,* 2350–2356.

Silverman, D. C. (1993). Psychosocial impact of HIV-related caregiving on health providers: A review and recommendations for the role of psychiatry. *American Journal of Psychiatry, 150* (5), 705–712.

Spiegel, L., & Mayers, A. (1991). Psychosocial aspects of AIDS in children and adolescents. *Pediatric Clinics of North America, 38* (1), 153–167.

Van de Ven, P., et al. (1996). Trends in heterosexual tertiary students' knowledge of HIV and intentions to avoid people who might have HIV. *AIDS Care, 8* (1).

PART VII

The Role of Technology in the Rearing of Children

7 / The Impact of Television on Children and Adolescents

Gail Ritchie Henson

Television has achieved 99% penetration into American households (Walker, 1996). Children and adolescents spend more time watching television than they do attending school. Before they are 18, they may see 200,000 violent acts and 14,000 sexual messages, not to mention thousands of advertisements (Derksen & Strasburger, 1994). MTV reaches 239 million viewers in 68 countries, most of whom are teens and young adults. Children and television wield enormous economic power, spending almost $100 billion a year on clothes, food, entertainment, and cosmetics (Strasburger & Hendren, 1995). The issue of television's effects on this vulnerable yet powerful population generates research, hot discussion, legislation, and much emotion.

Health care professionals, parents, public policy makers, and educators find themselves responding to issues of special concern that emerge from the television screen into the worlds inhabited by children and adolescents: alcohol, drug, and tobacco use; body image, eating disorders, images of beauty; obesity; gender roles, sexuality; and interpersonal behavior; posttraumatic stress disorder, risk-taking, violence, aggression, and suicide.

Public concern over the effects of television on children and adolescents is so great that policy makers and children's advocacy groups have not waited for the scientific community to produce empirical evidence linking television viewing to negative effects on children. The landmark Telecommunications Act of 1996 is a direct outgrowth of public outrage and concern over the sex, violence, and negative messages of television to children and adolescents. While the debates within the medical and scientific communities continue, legislators have required by this act specific actions to let television programming be blocked out with a v-chip and to rate television programs.

A discussion of television's effects on children and adolescents must start by noting that the term *television* today means far more than offerings from the major networks. Rather, children and adolescents have access to a wide variety of offerings through a television set: They can rent videos; tape programs playing during school hours or overnight; pick up a wide range of programs via cable and satellite; play video games; and see the regular offerings from network, public, and independent television stations. For the purposes of this discussion, therefore, the term *television* extends to the total offerings that a child or adolescent can experience with a television set.

Whether television is perceived to be a boob tube or a magic window, researchers and policy makers have tackled many issues relating children and adolescents to television because of the roles that television has assumed in their developing lives. Television may take on the role of teacher and propagandist, offering children and adolescents information, attitudes, and behaviors that may or may not be adopted. Television may serve as a surrogate parent to many children. Television's offerings of violence cause great concern among professionals and parents alike as they study the link between television violence and aggression. As an educator and propagandist, television provides a view of life and how to live it, a view carefully constructed in most instances by its writers, producers, and editors.

American Culture: Children and Youths

Children and adolescents are both active and passive consumers of television. They do not watch television like sponges waiting to soak up the mediated experience provided by television; instead, a reciprocal or bidirectional relationship exists in varying degrees between the television and young viewers.

Conditions that affect their vulnerability to television include at least these: the experiences they bring to television; their understanding of the technical forms that comprise a television experience; their stage of cognitive and behavioral development; their intellectual capacity; their motivations for and expectations from viewing; their family's attitude toward television; their family's educational status; their viewing pattern (i.e., do they watch television alone, with parents, with siblings, or with peers?); the immediate and larger cultures in which they live; and their total media environment. Thus television will have different effects on different children.

Children may view television long before they can make sense of it. Systematic viewing of television begins around 2.5 years of age, reaches a high level during preschool, and declines somewhat during adolescence (Anderson, Lorch, Field, Collins, & Nathan, 1986; Huston, Wright, Rice, 1990). Nevertheless, children watch a lot of television daily—3 hours and 7 minutes a day, and teens watch 3 hours and 2 minutes a day (Television and Video Almanac 1997, 17a).

Children's viewing habits vary, and those habits will affect a child's attention to television. When they watch television, they usually do not give it their full attention. Children ages 1 to 10 years watch television with an estimated 52% of their visual attention. Children ages 11 to 19 years watch television with an estimated 68.8% of their visual attention. These figures stand in contrast to adults, who watch with 63.5% of their visual attention (Anderson et al., 1986, p. 1026; Bordeaux & Lange, 1991). Children and adolescents usually view television primarily with someone else, most often a sibling. Lawrence reported that a child spends 65% of the time viewing with a family member (Lawrence, Tasker, Daley, Orhiel, & Wozniak, 1986). Considering that children do not give full attention to the television and have access to one or more individuals in the viewing environ-

ment, then measures of hours of television attended to are, at best, estimates. While the television is on, children may spend time doing homework, talking with others, working on the computer, playing games or with toys, reading, talking on the phone, as well as many other activities.

Children bring to the television set different levels of comprehension of the television form itself, circumstances which may affect a child's attention to, comprehension of, and response to the television content (Anderson, Lorch, Field, Collins, & Nathan, 1986; Bearinger, 1990; Blanchard-Fields, Coon, & Matthews, 1986; Campbell, Wright, & Huston 1987; Dorr & Kunkel, 1990; Ginsburg, Jenkins, Walsh, & Peck, 1989; Gortmaker, Salter, & Walker, 1990; Harwood & Weissberg, 1987; Paget, Kritt, & Bergemann, 1984; Pezdek, Simon, Stoeckert, & Kiely, 1987; Potter, 1986, 1987).

Children's programming and adult programming may differ in formal features, or those technical aspects that help to shape the content. Such differences may include special effects, use of music, cutting and editing of footage, and voice-overs, among others. Children's programming may be characterized by "animated film, second person address, character voice narration," and simpler language. Adult programming may have more "live photography, third-person address, and adult male narration with sedate background music" (Campbell, Wright, & Huston, 1987, p. 311). The formal aspects of television production comprise part of the symbolic code of television.

Children and adolescents encounter television forms with different cognitive and developmental capabilities to understand the narrative form of the actual program, the technicalities of the production, the language used, and the program as a construction of a mediated reality as opposed to whatever *reality* truly is (Abelman, 1995; Meadowcroft, 1989; Rolandelli, Wright, & Huston, 1991). Researchers examining various developmental aspects of television viewing and inferencing suggest differences between adolescent and adult viewing (Blanchard-Fields, et al., 1986).

Children and adolescents have different incentives for viewing. If it is true that children, and particularly adolescents, have more access to television than to parents, then using television to alleviate loneliness or boredom becomes a salient motive (Brown, Childers, Bauman, & Koch, 1990; Brown, Childers, & Waszak, 1990; Coles, 1986). Television provides information to children and adolescents that may accomplish a variety of needs. Television provides information, entertainment, and relaxation. Television provides a background for interpersonal interaction by providing a basis for conversation, an opportunity to be with other family members or peers (Alexander, 1985; Anderson et al., 1986). Television also displaces other activities, such as exercise, conversation, reading, and engagement in interpersonal activities (Mutz, Roberts, & Vuuren, 1993). Thus any discussion of television's impact on children and adolescents must be qualified by considering individual differences in development, motivation, and comprehension of the forms of television.

Parents and Television: Who Is Doing More Parenting?

As the majority of children and adolescents studied live with 1 or more parents, the interaction between the parents and their children figures into the discussion of television's impact on this population. Television can be considered a positive factor in family relationships, both with siblings and with parents.

The role of the parent as a mediator of the child's television experience may be more potent before adolescence than during adolescence, and recommendations from such organizations as the American Academy of Pediatrics and the American Psychological Associations encourage parents to take an aggressive role in the use of television in the home (1995, 1996). Research generally supports the notion that parents have more rules for children under the age of 10 and very few, if any, rules for children over 10 (Abelman, 1984; Bearinger, 1990; Rothschild & Morgan, 1987). Dorr noted that children watch less television when parents have more rules related to it (Dorr & Kunkel, 1990). Rothschild (1984) said that the decrease in parental control—in rules, firmness, and disciplinary style—during adolescence tends to increase television's impact on adolescents. As youths seek more freedom and independence from their parents, they turn more to their peers (Larson, Kubey, & Colletti, 1989).

One special population of children and parents is that of gifted children (Abelman, 1984, 1995). Parents of gifted children have fewer rules about television than other parents and are less likely to talk about what the children have viewed with them. These parents are "less likely to use television for punishment or reward than are parents of nongifted children" (Abelman, 1984, p. 116). He said that gifted children do not ask their parents as many questions about television content as do nongifted children (Abelman, 1995).

Television can provide opportunities for positive interactions between parents and children (AAP, "Children, adolescents, and television" 1995b). Parents and children may decide together what to watch and what not to watch. The content of the programming may reinforce parental values; if it does not, then the content may provide an opportunity for discussion and reflection. Television content may provide an opportunity for the parents to broach sensitive topics such as sex, alcohol, and drugs. For example, parents in one study indicated an 83% approval rate for condom advertisements on television, reflecting their perception that the current AIDS crisis is a life-and-death situation (Buchta, 1989). Parents' fears that their children may contract AIDS or a sexually transmitted disease may lead them to use television messages about AIDS or diseases as a jumping off point for discussion with their children.

Television may be a source of conflict for some parents and children. The research of Ellis-Schwabe and Thornburg (1986) suggests that television is a noticeable but not particularly severe area of conflict with adolescents. They conclude that conflict occurs between mothers and sons less often than between fathers and daughters.

On the other hand, Bearinger (1990) suggests that conflicts over television viewing may be low on a parent's priority list of things to argue about in light of other problems they may have with their children, including "areas where they need control such as dating, telephone use, drinking, and driving" (p. 73).

Various studies suggest that children are more vulnerable to television content when parents are absent (Bearinger, 1990; Brown et al., 1990; Coles, 1986). Parental absence—physical or emotional—may encourage children to turn to television for relief, emotional needs, or information. Brown et al. (1990) cited 1 study in which children spent only 10 minutes a day with fathers, and of those 10 minutes, half of that was spent viewing television. Dorr and Kunkel (1990) noted that when fathers are present in a house, less television viewing occurs.

Coles (1986) stated very clearly what makes sense:

I conclude that what children do with television, psychologically, depends really of the nature of their own lives, the quality of their family life. A child who is having a rough time of it personally—whose parents . . . are mostly absent, or indifferent to him or her, or unstable—will be much more vulnerable to the emotional and moral power of television; will find in the programs all too much comfort or stimulation. But it is the life that these children bring to their television watching that prepares them so sadly, so dismally for the troubles they soon enough have. (7)

The general consensus is that few parents talk about television with their children. With the reality of single-parent households and 2 working parents, there is little prospect for parents to take up more of a mediator's role in their children's and adolescents' consumption of television. The National Parent Teachers Association (Dykstra 1996), Singer (1985, 1989), and others have called for parents to have training or at least a curriculum to help them talk about television with their children. Such parent education would be a critical part of the family's response to television in their lives. The American Academy of Pediatrics policy statements on children, adolescents, and television call for pediatricians to advise parents to limit children's viewing to 1 to 2 hours a day, provide advice on the effects of television, and encourage parents to develop television substitutes such as reading, athletics, and physical conditioning (CA & TV, *Pediatrics* 96–786–787, 1995b). The AAP statements also call for family participation in the program selection process as well as watching television with children to interpret it. The television has been thrust into the role of parent in many instances, but persons in health care and other child-oriented professions should encourage parents to take an active part in their children's television experience.

Television as Educator and Propagandist

A growing body of health care literature concerns key areas as related to television and children. This discussion will address those areas, specifically children's and adolescents' learning about alcohol, drug, and tobacco use; gender roles, sexuality, and behavior; body image and perceptions of beauty; and obesity. A separate section deals with violence, suicide, and aggression.

Most parents, pediatricians, and mental health workers agree that children learn much about the world around them and how they are a part of it from television; their level of media literacy is very high by the time they finish high school. Children and youths model behavior, language, styles of dress, and attitudes that they observe on television. The learning can be positive or prosocial, engendering empathy, altruism, and helping actions. However, the learning also can be negative or antisocial, playing itself out in antisocial attitudes, nonverbal violence, and verbal or physical violence.

Television can serve as a educator and propagandist. Studies by the Surgeon General, the National Institute of Mental Health, the National Institutes of Health, the American Medical Association, the American Academy of Pediatrics, and the American Psychological Association over the last 30 years show television to be a salient force as an educator.

Television, Children, Adolescents: Tobacco, Alcohol and Drug Abuse

Television provides many opportunities for educating children and adolescents about tobacco, drug, alcohol, and other substance abuse. At special risk are adolescents who consider the content of television portrayals of alcohol and drugs. Most available research considers alcohol use, as advertising for tobacco and illegal drugs is not permitted. Content analysis of televised portrayals of such usage is not abundant. However, children and adolescents view advertisements for beer and wine; sports sponsorships of athletic events by tobacco and alcohol companies; public service announcements about tobacco, drug, and alcohol abuse; information from television newscasts about them; and portrayals of their use in adult television programming. Researchers seem to agree that youths learning from television and other media sources about drug and alcohol use is a 2-step flow: The youths attend to mediated messages and then communicate their messages to others; in other words, the interpersonal component of the communication process is an important force in the salience of the televised messages.

Tobacco products may not be advertised on television, having been banned in 1971. Nevertheless, tobacco consumption—cigarettes, smokeless tobacco, and cigars—continues to increase, causing 400,000 deaths per year (AAP, 1995a). Children still view tobacco messages through programming content and sports events. When they see that smoking or using smokeless tobacco products is the norm for certain sports figures or for certain lifestyles, they may believe that more people smoke than actually do and their tendency to begin smoking may increase (Hazan & Glantz, 1995).

Children and adolescents view nonstandard forms of messages from the tobacco industry through televised sports. Stadium signs, logos on race cars, giant inflatable beer cans or wine bottles, are familiar fare (Madden & Grube, 1994). The Joe Camel logo has great recognition among children as young as 3 years old, almost as great as that of Mickey Mouse (AAP, 1995a).

One study of 3 weeks of prime-time programming on the 3 networks found that 24% of the programs contained at least 1 tobacco event, and 92% of tobacco "events" were pro-tobacco (Hazan & Glantz, 1995). More men smoked than women; smokers were middle class, rather than rich or poor; more were in technical and professional jobs; "good guys" outnumbered bad buys; and high-status role models were more likely to smoke than people of low or medium status. Hazan and Glantz concluded that the more high profile and glamorized the characters are on television, the more likely they are to be copied by children.

Even though the child can learn information from television about tobacco usage and develop positive or negative associations due to the knowledge of its effects, the parent's role is still critical in smoking prevention and cessation (Flay, et al., 1995).

While tobacco usage among teens is on the increase, so is the use of alcohol. Teens begin to experiment with alcohol early, so the information, attitudes, and behaviors conveyed by television has the potential to affect their attitude toward and use of drugs, alcohol, and tobacco. The American Academy of Pediatrics Committee on Communications noted sobering statistics related to alcohol abuse by youths in its 1995 position paper *Children, Adolescents and Advertising*. The authors stated that 25% of teenage suicides and homicides involve alcohol, 14,727 young people ages 16–20 died in alcohol-related motor vehicle

crashes in 1991, and that the average American child sees nearly 2000 beer and wine commercials annually (1995, pp. 295–297).

Indeed, alcohol abuse is a leading cause of death in motor vehicle fatalities for youths between 15 and 20, despite the attempts by states to decrease fatalities by raising the minimum legal drinking age (Worsnup 1997, 230 and National Safety Council 1996, p. 86). To illustrate this further, in 1994, 57% of 15–17 year olds who were drivers in fatal car accidents were alcohol-involved; 64% of drivers 18–20, and 75% of drivers 21–24 (Wright 1995).

Despite proactive groups like Students Against Drunk Driving (SADD), high school students drink a lot. By ninth grade, 19% of students report using alcohol once a week or more; 36% of high school students say they have had five or more drinks in a row during the past two weeks; and 90% of American high school seniors have tried alcohol (DeFoe & Breed, 535; AAP, 1995a).

One concern about television's influence on alcohol use by adolescents is that drinking leads to other behaviors that may have negative outcomes; it is a gateway drug. Students who drink often begin to use cigarettes, then marijuana, and perhaps other harder drugs (DeFoe & Breed, 1988). Students who do not drink from the seventh through 11th grades rarely use illicit drugs (DeFoe & Breed, 1988). However, substance use is considerable: Two-thirds of high school graduates are regular drinkers, one-fourth smoke marijuana on a monthly basis, and 1 out of 6 has tried cocaine (Atkin, 1990).

Adolescents are television literate: Television is a vital text in their learning process, one whose forms they readily understand. The advertisements, counteradvertisements and public service announcements, and program portrayals of alcohol use serve as a ready text for them (AAP, 1995b). Television provides information and vicarious modeling of experiences to inexperienced and curious viewers. Legally, this population cannot purchase alcohol, so television opens up to them a window into a forbidden world.

Advertisements for beer and wine fulfill both entertainment and educational functions, using clever technical production to attract and retain youths' attention or to provide more sober information about caloric content. Atkin's study of television advertisements for alcohol and teen drinking concluded that such advertisements may have a slight impact on alcohol misuse and drunken driving. From advertisements, teens can easily learn about drinking practices, brands, symbols, slogans, celebrity endorsers, and themes. They also may learn about ingredients, calories, and how beer is made (Atkin, 1990). With the alcohol industry spending over $1 billion in advertising annually, teens are exposed to many messages about alcohol (Worsnop (1997), 222).

Television advertising of alcohol depicts pleasurable contexts for drinking: Young people are shown "to have more friends, greater prestige, more fun and greater sex appeal" as well as "psychologic benefits such as self-confidence, escape from problems, or intensified feelings of femininity . . . gregariousness, sexual disinhibition, or male bonding experiences" (AAP, 1995a, p. 296; Atkin, 1990; Greenberg, B. S., Brown, J., Buerkel-Rothfuss, N. L., 1993). Social learning theory would suggest that the repetition of alcohol advertisements would provide a ready text from which adolescents can learn.

Public service announcements (PSAs) ask viewers to be careful with alcohol, not to drink and drive, to have a designated driver, not to smoke during pregnancy, not to use drugs. They provide scenarios by which teens can see behaviors they may choose to model. For example, an announcement may show a child refusing to use marijuana, try crack, or drink with others. Such announcements provide information about what is healthy, socially acceptable or unacceptable, and may be considered as alternative behaviors. The announcement may suggest rewards for good behavior as well as punishment for socially unacceptable behavior (Atkin, 1990). An avenue of research on the effectiveness of these announcements should include studying messages aimed at youths and teens, while not specifically related to drug or alcohol use, nevertheless with "themes of alternative highs, self-esteem, enhanced decision-making skills, the importance of taking care of oneself, and other values approaches to health behavior" (Resnick, 1990, p. 26).

The chief educator about the use of and abuse of alcohol and drugs, however, comes in the content of television programming itself. Preadolescents and teens watch a lot of television each week. The context of the content is that of adult programming, particularly drama and action stories. It is estimated that 80% of what children by sixth grade view is aimed at adults (DeFoe & Breed, 1988; Singer, 1985). Atkin (1990) suggested that a young person views several thousand

portrayals of drinking in television programming each year. Since 1978 prime-time adult programs have depicted about 8 drinking acts per hour; one study tracked 8 seasons of prime-time offerings and found alcohol appeared in 9 to 14% of all scenes (DeFoe & Breed, 1988). A 17-year study (1969–1985) of programming indicated that references to alcohol occurred in half of programs, 60% of action-adventure programs contained such references, and 70% of general dramatic programs contained them (Signorielli, 1987b). These same programs contained high levers of violence and sexual references, one figure estimating 70% of dramatic programs contained violence and one-third contained sexual references as a major component of the plot and another that 50% of music concept videos contain violence and 75% contain sexual imagery (Signorielli, 1987b, Strasburger & Hendren, 1995). Programs containing strong references to drinking also provide messages about violence and sex. Studies of the links among television portrayals of alcohol, violence, and sexual behavior are salient to discussion of television and youths. Youths and teens may use television as a basis for some of their perceptions of the reality of and frequency of alcohol use and contexts, attitudes, and behaviors. Family attitudes toward and use of alcohol peer influence youth use of alcohol.

What does television tell youths about alcohol? Children see alcohol used as a background for conversation, for business deals, or as a prelude to sexual activity; they see it used to deal with crisis, escape loneliness, have camaraderie or romance, or relax physically (AAP, 1995a; Atkin, 1990; DeFoe & Breed, 1988; Resnick, 1990). They see more men using alcohol than women (Signorielli, 1987b). Television content largely depicts the positive consequences of drinking, linking alcohol use to self-enhancement, legitimizing its use, convincing the young audience that drinking is the norm and is a reasonable way to deal with problems.

Research supports the view that heavy viewing is associated with favorable beliefs about alcohol, even in children of elementary school age. Children in fourth grade perceive alcohol as appropriate for adult use, and at fifth and sixth grades, boys express favorable attitudes to alcohol use after viewing television programs with drinking (DeFoe & Breed, 1988; Futch, Lisman, Geller, 1984; Neuendorf, 1985). Youths associate drinking alcohol with being an adult (DeFoe & Breed, 1988). Television advertisements certainly paint a rosy, happy world enhanced by alcohol use (Lipsitz, Brake, & Vincent, 1993).

Generally the television content does not show negative consequences of drinking—embarrassment, injury, violence, disease, alienation, delinquency (Atkin, 1990; DeFoe and Breed, 1988; Signorielli, 1987). Negative consequences, if depicted, may be laughed at or depicted as funny (e.g. a comical drunk, college kids acting silly after drinking) (Lowry, 1981; Signorielli, 1987). Children and adolescents do not have as many opportunities to view televised content in which alcohol is depicted in a negative way, as possibly leading to antisocial behavior, as being a source of danger to themselves and to their health.

Researchers have called for more content analysis and effects analysis of drug and alcohol portrayals on television. The Adolescent Health Program Study Group on the impact of televised drinking and alcohol advertising on youths outlined four areas of content analysis for future research:

1. Analysis of attributes of characters who use drugs (e.g. demographic characteristics, wealth, stealth)
2. The apparent consequences of use: are they depicted as positive, negative, or nonexistent?
3. Examination of how motives for use of chemicals are portrayed and how motivation is tied to consequences
4. Analysis of the context of use: to what extent programming provides normative cues for use, such as associating recreation with beer, romance with champagne, family and/or peer celebrations with alcohol in general; for illicit drug use, to what extent wealth, glamour, and excitement are associated with the procurement, use, and distribution of drugs (Resnick, 1990, p. 25).

The Adolescent Health Project Study Group also calls for effects analysis on cognition, attitudes, and behavior, including consideration of effects analysis on minority audiences, and on the outcomes of television events sponsored by the alcohol industry (e.g., the Super Bowl) and tobacco industry (e.g., car racing events).

The 1992 and 1995 policy statements of the American Academy of Pediatrics call for pediatricians to support efforts to eliminate alcohol advertising on television and also encourage extensive counteradvertising.

Gender, Body Image, Sexuality, and Behavior

Television serves as an educator and propagandist to its young viewers in the messages it sends about gender, body image, and sexuality, through exposure to thousands of images of what men and women do and how they dress and behave with members of the same and opposite sex. Children and adolescents add a substantial amount of information, attitudes, and symbolic behavior to their mental repertoire. How much they attend to that information, comprehend, retain, or act on it varies among the youths themselves. However, to children and adolescents, television serves as a potent medium for communicating stereotypes about men and women.

GENDER

Television helps to socialize children and adolescents about gender through its portrayals of men and women. Children who are frequent viewers of television tend to accept sex-role stereotypes and sex-typed occupational choices (Beuf, 1974; Frueh & McGhee, 1979; Liebert, 1986; Luecke-Aleksa, Anderson, & Collins, 1995; Wright et al., 1995). Children too young to read can comprehend cartoons, situation comedies, and other forms of programming that depict men and women (Calvert & Huston, 1987). Older children and adolescents are bombarded with gender-typed messages from both adult programming content and commercials. Television content can reinforce roles youths see in their viewing environment as well as provide them new information.

Over the past 20 years, content analyses of gender typing on television confirm that such stereotyping is pervasive (Calvert & Huston, 1987; Gerbner, Gross, Signorielli, Morgan, & Jackson-Beck, 1979; Mackey & Hess, 1982; Smith, 1994; Strasburger & Hendren, 1995). Portrayals of gender roles on television have been stable, in being supportive of a traditional image of men and women and the division of labor. In terms of sheer volume, portrayals of men outnumber portrayals of women by 2 or 3 to 1 (Remafedi, 1990). Stereotypes about women tell children that women usually are subservient to men, less aggressive, employed in largely stereotypical female occupations, interested in attractiveness, sex objects of men, often victims of sexual violence, and not as competent, authoritative, or important as men. Stereotypes about men tell children that men are more aggressive, stronger, problem solvers, more knowledgeable, more powerful, more authoritative, and more important than are women (Blum, 1990; Calvert & Huston, 1987; Liebert, 1986). Children learn cues about attitudes and behaviors toward chores from television, as well (Signorielli & Lears, 1992). In recent years there has been some increase in the presentation of female characters and in the diversity of their careers.

While traditional sources of instruction about sex roles and behavior such as family, religious institutions, and schools influence a child's understanding of sex roles, television provides a series of text for the child to study. Research supports the hypothesis that those who watch more television have more sexist views (Signorelli, 1990). Little research has been done about the effects of portrayal of sex roles on films, reruns, and programming such as music videos available through cable or videocassettes. Since many adolescents do have access to cable and videocassette recorders, more research needs to be conducted in this area.

Children become aware of gender-typed behaviors in media portrayals (Signorielli, 1990; Zemach & Cohen, 1986). Children can identify television content that communicates "feminine traits (warmth, sensitivity, gentleness), masculine occupations (medicine, science, politics), and roles ... of money management, providing for the family and shopping for food." Children select programs featuring same-sex characters who behave in gender-typed ways (Signorielli, 1990, p. 52).

However, television content does provide alternatives to the stereotypes, a technique called "counterstereotyping," in which characters act contrary to the stereotypes descried. Depictions of women as physicians or plumbers or of males as nurses or house husbands can provide information that will affect the child's sex-role attitudes. The repetition of counterstereotypical images can diminish stereotyped beliefs (Signorielli, 1990).

Children who are heavy viewers of television and think that the world of television is realistic aspire to televised images of occupations, usually careers of higher status that yield higher income and are more glamorous (Wright et al., 1995).

Adolescents learn sex-role attitudes from television as well as notions of the number of children to have and when to start a family (Morgan, 1987; Rothschild & Morgan, 1987; Signorielli, 1990). Girls who believe in traditional gender-role stereotypes are reinforced significantly by television (Morgan, 1987; Wright et al., 1995).

Body Image

Not only does the television provide many images of gender roles and behaviors, but myriad images abound to tell young viewers how men and women should look. As adolescents asset their independence from parents and seek their own identity, television is one ever-present text on beauty and physical attractiveness to which they can turn. Exposure of young women to beauty commercials results in an increase in young women's valuing beauty and developing unrealistic stereotypes and idealized images of physical attractiveness (Brown et al., 1990).

Advertising and television content powerfully communicate cultural ideals of beauty and attractiveness to teenagers. Such ideals may be reinforced by other media forms, family, and peers. The Adolescent Health Project Study Group on Television reported the following sober information:

The extreme ideals of physical attractiveness and thinness, presented in television programming and advertising, may exacerbate the difficulties many adolescents have in accepting their bodies and their own and others' overall appearance and may contribute to the development of depression, excessive use of cosmetics, abuse of cosmetic surgery, preoccupation with weight loss, and more severe and potentially fatal eating disorders such as anorexia nervosa. Media researchers have only just begun to test these hypotheses. Content analyses show that the current standard of attractiveness portrayed on television and in magazines is slimmer for women than for men and that the standard portrayed now in magazines and in the movies is the slimmest it has been since the last epidemic of eating disorders occurred in the mid 1920s. (Brown b, page 63)

The preoccupation with beauty, whether due to television appeals for beauty or through peer endorsement of cultural ideals of beauty, translates into teenage young women spending billions of dollars a year on cosmetics, girls as young as 14 seeking surgery to reduce or enlarge breasts, and more than half of high school girls embarking on serious weight-reducing diets (Brown et al., 1990;

Graham & Hamdan, 1987). Serious diets and preoccupation with thinness as an ideal may lead to eating disorders. Adolescent girls, primarily white and upper middle-class girls, have an incidence of 10 to 14% of anorexia nervosa and bulimia (American College of Physicians, 1986).

Despite the cultural ideal of thinness, adolescent obesity is prevalent (Black-Williams, 1994; Dietz, 1993; Gortmaker, 1996; Klesges, Shelton, & Klesges, 1993; Kotz & Story, 1994; Taras, 1995; Wong et al., 1992). Between 15 and 30% of all adolescents are obese, with those watching television more than 5 hours of television per day being 4.65 more likely to be overweight than those watching zero to 2 hours per day (Desmond, Price, Hallinan & Smith, 1989; Gortmaker, et al., 1996). More females are obese than males. During the past 2 decades, obesity has increased 53% for blacks and 35% for whites. Desmond suggested that the increase in obesity in black adolescents may be accounted for by an acceptance of overweight as a cultural norm for this subgroup. Other data suggest the influence of a black subculture regarding eating patterns (Desmond et al., 1989). Inactivity among other minority groups, such as Hispanics and Asians, has been studied but not positively correlated to obesity (Wolf et al., 1993). Target marketing of food products to ethnic minority youths also may reinforce food preferences and encourage eating patterns that contribute to obesity (Wolf, 1993).

Children and adolescents receive mixed messages from television content, whether from advertising or other film and television content. On the one hand, they are encouraged to be physically fit, watch calories, be slim, have attractive hair, and adopt healthy lifestyles, and on the other, they observe a steady diet of advertising for junk food, fat- and sodium-laden food, cereals and snack products high in sugar, alcohol—all consumed by people who are thin and glamorous. The results observed are obesity on the one hand and eating disorders on the other.

The link between television viewing and obesity continues to be a matter of discussion by health care professionals (Gortmaker et al., 1996; Kotz & Story, 1994; Taras & Gage, 1995; Wong et al., 1992). Studies indicate that 60% of overweight incidence in the adolescent population ages 10 to 15 can be linked to excess television viewing time (Gortmaker et al., 1996). Most children do not actively exercise while viewing television. Televising viewing and obesity are associated by children eating more—both while watching television and by eating foods that are advertised—and reducing energy expended because of reduced time spent in more energy-intensive activities and alterations in metabolic rate (Dietz, 1990; Kotz & Story, 1994).

However, they do receive cultural images of beauty, body image, food consumption patterns, and fitness from television and other media. These media consistently convey negative messages about obesity, messages that adolescents internalize (Dietz, 1990). Research suggests that as early as age 7, children have learned what characteristics their culture deems attractive (Dietz, 1990; Feldman, Feldman, & Goodman, 1988), preferring lean figures over obese figures.

Heavy viewers of television will observe more characters or models who fit cultural norms of attractiveness, fitness, and beauty. Commercials rarely show obese characters, and television programs rarely show obese teens. Television characters are usually fit, with only 12% of characters being overweight or obese (Dietz, 1990). With 30% of the population being overweight and the television portrayals of men, women, and children not being very obese, young viewers in search of identity and body image may infer that obesity is a stigma and that something is wrong with them if they are overweight.

With the amount of food advertising shown to the young viewers, they also get the message that they can eat and not get fat (Ogletree, et al., 1990). Dietz (1990) concludes that "bulimia can be seen as the fullest adaptation to the food messages of television, because only a bulimic can eat all she wants and never become obese (p. 81).

Education programs to enlist parents, schools, health professionals, the food and entertainment industries all could work together to provide massive amounts of education for this population. However, children and adolescents have so much direct access to televised messages—in some cases more than do parents—that the power of these messages to affect their cognitive, affective, and behavioral responses is great.

SEXUALITY

Television indeed serves children and adolescents as an educator about body image and gender roles. Yet the learning does not stop there; television also provides information, attitudes, and behaviors about sexuality and sexual behavior for its young viewers to process. Teens view nearly 14,000 sexual references via television annually, with only 165 references concerning birth control, self-control, abstinence, or sexually transmitted diseases (AAP, 1995c). The popular MTV channel airs concept videos that involve sexual imagery 75% of the time, violence 50% of the time, and videos that combine violence and sex, usually violence against women, 80% of the time (Strasburger & Hendren, 1995). Soap operas—favorite fare among teen and preteen girls—depict sex between unmarried partners 24 times more than between spouses and rarely talk about contraception, disease, or AIDS as negative consequences.

The specter of AIDS has made sexuality as portrayed on television an issue of life and death. Teenage sexuality has increased dramatically. According to the American Academy of Pediatrics, half of all American females and two-thirds of all males have had sexual intercourse by the age of 17 (AAP, 1995c). Most teenage girls say their first experience was unplanned, and over 85% have sexual intercourse without seeking advice on contraception or sexually transmitted diseases (AAP, 1995). One in 10 teenage girls becomes pregnant; half of the babies are born, and half are aborted. One out of 7 sexually active teenagers has a sexually transmitted disease, and half of the 20 million cases of sexually transmitted diseases in the United States afflict teens (Brown et al., 1990).

Teenagers are more sexually active now than ever, but these teens are not necessarily looking to parents for information about sexuality (Csikszentmihalyi, 1996). In fact, most parents do not provide the information adolescents seek, for example, about the interpersonal aspect of sexuality (Silverman-Watkins & Sprafkin, 1983). As the parents detach themselves from the role of mediator of television content, they also abandon most, if not all, rules governing their child's viewing of television.

Social learning theorists contend that televised sexual content provides information, attitudes, and behaviors that young viewers can attend to, comprehend varying degrees, retain, and copy, given the right context. Observational learning theory suggests that television affects young viewers through exposure, acquisition, and acceptance (Silverman-Watkins & Sprafkin, 1983; Sprafkin, Gadow, & Grayson, 1987). The question is to what extent children and adolescents understand the sexual innuendoes they hear and the information about sex and sexual behaviors they see.

The content viewed by children and adolescents varies according to the individual, the time of day, the availability of cable and premium channels, and the use of videocassettes. They see informational public service announcements urging safe sex and the use of condoms (Buchta, 1990). They see fragile marriages in soap operas and dramas. They hear panels on afternoon talk shows that discuss extramarital affairs and all manner of sexual topics. They see sexual behavior associated with violence and power rather than in the context of love. They see traditional gender typing in the interpersonal relations between men and women, with men and being aggressive sexually and women taking on passive roles or being victims (AAP, 1995c; Brown et al., 1990; Silverman-Watkins & Sprafkin, 1983; Solderman, Greenberg, & Linsangan, 1988). Sex is used in advertising to sell beer, engines, waterbeds, lottery tickets—actually, anything. The 900-numbers by which viewers are invited to call women to assuage their loneliness or need for love or find a date constitute a form of interactive sexuality mediated by the television.

Research on the effects of televised portrayals on sex on preadolescent children is scarce. Also research with adolescents is difficult because of the parental consent needed to conduct it. Research on 900-numbers, sexual messages from music videos, cable sex offerings, and sexually oriented films viewed on videocassettes needs to be conducted. However, abundant studies suggest the effects of viewing televised content about sexuality and sexual behavior on adolescents.

The standard of beauty held up for young women by television messages is a difficult one for this adolescent population to achieve. Some implications of televised images of beauty and attractiveness as they relate to learning about sexuality bear noting. For young men repeatedly exposed to mediated pictures of sexual attractiveness, dissatisfaction with their girlfriends or girls in their environment has been documented (Weaver, Masland, & Zillman, 1984; Kendrick & Gutierres, 1980).

Tan (1985) conducted experiments with girls 16 to 18 to determine the effects of beauty commercials, those incorporating sex appeal, youth, beauty, or actors for whom sex appeal was a prominent feature. The girls who saw the beauty advertisements ascribed a higher importance rating to beauty characteristics as a means to "be popular with men."

Television viewing may have dramatic effects on both male and female adolescents' beliefs about sex. Disinhibition may be one effect, leading young viewers to become sexually callous to women or more readily accept the incidences of sexual activity, such as promiscuity, extramarital affairs, and rape (Brown et al., 1990). Brown et al. (1990) concluded that television tells youth that "sex is the province of the young and is used to initiate heterosexual interaction rather than to express affection in long-standing, intimate relationships; precautions against pregnancy or disease are never discussed or used" (Brown et al., 1990, p. 65).

Sexual activity on television has exploded since the 1950s, when Lucy and Ricky Ricardo had to sleep in separate beds. A Harris and Harris 1988 study of the sexual messages during the 1987–1988 season found 65,000 instances of sexual material during the 12:30–4:00 P.M. and 8–11 P.M. time slots, both times of adult programming with high action, drama, and situation comedies (Solderman et al., 1988). Peterson, Moore, and Furstenburg (1984) studied the correlation of television watching with early initiation of sexual activity among adolescents, and they found a positive relation for adolescent females but not males.

Sexuality on television is often portrayed in drama and action-adventure programs that also contain a significant amount of alcohol use and violence. Signorielli (1987b) has reported that sex on prime-time dramatic programs occurs in 9 out of 10 programs. She noted that 60% of programming depicts sex as incidental to the plot and 35% have sex as a major focus. One-third of situation comedies, popular with young adolescents, and action-adventure programs have sexual references as vital aspects of the plot. Twenty-five percent of sexual references are light or comic in nature, with comic sex prevailing in situation comedies and serious sex in action-adventure and general dramatic programs. Drinkers are more often portrayed as being involved in romantic relationships.

Television portrayals of sexual behavior concern adults, particularly as AIDS and sexually transmitted diseases continue to claim victims. On television, prostitutes and homosexuals get AIDS or sexually transmitted diseases, not ordinary people who engage in casual, unprotected sex. While television stations run public service announcements urging people to practice safe sex and use condoms, particularly on cable channels such as MTV, popular with older children and adolescents (AAP, 1995c). Few stations will air advertisements for contraceptive devices. However, one writer suggested that "it is possible that the appearance of one or two condom advertisements on Monday Night Football programs would do much more to

lower teenage pregnancy rates than five years worth of federally funded adolescent health programs" (Buchta, 1989, p. 223).

Television portrayals of sexuality and sexual behavior serve as powerful educators for young viewers. The high incidence of such references, the access children and adolescents have to television, and the decreasing role parents play as mediators of television content all serve as catalysts for continuing research about the effects such content has on children and adolescents.

However, television can be a powerful medium for promoting responsible sex, awareness of AIDS and sexually transmitted diseases, delaying sexual activity, and encouraging abstinence. The American Academy of Pediatrics recommends that the broadcast industry to endorse the Advocates for Youth's "Guide to Responsible Sexual Content in Television, Films, and Music"; use public service announcements that promote abstinence and use of condoms; and focus on responsible sexual behavior and decision making (AAP, 1995).

TELEVISION VIOLENCE

No discussion of television and its impact on children and adolescents is complete without an examination of television violence and its possible effects on this population. This discussion examines the nature of violence observed on television and questions related to violence, theories regarding televised violence and young people, and consequences of viewing television violence. Psychiatrists, parents, and health care givers play vital roles in assisting children and adolescents as they react to the televised images of violence—both real and fictional—that they see.

Televised violence abounds during hours that children and adolescents are watching. For almost 20 years, violence watchers have observed 5 to 6 acts of violence during adult prime-time shows. This contrasts with the 20 to 30 acts of violence during children's programming (APA, 1996; Friedrich-Cofer & Huston, 1986; Gerbner et al., 1979; Gerbner, Gross, Morgan, and Signorielli, 1980). Researchers are just starting to consider the violence presented by television reruns, music videos, and film videocassettes.

The issue of linkage between violence on television and violence or aggressive behavior in a child's life is an important one. The number of incidents of violence observed by children and adolescents is mind-boggling—200,000 before the age of 18 (Derksen & Strasburger, 1994).

However, televised violence has other effects on the lives of children and adolescents; the violence observed on television becomes of the other violence in their lives at school, on the streets, in their homes, and in their community (Tulloch, 1995). Making sense of violence is a challenge for young children who are distinguishing real violence from fictional violence and for adolescents who are developing life patterns of dealing with violence (Eron, 1995; Hoffner, 1995; Libow, 1992; Paik & Comstock, 1994).

Adolescents are in the midst of a variety of cognitive changes, particularly with regard to the capacity for abstract thought and moral judgment, which may render them especially susceptible to the influence of media portrayals of violence. Adolescents are both the perpetrators and the victims of a disproportionate number of antisocial acts relative to their proportion in the population. It is estimated that 15% of adolescents engage in repeatedly serious antisocial acts; a full one-third of all violent crimes are committed by adolescents. Suicide and homicide are two of the three leading causes of death among adolescents and young adults. By college age, as many as 22% of women have been raped, and half of all rape victims are less than 18 years old. (Hoberman, 1990, p. 45)

Children and adolescents observe playful violence, fantasy violence, object violence, nonphysical violence, and interpersonal violence. They see it in cartoons, soap operas, newscasts, situation comedies, music videos, videos they rent, and video games: Violence is everywhere. They see nightly stories of murder and drug-related crimes, police and suspects clashing, demonstrators clashing with police in local as well as international streets, children of war carrying assault weapons, not to mention violence in sports, interpersonal violence in political debates, and domestic violence. Often cited is the 1993 case of a 5-year old Ohio boy who set fire to his family's home, killing his 2-year-old sister, allegedly inspired by the MTV cartoon series *Beavis and Butthead.*

Children can observe in the media and then evaluate the following types of aggression: physical, playful physical, nonpayment, verbal, symbolic, and object (Gadow, Sprafkin, & Ficarrotto, 1987). *Physical aggression* involves hitting, punching, biting, kicking, tripping, pushing, or fighting; the recipient may respond negatively or be neutral. *Playful physical aggression* could be the same, except that the recipient might laugh or respond approvingly. *Nonpayment aggression* involves verbal, object-directed, or symbolic aggression. *Verbal aggression* may include verbal threats, teasing, and name calling. *Symbolic aggression* may take the form of gestures that threaten, chasing another child, attempting to hurt or threaten another in a nonverbal way. *Object aggression* may include damaging an object or throwing it to the floor (Gadow et al., 1987). The effects of violence—the pain caused by whatever kind of violence is viewed, the pain felt by the victim's family or friends—is rarely demonstrated (Price, Merrill, & Clause, 1992).

The questions raised by the medical community, social science researchers, public policy makers, parents, and the public boil down to this basic issue: Since television violence persists, so what? While broadcasters and scientists continue to debate the connection between children's viewing of violence via the television screen and becoming more aggressive and violent, physicians, psychologists, researchers, not to mention children's advocacy groups and lawmakers alike have concluded that television violence *does* teach antisocial behavior; desensitize children to violence; make them more prone to anxiety, sleep disorders, post-traumatic stress syndrome, and aggressive behavior; and lead them to condone violence as an acceptable means of conflict resolution, making them more fearful of the world around them; less sensitive to the pain and suffering of others; more prone to take risks, disobey class rules, and argue more; and more likely to behave in aggressive or harmful ways to others (APA, 1996; Baillie, 1994; Dykstra, 1997; Forbes & McClure, 1994; Friedlander, 1993; Sege & Dietz, 1994; Simons & Silveira, 1994).

Unwilling to wait for the scientific community to reach a conclusion, lawmakers and parents have taken matters in their own hands. Lawmakers addressed concern about the effects of violence on television in the 1996 Telecommunications Act, which called for the television industry to create a v-chip that would let parents block out shows they deem unacceptable and also to create a series of ratings similar to those used by the movie industry. Organizations such as the American Academy of Pediatrics and the American Psychological Association have issued statements and position papers related to the negative effects of television viewing. Parent groups such as the National Parent Teacher Association joined with lawmakers and scientists to lobby for legislation, content-based labeling and develop curriculum for parents and students to develop media literacy and awareness of negative effects of television (Dykstra, 1997).

These questions and others have been studied using a variety of approaches, including Freudian-based theories that humankind possesses violence in its psyche, a theory of catharsis; social learning theory; instigation and cue theory; and arousal theory, social cognition, and constructivist theory. Several meta-analyses of the vast literature (over 1,000 articles) on children and televised violence exist; these conclude that a positive relationship exists between exposure to television violence and aggressive, antisocial behavior (Comstock & Strausburger, 1990; Heath, Bresolin, & Rinaldi, 1989; Josephson, 1987; Paik & Comstock, 1994; Pearl, 1984; Tulloch, 1995).

The catharsis theory suggests that viewing violence on television may encourage people to act less aggressively. The word *catharsis* derives from Aristotle's *Poetics,* in which he suggested that drama, especially tragedy, has the power to move the viewer to fear and pity, purging the viewer of those emotions. For researchers who believed that human nature possessed a tendency to violence, such a theory seemed viable (Berkowitz, 1962; Comstock & Strausburger, 1990; Ellis, 1972; Feshback, 1979, 1972). To date, there has been no firm substantiation of the catharsis theory; rather, all available evidence tends to support Albert Bandura's social learning theory and its subsequent modifications.

Albert Bandura saw television violence's link with aggression through his theory of social learning (Bandura, Ross, & Ross, 1963; Bandura, 1973, 1983; Josephson, 1987). This theory has been modified and expanded over the decades. Social learning theory posits that children may learn behaviors from observing television, much the same way that they learn them from parents and other live sources. It proposes that children may reproduce behaviors they have witnessed, both prosocial and antisocial or violent acts. Estimates of the child's ability to copy behaviors, given the right circumstances or frustrations, after even a one-time exposure, range from 6 months to 2 years (Comstock & Strausburger, 1990; Josephson, 1987). The social learning approach to televised violence has been supported in laboratory experiments and field studies (Belson, 1978; Eron, 1982; Huesmann & Eron, 1963; Josephson, 1987; Lefokowitz, Eron, & Walder, 1977; Singer & Singer, 1981).

The theory of disinhibition, instigation, and cue theory suggests that viewing violence on television not only leads to learning specific attitudes and behaviors that can be copied but also enables children to generalize from the violence that they view and apply it, particularly when violence is rewarded. A change in attitude toward violent behavior occurs. Television violence triggers an aggressive response:

. . . when a subject had been provoked and was emotionally aroused or angered, exposure to violent programming could instigate an immediate aggressive response. Whether the depicted aggression is justified then becomes a crucial determinant in whether the modeled violent behavior will be adapted. Observing justified behavior is more likely to prompt aggressive behavior in the viewer. This theory is more sensitive to the idea that children learn aggressive attitudes from certain programs and may come to believe that violence is a necessary and acceptable solution to complex problems, as long as the good guys "triumph." (Comstock 1990, p. 34)

Researchers have conducted numerous studies to indicate that children who are heavy viewers of television perceive the world to be more violent and dangerous—or "mean and scary"—than it is and to accept or condone other children's acts of aggression (APA, 1996; Comstock & Strausburger, 1990; Gerbner, Gross, & Gross; 1980; Hoffer, 1994; Singer & Singer, 1984). Gerbner heads the Annenberg School of Communication program, which produces a violence profile each year. It measures perceptions of danger, a mean world index, and an index of alienation and gloom. Research from the project suggests that television viewing tends to cultivate a sense of danger, vulnerability, mistrust, and a general feeling of gloominess.

Yet another theory, the arousal theory, needs to be considered. Comstock and Strausburger (1990) stated that "Researchers after Bandura developed a theory that certain programming can evoke a generalized emotional arousal that could affect an individual's subsequent behavior, driving it beyond its normal threshold" (p. 95). They cited an increase in aggressive behavior and restlessness, even in preschoolers who watch *Sesame Street,* as exemplifying the arousal theory.

The constructivist view suggests that children construct their view of reality and make sense or meaning of it from a variety of sources. To be sure, institutionalized violence in the society comes to children via the television. The nightly fare of news brought the Challenger disaster in 1986, the Gulf War in 1991, and pictures of war in Ireland, the Middle East, and Central Europe. Interpersonal violence—verbal, nonverbal, and physical—is observed through soap operas, prime-time viewing, music videos, video games, and cartoons such as *Beavis and Butthead,* all of which the children see. Whether viewing one-time traumas such as the Challenger disaster or daily programming, children construct a view of the reality in which they live (Terr et al., 1996).

Variables such as sex, knowledge about aggression, disposition, production techniques, plot, cues for aggression, and patterns of social interaction among family and peer, family factors, hours of sleep, outdoor activity, and organized daily routine all account for responses to media violence (Berkowitz, 1984; Friedlander, 1993; Friedrich-Cofer & Huston, 1986; Heath, et al., 1989; Libow, 1992; Wiegman, Kuttschreuter, & Baarda, 1992; Wiley & Weiss, 1993; Wilson & Weiss, 1993). Singer (1989) stated that "parents' own viewing habits, their paucity of other cultural interests, and their lack of rules concerning television viewing may provide a home atmosphere that puts their children at risk" (p. 445). It might be asked if certain groups are more susceptible to televised violence than others, the extent to which demographic factors affect youths' reactions to television violence, how family values, attitudes toward violence and firearms, and patterns of interaction affect youths' reactions, and if youths with aggressive behavior are necessarily attracted to violent television control.

PERSONAL VIOLENCE: SUICIDE

One other form of violence needs to be mentioned here: suicide. Debates exist within medical literature about whether presentations of suicide on television newscasts, programs, or films shown on television cause an increase or clustering of suicides (Simkin et al., 1995). Teenage suicides are more prevalent among boys than girls (Kessler, Downey, Milavsky, & Stipp, 1988). The question is if television—through news reporting and fictional portrayals of suicides, their motives, and their methods—provides the script and opportunity for learning an activity.

Concern with the effect of mediated portrayals of suicide are old. Researchers referring to the "Werther effect" allude to a character by Goethe in his 1774 *The Sorrows of Young Werther,* a character who committed suicide, and suggested that copy behavior occurs (Berman, 1988; Schmidtke & Hafner, 1988). Other studies have found that suicides have increased following the fictional portrayal of deaths on television. One study found that railway suicides among 15- to 19-year-old West German boys increased sharply after a program showing a teenager jumping under a train; deaths from Russian roulette increased following release of *The Deer Hunter* (Videodrome, 1994).

Television news accounts about youth suicide have increased significantly over the past 30 years. Feature stories discussing youth suicide have also increased (Kessler et al., 1988). Phillips and Cartensen (1986) reported that clusters of teen suicides occurred nationally after news stories about youth suicides were aired. The number of suicides reaches a peak after national stories of suicides. The evidence presented suggests that the more publicity given to the suicide story, the greater the increase in suicides. Moreover, that increase in death occurs mainly in the geographic area where the story is publicized; single-vehicle crashes increase after such news stories. They suggested that the suicides may have precipitated suicides that would have occurred soon anyway, even in the absence of a news story. Their study also suggested that coroners may have misclassified ambiguous deaths, being influenced by the news stories themselves.

Kessler and his colleagues have conducted several comprehensive studies to suggest that there is no reliable association between news stories and suicides and adults; however, they found that a reliable association did exist among teenagers, news stories, and suicides between 1973 and 1980, but reversed itself by 1981.

Fictional portrayals of suicides may lead in some cases to imitative suicidal behavior among teenagers (Gould and Shaffer, 1986; Simkin, et al., 1995). Berman (1988) also studied fictional portrayals of suicides and concluded that there is no increase in suicide. However, he did find that among completed suicides, there was an increased imitation of the method of suicide depicted in fictional portrayals. He also noted that the effect of portrayals of suicide is interactive with the viewer. The impact of such portrayals depends on the viewer's character, the stimulus, and the condition of the viewer's environment.

The portrayal of nonfictional and fictional suicides may have a profound effect on young viewers. Health care workers, parents, and educators fear that adolescent suicides cause pacts of death, even an epidemic of suicides (Steede & Range, 1989). Adolescents' knowledge of a suicide may not be enough to influence suicidal behavior (Simkin et al., 1995; Steede & Range, 1989). Nevertheless, parents, educators, and some health care workers can provide anecdotal evidence of completed suicides imitating a televised portrayal of method, cause, and provocation. Suicide is a tragic form of violence to self, friends, and family. Continued research into the effects of television portrayals of suicides will benefit children and adolescents.

Regardless of the theories espoused, the question of effects or consequences of television violence unfold before health care givers, parents, educators, and public policy makers. First there are the short-term and long-term effects to consider. It can be said that short-term effects may occur from a one-time viewing of television. As Bandura's and others' research shows, a child can copy behavior viewed once on television up to 2 years later. Short-term effects such as one child hitting another child immediately after seeing a morning of fantasy violence on cartoons may be serious (such as the *Beavis and Butthead* incident).

Long-term effects of television violence are more difficult to measure. Some studies suggest that a child who sees considerable violence on television as early as the third grade will be more aggressive 20 years later (Comstock & Strausburger, 1990; Huesmann, 1982; Huesman, Eron, Lefwokitz, 1984).

If children and adolescents watch a significant amount of television, and if violence is an important component in that viewing, then they may be affected by the violence they see. The Study Group on Television Violence and Aggressive Behavior lists the following situations in which violence on television can trigger aggressive or antisocial behavior:

1. Reward or lack of punishment for the perpetrator of violence
2. Portrayal of the violence as being justified
3. Clues in the portrayal that mimic real life
4. Portrayal of the perpetrator as being similar to the viewer
5. Depiction of behavior that has vengeful motives
6. Depiction of violence without consequences—violence without pain, suffering, sorrow, or remorse
7. Real-life violence
8. Uncriticized violence
9. Violence that pleases the viewer
10. Violence without associated humor in the story
11. Abuse that includes physical violence as well as verbal abuse
12. Aggression against females by males engaged in sexual conquest
13. Portrayals—whether violent or not—that leave the viewer angry
14. Viewers who are angry or provoked before viewing a violent portrayal or who are frustrated afterward (Comstock & Strausburger 1990, p. 39)

Media violence has specific consequences. It teaches social scripts for violent response to specific environmental triggers; facilitates tendencies toward aggressive behavior, especially sexual aggression; modifies community attitudes toward accepting violence; stimulates emotional desensitization to violence; and fails to explore the social and political roots of observed violence.

Research on television programming about suicide should continue. Also, research should be conducted on the effects on children of popular sources of violence including interactive phone lines and 900 numbers, and cybercommunication. Research on posttraumatic stress syndrome as related to televised violence and children's awareness of real violence as seen in news and documentary accounts continues.

The federal government took a bold step in passing the Telecommunications Act of 1996 mandating the v-chip for blocking out violence and calling for industry-based ratings of television shows. Media decision makers struggle with ethical dilemmas about airing executions, scenes of police brutality, or victims of violence. Children and adolescents who see real violence process those experiences in a wide range of ways. The National Institutes of Mental Health, the American Academy of Pediatrics, and the American Psychological Association join with civic and consumer groups to alert the public of potential dangers of television violence to this vulnerable audience.

What can be done about television violence? First, it will not go away. Second, as cable and satellite services become increasingly available to young viewers, these viewers will have more opportunity to view violent programming. Third, it is likely that network programming will continue to offer more violent programming to try to keep its share of the viewing audience. Fourth, parents need to take an active role in helping their children understand what they are seeing on television. Limiting the number of hours children watch television will reduce the amount of violence seen. Sixth, media programmers should be encouraged to join with specialists in child and adolescent health care to develop programming that shows other means than violence to solve conflict.

Conclusion

Television touches the lives of children and adolescents in countless ways. As an educator and propagandist, it delivers many lessons to this vulnerable audience. It educates them about how they should look, dress, eat, talk, act, interact, feel, and treat the opposite sex.

This discussion has confined itself to broad areas that involve children and adolescents: alcohol, drug, and tobacco use; body image, gender roles, sexuality, AIDS, and sexually transmitted diseases; television violence and aggression. Professional organizations continue to express their concerns about these topics, as they have through the years. They have commissioned studies and issued statements regarding sexual messages, advertising, substance abuse, diet, and violence on television. The 1996 Telecommunications Act indicates the extent to which concern over the effects of television on children has reached the policy makers in this country.

Implications of research about television and its impact on children and adolescents suggest many things to health care professionals and all involved with children. First, children and parents need to be taught critical viewing skills. Children can learn about the technical and production aspects of producing television content. They also can benefit from instruction about reality and fantasy, or the *mediated* view of the world, its people, and their relationships. The National Parent Teacher Association has promoted media literacy and parent awareness programs (Dykstra, 1996), and more school systems are incorporating media literacy into their curricula to facilitate comprehension of televised and other mediated content.

Second, parents need to take an active role in their children's use of television. They need to watch television with their children, regardless of the age, and discuss its content. If parents tend to detach themselves from active involvement in their children's use of television after the age of 10, they should become encouraged to be more active participants, and therefore their children's primary source of information and attitudes.

Third, health care givers and people in related fields of social sciences, communication, and ethnography can continue to conduct studies on the effects of television on children and adolescents. Much is to be done to assess the learning available from nonnetwork sources of television fare; convergence is becoming a reality in the entire telecommunications industry, bringing the whole world of cyberspace to the television screen, not to mention cable programming, premium services that might bring pornography into the house, satellite offerings, interactive television services, music videos, video games, and film videocassettes. As the media environment for viewing is rapidly evolving, so research must trap into that new environment.

More attention needs to be devoted to television portrayals of sexuality and sexual behavior, gender roles, and youth perceptions of AIDS and sexually transmitted diseases. Also, more research is needed in the impact of television images of global violence and youths' perceptions of that violence and threats to themselves or their country.

Fourth, health care providers need to continue to use their findings and make them known to people in the entertainment industry and the government, continuing to lobby for programming and advertising context that does not hold up unreachable ideals of beauty and success; devalue children, women, or minorities; or lock persons into rigid gender roles.

As the technology of telecommunications is in a state of rapid change, so the impact of television on children and adolescents will continue to be of concern and fascination.

REFERENCES

Abelman, R. (1984, November). Television and the gifted child. *Roper Review*, 115–118.

Abelman, R. (1995). Gifted, LD, and gifted/LD children's understanding of temporal sequencing on television. *Journal of Broadcasting & Electronic Media, 39*, 297–312.

Abramowitz, R. H., Peterson, A. C., & Schulenberg, J. E. (1984). Changes in self-image during early adolescence. In D. Offer, E. Ostrov, & I. Howard (Eds.), *Patterns of adolescent self-image* (pp. 19–28). (New Directions for Mental Health Services, No. 22). San Francisco: Jossey-Bass.

Alexander, A. (1985). Adolescents' soap opera viewing and relational perceptions. *Journal of Broadcasting, 29*, 295–308.

American Academy of Pediatrics. Committee on Communications. (1995a). Children, adolescents, and advertising. *Pediatrics, 95*, 295–297.

American Academy of Pediatrics. Committee on Communications. (1995b). Children, adolescents, and television. *Pediatrics, 96*, 786–787.

American Academy of Pediatrics. Committee on Communications. Policy statement: The commercialization of children's television. (1992). *Pediatrics, 89:* 343–344.

American Academy of Pediatrics. Committee on Communications. (1995c). Sexuality, contraception, and the media. *Pediatrics, 95*, 298–300.

American Association of Family Physicians Commission on Special Issues and Clinical Interests. (1994). Family violence: An AAFP white paper. *American Family Physician, 50* (8), 1636–1640, 1644–1646.

American Psychological Association. (1996). *Violence on Television. What Do Children Learn? What Can Parents Do?* (brochure). Washington, DC: Author.

Anderson, D., Lorch, E., Field, D., Collins, P., & Nathan, J. (1986). Television viewing at home: Age trends in visual attention and time with TV. *Child Development, 57*, 1024–1033.

Atkin, C. (1990). Effects of televised alcohol messages on teenage drinking patterns. *Journal of Adolescent Health Care, 11*, 10–24.

Atkin, C. (1989). Television socialization and risky driving by teenagers. *Alcohol, Drugs and Driving, 5* (1), 1–11.

Atkin, D., Greenberg, B., & Baldwin, T. (1991). The home ecology of children's television viewing: Parental mediation and the new video environment. *Journal of Communication, 41* (Summer), 40–52.

Austin, E., & Meili, H. (1994). Effects of interpretations of televised alcohol portrayals on children's alcohol beliefs. *Journal of Broadcasting & Electronic Media, 38*, 417–435.

Austin, E. (1989). *Influence of family communication on children's television interpretation processes.* Paper presented at the International Communication association, San Francisco. (ERIC Document Reproduction Service No. ed 318 075).

Baillie, M., Thompson, A., Kaplan, C. (1994). The terror of television. Anxious children at greater risk, 308 (March 12) 714.

Bandura, A. (1973). *Aggression: A social learning analysis.* Englewood Cliffs, NJ: Prentice-Hall.

Bandura, A. (1983). Psychological mechanisms of aggression. In R. G. Green & C. I. Donnerstein (Eds.), *Aggression: Theoretical and empirical reviews. Vol. 1: Theoretical and methodological issues* (pp. 1–40). New York: Academic Press.

Bandura, A., Ross, D., & Ross, S. A. (1963). Vicarious reinforcement and imitative learning. *Journal of Abnormal and Social Psychology, 67*, 601–607.

Bauman, K., Brown, J., Bryan, E., Fisher, L., Paedgett, C., & Sweeney, J. (1988). Three mass media campaigns to prevent adolescent cigarette smoking. *Preventive Medicine*, 510–530.

Bearinger, L. (1990). Study group report on the impact of television on adolescent views of sexuality. *Journal of Adolescent Health Care, 11*, 71–75.

Bearison, D., Bain, J., & Daniele, R. (1982). *Social Behavior and Personality, 10* (2), 133–144.

Belson, W. (1978). *Television and the adolescent boy.* Westmead, England: Saxon House.

Berkowitz, L. (1962). *Aggression: A social psychological analysis.* New York: McGraw-Hill.

Berkowitz, L. (1984). Some effects of thoughts on anti- and prosocial influences of media events. A cognitive neoassociation analysis. *Psychological Bulletin, 95*, 410–427.

Berman, A. (1988). Fictional depiction of suicide in television films and imitation effects. *American Journal of Psychiatry, 145*, 982–986.

Beuf, A. (1974). Doctor, lawyer, household drudge. *Journal of Communication, 24*, 142–145.

Blanchard-Fields, F., Coon, R., & Mathews, R. (1986). Inferencing and television: A developmental study. *Journal of Youth and Adolescence, 15*, 453–459.

Blum, R. (1990). Executive summary. *Journal of Adolescent Health Care, 11*, 86–90.

Bordeaux, B., & Lange, G. (1991). Children's reported investment of mental effort when viewing television. *Communication Research, 18*, 617–635.

Brannon, B., Dent, C., Flay, B., Smith, G., Sussman, S., Pentz, M., Johnson, C., & Hansen, W. (1989). The television, school, and family project. The impact of curriculum delivery format on program acceptance. *Preventive Medicine, 18*, 492–502.

Brown, J., Childers, K., Bauman, K., & Koch, G. (1990). The influence of new media and family structure on young adolescents' television and radio use. *Communication Research, 17* (1), 65–82.

Brown, J., Childers, K. W., Waszak, C. S., (1990). Television and Adolescent Sexuality. *Journal of Adolescent Health Care, 11*, 62–70.

Buchta, R. (1989). Attitudes of adolescents and parents of adolescents concerning condom advertisements on television. *Journal of Adolescent Health Care, 10*, 220–223.

Calvert, S., & Huston, A. (1987, Winter). Television and children's gender schemata. In L. S. Liben & M. L. Signorella (Eds.), *Children's gender schemata. New Directions for Child Development*, 75–88.

Campbell, T., Wright, J., & Huston, A. (1987). Form cues and content difficulty as determinate of children's cognitive processing of televised educational messages. *Journal of Experimental Child Psychology, 43*, 311–327.

Cantor, J. (1996). *What parents want in a television rating system: Results of a national survey.* University of Wisconsin-Madison, National PTA, Institute for Mental Health Initiatives.

Centerwall, B. (1992). Television and violence. The scale of the problem and where to go from here. *Journal of the American Medical Association, 267*, 3059–3063.

Centerwall, B. (1993, Spring). Television and violent crime. *Public Interest*, 56–71.

Chandara, P., Conlon, P., Noh, S., & Field, V. (1990). The impact of AIDS education among elementary school students. *Canadian Journal of Public Health, 81*, 285–289.

Coles, R. (1986, June 21). What makes some kids more vulnerable to the worst of TV? *TV Guide, 34*, 4–7.

Comstock, G., & Strausburger, V. (1990). Deceptive appearances: Television violence and aggressive behavior. *Journal of Adolescent Health Care, 11*, 31–44.

Cook, T. D., Kendziersky, D. A., & Thomas, S. V.

(1983). The implicit assumptions of television. An analysis of the 1982 NIMH Report on Television and Behavior. *Public Opinion Quarterly, 47,* 161–201.

"Correspondence: Impact of Televised Movies about Suicide." Tanner, M.; Murray, J.; Phillips, D. & Paight, D. Letters from Tanner, M., Stroff, R. & Boyd, J.; Marks, A.; Mastroianni, G.; Phillips, David Castensent,L.

Csikszentmihalyi, M. (1986, Spring). The pressured world of adolescence. *Planned Parenthood Review,* 2–4.

Defoe, J., & Breed, W. (1988). Youth and alcohol in television stories, with suggestions to the industry for alternative portrayals. *Adolescence, 91,* 533–550.

Derksen, D., & Strasburger, V. (1994). Children and the influence of the media. *Primary Care: Clinics in Office Practice, 21* (4), 747–758.

Desmond, S., Price, J., Hallinan, C., & Smith, D. (1989). Black and white adolescents' perception of their weight. *Journal of School Health, 59,* 353–358.

Dietz, W. H., Strasburger, V. C. (1991). Children, adolescent, and television: Current problems in *Pediatrics,* vol. 21. Jan. 8–31.

Dietz, W. (1990). You are what you eat—what you eat is what you are. *Journal of Adolescent Health Care, 11,* 76–81.

Dietz, W. (1993). TV or not TV: Fat is the question. *Pediatrics, 91,* 499–501.

Dominick, J. (1984). Videogames, television violence, and aggression in teenagers. *Journal of Communication, 34,* 136–147.

Dorr, A., & Kunkel, D. (1990). Children and the media environment. Change and constancy amid change. *Communication Research, 17* (1), 5–25.

Dorr, A. *Television and children.* (1986). Beverly Hills, CA: Sage Publ., Inc.

Dykstra, J. (1997, January/February). How does TV rate? Ask parents. What parents want in TV ratings. *Our Children, 5,* 11.

Eastman, H. A., & Liss, M. B. (1980). TV preferences of children from four parts of the U.S. *Journalism Quarterly, 57,* 488–490.

Ellis-Schwabe, M., & Thornburg, H. (1986). Conflict areas between parents and their adolescents. *Journal of Psychology, 120* (1), 59–68.

Epstein, L. H., Valoski, A. M.; Vara, L. S.; McCurley, J.; Wisniewski, L.; Kalarchian, M. A.; Klein, K. R.; Shrager, L. R. (1995). Effects of decreasing sedentary behavior and increasing activity on weight change in obese children. *Health Psychology, 14* (2), 109–115.

Ernster, V. (1989). Advertising and promotion of smokeless tobacco products. *NCI Monographs, 8,* 87–94.

Eron, L. (1982). Parent-child interaction, television violence, and aggression of children. *American Psychologist, 37,* 197–211.

Eron, L. (1988, November/December). Aggression in middle childhood—a harbinger of future problems. *Canadian Journal of Public Health Supplement, 2* (79), S17–S21.

Eron, L. (1995). Media violence. *Pediatric Annals, 24,* 84–87.

Fedler, F., Phillips, M., Raker, P., Schefsky, D., & So-

luri, J. (1994). Network commercials promote legal drugs: Outnumber anti-drug PSA's 45-to-1. *Journal of Drug Education, 24* (4), 291–302.

Feldman, W., Feldman, E., & Goodman, J. T. (1988). Culture versus biology: Children's attitudes toward thinness and fitness. *Pediatrics, 81,* 1990–1994.

Feshbach, S. (1972). Reality & fantasy in filmed violence. In John Murray & Eli Rubenstein (Eds.), *Television & Social Behavior* (pp. 318–345). Rockville, MD: National Institute of Health.

Feshbach, S., & Singer, R. D. (1979). *Television and aggression.* San Francisco: Jossey-Bass.

Flay, B. R., Miller, T. Q., Hedeker, D., Siddiqui, O., Britton, C. F., Brannon, B. R., Johnson, C. A., Hansen, W. B., Sussman, S., Dent, C. (1995). The television, school, and family smoking prevention and cessation project. VIII. Student outcomes and mediating variables. *Preventive Medicine, 24* (1), 29–40.

Forbes, F., & McClure, I. (1994). The terror of television. Made worse by family stress. *British Medical Journal, 308,* 714.

Freedman, J. L. (1984). Effect of television violence on aggressiveness. *Psychological Bulletin, 96,* 227–246.

Freedman, R. J. (1984). Reflections on beauty as it relates to health in adolescent females. *Women's Health, 9,* 29–45.

Friedlander, B. (1993). Community violence, children's development, and mass media: In pursuit of new insights, new goals, and new strategies. *Psychiatry, 56* (1), 66–81.

Friedrich-Cofer, L., & Huston, A. (1986). Television violence and aggression: The debate continues. *Psychological Bulletin, 100,* 364–371.

Friel, J., Hudson, N., Banoub, S., Ross, A. (1989). The effect of a promotion campaign on attitudes of adolescent females toward breastfeeding. *Canadian Journal of Public Health, 80,* 195–199.

Frueh, T., & McGhee, P. E. (1975). Traditional sex role development and amount of time spent watching television. *Developmental Psychology, 11,* 109.

Funk, J., & Buchman, D. (1995). Video game controversies. *Pediatric Annals, 24,* 91–94.

Futch, E., Lisman, S., & Geller, M. (1984). An analysis of alcohol portrayal on prime-time television. *International Journal of the Addictions, 19,* 403–210.

Gadow, K., Sprafkin, J., & Ficarrotto, T. (1987). Effects of viewing aggression-laden cartoon on preschool-aged emotionally disturbed children. *Children Psychiatry and Human Development, 17,* 257–273.

Gerbner, G. (1972). Violence in television drama: Trends and symbolic functions. In G. A. Comstock & E. A. Rubenstein (Eds.), *Television and social behavior. Vol. 1. Media content and control* (pp. 28–187). Washington, DC: U.S. Government Printing Office.

Gerbner, G., Gross, L., & Gross, M., Signorielli, N. (1980). The "mainstreaming" of America: Violence Profile No. 11. *Journal of Communication, 30,* 10–29.

Gerbner, G., Gross, L., Signorielli, N., Morgan, M., & Jackson-Beck, M. (1979). The demonstration of power: Violence Profile No. 10. *Journal of Communication, 29,* 177–196.

Ginsburg, H., Jenkins, C., Walsh, R., & Peck, B. (1989).

Visual superiority effect in televised prevention of victimization programs for preschool children. *Perceptual and Motor Skills, 68,* 1179–1182.

Goodall, C. (1994). Child abuse. No smoke, no fire. *Nursing Standard, 8* (30), 93–4.

Gortmaker, S., Must, A., Sobol, A. M., Peterson, K., Colditz, G. A., Dietz, W. H. (1996). Television viewing as a cause of increasing obesity among children in the United States, 1986–1990. *Archives of Pediatric and Adolescent Medicine, 150,* 356–361.

Gortmaker, S., and Salter, C., & Walker, D. (1990, Winter). The impact of television viewing on mental aptitude and achievement: A longitudinal study. *Public Opinion Quarterly,* 594–604.

Gould, M., & Shaffer, D. (1986). The impact of suicide in television movies. Evidence of imitation. *New England Journal of Medicine, 315,* 690–694.

Gould, M., Shaffer, D., & Kleinman, M. (1988). The impact of suicide in television movies: Replication and commentary. *Suicide and Life-Threatening Behavior, 18* (1), 90–99.

Graham, L., & Hamdan, L. (1987). *Youth trends: Capturing the $200 billion youth market.* New York: St. Martin's Press.

Green, L. (1990). Editorial: TV and teens. *Journal of Adolescent Health Care, 11,* 91–92.

Greenberg, B. S.; Brown, J. D.; Buerkel-Rothfuss, N. L. (1993). *Media, Sex, and the Adolescent.* Cresskill, NJ: Hampton Press, 1993.

Grube, J., & Wallack, L. (1994). Television beer advertising and drinking knowledge, beliefs, and intentions among schoolchildren. *American Journal of Public Health, 84,* 254–259.

Harwood, R., & Weissberg, R. (1987). The potential of video in the promotion of social competence in children and adolescents. *Journal of Early Adolescence, 7,* 345–363.

Hazan, A., & Glantz, S. (1995). Current trends in tobacco use on prime time fictional television. *American Journal of Public Health, 85,* 116–117.

Healy, Jon. (1995, July 8). Proposed electronic 'V-chip' complicates the view. *CQ.* pp. 1994–1996.

Heath, L., Bresolin, L., & Rinaldi, R. (1989). Effects of media violence on children: A review of the literature. *Archives of General Psychiatry, 46,* 376–379.

Hellmich, Nanci. (1991, June 4). Children are filling up on junk-food TV ads. *USA Today,* 2D.

Hoberman, H. (1990). Study group report on the impact of television violence on adolescents. *Journal of adolescent Health Care, 11,* 45–49.

Hoffner, C. (1995). Adolescents' coping with frightening mass media. *Communication Research* 22, (June) 325–346.

Houle, R., & Feldman, R. (1991). Emotional displays in children's television programming. *Journal of Nonverbal Behavior, 15,* 261–271.

Huesmann, L. R. (1982). Television violence and aggressive behavior. In D. Pearl, L. Bouthilet, & L. Lazar (Eds.), National Institutes of Mental Health. *Television and behavior: Ten years of scientific progress and implications for the eighties* (DHHS Publication No. ADM 82–1195) (Vol. 2, pp. 220–256). Washington, DC: U.S. Government Printing Office.

Huesmann, L. R., & Eron, L. D. (1963). Factors influencing the effect of television violence in children. In J. Howe (Ed.), *Learning from television* (pp. 153–177). New York: Academic Press.

Hundt, R. (January 1996). *Television, kids, indecency, violence and the public interest.* Paper presented at the 27th Annual Administrative Law Conference of Duke Law Journal. Duke University School of Law, Chapel Hill, N.C.

Huston, A., Donnerstein, E. (1992). *Big world, small screen: The role of television in American society.* Lincoln: University of Nebraska Press.

Huston, A., Wright, J., & Rice, M. (1990). Development of television viewing patterns in early childhood: A longitudinal investigation. *Developmental Psychology, 26,* 409–420.

Jones, R. (1995). Use of smokeless tobacco in the world series, 1986–1993. *American Journal of Public Health, 85,* 117.

Josephson, W. (1987). Television violence and children's aggression: Testing the priming, social script, and disinhibition predictions. *Journal of Personality and Social Psychology, 53,* 882–890.

Kaufman, L. (1980). Prime time nutrition. *Journal of Communication, 30,* 37–46.

Kelly, A., & Spear, P. (1991). Intra-program synopses for children's comprehension of television content. *Journal of Experimental Child Psychology, 52,* 87–98.

Kendrick, D. T., & Gutierres, S. E. (1980). Contrast effects and judgments of physical attractiveness: When beauty becomes a social problem. *Journal of Personality and Social Psychology, 38,* 131–140.

Kessler, R., Downey, G., Milavsky, J., & Stipp, H. (1988). Clustering of teenage suicides after television news stories about suicides. *American Journal of Psychiatry, 145,* 1379–1383.

Klesges, R., Shelton, M., & Klesges, L. (1993). Effects of television on metabolic rate: Potential implications for childhood obesity. *Pediatrics, 91,* 281–86.

Kotz, K., & Story, M. (1994). Food advertisements during children's Saturday morning television programming: Are they consistent with dietary recommendations? *Journal of the American Dietetic Association, 94* (11), 1296–1300.

Kubey, R., & Larson, R. (1990). The use and experience of the new video media among children and young adolescents. *Communication Research, 17,* 107–130.

Kunkel, D., & Gantz, W. (1992). Children's television advertising in the multichannel environment. *Journal of Communication, 42,* 134–152.

Landau, S., Lorch, E., & Milich, R. (1992). Visual attention to and comprehension of television in attention-deficit hyperactivity disordered and normal boys. *Child Development, 63,* 928–937.

Lande, R. (1993). The video violence debate. *Hospital & Community Psychiatry, 44,* 347–351.

Larson, R., Kubey, R., & Colletti, J. (1989). Changing channels: Early adolescent media choices and shifting investments in family and friends. *Journal of Youth and Adolescence, 18,* 583–599.

Lawrence, F., Tasker, G., Daley, C., Orhiel, A., & Wozniak, P. (1986). Adolescents' time spent viewing television. *Adolescence, 82,* 431–436.

Lawrence, F., & Wozniak, P. (1989). Children's television viewing with family members. *Psychological Reports, 65,* 395–400.

Lefkowitz, M. M., Eron, L. D., & Walder, L. O. (1977). *Growing up too violent: A longitudinal study of the development of aggression.* New York: Pergamon Press.

Leung, A., Fagan, J., Cho, H., Lim, S., & Robson, W. (1994). Children and television. *American Family Physician, 50* (5), 909–912, 915–918.

Libow, J. (1992). Traumatized children and the news media: Clinical considerations. *American Journal of Orthopsychiatry, 62,* 379–386.

Liebert, R. (1986). Effects of television on children and adolescents. *Developmental and Behavioral Pediatrics, 7* (1), 43–48.

Liebert, R., Sprafkin, J. (1988). *The early window. Effects of television on children and youth* (3rd ed.). New York: Pergamon Press.

Lipsitz, A., Brake, G., & Vincent, E. (1993). Another round for the brewers: Television ads and children's alcohol expectancies. *Journal of Applied Social Psychology, 23,* 439–450.

List, S. (1992). The right place to find children. *American Demographics, 14,* 44–47.

Lowry, D. T. (1981). Alcohol consumption patterns and consequences in prime-time network TV. *Journalism Quarterly, 58* (1), 2–8.

Luecke-Aleska, D., Anderson, D., & Collins, P. (1995). *Developmental Psychology, 31,* 773–780.

Lynch, K. (1989). Medicine and society. Another perspective on television. *Delaware Medical Journal, 61,* 371–372.

Mackey, W. D., & Hess, D. J. (1982). Attention structure and stereotyping of gender on television: an empirical analysis. *Genetic Psychology Monographs, 106,* 199–215.

Madden, P. A., & Grube, J. W. (1994). The frequency and nature of alcohol and tobacco advertising in televised sports, 1990–1992. *American Journal of Public Health, 84* (2), 297–299.

Meadowcroft, J. M. and Reeves, B. (1989). Influence of Story Schemes Development on Children's Attention to TV. *Communication Research, 16,* (June 1989) 352–74.

Merskey, H. (1996). Influences of the media: A powerful what? *Lancet, 347,* 416.

Morgan, M. (1987). Television, sex-role attitudes, and sex-role behavior. *Journal of Early Adolescence, 7,* 269–282.

Morgan, M., Alexander, A., Shanahan, J., & Harris, C. (1990). Adolescents, VCRs, and the family environment. *Communication Research, 17,* 83–106.

Mortimer, Jeffery. (1994). How TV violence hits kids. *Profiles. The ISR Newsletter, 18,* 5–7.

Mutz, D., Roberts, D., & Vuuren, D. van. (1993). Reconsidering the displacement hypothesis: Television's influence on children's time use. *Communication Research, 20,* 51–75.

National Safety Council Accident Facts. (1996). Itasca, Il.: National Safety Council, p. 84.

National Institute of Mental Health. (1982). *Television and behavior: Ten years of scientific progress and implications for the eighties* (DHHS Publication No. ADM 82–1195). Washington, DC: U.S. Government Printing Office.

Neuendorf, K. A. (1985). Alcohol advertising and media portrayals. *Journal of the Institute of Socioeconomic Studies, 10,* 67–78.

Ogletree, S., Williams, S., Raffeld, P., Mason, B., Fricke, K. (1990). Female attractiveness and eating disorders: Do children's television commercials play a role? *Sex Roles, 22,* 791–797.

Paget, K., Kritt, D., & Bergemann, L. (1984). Understanding strategic interactions in television commercials: A developmental study. *Journal of Applied and Developmental Psychology, 5,* 145–161.

Paik, H., & Comstock, G. (1994). The effects of television violence on antisocial behavior: A meta-analysis. *Communication Research, 21,* 516–546.

Palmer, E. (1988). *Television and America's children: A crisis of neglect.* New York: Oxford University Press.

Palmer, P. (1986). *The lively audience. A study of children around the TV set.* Sydney: Allen and Unwin.

Pearl, D. (1984, September/October). Violence and aggression. *Society,* 17–22.

Pedzek, K., Simon, S., Stoeckert, J., & Kiely, J. (1987). Individual differences in television comprehension. *Memory and Cognition, 15,* 428–435.

Peterson, J., Moore, K. A., & Furstenberg, F. F. (1991). Initiation of sexual intercourse: Is there a link? *Journal of Homosexuality, 21,* 93–118.

Phillips, D., & Carstensen, L. (1986). Clustering of teenage suicides after television news stories about suicide. *New England Journal of Medicine, 317,* 685–689.

Phillips, D., & Paight, D. (1987). The impact of televised movies about suicide. A replicative study. *New England Journal of Medicine, 317,* 809–811.

Pingree, S. (1986). Children's activity and television comprehensibility. *Communication Research, 13,* 239–256.

Potter, W. (1986). Perceived reality and the cultivation hypothesis. *Journal of Broadcasting & Electronic Media, 30,* 159–174.

Potter, W. (1987). Does television viewing hinder academic achievement among adolescents? *Human Communication Research, 14,* 27–46.

Potts, R., Doppler, R., & Hernandez, M. (1994). Effects of television content on physical risk-taking in children. *Journal of Experimental Child Psychology, 58,* 321–331.

Potts, R., Huston, A., & Wright, J. (1986). The effects of television form and violent content on boys' attention and social behavior. *Journal of Experimental Child Psychology, 41,* 1–17.

Price, J., Merrill, E., & Clause, M. (1992). The depiction of guns on prime time television. *Journal of School Health, 62,* 15–18.

Rajecki, D., McTavish, D., & Rasmussen, J., Schreuden, M., Byer, D. C., Jessup, K. S. (1994). "Violence, Conflict, Trickery, and other story themes in TV ads for food for children." *Journal of Applied Social Psychology, 24,* 1685–1700.

Remafedi, G. (1990). Study group report on the impact of television portrayals of gender roles on youth. *Journal of Adolescent Health Care, 11,* 59–61.

Resnick, M. (1990). Study group report on the impact of televised drinking and alcohol advertising on youth. *Journal of Adolescent Health Care, 11,* 25–30.

Riedley-Johnson, R., Chance, J., & Cooper, H. (1984). Correlates of children's television viewing: Expectancies, age, and sex. *Journal of Applied Developmental Psychology, 5,* 185–202.

Rolandelli, D., Wright, J., & Huston, A. (1991). Children's auditory and visual processing of narrated and nonnarrated television programming. *Journal of Experimental Child Psychology, 51* (2), 90–122.

Rothschild, N., & Morgan, M. (1987). Cohesion and control: Adolescents' relationships with parents as mediators of television. *Journal of Early Adolescence, 7,* 299–314.

Rowe, D., & Herstand, S. (1986). Familial influences on television viewing and aggression: a sibling study. *Aggressive Behavior, 112,* 111–120.

Rudd, D. (1992). Children and television: A critical note on theory and method. *Media, Culture, and Society, 14,* 313–320.

Schmidtke, A., & Hafner, H. (1988). The Werther effect after television films: New evidence for an old hypothesis. *Psychological Medicine, 18,* 665–676.

Sege, R., & Dietz, W. (1994). Television viewing and violence in children: The pediatrician as agent for change. *Pediatrics, 94,* 600–607.

Selnow, G. (1986). Television viewing and the learning of expectations for problem resolutions. *Educational Studies, 12,* 137–145.

Signorielli, N. (1987a). Children and adolescents on television: A consistent pattern of devaluation. *Journal of Early Adolescence, 7,* 255–268.

Signorielli, N. (1987b). Drinking, sex, and violence on television: The cultural indicators perspective. *Journal of Drug Education, 17,* 245–260.

Signorielli, N. (1990). Children, television, and gender roles. Messages and impact. *Journal of Adolescent Health Care, 11,* 50–58.

Signorielli, N., & Lears, M. (1992). Children, television, and conceptions about chores: attitudes and behaviors. *Sex Roles, 27,* 157–170.

Silverman-Watkins, L., & Sprafkin, J. (1983). Adolescents' comprehension of televised sexual innuendoes. *Journal of Applied Developmental Psychology, 4,* 359–369.

Silverstein, B., Perdue, L., Peterson, B., Kelly, E. (1986). The role of the mass media in promoting a thin standard of bodily attractiveness for women. *Sex Roles, 14,* 519–532.

Silverstein, B., Peterson, B., & Perdue, L. (1992). Some correlates of the thin standard of bodily attractiveness for women. *International Journal of Eating Disorders, 5,* 5.

Simkin, S., Hawton, K. (1995). Media influence on parasuicide. A study of the effects of a television drama portrayal of paracetamol self-poisoning. *British Journal of Psychiatry, 167* (6), 754–759.

Simons, D., & Silveira, W. (1994). Post-traumatic stress disorder in children after television programmes. *British Medical Journal, 308,* 389–390.

Singer, D. G. (1985). Alcohol, television and teenagers. *Pediatrics, 76,* 668–674.

Singer, D. G. (1989). Children, adolescents, and television—1989. I. Television violence: A critique. *Pediatrics, 883,* 445–446.

Singer, D. G., & Benton, W. (1989). Caution: Television may be hazardous to a child's mental health. *Developmental and Behavioral Pediatrics, 10,* 259–261.

Singer, J., & Singer, D. (1981). *Television, imagination, and aggression: A study of preschoolers.* Hillsdale, NJ: Lawrence Erlbaum.

Singer, J., Singer, D., & Rapaczynski, W. (1984). Family patterns and television viewing as predictors of children's beliefs and aggression. *Journal of Communication, 34,* 73–89.

Smith, L. (1994). A content analysis of gender differences in children's advertising. *Journal of Broadcasting & Electronic Media, 38,* 323–337.

Sneed, C., Runco, M. (1992). The beliefs adults and children hold about television and video games. *Journal of Psychology, 126,* 2273–2284.

Sneed, D., Wulfemeyer, K., Riffe, D., & Van Ommeren, R. (1990). Promoting media literacy in the high school social science curriculum. *The Clearing House, 64,* 36–38.

Solderman, A., Greenberg, B., & Linsangan, R. (1988). Television and movie behaviors of pregnant and nonpregnant adolescents. *Journal of Adolescent Research, 3,* 153–170.

Sprafkin, J., Gadow, K., & Grayson, P. (1987). Effects of viewing aggressive cartoons on the behavior of learning disabled children. *Journal of Child Psychology, 28,* 387–398.

Steede, K., & Range, L. (1989). Does television induce suicidal contagion with adolescents? *Journal of Community Psychology, 17,* 166–172.

Story, M. (1990). Study group report on the impact of television on adolescent nutritional status. *Journal of adolescent Health Care, 11,* 82–85.

St. Peters, M., Fitch, M., & Huston, A. (1991). Television and families: What do young children watch with their parents? *Child Development, 62,* 1409–1423.

Strasburger, V. (1989). Adolescent sexuality and the media. *Pediatric Clinics of North America, 36,* 747–773.

Strasburger, V. (1992). Children, adolescents, and television. *Pediatrics in Review, 13* (4), 144–151.

Strasburger, V., & Hendren, R. (1995, February vol 24 2). Rock music and music videos. *Pediatric Annals,* 97–103.

Sussman, S., Dent, C., Brannon, B. R., Glowacz, K., Gleason, L. R., Ullery, S., Hansen, W. B., Johnson, C. A., Flay, B. R. (1989). The television, school, and family smoking prevention/cessation project IV. Controlling for program success expectancies across experimental & control conditions. *Addictive Behaviors, 14,* 601–610.

Tan, A. (1979). TV beauty ads and role expectations of adolescent female viewers. *Journalism Quarterly, 56,* 283–288.

Tan, A. (1985). *Mass communication theories and research.* New York: John Wiley & Sons.

Tannenbaum, P. H., & Zillman, D. (1975). Emotional arousal in the facilitation of aggression through communication. In L. Berkovitz, ed. *Advances in experimental social psychology* (Vol. 8, pp. 3–11). New York: Academic Press.

Taras, H., & Gage, M. (1995). Advertised foods on children's television. *Archives in Pediatric Adolescent Medicine, 149,* 649–652.

Taras, H., Sallis, J., Patterson, T., Nader, P., & Nelson, J. (1989). Television's influence on children's diet and physical activity. *Developmental and Behavioral Pediatrics, 10,* 176–180.

Television and Video Almanac, 42nd edition (1997), ed. James D. Moser. p. 17a New York: Quigley Publishing Co., Inc.

Terr, L. C., Bloch, D., & Michel, B. A., Shi, H., Reinhardt, J. A., Metayer, S. (1996). Children's memories in the wake of Challenger. *American Journal of Psychiatry, 153* (5), 618–625.

Tucker, L. (1986). The relationship of television viewing to physical fitness and obesity. *Adolescence, 84,* 797–806.

Tulloch, M. (1995). Evaluating aggression: School students' responses to television portrayals of institutionalized violence. *Journal of Youth & Adolescence, 24,* 95–115.

Turow, J. (1996). Television entertainment and the US health-care debate. *Lancet, 347* (9010), 1240–1243.

Valkenburg, P., Voort, T. van der. (1994). Influence of TV on daydreaming and creative imagination: A review of research. *Psychological Bulletin, 116* (2), 316–339.

Valkenburg, P., & Voort, T. van der. (1995). The influence of television on children's daydreaming styles: A 1-year panel study. *Communication Research, 22,* 267–287.

Vetro, A., Csapo, A., Szilar, J., & Vargha, M. (1988). Effect of television on aggressivity of adolescents. *International Journal of Adolescent Medicine and Health, 3,* 303–320.

"Videodrome." (1994, August 13). *The Economist,* 73–74.

Walker, C. (1996, May). Can TV save the planet? *American Demographics,* 42–48.

Ward, L. (1995). Talking about sex: Common themes about sexuality in the prime-time television programs children and adolescents view most. *Journal of Youth & Adolescence, 24,* 595–615.

Wartella, E., Heintz, K., Aidman, A., & Mazzarella, S. (1990). Television and beyond. Children's video media in one community. *Communication Research, 17,* 45–64.

Wass, H., Raup, J., & Sisler, H. (1989). Adolescents and death on television. A follow-up study. *Death Studies, 13,* 161–173.

Weaver, J. B., Masland, J. L., & Zillman, D. (1984). Effect of erotica on young men's aesthetic perception of their female sexual partners. *Perceptual Motor Skills, 58,* 929–30.

Wiegman, O., Kuttschreuter, M., & Baarda, B. (1992). A longitudinal study of the effects of television viewing on aggressive and prosocial behaviors. *British Journal of Social Psychology, 31,* 147–164.

Wiley, C., & Casey, R. (1993). Family experiences, attitudes, and household safety practices regarding firearms. *Clinical Pediatrics, 32,* 71–76.

Wilson, B., Weiss, A. (1993). The effects of sibling coviewing on preschoolers' reactions to a suspenseful movie scene. *Communication Research, 20,* 214–248.

Wilson, P. (1988). The impact of cultural changes on the internal experiences of the adolescent. *Journal of Adolescents, 11,* 271–286.

Wolf, A. M., Gortmaker, S. L., Cheung, L., Gray, H. M., Herzog, D. B., Colditz, G. A. (1993). Activity, inactivity, and obesity: Racial, ethnic, and age differences among schoolgirls. *American Journal of Public Health, 83,* 1625–1627.

Wong, N. D., Hei, T. K., Qaqundah, P. Y., Davidson, D. M., Bassin, S. L., Gold, K. V. (1992). Television viewing and pediatric hypercholesterolemia. *Pediatrics, 90,* 75–79.

Worblewski, R., & Huston, A. (1987). Televised occupational stereotypes and their effects on early adolescents: are they changing? *Journal of Early Adolescence, 7,* 283–297.

Worden, J. (1988). Development of a smoking prevention mass media program using diagnostic and formative research. *Preventive Medicine, 17,* 531–558.

Worsnop, Richard. (1997). Alcohol Advertising: the issues. *The CQ Researcher 7* (March 14) 219–224.

Wright, J., Huston, A., & Reitz, A. (1994). Young children's perceptions of television reality: determinants and developmental differences. *Developmental Psychology, 30,* 229–239.

Wright, J., Huston, A., Truglio, R., Fitch, M., Smith, E., Piemyat, S. (1995). Occupational portrayals on television: children's role schemata, career aspirations, and perceptions of reality. *Child Development, 66* (6), 1706–1718.

Wright, J. B. (1995). Update: "Alcohol-related traffic crashes and fatalities among youth and young adults-United States, 1982–1994." *Morbidity and Mortality Weekly, 44* (Dec 1), 869–875.

Zemach, T., & Cohen, A. A. (1986). Perception of gender equality on television and in social reality. *Journal of Broadcasting and Electronic Media, 30,* 427–444.

Zillmann, D., Bryant, J., & Huston, A. (Eds.). (1994). *Media, children, and the family: Social, scientific, psychodynamic, and clinical perspectives.* Hillsdale, NJ: Lawrence Erlbaum.

Zylke, J. (1988). More voices join medicine in expressing concern over amount, content of what children see on TV. *Journal of the American Medical Association, 260,* 1831–1832.

8 / The Impact of Computers on Children

Charles E. Holzer III and Christopher Paul Holzer

The purpose of this chapter is to introduce the reader to some of the mental health issues surrounding the use of computers by children. Computers have become an increasingly prominent feature of our society and reflect the full range of human endeavor (Turkle, 1984). This means that access to computers can facilitate children's access to the world around them, including both the good and the bad. The thesis of this chapter is that computers are carriers of culture and that it is the obligation of parents to guide access to that culture by facilitating the desirable and avoiding the not so desirable. In this chapter we introduce some general concepts about computing, discuss the different ways children use computers, and conclude with some suggestions regarding this use.

Computer Concepts

A computer was originally defined as any device that could do mathematical and logical computations. As commonly used today, however, the word "computer" implies a number of additional concepts. Present-day computers are generally assumed to be electronic and often are implemented in the form of microprocessor chips, which have become small and relatively inexpensive. Computers nowadays are assumed to use stored programs; thus they have the flexibility to perform a wide variety of tasks and are no longer limited to mathematics, even though mathematical logic remains essential to how computers work. Special-purpose computers have found their way into many different devices, ranging from automobiles, to wristwatches. General-purpose computers come in many different sizes: small, hand-held units for planning and taking notes (called personal digital assistants), portable and desktop personal computers, workstations, and multiuser computers used by businesses and universities. Children and adolescents are most likely to use personal computers (PCs) whether at home or at school. Most PCs can run many different kinds of programs, including calculators, spread-

sheets, word processors, databases, graphics, communication packages, and, of course, games.

The essence of every PC is the electronic microprocessor or central processing unit (CPU). This small electronic chip is mounted on a circuit board (the motherboard) with various support electronics, inside a box that includes a power supply and other components. In order to function, a computer needs main memory, called random access memory (RAM), in which programs are loaded and run. Because RAM is cleared when the computer is turned off, there must also be nonvolatile storage. This is found in several forms. The simplest is the diskette, a small magnetic disk, written to and read by the computer. Diskettes can be inserted and removed, so users can have a whole library of stored programs and data. Generally diskettes are relatively slow and are limited in amount of information they can hold. Therefore, most computers have a larger mass and faster storage device, called a hard disk, which can hold large amounts of data and can be accessed quickly by the microprocessor without a user having to change the disk. Most new computers have drives for reading compact discs (CD-ROMs), similar to music CD-audio discs, which can hold large programs, pictures, and even music.

All PCs have a keyboard, and most computers now have a mouse, track ball, or other pointing device. Many new computers have audio boards that can synthesize music or even speech. Most home PCs have modems, short for modulator/demodulator, which can connect them to the public telephone system and the Internet. Any given PC can contain more, or less, but otherwise all are similar in the kinds of things they do. Recently the price of computers with most of the features just listed has dropped below $1,000.

As prices have dropped, the availability of computers to everyone, including children, has increased. A 1993 survey by the U.S. Bureau of the Census indicates that the availability of computers in households has increased from 8.2% in 1984, to 15.0% in 1989, to 22.8% in 1993. For all children ages 3 to 17, 31.9% have a computer at home, but this slightly higher for teenagers (36.7–37.9%). Of those with a computer at home, the use by children as young as three years old is only 32.7% but increases to 75% by age 7 and peaks at 85.2% by age 12. Use at school starts for some at age 3 or younger, increases to 64.9% by age 7 and peaks at 76.9% by age 10. At age 10 as many as 76.8% reported using a computer somewhere. These numbers are influenced by household income with only 5.6% of children from the poorest households having access at home, but overall use is 42.6% in this group, mostly due to use at school. Increases in children's access to computers are likely to continue.

Computers and Children

Computers are intrinsically interesting as technology, but to most children the issue is: What do they do? From the child's point of view, the computer can be a toy, a tool, or a playmate. As a toy, the computer can present games and play them with the child or generate virtual playgrounds for the child. We return to the topic of games later. As a tool, the computer can be used in ways similar to adult usage.

The uses children make of computers and the specific types of programs they prefer change throughout childhood. In general, children need to have some reading and typing skills before they can use computers, although with the assistance of a more experienced person they can operate computers with a minimum of difficulty. *Home PC* magazine (September 1994) reviewed programs for children in categories based on school grade, starting with preschool through grade 3, grades 4 through 8, and grades 9 through 12.

PRESCHOOL TO GRADE 3

In the youngest category were programs for initial exploration of the computer. Programs at this level, which teach basic concepts of math and reading, mostly present material in cartoon or picture form, although the use of sound and synthesized speech is increasing. The most difficult task at this age is structuring the interaction so that the child's input controls the program. Typing skills or even knowledge of the keyboard cannot be assumed. Thus interaction is likely to emphasize simple questions answered with a single keystroke—yes or no, or a number. With increasing

availability of pointing devices such as a mouse, the interaction can involve pointing at a part of the picture. Early research with children showed the utility of the touch screen, which lets a program detect a finger touching the screen over some part of the picture or over a word. This is more direct than using the mouse or keyboard and thus easier for young children to learn. Touch screens, however, continue to be relatively expensive and thus are not often in home use. Some games and computers support special devices for interacting with games, such as joysticks, flight sticks, or game paddles, such as are found on video games. Many younger children do not usually have the psychomotor skills to use them effectively.

Why would a parent make a relatively expensive computer available to a young child? One reason parents encourage children to use computers is the widespread belief that using a computer will help children acquire psychomotor and intellectual skills that will help them perform better in school (Martin, 1991). This view is encouraged by the increasing use of computers as teaching tools at school. Another reason is that the computer can act as a baby-sitter or playmate. Certainly many children have a natural curiosity about computers and want to play with them, just like their parents. Even though there are many different possible motivations for encouraging children to use computers, parents must be clear about the motivations and be aware of the positive and negative elements in each kind of use, based on the child's age and skills. Parental judgment is required. More so, parents need actively to facilitate and participate in the young child's use of the computer. Facilitation is needed to prevent the computer from being frustrating or boring. Participation by adults is probably prudent for preservation of the equipment.

GRADES 4 TO 8

By the fourth grade, many children have the knowledge and skills to master programs of moderate complexity, whether games or tools. Generally they are not ready to use programs developed for adults, partly due to complexity and partly due to motivation or need. Computer games, on the other hand, are very attractive to this age group, just as this age group makes up a major segment of the video game market. Many computer programs are developed for children in this group, including, but not limited to, games.

The games for this age range from simulations of simple games of chance through complex action adventure games. Many games make use of the child's developing problem-solving skills to find treasure, avoid bad guys, and the like. Other games are based almost purely on eye-hand coordination. Although many of these games are simple entertainment, sometimes there is an effort to make games educational or even to make education fun, through presentation of adventures based on educational content. Many educational programs, ranging from simple drills for math and other subjects, through multimedia encyclopedias, are targeted at this age range.

Children in this age group start to have strong opinions about the kinds of games and other programs they want to use. Many of these opinions are influenced by those of peers and by television advertising. Often this produces some differences of opinion between child and parent. Parental participation is essential in the choice of programs and in maintaining a reasonable balance in time spent playing on the computer versus other age-appropriate activities.

GRADES 9 TO 12

By high school most children have been exposed not only to computer and/or video games but also to introductory forms of serious tools, such as word processors, spreadsheets, and programming languages. This level of introduction is part of a computer literacy requirement for an increasing number of school districts and/or states. At the high school level, adolescents' use of computers begins to differentiate. Some students are exposed mainly to word processing, others learn business applications, and others take commercial or scientifically oriented computer programming courses. At this stage some students gain access to the whole world of adult and professional computer software. They also may gain access to adult-oriented software with explicit content inappropriate to adolescents.

Educational Use of Computers

Education involves the availability of information in a usable form, motivation for the student to learn, and the opportunity to make use of that newfound knowledge. Computers have been used to support each of these elements of education with many kinds of subject matter, including information about computers themselves.

The potential for using computers in education was recognized early, and a number of different projects tested their value in that arena. These include project Plato at the University of Illinois, the development of Coursewriter by IBM, and various experiments making interactive computer terminals available in structured and unstructured settings. These efforts moved into the microcomputer age with the introduction of the Apple II computer, which was embraced by teachers and schools nationally. Overall, computers have been shown to be effective in supporting education. That effectiveness, however, depends on the availability of educational material, its appropriateness to the state or preparation of a particular child, and effective reinforcement of the outcomes.

The availability of educational material for the computer has varied widely for a number of technical and nontechnical reasons. In the earliest experiments with computer instruction, mainframe computers were linked to interactive terminals that were used to present text to students, who could respond by typing information in at the keyboard. Later developments added the ability to display graphic material and even sound.

Initial efforts to use PCs as teaching machines were limited by the lack of storage on PCs, the limitations of their displays, the lack of sound, and the speed of their processors. Therefore, during the 1980s the educational programs for PCs were largely limited to practice drills and programs that could operate from algorithms rather than having to store large amounts of data. Many programs could present math problems, language tests, and typing drills, but few provided new information in an effective format.

Current PCs have the computing capacity of early mainframes, better displays, and, with media such as CD-ROMs, can provide a tremendous amount of stored information. One question is how effective they are in producing learning. Another concern is the extent to which they can present some kinds of materials more effectively than other methods.

Issue of Reinforcement

Computer games/tutors may or may not be more effective than traditional review methods, such as flash cards. The issue, however, is whether the reinforcement a computer provides can be used to make programs more interesting and fun, causing children to want to study or practice more. Sometimes children may not even consider computer time to be study time. As a person who is learning by choice will learn "better" than one who is being forced to learn, the fact that computer games/tutors can be enjoyable translates to more effective and less stressful learning.

Ideally, computers provide evaluative feedback to the student for every performance. For simple drills this is quite easy. Present the question and check if the answer is correct. The computer can check spelling and catch some grammatical errors. For more complex performances, such as writing an essay or proving a theorem, current PCs are less than adequate as an evaluative tool.

Computers and Schools

Can computers help with schoolwork? The specific value of a home computer depends in large part on the orientation of teachers to the use of computers. Schools have introduced computers into many areas of the curriculum, including specific computer courses, usually in later grades, but also for English, math, science, and other subjects. This use is usually a formal part of the curriculum, often mandated by school district or entire state standards. Computer usage in schools varies widely across the country but is increasing in amount and is introduced in earlier grades. Usually when schools want to introduce computing, they supply computers to the schools and mandate the use of specific programs. The utility of the home computer for that specific learning may depend on the availability of the assigned programs for the computer at home. A family may be lucky and already have the program being used or acquire it specifically for that class. How much prior knowledge about computers will generalize to that situation depends on the specific programs used. Typing skills, of course, generalize well.

The advantage of computers for accomplishing homework varies widely too. Some teachers, particularly in the primary grades, are focused on developing specific skills such as handwriting, mental arithmetic, and spelling. In those situations, some teachers discourage use of computers at home because they want to emphasize practice of

the specific skills. Often teachers want to see handwritten papers and a series of handwritten drafts rather than a copy corrected on a word processor. Controversy exists about the need for paper-and-pencil techniques when a child has a computer and has learned how to use it for these tasks. Counterarguments include fairness for those without computers and the need for portable skills. The difficulty of verifying authorship on a typed paper or homework sheet has also been raised.

The educational benefits of computers have been studied in a variety of educational contexts, beyond the scope of the present review.

Computer Games

In the 1950s and 1960s computers were very big, very expensive, and not very accessible to children of any age. A very small number of students as well as researchers interested in human/computer interaction managed to gain access to the early computers at universities; as a result, games have been a part of computing almost from the beginning. For more on that phenomenon, see *Hackers* (Levy, 1984).

Children first began to have access to primitive computers as electronic processors, which began to appear in simple and then increasingly complex video games. Pong was one of the first; in it, a simple processor displayed a bouncing ball on a television screen and the player could move a simple control so that the ball would bounce against a movable barrier and be returned to the other side of the screen, similar to a game of Ping Pong. Missing the ball lost a point to the computer.

This electronic simulation of conventional games became one of the major themes that persists in children's use of computers. Electronic simulation of traditional games provided an easy market—most people were familiar with the game, and the electronic game always provided the player with an opponent, one who never got bored and quit even if defeated regularly. Those marketing such games learned that the skill level needed to be adjustable, or staged so that anyone could play. They also learned that sound, visual motion, color, and positive feedback kept players interested longer and sold more games. While that lesson was not new to makers of pinball machines and other arcade games, these electronic versions were smaller, cheaper (usually), and safer for children to play. There is now a huge market for all sizes of electronic games, ranging from single-program pocket games, through large and expensive systems using CD-ROMs. Game systems and the game programs to run on them can be bought at toy stores or rented at most movie rental outlets.

Video games are limited in several ways that computers are not. The graphics resolution on video games is limited to that of a television set, which is lower than that of the high resolution monitors on most recent computers. Computers have, as their control interface, a keyboard and usually a mouse or other pointing device. In comparison, most home video game systems have a "control pad" consisting of a simple joystick and a few control buttons. As far as games are concerned, this means that a computer can do almost anything a game system can do, only better; but a game system cannot do everything a computer can do. The reason home video game systems are omnipresent is that they are much less costly and are simpler to use.

Communications

One of the more interesting capabilities of PCs is their ability to communicate with other computers. For home computers this is accomplished most often through a dial-up modem that communicates over regular telephone lines. With a modem and a simple communications program, several different kinds of computers can be dialed up. The simplest is to call up a friend who also has a computer and a modem. Doing this makes it possible to send messages back and forth, to share files, and to play certain multiuser games. Chatting is a slow substitute for talking on the telephone. On the other hand, sharing files lets data files and programs be passed back and forth. This lets children send each other homework assignments and work together on homework problems. Parents may want to supervise sharing homework if it is supposed to be done individually and unaided. They also may want to supervise sharing of programs because most commercial programs are licensed to a single user so sharing is illegal. Worse, shared programs can carry computer viruses and wipe out everything.

Bulletin Board Systems (BBSs) were an early form of public computer network which continue to exist because of their low cost and minimal regulation. Anyone can create a bulletin board using a computer with a modem and software that is readily available. Many are created locally by amateurs, including teenagers, for fun or profit and become known by word of mouth, e-mail, or other informal means. Over the past decade there have also been large numbers of commercial BBSs, some of which are private and accessible only by registered users, and others that are open to the public. The greatest risk from bulletin boards is that some are poorly monitored or have unscrupulous operators who permit sharing of inappropriate material. These sites can be self monitoring and can be shut down by appropriate authorities if someone can document that laws have been broken. The growth of the Internet has provided technically better communication functions and thus many BBSs have been abandoned or recreated on the Internet, including all the potential problems of inappropriate use, which are discussed later in the context of the Internet. Some BBSs have continued because they can avoid the intense scrutiny being received by the Internet. Internet content can be monitored by Internet service providers and other authorities but BBSs continue to receive only minimal and ineffective monitoring.

Commercial network providers, such as CompuServe, Prodigy, and America Online, are the large-scale equivalents of BBSs. These national services offer information to dial-up consumers for a fee. They offer various packages that sell access for a fixed price, with additional services available on a fee-for-service basis. Most of these services provide telephone numbers for local access, at least in cities. These services provide all kinds of information and programs, some of which are aimed at children, such as encyclopedias. Most commercial networks are quite discreet about the content made available, but access to inappropriate material still may be possible, especially as the account is likely to be in an adult's name. Parents must supervise the use of such accounts, especially because some services may incur substantial additional charges.

The Internet is potentially the most interesting of all communication services. It is referred to by some as the National Information Highway or the Information Superhighway. It uses technology developed initially by the military, was sponsored by the National Science Foundation, but has grown through participation of both educational and commercial institutions (Krol, 1992). The Internet has grown from being primarily a tool for scientists and engineers to being used in nearly every sector of human endeavor from business to religion. Of primary relevance here is its use by children. With the growth of local Internet service providers and the addition of Internet access by the older online services, nearly every home computer in the U.S. can be connected to the Internet. Millions of parents make this access to the Internet available to their children of all ages. In his January 23, 1996, State of the Union Address, President Clinton stated that "every classroom in America must be connected to the information superhighway, with computers and good software, and well-trained teachers." Further, the administration has made knowledge of how to use the Internet a target for every twelve-year-old.

On the positive side, Internet access by children opens access to vast libraries of information and the opportunity to communicate with other children around the world. Ideally, such access will encourage learning and involvement about the world around them. Children can gain access to the Internet through schools, libraries, and some of the commercial networks. Once access is achieved, the Internet is generally free, and connects computers all over the world. It facilitates the sending and receiving of electronic mail as well as the exchange of files, programs, pictures, and even sounds. It has news servers, and public message boards. Because it connects everyone, it is intrinsically diverse, reflecting the world.

Resources for children and their parents are widely available on the Internet. Some of these are primarily educational while others are more diverse. The U.S. Department of Education (http://www.ed.gov) identifies many programs for teachers, parents, and children. There are also many networks focusing on children or their education. Kehoe and Mixon (1997) review a number of these. Examples are KIDLINK (http://www.kidlink.org) which serves over 50,000 children worldwide; the Information Infrastructure and Technology Administration (http://www.ietf.org); and Educational Resources Information Centers (e.g. http://ericir.syr.edu). These and many more child-oriented programs can be identified by calling up a web search engine and searching phrases such as "Children Internet Resources." Our search yielded a website named (http://www.econonet.com/children.html), which has listings of programs from libraries, museums,

and even individual children. Searching the Internet and connecting to the ever changing landscape of the web is a lot of fun for adults and children.

On the negative side, the Internet can expose a child to almost all of the risks of society, as well as the good. We address three of these risks. The first and most highly publicized risk of the Internet is that children may gain access to information which is inappropriate for them (and, perhaps, questionable for anyone else). The chief offenders are sites which include explicit portrayals of sex and/or violence. Access to such sites may be inadvertent, such as the unintended result of a search using a word with an ambiguous meaning. The access may also be intentional by a youth looking for "naughty" material. Both kinds of access have received much attention in the media and in legislative bodies (see Wallace and Mangan, 1997).

Clearly, the most extreme material, such as child pornography, is and has been illegal on the net, just as it has been in other media. There have been numerous attempts at the national, state, and local levels to regulate the content of the net in order to protect children as well as public morals. An example is the Communications Decency Act of 1996 which created penalties for making indecent material available in the Internet or other means of telecommunication. This act greatly increased restrictions on the types of material which could be posted beyond earlier definitions of obscene or pornographic material, which were already restricted. Elements of that law have been overturned by the Third Circuit Court of Appeals, pending a final decision from the Supreme Court.

The issue is that material which is inappropriate for children and offensive to many adults can, nonetheless, be appropriate and even protected speech for other adults. There is reluctance to restrict the entire Internet to material appropriate to a young child. The main mechanism available to a provider of adult material is to restrict access to information to those 18 or older. This is now commonly done in one of two ways. The simplest and least effective method is to label the site as restricted to adults and ask the user to click on statements acknowledging that he or she is eighteen or older and is not going to be offended by the adult material. Unfortunately, that is just an invitation to the inquisitive adolescent. The only way to verify that a user is age 18 or older is to require some form of mail-in registration or provision of a credit card number. Those requirements are more challenging to an adolescent but not always foolproof. However, they do establish that the site has made an effort to restrict underage users.

The advocates of openness for the Internet, such as the Electronic Frontier Foundation, argue that restriction of access to material inappropriate to children can be adequately carried out through the use of voluntary ratings of Internet web sites in conjunction with the installation of software on computers which would block the sites designated as inappropriate and permit access to sites rated as appropriate for the children in the household. This type of software is now widely available, is inexpensive and often free, and can be used by parents to control inadvertent and even intentional attempts by children to access inappropriate material. Examples of this kind of software include Cyber Patrol, Cybersitter, Net Nanny, SurfWatch, and many others (Kehoe and Mixon, 1997, Chapter 2). The issue is whether parents are willing or able to install the software, and whether the adolescent or child is clever enough to get around the software. (Although most are not, some are able to do so.) Thus, the debate continues.

A second and far more dangerous threat to children is in the availability of chat rooms and other interactive settings, which let the computer user have conversations with other persons. This means of communication has the potential for the child to become involved in conversations with persons who have ulterior motives, ranging from deceptive marketing to pedophilia (Furger, 1997). The problem is that a child may connect to someone who identifies themselves as a friend, creates a relationship, and then uses that relationship to obtain information which puts the child at risk. It is reported that pedophiles have managed to enter chat rooms pretending to be a child and then have enticed a child into meeting them in the real world. There is some attempt to control this type of problem by having "safe" chat rooms for children which are monitored. Yet, many conversations which start out looking safe can lead to private e-mail conversations which are less appropriate. Ultimately, the only solution is to have parental supervision of the activity.

A third risk of the Internet comes from the possibility for users, including children, to create web pages. A web page is a special file which can be downloaded and viewed by users of the Internet with World Wide Web browser software. Anything can be posted, including text, pictures, and sounds. This provides a great means of self expression, but also poses the risk that some of the information being posted is inappropriate. There may be names, addresses, telephone numbers, e-mail addresses, or even family matters that a parent would like to keep private. Things said about other people can be a serious problem if they are derogatory or invade their privacy. Even pages intended to be humorous can be a problem, as was discovered by a middle school student who posted a conspiracy theory about his school. In it, he parodied everything from food, to playgrounds, to administration. He was awarded a suspension for his efforts. Another common problem of Web publication is the posting of copyrighted information without appropriate permission from the author. Parental input on the appropriateness of postings to the web is in order, because once information is posted, it is nearly impossible to retrieve.

Some Additional Issues

SHOULD A COMPUTER BE BOUGHT FOR A CHILD?

The answer to this question is a trade-off between price and expected benefits. As noted, the price of personal computers has continued to drop since their introduction and is likely to continue to drop for the foreseeable future. There appears to be little real liability and much to be gained by providing children with access to computers.

AT WHAT AGE SHOULD CHILDREN BE INTRODUCED TO COMPUTERS?

There is very little problem with introducing children to computers at a very early age. The issue is to make sure that the programs are developmentally appropriate and that sufficient parental supervision is provided. If a computer is in the home, the parent has the choice between teaching the child to stay away from it or teaching the child how to use it correctly. The latter seems preferable. Generally, desktop computers are durable and not likely to be broken in normal use, even by a young child. Commercial software is available that can limit the child's access to only those areas made available by the parent. Laptop computers are a bit more fragile and a bit more expensive, so increased supervision is advised when they are involved.

WHAT ARE THE LIKELY BENEFITS FROM INTRODUCING A CHILD TO COMPUTERS?

Although many generalizations about the benefits of introducing a child to computers can be made, the first rule is that the benefits depend in large part on the nature of the experience the child has. Computers are a part of the present culture, which we learn to value or abhor depending on our experience with them. For children it is no different. The consequences of pushing computers at children probably has a parallel in piano lessons. Learning about computers at an early age may open the door for development of genius, whether literary or technical, but also has the risk of stifling any natural curiosity if pushed too hard. Computers can be very frustrating to adults, and certainly to children, when they do not work right for unknown reasons. It is estimated that quite a large number of computers in the United States have been relegated to garages or attics for just that reason. Therefore, introduction of children or persons of any age to computers needs to be structured and supported and ideally have a well thought out goal. The benefits depend on the goal.

Those who have or sell computers often state that having a computer will make Johnny or Jenny become smarter, do better in school, and grow up to be a technical wizard. It is clear that enriching a child's environment helps a child do better. In that regard, introducing computers into a child's home enriches the environment and increases the opportunity for intellectual development. This can be true at any age. But how much difference a computer can make depends on the child's social environment, including the roles of parents, peers, and teachers and the other sources of enrichment in the home.

Some Concerns about Computers for Children

IS COMPUTER USE ADDICTIVE?

One of the major concerns raised about computers is the extent to which they can pull youths into playing with them to the exclusion of almost all other activities, including doing homework, having a normal social life, exercising, eating, and sleeping.

The feedback provided by computers can be very reinforcing to children and adolescents. This happens most often with the introduction of a new game but can also happen with other computer-based activities. Examples include hours and hours spent to make something in the computer better, such as the amount of memory available, the colors and format of the display, and particularly the programs available. Some of these activities are motivated by the goal of winning a game, achieving a new level of mastery of the computer itself, or writing a new program. Sometimes the activity is competitive with peers, such as being the first to achieve a high score or solve a particular puzzle in a game. This kind of reinforcement often is understandable in terms of variable ratio operant conditioning. Game levels are set to be progressively more difficult so that winning is not assured. Solving difficult systems problems is also a variable reinforcement because every problem solved can be replaced by any number of other problems to solve or things to change. In fact, the code for at least one major system program, as well as many games, includes undocumented and hidden tricks that can be discovered only through persistent search.

Discovering these tricks makes the user feel like a knowledgeable insider in some communal secret. Often this is accompanied by a feeling of power and self-worth. Beyond the games, computers provide access to a very technical world that is too big for any single person to master. Further, it is not static but is continuously evolving, so that a programmer, of any age, can feel like he or she is on the cutting edge of technological change. The hacker mythology of the computer industry has taken advantage of this fact. Hackers—bright but "nerdy" young persons—can learn enough about computers by working with them night and day to discover or develop new technologies. Indeed, the computer industry brags about and makes heroes of some hackers. An implication of the hacker myth is that a person can break many of the social norms and still be special. The hacker phenomenon is well documented in a number of volumes, including *Hackers* (Levy, 1984). Yet the hacker world also has a dark side, including those who break into systems and disrupt or steal whatever they find.

Another element that reinforces computer use applies to a social aspect of computing. When a person signs onto computer bulletin boards or the Internet, his or her usual identity is hidden by the text-only communication and lack of visual identification. By convention, people identify themselves to these environments by made-up names or aliases. Although the system administrator usually needs to identify users in order to authorize access, the rest of those on the network do not. This fact makes it not only possible but common for participants to take on environment-specific personas that can be totally different from their real-life personas. Playing roles is expected in games, so why not on the Net? Anecdotal examples include misidentification of age, gender, and personality. Shy people can act out aggressive, bigger-than-life characters. Good people can play evil ones, and so on.

Unlike playing games against the computer, some games on bulletin boards or the Internet are multiuser role-playing games, such as multiuser dungeons (MUDs). These have all of the role-playing possibilities of the game Dungeons and Dragons except that they are played on the network. The Dungeon Master is played by the computer. Different networks provide other types of competitive games.

Shotton (1989) conducted a fairly comprehensive study of computer addiction in Great Britain. In her review she found reference to computer dependency as early as 1970. Her own study drew from a number of informants, including discussions with authors of earlier papers raising the alarm about possible computer addiction. She also interviewed 5 university students identified as computer dependent. Next she prepared a public solicitation for persons directly or indirectly familiar with computer dependency, which resulted in 180 responses. These people were sent a questionnaire; 151 responded, with 121 (84%) considering themselves to be computer dependent. Average time spent computing was 22.4 hours per week for those using the computer at home ($N = 120$) and 21.6 hours per week at work ($N = 69$), and a mean of 42.8 hours for the 68 people using computers in both settings. Shotton's preliminary conclusion was that a computer addiction syndrome existed, usually focusing on males who seemed to prefer the computer to people, who spent many hours interacting with the computers, and who often were not goal-directed in that interaction. Shotton's study included additional questionnaires and comparison with control groups, which helped her expand on her conclusions. The general conclusion was that computer dependency exists, but that at least within the age groups studied, it was relatively benign, often consistent with preexisting personality characteristics and often used to personal advantage, either instrumentally or to develop alternative so-

cial relationships. The general applicability of these findings to adolescents is uncertain due to the small numbers included ($N = 22$, ages 10–19), but continues to be of concern in the popular press.

While it would be unwise to overgeneralize from the limited work uncovered, it would seem wise for parents to exercise some supervision over computer use, at least to be sure that it does not displace other activities that are appropriate for normal educational and social development.

Computer Games and Violence

Computer and video game violence is an area hotly debated in both political and professional circles. Many parents, politicians, and professionals argue that computer and video games containing representations of violence either cause or promote aggressive and/or violent behavior in children and adolescents who play them. This debate is not confined to computers and video games but reflects a much broader concern about social values and violence as reflected in books, movies, television, and on the street.

The effect that playing computer games has on children and adolescents depends on several conditions. The first of these is the degree of violence represented in the game. Second is the child's ability to differentiate between the imaginary world of the game and reality. Third is the child's degree of impulse control, and fourth is the value context in which the child and game are embedded.

First, computer games vary widely in the type and amount of violence represented. One part of the portrayal of violence is the degree of abstraction of players, and another is the type of competitive action required. These can be used to describe a continuum from the least violent to the most violent games. The least violent games are nonadversarial strategy games. Among the least violent of adversarial games are checkers, chess, Pac Man, Space Invaders, and Star Trek. These are all violent in a very symbolic way in that players have to take the other player's pieces, but they are so abstract that they are unlikely to tap any of the primitive emotions related to fear or hate, which are prime motivators of aggression. Nonetheless, some of these games are likely to generate excitement as players seek to win, get a high score, and avoid losing. Yet it is very unlikely that any children could confuse these games with any aspect of their real lives. In the middle of the continuum are games that have confrontations with cartoonlike or vehicular opponents and which are dispatched through relatively simple actions. At the most violent end of the continuum are current games of personal combat, which provide an explicit representation of an opponent with human features and which require the player to engage in explicit acts of violence in order to overcome the opponent and win. For some games, combat is the sole object of playing. The games could be considered less violent if the player had some role other than combatant.

Second, the ability of the child to understand the game as distinct from reality is likely to limit its potential influence on the child's aggressive behavior. If the boundaries of reality are not maintained, then there is increased risk that the child will attempt to act out the game roles after playing, as an extension of the game into real life. It would seem that unreal games with abstract players would be least generalized into postgame behavior. More lifelike roles would seem to be harder to differentiate from real life, especially for younger players.

Third, the child's degree of impulse control should influence the apparent effects of playing a violent game. Playing any game can be exciting, especially one in which a player fights for the survival of his or her game character. This excitement may be reflected in greater activity levels after play even if there is no confusion of roles. The timing of game play should be structured so that any excess excitement can be channeled into other appropriate activities.

Fourth, playing a game puts the player in a context in which decisions are made and actions taken. In the absence of a social values context, the child may internalize the implicit or explicit value systems portrayed by the game. This would be offset if the child has a clear set of values about the game activities and even game-playing itself. The obvious lesson here is that parents should become part of the social context, helping the child to understand the game in relation to the social values that they wish to enculcate.

Empirical data on the degree to which computer and video games produce violence is mixed. A study by Silvern and Williamson (1987) suggests that the effects of video games are similar to those from watching cartoons. Other studies show physiological arousal (Winkle, Novak, & Hopson, 1987). Aggressive content in games also may lead to increased hostility, although this may be less from video games than some of the other media (Favaro, 1983). There is some suggestion that video games can be used as an adjunct to psychotherapy, by helping children to model and gain control of their behavior (Gardner, 1991).

REFERENCES

Favaro, P. J. (1983). *The effects of video game play on mood, physiological arousal, and psychomotor performance.* Unpublished doctoral dissertation, Hofstra University, New York.

Furger, Roberta (1997). "Your Children Are Talking to Strangers." *PC World,* June, p. 35.

Gardner, J. E. (1991). Can the Mario Bros. help? Nintendo games as an adjunct in psychotherapy with children. *Psychotherapy, 28* (4), 667–670.

Home PC. (1994). Special Back to School Issue. *Home PC,* CMP Publications, September.

Jabs, Carolyn. (1994). "Raising Computer Smart Kids: Parental Guidance Suggested." *Home PC,* CMP Publications, September.

Kehoe, Brendan and Mixon, Victoria. (1997). *Children and the Internet: A Zen Guide for Parents & Educators,* Prentice Hall, Upper Saddle River, New Jersey.

Krol, E. (1992). *The whole Internet users guide and catalog.* Sebastopol, CA: O'Reilly & Associates.

Levy, S. (1984). *Hackers: Heroes of the computer revolution.* New York: Dell.

Martin, R. (1991). "School Children's Attitudes Towards computers as a Function of Gender, Course Subjects, and Availability of Home Computers." *Journal of Computer Assisted Learning,* Vol. 7, No. 3, September.

Silvern, S. B., & Williamson, P. A. (1987). The effects of video game play on young children's aggression, fantasy, and prosocial behavior. *Journal of Applied Developmental Psychology, 8,* 453–462.

Shotton, M. A. (1989). *Computer addiction? A study of computer dependency.* London: Taylor and Francis.

Turkle, S. (1984). *The second self: Computers and the human spirit.* New York: Simon & Schuster.

U.S. Bureau of the Census (1993). *Current Population Survey, Series P23, No. 171.* (see http://www.census.gov/population/www/socdemo/computer.html Tables A,B,C).

Wallace, Jonathan and Mangan, Mark. (1997). *Sex, Laws and Cyperspace: Freedom and Censorship on the Frontiers of the Online Revolution.* Henry Holt and Company, New York.

Winkle, M., Novak, D. M., & Hopson, H. (1987). Personality factors, subject gender, and the effects of aggressive video games on aggression in adolescents. *Journal of Research in Personality, 21* (2), 211–223.

9 / Space Exploration: Influence on Children and Adolescents

Daryll Anderson

Children in grade school are offered a view of space exploration as a glorious American adventure illustrating the virtues of progress and science, wherein a few larger-than-life citizens risk their lives to enlarge the known world. The library provides ample further development of this theme to accommodate varying tastes: attractive pictures of planets, diagrams of spaceships, biographies of female astronauts and dead astronauts, predictions of colonies and businesses in space. I mentioned this topic—how space exploration has affected the view of the world held by today's youth—to a 24-year-old who knew today's children. He looked blank and replied, "It hasn't had any effect." I persisted, asking if he thought people would live in space one day, and he answered, "We have to. We've ruined the earth." That's a pretty dramatic noneffect. My informant was suspicious of the public image of space exploration taught in school but all the same accepted exploration of an infinite universe as too obvious to mention. His drawing of the universe was a labeled blank page, which he said showed that the universe goes on and on with no edges.

Since the moon landing in 1969, space exploration has for many adults faded to an assumption, with new territories of space and mind opening up for speculation, the view of the earth from the outside calling attention to its beauty and value and plight, the infinities and shifting borders of the universe reminding people that they like to know some boundaries. Our present climate of intolerance toward children and adults is an effort to reestablish boundaries, as a group of people band together against the unknown.

The Beginning of Space Exploration

Early space launchings were events of such moment that schoolteachers permitted black-and-white televisions to be tuned all day to a picture of a horizon, unmoving gray ground and gray sky with a little potential spaceship dead center, interrupted occasionally by a picture of a man in front of a panel of dials in Houston and an attempt to explain why it was still T-minus-10 and holding. Probably no event, and surely no mere rocket, could now so inspire imagination that television producers would trust children to watch such a slow-paced, visually boring, long program just to catch a view lasting less than a minute of a lengthening puff of exhaust. Television has changed, of course, and so have people's requirements for entertainment. But when space exploration first began, imagination could fill in the defects of the program because the idea or meaning of space exploration was powerful, powerful enough to override any objections, aesthetic, economic, moral.

Partly imagination was fueled with ideology. The Soviet Sputnik in 1957 intensified Americans' fear of communism. Cosmonauts watching from the sky were upsetting; and if *they* got to the moon first, it would be shattering proof that the United States was not the best in everything; the moon would become a transmitting station not only for plain propaganda, which right-thinking people could spot at a glance, but also for subtle totalitarian influences, which might be more difficult to eschew.

Not everyone took this partisan view. Hannah Arendt (1958), for instance, saw the *Sputnik* launch as the most important development in history, as an escape from imprisonment on earth, although she was ironic about just why people are so eager to escape. Her more international ideology has proven more durable. And mixed with the nationalistic competition of the space race announced in 1961 by President John F. Kennedy, its goal to reach the moon in a decade, many hoped for great progress in science, something humanitarian, something easier to be happy about than merely earth-bound bombs. The space program became a kind of modern cathedral, a work of art of enormous scope demanding concerted effort and vast amounts of money, an expression of what is important, an idea so compelling as to be above calculations of cost. Nigel Calder (1978) claimed that the poor like cathedrals, perhaps more than they like meals. The deaths of astronauts Virgil I. Grissom, Edward H. White, and Roger B. Chaffee on the first *Apollo* craft in 1967 gave pause, but only for 18 months, and the *Apollo II* fulfilled Kennedy's prediction by setting people on the moon in 1969. While this excited many children, the moon seemed static again when word got out that the astronauts' footprints will be there at least 10 million years.

Responses to Space Exploration: Something Lost, Something Gained

Much has happened since 1967 in space research—probes to planets, dozens of shuttles, Skylab—and information about the universe has multiplied many times. The first airplane flights inspired artists. The scope of human effort widened; possibilities suggested themselves right and left; progress was taking place. Artists did not respond in that way to space exploration.

The moon turned out to be rocks and dust, as predicted, no surprise. The craters so touchingly named *Mare Tranquilitatis* and *Mare Foecunditatis* were confirmed as accidental dents; no discernible creatures past or present, not even a miserable spore, greeted us; nothing propelled imagination or induced great art. This, our own planet's celestial body, seeming so meaningful in potential, turned to dust in actuality, and, except for a few wry works, artists fell silent in their disenchantment.

In "First Walk on the Moon," for example, May Swenson (1971) jabbed at the constricted language, movements, imagination, and feeling of the moonwalkers: "We felt neither hot nor cold." However, poets have a long tradition of protesting science. Elucidations of likable mysteries and rearrangements of reality, however elegant, meet poets' resistance. John Donne in the early seventeenth century wrote of the decline of everything, beginning with the Garden of Eden and picking up speed in modern times with the appearance of new stars in the immutable spheres, in "An Anatomie of the World":

> The Sun is lost, and th'earth, and no mans wit
> Can well direct him where to looke for it.
> And freely men confesse that this world's spent,
> When in the Planets, and the Firmament
> They seeke so many new; then see that this
> Is crumbled out againe to his Atomies.
> 'Tis all in peeces, all cohaerence gone.

C. P. Snow (1957) saw this when he called literary intellectuals "natural Luddites." Ursula LeGuin (1979) postulated a law that technology opposes fantasy, that all bums but no capitalists have read *The Lord of the Rings*. That's not the whole story.

In one aspect, in light of the weight and force of the traditions and metaphor and the wild freedom of boundless speculation, scientific advances seem to surround themselves with dead territory, infertile to imagination. Children, as a result, are not helped to delight in space fantasy. Science fiction writers, in deference to the known, had, long before the moon landing, left the dead moon for the more promising Venus, and when Venus's surface temperature came back as 477° C, they peaceably removed their worlds to other solar systems. Speculators turned their attention to astronomical wonders—the expanding and contracting and folding of infinite space, the marvels of black holes, anything to get back that feeling that the world is full of possibilities and its boundaries are elastic.

Mental gymnastics are one pathway to an exotic universe, an interesting place to live, and the flip side of the limits of matter is the limits of mind. Science fiction writers of the 1940s point to their accurate predictions of the 1960s as proof of their credibility, but with some regret that their remarkable ideas came true so fast. As Isaac Asimov (1981) said, those writers responded by changing their focus from technology to people. Asimov was referring to plots hinging on people's personalities and behavior rather than their machines, but that was in 1973, and since then science fiction has become populated with a bewildering variety of expanded minds, strange potentials, other consciousnesses, and deliberately odd points of view.

Commonly in early science fiction, aliens were enemies, monsters monstrous, and the plot circled around the kill. The film *King Kong*, in 1933, alerted people that other kinds of creatures may merit sympathy. (Kong was sympathetically killed, however.) The notion progressed to a vision of other creatures as superior to people, more humane than humans, by the 1950s with the movie *The Day the Earth Stood Still*—and became a fad around 1970 with *Stranger in a Strange Land* (novel by Robert Heinlein, published 1961). The children's version of this idea appeared in the movie *E.T.* (1982), although it became more a consumer item than a fad, a triumph of merchandising rather than of an idea. People in stories have progressed from reflexively squashing any different life-forms to asserting, at least, if not illustrating, a principle of tolerance and appreciation. Children are offered many books connecting space and understanding of others: an example is Umberto Eco's *The Three Astronauts* (1989), showing astronauts from Russia, the United States, and China finding common ground on Mars.

The other direction for human minds to expand is inward, within. Perhaps science fiction writers took a lesson from earlier literary experiments in stream of consciousness as a form. Such works, however poetic, are hard to read and not plotful and present machines that turn dreams into actual events and personalities into things that can be exchanged. The contents of the mind become as real as objects.

The contemplation of aliens in outer space redirected adults' attention to themselves, and, in parallel, exploration of other planets redirected attention to earth. Stewart Brand, publisher of *The Whole Earth Catalog* (1968), made a fuss until photographs of the earth, taken from space, were released. Now ecology has grown from a counterculture to a mainstream interest popular enough to keep business and government leaders walking on eggs. We have an environmentalist as a vice president. Space research showed us a fresh view of ourselves. We want to look good in the universe, and we want to avert the doom predicted by fiction writers and confirmed by statisticians with computers. Global home repairs may reverse or at least slow the trend toward extinction.

One current justification for further space research is also cast as helping out the earth. In response to those who prefer vistas of nature uncontaminated by people and their creations, or who hope that nature left alone will correct people's mistakes, space technologists now offer in rebuttal a way to open the closed system of earth and defy the statisticians with a hope of natural resources imported from space and of housing in space for surplus people on earth.

Gerard K. O'Neill (1977) has devoted much effort to promoting space colonies:

It is the hope of those who work toward the breakout from planet Earth that the establishment of permanent, self-sustaining colonies of humans off-Earth will have three vital consequences. First, it will make human life forever unkillable, removing it from the endangered species list, where it now stands on a fragile Earth overarmed with nuclear weapons. Second, the opening of virtually unlimited new land area in space will reduce territorial pressures and therefore diminish warfare on Earth itself. Third, the small scale of space colonies, the largest some tens of thousands of people, will lead to local governments that are simple in form, responsive to the desires of the people, and as reachable and intimate as were the New England town meetings of America's heritage.

This vision of little Edward Hicks paintings scattered around the sky (with the Pilgrims making a deal with the Indians in the background, perhaps) is not utopian, O'Neill says, because people will be free to leave the colony at any time they want, because they will choose their variety of government, and because there will be no policy prohibiting technological advances. That view seems utopian on its face and unlikely to take the direction predicted.

In these distant settlements, evolution will keep on improving our species. This is Frank White's (1987) vision of our future:

What kind of species will humanity be at that point? What will *Homo universalis* be like? Even the capacity to generate metaphors fails at this level, so we admit that we cannot know. However, we can be certain that they will be our children, and they will love us for being their parents, for having the courage to create the conditions for them to exist, and for exploring, for that is the human thing to do. (p. 192)

Contemplating Infinities

Space inspires preoccupation with infinities. Whether received opinion currently treats the universe as technically boundless or merely enormous, the idea of boundlessness always crops up. The distance to the star next door, a smallish number of light-years in astronomy, no matter how cleverly compared to time around the earth in reality-provoking exercises, remains hard to grasp, and probably many people give up trying to grasp such distances and just refer to them.

Large numbers are ordinary fare: 4 billion people living, increasing every moment; some trillions of dollars in the national debt (how many zeros is that?), and the debt similarly increases. Thirty thousand people dying in a landslide can seem like less a disaster than 1 or 2 dying, a phenomenon much exploited in the news, perhaps because 30,000 is too many and not appreciably different from 1,000 or 80,000. Peoples exist who do not consider numbers over 10: more than 10 are many, but not countable. Each person may have such a limit of understanding for numbers beyond which any number merely means *many*. Yet astronomy, along with any other science—and mimicked in business, politics, and scholarship— insists on the actuality of numbers that people cannot grasp.

Early scientists—or friends of science, their activities not being even a job, much less a profession—liked marvels. The *Philosophical Transactions* of the Royal Society beginning in 1660 reported monstrous births, rains of dust, trees with deadly shade. Robert Boyle, of thermodynamics, contributed many articles describing rotting mackerel shining in the dark. People particularly liked the science of what they could not explain. Perhaps continuously since the 17th century, but surely in ours, friends of science continue ingenuously to admire the marvels of nature and promote new wonders. The offshoots of marvels are unidentified flying objects, ancient astronauts, and parapsychology. One response to infinities is to enjoy them. Sitting in an armchair, looking forward to a good dinner, expecting that the armchair and the dinner probably will be around tomorrow, we can interpret as pleasure the ripple of unease that comes from stretching the mind around something very big. Joy in amazement does require some security, even for very young people.

Children often mention infinities in connection with space, usually as a source of distress. Infinities used to be the province of religion, and nature, for some, was its revelation. Despite bickering about science's threats to faith, many people find religious explanations a good template for accepting things that cannot be grasped, which

contemporary science produces by the dozens. Children's stories, without necessarily being too prettified, often show an ultimately benign universe, with supernatural elements hauled in from folklore or animate nature. Madeleine L'Engle's books show children with a religious worldview withstanding challenges in many arenas, including that of science, and finding the security in religion to contemplate the horizons suggested by science.

Any moderately alert youngster notices that scientific facts change (e.g., the chemically ideal breakfast menu) and that another response to infinities is to insist pigheadedly on one's own point of view. Independence of thought sounds pleasingly democratic, and after all, the principle that justified the 17th-century marvels was that nothing should be accepted on authority, because observation and not Aristotle was the source of knowledge. The Flat Earth Society, which was considering reconsidering after the moon landing, represents an extreme of this feeling of being entitled to one's own view. Some allegedly personal views develop traditional lines of argument. These are the topics college freshmen pick for expressing themselves: evolution, abortion, and so on. Announcing which of 2 well-delineated camps a person prefers is only minimally individual, and that stance easily develops into pigheadedness, which is a popular version of individuality, whether the view in question is widely shared or private and eccentric.

Selfhood and Subjectivity in the Space Age

Defining experience as subjective is another route to having one's own point of view. It might be largely a reaction to insistence, attributed to scientists, on the unique reality of matter, which disallows any discussion of attitudes, feelings, and other immaterial influences. In James Thurber's *Many Moons* (1943), a princess falls ill and will die unless she can have the moon. The king consults the lord high chamberlain, the royal wizard, and the royal mathematician, whose different descriptions of the moon all lead to the conclusion that she cannot have it. The court jester saves the day by asking the princess what she thinks the moon is. She thinks it is a half-inch circle of gold. Her blessed subjectivity saved the princess.

The loss of this subjectivity with the moon landing—the moon is now known to be just rocks and that is the only factual way to look at it—is what seemed so stultifying to poets. Knowing the party line about the moon, children now will be ridiculed if they think of the moon and green cheese during the same breath. In physics, relativity and uncertainty appeared almost a century ago, but remained somewhat esoteric for many years. Psychologists and philosophers have provided corroborating evidence for the value of one person's view even if it is divergent. Too, relativity and uncertainty have become common topics of speech, even among poets.

In its benign form, justifying the individual point of view (idiosyncratic though it may be) can be a sane response to the collectivism that has always been a feature of predictions. It may be a healthy retort to a world where a person's job can be to operate a self-service elevator. Carried farther, however, the individual is exalted, and people are lost in mental health. The endless exploration of the self, with life as material for therapy, art as therapy for artist and audience, and the quest for personal growth an industry (keeping psychiatrists in business despite insurance cutbacks), may not be so sane.

The version of individuality defined as one's inner experience independent of cultural or other outside influences, the "disinterested" subjectivity of Kant's aesthetics, is an effort to deny that individuality is forged in a culture and a family and to assert that one makes it out of nothing. Disorders of the self have become an important subject for speculation and research in parallel with widespread floundering to reestablish the importance of the individual.

Crystallizing a New Worldview

Space exploration has become mundane for contemporary youths. Some children still aspire to be astronauts, but their number is smaller than before. Astronauts are offered to children as heroes, but many of those heroes have gone on to write gloomy memoirs. Children subjected to the publicity about Christa McAuliffe, the schoolteacher in space, watched her disappear in the *Challenger* explosion in 1986 and had second thoughts. No longer a path to glory, trivial space is part of daily life. People are busy improving the earth, setting up space businesses, signing up for shuttle rides, getting on with work and play. Space is possessible: The earth or any celestial body can be had as a pillow, a poster, a sticker, a shower curtain, or even a work of art. Artists are coming to terms with space. Space research is back to warfare.

Historians of science fiction show it growing up. Early works (meaning those of the 1930s) were childish. C. M. Kornbluth (1969) describes the world of popular science fiction as "congruent with the attitudes and emotions of a boy seven or nine years old tearing off down an alley on his bike in search of adventure. The politics of this boy are vague, half-understood, overheard adult dogmatisms. His sex-life is a bashful, inhibited yearning for nonspecific contact. His cultural level is low" (p. 61). Critics interpret early science fiction in terms of infantile psychology. Currently, however, science fiction is supposed to be about adults; mating is allowed. Simple, childish plots are out. Everybody liked the special effects in the film *Star Wars* (1977), but the plot came under fire as puerile and old-fashioned and it remains so on re-release. No matter how many people laud a childlike perception of the world, people, including children, are supposed to be sophisticated enough to reject such psychologically transparent stuff. Complexity, mixed emotions, doubt—these are the markers for sophistication, and children are expected to come to terms with them early in their development.

The prevailing idea of the universe and the worldview that it implies have changed in other centuries and in our time, and, I guess, will change some more. Adapting to new situations and evaluating new ideas are skills given lip service but not much promoted in current psychiatry and education; few adults have themselves had great success with the complexities of subjectivity and cultural and moral relativity.

The United States, we learn in school, was initially settled by people who wanted religious freedom, and its government was designed by their descendants who wanted political freedom. Religious freedom in the colonies promptly stiffened into the freedom to exercise one's own variety of intolerance rather than be subjected to another's. Tolerating other ways of looking at things has not been a strong American tradition. Yet tolerance has caught on, after a fashion. Exotic aliens—well, all right. Chinese medicine—illuminating, perhaps. Black Africans—very socially acceptable. But black Americans lack social cachet, insights from China should not influence medicine, and exotic aliens remain hypothetical. What has evolved is more tolerance for people in another solar system or in another country than for the people met here. Many Americans feel privileged and bound therefore to help starving people in India or Somalia, but they believe that starving people in the United States choose to starve or even like starving. It is our history again: The ideal of tolerance is good; actually tolerating is not. Most children seem to understand this contradictory state, even in the space age.

Trying to make people behave with more laws and more prisons has gotten the United States the highest proportion of people in prison on earth, and politicians elected by landslides are urging ever tighter control, more people chosen for longer prison sentences, and everyone makes peace with the death penalty. The special treatment of children who commit crimes is thought to encourage more crimes, and the logical solution is to certify them to be tried and punished as adults. The hope that external controls will prevail over undesirable behavior justifies the environment of artificial and arbitrary consequences in adolescent psychiatry wards and can be expected to have parallel results. Our way of life requires the sacrifice of a great many people, many of them children, who are simply discounted and kept in separate locked-up buildings.

Authority-centered treatment of ideas as well as behavior in the American school, particularly in science education, ensures that few people develop any skill in evaluating information, despite the fact that information requiring evaluation continues to proliferate. Experiments are not something done in school to see what happens, and young students promptly see through the teacher's obligatory sop to honesty in research. The notion that the experimenter and not the experiment failed is established early and is reflected in all the scientific papers that conclude "That the experiment failed to support the hypothesis is no reason to believe that the hypothesis might be wrong." If an experiment is a formality designed to illustrate what is already believed, then if it illustrates something else, it should not be believed. Such a science education in the space age must be questioned.

The announcement, designed to quell troublemakers in 9th-grade science, that science is not concerned with values probably backfires. People who decline to consider values are at their mercy in the same way that people who do not consider emotions are at their mercy. In my first premedi-

cal course—biology—the teacher taught us that evolution following accidental formation of amino acids is the correct view of the universe and promptly forbade any remarks from the students. This point appeared on the true-or-false test, and quite a few people in the class marked it false on principle and lowered their scores. Pigheadedness begets pidheadedness, even though I can sympathize with a teacher who wishes to prevent too-lengthy discussions in which students announce what God thinks. It takes a lot of faith in humanity to ask people what they think and be able to stand their answers. But since everyone is bombarded with so much conflicting information, educators should address rather than avoid the question of how a person chooses to believe one fact rather than another. There are, however, few debates about space—only bafflement and awe.

Hannah Arendt, who saw space exploration as welcome liberation, acknowledged with regret that it diminishes people's importance in the universe, and this reciprocity may explain why, despite new ideas to capture imagination, new places for people to go, and wider knowledge of the variety of people on earth, we hear the clatter of minds clamping shut. Culture is conventional agreement about the acceptable range of activity, its boundaries and limits; culture is a framework that, like language, both liberates and restricts. Systems scientists point to the much-augmented power and scope of action in an organization compared to those of one of its parts on its own, while treating the lost potentials of separate persons as unimportant. But a larger universe probably does not mean that whole groups of people or faculties of people can be squeezed out as new agreements about limits are negotiated.

The United States alone has enough interest groups clamoring for consideration—and of varied enough ethical points of view—to baffle any policy maker. This messiness can be avoided by retreating to the laboratory, investigating only testable hypotheses and averaging disparate values. Or things can be tidied up with words, pretending that telling children not to have sex is an adequate public health intervention to eliminate both teenage pregnancy and AIDS, or venturing to solve the problem of alcoholism by telling young people not to drink. Similar simplifications take care of obesity, any cancer or other disease that can be shown to have a behavioral antecedent, and any problem resulting in undesirable behavior. Dictating correct behavior with fierce penalties for noncompliance is a way of squeezing these people out with consequences. Some of the consequences may be inherent and provide sufficient logic to impel the dictates; but the more devastating consequences come from stigma, which is totally optional.

When I was a teacher, the doctrine of teaching the whole person gained currency, and I found it daunting to suppose that a teacher could appreciate and respond to the entirety of 100 people's natures every 16 weeks. Teaching about the known universe also could be a big task. The much-lauded biopsychosocial model in medicine similarly has provided both a profusion of influences, factors, and causes of someone's catching a cold or going to the doctor and a paralyzing array of caveats for the doctor-patient relationship. Psy-

choanalysis should have warned us that tracing behavior down to its roots can go on until doomsday. Often in the past a proliferation of conflicting information has sorted itself into manageable form under the influence of a new idea. With or without new ideas, a person's dogmatic attempts to force ideas into manageable form by repeating his or her point in a louder voice may have succeeded in oppressing many people for a time, but ultimately it did not work. Somehow, we need to make room for people, including children, whether by our lights they behave properly or not. So this may well be an era of some tolerated brainstorming, ambiguity, and doubt. The new, larger earth revealed by space exploration cannot be compressed back to its old size.

REFERENCES

Arendt, H. (1958). *The human condition.* Chicago: University of Chicago Press.

Asimov, I. (1981). *Asimov on science fiction.* Garden City, NY: Doubleday.

Calder, N. (1978). *Spaceships of the mind.* New York: Viking Press.

Donne, J. (1952). An anatomy of the world: The first anniversary. (1910?). In C. Coffin (Ed.), *The complete poetry and selected prose of John Donne* (pp. 185–197, 207–213). New York: Modern Library.

Kornbluth, C. M. (1969). The failure of the science fiction novel as social criticism. In B. Davenport (Ed.), *The science fiction novel: Imagination and social criticism* (p. 61). Chicago: Advent Publishers.

LeGuin, U. (1979). *The language of the night: Essays on fantasy and science fiction.* New York: Putman's Sons.

O'Neill, G. K. (1977). *The high frontier: Human colonies in space.* New York: William Morrow.

O'Neill, G. K. (1987). Foreword. In F. White, *The overview effect: Space exploration and human evolution* (p. xiv). Boston: Houghton Mifflin.

Snow, C. P. (1957). *The two cultures and the scientific revolution.* New York: Cambridge University Press.

Swenson, M. (1971). First walk on the moon. *Antaeus, 2,* 130–132.

White, F. (1987). *The overview effect: Space exploration and human evolution.* Boston: Houghton Mifflin.

10 / The Impact of the Nuclear Threat on Children and Adolescents

Harris B. Peck

Studies of the impact of the nuclear threat on children and adolescents began to appear over 30 years ago and have involved adolescents, preadolescents, and a few younger children. In almost all instances, such studies have revealed considerably more awareness and concern by youngsters than had been recognized previously. In the United States, both children and adolescents appear to derive their information primarily from the media and particularly from television. Their concerns

are rarely shared with parents, and for the most part, there are only beginning efforts by parents or teachers to open the way. This chapter reviews some of the salient findings and gives some consideration to the implications for parents, teachers, and other caregivers.

The growth of the Cold War and the deteriorating relations between the United States and the Soviet Union have been linked to an ever-escalating arms race and an alarming growth in the number and destructiveness of the nuclear arsenals. The 13-kiloton bomb that destroyed Hiroshima was followed by stockpiling of approximately 50,000 weapons, most of which are 70 times or more destructive than those first weapons dropped on Japan.

To justify the nuclear buildup, our national administrations have stressed the need to deter the ever-present threat from a dehumanized enemy, often described in such terms as "the evil empire." In the 1950s there were the "duck-and-cover" drills conducted in schools, the encouragement to build backyard bomb shelters, and the establishment of a Civil Defense organization. We were told, on the one hand, that a nuclear war could be kept limited, and, on the other, that a protracted war could be won with only 30 or 40 million dead. As such information was disseminated in the media, it became increasingly accessible to adults, adolescents, and children. Various surveys and studies indicated that many, and perhaps most, American adults feared the possibility of an unsurvivable nuclear war. For the most part, however, it appeared that the typical reaction was to try not to think about the danger and rarely to talk about it to anyone.

Initially relatively few individuals or organizations were engaged in actions aimed at reducing or preventing the threat of nuclear war. In the last decade, however, a growing number of peace and antinuclear activists developed organizations of physicians and other professionals, scientists, and various religious denominations, all of who have begun to focus on nuclear issues. Also, many kinds of community groups now are engaged in attempts to raise the level of public awareness, provide a better understanding of the meaning of nuclear weapons, and encourage actions designed to curb the nuclear arms race. These efforts have been accompanied by a more extensive outpouring of information on the subject in the media and broadening participation of previously uninvolved segments of the public. Until recently, however, little attention has been paid to the impact of all of these developments on children and adolescents, and even fewer efforts to deal with it.

Some beginning research on these issues was initiated as early as 1961, but it is largely within the last decade, with the growth of the peace and antinuclear movement among adults, that more studies have appeared on the impact of the nuclear threat on children and adolescents.

The initial studies in the early 1960s (Escalona, 1965; Schwebel, 1965) were prompted by the growing concern around the building of the Berlin Wall and the Cuban missile crisis. In Schwebel's first 1961 study of adolescents (1965), approximately 45% stated that they expected a war to occur. In a comparable study, however, carried out in 1962 after the resolution of the Cuban missile crisis, only 23% of students expected war. It has been suggested that these results reflect the students' responsiveness to the course of events on the international scene. Schwebel notes that when students were asked specifically about the nuclear threat, their answers were emphatic and included such replies as: "anyone who doesn't fear it is insane"; "It keeps me awake at night"; and "It is so terrible, I try not to think about it."

In an effort to minimize bias that might be introduced by questions that were explicitly about war, Escalona asked students ranging in age from 10 to 17 to "think about the world as it may be 10 years from now. What are some ways in which it might be different?" (1965). She was startled to find that approximately 70% of the children spontaneously mentioned issues relating to their concerns about war.

More recently, Beardslee and Mack reported in 1983 on a survey of over 1,100 high school students in Massachusetts, California, and Maryland, in which they were asked questions specifically about nuclear issues such as: "What does the word 'nuclear' bring to mind?" "Have nuclear advances affected your way of thinking about the future?" "Your view of the world?" Responses indicated a great deal of awareness, often from an early age, and answers were filled with disturbing images of possibilities of world devastation. The authors concluded that "thoughts of nuclear annihilation had penetrated deeply into the consciousness of adolescents." Students doubted that a nuclear war could be limited and did not expect to survive it if it occurred. Seventy percent felt that their country would not survive a nuclear war.

Goldenring and Doctor (1986) studied over 900 students from ages 11 to 19 in 2 major California cities. Students were asked to list their 3 greatest worries in relation to a list of 20 worry items. "Death of parents" received the highest rating; "bad grades" was next; and "nuclear war" was third. Multiple-choice responses to questions dealing exclusively with nuclear issues revealed some of the following:

1. 51% said that they first heard of nuclear weapons at ages 5 to 10, 41% at 11 to 13
2. 33% thought of nuclear war often, 57% sometimes, 10% never
3. 51% talked to their parents about nuclear war not at all, 39% a few times, 10% often
4. 9% definitely thought that a nuclear war might occur between the United States and the Soviet Union in their lifetimes, 42% probably, 32% probably or definitely not
5. 64% did not think that they or their families would survive a nuclear war, 22% thought they might
6. 24% said that thinking about a nuclear war had affected their plans for the future; 60% said no
7. 42% said the amount of information that they had received about nuclear war in school was "not enough," 44% considered themselves very or somewhat uninformed, and only 10% thought they were very well informed

The students who were more worried about nuclear war tended to have better scores with respect to adjustment and self-esteem, talked more with their parents, and were more hopeful than the less worried students that nuclear war could be prevented.

Jeffrey Gould (1986) interviewed some 1,700 children from the 4th to 12th grades following the shooting down of the Korean airliner in August of 1983. Using the same questions Schwebel used following the Berlin Wall crisis in 1961, he found that 64% of the children believed there would be a war, as compared to 44% after the Berlin crisis. Forty-nine percent of 4th and 5th graders felt there would be a war; 69% of 9th graders and 65% of 12th graders felt that there would be a war. Although the style and extensiveness of replies differed, Gould found that essentially the same content was noted in the responses of a relatively privileged, higher socioeconomic level and the disadvantaged, lower-socioeconomic segments of the students. A number of students referred to loss as "total loss" or "global loss" and made comments about the fact that the whole world would be wiped out and that humanity would end and there would not be anything left of "us." This was actually a more common response than those who restricted themselves simply to comments about their personal fates. Gould was impressed with the fact that, in a relatively open-ended type of question, as many as 64% of the students felt that there would be a nuclear war, and 30% stated that it would result in "global loss" and in the destruction of humankind.

Judith Van Horne compared the attitudes and knowledge about nuclear issues of three groups in 1986: 13- to 17-year-old high school students; 18- to 22-year-old college students; and those over 22 years of age. Three questions were asked: (a) In the next 50 years, how likely do you think it is that the United States will be involved in a nuclear war with the Soviet Union? (b) In the next 50 years, how likely do you think it is that you will die from a nuclear blast or its fallout? (c) How often do you think of the possibility of a nuclear war? Differences among the age groups were not significant regarding the likelihood of a nuclear war, although younger respondents in small but significant numbers tended to believe that a nuclear war was somewhat more likely. Younger people believed it more likely that they would die in a nuclear war. Significant age differences were more consistent among items dealing with the personal reactions to the nuclear threat. The younger groups tended to think about the possibility of a nuclear war more often. Those over 22 years of age seemed to have a greater degree of pessimism about their own ability to take preventive action, whereas younger participants were more likely to have confidence in the efficacy of arms control. Van Horne suggested that younger subjects report thinking of nuclear war more often than older subjects and that "it does begin to look as if the young use less denial, less repression." Van Horne, in conclusion called attention to the similarities among age groups which she felt were more striking than the differences, but she suggested that "by the time children reach adolescence, their patterns of awareness and response closely parallel those of adults in their communities." She goes on to conclude that "as in other realms of life, children are well enculturated by societal patterns by the time they are adolescents."

Bachman (1983) reports on an ongoing national study, "monitoring the Future Project," which had the aim of surveying lifestyles and values of youths and young adults. Three of the items dealt directly or indirectly with nuclear war. The study is of particular significance because the survey was a nationally representative sample of adolescents over successive years from 1975 through 1982. The questions related to students' expectations of "global annihilation," their expectation of a "major world upheaval," and the frequency with which they worried about nuclear war. Students' concern about nuclear war showed a steady rise from 1975 through 1982, with those worrying increasing nearly fourfold, from 8% to 30%. Those who stated that they never worried about nuclear war decreased steadily from 1975 to 1982, from 23 to 6%.

Zeitlin (1987) interviewed Boston families with adolescent children to discover how they communicate about the threat of nuclear war. Videotaped discussions often portrayed the parents as avoiding discussion of nuclear issues. The children, especially in initial interviews, seemed to respond essentially by not bringing up their apprehensions. Although feeling troubled themselves, they seemed to be protecting their parents or to be apprehensive about what response they might get if they did mention their concerns. In some of the families there was little or no talk at all about the nuclear threat in the initial interview. In the second session, however, as parents became more comfortable and the adolescents more at ease with the interviewer, adolescents would begin to reveal the extent to which they were worried about the nuclear threat. In a number of instances they expressed resentment toward their parents because previously they had not seemed to receptive to hearing about the adolescents' concerns. For the most part adolescents responded positively when parents expressed clear viewpoints about specific aspects of the nuclear arms race or when they simply asked their children to share their ideas. Although the act of sharing initially appeared to raise anxiety, especially in the parents, it also led to an increased sense of connectedness among the family members.

Although there are fewer studies of younger children, almost all the reports suggest that young children do have a far greater awareness of the nuclear threat than was generally believed. Friedman (1984), in a study of 4-year-old preschoolers, observed the youngsters' play before and after a presentation of children's stories involving conflict. She found that 23% of the children spontaneously included references to nuclear weapons in their play and in their responses.

Eisenbud, Van Horne, and Gould (1986) reviewed the studies of adolescents in the Soviet Union, Finland, Sweden, and Canada and compared them with studies in the United States. The studies indicated that the large numbers of adolescents in these countries think about the risk of nuclear war and worry that it may, or believe that it will, take place in their lifetimes. American youths tended to consider the possibility of nu-

clear war most likely but also most survivable, while Soviet youths, on the other hand, considered war less likely and less survivable. The authors point out that even though young people tend to be fearful that nuclear war will occur, most feel that it is preventable, with Soviet youths considering prevention most likely.

Sommers, Goldberg, Levinson, Ross, and La-Combe (1984) sought to determine the impact on the emotional and psychological development of Canadian children and youths living in the nuclear age. Students included those in grades 6 to 13, and the research instrument incorporated questions about the nuclear issue along with other subjects. Of particular significance this study, 90% felt they had no personal influence and 62% only a little personal influence in preventing nuclear attack, and viewed their parents as just as powerless. Twenty-eight percent of these students reported that the nuclear threat had made them question "somewhat or a lot" whether to marry and have children, and 24% felt the nuclear threat led them "somewhat or a lot" to "live only for today." In their comprehensive review of the literature, Eisenbud et al. (1986) concluded that awareness of the nuclear realities aroused concern in many adolescents. They suggested that in some instances, greater awareness results from family discussion, but also it appeared that, at least in some families, young people's awareness about nuclear issues leads them to be the ones who initiate discussion in the home. For worried youths there does appear to be a correlation among frequent worry, sharing of concerns, and optimism. This finding suggests that thinking about the nuclear threat, coupled with support from others, is a prerequisite for contemplating and searching for solutions to the nuclear dilemma. The authors opined that "what needs to be prevented is the hopelessness that may result" when young people's awareness receives no support, or when "their legitimate concerns fail to be validated." If they believe that their parents are worried, but see no evidence of their readiness to share their concerns with them or to take meaningful action, this may feed into the hopelessness some children and adolescents experience. The authors particularly recommended encouraging adolescents to learn how to think critically and to learn about their power to influence the world around them by addressing problems that affect their communities. They believed that parents and educators can play an important role in this process.

If adults are to intervene in a useful and effective way in helping children to deal with their fears about the nuclear threat, it is important for them to know something about the nature of children's defenses against nuclear death. Lifton and Falk (1982) called attention to the people who knew "... that all that they had ever touched or know or loved could be extinguished in a single moment. Yet they and everyone else seemed to go about business as usual." They referred to this phenomenon as "living a double life." Wolper (N.D.) pointed out that the analysis of coping mechanisms of very young children "yielded no significant difference between defenses used to cope with everyday life and nuclear fears" and that "children employ the defenses available to them in response to nuclear war as they do to any other frightening situation." She goes on to note, however, that "the vacillations between fear of dying and certainty that it would never happen, between seeing nuclear weapons as dangerous and hoping they were safe" suggests that sixth graders were unable to maintain the "double life," referred to by Lifton and Falk, which most adults maintain. Wolper saw this problem in coping as related to the child's developmental level and notes, "If the child's parents either verbally or nonverbally demonstrate helplessness and despair about living under the threat of nuclear war, the child's sense of initial powerfulness and age-appropriate narcissism, self esteem and feelings of safety are also being compromised." Her anecdotal data, she believed, indicated that in the process of attempting to replace one defense with another, some children are unable to do so. She quotes children as saying "I try to get it off my mind so I wouldn't have the feeling when I'm trying to do other things, like when I try to concentrate on other things"; another child says, "I just put it into my mind that it won't happen. I just think that way. I keep on thinking that it won't happen if I try to get rid of the idea." She concluded that "children seem unable to lead a 'double life' in the way that adults can. They try to deny the possibility of a holocaust, but their fears continue to surface." Wolper also suggests that part of the difficulty young children have in coping or in living a "double life" seems to be "as much fear of abandonment as fear of their own deaths." This is reflected in such statements as "I feel scared about people. My parents could die. My family could die. Everything." Wolper suggests that one way parents may usefully respond to this kind of concern is by talking to their children about the nuclear threat. She

believes it is particularly important for parents to give their children some evidence that they are doing something about the threat in some specific way, thus modeling for their children a "coping style which promotes healthy development."

I have noted previously some investigators' observation of American youths "live-only-for-today" response to the threat. That this defense is shared by youths in other countries is illustrated by the report on Norwegian youth by Raundalen and Finny (1986), who studied more than 2,400 children between the ages of 11 and 19. Students were presented with 10 items called "future problems" and were asked to arrange them in order. The children also were given a blank sheet of paper and asked to write in greater detail about the problem that they had ranked as being of most concern. The authors noted how many respondents avoided the issue by writing about immediate events in their lives, with a "happy-go-lucky" attitude. Others wrote that they found it meaningless to invest in lengthy education or vocational training when they had no assurance that they would ever have a chance to make use of it. Still others focused on a wish to destroy nuclear weapons and feelings against the generation who were "playing with our future." "Many resorted to strong language and profanity to communicate their anger," say the authors, and they suggest that these youngsters were coping with depression and anxiety in this way.

Peck (1984) conducted workshops for American high school students; here teenagers were given an opportunity to discuss their reactions to the nuclear threat in a small group, facilitated either by one of their peers or by an adult with whom they felt comfortable. The kind of expressions just cited, of disgust with the way adults have "screwed up our world," and feelings of hopelessness and a sense that "we might as well have a good time now because we don't know how long it will last," were frequently expressed. In such discussion within the workshops, usually at least a few students were actively engaged in the peace and antinuclear movement. In response to such negative statements by their peers, they almost invariably cited the things that they were doing and that other students could do to reduce the likelihood of a nuclear war. It has been noted that, among adults, the movement toward relevant types of action seems to reduce the need for denial and the use of defenses, which are at best only partially effective. It would not be surprising if further studies of youths reveal similar patterns.

TABLE 10.1

"Of all the problems facing the nation, how often do you worry about nuclear war?"

	1982	1991
Never	6.5%	18.6%
Seldom	21.8%	40.0%
Sometimes	41.3%	31.3%
Often	30.3%	10.6%

"My guess is that this country will be caught up in a major world upheaval in the next ten years."

	1982	1991
Disagree	9.8%	15.0%
Mostly disagree	15.1%	15.0%
Neither	30.3%	37.5%
Mostly agree	28.2%	20.5%
Agree	16.5%	11.1%

"Nuclear or biological annihilation will probably be the fate of all mankind in my lifetime."

	1982	1991
Disagree	16.5%	28.0%
Mostly disagree	16.7%	20.2%
Neither	30.8%	34.0%
Mostly agree	21.1%	10.5%
Agree	14.9%	7.9%

Beginning in about 1990, the nuclear threat related to the possible confrontation between the United States and the former Soviet Union became significantly reduced as a result of new agreements and nuclear arms reductions. This seems to have been reflected in the general public's perception that the nuclear threat was no longer as great as it had been. Several researchers who published earlier reports on the response of children and adolescents to the nuclear threat are now at work on follow-up studies of comparable populations using instruments similar to those used in their earlier studies.

Bachman published a survey in 1983 on how American high school seniors viewed the military. In a recent personal communication he reported that he reused his 1982 instrument with a comparable population involving over 2000 high school seniors throughout the nation. Responses to three of the questions, presented in Table 10.1, illustrate some of the significant changes in attitude that have occurred.

This updated report will be published in the 1992 volume of *Monitoring the Future,* published by the Institute of Social Research at the University of Michigan.

Judith Van Horne has compared current responses in interviews with as many of the same individuals as she had interviewed as college students 10 years ago as she could locate. She found that most no longer feared the nuclear threat that had previously been posed by the competitive relationship between the United States and the Soviet Union.

Petra Hesse (1986) studied the way that German adolescents viewed "the enemy" in the mid-1980s. Their responses emphasized the nuclear threat and included drawings of the mushroom-shape cloud. In a personal communication she reported that, in recent interviews with a comparable group of German teenagers, mention of the nuclear threat as the prime enemy had been largely replaced by fears of environmental dangers.

Although the focus of this chapter has been on research that directly studied children and adolescents, attention also should be paid to the ways in which parents and other adults significant in the lives of youngsters are changing in their attitudes about the nuclear threat. Oliver (1990) used a questionnaire and interview to study young New Zealanders living in a nuclear-free zone. She was impressed by the importance of adult role models in facilitating children's belief in the power of anti-nuclear activities.

Lewis, Goldberg, and Parker (1989) conducted a national survey of Canadian adolescents' anxieties, concerns, and sources of information about the threat of nuclear war. Although students with activist parents showed more concern, family impact ranked below all media as a source of information.

There is clearly a need to update earlier studies of children's fears of nuclear war in particular as well as of other kinds of military, environmental, and other world threats.

It seems evident that children and adolescents are highly responsive to changes in the world that surrounds them. If we look to them and want to help them improve on the efforts of the generation that preceded them, we need to be actively engaged with them and remain knowledgeable about what they are thinking and feeling.

This presentation would not be complete without some attention to the criticism of studies of the kind that have been cited herein. Kleinberg (1986), an outstanding social scientist and clinician, deals with some of these issues. He addresses himself primarily to two articles, one by Adelson and Finn (1985) and another by Robert Coles (1985). Kleinberg deals incisively with both articles, which attacked the unscientific and "amateurish" nature of the research, and cites a list of distinguished scholars who have participated in this kind of research. He responded to Coles's statement that children react to the nuclear threat with not nearly the fear that some social scientists claim, questioning how widespread such fear is in the population. Kleinberg points out that there exists a "whole corpus of research which contains a great deal of material assembled with care in many countries (and populations) by well-qualified investigators with expertise in research . . ." We concede that methods of inquiry and possibly the nature of the sampling may have some impact on the proportion of children who are concerned, but noted that "the problem cannot be regarded as inconsequential, even if it is less widespread than is suggested."

Kleinberg's position is supported by a paper by Deutsch (1985), which, in reviewing research in the field, stated that "a number of excellent studies have been conducted and the results are reasonably consistent. They provide good grounds for asserting that a sizable number of children and adolescents in different countries are consciously concerned about and have fears or worries about the possibility of nuclear war."

In summary, the impact of the nuclear threat on children and adolescents is evidently both more widespread and more devastating than has been generally recognized. Many youngsters appear to be having considerable difficulty coping with their concerns. As the world political situation changes, new issues join the nuclear threat in causing significant anxieties among children and adolescents. Teachers, parents, other adults, and their institutions must become more responsive to the fears and concerns of these young people while doing all they can to lessen the reality of the threats themselves.

REFERENCES

Adelson, J., & Finn, E. (1985). Terrorizing children. *Commentary, 79* (4), 29.

Bachman, J. G. (1983). American high school seniors view the military: 1976–1982. *Armed Forces and Society, 1,* 86–104.

Beardslee, W. R., & Mack, J. D. (1983). Adolescents and the threat of nuclear war: The evolution of a perspective. *Yale Journal of Biology and Medicine, 56,* 79–91.

Coles, R. (1985, December 8). Children of the bomb. *New York Times Magazine.*

Deutsch, M. (1985, May). Impact of the threat of nuclear war on children and adolescents. *International Physicians for the Prevention of Nuclear War, 259.*

Eisenbud, M., Van Horne, J., & Gould, B. (1986). Children, adolescents and the threat of nuclear war: An international perspective. In B. Gould, S. Moon, & J. Van Horne (Eds.), *Growing up scared.* Berkeley: Open Books.

Escalona, S. K. (1965). Children and the threat of nuclear war. In M. Schwebel (Ed.), *Behavioral science and human survival* (p. 2). Palo Alto, CA: Behavioral Sciences Press.

Friedman, B. (1984). Preschoolers' awareness of the nuclear threat. California Association for the Education of Young Children *Newsletter, 12,* (2).

Goldenring, J. M., & Doctor, R. (1986). Teenage worry about nuclear war: North American and European questionnaire studies. *International Journal of Mental Health, Vp;/15. #1–3.*

Gould, J. (1986). Exploring youth's reaction to the threat of nuclear war. In B. Gould, S. Moon, & J. Van Horne, (Eds.), *Growing up scared.* Berkeley, CA: Open Books.

Hesse, P. (1986). *International Journal of Mental Health, 15.*

Kleinberg, O. (1986). Children and nuclear war: A methodological note. *International Journal of Mental Health, 15,* (1–3).

Lewis, C., Goldberg, S., & Parker, K. B. (1989). Nuclear worries of Canadian youth. *American Journal of Orthopsychiatry, 59.*

Lifton, R. J., & Falk, R. (1982). *Indefensible weapons.* New York: Basic Books.

Oliver, P. (1980). Nuclear freedom and students' sense of efficacy about the prevention of nuclear war. *American Journal of Orthopsychiatry, 60.*

Peck, H. B. (1984). Do you prefer life to death?: From denial to action. *Transactional Analysis Journal, 14,* (4).

Raundalen, M., & Finney, O. (1986). Children and teenagers' views of the future. *International Journal of Mental Health, 15,* (1–3).

Schwebel, M. (1965). Nuclear cold war: Student opinion and professional responsibility." In M. Schwebel (Ed.), *Behavioral science and human survival* (p. 1). Palo Alto, CA: Behavioral Sciences Press.

Sommers, F., Goldberg, S., Levinson, D., Ross, C., & LaCombe, S. (1984, June). Children's mental health and the threat of nuclear war: A Canadian pilot study.

Paper presented at the fourth Congress of International Physicians to Prevent Nuclear War, Helsinki, Finland.

Van Horne, J. (1986). Facing the threat: Comparison of adolescents and adults. In B. Gould, S. Moon, & J. Van Horne (Eds.), *Growing up scared*, Berkeley: Open Books.

Wolper, M. L. (N.D.). *Coping mechanisms of preadolescents around the threat of nuclear war.* Unpublished manuscript.

Zeitlin, S. (1987). *No reason to talk about it: Families confront the nuclear taboo.* New York: W. W. Norton.

11 / Children and Reproductive Biotechnology: An Essay into the Unknown

Nada L. Stotland and Bryna Harwood

This chapter focuses on one subset of the technological revolution in medicine and its effects on children and adolescents. For readers unfamiliar with the fast-growing domain of reproductive technology, a brief definition and description may be helpful. The term "reproductive technology" has been used to cover a wide array of interventions. They range from the kitchen-table insemination of a lesbian woman with the sperm of a male friend via a turkey baster, to procedures involving the hormonal synchronization of the menstrual cycle phases of 2 women so that an ovarian follicle of 1 can be located by ultrasound imaging and an egg "retrieved" or "harvested," fertilized in vitro, and then implanted in the other. Perhaps the reason some of these relatively methodologically crude methods have been included as "technologies" is the marked contrast between them and the traditional means of conception. Some readers may be surprised to learn that there are sperm banks that have assembled scrapbooks with pictures and descriptions of the physical attributes, accomplishments, and interests of the men whose sperm can be purchased. They advertise that Nobel Prize winners are numbered among them.

Premium on the Unborn Child

It is ironic that most reproductive technology has been developed to create children, because little if any attention has been lavished on those children after they are delivered, on children who are their social and/or biological siblings, or on other children affected by their birth. Medicine has performed the equivalent of the parents' counting of fingers and toes and exclaiming over the likeness of the newborn to this or that relative. There are few [no?] systematic studies of the psychological impact of having been conceived by some method that bypasses or intrudes upon the intimate physical connection of one's genetic parents. Lest we hasten to accept the argument that the emotional well-being of those children is not of concern, we must remember that they are conceived because of the psychological needs of adult people who wish to become genetic, biological (the two are no longer identical), and/or social parents. The medical interventions are merely the means by which those wants are satisfied.

There has been considerable study of the psychological concomitants of infertility and childlessness for would-be parents, from the causal hypotheses of the classical psychoanalysts to the more recent focus on the effects of both the conditions and the treatments. Self-help and support groups exist. Organized groups, in concert with medical experts in fertility, have successfully lobbied to achieve the passage of legislation mandating health insurance coverage for costly technological interventions. The complexity of some of the procedures currently in use puts them out of the reach of the poor and unsophisticated and becomes the predominant organizer of the budgets and daily schedules of members of the middle classes.

Facts Remain Occult

The literature seldom explains why various subjects have not been written about. In this chapter, it is necessary to consider and hypothesize about the reasons for the comparative lack of attention to the psychological relations between children and reproductive biotechnology as well as about those relations themselves. Why do we know so little—why have we tried so little to know—how it feels and what it means to have been conceived in a laboratory flask or via a turkey baster, to have been gestated inside a woman who is neither one's genetic nor social mother, to be the survivor of a multiple pregnancy in which the number of embryos was "reduced" to increase the likelihood of the delivery of 1 or more healthy children?

For one thing, society is not given to questioning the benefit of having been conceived and born, at least not unless the resulting infant is disabled or in physical pain. Whatever lip service is paid to the welfare of children, society is run by adults, who are likely to be most empathic and responsive to the feelings and needs of other adults. Within the medical community, many scientists and clinicians are uncomfortable with psychological issues. There is a fascination with the intellectual challenge and emotional power of facilitating the creation of human life, of deciphering, re-creating, and manipulating the conditions under which ovulation, fertilization, implantation, and development occur and come to fruition in childbirth.

It is perhaps too much to expect that scientists/clinicians who must master the knowledge and technical and administrative skills necessary to accomplish these feats also should be conversant and comfortable with their psychological aspects. Psychological evaluation and intervention are equally specialized and demanding. Gynecologists and infertility experts often are uncomfortable with the language of the mental health professions and skeptical about their knowledge base. Despite, or because of, the exhaustive array of medical tests and examinations that treatment entails, they are reluctant to impose requirements for psychological assessment and care. Psychological issues, if addressed at all, are likely to be handled clinically by a non-M.D. mental health practitioner. Studies, if any, are based on standardized instruments so as to generate seemingly "hard" numerical data.

Many busy infertility clinics offer little time for ordinary conversation and supportive interactions, much less the opportunity to address conflicts and ambivalence. Nor is there any incentive for practitioners to do so. With 10% of couples in the United States suffering from infertility problems, there are more than enough patients, and patients are loath to complain for fear of exclusion from treatment. Practitioners heavily invested in these procedures also may fear the revelation of psychological variables and outcomes that might weigh against the growing practice of biotechnology in human reproduction. Some fear that attention to psychosocial factors might expose them to legal liability, either from disgruntled individuals who were refused treatment or from those dissatisfied with outcome.

The focus on infertility here is not insignificant. Most reproductive technology has been developed to overcome the inability of couples or individuals to conceive pregnancies through sexual intercourse. Infertility is a major blow to self-image, self-esteem, sense of sexual adequacy, and gender identity. When a couple is involved in the evaluation and treatment, as is usual, it is also a strain on the relationship. The medical workup tends to place the "blame" for the fertility problem on one partner or the other, leading to a complex web of feelings. The "responsible" partner feels jealous, guilty, and wary toward the "fertile" partner, who could have "children of his or her own" with another partner. The partner diagnosed as unimpaired may feel guilty, resentful, and/or trapped, but usually feels an obligation to deny those feelings in an effort to support the "affected" partner. A sense of deficit hangs over the following treatment and outcome.

The child who is born after technological fertility enhancement may be a living reminder of that deficit and of the physical and emotional pain of the treatment. There is evidence in the adoption literature that that is true and that it has an impact on the child. Another factor impeding the gathering of data about the effect of reproductive biotechnology on children is the fact that the families involved nearly always desire nothing more than to forget or deny the necessity for technological intervention in their children's creation. They wish to blend imperceptibly into the "normal" population. It is also reasonable to hypothesize that anxiety about the circumstances of a child's conception and gestation may prompt parents to scrutinize that child with extra care and to invest him or her with special value.

Aside from these general concerns about the

child's normalcy and health, the use of technological intervention may reflect intense parental needs or wishes for a child with specific traits. Prominent among these is the wish to reproduce one's own and one's family's genetic traits. Families carrying genes for major disabilities may choose technologically assisted conception in order to avoid their reproduction. Couples carrying genes for sex-linked diseases and those determined to have only a child of 1 gender (usually, but not always, male) may take advantage of prenatal genetic testing to learn the sex of an embryo and undertake abortion to end pregnancies in which the result is not what they desire. The expectations of those who buy the sperm of Nobel Prize winners are fairly blatant. Since Nobel Prizes do not "run in families," and the somatic, intellectual, and artistic expression of cellular genetics is unpredictable, children born under all these circumstances may feel pressured to live up to unrealistic and unattainable standards.

Of course, parents do have powerful expectations of children conceived in the usual way. People who are able to achieve parenthood without medical and legal intervention are not subject to screening or scrutiny and cannot be supposed to be uniformly "normal," whatever that condition might entail. The psychosocial factors, even the biological factors, contributing to conception and delivery have been little studied. There is dispute as to whether most children are conceived with conscious or unconscious intent or are the unintended by-product of the fulfillment of sexual desire. And aside from anecdotal reports from extreme situations, nothing is known about the effect of adults' conceptional volition on children.

Children Know of Some Technology

Children's experiences with reproductive technologies range from ultrasound photographs of themselves in utero to bitter custody battles. It is probably safe to hypothesize that the former experiences are benign and the latter potentially damaging, but situations more ambiguous than these are more common and more difficult to prognosticate about. One issue running through most of them is secrecy. What and when should children know about technologies used in their conception and about discrepancies between their social and bio-

logical parentage? The genetic, gestational, and social mothers may be 3 different women. The genetic father may be an anonymous or chosen sperm donor, and the social immediate family may include the mother's husband or male partner, the mother alone, the mother and her lesbian lover, or any other combination. Very few states have enacted laws governing the maintenance of records of genetic and gestational parenthood or the provision of that information to the children.

Anonymity is crucial to some sperm donors, who require assurance that no legal or social encumbrance will result from their genetic participation in parenthood. (Few studies have been performed to determine the long-term impact of this decision on them.) Siding with these males are those who argue that genetics should not play a central role in parenthood and that the children who would not otherwise exist are fortunate to have been wanted and cared for. However, there is reason to believe that family secrets arouse uncertainty and insecurity in children and that secrets are difficult, if not impossible, to keep. How is the parent to respond to the child's inevitable queries about the family origin of freckles or musical talent? Do the parents construct an elaborate falsehood? Can they be open and spontaneous parents if they are braced constantly to avoid a telltale flinch or facial expression? If questions of genetically transmitted disabilities arise, should the adult child be permitted to believe and act on an inaccurate version of his or her genetic parenthood?

Nor is disclosure an uncomplicated matter. No one knows how central the experience of having the same, known, man and woman as biological and social parents is to human development and psychology. While physical presence and biological relatedness do not assure optimal parenting, and both social and biological parents sometimes desert and abuse children and spouses, there is little precedent for the emotional integration of conception by a disconnected gamete rather than a person. We do not know whether the resulting children, if so informed, will experience a psychic void, a sense of absence, a painful curiosity about the person who is the source of half their genetic heritage, or simply a sense that the family structure into which they were born is the natural one. The connection between human intimacy and conception is critical to attachment. If and when there is an attempt to study these questions, the confounding variables will be many and will include the satisfaction of the social parent(s) with the family structure and the ethos of the culture and subculture in which they live.

Questions may intensify for these children, as they seem to do for those who are adopted, when they enter adolescence and contemplate their own sexuality, fertility, and future parenthood. Children who have felt deprived of traditional families may hasten to form traditional families of their own; children who have internalized the family structure with which they are familiar may gravitate toward the re-creation of that structure in the next generation.

Surrogate Motherhood

So-called surrogate motherhood raises another set of emotional challenges as well. The term "surrogate" has been used whenever a woman undertakes to gestate a child intended to be the social child of another woman. The maternal genetic material may originate with her, with the intended social mother, or with another woman who donates an egg. The sperm contributor is generally the intended social father but could be an "outside" donor. During pregnancy, whatever its genetic origins, the embryo/fetus is bathed in and nourished by the bodily fluids, nutritional intake, and hormones of the gestational mother, hears her voice, is entrained to her cardiac and diurnal rhythms. The effects of these influences is unknown. Surrogate mothers report that they experience the child as not their own throughout. Nevertheless, there is a strong belief in most cultures that the experience of pregnancy and childbirth is a significant factor in maternal attachment.

Surrogacy relationships within friendships and families raise other complex issues. Most commonly, the sister of a woman unable to bear children agrees to be inseminated with her brother-in-law's sperm. Sometimes the infertile woman lacks only a uterus; with the aid of technology, she and her husband or partner can produce fertilized eggs, which are introduced into the reproductive tract of the volunteer. Either arrangement allows for the maximum genetic similarity to the intended social parents and provides assurance that the pregnancy will take place under optimal biological and social circumstances. The child's biological and social families will overlap. However,

the child's social aunt will be his or her gestational, and possibly genetic, mother. Many or most family relationships are ambivalent and changeable; jealousy, conflict, and divided loyalties may ensue.

Other Issues

Combinations of new technologies have made possible other new and widely publicized developments that raise psychological questions for children. The increasing success of bone marrow transplantation in the treatment of several malignancies has led to cases in which the bone marrow of children is sought in an attempt to save the lives of their afflicted relatives. In one case, the mother refused to allow the aspiration of bone marrow from her young child to be used for her ex-husband's child by another woman. In another, a couple conceived a child solely in the hope of producing a compatible bone marrow donor for their terminally ill daughter. In neither of these cases is the potential donor child yet old enough to express feelings about these events. The use of hormones to re-create and prolong fertility after natural menopause has made it possible for mothers to conceive and/or gestate children for their infertile daughters to rear as their own. These women are those children's gestational and/or genetic mothers as well as their grandmothers.

Last, we must consider the impact of reproductive technologies on children other than those directly involved. The most obvious group are siblings and potential siblings, including the children of women who serve as surrogates. (Most surrogacy programs require that potential volunteers already have borne children.) These mothers assume the risks, disabilities, and discomforts of pregnancy for financial gain, family loyalty (or pressure), and/or the psychological gratification of childbearing. Their existing children endure whatever minor or major deprivations their pregnancies entail, observe as babies grow within their mothers, and then witness the delivery of their siblings to other families. Even where children are given a nominal say in the proceedings, it is unlikely that their consent is either informed or free of inherent constraint. In cases of secondary infertility, children already born must be affected by the economic, physical, time, and psychological demands of the parents' attempts to produce more children. It may be that learning of the existence of reproductive technologies raises anxieties in children—but then, the "primal scene" and the Oedipus complex, both closely associated with nontechnological reproduction, have been thought to do so for some time.

Conclusion

This has been a chapter about questions. In the absence of answers, it may help those who work with children and their families to identify areas of interest and concern. Families that have used or who contemplate using reproductive biotechnology deserve to know not only what has been accomplished but also what is yet to be learned, especially about the impact on the children involved. Despite the lack of information, families find discussion of the potential problems very useful. It is also hoped that the issues raised here may inspire scientific curiosity and help to frame research questions. The absence of follow-up data on this massive human experiment is unconscionable. Data are sorely needed not only to inform our clinical interventions but to assist our legislators and judges in their deliberations about Solomonic problems. Our increasing control over the technical aspects of reproduction exposes our profound ignorance about its human meanings. The gift of life is precious, but ever more complicated.

PART VIII

What Does a Multiethnic, Pluralistic Society Mean for Youths?

Ernest A. Kendrick and Pedro Ruiz

In this chapter we focus on what it means for youths to grow up in the United States. In so doing, we plan to discuss youths as they relate to present-day society. We premise that the United States has almost become a multiethnic society. Such a pluralistic society offers a better outcome for the ethnic minorities than did the melting pot. In many ways, a multiethnic, pluralistic society is less xenophobic and offers more tolerance and acceptance of people of different cultures, races, and ethnicity.

Here we primarily address issues and problems relating to urban America. While multiethnic issues are also present in rural America, these problems are far less prominent than in urban areas. Nevertheless, in certain rural areas throughout the United States large pockets of ethnic minority populations can be found. This is particularly true in the southern, southwestern, western, and midwestern sections of the United States, where there are large populations of African Americans, Mexican Americans, Native Americans and Asian Americans. Focusing on ethnic minority issues is extremely important, but looking at youths from a broader perspective, including youths from the majority culture, is also relevant. In this context, we review and discuss the meaning of pluralism, identity consolidation, youth culture, drugs and violence, sex and intimacy, and the transition to adulthood. When appropriate, we review specific ethno-cultural issues as they relate to the previously mentioned areas of discussion.

The authors thank Aziza D. Kendrick for her contributions in the conceptualization of the content of this chapter. They also thank Mary desVignes-Kendrick, M.D., for her review of the manuscript.

What Pluralism Means

It is important first to clarify the concept of pluralism as we use it. Conceptually, we perceive pluralism as encompassing the following elements:

- The existence within a country or society of groups from different ethnic origins and/or with different cultural norms and religious beliefs
- The intrinsic policy of maintaining and preserving these different ethnic groups within a nation and/or a society
- The acceptance within a nation or society of groups of people with different languages
- The belief that all ethnic groups residing within the boundaries of a nation, society, or geographical area must be willing to interrelate with each other with the hope that the social distances between them will be diminished and/or abolished
- The right of any ethnic group member to be upwardly mobile socially, to occupy any public office in the nation, to have equal access to education and health care, and to be given the same respect and recognition that any other person residing in this nation and/or sharing this society is given
- Recognition that gender, age, or physical/mental disabilities should not play a discriminatory role in society; that is, that any member of the society should be guaranteed equal rights in every respect

It is imperative, however, that we acknowledge that, culturally speaking, all ethnic groups are *not* treated equally. It is also important to realize that prejudice (racial, sexual, and other) still plays a major role in the everyday interactions among people in the United States. While conceptually it is ideal to view American youths from a more ethnically neutral point of view, this position is unrealistic. Youth issues must be addressed within the context of racism, sexism, and discrimination. In these circumstances, discrimination also includes socioeconomic conditions, since ethnic minority youths have to face and overcome all the problems confronted by youths in general as well as problems inherent in being members of an ethnic minority. This country, while striving to become more pluralistic, still is embued with stereotypes, prejudice, and racism. In many ways, we can hypothesize that any ethnic minority youths who are able to move forward and succeed in the United States may have to call upon greater strength than their counterparts from the majority culture. This also applies to majority culture youths growing up in areas where they are a minority population.

Identity Consolidation

Of the problems that youths must face and overcome, that of consolidating their identity is perhaps the most important. The strength and quality of the foundation that forms the basis for identity development will determine their later success in life. Additionally, it may influence a myriad of pathological conditions that can arise not only during the adolescent years but later in life as well. During youth, development of a good self-image is a key task. Within this context, ethnic minority youths face major challenges during the process of self-image development. Indeed, many ethnic minority youths have to resort to atypical means to accomplish this task. For instance, some Hispanic American youths form gangs as a way of achieving identity consolidation. The role of machismo is a major factor in these circumstances. This situation is particularly relevant with the Mexican American youths in Los Angeles, California. For example, a Hispanic American male may intend to find his identity within a healthy environment but see few to no opportunities in society to channel its appropriate consolidation. Often this is due to high unemployment and/or lack of educational opportunities. Unfortunately, this situation may then lead to personal frustration, to group alienation, and ultimately to violence as the only perceived viable pathway to follow. The same situation can be observed with other ethnic minority youths, such as Asian Americans and African Americans. Of course, with other ethnic minority youths, the dynamics that interplay with violent behavior may arise from different origins. For instance, while machismo is culturally prevalent among Hispanic Americans, it does not necessarily play a similar role among other ethnic groups.

For African Americans, the human frustration youths face finds other means of expression. African American youths who become totally alienated by society's inability to offer them opportunities to mature and achieve a place in life will definitely confront major problems in developing and consolidating their identity. This is currently very relevant for African American male youths. The outcome of poor access to educational opportunities during early childhood years, coupled with high unemployment rates, combine to produce an environment that leads to despair, frustration, and aggressive behavior. Of course, child-rearing deficits and familial pathology also may play a role in this regard. Unfortunately, for African American youths, this aggression often finds its expression in homicidal behavior. This situation has been well addressed and researched in the past (Griffith & Bell, 1989). For years we were unable to understand why young African Americans, particularly males, had lower rates of suicide in comparison to the majority population (Group for the Advancement of Psychiatry, 1989). However, the increase of homicidal behavior among African Americans offers a very good hypothesis toward explaining this phenomenon.

It has been observed that a rise in epidemic suicidal behavior among majority youths has occurred in certain geographical areas, such as Dallas and Clear Lake, Texas. Within the context of the majority youth's culture, it appears that continuous and frequent migration from place to place is a major concomitant of suicidal behavior among adolescents. For youngsters who have to change their social network systems and their familiar environmental settings frequently, the opportunities to consolidate their self-image and identity become impaired, thus leading to alienation and self-destructive behavior (Shaffer, Garland, Gould, Fisher, & Trautman, 1988). Since the phenomenon of social migration resulting from the need for economic survival has been increasing during recent years, this suicidal epidemic behavior by majority youths may be seen again in various areas of the country.

In achieving identity consolidation, it is most important that youths become aware of their ethnic roots—that is, from where they came from. While this notion is relevant to all youths, it is even more so with certain ethnic minority youths.

For instance, for African Americans, where the forced uprooting from Africa to the United States during the slave trade was quite destructive, the conceptualization of where you came from becomes more difficult. This factor has been further complicated by the forced destruction and fragmentation of the African American family that took place in the United States during the slavery period. The difficulties faced by African American youths will in turn influence their perception of who they are. In these circumstances, it is expected that for some African American youths, appropriate consolidation of their identity may be impaired.

For Hispanic Americans, this situation is somewhat different. The Hispanic American groups in the United States have increased significantly during the last 40 to 50 years. This has been particularly true after World War II for Puerto Ricans, after Castro for Cubans, and more recently for Dominicans, Salvadorans, Guatemalans, and Nicaraguans. For these Hispanic American groups, identity formation was, by far, already established in their countries of origin. Therefore, this problem was not crucial insofar as first-generation Hispanic Americans were concerned. For these Hispanic American groups—and here we must include the Mexican Americans—the problem of achieving identity consolidation predominantly affects the second and third generation.

In general, ethnic identity is impacted by the influence of the host society as well as by the length of exposure to the new environment. For Hispanic Americans, and in particular Puerto Ricans, education and age of arrival into the United States have important and independent effects on the ethnic identity of mothers, fathers, and children. Further, the child's education and age of arrival to the host society are not only significant but also are independently related to changes in the family's ethnic identity (Rogler, Cooney, & Ortiz, 1980). Children who arrive in the host nation at a younger age have more limited previous social experiences in their native country; therefore, their sense of ethnic identity is less firmly established. Similarly, more education weakens ethnic identity, since it expands cognitive life beyond the native ethnic group by exposure to new and different values and lifestyles. This is true whether the education was secured in the native country or in the host nation. In this context, Hispanic American males tend, so far, to have weaker ethnic identities than Hispanic American women. This is due,

in part, to their higher ability to be employed and be away from home, thus increasing their relationships with other ethnic groups and cultures. Moreover, family cohesion, which leads to a strong positive interaction between parents and children, helps promote the development of a strong ethnic identity.

Insofar as the Mexican Americans are concerned, the issue of ethnic identity is most complex. Many states that currently form part of the United States of America (Texas, New Mexico, Arizona, and California) were part of Mexico in the past. For this reason, it must be difficult for many Mexican migrants or even Mexican Americans to consider themselves foreigners in these states. In many of these cases, Mexican Americans have to give up their Mexican identity to achieve a new synthesis of being both Mexican American and American. This situation affected prior Mexican American generations and will have an impact on future generations as well. This phenomenon becomes even more complicated when we see "Chicanos" and "Niuyoricans" not accepted and/or rejected when they visit and try to reestablish bonds in their native countries (Mexico and Puerto Rico).

For Asian Americans, we must address the situation confronted by the Japanese Americans during World War II. During this period, many Japanese Americans were stripped of legal papers, uprooted from their homes, separated from their families, and interned in camps. Many Japanese American youths who were exposed to such unfair treatment were negatively affected in the consolidation of their ethnic identity. Furthermore, this historical tragedy still affects many current Japanese American youths through their ongoing contacts with their family members. It must have been very difficult for Japanese Americans who were able to consolidate their identity as Japanese Americans during that period to be told that they were no longer Japanese Americans but merely Japanese as well as potential traitors to the United States. Undoubtedly this situation still has much influence insofar as current Japanese American youths are concerned.

Such historical catastrophes raise the question of the existence of a truly pluralistic society in the United States. This is why, earlier in this chapter, we placed a great deal of emphasis on defining what pluralism means. Ideally, it will be very advantageous if all ethnic minority groups that reside in the United States were to become acculturated through an intergrational process rather than becoming assimilated, separated, or marginalized. Integration has proven to be beneficial for migrant groups entering a host nation (Berry & Kim, 1988).

Youth Culture

From a pluralistic point of view, the United States has become a mosaic nation. The constant migration of different ethnic groups, such as Asians and Pacific Islanders, Hispanics from the Caribbean and Central/South America, blacks from the West Indies and Africa, the more traditional European migrants, and Middle Easterners from the Arabic countries have all contributed to the patchwork of minority groups residing in this country. Despite these multiethnic influences, we can still observe some core themes that are unique to most youths' culture. For instance, rock music has been at the center of American youth culture for over 2 decades. This is not to say, however, that there have been no influences from the different ethnic minority groups residing in the United States. The experience with "lambada," which originated in Brazil, is a good example of these influences among some sectors of Latin American youths in the United States. Similarly, Tex-Mex music has greatly influenced American youths' culture in the Southwest region of the United States. Likewise, dress codes also have unique connotations among certain youths. Dress codes definitely have great impact in defining youth culture, and ethnic minority values have greatly influenced the dress codes currently in use among American youths.

We, however, need to understand that the U.S. culture at large, and the youth culture in particular, is constantly changing because of recent technological advances. A good example of these changes may be observed in the influence and role of the media in the shaping of culture. Television has exercised a major influence in society at large and with youths in particular. As a result, geographic and ethnic barriers are rapidly becoming a thing of the past. Nowadays, nationally aired television programs focus on ethnically oriented themes. Several black-oriented, Hispanic-related, and even Asian-influenced youth shows may now be observed on television. The experiences produced by the media have fostered a better multiethnic image of this country. Additionally, they have helped to promote an understanding between ethnic groups and the recognition of related cultural values among the different population subgroups of this nation. The technological advances related to the news media have been of such a magnitude that we now observe their impact in all youth groups in this country. For instance, cable television now allows youths to see on a 24-hour basis several channels specially targeted for them. Music, in particular, is highly widespread through cable television among all youth groups.

From a different perspective, athletics and sports-related activities are now becoming more pluralistic in nature. A few decades ago certain sports, such as baseball, were under the complete hegemony of the majority culture. Nowadays, however, all sports and athletic activities include almost all ethnic minority groups. However, some improvement is needed insofar as certain ethnic minority groups are concerned. For instance, Asian Americans are insufficiently represented in sports-related activities throughout the nation. The video games attraction that has spread nationwide among all ethnic groups is an excellent example of what constitutes a core cultural recreational activity for youths.

We must address the stereotypes that still exist in relation to ethnic minority youths in this nation. For instance, tall, blond, and blue-eyed youths continue to symbolize ideal characteristics for American males. Also, slender, tall, and blond youths personify the ideal features for American females. However, these stereotypes are rapidly changing and, therefore, the image of the ideal male/female American will soon have different skin color and more ethnically acceptable connotations. Gloria Estefan, Michael Jackson, Paula Abdul, and other important ethnic minority role models are all now contributing to the creation of a new synthesis of what soon will constitute the ideal American youth.

Some recent historical events have, however, fostered ethnic individualism rather than ethnic pluralism. For instance, the Vietnam War during the late 1960s and early 1970s led to large numbers of African Americans killed or wounded when compared with the majority culture. The socioeconomic conditions prevailing in this country forced large numbers of ethnic minority youths, particularly African Americans, to enlist in the armed forces. Concurrently, many white youths had the necessary resources to obtain deferments or leave the country, thus avoiding being drafted into the military. While there is still a disproportionate number of ethnic minorities, particularly African Americans, in the armed forces, it is hoped that the current trend toward a more multiethnic society will not permit these unfortunate circumstances to prevail in the future.

Drugs and Violence

From a multiethnic point of view, most youths in the United States are facing nowadays a major challenge with respect to drugs and violence. It is important to note, however, that insofar as drugs are concerned, youths from the majority culture have also been affected a great deal. As a result, the federal government recently has developed major initiatives to combat drug addiction. This decision on the part of governmental agencies is highly beneficial to the ethnic minority youths as well. For years it was felt that drug-related problems were encountered primarily in ethnic minority groups. Nowadays, however, it is clear that drug-related problems have reached out to every segment of society. This is not to say, however, that ethnic minority youths have fewer problems than majority culture youths. For instance, insofar as crack cocaine is concerned, African American and Hispanic American youths are much more affected than the white youths of this country. In this respect, the National Household Survey on Drug Abuse of 1993 shows that in the United States, the lifetime use of crack among the African American population is estimated to be 3.4%; among the Hispanic American population, 2.0%; and among the white population, 1.6%. With respect to heroin, the same survey shows that the lifetime percentages in the United States are about 2.1% for African Americans, 1.4% for Hispanic Americans, and 0.9% for whites. Alcohol in this survey, however, shows a lifetime percentage of 86.4% among the white population, 77.0% among the Hispanic American population, and 75.2% among the African American population. The results are similar for marijuana; the rates of use are 35.6% among whites, 30.7% among African Americans, and 28.1% among Hispanic Americans.

What makes for an even worse situation regarding the drug problem is the fact that a large number of treatment programs are either irrelevant or of inferior quality. For instance, only a little more

than half of Puerto Rican addicts in New York City become involved in some form of treatment. Even more important, many of them leave treatment prior to its completion (Langrod, Ruiz, Alksne, & Lowinson, 1978).

Insofar as drug use is concerned, it is of interest to note some current trends and characteristics in the use and abuse of drugs among specific ethnic groups. For instance, the findings of the Hispanic Health and Nutrition Examination Survey (1987) show that Puerto Ricans have a higher lifetime percent use of marijuana (42.7%) than either Mexican Americans (41.6%) or Cuban Americans (20.1%). The same holds true for cocaine, where use is found to be higher among Puerto Ricans (21.5%) than either Mexican Americans (11.1%) or Cuban Americans (9.2%). Inhalants, however, are more widespread among Mexican Americans (6.4%) than among Puerto Ricans (5.8%), primarily among the youth group.

Concerning treatment outcome, it is noteworthy to mention the work of Szapocznik et al. (1988) regarding the engagement of Hispanic American adolescents in treatment. Their work has pointed out the effectiveness of a strategy to engage adolescent drug users and their families in treatment. The interventions in which this treatment is based focus primarily on strategic and structural systems concepts. Based on this approach, the identified patterns of interactions that interfere with entry into treatment are isolated and restructured. The subjects involved in their study were engaged at a rate of 93%, in comparison to 42% for those not involved in this type of treatment approach. Additionally, 77% of the adolescents involved completed their treatment program, while only 25% of those treated with other conventional treatment approaches were able to complete their treatment program. These types of interventions, which have proven to work well with Hispanic American youths, also should be used when treating adolescent substance abusers and their families from other ethnic minority groups. When it comes to drugs, the youths of the United States show less of a multiethnic trend and more of an individually oriented pattern. However, as pluralism develops in this nation, we expect to see more common trends among all the ethnic minority youth groups residing. When it comes to violence/aggression, this ethnically individualistic trend becomes even more pronounced among the ethnic minority youth groups. In this regard, Hispanic Americans, particularly Mexican Americans, have taken the lead in gang organization and violence. Asian Americans also have displayed great violence in their neighborhoods. From a pluralistic point of view, issues such as "being cool," peer pressure, escape from problems, and dealing with boredom are some of the most important etiological factors concerning drug use and abuse among youths in this country. Logically, any preventive efforts must be tailored toward these causative factors. Further, we believe that much of the violence seen among youths is directly related to the sale and use of recreational drugs.

The interrelationship between crime and drugs has been well established. Many illicit drug users commit crimes, such as robbery, burglary, drug dealing, prostitution, and gambling, to earn enough money to maintain their drug habit. Further, young persons under the influence of drugs such as cocaine and alcohol also commit acts of aggression and violence. U.S. Department of Justice statistics (1987) show that 54% of all jail inmates during 1983 reported having used alcohol just before they committed their criminal offense. Furthermore, the U.S. Department of Justice statistics (1989) also demonstrate that during 1986, most prisoners in state penitentiaries convicted of arson as well as violent crimes, such as murder, involuntary manslaughter, and rape, were far more likely to be under the influence of alcohol and/or drugs when they committed their crimes. The relationship between drugs and crime is currently of such a magnitude that drug legalization has been recommended as a potential solution (Nadelmann, 1989).

Sex and Intimacy

Sex and intimacy play key roles in the social and emotional development of all youths. The so-called sexual revolution initiated in the 1960s created an environment for open discussion and better acceptance of sexuality in the United States. However, it also enhanced many of the sexual problems confronted by today's youths. Hand in hand with an alarming rise in unplanned pregnancies and in venereal diseases goes much ignorance and anxiety regarding human sexuality. In recent years, adolescent pregnancy has become a psychosocial and health problem of crisis proportions. In the 1960s many unwed women who be-

came pregnant were married prior to delivery. However, at the present time, 1 of every 4 women who give birth to a child is unmarried. Also, 2 of every 3 teenagers who deliver a child are single. Further, among African American teenage mothers, only 1 in 10 are married ("Science and Society," 1991). It must be noted here that childbirth among adolescents undoubtedly would have been more numerous without the recent liberalization of legal abortions and the increased availability of contraceptives to teenagers.

Anyone considering the widespread occurrence of teenage pregnancies must keep in mind certain physiological, psychosocial, and social factors. To begin with, today's females mature earlier physiologically. Additionally, there is considerable speculation whether today's adolescent pregnancies are largely a result of ignorance regarding sexuality and contraception, or whether they are an expression of a conscious or an unconscious wish to have a baby, thus representing a distorted assertion of adulthood, an act of rebellion, or an attempt to escape from societal expectations and find solace in vicarious mothering.

From a social point of view, the welfare system with its penalties for working parents, plays a major role in early conception. While there are no final answers to this complex problem, our experience suggests that many pregnant teenagers are ambivalent about becoming mothers. Most of these teenage girls choose not to use contraceptives due to a lack of reliable information, to psychosocial problems about their sexuality, and, especially, to a lack of concern by their male youth partners.

The younger teenagers, and particularly those with second pregnancies, are especially vulnerable to serious medical complications. For these female youths, a higher incidence of obstetrical problems, insufficient prenatal and postnatal care, and even maternal death are the rules rather than the exceptions. Extrinsic factors such as poor nutrition and poverty play a major role in this heightened risk. Teenage females who bear children have less access to schooling and education than their peers who become mothers later in life. Furthermore, teenage females who bear children while still in high school are more likely to drop out and, therefore, not to attain their educational goals in comparison to their classmates who do not have to face such a situation. Lower educational attainments undoubtedly lead to unemployment, lower income, and poverty. These factors also play a major role in contributing to unwed teenage pregnancies, thus creating a vicious cycle. Adolescent pregnancy is almost invariably associated with unstable family patterns characterized by illegitimacy, unstable marriages, and divorce. What is puzzling is the fact that ethnic minority youth females, especially African American female youths, who have children are more susceptible to additional pregnancies. Compounding the tragic psychosocial problems for these unwed teenagers is the bleak future that lies ahead for their offspring, who often face, among other conditions, prematurity, low birthweight, poor nutrition, and high perinatal mortality. The added stress of an infant facing these problems will certainly further exacerbate this difficult psychosocial problem.

From a psychological point of view, these unwed teens have serious difficulties in attaching themselves to their children because they did not have the opportunity to separate successfully themselves from their parents and families. As adolescents, they are still in the process of securing their identity and independence. Perhaps becoming pregnant and having a baby is not a traumatic event for adolescents in societies that have built-in institutional support to help the new family nucleus, but in our society this is not so.

In this country, we have a dual set of risks. On one side, we have to address the emotional well-being of the adolescent parent. On the other side, the physical and emotional well-being of their children must be considered. It is not at all surprising that adolescent mothers occasionally are suspected of child neglect and abuse as well as involvement with substance abuse. While there is an urgent need for secondary prevention in these cases, primary prevention is certainly much more important. In the long term, it also may prove to be less expensive. Comprehensive sex education offered to all youths by societal institutions such as the family and the school system certainly will represent a very appropriate primary prevention approach. In this respect, we should focus on both family planning and sex education. Unfortunately, sex education efforts have proven to be insufficient and inadequate due to the school climate and the political biases that currently besiege the U.S. society. Parents, in particular, need to strengthen and improve their roles as primary sex educators for their children. In so doing, they need to secure a better understanding of their children's sexuality, they need to accept that it is healthy for their children to be sexually educated, and they need to be reassured that this enhanced knowledge presents no increased danger for sexual experimentation among youth.

Interestingly, some parents prefer that the school system take responsibility for the sex education of their children rather than themselves. Unfortunately, many school programs in sex education leave much to be desired, particularly those in urban ghetto schools. Even in schools where sex education currently is taking place, many teachers frequently are inadequately prepared. In this respect, child and adolescent mental health specialists could play a significant role by being consultants to the school system, particularly in public schools and to parent/teacher organizations. In order for this approach to be meaningful, these mental health specialists must go beyond the presentation of facts of sex education and become involved in important matters such as self-esteem development, revision of societal and individual values, and focus on issues related to personal responsibility and judgment. In addition, and most important, these issues also must be addressed from a public policy point of view. For instance, it would be very beneficial to ensure reimbursement from third-party payors for preventive interventions in the area of teenage pregnancy and breast cancer prevention.

In discussing sex and intimacy issues among American youths, it is also imperative to address HIV and AIDS. Up to now, most adolescents have become infected with HIV via sexual intercourse and intravenous drug use. In comparison to adults, most adolescents suffering from AIDS are female and of minority status and have acquired the infection heterosexually (Brooks-Gunn, Boyer, & Hein, 1988). Current statistics show that over 50% of female youths in high school have had sexual intercourse and also that 1 out of 6 female youths in high school has had more than 4 sexual partners (Belfer, Krener, & Miller, 1988). Additionally, close to 50% of all youths in the United States do not use contraceptive methods when they have sexual intercourse for the first time; therefore, they are more vulnerable to pregnancy, HIV infection, and a host of other sexually transmitted illnesses (Zelnik & Shah, 1983). It is quite common to see adolescents behaving as if they were omnipotent and, thus, invulnerable to illnesses, including AIDS. As a result, they do not see the need to protect themselves against sexually transmitted diseases. Many American youths have many misconceptions about HIV and its mode of transmission. For instance, even after being exposed to sexually related information, adolescents prefer not to change their sexual behavior and their use of contraceptive methods (Kegeles, Adler, & Irwin, 1988). Definitely, all American youths are at high risk for sexually transmitted diseases, particularly HIV/AIDS. However, ethnic minority youths are at a much higher risk for acquiring these illnesses. For instance, many ethnic minority group members believe that AIDS is a disease of gay white males and thus do not consider themselves to be at risk. Racial minorities are definitely among the faster-growing groups of HIV-infected persons in this country. Forty-four percent of all African American and Hispanic American adult/adolescent males suffering from AIDS are intravenous drug users, in comparison to only 17% of white adult/adolescent males (Centers for Disease Control and Prevention, 1996). African American and Hispanic American drug users have a higher probability of using intravenous methods when abusing drugs in shooting galleries and of sharing needles. This type of behavior places individuals at high risk of becoming infected with HIV.

Homosexuality and bisexuality within minority populations tend to be taboo subjects, and because they are not discussed, the possibility of acquiring sexually transmitted diseases increases. For instance, African American and Hispanic American males tend to not easily acknowledge their homosexual behavior (Peterson & Marin, 1988). Language barriers, cultural differences, and prejudice could place ethnic minority youths at a disadvantage when it comes to securing the necessary information regarding sexually transmitted diseases. This situation is certainly deleterious with respect to health promotion. Unfortunately, the role of the church in this regard has not been strong enough. Religious institutions play a major role in many aspects of life among African American and Hispanic American populations. However, so far the church has not been as actively involved in AIDS prevention and sex education as it could be (Mays & Cochran, 1987).

With respect to ethnic minorities, HIV information should be presented in a culturally sensitive manner and, preferably, by a member of the ethnic group to whom the information is being presented. Otherwise, it may be perceived as demeaning and prejudicial in nature. Then AIDS education may become counterproductive, caus-

ing youths to underutilize HIV testing and related services (Bing et al., 1990).

Recent statistics related to sexual practices among U.S. youths are not only a cause for alarm but also are appalling. For instance, half of high school students receive no AIDS instruction, only 26% of sexually active 12th graders always use condoms, 34% of college males claim they have lied about their sexual habits in order to have sex, and 63% of venereal disease cases occur among those under 25 years old ("Teenage Sex," 1991). It is imperative that we face, appropriately and expeditiously, the need for sex education and HIV prevention among American youths by encouraging school boards to work with HIV prevention plans, AIDS education programs, and sex education courses. Outreach efforts directed toward better involvement by the community and its institutions also may be salutary. Additionally, epidemiological studies concerning attitudes and behavior in the area of sexual practices should be further encouraged and financially supported. Only through these efforts as well as through public awareness we will be able to master the major challenge that we are now facing regarding HIV prevention and AIDS treatment.

While we have primarily addressed the issue of sex and intimacy from a multiethnic point of view, we must acknowledge that in the United States, when it comes to marriage, dating, intimacy, and sex, we are not a homogeneous culture. We hope that, as this nation becomes more pluralistic in nature, these barriers will slowly disappear.

Transition to Adulthood

Nowadays, maturing successfully into adulthood represents a major challenge for youths in the United States. This is due, among other circumstances, to some of the socioeconomic problems currently facing this nation, particularly among for ethnic minority youths. For instance, 47.8% of African American households are headed by females, in comparison to only 11.4% for non-Hispanic whites. Eighty percent of white youths complete high school, in comparison to only 67% of African American youths. The number of African American families below the poverty level is 32%, in comparison to only 12% of white families (U.S. Bureau of the Census, 1991). For the Hispanic American population residing in the United States, a similar picture is also observed. According to the 1990 Census (U.S. Bureau of the Census, 1991), 26.2% of the population below the poverty level was Hispanic American, while for the total U.S. population the rate was only 12.8%. Concomitantly, only 41.2% of the Hispanic American population were homeowners, compared to 64.1% among the total U.S. population.

These statistics and their related consequences depict well the difficulties faced nowadays by American youths, particularly ethnic minority youths, who must overcome and master these difficulties in order to achieve competency and maturity.

However, recent reports clearly demonstrate that today's youths are not only aware of the financial difficulties that lie ahead but are able to master the situation fairly well. For instance, it has been reported that among high school juniors and seniors, 65.9% have savings accounts, 24% have checking accounts, and 24% own cars in their names. Of course, many of these initiatives were encouraged or guided by their parents. In this group of students, 43% reported that their source of income was wages or salary ("Many Teens Work Hard," Houston Chronicle, 1991). While promising, this body of data does not address such important issues as the high level of unemployment among African American male youths. Although there was a 52% increase in the number of African American managers, professionals, technicians, and government officials during the last decade, the gap in median income between African Americans and whites is now wider than it was in the late 1970s. Furthermore, rather than welcoming African Americans into the mainstream of this country, some whites feel threatened by and thus tend to reject them ("Between Two Worlds," 1989). Not infrequently, affluent African Americans face difficulties when they try to buy homes in predominantly white neighborhoods. Along these lines, 2 to 3 decades ago many African American youths were not interested in matriculating in historically black colleges and universities and preferred to attend Ivy League academic institutions. More recently, however, African American youths have begun to return to historically black institutions due to the surge in prejudicial and racist behavior in Ivy League and other predominantly white colleges and universities. To complicate things more, the below-average educational level of achievement that predominates

among the ethnic minority youth groups reflects in less favorable occupational status/accomplishment. For instance, among the total U.S. population, 56% of all employed persons fell either in the managerial/professional or technical/sales categories. However, Hispanic Americans make up only 38% of these 2 highest occupational categories (Ginzberg, 1991). Certain cultural characteristics make this situation much worse for Hispanic American female youths. Some tend to stay at home and take care of the family, while most Hispanic American male youths are encouraged to pursue business and professional careers (Gomez, Gomez, & Ruiz, 1983). However, this situation is rapidly changing, particularly for subsequent-generation Hispanic American females.

The vocational and educational goals for today's ethnic minority youths are certainly restricted and limited. Acknowledging this fact, we think, constitutes an important step toward finding solutions to these problems. It is hoped that through interactions with the members of the majority culture and by mastering their external world and environment, ethnic minority youths will achieve better outcomes in the future. Establishing independence and maturity, beginning a family, and becoming adults will undoubtedly depend on finding an appropriate job, retaining it, and moving up in the socioeconomic ladder. Unless this can be achieved, drug abuse, alcoholism, crime, homicide, and suicide will be prevalent among the poverty-stricken youths of this nation.

Conclusion

Today's youths face unique challenges and opportunities in the United States. Interestingly, the appropriate resolution of the dilemma currently faced by America's youths is directly related to the achievement of a pluralistic society in this nation. As we have shown, while this country has become a multiethnic mosaic, it still is far from becoming a truly pluralistic society. We hope that this goal will be achieved eventually. Herein we have focused on all of the current important and relevant problems faced by America's youth and have noted the special challenges faced by ethnic minority youths.

We hope that our discussion will call additional attention to the needs and problems of the nation's youths. If this call for attention is amplified in communities across the nation by the public and private sectors, soon we should expect to see more consideration paid to research and investigational efforts focusing on creating and implementing solutions to these compelling youth needs. Ultimately these problems will be remedied and/or corrected through the generation and synthesis of new knowledge from original and innovative thinking. Definitely, American youths represent the future of this nation.

REFERENCES

Belfer, M. L., Krener, P. K., & Miller, F. D. (1988). AIDS in children and adolescents. *Journal of the American Academy of Child and Adolescent Psychiatry, 27* (2), 147–151.

Berry, J. W., & Kim, U. (1988). Acculturation and mental health. In P. Dasen, J. W. Berry, & N. Sartorius (Eds.), *Health and cross-cultural psychology: Toward applications.* London: Sage Publications, 207–236.

"Between Two Worlds." (1989, March 13). *Time,* p. 58.

Bing, E. G., Nichols, S. E., Goldfinger, S. M., Fernandez, F., Cabaj, R., Dudley, R. G., Krener, P., Prager, M., & Ruiz, P. (1990). The many faces of AIDS: Opportunities for intervention. In S. M. Goldfinger (Ed.), *Psychiatric aspects of AIDS and HIV infection, New directions for mental health services* (pp. 69–81). San Francisco: Jossey-Bass.

Brooks-Gunn, J., Boyer, C. B., & Hein, K. (1988). Preventing HIV infection and AIDS in children and adolescents. *American Psychologist, 43* (11), 958–964.

Centers for Disease Control and Prevention. (1996). *HIV/AIDS Surveillance Report, 8* (1), 1–33.

Ginzberg, E. (1991). Access to health care for Hispanics. *Journal of the American Medical Association, 265* (2), 238–241.

Gomez, G. E., Gomez, E. A., & Ruiz, P. (1983). Mental health care of Hispanic-Americans in the United States: A cultural and clinical perspective. *World Journal of Psychosynthesis, 15* (1), 19–23.

Griffith, E. E. H., & Bell, C. C. (1989). Recent trends in suicide and homicide among blacks. *Journal of the American Medical Association, 262* (16), 2265–2269.

Group for the Advancement of Psychiatry. (1989). *Suicide and ethnicity in the United States.* (Report No. 128). New York: Brunner/Mazel.

Kegeles, S. M., Adler, N. W., & Irwin, C. E. (1988). Sexually active adolescents and condoms: Changes over one year in knowledge, attitudes, and use. *American Journal of Public Health, 78* (4), 460–461.

Langrod, J., Ruiz, P., Alksne, L., & Lowinson, J. (1978). Understanding cultural conflict in community-based treatment for the Hispanic addict. In A. Schecter, H. Alksne, & E. Kauffman (Eds.), *Drug abuse: Modern trends, issues and perspectives* (pp. 837–848). (Proceedings of the Second National Drug Abuse Conference.) New York: Marcel Dekker.

"Many Teens Work Hard, Save Hard." (1991, December 15). *Houston Chronicle,* p. 3F.

Mays, U. M., & Cochran, S. D. (1987). Acquired Immunodeficiency Syndrome and Black Americans. Special psychosocial issues. *Public Health Reports, 102* (2), 224–231.

Nadelmann, E. A. (1989). Drug prohibition in the United States: Costs, consequences, and alternatives. *Science, 245,* 939–946.

National Health and Nutrition Examination Survey. (1987). *Use of selected drugs among Hispanics: Mexican Americans, Puerto Ricans and Cuban Americans.* Findings from the National Health and Nutrition Examination Survey, National Institute of Drug Abuse.

National Household Survey on Drug Abuse. (1993). *National Household Survey on Drug Abuse: Population Estimates 1993.* Washington, DC: (DHHS Publication No. [SMA] 94-3017).

Peterson, J. L., & Marin, G. (1988). Issues in the prevention of AIDS among black and Hispanic men. *American Psychologist, 43* (11), 871–877.

Rogler, L. H., Cooney, R. S., & Ortiz, V. (1980). Intergenerational change in ethnic identity in the Puerto Rican family. *International Migration Review, 14* (2), 193–214.

"Science and Society." (1991, December 16). *U.S. News & World Report, 3* (25), p. 38.

Shaffer, D., Garland, A., Gould, M., Fisher, P., & Trautman, P. (1988). Preventing teenage suicide: A critical review. *Journal of the American Academy of Child Adolescent Psychiatry, 27* (6), 675–687.

Szapocznik, J., Perez-Vidal, A., Brickman, A. L., Foote, F. H., Santiesteban, D., Hervis, O., & Kurtines, W. M. (1988). Engaging adolescent drug abusers and their families in treatment: A strategic structural system approach. *Journal of Consulting and Clinical Psychology, 56* (4), 552–557.

"Teenage sex, after Magic." (1991, December 16). *U.S. News & World Report, 3* (25), pp. 90–92.

U.S. Bureau of the Census. (1991). *Current Population Reports* (Series P-20, No. 449). Washington, DC: Author.

U.S. Department of Justice. (1987). *Sourcebook of criminal justice statistics, 1986.* Washington, DC: Bureau of Justice Statistics.

U.S. Department of Justice. (1989). *Sourcebook of criminal justice statistics, 1987.* Washington, DC: Bureau of Justice Statistics.

Zelnik, M., & Shah, F. K. (1983). First intercourse among Americans. *Family Planning Perspectives, 15* (2), 64–70.

SECTION III
Prevention and Risk Factors

12 / Risk and Protection Factors in Child and Adolescent Psychiatric Disorders

John F. McDermott Jr.
Professor Emeritus

Risk factors for mental disorder are those characteristics of a group of children or adolescents that increase the odds or probability that they will incur a mental disorder. Protective factors, on the other hand, are those characteristics that decrease the odds or probability of mental disorder. Often protective factors are simply the opposite of risk factors—for example, family support versus lack of family support. Risk and protective factors can be either internal (constitutional) or external (environmental).

What we consider risk factors for mental disorder today were, for centuries, a natural part of childhood existence. There was no place for childhood in medieval times. The only stages of life that were recognized were infancy and adulthood. Those who fell in between these stages were considered nonpersons and experienced neglect and abuse as a way of life. Children were sold or indentured or wandered homeless in a nomadic society until a major restructuring sanctioned the family as the basic unit of society and some stability for human life was finally achieved. This family unit offered the necessary protection for the period that we know as childhood. Next, the addition and institutionalization of formal schooling marked the second boundary separating childhood from adulthood; with it arose the possibility of a distinct developmental atmosphere for childhood as a separate stage between infancy and adulthood in the life cycle.

Yet this stabilization of society through the family unit was not the final answer. Children continued to be abused. Evil now became the principal risk factor believed to cause mental illness. Regular beatings to suppress the animal side of the child and allow the human side to emerge were sanctioned in the family. Orphanages and workhouses became huge dumps for unwanted children until social reformers in 19th-century Dickensian England came to recognize neglect and abuse as evils themselves.

Concern by early 20th-century social activists over the mortality and morbidity rates in these overcrowded institutions eventually led to the first scientific studies of the constricting effects of institutionalization on the development of human intelligence and personality. The high rates of death and developmental retardation among infants raised in institutions, when compared to those raised in homes, were convincing. Parenting was implicated as the key variable, with the quality of attachment, or bonding, its mediator. Lack of parenting was clearly the major risk factor for psychiatric disorder. But what about those children reared in hospitals and orphanages who seemed so much less affected by the lack of adequate parenting? Some individuals must be more vulnerable to stress than others. Protective factors must be operating as well as risk factors.

Components of "good" and "bad" parenting needed to be identified. The focus for study was a sample of convenience, the retrospective accounts of adult psychiatric patients about their own child rearing. Child-rearing practice was assumed to have exerted a powerful influence on the development of their mental illness; if we could learn enough about bad practice, education and training for parenthood, perhaps, could influence it for the better. A method had been found which, it was believed, actually could prevent mental illness or at least ameliorate it.

The mid-20th century became an era of optimism that gave rise to exaggerated hopes. During this time most mental disorders were assumed to be largely determined by the experience of being raised, rather than from the combination of external *and* internally derived, genetic factors. As we later found, child-rearing practice could shape development but could not prevent many forms of true mental disorder.

Meanwhile, after World War II, a new science was developing in the United States that had its origins in public health, rather than in medicine. Epidemiology emerged as the scientific study of the distribution of disease; from knowing a disease's distribution, the factors that determine it could be found. Longitudinal follow-up of large populations over time revealed the natural history of disease—its development and course, its prognosis, and, ultimately, an understanding of the risk and protective factors that differentiated those who became ill from those who did not. This method led to the great medical triumphs over infectious disease, from cholera, to tuberculosis. It was now brought to bear on cardiovascular disease through the identification of specific risk factors—smoking, high blood pressure, obesity, and cholesterol. A person's chances of getting heart disease could be reduced by influencing one or more of these risk factors. Could this method be brought to bear on psychiatric disorder in adults, adolescents, and children? Perhaps.

Epidemiological longitudinal studies utilize large community populations rather than clinical cases, are prospective rather than retrospective, and are health rather than disease oriented, with prevention rather than treatment as the ultimate goal. They could identify not only risk factors but also the major principles in the operation of those risk factors in psychiatric illness: which risk factors are intrinsic or genetic, and which are extrinsic or environmental; which ones interact with each other and how—that is, the degree by which each interacting risk factor changes the odds of contracting a psychiatric illness.

But there was a problem. Epidemiological studies of the natural history of illness needed a precise diagnostic system that is criterion-based to give them reliability. And the distortions and biases in open-ended clinical interviews had to give way to assessment instruments derived from such a criterion-based diagnostic system, instruments that could be administered inexpensively in large-scale studies by lay assistants rather than mental health professionals. At the same time that the epidemiological method became available to researchers in the field, child and adolescent psychiatry was shifting from a continuous model of psychopathology in which the normal and the abnormal fell in the same spectrum of symptom development, to a new conceptual model. The third edition of the *Diagnostic and Statistical Manual of Mental Disorders* (*DSM-III*) employed "caseness," which defined a distinct boundary between normal and abnormal, and established a categorical separation between ordinary developmental variation and clinical disorder. With such a new diagnostic system and with the advent of standardized *DSM-III* diagnostic instruments structured interviews such as the Diagnostic Interview

Schedule for Children (DISC), and the Schedule for Affective Disorder and Schizophrenia for School-Age Children (K-SADS), or the Diagnostic Interview for Children and Adolescents (DICA) (Costello, Edelbrock, Dulcan, Kalas, & Klaric 1984; Orvaschel & Puig-Antich, 1987; Shaffer et al., 1988; Welner, Reich, Herjanic, Jung, & Amado 1987), epidemiological longitudinal studies became available as a scientific method for testing our theories and concepts as never before. They have been improved as we have moved to DSM IV and now give us the means to map the beginnings of mental illness in childhood, to follow its natural history through adolescence into adulthood, and to define the risk and protective factors that influence its onset and course in a vulnerable population. The evolution of this empirically derived knowledge base is the foundation for a new model of developmental psychopathology that outlines the continuities and discontinuities in development and the origin and course of psychopathology in childhood.

Risk Factor Research

The 1970s saw the dawn of the epidemiological era in child and adolescent psychiatry, but before the new diagnostic system and structured interviews were established, 2 landmark studies set the pace for subsequent investigations and placed us firmly in the new age of scientific discovery. Both were longitudinal studies, examining all youngsters born in a single year in a defined geographic region and following them chronologically. The first, known as the Children of Kauai Study (Werner, Bierman, & French, 1971), set out to examine the sequelae of prenatal and perinatal birth complications, which were hypothesized to be important risk factors for the development of mental illness in childhood and adolescence. To everyone's surprise, the findings from that study proved otherwise. While there did appear a spectrum of organic impairment of intellectual and social development in affected infants at 20 months of age, that spectrum became largely invisible by 10 years of age, except for the most severely damaged children. On the other hand, a new set of risk factors—poverty, family discord, and parental psychopathology—appeared, which accentuated the effects of these organic deficits at *all* ages. Several of these new risk factors were found associated with serious learning or behavior problems at age 10 and with delinquency or serious psychiatric problems at age 18. In other words, psychosocial factors were discovered to be more powerful determinants of maladjustment than biological ones. As a result of these findings, the impact of neonatal anoxia was reevaluated and family influences became identified as critical risk *and* protective factors for later psychiatric illness. In subsequent work the investigators (Werner & Smith, 1982, 1977) have further refined their initial findings and suggested that this interaction of risk and protective factors is a developmental phenomenon—that internal biological factors are more important as risk factors during infancy and childhood, with external or interpersonal factors more important in adolescence.

The second landmark study, the Isle of Wight Study (Rutter, Tizard, Yule, et al., 1976) carried these early impressions further. From a large sample of 10-year-old children studied from birth to adolescence, Rutter and his investigators were able to pinpoint 6 specific risk factors for psychiatric disorder: (1) severe marital distress, (2) low social status, (3) overcrowding or large family size, (4) paternal criminality, (5) maternal psychiatric disorder, and (6) admission to care (foster home placement). Furthermore, this study quantified the cumulative impact of risk—a child with 1 of these 6 factors had a 2% chance of disturbance; that probability increased to 6% with 2 to 3 factors and to over 20% with 4 risk factors.

Thus, between the 1940s and the 1980s, empirical studies changed the risk factor concept from a 1-dimension theory in which mother-child interaction was the single key factor in the development of mental illness in childhood and adolescence, to one in which a series of specific family-related categories could be identified. One of them, Rutter's sixth category, called "admission to care," or foster placement, allows a specific focus on separation from parents, the previously most accepted risk factor.

How have more recent epidemiological longitudinal studies using the modern technology of structured interviews added to the knowledge base of the natural history of mental disorder as we approach the year 2000? The rest of this chapter addresses this question and summarizes what is known for early, middle, and late childhood as we attempt to integrate this new conceptual model of the at-risk population into our current understanding of psychiatric disorder in children and adolescents.

Early Childhood

The concept of biological risk has changed dramatically from brain damage to genetic vulnerability. First, the notion that varying degrees of perinatal injury or hypoxia produce a continuum of intellectual and behavioral disorder later in childhood was not confirmed (Werner, Bierman, & French, 1971). The effects washed out with strong family support, clearly a powerful protective factor. However, the story was not complete. A longitudinal study of over 1,000 children born in the same year in Dunedin, New Zealand, continued to examine the findings of the Kauai Study more closely (Silva, McGee, & Williams, 1984). It found that infants who were born prematurely in time did not develop lower IQs and increased behavior problems, whereas those born prematurely by weight did. In other words, it was better to be born too early than too small. The smallest end of the gestational age–weight spectrum does seem to be at risk for disorder, with the lowest 10% of infants by birthweight most susceptible to developing later psychiatric symptoms.

Meanwhile, newer forms of biological risk factors, called temperamental characteristics (Earls & Jung 1987), were related to higher levels of psychopathology in childhood, and a new continuum of reproductive casualty replaced the old hypothesis of a perinatal continuum of risk. Maternal alcohol consumption, especially during early pregnancy, results in a characteristic physical and behavioral intellectual deficit in the child called fetal alcohol syndrome. In its classic form, diagnostic facial stigmata are accompanied by mental retardation and hyperactivity, most often expressed as attention deficit hyperactive disorder. There is increasing evidence that less severe forms of this condition appear as variants of behavior and intellectual disorder in early childhood. Other drugs such as cocaine, when used during pregnancy, also have been implicated in psychiatric disorders of infancy and childhood.

Findings from family genetic studies in the 1980s and 1990s have revolutionized our understanding of the biological determinants of mental illness. Major advances have been made in uncovering the genetic vulnerability for mental disorder. For example, twin and family studies have demonstrated a significant increase in the risk for autism in those families with a positive history (Bailey, LeCouteur, Gottesman 1995; Ritvo, Freeman, Freeman, Pingree, et al., 1989; Ritvo, Jorde, et al., 1989).

But beyond biological risk, the picture has changed even more for other forms of family risk factors. What, for example, ever happened to the "original" risk factor of the 20th century, deficits in the parent-child interaction? And what of its associated protective factors? The woman's movement of the 1970s and 1980s modified our view of separation from parents as the major risk factor for children. Many working mothers could not continue to serve as the sole or even the primary caregiver from birth until the school years. Economic necessity forced most women to return to work soon after their babies were born and demonstrated that such early partial separation from a full-time mothering person was not detrimental to development as long as suitable alternatives were available. In other words, infants were found to adjust to multiple caregivers much earlier than previously thought. Longitudinal researchers discovered a corollary to these impressions from social and economic changes. Breast-feeding of infants, previously believed to be an important protective factor for healthy development, was found to have no direct connection with personality development (Silva, Buckfield, & Spears, 1978).

The risk factor of early separation from parents also has changed in its form and its influence. For example, the premature death of a parent did not turn out to be predictive of disorder unless it resulted in loss of care and affection, while divorce, another form of separation from parents, came to assume a much larger role. Studies of the children of divorce have confirmed that divorce is a significant risk factor for disorder, its effects spanning the developmental spectrum from early childhood through adolescence. A large-scale national study demonstrated that children who had experienced marital dissolution were significantly worse off than those who had not with respect to problem behavior, academic performance, and psychological distress, differences that persisted when controlled for age, race, sex, and mother's education (Furstenberg & Nord, 1985; Furstenberg, Peterson, Nord, & Zill, 1983). The early years are a particularly vulnerable period because marital problems and disruption directly affect the security of preschool children, while, at the same time, their cognitive development is not yet adequate for coping. The reactions of younger children whose parents had separated when they were in preschool are more severe than those affected later in childhood. In other words, it is clear that a significant number of children who experience parents' divorce as preschoolers enter adolescence severely at risk for disorder (Wallerstein, 1991).

In summary, the longitudinal studies of the 1980s have confirmed and further developed earlier findings of the importance of family functioning as a major contributing factor to the development of psychiatric disorder in childhood (Offord, et al., 1987; Silva et al., 1978). Those family factors are now being defined further. In addition, disorder-specific genetic vulnerability is being unraveled so that children at biological risk can be identified more clearly.

Middle Childhood

Since it is clear that family factors play a significant role as both risk and protective factors for psychiatric disorder in early and middle childhood, the study of dysfunctional families has been in the research spotlight since the 1960s, when the rate of divorce, the legal term for family disruption, began to affect a significant number of children. Divorce originally was thought to be a short-lived crisis, one that could be understood within the familiar framework of crisis management. This theory is not adequate to account for the findings from longitudinal studies of children of divorce. Divorce significantly affects acting-out behavior and distractibility in boys, key symptoms in the diagnosis of disruptive behavior disorders in middle childhood (Hetherington, Cox, & Cox, 1985; Hodges, Tierney, & Buchsbaum, 1984; Kalter, Kloner, Schreier, & Okla, 1989; Portes, Haas, & Brown, 1991). Girls appear to be protected from acute disturbance as an immediate reaction to divorce but may have more difficulty later (Wallerstein, 1991), a phenomenon that is considered further in the section on late childhood.

This finding illustrates the developmental shift of gender as a risk and protective factor in itself. Throughout the first decade of life, boys exceed girls in the development of psychiatric disorders by a ratio of 3 or 4 to 1. However, during the second decade, the ratio reverses, and after the age of 18, it evens out. Over the entire span, boys are more prone to externalizing illness and girls to internalizing disorder.

So much for gender. What about socioeconomic status as a risk factor for mental disorder? Poverty traditionally has been associated with emotional and behavioral problems, a relationship found to be stronger in younger children than in adolescents (Rutter, 1989). The overwhelming majority of youths with a record of delinquency and/or psychiatric problems have grown up in childhood poverty (Werner, 1990). There is no question that low income has a significant effect in predicting later onset of psychiatric disorder (Offord et al., 1992). But just how this risk factor of poverty is mediated is unknown. Poor neighborhoods that are organized, often around church-related activities, may have much lower rates of disorder than neighborhoods that are just as poor but are disorganized and chaotic. Furthermore, the effects of poverty may be mediated as much through genetic transmission of mental illness as through inadequate parenting (Jensen, Bloedau, Degroot, Ussery, & Davis, 1990). Thus, while most of the evidence supports a qualified confirmation of the notion of low socioeconomic status as a risk factor, economic disadvantage by itself is not sufficient. It must be associated with other risk factors and mediated by family as well as individual characteristics (e.g., low IQ, reading disability) in the children themselves (Werner, 1990).

Another of the 6 risk factors originally identified in the Isle of Wight Study, overcrowding or large family size, is related to socioeconomic status as well. It now appears that it is associated with increased rates of conduct disorder and delinquency in boys but not in girls (Jones, Offord, & Abrams, 1980). Again, however, the relationship between large family size and overcrowding to psychiatric disorder is most marked in families that are both economically disadvantaged and disrupted or disorganized (Wadsworth, 1979).

Specific risk factors occurring within the family have long been known—child abuse and neglect. Children with a history of being abused are more likely than others to exhibit depressive symptomatology, both major depressive disorder and dysthymia (Kaufman, 1991). Maltreated children present with a significant incidence of psychotic symptomatology as well as personality and adjustment disorders (Famularo, Kinscherff, & Fenton, 1992). An abuse history is invariably present in violent, conduct-disordered youths (Lewis, 1992). Clinical impressions of adult patients also suggests that persons with specific disorders—multiple personality and borderline disorders—have a high rate of physical and sexual abuse in early childhood.

While abuse and neglect have long been known as risk factors for disorder, psychic trauma has been largely overlooked throughout history. Recent systematic studies provided evidence for posttraumatic stress disorder as a significant outcome of psychic trauma (Terr, 1979). Children exposed to violence; who witness the rape, murder, or suicide of a parent; who are kidnapped (most often parental kidnapping in contested custody cases); or who are victims of airplane and automobile accidents or other major disasters are all at high risk for developing posttraumatic stress disorder. One thing is clear. Trauma of human design cause more severe and longer disturbance than those from natural disaster.

Chronic physical illness has been found to be a risk factor for mental disorder. Leukemia, diabetes mellitus, asthma, cystic fibrosis, and epilepsy as well as sensory deficits including deafness and blindness, carry with them a 25% risk for one or more psychiatric disorders, twice the usual rate for children in middle childhood (Bird, Gould, Yager, Staghezza, & Canino, 1989). Newer conditions such as AIDS and organ transplant with accompanying immunosuppressant agents that can damage the central nervous system also have produced behavioral and emotional problems and are likely to be identified as specific risks as more studies of their effects emerge. Finally, genetic studies have positively identified increased biological risk factors for several disorders that typically emerge in middle childhood. Attention deficit disorder (Biederman, Munir, & Knee, 1987; Levy, Hay, McStephen, Wood, Waldman, 1997), perhaps the most common disorder in childhood, has a familial risk. So does reading disability (Decker & DeFries, 1980; DeFries & Decker, 1981) and its subtypes, the other most commonly found disorders among school-age children, and Tourette's disorder, (Curtis, Robertson & Gurling 1992) less common but clearly transmitted vertically within families. These conditions are heterogeneous, not single-gene disorders, but the increased risk to a child can be estimated when the family incidence is known.

Late Childhood

During adolescence, family factors continue to be a most important cluster of risk factors for psychiatric disorder, with divorce once again placing adolescents at risk, but in a different way. On the one hand, adolescents are more resilient to family breakup because they are separating from the family and have newer outside attachments, making them less vulnerable to the loss of parents than younger children. As described earlier, school-age boys show acute reactions to the breakup of the family, while girls display "sleeper" effects, often found in relationships later in life (Wallerstein, 1991). Indeed, the effects of divorce in girls often are manifested many years after the event, in late childhood or adolescence. Hetherington 1989; Hetherington et al., 1985) found 3 clusters representing the outcome of divorce in adolescence. One, called "maladaptive," is composed of aggressive, insecure youngsters who show problems in many domains, are likely to be impulsive, and are socially withdrawn. A second cluster has been labeled "opportunistic and competent," often with short-lived relationships. The third group, "caring and competent," was composed almost entirely of girls. Girls, then, illustrate both vulnerability to the effects of divorce and resilience well.

Children of divorce are at risk for higher rates of psychopathology, but there are other contributing factors as well. They include the marital conflict preceding and following the divorce as well as the loss of a parent, the lowering of socioeconomic status that often occurs after divorce, and the single-parent dysfunction that occurs from the stress of doubled family responsibility. Thus the event of divorce itself should be viewed cautiously as a single risk factor leading to mental disorder in childhood or adolescence.

Delinquency, the social expression of conduct disorder, reaches a peak in adolescence and has long been associated with low socioeconomic status. However, we may now conclude that low socioeconomic status, like divorce, does not act by itself but does so in combination with other risk factors. Its effects are most clear when associated with disrupted or disturbed family relations, with disorganized and chaotic neighborhoods—neighborhoods without structure. Protective factors against the development of delinquency appear to be strong religious affiliation as well as an intact family. However, if there is not an intact family, access to an elder (grandparent, aunt or uncle) who provides structure and stability in children's lives is a significant protective factor (Werner & Smith, 1982). In other words, socioeconomic status does not have a 1-to-1 linear relationship with psychopathological outcome. A combination of several risk factors must be present before an adverse outcome occurs. For example, low socioeconomic status coupled with low IQ (below 90) sharply increases reported deviant behavior (Miller, Hampe, Barrett, & Noble, 1971).

As suggested earlier, the interaction of risk and protective factors constitutes a balance through which different risk factors assume varying degrees in importance at different developmental stages. Protective factors are the opposite of risk factors—easy rather than difficult temperament, family support rather than family distress. Protective factors have been identified most specifically in adolescence. Like risk factors, they consist of 3 broad categories: (1) inherent attributes of the child such as positive temperament, hardiness, autonomy, sociability, and positive self-esteem; (2) attributes of the family including family cohesion, warmth, harmony, and the absence of neglect; and (3) attributes of the extrafamily social environment, including the availability of external resources and extended social supports (Garmezy, 1985). These last 2 categories, family and social relationships, become the most important protective factors in adolescence. Interpersonal protective factors significantly related to psychiatric disorder have been identified as getting along with others, being a good student, and participating in 2 or more activities. When deficient, these same peer relationships combine with family problems to place youngsters at significant risk for psychiatric disorder (Rae-Grant, Thomas, Offord, & Boyle 1989).

What are the significant biological factors in the risk for disorder in adolescence? Just as family history for autism, attention deficit hyperactivity disorder, and Tourette's was a risk factor for those disorders in earlier childhood, a positive family history for affective disorder or schizophrenia is a risk factor for those disorders in adolescence (Rae-Grant et al., 1989; Rutter et al., 1976; Kovacs, 1997; Strober et al., 1988). Of all the disorders studied in families, maternal depression has most often been noted to place youngsters at risk for developing depression themselves (Beardslee, Bemporad, Keller, & Klerman, 1983; Weissman, Fendrich, Warner, & Wickramaratne, 1992). Perhaps depression is more common in adolescence than in early or middle childhood, as a result of hormonal forces at puberty triggering the genetic predisposition (Kutcher et al., 1991). In any case, while depressive *symptoms* are common throughout childhood, major depressive disorder similar to that found in adults is seen most commonly in adolescence and is familial, with a higher risk for teenagers from families with a clear history.

While schizophrenia also has its major onset in adolescence and is thought to be inherited, it also illustrates the problem in interpreting such findings. Offspring of schizophrenic parents run a 10-fold increased risk for developing schizophrenia compared with the general population. However, only 10 to 15% of the offspring of a single schizophrenic parent and 40 to 50% of the offspring of 2 schizophrenic parents develop schizophrenia themselves (Holzman, 1982). Furthermore, 40% of the children of schizophrenic parents develop psychopathology that is *not* along the schizophrenic spectrum (Mednick & McNeil, 1968). And the main point to remember is that most schizophrenics do not themselves have schizophrenic parents. The same is true for affective disorder. Why? The answer is that there is not likely to be a single-gene mental disorder but only a genetic vulnerability that must interact with other risk factors to be expressed.

In sum, while there is growing evidence for genetic risk factors (Kovacs, 1997), especially in the genetic transmission of serious mental disorder, there is also a considerable lack of specificity associated with these risk factors. They are cumulative in the sense that a higher certainty of illness is related to the number of risk factors present and how they facilitate each other (internal genetic vulnerability interacting with external family support). It is likely that protective factors, like risk factors, also operate in a general way and are nonspecific. In other words, no single risk or protective factors known to date operate to produce a vulnerable or invulnerable child.

Conclusion

The scientific method of epidemiology, through large-scale longitudinal studies, has provided us with a new body of knowledge in which risk and protective factors are becoming better defined in populations that develop psychiatric illness. One way of grouping risk factors is to consider them to fall into 2 categories: (1) internal or systemic to the child, such as inborn temperament, genetic predisposition, very low birthweight, or chronic physical illness; or (2) external or environmental, such as low socioeconomic status, abuse and neglect, major trauma, prenatal drug or alcohol toxicity, and family dysfunction or disruption. While it is difficult to tease apart the interaction of these multiple factors, to define their interactions, or to assign weights to them with our present state of knowledge, it is clear that some are more powerful than others and that they do not act singly but are cumulative.

Epidemiological studies are drawing a new map of developmental psychopathology. By following the course of illness from infancy through adolescence, they show us a better outline of the natural history of mental illness. However, in order to focus in on the specific risk factors that predispose to specific mental disorders, we must proceed from the stage in which we observe large populations to a second stage in which small subgroups of high-risk youngsters taken from these broad surveys are followed closely. The intensive study of smaller high-risk groups from these larger surveys offers the hope of isolating specific risk factors for specific disorders.

This most recent risk factor research is moving toward the identification of "markers," which will identify groups of children at increased risk for particular disorders. The objective is to find a specific marker that identifies those at risk for a specific illness. For example, catecholamine research in child and adolescent psychiatry eventually may discover a marker for those at risk for depression, much as serum cholesterol now does for millions of Americans at risk for coronary artery disease.

Nevertheless, we must never forget that while markers such as elevated cholesterol can identify *groups* at risk, they cannot pinpoint precisely which *individuals* in these groups will be affected. That is a matter for individual clinical judgment. Just as we once falsely assumed that reports of individual clinical cases would tell us about the population at large, we should not now assume that studies of the population at large will define individual clinical cases. Group data cannot substitute for good clinical judgment. But it can provide practitioners with a set of odds, so that they can outline the prognosis for their patients more scientifically and discuss intervention options with families at risk for psychiatric illness with more certainty.

REFERENCES

Bailey, A., LeCouteur, A. & Gottesman, I. (1995). Autism as a strongly genetic disorder: Evidence from a British twin study. *Psychological Medicine, 25,* 63–77.

Beardslee, W., Bemporad, J., Keller, M., & Klerman, G. (1983). Children of parents with major affective disorder: A review. *American Journal of Psychiatry, 140,* 825–832.

Biederman, J., Munir, K., & Knee, D. (1987). Conduct and oppositional disorder in clinically referred children with attention deficit disorder: A controlled family study. *Journal of the American Academy of Child and Adolescent Psychiatry, 26,* 724–727.

Bird, H. R., Gould, M. S., Yager, T., Staghezza, B., & Canino, G. (1989). Risk factors for maladjustment in Puerto Rican children. *Journal of the American Academy of Child and Adolescent Psychiatry, 28,* 847–850.

Costello, A. J., Edelbrock, C. S., Dulcan, M. K., Kalas, R., & Klaric, S. H. (1984). *Development and testing of the NIMH Diagnostic Interview Schedule for Children in a clinic population.* Final report (Contract #RFP-DBB-81-0027) submitted to the Center for Epidemiologic Studies at the National Institute of Mental Health, Rockville, MD.

Curtis, D., Robertson, M. M. & Gurling, H. M. (1992). Autosomal dominant gene transmission in a large kindred with Gilles de la Tourette's syndrome. *British Journal of Psychiatry, 160,* 845–849.

Decker, S. N., & DeFries, J. C. (1980). Cognitive abilities in families with reading disabled children. *Journal of Learning Disabilities, 13,* 53–58.

DeFries, J. C., & Decker, S. N. (1981). Genetic aspects of reading disability: The Colorado family reading study. In P. G. Aaron & M. Malatesha (Eds.), *Neuropsychological and neuropsycholinguistic aspects of reading disability.* New York: Academic Press.

Earls, F., & Jung, K. G. (1987). Temperament and home environment characteristics as causal factors in the early development of childhood psychopathology. *Journal of the American Academy of Child and Adolescent Psychiatry, 26,* 491–498.

Famularo, R., Kinscherff, R., & Fenton, T. (1992). Psychiatric diagnosis of maltreated children. *Journal of the American Academy of Child and Adolescent Psychiatry. 31,* 863–867.

Furstenberg, F., & Nord, C. (1985). Parenting apart. *Journal of Marriage and the Family, 47,* 893–904.

Furstenberg, F., Peterson, J., Nord, C., & Zill, N. (1983). The life course of children of divorce. *American Sociological Review, 48,* 656–668.

Garmezy, N. (1985). Stress resistant children: The search for protective factors. In J. Stevenson (Ed.), *Recent research in developmental psychopathology* (*Journal of Child Psychology and Psychiatry* Book Supplement 4) (pp. 213–233). Oxford: Pergamon Press.

Hetherington, E. (1989). Coping with family transitions. *Child Development, 60,* 1–14.

Hetherington, E., Cox, M., & Cox, R. (1985). Long-term effects of divorce and remarriage on the adjustment of children. *Journal of the American Academy of Child and Adolescent Psychiatry, 24,* 518–530.

Hodges, W. F., Tierney, C. W., & Buchsbaum, H. K. (1984). The cumulative effect of stress on preschool children of divorced and intact families. *Journal of Marriage and the Family, 46,* 611–617.

Holzman, P. (1982). The search for a biological marker of the functional psychoses. In *NIMH Preventive Intervention in Schizophrenia: Are We Ready?* (pp. 19–38) (DHHS Publication No. 82-1111). Washington, DC: U.S. Government Printing Office.

Jensen, P. S., Bloedau, L., Degroot, J., Ussery, T., & Davis, H. (1990). Children at risk: I. Risk factors and child symptomatology. *Journal of the American Academy of Child and Adolescent Psychiatry, 29,* 51–59.

Jones, M. B., Offord, D., & Abrams, N. (1980). Brothers, sisters, and antisocial behavior. *British Journal of Psychiatry, 136,* 139.

Kalter, N., Kloner, A., Schreier, S., & Okla, K. (1989). Predictors of children's postdivorce adjustment. *American Journal of Orthopsychiatry, 59,* 605–618.

Kaufman, J. (1991). Depressive disorders in maltreated children. *Journal of the American Academy of Child and Adolescent Psychiatry, 30,* 257–265.

Kovacs, M. (1997). Depressive disorders in childhood: An impressionistic landscape. *Journal of Child Psychology and Psychiatry, 38,* 287–298.

Kutcher, S., Malkin, D., Silverberg, J., Marton, P., Williamson, P., Malkin, A., Szalai, J., & Katic, M. (1991). Nocturnal cortisol, thyroid stimulating hormone, and growth hormone secretory profiles in depressed adolescents. *Journal of the American Academy of Child and Adolescent Psychiatry, 30,* 407–414.

Levy, F., Hay, D., McStephen, M., Wood, C. & Waldman, I. (1997). Attention deficit hyperactivity disorder: A category or a continuum? Genetic analysis of a large-scale twin study. *Journal of the American Academy of Child and Adolescent Psychiatry, 36,* 737–744.

Lewis, D. O. (1992). From abuse to violence: Psychophysiological consequences of maltreatment. *Journal of the American Academy of Child and Adolescent Psychiatry, 31,* 383–391.

Mednick, S., & McNeil, T. (1968). Current methodology in research on the etiology of schizophrenia: Serious difficulties which suggest the use of the high risk group method. *Psychological Bulletin, 70,* 681–693.

Miller, L. C., Hampe, E., Barrett, C. L., & Noble, H. (1971). Children's deviant behavior within the general population. *Journal Consultation Clinical Psychology, 37,* 16–22.

Offord, D., Boyle, M., Ricine, Y., Flemming, J., Cadman, D., Blum, H., Byrne, C., Links, P., Lipman, E., MacMillan, H., Grant, N., Sanford, M., Szatmari, P., Thomas, H. & Woodward, C. (1992). Outcome, prognosis and risk in a longitudinal follow-up study. *Journal of the American Academy of Child and Adolescent Psychiatry, 31,* 916–923.

Offord, D. R., Boyle, M. H., Zatmari, P. (1987). Ontario

child health study II. *Archives of General Psychiatry, 44,* 832–836.

Orvaschel, H., & Puig-Antich, J. (1987). *Schedule for Affective Disorder and Schizophrenia for School-Age Children Epidemiological Version Kiddie-SADS-E (K-SADS-E)* (4th version).

Portes, P. R., Haas, R. C., & Brown, J. (1991). Identifying family factors that predict children's adjustment to divorce: An analytic synthesis. *Journal of Divorce and Remarriage, 15,* 87–103.

Puig-Antich, J. (1987). Affective disorder in children and adolescents: diagnosis, validity and psychobiology. In H. Y. Meltzer (Ed.), *Psychopharmacology: The third generation of progress.* New York: Raven Press.

Rae-Grant, N., Thomas, B. H., Offord, D. R., & Boyle, M. H. (1989). Risk, protective factors, and the prevalence of behavioral and emotional disorders in children and adolescents. *Journal of the American Academy of Child and Adolescent Psychiatry, 28,* 262–268.

Ritvo, E. R., Freeman, B. J., Pingree, C., Mason-Brothers, A., Jorde, L., Jenson, W. R., McMahon, W. M., Petersen, P. B. Mo, A., & Ritvo, A. (1989). The UCLA-University of Utah epidemiologic survey of autism: Prevalence. *American Journal of Psychiatry, 146,* 194–199.

Ritvo, E. R., Jorde, L., Mason-Brothers, A., Freeman, B. J., Pingree, C., Jones, M. B., McMahon, W. M., Petersen, P. B., Jenson, W. R. & Mo. A. (1989). The UCLA-University of Utah epidemiologic survey of autism: Recurrence risk estimates and genetic counseling. *American Journal of Psychiatry, 146,* 1032–1036.

Rutter, M. (1989). Isle of Wight revisited: 25 years of child psychiatric epidemiology. *Journal of the American Academy of Child and Adolescent Psychiatry, 28,* 633.

Rutter, M., Tizard, J., & Whitmore, K. (1970). *Education, health and behaviour.* London: John Wiley & Sons.

Rutter, M., Tizard, J., Yule, W., Graham, P. & Whitmore, K. (1976). Isle of Wight studies 1964–1974. *Psychological Medicine, 6,* 313–332.

Shaffer, D., Schwab-Stone, M., Fisher, P., Davies, M., Piacentini, J., & Gioia, P. (1988). *A revised version of the Diagnostic Interview Schedule for Children (DISC-R)—Results of a field trial and proposals for a new instrument (DISC-2).* Report submitted to the Division of Epidemiology and Biometrics at the National Institute of Mental Health, Washington, DC.

Silva, P. A., Buckfield, P., & Spears, G. F. (1978). Some maternal and child developmental characteristics associated with breast feeding: A report from the Dunedin multidisciplinary child development study. *Australia Paediatric Journal, 14,* 265–268.

Silva, P. A., McGee, R., & Williams, S. (1984). A longitudinal study of the intelligence and behavior of preterm and small for gestational age children. *Developmental and Behavioral Pediatrics, 5,* 1–5.

Strober, M., Morrell, W., Burroughs, J., Lambert, C., Danforth, H., & Freeman, R. (1988). A family study of bipolar I disorder in adolescence: Early onset of symptoms linked to increased familial loading and lithium resistance. *Journal of Affective Disorders, 15,* 255–268.

Terr, L. (1979). Children of Chowcilla: A study of psychic trauma. *Psychoanalytic Study of the Child, 34,* 547–623.

Wadsworth, M. (1979). *Roots of Delinquency: Infancy, Adolescence, and Crime.* New York: Barnes and Noble Books.

Wallerstein, J. (1991). The long-term effects of divorce on children: A review. *Journal of the American Academy of Child and Adolescent Psychiatry, 30,* 349–360.

Weissman, M., Fendrich, M., Warner, V., & Wickramaratne, P. (1992). Incidence of psychiatric disorder in offspring at high and low risk for depression. *Journal of the American Academy of Child & Adolescent Psychiatry, 31,* 640–648.

Welner, Z., Reich, W., Herjanic, B., Jung, K., & Amado, H. (1987). Reliability, validity, and parent-child agreement studies of the Diagnostic Interview for Children and Adolescents (DICA). *Journal of the American Academy of Child & Adolescent Psychiatry, 26,* 649–653.

Werner, E. (1990). *Antecedents and consequences of deviant behavior.* Unpublished manuscript.

Werner, E. E., Bierman, J. M., & French, F. E. (1971). *The children of Kauai: A longitudinal study from the prenatal period to age 10.* Honolulu: University of Hawaii Press.

Werner, E. E., & Smith, R. S. (1977). *Kauai's children come of age.* Honolulu: University of Hawaii Press.

Werner, E. E., & Smith, R. S. (1982). *Vulnerable but invincible: A longitudinal study of resilient children and youth.* New York: McGraw-Hill.

13 / Demographic and Epidemiologic Studies in Child and Adolescent Psychiatry

Charles E. Holzer III and Christopher R. Thomas

The aim of this chapter is to examine recent progress in identifying sociodemographic risk factors for specific childhood psychiatric disorders. Current epidemiologic work in child disorders is in a state of transition from earlier work, which focused largely on assessment of distributions of symptomatology and developmental problems toward structured diagnostic assessments of specific disorders as defined by the *Diagnostic and Statistical Manual of Mental Disorders, Fourth Edition* (DSMIV), published by the American Psychiatric Association. It is also moving from studies of clinic populations toward school and community household populations.

This transition has been accompanied by a great deal of concern regarding the reliability and validity of alternative assessment procedures and, more fundamentally, a concern for the theoretical and empirical basis for criterion sets used to achieve particular diagnostic categorizations. Over the past decade there has been a great deal of substantive progress, but work on instrumentation continues. Some efforts also have been directed to place classification in a developmental framework with use of longitudinal studies and comparison age groups. Most interesting is ongoing multisite study of Mental Health Services Need, Outcomes and Costs for Children and Adolescent Populations (UNOCAP), funded by the National Institute of Mental Health (NIMH). It is examining epidemiologic and services questions in a large national sample.

Issues in Assessment

ISSUES OF DIAGNOSTIC CRITERIA

Robins and Guze (1970) have described 5 phases for establishing the validity of a diagnostic classification: clinical description, laboratory studies, delimitation from other disorders, follow-up studies, and family studies. The various Diagnostic and Statistical Manuals have been developed

to maximize the utility of diagnosis for both clinical and research purposes.

MEASUREMENT INSTRUMENTS

Current epidemiologic knowledge in child and adolescent psychiatry is based on two kinds of assessment, the first using symptom and behavioral rating scales, and the second using structured diagnostic assessments. Rutter, Tuma, and Lann (1988) have edited a volume reviewing issues of assessment and diagnosis.

Rating Scales: Barkley (1988) reviews a number of checklists and rating scales and identifies assumptions of the rating process, particularly that the rater shares with the researcher some common understanding of the attributes being rated, the corresponding observable behaviors, and the reference points for making ratings. Also at issue is the choice or set of raters, which is typically the parent and/or teacher for children and also may include adolescent self-ratings. When multiple raters are used, the differences in the quality of information from each source must be considered and weighted differentially in combining items into a single assessment. Generally, rating scales can provide acceptable levels of reliability and validity for the constructs they measure, but most do not attempt to provide diagnostic assessments.

A typical set of rating instruments, often used in epidemiologic work, is the Child Behavior Checklist (CBCL) (Achenbach & Edelbrock, 1983), which consists of 118 behavior problem items and 20 social competence items, which are rated by a parent for children ages 4 through 18. A version for ages 2 to 3 is also available. The companion Teacher Report Form (TRF) (Edelbrock & Achenbach, 1984) is designed for ages 5 through 18. The Youth Self Report (YSR) (Achenbach, 1988) which covers similar items, depends on responses from the child, and is considered valid only for ages 11 through 18. The CBCL norms permit comparison to clinical and non-clinical populations within sex and age groups. Multifactorial analysis defined symptom clusters that has served as the basis for describing certain profiles for all symptoms. Further research has been performed comparing these symptom factors to clinically defined disorders. Sometimes self-report instruments developed for adults are also used with adolescents. Examples are the Center for Epidemiologic Studies Depression Scale (CES-D) developed by Radloff (1977) and a child version, the CES-DC developed by Fendrich, Weissman, and Warner (1990). See also Garrison, Addy, Jackson, McKeowan, and Waller (1991).

Diagnostic Interviews: Within adult psychiatric research, the improved reliability and validity of using structured diagnostic assessments, as compared to unstructured interviews, has been well established. Some adult interviews are designed for use by experienced clinicians, such as the Schedule For affective Disorders and Schizophrenia (SADS) and the Structured Clinical Interview for *DSM-IV* (SCID), while others have been designed for use by lay interviewers, such as the Diagnostic Interview Schedule (DIS) and the Composite International Diagnostic Interview (CIDI).

Diagnostic assessment for children and adolescents has followed a parallel course, although it is made more difficult because young persons are less familiar with the concepts and terminology used to describe psychiatric symptomatology. This makes young children very difficult to interview effectively, and questions for adolescents must be stated in familiar terms. Parents and/or teachers typically are used as informants for children and adolescents, although adolescents typically are interviewed as well. The relative validity of the information from these different sources has been a point of much attention (Herjanic, Herjanic, Brown, and Wheatt, 1975) and the rules for combining information from different sources have been hotly debated.

Edelbrock and Costello (1988) and Hodges (1993) have provided reviews of structured psychiatric interviews for children and adolescents, although continuing revisions of the instruments makes such reviews rapidly outdated. As with adult instruments, clinician and lay instruments are available. The Schedule for Affective Disorders and Schizophrenia for School-Aged Children (Kiddie SADS) (Puig-Antich & Chambers, 1978) is typical of the clinician instruments and is modeled on an adult counterpart, which used the Research Diagnostic Criteria. An epidemiologic version, the Kiddie-SADS-E, is available for lifetime diagnosis (Orvaschel, Puig-Antich, Chambers, Tabrizi, and Johnson, 1982). Herjanic and Campbell

(1977), and Herjanic and Reich (1982) developed a structured diagnostic instrument, modeled on the DIS, and for use by lay interviewers. Reich (1991) has developed more recent version of the Diagnostic Interview for Children and Adolescents (DICA), with parent and adolescent versions, as well as a computer administered version. Another diagnostic interview is the Child Assessment Schedule (CAS) (Hodges, McKnew, Cytryn, Stern, & Kline, 1982).

The Diagnostic Interview Schedule for Children (DISC) is another structured instrument that can be administered by trained lay persons. It grew out of an expert advisory panel at the National Institute of Mental Health, Division of Biometry and Epidemiology. The initial draft was produced by Herjanic and colleagues with a first set of revisions and evaluation by Costello, Edelbrock, Kalas, Kessler, and Klaric (1982). Costello's revisions included child and parent versions and a computer program for administration and scoring. Comparisons were also made between psychiatric and pediatric referred samples (Costello, Edelbrock, & Costello, 1985). From 1985, Shaffer and colleagues undertook additional evaluation of the DISC leading to revisions DISC-R (1988) and a new version, DISC-2 (Fisher, Wicks, Shaffer, Piacentini, and Lapkin, 1992). Further development of the DISC-2 was sponsored by NIMH as part of the Cooperative Agreement for Methods for the Epidemiology Child and Adolescent of Mental Disorders (MECA). This program has included field testing of DISC-2, Version 2.3 at 4 sites and is described below. Version 2.3 of the DISC is described by Shaffer et al. (1996). Schwab-Stone et al. (1996) report "moderate to good validity across a number of diagnoses," and "some specific diagnostic areas in which further revision of the DISC is warranted." The current revision is DISC-IV, which has been modified for *DSM-IV* and for use in the UNOCAP study. A computer program is available to support administration and scoring of the DISC.

Selective Review of Community Surveys

Vikan (1985) has provided a review of 11 epidemiologic studies of psychiatric disorder in children published during the period from 1958 to 1978.

Among these was the study by Rutter, Tizard, and Whitmore (1970) in the Isle of Wight, which reported relatively low prevalence of 6.8% for children ages 10 to 11, based on parent, teacher, and child information. This contrasted with Rutter's London study, which had a much higher prevalence of 25.4% based primarily on teacher reports. Other studies in Vikan's review provided prevalences ranging from Rutter's 6.8% to a maximum of 29.8%, with a median of approximately 18%. This wide range of variability is seen as resulting from the differing criteria (before the *DSM-III*), instruments, informants, ages of children, and national or geographical settings.

Brandenburg, Friedman, and Silver (1990) have reviewed a more recent generation of 8 studies conducted from 1978 through 1986. These include: Connell, Irvine, and Rodney (1982), Verhulst, Akerhuis, and Althaus (1985), Vikan (1985), Anderson, Williams, McGhee, and Silva (1987), Cohen, Velez, Kohn, Schwab-Stone, and Johnson (1987), Kashani, Orvaschel, Rosenberg, and Reid (1987), Offord et al. (1987), and Bird et al. (1988). Although these studies vary in methodology and instrumentation, 6 of the 8 adopted *DSM-III* criteria, with the remaining 2 using Rutter's classification. Instruments for assessing *DSM-III* criteria in these studies included: the CBCL (n = 4), the DICA (n = 1), the DISC (n = 2), and the CAS (n = 1). The CBCL was sometimes used as a screener to identify cases for later diagnostic interview (e.g. Bird, et al., 1988) and other times for assessing specific *DSM-III* criteria (Offord et al., 1987). Age ranges varied by study, but were as low as 4 and as high as 19. Within this set, overall prevalence rates range from a low of 5.0% (Vikan, 1985), through a high of 26.0%, when moderate and severe criteria were combined (Verhulst, Berden, and Sanders-Woudstra, 1985). Again, age of child, specific instrumentation, type of informant, and location vary among the studies. Now we turn to an in depth examination of some of these studies.

THE QUEENSLAND STUDY

Connell, Irvine, and Rodney (1992) screened 779 children 10 to 11 years of age in schools in Queensland, Australia, by administering the Rutter A and B scales to parents and teachers, and following the 176 who screened positive with semistructured interviews of parents and their children. Overall prevalence was 14.1%. Rates were only slightly higher for girls (7.2% than for

boys (6.9%). Highest rates were found for metropolitan areas (18.4%), with intermediate rates for urban (15.1%) and lowest for rural areas (10.0%). This finding parallels Rutter's comparison of the Isle of Wight with London. The higher rates for metropolitan areas as compared to rural areas was found for each of three diagnostic categories: emotional disorders (9.2% vs 3.7%), conduct disorder (8.3% vs 5.7%), and other (0.9% vs 0.7%).

THE NETHERLANDS STUDY

Verhulst, Akerhuis, and Althaus (1985) obtained a school based sample of children ages 8 and 11 years from which they solicited CBCLs from 334 parents and TRFs from 292 teachers. Of these they selected and interviewed subsamples of 78 children scoring high and 75 scoring low. They used Hodges' Child Assessment Schedule (CAS) for the interview. Based on the CBCL and TRF scores, the overall prevalence for severe disorder was 7% and 26% for moderate and severe combined. Among 8 year old children, 13% were identified with severe and 27% with moderate and severe disorder. For children age 11, the corresponding prevalence rates are 4% for severe and 24% for severe plus moderate disorder. Approximately twice as many boys as girls (2.4:1) were diagnosed. Within subtypes of disorder, attention deficit disorder with hyperactivity was most common for boys and overanxious disorder for girls. With regard to risk factors, the authors stated that "poor marital relationships, parental lack of empathy, maternal hostility, and frequent conflicts with the child were highly associated with psychiatric problems in the child" (pg. 40). In a later study of international adoptees, Verhulst, Althaus, and Versluis-den Bieman (1992) indicated that damaging backgrounds similar to those above, and additionally physical abuse were associated with poor adjustment.

THE NORWAY STUDY

Vikan (1985) conducted a study of 1510 children born in North Trondelag County of Norway. Initial data were collected by questionnaires mailed to parents and returned through the schools, with additional questionnaires for teachers and school nurses. These were based on the work of Rutter, Tizard, & Whitmore (1970). Interviews with parents and children were obtained for those above Rutter's cutoff scores. When combined, the ratings provided an overall prevalence of 5% for problems primarily psychological in nature and an additional 3% for other problems, such as mental retardation and hyperkinesis. The estimate of 7% is regarded as low in comparison to other studies. The low rates are in part attributed to the homogeneous, stable, rural nature of the county being examined and the initial selection of a cohort born in the county. This is supported by the lower rate of 4.6% for lifelong residents and 6% for migrants.

THE NEW ZEALAND STUDY

Anderson, Williams, McGee, and Silva (1987, 1989) interviewed 792 eleven year old children from a birth cohort in Dunedin, New Zealand, using the original Child Version of the DISC and administered the Rutter Child Scale A to parents and the Rutter B scale to teachers. Overall, 17.6% of the sample met diagnostic criteria, with 7.3% having criteria confirmed by 2 or more informants. More than half (55%) of those diagnosed had more than one disorder.

Boys had nearly twice as many disorders as girls, a ratio of 1.8 to 1. Among boys, attention deficit disorder was most common (n = 45, 10.8%), followed by oppositional disorder (n = 32, 7.8%) and conduct disorder (aggressive) (n = 21, 5.0%). For girls, separation anxiety was most common (n = 19, 5.0%), followed by oppositional disorder (n = 13, 3.5%) and simple phobia (n = 12, 3.2%). Interestingly, depression/dysthymia was more common in boys (n = 12, 2.8%) than girls (n = 2, 0.5%), a contrast to adult ratios.

In further analyses by Anderson, Williams, McGee, and Silva (1989), externalizing disorders were identified as more frequent for boys, and internalizing disorders were about even for boys and girls. Poor peer socialization was identified as a correlate of having multiple disorders. Further, those with multiple disorders and those with conduct disorders, particular aggressive children, were identified as having more disadvantaged families than those without disorders.

McGee et al. (1990) describe the extension of this study of 11-year-old children with interviews at age 13 and 15. They report on 962 adolescents interviewed at age 15 using a shortened version of the DISC child interview. Most children had been interviewed at age 11 along with a parent and a teacher, but some additional respondents from the same birth cohort also were interviewed. At age 15 as many as 22% had 1 or more disorders, an increase from the 17.6% initially diagnosed.

Significantly more females (25.9%) had a disorder as compared to males (18.2%). The most common disorders for females and males were overanxious disorder (5.9%), conduct disorder-nonaggressive (5.7%), simple phobia (3.6%), attention deficit disorder (2.1%), and separation anxiety (2.0%). Major depression was less common (1.9%), as was dysthymia (1.1%). Major depression had the highest female-to-male sex ratio, while conduct disorder-aggressive (1.6% overall) was present only for boys.

McGee, Feehan, Williams, and Anderson (1992) have examined the cohort with data both at ages 11 and 15. They specifically note the reversal of the boy-to-girl sex ratio from 1.3 to 1 at age 11 to 0.7 to 1 at age 15. However, substantial change occurred among which children were identified as having disorders. Of the 66 with disorder at age 11, only 28 (42%) had a disorder at age 15. Similarly, of the 147 having a disorder at age 15, only 28 (19%) had a disorder at age 11; (81%) did not. Family disadvantage was significantly associated with the occurrence of new disorder.

THE NEW YORK STUDY

Velez, Johnson and Cohen (1989) presented results from a longitudinal study in upstate New York that began in 1975 with 976 mothers with at least one child between the ages of 1 and 10 years. Structured interviews collected data about the health status of the child as well as various risk factors. In 1983 and again in 1985 the mothers were reinterviewed and the children interviewed using the Costello's version of the DISC-I. The data from mother and child were combined through the original Costello scoring program and a revised set of *DSM-III-R* based algorithms (Cohen, Velez, Kohn, Schwab-Stone, and Johnson, 1987). This algorithm considered both sources of information for individual symptoms and combined them into diagnoses, resulting in diagnoses that were more strongly to risk factors.

Prevalence rates (Velez et al., 1989) were reported by age group and year of interview. Overall prevalence of 1 or more severe diagnoses in 1983 was 19.4% for ages 9 to 12; it was 16.4% for ages 13 to 18. For 1985 those 11 to 14 years of age had a prevalence of 15.6%; those 15 to 20 had a prevalence of 16.0%. The inclusion of probable as well as severe diagnoses would have produced much higher estimates.

The examination of specific disorders includes

severe and probable diagnoses. The highest estimates for specific disorders included separation anxiety, which was 25.6% for ages 9 to 12 in 1983, and decreased to 15.3% by 1985. The prevalence of separation anxiety was 6.8% for those 13 to 18 years of age in 1983, and decreased to 4.4% by 1985. Overanxiety (19.1%), attention deficit disorder (16.6%), oppositional disorder (15.6%) and conduct disorder (11.9%) were all relatively high for those 9 to 12 years of age in 1983. For both age groups, most of these disorders decreased in prevalence by the 1985 interview, with the exception of oppositional disorder which increased from 15.6% to 22.5% for those 9 to 12 years of age in 1983, and major depression which was unchanged at 2.5% in the same age group.

Although sex-specific rates were not presented, a higher prevalence was found for males in the younger age group for attention deficit disorder and conduct disorder 1983 and for conduct disorder in 1985. A female preponderance was found for overanxiety in the older age group in 1983 and 1985. Major depression was significantly more common for females in the older age group in 1983 and the younger age group in 1985, but not elsewhere. This appears to anticipate the emergence of the 2 to 1 female-to-male sex ratio found for depression in adults (Weissman, Leaf, Holzer, Myers, and Tischler, 1984).

In an initial analysis of the stability of these childhood problems from 1975 to 1983, Cohen and Brook (1987) indicated that, "On the whole, long-term risk tended to be associated with the characteristics of the family not limited to the parent-child relationship-poverty, poor housing, family instability, and family sociopathy" (p. 344). Stability over that long a period was moderately low, being 0.44 for behavior problems, 0.48 for immaturity, 0.46 for anxiety, and only 0.23 for affective problems.

In a later analysis, risk factors from the 1975 interviews were examined for their association with prevalence in 1983 and risk factors from 1983 were compared with 1985 prevalence. Low socioeconomic status factors such as income and education were associated with conduct disorder, attention deficit disorder, oppositional disorder, overanxiety, and separation anxiety, but not generally with major depression. Family structure, such as the mother having never been married or divorced, was associated with conduct disorder and oppositional disorder. Being non-white was associated with separation anxiety in 1983 and conduct disorder in 1985, but not otherwise. Socio-

pathy in the parents was associated with conduct disorder, attention deficit disorder, and oppositional disorder (externalizing disorders) in 1983 and conduct and attention deficit disorders in 1985. Child characteristics such as repeating a grade, mental health treatment, and stressful life events were associated with all 1985 disorders except separation anxiety.

As an additional methodological evaluation, 100 of the mother-child pairs from the longitudinal study were reinterviewed using The Schedule for Affective Disorders and Schizophrenia for School-Aged Children (Kiddie SADS), with clinician and algorithm based diagnoses compared to DISC possible and probable diagnoses (Cohen, O'Conner, Lewis, Velez, & Machowski, 1987). This comparison resulted in significant but only moderate agreement between K-SADS (possible) and DISC (probable) diagnoses. Kappas were highest for oppositional disorder ($\kappa = 0.38$), and moderately less for conduct disorder and separation anxiety. Agreement was poor for major depression. Agreement with DISC possible diagnoses was lower and the prevalence rates were thought to be excessive.

THE MISSOURI STUDY

Kashani and colleagues (Kashani, et al., 1987; Kashani, Daniel, Sulzberger, Rosenberg, and Reid, 1987; Kashani & Orvaschel, 1988) drew a stratified random sample from the school system with equal numbers of girls and boys in each age group from 14 to 16 years. Parents were administered the CBCL and the DICA-Parent version. Children completed the DICA and a set of questionnaires, including the Piers-Harris Children's Self-Concept Scale. Cases were defined according to *DSM-III* and based on combined parent and child information. Sixty-two (41.3%) of the adolescents had at least one *DSM-III* diagnosis based on the DICA. When additional criteria for impairment and need for treatment were added via the psychiatrist review, prevalence dropped to 18.7%, with 16% of boys and 21% of girls being positive. The most common diagnoses for girls were anxiety disorder (13.3%) and depression (including major depression and dysthymia) (13.3%), followed by oppositional disorder (8.0%). For boys, conduct disorder (9.3%) was most common, followed by substance abuse (6.7%).

In a later study, Kashani and Orvaschel (1990) sampled 210 children ages 8, 12, and 17 years. These were assessed using Hodges' Child Assessment Schedule and the Revised Children's Manifest Anxiety Scale. Overall 21% of the sample was identified as having an anxiety disorder, with 25.7% for age 8, 15.7% for age 12, and 21.4% for age 17. Separation anxiety was most common in the youngest age group (18.6%) and overanxious disorder in the 2 older groups (17.1% and 9.5%). More girls had anxiety disorders (28.6%) than boys (13.3%), with separation anxiety and overanxious disorder being the most common in both groups.

THE ONTARIO STUDY

Offord and colleagues (Boyle et al., 1987; Offord et al., 1987; Offord, Boyle and Racine, 1989; Links, Boyle and Offord, 1989; Bowen, Offord, & Boyle, 1990; Boyle & Offord, 1991) conducted a survey of 2679 children age 4 to 16 sampled from households throughout the province of Ontario. Data collection included interviews and questionnaires based primarily on Achenbach's CBCL, TRF, and YSR. Assessment focused primarily on conduct disorder, hyperactivity (attention deficit disorder with hyperactivity), emotional disorder, and somatization. *DSM-III* disorders were based on items selected from the CBCL plus six additional items, and were for a 6-month prevalence period. The overall prevalence estimate was 18.1% with a 95% confidence bound of plus or minus 1.7%. Prevalence varied from 15.5% to 19.5% among 4 geographical regions, but was not significant. Overall disorder varied significantly by urban-rural residence and age and sex, with rates (19.5%) for boys 4 to 11 years of age being higher than the rates (18.8%) for boys 12 to 16 years of age, and the rates (21.8%) for older girls being greater than the rates (13.5%) for younger girls.

In considering specific disorders, rates of conduct disorder were higher among older boys (10.4%) as compared to younger boys (6.5%) and greater than either older (4.1%) or younger (1.8%) girls. Hyperactivity was more frequent for both younger boys (10.1%) and older boys (7.3) than for girls of the same ages (3.3% and 3.4%) respectively. Rates of emotional disorder were higher for older girls (13.6%) than for younger girls (10.7%), but higher for younger boys (10.2%) than for older boys (4.9%). Somatization was 10.7% in older girls and 4.5% in older boys. It was noted that psychiatric disorders did not cluster in households where multiple children were studied, although service utilization did cluster. Mental health or social services were received by

16.1% of the children with disorder as compared to only 4.3% of children without disorder. In a later analysis, Bowen, Offord, and Boyle (1990) used items from the original survey to estimate prevalence for *DSM-III-R* overanxious disorder as 3.6% and the prevalence of separation anxiety disorder as 2.4%.

In 1987 follow up interviews were conducted with 652 adolescents who had been 13–16 years of age in the original 1983 survey (Boyle, Offord, Racine, and Catlin, 1991; Fleming, Boyle, and Offord, 1993). Adolescents were asked to complete a self-report instrument based on the Diagnostic Interview Schedule of Robins, with *DSM-III* criteria used to generate diagnoses. Data from the 1983 survey were used to approximate *DSM-III* criteria for major depressive syndrome and conduct disorder. The effect of using information from parent only, youth only, both, or either was considered, with the more liberal either-informant positive approach resulting in a prevalence of 5.4% for major depressive syndrome and 5.2% for conduct disorder. In the 1983 data, major depression was more common in girls (6.9%) than boys (3.9%), while conduct disorder was more common in boys (9%) than girls (0.6%). Only 25% of those who met the approximate criteria for major depressive syndrome in 1983 met criteria for major depressive syndrome in 1987, as compared to 6.9% of those who initially had neither major depressive syndrome or conduct disorder. Of those identified with conduct disorder in 1983, 12.5% reported antisocial personality in 1987, as compared to 0.7% without initial conduct disorder, and 23.1% reported substance abuse as compared to 2.1% without initial conduct disorder. This comparison suggests that some but not the majority of "cases" in 1983 had persistent illness, while remission was the norm.

THE PUERTO RICO STUDY

Bird, and colleagues (Bird et al., 1988; Bird et al., 1990) collected data on 777 children 4 to 17 years of age who were identified in a larger survey of households in 210 areas of Puerto Rico. One child was selected at random where more than 1 child was present. The study used a 2 stage psychiatric evaluation, with the first stage (n = 777) being based on interviewer administration of the Achenbach's Child Behavior Checklist to a parent, usually the mother. Additional information about the child and household was collected in that interview. For children 6 to 16 years of age, the

Teacher Report Form was administered to the child's homeroom teacher as part of the first stage.

The second stage assessment (n = 386) was offered to a random sample of 20% of those in the first stage and all those who scored over published cutoff ranges for either the CBCL or TRF. The second stage was carried out by 1 of 4 board certified psychiatrists who administered Costello's 1985 version of the Diagnostic Interview Schedule for Children (DISC) to the child and a parent. Using clinical judgment and all information available the psychiatrists made *DSM-III* diagnoses. Additionally the psychiatrists rated the Child Global Assessment Scale (CGAS) (Shaffer et al., 1983) based on their interview information. Psychiatrists were not provided the CBCL data from stage 1, although they had contact with the parent who provided it.

In the first stage, 37.8% of children were rated above the cutoff by their parent and 23.2% by their teacher. This resulted in 45.2% (weighted) being identified as positive on the screen, with parent and teacher agreeing on 14.7% of the total positives. Next the second-stage positives were weighted based on the first and second stages, resulting in prevalence rates based on the DISC interviews separately and in conjunction with the CGAS ratings. Those with a positive DISC diagnosis and a CGAS rating below 61 were considered definite cases, providing a weighted prevalence of 17.9%. Those with DISC diagnosis and CGAS rating of 61–70 were considered to have possible diagnoses, for a prevalence of approximately 16.0%. The overall prevalence of those with DISC diagnoses was 49.5%.

Specific prevalence rates are presented with CGAS scores as an indication for impairment. For CGAS scores below 61, identified as definite cases, specific rates are: oppositional disorder, 9.9%; attention deficit, 9.5%; depression/dysthymia, 5.9%; separation anxiety, 4.7%; functional enuresis, 4.7%; adjustment disorder, 4.2%; and simple phobias, 2.6%. Rates are substantially higher when a less restrictive measure of impairment is used. The need for this additional criterion of impairment is developed by Bird et al. (1990), and the reliability of the CGAS is examined by Bird et al. (1987).

Risk factors are also assessed for this sample. Generally, the presence of any disorder was greater for males than females and for the lowest socioeconomic status (SES) group. Oppositional disorder was greater for males and low SES chil-

dren. The prevalence of attention deficit disorder was greater for older, male, and lower SES children. The prevalence of depression was greater in the older and in the low SES children. The prevalence of separation anxiety was higher in the middle age group and in the low SES group. Phobias were more common in the low SES group.

A potential risk factor for childhood disorder is the presence of disorder in 1 or more parents. This was assessed in an analysis by Canino, Bird, Rubio-Stipec, Bravo, and Alegria (1990) by matching up children with assessments of their parents in the corresponding adult mental health survey (Canino, Bird, Shrout et al., 1990). This comparison was based on the first stage CBCL, TRF, and YSR ratings. Generally, total problem behaviors, internalizing and externalizing scores on both the CBCL and the YSR were significantly higher for children of parents with a diagnosis. Differences on the same scales of the TRF were smaller and non-significant.

THE MECA STUDY

In preparation for a planned national epidemiologic study, the National Institute for Mental Health (NIMH) initiated a multisite methodological collaborative agreement called the Methods for the Epidemiology of Child and Adolescent Mental Disorders Study (MECA) (Shaffer et al., 1996). The participants in the study were Emory University, the New York State Psychiatric Institute, Yale University, and the University of Puerto Rico, in addition to NIMH. The design used samples of children 9 to 17 years of age, who were representative of the four study sites, with a total sample size of 1,285. In each household the child and a parent or guardian were interviewed by lay interviewers using the respective child or parent versions of the DISC Version 2.3, and additional instruments for ascertaining functional impairment, demographic background, services utilization, and other characteristics likely to be risk factors for mental illness. The DISC parent interviews averaged 1 hour in duration and child interviews averaged 70 minutes, exclusive of other interview components.

Prevalence rates are reported for 4 different conditions, including: (1) met *DSM-III-R* criteria, (2) met *DSM-III-R* criteria and had a Childrens' Global Assessment Score (CGAS) below one of three specified thresholds, (3) met DSM-III-R criteria and met diagnosis specific impairment criteria, and (4) met *DSM-III-R*, CGAS, and diagnostic specific criteria simultaneously (Shaffer et al., 1996, pg 870). The prevalence rates are reported for specific disorders and for summary groups. The prevalence for any of the DSM-III-R disorders assessed, when no impairment criteria were imposed, was 30.3% from parent information, 32.2% from youth information, and 50.6% when both sources were combined. Imposition of diagnostic specific impairment criteria brought the dual informant rate down to 32.8%. Additionally, imposition of CGAS functional impairment criteria lowered the prevalence of any disorder to 20% for CGAS ≤ 70, 11.5% for CGAS ≤ 60, and only 5.4% for CGAS ≤ 50. Thus it becomes clear that functional impairment criteria are as important in determining prevalence rates as the standard *DSM-III-R* criteria. Moreover, this pattern is replicated within each of the specific disorders. For major depression the rate based on *DSM-III-R* criteria alone is 7.1% for combined child and parent reports, but decreases to 5.6% when diagnosis specific impairment criteria are imposed, and drops to only 1.9% when a CGAS ≤ 50 is also required.

Achieving consensus on these additional measures of functional impairment remains one of the major challenges for the epidemiology of child psychiatric disorders. Further, the discrepancies in prevalence rates based on child and parental reports make the source of information and the means by which it is combined very important. Finally, Schwab-Stone et al. (1996) report on the validation component of the MECA study. Of the original 1,285 children studied, 134 who screened positive for disorder and 113 who screened negative for disorder received clinician administered DISC validation interviews an average of 12.6 days after the initial lay interview. Test-retest validity is identified as moderate to good, with evidence presented for more validity for parent reports and less validity for child reports. The disorders with the highest validity for parent reports were attention deficit, oppositional, and conduct disorders. Anxiety disorders had the least test-retest validity for both child and parent informants and for their information combined.

COMMENT

In this section we have reviewed a representative selection of the general community studies looking at mental disorder in children, emphasiz-

ing studies assessing multiple disorders and *DSM-III* or later diagnostic categorizations. We have emphasized substantive findings instead of the methodologic issues that abound at this stage of development of the field. A number of consistent as well as many contradictory substantive patterns have emerged. For example, overall prevalence of disorder seems to increase somewhat with age from childhood through adolescence and perhaps into early adulthood. On the other hand, this pattern does not hold for each of the specific types of disorder, as will be discussed later. Further, there is some indication that sex ratios may change with age and the specific disorders considered. In the Ontario study, young boys had more disorder than young girls, but by adolescence, this finding was reversed. Some of these inconsistencies make better sense within the context of specific disorders, for example depression, anxiety disorders, and conduct disorder.

Related to age distributions is the extent to which disorders are transient or persist and develop over time. Historically, many researchers have thought that childhood disorders are sufficiently transient that formal diagnoses are inappropriate or not particularly useful. The longitudinal studies suggest much greater continuity over time, particularly for conduct disorder and possibly depression. The studies reviewed tended to make urban-rural or other geographic comparisons, with somewhat higher rates generally reported for urban areas. In such comparisons, issues such as access to care may influence both treatment and familiarity with the concepts used.

Given the diversity of locations studied, there is naturally interest in race, ethnicity, and other cultural factors. These factors usually are confounded with socioeconomic status as well as minority status. Socioeconomic status generally appears to be more strongly related to externalizing and specifically conduct disorders than to internalizing disorders. Although not addressed by the studies discussed, general health and physical abuse are also factors in child and adolescent emotional health. Specific studies include: Verhulst, Akerhuis, and Althaus, (1985); Verhulst, Berden, and Sanders-Woudstra (1985); and Verhulst, Althaus, and Versluis-den Bieman (1992). Canino's work provides evidence for parental illness as a risk for child illness.

TABLE 13.1

Estimates of Child and Adolescent Major Depression from Community Surveys

Ages	Prevalence (%)	Time Frame	Instruments	Reference
4–16	5.9°	Past 6 mos.	CBCL,DISC,CGAS	Bird et al.(1988)
6–16	5.9	Past 6 mos.	SDI	Fleming et al.(1989)
7–11	0.4child/0.6parent°°	Past Year	CBCL,DISC	Costello et al.(1988)
7–12	1.9	Current	Interview	Kashani & Simonds(1979)
8	1.4child/0.7parent	Current	CAS	Kashani et al.(1989)
9	1.8	Current	Symptoms,KSADS-E	Kashani et al.(1983)
9–17	4.8child/3.1parent	Past 6 mos.	DISC	Shaffer et al.(1996)
9–18	6.4child/1.0parent	Past 6 mos.	DISC	Velez et al.(1989)
11	0.5	Past Year	DISC,RCS	Anderson et al.(1987)
11–17	4.4	Current	CES-D	Garrison et al.(1989)
12	5.7child/2.9parent	Current	CAS	Kashani et al.(1989)
12–16	2.9	Current	CES-D	Schoenbach et al.(1982)
13	0.4	Current	DISC,RBPC	McGee & Williams(1988)
14–16	4.7	Current	DICA	Kashani et al.(1987a,b)
16.6 avg.	2.6	Current	KSADS-E/P	Roberts et al.(1995)
16–19	8.3	Lifetime	DIS	Deykin et al. (1987)

°Includes depression and dysthymia with CGAS<61.
°°Separate prevalence rates derived from child and parent reports.
Adapted from Tables 1, 2, and 3 in Fleming and Offord (1990:572–574).

Review for Mood Disorders

PREVALENCE ESTIMATES

The epidemiology of childhood and adolescent depression and other mood disorders has been reviewed by: Angold (1988 a,b); Stavrakaki and Gaudet (1989); Kutcher and Marton (1989); Fleming and Offord (1990); and Birmaher et al. (1996). Angold (1988) emphasized the need for specificity in what is meant by the term *depression* and has summarized symptom prevalence where available. For 13 studies reporting prevalence for depression, rates ranged from a low of 0.14% to a high of 49%, with a median of 15%. Fleming and Offord (1990) reviewed a slightly later set of studies based primarily on *DSM-III* criteria and found a range from 0 to 8.3% for major depression, 0.6 to 8.0% for dysthymia, and a maximum based on a scale score of 15 to 28%. See Table 1, which is adapted from Fleming and Offord (1990) with two additional citations. Rates were generally higher for older respondents, and for lifetime versus current prevalence. The highest estimate for any depressive disorder was 15–18%, which came

from an index of 6 depressive symptoms (Kandel and Davies, 1982). The high variability in rates is due largely to differences in methodology, particularly case definition, the prevalence period, and the informants used.

Before proceeding with an examination of demographics, we want to note 2 sets of studies that show alternatives to the more comprehensive community studies just noted. The first of these is the work of Kovacs (Kovacs, Gatsonis, Paulauskas, and Richards, 1989; Kovacs, Paulauskas, and Richards, 1988; Kovacs, Feinberg, Crouse-Novak, Paulauskas, and Finkelstein, 1984; Kovacs, Feinberg, Crouse-Novak, Paulauskas, Pollock, and Finkelstein, 1984; and Kovacs, Goldston, and Gatsonis (1993). Kovacs' study is based on 142 depressed and 49 nondepressed outpatients, who were followed for up to 12 years. They showed some stability in the presence and development of depressive disorder, a consistent pattern of suicidal ideation, and a general increase in suicide attempts with age. Methodologically, the prospective study is to be commended, because it helps to answer questions about the transition from childhood to adult depressive disorder.

The work of Garrison is also mentioned because it represents an adaptation of the 2-stage model to depressive disorder. Garrison, Schluchter, Schoenbach, & Kaplan (1989) used the CES-D (Radloff, 1977) and a demographic questionnaire to screen 677 junior high school students. In the next 2 years the CES-D was readministered in the same school, resulting in a panel of 550 individuals who participated in all 3 years of the study. Among the major findings were higher depression scores for blacks than whites. This is consistent with some other studies (e.g. Warheit, Holzer, and Schwab, 1973) but does not consider the influence of socioeconomic factors or ethnic differences for lifetime versus current depression and dysthymia in the Epidemiologic Catchment Area project (Weissman, Bruce, Leaf, Florio, & Holzer, 1991). Higher scores were found for females than for males, which is also consistent with other reports and with the sex ratio found in most studies of adult depression (Weissman et al., 1984). Over the 3 years of follow up, Garrison found only moderate stability in depression scores. Although 90% of the low scorers continued to have low scores, only 30% of high scorers remained high over a year. In comparison, Edelsohn et al. (1992) found stability in depressive symptoms over a 4 month period, even for first graders. Kandel and Davies (1982; 1986) showed relative stability of scores on a brief depression scale over 8 years. More recently, Garrison et al. (1997) have reported a 1 year incidence of 3.3% for ages 11 to 16.

Garrison et al. (1991) report a validation study in which 332 mother-adolescent pairs from the longitudinal study were interviewed by nurse clinicians who administered the K-SADS-E. This analysis suggests that the CES-D performed only moderately well when compared to the K-SADS-E, although it should be noted that the K-SADS-E is designed primarily as a lifetime instrument and the CES-D focuses on the past week. Analyses yielded better sensitivity and specificity for females than males at several different cutting points, and Receiver Operating Curve analyses suggested the need for a higher cutting point (e.g., 20) for adolescents than the score of 16 typically used with the CES-D for adults.

DEMOGRAPHIC AND OTHER RISK FACTORS FOR DEPRESSION

Age appears positively associated with depression, with lower rates for children, increasing into adolescence, when the rates stabilize. In childhood, there is some evidence that depression is more prevalent in boys than in girls. However, depression is more prevalent in females than in males during adolescence, as is found for adults. There continues to be some question as to the age at which the adult pattern arises, although Angold (1988a,b) suggests that the issue may be the onset of puberty rather than age per se. The relationship of socioeconomic status (SES) to depression in children and adolescence is less well established. Adult findings from the ECA show a modest relationship between depression and SES (Holzer et al., 1986).

Race also bears an uncertain relationship to depression. Higher symptom scores for blacks than whites have been reported by Garrison et al. (1989), but not in most other studies. A binational study in south Texas and northern Mexico (Swanson et al., 1992) found CES-D scores to relate to perceived poverty, and to be lower in Mexican nationals than in the Mexican Americans living in Texas. In contrast, another study in the same area found higher CES-D scores in Mexican Americans than in non Hispanic whites. African American girls in the same sample had lower scores than the Mexican American girls, but African American boys had somewhat higher scores than their Mexican American counterparts. Thus, much more work needs to be done to understand race and/or ethnicity in this context.

Family dysfunction appears to contribute to depression in children and adolescents (Bird, et al. 1988, Garrison, Schoenbach, and Kaplan, 1985, Garrison et al., 1997, Kandel and Davies, 1982, and Kashani and Orvaschel, 1988). The presence of disorder in the parents appears to contribute to depression in children and adolescents. This is seen as association between parental disorder and CBCL scores (Canino et al., 1990) and also as increased risk for depressive disorders in relatives of depressed probands (Weissman, 1988).

Conclusion

Child epidemiologic surveys have documented significant and discrete mental disorders in children and adolescents. Surveys have shown some of these disorders to be stable over time and predictive of adult outcome. As in adult studies, significant differences are found based on sex, age, socioeconomic status, culture, and familial factors, including parental disorder. Standardized instruments utilizing a variety of information sources have been developed encompassing most childhood disorders. Even so, there is a great deal of methodological work under way and yet to be done to refine the diagnostic categories and the instrumentation to assess these disorders. Improved procedures for taking into account the information from multiple informants must be found. Recent and ongoing studies show an appropriate emphasis on dealing with these methodological issues. Further, we expect the UNOCAP project or equivalent large surveys to ascertain prevalence rates with greater precision, their association to current and developmental risk factors, and ideally the course of disorder over time. Greater emphasis on longitudinal studies is needed to define developmental differences in the expression and course of specific disorders. Longitudinal studies will reveal the influence of risk factors in a developmental framework, as they relate to the incidence of disorder and not just its prevalence.

REFERENCES

Achenbach, T. M. (1988). *Youth Self Report*. Burlington, VT: University Associates in Psychiatry.

Achenbach, T. M. & Edelbrock, C. (1983). *Manual for the Child Behavior Checklist and Revised Child Behavior Profile*. Burlington, VT: Thomas M. Achenbach.

Anderson, J., Williams, S., McGee, R., & Silva, P. (1987). DSM-III disorders in preadolescent children. *Archives of General Psychiatry, 44,* 69–76.

Anderson, J., Williams, S., McGee, R., & Silva, P. (1989). Cognitive and social correlates of DSM-III disorders in preadolescent children. *Journal of the American Academy of Child and Adolescent Psychiatry, 28* (6), 842–846.

Angold, A. (1988a). Childhood and adolescent depression I. Epidemiological and aetiological aspects. *British Journal of Psychiatry, 152,* 601–617.

Angold, A. (1988b). Childhood and adolescent depression II. Research in clinical populations. *British Journal of Psychiatry, 153,* 476–492.

Barkley, R. A. (1988). Child Behavior Rating Scales and Checklists. In M. Rutter, A. H. Tuma, & I. S. Lann (Eds.), *Assessment and diagnosis in child psychopathology.* New York: Gilford Press.

Bird, H. R., Canino, G., Rubio-Stipec, M., Gould, M. S. Ribera, J., Sesman, M., Woodbury, M., Huertas-Goldman, S., Pagan, A., Sanchez-Lacay, A., & Moscoso, M. (1988). Estimates of the prevalence of childhood maladjustment in a community survey in Puerto Rico: The use of combined measures. *Archives of General Psychiatry, 45,* 1120–1126.

Bird, H. R., Canino, G., Rubio-Stipec, M., & Ribera, J. C. (1987). Further measures of the psychometric performance of the Children's Global Assessment Scale. *Archives of General Psychiatry, 44,* 821–823.

Bird, H. R., Yager, T. J., Staghezza, B., Gould, M., Canino, G., & Rubio-Stipec (1990). Impairment in the epidemiologic measurement of childhood psychopathology in the community. *Journal of the American Academy of Child and Adolescent Psychiatry, 29* (5), 796–803.

Birmaher, B., Ryan, N. D., Williamson, D. E., Brent, D. A., Kaufman, J., Dahl, R. E., Perel, J., & Nelson, B. (1996). Childhood and adolescent depression: A review of the past 10 years. Part I. *Journal of the American Academy of Child and Adolescent Psychiatry, 35* (11), 1427–1439.

Bowen, R. C., Offord, D. R., & Boyle, M. H. (1990). The Prevalence of overanxious disorder and separation anxiety disorder: Results from the Ontario Child Health Study. *Journal of the American Academy of Child and Adolescent Psychiatry, 29* (5), 753–758.

Boyle, M. H., Offord, D. R., Hofmann, H. G., Catlin, G. P., Byles, J. A., Cadman, D. T., Crawford, J. W., Links, P. S., Rae-Grant, N. I., & Szatmari, P. (1987). Ontario Child Health Study, I. Methodology. *Archives of General Psychiatry, 44* (9), 826–831.

Boyle, M. H. & Offord, D. R. (1991). Psychiatric disorder and substance abuse in adolescence. *Canadian Journal of Psychiatry, 36* (10) 699–705.

Boyle, M. H., Offord, D. R., Racine, Y. A., & Catlin, G. (1991). Ontario Child Health Study Followup: Evaluation of sample loss. *Journal of the American Academy of Child and Adolescent Psychiatry, 30* (3), 449–456.

Brandenburg, N. A., Friedman, R. M., & Silver, S. E. (1990). The epidemiology of childhood psychiatric disorders: Prevalence findings from recent studies. *Journal of the American Academy of Child and Adolescent Psychiatry, 29* (1), 76–83.

Canino, G. J., Bird, H. R., Rubio-Stipec, M., Bravo, M., & Alegria, M. (1990). Children of parents with psychiatric disorder in the community. *Journal of the American Academy of Child and Adolescent Psychiatry, 29* (3), 398–406.

Canino, G. J., Bird, H. R., Shrout, P. E., Rubio-Stipec, M., Bravo, M., Martinez, R., Sesman, M., & Guevara, L. M. (1990). The prevalence of specific psychiatric disorders in Puerto Rico. *Archives of General Psychiatry, 44,* 727–735.

Cohen, P., & Brook, J. S. (1987). Family factors related to the persistence of psychopathology in childhood and adolescence. *Psychiatry, 50,* 332–345.

Cohen, P., O'Connor, P., Lewis, S., Velez, C. N., & Malachowski, B. (1987). Comparison of DISC and K-SADS-P interviews of an epidemiological sample of children. *Journal of the American Academy of Child and Adolescent Psychiatry, 26* (5), 662–667.

Cohen, P., Velez, N., Kohn, M., Schwab-Stone, M., & Johnson, J. (1987). Child psychiatric diagnosis by computer algorithm: Theoretical issues and empirical tests. *Journal of the American Academy of Child and Adolescent Psychiatry, 26* (5), 631–638.

Connell, H. M., Irvine, L., & Rodney, J. (1982). Psychiatric disorder in Queensland primary schoolchildren. *Austtralian Paediatric Journal, 18,* 177–180.

Costello, E. J., Edelbrock, C. S., & Costello, A. J. (1985). Validity of the NIMH Diagnostic Interview Schedule for children: A comparison between psychiatric and pediatric referrals. *Journal of Abnormal Child Psychology, 13* (4), 579–595.

Costello, E. J., Edelbrock, Kalas, C., Kessler, M. D., & Klaric, S. H. (1982). *Diagnostic Interview Schedule for Children (DISC).* Unpublished interview schedule, Department of Psychiatry, University of Pittsburgh.

Costello, E., Costello, A., Edelbrock, C., Burns, B., Dulcan, M., Brent, D., & Janiszewski, S. (1988). Psychiatric disorders in pediatric primary care. *Archives of General Psychiatry, 4* (12), 1107–1116.

Deykin, E. Y., Levy, J. C., & Wells, V. (1987). Adolescent depression, alcohol and drug abuse. *American Journal of Public Health, 77,* 178–182.

Edelbrock, C., & Achenbach, T. M. (1984). The teacher version of the Child Behavior Profile: I. Boys aged 6–11. *Journal of Consulting and Clinical Psychology, 52,* 207–217.

Edelbrock, C., & Costello, A. J. (1988). In M. Rutter, A. H. Tuma, & I. S. Lann (Eds.), *Assessment and diagnosis in child psychopathology.* New York: The Guilford Press.

Edelsohn, G., Ialongo, N., Werthamer-Larsson, L., Crockett, L., & Kellam, S. (1992). Self-reported depressive symptoms in first grade children: Developmentally transient phenomena? *Journal of the American Academy of Child and Adolescent Psychiatry, 31* (2), 282–290.

Fendrich, M., Weissman, M. M., & Warner, V. (1990). Screening for depressive disorders in children and adolescents: Validating the Center for Epidemiologic Studies Depression Scale for Children. *American Journal of Epidemiology, 131* (3), 538–551.

Fisher, P., Wicks, J., Shaffer, D., Piacentini, J., & Lapkin, J. (1992). *NIMH Diagnostic Interview Schedule for Children, users manual.* New York: Division of Child and Adolescent Psychiatry, New York State Psychiatric Institute.

Fleming, J. E., Boyle, M. H., & Offord, D. R. (1993). The outcome of adolescent depression in the Ontario Child Health Study follow-up. *Journal of the American Academy of Child and Adolescent Psychiatry, 32* (1), 28–33.

Fleming, J. E., & Offord, D. R. (1990). Epidemiology of childhood depressive disorders: A critical review. *Journal of the American Academy of Child and Adolescent Psychiatry, 29* (4), 571–580.

Fleming, J. E., Offord, D. R. & Boyle, M. H. (1989). Prevalence of childhood and adolescent depression in the community: Ontario Child Health Study. *British Journal of Psychiatry, 155,* 647–654.

Garrison, C. Z., Addy, C., Jackson, K. L., McKeown, R., & Waller, J. L. (1991). The CES-D as a screen for depression and other psychiatric disorders in adolescents. *Journal of the American Academy of Child and Adolescent Psychiatry, 30* (4), 636–641.

Garrison, C. Z., Schluchter, M. D., Schoenbach, V. J., & Kaplan, B. K. (1989). Epidemiology of depressive symptoms in young adolescents. *Journal of the American Academy of Child and Adolescent Psychiatry, 28,* 343–351.

Garrison, C. Z., Schoenbach, V. J., & Kaplan, B. K. (1985). Depressive symptoms in early adolescence. In A. Dean (Ed.), *Depression in multidisciplinary perspective,* pp. 60–82. New York: Brunner Mazel.

Garrison, C. Z., Waller, J. L., Cuffe, P., McKeown, R. E., Addy, C. L., Jackson, K. L. (1997). Incidence of Major Depressive Disorder and Dysthymia in Young Adolescents. *Journal of the American Academy of Child and Adolescent Psychiatry, 36* (4), 458–465.

Herjanic, B., & Campbell, W. (1977). Differentiating psychiatrically disturbed children in the basis of a structured interview. *Journal of Abnormal Child Psychology, 5,* 127–134.

Herjanic, B., & Reich, W. (1982). Development of a structured psychiatric interview for children: Agreement between child and parent on individual symptoms. *Journal of Abnormal Child Psychology, 10* (3), 307–324.

Herjanic, B., Herjanic, M., Brown, F., & Wheatt, T. (1975). Are children reliable reporters? *Journal of Abnormal Child Psychology, 3* (1), 41–48.

Hodges, K. (1993). Structured interviews for assessing children. *Journal of Child Psychology and Psychiatry, 32* (1), 49–68.

Hodges, K., McKnew, D., Cytryn, L., Stern, L., & Kline, J. (1982). The Child Assessment Schedule (CAS) diagnostic interview: A report on reliability and validity. *Journal of the American Academy of Child and Adolescent Psychiatry, 21,* 468–473.

Holzer, C. E., Shea, B. M., Swanson, J. W., Leaf, P. J., Meyers, J. K., George, L., Weissman, M. M., & Bednarski, P. (1986). The increased risk for specific psychiatric disorders among persons of low socioeconomic status. *The American Journal of Social Psychiatry, 4* (4), 259–271.

Kandel, D., & Davies, M. (1982). Epidemiology of depressive mood in adolescents. *Archives of General Psychiatry, 39,* 1205–1212.

Kandel, D. B., & Davies, M. (1986). Adult sequelae of adolescent depressive symptoms. *Archives of General Psychiatry, 43,* 255–262.

Kashani, J. H., Beck, N. C., Hoeper, E. W., Fallahi, C., Corcoran, C. M., McAllister, J. A., Rosenberg, T. K., & Reid, J. C. (1987a). Psychiatric disorders in a community sample of adolescents. *American Journal of Psychiatry, 144* (5), 584–589.

Kashani, J. H., Carlson, G. A., Beck, N. C., Hoeper, E. W., Corcoran, C. M., McAllister, J. A., Fallahi, C., Rosenberg, T. K., & Reid, J. C. (1987b). Depression, depressive symptoms, and depressed mood among a community sample of adolescents. *American Journal of Psychiatry, 144* (7), 931–934.

Kashani, J. H., Daniel, A. E., Sulzberger, L. A., Rosenberg, T. K., & Reid, J. C. (1987). Conduct disordered adolescents from a community sample. *Canadian Journal of Psychiatry, 32* (9), 756–60.

Kashani, J. H., McGee, R. O., Clarkson, S. E., et al. (1983). Depression in a sample of 9-year-old children. *Archives of General Psychiatry, 40,* 1217–1223.

Kashani, J. H., & Orvaschel, H. (1988). Anxiety disorders in mid-adolescence: A community sample. *American Journal of Psychiatry, 145* (8), 960–964.

Kashani, J. H., & Orvaschel, H. (1990). A community study of anxiety in children and adolescents. *American Journal of Psychiatry, 147* (3), 313–318.

Kashani, J. H., Orvaschel, H., Rosenberg, T. K., & Reid, J. C. (1989). Psychopathology in a community sample of children and adolescents: a developmental perspective. *Journal of the American Academy of Child and Adolescent Psychiatry, 28,* 701–706.

Kashani, J. H., & Simonds, J. F. (1979). The incidence of depression in children. *American Journal of Psychiatry, 136,* 1203–1205.

Kovacs, M., Feinberg, T. L., Crouse-Novak, M. A., Paulauskas, S. L., & Finkelstein, R. (1984). Depressive disorders in childhood. I. A longitudinal prospective study of characteristics and recovery. *Archives of General Psychiatry, 41,* 229–237.

Kovacs, M., Feinberg, T. L., Crouse-Novak, M. A., Paulauskas, S. L., Pollock, M., & Finkelstein, R. (1984). Depressive disorders in childhood. II. A longitudinal study of the risk for a subsequent major depression. *Archives of General Psychiatry, 41,* 643–649.

Kovacs, M., Gatsonis, C., Paulauskas, S. L., & Richards, C. (1989). Depressive disorders in childhood. IV. A longitudinal study of comorbidity with risk for anxiety disorders. *Archives of General Psychiatry, 46,* 776–782.

Kovacs, M., Goldston, D., & Gatsonis, C. (1993). Suicidal behaviors and childhood-onset depressive disorders: A longitudinal investigation. *Journal of the American Academy of Child and Adolescent Psychiatry, 32* (1), 8–20.

Kovacs, M., Paulauskas, S., & Richards, C. (1988). Depressive disorders in childhood. III. A longitudinal study of comorbidity with and risk for conduct disorders. *Journal of Affective Disorders, 15,* 205–217.

Kutcher, S. P., & Marton, P. (1989). Parameters of adolescent depression. *Psychiatric Clinics of North America, 12* (4), 895–918.

Links, P. S., Boyle, M. H. & Offord, D. R. (1989). The prevalence of emotional disorder in children. *Journal of Nervous and Mental Disorder, 177* (2), 85–91.

McGee, R., Feehan, M., Williams, S., & Anderson, J. (1992). DSM-III disorders from age 11 to age 15 years. *Journal of the American Academy of Child and Adolescent Psychiatry, 31* (1), 50–59.

McGee, R., Feehan, M., Williams, S., Partridge, F., Silva, P. A., & Kelly, J. (1990). DSM-III disorders in a large sample of adolescents. *Journal of the American Academy of Child and Adolescent Psychiatry, 29* (4), 611–619.

McGee, R., & Williams, S. (1988). A longitudinal study of depression in nine-year-old children. *Journal of the American Academy of Child and Adolescent Psychiatry, 273,* 342–348.

Offord, D. R., Boyle, M. H., & Racine, Y. (1989). Ontario Child Health Study: Correlates of disorder. *Journal of the Academy of Child and Adolescent Psychiatry, 28,* 856–860.

Offord, D. R., Boyle, M. H., Szatmari, P., Rae-Grant, N. I., Links, P. S., Cadman, D. T., Byles, J. A., Crawford, J. W., Blum, H. M., Byrne, C., Thomas, H., & Woodward, C. A. (1987). Ontario Child Health Study. II. Six-month prevalence of disorder and rates of service utilization. *Archives of.General Psychiatry, 41,* 832–836.

Orvaschel, H., Puig-Antich, J., Chambers, W., Tabrizi, M. A., & Johnson, R. (1982). Retrospective assessment of prepubertal major depression with the Kiddie-SADS-E. *Journal of the American Academy of Child Psychiatry, 21,* 392–397.

Puig-Antich, J., & Chambers, W. (1978). *The Schedule for Affective Disorders and Schizophrenia for School Aged Children.* Unpublished interview schedule, New York Psychiatric Institute.

Radloff, L. (1977). The CES-D Scale: A self-report depression scale for research in the general population. *Applied Psychological Measurement, 1* (3), 385–401.

Reich, W. (1991). *Diagnostic Interview for Children and Adolescents-Revised.* St. Louis: Washington University.

Roberts, R. E., Lewinsohn, P. M., & Seeley, J. R. (1995). Symptoms of *DSM-III-R* Major Depression in adolescence: Evidence from an epidemiological survey. *Journal of the American Academy of Child Psychiatry, 34,* 1608–1617.

Robins, E., & Guze, S. B. (1970). Establishment of diagnostic validity and psychiatric illness: Its application to schizophrenia. *American Journal of Psychiatry, 126,* 983–987.

Rutter, M., Tizard, J., & Whitmore, K. (Eds). (1970). *Education, health, and behavior.* London: Longmans.

Rutter, M., Tuma, A. H., & Lann, I. S. (1988). *Assessment and Diagnosis in Child Psychopathology.* The Guilford Press, New York.

Schoenbach, V. J., Grimson, R. C., & Wagner, E. H. (1982). Prevalence of self-reported depressive symptoms in young adolescents. *American Journal of Public Health, 73,* 1281–1287.

Schwab-Stone, M. E., Shaffer, Dulcan, M., Jensen, P. S., Fisher, P. M., Bird, H. R., Goodman, S. H., Lahey, B. B., Lichtman, J. H., Canino, G., Rubio-Stipec, M., & Rae, D. S. (1996). Criterion Validity for the NIMH Diagnostic Interview Schedule for Children Version 2.3 (DISC-2.3). *Journal of the American Academy of Child and Adolescent Psychiatry, 35* (7), 878–888.

Shaffer, D., Fisher, P., Dulcan, M., Davies, M., Piacentini, J., Schwab-Stone, M. E., Lahey, B. B., Bourdon, K., Jensen, P. S., Bird, H. R., Canino, G., & Regier, D. A. (1996). The NIMH Diagnostic Interview Schedule for Children Version 2.3 (DISC-2.3): Description, acceptability, prevalence rates, and performance in the MECA Study. *Journal of the American Academy of Child and Adolescent Psychiatry, 35* (7), 865–877.

Shaffer, D., Gould, M., Brasic, J., Ambrosini, P., Fisher, P., Bird, H., & Aluwahlia, S. (1983). A Children's

Global Assessment Scale (CGAS). *Archives of General Psychiatry, 40,* 1228–1231.

Stavrakaki, C., & Gaudet, M. (1989). Epidemiology of affective and anxiety disorders in children and adolescents. *Psychiatric Clinics of North American, 12* (4), 791–802.

Swanson, J. W., Linskey, A. O., Quintero-Salinas, R., Pumariega, A. J., & Holzer, C. E. (1992). A binational school survey of depressive symptoms, drug use, and suicidal ideation. *Journal of the American Academy of Child and Adolescent Psychiatry, 31* (4), 669–678.

Velez, C. N., Johnson, J., & Cohen, P. (1989). A longitudinal analysis risk factors for childhood psychopathology. *Journal of the American Academy of Child and Adolescent Psychiatry, 28* (6), 861–864.

Verhulst, F. C., Akerhuis, G. W., & Althaus, M. (1985). Mental health in Dutch children: I. A cross-cultural comparison. *Acta Psychiatrica Scandinavica, 72* (Suppl. 323), 1–108.

Verhulst, F. C., Althaus, M., & Versluis-den Bieman, H. J. M. (1992). Damaging backgroups: Later adjustment of international adoptees. *Journal of the American Academy of Child and Adolescent Psychiatry, 31* (3), 518–524.

Verhulst, F. C., Berden, G. F. M. G., & Sanders-Woudstra, J. A. R. (1985). Mental health in Dutch children: II. The prevalence of psychiatric disorder and relationship between measures. *Acta Psychiatrica Scandinavica, 324* (72), 1–43.

Vikan, A. (1985). Psychiatric epidemiology in a sample of 1510 ten-year-old children: I. Prevalence. *Journal of Child Psychology and Psychiatry, 26* (1), 55–75.

Warheit, G. J., Holzer, C. E., & Schwab, J. J. (1973). An analysis of social class and racial differences in depressive symptomatology: A community study. *Journal of Health and Social Behavior, 14* (4), 291–299.

Weissman, M. M. (1988). Psychopathology in the children of depressed parents: Direct interview studies. In D. L. Dunner, E. S. Gershon, & J. E. Barrett (Eds.), *Relatives at risk for mental disorder* New York: Raven Press, (pp. 143–159).

Weissman, M. M., Bruce, M. L., Leaf, P. J., Florio, L. P., & Holzer, C. E. (1991). Affective Disorders. In L. Robins & D. Regier (Eds.), *Psychiatric disorders in America: the Epidemiologic Catchment Area Study.* New York: The Free Press.

Weissman, M. M., Leaf, P. J., Holzer, C. E., Myers, J. K., & Tischler, G. L. (1984). The epidemiology of depression: An update on sex differences in rates. *Journal of Affective Disorders, 7,* 179–188.

14 / **Parenting and the Development of Children**

Klaus K. Minde and Regina Minde

Parents all over the world want their children to become happy, independent, responsible adults who participate fully in the life of their respective societies (LeVine, 1977). The ever-growing number of popular books and magazines devoted to the task of raising children attests to parents' willingness to accept guidance. While traditionally, child-rearing practices vary widely between and within societies, there are nevertheless gross similarities in the caregiving practices toward infants and young children in different cultures (Ainsworth, 1957).

Given these similarities, evolutionary theory also predicts conflict between parents and their offspring based on their different genetic make-ups and needs (Trivers, 1974). Not only are some parental behaviors not optimal for their children at all times, various external or internal events can further increase the disparity between the parents' caregiving activities and the needs of their children. This chapter examines the degree to which the ensuing conflicts can affect the development of children.

The Evolution of Parenting

Parenting in higher primates is associated with the offsprings' long nutritional dependence on breast feeding. Hence, the male's role in day-to-day nurturance is minimal, and low birth rates reflect the fact that a female can nourish only one young at a time. Anthropologists believe that the family structure of *Homo sapiens* evolved because human children need even longer care and supervision than those of other primates. To allow mothers to have more children, fathers had to become more actively involved in the care of their young.

There are 2 basic sets of theories about parenting. One is based on the assumption that parents are innately sensitive to their children—that there is a universal concept of attachment associated with later social and cognitive development (Bowlby, 1969). Proponents of a competing theoretical concept see parenting as the process through which a unique cultural perspective is transmitted from generation to generation (LeVine, 1988). While studies supporting the latter hypothesis often do not provide good data that specify how the distant goal of cultural adjustment is translated into early caregiving, LeVine traces the effects of cultural variables on overall parenting by examining sample families in the Yucatan, Kenya, Italy, Boston, and the Fiji Islands. He concludes that cultures with a high infant mortality rate, as in Kenya, have elaborate customs to ensure the survival of the children but provide little initial encouragement for learning. In cultures with poor subsistence, as in the Yucatan, child training is given more emphasis so as to train competent proponents of the culture. Likewise, in agrarian countries, caregiving strategies are geared toward having many surviving children, and parents invest much time in their children early on in their lives. In contrast, in urban industrial countries, parental commitment is generally more intense later on in life. In such societies parents also talk more to their children. Thus parenting has an important developmental component, and the adequacy of an individual parent may change in relation to a youngster's changing needs over time.

Views of what constitutes good or poor parenting also have changed over time. For example, in the 17th and 18th centuries, it was common in southern and western Europe to send children away to be cared for by wet nurses during the first few years of life (deMause, 1974). A statistic compiled by the chief of police in Paris in 1780 estimated that of 21,000 infants born in that city per year, 17,000 were sent out into the country to live with professional wet nurses; others were placed in suburban nursery homes; only about 1,400 infants were cared for at home, and of these only about half were nursed by their own mothers (Kessen, 1965; Robertson, 1974). This finding suggests that the practice of early separation of mothers and infants was common in all social classes at that time.

Still other management practices existed that would be unacceptable today. For example, for almost 1,000 years, infants and young children who cried too much or had trouble falling asleep were given soothing syrups containing opium (Peiper, 1966). The extent to which these drugs were in general use can be seen from the report of an English physician presented to a parliamentary committee in 1871. According to this document, 3,000 children in Coventry alone were treated at that time with Godfrey's Cordial, a concoction of opium, treacle, and sassafras (Langer, 1973–74).

The question of whether children were disciplined more harshly in previous centuries has been much debated (Pollock, 1983). Whereas the 17th-century philosopher John Locke wanted parents to steel their children to cope with hardships and pain by withholding what they cried for, Jean-Jacques Rousseau, in the 18th century, advocated that children should be allowed to explore the world on their own and receive little direct guidance early on (Minde & Minde, 1986).

More recently, parenting practices have been associated with specific theoretical models of development, such as behaviorism and psychoanalytic theory. For example, Luther Emmett Holt (1855–1924), the first noted American pediatrician, espoused surprisingly harsh behavioral principles. He advised parents never to give a child what it cried for, and warned mothers not to play with babies under 6 months and in general "the less of it at any time the better" (Holt, 1902). Holt's opinions had an immense impact on parenting practices, as witnessed by the fact that his book, *The Care and Feeding of Children,* first published in 1894, went through 75 printings in the subsequent 49 years. The behaviorist John B. Watson (1878–1958) was an admirer of Holt's principles. He considered affectionate mothers their children's worst enemies and called "mother love" a "dangerous instrument" that could lead to all kinds of troubles, including unhappy marriages (Watson, 1928).

Psychoanalytic theory has propagated a more compassionate and sensitive model of parenting by devoting much attention to the emotional development of children. Mothers and other key caregivers were accepted to be essential reference points for the normal emotional and cognitive development of their children (Bowlby, 1969; A. Freud, 1965). Psychoanalysts learned from their adult patients about problematic parenting experience and associated them with these patients' conflicts later on. Examples here are Freud's (1958) concerns about parental prohibition of masturbation in young children. Anna Freud (1946) and others later extended these views by discussing how particular parental attitudes, such as overindulgence or rejection, cause children to develop specific defense mechanisms that would compromise their later development.

It should be stressed that this theory-driven literature initially provided few empirical data. However, as children started to become objects of studies and investigators used contemporary scientific techniques, we have learned much about the effects families have on the psychological well-being of children. In the remainder of this chapter, we define developmentally appropriate parenting and examine the contribution of particular parenting constellations or techniques, in conjunction with specific child characteristics, on the development of children. We also describe some programs designed to teach parenting skills and assess their efficacy.

Developmentally Appropriate Parenting: What It Is and How It Comes About

Parenting is the task of raising children—that is, of providing them with the necessary material and emotional care to further their physical, emotional, cognitive, and social development.

Several broad parameters have been identified as contributing to developmentally appropriate parenting. Some of them reside primarily within the parents, others reflect the characteristics of the child, and a third group describes the societal context in which parents and their children live.

THE PARENT-CHILD DYAD

Parenting is always a direct reflection of the unique qualities of each individual parent-child dyad (Minde, 1986). Emde (1989) suggests that the initial tie a parent develops with his or her infant is an important determinant of their subsequent relationship. Bowlby (1969, 1979), who first described this tie and named it "attachment," has convincingly shown that all children are biologically primed to develop attachments to selected adults. The quality of these attachments, however, is unique to each dyad and reflects, among other things, the parent's empathic responsiveness toward the child's overall adaptive needs (Ainsworth, Blehar, Waters, & Wall, 1978; Bretherton, 1985). It has now been established that the quality

of this attachment plays an important part in the child's overall social and cognitive development. Children who feel that they can trust their mother or father to help them if they get in trouble dare to explore the world around them more freely and consequently will advance cognitively. It also has been found that attachment has an intergenerational component and that the adults' understanding of their early experiences with their own parents significantly predicts the kind of attachment they will form with their children (Main & Goldwyn, 1984; Main & Hesse, 1990). In other words, there is evidence that both our interpretation of our children's behavior and how we respond is determined by the way we have learned to interpret the world through past experiences with our own caregivers.

PARENTAL MENTAL HEALTH

An extensive literature, reviewed by Minde (1996), describes how specific psychiatric or medical conditions can influence the parenting style of an individual caregiver. The available data leave no doubt that the overall psychosocial functioning of parents is an essential contributor to the quality of parenting they can provide. For example, emotionally disturbed individuals are generally more preoccupied with themselves. This compromises their sensitivity and responsiveness to their children and affects the support and discipline these youngsters receive.

Nevertheless, the data often ignore that the association between parental and child behavior is bidirectional. Thus some children of a depressed parent, to take just one example, may have a particular genetic predisposition to be affected by their parent's mood, while children without such a genetic vulnerability may respond very differently to the same stresses.

Another shortcoming of studies describing the effect of psychiatrically compromised parents on their offspring is that they often limit themselves to identifying the incidence of depression or conduct disorders in the offspring without examining closely the processes by which these associations come about.

PREVIOUS PARENTING EXPERIENCE

There is much to suggest that parenting competence is a function of experience. Mothers of later-born children are more patient, sensitive, and competent than are mothers of firstborn children (Rutter, 1981). Interestingly, this is also true for monkeys (Goodall, 1990; Suomi, Harlow, & Novak, 1974). Older mothers also have been shown to provide more appropriate stimulation, possibly reflecting their higher sensitivity to their children's developmental needs (Jones, Green, & Krauss, 1980; Ragozin, Basham, Cronic, Greenberg, & Robinson, 1982).

PARENTING AS A REFLECTION OF FAMILY AND SOCIAL SYSTEMS

Parenting, in addition to being reflected in the individual relationship of caregiver and child, also is embedded within a broader social nexus. This may be demonstrated by looking at the interaction between external stresses, such as unemployment or single parenthood, versus the support structures available to parents, such as supportive friends or grandparents (Belsky & Vondra, 1989). Individual family dynamics represent another level of analysis (Hetherington, Cox, & Cox, 1982; Wynne, 1984). An absent father, to take just one example, will not only influence a child's life because he or she now lacks direct contact with a male caregiver but also because the now-single mother is deprived of spousal support and may change her parenting style as a direct result of this event (Clarke-Stewart, 1978; Steinhauer, 1984). The differences in parenting related to cultural factors, as mentioned earlier, reflect a yet more generalized frame of reference to looking at determinants of parenting behavior.

While family function has long been known to reflect wider cultural values, clinicians always have felt a need to obtain reliable assessments of families and their effect on children's development. To account for the complexity, some authors (Olson, Sprenkle, & Russel, 1979) suggest that families should be assessed on their levels of cohesion and adaptability. According to them, cohesion varies from a pathological high "enmeshment" to an equally problematic low "disengagement," with "respectful caring" being in the middle. Adaptability, in turn, refers to the way a family meets a child's changing developmental needs. Scores here range from rigidity to total disorganization.

Others assess families by the roles members are given and how well specific developmental tasks, such as individuation, are accomplished. Additional criteria are the quality of communication among family members, the sharing of affect, and the maintenance of established family and cultural norms (Minuchin, 1985; Skinner, Steinhauer, & Santa Barbara, 1983). Failure in any one or more of these functions is seen as cause for children's behavioral dysfunction.

DIRECT CAREGIVER-CHILD INTERACTION

The actual interactions between parents and their children can provide a powerful demonstration of individual caregivers' parenting style and have long been used as a major instrument for assessing parenting competence. However, a number of investigators have pointed out that parenting is affected by the characteristics of both the child and the parent (Maccoby & Martin, 1983). For example, an individual child's temperament and physical and mental intactness can be important determinants of the parents' behaviors toward the child. Those born prematurely or diagnosed as hyperactive are good examples here, as they require a more structured interactional style from their parents in response to demands or distress than do other children (Minde, 1992, 1993). As a consequence, the assessment of parent-child interactions for research purposes has become more sophisticated. Rather than, as previously, counting the number of positive or negative statements a mother would make within a certain time unit or recording smiles and touches, investigators now focus on her empathic responsiveness to the child's overall adaptive needs or on the mutual regulation of affect between the dyad (Bretherton, 1985; Emde, 1989). The advantage of this type of assessment is its flexibility, since the observed characteristics apply equally to, for example, hyperactive and nonhyperactive youngsters and reflect more realistically how parents deal with the resolution of interpersonal conflicts and the overall behaviors and demands of their children within the context of their developmental needs (Rutter, 1989; Shure & Spivack, 1978).

Parental Psychiatric Disorders

Professionals have long been interested in how specific psychiatric conditions influence a person's ability to parent. While much of the history of this association has come from individual case descriptions, empirical studies also go back to the beginning of the century. Janet was the first to report, in 1925, that mental disorders of parents, because of their pervasive influence on the overall social life of the family, have a negative effect on the children. He had observed how a mental illness could affect the biological as well the nonbiological children who lived with a mentally ill mother or father and described cases where children had done well, possibly because they had been removed from their homes early in life. Canavan and Clark (1923a,b) undertook the first controlled study, where they compared 463 children of 136 married patients diagnosed with schizophrenia with 581 youngsters of 145 families attending an outpatient clinic. Interestingly, the main difference between the 2 samples was found to be the higher rate of conduct disorders in the offspring of schizophrenics (9.5% vs. 1.6%).

Subsequent studies (Preston & Antin, 1933) confirmed these findings. They indicate that the children of schizophrenic parents rarely showed psychotic symptoms themselves but exhibited more general dysfunctional symptomatology (Canavan & Clark, 1936). This nongenetic model of intergenerational transmission of psychiatric illness was challenged by Rutter's 1966 monograph. In this study Rutter examined the records of 922 children who had attended the Maudsley Hospital Children's Department in 1955 and 1959. From this sample, he selected a subsample of 137 youngsters who had at least 1 parent with a mental illness, 85 who had lost a parent, and 190 who had parents with either a chronic or recurrent physical disease. The following findings are most relevant to the questions posed in this chapter:

1. There is a strong association between parental illness and psychiatric disorder in children.
2. This is true for both psychiatric and physical illness in the parent.
3. Parental illness usually precedes the onset of the child's disorder, suggesting a parent-child effect.
4. A mental or chronic physical disorder in the parent is most likely to be followed by behavioral disturbances in children when the parent exhibits a "long-standing abnormality of personality."

Rutter's findings have led to a number of subsequent investigations by his own group and by others who have attempted to delineate more precisely the relationship between specific psychiatric conditions and problems of parenting. These studies have explored a number of questions.

One question was whether the impact of a parent's psychiatric disorder on his or her child's development or behavior was a reflection of the actual diagnosis, and if so, what the expected rate of disturbance in these youngsters was. A study (Rutter & Quinton, 1984) in which the authors looked at 137 newly referred psychiatric adult patients with 292 children up to 15 years of age suggests that a conduct disorder in 1 parent is the single most significant factor predicting psychopathology in the children. Forty-five percent of all the children with such a parent showed a disturbance on a teacher questionnaire and 48% during a psychiatric interview. This was more than double the rate shown by children whose parents suffered from schizophrenia or an affective psychosis (21%). Furthermore, children who had 1 healthy and 1 psychotic parent did not differ from a matched control group in their later psychiatric risk (20%). However, in most families with 1 mentally ill parent, the other parent also was disturbed and the rate of problems in the children, as determined during a psychiatric interview, was very high (54%).

Similar findings were obtained from the well-known schizophrenia project in Rochester where boys ages 7 to 10 who had parents with a nonpsychotic psychiatric disorder had far more problems than those with schizophrenic or affectively ill parent (Harder, Kokes, Fisher, & Strauss 1980; Kokes, Harder, Fisher, & Strauss 1980).

It is important to assess the effect a psychiatric illness has on children not only at the time of diagnosis but also during the ongoing course of the condition. The study by Rutter and Quinton (1984) is important here since all children were followed for 4 years and subcohorts of different age groups could be established. The well-known Minnesota study of Garmezy and Devine (1984) also followed 9- to 11-year-old children of schizophrenic and internalizing (primarily depressed) mothers for 7 years, using peer and teacher ratings as well as school records. Both these studies established that the incidence of disorders in the children changed over time. For example, in the Minnesota study, children of the "internalizing mothers" initially looked very much like their control peers; seven years later, however, 52% showed difficulties compared to only 18% of the controls. Both groups of investigators agreed that more than the psychotic illness of the initially selected parent was responsible for the continuing psychiatric disorder in the child. Rutter and Quinton (1984) identified the child's exposure to hostile parental behaviors to be the most specific risk for ongoing difficulties, especially in boys. Thus 17% of the boys with nonhostile fathers and mothers versus 40% with hostile mothers and 71% with hostile fathers showed a persistent disturbance.

Another question explored was whether the children's age or gender matters in their susceptibility to the parents' mental illness. It could be argued that young children with emotionally ill mothers may be more severely affected by their parent's illness than adolescents, who potentially can find alternative resources for some of the caregiving they require. On the other hand, it might be hypothesized that older children are more aware of the potential peculiarities or deficits mentally ill parents may show and therefore may be more strongly affected than preschool youngsters. Likewise, girls may be more handicapped by a mother's illness because of the compromised role modeling they are exposed to.

The question of age has never been examined directly, but findings from related areas suggest that developmental differences are relevant. We know, for example, that repeated hospitalizations are especially stressful for children between 6 months and 5 years because they cannot yet understand that the separation from their family is only temporary (Quinton & Rutter, 1976).

These and other similar data suggest that young children of different ages may be affected by different aspects of a parent's emotional illness. While some areas of parental dysfunction, such as hostility and marital discord, are problematic at any age, delusional thinking is more traumatic for older children. A mother's frequent hospitalizations for a mental illness, on the other hand, may be especially disruptive for a preschooler.

As far as gender is concerned, the data are not altogether clear. It is known that boys are more susceptible to all types of psychosocial stressors (Maccoby & Martin, 1983). However, their persistent emotional and behavioral disturbance may be due partly to the overpowering negative effect of hostile interpersonal child-rearing practices. As personality disorders are more common in men, boys simply may be the victims of such a parenting style more often.

Rutter and Quinton (1984) confirmed that children who have the same sex as the mentally ill parent are more profoundly affected. Judged by teachers' ratings, 40% of the boys compared to only 23% of the girls had difficulties when their father was mentally ill, while 11% of daughters and none of the sons of mentally ill mothers were seen as abnormal.

Still another question examined was the degree to which problem behaviors in children of mentally ill parents reflect the common gene pool between the generations. Available evidence suggests that the picture is more complex than previously imagined. On the one hand, we know that both schizophrenia and major depressive illness have a significant genetic component. There are even adoptive studies that report equal rates of schizophrenia in adopted and nonadopted children of schizophrenic parents (Gottesman & Shields, 1982). This finding in itself, however, carries a different significance today since we have become more aware that adopted-away children come from more disturbed schizophrenic parents than do those who remain with their biological families (Sameroff & Zax, 1978). The additional disturbance often is based on the presence of a conduct or substance abuse disorder. These conditions, which appear as comorbid with schizophrenia, had their own genetic inheritance pattern but make both the diagnosis and treatment of schizophrenia or major depression more complex and difficult. They also prove that a direct comparison between adopted and nonadopted children should not be used to measure the genetic penetrance of a specific mental disorder.

The traditional concept of straightforward genetic transmission of mental disturbances has been challenged by that of shared and nonshared environmental influences, developed by Plomin and his colleagues (Plomin & Daniels, 1987). This concept is based on persuasive data that show that families are experienced very differently by individual family members at any one time; and family environments change over time, and children born during various periods of the family's natural history have few shared experiences.

The reasons why we experience an identical event so differently are complex. For example, children in family X may vary in their assessment of their father's psychotic decompensation because of their different ages, intelligence, previous relationship with their father, or differential vulnerability toward a schizophrenic illness. All these factors make up the "nonshared" aspect of family X member's life at home and account for up to 85% of the variance in any personal experience (Plomin & Daniels, 1987). Reitsma-Street, Offord, and Finch (1985) provide a vivid example of this hypothesis in their study of 71 antisocial Canadian adolescents with same-sex siblings 2 years younger to 5 years older who had not been involved in antisocial activities. The authors found that the nondelinquent siblings had been different long before their brothers or sisters began

their antisocial activities. For example, the nondelinquent siblings always had had a better relationship with their mothers and had on average been
2 years younger when their parents had separated
initially. They also had experienced more medical
illnesses and possibly, as a consequence, received
more care from their mothers because of this. The
notion, first suggested by Mednick and Schulsinger (1968), that a history of perinatal insults
differentiates delinquent from nondelinquent
children in the same family was not supported.

In summary, there is good evidence that children are adversely affected by parents with psychiatric illness. However, their vulnerability is
related primarily to the pervasiveness with which
the illness affects the parents' actual caregiving
practices. Thus additional personality disorders in
parents are more difficult for children to cope
with than, say, an intermittent psychotic illness in
a parent. Age and sex differences in susceptibility
exist but vary at different developmental stages.

DEPRESSION

Depression is a condition that is comparatively
common in women of childbearing age. The overall prevalence of depression in women ages 20 to
40 is said to be about 30%—double the rate seen
in men (Rutter, 1986). In fact, Boyd and Weissman (1981) reported that 9% of all young women
experience a moderate to severe depression every
year. Brown and Harris (1978) in their London
surveys found that 17% of women were definite
"cases" and a further 19% were "borderline."

In spite of this overall high prevalence and incidence, many psychosocial factors are associated
with depression. For example, Richman, Stevenson, and Graham (1982) claimed that depressive
symptoms are higher in nonworking than working
mothers of young children (40% vs. 20%). Depression also increases during unemployment and
is higher in lower-class women, especially if they
lost a parent before the age of 10 (Brown, Harris,
& Bifulco, 1986). All these data suggest that a
large number of children live with a depressed
parent during their early formative years.

The effects of depression on children have
been described by various authors (Beardslee,
Bemporad, Keller, & Klerman, 1983; Cox, Puckering, Pond, & Mills, 1987; Puckering, 1989).
Findings suggest a wide range of behavioral problems in the children, from depression to conduct
disorders or hyperactivity.

Intergenerational Transmission of Depression:
There are basically 3 ways by which parental depression can be associated with child psychopathology.

The most elementary proposition is that depression is a genetic disorder and will be transmitted
in a predetermined manner.

Second, depressed individuals may marry more
disturbed spouses (assortative mating), leading to
compromised marital and overall problematic
family functioning.

Finally, problems in the children may be a reflection of difficulties in the social supports or of
a high number of stressful life events. This would
suggest that the children's difficulties are related
to the context in which the family lives.

The available data are complex and suggest
multiple pathways of intergenerational transmission. It has been found that children who have
parents with bipolar disorders show more disturbed behavior than do those whose parents have
a unipolar disorder (43% vs. 20%); children with
1 affected parent also do better than those who
have 2 affected parents (Gershon et al., 1982;
Puig-Antich et al., 1985; Weissman et al., 1984).
How much of these differences is due to environmental stresses in these high-risk groups is not
yet clear.

Preliminary data by Sameroff and his group
(Sameroff, Dickstein, Hayden, & Schiller, 1993)
also suggest that depressed women more often
marry or live with depressed or otherwise psychiatrically disturbed men than do women with obsessive compulsive disorders. This fact suggests
that assortative mating takes place in this population. The same group also found that overall functioning in depressed families is compromised only
when mothers are symptomatically depressed and
not when they are in between depressive episodes. However, we have data that indicate that a
substantial number of children of depressed
mothers tend to maintain their abnormal behavior
even after their parent's illness has remitted (Cox
et al., 1987; Richman et al., 1982). In Richman's
longitudinal study, for example, 58% of youngsters who had shown behavioral problems at age
3 still did so at age 8 even though their mother's
depression had ended long before. This finding
suggests that parent-child interactions taking
place during an acute depressive episode change
a youngster's inner world to such a degree that he
or she later may continue to exhibit behavioral abnormalities even in the absence of grossly abnor-

mal parenting practices. Looking at the actual parenting behaviors of depressed individuals, a number of observations have been made. Richman et al. (1982), who followed a community sample of nearly 200 children from age 3 to 8, found that depressed mothers would read very little to their children, leaving them with a significantly decreased reading level at age 8. Other investigators have suggested that depressed mothers are more preoccupied with themselves and therefore less sensitive to the needs of their children (Billings & Moos, 1983; Cox et al., 1987; Zekoski, O'Hara, & Wills, 1987). They also are less consistent in their disciplining (Cox et al., 1987), tend to use a more controlling way of speech, and are less able to compromise (Kochanska, Kuczynski, Radke-Yarrow, & Welsh, 1987).

Depression and Attachment: Another important area of recent research has been the effect of maternal depression on children's attachment patterns. As discussed elsewhere in this volume, the type of attachment children show during infancy predicts to a significant degree how they will relate to their peers during later childhood and in what fashion they will explore the world around them (Bretherton, 1985). As the way children interact with the world is significantly dependent on the models they have been exposed to early on in life, the effect of maternal depression on this process naturally has been of interest to investigators. Findings suggest that the children of depressed mothers more often display an insecure attachment than do children in control populations (65% vs. 35%) (Radke-Yarrow, Cummings, Kuczynski, & Chapman, 1985). In the above-mentioned study by Sameroff et al. (1993), only actively depressed mothers had insecurely attached children. However, these findings must be taken with caution as mothers who present with sleep-disturbed youngsters or those with failure to thrive also show an unduly high rate of insecure attachment patterns (Benoit, Zeanah, & Barton, 1989; Benoit, Zeanah, Boucher, & Minde, 1992; Minde, Corter, Goldberg, & Jeffers, 1990). Hammon and colleagues suggest that such negative representations about one's self worth, expressed in an insecure attachment pattern, may function as a mediator for later experiences which are then interpreted as confirming, in conjunction with a depressive pre-disposition, this assessment of the self (Hammon, Gordon, Burge, Adrian, Jaenicke, & Hiroto, 1987).

In summary then, there is support for the notion that parental depression is a risk factor for the mental health of children and that at least some of intergenerational continuity of this condition is a direct consequence of the parenting these children are exposed to. There is evidence, however, that depressed parents overall show a wide range of interactional patterns and that some are found to be warm and very caring with their children (Cox et al., 1987).

Other Psychosocial Abnormalities in Parents

Parenting patterns can be affected profoundly by other than the traditional mental disorders of schizophrenia and depression. Institutionalization, parental criminality, abusive practices, and specific social risk factors such as poor housing and unemployment have been thoroughly investigated and warrant separate discussions.

INSTITUTIONALIZATION AND OTHER PARENTING DISRUPTIONS

Children who have been placed in foster care and/or institutions have long been considered to be at risk for developing parenting problems later on in life. This assumption is based on the concept that parenting is both an input or independent as well as an output or dependent variable. Thus the parenting skills of a mother reflect what will happen to her child in the future (input) and are at the same time a result of her own problems and/or her current social conditions (output). Quinton and Rutter (1988), in an extensive retrospective and prospective study, have examined this issue in great detail. They looked at 48 mothers whose children had been placed in care between the ages of 5 and 8 because of these women's inability to care for them and compared them to 47 families who came from the same social class but whose children had never been placed outside their homes (retrospective study). They also examined a sample of 81 women 21 to 29 years of age who 12 years earlier had been living in 1 of 2 children's homes, assessed their current parenting competence, and compared them to a control sample of 51 women (prospective study).

The retrospective study showed, among other things, that the in-care group of mothers had been exposed to more criminal behavior and alcohol abuse in their own families (20% vs. 5%). They also had often been in care themselves (25% vs. 7%) and been exposed to unusually harsh punishment by their mothers (42% vs. 10%). The in-care mothers also had been more unhappy in school, had left home by age 19 (65% vs. 26%), and more were pregnant by this time (61% vs. 23%). The fathers of their children likewise tended to have deviant histories. For example, 55% (vs. 13%) had been on probation or in prison and 58% (vs. 18%) had a current psychiatric disorder.

While the in-care mothers showed an unduly high number of past adversities, the control families had been exposed to a good number of negative events as well. This raised the question to what extent parenting breakdown (i.e., the need to have one's child placed in care) versus difficulties in handling children is associated with early family adversities and how family environment hardships perpetuate or attenuate such difficulties.

A close review of Rutter and Quinton's data suggests the following mechanisms underlying intergenerational continuities in parenting problems: In-care mothers had more often experienced childhood adversities with both parents; 3 times as many in-care mother also had experienced both parental deviance (defined as alcoholism, psychiatric disorder, conviction of indictable offenses of 1 or both parents) and adverse childhood experiences (defined as harsh disciplining, marital discord, and rejection). When there was only 1 type of problem, adverse childhood experiences were more often present in the in-care mothers.

The fact that these women had been exposed to multiple stresses came up again in the effect teenage difficulties had on their later parenting ability. Thus most in-care mothers had experienced both early childhood and teenage problems (defined as marked unhappiness in school; persistent truancy and marked negative experiences with 1 or both parents). When there was only 1 type of adversity, problems occurring early on in life were more predictive of poor parenting skills than those that happened during adolescence. Disadvantaged current circumstances (e.g., poor housing) could not explain the association between childhood adversities and parenting breakdown, although they were related to these early adversities. However, the presence or absence of marital support for a spouse made an independent contribution to parenting competence, especially in families where parents had grown up in reasonably harmonious circumstances.

In summary, the retrospective part of Quinton and Rutter's study suggests that parenting breakdown occurs most often in families that had experienced multiple past disadvantages and does not occur only as a direct effect of current social problems. Furthermore, a series of early adversities in childhood does not necessarily lead to later parenting breakdown by, for example, causing children to become mentally disordered individuals who later get themselves into social trouble. In fact, some problem mothers functioned quite well as teenagers despite adverse early childhood experiences, but nevertheless they were unable to care for their own children.

The study also showed that we have to differentiate between parenting breakdown (i.e., the need to place children) and mild to moderate parenting difficulties. The latter are relatively common; can occur in the absence of personality disorders; and can be associated either with current psychosocial adversities only or with the experience of early childhood adversities. Parenting breakdown, on the other hand, is more consistently a direct result of multiple early traumatic experiences.

Concerning the prospective aspect of Quinton and Rutter's investigation, the following results appear relevant for our discussion. Only 35% of the women who had spent time in an institution during their childhood later experienced permanent or temporary separation from 1 or all of their children. Their firstborns were more likely to be taken into foster care; many of the women were better with subsequent children.

When these "ex-care" mothers were observed in interactions with their children, they ignored them more; showed more negative affect embedded within other interactions; and showed less overall sensitivity and reconciled fewer disputes. They also disciplined through their irritation rather than by teaching their children concepts of behavior. In contrast to the control mothers, initially they did not respond positively to their children's demands and hence did not acquire the necessary "disciplinary currency" needed to provide their children with appropriate skills of conflict resolution.

The investigators also found that parenting ability was higher in those women who had returned from the institution to a harmonious home setting and among those who had good experiences in school (79% vs. 41%).

In summary, these and other analyses suggest that childhood adversities lead to poor parenting behavior later in life through 2 main mechanisms.

The first is the chain of events that increases the likelihood of limited later opportunities—affected children go to poor schools, get pregnant early on by someone equally disadvantaged, have no occupational skills, and so on. The other mechanism concerns an apparent vulnerability in previously institutionalized women to poor social circumstances or a lack of marital support. These individuals seem to have a sense of hopelessness and helplessness not found in women who did not grow up in institutions.

PARENTAL CRIMINALITY

A large number of investigations have documented that criminality in parents is associated with delinquency as well as conduct disorders in children (McCord & McCord, 1959; Wadsworth 1979; West & Farrington, 1973). This has been true in different ethnic and cultural groups (Minde, 1975; Rohner, 1975; Werner, 1979). The rate of delinquency in boys of criminal parents is more than double that of control populations (39% vs. 16%) (West & Farrington, 1973) and even more so if both parents are criminals (Robins, West, & Herjanic, 1975).

The caregiving ingredients especially compromised in such populations have been identified in the meta-analysis by Loeber and Stouthamer-Loeber (1986) as inadequate supervision, open conflict, deviant values, and family discord.

Inadequate supervision and neglect are strongly correlated with later conduct disorders. This finding confirms data reported half a century ago by Glueck and Glueck (1944) in their prospective observational studies of delinquent youngsters.

Antisocial parents have difficulties in negotiating disciplinary arrangements with their children, leading to open conflict much of the time. They themselves see the world as a place where one either wins or loses and where compromise or trust in each other or in another person seems impossible. As a consequence, parents get involved in long sequences of coercive interchanges (Patterson, 1982). They are aware of their children's disobedience but cannot set appropriate limits or modify their abnormal behavior in a nonaggressive manner. As a result, the children's behavior fails to improve. This leads to an escalation of parental manipulative efforts, which in turn increases the children's evasiveness. In the end, both parties may see each other as enemies and totally cease to be interested in working together. While there may be a genetic aspect to the ten-

dency of these children to struggle against any requests that originate from outside themselves, the main deficit appears to be the parents' insensitivity to their children's emotional needs, especially in regard to their overall behavioral regulation. This makes the children feel rejected and suggests to them that the world is a place that cannot be trusted and where one has to fight. The detailed interactional analyses of mothers who were raised in institutions (Quinton & Rutter, 1988) provide a very similar flavor.

Parents with criminal records often condone abnormal behaviors and therefore may serve as models of deviant problem solving. This is supported by the observation that delinquency in children is more highly associated with deviant adult behaviors of their parents than with difficulties these parents had during their own adolescence (Robins et al., 1975).

Families with a history of criminal behavior show much family discord (Rutter & Giller, 1983; West, 1982). Thus children in these families frequently witness quarrels between their parents and are subjected to unpredictable separations because of these arguments. Moreover, they often experience the effects of alcohol and drug abuse, and live within a context where events are unpredictable and violence is an everyday companion. It is of interest that the exposure to behaviors defined as family discord is the most predictive of recidivism within delinquent groups (Clarke & Cornish, 1978).

CHILD ABUSE

Child maltreatment, including physical as well as sexual abuse, is by definition the most obvious syndrome of deviant parenting. It is a complex problem that cuts across social class despite its preponderance among poor families (Pelton, 1978). Since child abuse is discussed elsewhere, we will limit ourselves to raising only a few general issues.

In the contemporary literature, child abuse often is seen as a result of highly maladaptive interactions between a child and his or her parent (Cicchetti & Rizley, 1981). It is therefore not only a reflection of parental deviance but also of a balance of risk and compensating factors within an individual family unit (Belsky & Vondra, 1989). Others see child maltreatment as a reflection of highly abnormal parenting that at different developmental levels can lead to failure to thrive, physical and sexual abuse, or even deliberately created iatrogenic conditions such as seen in the Munchausen by proxy syndrome (Rutter, 1989). However, a number of parental characteristics have been consistently identified in the families of abused children.

Younger rather than older mothers tend to abuse their children (Ragozin et al., 1982). Thus psychological maturity and age in parenting competence do go together. An empirical study of 267 economically deprived families found that the abusing parent scored lower on scales assessing aggression, locus of control, suspicion, and defensiveness (Brunquell, Crichton, & Egeland, 1981). An investigation of 170 German families with abusing parents found abuse to be associated with unfavorable early socialization experiences of the parent leading to heightened irritability, anger, and harsh punishment of the children (Engfer & Schneewind, 1982).

Yet not all parents who have experienced abnormal socialization or abuse become maltreating parents. For example, in a prospective study in which 282 parents of newborns admitted to an intensive neonatal care unit were followed for 1 year, only 18% of the mothers who had reported having been abused in the past repeated the abuse with their children (Hunter & Kilstrom, 1979). Other research confirms these figures (Kaufman & Zigler, 1987).

While the mechanisms by which maltreatment is transmitted from one generation to the next have yet to be established, it is obvious that the process must allow for a significant discontinuity of transmission to account for the majority of at-risk parents who do not become abusers. Concurrent psychosocial stresses as well as biological characteristics of the child may be important in triggering actual abusive episodes in the parent.

Nevertheless, since most survivors of discord or violence in their childhood families do not become abusers themselves, there is hope that much of the pain and misunderstanding we see around us will not perpetuate from generation to generation.

Clinical Manifestations of Disordered Parenting

Earlier we discussed the skills and attitudes that appear to be associated with successful parenting. Here we focus on 2 specific strategies or parenting

categories that have consistently been associated with behavioral difficulties in children: an unemotional, unresponsive, or insensitive attachment and a parental behavior strategy that combines hostility, rejection, and harsh discipline.

LACK OF ATTACHMENT AND INSENSITIVITY

Children whose parents do not seem to be interested in their feelings and concerns feel misunderstood, rejected, and abandoned. The consequence of these feelings for the later cognitive and social functioning of children has been carefully examined (Bifulco, Harris, & Brown, 1992; Sroufe, 1983). It appears that a secure attachment between a child and his or her primary caregivers will lead to a generally superior sense of competence and mastery in the youngster (Cicchetti, Cummings, Greenberg, & Marvin 1990). This sense of mastery creates a resilience toward later stressful events. In contrast, early parental detachment, neglect, or insensitivity leads to helplessness and later depression (Brown et al., 1986).

It is of interest that this sense of inadequacy or helplessness may not be present at all times but become obvious only when the adult experiences new losses or disappointments, such as unemployment or bereavement. Such an event will then cause depressive episodes, which, in turn, may lead to a change in parenting competence (Conger et al., 1992).

This concept also has been found useful in other areas of research. For example, Minde, Corter, Goldberg, and Jeffers (1990) showed how maternal sensitivity to social cues of premature twins within 3 weeks after birth predicted which of the twins was preferred by the mother 4 years later.

Rutter, in his studies on women who had been reared in institutions, also showed that a placement before age 2 was associated with a far higher rate of personality disorder later on in life than was a later placement (82% vs. 6%).

One other study highlights the importance of parental sensitivity on normal development. Tizard and her associates studied 65 children who had been placed in 2 well-run institutions shortly after birth in the 1960s. Twenty-four of these children were adopted before age 4, and most of the other youngsters had returned to some type of family by age 16. In an early follow-up study, the authors found that most of the early-adopted youngsters had developed stable affectionate relationships with their adoptive parents by age 8. However, those adopted between age 4 and 8 had poorer relationships with peers and others (Tizard & Hodges, 1978). In a later follow-up of the same sample at age 16, these authors report that children who returned to their biological parents after age 2 showed far more psychiatric disorders during adolescence than did those adopted early on, possibly because they had returned to a very disadvantaged environment. However, even the "successful" adoptees during their adolescence were perceived to have fewer close relationships, to confide less in others, and to be more indiscriminately friendly than were the controls, although there were no differences among the groups in their academic functioning (Hodges & Tizard 1989a,b). This suggests that a lack of early sensitive caregiving left a mark on the quality of social and interpersonal relationships these children had in adolescence despite normal academic functioning.

PARENTS WHO CONTROL THROUGH HOSTILE, REJECTING, HARSH DISCIPLINE

The strategies used by parents to control their children have long been seen as important predictors of children's later social and intellectual competence (Maccoby & Martin, 1983). Earlier we described the effects personality disorders, especially in fathers, have on the children's later functioning. The actual parent-child interactions observed in these families are characterized by an autocratic or authoritarian parenting style and excessive physical punishment. This prevents children from expressing their thoughts and feelings (Patterson, 1982; Rutter, 1989). Observations indicate that such children become passively hostile in early childhood but later on often turn into aggressive and even antisocial adults. To some extent this seems to stem from the fact that harshly disciplined children do not learn appropriate social information skills and tend to misidentify social situations that require an aggressive and hostile response (Weiss, Dodge, Bates, & Pettit, 1992).

Baumrind (1967, 1971, 1989), in an extensive study of 134 children, differentiated between families with permissive and authoritarian parenting styles. She found that children with permissive and authoritarian parents experienced little personal warmth. A third type of parenting, called authoritative, in later work was associated with the best behavioral outcome and highest school achievement right through adolescence (Steinberg, Elmen, & Mounts, 1989).

The authoritative parenting style is described as combining parental warmth and acceptance or involvement with an index of parental control or strictness. This combination seems to give children a feeling that their parents take them seriously and will help them when they need their assistance, but that at the same time these parents also have clear expectations of their youngsters.

In more recent work, the permissive category has been subdivided into indulgent and neglectful permissiveness (Lamborn, Mounts, Steinberg, & Dornbusch, 1991). This division was based on the notion that some parents employ a low level of control because of their ideological orientation (i.e., they have democratic principles and trust their children), while in others it reflects a disengagement from child-rearing responsibilities.

Whereas earlier studies suggested that the primary mediating factor between authoritarian and permissive parenting styles and later child dysfunction was the child's low self-esteem, the more recent studies indicate that youngsters from authoritarian homes are also comparatively well adjusted, achieve well in school, and experience little psychological distress. Children of indulgent and neglectful parents, on the other hand, are relatively disengaged from school and tend to use drugs more often than do children from authoritarian or authoritative families. However, the indulged children showed a high degree of self-competence and a low rate of delinquency; children from authoritarian and neglectful families fared much worse on these characteristics.

It must be pointed out that these parenting styles were found in nonclinical populations and that the associations between developmental outcome and parenting styles are far more striking in clinical samples. For example, Patterson (1982) has identified a strong relationship between an authoritarian parenting style and later childhood aggression. He pointed out that children in authoritarian families receive far more punishment for an aggressive act than do children of nonauthoritarian parents, highlighting the coercive aspects of such relationships.

Minde (1992) also has shown the association between parenting style and the presence of aggressive behavior in clinically referred preschool children over an 18-month period and pointed out the difficulties inherent in changing the parenting style in these families.

Parent Education

Educating parents in the task of raising children has long been a concern of professionals (Croake & Glover, 1977). It appears that the first serious activities in this area in North America took place in 1815, when mothers in Portland, Maine, began to meet regularly in study groups, called "maternal associations," to talk about child-rearing problems (Bridgman, 1930). Their discussions were informal and focused on the religious and moral improvement of their children (Sunley, 1955).

In the 1830s the first parent magazines were published in North America. For example, *Mother's* magazine had its first volume in 1832, *Parent's* in 1840 and *Mother's Assistant* in 1841.

In 1909 the first White House conference on child welfare was held; the Children's Bureau was established in 1912. This led to a definition of "homemaking" as a basic vocation for women and allowed federal support for health-oriented programs of parent education. During the 1930s thousands of adults participated in parent education groups all over the United States, and several volumes of research were published (e.g., Hattendorf et al., 1932).

The more recent interest in parent education is both an outgrowth of the Head Start program as well as of Gordon's Parent Effectiveness Training (PET) program (Gordon, 1970). According to Brown (1976) the PET program had reached over 250,000 parents by 1976 and 8,000 formal instructors had been trained. Since then interest has continued to grow, and many parents have been seeking out information and trying to acquire effective parenting skills, reflecting most parents' belief that raising children today is harder than in the past (Greer, 1986).

The proliferation of parenting programs also has raised questions for the concerned clinician and researcher because a variety of professional and nonprofessional groups have claimed to be the ultimate specialists in parent education (Fine & Brownstein, 1983; Fine & Henry, 1989). It is difficult to substantiate specific assumptions made by certain groups of parent educators in regard to the effect of their respective programs and has hindered empirical studies evaluating parent education.

The parent education programs focus on 1 or more of the following areas:

- Information sharing: This consists of providing knowledge about developmental expectations, legal rights of parents and children, and other factual information. Lectures, printed materials, or group discussions often are used to reach parents.
- Improving self-awareness: This aspect stresses the need for parents to reflect on their own behaviors and bring insight into how their actions may influence their children. Group discussions, specific individual activities, or the use of a diary or log are the most common instructional methods.
- Skill acquisition: Here parents learn ways to manage children's behavior appropriately. Parent trainers use group discussions or direct practice feedback demonstrations.
- Problem solving: This relates to the utilization of more constructive strategies in situations that previously may have led to conflicts and arguments. These skills are taught by using feedback from reported actual events at home or from direct observations within group sessions as well as video- or audiotapes.

What then are the most common models of parent training and how effective are they?

There are 3 major models of parent education programs: reflective counseling, behavior management courses, and Alderian counseling. Each is based on different aspects of developmental theories and, despite common features, addresses different areas of child and caregiver behavior.

Reflective counseling programs are based on Carl Roger's teaching and emphasize the understanding and acceptance of the child's feelings. Parent effectiveness or PET programs (Gordon, 1975) is a good example of this approach. Reflective counseling also helps parents to become more authoritative in their interactions with their children.

Behavioral management courses teach parents to manage children's actual behavior through behavioral analysis. Examples are the Responsive Parenting Program (Clark-Hall, 1978) and the Family Learning Series (Patterson & Forgatch, 1975). These programs emphasize information sharing and skill training and devote less attention to improving parental self-awareness.

Adlerian education programs emphasize that parents must understand the goals and meanings of their children's misbehavior in order to deal with it successfully. They aim to establish a more cooperative family environment and use logical consequences to control behaviors. The best known proponent of this approach is Dreikurs (Dreikurs & Soltz, 1964). As Adler was both a psychoanalyst and an educator, this teaching is based on self-analysis and increased self-awareness (McKay & Hillman, 1979).

Evaluations of individual programs must be treated with caution. As Medway (1989) observes, few studies in this area have used clearly defined methodologies, objective measurements, matched samples of control populations, and adequate follow-up evaluations. Furthermore, different programs demand varying degrees of training and sophistication from their respective leaders and therapists. For example, Dreikurs and Soltz (1964) state that all parents can become group leaders after reading their manual. Leadership in Gordon's PET program is also seen as open to anyone without formal previous training (Dinkmeyer & McKay, 1976). It is of interest in this context that far more parents drop out of PET programs than of those stressing insights (28% vs. 7%), possibly because of the lack of professional sophistication of many PET leaders (Medway, 1989). On the other hand, more recent programs such as Active Parenting (Popkin, 1983) include sophisticated training components and present parent training as a professional endeavor.

Outcome studies are hampered by other confounding problems. For example, parents of young children need different skills from parents of adolescents, and the educational emphasis of programs may have to match these differing developmental needs. Furthermore, new attitudes may be best taught in nonbehavioral programs while direct behavioral change of a child may more quickly follow a behavioral management course.

Despite these difficulties, a number of studies have attempted to assess the effectiveness of parent education (Hinkel, Arnold, Croake, & Keller, 1980; Patterson, Chamberlain, & Reid, 1983; Webster-Stratton, 1984). In addition, the 24 scientifically most acceptable programs have been analyzed in a meta-analysis by Medway (1989). The analysis included 12 studies evaluating behavioral training, 5 PET programs, and 7 Adlerian training programs. Medway reports that all programs were effective in that children and parents showed an average of 62% more improvement than did their respective control populations. A few of these studies followed their sample for up to 6 months, and results indicated that gains were enduring. While outcome results were similar between the different types of programs, Medway suggests that behavioral management courses seem to improve child behavior more rapidly than programs using the reflective or the Adlerian model.

In summary then, there is some evidence that parents' training can be helpful to adults who are interested and committed to improve their parenting skills. While parent education programs have been based on at least 3 distinct developmental models, there are few if any differences between them concerning the outcome as reported by participants. This suggests that behavioral change in children can be elicited both by parental insight and through direct behavioral intervention by the parent. However, the long-term effect of such changes as well as their relationship to more global behavioral variables, such as general problem solving or social skills behaviors, has not yet been established.

Conclusions and Questions for Future Research

Evidence from the studies referred to in this chapter shows the great complexity of the parenting process in general. This chapter is an attempt to organize the data by suggesting the possible psychological processes behind the numerous research findings. It clearly documents that disorders of parenting are not single unidirectional events but reflect interactions between internal representation within parents and genetic vulnerabilities in both parents and children as well as family and community support structures.

While some of the available data provide a valid empirical base to teach those who come to see us for advice, many of our hypotheses still need elaboration and confirmation. For example, we still know little about how marital discord gets transferred to child psychopathology and how the parents "making up" after a fight or an argument can modify the impact of such stressful experiences for children later on. We also still poorly understand the effect of child-centered mediating variables in the intergenerational transmission of parenting problems. For example, does the possible genetic contribution children make to the parenting they receive operate through temperamental features, an overall vulnerability to stress, or through ways in which the child selectively perceives aspects of the environment? The difference that sex or the presence of older or younger siblings makes on susceptibility of children to abnor-

mal parenting also is not yet well understood. However, it is well recognized in child psychiatry today that developmental pathways show both continuities and discontinuities and that there are few experiences that are unalterable later on in life. This makes the study of parenting competence central in the development of preventive and therapeutic interventions.

REFERENCES

Ainsworth, M. D. (1957). *Infancy in Uganda: Infant care and growth of love.* Baltimore, MD: Johns Hopkins University Press.

Ainsworth, M. D., Blehar, M. C., Waters, E., & Wall, S. (1978). *Patterns of attachment: A psychological study of the strange situation.* Hillsdale, NJ: Lawrence Erlbaum.

Baumrind, D. H. (1967). Child care practices anteceding three patterns of preschool behavior. *Genetic Psychological Monographs, 75,* 43–88.

Baumrind, D. H. (1971). Harmonious parents and their preschool children. *Developmental Psychology Monographs, 4,* 99–123.

Baumrind, D. H. (1989). Rearing competent children. In W. Dounon (Ed.), *Child development today and tomorrow* (pp. 349–378). San Francisco: Jossey-Bass.

Beardslee, W. R., Bemporad, J., Keller, M. B., & Klerman, G. L. (1983). Children of parents with major affective disorder: A review. *American Journal of Psychiatry, 140,* 825–831.

Belsky, J. (1984). The determinants of parenting: A process model. *Child Development, 55,* 692–705.

Belsky, J., & Vondra, J. (1989). Lessons from child abuse: The determinants of parenting. In D. Cicchetti & V. Carlson (Eds.), *Child maltreatment: Theory and research on the causes and consequences of child abuse and neglect* (pp. 153–202). Cambridge: Cambridge University Press.

Benoit, D., Zeanah, C. H., & Barton, M. L. (1989). Maternal attachment disturbances in failure to thrive. *Infant Mental Health Journal, 10,* 185–202.

Benoit, D., Zeanah, C., Boucher, C., & Minde, K. (1992). Sleep disorders in early childhood: Association with insecure maternal attachment. *Journal of the American Academy of Child and Adolescent Psychiatry, 31,* 86–93.

Bifulco, A., Harris, T., & Brown, G. W. (1992). Mourning or early inadequate care? Re-examining the relationship of maternal loss in childhood with adult depression and anxiety. *Development and Psychopathology, 4,* 433–449.

Billings, A. G., & Moos, R. H. (1983). Comparisons of children of depressed and non-depressed parents: A social-environmental perspective. *Journal of Abnormal Child Psychology, 11,* 463–485.

Bowlby, J. (1969). *Attachment and loss. Vol. 1: Attachment.* New York: Basic Books.

Bowlby, J. (1979). *The making and breaking of affectional bonds.* London: Tavistock Publications.

Boyd, J. H., & Weissman, M. M. (1981). Epidemiology of affective disorders: A re-examination of future directions. *Archives of General Psychiatry, 38,* 1039–1046.

Bretherton, I. (1985). Attachment theory: Retrospect and prospect. In I. Bretherton & E. Waters (Eds.), *Growing points of attachment theory and research* (pp. 3–38). *Monographs of the Society for Research in Child Development, 50* (Serial No. 209).

Bridgman, R. O. (1930). Postwar progress in child welfare. *Annals of the American Academy of Political and Social Sciences, 151,* 32–45.

Brown, C. C. (1976, November). It changed my life. *Psychology Today.*

Brown, G. W., & Harris, T. O. (1978). *Social origins of depression.* New York: Free Press.

Brown, G. W., Harris, T. O., & Bifulco, A. (1986). Long-term effects of early loss of parent. In M. Rutter, I. E. Tizard, & P. B. Read (Eds.), *Depression in young people* (pp. 251–296). New York: Guilford Press.

Brunquell, D., Crichton, L., & Egeland, B. (1981). Maternal personality and attitude in disturbances of child rearing. *American Journal of Orthopsychiatry, 51,* 680–691.

Canavan, M. M., & Clark, R. (1923a). The mental health of 463 children from dementia praecox stock (I). *Mental Hygiene, 7,* 137–149.

Canavan, M. M., & Clark, R. (1923b). The mental health of 581 offspring of non-psychotic parents. *Mental Hygiene, 7,* 770–780.

Canavan, M. M., & Clark, R. (1936). The mental health of 463 children from dementia praecox stock (II). *Mental Hygiene, 20,* 463–469.

Cicchetti, D., Cummings, E. M., Greenberg, M. T., & Marvin, R. S. (1990). An organizational perspective on attachment beyond infancy. Implications for theory, measurement and research. In M. T. Greenberg, D. Cicchetti, & E. M. Cummings (Eds.), *Attachment in preschool years: Theory, research and intervention* (pp. 3–49). Chicago: University of Chicago Press.

Cicchetti, D., & Rizley, R. (1981). Developmental perspectives on the etiology, intergenerational transmission, and sequelae of child maltreatment. In R. Rizley & D. Cicchetti (Eds.), *Developmental perspectives on child maltreatment. New directions for child development, 11,* 33–55. Chicago: University of Chicago Press.

Clarke, R. V. G., & Cornish, D. B. (1978). The effectiveness of residential treatment. In L. A. Hersov, M. Berger, & D. Shaffer (Eds.), *Aggression and antisocial behaviour in childhood and adolescence* (pp. 143–159). Oxford: Pergamon.

Clark-Hall, M. (1978). *Responsive parenting manual.* Lawrence, KS: H. & H. Enterprises.

Clarke-Stewart, K. A. (1978). And daddy makes three: The father's impact on mother and the young child. *Child Development, 50,* 466–478.

Conger, R. D., Conger, K. J., Elder, G. H., Lorenz, F. O., Simons, R. L., & Whitbeck, L. B. (1992). A family process model of economic hardship and adjustment of early adolescent boys. *Child Development, 63,* 526–541.

Cox, A. D., Puckering, C., Pond, A., & Mills, M. (1987). The impact of maternal depression in young children. *Journal of Child Psychology and Psychiatry, 28,* 917–928.

Croake, J. W., & Glover, K. E. (1977). A history and evaluation of parent education. *Family Coordinator, 26,* 151–158.

deMause, L. (1974). *The history of childhood.* New York: Psycho-history Press.

Dinkmeyer, D., & McKay, G. (1976). *Systematic training for effective parenting.* Circle Pines, MN: American Guidance Service.

Dreikurs, R., & Soltz, V. (1964). *Children: The challenge.* New York: Hawthorn.

Emde, R. N. (1989). The infant's relationship experience: Developmental and affective aspects. In A. Sameroff & R. N. Emde (Eds.), *Relationship disturbances in early childhood: A developmental approach* (pp. 33–51). New York: Basic Books.

Engfer, A., & Schneewind, K. (1982). Causes and consequences of harsh parental punishment. *Child Abuse and Neglect, 6,* 129–139.

Fine, M. J., & Brownstein, C. (1983). Parent education: Problems, promises and implications for school social workers. *Social Work in Education, 6,* 44–55.

Fine, M. J., & Henry, S. A. (1989). Professional issues in parent education. In M. J. Fine (Ed.), *The second handbook on parent education* (pp. 3–20). New York: Academic Press.

Freud, A. (1946). *The ego and the mechanisms of defence.* New York: International Universities Press.

Freud, A. (1965). *Normality and pathology in childhood.* New York: International Universities Press.

Freud, S. (1958). Analysis of a phobia in a five-year-old boy. In J. Strachey (Ed. & Trans.), *The standard edition of the complete psychological works of Sigmund Freud* (Vol. 10, pp. 3–148). London: Hogarth Press. (Originally published 1909.)

Garmezy, N., & Devine, V. (1984). Project competence: The Minnesota studies of children vulnerable to psychopathology. In N. Watt, J. Rolf, & E. J. Anthony (Eds.), *Children at risk for schizophrenia* (pp. 289–303). London: Cambridge University Press.

Gershon, E. S., Hamovit, J., Guroff, J., Leckman, J., Sceery, W., Targum, S. D., Nurnberger, J. I., Jr., Goldin, L., & Bunney, W. E., Jr. (1982). A family study of schizoaffective, bipolar I, bipolar II, unipolar probands and normal controls. *Archives of General Psychiatry, 39,* 1157–1167.

Glueck, S., & Glueck, E. T. (1944). *After-conduct of discharged offenders.* London: Macmillan.

Goodall, J. (1990). *Through a window.* Boston: Houghton Mifflin.

Gordon, T. (1970). *Parent Effectiveness Training.* New York: Wyden.

Gordon, T. (1975). *P.E.T.: Parent effectiveness training.* New York: American Library.

Gottesmann, I., & Shields, J. (1982). *Schizophrenia the epigenetic puzzle.* Cambridge: Cambridge University Press.

Greer, K. (1986, October). Today's parents: How well are they doing? *Better Homes and Gardens,* pp. 36–46.

Hammon, C., Gordon, D., Burge, D., Adrian, C., Jaenicke, C., Hiroto, D. (1987). Maternal Affective Disorders, Illness and Stress: Risk for Children's Psychopathology, American Journal of Psychiatry, 144: 736–741.

Harder, D. W., Kokes, R. F., Fisher, L., & Strauss, J. (1980). Child competence and psychiatric risk. IV. Relationship of parent diagnostic classification and parent psychopathology severity to child functioning. *Journal of Nervous and Mental Disorders, 168,* 343–347.

Hattendorf, K. W., Ojemann, R. H., Shaus, H. S., Jack, L. M., Nystrom, G. H., & Remer, L. L. (1932). *Researches in parent education* (Vol. 1). Iowa City: University of Iowa Press.

Hetherington, E. M., Cox, M., & Cox, C. R. (1982). Effects of divorce on parents and children. In M. Lamb (ed.), *Nontraditional families* (pp. 233–288). Hillsdale, NJ: Lawrence Erlbaum.

Hinde, R. A., & Stevenson-Hinde, J. (eds). (1988). *Relationships within families: Mutual influences.* Oxford: Clarendon Press.

Hinkel, D. E., Arnold, C. F., Croake, J. W., & Keller, J. F. (1980). Adlerian parent education: Changes in parents' attitudes and behaviors, and children's self-esteem. *American Journal of Family Therapy, 8,* 32–43.

Hodges, J., & Tizard, B. (1989a). Social and family relationships of ex-institutional adolescents. *Journal of Child Psychology and Psychiatry, 30,* 53–75 & 77–97.

Hodges, J., & Tizard, B. (1989b). IQ and behavioural adjustment of ex-institutional adolescents. *Journal of Child Psychology and Psychiatry, 30,* 53–75.

Holt, L. E. (1902). *The care and feeding of children.* New York: Appleton.

Hunter, R., & Kilstrom, N. (1979). Breaking the cycle in abusive families. *American Journal of Psychiatry, 136,* 1320–1322.

Janet, P. (1925). *Psychological healing* (Vol. 1). (E. Paul & C. Paul, Trans.). London: Allen & Unwin.

Jones, F. A., Green, V., & Krauss, D. R. (1980). Maternal responsiveness of primiparous mothers during the postpartum period: Age differences. *Pediatrics, 65,* 579–584.

Kaufman, J., & Zigler, E. (1987). Do abused children become abusive parents? *American Journal of Orthopsychiatry, 57,* 186–192.

Kessen, W. (1965). *The child*. New York: John Wiley & Sons.

Kochanska, G., Kuczynski, L., Radke-Yarrow, M., & Welsh, J. D. (1987). Resolution of control episodes between well and affectively ill mothers and their young children. *Journal of Abnormal Child Psychology, 15,* 441–456.

Kokes, R. F., Harder, D. W., Fisher, L., & Strauss, J. (1980). Child competence and psychiatric risk. V. Sex of patient parent and dimensions of psychopathology. *Journal of Nervous and Mental Disorders, 168,* 348–352.

Lamborn, S. D., Mounts, N. S., Steinberg, L., & Dornbusch, S. M. (1991). Patterns of competence and adjustment among adolescents from authoritative, authoritarian, indulgent, and neglectful families. *Child Development, 62,* 1049–1065.

Langer, W. (1973–1974). Infanticide: A historical survey. *History of Childhood Quarterly, 1,* 354–365.

LeVine, R. A. (1977). Child rearing as a cultural adaptation. In P. H. Leiderman, S. R. Tulkin, & A. Rosenfeld (Eds.), *Culture and infancy, variations in the human experience* (pp. 15–27). New York: Academic Press.

LeVine, R. A. (1988). Human parental care: Universal goals, cultural strategies, individual behavior. In R. A. LeVine, P. M. Miller, & M. Maxwell-West (Eds.), *Parental behavior in diverse societies* (pp. 3–12). San Francisco: Jossey-Bass.

Loeber, R., & Stouthamer-Loeber, M. (1986). Family factors as correlates and predictors of juvenile conduct problems and delinquency. In M. Tonry & N. Morris (Eds.), *Crime and justice* (Vol. 7, pp. 29–149). Chicago: University of Chicago Press.

Maccoby, E., & Martin, J. (1983). Socialization in the context of the family: Parent-child interaction. In E. M. Hetherington (Ed.), P. H. Mussen (Series Ed.), *Handbook of child psychology. Vol. 4: Socialization, personality, and social Development* (pp. 1–101). New York: John Wiley & Sons.

Main, M., & Goldwyn, R. (1984). Predicting rejection of her infant from mother's representation of her own experience: Implications for the abused abusing intergenerational cycle. *Child Abuse and Neglect, 8,* 203–270.

Main, M., & Hesse, E. (1990). Parents' unresolved traumatic experiences are related to infant disorganized attachment status: Is frightened and/or frightening parental behavior the linking mechanism? In M. Greenberg, D. Cicchetti, & M. Cummings (Eds.), *Attachment in the preschool years* (pp. 161–182). Chicago: University of Chicago Press.

McCord, W., & McCord, J. (1959). *Origins of crime: A new evaluation of the Cambridge-Sommerville Study*. New York: Columbia University Press.

McKay, G. D., & Hillman, B. W. (1979). An Adlerian multimedia approach to parent education. *Elementary School Guidance and Counselling, 14,* 23–25.

Mednick, S. A., & Schulsinger, F. (1968). Some premorbid characteristics related to breakdown in children with schizophrenic mothers. In D. Rosenthal & S. S. Kety (Eds.), *The transmission of schizophrenia* (pp. 267–291). London: Pergamon Press.

Medway, F. J. (1989). Measuring the effectiveness of parent education. In M. J. Fine (Ed.), *The second handbook on parent education* (pp. 237–255). New York: Academic Press.

Minde, K. (1975). Psychological problems in Ugandan school children: A controlled evaluation. *Journal of Child Psychology and Psychiatry, 16,* 49–59.

Minde, K. (1986). Bonding and attachment: Its relevance for the present-day clinician. *Developmental Medicine & Child Neurology, 28,* 803–813.

Minde, K. (1991). The effect of disordered parenting on the development of children. In M. Lewis (Ed.), *Child and adolescent psychiatry. A comprehensive textbook* (pp. 394–407). Baltimore, MD: Williams & Wilkins.

Minde, K. (1992). Aggression in preschoolers: Its relation to socialization. *Journal of the American Academy of Child and Adolescent Psychiatry, 31,* 853–862.

Minde, K. (1993). Prematurity and serious medical illness in infancy: Implications for development and intervention. In C. Zeanah (Ed.), *Handbook of infant mental health*. New York: Guilford Press.

Minde, K. (1997). Sleep disorders in young children. In J. D. Noshpitz (Ed.), *Handbook of child and adolescent psychiatry* (Vol. 1, pp. 492–507). New York: John Wiley & Sons.

Minde, K., Corter, C., Goldberg, S., & Jeffers, D. (1990). Maternal preference toward premature twins: Stability and effect on behavior over four years. *Journal of the American Academy of Child and Adolescent Psychiatry, 29,* 367–374.

Minde, K., & Minde, R. (1986). *Infant psychiatry: An introductory textbook*. London: Sage Publications.

Minuchin, S. (1985). Families and individual development: Provocations from the field of family therapy. *Child Development, 56,* 289–302.

Olson, D. H., Sprenkle, D. H., & Russel, C. S. (1979). Circumplex model of marital and family systems. I. Cohesion and adaptability dimensions, family types, and clinical applications. *Family Process, 18,* 3–28.

Patterson, G. R. (1982). *Coercive family processes*. Eugene, OR: Castalia.

Patterson, G. R., Chamberlain, P., & Reid, J. B. (1983). A comparative evaluation of a parent-training program. *Behavior Therapy, 13,* 638–650.

Patterson, G. R., & Forgatch, M. S. (1975). *Family learning series* (Cassettes 1 & 2). Champaign, IL: Research Press.

Peiper, A. (1966). *Quellen zur Kinderheilkunde*. Bern: Huber.

Pelton, L. (1978). Child abuse and neglect: The myth of classlessness. *American Journal of Orthopsychiatry, 48,* 608–617.

Plomin, R., & Daniels, D. (1987). Why are children in the same family so different from one another? *Behavioral and Brain Sciences, 10,* 1–60.

Pollock, L. A. (1983). *Forgotten children: Parent-child relations from 1500–1900*. Cambridge: Cambridge University Press.

Popkin, M. (1983). *Active parenting handbook*. Atlanta, GA: Active Parenting.

Preston, G., & Antin, R. (1933). A study of the children

of psychotic parents. *American Journal of Orthopsychiatry, 2,* 231–239.

Puckering, C. (1989). Maternal depression. *Journal of Child Psychology and Psychiatry, 30,* 807–817.

Puig-Antich, J., Lukens, E., Davies, M., Goetz, D., Brennan-Quatrock, J., & Todak, G. (1985). Psychosocial functioning in prepubertal major depressive disorders. *Archives of General Psychiatry, 42,* 500–507.

Quinton, D., & Rutter, M. (1976). Early hospital admissions and late disturbances of behavior. *Developmental Medical Child Neurology, 18,* 447–459.

Quinton, D., & Rutter, M. (1988). *Parenting breakdown: The making and breaking of intergenerational links.* Avebury: Gower Publishing Co., Aldershot.

Radke-Yarrow, M., Cummings, E. M., Kuczynski, L., & Chapman, M. (1985). Patterns of attachment in two and three year olds in normal families and families with parental depression. *Child Development, 56,* 884–893.

Ragozin, A. S., Basham, R. B., Crnic, K. A., Greenberg, M. T., & Robinson, N. M. (1982). Effects of maternal age on parenting role. *Developmental Psychology, 18,* 627–634.

Reitsma-Street, M., Offord, D. R., & Finch, T. (1985). Pairs of same-sexed siblings discordant for antisocial behaviour. *British Journal of Psychiatry, 146,* 415–423.

Richman, N., Stevenson, J., & Graham, P. J. (1982). *Preschool to school: A behavioural study.* London: Academic Press.

Robertson, P. (1974). Home as a nest: Middle class childhood in nineteenth century Europe. In L. deMause (Ed.), *The history of childhood* (pp. 407–431). New York: Psychohistory Press.

Robins, L., West, P. A., & Herjanic, B. L. (1975). Arrests and delinquency in two generations: A study of black urban families and their children. *Journal of Child Psychology and Psychiatry, 16,* 125–140.

Rohner, R. P. (1975). *They love me, they love me not: A worldwide study of the effects of parental acceptance and rejection.* New Haven, CT: H.R.A.F. Press.

Rutter, M. (1966). Children of sick parents: An environmental and psychiatric study. *Institute of Psychiatry Maudsley Monographs* (No. 16). London: Oxford University Press.

Rutter, M. (1981). *Maternal deprivation reassessed* (2nd ed.). Harmondsworth: Penguin.

Rutter, M. (1986). The developmental psychopathology of depression: Issues and perspectives. In M. Rutter, C. E. Izard, & P. B. Read (Eds.), *Depression in young people: Developmental and clinical perspectives* (pp. 3–30). New York: Guilford Press.

Rutter, M. (1989). Intergenerational continuities and discontinuities in serious parenting difficulties. In D. Cicchetti & V. Carlson (Eds.), *Child maltreatment: Theory and research on the causes and consequences of child abuse and neglect* (pp. 317–348). Cambridge: Cambridge University Press.

Rutter, M., & Giller, H. (1983). *Juvenile delinquency: Trends and perspectives.* Harmondsworth: Penguin.

Rutter, M., & Quinton, D. (1984). Parental psychiatric disorder: Effects on children. *Psychological Medicine, 14,* 853–880.

Sameroff, A. J., Dickstein, S., Hayden, L. C., & Schiller, M. (1993, March). *Effects of family process and parental depression on children.* Paper presented at 60th meeting of the Society for Research in Child Development, New Orleans, LA.

Sameroff, A. J., & Zax, M. (1978). In search of schizophrenia: Young offspring of schizophrenic women. In L. C. Wynne, R. L. Cromwell, & S. Mathysse (Eds.), *The nature of schizophrenia: New approaches to research and treatment* (pp. 85–102). New York: John Wiley & Sons.

Shure, M. B., & Spivack, G. (1978). *Problem-solving techniques in child rearing.* San Francisco: Jossey-Bass.

Skinner, H. A., Steinhauer, P. D., & Santa Barbara, J. (1983). The family assessment measure. *Canadian Journal of Community Mental Health, 2* (2), 91–105.

Sroufe, L. A. (1983). Infant-caregiver attachment and patterns of adaptation in preschool: The roots of maladaptation and competence. In M. Perlmutter (Ed.), *The Minnesota symposium on child development* (Vol. 16, pp. 41–83). Hillsdale, NJ: Lawrence Erlbaum.

Steinberg, L., Elmen, J. D., & Mounts, N. S. (1989). Authoritative parenting, psychosocial maturity, and academic success among adolescents. *Child Development, 60,* 1424–1436.

Steinhauer, P. (1984). Clinical applications of the process model of family functioning. *Canadian Journal of Psychiatry, 29,* 98–111.

Sunley, R. (1955). Early nineteenth century American literature on child rearing. In M. Mead & M. Wolfenstein (Eds.), *Childhood in contemporary cultures* (pp. 150–167). Chicago: University of Chicago Press.

Suomi, S. J., Harlow, H. F., & Novak, M. A. (1974). Reversal of social deficits produced by isolation rearing in monkeys. *Journal of Human Evolution, 3,* 527–534.

Tizard, B., & Hodges, J. (1978). The effect of early institutional rearing on the development of eight-year-old children. *Journal of Child Psychology and Psychiatry, 19,* 99–118.

Trivers, R. (1974). Parent-offspring conflict. *American Zoologist, 14,* 249–264.

Wadsworth, M. (1979). *Roots of delinquency: Infancy, adolescence and crime.* Oxford: Martin Robertson.

Watson, J. B. (1928). *Psychological care of infant and child.* New York: W. W. Norton.

Webster-Stratton, C. (1982). Randomized trial of two parent-training programs for families with conduct-disordered children. *Journal of Consulting and Clinical Psychology, 52,* 666–678.

Weiss, B., Dodge, K. A., Bates, J. E., & Pettit, G. S. (1992). Some consequences of early harsh discipline: Child aggression and a maladaptive social information processing style. *Child Development, 63,* 1321–1335.

Weissman, M. M., Gershon, E. S., Kidd, K. K., Prusoff, B. A., Leckman, J. F., Thompson, W. D., Pauls, D., Dibble, E. D., Guroff, J. J., & Hamovit, J. (1984). Psychiatric disorders in the relatives of probands with affective disorders: The Yale-NIMH Collaborative Family Study. *Archives of General Psychiatry, 41,* 13–21.

Werner, E. E. (1979). *Cross-cultural child development: A view from the planet earth.* Monterey, CA: Brooks/Cole.

West, D. J. (1982). *Delinquency: Its roots, careers and prospects.* London: Heinemann.

West, D. J., & Farrington, D. P. (1973). *Who becomes delinquent?* London: Heinemann.

Wynne, C. (1984). The epigenesis of relational systems: A model for understanding family development. *Family Process, 23,* 297–318.

Zekoski, E. M., O'Hara, M. W., & Wills, K. E. (1987). The effects of maternal mood on mother-infant interaction. *Journal of Abnormal Child Psychology, 15,* 361–378.

15 / **Prevention in Child and Adolescent Psychiatry**

Morton M. Silverman

Historical Perspectives

Two physicians, Hugh Leavell and E. Gurney Clark (1953), defined 3 levels of prevention that mirrored epidemiological concepts of infectious disease prevention. Their conceptualization of prevention has been applied to the domain of psychiatric disorders and dysfunctions, albeit with some modifications (Caplan, 1961, 1964). The initial concept of prevention was rooted in a public health (community) perspective, and so "pure" prevention, specifically "primary prevention," was aimed at groups and communities believed to be at increased risk for the development of a disorder or dysfunction.

Many authors have pointed out that the mental health field's claims about prevention have fallen short, that promises have been unfulfilled and conclusions have been stated without sufficient empirical evidence. Pardes, Silverman, and West (1989) have stated:

During the first half of the century, primary prevention was achieved with traditional public health approaches for at least two illnesses with psychiatric components: pellagra and general paresis. The discovery that infection with measles, during a woman's first trimester, puts the fetus at risk for brain dysfunction also resulted in the application of primary prevention techniques for women in their child-bearing years. In the past decade, with new techniques (including methods developed by other disciplines, such as neurology and genetics), psychiatric epidemiologists have been working to identify antecedent factors that may provide a basis for other primary prevention strategies.

Nevertheless, the application of public health methods to mental health problems has been a complex proposition. The classic public health model, conceptualizing illness in terms of host, agent, and environment, does not "fit" most psychiatric disorders. The difference now, in psychiatry and behavioral science, is the mounting evidence for a biological substrate in many mental disorders. Environmental and social factors are now regarded—more widely than in the past—as critical determinants of whether an illness will be expressed in a biologically vulnerable individual, rather than as exclusive causes in themselves. Recognizing this distinction may make public health approaches, both to major mental illnesses and to behavioral dysfunctions, much more feasible. Connections among biology, environment, and psychopathology can be analyzed in much more specific terms. (p. 405)

In their review of the status of past preventive intervention efforts, the American Psychiatric Association's Task Force on Prevention Research (1990; hereafter cited as APA) highlighted the unkept promises and disappointments of early efforts:

As Shaffer (1989) has pointed out, for most of the last 100 years, there has generally been a humane and optimistic view about preventing children's unhappiness and disturbed behavior. However, it is also true that until recently, any psychiatric disorder in a child was predominantly viewed solely as a distortion of normal development. Thus, it was held that if parents avoided being too repressive, thus preventing the child's expression of normal wishes or impulses, and if they attended to the principles of learning theory and reinforcement, their child would not develop significant disturbances or psychopathology. Later it was felt that if parents could be educated more intensively, if prenatal care could be extended to all women, and if parents and children had more access to medical resources and housing, a happy and productive childhood would almost universally be ensured. However, as pointed out by

Eisenberg (1989), the "IOUs" issued in the early days of the mental hygiene movement, which promised that "mental illness" would be eliminated by education about human relationships, proved to be unredeemable. Thus, some of the widespread disbelief or skepticism regarding preventive psychiatry can be traced directly to early assertions that preventive interventions such as education, support, and reasonable child-rearing practices would together prevent child psychopathology. (p. 1701)

The APA Task Force members (APA, 1990) also identified inherent problems associated with conceptualizing mental disorders in public health and epidemiological terms:

As Earls (1979) has pointed out, confusion has also arisen because risk factors have not been restricted to causes or even correlates of the disorder; erroneously, even consequences have been designated as risk factors. Furthermore, attributes such as age and sex have been designated risk factors. Appropriate use of the term "risk factors" is most important when one moves from descriptive studies to experimental interventions, where risk factors should be restricted to variables that can be manipulated (attributes usually cannot be manipulated). Prevention research in psychiatry has progressed substantially from assertions of causal relationships based solely on theoretical positions and not on solid epidemiologic, prospective, or longitudinal data. Our data have been gathered from complementary studies of the most salient risk factors in various mental disorders, but they are uneven. We have more complete information about childhood conduct disorder and adult antisocial behavior than about effective disorders or schizophrenia. However, this unevenness of solid data across the diagnostic spectrum is no worse in psychiatry than it is in other medical specialties. (pp. 1702–1703)

It is against this background of good intentions and poor outcomes that we take a harder look at issues of using more precise definitions, more refined concepts, and more specific preventive intervention approaches to address more rigorously defined disorders and dysfunctions. In the process, we will see that the challenges are great, the complexities many, but the potential possible.

Definitions

Gerald Caplan (1964), a child psychiatrist and student of Erich Lindemann, defined primary prevention in mental health as ". . . lowering the rate of occurrence of new cases of mental disorder in a population . . . by counteracting harmful circumstances before they have had a chance to produce illness. It does not seek to prevent a specific person from becoming sick. Instead, it seeks to reduce the risk for the whole population so that although some may become ill, their numbers will be reduced" (p. 26).

The key reformulation and emphasis here is on a community or population-based approach, whereby the preventive actions are directed at a "healthy" population to assist in keeping groups of individuals on normal developmental and psychological trajectories. Concepts of prevention always have held a particular fascination for those working with children and adolescents. The potential for interfering, modifying, averting, or preventing the development of dysfunctional behaviors and pathways (or for promoting healthy functioning) fit well with the general focus on charting developmental trajectories and assessing the acquisition of stage and phase appropriate behaviors.

Primary prevention refers to measures directed at averting the development and appearance of disease. The goal of primary preventive interventions are to prevent the onset of a disease or disorder, thereby reducing its incidence (number of new cases occurring in a specific period of time). As Table 15.1 suggests, this can be accomplished by eliminating causative agents, interfering with the mode of disease transmission, reducing risk factors, enhancing host resistance, or protecting health through environmental and ecological measures. In essence, primary prevention may be dichotomized into 2 main endeavors: (1) actions designed to prevent the development of psychiatric disorders (specific protection); and (2) interventions designed to promote well-being as an inoculant against dysfunction (health promotion).

Secondary prevention is defined as early intervention and prompt treatment of the early signs and symptoms of an emerging illness or disorder, with the goal of reducing the *prevalence* (total number of existing cases) of the condition by decreasing its duration. Hence, the goal is to reduce symptoms (diminish suffering), limit sequelae, and minimize any possible contagion. According to Cowen (1983), there are 2 distinct pathways to secondary prevention: "(1) identify prodromal signs of serious disorder early, so that prompt effective steps can be taken to avert dire psychological consequences, and (2) identify signs of dysfunction as soon as possible in a person's (child's)

TABLE 15.1

Prevention Concepts: Focus on Child and Adolescent Mental Health

Type	Goal	Methods	Examples
Primary	Reduce incidence	Disease/disorder prevention	Prenatal and postnatal screening for genetic defects
			Counseling pregnant women about the fetal alcohol syndrome
		Health promotion and enhancement	Alcohol and other drug use public education programs
			Parent education programs on child development and nutrition
		Health protection (modifying agent/environment)	Protection from hazardous environmental conditions (seat belts, lead, gun control)
			Labeling of alcoholic beverages
		Health maintenance	Educational programs on exercise, stress management, relaxation techniques
			Regular physical checkups including mental status assessments
Secondary	Reduce prevalence	Early intervention and treatment	Early detection, referral, and treatment of adolescent drug abusers
			Screening and remediation for childhood emotional dysfunctions
Tertiary	Reduce disability/ dependence	Rehabilitation programs	Treatment services for youths in criminal detention facilities
		Community support programs	Shelters and programs for battered women and their children
		Treatment for the chronically ill	Integrating continuing care systems in the community

life history and use the best available tools to short-circuit later, more serious problems" (p. 11–12).

Tertiary prevention is the reduction of the prevalence of residual defects or existing disability secondary to the presence of an illness or disorder (often of chronic nature and duration). It refers to rehabilitative efforts to enable those with long-standing or chronic mental disorders or disabilities to function at their highest possible physiological and psychological level. This may well mean focusing on appropriate social skills and job effectiveness.

In an attempt to translate epidemiological terms and public health concepts into understandable psychosocial concepts, Albee (1982) developed an equation to define the roles of community, professional, and individual efforts in accomplishing the goal of reduced incidence of mental disorders or behavioral dysfunctions. (See Figure 15.1.) Albee argues that the reduction in

the incidence of mental disorders and behavioral dysfunctions can come about either by reducing the numerator or by increasing the denominator, or by doing both. For Albee, decreasing stress and increasing the triad of coping skills, self-esteem, and social support would all lead to a decrease in the incidence of mental dysfunctions among children and adolescents.

Naomi Rae-Grant (1983), a noted Canadian child and adolescent psychiatrist, has identified different levels at which these multiple preventive interventions may occur. (See Table 15.2.) Among her many contributions is to highlight the expansion of individual intervention approaches to incorporate those at the familial, sociocultural, and sociopolitical level. This provides a much richer tapestry and opportunity in which to intervene. To ignore the potential of legislation, federal funding, and legal mandates for the implementation of targeted preventive interventions is to ignore some

$$\text{Incidence} = \frac{\text{Organic Factor} + \text{Stress}}{\text{Coping Skills} + \text{Self Esteem} + \text{Support Groups}}$$

FIGURE 15.1

Community Psychology Definition of Incidence

TABLE 15.2

Preventive Interventions at Different Levels

Intervention Target	Level	Nature of Intervention
Individual child and/or family	Case level	Intrapsychic Intrafamilial Interpersonal
Group (type) of children or families	Class level	Familial/subcultural
Local environment (e.g., institutions, agencies, neighborhoods)	Community level	Sociopolitical
Wider environment areas (e.g., national)	Central level	Sociopolitical

NOTE: From "Prevention," by N. Rae-Grant, in P. Steinhauer and Q. Rae-Grant (Eds.), *Psychological Problems of the Child in the Family* 1983, New York: Basic Books. Copyright 1983 by Naomi Rae-Grant. Adapted with permission.

of the major facilitative tools for change that are currently available. Some examples include enactment of seat belt laws, server liability laws, warning labels on tobacco products, and eliminating lead levels in paint.

The Science of Prevention

A comprehensive definition of prevention highlights the importance of recognizing the role of biological, environmental, and behavioral factors in the development and implementation of preventive interventions. In moving from prevention definitions to developing preventive interventions, many disciplines and basic research findings must be coordinated and integrated. Figure 15.2 illustrates the essential building blocks of preventive intervention research and suggests an interplay and interdependence of various disciplines and research paradigms (Silverman & Koretz, 1989). Such research, if well designed, well executed, and well evaluated, has the potential to help answer a number of related questions about:

1. The etiology and pathogenesis of disorder
2. The who, when, where, what, and how of interventions

3. The essential ingredients of an intervention, the relative roles of components of an intervention, and the significance of timing, frequency, duration, and intensity
4. The role and function of mediating variables in the development of a disorder, the maintenance of a disorder, or the interruption in the development and expression of a disorder
5. The interplay among subject variables, intervention/mediating variables, and outcome variables

Hence, the essential ingredients for developing a preventive intervention is the identification of a: (1) well-defined population at risk for a disorder; (2) well-defined disorder and/or dysfunction that is present in the population and is resulting in a general level of distress; (3) well-defined theory/ hypothesis of the etiology and pathogenesis (pathophysiology, psychopathological process) of the disorder; and (4) well-reasoned intervention that conceptually takes into account the previous 3 points.

Such an orientation allows for a range of preventive interventions to be tested in specific settings, with specific at-risk populations, and aimed at specific targeted disorders. However, often it is not clear that these criteria (or essential ingredients) have been rigorously addressed in the development and implementation of preventive intervention programs. (Silverman, 1996).

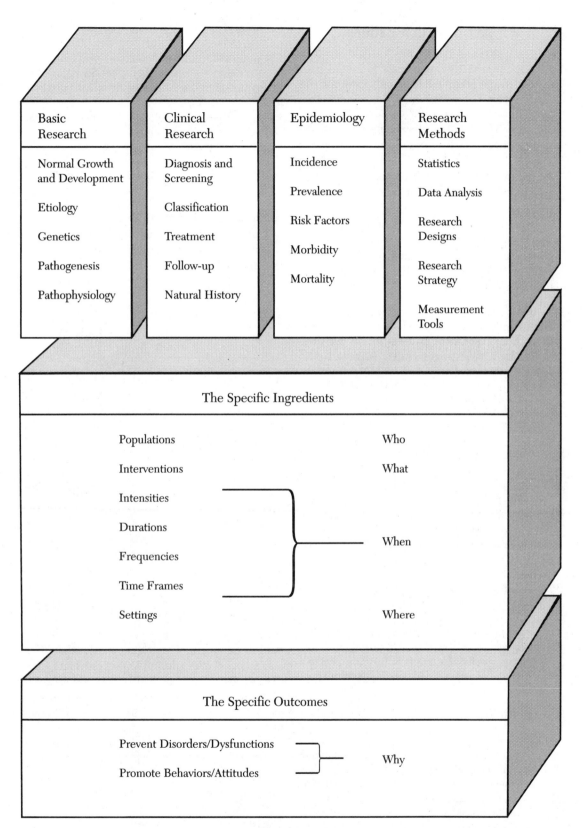

FIGURE 15.2

Preventive Intervention Research:
The Final Common Pathway

Models of Risk for Illness

As Shaffer (1989) pointed out, we do not know how to prevent the initial appearance of any psychiatric disorder, except for certain disorders of childhood. There is also a developing consensus in our field that most disorders cannot be explained solely as the result of stresses imposed on normal developmental processes. This model was essentially founded on the belief that all individuals have a universal potential for disturbance, and it deemphasizes or ignores the observation that some people are at substantially greater risk for specific disorders than are other people.

The APA Task Force on Prevention Research (1990) identified the dilemma:

The concept of universal, nonspecific vulnerability for illness is no longer widely held in psychiatry; we have learned from a number of excellent studies that there are significant differences in vulnerability to certain psychiatric disorders. Earls (1979, 1989) has divided the data about differential risk into two types of epidemiologic studies. The first type addresses the prevalence of disorders in parents and other adult relatives of children, and the second is longitudinal studies of impaired children that evaluate the risk for later development of adult disorders. Both types of studies have contributed greatly to our understanding of risk factors in vulnerable children.

Nevertheless, it is also clear that many mental health professionals mistrust the medical-illness model of child and adolescent psychopathology. There is tension between those who focus on specific risk factors as antecedents for psychopathology and those who do not support this specific-etiology model. The latter group finds that an antecedent-condition model applies across a wide range of emotional and behavioral dysfunctions. These observers argue that nonspecific predisposing factors and precipitating conditions may be responsible for the expression of many disorders, moving away from the focus on specific risk factors to the possibility of a more universal potential for disturbance in various populations. (p. 1702)

Felner and Silverman (1989) have elaborated on this controversy as follows:

At this point, a key debate in the prevention literature becomes salient if we are to decide how and when to move from "risk factors" to programs. We need to be clear on how we answer the questions: (a) Do we attempt to tailor primary prevention programs to the prevention of a specific disorder, or (b) do we develop programs which are effective in alleviating a number of conditions that are antecedent to a range of emotional and physical problems, including, but not limited to the target problem?

The "specific disorder prevention" model rests heavily in a classic medical-public health paradigm which views diseases as caused by specific conditions that interact with individual vulnerabilities, again, specifiable. In contrast, the antecedent condition model argues that at least for a wide range of emotional and behavioral disorders, particularly those related to stress and other elements of the normal life-course, the specific etiology model is not appropriate. (Goldstein, 1985, p. 25)

Consequently, one of the current conceptual controversies relates to the appropriate selection of a testable hypothesis and model or models on which to base the implementation of a preventive intervention.

Developmental Perspectives

A developmental perspective is best suited for explicating pathways to disorder that are congruent with prevention's tasks, assumptions, and defining characteristics (Sameroff & Fiese, 1989; Seidman, 1987). This view is based on emerging research that suggests that the principles of normal development also can be applied to understanding the emergence of disorder (Sroufe & Rutter, 1984). The implication is that processes that are the primary targets of preventive efforts should be those deviations in normal developmental processes that are experienced by the target population and lead to the outcomes that are targeted for prevention.

Thus developmentally based preventive interventions start by identifying those developmental processes that relate to "healthy" forms of the outcomes of concern. They then consider the differences between the desirable processes and those that are being experienced by the population of concern. Preventive interventions are aimed at closing this "gap" in the desired direction (Felner, Silverman, & Felner, in press). The outcomes of concern are now seen as predictable and even "normal" results of the deviations in developmental conditions, since the mechanisms that lead to problematic developmental outcomes are the same as those that lead to positive ones.

Historically, a major dimension on which most prevention efforts can be categorized reflects 2 quite different assumptions about the specificity and uniqueness of developmental pathways. Single-outcome focused programs, such as those targeted to substance abuse, delinquency, school failure, depression, youth suicide, and teenage pregnancy, reflect a specific disease prevention model that rests heavily on classical medical paradigms of disorder. These paradigms hold that dysfunction is caused by specifiable disease agents or germs that interact with individual, identifiable vulnerabilities.

A contrasting perspective to this position is one that holds that there is a need for a comprehensive, multicausal, nonspecific developmental pathway approach (Felner & Felner, 1989; Felner & Silverman, 1989). This model recognizes that: (1) most of the disorders we seek to prevent have a large number of common risk factors; (2) conditions that protect against one disorder generally also protect against others; and (3) nonspecific, personal vulnerabilities increase an individual's susceptibility to the onset of a wide array of dysfunctions. The pathways to most of the social, emotional, and adaptive difficulties with which we are concerned are generally complex and shared by more than 1 disorder. Hence, for a wide range of developmental outcomes and pathologies, it appears that efforts to identify specific and unique etiological "causal agents" are not appropriate (Felner et al., in press).

A number of studies are highly supportive of this view. In studies of the adaptive impact of a wide array of developmental circumstances, common developmental antecedents, including family resources and interaction patterns, economic and social deprivation, other life stressors, powerlessness, personal competencies, and an array of nonspecific protective resiliency factors (e.g., social support, self-sufficiency, self-efficacy, hope) relate to the probability that persons in a population will develop an extraordinary variety of mental and physical disorders (Felner et al., 1983; Kellam & Brown, 1982; Sameroff & Fiese, 1989; Silverman, 1989). Converging with this developmental evidence, others who have focused on the epidemiology of serious disorders (Cantwell & Baker, 1989; Dryfoos, 1990; Rutter, 1989a) have pointed to the high levels of comorbidity among such disorders. These authors have underscored the fact that they appear to share a common constellation of antecedent developmental experiences and "root causes" in their emergent pathways of disorder and dysfunction.

The nonlinear and overlapping nature of pathways to disorder is further underscored by a third set of studies of the stability of the developmental course of such difficulties. Cantwell and Baker (1989) examined the "stability" of clinical levels of disorder in children and adolescents and found that "four years after the time of initial diagnosis for some disorders, 100% of those who were diagnosed as previously showing clinical levels of dysfunction were now symptom-free" (p. 16). Additionally, among those children who had an initial diagnosis and who still had a diagnosable condition at follow-up, across conditions, only 30–50% were still found to have the original condition, while the remainder manifested quite different clinical conditions than had been originally diagnosed.

Rutter (1989a) reviews recent studies of child psychiatric epidemiology and concludes, "perhaps the most striking finding to emerge from all developmental epidemiological studies undertaken up to now has been extremely high levels of comorbidity" (p. 645). Sameroff and Fiese (1989) state that "while clear linkages have been found between some 'germs' and specific biological disorders, this has not been true for behavioral disorders . . . (p. 24)." What is missing in our armamentarium of preventive intervention efforts is an integrative theoretical framework that allows us to design interventions that can address the multicausal and multidimensional pathways of disorder and dysfunction.

Table 15.3 highlights some targets for primary preventive interventions during early developmental stages. These targets for intervention are not causally linked to specific disease or disorder outcomes but rather represent critical foci to monitor when concerned about maintaining and promoting healthy developmental trajectories.

Further Complexities

The complex etiology and pathogenesis of most psychiatric disorders has several important implications. It implies that no single, comprehensive solution will prevent all forms of a particular disorder at all developmental stages or phases. Those who seek to identify the one "real" cause of a particular type of disorder (in order to design the one, comprehensively effective preventive intervention) will inevitably be disappointed, since no

TABLE 15.3

Preventive Interventions: Focus on Developmental Trajectories

Prenatal and Natal	Postnatal and Infancy	Childhood	Adolescence
Adequate nutrition during pregnancy	Parent training courses in child rearing, development, nutrition, etc.	Nurturing and protective institutional settings (schools)	Nutrition and exercise programs
Abstinence from alcohol and other drugs (tobacco)	Improved day care regulations and availability	Periodic screenings for developmental delays/ physical disabilities	Alcohol and other drug use education and early intervention
Genetic screening			
Genetic counseling	Screening for inborn errors of metabolism (PKU)	Child abuse laws and monitoring	Nurturing a sense of hope in the future
Amniocentesis			
Regular obstetrical examinations with risk monitoring (toxemia, systemic illnesses)	Consistent and competent caregiving/nurturing practices	Interpersonal cognitive problem solving skills development	Competency building
			Self-esteem enhancement
Social support for pregnant mothers	Regular schedule of immunizations and pediatric exams	Head Start programs	Anticipatory guidance programs
		Enlightened policies and procedures for adoption, separation and divorce that protect rights of children	Crisis intervention support networks
Improved obstetrical monitoring and delivery practices			
Seat belts	Seat belts	Seat belts	Seat belts
		Fostering positive attitudes toward learning	Education about sexually transmitted diseases and prevention of teen pregnancy
		Environmental safety legislation	
		Lead elimination laws	

single factor is a necessary component in the etiology of all symptoms or signs of a major psychiatric disorder, emotional disturbance, or behavioral dysfunction (Department of Health and Human Services, 1992; hereafter cited as DHHS).

The following paragraph from "Prevention of Violence and Injuries Due to Violence" submitted to the Third National Injury Control Conference highlights the opportunities for creative thinking applied to the development and implementation of preventive interventions for all psychiatric and behavioral disorders, not just those related to violence and injury:

This dilemma has an encouraging flip side: because the causes of violent injuries are complex and multifaceted, there are multiple points in the causal chain where preventive interventions could be applied. Having recognized that no single type of intervention is likely to be universally effective, we can turn our attention to a much more appropriate question: Which combination of the many potential interventions is likely to be most effective (as well as feasible) in preventing violent injuries? This question can be broken down into a series of more specific questions: Which points in the causal chain are particularly vulnerable to interruption? Which interventions are likely to contribute to the prevention of a large proportion of a given type of violent injury? Which are likely to be effective across different types of violent injuries? What sorts of interventions will result in immediate reductions in such injuries? In long-term reductions? Which of the potential interventions are feasible and most readily adopted? Finally, what are the costs of the various promising interventions, relative to their likely effectiveness? (DHHS, 1992, p. 169)

Primary Prevention Targets

Primary prevention efforts may be aimed at 4 primary targets (Goldston, 1977). The first target is mental illnesses of known etiology, caused by such factors as: (1) poisoning (e.g., lead poisoning); (2) infections such as encephalitis and rubella; (3) genetic disorders such as phenylketonuria; (4) malnutrition disorders such as pellagra; (5) general systemic diseases such as juvenile onset diabetes; and (6) accidents or trauma.

The essence of such interventions is specification of relevant antecedents and, in most cases, either environmental modifications, resulting in a reduction of pathogens, or the initiation of appropriate physical, physiological, or behavioral (e.g., exercise programs) interventions.

A second target is mental illnesses of unknown etiology (e.g., functional psychoses, neuroses, and personality disorders). Although this category of potential targets represents perhaps the most seductive focus for primary prevention interventions, it is also the one most fraught with potential for disaster. By definition, the exact causes of such disorders are as yet unknown. Once determined, they will, in all likelihood, reflect the complex interaction of multiple biopsychosocial factors. At present, predicting their onset with any accuracy is an unachieved goal. At best, we can adopt available epidemiological strategies and identify which groups are at highest risk for specific dysfunctions (e.g., physically abused children, children of emotionally disturbed parents, children with chronic physical handicaps, and persons experiencing high levels of stress) and attempt to promote mental health in these groups. Given the lengthy gestation period characteristic of most of these disorders, intervention prior to their onset is obviously problematic and, in most cases, directed to populations of early and middle-childhood age (Silverman 1985, 1989).

If we identify critical life events as significant stress-related precursors of at least a fraction of the disorders within this category, a number of alternative strategies become possible: (1) stressor management (e.g., controlling the level of competition in children's sports); (2) stressor avoidance (e.g., changing schools); (3) stress resistance building (Parent Effectiveness Training); and (4) stress reaction management (workshops for the recently bereaved or newly divorced).

Another target category is emotional distress, maladaptation, and maladjustment. This category of disorders may represent, at present, the most viable target for primary prevention efforts. However, its success or failure may well depend on how rigorously these terms are defined and how explicitly the interventions are administered. It entails the adoption of psychological, sociological, cultural, and educational approaches in which crisis theory, crisis intervention, and anticipatory guidance are particularly relevant. The overarching goal of these efforts is to reduce emotional distress that becomes incapacitating to a community.

A fourth category is promotion of personal, social/interpersonal, and functional competency. This category involves maximizing the positive, health-related capabilities of individuals in order to improve the quality of their lives and consequently their general state of mental health. These individuals are likely to have a positive influence on those with whom they interact and, therefore, have the potential for producing an exponential extension of the impact of such efforts. Although individuals may appear to be the recipients of the interventions, in fact the focus is on enhancing the overall level of functioning of individuals within group settings. The interventions are therefore group-focused.

A major thrust in this area involves the introduction of curriculums promoting social problem-solving skills within elementary and secondary schools. Stress management workshops also fit within this category. The creation of a warmer, more supportive and understanding interpersonal, educational, and occupational environment may, in the long run, be one of the major contributions of these preventive efforts.

Children of Psychiatrically Ill Parents: A Case in Point

Psychiatric genetic researchers have found increased expression of psychiatric illness in the children and first-degree relatives of probands with unipolar affective disorders (Weissman, et al., 1984), bipolar affective disorders (Gershon, et al., 1982), schizophrenia (Gershon, 1983), alcoholism (Goodwin, 1985), personality disorder (Cadoret, Cain, & Crowe, 1983), and panic disorder (Crowe, Noyes, Pauls, Slymen, 1983). Epidemiological and life events literature also have identified intervening variables that can modify individual risk, such as the presence of social supports, significant recent life events, the individual's perception of stress, and the individual's temperament and personality traits (Rutter & Quinton, 1984).

The degree of psychiatric disturbance in children of psychiatrically ill parents can be seen as a function of the intensity, frequency, duration, and severity of parental dysfunction; the degree of genetic loading for a specific disorder; the availability of a healthy alternate caregiver; the intensity and duration of exposure to the parental dysfunctional behavior; and the degree of psychosocial stress experienced by the child (Garmezy & Rutter, 1983).

Genetic predisposition is not synonymous with expression of disease, and environmental stresses do not affect all people similarly. Some children of psychiatrically ill parents, especially those of schizophrenic parentage, do exceedingly well ("superkids") (Rutter, 1985), in part due to positive influences in their environment independent of their parent's illness. The combination of genetic predisposition and chronic stressful environment ("double loading") now identifies a person as being *at high risk* rather than just *at risk,* and may well predict certain degrees of dysfunction, but it does not guarantee dysfunction (Weinberger, 1987).

Although parental psychiatric illness confers increased risk on offspring, the risk may be genetically, biologically, or psychosocially mediated. Genetic factors appear to play less of a role in transmission than the characteristics of the child and the environmental consequences of the parent's illness (Cantwell & Baker, 1984; Rutter, 1989b).

Some of the risk factors may be modifiable (poor communication patterns, exposure to ineffective parenting, and exposure to chaotic environments), and others nonmodifiable (age, sex, race, and genetic loading). Current prevention research is addressing whether we know enough to intervene and what might be the appropriate type, duration, and time in the developmental sequence for intervention.

A key factor in the likelihood of expressed psychopathology is the child's ability to recognize, react to, and make allowances for exposure to such risks. Some children display early premorbid signs and symptoms of dysfunction, such as cognitive deficits, soft neurological signs, and other behavioral abnormalities that result in their inability to fully comprehend and accurately engage in constructive and meaningful interactions with parents and other significant adults (Marcus, et al., 1987). Preventive interventions addressing these deficits may be feasible and beneficial.

An objective for prevention research is to establish which vulnerability markers, causal factors, and risk factors can be modified and whether such modifications affect the expression of symptoms, the cognitive and social functioning of the child at risk, or the intrafamilial and environmental processes that may contribute to the expression of psychopathology. Prevention specialists must determine which clinical tools and techniques can be adapted to their focus and must create new interventions. Although the amount of literature on effective research-based preventive interventions is growing, many areas remain promising but speculative (Price, Cowen, Lorion, & Ramos-McKay, 1988; Steinberg & Silverman, 1987).

To improve precision in the field, researchers must target specific psychiatric disorders for preventive efforts. For example, the prevention of depression would significantly decrease the morbidity and mortality associated with it. One of the obvious methods of preventing suicide is to prevent depression. Mortality from suicide approaches 15% in the more severe forms of depression, and suicide from depression accounts for approximately 80% of all suicides in the United States (Tanney, 1992). Decreasing the incidence and prevalence of alcohol use, misuse, and abuse in the country would improve the economy and decrease health care expenditures. Major federal prevention efforts are already under way to reduce illicit drug use, especially among our youth (Bell & Battjes, 1986).

A truly primary preventive intervention for the expression of psychopathology secondary to psychogenetic factors in children of psychiatrically ill parents would be to successfully identify, treat, and monitor all forms of expressed psychopathology in the affected parent or parents. The early identification of psychopathology in the adult population depends on broad-based public mental health education (with an attendant reduction in stigma) coupled with easy access to treatment facilities. The coordinated provision during treatment of social and economic supports to affected persons and their families also is critical.

Education and training of family members, including the affected parents, about the nature and expression of the parental psychopathology is essential to ensure management of the illness and its psychosocial manifestations. Family members' awareness of their vulnerabilities allows them to develop specific individualized coping skills, adaptational modes, and resistances to the effects of parental psychopathology.

Family awareness also facilitates early identification of psychopathological signs and symptoms in the children at risk. Inability of such children to adapt, adjust, or cope in their environment or to reach developmental milestones are signals of distress. Early intervention may be simple and of short duration or may be the first of many carefully timed and implemented interventions. The dynamic interaction among the affected parent, the child at risk, and other family members allows the stratified involvement of many health care professionals.

Goldstein (1986) suggested 4 areas in which preventive interventions might be attempted for children at risk for schizophrenia. Studies of high-risk infants have identified the need for special attention to prenatal nutrition, prenatal counseling, postnatal bonding, and to decreasing birth complications in the prenatal–early infancy period.

During the middle-childhood developmental phase, the goals of interventions should be increasing the child's ability to process information and to pay attention to appropriate external and internal signals. Many promising techniques have been developed to improve a child's ability to work toward effective cognitive problem solving in an interpersonal sphere (Shure & Spivack, 1987). Social skills training also has been effective in altering the shy, withdrawn behavior of some children at risk for schizophrenia.

The third major area for preventive intervention is addressing patterns of communication within family units. Recent research has identified the need to decrease communication deviance, improve affective styles, and change patterns of inappropriately expressed emotion in families at risk (Doan, Falloon, Goldstein, Mintz, 1985).

Goodman and Isaacs (1984) cited 3 general goals for preventive interventions with children of psychiatrically ill parents: to improve the stability of the family system, to foster the ability of the caregiver to meet the child's needs, and to minimize the pathology to which the child is exposed. Family system stability can be improved by decreasing marital discord and separation, developing better and more consistent child-rearing techniques, and increasing the availability of community resources and social support networks for the parents. The specific abilities of the primary caregiver can be fostered through improving skills in parenting, problem solving, coping, communication and listening, interpersonal and social interaction, and self-help.

Controversial Issues

The field of primary prevention must make significant strides before it becomes a major component of the nation's armamentarium against emotional disorders and behavioral dysfunctions. To do so, it must develop on 2 fronts simultaneously. First, it must create a series of *reactive* strategies focused on populations at risk for identifiable mental disorders. Determination of risk represents, in and of itself, a formidable challenge that will test both the predictive accuracy of state-of-the-art epidemiological strategies and the existing knowledge bases in the behavioral sciences. Risk determination is a statistical concept that is based on prediction and probability. In addition, risk determination must encompass an awareness and sensitivity to risk and protective factors in the development of psychopathology (Kellam et al., 1983; Rolf et al., 1990; Rutter, 1987).

Speculation about the etiology of dysfunction must be replaced by a rigorous understanding of its individual, familial, sociocultural, and environmental determinants. Simple-minded univariate conceptions of cause and effect must give way to complex transactional-ecological and diathesis-stress models of psychopathology, which will enable us to determine who is at risk for what dysfunctions under what specific conditions Felner & Silverman, 1989). Primary preventive efforts may then be designed either to modify the "whos," in order to fortify them against potential pathogens and pathological processes, or to modify the pathogenetic conditions, in order to remove them from the environment. We must accept the challenge of learning about the ecology of health and pathology in order, ultimately, to engineer environments, social as well as physical, that minimize negative emotional states and promote positive adaptive coping styles.

Another direction for primary prevention efforts to take is toward promotive or *proactive* interventions, which focus not on the alleviation of pathology per se but on the development of positive, adaptive, adjustive capacities and skills as ends in and of themselves. In essence, proactive efforts carry the promise of allowing the mental health professions finally to focus on that very outcome: mental health.

Regardless of whether the focus of the primary prevention activity is reactive or proactive, it is essential that it be characterized by specific actions directed at specific populations for specific purposes. Each of these facets must be operationally defined so that the intervention process can be monitored and its impacts objectively assessed, whether they are reactive or proactive. It is equally important, given the population-focused nature of such efforts, that public health strategies of education, community organization, and coordination of the major social systems be integral components of the specific interventions affecting the target population (Silverman, 1985).

Pardes, Silverman, and West (1989) characterize the state of our field as follows:

For most mental illnesses, we still have no cures. For others, we do not even have effective treatments. Some investigators argue that these most recalcitrant disorders should be the first target of prevention research, via studies aimed at learning their basic mechanisms and causes.

On the other hand, there are disorders for which we can offer good interventions—fetal alcohol syndrome, failure to thrive, postpartum depression, school anxiety, adjustment disorders, bereavement and grief—largely because we have research-based evidence of what causes them. Some in the field believe that these seemingly more accessible disorders should be the chief focus on prevention research, because, given additional knowledge, there seems to be a better chance of developing more widely applicable interventions.

. . . It is also sometimes debated whether to apply an intervention after a trial has yielded suggestive findings, even if some problems are left unsolved (or new ones are raised). . . . Not only is it necessary to use limited resources carefully, but it is also crucial to avoid negative effects. Another source of controversy is the fact that some of the most troubling disorders of behavior faced by mental health and public health professionals alike—including all forms of violence—may indeed respond to intervention on an individual basis. However, large-scale remediation efforts would require major societal changes and allocation of resources to provide either one-on-one interventions or wide-ranging population-based interventions. (p. 413)

Conclusion

The prevention of psychiatric and emotional disorders and dysfunctions is based on a fundamental knowledge of the neurobiological and behavioral foundations of mental illness and of predisposing, precipitating, perpetuating, exacerbating, and mediating factors. The explosion of interest in biobehavioral and neurobiological research (including epidemiology, statistics, and developmental psychopathology) is making such knowledge available at an unprecedented rate. Genetic and biochemical research is beginning to link specific biological markers to subsequent signs and symptoms of specific psychiatric illness. Epidemiological and life-events research is clarifying the roles of mediating and precipitating variables in the expression, maintenance, and exacerbation of psychiatric illness. The challenge for preventive intervention efforts is to identify the specific effects of modifiable risk factors during various developmental periods and then link them to the development or expression of psychopathology (Silverman, 1989, 1996).

Researchers must test which specific interventions affect the development of specific psychiatric disorders in the different populations at risk. Determining why certain interventions make a difference in specific cases would enable clinicians to design large-scale public preventive intervention programs (Felner & Felner, 1989).

Clinical and legal disciplines alike are addressing ethical issues regarding early preventive interventions for children at risk. Ethical problems include labeling children before they express signs or symptoms of psychopathology, intervening for a problem that has yet to express itself, and obtaining informed consent for a procedure from a minor (Weithorn, 1987). Ethics also require clinicians to ensure that a preventive intervention has no negative side effects or untoward future negative outcomes (Lorion, 1987). Children deserve to develop in an environment free of the stigma of being labeled "at risk" for psychopathology. However, when the specific tools and techniques for successful interventions are refined, it may be incumbent on all health care professionals to identify persons who could best benefit from exposure to valid and reliable preventive interventions. As psychiatry enters the 21st century, it may well focus more on those who are at risk than on those who already exhibit psychiatric disorders and dysfunctions.

REFERENCES

Albee, G. W. (1982). Preventing psychopathology and promoting human potential. *American Psychologist, 37*, 1043–1050.

American Psychiatric Association Task Force on Prevention Research. (1990). Report of the APA task force on prevention research. *American Journal of Psychiatry, 147*, 1701–1704.

Bell, C. S., & Battjes, R. (1986). *Prevention research: Deterring drug abuse among children and adolescents.* National Institute on Drug Abuse Research Monograph No. 63. (DHHS Publication No. ADM-86-1334). Washington, DC: U.S. Government Printing Office.

Cadoret, R. J., Cain, C. A., & Crowe, R. (1983). Evidence for gene-environment interaction in the development of adolescent antisocial behavior. *Behavioral Genetics, 13*, 301–310.

Cantwell, D. P., & Baker, L. (1984). Parental mental illness and psychiatric disorders in "at risk" children. *Journal of Clinical Psychiatry, 45*, 503–507.

Cantwell, D. P., & Baker, L. (1989). Stability and natural history of DSM-III childhood diagnoses. *Journal of the American Academy of Child and Adolescent Psychiatry, 28*, 691–700.

Caplan, G. (1961). *Prevention of mental disorders in children.* New York: Basic Books.

Caplan, G. (1964). *Principles of preventive psychiatry.* New York: Basic Books.

Cowen, E. L. (1983). Primary prevention in mental health: Past, present, and future. In R. D. Felner, L. A. Jason, J. N. Moritsugu, & S. S. Farber (Eds.), *Preventive Psychology: Theory, Research and Practice* (pp. 11–25). New York: Pergamon Press.

Crowe, R. R., Noyes, R., Pauls, D. L., Slymen, D. (1983). A family study of panic disorders. *Archives of General Psychiatry, 40*, 1065–1069.

Department of Health and Human Services. (1992). *The third national injury control conference.* (DHHS Pub. No. 1992-634-666). Washington, DC: U.S. Government Printing Office.

Doane, J. A., Falloon, I. R. H., Goldstein, M. J., & Mintz, J. (1985). Parental affective style and treatment of schizophrenia: Predicting course of illness and social functioning. *Archives of General Psychiatry, 42*, 34–42.

Dryfoos, J. G. (1990). *Adolescents at risk: Prevalence and prevention.* New York: Oxford University Press.

Earls, F. (1979). Epidemiology and child psychiatry: Historical and conceptual development. *Comprehensive Psychiatry, 20*, 256–269.

Earls, F. (1989). Epidemiology and child psychiatry: Entering the second phase. *American Journal of Orthopsychiatry, 59*, 279–284.

Eisenberg, L. (1989). Public policy: Risk factor or remedy? In D. Shaffer, I. Philips, N. Enzer, M. Silverman, & V. Anthony (Eds.), *Prevention of mental disorders, alcohol, and other drug use in children and adolescents* (pp. 125–156). (DHHS Pub. No. ADM 90-1646). Washington, DC: U.S. Government Printing Office.

Felner, R. D., & Felner, T. Y. (1989). Primary prevention programs in the educational context: A transactional-ecological framework and analysis. In L. Bond & B. Compas (Eds.), *Primary prevention and promotion in the schools.* Newbury Park, CA: Sage Publications.

Felner, R. D., Jason, L. A., Moritsugu, J. N., & Farber, S. S. (Eds.). (1983). *Preventive psychology: Theory, research, and practice.* New York: Pergamon Press.

Felner, R. D., & Silverman, M. M. (1989). Primary prevention: A consideration of general principles and findings for the prevention of youth suicide. *Report of the Secretary's Task Force on Youth Suicide. Vol 3: Prevention and Interventions in Youth Suicide* (pp. 23–30). (DHHS Pub. No. ADM 89-1623). Washington, DC: U.S. Government Printing Office.

Felner, R. D., Silverman, M. M., & Felner, T. Y. (in press). Prevention in mental health and social intervention: Conceptual and methodological issues in the evolution of the science and practice of prevention. In J. Rappaport & E. Seidman (Eds.), *Handbook of community psychology.* New York: Plenum Press.

Garmezy, N., & Rutter, M. (1983). *Stress, coping, and development in children.* New York: McGraw-Hill.

Gershon, E. S. (1983). Genetics of the major psychoses. In S. S. Kety, L. P. Rowland, R. L. Sidman, S. W. Matthysse. (Eds.), *Genetics of neurological and psychiatric disorders.* New York: Raven Press.

Gershon, E. S., Hamovit, J., Guroff, J., Dibble, E., Leckman, J. F., Sceery, W., Targum, S. D., Nurnberger, J. I., Jr., Goldin, L. R., Bunney, W. E., Jr. (1982). A family study of schizoaffective, bipolar I, bipolar II, unipolar, and normal control probands. *Archives of General Psychiatry, 39*, 1157–1173.

Goldstein, M. (1985). Comments on the possibility of primary prevention in mental health. In R. L. Hough, P. A. Gongla, V. B. Brown, & S. E. Goldston (Eds.), *Psychiatric epidemiology and prevention: The possibilities* (pp. 65–70). Rockville, MD: National Institute of Mental Health.

Goldstein, M. J. (1986). Prevention of schizophrenia: What do we know? In B. B. Long (Ed.), *The prevention of mental-emotional disabilities: Resource papers to the report of the national mental health association commission on the prevention of mental-emotional disabilities.* Alexandria, VA: National Mental Health Association. pp. 223–239.

Goldston, S. E. (1977). An overview of primary prevention programming. In D. C. Klein & S. E. Goldston (Eds.), *Primary prevention: An idea whose time has come* (pp. 23–40). (DHHS Publication No. ADM 80-447). Washington, DC: U.S. Government Printing Office.

Goodman, S. H., & Isaacs, L. D. (1984). Primary prevention with children of severely disturbed mothers. *Journal of Preventive Psychiatry, 2*, 387–402.

Goodwin, D. W. (1985). Alcoholism and genetics: The sins of the fathers. *Archives of General Psychiatry, 42*, 171–174.

Kellam, S. G., & Brown, C. H. (Eds.). (1982). *Social, adaptational, and psychological antecedents of ado-*

lescent's psychopathology ten years later. Baltimore, MD: Johns Hopkins University Press.

Kellam, S. G., Brown, C. H., Rubin, B. R., & Ensminger, M. E. (1983). Paths leading to teenage psychiatric symptoms and substance abuse: Developmental epidemiological studies in Woodlawn. In S. B. Guze, F. T. Earls, & J. E. Barrett (Eds.), *Childhood psychopathology and development.* New York: Raven Press.

Leavell, H., & Clark, E. G. (1953). *Preventive medicine for the doctor in his community.* New York: McGraw-Hill pp. 17–51.

Lorion, R. P. (1987). The other side of the coin: The potential for negative consequences of preventive interventions. In J. A. Steinberg & M. M. Silverman (Eds.), *Preventing mental disorders: A research perspective* (pp. 243–250). (DHHS Pub. No. ADM 87-1492). Washington, DC: U.S. Government Printing Office.

Marcus, J., Hans, S. L., Nagler, S., Auerbach, J. G., Mirsky, A. F., Aubrey, A. (1987). A review of the NIMH Israeli kibbutz-city study and the Jerusalem infant development study. *Schizophrenia Bulletin, 13,* 425–438.

Pardes, H., Silverman, M. M., & West, A. (1989). Prevention and the field of mental health: A psychiatric perspective. In L. Breslow, J. E. Fielding, & L. B. Lave (Eds.), *Annual review of public health* (Vol. 10, pp. 403–422). Palo Alto, CA: Annual Reviews Inc.

Price, R. H., Cowen, E., Lorion, R. P., & Ramos-McKay, J. (Eds.). (1988). *Fourteen ounces of prevention: A casebook for practitioners.* Washington, DC: American Psychological Association.

Rae-Grant, N. (1983). Prevention. In P. Steinhauer & Q. Rae-Grant (Eds.), *Psychological problems of the child in the family* (2nd ed., pp. 591–610). New York: Basic Books.

Rolf, J., Masten, A. S., Cicchetti, D., Nuechterlein, K. H., & Weintraub, S. (Eds.). (1990). Risk and protective factors in the development of psychopathology. New York: Cambridge University Press.

Rutter, M. (1985). Resilience in the face of adversity; protective factors and resistance to psychiatric disorders. *British Journal of Psychiatry, 147,* 598–611.

Rutter, M. (Ed.). (1987). *Developmental psychiatry.* Washington, DC: American Psychiatric Press.

Rutter, M. (1988). Epidemiological approaches to developmental psychopathology. *Archives of General Psychiatry, 45,* 486–495.

Rutter, M. (1989a). Isle of Wight revisited: Twenty-five years of child psychiatric epidemiology. *Journal of American Academy of Child and Adolescent Psychiatry, 28,* 633–653.

Rutter, M. (1989b). Psychiatric disorder in parents as a risk factor for children. In D. Shaffer, I. Philips, N. Enzer, M. M. Silverman, & V. Anthony (Eds.), *Prevention of mental disorders, alcohol, and other drug use in children and adolescents* (pp. 157–190). (DHHS Pub. No. ADM 90-1646). Washington, DC: U.S. Government Printing Office.

Rutter, M., & Quinton, D. (1984). Parental Psychiatric Disorder: Effects on children. Psychological Medicine 14, 853–880.

Sameroff, A. J., & Fiese, B. H. (1989). Conceptual is-

sues in prevention. In D. Shaffer, I. Philips, N. Enzer, M. Silverman, & V. Anthony (Eds.). *Prevention of mental disorders, alcohol, and other drug use in children and adolescents* (pp. 23–54). (DHHS Pub. No. ADM 90-1646). Washington, DC: U.S. Government Printing Office.

Seidman, E. (1987). Toward a framework for primary prevention research. In J. A. Steinberg & M. M. Silverman (Eds.), *Preventing mental disorders: A research perspective* (pp. 2–19). (DHHS Pub. No. ADM 87-1492). Washington, DC: U.S. Government Printing Office.

Shaffer, D. (1989). Prevention of psychiatric disorders in children and adolescents: A summary of findings and recommendations from Project Prevention. In D. Shaffer, I. Philips, N. Enzer, M. Silverman, & V. Anthony (Eds.), *Prevention of mental disorders, alcohol, and other drug use in children and adolescents* (pp. 443–456). (DHHS Pub. No. ADM 90-1646). Washington, DC: U.S. Government Printing Office.

Shure, M. B., & Spivack, G. (1987). Competence-building as an approach to prevention of dysfunction: The ICPS model. In J. A. Steinberg & M. M. Silverman (Eds.), *Preventing mental disorders: A research perspective* (pp. 124–139). (DHHS Pub. No. ADM 87-1492). Washington, DC: U.S. Government Printing Office.

Silverman, M. M. (1985). Preventive intervention research: A new beginning. In T. C. Owan (Ed.), *Southeast Asian mental health treatment, prevention, services, training and research* (pp. 169–182). (DHHS Pub. No. ADM 85-1399). Washington, DC: U.S. Government Printing Office.

Silverman, M. M. (1989). Children of psychiatrically ill parents: A prevention perspective. *Hospital and Community Psychiatry, 40,* 1257–1265.

Silverman, M. M., & Koretz, D. S. (1989). Preventing mental health problems. In R. E. K. Stein (Ed.), *Caring for children with chronic illness: Issues and strategies* (pp. 213–229). New York: Springer Publishing Company.

Silverman, M. M. (1996). *Approaches to Suicide Prevention: A Focus on Models.* (Chapter 2- pp. 25–94). In: Richard F. Ramsay & Bryan L. Tanney (Eds): *Global Trends in Suicide Prevention: Toward the Development of National Strategies for Suicide Prevention.* Mumbai, India: Tata Institute of Social Sciences.

Sroufe, L. A., & Rutter, M. (1984). The domain of developmental psychopathology. *Child Development, 83,* 173–189.

Steinberg, J. A., & Silverman, M. M. (Eds.). (1987). *Preventing mental disorders: A research perspective.* (DHHS Pub. No. ADM 87-1492). Washington, DC: U.S. Government Printing Office.

Tanney, B. L. (1992). Mental disorders, psychiatric patients, and suicide. In R. W. Maris, A. L. Berman, J. T. Maltsberger, & R. I. Yufit (Eds.), *Assessment and prediction of suicide* (pp. 277–320). New York: Guilford Press.

Weinberger, D. R. (1987). Implications of normal brain development for the pathogenesis of schizophrenia. *Archives of General Psychiatry, 44,* 660–669.

Weissman, M. M., Gershon, E. S., Kidd, K. K., Prusoff, B.A., Leckman, J. F., Dibble, E., Hamovit, J., Thompson, W. D., Pauls, D. C., Guroff, J. J. (1984). Psychiatric disorders in the relatives of probands with affective disorders: The Yale-NIMH collaborative family study. *Archives of General Psychiatry, 41,* 13–21.

Weithorn, L. A. (1987). Informed consent for prevention research involving children: Legal and ethical issues. In J. A. Steinberg & M. M. Silverman (Eds.), *Preventing mental disorders: A research perspective* (pp. 236–242). (DHHS Pub. No. ADM 87-1492). Washington, DC: U.S. Government Printing Office.

SECTION IV
Consultation and Child and Adolescent Psychiatry

16 / The Process of Consultation in Child and Adolescent Psychiatry

Larry K. Brown and Gregory K. Fritz

Despite having had little formal exposure to consultation work during training, in practice, most child and adolescent psychiatrists consult to an organization such as a hospital, school, or court (American Academy of Child Psychiatry, 1983). Subsequent chapters describe the elements important for a psychiatrist in consulting to each of these particular systems. This chapter focuses on the processes that are common to consultation across all settings. Here we review the history of consultation in child and adolescent psychiatry, theoretical models used by the field, principles of practice, and specific advice concerning this work.

History of Consultation

Consultation by mental health professionals to other human service workers has been recognized as a useful function since the 1930s. Initially, consultation was seen as a way to educate workers who lacked mental health training or to provide professional input on difficult cases (Sloane, 1936). Prevention was of central importance to the community mental health movement, and consultation was the main form of outreach employed to expand the availability of mental health expertise to the network of community agencies. Berlin (1964) summarized several decades of consultation experience and advocated formal training for psychiatrists, psychologists, and other mental health professionals in the process of consultation.

In the medical realm, the roots of consultation-liaison psychiatry also extend back to the 1930s. An extensive literature describes clinical issues, organization of services, evaluation techniques, and—to a degree—relevant empirical research. The role of the psychiatric consultant in the medical setting has been extensively debated and frequently bemoaned for its frustrations (Lipowski, 1986). In the past decade, the primacy of consultation—direct patient evaluation in the medical model that is common to other medical specialties—versus liaison—education and support focused on the other professionals and the medical system rather than the patients directly—has been argued. At times the debate has become quite contentious and polarized, but the utility of both activities in specific situations is acknowledged—hence, the term "consultation-liaison service." In practice, many consultation-liaison psychiatrists serve more often as a consultant rather than as a liaison expert, since many managed care programs will reimburse only for direct patient contact.

Overall, mental health professionals have developed many approaches to providing consultation in various settings, and no single method is seen as universally applicable. Experience over the years has resulted in the goals of mental health consultation to particular groups or agencies becoming more focused, as reflected in a recent monograph by Fritz, Mattison, Nurcombe, and Spirito (1993). Outcome research and financial pressures have curtailed some of the grandiosity that characterized consultative efforts in the heyday of the community mental health movement, but the total number of psychiatrists and psychologists involved in some form of consultation has never been greater.

Theoretical Models

Diverse theoretical models have been applied in order to understand and inform consultation work done by psychiatrists. Generally, these models were developed for use in other domains of psychiatry and subsequently were incorporated into consultation work, with variable results. None was developed specifically to address the realities faced by child and adolescent psychiatrists in this area. Even if the field continues to lack a central, organizing theory to which all practitioners agree, each of the models has shown some utility and has left its imprint on modern methods of practice. The following models will be reviewed briefly:

consultee model, psychoanalytically informed consultation (Caplan, 1963, 1970), Bion's group theory, organizational theory, the social systems model, and the biopsychosocial model. The references provide information on more detailed reviews of each model.

CONSULTEE MODEL

Schiff and Pilot (1959) described the consultee model of consultation. Their report noted that often there was a discrepancy between the referring physician's definition of the major problem for each case and the psychiatric consultant's. In fact, generally the physician's most pressing and cogent concerns were not explicitly stated in the initial request for consultation. The authors suggested that the physician's anxiety and discomfort with the patient were the prime factors motivating consult requests. The major goal of the consulting psychiatrist was to recognize and resolve this anxiety. A hallmark of consultation work is examining the emotional reaction of those with whom one is consulting. However, forces other than anxiety prompt the need for consultation, and the consultee's anxiety, even if present, may not be irrationally based. In extreme cases, consultees can perceive a central focus on emotional reactions as intrusive, unwarranted, and "unwanted psychoanalysis."

PSYCHOANALYTICALLY INFORMED CONSULTATION

Caplan (1963, 1970) provided a comprehensive model of mental health consultation based on years of experience in the community mental health movement. He proposed that two factors distinguish four basic types of consultation: *focus* and *content*. *Case consultation* and *administrative consultation* both focus on the particular patient or program, taken at face value, which constitutes the content of discussions. *Consultee-centered consultation* and *systems consultation* focus on the individual or group of consultees; the content is only the "grist for the mill" the consultant uses to help consultees become more objective, less impeded by their own intrapsychic conflicts, and more confident and effective in their professional work. Caplan's consultee-centered consultation is similar in many respects to Schiff's model, and both have obvious roots in the psychoanalytic tradition. Caplan's detailed descriptions of other types of consultation, the various stages of consultation, and the process of problem-solving are enduring contributions to the theory of mental health consultation. Although Caplan explicitly distinguished consultee-centered consultation from psychotherapy, there is a risk of the difference becoming more semantic than real. The stages of consultation, in fact, closely approximate the stages of psychoanalytic psychotherapy. In addition, a central component of Caplan's problem-solving process is "theme interference reduction," which is remarkably similar to the analysis of transference, except that it stays within the metaphor of the work-related problem.

BION'S GROUP THEORY

Bion's group theory has been utilized by psychiatrists as they consult to groups (Bion, 1961; Kernberg, 1983; Rioch, 1970). Wilfred Bion who adapted Kleinian principles to small groups in the 1950s, felt that every group had a primary task. In an emergency room, for example, the primary task might be defined as turning emergently ill patients into nonemergencies. Groups, when functioning normally, proceed rationally, and members have clear roles in achieving their primary task. A variety of events can disrupt the normal functioning of a group, such as loss of the leader or ambiguity in members' roles. Bion felt that such disruption was accompanied by degeneration of normal group functioning, loss of the primary task, and regression, characterized by members acting on the basis of shared irrational assumptions. Three characteristic assumption patterns have been described: dependency (group is passive and dependent on a controlling, paternalistic leader), fight/flight (members are ready to struggle or disband), and pairing (group is focused on a "couple" that channels much of the available emotional energy). While it is seldom useful for the consultant to interpret these assumption patterns directly, his or her recognition of them can highlight the need to marshal forces to counteract the disruptive influences. For example, in one case the retirement of a pediatric unit's head nurse occurred in conjunction with a hospital-wide nursing restructuring, leading to a fight/flight reaction in a unit's remaining nurses. Nurses and support staff perceived all attending staff and consultants as either unavailable or overly demanding. A plan for interim nursing leadership that was endorsed by both nurses and physicians allowed staff to resume collaboration on their primary task, patient care. Although Bion's theory is a useful description of leaderless, "irrational" groups, it omits processes often crucial in consultation work such as the functioning of an individual within the group and dysfunctional patterns that may arise in groups even though a leader exists and members' roles are clear.

ORGANIZATIONAL THEORY

Theories first used to describe industrial organizations also have been applied to psychiatric consultation (Miller, 1976; Newton & Levison, 1973; Rice, 1965, 1969; Woolston, 1994). Organizational theory is concerned with the inputs and outputs of open systems, the boundaries within the system, and the divisions of labor and authority. Although these terms initially sound quite foreign to psychiatric ears, such principles are useful in examining chronic or acutely dysfunctional patterns of social institutions. For example, nearly every system has an input (an admission on a medical unit) and an output (a discharge). On a pediatric unit, the input is not only sick children but their families as well, whose needs and reactions are routinely assessed. On rare occasions, our adult surgical intensive care unit admits adolescents. In such cases staff members, unaccustomed to working with children, often are unaware that an entire family, rather than a single patient, is the "input." The consultant thus works to have the family included in the system. Other useful concepts concern boundaries and the division of labor within the organization. Boundaries are not barriers but rather means of identifying group membership and role, such as title, academic degree, dress (white coats for physicians), or salary. Consultants need to be aware of the degree to which they are seen as a member of the group (wearing white coats) and the extent of their prescribed labor (work expected of them by other members).

SOCIAL SYSTEMS THEORY

Social systems theory, based on the work of Kurt Lewin, provides another view of important psychological forces within a group (Karasu & Hertzman, 1974). A group's mythology stems from partial truths about the ideal world. For example, such shared "truths" in a school system might be that students are interested in learning, always prepared, and committed to hard work. These truths resemble a Norman Rockwell painting that describes group values and ideals, although generally it is acknowledged not to be an accurate picture of the reality for any one individual. If these myths are challenged too greatly, the system becomes chaotic. The consultant works to stabilize the system (restoring the myths) rather than to interpret the loss of belief in the myth. For example, a medical resident mistakenly injected an antineoplastic medication in a child's artery rather than the vein, causing necrosis and eventual loss of several digits. With the child still hospitalized, the family began litigation proceedings, and psychiatric consultation was requested by the staff. Since the medical resident was well liked, staff members were unable to displace the error onto a scapegoat. One nurse commented, "I feel like I made the mistake, not him." The consultant realized that two prime medical myths had been disrupted: Medical personnel cure rather than harm patients, and patients, in turn, are always grateful rather than adversarial. The consultant assisted staff members in focusing on ways in which they could continue to care for the patient (neither being distant nor overly solicitous) and to be able to include the family in their decision making, despite the tragedy.

THE BIOPSYCHOSOCIAL MODEL

The biopsychosocial model is the most comprehensive of models that has found utility in the consultation field. Engel (1980) has eloquently described the manner in which any event has ramifications at many different systemic levels, such as molecular, tissue, organ, person, family and community. In his classic paper, he illustrated how an unsuccessful attempt at arterial puncture in a man with chest pain led to increased myocardial ischemia, mobilization of the nervous system's fight-or-flight response, reactive anger and loss of confidence in staff, distancing by medical staff, and family strain. This model, if thoroughly applied in consultation, ensures that the reactions and stresses in all possible systems are considered. The model is useful for organizing data into different hierarchies of systems (e.g., family, person) but, since it is not a theory, does not offer new explanations for conflicts in any given system. For an individual case, the consultant often chooses to focus the consultation work on 1 or 2 systems, rather than comprehensively cataloging and attending to the full range. AIDS, for example, may be the quintessential biopsychosocial disease. For every patient with AIDS, there are important considerations from the cellular to the societal level of functioning. At a particular moment, though, the consultant may be most concerned with only 1 level (e.g., onset of dementia, discrimination at the jobplace, transmissibility of HIV to the sexual partner).

Consultation-Liaison in Practice

Despite consultants' diverse theoretical orientations and the equally diverse settings in which they work, a number of principles are held in common. Here we review methods of practice that apply to the consultant's roles in system formulation, case evaluation, and intervention. Consultation, strictly defined, involves someone requesting specific advice from the consultant about one particular matter. Liaison work, in contrast, describes an ongoing relationship between the consultant and an organization or group, with the goal of improving the group's total effort. Although psychiatrists need to be mindful of the role they have been asked to play, the clear distinction between consultation and liaison activities is seldom so precise. Most often psychiatrists are requested to consult on specific cases but do so repeatedly to the same organization (e.g., medical ward, school) over time. With repeated contact, the consultant's role evolves. This review of practice principles assumes the conditions in which most psychiatrists work: a case consultation to 1 organization, with vague interest by the organization in issues beyond the specific case.

Knowledge about the system to which one is consulting is a prerequisite for effective work. (Other chapters in this volume describe elements and methods unique to particular settings.) One becomes more familiar with the system over time, so each case consultation becomes an opportunity to gather more information about the workings of the organization. It may seem self-evident that the consultant is concerned with the organization's members, their roles, their skills, and their powers. Unfortunately, the psychological roles of staff members seldom correspond to their place on an organizational tree. For example, a consultant to a residential treatment facility was presented with

an angry, suicidal adolescent who had eloped from the facility several times. An apparently sound psychological plan to explore the boy's current frustrations, address his chronic sadness, and firmly control his behavior was agreed to by his therapist, case worker, milieu workers, and administrative staff. Unfortunately, the plan failed. Because of violent behavior, the boy was next interviewed in restraint in his cottage rather than the consultant's office. It was discovered that the only nurturant model for this minority boy was a minority food service worker who had "adopted" him. Once she was included in the treatment plan, the case proceeded routinely.

Likewise, the consultant often is advised to negotiate his or her contract carefully and explicitly (i.e., duties, responsibilities, confidentiality, legal liabilities) with the person "in charge." It should be remembered that the person with authority to negotiate money and space (e.g., school superintendent) may have different views on consultation from the staff (e.g., teachers, school psychologist) with whom the consultant more closely works. Such discrepancies are common, and their resolution is the first step in ongoing consultation. Last, even when operating in familiar, well-known territory, the consultant should be mindful of the fact that roles change, status shifts, and new priorities emerge. Some elements of every system are continuously in flux, so interventions need to be reconsidered freshly with each new case.

In the evaluation phase of each case consultation, the consultant gathers enough information to form an effective intervention. Initially he or she works to understand the immediate precipitants to the request and both the overt and the covert wishes of the important parties. For example, what prompted a school principal at a particular moment to request consultation on a young girl after 2 years of elective mutism? To what degree do school personnel hope that the consultant will assist the girl in talking, improve her academic functioning, decrease other disruptive behavior, assist the school in avoiding a lawsuit, or garner further support for dismissing an incompetent teacher? In evaluating these spoken and unspoken requests, the consultant is attuned to stresses in the system that are unrelated to the specific case. For the girl with elective mutism, the stresses included the loss of a teacher's aide within the classroom, a fear of job termination by several teachers because of a plan for school redistricting, a concurrent lawsuit against the principal by another family over an unrelated matter, and the teacher's prior experience with a suicidal student. Last, because of the evaluation, the consultant may become aware of issues and problems that have not yet been identified by the system. For example, the psychiatric consultant may be the first one to discuss the ethical, moral, or humanistic issues that the case raises. In the case described, the consultant discussed with school personnel the potentially coercive nature of their plans to "force" the girl's depressed mother into therapy and to use a "behavioral approach" with the child that would make her stand in a corner when she refused to talk.

With the evaluation smoothly and expediently done, interventions should follow logically. In reality, intervention is the art of balancing inadequate data, scarce resources, inevitable constraints, and multiple, conflicting demands with the potential for a positive outcome. Nevertheless, consultants can proceed with a view toward both short-term and long-term goals.

The typical short-term goal for a single-case consultation is resolution of the problem for the identified case and the organization. The consultant hopes to return the system to its normal, baseline level of functioning so the organization's primary task can continue. Techniques that are commonly used stem from crisis intervention paradigms. Existing resources may be supported, tentative approaches amplified, or the problem redefined. (For example, curing a parent's character pathology is not a reasonable goal of a brief, pediatric hospitalization.) At this point, the system is fixed only to the degree required by the identified case, even if the consultant recognizes that the problem presented by the case is symptomatic of larger, ongoing difficulties. The heat of the crisis generally is an inopportune time to attempt larger-scale change, as most people are unable to tolerate dispassionate introspection in the face of turmoil.

Long-term goals involve change in fundamental organizational structure. Such change may be prompted by interventions that include didactic presentations, psychosocial rounds, case conferences, team meetings and conflict mediation (DeMaso and Meyer, 1996). Other creative interventions include a discussion group for trainees in an intensive care setting, a joint research project between the organization and the consultant, and placement of the consultant on the organization's board of trustees. The consultant may assist staff in formulating new institutional programs, advocating with other agencies, or establishing new institutional procedures. Fundamental organizational changes also may require a change in the consultant's basic contract, lest roles and boundaries become ambiguous. Consultants must never overlook their contract. Expectations should be explicit to minimize subsequent problems and disappointments on both sides.

CONSULTATION DOS AND DON'TS

Even with an adequate formulation of the case, a good knowledge of the organization, achievable short- and long-term goals, and a feasible intervention, consultation may fail if it falls on "deaf ears." Form matters. The psychiatric consultant to any system should avoid jargon, preaching, and proselytizing. Although liaison work sometimes has been imbued with an aura of missionary work, in fact, most staff are unwilling to adopt the consultant's worldview. Our enthusiasm for consultation should not lead us to oversell it. The experiences of the community mental health movement are a poignant reminder of the inability of mental health professionals to remake society.

Consultation must "fit" the system. The consultant's actions should be prescribed by the basic contract, be understandable by staff, and be approved by the organization. Although consultants should be knowledgeable, they should avoid interpreting directly staff members' psychological reactions or "taking over" the case. Likewise, the consultant's attention to multidisciplinary staff and elucidation of multiple systems of information cannot be an excuse to avoid responsibility. Committees are notoriously poor decision makers. Despite the covert pressure of some systems, the consultant should never unwittingly support passive, nondecision situations. The consultant who has carefully elucidated a specific request should be mindful of answering it in terms that are understandable and useful to staff (Lewis, 1994). In short, the consultant should strive to be prompt, practical, and pithy.

Last, no psychiatrist should be *only* a consultant. The psychiatrist needs to continue to be on the front line in some portion of his or her professional life. The experience of being under pressure, busy, challenged by the limits of one's expertise and confronted by atypical "untreatable" cases is essential in promoting an effective consultant's empathy, humility, and practicality. In addition, the emotional and intellectual demands of consultation are unique and cumulative. Thus, most psychiatrists find that consultation is a welcome contrast to other clinical or academic work but that it could rarely constitute their complete professional life.

Consultation Truisms

• "When in doubt, get more data." Although we may need to "shoot from the hip" in consultation work, significant ambiguity in the consultant's mind should prompt a search for further information in the case.

• "When still in doubt, act." Data collection, though, should not become an end unto itself. When the consultant understands the general system, the precipitants, the covert and overt requests, and the case dynamics, then only action awaits. The stereotype of an obsessively analyzing psychiatrist who is loath to act is distressingly common. Often appreciated is the consultant's practical ability to suggest a specific response, help develop a behavioral contingency program, intervene with a family, or recommend a pharmacologic treatment. Action, even if imperfect, reveals the necessary clues to a more effective solution.

• "When all anxiety is directed at you, call a meeting." Groups may channel all of their anxiety about a crisis into the consultant's lap. Requests that the case be handled immediately, frequent urgent phone calls, and expectations that the consultant handle aspects of the case normally dealt with by staff members are all clues that such a process is operative. A meeting of everyone with any connection to the case, to discuss contrasting views and redefine expectations, often quickly resolves this problem. Further, the pooled observations and wisdom of multiple professionals dealing with the patient can provide enough of the pieces of the puzzle to make the picture clear or at least comprehensible rather than confusing or hopeless.

• "If over your head, call *your* consultant." A child and adolescent psychiatrist need not be all-knowing. Calmly admitting the limits of your knowledge provides a model of mature, sincere behavior for staff members. "I don't know but I'll find out" often has begun a process that proves helpful to both the consultant and staff.

• "Quotable is notable." Sometimes the essence of the consultation can be summed up in a memorable phrase. Such a clear, easily understood statement becomes a touchstone for staff members as they work to more fully incorporate the pieces of a consultant's intervention. Useful phrases generally arise from a specific event rather than from a well-stocked catalog. In our consultations, however, among the most useful, lasting lines have been "Knowledge is power," "Sad not mad," and "Seek peace, not power."

It is easy to imagine the role that these lines have played in their respective cases to explain the need for a child to know his or her diagnosis, to redefine noncompliant behavior, and to encourage a more collaborative relationship with an oppositional teenager.

REFERENCES

American Academy of Child Psychiatry. (1983). *Child psychiatry: A plan for the coming decades.* Washington, DC: Author.

Berlin, I. N. (1964). Learning mental health consultation: history and problem. *Mental Hygiene, 48,* 257–266.

Bion, W. R. (1961). *Experiences in groups.* New York: Basic Books.

Caplan, G. (1963). Types of mental health consultations. *American Journal of Orthopsychiatry, 33,* 470–481.

Caplan, G. (1970). *The theory and practice of mental health consultation.* London: Tavistock Publications.

DeMaso, D., & Meyer, E. (1996). A psychiatric Consultant's survival guide to the pediatric intensive care unit. *Journal of the American Academy of Child and Adolescent Psychiatry, 34,* 1411–1413.

Engel, G. (1980). The clinical application of the biopsychosocial model. *American Journal of Psychiatry, 137,* 535–544.

Fritz, G. K., Mattison, R., Nurcombe, B., & Spirito, A. (1993). *Child mental health consultation in hospitals, schools and courts.* Washington, DC: American Psychiatric Press. 1–89.

Karasu, T., & Hertzman, M. (1974). Notes on a contextual approach to medical ward consultation: The importance of the social systems mythology. *International Journal of Psychiatry and Medicine, 5,* 41–49.

Kernberg, O. F. (1983). Psychoanalytic studies of group processes: Theory and applications. In L. Grinspoon

(Ed.), *Psychiatry update: The American Psychiatric Association annual review* (Vol. 2). Washington, DC: American Psychiatric Press. 21–36.

Lewis, M. (1994). Consultation process in child and adolescent psychiatric consultation—Liaison in pediatrics. *Child and Adolescent Psychiatric Clinics of North America, 3:* 439–448.

Lipowski, Z. J. (1986). Consultation-liaison psychiatry: The first half century. *General Hospital Psychiatry, 8,* 305–315.

Miller, E. J. (1976). *Task and organization.* New York: John Wiley & Sons.

Newton, P., & Levinson, D. (1973). The work group within the organization. *Psychiatry, 36,* 115–141.

Rice, A. K. (1965). *Learning for Leadership.* London: Tavistock Publications.

Rice, A. K. (1969). Individual, group, and intergroup processes. *Human Relations, 22,* 565–589.

Rioch, M. (1970). The work of Wilfred Bion on groups. *Psychiatry, 33,* 56–66.

Schiff, S., & Pilot, M. (1959). An approach to psychiatric consultations in the general hospital. *Archives of General Psychiatry, 1,* 115–141.

Sloane, P. (1936). The use of a consultation method in casework therapy. *American Journal of Orthopsychiatry, 6,* 355–361.

Woolston, W. (1994). General systems issues in child and adolescent consultation and liaison psychiatry. *Child and Adolescent Psychiatric Clinics of North America, 3:* 427–437.

---

17 / **Pediatric Consultation Liaison**

Michael S. Jellinek and David B. Herzog

Child psychiatric consultation, paralleling other medical subspecialties, provides the referring physician, child, and family with an expert medical opinion regarding psychiatric and developmental aspects of the child's response to illness. In some pediatric training centers, the impact of the child psychiatric consultation service is broadly felt; it may encompass seminars, rounds, teaching pediatric residents, psychiatric residents, psychiatrists, nurses, medical students or elective rotations; hospital administrators contributing to policy decisions; and guidance for pediatric residents and nursing staff as they face the anguish of acutely ill, chronically ill, and emotionally troubled children and families (Jellinek & Herzog, 1990, 1992; Reinhardt, 1979).

In the first half of this century, pediatricians focused on the serious morbidity and mortality of infectious diseases, and a recognition of psychosocial issues was only beginning to evolve (Jellinek, 1982; Kessel & Haggerty, 1968). What we now accept as routine—parents having 24-hour access and "rooming in," the need for preoperative teaching, the emotional impact of illness, and the role of play in helping children cope with the experience of hospitalization—was essentially unknown. Hospital staff interpreted the quiet and withdrawn state of young children as "settling in" rather than the inevitable despair when children were forced to separate from their parents. Grad-

ually the advances in psychoanalytic and developmental theories became integrated into practice. Contemporaneous with the development of antibiotics and immunizations, there emerged a growing appreciation of children's reaction to chronic disease and hospitalization. By the 1960s children's psychosocial issues, both inpatient and outpatient, were deemed as clinically relevant as infectious disease (Task Force on Pediatric Education, 1978). Where welcomed and available, child psychiatrists consult on a wide range of clinical issues, including failure to thrive, poor compliance with essential treatment, adaptation to chronic disease (leukemia, cystic fibrosis, transplantation), depression/suicide, psychosomatic disorders, anorexia nervosa, abuse/neglect, the dying child, and so on.

Currently the status of child psychiatric consultation to hospitalized children is site-specific and dependent on multiple factors. The chiefs of general psychiatry, child and adolescent psychiatry, and pediatrics all must be supportive, as often the first two provide the departmental resources to have a qualified consultant available; in addition, the pediatric chief must at least tolerate if not encourage multidisciplinary, comprehensive care. Even if the three chiefs agree, third parties must provide some reimbursement, and pediatric residents must have sufficient training to appreciate the need for and to help implement psychosocial recommendations. Despite all we now know about children's emotional needs, such basic services as preoperative preparation or psychiatric consultation often are not routinely available. However, when children's needs are recognized, upward of 5% of all admissions will receive child psychiatric consultation, and many more will benefit from the psychosocially informed care of residents and staff.

Prevention

Much can be done to ease children's anxiety and thus reduce the need for consultation. Parents can be well informed and supported as they stay with and help care for their child. The hospital environment can be child oriented in procedures, design, and program. Child life services, preoperative or preprocedure preparation, and age-appropriate explanations can help children understand and cope with illness and hospitalization. Primary care nursing in cooperation with parental care makes children feel safe despite being in an alien, often painful, setting. Permitting children some control, when possible, over diet, scheduling of procedures, and pain management will further reduce anxiety, enhance coping, and ease their and their parents' suffering. Creating a sensitive, supportive, and understandable setting in conjunction with high-quality pediatric care is common sense—how we and our children would like to be treated—and will result in better utilization of the available child psychiatric resources.

The concept of prevention can be expanded to those children and families at high risk or likely to experience emotional distress. If resources permit, child psychiatric consultation can be helpful at the time of initial diagnosis of a serious illness, such as cancer, diabetes, or cystic fibrosis, after trauma, or pretransplant. When early consultation is built into the care of hospitalized children and the thinking of the pediatric team, early on the child and family receive direct service and assessment of potential areas of difficulty, as with family discord or compliance issues.

Prevention also can include availability to pediatric house staff who, as individuals and in teams, face serious stresses and are at a substantial risk for depression during their residency training (Jellinek, 1986; Small, 1981). The child psychiatrist can work within the pediatric curriculum to participate in "retreats" and "vent rounds," consult to dysfunctional teams, and facilitate treatment for individual houseofficers.

General Approach to Diagnosis

The age and developmental level of the child serve as the basic framework for the consultation. Given current very short lengths of hospital stays, the consultant must understand the in-hospital "snapshot" evaluation in the context of a longer-term perspective. For example, after suffering an accident, a child seen in the hospital may be in a regressed state marked by depression or unusual anxiety and/or some bizarre ideational content; the child may demonstrate better psychological resources when the consultant reviews recent functioning and behavior or sees him or her on follow-up in an outpatient setting. There is increasing pressure from third party payors to do the minimum necessary on an inpatient basis and expect outpatient follow-up to complete the consultation; however, there is a risk that outpatient work will be limited by reimbursement, delays, and a decreased sense of urgency.

The age-specific effects of hospitalization parallel the concept of age-appropriate developmental expectations or norms (Bergman, 1965). For the infant, the psychological impact of hospitalization (in addition to the illness) is separation from the mother or main caregiver. Despite the best efforts at continuity of care, the infant is handled by numerous different medical and nursing personnel and, unless the mother is available at all times, has to face repeated separations. Bowlby's observations (1960) of separation anxiety are clearly seen in infants, and elements of his model are evident in the regressed behavior of older children as they cope with illness and the alien environment of a hospital. Bowlby's classic observations concerning the 3 stages of separation are relevant and worthy of a brief review:

The first stage is protest. The infant or toddler cries and thrashes in an attempt to prevent the mother's leaving or recapture the mother. In the older child this phase may appear as clinging and bargaining as a parent is about to leave, or negative behavior directed at nurses.

Despair marks the second stage. The infant or toddler withdraws and appears hopeless. Sometimes the withdrawal phase is misleading, as caregivers welcome the quiet and project their own hopes that the child is settling in.

The third stage is detachment. The young child seems more alert and too accepting of nursing care. However, these new attachments are superficial and may predict the child's future difficulty with trust and intimacy; often there is a history of poor continuity of care (foster placements), multiple hospitalizations, or an emotionally unavailable mother. More recent work by Tronick (1978) found antecedents of Bowlby's 3 phases of separation in the first weeks of life.

Anna Freud's classic work on defenses (1952) emphasizes regression, especially in the toddler. The normal child between the ages of 2 and 4 years might lose autonomous functioning (bladder and bowel control, body movement, ego autonomy) under the stress of physical illness and with the family's lower expectations of the child during hospitalizations. Prugh et al. (1953) found that hospitalized children experience a wide variety of reactions. Virtually all children are anxious—some seriously so. Older children tend to be irritable, restless, and withdrawn.

Children, especially of younger school age, may feel that their illness is a punishment for angry thoughts or misbehavior. This sense of guilt stems from the development of a conscience and from an egocentric view of causation.

The school-age child may share some of the separation phases but in general develops multiple, often magical fears about the nature of the illness. Children, especially in the initial interview, may be reluctant to verbalize their fears or fantasies. The Draw-a-Person test sometimes is useful in estimating the child's developmental level and anxiety about his or her illness. Children may draw an immature figure with distortion or shading of an area that reflects their anxiety about their illness. Drawings with irregular curved lines, awkward placement of extremities, wavy lines or lines that do not meet may reflect cognitive deficits (Koppitz, 1968). Several drawings over time may demonstrate the child's neurologic and psychological recovery from trauma, surgery, or head injury.

The hospitalized adolescent is concerned about maintaining a recently won sense of autonomy. Because of the adolescent's tentative identity formation and investment in peer acceptance, physical stigmata or limitations in daily activity arouse significant anxiety. Invariably the illness awakens dependency needs that may be defended against by aggressive assertiveness, denial, or refusal to follow medical regimens.

Serious or chronic illness in a child is among the most stressful events in a family's life (Perrin, 1991). The parents must cope with uncertainty and a seemingly endless series of highs and lows. Abnormal laboratory results, adverse reactions, life-threatening crises, limitations on the child's future, and fear of the child's death are all too often recurrent realities. Other members of the family, such as siblings or grandparents, also are involved; each may have a different style of coping—withdrawal, anger, manipulation, depression, anxiety, or denial. Clearly the family's reaction is the critical mirror that serves as the child's most trusted resource. The stress of the child's illness may well either increase family cohesiveness or exacerbate areas of conflict.

In general, the premorbid quality of the child's relationship to his or her parents and the maturity of a child's defensive style may help in coping with anxiety; however, defensive patterns are complex. The defense of denial, especially with some isolation and intellectualization, may modulate anxiety very successfully. Denial, particularly in a withdrawn child, sometimes can obscure psychopathology and prevent psychiatric referral. The consultant must use a developmental perspective in understanding the normal range of responses to hospitalization and then apply this perspective in the evaluation of a child's behavior, emotional state, and defensive style.

Hospitalized children frequently have psychiatric disorders and psychosocial problems. Mutter and Schliefer (1966) studied latency-age children hospitalized with "nonpsychosomatic" illness and compared them to nonill children. The hospitalized children had more disorganized families and had suffered more frequent and threatening changes in their environment. Stocking et al. (1972) found that 64% of children on their pediatric wards had emotional problems that warranted psychiatric consultation, even though only 11% were referred for such consultation. Lloyd (1995) found that 13% of pediatric inpatient unit were dysfunctional based on Pediatric Symptom Checklist screening.

Given the current common inpatient diagnoses—chronic diseases, accidents, intensive care—the child psychiatric consultant often confronts difficult differential diagnostic decisions regarding the primary effects of the chronic illness or trauma, the side effects of treatments, and depressive or reactive symptoms. Aggressive, life-saving treatments such as bone marrow transplantation or extracorporeal membrane oxygenation contribute to stress and potentially to psychosocial morbidity. Parents often feel helpless and guilty as they see their child, especially if he or she has a chronic disease and undergoes multiple hospitalizations, suffering over a period of years. As part of their mission and dedication, primary nurses become highly invested in these patients and families and thus share a substantial burden. House staff are frustrated by illnesses that do not easily yield to their interventions and often require them to perform painful procedures; in addition, they must face the anguish of the family several times a day.

The most common problems that are referred for consultation include: (1) depression, (2) concerns about the child's reaction to illness and hospitalization, (3) psychosomatic disorders, (4) suicide gestures, (5) familial grief, (6) behavior problems, (7) problems specific to the preschool child, and (8) neonatal and pediatric intensive care issues (Jellinek, Herzog, & Selter, 1981).

DEPRESSION

Depression is a frequent disorder in hospitalized children. It may be a secondary adjustment reaction to acute or chronic illness, or it may be primary and present with psychosomatic symptoms and behavior problems. What aspects of the child's mood is an "adjustment reaction" to being in the hospital, undergoing procedures, or in pain? What is a grief reaction to the loss of feeling well, playing a sport, or being with friends (Bowlby, 1961)? Finally, what depressive symptoms are features of a "true" depression? Until recently, depression was a neglected area in child psychiatry, and some still question its existence, particularly in the very young child. Childhood/adolescent depression has the typical features of adult depression with the exceptions that there is more irritability than sadness and there are less neuro-vegetative signs. If depression is a serious concern, possibly stemming from several sources, then specific treatment may be indicated. Antidepressants used in conjunction with psychotherapy and social skills programs may improve and hasten the relief of symptoms in ill, depressed school aged children (Biederman et al; Emslie et al. In press, 1977). Fluoxetine has recently become the first FDA approved psychotropic medication for depression in children. Future research may demonstrate complex interrelationships between mood disorders and children's immunological or physiological state. It is likely that, as in adults,

psychological stress and mood may alter the outcome if not the survival of children with serious illness.

REACTIONS TO ILLNESS OR HOSPITALIZATION

A substantial number of patients are referred by their primary physician because they respond to illness in ways that interfere with medical treatment or psychosocial development. In our tertiary facility over one-third of the children in this group have an invasive malignancy. Differential diagnosis requires a careful assessment of central nervous system functioning, side effects of medication, nutritional state, and psychodynamic factors. These children commonly have depressive symptoms. Like depression, chronic illness often is manifested by weight loss, insomnia, dysphoric mood, and anhedonia. The psychodynamic issues may include understanding the illness as a punishment or excessive concern about the pain the child is causing the family. Fears of intolerable pain and death are common. These children may substantially distort the surgeries they have had or are about to have. The consultant functions in several ways, to help these children: cope with the diagnosis; follow their medical regimen (including invasive procedures); and continue to master their developmental tasks. In almost every case of severe chronic disease, the consultant works with the staff and with the patient's family concerning their feelings of anger, impotence, and helplessness in the face of the relentless course of the child's illness. The consultant helps the child bear the stress of the illness and its impact on his or her life.

PSYCHOSOMATIC DISORDERS

A hallmark of psychosomatic disorders is the great pressure from families on the doctor to define the disorder in biomedical terms and to do so without a total medical evaluation of the child, specifically without exploring the child's emotional or family life (Herzog & Harper, 1981). The families are characterized by their inability to speak in psychological terms and their denial of family involvement in the child's symptoms. They prefer to talk about their daughter's amenorrhea and the need for a laparotomy rather than what the daughter was experiencing as a result of poor school performance due to a recently identified learning disability. They deny any possible relationship between the child's symptoms and even the most painful issues in family life, such as threatened parental separation or extramarital affairs. These families overemphasize anything medical, including borderline test results, and pressure the doctor constantly.

The consultant may help the pediatrician to define a rational approach to assessment and treatment. The rule-out approach in these disorders is problematic because it reinforces the family's biomedical tunnel vision and delays their obtaining effective help with the denied or ignored psychosocial issues. When excessive anxiety is noted in the family's communication about the child's illness, the concept of displacement may be applied as a way of understanding and managing this anxiety for the family. Some helpful tools for making these diagnoses include:

- Watchful waiting: It is not necessary to make the whole diagnosis the first day, week, or month, despite the wishes of the family.
- Judicious disregard: Use of restraint in the pursuit of equivocal organic findings.
- Multiple diagnoses: It is not necessary to reduce the symptoms to one disorder. (A child may have atypical asthma, family tension, and a depressive disorder at the same time.)
- Diagnosis in context: Children often have shifting levels of functioning in different settings.

Therapeutic interventions for the patient include a medical-psychiatric team approach. Such an approach often helps directly; at other times, at least initially, it serves as a graceful way out of a tense situation. The development of the relationship between the med-psych team with the child and family is critical. Children with these kinds of symptoms are at risk for medical abandonment, especially after psychiatric referral. Pediatric reexaminations and ongoing comanagement are useful. Since the child's symptoms frequently serve to stabilize the family or "solve" some family problem, the family often needs therapy so that the child may become free to move beyond the sick role. Family therapy frequently helps parents reestablish themselves as a couple and remove the child's symptoms as the focus on their relationship. Developmentally appropriate activities can increase the child's sense of mastery and self-esteem. But implementation of such activities may require prescription by the pediatrician and enforced mobilization by the staff. A nutritional rehabilitation program may be necessary for the child with anorexia or failure to thrive; a physical rehabilitation program may be a neces-

sary component for the child with the "clenched fist syndrome." At the extreme of psychosomatic families is probably a larger than expected number of Munchausen by proxy. These families, often headed by a single mother, have children repeatedly hospitalized for vague, contradictory, and sometimes life-threatening symptoms. The children are at risk for repeated invasive procedures and possibly murder secondary to the illnesses induced by their parents. Diagnosis requires awareness and often elaborate efforts at detection (Rosenberg, 1987; Sugar, Belfer, Israel, & Herzog, 1991).

SUICIDE GESTURES

Suicide is the third leading cause of death among males and the fourth leading cause of death among females in the United States. (See Chapter 25.) Furthermore, suicide attempts among adolescents have increased sharply. Although the incidence of completed suicide among children ages 6 to 12 years may be relatively low, suicidal threats and attempts by children in this age group are not uncommon. Almost without exception all children who have made a suicide gesture should be admitted for pediatric (or, if indicated, psychiatric) hospitalization. A brief pediatric hospitalization gives the staff sufficient time to complete a thorough evaluation and arrange disposition. Specific suggestions for the assessment of the suicidal child include gathering a very detailed review of the suicide attempt, pursuing the child's understanding of death and his or her funeral, exploring why the attempt was not successful, and conducting 1 or more family interviews.

The assessment of a suicidal child or adolescent should address the following issues:

- The risk of the attempt
- The wish and efforts to be rescued
- Whether a plan was present to kill him-/or herself
- Feelings of hopelessness, helplessness, and despair
- Psychosis or drug or alcohol abuse
- Previous suicide attempts
- Identification with someone who has committed suicide
- The intensity of the anger or depression
- The presence of support systems
- Vulnerability to impending losses
- Ability to use help

Family issues that should be assessed include a family history of depression, whether a family is "modeling" suicide, interpersonal tension, and real or imagined rejection of the suicidal child by the parents. Initially the consultant is asked to decide the appropriate ward management for the suicidal child—whether the child needs 1-to-1 staffing, 4-point restraints, sedation, or none or some or all of the above. The consultant then needs to determine, often within 24 to 48 hours, whether the child or adolescent can be managed as an outpatient living at home, needs psychiatric hospitalization, or requires a more temporary shelter, pending further evaluation of the family.

The Department of Nursing and increasingly third-party payors often put pressure on the consultant to make a rapid decision about disposition. Nursing departments often are forced to provide the funding for 1-to-1 staffing, which may not be allocated adequately in their budget. Many times communication with nursing administration is critical to avoid resentment toward the patient; a thoughtful approach will limit the pressure of those emphasizing financial considerations to push the psychiatric consultant for an unduly hasty decision.

FAMILIAL GRIEF

The families referred for consultation often are overwhelmed by their child's severe illness or death and require careful assessment and observation. If unable to withstand their child's stormy course, some of these families become abusing, devaluing or splitting the staff into arguing factions (Beresin, Jellinek, & Herzog, 1990). The assessment should include how families have responded to traumatic events in the past, whether they are chronically grieving, whether there is a history of psychiatric problems, whether a current family member has a depressive disorder, and what marital supports are available. Occasionally a family member will require psychiatric hospitalization or a mild sedative. If a child dies, many centers have group programs to help parents, and most family members are appreciative and responsive to the consultant's effort to follow up by phone or personal interview. Such efforts often are most helpful between 6 and 18 months after the death.

BEHAVIOR PROBLEMS

Some children are referred for consultation for excessive activity, agitation, verbal or physical threats to staff and other children, seizurelike episodes, and temper tantrums. A careful assessment, including medical, developmental, psycho-logical, and social histories from the child and family, a neurologic examination, nursing observations, and school reports, is needed. When attention deficit disorder with hyperactivity is diagnosed, the child may respond quite dramatically to the prescription of stimulants or an antidepressant. Occasionally an underlying psychosis is discovered; if so, the appropriate antipsychotic agent should be instituted. At times a neuropsychiatric disorder, such as partial complex seizures, are noted, and anticonvulsants are begun. Patients with behavioral problems also should be assessed for poorly controlled pain. Pediatric pain management, including pain management in neonates, is an overlooked source of suffering and problematic behavior (Anand & Hickey, 1992; Lebel-Schwartz, 1990).

Ward issues arise around such patients. Staff and patients may feel unsafe and need to be reassured. Issues of control, explaining what the patient's needs are and what the staff's needs are, often need to be addressed. There may be disagreements between staff members concerning the management of a given child, and the child may be acting out this disagreement. A team meeting with various staff members may reduce the extent of this symptomatology. Sometimes these children cannot be managed on a pediatric ward and require placement in a setting that has the staffing necessary to manage emotionally disturbed children.

PROBLEMS SPECIFIC TO THE PRESCHOOL CHILD AND INFANT

Referrals specific to preschool children usually involve failure to thrive, developmental delays, or suspected or confirmed sexual and/or physical abuse. Evaluation of the child's physical, intellectual, and emotional involvement; themes in play; and interaction with family, staff, and consultant form the foundation of the assessment. The use of dolls may be helpful in such an evaluation to understand the child's concern about abuse or aggression. The consultant also may note the child to be hypervigilant and to have great difficulty trusting anyone. It is important to assess attachment behavior with such children. Does the child have a special attachment to a parent, or does the child attach the same to all providers? Assessing the parent is equally important.

With the parent, the consultant addresses past and present feelings of hate and anger, and how the infant contributes to these feelings. Treatment intervention often includes a family perspective that ranges from therapy to the filing of a statement of concern for the child's welfare with the appropriate state agency. The child may need medical interventions (i.e., nutrition), play therapy, or a child-stimulation program including physical therapy, occupational therapy, and speech therapy.

THE NEONATAL INTENSIVE CARE UNIT

In the neonatal intensive care unit, the basis for referral is the reaction of either the parents or staff members to the infant's serious illness. Parents may be overwhelmed at the sight of their newborn lying passively while attached to multiple life-sustaining equipment. Although many parents adjust, some, especially those with poor social support or a history of psychiatric disorder or a painful loss, may need social service or psychiatric intervention. Inevitably some babies die; psychiatric consultation should be available for parents and staff both acutely and, for those parents at risk for developing clinical depression as part of prolonged grieving, over time (Jellinek, Catlin, Todres, & Cassem, 1992).

THE PEDIATRIC INTENSIVE CARE UNIT

The pediatric intensive care unit bears no resemblance to home or school and denies the patient any sense of control over his or her surroundings (Herzog, Jellinek, & Todres, 1990). Children often react to intensive care hospitalization with confusion, withdrawal, or anxiety. The use of familiar toys, blankets, photos, and accessories may be helpful in such reactions.

Conscious children usually are solemn and preoccupied with their physical condition. They experience adjustment problems related to control, protection, and pain. They want to know "Where am I?" and "What is happening to me?" "Who is here to protect and care for me?" These children need to know that someone caring and familiar is close by. Their coping strategies usually include dependence on the parenting figure, and thus open parental visiting and vigil are encouraged. Children are also in acute fear of pain. Adequate local anesthesia or intravenous anesthesia should be used for painful procedures. Sedation may be indicated as well.

Psychiatric consultation in the pediatric intensive care setting has several features: urgency, constant availability, minimal privacy, considerable noise and distraction, and pressure to make major changes immediately. Reasons for referral to the psychiatrist in such a unit include depression, suicide attempts, postoperative nightmares, psychosis, delirium, and developmental assessment. In a psychotic or delirious child, the differential diagnosis includes hypoxia, hypoglycemia, meningitis, and drug ingestion. Postoperative nightmares are common in the intensive care setting. Often the comfort of a familiar figure is all that is needed to alleviate the problem. However, for some children the nightmares are chronically accompanied by agitation. Often their nightmares involve misconceptions of what their surgery involved; occasionally uncontrolled pain is a hidden factor.

An "intensive care unit syndrome" has been noted in children, primarily those 18 months to 6 years. The syndrome refers to a transient psychotic state and delirium, characterized by depression, confusion, disorientation, hallucinations, and/or paranoid delusions. Some children become withdrawn, do not speak, and are passive. Others are hostile and agitated. Contributing factors include sleep and sensory deprivation, inappropriate parental reactions, and overstimulation. The syndrome is generally alleviated by increased parental contact, familiar toys, reduced lighting, and decreased noise to facilitate sleep. The child may need to be relocated to a less noisy or less frightening area, with increased parental visitation and a more active play program. In rare circumstances the administration of haloperidol may be helpful.

Staff and trainees are under unique stress in the intensive care environment. Jellinek, 1992, outlined these stresses in "The Dark Side of Intensive Care Training" and noted potentially high levels of anger and guilt among physicians.

Initial Steps in the Consultation Process

After the referral is received, the consultant should contact the pediatrician and, if necessary, clarify or explore the question being asked. Some pediatricians are especially sensitive to psychological concerns and have known the patient and family for several years. In university-affiliated hospitals, the consultant often deals with less experienced house staff on monthly rotating schedules; in such cases discussion with the "referring physician" will be shifted toward teaching. A crucial function of ongoing consultation is the trust relationship that should develop among pediatrician, ward personnel, and consultant. This trust creates an atmosphere in which the psychological needs of children are recognized and the consultant's recommendations are carried through even when they take considerable time and effort.

In reviewing the medical record, the consultant must pay special attention to the notes made in the chart by ward personnel. The pediatric nurse's observations may be the most helpful in a number of areas. The nurse usually makes the most careful observations of the child's level of anxiety, state of aggression, and temperamental characteristics. The nurse's notes may be supplemented by observations from additional personnel, such as a child life worker. The role of the child life worker, trained in child development, is to help children cope with the stress of hospitalization. By organizing group activities in the playroom or by celebrating a birthday on the ward, the child life worker may make significant observations about the child's ability to interact with peers. Last, some inpatient services have a social worker who reviews all admissions; the expanded social history such a worker can provide may be very helpful before the consultant meets the family and child.

Techniques of Child Psychiatric Consultation

The child and family should be prepared for the consultation (Jellinek & Herzog, 1988). It is essential that the referring physician discuss the reasons for the referral with both the child and the parents so that the child feels more included and does not feel that information is being withheld. The psychiatric consultant should interview parents of a preschool and young school-age child (generally less than 8 years old) before interviewing the child.

The interview of the young child requires largely nonverbal means for the expression of feelings and concerns. In the initial interview the psychiatrist needs to create as normal an environment as possible to facilitate beginning to get to know the child. The consultant's attitude should be active, interested, and playful. The room should contain familiar items and not be the setting associated with the painful procedures. First, the consultant should perform an eyeball examination and then a gross developmental assessment. In the child under 3 years of age, observations of the parent-child dyad are crucial. What is the eye contact like between parent and child? Does the parent respond to cues in the child and vice versa? What is the child's temperament like, and how does the parent handle frustration, whether it occurs as a result of the child's inactivity or excessive activity? How do the child and parent handle separation? How does the child respond to strangers? The psychiatrist needs to be well equipped to perform such an evaluation. The minimal equipment includes a toy doctor kit, puppets, and some doll furniture.

The 3- to 6-year-old child may require that a parent be present throughout the interview. That request should be respected, although at some point in the interview an attempt should be made to have the parent leave the room. Developmental assessment, including language, social interaction, and gross and fine motor coordination, is a mandatory part of the interview. Drawings become a more important tool for expressing troublesome thoughts and feelings. The psychiatrist should not expect to complete the evaluation in one visit, and the length of each visit likely will be less than an hour.

The latency-age child can be a more verbal participant in the interview. The child should be questioned about current and previous school attendance, school behavior, school performance, after-school activities, friends, health (including mental health) of family members, family problems, and interaction of family members in response to traumatic events. The consultant's approach should be flexible depending on the child's way of relating. The active verbal child can be approached in the more traditional interview. The shy child may be engaged through drawings or games such as checkers or video arcade games. These activities can prove helpful in facilitating an alliance and in demonstrating organic deficits. The first few sessions with a child suffering from a chronic disease may be brief and consist of supportive comments; gross developmental assessment (past and current); assessment of several symptoms, including pain, anorexia, and insomnia; assessment of the usual coping strategies; and suggestions for ways to deal with symptoms and feelings. The role of the psychiatric consultant for these children has many features of a "professional friend"; after a few sessions, the consultant may drop in only for several minutes during rounds.

Interviewing an adolescent can pose a true challenge. Some adolescents will flatly refuse to talk, and others will substantially distort their psychosocial histories. They are often labile and experience emotions intensely. How does the consultant proceed with the silent adolescent? Often the adolescent's initial anxiety and resistance are difficult to surmount. The consultant should not become discouraged and interpret silence in response to a question as a personal blunder. The adolescent should be given a thorough explanation and reason for the referral. Often it is helpful to reassure the adolescent about the consultant's knowledge of his or her physical problems and clinical procedures. The limits and expectations of the interview should be clarified and the necessary information gathered to understand what may be bothering the adolescent and how to best approach helping him or her. The adolescent should be told how long the interview will last and that although it is preferable to talk about feelings, periods of silence are also acceptable. Confidentially should be assured, and interviews should take place in a private setting. In general, the consultant should be patient and easygoing. It may be necessary to initiate the conversation with some safe topic that the adolescent can relate to easily, such as a sporting event, a rock group, or a television program. The consultant should visit the adolescent frequently, if only for brief periods. Most introductory sessions do go smoothly. Over time, questions about body image, school, family relationships, friendship patterns, goals, and sexuality need to be addressed.

The role of the family interview as the initial interview for the assessment of a child is somewhat controversial. Some clinicians feel that a family evaluation is mandatory in order to understand the child. A family evaluation for certain disorders, specifically psychosomatic disorders (anorexia nervosa, school phobia, recurrent abdominal pain) is essential where family interaction may either precipitate or maintain the symptoms. In the pediatric intensive care unit, all families should be screened, often by a social worker. Families of seriously ill children need to express their feelings about hospitalization and obtain emotional support. Siblings often have distorted concepts of their brother's or sister's illness that need to be corrected. A family meeting can clarify distortions, reduce family turmoil, improve coping skills, and dispel conflicts between family and staff. During the meeting the ward staff or the psychiatrist should evaluate the family's psychological state, including coping mechanisms, anxiety level, available support, and ability to comprehend information.

Liaison Functions

Child psychiatric consultation almost always involves more than the patient and referring physician. Parents give critical information and will need to be actively involved in implementation of recommendations; nurses serve in loco parentis; the ward rather than the child's room is the temporary home; and behavior has an impact on many other patients and staff. Children are likely to evoke intense feelings in the staff. Since many pediatric units encourage parental visitation and even live-in, the potential impact of a distraught or disturbed parent on the entire ward is substantial. As there are fewer pediatric units than adult units and since they usually are defined by age level, a given patient may return to the same floor over a 5- or 10-year period. Thus many children become well known to staff members, and the depth of their involvement with the children grows over the years. Child psychiatric consultation includes an essential liaison role that is relevant to patient and family care, interstaff tensions, and individual staff stress.

A key stressor is inherent to primary nursing. Primary nursing encourages continuity of care, as 1 or 2 nurses are assigned to the child during the hospitalization and often for repeated admissions. Primary nursing is beneficial for the child's sense of trust, makes the nurse's role more personally satisfying, and can add a needed perspective if too many subspecialists forget the whole child's needs. Unavoidably and happily, primary nurses become intensely involved in the child's personal and family life; thus they have critical information and share the stress of the child's illness. The child psychiatrist can provide suggestions and supervision for dealing with difficult families or crises, review when psychiatric referral is indicated, and help in understanding the painful issues of chronic disease, suicide, and terminal illness.

A basic stressor for house staff is being relatively inexperienced and yet forced to deal with complex medical and psychological circumstances. The source of stress is clearest in the intensive care unit, where frustration mounts rapidly as children do not respond to treatment or suffer lifelong physical and neurologic damage. The consequences of multiple stresses—frustration with the patient's course, lack of sleep, and feeling incompetent—may lead to depression, substance abuse, or bitter tensions without house staff or nurses.

Part of the child psychiatrist's liaison function is to attend rounds, be aware of difficult clinical and family situations, get to know nurses and house staff through teaching and informal discussion concerning patients, and be aware of the early signs of behavior destructive to patient care and fellow staff.

Ethical Issues

In addition to adhering to the established medical ethical standards of confidentiality, "do no harm," "duty to warn," and so on, the consultant often has to face the difficult position of serving more than one master. The consultant serves the referring pediatrician, the child and family, the hospital, and society. These several "masters" may be in conflict with regard to patient confidentiality, suspicion of child abuse, and acknowledgment of "secrets" within the family or errors in medical care (Bloomberg, Wozniak, Fost, Medearis, & Herzog, 1992). Although facing these ethical dilemmas can

be tortuous, ultimately the child psychiatric consultant should serve the best interests of the child.

Conclusion

Psychiatric consultation faces major barriers because of inadequate funding, too few qualified child psychiatrists, and the level of cooperation needed between departments of pediatrics and psychiatry. Reimbursement guidelines do not recognize multiple evaluation visits or the time spent gathering data from other sources. The intervention, although critical to control behavior, enhance compliance, support the family, and even improve medical outcomes, is still considered vague and harder to quantify than more technical procedures. The future of inpatient psychiatric consultation to children depends on recognition by third-party payors that this is a necessary service and that it must be supported financially in all its facets. Under managed care and capitation, short lengths of stay and financial disincentive to obtain consultation will require thoughtful protocols between pediatricians and child psychiatrist that span inpatient and outpatient care. As in other areas, pediatric consultation also suffers from a shortage of child psychiatrists, which results in overwork, burnout, unavailability, and inadequate research. The needs of children hospitalized on pediatric services and the educational needs of pediatric house staff are quite clear. It is hoped that those needs can be met in the future.

REFERENCES

Anand, K. J. S., & Hickey, P. R. (1992). Halothane-morphine compared with high-dose sufentanil for anesthesia and postoperative analgesia in neonatal cardiac surgery. *New England Journal of Medicine, 326,* 1–9.

Beresin, E. V., Jellinek, M. S., & Herzog, D. B. (1990). The difficult parent. In M. Jellinek (Ed.), *Psychosocial aspects of ambulatory pediatrics* (Vol. 20, pp. 620–633). Chicago: Mosby-Year Book.

Bergman, T. (1965). *Children in the hospital.* New York: International Universities Press.

Bloomberg, J., Wozniak, J., Fost, N., Medearis, D. N., & Herzog, D. B. (1992). Grand rounds: Ethical dilemmas in child and adolescent consultation psychiatry. *Journal of the American Academy of Child and Adolescent Psychiatry,*

Bowlby, J. (1960). Separation anxiety. *International Journal of Psycho-Analysis, 41,* 89–113.

Bowlby, J. (1961). Childhood mourning and its implication for psychiatry. *American Journal of Psychiatry, 118,* 481–498.

Freud, A. (1952). The role of bodily illness in the mental life of children. *The Psychoanalytic Study of the Child, 7,* 69–81.

Herzog, D. B., & Harper, G. (1981). Unexplained disability: Diagnostic dilemmas and principles of management. *Clinical Pediatrics, 20,* 761–768.

Herzog, D., Jellinek, M. S., & Todres, I. D. (1990). The intensive care units. In M. S. Jellinek & D. B. Herzog (Eds.), *Massachusetts General Hospital: Psychiatric aspects of general hospital pediatrics* (pp. 41–50). MA: Year Book Pubs.

Jellinek, M. S. (1982). The present status of child psychiatry in pediatrics. *New England Journal of Medicine, 306,* 1227–1230.

Jellinek, M. S. (1986). Recognition and management of discord within house staff teams. *Journal of the American Medical Association, 256* (6), 754–755.

Jellinek, M. S., Catlin, E., Todres, I. D., & Cassem, E. H. (1992). Facing tragic decisions with parents in the NICU: Clinical perspectives. *Pediatrics,*

Jellinek, M. S., & Herzog, D. B. (1988). The child. In A. Nicholi (Ed.), *The new Harvard guide to psychiatry* (pp. 607–636). Cambridge, MA: Harvard University Press.

Jellinek, M. S., & Herzog, D. B. (1992). Psychiatric consultation in pediatrics. In N. H. Cassem (Ed.), *Massachusetts General Hospital handbook of general hospital psychiatry* (3rd ed.). MA: Mosby-Year Book.

Jellinek, M. S., & Herzog, D. B. (Eds.). (1990). *Massachusetts General Hospital: Psychiatric aspects of general hospital pediatrics.* MA: Year Book Pubs.

Jellinek, M. S., Herzog, D. B., & Selter, L. F. (1981). Psychiatric consultation to hospitalized children at Massachusetts General Hospital. *Psychosomatics, 22* (1), 29–33.

Kessel, S. J., & Haggerty, R. J. (1968). General pediatrics: A study of practice in the mid-1960's. *Journal of Pediatrics, 73,* 271–279.

Lebel-Schwartz, A. (1990). Pain management in children. In M. S. Jellinek & D. B. Herzog (Eds.), *Massachusetts General Hospital: Psychiatric aspects of general hospital pediatrics* (pp. 98–113). MA: Year Book.

Lloyd, J., Jellinek, M. S., Little, M., Murphy, J. M., Pagano, M. (1995). Screening for psychosocial dysfunction in pediatric inpatients. *Clinical Pediatrics, 34:* 18–24.

Mutter, A. Z., & Schliefer, M. H. (1966). The role of psychological and social factors in the onset of somatic illness in children. *Psychosomatic Medicine, 28,* 333–343.

Perrin, J. M. (1991). Children with chronic illness. In R. E. Behrman, *Nelson textbook of pediatrics* (14th ed., pp. 91–94). Philadelphia: W. B. Saunders.

Prugh, D. G., Staub, E. M., Sands, H. et al. (1953). A study of the emotional reactions of children and families to hospitalization and illness. *Am Journal Orthopsychiatry, 23:* 70–106.

Reinhardt, J. B. (1979). Direct consultation to the pediatric service. In J. D. Noshpitz (Ed.), *Basic handbook of child psychiatry* (Vol. 1, pp. 648–653). New York: Basic Books.

Rosenberg, D. (1987). Web of deceit: A literature review of Munchausen syndrome by proxy. *Child Abuse and Neglect, 11,* 547–563.

Small, G. W. (1981). House officer stress syndrome. *Psychosomatics, 22,* 860–869.

Stocking, M., Rothney, W., Grosser, G., et al. (1972). Psychopathology in a pediatric hospital: implications for the pediatrician. *American Journal of Public Health, 62:* 551–556.

Sugar, J. A., Belfer, M., Israel, E., & Herzog, D. B. (1991). A three year old boy's chronic diarrhea and unexplained death. *Journal of the American Academy of Child and Adolescent Psychiatry, 30* (6), 1015–1021.

Task Force on Pediatric Education. (1978). *The future of pediatric education.* Evanston, IL: American Academy of Pediatrics.

Tronick, E., Als, H., Adamson, L., et al. (1978). The infant's response to entrapment between contradictory messages in face to face interaction. *Journal of the American Academy of Child Psychiatry, 17,* 1–13.

18 / **School Consultation**

Irving H. Berkovitz

This chapter presents principles that will help child and adolescent psychiatrists to (1) relate more effectively to school personnel when treating a child (an area I call case management); (2) consult generally to school systems and personnel, including case, program, administrative, and system consultation; and (3) consult specifically to programs for children designated learning disabled (LD) and seriously emotionally disturbed (SED) according to Public Laws 94-142, 99-457, and 101-476. These laws will be discussed more in detail later.

Importance of School to Children

Next to the family, schools are one of the most influential areas of learning and development for the majority of children. Experience in schools can help children to develop cognitive abilities and social skills with peers, reinforce self-esteem, lessen attachment to and dependence on family, and expand ability to relate to adults, other than parents and relatives (Hanson, 1997).

Unavoidably, children entering school will demonstrate to parents and the school personnel any developmental lags and deficiencies that may be present. These may include difficulties separating from parents or caregivers, inappropriate aggression toward other children, oppositional behavior, difficulty sharing, bizarre rituals, symptoms of attention deficit hyperactivity disorder (ADHD), and so on. Some of these reactions may have been seen already in preschool, but are more likely to occur in the larger kindergarten or first grade. Some parents take information regarding this behavior quite personally, as if they are getting a negative report card on their parenting abilities. Many practice denial but most seek remediation.

Approximately, 25% of referrals to mental health agencies and private practitioners have come after parents have been alerted to their children's needs by school personnel. Consultation to school personnel can often be of crucial value in developing appropriate referral and providing empathic educational help to these children in schools, before or after psychotherapy is initiated.

History of School Consultation

Assistance to teachers and other school personnel in regard to the mental health and behavior of children in schools worldwide probably began soon after the first schools were established. The earliest published report in the United States by a mental health professional was by Witmer (1896), a psychologist. He consulted to a teacher regarding the classroom management of a mentally retarded child. Anna Freud (1930), herself a teacher before becoming a psychoanalyst, consulted with teachers in Vienna in the 1920s.

After World War II, the community psychiatry movement in the United States emphasized mental health consultation to all agencies, including schools, as a way of reducing mental health casualties and admissions to hospitals and clinics. Several psychiatrists were active in formulating and advocating this type of intervention (Berlin, 1980; Caplan, 1970). In the 1960s and 1970s federally funded community mental health centers were required to have a consultation component, devoted to all agencies, but especially to schools. Since then the amount of consultative activities to other agencies has decreased considerably, but some consultation to schools still survives.

The preventive focus favored in the 1960s and 1970s usually deemphasized direct service to children, hoping instead to improve the educators' skills so that they could better help children's incipient and existing mental health problems. Caplan (1970) defined mental health consultation as a "process of interaction between two professional persons—the consultant who is a specialist, and the consultee, who invokes the consultant's help in regard to a current work problem" (p. 19). The consultant accepted no direct responsibility for implementing remedial action. Despite this emphasis, many consultative programs did include direct service to children. Since then many more programs do include direct services.

In the 1980s and 1990s, the implementation of Public Law 94-142 (now Public Law 101-476) increased the number of psychiatrists consulting to programs for emotionally and mentally disturbed children (APA, 1993). (The mandates of these laws will be discussed later.) These children and adolescents comprise about 1 to 2% of the school population. Since medical diagnosis, medication, and family treatment is very often necessary with this group, more psychiatrists are directly evaluating and treating these children as well as consulting with the school personnel who are educating and counseling them.

School psychological services and more general consultative services to the 90% of the school system containing the nondisabled students have decreased markedly as a result of this shift of funds to special education. However, as school districts try to lessen the costs of special education programs, some districts are returning to the use of more general consultative assistance to improve the classroom milieu for all children (Knitzer, Steinberg, & Fleisch, 1990). Thus, they hope to lessen the worsening of emotional and mental disorders of the children in regular classes and reduce the numbers needing referral to special education.

Consultation Models

Several models of consultation have been used in schools: (1) *child-focused,* or case consultation, (a) pertaining to a child one is seeing in therapy (case management), or (b) pertaining to children not seen in therapy by the consultant; (2) a child focused consultation to *special education programs,* especially those for children designated seriously emotionally disturbed (SED) according to Public Laws 94-142, 99-457 and 101-476. This may include also elements of educator and/or system focused consultation; (3) *school, or educator, focused* consultation. Here the goal is to improve the educator's skills in dealing with current and future interactions with children and adolescents, whether these are disturbed or not. This category may include program, administrative, and system consultation. In this category there is usually minimal contact with the students.

Some effective consultation does occur 1 to 1, but usually consultation is conducted in groups of 3 to 15 educators. Here the input from the consultant can reach a larger number, and the group process can facilitate exchange of knowledge and attitudes between the consultees. Since most elementary schools often contain no more than 10 to 20 teachers, at times this type of consultation can beneficially affect an entire milieu for the 600 to 800 children who attend the school (APA, 1993; Jellinek, 1990). Teachers usually need to meet after school, while psychologists, counselors, and administrators may be able to meet during the school day.

This type of intervention has a protocol and process similar to, but also different from, consultation in general. Consultation in general is a broader activity, pertaining especially to children not being seen therapeutically by the consultant.

Attitudinal Factors to be Considered in Relating to School Personnel

Before discussing any contact with school personnel, it is crucial to consider attitudinal positions in both the educator and the consultant.

ATTITUDES OF EDUCATORS

It is important to keep in mind that most school personnel have ambivalent feelings about a mental health professional entering the school domain. There can be a mixture of awe, overexpectation, resentment, fear, envy, and, at times, even disdain. The mental health person is on the educator's "turf" and needs to act considerately as "a guest" in the school. Most mental health consultants will be unfamiliar with educational jargon or practices.

Educators, for the most part, pay more attention to achievement and the coping parts of a child's behavior and thinking than to pathology. They generally avoid the term "therapy" in favor of the term "counseling." Most teachers want the disturbed/disturbing child to be removed from their class as soon as possible. Today's public schools often contain more disturbed and disturbing children than in previous years, causing stress to teachers. Also, the greater number of non-English-speaking children in many urban schools especially adds to teacher difficulties. Many experienced teachers and those in special education may be less concerned by a symptomatic child and accept the challenge of trying to help him or her, providing there are not too many in the class. Such teachers welcome working with a consultant and become receptive, collaborative consultees.

Giving advice or recommendations to a teacher or other educator on the phone, or even in a letter, may result in misunderstanding, frustration, or confusion and no benefit to the student patient. For example, recommending to a teacher that a patient needs more individualized nurturing attention and positive support may be appropriate, but not possible for the teacher to do consistently in a classroom of 20 to 30 students. Such a recommendation may increase the resentment and/or guilt of an already overtaxed young teacher, who may feel that he or she is already giving too much attention to that particular child. Yet at times a word of advice or explanation can correct and lessen a teacher–student conflict. This may even reduce or interrupt a student's increasing disability.

Ideally, if a face-to-face meeting is possible, the therapist can evaluate the sophistication and/or biases of the particular teacher and decide on how best to present a recommendation without wounding his or her self-esteem or increasing his or her guilt. Parents and/or some insurance plans often reimburse for such meetings. Additionally, a teacher can usually provide data about a child's peer relations, judgment, social skills or deficits, and coping skills, which can advance the psychotherapy.

ATTITUDES OF CONSULTANTS

On the other side of the interaction, attitudes of some consultants need consideration. Some consultants may have conscious, or unconscious, disrespectful, depreciatory, or pessimistic attitudes about public education and educators, often influenced by their own negative experiences in past schooling. Certainly some areas of current public education can generate pessimism and criticism, but most educators are sensitive to such prejudices and will withdraw from these attitudes, either by attending the consultation sessions only sporadically or by discontinuing the service entirely. The consultant will need to exercise self-scrutiny to minimize the prevalence of such biases. As much as possible a coequal relationship should prevail, where there is mutual respect for each other's expertise.

Most educators are conscientious and hardworking, despite the too frequent lack of societal appreciation and adequate financing of school resources or salaries. Managing interpersonal events in a classroom of 20 to 30 children requires different skills from those required to do psychotherapy, where one is relating only 1 to 1 or, in group therapy, 1 to 6 or 8. Considering a teacher as primarily a therapist is inappropriate. However, many beneficial therapeutic interactions can, and do, take place in classrooms between teachers and students. For example, teachers can help children develop skills for friendship making, dealing with feelings, developing alternatives to aggression, and ways to deal with stress. Unfortunately, also some harmful interactions do occur in classrooms. Some of these may come into the consultative discussion and be remedied.

Berlin (1980) cautions that since consultation "is not a casework, patient or client relationship, certain gratifications and rewards inherent in direct work may be missing and may initially make consultation less satisfying. Consultees who are helped to work more effectively usually do not express gratitude. They often may not recognize that they have been helped" (p. 2254). A support group where the consultant can confer with other consultants to give added perspective helps to lessen some of the occasional discouragement. Often more has been accomplished than the consultant realizes.

Categories of School Personnel

When consulting to a school, it is important to understand the several different categories of school personnel. Figure 18.1 presents an organizational chart of a typical school district. Each category will have different functions and may have different needs in consultation.

Primary is the regular teacher, often with classroom aides. In special education, there is the special education teacher and the resource room specialist teacher. These have the most contact with the children. The principal is the gatekeeper, especially in elementary schools, and needs to be consulted regarding anything going on in the school, including consultation (Berkovitz, 1977). When a school contains over a certain number of pupils, there may be one or two assistant principals. The supportive services, or helping personnel, are the psychologist, counselor, and nurse. Some districts have school physicians, home-school coordinators, and/or social workers. The superintendent and assistant superintendents sometimes may want to meet the consultant, but usually remain uninvolved, except in smaller districts. Junior and senior high schools are bigger and may have several layers of administrative personnel.

Stages of School Consultation

The following five-stage process (Berlin, 1974, pp. 737–739) is applicable especially to an ongoing consultation with a discrete group of personnel, such as teachers, counselors, principals, nurses, or other personnel.

1. "Develop a good working relationship, allaying suspicions that the consultant will try to uncover unconscious motivations or pry into personal problems"; avoid psychiatric terminology.
2. "Try to reduce consultee's anxieties and self-blame, feelings of failure, frustration, anger and hopelessness"; often these attitudes will be expressed in early sessions.
3. Keep the collaboration task-oriented; consider etiological factors in the child's troubles or personnel problem, and "appraise consultee's ego strengths to focus on the first step to be taken by consultee to help the child; consultant needs to be wary of making unilateral recommendations or being seduced into prescriptions about the educative process in which the educator is the expert"; solicit opinions from the educators.
4. Schedule follow-up meetings to evaluate, reconsider, modify, and try new approaches in the light of the educator's experiences and the changes in the child (or situation).

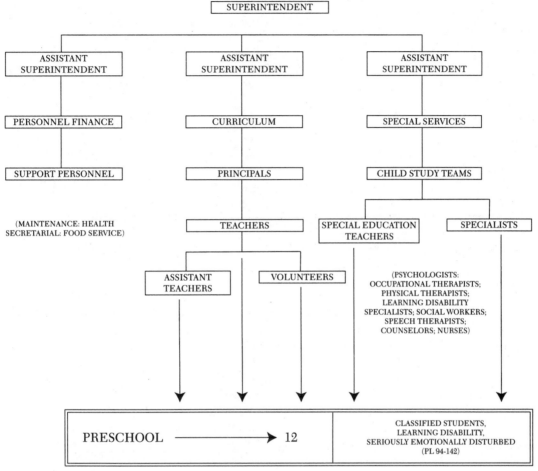

BOARD OF EDUCATION

SUPERINTENDENT

ASSISTANT SUPERINTENDENT   ASSISTANT SUPERINTENDENT   ASSISTANT SUPERINTENDENT

PERSONNEL FINANCE   CURRICULUM   SPECIAL SERVICES

SUPPORT PERSONNEL   PRINCIPALS   CHILD STUDY TEAMS

(MAINTENANCE: HEALTH SECRETARIAL: FOOD SERVICE)   TEACHERS   SPECIAL EDUCATION TEACHERS   SPECIALISTS

ASSISTANT TEACHERS   VOLUNTEERS   (PSYCHOLOGISTS: OCCUPATIONAL THERAPISTS; PHYSICAL THERAPISTS; LEARNING DISABILITY SPECIALISTS; SOCIAL WORKERS; SPEECH THERAPISTS; COUNSELORS; NURSES)

PRESCHOOL ⟶ 12   CLASSIFIED STUDENTS, LEARNING DISABILITY, SERIOUSLY EMOTIONALLY DISTURBED (PL 94-142)

FIGURE 18.1

Organizanal Chart of a School System

(American Psychiatric Association, 1993)

5. "Consolidation and disengagement from consultation: as consultee works more effectively and feels more secure in his [or her] capacity to work and help a wider variety of disturbed children, he [or she] needs the consultant less and feels more competence as teacher, counselor or administrator."

In some cases, consultation may go on for several years, involving, for example, different groups of personnel in the same school district. Disengagement may occur from some groups, but consultation may begin or continue with others (Jellinek, 1990). Consultation to special education programs where direct service, case, and program consultation may be occurring, may go on productively for years.

Child-Focused Consultation

Case management refers to a psychiatrist intervening with school personnel, in one way or another, around the treatment of a child being seen in the office. Often, this will consist only of a letter to the school (if parents are willing), where information is requested about school grades, behavior, test results, and social histories, if these have been done. School records and personnel very often have data that can be useful in a child's therapy. If the child's problem does involve school behavior and/or performance to a major degree, a visit to observe or confer with involved staff may be in order, if parents and the child are willing.

When done judiciously and with respect for the child's and the school staff's feelings, such an intervention can be very helpful to the treatment and the welfare of the child.

One consultant had all the sessions with child, family, and school personnel in the public school rather than at the clinic. He reported positive results in the child's behavior and symptoms, the family behavior, and especially increased understanding and assistance to the child by school personnel (Aponte, 1976). Such a visit is often easier to arrange and manage in a small private school than in a larger public school.

Case consultation generally refers to helping school personnel especially with children not being seen therapeutically by the consultant. This can involve listening to the teacher's (or psychologist's or counselor's) account of the child's difficulties and the problems with educating the child in a classroom setting. In a group consultation, especially in the average elementary school, several personnel may have knowledge of the parents and/or siblings, and often a composite view of the student's problem can be constructed. At times, social histories or home visit data is available from the nurse or social worker (if there is one). Rather than expound in psychiatric terminology on the differential diagnosis, DSM IV category, or psychodynamics (unless the severity of the problem justifies clinical referral), jargon-free discussion by the consultant should center on measures that can be used in the school milieu. Often some of the consultees will have suggestions, based on their own experience with similar children. Facilitating this exchange of information can be one of the most enduring contributions of a group consultation.

An example of a consultant tactfully encouraging a change of attitude to a troublesome student is the following.

CASE EXAMPLE

A very greedy child, whose incessant efforts to grab everything—food, supplies, adult attention—arouses a withholding attitude on the teacher's part. To maintain her own defenses, she is unreasonably depriving to the child. It was inappropriate and ineffective to deal with the teacher's psychological problems directly, as might be done with a psychiatric supervisee or patient. [The consultant] decided he would try to use the teacher's underlying identification with the child to promote

more tolerance for him. [The consultant] was able to point out how "starved" and anxious the child was, how difficult it was to deal with him since all of us, including himself, had a distaste for such behavior and wondered speculatively whether it was possible ever to gratify such a child. Such discussion served to promote the teacher's empathy with the child, intellectual interest in the problem, and identification with the consultant's greater willingness to try to satisfy the youngster. (LaVietes and Chess, 1969, p. 90)

In another situation the consultant was more active in intervening in the classroom management and was able to engage the teacher as a collaborator. A 9-year-old girl, Brigitta, was referred because she never talked at school after two months. She had been teased about her foreign accent and slight difficulties in pronunciation. "It was decided to use a behavioral approach in which things should be organized to give maximum encouragement for speaking at school . . . there were a series of meetings with the child, with the parents and with the schoolteacher, to work out how to do this" (Rutter, 1975, p. 227). A program was developed in the classroom to help reinforce Brigitta's willingness, pleasure, and freedom to talk. "The main onus in treatment fell on Brigitta's class teacher who proved very adept at judging how hard to press Brigitta and when to let her be" (p. 227).

In other cases, the children may be too severely troubled to be helped in the classroom setting and may need referral to special education classes or community clinical facilities. Occasionally, school personnel need to be told by a consultant that a child is too ill to be helped only in the educational setting and needs referral to a clinical setting. Some teachers, counselors, or psychologists become invested in helping a child and do not wish to refer. Especially during individual consultation, conscious or unconscious biases in the school personnel to the student may be detected. These may be interfering with optimal help to the student, as in the previous example of the "greedy child." Tactful reworking of attitudes may help to correct the bias.

Individual children discussed in consultation sessions may include those with conduct or behavior disorders, chronic or transient, often involving aggression or defiance. These are the most troublesome to educators and often provoke frustrated, punitive, disciplinary reactions. Many teachers have not been trained to use a psychological frame of reference within which to understand a child's behavior. Consultative help at this stage can ameliorate some problems before they escalate to the need for referral to special education. Many children, already on the edge of alienation from the educational and social process in the school, can be rescued from being pushed into developing a more negative identity in the particular school milieu.

CASE EXAMPLE

A 14-year-old girl had been hospitalized for anorexia. She was reluctant to return to her former school because of fear of the questions her classmates would ask, and that would label her as "crazy." A consultant in the school was able to explain anorexia to the teachers and the principal in a way that avoided the stigma of "craziness." Discussion focused on specific difficulties this girl would have in getting back to the primary task of learning her subjects because of continued preoccupation with food. Stimulated by the consultation, the teachers themselves devised special approaches. As a result, the reentry was accomplished smoothly. In contrast, another patient with anorexia returned to a school that did not receive this assistance. Within 3 weeks she reported that she felt that the teachers "don't understand me and I think they hate me." She refused to return to the school and had to be transferred to 2 other schools before her education could resume. (L. Newman, personal communication, 1980)

The less disruptive, passive, depressed child often receives lesser attention. Sensitive teachers may want to discuss this type of child as well, depending on the attention demanded by the preponderance of aggressive, angry children in their class. A large range of more internalized psychopathology will also be of concern, especially in secondary schools. Among these are suicide attempts (or completions), eating disorders, drug abuse, alcoholism, or school dropout. Aggressive adolescents in junior and senior high schools present more frightening problems. Their size and strength and the prevalence of violence and weapons on campuses engender fear and/or counteraggressive reactions by many educators. Truancy or school dropout is causing greater concern in many regions. Case consultation is often of value here for the school personnel involved with school attendance. Some districts have special committees to consider this, and a consultant attending these meetings can offer useful input. A consultant can-

not be expected to provide solutions for this myriad of problems. In a skillfully facilitated discussion, emotional interferences with problem solving can be identified and reduced and school personnel be helped to find new solutions. In some instances case consultation may need to move into system or program consultation.

Another issue in schools of the 1990s is the growing enrollment of immigrant, usually non-English-speaking, children. Many of these children have come from countries where they have been the victims or witnesses of horrendous atrocities. Many suffer symptoms of post-traumatic stress disorder, which interferes with healthy development as well as effective learning or ability to be comfortable in the classroom. Educators welcome the entry of a consultant and refer gladly, often for psychotherapy. An in-class consultative program for detecting and providing relief for some of these children exposed to traumatic situations, recently or in the past, has proven useful (Eth et al., 1985; Wang, 1985). When non-English-speaking students are involved translators may be necessary, unless the consultant speaks the language(s) needed.

Consultation in Secondary Schools

Consultation in junior/middle or senior high schools is very different from consultation in elementary schools due to the size and complexity of the schools as well as the older age of the children. Junior high schools (grades 7 to 9) or middle schools (grades 6 to 8) will usually have 800 to 1,500 students. High schools (grades 9 to 12) may contain 800 to 3,000 students. In the elementary schools, children have 1 or 2 teachers each day and a class of 20 to 30. In secondary schools, the adolescents have 5 to 6 teachers per day and classes often contain 35 to 50 students. High school personnel (and students) are subject to special stresses. They feel the community's demands for academic achievement, high SAT scores, no dropouts, and college acceptances. Additionally they are often expected to decrease violence, drug and alcohol abuse, teenage pregnancy, suicide attempts and completions, and to endure gang problems and violence on campus (Jellinek, 1990; Berkovitz, 1985).

In this setting, the psychiatric consultant can work with individual teachers, small groups of faculty, and/or administrators to discuss these pressures, conduct case consultation, and help create a more supportive environment as well as to reenforce existing resources or introduce new programs to address some of these problems. Some consultants have also met with students and parents to discuss mental health or school issues (Kandler, 1979). Group counseling has been more prevalent in many schools, elementary and secondary, but especially in secondary (Berkovitz, 1987). Here the consultant can be very useful as inservice trainer, supervisor, or at time modeling as a coleader. This modality has proven very helpful to many students, even when experiencing severe mental health difficulties.

Many school systems, depending on their size, have units that address special problems, especially for adolescent students. These include, for example:

1. The continuation high school containing 100 to 200 students who have been found less able to cope with the larger high school campus.
2. A special school for pregnant adolescents.
3. A special school for students with behavior problems or those who have been suspended for infractions on campus.
4. Special schools for children with deafness, blindness, or with other exceptionalities.
5. Magnet schools, at elementary and secondary levels, for business, science, medical studies, performing arts, fashion design, or the gifted. A consultant can be especially useful in these schools (Berkovitz, 1995). Knowledge of the social makeup of the school campus and the varieties of adolescent behavior, dress, affiliations, and so on are indispensable to the psychiatrist treating adolescents or consulting in secondary schools (Berkovitz, 1997).

In recent years, over 400 school-based clinics have been established especially on high school campuses in the United States, primarily to treat minor medical problems, such as acne, diabetes, sexually transmitted diseases and others. Some clinics will provide sexual counseling, but not abortions (Adelman & Taylor, 1991). Over 20% of the adolescents requesting services have been referrals for psychological evaluation and/or psychotherapy (Pearson, 1997). Here direct services are needed, but a psychiatric consultant can provide supervision of and training for other personnel.

Program and System Consultation

While case consultation is more common and in demand in most schools, sometimes a district calls on a consultant for program consultation. This is especially so if the consultant has been known to the district or has demonstrated useful expertise over the course of several case consultations. In program consultation an administrator may request that the consultant meet with several personnel and/or visit parts of the system to help develop a program to deal with problems troubling the district. Some examples may be programs to improve racial desegregation, to reduce drug abuse or violence, for prevention of and postvention after suicides, to reduce the stresses of closing a school, to redesign a crisis team program, or to improve staff and/or student morale.

System consultation involves consulting with several different levels of the personnel in the organization, focusing on communication problems as well as possibly on program issues (Jellinek, 1990). For example, one elementary school was facing enormous pressures and a divided faculty.

The principal felt under siege by parents and some of the faculty. Many of the teachers felt passive and alienated. The consultant, already active in the district, was asked to lead a faculty meeting "to help morale." At this meeting many previously covert feelings were exposed and given some credibility. The entire faculty argued amongst themselves about next steps. Slowly positions began to ease and a schoolwide "action" plan was developed. The faculty pulled together by focusing on the new "action plan," which included establishing committees to study a list of relevant issues. [The consultant] tried to empower the faculty's and principal's professional ability to set standards and, once done, to withstand parental pressure. Six months later the faculty was calmer and better integrated. Parental pressure and intrusiveness had decreased, and the tone of the school was gradually improving. (Jellinek, 1990, p. 314)

At times during the course of case consultations, the consultant may become aware of frictions between personnel, longstanding feuds, or poor communication that is interfering with the efficient working of the school program. The consultant may feel the need to call this to the attention of the appropriate personnel. This would need to be done tactfully, without violating confidentiality or placing blame. If qualified, the consultant may suggest this need and offer to conduct program or system consultation.

Administrative Consultation

While the administrators—principal, vice-principal, department heads, occasionally superintendents and assistant superintendents—often are included in consulting with teachers or other consultees, at times they need to have separate meetings involving only their peers, to consider their special role in the school hierarchy. They are less interested in case consultation about students but more interested in problems of managing personnel, establishing job priorities, and reducing job stress. Most clinicians are not experienced in consulting on such middle-management issues. However, this level of consultation can effect significant changes in a school district's mental health attitudes and practices. The administrator's manner and tone of relating to teachers (and principals) often has repercussions on a teacher's behavior with the children in the classroom.

"It may be that the consultant's best attitude on entry [to a school or school district] is to let the principal or the superintendent know that he [or she] will help advance any program of mental health that he or she is interested in implementing" (Berkovitz, 1977, p. 95). The places that a consultant often meets with administrators are as follows:

1. In sessions including faculty.
2. In conference about a child with school psychologist, nurse, counselor, and possibly parent.
3. In guidance committees or on pupil service teams, set up to consider the best steps needed to help a child, including referral for medical examinations or referral to special education.
4. In groups for principals around crisis issues, or issues of child development, administrative management, communication improvement, and/or increased personal awareness.

Some of the benefits reported by several different principals who were involved in series of sessions of ongoing consultation are as follows:

1. "Improved ability to listen and communicate with others."
2. "I believe I take more time to help children with problems and am less quick to make judgments."
3. "I can take criticism more easily. Partly as a result of this, I have involved my staff in decisions affecting the school, for example, the selection of teacher aides."

4. "Reading scores in my school have increased 26% to 62%, partly as a result of better teacher and principal interaction." (Berkovitz, 1977, pp. 104–106)

Consultation to Nursery Schools and Parenting Programs

An important school area for early prevention is mental health consultation to nursery schools. Aruffo (1997) describes holding weekly conferences in one nursery school. He states, "We talk about individual children, usually children who are problems to the teachers. The conferences have teachers present, the principal present, and sometimes parents are invited. A few words from a consultant does not basically alter the psychopathology from a parent, but often parents change just enough to allow the child to grow" (p. 3). One program has developed consultation for preschools where exclusion of a disturbed child has occurred or is being contemplated (Farley, A., 1997, personal communication). The Furmans (1992) have trained many professionals who are consulting to nursery schools around the United States (Lipkowitz, 1992).

Parenting training programs are offered by many school districts, often with the participation of mental health professionals from outside the schools. A mental health team in Philadelphia developed parenting education courses also for middle school classes, grades 5 to 8 (Parens et al., 1990). A followup study done 20 years after the onset of the program for the adult parents showed in a group of 17 children born during the 6 years of the program, "no trouble with the law, less drug abuse, more school continuation (lower dropout rate), and reduction of anger, passive aggressiveness, and violence potential in the experimental group, compared with 400 "normal adolescents" (APA, 1993, p. 83).

Consultation to Special Education Programs

In the 1980s and 1990s the biggest demand for psychiatric consultation is involved with children being educated under several special education laws. This is a special type of case consultation with some program and system elements. Public Law 94-142 was first passed by the U.S. Congress in 1975 and mandated services for learning disabled and "seriously emotionally disturbed" children in school. The law applies to all exceptionalities, including blindness, deafness, aphasia, orthopedic handicaps, mental retardation, autism, and others. This includes over 4 million children in the United States, constituting approximately 10% of the school population. This represents over 4 billion dollars in the federal budget.

Mental health factors are relevant to all of them, but specifically about 10% of these, or 1 to 2% of the total school population are classified learning disabled or seriously emotionally disturbed. The numbers of identified children differ from state to state. Many of these students usually attend a resource specialist room for 1 to 2 hours per day or are in all-day classes, especially those classified seriously emotionally disturbed. Those students who cannot be served in these locations can be placed in nonpublic schools paid for by the student's home school district. Each child is provided with an individual educational plan (IEP), which specifies the services each is to receive, for example, help with math, reading, social relating, or aggression control. Often counseling by school personnel, usually a half hour per week, is specified in the IEP.

Public Law 99-457, passed in 1986, extended the benefits of this service to handicapped infants and toddlers, ages birth through 2 years. Early intervention had to include a multidisciplinary assessment and a written individualized Family Service Plan. Public Law 101-476, passed in 1990, amended Public Law 94-142. It substituted the word "disabled" for "handicapped" and added autism and traumatic disabilities. It also added rehabilitation counseling and social work services, and mandated that schools help disabled students plan for when they leave school.

Different than the case consultations described above, these children have already been identified and evaluated by school psychological personnel. The seriously emotionally disturbed children are among the more disturbed children in the system, who have not been able to learn or allow others to learn in the larger regular classes of 35 to 40 students. School districts are using psychiatrists to (1) evaluate children usually for disability according to the criteria used by schools to classify children for serious emotional disturbance, for example, to diagnose depression, psychosis, family-school conflict, behavior disorder with and without depression, and so on; (2) recommend interventions and monitor the child's progress; (3) provide or supervise therapy; and (4) consult to the school personnel (Mattison, 1993). While this law has improved school services for the 400,000 seriously emotionally disturbed children in American schools, unfortunately, it has also reduced the funds available for psychological assistance to the other thousands of less disabled children, who also need services. Due to the rising costs for the care of these children in special education, many school districts restrict entry to special education or try to provide preventive measures that may reduce the severity of symptoms in at-risk children so that they might not require entry to special education (Knitzer et al., 1990).

One dilemma is that what the clinician will consider "severely emotionally disturbed" is not always what school personnel will call "seriously emotionally disturbed." School criteria are more narrow. They try to exclude conduct or behavior disorder and attention deficit hyperactivity disorders, even though often these diagnoses do involve covert depression. School criteria for the classification seriously emotionally disturbed are defined as at least two of the following:

1. An inability to achieve adequate academic progress that cannot be explained by intellectual, sensory, or health factors.
2. An inability to build or maintain satisfactory interpersonal relationships with peers and teachers.
3. Inappropriate types of behavior or feelings under normal circumstances.
4. A general pervasive mood of unhappiness or depression.
5. A tendency to develop physical symptoms or fears associated with personal or school problems.

In the individualized educational plan (IEP) meeting, the school psychological personnel, with or without outside professional consultation, determine the status and eligibility of the child and prescribe a program within the school system, if available. If it is not available or is insufficient, approval may be given for entry into a nonpublic school or residential program, nearby or occasionally even in another state. However, to reduce costs of such nonpublic school programs, larger school systems offer smaller classes of 8 to 10 students to serve seriously emotionally disturbed children.

For example, one large school district with over 600 thousand children (total enrollment) offers over 60 such classes. Since the special education teachers in these classes, for the most part, are not fully trained to deal with such disturbed children, the psychiatric consultant can be especially useful here to help teachers understand the children's behavior, as well as to be able to accept their own unavoidable feelings of frustration and failure. Some programs, often in conjunction with local public mental health agencies or clinics, offer family therapy as well. The clinician consultant can often help the teacher and/or school mental health personnel to decide which children need this type of referral. Medication is prescribable by consultants in some districts, by special arrangement, but for the most part the family's private or clinic physician is the only one who can prescribe. The school nurse or, at times, the classroom teacher will dispense this to the student during the school day.

When parents and school authorities disagree about the program suitable for a child, arbitration, or fair hearing, may be used. The psychiatrist may need to testify to represent the child's needs. Despite the limitations of these special education programs, which vary from state to state in the United States, much good for disabled children in schools has been provided, especially compared to what existed prior to 1975. Many child psychiatry training programs provide placement of trainees in the school programs for seriously emotionally disturbed children. In one, the residents are allowed to prescribe the psychopharmacology regimen for the children needing this, for example, attention deficit hyperactivity disorder, psychotic, and/or depressed children. In other districts the psychiatrist visits these classes to advise the teacher and psychologist on how to handle the severe behavior problems, or at times even models or helps the teacher conduct group counseling.

An example of consultation to such a class is the following:

CASE EXAMPLE

Jessica was a 14-year-old eighth grader who had been in special education classes since third grade. Her present class consisted of herself and eight aggressive boys. The teacher had two aides. Jessica was felt to be above average in intelligence, but would not make eye contact. Socially she had no friends. She didn't take care of her hygiene, clean, or groom herself. Her mother had similar habits. Two younger siblings were clean. Jessica raised mice at home and when one died, she showed no compassion. Her father had tried to abort the pregnancy with Jessica and she was born premature. She had been neglected as an infant and later was a victim of child abuse.

The consultant and the school staff recognized Jessica's severe depressive pathology. Referral to an inpatient setting was unlikely, especially because of the family's rejection of Jessica. The last resort was this classroom. The consultant suggested that the staff pay attention to her grooming. The female teacher and the female aide had not seen that as an appropriate role, but were happy to get permission from an authority figure to do this. Five months later, Jessica showed some improvement in grooming, such that she was less offensive to peers. She was beginning to have more pride in herself and higher self-esteem. She was able to be more assertive to the aggressive boys in the class. She was then given the responsibility of acting as a learning assistant in a remedial class of younger children. This added further to her self-esteem. The consultant's input may have seemed minimal, but aided a crucial turning point in her management. Her future is still uncertain. Hospitalization and/or removal from the family may still be necessary. If her parents had been more cooperative, the consultant could have recommended that they request antidepressant medication from the family pediatrician.

Mattison and Spirito (1993) have recommended a model of psychiatric consultation for evaluation of children prior to or after referral to special education programs. This would apply especially when the consultant is not already part of a classroom visiting team.

1. Review of referral information (15 minutes).
2. Initial meeting with school multidisciplinary team (30 minutes).
3. Student interview (45 minutes).
4. Parent(s) interview (45 minutes).
5. Feedback to the team and collaborative treatment planning (30 minutes).
6. Feedback to parent(s) and student (15 minutes).
7. Report preparation (30 minutes) (p. 110).

Full-Service Schools

In recent years schools and surrounding communities have worked together developing structures that allow schools to work more productively with the needs of families in the school community.

This movement is called full-service schools. Dryfoos (1994) describes this as a "movement to create an array of integrated support services in schools that respond to the declining welfare of many American families and the rising 'new morbidities' of sex, drugs, violence, and stress among youth" (book jacket). The movement in a sense is the transition from school-based clinics, where health services are delivered to all students, and especially those from low income families. In full-service programs parents and other community members have a more active participating and governing role alongside the school personnel. Psychiatrists may be called on to consult in such programs, but these programs are new and not prevalent enough for a role for the mental health professional to be clearly determined—other than the familiar case consultation model or as an interested community member.

Comer (1980) is a consultant who has been in the forefront of bringing parents onto the campus to play a part in designing programs for the children and the school, working collaboratively with school personnel. His program does not always include full social services, but could move to that scope if the consultees request it. This program and the full-service programs are system-oriented, including the community as well as the school, and promise constructive changes in delivery of health services, especially to lower socioeconomic communities.

Evaluation

In a complex system such as a school and its surrounding community, it is difficult to construct an evaluative study free of confounding variables. Yet some degree of accountability has been desired to justify expenditures of funds for consultative projects. One of the more extensive efforts was that of Mannino and Shore (1975). They reviewed 35 studies reported during 1958 to 1972 that attempted to measure the effect of consultation practice, that is, outcome studies. These studies included those focusing on consultee, clients, and systems, and combinations of all three. They found that "positive change of some kind was demonstrated in 24, or approximately 69%. Of the 23 studies that focused on consultee change either separately or in combination with other factors, 17

(approximately 74%) showed statistically significant change. Of the 19 studies that focused on change in the client, either separately or in combination with other factors, 11 (approximately 58%) reported positive change. Finally, positive change was shown in 2 of the 4 studies which focused on system change" (p. 17).

Cowen and his group (Weissberg et al., 1983) have conducted over 30 years of case-oriented consultation and direct service to children and teachers throughout the United States, in grades 1 and 2 especially. These interventions have been statistically evaluated by having teachers, parents, and child aides fill out extensive questionnaires pre- and post-intervention. Interventions consisted of discussion with the teacher by consultant and school psychologist. Then the identified child and the aide met 1 to 3 times per week—1 to 1—in a 30- to 40-minute play session. They concluded "the findings suggest that the intervention reduced acting-out, shy-anxious, and learning problems, and promoted competencies such as adaptive assertiveness, peer sociability, and frustration tolerance. The program's positive effects were least strong in terms of reducing children's acting-out, aggressive behaviors" (p. 103).

In regard to consultation programs directed to this acting-out problem in children, a department of pediatrics (Grossman et al., 1997) consulted to several elementary schools. They evaluated "the efficacy of a widely used violence prevention curriculum designed to prevent aggressive behavior by increasing prosocial behavior. Prosocial behavior reflects competence in peer interactions and friendships and in interpersonal conflict resolution skills" (pp. 1605). They concluded from data of 790 students in 49 classrooms that there were "modest reductions in levels of aggressive behavior and increases in neutral/prosocial behavior in school among second and third graders" (pp. 1611) persisting for 6 months following the exposure. They could not evaluate behavior outside the school.

Active Intervention Programs

Several consultants actively enter the school milieu and introduce new programs. This entry has often been preceded by periods of discussion with key school personnel to arrive at maximal understanding and implementation. Murphy, Pynoos, and James (1997) in Southern California helped form and monitor trauma grief focus groups in an elementary school, which is located in a community beset with poverty, violence, and deaths. In New York State a coalition of 17 organizations was founded by a member of the local psychiatric society. They introduced a volunteer improvisational dramatic group to fifth-grade students at an elementary school with the goal of destigmatizing mental health issues. The dramatic group portrayed "a student struggling with attention/deficit disorder (ADHD), a child saddened by his mother's depression, and a child struggling with the emotional turmoil of his parent's divorce. Mental health professionals served as moderators and fielded questions from the audience. About 10 coalition members visited fifth-grade classrooms in pairs a few days later to discuss the students' reactions to specific skits and their art work. This gave the students a chance to talk about negative feelings they were experiencing and be aware that help is available. Later a coalition member met with the elementary school's principal, the psychologist and fifth-grade teachers to discuss mental health problems among the students" (*Psychiatric News,* 1997, p. 11). "Furthermore, the New York State Commission on Quality Care has expressed interest in working with the coalition on a school-based mental health curriculum" (p. 25).

These types of active interventive consultations are becoming more frequent in recent years. There are also efforts by some consultants to make mental health services, including consultation, a more durable and established part of the school administrative structure, so that it is not always regarded as an add-on, which is then considered dispensable when fiscal problems occur in the district (UCLA school mental health project, 1997).

A note in favor of direct service models is sounded by Salzer and Bickman (1997). They conclude that while systems of care produce important system-level changes, early results suggest that systems changes do not impact clinical outcomes. They argue that the primary direction to improving children's mental health services should be through effectiveness research, in contrast to continued large-scale investments in systems research and development.

No doubt many other types of consultation and intervention have been developed in schools around the world. One that needs to be mentioned here is mental health consultation performed in schools of education. This can be in the form of discussion groups and/or lectures, especially with teachers in training and at times with administrators in training. This early exposure for educators can have long-term benefits, and encourage later use of mental health consultation by those educators in their schools.

Conclusion

Each mental health professional who is treating children and adolescents should provide mental health consultation to school personnel. The range of such consultation may include intervening for one's own patients, discussing teacher-student interactions for children generally, program development, administrative/system issues, or consulting to federally mandated programs for disabled students.

Many child psychiatry training programs in the United States offer training for visiting or consulting in schools (APA, 1993). This training helps psychiatrists and other mental health professionals to become acquainted "in vivo" with the ranges of behavior and attitudes of "normal" children. In addition, these experiences acclimatize the mental health professional to the very nonclinical world of the schools and thus to be more effective communicating with school personnel. In the future, especially if clinical facilities for children in the community continue to decrease, services for disturbed children in schools will need to increase. Like it or not, the schools are the places of last resort for many emotionally disturbed children and families, in the United States and worldwide. In many countries, school personnel are often the only professionals available to parents. They provide valuable assistance to families and children (WHO, 1993), even in the absence of consultation. With consultation this assistance can be greatly improved and better sustained.

REFERENCES

Adelman, H. S., & Taylor, L. (1991). Mental health facets of the school-based health center movement: Need and opportunity for research and development. *Journal of Mental Health Administration, 18,* 272–283.

American Psychiatric Association Report: *Psychiatric Consultation in Schools* (1993). Washington, D.C.: American Psychiatric Press.

Aponte, H. J. (1976). The family school interview: An ecostructural approach. *Family Process, 15,* 303–312.

Aruffo, R. (1997). Association of Child Psychoanalysis Newsletter, p. 6. Editor, P. M. Brinich, Chapel Hill, North Carolina.

Berkovitz, I. H. (1977). Mental health consultation for school administrators. In S. C. Plog & P. I. Ahmed (Eds.), *The Principles and Techniques of Mental Health Consultation* (pp. 93–118). New York: Plenum.

Berkovitz, I. H. (1980). School interventions: Case management and school mental health consultation. In G. P. Sholevar, R. M. Benson & B. J. Blinder (Eds.), *Treatment of emotional disorders in children and adolescents* (pp. 501–520). New York: Spectrum Publications.

Berkovitz, I. H. (1985). The adolescent, schools and schooling. *Adolescent Psychiatry, 12,* 162–176.

Berkovitz, I. H. (1987). Value of group counseling in secondary schools. *Adolescent Psychiatry, 14,* 522–545.

Berkovitz, I. H. (1995). The adolescent in the schools: A therapeutic guide. *Adolescent Psychiatry, 20,* 343–363.

Berkovitz, I. H. (1997). Junior high/middle school and high school life. In J. D. Noshpitz, L. T. Flaherty & R. Sarles (Eds.), *Handbook of child and adolescent psychiatry,* Vol. 3. (pp. 233–242). New York: John Wiley & Sons.

Berlin, I. N. (1974). Mental health programs in schools. In S. Arieti (Ed.), *American handbook of psychiatry* (pp. 735–748). New York: Basic Books.

Berlin, I. N. (1980). Psychiatry and the school. In H. I. Kaplan, A. M. Freedman, & B. J. Sadow (Eds.), *Comprehensive textbook of psychiatry II, second edition,* (pp. 2253–2255). Baltimore: Williams and Wilkins.

Caplan, G. (1970). *The theory and practice of mental health consultation.* New York: Basic Books.

Comer, J. P. (1980). *School power.* New York: Free Press.

Dryfoos, J. G. (1994). *Full-service schools.* San Francisco: Jossey-Bass.

Eth, S., Arroyo, W., & Silverstein, S. (1985). A psychiatric crisis team response to violence in elementary schools. In Berkovitz, I. H. & Seliger, J. S. (Eds.), *Expanding mental health interventions in schools.* Dubuque, IA: Kendall/Hunt.

Farley, A. (1997). Personal communication.

Freud, A. (1930). The relation between psychoanalysis and education. In *The writings of Anna Freud,* Vol. 1 (pp. 121–133). New York: International Universities Press.

Furman, R. A. (1992). What is day care? In *Child Analysis: Clinical, Theoretical & Applied,* Vol. 3 (pp. 24–28). Cleveland Center for Research in Child Development.

Grossman, D. C., Neckerman, H. J., Koepsell, T. D., Liu, P., Asher, K. N., Beland, K., Frey, K., & Rivara, F. P. Effectiveness of a violence prevention curriculum among children in elementary school. *Journal of the American Medical Association, 277,* 1605–1617.

Hanson, G. (1997). The role of school in the psychotherapy of the child or adolescent. *Child and Adolescent Psychiatric Clinics of North America, 6,* 197–208.

Jellinek, M. S. (1990). School consultation: Evolving issues. *Journal of American Academy of Child and Adolescent Psychiatry, 29,* 311–314.

Kandler, H. O. (1979). Comprehensive mental health consultation in high schools. *Adolescent Psychiatry, 7,* 85–111.

Knitzer, J., Steinberg, Z., & Fleisch, B. (1990). *At the schoolhouse door.* New York: Bank Street College of Education.

LaVietes, R. L., & Chess, S. (1969). A training program in school psychiatry. *Journal of American Academy of Child Psychiatry, 8,* 84–96.

Lipkowitz, A. (1992). Practical application of psychoanalytic principles in an outreach setting. In *Child analysis: Clinical, theoretical & applied* (pp. 93–98). Cleveland Center for Research in Child Development.

Mattison, R. E., & Spirito, A. (1993). School consultation. In G. K. Fritz, R. E. Mattison, B. Nurcombe, & A. Spirito (Eds.), *Child and adolescent mental health consultation in hospitals, schools and courts* (pp. 93–183). Washington, D.C.: American Psychiatric Press.

Mannino, F. V., & Shore, M. F. (1975). The effects of consultation. *American Journal of Community Psychology, 3,* 1–21.

Murphy, L., Pynoos, R. S., & James, C. B. (1997). Trauma, grief focus group: Psychotherapy module of elementary school-based violence prevention/intervention program. In J. D. Osofsky, *Children in a Violent Society* (pp. 223–255). New York: Guilford Press.

Newman, L. (1980). Personal communication.

Parens, H., Scattergood, E., Duff, A., et al. (1990). Parenting education for emotional growth: A curriculum for students in grades K through 12. Philadelphia, PA. (unpublished manuscript).

Pearson, G. (1997). School-based mh services improve student behavior. *American Psychiatric Association Psychiatric News* May 2, 1997, p. 44. Washington, D.C.

Psychiatric News of the *American Psychiatric Association.* May 16, 1997, p. 11 & 25.

Rutter, M. (1975). *Helping troubled children.* New York and London: Plenum.

Salzer, M., & Bickman, L. (1997). Delivering effective children's services in the community: Reconsidering the benefits of system interventions. *Applied & Preventive Psychology, 6,* 1–13.

UCLA School Mental Health Project, (1997). H. Adelman, University of California, Los Angeles, CA.

Wang, A. (1985). Helping the immigrant Asian child in the schools. In Berkovitz, I. H. & Seliger, J. S. (Ed.), *Expanding Mental Health Interventions in Schools.* Dubuque, IA: Kendall/Hunt.

Weissberg, R. P., Cowen, E. L., Lotyczewski, B. S., & Gesten, E. L. (1983). The primary mental health project: Seven consecutive years of program out-come research. *Journal of Consulting and Clinical Psychology, 51,* 100–107.

World Health Organization, (1993). Division of Mental Health, *Mental health programmes in schools,* R. Hendren, R. B. Weisen, J. Orley. Geneva, Switzerland.

Witmer, L. (1896). Practical work in psychology. *Pediatrics 2,* 462–471.

19 / **Principles of Child Forensic Psychiatry Consultations**

Diane H. Schetky

This chapter provides an introduction to the field of child forensic psychiatry with a focus on principles. The chapter also touches upon legal issues, such as consent and confidentiality, that impact upon practice.

Child forensic psychiatry is a subspecialty of child psychiatry that utilizes our knowledge of child development and child and family psychopathology in the service of resolving legal issues affecting children. In contrast to the usual diagnostic evaluation, the intent of a forensic evaluation is not therapeutic; rather it is to help answer the legal question at hand. The issue of psychiatric diagnosis often is secondary. Another major difference is that the forensic evaluation is performed for the court or an attorney and is not confidential. The evaluation performed for an attorney becomes part of that attorney's work product; the attorney, if not satisfied with it, need not use it.

In performing forensic evaluations, it is essential to strive for objectivity. Much is at stake in the outcome of these cases, and, in contrast to psychotherapy, we do not have the opportunity to redress mistaken impressions. Access to as much information as possible helps the child psychiatrist to attain a balanced view. Typically, in this sort of evaluation the examiner seeks corroborating information from numerous sources such as police reports, school and medical records, and prior evaluations, when indicated. Being court appointed may confer more neutrality on the child psychiatrist, but these evaluations may also be conducted when an expert has been agreed upon by parents and their attorneys. The child psychiatrist must guard against bias and be aware of countertransference reactions that may color his or her responses to a particular case (Schetky & Devoe, 1991).

The forensic evaluation should be separated from treatment whenever possible. The psychiatrist involved in a treatment relationship loses a certain amount of objectivity and also becomes invested in the outcome of the case. Getting entwined in legal issues may derail therapy, undermine confidentiality, and even be detrimental to therapy (Strasburger et al 1997). If treating a child whose parents become involved in a custody battle, the child psychiatrist may insist that another clinician perform the custody evaluation. The forensic examiner may confer with the treating psychiatrist but is spared having to make custody recommendations. A corollary is that generally it is not wise to accept into treatment a patient seen for a forensic evaluation. Therapeutic neutrality is lost once a forensic opinion is rendered and, particularly in divorce cases, one or both parents may have become alienated from the psychiatrist who performed the evaluation. Further, there is always risk of relitigation at a later date. It also may appear self serving if the forensic child psychiatrists self refers a child for treatment.

The Expert Witness

Ultimately, the court decides if a witness has sufficient qualifications to provide expert testimony. The expert is generally considered to possess specialized knowledge that will assist the trier of fact (judge or jury) to understand evidence or determine the facts at issue. The subject matter in which the expert testifies must not be within the common knowledge of the trier of fact and must provide some insight beyond the kind of judgment an ordinarily intelligent person can offer. The expert witness, in contrast to the factual witness, is allowed to give opinion testimony.

Various types of testimony may be permitted, ranging from hypothetical testimony intended to educate a judge or jury, testimony as to standard of practice or evaluation, rebuttal testimony to statements such as "children never lie," or testimony based on the actual evaluation of children and their parents.

The expert needs to be aware that the standard of evidence varies according to the type of legal proceeding. Dependency, neglect, and civil proceedings require only a preponderance of evidence, 51% certainty. A higher standard of clear and convincing evidence (about 75% certainty), is required in termination of parental rights and civil commitment. Criminal proceedings require the highest standard, beyond a reasonable doubt (about 95% certainty).

Standards for the admissibility of scientific testimony have changed as of the 1993 *Daubert v. Merrell Dow Pharmaceutical, Inc.* (113 S. Ct. 2786, 1993) decision. Most states had been guided by *Frye v. U.S.* (293F 1013 D.C. App., 1923) or their own case law. Under *Frye*, opinions had to be based on scientific techniques which were generally accepted in the relevant scientific community. The *Daubert* decision calls for the expert's testimony to be scientific, reliable and relevant. In contrast to *Frye*, reliability is based on scientific reliability rather than the community acceptance standard. Inasmuch as *Daubert* is a federal case, it is not binding in state courts although many have chosen to follow it.

Ethical Dilemmas

The expert witness needs to guard against conflict of interest, which may occur when he or she has prior ties to any of the parties in a legal proceeding. It also may occur if the psychiatrist deviates from a position of neutrality and uses the patient in any way for his or her own self-gratification— for example, making disclosures to the press out of a wish for notoriety. Another example of conflict of interest is double agentry which occurs when the psychiatrist must serve 2 masters. For instance, in doing an evaluation for a juvenile court, the interests of the juvenile may conflict with the interests of the court. The expert needs to clarify with the juvenile for whom he or she is working and explain the lack of confidentiality.

The expert must resist the temptation to skew a report or testimony to the desired outcome. Additional pressures may come from attorneys and getting caught up in the adversary system and in the need to win. Experts must not exceed their data bases in arriving at conclusions and recommendations and must be able to admit to the limits of their knowledge. The psychiatrist's testimony should be essentially the same regardless of which side hired him or her.

Expert witnesses need to exert extreme caution in commenting on parties they have not examined in person. They should refrain from making custody recommendations unless they have seen both parties.

An unfortunate ethical dilemma arises when treating psychiatrists are subpoenaed to testify. Patients who raise their mental health as an issue in medical malpractice or tort litigation automatically tender their records so that privilege becomes a moot point. However, the issue also may arise in divorce litigation where surrendering of records is often not in the best interests of the patient. The American Psychiatric Association (Task Force on Disclosure of Psychiatric Treatment Records in Child Custody Disputes) recommends that the court deciding custody should permit the disclosure of confidential information revealed in psychiatric treatment only when such information is relevant to parental fitness and is not available from other sources. When necessary such a determination can be made by an independent court appointed psychiatrist. Therapists who choose to resist a subpoena for patient records have several recourses. They should first determine whether or not the patient has authorized release of records and information. If so they may then contact the attorney who subpoenaed them and explain why it is not in the client's best interest to release the records, even if a waiver has been signed. They also may contact their own attorney or the hospital's or may appeal to the judge or guardian ad litem for the child in an attempt to quash the subpoena and determine the relevancy of the records. If ordered to testify by the court, they should do so in as narrow a fashion as possible.

Psychiatrists usually charge more for forensic evaluations, and it is customary to ask for a retainer fee. In addition to ensuring that the psychiatrist gets paid, the retainer infers that the expert is being paid for time away from practice rather than for his or her opinion. It is unethical to accept a case on a contingency fee. Contingency fees, while acceptable in the legal profession, create an undue investment in the outcome of the case, which destroys the expert's neutrality.

Developmental Concepts and Considerations

THE CHILD'S BEST INTERESTS

The concept of making legal decisions in accord with "the child's best interests" was first introduced in the custody case of *Finlay v Finlay* (148 NE 624 NY) in 1925. In this landmark case, Judge Benjamin Cardozo stated that the court's role is to serve as parens patriae and do "what is in the best interests of the child." Prior to this time children were viewed as property, often their rights were thought to be synonymous with those of their parents, and they were not entitled to independent legal representation.

The concept of the child's best interest was taken a step further by Goldstein, Freud, and Solnit's publication of *Beyond the Best Interests of the Child* in 1979. These authors applied psychoanalytic concepts to the resolution of custody conflicts, stressing the child's need for permanency, the concept of the "psychological parent," and the need to consider developmental needs in making custody decisions. They authors noted the need to take the child's timetable in consideration in making custody decisions. For example, expecting a 1-year-old to wait a year for parental reunification may be much more disruptive and stressful than asking an 8-year-old who has concepts of time and object constancy to wait that long.

Another shift in thinking has been moving away from the tender years presumption, which prevailed in the early 20th century and which automatically awarded custody to mothers, to assessing each case individually. Belatedly, child psychiatry and the courts are beginning to appreciate the role of the father in early child development, and the traditional biases against father custody are gradually being overcome.

Weighing parental interests against those of the child continues to be difficult. For instance, joint custody, now the presumption in many states, has been popular because it is equitable and encourages ongoing involvement and access by both parents. However, we know that it can be particularly stressful for very young children and that teenage children often begin to resist it (Steinman, 1981).

Courts have responded to the interests of children by appointing guardians ad litem and sometimes attorneys for them in custody disputes and child protection proceedings. The guardian ad litem is charged with representing and protecting the child's interests and acts as an independent advocate for the child. The guardian serves a unique role; it may include being a fact finder, legal representative, case monitor, mediator, and facilitating support systems and disposition. A study by the U.S. Department of Health and Human Services (Duquette, 1990) found that volunteer court appointed special advocates (CASAs) were more effective than attorneys with no special training in representing children.

How much weight an advocate, expert witness, or the court should give to the child's stated wishes as opposed to the child's best interests will depend on the child's chronological age and relative maturity. The child's wishes should be voiced, but the reasons behind them also must be explored. For instance, a 5-year-old girl may say she wants to live with her father because he has promised her a pony. A 10-year-old boy might wish to remain with an alcoholic mother because he feels a need to protect and care for her. The clinician may further aid the court by conveying a sense of where the child is developmentally. Generally, courts will give some consideration to the expressed wishes of school-age child and considerably more weight to the expressed preference of an adolescent. Cognitive development research by Weithorn (1984) supports the notion that children ages 12 to 14 have the capacity to conceptualize custodial alternatives and consider consequences of each alternative.

COMPETENCY IN CHILDREN

"Competency" is a relative term that legally refers to the ability to perform a certain task. The competency of a child to be a witness is a determination made by the court. However, child psychiatrists sometimes may be asked to aid the court in making these determinations. Competency takes into consideration the child's capacity at the time of the event in question to observe, accurately register the event, have memory sufficient to retain an independent recollection of the event, and current ability to communicate this memory. Many states also require that the child be capable of taking an oath and understand the duty to tell the truth. Adults are presumed competent to be witnesses whereas many jurisdictions require competency hearings for children beneath a certain age. A few states permit all alleged victims of sexual abuse to testify regardless of age (Myers, 1987).

A review of the burgeoning literature on memory in children and their capacity to be witnesses is beyond the scope of this chapter. In general, very young children have more difficulty with free recall than do adults and lack the prior knowledge needed to organize their memories. They may confuse the source of their memories and they tend to make more errors of omission than commission (Goodman and Reed, 1989). Retrieval strategies seem to improve between ages 5 and 10 (Brown, 1979) and memories are apt to be most accurate when related in narrative form. Studies by Chance and Goldstein (1984) suggest that children perform poorly on eyewitness testimony with only 35 to 40% accuracy among kindergarten children in a laboratory situation. By age 12–14 accuracy reaches the adult range of 70 to 80%.

Children may attempt to fill in the blanks by confabulating or incorporating leading information (Loftus and Davies, 1984). Post-event information may compete with the original information or alter subsequent recollection of events (Leichtman, Ceci & Morse, 1997). Research has demonstrated the suggestibility of children to repeated leading questions and misinformation (Hyman & Loftus, 1997), Ceci, Ross & Toglia (1987), Ceci & Bruck (1993), Ceci, Leichtman & Bruck, Loftus (1994). The implications of these studies have important bearing on how we question children. Multiple interviews and repeated questions, particularly leading ones, may be hazardous. Other factors affecting suggestibility include the strength of the trace memory, the authority of the person questioning the child, and the child's age. The affective affective state of both interviewer and child will also affect the child's performance on memory tasks (Bartlett and Santrock, 1979).

ISSUES OF CONSENT

Minors are not capable of giving informed consent for decisions regarding medical or psychiatric treatment. With a few exceptions, consent is required from the custodial parent or the child's guardian. In cases of shared custody, consent must be obtained from at least 1 parent. Inasmuch as most shared custody arrangements stipulate shared decision making in matters of health care, usually it is prudent to attempt to get at least verbal consent from both parents. In most jurisdictions, treatment without parental consent may occur in emergencies, in regard to birth control and treatment of venereal disease, and when the patient is emancipated. Emancipation may occur when adolescents are living on their own, supporting themselves, and are considered sufficiently mature to enter into contracts. Some states have a "mature minor" rule that allows for certain minors to make decisions about health care without parental consent if they exhibit sufficient cognitive maturity. Clinicians should be aware of statutes in their states as they pertain to treatment of minors. For instance, some states permit minors to consent to treatment for substance abuse or mental illness over parental objection.

For consent to be legal, it must be informed. This means that the language of the consent is at a level commensurate with the consenters' ability to understand. The clinician should discuss the nature of the condition being treated and the risks and benefits of the proposed treatment, and also outline alternative treatments. A notation should be made in the chart as to what has been discussed with the child and parents. Children under 18 cannot give legal consent but often it is both tactful and therapeutic to ask for their assent to treatment or participation in a research protocol. Their refusal to consent may amount to veto power. It is always helpful to get feedback on the child's perceptions of what has been said and correct them when indicated.

CONFIDENTIALITY AND PRIVILEGE

"Privilege" refers to rules of evidence that govern the disclosure of information obtained through treatment to the court. Privilege belongs to, and in most instances may be waived, only by the patient. In contrast, confidentiality refers to the clinicians's obligation not to divulge information disclosed in therapy and governs the communication of information about the patient to others not involved directly in the patient's care. As noted by MacBeth (1991) in her extensive discussion of these issues, the legal status of minors greatly complicates the rules of confidentiality that apply to adults. Parents may seek information that minors do not wish to disclose. Inasmuch as they, rather than their minor children, have given consent for treatment, legally they may be entitled to it. Too much disclosure obviously threatens the child's alliance with the therapist; thus it is wise to lay out ground rules at the onset of therapy. When disclosure is indicated, as around self-destructive behavior, the therapist should generally advise the patient to make the disclosure or seek the patient's permission to inform the parents.

Parents, rather than the minor patient, must give consent to release information to third parties. However, in most cases, the therapist will choose to discuss this first with the patient.

Physicians and other therapists are mandated to report suspected child abuse and may be subject to penalties if they fail to do so. In most instances, the family should be informed that a report is being filed.

Practical Advice

GETTING STARTED

The novice should not feel intimidated by doing forensic evaluations and testifying in court. If the basic principles are mastered, it easy to gradually gain experience and, in turn, confidence. The author, who is largely self taught, acquired her early experience through testifying in many child protection proceedings, talking with attorneys, auditing law courses, watching others testify in court, and her own mistakes. Nowadays, trainees have access to a considerable body of literature in the area of child forensic psychiatry, continuing medical education seminars that address forensic issues, and, if they are fortunate enough, mentors with experience in the area and some curriculum in child forensic psychiatry.

Before embarking on a forensic evaluation, it is important that the psychiatrist to be clear what the legal issue is and what the purpose of the evaluation is. It is also important to know who it is the referring attorney represents. Referrals may come directly from the court or from a guardian ad litem, as well. The psychiatrist needs to be candid regarding his or her expertise in the particular area. Lack of experience is not necessarily a reason to turn down a case as knowledge in one area; for example knowledge of child sexual abuse dynamics may be readily transferred to a malpractice case involving sexual misconduct between therapist and patient. Similarly, a child psychia-

trist with expertise in posttraumatic stress disorder but with minimal exposure to tort law need not shirk from a case alleging psychic trauma in which a child was bitten by a dog. Rather, the psychiatrist can turn to literature or the referring attorney to become acquainted with the relevant principles.

Child psychiatrists should attempt to maintain control of the forensic evaluation by stating what information they need to review, which parties they wish to see, and the terms of payment. Forensic psychiatrists should never feel forced to do something which they believe is unethical such as withholding an important, but unfavorable, piece of information from their report. Time tables are important in forensic evaluations as deadlines must be set for discovery, and dates for deposition and trial often are set up many months in advance. Experts should not undertake a case unless they have sufficient time to invest in it. Shortcuts are costly, and evaluations should not be done in haste under the wire. Experts will usually be required to testify in court if their testimony is used. Most courts will attempt to accommodate a psychiatrist's schedule when it comes to scheduling testimony. Many cases of civil litigation will settle out of court, but this cannot be anticipated in advance. In contrast to custody and child protection cases, tort litigation cases tend to linger on for years.

THE CLINICAL EVALUATION

Parties need to be appraised as to which side has retained the psychiatrist's services, the purpose of the evaluation, and the fact that it is not confidential. Waivers should be signed at the onset. How much the children should be told about a forensic evaluation should be scaled down to their ages. For instance, it may suffice to tell young children in custody evaluations that the examiner will be helping the judge understand how they feel about what is happening in their families. Sometimes, it is helpful to ask children if there is anything they would like the judge to know about them.

How much is spent with various parties will depend on what the issue is and how complex the case is. Generally, at a minimum 2 hours will be required with each party. The pros and cons of whether to videotape sessions as in child abuse evaluations is a complex one for which the reader is referred to Quinn and White (1991). It is important to record the statements of very young children and note how questions were phrased so as to avoid being charged with asking leading questions. Whenever possible, leading questions should be avoided as they may contaminate the interview. They may be unavoidable with infants and toddlers who lack sufficient abstract thinking to be able to deal with open ended questions (Schetky, 1991). If custody is at issue, it is useful to observe the child with each parent in a free-play situation.

THE WRITTEN REPORT

Attorneys may or may not request a written report. If the psychiatrist is asked to prepare one, the report should reflect who retained them, the circumstances of the evaluation, who was seen, where when and for how long, and other sources of information relied upon in forming opinions.

The written report is the psychiatrist's work product and if thoroughly and thoughtfully done often may lead to an out of court settlement. If the case does not settle out of court, the report then becomes the basis for the expert's testimony in court. Reports should be free of psychiatric jargon. The challenge is to communicate findings and recommendations in such a way that they are readily understood by a lay person. Judgmental and pejorative statements should be avoided as they may inflame and create the impression of possible bias. First hand information will hold more weight than hearsay. Observations should be fortified with direct quotes which serve to bring the case to life and refresh the psychiatrist's memory. Balance should be sought by addressing the strengths as well as the weaknesses of the parties seen. The foundations for conclusions should be laid out carefully and speculative comments or psychoanalytic interpretations should be avoided as they are not useful in court. Judges and attorneys will assess reports in terms of whether they appear to be fair and unbiased and whether recommendations are reasonable and feasible. When completed the report should be sent to the retaining attorney and/or to the court.

DEPOSITIONS

Depositions are standard in civil litigation and sometimes may occur in other proceedings if a witness is unavailable to testify. Depositions usually occur in the expert witness's office and are conducted by the attorney for the opposing side as part of preparation for trial. The attorney who

retained the psychiatrist will prepare him or her for the deposition and be present during it. A stenographer records the deposition. Plaintiffs or defendants may choose to attend but no judge is present. The attorney conducting the deposition will attempt to determine the nature of and the strength and weaknesses of the expert's testimony. As in testifying in court, it is important to listen carefully to questions and think though answers before giving them. Depositions should be proofed for errors and signed and reviewed again prior to testimony. Experts should bill for time spent in giving a deposition.

TESTIFYING IN COURT

Anxiety prior to testifying in court is normal and useful. It is best dealt with through careful preparation which involves reviewing notes, meeting with the attorney ahead of time to anticipate lines of questioning, and in some instances rehearsing testimony. Attorneys rarely pose questions to their experts unless they know how they will be answered. Psychiatrists who have not testified before may wish to observe a colleague testify in court or watch a video of a mock trial. Direct examination is usually benign and consists of the attorney having his or her expert review findings. The other side will frequently interrupt with objections based on rules of evidence. If this occurs, the expert should pause and wait until the judge says it is alright to continue. Everything said in court is recorded by the stenographer so the expert needs to avoid saying "uhm" and nodding the head, and it is important to carefully articulate, and when necessary, spell out terms.

The purpose of cross-examination is to discredit the expert's testimony. Lest this be perceived as a personal attack, it is important to remember that the expert is not on trial. It is extremely important to listen carefully to questions and not to respond to nonsensical ones. If is a question is confusing the expert may ask to have it repeated or rephrased. Witnesses should keep responses brief and not volunteer more than is asked for. They should admit when they do not know the answer to a question. If new information is introduced in court that might alter the expert's opinion, he or she must say so, if asked. Humility goes a long way. Arrogance, on the other hand, may undermine effective testimony and is likely to alienate a jury. Witnesses should be respectful and avoid sarcasm or anger. If the opposing attorney's questioning becomes overly aggressive it may mean that he or she does not have a good case. The expert witness should stay calm at all costs. If he or she is indeed being harassed or questions are becoming too personal, it is possible to appeal to the judge.

Cross-examination is followed by redirect examination in which both attorneys have the opportunity to seek clarification on testimony that has been given. The judge may choose to ask questions before excusing the witness.

It is useful for experts to get feedback on their testimony from the retaining attorney. Follow up on the outcome of the case is also important. Experts should not take it too personally if their recommendations were not followed. Often, an expert witness is often but one cog in the wheel and the adversary system sometimes operates in ways which are difficult for the psychiatrist to understand.

persons who are an integral part of the judicial process for example, case workers and probation officers. Experts acting without court order may claim absence of a doctor-patient relationship, in that they were not consulted by the patient for diagnosis and treatment, but rather by the attorney in regard to a specific legal issue. At present this issue is not well defined by case law. Suits filed by parties unhappy with the outcome of a case are often spurious, without merit, and will never get to court. Nonetheless, they pose any unnecessary stress on the clinician and may take years to resolve.

Anyone who engages in court work is advised to take advantage of legal consultation plans offered by their liability insurance carrier. For additional reading on malpractice issues, see Applebaum and Gutheil (1991), Nurcombe, B. & Partlett, D. (1994) and Simon and Sadoff (1992).

Areas of Liability for the Expert Witness

As our society becomes more litigious, we hear of child psychiatrists being sued for failure to diagnose sexual abuse, for faulty diagnosis of sexual abuse, and for inducing false memories of abuse. Psychiatrists who are engaged in forensic child psychiatry do seem to be at greater risk for being sued than those who are not. Court appointed psychiatrists are considered to be acting in a quasi-judicial capacity and as such they are afforded absolute immunity (*Lalonde v. Eissner,* Mass. Sup. Jud. Ct, 405 Mass 207, 6/19/89) from being sued. Some courts have extended this to

Conclusion

Forensic child psychiatry is an exciting area that is often on the cutting edge and confronts the clinician with provocative and novel questions. It affords the opportunity to be an advocate for children and encourage courts to make decisions in keeping with the child's best interests. It is also a field in which one is continually learning from colleagues and attorneys. Being challenged by the adversary system can improve our thinking and refine our ability to communicate with the rest of the world. Rather than shirk from the unknown turf of the legal world child psychiatrists are encouraged to make forays, familiarize themselves with the issues, and leave their mark.

REFERENCES

Appelbaum, P. S., Gutheil, T. G. (1991). *Clinical handbook of psychiatry and the law* (2nd ed.) Baltimore, MD: Williams & Wilkins.

Bartlet, J., Santrock, J. (1979). Affect-dependent episodic memory in young children. *Child Development 50:* 513–518.

Brown, A. K. (1979). Theories of memory and the problem of development: Activity, growth and knowledge. In L. Cermak & FIM Craik (Eds.) *Levels of processing in memory.* Hilldale, NJ: Lawrence Erlbaum, pp. 225–258.

Ceci, S. J., Ross, D. F., Toglia, M. P. (1987): Suggestibility of children's memory: psycholegal implications. *Journal Experimental Psychology* Gen. 116:38–49.

Ceci, S. J., Bruck, M. (1993). Suggestibility in the child witness: a historical review and synthesis. *Psychology Bulletin* 133:403–409.

Ceci, S. J., Loftus, E., Leichtman, M., Burck, M. (1994). The possible role of source attribution in creation of false beliefs among preschoolers. *International Journal Clinical Hypnosis 42:* 304–320.

Chance, J. E. & Goldstein, A. F. (1984). Face recognition memory: Implications for children's eyewitness testimony. *Journal of Social Issues 40 (2),* 69–85.

Duquette, D. (1990). *Advocation for the child in protection proceedings.* Lexington, MA: Lexington Books.

Goldstein, J., Freud, A., & Solnit, A. (1976). *Beyond the best interests of the child.* New York: Free Press.

Goodman, G. S. & Reed, R. S. (1986). Age differences in eyewitness testimony. *Law and Human Behavior 10:* 317–322.

Hyman, I. & Loftus, E. (1997). Some people recover memories of childhood trauma that never really happened. P. Appelbaum, L. Uyehara, & M. Elin (Eds.): *Trauma and memory: Clinical and legal controversies.* NY: Oxford U. Press.

Leichtman, M., Ceci, S., Morse, M. (1997): The nature and development of children's event memory. In P. Appelbaum, L. Uyehara & M. Elins (Eds.) *Trauma and memory: Clinical and legal controversies.* NY: Oxford U. Press pp. 158–187.

Loftus, E. F. & Davies, G. M. (1984). Distortions of memory of children. *Journal of Social Issues 40:* 51–67.

MacBeth, J. (1991). Legal issues in the psychiatric treatment of minors. In D. H. Schetky & E. P. Benedek (Eds.), *Clinical handbook of child psychiatry and the law.* Baltimore: Williams & Wilkins. pp. 53–74.

Myers, J. E. B. (1987). *Child witness: Law and practice.* New York: John Wiley & Sons.

Nurcome, B. & Partlett, D. (1994). *Child mental health and the law.* New York: Free Press.

Quinn, K. & White, S. (1991). Interviewing children for suspected sexual abuse. In D. H. Schetky & E. P. Benedek (Eds.): *Clinical handbook of child psychiatry and the law.* Baltimore, MD: Williams & Wilkins. pp. 119–144.

Schetky, D. H. (1991). The sexual abuse of infants and toddlers. *Annual review of psychiatry (Vol. 10).* Washington, DC: American Psychiatric Press, Inc. pp. 332–343.

Schetky, D. H. & Devoe, L. H. (1992). Countertransference issues in child forensic psychiatry. D. H. Schetky & E. P. Benedek (Eds.): *Clinical handbook of child psychiatry and the law.* Baltimore, MD: Williams & Wilkins. pp. 230–248.

Simon, R. & Sadoff, R. (1992). *Psychiatric malpractice.* Washington, DC: American Psychiatric Association Press, Inc.

Steinmen, S. (1981). The experience of children in joint custody arrangement: A report of a study. *American Journal of Othopsychiatry, 51:* 403–424.

Strasburger, L., Gutheil, T. & Brodsky, B. (1997). On wearing two hats. *American Journal of Psychiatry, 154 (4):* 448–455.

Task force on disclosure of treatment records in child custody disputes. Report #31. (1991). Washington, DC: American Psychiatric Association.

Weithorn, L. A. (1984). Children's capacities in legal contexts. In Repussi, L. A., M. P. Weithorn, Mulvey, & J. Monahan (Eds.). *Mental health, law and children.* Beverly Hills: Sage Publications.

20 / Clinical Consultation to Mental Health Agencies and Practitioners

Donald S. Gair

This chapter focuses on concepts and attitudes that are essential for effective clinical consultations to psychiatric hospitals, residential treatment centers, mental health centers, individual therapists, and peer groups.

Because of the relatively small number trained in child and adolescent psychiatry (now approximately 7000) and the breadth of its mission, clinical consultation has been recognized as a primary means by which to pursue the goals of our specialty since Caplan's pioneering work in the 1940s. Ranking with educational, interprofessional, and political approaches in importance in improving child rearing and therapeutic practices, consulta-

tion differs from these because of its immediate impact in helping resolve current crises with patient care.

Definitions and Roles in Consultation

Consultation is an interpersonal activity whose manifest rationale is the immediate benefit of consultees and, through them, to patients directly under their care or treated in programs under their management. A major motivating benefit to

338

the child and adolescent psychiatric consultant is the opportunity to influence for the better services to children and families.

Caplan's classic frames of reference (Caplan, 1963) clearly delineate the manifest reasons given for consultation: Consultants may be asked to focus on clinical problems ("client" [patient]-centered or program-centered consultation) or to focus on consultee's problems (consultee-centered, whether the clinical subtext is patient or program). These categories will not be the framework of this chapter, however, since I find that the separable aspects are always intertwined. Consultants must cultivate a multilensed eye, scanning all frames of reference for clues to the problematic areas that the consultees have lost sight of. The major challenge is translating the impressions gleaned into useful expansions of the consultee's perspective.

Consultants are valuable to the degree that consultees (individual practitioners or managers and members in a clinical organization) have become frustrated, anxious, and in conflict over patients' lack of improvement, violence, suicidality, clinical disagreements, and doctor/patient tensions.

Inpatient clinicians have special concerns about stormy hospital stays, pressures for discharge, limitations on insurance coverage or allotted lengths of stay, risks of premature discharge, and loss of staff.

Special outpatient concerns include deterioration of patient's self-control, competence for self-care, the capability of caretaking parents/guardians and community schools and agencies, duty to warn, whether to remove a patient from the home and admit to a hospital, and how to manage what the consultee sees as too few pre-approved appointments for a given patient.

Intrinsic Consultee Resistance

To be successful, a consultant must somehow transcend the consultee's conflict—wanting help but fearing exposure. Consultees often have the nagging fear that they are "missing something." In treating complex and difficult patients, clinicians can lose sight of one or another aspect of the problem. For instance, family approaches may have obscured aspects that can be better approached individually, or dynamic aspects in general may

have deflected attention from biologic determinants. The consultant's objective vantage point can help restore more inclusive perspectives. The essential product of successful consultation is restoration of a balanced view.

However, self-protective reflexes can neutralize consultative help by minimizing the newness or importance of perspectives the consultant suggests. Maintaining a clear distinction between consultee's views before the consultation and those that arise in the process may not be easy. The consultee's defensive stance sometimes can be lessened by outlining in advance generic preconceptions the consultant has that might fit the manifest presenting problem, before any details emerge. Overall, however, the most important factor in preempting defensive tendencies is the establishment of genuine trust and rapport.

Earning and maintaining access to influence is more exacting in consultation than in any other clinical role. Although the psychiatrist's role in consultation is analogous to that in psychotherapy, teaching, supervision, and evaluation interviews or surveys, there are crucial differences. Clinical consultants carry no concrete authority, rewards, or penalties, such as do these other clinical/administrative roles that lead patients, students, trainees, subordinate clinicians, or those being surveyed for approval to be attentive and compliant, however grudgingly.

Both the leader in the field who has been enthusiastically recruited as a consultant and the assigned resident who feels self-conscious and underqualified have to maintain their value to the consultee by their manner of relating and their approach to the problems presented. Essentials of the consultant/consultee relationship are discussed later.

In this chapter the terms "clinical consultation," "consultant," and "consultee" refer exclusively to those situations in which the psychiatrist's overriding responsibility is to the consultee and not to the patient or family (even if patient and family members are interviewed), or to the program, if that is the basic focus. Although some authors (Group for the Advancement of Psychiatry, 1979; Rutter, Sawyer et al. (p. 66) say that the psychiatrist's primary responsibility is to report findings and recommendations to the consultee rather than to the patient and family, I believe it is self-evident that such clinical work constitutes the actual practice of medicine with direct responsibility to the patient and family and inescapable liability for poor outcome. To classify this as consultation would be the same as labeling all psychiatrist/patient treatment relationships as consultations.

Consultants must emphasize that they are not taking over the clinical situation. Clinical and administrative authority for treatment and management of the patient, family, or mental health organization remains in the consultee's hands, and the consultee is under no obligation whatever to follow any recommendations made or implied. (Steinberg and Yule, p. 914).

The explicit absence of responsibility for the treatment and its outcome distinguishes consultation not only from treatment but also from supervision (of residents or other clinical trainees), which it resembles. When faced with diagnostic and treatment problems, clinicians automatically assume the "treating physician" mindset. However, upon becoming a consultant, one must transmute the urge to treat into an urge to expand the consultee's concepts and confidence.

Difficulty distinguishing between treating and consulting is dramatically evident in the Consultation Section of the Examinations in Child and Adolescent Psychiatry of the American Board of Psychiatry and Neurology. Some candidates describe how they would treat patients in sample problems rather than how they would function as consultants to those who are treating or managing the problem, which is what the exam is calling for.

Establishing Effective Relationships with Consultees

THE BASIC MODEL

Essentially the same core attitudes and skills are required in all clinical consultation situations that succeed on the basis of shared interest and respect. Recognizing the personal distress that underlies the consultee's need for consultation dictates that consultants be seen as accepting, understanding, usefully competent allies. The basic consultative model is a natural discourse between two companions intensely concerned about a current problem that one of them faces. The two are either true peers or one is more experienced in some area. In either case, each holds the other in sufficient regard for one to welcome clarification,

direction, and/or advice and the other to make the effort to be of help in the matter at hand.

This type of model is essential to gaining trust and eliciting useful information in peer-review settings and in the institution-wide observations and discourses necessary to consultations in response to organizational difficulties, even though those discussions are not primarily one to one. It is, after all, through personal impact on human ears, eyes, and minds that individuals influence organizations.

Some writers have warned consultants about the risk of fostering dependency in consultees by providing support, advice, or insight (Steinberg & Yule, 1986). I think it is impossible to consult successfully without all three. Furthermore, excessive caution in editing one's professional opinions and instincts blocks spontaneity and projects a patronizing attitude, which undermines confidence. It is far better to be open, encouraging free exchange, even argument—a "brainstorming" approach—always, however, staying within one's natural feelings, not play-acting an attitude deemed correct. While the consultant's views are, and should be, influential, they do not replace the primary message to the consultee: Responsible clinicians should never do anything within their "sphere of responsibility that is not within the limits of what the therapist thinks and believes to be right and necessary" (Gair, Hersch, & Weisenfeld, 1980, p. 267).

THE NEED FOR SUPERIORITY IN KNOWLEDGE

The necessity of consultant superiority in experience or specialized knowledge has been overstressed (GAP, 1979). Evidence to the contrary includes senior clinicians who receive unanticipated helpful new perspectives from ad hoc junior consultants when presenting summaries of their own patients as illustrative cases, and many professionals who get excellent consultative advice about thorny impasses in their work from friends or spouses who are not even in the same field. However brilliant a consultant's flash of insight may be, it will have no value if the consultee is resistive because the bright idea is felt to be intrinsically critical.

Caplan (1963) emphasized many years ago that the more a consultee seeks and appears to need primarily technical information (such as psychopharmacological advice), the more purely educational approaches are indicated. The effective relaying of this conclusion may require tact and strategy; however, the presentation of educational programs to client organizations is not the focus of this chapter.

This is not to say that there are no teaching aspects to consultation, rather that what is "taught" or modeled is an approach to clinical self-monitoring, not academic information.

USE OF CONSULTANT'S PAST ERRORS AS CLINICAL EXAMPLES

The clinical mentor who has never blundered makes a poor teacher and an impossible model. The most effective clinical examples are the consultant's own errors, with discussion of their outcome and what might have been better. These are not only instructive anecdotes in themselves, but they also emphasize that the consultant shares in the universal lack of absolute clinical certainty.

Such humility should not be merely a useful pose to put consultees at ease; rather it is a necessary recognition of the truth that all clinicians struggle to manage serious crises with meager information. We all find it difficult to tolerate our limited power to affect the course of grievous difficulties in our patients, tend to mistake our fallibility for incompetence, and have a reflex tendency to shift blame. We must do what we feel is best under the circumstances, recognizing the elusiveness of certainty. "Life is short, the art long . . ." was not written just for young physicians.

Legal Liability

In clinical consultation the duty is to the consultee, not to the patient. Unless the patient is interviewed, all of the consultant's activities can be viewed as responses to hypothetical questions, which do not constitute the practice of medicine. In fact one does not need a medical license to consult (some valued consultants have given up their medical licenses).

In clinical consultative interviews the responsibility for staying within acceptable interviewing protocol is self-evident. Demonstrably damaging conduct of an interview may become grounds for malpractice. If the interview is managed acceptably, immunity from liability will remain.

However, if a consultant gives a patient reason to believe that medical advice is being provided, he or she may well become as liable as a member of the treatment team. It is therefore essential that consultants scrupulously avoid giving the patient or parents/guardians any such impression. The consultant must refer all questions about treatment back to the treating physician, or other responsible clinician or team.

Hierarchy, The Status Quo, and Organizational Consultations

It is essential to know who is in charge of the case in which consultation takes place, who authorizes the consultation, who will be responsible for payment, and what the roles are of the all those with whom the consultant will come in contact. The chief of the organization in which a consultation takes place is the generic consultee whether he or she participates in the sessions or not; the consultant must maintain open communication with this person. In cases presenting as individual consultations, it is always wise to explore the possibility of a connection with a significant hierarchy that should be apprised of the consultant's activities, lest the effort become fruitless.

All activities to any extent connected with organizations are influenced by their hierarchy. Whatever its drawbacks, Jaques (1990) convincingly points out, ". . . managerial hierarchy is the most efficient, the hardiest, and in fact the most natural structure ever devised for large organizations. Properly structured, hierarchy can release energy and creativity . . . and improve morale." (p. 127)

As perennial advocates, our goal is certainly to change the status quo for the better wherever we can; however, as consultants we can be neither autocrat nor rebel. Because consultees necessarily retain full clinical authority, we can achieve our goals only by working within the status quo. If we do not, we lose our access to consultative influence. This implicit truth is worth pondering since it runs counter to the preponderantly liberal political bias of child and adolescent psychiatrists who are not characteristically known as establishment zealots or bureaucrats with button-down collars.

Consultation to Psychiatric Hospitals and Residential Treatment Centers

The two organizational consultations summarized in this section each required several weeks to complete. Even at that, they still were not nearly as thorough as a true organizational diagnosis, such as those by Levinson (1972) and Edelson (1970), would be. For example, the list of topics covered in Levinson's investigative procedure takes 11 pages (pp. 56–65), and all of that information is needed in order to fully understand how an institution functions and malfunctions. The process Levinson outlines for his studies of large organizations takes far longer than the time available for the majority of clinical consultations. The complexity of the issues, however, are as great in smaller organizations as in large ones, and clinical consultants have less complete access to all participants than that described by Levinson in which his entire list of relevant topics can be explored. It is therefore most desirable that consultants qualify their opinions as surmises and that they support their impressions with relevant evidence whenever possible.

RESOLUTION OF ADMINISTRATOR/ THERAPIST CONFLICT

At the time of the consultation summarized here, a psychiatrist administrator in a private hospital had such questions about the therapy of an 18-year-old adolescent boy on the psychiatric inpatient unit that she had made an implicit threat to report the treating psychiatrist to the Board of Registration in Medicine if he did not withdraw from treatment and "allow" transfer of the patient. The adolescent had already been hospitalized for over 2 years while the average length of stay on the unit was 3 weeks.

The problematic treatment had begun when the patient was admitted from the emergency ward following a serious suicide attempt after precipitant discharge from a previous psychiatric hospitalization, one of numerous previous admissions to many psychiatric services since age 12 for recurrent depressions with suicide attempts, borderline personality, and anorexia nervosa. Several previous initiations of therapy, some of which showed promise, had been interrupted by discharges from hospitals when insurance coverage ran out.

The treating psychiatrist had assessed the patient on admission as treatable but untrusting. He established a close and nurturant treatment relationship. In addition to psychotherapy 3 or more times a week (sessions often extending beyond the standard 50 minutes), and medication, the psychiatrist related to the adolescent much as would a big brother. They would, for instance, play tennis on afternoon outings and go to Burger King afterward. The psychiatrist also gave the patient permission to call him at home when he felt the need. The psychiatrist was aware that these approaches were not usual practices. He documented his rationale and shared his thinking with nursing staff, some of whom, however, resenting what they saw as overindulgent "special treatment," complained to the psychiatrist-administrator.

Treatment had shown signs of success—the adolescent had gained weight for the first time in 4 years, ate spontaneously (starting at the fast-food restaurant), and expressed a positive wish to live rather than his previous consistent wish to die. Both the adolescent and his family endorsed the treatment and the psychiatrist.

In response to several dates for "obligatory discharge" set by the psychiatrist administrator, the treating psychiatrist protested suicidal danger and invited several consultants, who agreed. The administrator was progressively exasperated as the patient remained while generations of other admissions came and went. She invited other consultants who supported her position. When one of these questioned the ethical acceptability of the "special treatment" and cited the "anaclitic relationship" as beyond proper patient/doctor boundaries, the threat of reporting to the medical board was raised. The treating psychiatrist persuaded the administrator to accept one last consultant, another child and adolescent psychiatrist.

The final consultation broke the impasse. Its support of the treatment was balanced by recognition of the administrative difficulties and the suggestion that therapist and administrator work jointly on the problem of need to be in the hospital. The report stated, in part:

Treatment of such patients always creates tension between therapeutic perspectives and "realistic" demands of hospital and society—laws of commitment, civil rights, reimbursement factors, hospital regulations about lengths of stay, patient behavior, and census limits. No therapist can be totally in charge of everything that happens around a patient and no administrator can legitimately act in total isolation from the valid clinical opinions of a therapist. The longer and more intense the treatment and the higher the clinical stakes (e.g., risk of suicide) the more likely is administrative/therapist conflict.

Recognizing that there is no absolute method to prevent such mismatches of patient need and hospital policy, the report suggested that the hospital and attending staff psychiatrists work out a clear protocol for dealing with such events in the future so as to avoid the profitless and near-disastrous escalation of confrontational mutual scapegoating between people who actually are clinical partners.

This consultation succeeded because it concentrated on the shared values and interests of administration and treating psychiatrist. The consultant stressed how patient, staff, treating psychiatrist, and administration were all trapped by the patient's serious illness and the real impossibility of transfer. By recognizing that the source of the tension was neither the therapist's nor the administrator's fault, mutual scapegoating was neutralized. In contrast, the previous consultations had been partisan to one "side" or the other and succeeded only in adding to the dangerously mounting polarization that had developed.

No charges were brought, treatment continued with much less staff conflict, and the patient was ultimately transferred successfully to a nonhospital setting. The hospital absorbed the bulk of the cost of the continued hospitalization. The consultant's role as mediator, exemplified in this example between therapist and administrator, also applies to analogous polarizations between collaborating agencies.

CONTROVERSY OVER USE OF SECLUSION

A legislator opposed to hospitalization of children demanded an investigation of a state hospital adolescent program that had placed a 15-year-old seriously assaultive adolescent boy with conduct disorder in prolonged seclusion. The patient had been assigned to live in a locked room from which he was released only on a specified schedule with adequate personnel on hand to ensure safety and with the duration of time outside of the room being extended as the patient demonstrated increasing self-control. This program had been initiated after several months of increasingly violent behavior by this adolescent, which had culminated in assaults on staff causing serious injury.

The Department of Mental Health selected a child and adolescent psychiatrist with extensive inpatient experience to do a consultative evaluation.

The ward staff felt under attack and defensive especially after the consultant admitted to a mild bias against seclusion. However, her openness and also her expressed sympathy with the difficulties presented by the patient overcame much initial mistrust. Her disclaimer of any doctrinaire certainty of what she expected to recommend became more believable each day as her collegial manner created open exchanges in individual and group interviews.

Her final report endorsed the treatment procedures as justified. The report also commented on the overcrowding/understaffing that had contributed to the difficulties in managing the patient on this professionally well-regarded state hospital program for adolescents.

This consultant's manner led to a productive exit interview with staff and leadership in which she deftly facilitated recognition of some problems that probably had prevented an earlier intervention with less development of violence. Her impact went far beyond the official report she dutifully filed, helpful as that was.

What became clear was that the pressures of overcrowding had interfered with adequate communication between different shifts, between school and ward, and between different disciplines. As a result, divergent views did not get aired and resolved. Instead, they festered in isolation and led to increasing antagonisms and mutual blaming, or scapegoating. This extended to the family; one result was their loss of rapport, which led them to complain to the legislator who demanded the investigation. Due to the consultant's skill, this understandable sequence ended up with genuine help. Recognition of the fragmentation that had developed led to resumption of adequate staff communication and a strengthening of lines of access to the support of senior management and hierarchical monitoring. In this instance it led to reestablishment of staff cohesion and a significant rate of improvement in the patient's self-control, although he ultimately had to be transferred to another secure facility.

Consultants must be on the alert for similar problems whenever seriously ill patients are being treated. Persistent suicidal risks, violence to others, and disheartening lack of progress in patients without dangerous behavior can lead to staff fragmentation and mutual scapegoating with acrimonious disagreements about diagnosis, treatment procedures, and theories. The commonplace occurrence of staff jointly scapegoating parents of seriously ill patients is a related problem.

Clinical Consultation to a Solo Practitioner

BOUNDARY CONCERNS

A child and adolescent psychiatrist was treating a 12-year-old boy with school avoidance and conduct disorder, whose parents had been divorced for 3 years. The boy had improved dramatically until father remarried and moved away. Father also then questioned the need for continued treatment since the boy was doing well. He refused to pay pending a joint meeting, and mother had arranged to pay a reduced fee—"all she could afford." The psychiatrist had to attend several school conferences with mother because of behavioral crises. In several treatment sessions the boy stormed out to the car but was persuaded to come back by the psychiatrist who had followed him out.

This period of therapy was reviewed along with other cases in consultation appointments with a senior colleague. The treating psychiatrist, a single man, reported sympathy for mother's plight and also that he felt attracted to her. The consultant underscored the need for hyperalertness to such feelings, clarity about limits, and minimizing seductive overtones. They discussed the real possibility of disastrous lapses in these situations if their potential is not recognized. The advisability of individual therapy for the consultee was discussed. (He was already in personal psychotherapy.) The consultant talked about how she had managed some positive countertransference problems of her own.

Several sessions later, the mother appeared for an appointment without bringing her son. She expressed gratitude for all of the psychiatrist's help and said she was attracted to him and wanted to "have a relationship with him." The psychiatrist responded gently, explaining that as a physician he had given up the right to pursue personal relationships with any patient or relative of a patient. He said that her feelings were understandable in view of his role as her son's psychiatrist; in it he had been and would continue to try to be realistically helpful and supportive. Therapy continued with ultimately satisfactory results.

Had this child and adolescent psychiatrist not been reviewing his work with a consultant, an unethical and (in some states unlawful) overt relationship with mother might have taken place. The likelihood of such an occurrence was sharply reduced by this discussion, which allowed the consultee time to react with forethought.

Less formal consultation with peers often provides the useful support and perspective gained in this instance by contracted consultation.

Adolescent Psychiatric Ward in a Private General Hospital

STAFF CONFLICT ABOUT RESPONSE TO INCESTUOUS ALLEGATIONS

On an adolescent unit in a general hospital serious issues arose about how to respond to a series of currently unproven allegations of sexual abuse of adolescent girls by male family members. Dr. C, who had had extensive professional experience with male perpetrators, dominated the team's approach by insisting that all allegations be recognized as disclosures and all accused men recognized as guilty. Insisting that denial was all but universal among perpetrators and virtual proof of guilt, he referred to these accused men as "perps." Others felt dishonest in fully believing something of which they were in fact unsure. Dr. C countered that if staff does not profess total belief, the girl who discloses will reexperience the trauma of mother's disbelief, feel betrayed and alone, and become more of a suicidal risk. The issue was disruptive to this cohesive and mutually supportive group of professionals.

The consultant talked about everyone's discomfort in dealing with uncertainty. She said she expected that many shared her inner worry that if one does not take a clear-cut distancing and accusatory position against the accused, one seems to condone or endorse egregious behavior.

The group, including Dr. C, ultimately agreed that they could provide honest and sympathetic support to the adolescent girl accusers ("disclosers") without expressing a certainty they did not possess. They agreed they could say that although they could not be sure of what happened they believed the distress and would work to prevent any future risk of abuse. Similarly honest dealings with the accused, however difficult, were seen as preferable to the spurious comfort of assumed certainty. The consultant's viewpoint is supported by Beahrs: "No data . . . support the . . . claims sometimes made by memory recovery therapists that the therapeutic alliance depends on uncritical affirmation of patients' narratives as historical truth." (page 51).

Mental Health Center Outpatient Peer Review Group

CONSULTANT CONCERNED ABOUT TREATMENT TEAM JUDGMENT

A suicidally preoccupied 18-year-old adolescent boy who had professed a wish to be a female since latency, in outpatient individual and family therapy in a mental health center for the preceding year, was brought up at peer review because of recent increase in suicidal preoccupation and poor school performance.

Although in a heterosexually active friendship with a high school classmate for 6 months, he had, several months earlier, in a family meeting threatened his mother with cutting off his own penis if she did not support his wish to pursue a transsexual procedure. The outpatient therapist, a member of this peer review group, had encouraged this boy's membership in a self-help group of transsexuals and also had arranged a consult with a team at a general hospital that evaluated applicants for transsexual procedures.

The boy had become more depressed and had stopped doing previously excellent schoolwork shortly after the general hospital's transsexual team had announced that he was an acceptable candidate for the period of hormonal treatment anticipating surgery. The members of the peer review group, although uncomfortable about what was happening, felt strongly that to question the boy's plans in any way would both violate his civil rights and threaten the therapeutic alliances that he had established.

The consultant expressed a categorical objection to treating this 18-year-old boy as a fully mature candidate for irreversible transsexual alteration. He thought it was inappropriate to endorse the judgment of an immature and unusually troubled adolescent in dealing with such serious, complex, and problematic questions. The consultant worried about the limited recognition by the ther-

apist and his peers of what seemed an obvious coincidence between the adolescent's recent academic collapse and increase in suicidality and the go-ahead signal from the transsexual team. He thought this was a clear indication of real conflict in this young man about the idea of moving ahead with transsexual surgery. The consultant also stressed the incongruity of the patient's significant heterosexual relationship, which also suggested major unrecognized conflict in this young man.

If delaying patient's plans intensified his suicidality, the consultant suggested the staff consider hospitalization as they would for any suicidal adolescent whose level of risk merited that response.

Although taken aback by the consultant's uncharacteristically confrontational stance, the staff's confidence in him led the group to reconsider their tacit support of the plans for the transsexual procedure.

Resigning from a Consultative Relationship

Before embarking on a consultation (unless one is obligatorily assigned, as a resident), it is advisable to get as much information as possible about the nature of the person or site of the consultation. Most assigned consultative arrangements usually allow sufficient prescreening to ensure a reasonable compatibility between consultant and consultee. Nonetheless, on rare occasions, bad misfits occur. It is never pleasant to call a relationship a failure, but it is always better to end nonproductive consultations.

As in all professional activities, we are always responsible to our judgment and ethical positions. We can never be under an obligation to support and encourage programs or practices that we believe to be unethical or examples of poor medical or child and adolescent psychiatric practice, unredeemable by our best efforts. Although, as has been strongly underlined, our roles in consultation are not in the line of treatment, and we do not have clinical responsibility or liability, we still lend our implicit support and tacit approval to the functioning of a psychiatrist, peer group, hospital, or other organization to whom we regularly consult. Consultants have an implicit alliance with and endorsement of consultees.

If we find that in our consultative role we cannot provide the kind of support and assistance in problem-solving that we believe minimally acceptable, we should withdraw, communicating our intent in a letter to the responsible person in charge as well as to consultative participants. If major problems are worrisome (reportable if there is direct information), we must inform in detail the responsible senior person. If we are directly aware of reportable problems, we must report them. If we are in doubt about reportability, we can consult the local office of the agency to which such reports are properly made for advice.

More than in any other area of training, adequate supervision and support to residents is essential in the consultative experience. When settings to which residents are assigned are underfunded and overcrowded, optimum clinical outcomes are rare. Residents often become deeply conflicted because they feel at ethical odds with these programs. On the other hand, such settings are in greatest need of the help that can come from consultation. It is the supervisor's task to maximize the possibility of the resident's providing such help without demoralization or compromise of ethics. Resigning from consultative relationships should be reserved for those situations that are truly unredeemable.

REFERENCES

Beahrs, J. O., Cannell, J. J., & Gutheil, T. G. (1996). Delayed traumatic recall in adults: A synthesis with legal, clinical, and forensic recommendations. *Bulletin American Academy Psychiatry Law, 24:* 45–55.

Caplan, G. (1963). Types of mental health consultation. *American Journal of Orthopsychiatry, 33,* 470–481.

Edelson, M. (1970). *The practice of sociotherapy.* New Haven, CT: Yale University Press.

Gair, D. S., Hersch, C., & Weisenfeld, S. (1980). Successful psychotherapy of severe emotional disturbance in a young retarded boy. *Journal of the American Academy of Child Psychiatry, 19,* 257–269.

Gair, D. S., Hersch, C., & Weisenfeld, S. (1984). Child psychiatric consultation concerning childhood psychosis. In N. R. Bernstein & J. N. Sussex (Eds.), pp. 331–353, *Handbook of psychiatric consultation with children and youth.* New York: Spectrum Publications.

Group for the Advancement of Psychiatry. (1979). *Psychiatric consultation in mental retardation* (Publication 104). New York: Author.

Jaques, E. (1990). In praise of hierarchy. *Harvard Business Review, 90,* 127–133.

Levinson, H. (1972). *Organizational diagnosis.* Cambridge, MA: Harvard University Press.

Sawyer, D. A. & Huessy, H. R. (1993). A model of inpatient child and adolescent care using a consulting psychiatrist. *Hospital & Community Psychiatry, 44:* 66–68.

Steinberg, D. & Yule, W. (1986). Consultative work. In M. Rutter & L. Hersov (Eds.), *Child and adolescent psychiatry: modern approaches* (pp. 914–926). Oxford: Basel Blackwell.

SECTION V
Emergency Assessment and Intervention

21 / Emergency Assessment

Marilyn Benoit

Psychiatric emergencies in children and adolescents are defined by adults in the immediate environment (Sadka, 1995). Shafii, Whittinghill, and Healy (1979) defined psychiatric emergencies in children as "situations in which the life of the child or of someone else is in danger or the child is at high risk for a catastrophic trauma. These patients are seen within 24 hours because the family and community support systems can no longer cope with the situation" (p. 1600). A comprehensive list of the spectrum of psychiatric emergencies includes:

1. Suicidal, self-destructive, or marked depressive behavior, suicide attempts or gestures, active suicidal thoughts, marked depression, severe withdrawal, and self-harming and self-destructive behaviors.

2. Harmful or destructive behavior to others—attempting to harm or actually harming others: threatening to kill or seriously harm others; violent destructive behaviors; fire-setting; being beyond the control of parents, teachers, or other authority figures; and serious antisocial behavior, including sexual assault on others.

3. Abuse or neglect—severe neglect, physical abuse, sexual abuse, molestation, and incest.

4. Phobic or extremely anxious behavior—severe school phobia, other severe phobias, school refusal, panic reactions, and severely anxious and agitated behavior.

5. Psychotic behavior—acute psychotic episodes and other severe forms of psychotic confusion.

6. Runaways—a high risk of running away from home (based on past history of runaway behavior).

7. Medical-psychiatric emergencies—severe anorexia nervosa, diabetes with refusal to take insulin, other serious physical conditions aggravated by emotional problems.

8. Drug and alcohol abuse—severe abuse of toxic agents such as glue, paint, and gasoline as well as severe alcohol or drug intoxication.

9. Others—severe family crisis, war trauma, multiproblem crises, and extreme emotional fragility. (Shafil et al., p. 1600)

Suicidality

Pfeffer et al. (1979) reported a study that they conducted on 58 latency-age hospitalized children who were evaluated for suicide potential. The study was designed to identify high-risk factors correlated with suicidal behavior in that age group. The authors determined that as many as 72% of those children evaluated had "suicidal ideas, threats, or attempts" (p. 683). Eighty percent of those making threats at that time proposed to commit suicide by jumping. The 1990s have been an era of increased availability of firearms, which are increasingly used in suicide deaths. The stresses that Pfeffer et al. identified as being most common for this group were concerns about school failure, difficulty with peers, fear of being punished by parents, and significant changes that had occurred in the school and/or family.

A family-related crisis (Ellison et al., 1989; Gutstein, Rudd, Graham, & Rayha, 1988), which often may be disciplinary in nature (Shaffer, 1974), is the most frequent precipitant of suicidality.

Danto (1980) made the following observations about the reasons for suicidality in both the latency- and adolescent age groups: "The latency age child appears to commit suicide out of a sense of frustration over his inability to establish peer ties and relationships" (p. 24). Based on clinical experience, this author also would include unwanted teenage pregnancy and reaction of being HIV positive as precipitants for suicidal behavior.

Several authors have discussed the phenomenon of suicide contagion (Brent et al., 1989; Gould & Shaffer, 1986; Phillips & Carstensen, 1986; Robbins & Conroy, 1983) presenting as a community psychiatric emergency in the adolescent population. Brent et al. (1989) have well summarized the consensus on this issue: "The risk for suicidality appears to be greatest among those with psychiatric vulnerability antedating the exposure, particularly past or current affective disorder and past suicidality. Those who were close friends of the victims may also be at risk, even if they do not have current or past psychopathology" (p. 923).

Child Abuse/Neglect

As revealed by the Third National Incidence Study (1996) by the U.S. Department of Health and Human Services, child victimization is a major public health issue in the United States. With more attention being given to this issue in the national media, there is no doubt that an increased index of suspicion has contributed to the phenomenal increase in the number of cases being reported. As many as 2.7 million cases a year are reported and about 2,000 children die as a result of abuse each year.

In 1974 the Child Abuse Prevention and Treatment Act became law in all 50 states. When the child psychiatrist suspects victimization by sexual assault, physical abuse, or neglect, he or she has a legal obligation to report to the agency designated for receiving and investigating such reports. The child's immediate protection must be ensured first. Once such protection has been accomplished, a multidisciplinary child protection team should do the necessary physical, laboratory, and mental health and psychosocial evaluations (Altieri, 1990). In cases where the child psychiatrist is the first professional to be aware of the possibility of abuse/neglect, he or she also will have the difficult task of dealing with the parental reaction to the allegation of abuse. These reactions may vary from relief (that help will be offered), disbelief (in cases where parents have never suspected the problem), denial, threatening behavior, and even violent outrage about being found out. Where a team approach is available (Benoit, 1992), designating specific tasks to various team members expedites the handling of family members.

Sexual abuse cases are the most difficult cases of victimization. Unless it presents as a sexually transmitted disease in the child (Hammerschlag, 1988), sexual victimization is easy to miss. Boys are the likely victims of homosexual victimization (Adams-Tucker, 1984; Vander Mey, 1988). The child usually knows the perpetrator (a family member, other relative or family friend, babysitter, teacher), and usually he or she is sworn to secrecy under threats of harm to self or to a loved one. When doing any psychiatric assessment, the child psychiatrist must ask specific questions about both physical and sexual victimization.

All child and adolescent psychiatrists should be aware of the characteristics Adams-Tucker (1984) has identified in incestuous sexual abuse:

1. Girls more than boys are known victims.
2. Fathers and father surrogates more than mothers are abusers. Hence homosexual victimization is most likely for boys; heterosexual victimization for girls.
3. Noncoercive and conning forms of assault are more likely than brutal, violent abuse.
4. Infants through young adults are equally likely to be victimized.
5. Incest has a prevalence rate equal to or greater than that of schizophrenia—1 to 4%. One in 6 girls is an incest victim by 18 years of age.
6. Younger children are more credible reporters of incest than are older youngsters (those over 12 years).
7. Any and all symptom complaints are possible, including none.
8. Incest occurs among all economic and occupational strata, in families of all religious persuasions, and among all ethnic groups. (p. 508)

It is important to note that although males are more often the perpetrators of sexual abuse, women also have been identified as perpetrators (Wilkins, 1990).

Violence

Suicide and violence account for the majority of psychiatric emergencies (Sadka, 1995). With the increasing awareness of the exposure of American children to violence both through the media (Eron, 1986; Heath, Bresolin, & Renaldi, AMA, 1996 National Television Violence Study (ND) 1989) and, for some youngsters, on the street by reason of drug-related violence in the cities (Benoit, 1993; Martinez & Richters, 1993; Richters & Martinez, 1993; Eth-Pynoos, 1994), more attention is being paid to the impact of violence on our youth.

When dealing with violence as a psychiatric emergency, the most important intervention is to provide external controls (Lehmann, Padilla, Clark, & Loucks, 1983; Miller, Walker, Friedman,

1989) to stop the violent behavior. This may mean using personnel trained in restraining violent patients; medication; physical restraints; and/or quiet isolation rooms, either singly or combined, depending on the specific circumstances.

Assessment of the patient's medical status will shed light on the possibility of an organic etiology, for example, drug intoxication, central nervous system problems, metabolic/endocrine problems (Benoit, 1988b). Phencyclidine (PCP) psychosis is well known as a cause of severe violent behavior. Psychiatric conditions that may result in violent behavior run the gamut from severe attention deficit disorder with hyperactivity, conduct disorders and acute anxiety states, to paranoid and other psychotic states, impulse control disorders, and severe personality disorders.

The issue of violence cannot be discussed without attending to the impact of the Tarasoff decision, initially conceived as a duty to warn a potential victim identified by a patient during a psychiatric interview (Mills, Sullivan, & Eth, 1987) on the clinical practice of emergency psychiatry. The authors specifically state: "Tarasoff II mandates a duty to protect, not specifically to warn. Protecting includes conventional clinical interventions such as reassessment, medication changes, or hospitalization designed to relieve the patient's symptoms" (p. 71).

In summary, the critical issues involved in the handling of the violent child or adolescent presenting as a psychiatric emergency are:

- Ensure safety of the clinician(s) and the patient.
- Control behavior immediately by appropriate means (restraints, medication, isolation).
- Assess the etiology of violent behavior.
- Provide appropriate treatment/disposition planning based on etiology (e.g., crisis intervention psychotherapy, use of medication, medical vs. psychiatric hospitalization, release to law enforcement authorities).
- Maintain awareness of legal duty to protect any identified potential victim(s) of patient's violence and take appropriate protective actions.

Involuntary Commitment

At times a child or adolescent will have to be hospitalized against the patient's or the parents' wishes. All child and adolescent psychiatrists must be familiar with the legal stipulations for involuntary psychiatric hospitalization in the jurisdictions in which they practice. Involuntary hospitalization of minor children presents some complicated legal issues, and psychiatrists must understand the statutes in the jurisdiction where they practice.

Substance Abuse

Substance abuse among adolescents remains a troubling problem (Bailey, 1989; Carter & Robson, 1987). The most common pattern of abuse is polydrug abuse. The San Diego Study on young suicide cases (Fowler, Rich, & Young, 1986) reported that in 133 suicides studied, substance abuse was a principal diagnosis in 53% of the cases. Based on findings of parallel increases in substance abuse and the suicide rate over time, that study concluded that "suicide is a late manifestation of substance abuse disorders. . . . the finding does suggest that, with respect to suicide, there is time for intervention early in the course of the illness" (p. 965). In fact, in many emergency rooms adolescent psychiatric admissions are precipitated by the discovery of substance abuse; if not the principal presenting problem, often it is part of a dual diagnosis in adolescents (Brent, 1995; Bailey, 1989). Violent behavior, especially related to phencyclidine (PCP) abuse, involving destruction to property and/or physical attack, is not an unusual presentation. Strange behavior (e.g., perceptual distortions, visual hallucinations secondary to psychedelic drug use, and psychotic behavior secondary to stimulant abuse) that is frightening to the observer also can precipitate an emergency psychiatric visit.

Farley, Echardt, and Herbert (1986), in their *Handbook of Child and Adolescent Psychiatric Emergencies and Crises,* include an excellent chapter on acute drug abuse. They advise that:

1. The patient should be seen in a quiet area.
2. The clinician should frequently reorient the patient.
3. The clinician should, if at all possible, get the patient to talk about what he or she is experiencing.
4. Friends or family should be allowed to stay with the patient.
5. Medication (haloperidol, diazepam) (Clinton, Sterner, Stelmachers, & Ruiz, 1987) for agitation should be administered if appropriate. In general,

if at all possible, medication use should be avoided, both to avoid complicating the clinical course and to decrease the likelihood of adverse drug interactions. Remember that with diazepam, disinhibition of aggression may occur.

Anxiety States, Phobias, and Panic Attacks

The expression of anxiety in children and adolescents varies in symptom formation and intensity. The diagnostic categories range from adjustment disorder with anxious mood, overanxious disorder of childhood, and separation anxiety disorder to simple phobias, school phobias, panic attacks, and obsessive compulsive disorder. All these may represent a continuum of psychopathology (Black & Robbins, 1990), perhaps having some common biological underpinnings.

School phobia also school refusal (Last & Strauss, 1990) is a psychiatric emergency because, if not aborted quickly, it can become a chronic problem that results in severe dysfunction (McAnanly, 1986). The prescribed intervention is as follows:

1. Get the child/adolescent back to school immediately unless it is determined that a good reason (Leung, 1989) e.g. abuse exists to account for the child's behavior.
2. Counsel and educate parents about the intervention, and pay attention to their anxiety.
3. Be sure to refer for a pediatric evaluation, if one has not been done.
4. Use medication (e.g., imipramine, nortryptiline, propanolol benzodiazepine) if deemed appropriate.

Panic disorder in the child and adolescent population is recognized as a distinct clinical entity (Black & Robbins, 1990; Ballenger, Carek, Steele, & Cornish-McTighe, 1989; Smith et al., 1988). Patients present with acute somatic complaints such as stomach pain, headaches, nausea, palpitations, light-headedness, diaphoresis, sense of impending doom, fears of getting out of control, being "crazy."

The immediate pharmacologic treatment used successfully was a combination of alprazolam (or other benzodiazepine) and imipramine (or desipramine), with alprazolam being tapered off after a consistent period of symptom abatement. Response to discontinuation of imipramine has to be monitored cautiously; discontinuation can result in a relapse.

In summary, the major emergency intervention strategies in dealing with the anxiety states focus on interrupting the cycle of anxiety and the increasing reinforcing power of that anxiety. It may mean dealing with the feared object (such as school) immediately, using support and desensitization, and/or may require judicious use of anxiolytic medication.

Psychosis

When a child or adolescent presents with a psychotic symptom complex, the medical history guides the clinician in determining the etiology of the psychosis (Robinson, 1994). Organic causes must be considered and necessary laboratory work completed in order to guide the treatment. Treatment of drug-induced psychoses vary depending on the offending agent.

When the patient is agitated, delusional, and unable to participate in his or her own care, hospitalization may be necessary. In cases where the family is stable and reliable, the patient may be able to be treated on an outpatient basis, with crisis intervention with medication, frequent reassessment, and environmental manipulation provided.

Delirium

Delirium is an acute and reversible alteration in mental status that presents with disturbed orientation, fluctuating consciousness, and mental confusion (Tavani-Petrone, 1986). There often are perceptual disturbances varying from illusions to delusions and hallucinations (Farley et al., 1986). The patient may be agitated, uncooperative, labile, and unpredictable. Causes of delirium are many—heat stroke, infection, trauma, metabolic changes, drug toxicity, malignancy, endocrine dysfunction, and HIV. In the pediatric population, one of the more common causes of drug-induced delirium is cold/and or asthma medications (Tavani-Petrone, 1986).

It is advisable to avoid treating cases of anticholinergic intoxication (Feldman 1986) with neuroleptics because of their high anticholinergic activity.

One delirious state that should be of particular concern for psychiatrists is the neuroleptic malignant syndrome. This iatrogenic, life-threatening condition with autonomic dysfunction results from the use of neuroleptics (Frances & Susman, 1986). Diamond and Hayes (1986) reported a case of an adolescent male with neuroleptic malignant syndrome. They reported that "Within hours of admission, the patient became comatose and was unresponsive to painful stimuli" (p. 420). Within 24 hours of a second intramuscular dose of fluphenazine, the patient was combative and had fluctuating levels of consciousness, elevated temperature, tachycardia, blood pressure of 140/90, and a white blood cell count of 23, 700 per millimeter. He responded to supportive care and was discharged on the 12th day. It is not unusual for children to be prescribed the phenothiazine prochlorperazine (Compazine) as an antiemetic, say Frances and Susman. Another drug, droperiderol, which is used by anesthesiologists as an adjunctive agent, is structurally related to haloperidol and therefore has the potential of precipitating neuroleptic malignant syndrome.

Sleep Disorders

Night terrors, or pavor nocturnis, is the sleep disorder most disturbing to parents. This is a disorder of arousal in stage IV sleep when the child, usually a boy, awakens, usually screaming, as if terrified (Linscheid & Rasnake, 1990). Autonomic overactivity causes the child to be diaphoretic, tachycardic, and tachypneic. To make matters worse for the parents, the child is unresponsive to any parental attempts to provide comfort. Parents can be reassured that this condition results from a neurophysiological maturational lag that generally remits without specific treatment. Child psychiatrists should inquire about specific psychosocial stressors in the life of the child and family and to minimize those factors with appropriate intervention.

Conversion Disorders

Conversion disorders are believed to be rare in children (Farley et al, 1986). Most conversions, however, do not present as psychiatric emergencies. Because conversion symptoms raise anxiety about serious medical illness, patients usually are seen by nonpsychiatric physicians. Should the child psychiatrist be the first physician to see a case of suspected conversion disorder, it is absolutely imperative, even if he or she is convinced that indeed it is conversion, to refer for a medical workup to rule out an organic basis for the symptom(s). One particularly interesting case of conversion disorder with which this author is familiar presented with intractable coughing spells of several weeks' duration, which were determined not to be of organic etiology after an exhaustive medical workup. The spells prevented the child from attending school and disrupted the parents' work schedules. The youngster was seen in an emergency psychiatric walk-in service, taken through an immediate session of relaxation and hypnosis, and scheduled for a follow-up appointment. The parents called to cancel the second appointment because the symptom remitted after the single emergency visit.

Posttraumatic Stress Disorder

Terr (1979, 1989) and Eth and Pynoos (1985) have made significant contributions to the understanding of posttraumatic stress disorder in children. Its causes in children and adolescents are myriad. Some common stressors are domestic violence, witnessing of murders, being involved in a motor vehicle accident (especially where a parent or sibling has died), hostile separation and divorce, child victimization, and catastrophic events of nature. The presenting symptoms include reexperiencing of the trauma e.g. flashbacks, psychological numbing/avoidance, and hyperarousal. Eth and Pynoos (1985) have developed special interview techniques to be used during the acute posttrauma phase. These techniques are designed to enable the repetitive work that must be done after the trauma and to develop active coping skills, thus promoting psychological mastery over the traumatic event.

The essential interventions for emergency psychiatric treatment of posttraumatic stress disorder are:

1. Protect the child/adolescent from reexposure to the trauma (e.g., do not return to an abusive home situation).
2. Provide psychotherapeutic crisis intervention to facilitate discussion of the trauma and develop psychological mastery.
3. Consider use of medication.
4. Counsel parents/guardians of the child.
5. Hospitalize the more severely symptomatic child.

Disposition Considerations in Child and Adolescent Emergency Psychiatry

The family situation is the most critical variable in determining the disposition of the child or adolescent patient from the emergency room. If the family is stable and reliable, shows an ability to understand a clearly stated formulation of the problem, and demonstrates a capacity to follow through with the treatment planning, the likelihood of discharge to home is markedly increased. Conversely, severely dysfunctional families which cannot provide a safe environment are not likely to cooperate with outpatient treatment.

A follow-up appointment allows the child psychiatrist to assess how well regrouping has taken place both in the identified patient and in the family system, how motivated all parties are for further treatment, and, in general, whether the crisis triggered a regressive trend or has served as an impetus for constructive change. Initial disposition plans then can be modified based on reassessment. Helping a family to utilize available community resources can assist in decreasing psychosocial stressors that may compromise their coping ability.

The major disposition alternatives to consider

when discharging a patient from the emergency room are:

1. Administer medical treatment when warranted.
2. Discharge to home (with or without medication) and with outpatient follow-up. (A stable, reliable family is essential.)
3. Hospitalize, either voluntary or involuntary.
4. Place out of the home—such as through child protective services if parents unavailable or unfit.
5. Remain available for further consultation.

Conclusion

Child and adolescent psychiatric emergencies trigger tremendous anxiety in families and in nonpsychiatric health care providers. The child psychiatrist's intervention must address that anxiety and result in a calming-down, not an escalating of, the anxiety in the system.

Any emergency evaluation must include an assessment of the integrity of the family environment (Perlmutter, 1985), which is critical in the management of emergencies in child and adolescent psychiatry.

The importance of the mental status examination and the medical and psychosocial history cannot be overemphasized. Diagnosis, treatment, and disposition planning all depend on results of that examination and the histories.

The child psychiatrist, as a physician, is well trained to assess the medical causes of the presenting symptoms in an emergency and request consultations where necessary. As a mental health expert with special training in child development, adult psychopathology, and family functioning, the child psychiatrist can do the necessary assessment of the child and family variables contributing to the emergency situation. And the child psychiatrist's psychotherapeutic skills, psychopharmacologic knowledge, and familiarity with community resources equip him or her to make the necessary and effective interventions.

REFERENCES

Adams-Tucker, C. (1984). Early treatment of child incest victims. *American Journal of Psychotherapy, 38*, 505–516.

Altieri, M. F. (1990, February). Child abuse. When to be suspicious and what to do then. *Postgraduate Medicine, 87*, 153–156, 161–162.

American Medical Association, (1996). *Physician guide to media violence.* AMA Press, Chicago, IL.

Bailey, G. W. (1989). Current perspectives on substance abuse in youth. *Journal of the American Academy of Child Psychiatry, 28,* 151–162.

Ballenger, J., Carek, D., Steele, J., & Cornish-McTighe, D. (1989). Three cases of panic disorder with agoraphobia in children. *American Journal of Psychotherapy, 146,* 922–924.

Benoit, M. B. (1988a). The role of the mental health practitioner in child advocacy in the school system. In J. Spurlock & A. Coner-Edwards (Eds.), *Black families in crisis* (pp. 139–146). New York: Brunner/Mazel.

Benoit, M. B. (1988b). Physical illness presenting with psychological symptoms. In J. Spurlock & A. Coner-Edwards (Eds.), *Black families in crisis* (pp. 149–156). New York: Brunner/Mazel.

Benoit, M. (1992). "Is there a role for the child psychiatrist on child abuse teams?" *Pediatric Annals 21:* (8) 508–511.

Benoit, M. (1993). Impact of violence on children and adolescents: Report from a community-based child psychiatry clinic. *Psychiatry 56:* 124–6.

Black, B., & Robbins, D. (1990). Panic disorder in children and adolescents. *Journal of the American Academy of Child Psychiatry, 29,* 36–44.

Brent, D., Kerr, M., Goldstein, C., Bozigar, J., Wartella, M., & Allan, J. (1989). An outbreak of suicidal behavior in a high school. *Journal of the American Academy of Child Psychiatry, 28,* 918–924.

Brent, D. (1995). Risk factors for adolescent suicide and suicidal behavior: Mental and substance abuse disorders, family environmental factors, and life stress. *Suicide and Life-Threatening Behavior 25 (Supplement):* 52–63.

Carter, Y. H., & Robson, W. J. (1987). Drug misuse in adolescence. *Archives of Emergency Medicine, 4,* 17–24.

Clinton, J. E., Sterner, S., Stelmachers, Z., & Ruiz, E. (1987). Haloperidol for sedation of disruptive emergency patients. *Annals of Emergency Medicine, 16,* 319–322.

Danto, B. L. (1980). An overview of suicide. *American Journal of Forensic Medicine and Pathology, 1,* 23–27.

Diamond, J. M., & Hayes, D. D. (1986). A case of neuroleptic malignant syndrome in a mentally retarded adolescent. *Journal of Adolescent Health Care, 7,* 419–422.

Ellison, J. M., Hughes, D., & White, K. (1989). An emergency psychiatry update. *Hospital and Community Psychiatry, 40,* 250–259.

Ellison, J. M., Jacobs, D. (1986). Emergency psychopharmacology: A review and update. *Annals of Emergency Medicine, 15,* 962–968.

Ellison, J. M., Wharff, E. (1985). More than a gateway: The role of the emergency psychiatry service in the community mental health network. *Hospital and Community Psychiatry, 36,* 180–185.

Eron, L. D. (1986). Interventions to mitigate the psychological effects of media violence on aggressive behavior. *Journal of Social Issues, 42,* 155–169.

Eth, S., & Pynoos, R. (Eds.). (1985). *Posttraumatic stress disorder in children.* Washington, DC: American Psychiatric Press.

Eth, S., & Pynoos, R. S. (1994). Children who witness the homicide of a parent. *Psychiatry 57:* 287–307.

Farley, G. K., Echardt, L. O., & Herbert, F. B. (1986). Handbook of child and adolescent psychiatric emergencies and crises. 2nd ed., New York, N.Y.: Medical Examination Pub. Co.

Feldman, M. D. (1986). The syndrome of anticholinergic intoxication. *American Family Physician, 34,* 113–116.

Fowler, R. C., Rich, C. L., & Young, D. (1986). San Diego suicide study. *Archives of General Psychiatry, 43,* 962–965.

Frances, A., & Susman, V. L. (1986). Managing an acutely manic 17-year-old girl with neuroleptic malignant syndrome. *Hospital and Community Psychiatry, 37,* 771–772.

Gould, M., & Shaffer, D. (1986). The impact of suicide in television movies. *New England Journal of Medicine, 315,* 690–693.

Gutstein, S., Rudd, M., Graham, J., & Rayha, L. (1988). Systemic crisis intervention as a response to adolescent crises: An outcome study. *Family Process, 27,* 201–211.

Hammerschlag, M. R. (1988). Sexually transmitted diseases in sexually abused children. *Advances in Pediatric Infectious Disease, 3,* 1–18.

Heath, L., Bresolin, L., & Renaldi, R. (1989). Effects of media violence on children. A review of the literature. *Archives of General Psychiatry, 46,* 376–379.

Last, C., & Strauss, C. (1990). School refusal. *Journal of the American Academy of Child and Adolescent Psychiatry, 29,* 31–35.

Lehmann, L., Padilla, M., Clark, S., & Loucks, S. (1983). Training personnel in the prevention and management of violent behavior. *Hospital and Community Psychiatry, 34,* 40–42.

Leung, A. K. C. (1989). School phobia. Sometimes a child or a teenager has a good reason. *Postgraduate Medicine, 85,* 281–282, 287–289.

Linscheid, T. R., & Rasnake, L. K. (1990). Sleep disorders in children and adolescents. In *Psychiatric disorders in children and adolescents* (pp. 359–371). Philadelphia: W. B. Saunders. Eds. Garfinkel, B., Carlson, G. A., Weller, E. B.

Martinez, P. & Richters, J. E. (1993). The NIMH community violence project: II Children's distress symptoms associated with violence exposure. *Psychiatry 56:* 22–35.

MaAnanly, E. (1986). School phobia: The importance of prompt intervention. *Journal of School Health, 56,* 433–436.

Miller, D., Walker, M. C., & Friedman, D. (1989). Use of a holding technique to control the violent behavior of seriously disturbed adolescents. *Hospital and Community Psychiatry, 40,* 520–524.

National Television Violence Study, Executive Summary 1994–1995. Mediascope, Inc., Studio City, CA.

O'Shanick, G. J. (1984). Emergency psychopharmacology. *American Journal of Emergency Medicine, 2,* 164–270.

Payton, J. B., Krocker-Tuskan, M. (1988). Children's reaction to loss of parent through violence. *Journal of the American Academy of Child Psychiatry, 27,* 563–566.

Peck, M., & Berkovitz, I. (1987). Youth suicide: The role of school consultation. *Adolescent Psychiatry, 14,* 511–521.

Perlmutter, R., & Jones, J. (1985). Assessment of families in psychiatric emergencies. *American Journal of Orthopsychiatry, 55,* 130–139.

Pfeffer, C. R., Conte, H. R., Plutchik, R., Jerrett, I. (1979). Suicidal behavior in latency-age children: An empirical study. *Journal of the American Academy of Child Psychiatry, 18,* 679–692.

Pfeffer, C. R., Conte, H. R., Pultchik, R., Jerrett, I. (1980). Suicidal behavior in latency-age children: An outpatient population. *Journal of the American Academy of Child Psychiatry, 19,* 703–710.

Pfeffer, C. R. (1984). Modalities of treatment for suicidal children: An overview of the literature on current practice. *American Journal of Psychotherapy, 38,* 364–373.

Pfeffer, C. R., Conte, H., Plutchik, R., & Jerrett, I. (1986). Suicidal behavior in latency-age children. An empirical study. *American Journal of Academy Child Psychiatry,* 679–692.

Phillips, D., & Carstensen, L. (1986). Clustering of teenage suicides after television news stories about suicide. *New England Journal of Medicine, 315,* 685–689.

Piersma, H., & Winger, S. (1988). A hospital-based crisis service for adolescents: A program description. *Adolescence, 22,* 493–500.

Pynoos, R. S., & Nader, K. (1990). Children's exposure to violence and traumatic death. *Psychiatric Annals, 20,* 334–344.

Richters, J. E., & Martinez, P. (1993). The NIMH community violence project: I. Children as victims and witnesses to violence. *Psychiatry 56:* 7–21.

Robbins, D., & Conroy, R. (1983). A cluster of adolescent suicide attempts: Is suicide contagious? *Journal of Adolescent Health Care, 142,* 588–592.

Robinson, J. E. (1994). Emergencies I in *Manual of Clinical Child and Adolescent Psychiatry,* pp. 251–181, Revised Edition. Robson, K. (ed.). American Psychiatric Press, Inc., Washington, DC.

Sadka, S. (1995). Psychiatric emergencies in children and adolescents. *New Directions for Mental Health Services 67:* 65–74.

Schilling, W. D. (1984). Child abuse prevention and intervention. *Pediatric Annals, 13,* 766–770.

Seiden, R. (1984). Death in the West—A regional analysis of the youthful suicide rate. *The Western Journal of Medicine, 140,* 969–973.

Shaffer, D. (1974). Suicide in childhood and early adolescence. *Journal of Child Psychology and Psychiatry, 15,* 275–291.

Shafii, M., Whittinghill, R., & Healy, M. (1979). The pediatric-psychiatric model for emergencies in child psychiatry: A study of 994 cases. *American Journal of Psychiatry, 136,* 1600–1601.

Siegel, C. (1987). Why should educators be concerned? *Public Health Review, 15,* 242–255.

Slaby, A., & Perry, P. (1980–81). Use and abuse of psychiatric emergency services. *International Journal of Psychiatry and Medicine, 10,* 1–8.

Smith, R. G., O'Rourke, D. F., Parker, P. E., Ford, C. V., Guggenheim, F. G., & Livingson, R. L. (1988). Panic and nausea instead of grief in an adolescent. *Journal of the American Academy of Child and Adolescent Psychiatry, 27,* 509–513.

Surles, R., & McGurrin, M. (1987). Increased use of psychiatric emergency services by young chronic mentally ill patients. *Hospital and Community Psychiatry, 38,* 401–405.

Tavani-Petrone, C. (1986). Psychiatric emergencies. *Primary Care, 13,* 157–167.

Terr, L. (1979). Children of Chowchilla. A study of psychic trauma. *Psychoanalytic Study of the Child, 34,* 547–629.

Terr, L. (1989). Family anxiety after traumatic events. *Journal of Clinical Psychiatry, 50,* 15–19.9. Third National Incidence Study. (1996). U.S. Department of Health and Human Services. Washington, D.C.

Vander Mey, B. J. (1988). The sexual victimization of male children: A review of previous research. *Child Abuse and neglect, 12,* 61–72.

Walker, B., & Mehr, M. (1983). Adolescent suicide—A family crisis: A model for effective intervention by family therapists. *Adolescence, 18,* 285–292.

Wilkins, R. (1990). Women who sexually abuse children. *British Medical Journal, 5,* 1153–1154.

22 / Emergency Assessment and Treatment of the Child Who Has Witnessed Homicide or Violence

Spencer Eth

Throughout the world, children are exposed to scenes of interpersonal violence. In most instances, these children struggle alone to cope with their memories of bloodshed. This chapter focuses on those children who are fortunate enough to receive professional assistance. First the initial psychiatric consequences of witnessing violence is reviewed, and then a technique targeted to the emergency evaluation and treatment of these symptoms is presented.

Psychiatric Consequences of Witnessing Violence

Observing catastrophic violence causes a profound feeling of helplessness in the face of overwhelming danger, anxiety, and arousal. During the relatively brief period of the violence itself, the child may appear stunned, dazed, terrified, unresponsive, or even elated. Disorganized thoughts and behaviors, autonomic dysfunction, and psychological regression also may be characteristic, although these immediate phenomena have not been well studied contemporaneously and later accounts are prone to retrospective distortion and suppression.

Over the ensuing days, the recently traumatized child generally seems frightened and unable to adapt to novel situations and unfamiliar people (Terr, 1991). The presence of visual, and perhaps auditory, misperceptions and hallucinations reflects a transitory disturbance of reality testing. Time sense also may be compromised, with distortions in the duration and sequencing of temporal events. Some children may seek to overcome the passivity and helplessness inherent in the traumatic situation and attempt to regain a sense of control by actively re-creating some aspect of the overwhelming experience. When these reenactments take a form involving weapons or accident-prone behavior, the child may be exposed to considerable danger.

Posttraumatic dreams constitute a group of typical early responses to violence. Some children report repetitive dreams of the trauma that will resemble the intrusive, painful memories of the awake state, while others experience modified dreams or nightmares. Clinicians should be alert to 2 prototypic dream forms that can be deeply troubling to the child. In one, the child views his or her own premature death. In the second, the dream is felt to be prophetic, much as the awake child often searches for omens to predict and control the future. Over the course of the first few weeks, some traumatized children become increasingly fearful and hypervigilant of trauma-related and mundane items and of a recurrence of the violence. In severe instances the child may develop panic symptoms with anticipatory anxiety and reluctance to separate from a parent or leave the home.

Following the witnessing of violence, children may be expected to exhibit some or all of the signs and symptoms of posttraumatic stress disorder (Eth, 1990). The hallmarks of this disorder are 3 clusters of symptoms encompassing reexperiencing of the trauma, psychic numbing, and increase arousal. The trauma is repeatedly reexperienced by recurrent, intrusive, and markedly dysphoric memories and dreams of the violent incident. Young children also may exhibit repetitive, joyless play sequences in which themes or aspects of the trauma are expressed.

Psychic numbing refers to a group of related symptoms that range from an isolated inability to remember an important feature of the trauma (psychogenic amnesia) to a pervasive erosion of interest in life; in very young children this may present as a regressive loss of acquired skills. Psychic numbing also may present as constricted affect, interpersonal detachment, and pessimism about the future. In the context of violence, a depressive mood may be seen. Suppression of thoughts and feelings, as well as attempts to avoid activities or situations reminiscent of the traumatic event may be understood as common, although usually unsuccessful efforts to control the subjective distress intrinsic to the disorder.

The third diagnostic cluster of posttraumatic stress disorder symptoms are the indicators of pathologic psychophysiologic arousal. Irritability, exaggerated startle reactions, and poor concentration are readily observable, elicited by audiovisual stimuli, and can be measured in the laboratory, thereby providing an objective method of validating the disorder and monitoring its response to treatment.

Technique for Emergency Evaluation and Treatment

A focused therapeutic interview technique has been developed specifically for use with the child who has recently witnessed violence (Pynoos & Eth, 1986). This 3-stage, semistructured protocol facilitates a spontaneous and complete exploration of the child's subjective experiences, and allows for support and closure within a 2-hour time frame. Before meeting with the child, the clinician is well advised to obtain information from the referring source and family about the circumstances of the event and the child's emotional and behavioral responses in order to be alert to significant references or omissions in the child's account.

OPENING PHASE

The first or opening stage of the interview begins when the child is greeted by the therapist. It is helpful for the therapist to mention that he or she wishes to know what it was like for the child to have gone through the recent events. By so doing the focus of the interview is established, and the child is informed that he or she will not be alone in contending with the painful memories of the violence. The child is immediately given art materials and asked to draw a picture of anything at all. Children invariably participate in this assignment, as it provides a less threatening alternative to speaking directly with the therapist. When the drawing is completed, the child is asked to make up a story to accompany the picture or to explain what it is about. This free drawing task initiates the active process of therapy by countering the traumatized victim's passive, helpless stance and by producing useful clinical material for the session.

TRAUMA PHASE

The intrusive nature of the violent incident or its association is usually reflected somewhere in the drawing or story. The second stage of the interview commences when the therapist identifies this traumatic reference and links it to the child's own art product. For example, if the drawing contains the figure of a sheriff, the therapist could indicate that "It would have been so much better if a sheriff had been there to prevent the violence from happening." This comment may trigger a powerful emotional response in the child. The therapist would then seek to comfort and reassure the traumatized child that he or she will not be overwhelmed with emotion.

After the child has regained composure, the therapist can suggest that "Now is a good time to tell me everything that happened." This direction promotes a thorough recounting of the entire episode of violence, which is critical to achieving mastery of the trauma. The child may respond with a verbal description of the traumatic incident or may reenact the events in play or in art. The therapist's role in the second stage of the interview is to facilitate a full description of the violence, its antecedents, and its aftermath. The child may need to be questioned carefully in order to explore the entire series of events and its consequences. This work may be exhausting for both parties, and the child may benefit from brief rest periods or even snacks to feel adequately cared for during the emotional challenge of the session.

During the child's description of the violence, attention is refocused on the central action that embodies the continued intrusive imagery and traumatic reminders. Although an increase in anxiety may accompany this material, afterward the child is emboldened in his or her resolve to overcome these painful memories. The therapist may inquire about what the child considers was the worst moment of the violence. Often surprising details are revealed that may portend identifications with the victim or aggressor. For example, one teenager was horrified when she noticed that her mother was wearing her own dress at the time she was shotgunned to death. The child's sensory experiences during and after the violence should be addressed. This may be elicited by such questions as "What did it feel like at the time?" or "Where exactly did it hurt?" (i.e., headache, chest pain, etc.). School-age children commonly complain of somatic aches and pains in the aftermath of violence, perhaps as physical concomitants to the recurrent memories of the violence.

The child should be encouraged to verbalize any feelings of fear of harm by the perpetrator and to express any wishes for revenge. A useful observation by the therapist might be that "It can feel good to imagine getting even with the bad man now, even though it was impossible to have stopped him then." If the criminal has not been captured, then the child's apprehension as an eyewitness in danger may be appropriate and consultation with the police is advisable. The issues of violence and revenge implicitly call into question the child's own ability to control aggressive impulses. It could be important to ask the child what he or she does when angry and if that has changed since the violent event. Some children also may be absorbed with feelings of self-reproach for not having acted successfully to prevent the violence, when in fact nothing more could have been done. The therapist can assist the child in restoring a more realistic sense of self-efficacy, thereby diminishing feelings of guilt.

CLOSURE PHASE

The final or closure stage centers on the sensitive, crucial process of terminating the interview and separating from the child. It is helpful in preparation for the session's end to review and summarize the preceding discussion. By emphasizing how understandable, realistic, and universal their responses have been, children come to feel less stigmatized and isolated and more willing to accept support from others. It may be convenient to return to the child's drawing or story in order to underscore a point or to articulate the continuity of the session. Some children will feel relieved by knowing what is expectable as they progress through the course of a posttraumatic syndrome. For instance, a child may be told that "Since the violence/loud noises make you jittery, but that this uncomfortable feeling should decrease over time."

Contrary to the usual practice of psychotherapy, it may be valuable to compliment children on their bravery during the violence and their courage in sharing their thoughts and feelings in the session. These children's beleaguered self-esteem needs support, and they usually swell with pride upon hearing these kind and truthful words. Children should be informed as to whether they will be seen again. However, even if the interview is a one-time consultation, it is advisable to hand the child a business card or telephone number and provide assurance that the therapist can be reached if necessary. Children rarely call but do treasure the knowledge of the therapist's availability and concern.

The step-by-step narration of the interview technique is not meant to suggest a rigid structure; rather, the format is intended to allow for a natural flow of material following as closely as possible the child's lead. What is most important is that the child be encouraged to confront directly the violence in the session secure in the knowledge that it can be done successfully. It is a countertransference-induced error to collude with the child's resistance to explore the traumatic source of the anxiety.

DEVELOPMENTAL FRAMEWORK

Notable differences in the phenomenology of psychic trauma according to the child's developmental phase influence the conduct of the clinical interview (Eth & Pynoos, 1994). The capacity to encode and retrieve a verbal memory of a traumatic experience begins between 30 and 36 months of age. Prior to that time infants may react to traumatic stimuli, but the ensuing symptoms are nonspecific, and confirmation of their etiology by interview is doubtful. Preschool-age children are particularly helpless when confronted by great danger and will readily respond to parental anxiety with an intensification of their own distress. More than any other age group, preschool children initially can appear as withdrawn, subdued, or even mute. Many children maintain a stance of silent aloofness, refusing to speak of the traumatic event except to trusted persons. In the session, very young children may find modeling clay, collage, or puppets more suitable creative media than paper and crayons.

The school-age child exhibits a wider range of cognitive, behavioral, and emotional responses to psychic trauma. In the cognitive domain, these children may display a dullness and functional impairment of intelligence that can be evident in a decline in school performance. Some school-age children spend considerable time discussing the fine details of the traumatic incident. By so doing, they may be temporarily protected from feelings of anxiety and fear. This obsessional defense can be appreciated when it leads to an unemotional, journalistic account in the interview. The reverse is also possible, where children remain in a perpetual state of anxious arousal, as if to prepare for imminent danger. This hypervigilance may permit the children to replace memories of the actual trauma with self-initiated fantasies of some future threat. School-age children display a diversity of behavioral alterations in the aftermath of trauma. Parents and teachers complain that these children seem both different and inconsistent, and these changes can markedly affect peer relationships and their own self-esteem.

The manifestations of psychic trauma during adolescence begin to resemble the adult syndrome (Eth, 1989). However, teenagers are especially prone to embark on a period of acting-out behavior characterized by truancy, sexual indiscretion, substance abuse, and delinquency. These adolescents adopt a rebellious attitude that is seemingly impervious to intervention by authority figures or the examiner. Because of their access to automobiles and weapons, the combination of impaired impulse control, poor judgment, and reenactment behavior can be life-threatening. Adolescents may explain their use of illicit drugs as a way to relieve the trauma induced dysphoria. They also may engage in self-destructive activities in order to expiate feelings of guilt. Adolescents may feel self-conscious in a playroom setting and may prefer to dispense with drawings and stories.

FAMILY EFFECTS

The child's present life concerns should be assessed during the session. Violence can result in disruptions in family relationships, changes in home or school, notoriety from media coverage, and ongoing involvement in legal proceedings. All of these reality-based issues will contribute to the child's distress and complicate the path to recovery. The most salient of these life events is major change in family structure and composition.

Homicide is an act that results in the death of a person. As such the child witness may suffer grief for a lost parent or close family member. It is widely accepted that children display a range of grief responses that vary as a function of maturity, personality, and cultural milieu. The tasks of mourning for the child, as for the adult, are to accept the loss through reality testing and tolerate the pain of grief, which may involve feelings of sadness, anger, guilt, confusion, and somatic discomfort. The trauma of witnessing a violent death can impair grief work and increase the likelihood of pathological grief. Under these circumstances, it is critical that the child be helped to master the traumatic memories associated with viewing the homicide so that mourning can proceed without compromise.

Interpersonal violence inevitably raises the issue of human accountability. Although some children prefer to refer to the incident as an accident, there usually lurks an awareness and conflict over responsibility. The therapist may wonder aloud, "What could make someone do such a thing?" When the perpetrator is a stranger, it is easier for the child to assign blame than in cases of intrafamilial violence. Under these circumstances the child may feel ambivalent over divided loyalties to both victim and assailant, and the assignment of responsibility may vary during the session. Young witnesses to family violence often are confused, frightened, and in need of protection (Hurley & Jaffe, 1990). The therapist can help the child distinguish unacceptable violence from angry arguments that may be normative ways of resolving family conflict. It is sometimes necessary to address basic safety skills to prepare the child for future family crises. Explicit discussion about the possibility of having the child telephone the police as needed may be in order.

DISPOSITIONAL ISSUES

Witnessing homicide or major violence has a potentially serious psychopathological impact for the child. However, most children will respond with considerable relief to a brief therapeutic intervention predicated on a thorough exploration of the traumatic event and its emotional consequences. The clinical interview is also useful to identify children and adolescents who exhibit severe symptoms of posttraumatic stress disorder, major depression, and other critical psychiatric conditions, including suicidal or homicidal ideation and substance abuse. These children require further psychiatric services (Pynoos & Nader, 1988). In those cases in which the child is referred to another clinician for individual psychotherapy, the interview protocol should facilitate the child's subsequent entry into treatment.

For children whose lives have been disrupted by major episodes of intrafamilial violence, close attention to the adequacy of care in the home is indicated. The evaluation of the family milieu is a separate task that may require the assistance of other professionals. Surely the clinician would wish to know at the least whether the remaining caregivers will be able to provide a supportive and holding environment for the child over time. Contacts with social service agencies are important components of any therapeutic intervention.

The emergency assessment and treatment of the child who has witnessed homicide or violence is not intended to, nor could it ever, erase the painful memories of the trauma, but it can help to minimize lasting distress and disability. Further, with enhanced trauma mastery, these children will be empowered to function as their own advocates so that their needs and interests become known and are met.

REFERENCES

Eth, S. (1989). The adolescent witness to homicide. In E. P. Benedek & D. G. Cornell (Eds.), *Juvenile homicide* (pp. 87–113). Washington, DC: American Psychiatric Press.

Eth, S. (1990). Post-traumatic stress disorder in childhood. In M. Hersen & C. G. Last (Eds.), *Handbook of child and adult psychopathology* (pp. 263–274). New York: Pergamon Press.

Eth, S., & Pynoos, R. S. (1994). Children who witness the homicide of a parent. *Psychiatry, 57,* 287–306.

Hurley, D. J., & Jaffe, P. (1990). Children's observations of violence: II. Clinical implications for children's mental health professionals. *Canadian Journal of Psychiatry, 35,* 471–476.

Pynoos, R. S., & Eth, S. (1986). Witness to violence: The child interview. *Journal of the American Academy of Child Psychiatry, 25,* 306–319.

Pynoos, R. S., & Nader, K. (1988). Psychological first aid and treatment approach to children exposed to community violence. *Journal of Traumatic Stress, 1,* 445–473.

Terr, L. C. (1991). Childhood traumas: An outline and overview. *American Journal of Psychiatry, 148,* 10–20.

23 / Emergency Assessment and Response to Child Physical and Sexual Abuse

Sandra Kaplan and Elizabeth Pinner

Child abuse is a significant health problem in the United States. Caregivers must know how to proceed when a physically and/or sexually abused child comes for help in an emergency situation.

Definitions

The U.S. Department of Health and Human Services (1988) has provided definitions for child physical and sexual abuse. Physical abuse is defined as the nonaccidental physical harm to a child under 18 years old, causing injury or substantial risk of death, disfigurement, impairment of bodily functioning, or other serious or moderate physical injury. This may include loss of consciousness, excessive burns, cessation of breathing, broken bones, bruises, and other observable forms of pain for 48 hours. Sexual abuse is defined as the sexual assault of a child under 18 years old resulting in harm or injury by: penile penetration of the genitals, mouth, or anus; genital contact molestation (e.g., fondling); pornographic depiction of the child for financial gain; or the prostitution of a child.

Assessment of Sexual Abuse

The main purpose of the evaluation is to determine whether abuse has occurred and whether the child is in need of protection, physical health treatment, and/or psychiatric treatment. Clinical guidelines for this assessment have been developed by the American Academy of Child and Adolescent Psychiatry (AACP, 1990). These guidelines suggest the following procedures.

When interviewing the child, the optimal condition is to do so in an uninterrupted, private, and calm environment without other family members present. As the perpetrator is most often a close relative, privacy may help to assist disclosure. It is important to keep the number of interviews with the child to a minimum. It is critical to avoid leading questions so as not to interfere with judicial case proceedings. The interviewing clinician should be an experienced child or adolescent psychiatrist or psychologist with a background or knowledge base in child development, family dynamics associated with sexual abuse, and the effects of sexual abuse on children; he or she must be willing to testify in court.

There are several useful methods for interviewing the child victim. For children, a doll's house with dolls representing the various family members may shed light on the family's sleeping arrangements. Anatomically detailed, racially specific dolls are helpful in facilitating the disclosure of possible sexual abuse, and the use of toy telephones between interviewer and child also may aid in disclosure. (This technique is helpful with preschool children.) Providing drawing materials to adolescents and preadolescents is facilitating. Often drawings by a sexually abused child or adolescent are very revealing for the clinician and may show sexual immaturity or hypermaturity, which has been found to be more frequent in sexually abused than non–sexually abused children (Aiosa-Karpas, Karpas, Pelcovitz, & Kaplan, 1991).

Several elements are of import when gathering historical information. During assessment, it is necessary to:

- Determine the child's developmental history
- Note any history of abuse or other traumas
- Take the relevant medical history
- Discovery any history of any abuse of parents during their childhoods
- Determine the family's attitudes toward sex
- Take a psychiatric history of parents and child
- Make a child cognitive assessment
- Determine allegiances to respective parents
- Discover any changes in child behavior
- Assess the child's credibility (i.e., appropriate language, appropriate anxiety, consistency of report over time, behavioral changes consistent with abuse)
- Review previous reports (e.g., school, medical, police, and any information from others) (AACP, 1990)

Physical Examination for Sexual Abuse

The physical examination should be performed by a physician known to the child, if possible. If this is not possible, the examining physician should be a pediatric gynecologist with special training. With regard to forensic evidence, the examination should take place within 72 hours of the reported abuse. To reduce the trauma of the physical exam, genitalia and anal examinations should be done in the context of the overall physical examination and a known, trusted, and understanding adult should be present with the child during the physical examination (AACP, 1990).

Guidelines developed by the American Academy of Pediatrics (1991) for the physical examination of sexual abuse include special attention paid to growth parameters and sexual development of the child and the documentation of all evidence of trauma. Particular areas of concern are the mouth, breasts, genitals, perineal region, buttocks, and anus, as these are typically areas involved in sexual activity. Reporting sexually transmitted diseases is also suggested. Common sexually transmitted diseases associated with pre-

pubertal sexual abuse (if not perinatally acquired) are gonorrhea, syphilis, chlamydia, condylomata acuminatum, herpes1 (genital) without clear indication of a history of autoinoculation, and herpes2. The guidelines suggest medical follow-up for bacterial vaginosis and candida albicans.

The following have been found to be consistent with, but not necessarily diagnostic of, sexual abuse in females: chafing, abrasions, or bruising of the inner thighs and genitalia; scarring, tears, or distortion of the hymen or labia minora; scarring or other injury to the posterior fourchette; and enlargement of the hymenal opening. Male children should be examined for bruises, scars, chafing, bite marks, and discharge in the thighs, penis, and scrotum (American Academy of Pediatrics, 1991).

For both the vaginal and anal examination, the position of the child (supine, lateral, knee-chest) and the amount of time taken may influence the anatomy. Additionally, the presence of bruises around the anus, in males and females, and anal dilation need to be noted (American Academy of Pediatrics, 1991).

Crisis Intervention for Sexual Abuse

In the case of child sexual abuse, the assessment of whether the abuse was incest or extrafamilial is critical, for crisis intervention differs for the two types of abuse. When the sexual abuse has occurred in the family, intervention includes protection from future abuse—usually the government agency responsible for child protection requires the perpetrator to leave the home—support of the child and family (nonoffending members) by facilitating care for acute psychiatric problems of alleged perpetrators, and monitoring the child's suicide potential. In addition, linkages with the government agencies managing protection is essential in case management to assure child protection. In the case of extrafamilial abuse, support for the child and parents without separation of child from parents is vital. Furthermore, it is important to prepare the child and family to work with law enforcement and legal (particularly district attorneys) and social agencies. In extrafamilial abuse particularly, nonleading questions by clinicians and issues of the use of treatment groups for children may impact on legal prosecution of the case.

Assessment of Physical Abuse

When interviewing the child for possible physical abuse, the history taking needs to include specific questions regarding the way in which the family resolves conflict, disciplinary practices, and the origin of injuries.

The American Medical Association (1992) has suggested guidelines for gathering historical information from the possible child abuse victim. The clinician needs to establish an empathic, trusting relationship with the child. In so doing, whoever is interviewing the child should do so in a private space (but without the child being left unattended in a room), without the presence of possibly abusive caregivers. The physician should sit close to the child, explain the purpose of the interview clearly and in age-appropriate language, avoid any display of horror or shock, remind the child constantly that he or she is not to be blamed, and use, whenever possible, the child's own language.

Physical Examination for Physical Abuse

The American Medical Association (1992) provides diagnostic and treatment guidelines for child physical abuse. According to these guidelines, physical signs of abuse include: bruises and welts of the face, ears, eyes; neck, head, lips, mouth, trunk, back, buttocks, thighs, or extremities; soft tissue forming regular patterns (i.e., of the object used in the abuse); multiple body tissue; burns from cigarettes or cigars (on soles, palms, back, or buttocks, in particular); immersion burns (stocking- or glove-shaped on extremities, doughnut-shaped on buttocks or genitals); burns with patterns resembling electrical appliances (e.g., iron, grill); lacerations; abrasions; fractures of the nose, ribs, skull, long bones, or facial structure (may be in various stages of healing); rope burns to ankles, neck, torso, wrists, mouth, lips, gums, eyes, palate, ears, or external genitals; retinal hemorrhage; ruptured blood vessels; kidney, bladder, or pancreatic injury; intestinal perforation; ruptured liver or spleen; central nervous system injuries including subdural hematoma (i.e., from blunt trauma or violent shaking); subarachnoid hemorrhage (also reflective of shaking) (Council on Scientific Affairs, 1985). Furthermore, "Characteristically, the injuries are more severe than those that could be reasonably attributed to the claimed cause" (Council on Scientific Affairs 1985).

Photographs may be helpful as evidence. When possible, photographs should be taken before medical treatment has been administered. It is helpful to hold a small object (e.g., a coin) next to the injured area so as to better indicate the size of the injury. Color film should be used and two pictures of each area should be taken. The child's face should appear in at least one picture, and all should be marked with the child's name, date, location of injury, and the name of the person who took the photograph and any witnesses present (American Medical Association, 1992).

Crisis Intervention for Physical Abuse

As in sexual abuse intervention, assessment of abuse and of mental status, protection from further abuse, and intervention for acute psychiatric disorders of both victim and other family members need to occur quickly. Suicide risk around the time of disclosure is an important concern, particularly with adolescent physical abuse and sexual abuse victims (Deykin, 1989).

Supportive interventions are needed to allay anxiety about separations required for child protection and about loyalty conflicts about family that surround disclosure. In addition, acute intervention with family members is indicated to avoid victim scapegoating surrounding abuse disclosure.

In addition to treating the victim's and family's acute physical and mental disorders, crisis intervention strategies require knowledge of referral resources. Facilitation is also necessary if referral for continued mental health treatment and abuse specific related advocacy is needed. Adolescent and child mental health treatment resource lists and phone numbers need to be readily available at case emergency management sites. Phone numbers and contact persons of pertinent child protection agency, law enforcement, legal resources, and abuse advocacy groups such as the local coalitions against child abuse and domestic violence also should be readily available.

The need for quick access to referral resources for treatment and other case management pertains to both the emergency management of child and adolescent sexual and physical abuse.

REFERENCES

Aiosa-Karpas, C., Karpas, R., Pelcovitz, D., & Kaplan, S. (1991). Gender identification and sex role attribution in sexually abused adolescent females. *Journal of the American Academy of Child and Adolescent Psychiatry, 30* (2), 226–271.

American Academy of Child and Adolescent Psychiatry. (1990, December).

American Academy of Pediatrics, Committee on Child Abuse and Neglect. (1991). *Guidelines for the evaluation of sexual abuse of children.*

American Medical Association. (1992). *Diagnostic and treatment guidelines on child physical abuse and neglect.*

Deykin, E. Y. (1989). The utility of emergency room data for record linkage in the study of adolescent suicide behavior. *Suicide and Life-Threatening Behavior, 19,* 90–98.

U.S. Department of Health and Human Services. (1988). *Study of the national incidence and prevalence of child abuse and neglect.*

24 / Emergency Assessment and Intervention with a Child or Adolescent Who Has Experienced a Catastrophe

Sherry L. Thaggard

According to *Webster's Third New International Dictionary,* "catastrophe" is defined as "a momentous, tragic, usually sudden event marked by effects ranging from extreme misfortune to utter overthrow or ruin." Natural disasters such as earthquakes, tornadoes, hurricanes, and floods, and human-induced calamities such as sniper attacks, kidnapping, and structural collapse are catastrophes that profoundly affect children and adolescents who experience them. This chapter describes common reactions of preschoolers, latency-age children, and adolescents to catastrophic events, discusses factors that influence a child's reaction to catastrophe, and outlines strategies for emergency intervention.

Common Reactions of Children to Catastrophe

The most common short-term reactions of children across a range of disastrous events include sleep problems and nightmares, persistent thoughts of the event, belief that another such event will occur, conduct disturbances, hyper-alertness with exaggerated startle response, deliberate avoidance of situations and stimuli symbolic of the event, and developmentally regressive behaviors (Frederick, 1985). Terr (1991) describes 4 particularly significant symptoms characteristic of traumatized children regardless of their age or of the time elapsed since the event:

1. Vividly visualized or otherwise repeatedly perceived memories of the event that are stimulated most strongly by reminders of the event but also may occur unbidden, when the child is at leisure.
2. Repetitive behaviors, including posttraumatic play, which is defined by the players as "fun" and is grim, long-lasting, and contagious to other children, and behavioral reenactments that repeat aspects of the traumatic event without the element of fun.
3. Trauma-specific fears, some of which gradually dissipate through spontaneous desensitization and some of which tend to linger into adulthood.
4. Changed attitudes about people, life, and the future, including a sense of profound vulnerability and a view of the future as severely limited.

Although a number of symptoms are common to children of any age who have experienced a catastrophe, preschool children, latency-age children, and adolescents may present distinct clinical pictures on assessment.

PRESCHOOL CHILDREN

The security of preschool children is based on a predictable routine carried out by dependable adults in a stable environment. When catastrophe disrupts this familiar world, the children likely will exhibit emotional distress related to the degree of disruption and the severity of the trauma. Because children in this age group generally lack the verbal and conceptual skills to cope effectively with overwhelming stress, symptoms are commonly nonverbal/behavioral manifestations of their anxiety, fear, and confusion. Excessive clinging and separation anxiety can be expected immediately following the trauma, as can sleep disturbances (Frederick, 1985), which may include nightmares, night terrors, inability to sleep alone or without a light, and frequent awakening. Regressive behaviors are prominent in this age group, including crying and whining, thumbsucking, bedwetting, loss of toilet skills, and an increase in dependent behaviors, such as wanting to be dressed or fed by an adult. Young children commonly experience a resurgence of old, mundane fears (darkness, animals, strangers) as well as new catastrophe-related ones. Psychosomatic complaints and excessive startle reactions also are reported frequently.

Even very young children retain accurate behavioral memories, apparently based on visual memories of traumatic events. These will be manifested in posttraumatic play and reenactment as the children attempt to master the associated anxiety. Children under age 2½ to 3 years at the time of the trauma will be able to verbalize their experiences only partially or not at all. However, when traumatized after that age, children are able to store and retrieve verbal memories of the traumatic event. Single, short, surprising traumas are most likely to be remembered verbally, and girls tend to better verbalize traumatic experiences earlier than boys (Terr, 1988).

LATENCY-AGE CHILDREN

Fears and anxieties are prominent symptoms among latency-age children and may include reality-based fears, reflecting an awareness of the danger to self, loved ones, and environment, and unrealistic fears that may seem unrelated to the catastrophe. Sleep disturbances and nightmares are common, as are regressive behaviors, including bedwetting, excessive dependency behaviors, and separation anxiety. Children may be irritable, sad, or disobedient, and complain of psycho-

somatic symptoms such as headache and nausea. Loss of pets and prized possessions may be particularly traumatic for children of this age group.

Children of latency age also experience reactions pertinent to school and peers. These may take the form of school refusal, distractibility, poor concentration, declining academic performance, and behavior problems. In the attempt to master traumatic experiences in their concrete cognitive style, children of this age group may choose topics such as natural phenomena, weather, and safety precautions as topics for school reports and science projects. With peers, these children may withdraw, become aggressive, or engage one another in posttraumatic play.

ADOLESCENTS

Adolescents typically are coping with internal physiologic changes, struggling to achieve independence from family, and attempting to establish a separate identity in the outside world. A catastrophe may threaten adolescents' progress in these various tasks. It may provoke fears related to physical injury, bodily function, and personal appearance as well as those concerning loss of family members. Disaster may disrupt peer relationships and slow emancipation from the family because of the crisis-induced need for the family to function as a tighter unit. Many adolescents are capable of abstract thought and may dwell on the existential and philosophical aspects of catastrophe to varying degrees.

The clinical picture of adolescents traumatized by catastrophe frequently includes a combination of physical complaints, anxiety symptoms, and changes in social behavior. Sleep disorders, which may include insomnia or hypersomnia and nightmares, are frequent problems, as are changes in appetite and psychosomatic symptoms. Catastrophe-specific fears and more generalized anxieties are common, and regressive fears are seen occasionally. Adolescents may describe feelings of anger, sadness, apathy, and isolation. There may be school problems, both academic and behavioral, and a decline in previously responsible behavior.

In situations of communitywide disaster, adolescents seem particularly vulnerable to the loss of communality. Following the Buffalo Creek, Ohio flood disaster, adolescents often seemed compelled to choose between rebellious predelinquent behavior and compliant social withdrawal (Newman, 1976). A study of the psychological impact of the Mount St. Helen's volcanic eruption revealed posteruption increases in juvenile criminal bookings, vandalism/malicious mischief charges, and charges of disorderly conduct over baseline date obtained prior to the disaster (Adams and Adams, 1984).

Factors Affecting Reaction to Catastrophe

A number of factors besides developmental level influence children's reaction to a catastrophe. The most significant of these is the degree of exposure to the traumatic event. Exposure may include physical proximity, life threat, personal injury, witnessing an injury or death, loss of a family member, and property and financial loss.

Following a fatal sniper attack on a Los Angeles elementary school playground, Pynoos et al. (1987) found that posttraumatic stress symptoms increased as the degree of exposure increased. One month after the event, the most frequent reaction of children who were on the playground during the attack was severe posttraumatic stress disorder; the modal reaction for children who were in the school building was moderate posttraumatic stress disorder; for those not at school, no such disorder was found. Of particular note was the effect proximity to the violence had on the children's memories of the event. In describing the attack, the most endangered group reduced their own life threat by not mentioning their own injuries, by increasing their distance from the injured or dead, by not mentioning moments of direct danger, or by placing themselves in a safe location. The least threatened group, however, tended to increase their life threat in the telling by placing themselves closer to the danger or by bringing the danger closer to them. Guilt feelings and knowing a child who was killed by the sniper were associated with increased posttraumatic symptoms. Fourteen months after the attack, however, the level of exposure remained the primary predictor of ongoing posttraumatic stress reactions in these children (Nader, Pynoos, Fairbanks & Frederick, 1990). The degree of exposure has been found to be significantly associated with psychiatric morbidity in studies of natural disasters as well (Burke, Moccia, Borus, & Burns, 1986; Newman, 1976; Shaw et al, 1995). Terr (1979, 1983) studied the 26 children who endured the Chowchilla school bus kidnapping and found the incidence of psychic trauma to be 100%. Thus it seems that given a directly experienced trauma of sufficient severity, any child would suffer psychic trauma.

Another variable that affects children's reaction to disaster is that of human accountability. Posttraumatic stress reactions are more severe and persistent following tragedies perceived as manmade than purely natural disasters; this is particularly true of acts of violence (Pynoos et al., 1987; Terr, 1979).

Predictability of the disaster is also an influential factor. In the aftermath of Hurricane Hugo, Austin (1991) found very few cases of posttraumatic stress disorder, as defined by the third edition of the *Diagnostic and Statistical Manual of Mental Disorders Revised*. This finding contrasts with those following unpredictable disasters, such as the San Francisco earthquake (Gilette, 1991) and the Huntsville Alabama tornado of 1989 (Thaggard, 1991). The ability to prepare for oncoming disaster allows for a greater sense of mastery over the experience and less severe subsequent morbidity.

Chronicity of the trauma is another factor pertinent to children's response. Terr (1991) has labeled more typical, unexpected, single-blow trauma Type I and the multiple or long-standing traumas Type II. Type I traumas do not appear to breed massive denial, psychic numbing, self-anesthesia, or personality problems as do the multiple, long-standing Type II traumas. The defenses and coping mechanisms called into play in Type II traumatic conditions may result in profound and lasting character changes in children. Cross-over conditions may occur when one blow creates a series of traumas, such as traumatic disfigurement or disability.

Another major factor affecting children's response to catastrophe is their parents' reaction. In World War II in England, Anna Freud and Burlingham (1943) found that parental fears precipitated more emotional difficulty for children than the explosion of bombs. Following an Australian brushfire, McFarlane (1987) found mother's responses to the disaster were better predictors of posttraumatic phenomena in children than the children's direct exposure to the disaster. This was attributed to maternal preoccupation with the disaster, a more overprotective parenting style, and changed family functioning.

Diagnosis

In the aftermath of catastrophe, children and adolescents may meet the diagnostic criteria for any of a number of disorders. Frederick (1985) found in a study of children exposed to disaster the following diagnoses to be most common, in order of relative frequency of occurrence.

1. Avoidant disorder of childhood and adolescence
2. Separation anxiety disorder
3. Sleep-terror disorder
4. Overanxious disorder
5. Simple phobia
6. Agoraphobia without panic
7. Posttraumatic stress disorder, acute
8. Posttraumatic stress disorder, chronic
9. Attention deficit disorder with hyperactivity
10. Attention deficit disorder, residual type

Different exposure factors have been found to correlate with specific forms of morbidity (Pynoos et al., 1987). The experience of personal life threat and the witnessing of injury or death of others correlate highly with the incidence of posttraumatic stress disorder. The death of a significant other is correlated with the presence of an adjustment reaction or single depressive episode. Sudden separation from a significant other or worry about a significant other is correlated highly with continued anxiety regarding the whereabouts and safety of significant others.

As previously discussed, the more severe and directly experienced the trauma, the more likely the diagnosis of posttraumatic stress disorder. Although there is no separate set of criteria to diagnose that disorder in children, a number of references specific to children are included in the fourth edition of the *Diagnostic and Statistical Manual of Mental Disorders*. Repetitive play may replace recurrent, intrusive recollections of trauma, and reenactment may be noted as a form of reexperiencing the trauma. A sense of foreshortened future has specific applicability to children and adolescents as they may believe their life will not extend to adulthood. The frequently seen adult symptoms of flashbacks and numbing of responsiveness are not typically seen in children. Children report reexperiencing trauma in the form of dreams and the intrusion of a specific vivid image more commonly than true flashbacks. Rather than feeling numb, they may complain of lessened interest in play, feeling more distant from their parents, and the desire not to be aware of their feelings (Pynoos & Nader, 1988).

Intervention

In the aftermath of a catastrophe, it may be difficult to determine how best to allocate limited psychiatric resources. A working strategy, based on triage principles, should first address the needs of those with the greatest degree of exposure and the highest likelihood of developing significant trauma-related symptoms (Pynoos & Nader, 1988). Often in situations of major disaster, those most affected are too overwhelmed with the details of survival to seek psychiatric help in the early days after the event. Therefore, community outreach in the initial postdisaster phase is essential, and might include mental health workers in disaster aid stations, shelters, hospitals, churches, and schools (Thaggard, 1991; Ponton & Bryant, 1991). During this time a great deal of media attention will be focused on the catastrophe, and a psychiatric perspective almost certainly will be welcome. The media can provide invaluable opportunities to educate the public and disseminate information about programs and resources (Cole, 1991).

Programs during the outreach phase might include a disaster hotline staffed by mental health professionals (Blaustein, 1991) and a series of catastrophe-related talks in the community. These talks should provide a vocabulary to describe reactions to the disaster and to legitimize and normalize responses, and encourage open expression of feelings in the community (Austin, 1991). When possible, larger, more general groups should be addressed first, then smaller, more focused groups, then individuals, weeding out along the way those whose needs can be met with less intensive services (Thaggard, 1991).

One intervention that can be particularly effective in reaching children is consultation to schools. Such consultation can include planning a comprehensive program with administrators, meeting with parent groups, providing guidance and therapeutic approaches to teachers and counselors, and working directly with the children, individually and in groups (Ponton & Bryant, 1991; Pynoos & Nader, 1988; Thaggard, 1991).

A variety of treatment techniques have been used with children in catastrophic situations, most of which can be adapted to group or individual settings. Necessary for each technique is the presence of a supportive adult and the creation of a safe environment permitting the reworking of the trauma and the reduction of anxieties (Frederick, 1985). Specific techniques include play therapy, role play, educational sessions, and the use of drawings. Frederick (1985) reports that for therapeutic and diagnostic purposes, it is important to help children reach the point that they can produce a drawing directly related to the catastrophe. They then should be encouraged to discuss the drawing, promoting catharsis and desensitization. However, when severe posttraumatic stress disorder is present, more intensive incident-specific treatment is necessary. It should involve reenactment of the trauma, either literally in vivo or through imagery, allowing for clarification of events, expression of conflicting emotions, working through of fears, and eventual mastery of the specific trauma the child experienced.

Following a devastating earthquake in Italy, Galante and Foa (1986) devised a small-group treatment program for elementary school students consisting of discussion, drawing, education, role play, and reenactment of the earthquake in a model of their community. After one year of monthly sessions, they found a dramatic drop in earthquake-related fears from initial levels and as compared to children who received no intervention.

Finally, the psychiatrist faced with a catastrophic situation should take advantage of organizational resources such as the American Academy of Child and Adolescent Psychiatry, the American Psychiatric Association, and local psychiatric associations. These groups frequently can provide names of psychiatrists who have dealt with similar situations as well as pertinent literature and handouts.

REFERENCES

Adams, P. R., & Adams, G. R. (1984). Mount Saint Helen's ashfall: Evidence for disaster stress reaction. *American Psychology, 39,* 252–260.

Austin, L. S. (1991). In the wake of Hugo: The role of the psychiatrist. *Psychiatric Annals, 21* (9), 520–524.

Blaustein, M. (1991). Earthquake hotline. *Psychiatric Annals, 21* (9), 533–535.

Burke, J. D., Moccia, P., Borus, J., & Burns, B. (1986). Emotional distress in fifth grade children ten months after a natural disaster. *Journal of the American Academy of Child Psychiatry, 25* (4), 536–541.

Cole, A. R. (1991). The San Francisco earthquake and the media. *Psychiatric Annals, 21* (9), 536–538.

Frederick, C. J. (1985). Children Traumatized by Catastrophic Situations. *Post Traumatic Stress Disorder and Children.* Spencer, E., Pynoos, R. S., eds. Washington, D.C.: American Psychiatric Press.

Freud, A., & Burlingham, D. T. (1943). *War and children.* New York: Medical War Books.

Galante, R. & Foa, D. (1986). An Epidemiological Study of Psychic Trauma and Treatment Effectiveness for Children after a Natural Disaster. *Journal of the American Academy of Child Psychiatry, 25* (3), 357–363.

Gilette, J. R. (1991). Santa Cruz county: Report from the epicenter. *Psychiatric Annals, 21* (9), 550–552.

McFarlane, A. C. (1987). Post traumatic phenomena in a longitudinal study of children following a natural disaster. *Journal of the American Academy of Child and Adolescent Psychiatry, 26* (5), 764–769.

Nader, K., Pynoos, R., Fairbanks, L., & Frederick, C. (1990). Children's PTSD reactions one year after a sniper attack at their school. *American Journal of Psychiatry, 147,* 1526–1530.

Newman, C. J. (1976). Children of disaster: Clinical observations at Buffalo Creek. *American Journal of Psychiatry, 133* (3), 306–312.

Ponton, L. E., & Bryant, E. C. (1991). After the earthquake: Organizing to respond to children and adolescents. *Psychiatric Annals, 21* (9), 539–546.

Pynoos, R. S., Frederick, C., Nader, K., Arroyo, W., Steinberg, A., Eth, S., Nurex, F., & Fairbanks, L. (1987). Life threat and post traumatic stress in school-age children. *Archives of General Psychiatry, 44,* 1057–1063.

Pynoos, R. S., & Nader, K. (1988). Psychological first aid and treatment approach to children exposed to community violence: Research implications. *Journal of Traumatic Stress, 1* (4), 445–473.

Pynoos, R. S., & Nader, K. (1989). Children's memory and proximity to violence. *Journal of the American Academy of Child and Adolescent Psychiatry, 28* (2), 236–241.

Shaw, J., Applegate, B., Tanner, S., Perez, D., Rothe, E., Campo-Bowen, A. & Lahey, B. (1995). Psychological Effects of Hurricane Andrew on an Elementary School Population. *Journal of the American Academy of Child and Adolescent Psychiatry, 34,* (9), 1185–1192.

Terr, L. (1979). Children of Chowchilla. *Psychoanalytic Study of the Child, 34,* 547–623.

Terr, L. (1982). Chowchilla revisited. *American Journal of Psychiatry, 140,* 1543–1550.

Terr, L. (1988). What Happens to Early Memories of Trauma? A Study of Twenty Children Under Age Five at the Time of Documented Traumatic Events. *Journal of the American Academy of Child and Adolescent Psychiatry, 27,* 1:96–104.

Terr, L. C. (1991). Childhood traumas: An outline and overview. *American Journal of Psychiatry, 148,* 10–20.

Thaggard, S. L. (1991). The Huntsville tornado of 1989: A psychiatrist's perspective. *Psychiatric Annals, 21* (9), 553–555.

25 / Suicide Assessment in Child and Adolescent Emergency Psychiatry

Marilyn B. Benoit

Suicide in children and adolescents is very dis-tressing. The traumatic experience for the parents and families left behind, the loss of young life with the potential it represents, the sense of never quite comprehending why a young person elects suicide as a preferred alternative, all leave the av-erage person very troubled. For those of us who are child and adolescent psychiatrists, the prob-lem of youth suicide is very troublesome because upon us falls the difficult task of making scientific sense out of an issue that is so very complex as well as making rapid clinical assessments and decisions that affect outcomes in our patients. Pfeffer (1986) cautions clinicians to be aware of their feel-ings about death and about suicidality in children before doing psychiatric evaluations on children. Researchers and clinicians in child and adolescent psychiatry have made serious and diligent efforts to understand the psychological, biological, famil-ial, social, and environmental factors related to suicide and suicidality in the young. This chap-ter is not intended to address the entire field of youth suicidology. Rather, the goal is to discuss the assessment of suicidality in the clinical set-ting when a youngster presents in a psychiatric emergency.

Brief Overview of Statistics

Over the past 20 years the suicide rate has shown an increasing trend in the latency-age and adoles-cent populations. Pfeffer (1990) reported that in the 5- to 14-year-old population, there was a 100% increase in the rate of completed suicides from 1979 to 1986, from 0.4 per 100,000 in 1979 to 0.8 per 100,000 in 1986. According to Danto (1979), . . . children between the ages of 10 and 19 have become a high risk suicide group. By 1990 children between 15 and 19 years showed an increased rate of suicide to 11.1 per 100,000. Shaffer (1974) reported that "between 7 and 10 percent of all referrals to child psychiatric clinics

are for threatened or attempted suicide, and . . . such referrals form an even larger proportion of cases seen as psychiatric emergencies" (p. 275). The latter claim is indeed supported by the data analysis of Shafii, Whittinghill, and Sealey (1979) of their 994 emergency child and adolescent pa-tients; 34.2% of the patients presented with sui-cidal, self-destructive, or marked depressive behavior. Ellison, Hughes, and White (1989) re-ported that in their sample of patients of all ages presenting to their psychiatric emergency service, "suicide attempts, gestures and ideation and self-destructive behavior" were twice as common among adolescents as in adults. What these data tell us is that suicide in the young is a significant problem in society.

Evaluation

All children and adolescents seen for a psychiatric evaluation should be assessed for suicidality as a routine part of a mental status examination. For those above 8 years of age, the Kovacs Child De-pression Inventory is a very useful and sensitive instrument that can be administered in a short time. This inventory, of course, is to be used as part of, not instead of, a comprehensive clinical evaluation. In fact, the answers to the items can provide a stimulus for further clinical exploration with youngsters who are somewhat difficult to draw out. As in all evaluations, the standard fam-ily, medical, social, school, and personal history must be obtained. The mental status exam, an as-sessment of the premorbid coping skills, plus an evaluation of the patient's psychosocial environ-ment must be performed. In suicidal patients, the psychiatrist must rigorously evaluate precipitating events, specific risk factors, and protective factors (Garmezy, 1983; Brent, 1995) in order to make an informed clinical decision as to the likelihood of the patients following through on a suicide threat in the near term.

Precipitants of Suicidal Behavior

The most frequently identified precipitant of suicidality is a family-related crisis (Ellison et al., 1989; Gutstein, Rudd, Graham, & Rayha, 1988), which often may be disciplinary in nature (Shaffer, 1974). In a study done at Children's National Medical Center in Washington, D.C. (Lyon, Benoit, Getson, Walsh, & O'Donnell, 1990) where data systematically collected (Lyon, 1987, Appendix A) on African American children and adolescents presenting with suicidality to the emergency room, it was concluded that the single most significant factor acting as a precipitant of suicidal behavior was a real or perceived threatened abandonment by a significant adult. Danto (1979) studied the reasons for suicidality in both latency-age and adolescent groups; he found that:

- Latency-age children appear to commit suicide out of a sense of frustration over their inability to establish peer ties and relationships.
- Older children seem to react with depression to family disruption caused by parental death or divorce and become frightened about the future.
- Some children react with suicidal behavior because of a sense of failure for not winning parental approval for expected social and academic achievements.
- Adolescents may react with depression and disappointment if a romance has not turned out well.
- Loss of face among peers can be a precipitant in adolescence.

This author, from clinical experience, also suggests that unwanted teenage pregnancy and knowledge of HIV-positive status can be precipitants for self-destructive behavior in adolescents. A recent phenomenon that is emerging among African American female teenagers seen at our emergency walk-in clinic in Washington, D.C., is suicidality related to the wish to join a teenage boyfriend murdered in the wave of violence that has plagued our city.

Several authors have discussed the phenomenon of suicide contagion (Brent et al., 1989; Gould & Shaffer, 1986; Phillip & Carstensen, 1986; Robbins & Conroy, 1983) presenting as a community psychiatric emergency in the adolescent population. Brent and colleagues well summarize the consensus on this issue: "The risk for suicidality appears to be greatest among those with psychiatric vulnerability antedating the exposure, particularly past or current affective disorder and past suicidality. Those who were close friends of the

victims may also be at risk, even if they do not have current or past psychopathology" (p. 923).

Risk Factors for Suicidality

There is some degree of overlap in precipitating factors and risk factors. For example, with the issue of suicide contagion, the completed suicide of the adolescent acquaintance is both a precipitant and risk factor for the teenage friends. Space does not permit a full discussion of all risk factors. I discuss a few major ones and cover others in outline form. Pfeffer, Conti, and Plutchit (1979) reported a study that they conducted on 58 latency-age hospitalized children who were evaluated for suicide potential. That study was designed to identify high-risk factors correlated with suicidal behavior in that age group. Affective and conduct disorders were associated with high suicide risk. The authors described significant feelings of hopelessness and worthlessness in the high-risk children in their study and determined that as many as 72% of them had "suicidal ideas, threats, or attempts," (p. 683) and 80% of those proposed to commit suicide by jumping. Martunnen, Aro, Henriksson and Lonnqvist (1991) reported a 32% prevalence of personality disorders in their suicide study on adolescents in Finland. They concluded that depression, antisocial behavior, and substance abuse in adolescents should trigger the need for aggressive suicide prevention intervention. Among adolescents, the methods used in suicide attempts, in decreasing order, are firearms and explosives, hanging and strangulation, and ingestion (Frederick, 1984).

The role of alcohol use/abuse in suicidal behavior has been well documented. Based on data acquired from the Suicide Prevention and Drug Information Center, Danto (1979) wrote: "What seems to be universally true is that in about 50% of the cases [suicides], heavy drinking preceding suicide and suicide itself seem to be associated" (p. 23). Martunnen et al. (1991) reported that 33% of suicide victims in their study had alcohol-related diagnoses and 50% had a detectable blood-alcohol level at the time of suicide. With alcohol being the mind-altering substance most abused by adolescents, it must be concluded that any alcohol-abusing adolescent who presents with a psychiatric emergency must be carefully evaluated for suicidality. It should be of particular concern if such a youngster operates a vehicle, because 30 to 50% of traffic fatalities involve alcohol (Frederick, 1984).

The exploration of a history of abuse, and especially of sexual abuse, is important as part of an evaluation of suicidality. One of the psychological dynamics of sexually abused children or adolescents is the sense that they are inherently bad. This negative sense of self can become so intolerable that the youngsters can decide that elimination of the bad self by suicide is the only option. In a study of life events and their relationship to suicidal behavior in adolescents, De Wilde, Kienhorst, Kiekstra, and Wolters (1992) found that "Suicide attempters differed from normal adolescents in that they reported more sexual abuse" (p. 48). In a highly publicized case in the Washington, D.C., metropolitan area where a teenage girl suicided, she left behind a journal detailing a sordid and distressing history of sexual abuse by her stepfather, who was convicted on the basis of her writings and reports she had made to a girlfriend. In a case of a borderline, suicidal teenager seen by this author, sexual abuse by the mother was disclosed during a hospitalization. It has been this author's experience that a major barrier to investigation of sexual abuse is the difficulty the clinician has in pursuing this line of inquiry. We owe it to our patients to overcome this barrier in order to make them feel less inhibited about discussing what is a horrific event in their lives, and one that carries significant morbidity and, perhaps, ultimately for some, mortality.

The reader is referred to Volume 5 of this *Handbook* for a more comprehensive treatise on suicide. For the purpose of a focused clinical assessment of a suicidal child or adolescent, the following risk factors, divided into intrinsic and extrinsic and summarized for clarity, must be explored:

1. Intrinsic suicide risk factors:
   a. Gender—three times as many girls as boys attempt suicide (Garfinkel, Froese, & Hood, 1982); boys are more successful completers.
   b. Preexisting and current psychopathology (especially affective disorder with comorbid conduct or personality disorder), and substance use/abuse
   c. Previous suicide attempt
   d. Unwanted pregnancy
   e. Medical illness and its meaning to the patient (e.g., HIV-positive status, AIDS)
   f. ideation vs. intent (Brent et al., 1988) concluded that "suicidal intent is one of the most

potent discriminative and predictive variables for completed suicide" (p. 586)
   g. Psychodynamic meaning of suicide to patient (Hendin, 1991)
   h. Premorbid coping skills (degree of resilience, prosocial vs. antisocial adaptation)
   i. Capacity to engage in psychotherapeutic encounter—risk increases with resistance
   j. Capacity to tolerate painful affects—risks increases with low tolerance (Hendin, 1991)
   k. Degree of hope vs. despair—risk increases with increase in hopelessness

2. Presence of extrinsic suicide risk factors: (Brent, 1995; Wagner, Cole, and Schwartzman, 1995; Gabarino, Guttman, & Sealy, 1986)
   a. Family crisis (e.g., separation, divorce, serious medical illness, financial crisis)
   b. Family psychopathology, substance abuse
   c. Recent or threatened loss of significant love object
   d. Narcissistic wound experienced as intolerable (e.g., school failure, rejection by peers)
   e. History of recent suicide of someone known to the patient
   f. Physical/sexual abuse history
   g. Availability of means to perform self-destructive act
   h. Lethality of means (e.g., firearms, jumping, strangulation vs. ingestion of vitamin or birth control pills)
   i. Availability of reliable adult supervision

Protective Factors

Factors that play a role in protecting children and adolescents from suicidal risk also must be evaluated to determine the degree of risk to which any given patient is exposed. Because of their cognitive immaturity and their dependence on family, children are at lower risk than adults for completing suicide (Shaffer & Fisher, 1981). The extent to which a family can be assessed as being functional will determine the safety net it will provide for the child (Garmezy, 1983). Where family supports may be lacking, secondary relationships in the child's life should be explored in order to determine what, if any, protective function they can play. Heacock (1990) suggests that black females are protected from suicide by having closer ties (than whites) to mother and grandmother. He also reported that a protective factor for Hispanic females was the low lethality of their suicide attempts. Temperament continues to emerge in study after study as a critical variable in any child's adaptation to stress. Children's capacity to engage others on their own behalf will, in part, be due to the level of ease or difficulty of their temperament. Their ability to regulate and contain intense affects—that is, not "act out"—will allow them to tolerate suicidal ideation without acting on the thoughts. Such children will most likely have a good capacity to engage in psychotherapy. In adolescents a network of close friendships functions as a protective barrier against suicidal acting out (Fawcett et al., 1987). Socially isolated adolescents should be considered to be at significant risk. Being African American, especially in the southern United States, appears to confer some degree of protection against suicide; however, Frederick (1984) has pointed out that the rate of increase of suicide among nonwhites has shown a remarkable 75% rise in the 15- to 19-year-old group; this compared to a 70% increase among whites. Some religious beliefs may function as a protective factor, as among Roman Catholics, whose religion has a powerful sanction against suicide. Evaluating the meaning of suicide within the context of the patient's religion is important to decide whether a specific religion serves a protective function or not.

Conclusion

The medical profession is plagued with the unenviable task of making "clinical judgments" that have far-reaching effects. In the majority of cases the data is clear enough to make such judgment without undue agonizing. However, in issues that involve life and death, and when the specter of malpractice suits looms overhead, as with suicidal cases, such clinical decision making can be rather difficult.

Currently there is no way to assess exactly the degree of suicidal risk. After the major factors just outlined have been evaluated, the psychiatrist is faced with the difficult task of having to weigh the relative valence of risk factors against protective factors. In other words, a clinical judgment must be made about suicidal risk at the time of assessment. In several pediatric medical specialties outcome studies show that children with the best outcomes are those with stable, nurturing, functional families. In child and adolescent psychiatry as well, a functional family provides the most critical protective factor for a suicidal youngster. In the final analysis, the ultimate disposition of a suicidal patient will hinge on the psychiatrist's assessment and a determination of the amount of containment that is necessary to neutralize the patient's suicidal impulses. If the family cannot provide such containment, an alternative safe holding environment must be made available for the patient. Where hospitalization may not be available, some jurisdictions will allow therapeutic home placement or clinical supervision (i.e., 24-hour in-home psychiatric nurse placement). The child psychiatrist dealing with noncompliant parents or guardians may have to appeal to the courts for a ruling of medical neglect or involuntary commitment of the patient. Because such drastic intervention may indeed be necessary, the assessment of suicidality must be comprehensive and must weigh carefully the balance of risk and protective factors.

REFERENCES

Berman, A., Jobes D. (1995). Suicide Prevention in Adolescents (Age 12–18). *Suicide and Life-Threatening Behavior, 25:* 143–154.

Brent, D., Kerr, M., Goldstein, C., Bozigar, J., Wartella, M., & Allan, M. (1989). An outbreak of suicidal behavior in a high school. *Journal of the American Academy of Child Psychiatry, 28,* 918–924.

Brent, D. (1993). Depression and Suicide in Children and Adolescents. *Pediatric Review. 14:* 380–388.

Brent, D. (1995). Research in Adolescent Suicide: Implications for Training, Service Delivery, and Public Policy. *Suicide and Life-Threatening Behavior. 25:* 222–230.

Brent, D. (1995). Risk Factors for Adolescent Suicide and Suicidal Behavior: Mental and Substance Abuse Disorders, Family Environmental Factors, and Life Stress. *Suicide and Life-Threatening Behavior. 25* (Supplement): 52–63.

Brent, D. A., Perper, J. A., Goldstein, C. E., Kolko, D. J., Allan, M. J., Allman, C. J., & Zelnek, J. P. (1988). Risk factors for adolescent suicide: A comparison of adolescent suicide victims with suicidal inpatients. *Archives of General Psychiatry, 45,* 581–588.

Centers for Disease Control and Prevention. (1995). Suicide among Children, Adolescents and Young Adults; United States, 1980–1992. *Journal of the American Medical Association, 274:* 451–452.

Danto, B. (1990). An overview of suicide. *American Journal of Forensic Medicine and Pathology, 1,* 23–27.

De Wilde, E. J., Kienhorst, I. C. W. M., Kiekstra, R. F. W., & Wolters, W. H. G. (1992). The relationship between adolescent suicidal behavior and life events in childhood and adolescence. *American Journal of Psychiatry, 149,* 45–51.

Ellison, J., Hughes, D., & White, K. (1989). An emergency psychiatry update. *Hospital and Community Psychiatry, 40,* 250–259.

Fawcett, J., Scheftner, W., Clark, D., Hedeker, D., Gibbons, R., & Coryell, W. (1987). Clinical predictors of suicide in patients with major affective disorders: A controlled prospective study. *American Journal of Psychiatry, 144,* 35–40.

Gabarino, J., Guttman, E., & Wilson, J. W. (1986). *The psychologically battered child.* San Francisco: Jossey-Bass.

Garfinkel, B. D., Froese, A., & Hood, J. (1982). Suicide attempts in children and adolescents. *American Journal of Psychiatry, 139,* 1257–1261.

Garmezy, N. (1983). Stressors of childhood. In N. Garmezy & M. Rutter (Eds.), *Stress, coping and development in children.* New York: McGraw-Hill.

Gould, M., & Shaffer, D. (1986). The impact of suicide in television movies. *New England Journal of Medicine, 315,* 690–693.

Gould, M., Fisher, P., Parides, M., Flory, M., Shaffer, D., (1996). Psychosocial Risk Factors of Child and Adolescent Completed Suicide. *Archives of General Psychiatry, 55,* 1155–1162.

Green, A. H. (1968). Self-destructive behavior in battered children. *American Journal of Psychiatry, 135,* 579–582.

Heacock, D. R. (1990). Suicidal behavior in black and Hispanic youth. *Psychiatric Annals, 20,* 134–142.

Hendin, H. (1991). Psychodynamics of suicide, with particular reference to the young. *American Journal of Psychiatry, 148,* 1150–1158.

Lyon, M., Benoit, M., Getson, P., Walsh, T., & O'Donnell, R. (1990). *The expendable child: Risk factors associated with black adolescent attempts.* Unpublished manuscript.

Martunnen, M. J., Aro, H. M., Henriksson, M. M., &

Lonnqvist, J. K. (1991). Mental disorders in adolescent suicide: Axis I and Axis II diagnoses in suicides among 13- to 19-year-olds in Finland. *Archives of General Psychiatry, 48,* 834–839.

Pfeffer, C. R., Conti, H. R., & Plutchit, R. (1979). Suicide behavior in latency age children: An empirical study. *Journal of the American Academy of Child Psychiatry, 18,* 679–692.

Pfeffer, C. R., Conti, H. R., & Plutchit, R. (1981). Suicidal behavior of children: A review with implications for research and practice. *American Journal of Psychiatry, 138,* 154–159.

Pfeffer, C. R., Conti, H. R., & Plutchit, R. (1986). *The suicidal child.* New York: Guilford Press.

Pfeffer, C. R., Conti, H. R., & Plutchit, R. (1990). Clinical perspectives in treatment of suicidal behavior among children and adolescents. *Psychiatric Annals, 20,* 143–150.

Phillips, D., & Carstensen, L. (1986). Clustering of teenage suicides after television news stories about suicide. *New England Journal of Medicine, 315,* 685–689.

Robbins, D., & Conroy, R. (1983). A cluster of adolescent suicide attempts: Is suicide contagious? *Journal of Adolescent Health Care, 3,* 253–255.

Shaffer, D. (1974). Suicide in childhood and early adolescence. *Journal of Child Psychology and Psychiatry, 15,* 275–291.

Shaffer, D., & Fisher, P. (1981). The epidemiology of suicide in children and young adolescents. *Journal of the American Academy of Child Psychiatry, 20,* 545–564.

Shaffer, D., Gould, M., Fisher, P., Trautman, P., Moreau, D., Kleinman, M., Flory, M. (1996). Psychiatric Diagnosis in Child and Adolescent Suicide. *Archives of General Psychiatry, 53,* 339–348.

Shafii, M., Whittinghill, R., & Sealey, M. (1979). The pediatric-psychiatric model for emergencies in child psychiatry: A study of 994 cases. *American Journal of Psychiatry, 136,* 1600–1601.

Wagner, B., Cole, R., Schwartzman, P. (1995). Psychosocial Correlates of Suicide Attempts Among Junior and Senior High School Youth. *Suicide and Life-Threatening Behavior, 25,* 358–372.

26 / Violent and Homicidal Children and Adolescents: Emergency Assessment and Intervention

Norman E. Alessi and Mohammad Ghaziuddin

Aggressive behavior is a common occurrence in childhood and adolescence. The first question that arises concerning this topic is "When does an act of aggression by a child or an adolescent constitute an emergency?" Aggression during these periods of life is ubiquitous (Kazdin, 1987; Letkowitz et al.,). Temper tantrums are especially common among the young (Leung & Fagan, 1991). Numerous reports have documented not only the presence of aggression in children and adolescents but both its increase in recent years and alteration in frequency of distribution among different groups (Inamdar et al., 1986; Pfeffer, 1985; Pfeffer et al., 1985). While minor tempertantrums and aggressive behavior are common in early childhood, the presence of deliberate, severe, and explosive aggression toward self or others is poorly tolerated and needs to be curtailed urgently. Despite the confusion surrounding the definition and the boundaries of aggressive behavior (Ghaziuddin, Tsai, & Ghaziuddin, 1991), the fact remains that the presence of severe aggression is one of the most important and frequent reasons for a child or adolescent to be referred for an emergency assessment. This chapter presents an overview of the steps necessary to undertake an emergency assessment and management of this type of aggression in children and adolescents.

Four steps need to be taken when confronted with a violent youth. (See Figure 26.1.) These are:

1. Define the degree of seriousness of the aggressive outburst.
2. Reduce the risk of danger to self or others.
3. Define the scope of the aggression and, when possible, determine the cause.
4. Arrange follow-up.

Identification of Emergency

Despite the prevalence of aggression, there are no clear guidelines as to when it can be regarded as having reached such serious proportions as to require professional assistance. The degree of subjectivity and tolerance, apart from personal and social tolerance, determines to a great degree when an act is defined as significant. Consequently, any contact made concerning aggressive children or adolescents should be explored, assuming that regardless of the severity, an intervention might be necessary. Obviously, to qualify as an emergency, aggressive acts require an acute onset with rapid escalation that do not respond to familial interventions.

Some aggressive acts that cannot be tolerated at any level of child development include:

- *Preschool:* Repetitive biting of caregivers, peers, and siblings. Breaking all toys, whether their own or others.

- *School-age:* Using objects as weapons or weapons as such. Hitting; biting caregivers, peers, friends, or peers. Destroying toys, their own or others and others' valuables.
- *Middle and High School:* Same as above, with the presence of overt violence and aggression toward others, property, and so on. In this age group the use of weapons, and the danger associated with them, increases.

These acts are characterized primarily by physical aggression against self, objects, and other people. Clearly, if these actions are severe and recurrent, they would constitute aggression requiring interventions. A notable attempt to document aggression systematically is the "Overt Aggression Scale" (Yudofsky et al., 1986). As shown in Table 26.1, this scale provides a checklist by which aggression—divided into verbal and physical aggression against self, objects, and other people—can be documented as well as the time and duration of the incident.

Reduce the Risk of Danger to Self or Others

Children or adolescents presenting due to aggression may or may not still be actively aggressive. In cases of actively aggressive youths, all attempts should be made to calm and settle them. This may vary from verbal support and acknowledgment of the difficulties the youths are having, to using either physical or psychopharmacological restraints. A number of factors may make consoling children or adolescents difficult to impossible, including a thought disorder, an affective disorder, limited intellectual or perceptual capabilities, a developmental disorder, overwhelming fear and concern due to fears of retaliation, an organic disorder, a severe personality disorder, the use of substances such as drugs or alcohol, or a combination of any of these factors (Jacobs, 1983; Rice & Moore, 1991). If youths appear not to respond to support and gentle questioning, one should assume that such is at play. One should not assume that such acts are for attention and either ignore or not take them seriously.

Regardless of etiology, if the aggression or the threats of such continues, immediate steps must

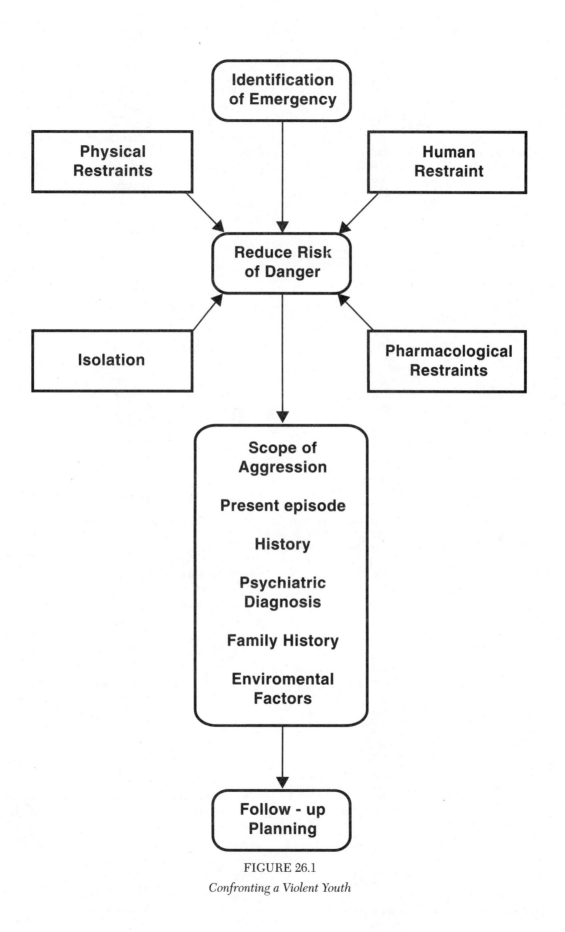

FIGURE 26.1

Confronting a Violent Youth

TABLE 26.1

Characterization of Aggressive Behavior

Verbal Aggression	Physical Aggression Against Self
Makes loud noises, shouts angrily.	Picks or scratches skin, hits self, pulls hair (with no or minor injury only).
Yells mild personal insults, e.g., "You're stupid!"	Bangs head, hits fist into objects, throws self onto floor or into objects (hurts self without serious injury).
Curses viciously, uses foul language in anger, makes moderate threats to others or self.	Small cuts or bruises, minor burns.
Makes clear threats of violence toward others or self ("I'm going to kill you") or requests to help to control self.	Mutilates self, causes deep cuts, bites that bleed, internal injury, fracture, loss of consciousness, loss of teeth.
Physical Aggression Against Objects	**Physical Aggression Against Other People**
Slams door, scatters clothing, makes a mess.	Makes threatening gesture, swings at people, grabs at clothes.
Throws objects down, kicks furniture without breaking it, marks the wall.	Strikes, kicks, pushes, pulls hair (without injury to them).
Breaks objects, smashes windows.	Attacks others, causing mild-moderate physical injury (bruises, sprain, welts).
Sets fires, throws objects dangerously.	Attacks others, causing severe physical injury (broken bones, deep lacerations, internal injury).
Time incident a.m. began: __ __ : __ __ p.m. (hours:minutes)	Duration of incident: __ __ : __ __ (hours:minutes)

NOTE: From "The Overt Aggression Scale for the Objective Rating of Verbal and Physical Aggression," by S. C. Yudofsky, J. M. Silver, W. Jackson, et al., 1986, *American Journal of Psychiatry, 143*, pp. 35–39.

be taken to reduce the risk and calm the children or adolescents. Primary methods of decreasing the risk of aggression can take 1 of 4 approaches: isolation and decrease of stimuli, human restraint, physical restraint, and pharmacological restraints.

DECREASE OF STIMULI AND/OR SECLUSION

Placement in a reduced-stimulation environment, away from family and the noise of an assessment situation, may help. If in the psychiatrist's own office, this may prove difficult. Yet reduction of stimuli-noise/sound, light, the confusion of a crowd or a group can help deescalate the aggression of a situation. Seclusion can be particularly effective on inpatient psychiatric units as a way to prevent the escalation of aggression and as a way to control aggression, although an appreciation of milieu factors can be just as effective (Erikson & Realmuto, 1983).

HUMAN RESTRAINT

When necessary, children or adolescents may need to be restrained physically by an adult. "Therapeutic holding" has been thought to have the advantage of allowing patients to regain control themselves and requiring a shorter intervention than seclusion (Miller, Walker, & Friedman, 1989). Patients for whom this was found to be most effective were younger, smaller, and with longer stays on the units.

PHYSICAL RESTRAINT

In some situations "physical restraints"—leather/mechanical restraints—will be required. Such restraints should be used only in settings where trained personnel can closely monitor time and degree of restraint to reduce possible injury and where clear guidelines have been developed (Splawn, 1991; Stilling, 1992). As with any other therapeutic technique, definable indications ("dosages," contraindications, and side effects) must exist if restraint is to be used, otherwise "abuse" can occur (Guirguis, 1978; Rosen & DiGiacomo, 1978).

PHARMACOLOGICAL RESTRAINTS

If the previous approaches are neither available nor effective, pharmacological interventions may be required. No literature on "rapid tranquilization" of children is available. Most if not all the existing literature concerning pharmacological interventions with aggressive children and adolescents concerns long-term interventions with chronic aggressive conditions (Campbell, Cohen, & Small, 1982). These include lithium carbonate, propranolol, carbamazepine, and halo-

TABLE 26.2

Dosages of Medications Rapid Tranquilization of Children and Adolescents

Medication	Dosage°	Maximum Dose per 24 hours
Neuroleptics		
Haloperidol (Haldol)	0.5 mg po/im every one-half to one hour	2–4 mg
Chlorpromazine (Thorazine)	10–50 mg po every one-half to one hour	20–400 mg
	10–25 mg im; repeat every half hour	
Lorazepam (Ativan)	0.5–1.0 mg either po/im repeat every 15–60 minutes as needed	1–2 mg
Trazadone	25–50 mg po per hour with monitoring of blood pressure and vital signs	25–50 mg

°Doses should be adjusted based on the patient's age, weight, debilitation, and other clinical consideration.

peridol. This appears to reflect the predominant views to date about child and adolescent aggression, and the lack of need to intervene aggressively. The following information is based on the existing literature, primarily dealing with adult psychiatric cases (Dubin, 1988; Dubin & Feld, 1989; Sadow, & Amanth, Solano 1989; Tardiff, 1982); Table 26.2 lists the medications and dosages that should be considered for aggressive children and adolescents.

In addition to dosage, other considerations should include time intervals and side effects. Depending on the medication selected, the side effects may include, but not be limited to, dystonia, akathisia, hypotension, drowsiness, sedation, and seizures.

Define the Scope of the Aggression

Once children or adolescents have been quieted, and the immediate danger of aggression has sub-

sided, then an assessment should follow to determine the severity and chronicity of the aggression and whether the youngsters can be managed in a less restrictive setting. Child and adolescent psychiatrists should examine the present episode and the patient's history and family history, should determine whether a psychiatric disorder exists, and should consider environmental factors (Alessi Wittekindt, 1990).

PRESENT EPISODE

How frequent are the aggressive episodes? How long do they last? Do specific circumstances trigger the incidents? If so, are they related to a specific setting, specific person, and the like? Where do the incidents occur, and with whom? Are they general; or are they specific to a person or place? If present before, what makes this incident different that required an emergency assessment and intervention? What are the specific details of the incident? Gather details from as many people as possible.

HISTORY

Is there history of previous episodes? At what age did they begin, and what help has been sought? If precipitous, evaluate for closed head injury, physical or sexual abuse, or other traumatic incidents.

FAMILY HISTORY

How do the parents set limits? Are they punitive? Do the parents use physical punishment? Are they consistent? Do the parents set limits together, or is one parent the sole disciplinarian? Is there a family history of child abuse (either sexual or physical), depression or suicide, alcoholism, criminal conduct, or childhood aggressive behaviors? Are the parents currently experiencing any of these difficulties? How do they deal with aggression with the child and their peers? Are the parents moody? Are they emotional and labile? Is there spouse abuse, alcoholism, or drug abuse in the home?

DETERMINE PRESENCE OF PSYCHIATRIC DISORDER

Is there evidence of any of the following psychiatric disorders: depressive disorders (major depressive disorder or dysthymia); bipolar disorder;

psychoses including childhood schizophrenia; autism or pervasive developmental disorder; mental retardation; organic brain syndrome, including substance abuse, closed head injury, other medical disorders.

If the child has been identified as having a psychiatric disorder, review the previous treatments. What medications have been tried? Were the medications given in doses that were within a therapeutic range? Did the medications worsen the aggressive behavior?

ENVIRONMENTAL FACTORS

In what type of neighborhood does the child live? Is there environmental support for aggressive behavior—that is, gangs or other youths with reputations for aggressive behavior?

Provide Follow-up Planning

Several decisions need to be made when confronted with aggressive children or adolescents. If they are seen in a setting other than a psychiatric hospital, the psychiatrist has to determine whether patients can and should return home. Attendant to this fact is how stable the patients are and how violent. Any associated or underlying psychiatric disorder also must be considered. Both for safety and in order to complete a detailed exam, patients may require hospitalization (Mandoki, Sumner, & Matthews-Ferrari, 1992).

Conclusion

Aggressive behavior can be found as a normal developmental variant at all ages in both sexes. This fact and the lack of clear guidelines in determining the point at which normal aggression becomes pathological makes the clinical management of childhood aggressive behaviors very difficult. Nevertheless, when confronted with such a case, a clinician must intervene to ensure the safety of the patient and others and to decrease the risk of harm and destruction. Once stabilized, the patient must be assessed to determine the extent of the aggressive behavior and its etiology. Care of aggressive behavior may and, if necessary, must entail a range of options, both acutely and chronically, involving the child, his or her siblings, and parents.

REFERENCES

Alessi, N. E., Wittekindt, J. (1990). Childhood aggressive behavior. *Pediatric Annals, 18,* 94–101.

Campbell, M., Cohen, I. L., & Small, A. M. (1982). Drugs in aggressive behavior. *Journal of the American Academy of Child Psychiatry, 21,* 107–117.

Dubin W. R. (1988). Rapid tranquilization: Antipsychotics or benzodiazepines? *Journal of Clinical Psychiatry, 49* (Suppl.), 5–12.

Dubin, W. R., & Feld, J. A. (1989). Rapid tranquilization of the violent patient. *American Journal of Emergency Medicine, 7,* 313–320.

Eichelman, B. (1988). Toward a rational pharmacotherapy for aggressive and violent behavior. *Hospital and Community Psychiatry, 39,* 31–39.

Erickson, W. D., & Realmuto, G. (1983). Frequency of seclusion in an adolescent psychiatric unit. *Journal of Clinical Psychiatry, 44,* 238–241.

Ghaziuddin, M., Tsai, L., & Ghaziuddin, N. (1991). Violence in Asperger syndrome: A critique. *Journal of Autism and Developmental Disorders, 21*(3), 349–354.

Guirguis, E. F. (1978). Management of disturbed patients: An alternative to the use of mechanical restraints. *Journal of Clinical Psychiatry, 39,* 205–209, 303.

Harry, B. (1985). Violence and official diagnostic nomenclature. *Bulletin of the American Academy of Psychiatry and the Law, 13,* 385–388.

Inamdar, S. C., Darrell, E., Brown, A., et al. (1986). Trends in violence among psychiatrically hospitalized adolescents: 1969 and 1979 compared. *Journal of the American Academy of Child Psychiatry, 25,* 704–707.

Jacobs, D. (1983). Evaluation and management of the violent patient in emergency settings. *Psychiatric Clinics of North America, 6,* 259–269.

Kazdin, A. E. (1987). *Conduct disorders in childhood and Adolescence.* Beverly Hills, CA: Sage Publications.

Letkowitz, M. M., Eron, L. D., Walder, L. O., et al. (1977). *Growing up to be violent: A longitudinal study of aggression.* Oxford: Pergamon Press.

Leung, A. K. C., & Fagan, J. E. (1991). Temper tantrums. *American Family Physician, 44,* 559–563.

Mandoki, M. W., Sumner, G. S., & Matthews-Ferrari, K. (1992). Evaluation and treatment of rage in children and adolescents. *Child Psychiatry and Human Development, 22,* 227–235.

Miller, D., Walker, M. C., & Freidman, D. (1989). Use of a holding technique to control the violent behavior of seriously disturbed adolescents. *Hospital and Community Psychiatry, 40,* 520–524.

Pfeffer, C. R. (1985). Self-destructive behavior in children and adolescents. *Psychiatric Clinics of North America, 8,* 215–226.

Pfeffer, C. R., Solomon, G., Plutchik, R., et al. (1985). Variables that predict assaultiveness in child psychiatric inpatients. *Journal of the American Academy of Child Psychiatry, 26,* 775–780.

Rice, M. M., Moore, G. P. (1991). Management of the violent patient. Therapeutic and legal considerations. *Emergency Medicine Clinics of North America, 9,* 13–30.

Rosen, H., & DiGiacomo, J. N. (1978). The role of physical restraint in the treatment of psychiatric illness. *Journal of Clinical Psychiatry, 39,* 228–232.

Solano, O. A., Sadow, T., & Ananth, J. (1989). Rapid tranquilization: A reevaluation. *Neuropsychobiology, 22,* 90–96.

Splawn, G. (1991). Restraining potentially violent patients. *Journal of Emergency Nursing, 17,* 316–317.

Stilling, L. (1992). The pros and cons of physical restraints and behavior controls. *Journal of Psychosocial Nursing, 30,* 18–20.

Tardiff, K. (1982). The use of medication for assaultive patients. *Hospital and Community Psychiatry, 33,* 307–308.

Yudofsky, S. C., Silver, J. M., Jackson, W., et al. (1986). The overt aggression scale for the objective rating of verbal and physical aggression. *American Journal of Psychiatry, 143,* 35–39.

Zubieta, J., & Alessi, N. E. (1993). Serotonin and its potential role in disruptive behavior disorder: A critical literature review. *Journal of Child and Adolescent Psychopharmacology, 3,* 11–35.

27 / Psychiatric Emergency Evaluation and Intervention with Runaway and Homeless Youngsters

David G. Inwood

Until the mid-1980s the youngsters, children and adolescents, who lived on the streets of urban America were typically and correctly considered to be runaways. However, an enormous increase in the number of homeless people occurred in the mid-1980s throughout cities and mid-size communities. Perhaps for the first time since the Great Depression of the 1930s, people lived and slept in railroad and bus stations, park benches and piers, streets and doorways of office buildings and department stores.

When the living conditions of so many people become unacceptable, municipalities opened up large military-style dormitories, shelters, and rental apartments in decaying hotels. Often these facilities were located in marginal, decrepit, and dangerous areas of the community.

Initially the homeless were thought to be predominantly comprised of men or mentally ill adults. However, during the late 1980s large numbers of undominciled families, often comprised of a single parent and several children, seemed to emerge. Additionally, older emancipated minors in their mid-to late teenage years began to be seen

with great frequency living on the streets (Bass, 1992).

As many as 900,000 of these teenage boys and girls were procured into rings of prostitution, and many suffered the ravishes of sexually transmitted illnesses including AIDS. Many of these youngsters also abused drugs and alcohol. Their plight soon drew the attention of the national media, social welfare authorities, the judicial system, and eventually the mental health system (Tomb, 1991).

This combination of adverse social and economic conditions and family dysfunction in impoverished lower socioeconomic populations led to the emergence of a large number of homeless families and undomiciled youngsters. Many youngsters ran away or were thrown away from their homes. Other youngsters, victims of physical or sexual abuse and general family dysfunction, were placed in foster care or group homes. A disproportionately large number of these youngsters would intermittently run away from placements and would live on the streets (Finkelhor, Hotaling, & Sedalak, 1990).

The societal safety net was breached. Children

and adolescents of these vulnerable families were at high risk for school failures, status offenses, criminal behavior, and the emergence of frank psychiatric illnesses. Many of these youngsters were referred for emergency psychiatric evaluations by the police, social welfare agencies, school officials, and on some occasions by the families themselves.

In certain inner-city child psychiatric clinics, up to 40% of the children were either in foster care or undomiciled. These patients challenged the customary model of psychiatric evaluation and intervention, which commonly assumes that the child lives in a family setting with at least 1 parent (Adnopoz, Grigsby, & Nagler, 1991).

Despite the strains that homeless and runaway youngsters present, there exists a body of knowledge that will enable clinicians to make an effective psychiatric evaluation and intervention.

Clinicians must be able to differentiate which youngsters are exhibiting chronic juvenile status offenses from those who are manifesting potentially life-threatening psychopathological phenomena. They must know which youngsters can safely be referred to social agencies or to their parents and which youngsters require psychiatric hospitalization or crisis intervention (Grigsby, 1991).

Definitions

The United States Department of Health and Human Resources (1990) defines A runaway as "a youth away from home at least overnight without permission of his parents or legal guardian." A homeless youth is "a person who has no home, not living with his family unit, and requires services and shelter to receive supervision and care" (Finkelhor et al., 1990).

Kurtz, Jarvis, and Kurtz (1991) discuss five types of problems that have caused homelessness:

1. Youngsters who leave or become separated from homeless families
2. Youngsters who run away from home because of physical or sexual abuse
3. Children who are thrown out of the home by parents or surrogates
4. Children who are removed from their home and then run away from placement
5. Youngsters who emigrate to the United States without their parents

Juvenile status offenders often are brought by their parents, police, or mental health workers to psychiatric emergency rooms for evaluation. By definition they are young people under the age of 18 who have committed offenses, not crimes. These offenses include violations of parental or societal norms, including breaking curfews, truancy, possession of alcohol and/or small amounts of drugs such as marijuana, promiscuous sexual behavior, and child parent verbal and physical altercations. If the person is older than 18 years of age, many of these issues would not be considered criminal but instead would reflect lifestyle choices (Tomb, 1991).

Epidemiology

Estimates of runaway and homeless youths in the United States range between 1.3 million and 1.5 million. These numbers do not include those children who run away from foster home or group home placements (Systemetrics/McGraw-Hill, 1989).

Whenever any child runs away, it is always necessary to investigate why, when, from where, and to where the youngster goes. In retrospect, the reasons for running away often may seem trivial. Many of the precipitants relate to parents attempting to enforce discipline on a child who impulsively leaves the home and then goes off to a friend or relative who lives nearby. By the next morning, the youngster and the family often resolve the incident. Outside authorities are never notified and the youngster is never labeled as a runaway. Regardless of how many times the youngster leaves the house, the incident may never become a statistic.

Nonetheless, once the youngster is defined as being a "runaway" and is brought to the psychiatric emergency room, the matter becomes significant and requires a thorough evaluation. Once the child is registered in the emergency room, the physician has the legal and medical responsibility to perform a comprehensive evaluation that may lead to returning the child to the family or a social welfare facility, to hospitalization, or to temporary placement at a shelter (Robinson, 1994).

According to recent surveys, more than 20% of runaways are homeless children who are running from foster homes or group home placements. Almost 40% of the runaway population have been in foster care placements during the previous year.

About 10% of youngsters run away from specifically designated shelters for this type of child. In sum, these youngsters reject those institutions created to serve, supervise, and protect them. When considering disposition, this fact makes the work of the emergency room physician and staff even harder (Bass, 1992).

Community Resources and Referrals

Youngsters who run away from home or foster care placements, as well as homeless youths, are eligible to attend specially funded youth shelters. The United States government funded the Run Away Youth Program in 1974 as part of the Juvenile Justice and Prevention Act of 1974 (Public Law 93–415). The program supplements services provided by the juvenile justice system and by the child welfare system.

There were established short-term, 15-day crisis-oriented, intervention services for youths who had not been placed in shelters by the courts. In other words, children who have not been arrested and who have not been previously in placement can attend these 15-day centers, which were established throughout the country. Professional services are provided by a multidisciplinary team often staffed on a social work model but with available psychiatric consultation and backup for those youngsters who require more extensive evaluation (Grigsby, 1991).

In the 1970s there was a large wave of interstate runaways. Children often ran away from rural and suburban homes to large urban centers, such as New York, Chicago, and Los Angeles. Many of these youngsters soon fell into illegal activities, such as male and female child prostitution and drug procurement and sales shortly after their arrival in the urban areas. The local police could not locate, detain, and/or reunite these youngsters with their estranged families. Since many of these youngsters had crossed state jurisdictions, it seemed natural and sensible for the federal government to intervene to bring help to these runaway children.

Congress ambitiously hoped that the public law program would reunite the children with their families, would stabilize family dysfunctions, and would prevent future runaway episodes. Approximately 66,000 children are served by the program each year. It must be noted that that number reflects but a tiny fraction of the 1.5 million runaways and homeless youngsters in need. The programs focus on crisis intervention, identification of aftercare needs, and family reunification. These modalities are appropriate and most useful for youngsters who have mild parent-child conflicts or mild juvenile status offenses of relatively recent onset. These centers are excellent for intervening with children who have left the home for a night or two and for those who have a competent parent or guardian, or adequate shelter to return to.

However, a large number of children are chronic runaways and essentially become both emancipated and homeless. Authorities recognize that not all runaways or homeless youths are delinquents. Indeed, many of these children have fled intolerable home conditions, and they should *not* be reunited with their parents (Yates, 1991).

Thus, Congress in 1988 passed the Transition Living Program for older, emancipated adolescents who were unlikely to be reunited with their families. A model of long-term, not short-term, crisis intervention was adopted and funded. The program provides supervised apartments, group homes, or host family settings for youngsters in transition. These adolescents received social and work skill training. Care for medical and emotional problems was offered. Comprehensive outreach program to youngsters on the street were developed.

Survey of Psychopathology in Runaway and Homeless Children and Their Parents

The National Association of Social Workers Survey of 1991 provides clinicians with the most comprehensive information available about the incidence of psychopathology among homeless youngsters and their parents. Participating in the survey were 360 agencies throughout the country that provide basic shelter, crisis intervention, transitional services, and independent living services. Key findings regarding parental and family psychopathology include the following:

1. More than 60% of the youths had been sexually or physically abused by their parents.
2. About 50% of families had absentee fathers.
3. About 30% of parents abused alcohol.

4. About 25% of parents abused drugs.
5. About 25% had experienced violence perpetrated by other family members or friends.
6. About 20% of parents had diagnosable mental illnesses.

Key findings regarding the psychopathology of youngsters include:

1. About 50% had school problems.
2. About 40% were in foster care.
3. About 30% were in the juvenile justice system because of conduct problems (Bass, 1992).
4. About 25% had diagnosable mental illnesses.
5. About 25% abused drugs.
6. About 20% abused alcohol.
7. About 20% had attempted suicide.

Severe psychopathology occurs in these youngsters and families at least 2 to 3 times to 10 times as often as in the general population. Clinicians working with this population must recognize and take into consideration when performing psychiatric interviews and establishing treatment plans for these youths and their families/caregivers.

Simply, many of these youths and their parents suffer from significant, chronically debilitating psychopathology. Many of these parents lack adequate resources and may not be able to care for their children (Adnopoz et al., 1991).

Psychiatric Evaluation

Given the nature of the widespread psychopathology that may be found in both parents and children, the clinician must be forewarned that neither parent nor child will find it easy to be fully candid during the initial part of the evaluation. Given the high prevalence of physical and/or sexual abuse and alcohol and drug abuse, we can assume that many of these youngsters have been chronically traumatized and may be reluctant to communicate detailed descriptions of their present and past lives. At the same time, since clinicians are legally required to report to appropriate municipal and state agencies allegations of alleged child maltreatment, it is crucial that clinicians maintain professional neutrality when exploring sensitive issues. It will be essential, at some point, to verify whatever the family or youngsters confides or alleges. It will be necessary to obtain records and information from social welfare agencies, the judicial system, schools, and the youngster's street network. At the same time, clinicians need to remember that whatever they write into the medical record may, at a future point, be subpoenaed.

Obviously, this type of evaluation takes a great deal of time and probably involves the collaborative assistance of colleagues from multiple disciplines. This type of work is best done during traditional daytime work week hours since so much interagency communication is required. Unfortunately, a great number of these children and families will present in evening and/or weekend hours. At those times, a clinician often is on his or her own and must manage to at least perform a traditional psychiatric evaluation. A more extensive evaluation may just have to wait.

The traditional psychiatric evaluation, as always, covers the chief complaint, presenting symptoms, present and past psychiatric illnesses, developmental history, family and school history, medical illnesses, and substance abuses. A mental status with particular focus on suicidal or homicidal behavior as well as evidence of psychotic thinking is crucial. A thorough physical examination with careful observation of any signs of physical and/or sexual maltreatment is necessary. Comprehensive blood tests including screening for sexually transmitted diseases as well as urine tests for drug use should be taken (Krugman, 1991).

Recommendations for practical guidelines include:

1. The clinician should be able to make Axis I, II, and III diagnoses from the fourth edition of the *Diagnostic and Statistical Manual of Mental Disorders* for the child and, when appropriate, for the parent.
2. Axis IV usually will reveal severe or extreme stresses.
3. Axis V usually will show a severely impaired youngster and/or family situation.
4. The clinician must make a differential diagnosis that will reflect the multifactorial nature of the child's difficulties. This includes major psychiatric psychopathology, personality disorders, learning or intellectual impairments, and medical illnesses.
5. The clinician must make immediate decisions, such as:
   a. Whether the youngster is at risk for running away from the emergency room during this evaluation period. If so, security may have to be called and the youngster may have to restrained physically or chemically.
   b. Whether the youngster is suicidal or violently aggressive and therefore may have to be hospitalized.

c. Whether the youngster has been so abused physically or sexually or is so medically ill that he or she will have to be transferred to the Department of Pediatrics for urgent care (Robinson, 1994).

During the psychiatric interview, the clinician must thoroughly search to uncover in the youngster present or past suicidal ideation or behaviors. About 2,000 adolescents commit suicide each year, and the incidence has increased almost 30-fold over the past 40 years (Fawcett, Clark, & Busch, 1993).

In general, the clinician needs to know that there exists a high comorbidity between the prevalence of certain major psychiatric disorders and the emergence of suicidal ideation and behavior. In the adolescent as well as the adult, successful suicidality typically occurs in the presence of untreated major depression, anxiety impulse disorder, and alcohol-substance abuse. Other conditions in which there is a high incidence of suicidality included bipolar mood disorders, schizophrenia, and borderline states. New findings have indicated that youngsters who have sexual identity conflicts are at higher risks for killing themselves (Clark, 1993).

Truisms include the fact that the presence of a lethal mechanism, such as the availability of guns, automobiles, and alcohol, leads to enhanced likelihood of death. Indeed, 46% of all adolescents who committed suicide were found to have blood-alcohol levels above the legal limit. Guns are the number-one cause of death by suicide. (Homicide using a gun also is a leading cause of death of young people ages 15 to 24.) Therefore, the clinician must inquire if a gun is available to the youngster. If so, that gun must be disposed of in order to reduce the probability that the youngster will fatally injure him-self or her-self or someone else during a moment of despair, anger, inebriation, or impulsivity (Callahan, 1993).

As is well known, males are more successful at suicide than females. Whites and Hispanics have higher rates of suicide than African Americans. African Americans have the highest rate of homicides both as victims and perpetrators. Homicides in inner cities often are related to drug warfare. Screening for drug and alcohol use can alert the clinician to youths at high risk (Cambor & Millman, 1991).

It is important for the clinician to know that 83% of suicide completers talked about suicide within 1 week of their deaths. However, approximately one-half of these youngsters spoke only to siblings and/or to peers, not to adults. Most frighteningly, at least half of all adolescent suicide victims never made a prior attempt at suicide or sought help from any mental health professional. Since we are dealing with large numbers of youngsters who do not typically or easily communicate their plans to adults, mental health professionals need to recognize how focused their interviews must be; they must attempt to develop a working alliance with the youngster and to assess the potential for lethality. Interviewers must be skillful in asking questions about previous and present occurrences of sexual and physical abuse. They must be knowledgable about street drugs and substance use in undomiciled youngsters (Bailey, 1994).

Interventions

The major intervention that a mental health professional has to make is to decide whether the youngster can safely return to his or her parent's home and then obtain further treatment, or whether the situation is so unstable and potentially dangerous that the youngster requires some kind of placement. The literature states that 50% of runaway youngsters go home. This author believes that for simple status offenders, of relatively recent onset, and where the family or caregivers appear to be caring and competent, returning home is a justifiable decision. However, many of these youngsters and families need to offered follow-up services in their home communities because it is evident that parent and child are having problems. At the same time it may be necessary to inform the local child welfare agency of the youngster's difficulties so that proper monitoring will put in place (Green, 1991).

However, when there is evidence of chronic running away, severe mood disturbance, sexual and/or physical abuse, alcohol and/or drug abuse, or suicidal or homicidal ideation, the child should not be returned to his or her home immediately. Such youngsters need to undergo a full and thorough evaluation in the light of the day, not in the pressure of an emergency situation. Even the most conscientious and experienced of mental health professionals are at risk for making errors in judgment when they base their decisions on insufficient available data or limited revelations from youths and their families. Therefore, the youngster either should be referred to a high-quality professionally staffed community-based shelter or should be hospitalized for a throughout assessment (Dickstein Hinz, & Eth, 1991).

If it is decided that the youngster requires a psychiatric hospitalization, he or she should be stabilized with standard mileau therapy, observation, medication, and psychological assessment. Pediatric care for any medical illness, including sexually transmitted diseases, AIDS, or tuberculosis, may be necessary. On occasion, a youngster may be on a dually diagnosed unit for substance abuse or developmental disabilities.

Only after the youngster is stabilized and no longer engaging in dangerous behaviors for self or others may he or she be released to a shelter or carefully chosen foster or group home. Meanwhile, in cases of blatant abuse or neglect, the child welfare system and/or the courts may have evaluated the members of the youngster's family. Similarly, if other family members are impaired, they need to receive appropriate medical, psychiatric, or economic assistance (Dickstein et al., 1991).

Even if the family is reasonably well functioning, in all probability the parents still need special help and training in dealing with runaway psychiatrically impaired youngsters. After these issues have been resolved and while the parents and child are receiving regular professional supervision it is time to consider if they should be re-united. Some families are unable to provide the level of supervision that very disturbed youngsters may require. These youngsters need to be referred to foster or group homes and later receive supervised experiences in independent living (Adnopoz et al., 1991).

Many youngsters will be able to master and overcome the trauma of living on the streets either as runaways or as homeless persons. For other more vulnerable and less resilient youngsters, life on the street becomes one more experience in a lifetime of adversity and despair. Despite all efforts of rescue and support by a series of devoted and caring professionals, these youngsters face the tragic outcome of an early and premature death (Tomb, 1991).

Emergency Resources

The following agencies can be very helpful:

Covenant House (New York) hotline: 1–800–999–9999 ("nine-line")

Florida Runaway Network Hotline: 1–800-RUN-AWAY

National Center for Missing and Exploited Children: 1–800–843–5678

National Runaway Switchboard: 1–800–621–4000 (HIT-HOME)

REFERENCES

Adnopoz, J., Grigsby, K., & Nagler, S. (1991). Multiproblem families and high risk children and adolescents: Causes and management. In M. Louis (Ed.), *Child and adolescent psychiatry: A comprehensive textbook* (pp. 1059–1066). Baltimore, MD: Williams & Wilkins.

Bailey, G. (1994). Alcohol and substance abuse. In K. Robson (Ed.), *Manual of clinical child and adolescent psychiatry* (rev. ed.). Washington, DC: American Psychiatric Press.

Bass, D. (1992). *Helping vulnerable youths: Runaway and homeless adolescents in the United States,* Washington, DC: NASW Press.

Callahan, J. (1993). Blueprint for an adolescent suicidal crisis. *Psychiatric Annals, 23* (5), 263–270.

Cambor, R., & Millman, R. (1991). Alcohol and drug abuse in adolescents. In M. Lewis (Ed.), *Child and adolescent psychiatry: A comprehensive textbook* (pp. 736–755). Baltimore, MD: Williams & Wilkins.

Child abuse. (1993). Parts I, II, III. *Harvard Mental Health Letter, 9* (11), (1–4); 9:12, 1:3, 10:1–5.

Clark, D. (1993). Suicidal behavior in childhood and adolescence: Recent studies and clinical implications. *Psychiatric Annals, 23* (5), 271–283.

Dickstein, L., & Hinz, L., & Eth, S. (1991). Treatment of sexually abused children and adolescents. In A. Tasman & S. Goldfinger (Eds.), *Review of psychiatry* (Vol. 10, pp. 345–366). Washington, DC: American Psychiatric Press.

Fawcett, J., Clark, D., & Busch, K. (1993). Assessing and treating youngsters at risk for suicide. *Psychiatric Annals, 23* (5), 244–255.

Finkelhor, D., Hotaling, F., & Sedlak, (1990). *Runaways.* In *Missing, abducted, and throwaway children in America: Numbers and characteristics* (NC) No. 123667 (pp. 171–225). Washington, DC: U.S. Department of Justice, Office of Juvenile Justice and Delinquency Prevention.

Green, A.(1991). Child physical abuse. In J. M. Wiener (Ed.), *Textbook of child and adolescent psychiatry* (pp. 477–485) Washington, DC American Psychiatric Press.

Grigsby, R. (1991). Consultation with youth shelters, group homes, and Big Brothers/Big Sisters programs. In M. Lewis (Ed.), *Child and adolescent psychiatry: A comprehensive Textbook* (pp. 909–914). Baltimore, MD: Williams & Wilkins.

Guger, M. (1991). Psychiatry, law and child sexual abuse. In A. Tasman & S. Goldfinger (Eds.), *Review of psychiatry*, (Vol. 10, pp. 367–390). Washington, DC: American Psychiatric Press.

Krugman, R. (1991). Physical indicators of child sexual abuse. In I. A. Tasman & S. Goldfinger (Eds.), *Review of psychiatry* (Vol. 10, pp. 336–344). Washington; DC: American Psychiatric Press.

Kurtz, D., Jarvis, S., & Kurtz, G. (1991). Problems of homeless youths: Empirical findings and human service issues. *Social Work, 36* (4), 309.

Pfeffer, C. (1991). Suicide and suicidality. In J. M. Wiener (Ed.), *Textbook of child and adolescent psychiatry* (pp. 507–514). Washington, DC: American Psychiatric Press.

Robinson, J. (1994). Emergencies I. In K. Robson (Ed.), *Manual of clinical child and adolescent psychiatry* (rev. ed.) Washington, DC: American Psychiatric Press.

Systemetrics/McGraw-Hill. (1989). *A partial listing of problems facing the american child, youth and families.* Lexington, MA: U.S. Department of Health and Human Services.

Tomb, D. (1991) The runaway adolescent. In M. Lewis (Ed.), *Child and adolescent psychiatry: A comprehensive textbook* (pp. 1066–1077). Baltimore, MD: Williams & Wilkins.

Yates, A. (1991). Child sexual abuse. In J. M. Wiener (Ed.), *Textbook of child and adolescent psychiatry* (pp 486–495). Washington, DC: American Psychiatric Press.

28 / Emergency Assessment and Treatment of the Anxious Child

Daniel R. Fisher and Harold S. Koplewicz

Separation anxiety disorder has its onset as early as preschool, but patients have presented with the full-blown clinical syndrome in adolescence. It is equally prevalent in both sexes and has its period of peak onset at changes of schools, such as first grade, start of middle school and high school (Gittelman-Klein, 1975). Often exacerbations are seen after school vacations. Its causes are multifactorial and involve psychosocial, dynamic, learning, ethological, and biological/genetic determinants (Kaplan & Saddock, 1991). In its most extreme form, separation anxiety disorder will manifest in a veritable psychiatric emergency, school refusal. Indeed, approximately 80% of school phobics are actually separation anxiety disorder sufferers (Gittelman & Klein, 1985). This chapter addresses the specific process involved in the clinical assessment and treatment of children with this debilitating disorder.

Assessment

CLINICAL VIGNETTE

Jennifer is a 15-year-old white female who presented to the pediatric emergency room on a Sunday night with a chief complaint of headaches and feeling anxious and worried. Her specific worries are about her and her parents' health.

History of Present Illness: For the past six weeks since the start of the academic year in a new high school and neighborhood, Jennifer has had physical complaints on Sunday nights and weekday mornings. They have consisted of a headache, lightheadedness, and a racing heartbeat. Jennifer admits to worries about harm befalling herself, concerns about her parent's health, and, in particular, her father's safety while he is at work.

Mental Status Examination: The patient is a well-developed, well-nourished, attractive white female appearing her stated age. She is tearful and sobbing intermittently. She denies any suicidal or homicidal ideation as well as any auditory or visual hallucinations. She denies any substance or alcohol use. Her speech is coherent and her mood and affect appear anxious and depressed.

Physical Examination: Her blood pressure, pulse, and electrocardiogram are within normal limits, and her physical examination is unremarkable. Complete blood panels as well as blood and urine drug screens are negative.

Past History: Jennifer is the product of a full-term pregnancy and normal delivery. Developmental milestones were normal. She had some transient separation difficulties when she started kindergarten. The parents state that she has always had difficulty separating from them and that sleepover dates outside the house were stressful and terminated early. She did not participate in any sleepaway camp experience. The parents state that the patient was always a sensitive child. Five years ago when her grandmother died, she mourned her death with greater intensity than the rest of the family. The death of a pet bird 7 months ago was exceptionally upsetting to Jennifer who was weepy and distressed for more than ten days afterward.

Jennifer and her family moved to a new neighborhood 3 months before the start of the academic year. Jennifer adjusted well to her new neighborhood. While she missed her old friends and was upset to leave her old bedroom, she was friendly and quickly developed a social network in her new neighborhood. She particularly enjoyed hanging out on the front lawn of the family's home talking with the other neighborhood kids.

Her parents report that every schoolday morning Jennifer complains of headaches and other physical symptoms and has to be encouraged, and at times forced, to attend school. In the past, Jennifer has exhibited hypochondriacal behavior, specifically a virus or another ailment that would require several extra days before she felt well enough to return to school. This is the first time that Jennifer has voiced direct complaints about going to school and overt fears about her and her parent's safety.

CLINICAL FEATURES

School phobia is only one symptom of separation anxiety disorder, which can have multiple behavioral consequences and cognitive manifestations (Gittelman-Klein, 1975). According to the fourth edition of the *Diagnostic and Statistical Manual of Mental Disorders*, (DSM-IV), the disorder's essential feature is an inappropriate and excessive anxiety revolving around separation from home or from those to whom the child is attached (American Psychiatric Association [AP], 1994). There are 8 "symptoms," of which 3 need to exist to make the diagnosis. Mother's accessibility is of primary concern; hence, the child is reluctant to attend school, a threatening place where separation is forcibly imposed for a fixed period of time (Gittelman-Klein, 1975). There is fear of possible harm befalling attachment figures (i.e., fear of accidents or illness). These children often display morbid dread of their own harm or kidnapping. Anticipatory anxiety at the prospect of leaving home for school, camp, or "sleepovers" is common, with frank panic or pervasive anxiety (e.g., homesickness) overwhelming children with the disorder upon actual separation. Sunday nights often are difficult for such children because of anticipatory anxiety.

Somatic symptoms such as stomachaches and nausea are frequently the markers of separation anxiety disorder and, not unlike the diurnal mood variation of melancholia, have their own daily fluctuations. The gastrointestinal symptoms plaguing a child on schoolday mornings commonly are absent on Saturday and Sunday mornings (Koplewicz, 1989). Adolescent sufferers complain of more cardiovascular or respiratory symptoms than gastrointestinal symptoms. Somatic symptoms or anxiety are also prominent at night for 2 reasons: anticipation of attending school the next morning, and fear of sleeping alone. Bedtime carries the perceived attendant risk of isolation and abandonment (Gittelman-Klein, 1975). Nightmares with themes of separation also make sleeping alone a daunting task, and children with separation anxiety disorder often attempt to sleep with parents. Intrusive, clinging behavior and demands for attention exacerbated by an imminent separation is common as well.

DIFFERENTIAL DIAGNOSIS

School refusal is a frequent and severe symptom of separation anxiety disorder; however, it is not pathognomonic (Kaplan & Saddock, 1991). In conduct disorder, truancy is common, yet these children avoid home as well as school and do not worry about the well-being of or separation from their caregivers. Physical violence, while common in patients with disruptive disorders, actually can be seen in separation anxiety disorder when the anxious, school-refusing adolescent is forced to separate prompting an irritable, sometimes aggressive reaction. Disorders that specifically interfere in successful school functioning, such as attention deficit hyperactivity disorder, learning disabilities, and avoidant disorder, may manifest in a phobic avoidance of school (Koplewicz, 1989). Despite the fact that separation anxiety may accompany the more globally debilitating disorders of schizophrenia and pervasive developmental disorder, their preexistence precludes the diagnosis of separation anxiety disorder, according to *DSM-IV* (APA, 1994).

Separation anxiety disorder and major depressive disorder frequently exist as comorbid conditions; indeed, both diagnoses may be given concurrently if criteria are met. In a study of adolescents with major depressive disorder, nearly half of the group had a comorbid diagnosis of separation anxiety disorder, and in 84% of these patients the anxiety disorder had the earlier onset (Koplewicz, 1990). However, depressive symptoms often may be secondary to separation anxiety disorder. A dysphoric mood, appetite and sleep disturbance, impaired concentration, and somatic complaints may exist while the child is away from home or the attachment figure and remit when reunited with the parents. Although panic disorder and agoraphobia in adults are postulated to be associated with childhood separation anxiety, they are uncommon before age 18 (Gittelman-Klein, 1985).

INFORMATION GATHERING

When a child is brought to the attention of a mental health professional with the presenting problem of school refusal, the clinician must keep the differential diagnoses in mind throughout the assessment. The following are general guidelines for the completion of a comprehensive evaluation. A cardinal rule in this evaluation is the use of multiple sources including parents, teachers, other health professionals as well as the child him/or herself.

On first presentation to the child and adolescent psychiatrist, the following information should be collected: history of present illness, developmental history, school history, medical and prior psychiatric history and associated treatments and outcome, medication history with doses, duration of trials and side effects, family history assessing for psychiatric illness with genetic or familial determinants, and mental status exam (Koplewicz & Williams, 1988).

Various useful diagnostic interviewing instruments exist. The Kiddie-SADS-Lifetime (Schedule for *Affective Disorders and Schizophrenia for School-Age Children-lifetime*) is a semistructured interview utilizing *DSM-IV* criteria for child and adolescent psychiatric disorders with exclusion criteria and a newly added section that addresses onset and course of each disorder over time. This is a useful tool to increase the reliability of a diagnosis and to screen for the presence of separation anxiety disorder and/or other diagnoses. The Diagnostic Interview for Children and Adolescents (DICA), like the Kiddie-SADS, has questions organized around specific disorders, allowing the clinician to select only relevant sections if desired (Gittelman-Klein, 1988).

Self-rating anxiety scales administered to the patient are efficient, quick, and cheap ways to provide further information and provide a measure of subjective improvement at follow-up visits. The Children's Manifest Anxiety Scale (Castaneda, McCandless, & Palermo, 1956) and its revised version by Reynolds and Richmond (1978) consist of 42 and 37 yes/no items, respectively, with a lie scale built in. It measures 3 factors: physical signs of anxiety, worry and oversensitivity, and fear/concentration.

Treatment

Once information is gathered and a diagnosis is established, the clinician sets a therapeutic agenda. As with the evaluation process, treatment efforts for separation anxiety disorder in general and school refusal in particular must include parents, school, and the child. The teacher, guidance counselor, and principal are involved as they monitor treatment efficacy and often need to modify school regulations for the child during the process (Gittelman-Klein, 1975). Most successful treatment efforts combine behavioral/cognitive therapies with psychopharmacology.

BEHAVIORAL THERAPY

The primary goal of the intervention is to get the child back to school expeditiously, as delays can exacerbate the problem. A combination of classical and operant methods are used. The former involves systematic desensitization, exposure, and flooding; the latter involves rearranging contingencies in the family and school settings in order to facilitate attendance (Bernstein & Borchardt, 1991). The clinician instructs the parents to encourage and at times insist that the already anxious child sustain further anxiety in making incrementally bolder steps toward return to full attendance. The parents have the equally important task of reassuring the child that his or her fears, while distressing, are unsubstantiated.

In structured sessions with the therapist, child, and parents, clear goals and expectations are set forth as to what the child will attempt to accomplish prior to the next meeting. The tasks are written out in the form of a "contract" with the child and involve ever-increasing degrees of separation. The child is rewarded for successfully completed tasks with points or stars that can be redeemed for some desirable treat. Interestingly, tangible rewards often are not even necessary, as children usually are internally motivated to get better; however, such rewards can be very helpful for younger children. Punishments per se for failure to reach the contracted goals should be avoided. The therapist should "accept" responsibility for a failed contract to avoid increasing the guilt of parents and child. Special gains that may be afforded to the school refuser while at home during the school day should be carefully avoided. *Home instruction, albeit tempting to the parent who fears the child's "falling behind," should not be allowed as it implicitly validates the nonattendance.* The child should have input in formulating weekly goals; this will minimize a sense of coercion. Goals should be well defined and not open to interpretation by the child or parents. Contract review assessing success and distribution of rewards should be done only with the therapist.

PHARMACOTHERAPY

Given that a significant proportion of school refusers will respond after a brief (1- to 2-week) behaviorally oriented psychotherapy trial, medication need not be administered until this trial is attempted. However, patients who present emergently to the clinician or in the emergency room often require immediate psychopharmacological intervention to address their agitated state and phobic fear of return to school. The benzodiazepines, in particular alprazolam, are useful in these situations. Initial dose of 0.25 milligrams three times a day titrated to a maximum daily dose of 3 mg should be utilized. These medications are effective in alleviating anticipatory anxiety as well as separation anxiety (Gittelman & Koplewicz, 1986). However, they should be seen as short-term interventions and part of a comprehensive treatment plan that includes behavioral intervention as well as the initiation and titration of an antidepressant medication.

The tricyclic antidepressant imipramine is the most studied agent to date in separation anxiety disorder and school refusal in particular. Based on the observation that a majority of adults with panic attacks with agoraphobia had suffered separation anxiety as children, Klein (1964) theorized that it would have potential therapeutic effect. Klein felt these two disorders to be related to the same underlying dysregulation of the biological mechanisms modulating the anxiety associated with separation experiences. Imipramine already had been shown to have powerful effects on panic disorder with agoraphobia.

Studies using imipramine thus far have provided mixed results. A double-blind, placebo-controlled 6-week study of imipramine in 7- to 15-year-olds who were school refusers showed a significant medication effect. Imipramine was used in doses up to 200 mg per day with an average of about 150 mg. The children chosen for the study were those who had failed a brief trial of behaviorally based psychotherapy. This psychotherapy was continued throughout the medication trial. Imipramine aided in school attendance and in reducing other symptoms associated with separation anxiety disorder, such as somatic complaints. Depressive symptoms also were improved in those who manifested them, yet the presence of depression and its subsequent alleviation is not a necessary prerequisite in imipramine's antianxiety effect (Gittelman-Klein & Klein, 1971, 1980). A more recent study (Klein, Koplewicz, & Kanner, 1992) failed to replicate the previous findings. This latter study investigated imipramine's effect on separation anxiety disorder using criteria, from the third revised edition of *DSM*, not school refusal in particular.

Children tolerate tricyclic antidepressants relatively well; sedation and dry mouth are the most prominent albeit insignificant side effects. Disinhibition consisting of temper tantrums can occur. Of greatest concern is cardiac toxicity, which can involve arrhythmias and heart failure in overdose situations. The potential for conduction changes necessitates obtaining a baseline electrocardiogram, repeated with every 50 mg increase in dose. The Food and Drug Administration's recommended maximum dose is 5 mg per kilogram per day. The initial dose should start at 25 mg at bedtime; it can be raised by 25 mg every 4 to 7 days. As with depression, the therapeutic effect may take 4 to 6 weeks to develop. Tapering the medication gradually (25 mg per week) should be attempted after a 3-month period of symptom remission (Koplewicz and Williams, 1988).

Fluoxetine, one of the selective serotonin-reuptake inhibitors, in doses of 20 mg per day, has had some reported success in separation anxiety disorder. A safer medication than the tricyclic antidepressants without the cardiac effects, it does not require electrocardiograms monitoring (Popper, 1993).

Conclusion

In summary, Separation anxiety disorder (SAD) is prevalent and often quite debilitating. Its most extreme behavioral sequela, school refusal, is a critical challenge for the clinician and often requires urgent intervention. A combination of behavioral and psychopharmacologic modalities make the disorder an eminently treatable condition. Further controlled studies, especially of the newer antidepressant agents (selective serotonin-reuptake inhibitors), are needed to further elucidate better, improved, and safer treatments.

REFERENCES

Albano, A., Chorpita, B. F. (1995). Treatment of anxiety disorders of childhood. *Psychiatric Clinics of North America, 18 (4),* 767–784.

American Psychiatric Association. (1987). *Diagnostic and statistical manual of mental disorders* (3rd ed., rev.). Washington, DC: Author.

American Psychiatric Association. (1994). *Diagnostic and statistical manual of mental disorders* (4th ed.). Washington, DC: Author.

Bernstein, G. A., & Borchardt, C. M. (1991). Anxiety disorders of childhood and adolescence: A critical review. *Journal of the American Academy of Child and Adolescent Psychiatry, 30,* (4), 519–532.

Castaneda, A., McCandless, B., & Palermo, C. (1956). The children's form of the Manifest Anxiety Scale. *Child Development, 27,* 317–326.

Gittelman, R., & Klein, D. F. (1985). Childhood separation anxiety and adult agoraphobia. In A. H. Tuma & J. D. Maser. (Eds.), *Anxiety and the anxiety disorders* (pp. 389–402). Hillsdale, NJ: Lawrence Erlbaum.

Gittelman-Klein, R. (1975). Pharmacotherapy and management of pathological separation anxiety. *International Journal of Mental Health, 4,* 255–271.

Gittelman-Klein, R. (1988). Childhood anxiety disorders. In C. J. Kestenbaum, & D. T. Williams, (Eds.), *Handbook of clinical assessment of children and adolescents* (pp. 722–741). New York: New York University Press.

Gittelman-Klein, R., & Klein, D. F. (1971). Controlled imipramine treatment of school phobia. *Archives of General Psychiatry, 25,* 204–207.

Gittelman-Klein, R., & Klein, D. F. (1980). Treatment methods in school refusal: Drug therapy. In L. Hersov (Ed.), *School Refusal.* New York: John Wiley & Sons.

Gittelman, R., & Koplewicz, H. S. (1986). Pharmacotherapy of childhood anxiety disorders. In R. Gittelman, (Ed.), *Anxiety disorders of childhood* (pp. 188–203). New York: Guilford Press.

Kaplan, M. I., & Saddock, B. J. (1991). *Synopsis of psychiatry (6th ed.),* Baltimore, MD: Williams & Wilkins.

Klein, D. F. (1964). Delineation of two drug-responsive anxiety syndromes. *Psychopharmacologia, 5,* 397–408.

Klein, R. G., Koplewicz, H. S., & Kanner, A. (1992). Imipramine treatment of children with separation anxiety disorder. *Journal of the American Academy of Child and Adolescent Psychiatry, 31,* (1), 27–28.

Koplewicz, H. S. (1989). Separation anxiety disorder. *Children's Hospital Quarterly, 1,* (4), 335–338.

Koplewicz, H. S. (1990, May). *Preliminary data of a study of the efficacy of desipramine in the treatment of adolescents with major depressive disorder.* Paper presented at the 30th annual meeting of the New Clinical Drug Evaluation Unit, Key Biscayne, FL.

Koplewicz, H. S., & Williams, D. T. (1988). Psychopharmacological treatment. In C. J. Kestenbaum, & D. T. Williams, (Eds.), *Handbook of clinical assessment of children and adolescents* (pp. 1084–1110). New York: New York University Press.

Popper, C. W. (1993). Psychopharmacologic treatment of anxiety disorders in adolescents and children. *Journal Clinical Psychiatry, 54,* (5, Suppl.), 52–63.

Reynolds, C. R., & Richmond, B. O. (1978). What I think and feel: A revised measure of children's manifest anxiety. *Journal of Abnormal Child Psychology, 6,* 271–280.

29 / The Emergency Assessment and Response to the Acutely Psychotic Child and Adolescent

Joseph I. Sison and Lois Flaherty

Introduction

Psychoses refer to a group of disorders characterized by specific symptoms as well as gross disorganization of mental functioning. These disorders include schizophrenia and schizophreniform disorder, brief reactive psychoses, and psychoses associated with affective disorders. In addition, psychotic symptoms may be present in various types of organic brain syndromes, secondary to trauma or metabolic derangements. Although not the most frequent psychiatric emergency seen, psychotic children or adolescents may present in crises that pose challenges to the clinician. The form of presentation is variable, and psychotic symptoms range from the more obvious positive symptoms, such as hallucinations, delusions, and thought disorder, to more subtle negative symptoms of anergy, paucity of speech, and mild changes in affect (Andreasen, Flaum, Swayze, Tyrrell, & Arndt, 1990). These symptoms may in turn be overshadowed by other behavioral problems.

Acutely psychotic children and adolescents seen in emergency settings either have an acute exacerbation of a chronic disorder, such as schizophrenia, or present de novo. In cases where there is a known chronic psychotic disorder, the major task is to evaluate the reason for the decompensation and to determine whether the crisis can be handled on an outpatient basis or whether hospitalization is needed. This approach is essentially the same as to any psychiatric emergency once a diagnosis has been made: Multiple factors must be assessed and a treatment plan developed. These factors include severity of disturbance, psychodynamic and interpersonal influences, adequacy of community resources, family and social supports, and possibility of immediate psychosocial intervention. Many communities are experimenting with innovative new forms of intervention specifically designed to provide alternatives to hospitalization for children with severe psychiatric disorders, including psychotic disorders (Burchard & Clarke, 1990).

Assessment

The child who presents with psychotic symptoms without a previously diagnosed psychiatric disorder presents a different and difficult challenge. In children and adolescents, psychotic symptoms can have multiple causes, ranging from disorders considered "functional"—that is, without an identifiable organic etiology (although many are considered to have a neurobiological basis)—to those based on an identifiable neurological or systemic derangement. Functional disorders include schizophrenia, schizoaffective disorder, bipolar disorder, major depressive disorder, personality disorder, stress-related disorders, episodic dyscontrol, autism, and mental retardation. Organically, based disorders include neurologic, endocrine, substance induced, metabolic, and deficiency states; postoperative states; systemic illnesses; and abstinence phenomena (Groves & Manschreck, 1987). Because of the possibility of an acute and life-threatening etiology of the psychosis, as well as the danger posed by the patient's behavior to self and/or others, acute psychosis is a medical emergency. The immediate goals are to determine a working diagnosis and the need for hospitalization and to set the foundation for treatment by the approach to the patient and family.

Often, in an emergency setting, it is impossible to arrive at diagnostic certainty. The key question is whether an organic factor is involved. The physician's immediate task is thus to obtain as complete a history as possible and to perform a thorough physical exam as well as to perform simple diagnostic procedures to help in ruling out drug intoxication or metabolic, infectious, or traumatic etiologies of psychotic disorders. Symptoms pointing to organic etiology include: disturbances in memory, orientation, alertness, or level of consciousness; autonomic instability; and gross neurological deficits, such as gait changes and abnormal response of the pupils. In addition, one should gather as much information as possible about past medical history. Initial diagnostic procedures that can be done in the emergency room are a complete blood count, electrolytes, glucose, and urinalysis and urine toxicology screen. Arterial blood gases, spinal tap, or electroencephalogram should be obtained if hypoxia, intracranial mass or infection, or seizure disorder, respectively, are suspected (Ellison, 1985). It is important to remember that these are basically screening tests that can help identify an immediately life-threatening situation but are not definitive. Additionally, even if all evidence points toward a nonorganic etiology, symptoms such as hallucinations alone are not pathognomic of a psychotic disorder (Pilowsky & Chambers, 1986). Both of these facts argue in favor of initially withholding neuroleptic medication, useful primarily in schizophrenia and mood disorders with psychotic features, until a more certain diagnosis can be determined.

The second goal is to determine the need for hospitalization, and facilitate this. Hospitalization usually is indicated for diagnosis and/or treatment of acute psychotic disorders. Nearly all children and adolescents with these disorders would meet the criteria outlined by the 1986 Committee on Peer Review of the American Academy of Child and Adolescent Psychiatry (Stevenson & Duprat, 1987): "Patients requiring acute inpatient psychiatric treatment have impaired cognitive, emotional, physiological, physical, academic, family and/or social functioning, have not improved or cannot be managed in treatment at the primary level, and may be a danger to property, self and/ or others." Hospitalization allows for further evaluation, stabilization, and treatment. The decision to hospitalize an acutely psychotic child is clear when the child presents with flagrant psychotic symptoms as illustrated by the following case:

A 12-year-old boy with a history of precocious puberty presented with a 2-week history of auditory hallucinations and complaints of neighbors spying on him. In addition, he was reported by his mother to have suffered "sleeping spells" for approximately 1 year when he was 9 years old. Upon initial examination, the child was noted to be withdrawn and isolated with blunted affect. He reported "hearing voices" of 2 friends who had broken off their friendship with him several months ago. In addition, he seemed preoccupied with television celebrities with whom he thought he had a special relationship.

The acute psychotic symptoms, together with the history of precocious puberty and possible narcolepsy, raised concern about an organic etiology. Organic workup revealed a consistently elevated estradiol level and a mildly suspicious pituitary gland, but no specific endocrine dysfunction was identified. Although the auditory hallucinations and delusions resolved with neuroleptic treatment, the child continued to manifest negative symptoms of his illness—withdrawal, isolation, and blunted affect.

Many children present to outpatient clinics or to the emergency room with subtle symptoms of social isolation; withdrawal; impairment in personal hygiene and grooming; blunted, flat, or inappropriate affect; digressive, vague, overelaborate, circumstantial, or metaphorical speech; and odd or peculiar behavior. As a result, a diagnosis of a psychotic illness sometimes is missed until the more flagrant symptoms appear, as illustrated in the following example:

A 16-year-old high school student was referred by his family physician because of a history of withdrawal and increasing psychological dysfunction over the past year. His grades dropped although he continued to attend school regularly. Recently the parents became aware of his increasing concern and anxiety over his body, noting how much time he spent in front of the mirror. Also he confided to his parents that people were talking about him behind his back and saying he was "gay." The patient presented as a thin, pale, slightly disheveled-appearing teenager who avoided eye contact. He insisted that he had no psychological problems and did not wish treatment, although he acknowledged conflict with his parents. When asked him to elaborate on this he laughed and said, "They're trying to kill me." He was convinced he had an enlarged heart and this is why people think he is gay.

Acute Management

It is essential that the environment in which the patient is seen initially is safe, structured, and calm enough to minimize the possibility of dangerous or self-injurious behavior. If it is known ahead of time that a patient likely is acutely psychotic, arrangements should be made to have him or her brought to an emergency room setting where additional personnel and seclusion and restraint are available if needed. If such a patient presents in an office or clinic setting, safety concerns may indicate rapid removal to an emergency room before the evaluation is begun, as deterioration may occur in the course of an evaluation and/or at the point at which hospitalization is recommended. The emergency room should be equipped with a seclusion room or at least a "quiet room" out of the way of the main traffic where furnishings and equipment are kept to a minimum. In addition to the physical environment, the physician's approach can provide reassurance; patients and families may need to be told at the outset that dangerous or self-injurious behavior will be prevented. The initial approach should be verbal; physical restraint may be necessary and, in the case of an agitated and terrified patient, will be calming. Psychotropic medication can be used, but if the patient is to be admitted to the hospital immediately it is better to wait, as part of the evaluation in the inpatient setting should include observation of the patient in his or her baseline state. If necessary, agitation and extreme anxiety can be controlled effectively with major tranquilizers such as chlorpromazine, thioridazine, or haloperidol (Robinson, 1986). The use of neuroleptic treatment of children and adolescents with acute psychosis is basically similar to that in adults; neuroleptics can be used in acute situations to control extreme agitation and will have a nonspecific tranquilizing effect. According to Teicher and Glod (1990), a drug such as haloperidol should be initiated at a daily dose of 0.01 to 0.05 milligrams (mg) per kilogram per day (approximately 0.25–0.5 mg haloperidol or 15–50 mg of chlorpromazine equivalents for the average child) in divided dosages (usually twice-a-day dosing). Dosage then can be gradually increased by 0.25 to 0.5 mg haloperidol per day every 3 to 4 days until clinical response is obtained or side effects present themselves. The medication is increased gradually for several weeks until the target symptoms become minimized or resolved to a point that the patient's overall functional capacity is brought back or close to baseline. A daily divided dose of 0.5 to 4 mg haloperidol or 30 to 250 mg chlorpromazine usually is effective in children or adolescents, but some may require considerably higher doses. In addition to the older agents, newer "atypical" neuroleptics (clozapine, risperidone, and olanzapine) have become available in the general treatment of psychotic behaviors. Although there are limited data in their general use in children (Hardan, Johnson, Johnson, and Hrecznyj, 1996; Lombroso, Scahill, King, Lynch, Chappell, Peterson, McDougle, and Leckman, 1995; Quintana and Keshavan 1995; McKenna, K., Gordon, C., and Rapoport, J., 1994; Toren, Samuel, Weizman, Golomb, Eldar, and Laor, 1995), their use in the acute management of psychosis in this population is yet to be thoroughly investigated.

"Rapid tranquilization"—the administration of hourly, higher-than-usual doses of neuroleptic medication (5–10 mg haloperidol or 50–100 mg chlorpromazine), usually intramuscularly, under close supervision—is a technique that has been widely used to control agitated, threatening, and hyperaroused behavior in adults. The superiority of this technique over a standard approach has been questioned, and concerns have been raised about the danger of side effects, such as neuroleptic malignant syndrome, tardive dyskinesia, and severe extrapyramidal symptoms (Solano, Sadow, & Ananth, 1989). Because of these concerns, together with the absence of studies of rapid tranquilization in children and adolescents, this method cannot be recommended for them.

Benzodiazepines have been shown to be effective in controlling the agitated and hyperaroused state of acutely psychotic adults and have been recommended particularly when the diagnostic picture is unclear. However, most of the literature suggests that benzodiazepines worsen symptoms in psychotic children and may have a negative disinhibiting effect on children and adolescents who have significant impulsive and aggressive behavior and environmental stress (Green, 1991). In addition, benzodiazepines are not without risk of side effects, such as ataxia, nausea, vomiting, and cognitive impairment. Thus clinicians should be cautious when considering the use of benzodiazepines in children and adolescents in general and in psychotic and impulsive children in particular.

In spite of confusion and disordered thinking, acutely psychotic patients are very aware of their surroundings, although often in a distorted way. The initial approach can set the foundation for the development of a therapeutic alliance that is crucial to treatment. Even in the case of fairly young children who may seem unable to understand what is happening, it is important to offer simple explanations and information about what is planned. It is important to attempt to elicit the child's or adolescent's own story about what has happened to him or her, and how it is perceived.

Some reassurance, such as "The voices aren't real, even though they seem real," or "We won't allow anyone to hurt you" are appropriate. Providing a balance between being concerned without being intrusive to the patient is crucial. Communications need to be clear and simple. Children rarely will object to decisions about hospitalization if their parents are in agreement, although severe separation anxiety is not infrequent. With adolescents, who may manifest the kind of denial and lack of insight sometimes seen in psychotic adults, as well as perceive hospitalization as a threat to their autonomy, every attempt should be made to enlist the patient's agreement, although in some cases it may be necessary to impose a decision for hospitalization against the adolescent's will. In the course of listening to the patient's story, usually it is possible to identify some problem that the adolescent agrees could be worked on, such as family conflicts.

Since most children and adolescents will be brought for treatment by their families, and since it is the families who are on the front lines, in most cases, in dealing with the manifestations of the psychotic disorder, they must be involved in every aspect of the diagnostic and treatment process. A useful approach is to interview parents together with the child or adolescent briefly at first, then see the patient alone, then meet with the parents to hear their concerns in more detail, and then meet with the family together to discuss treatment recommendations. Families are likely to be very anxious and are in need of as much information about diagnosis and treatment recommendations as it is possible to give.

The physician should keep in mind that continued compliance by the patient and family will be essential in ultimately providing effective long-term treatment. The experience of unanticipated side effects with an initial dose of neuroleptic medication may interfere with subsequent compliance. Some clinicians recommend routine administration of antiparkinsonian medication with a neuroleptic; another option is careful monitoring of medication reactions and explanation to the patient of what to expect and reassurance that side effects can be controlled.

Conclusion

The assessment and response to the acutely psychotic child or adolescent encompasses many different facets that include various diagnostic and treatment considerations. In addition to reducing the patient's hyperaroused and agitated state, the physician also needs to address associated psychological components that may be occurring simultaneously. This includes paying attention to the physician-patient alliance, the family, and the patient's social support system besides prescribing psychopharmacologic treatment.

REFERENCES

Andreasen, N. C., Flaum, M., Swayze, V. W., Tyrrell, G., & Arndt, S. (1990). Positive and negative symptoms in schizophrenia. *Archives of General Psychiatry, 47,* 615–621.

Burchard, J. D., & Clarke, R. T. (1990). The role of individualized care in a service delivery system for children and adolescents with severely maladjusted behavior. *Journal of Mental Health Administration, 17,* 48–60.

Ellison, J. M. (1985). Emergency treatment of acute psychosis, agitation, and anxiety. *Hospital and Community Psychiatry, 36,* 351–352.

Green, W. H. (1991). *Child and adolescent clinical psychopharmacology.* Baltimore, MD: Williams & Wilkins.

Groves, J. E., & Manschreck, T. C. (1987). Psychotic patients. In T. P. Hackett & N. H. Cassem (Eds.), *Massachusetts General Hospital handbook of general hospital psychiatry* (pp. 208–226). Littleton, MA: PSG Publishing Company.

Hardan, A., Johnson, K., Johnson, C., and Hrecznyj, B. (1996). Case Study: Risperidone Treatment of Children and Adolescents with Developmental Disorders. *Journal of the American Academy of Child & Adolescent Psychiatry, 35(11),* 1551–1556.

Lombroso, P, Scahill, L, King, R., Lynch, K, Chappell, P, Peterson, B., McDougle, C., and Leckman, J. Risperidone (1995). Treatment of Children and Adolescents with Chronic Tic Disorders: A Preliminary Report. *Journal of the American Academy of Child & Adolescent Psychiatry, 34(9),* 1147–1152.

McKenna, K., Gordon, C., and Rapoport, J, (1994). Childhood-Onset Schizophrenia: Timely Neurobiological Research, *Journal American Academy Child & Adolescent Psychiatry, 33,6,* 771–781.

Pilowsky, D., & Chambers, W. (1986). *Hallucinations in children.* Washington, DC: American Psychiatric Press.

Quintana, H., and Keshavan, M. (1995). Risperidone in Children and Adolescents with Schizophrenia. *Journal of the American Academy of Child & Adolescent Psychiatry, 34(10),* 1292–1296.

Solano, O. A., Sadow, T., & Ananth, J. (1989). Rapid tranquilization: A reevaluation. *Neuropsychobiology, 22,* 90–96.

Stevenson, K., & Duprat, M. M. (1987). *Child and adolescent psychiatry: Guidelines for treatment resources, quality assurance, peer review and reimbursement.* Washington, DC: Academy of Child and Adolescent Psychiatry.

Teicher, M. H., & Glod, C. A. (1990). Neuroleptic drugs: Indications and guidelines for their rational use in children and adolescents. *Journal of Child and Adolescent Psychopharmacology, 1,* 33–56.

Toren, P., Samuel, E., Weizman, R., Golomb, A., Eldar, S., and Laor, N. (1995) Case study: Emergence of transient compulsive symptoms during treatment with clothiapine. *Journal American Academy Child & Adolescent Psychiatry, 34, 11,* 1469–1472.

30 / The Emergency Assessment and Response to the Substance Abusive Child and Adolescent

Mary Lynn Dell and Steven L. Jaffe

Substance-Related Morbidity and Mortality

The use of psychoactive drugs and resultant medical, psychiatric, and behavioral complications remain significant factors in most child, adolescent, and young adult emergency room visits each year. Although some studies indicate that substance abuse among American high school seniors has been gradually declining since the late 1970s, an estimated 50 to 80% of children have used alcohol or illegal drugs by their 18th birthday. Emergency treatment may be sought for problems related strictly to drug use, such as intoxication, overdose, withdrawal, delirium, or psychosis, or for situations associated with abuse. Substance intoxication frequently precedes trauma from motor vehicle accidents, violence, and drownings. Cocaine, alcohol, and marijuana are most often associated with traumatic injury, and cocaine in some geographic locations has surpassed alcohol as the chief culprit in drug-related emergencies (Hoffman and Goldfrank, 1990).

ASSOCIATED MORBIDITY AND MORTALITY

Substance abuse increases the risk of suicidality and aggressivity toward others. Suicide is the second leading cause of death in the 15- to 24-year-old age group, the peak years for illicit chemical use. Rich, Young, and Fowler from the San Diego Suicide Study reported in 1986 that 70% of suicides of individuals 30 years and younger involved a substance abuse diagnosis. Many suicide victims have measurable blood alcohol levels at the time of death, and intoxicated adolescents are more likely to choose guns as the means of suicide. Numerous studies have shown correlations between substance abuse and property destruction, robbery, assault, and homicide (Hoffman and Goldfrank, 1990).

General Approach to the Intoxicated Patient

In the emergency setting, the primary objectives are to keep the patient from harming self or others and to initiate appropriate life-support measures and medical management. Most intoxicated individuals respond well to calm, understanding but firm caregivers experienced with a range of psychiatric and medical emergencies. More often than not, agitated and anxious adolescents can be reassured and "talked down" in a quiet environment where chaos and unexpected surprises are minimized. The need for benzodiazepines, neuroleptics, and physical restraint is less frequent than commonly believed, although physicians and emergency personnel should be able to implement these strong interventions immediately if required to do so. Disruptive behaviors may be impulsive, intentional, or due to sensory distortions caused by the particular substances used.

Cardiorespiratory failure is the leading cause

of morbidity and mortality associated with drug abuse. The airway must be maintained and respiration supported. Depending on the substance ingested, endotracheal intubation may exacerbate laryngospasm and compromise respirations further; however, it may be necessary for airway preservation if the gag reflex is compromised or if gastric lavage is indicated. Pneumonia is the most frequent complication of child and adolescent substance abusers who require transfer to intensive care units. (Feltner, Izsak and Lawrence 1987, Kaminer 1991, Slaby and Martin 1991).

Proper treatment rests on accurate identification of the specific chemicals used by the patient. If possible, a complete, thorough history should be obtained from the patient, parents, and companions about the substances used, time and route of administration, length and nature of past drug experiences, in addition to a comprehensive medical and psychiatric history. The patient's belongings and clothes should be examined carefully for clues, especially if he or she is disoriented, comatose, or alone. Good histories and physical examinations are crucial, but many studies have documented poor correlations of patient reports with actual abuse practices and information obtained on toxicology screens. Familiarity with current local patterns of abuse may give an edge to clinicians making decisions about diagnosis and treatment. However, basic toxicology screens and laboratory tests are needed to assure that the presenting behavioral or medical problems are due to foreign chemicals, not medical or metabolic disorders or more traditional psychiatric illnesses, such as schizophrenia or bipolar disorder. Laboratory tests most helpful in the evaluation of intoxicated youths include serum and urine drug screens, serum electrolytes, blood urea nitrogen (BUN), creatinine, arterial blood gases, blood glucose, and routine urinalysis for ketones and glucose. Occasionally serum ketones and osmolality and liver function tests may be helpful. Urine and serum toxicology screens vary considerably in specificity, sensitivity, and ultimate clinical utility. Negative screens may be in total error or not even test for the culprit chemical. Similarly, positive screens do not automatically mean the clinical picture can be explained totally by the results or that another medication or blood constituent is not giving a false positive reaction. Toxicology screens used in emergency settings must be considered to render presumptive results until confirmed by more reliable and definitive methods such as mass spectrometry or gas chromatography. Unfortu-

nately, these modalities are extraordinarily expensive and time-consuming, forcing the clinician to rely on clinical management skills and the less-than-perfect toxicology screens for diagnosis and treatment. (Boehnert et al 1985, Verabey and Turner 1991)

CARDIOVASCULAR STABILIZATION AND GASTROINTESTINAL EVACUATION

After respirations have been stabilized and while efforts are in progress to identify the responsible substance, an intravenous line should be established, especially if the patient is in shock, is hypotensive or hypertensive, or is in convulsions. Information on the specific treatments for these complications is available elsewhere in appropriate medical and pediatric emergency literature and is known to personnel of mobile rescue services and hospital emergency rooms. To minimize unpredictable drug interactions and idiosyncratic responses, additional medication should not be administered, if possible. After the airway has been secured in individuals either known or strongly suspected to have orally ingested compounds, upper gastrointestinal evacuation may be attempted by gastric lavage. Ipecac frequently is used to induce vomiting but carries significant risk in patients who are not fully alert and cooperative or who have compromised protective airway reflexes. Activated charcoal, 0.5 to 1.0 grams per kilogram, may be given at varying time intervals to bind the drug and enhance excretion. In some cases, a laxative or cathartic also may be given to shorten gastrointestinal transit time. The latter 2 treatments may be beneficial in acute and chronic ingestions and perhaps in some cases of parental substance toxicity but are not without risk and must be medically supervised (Ferry and Yeager, 1987, Saechettie et al 1987, Thorpe 1987).

DIAGNOSTIC CLASSIFICATION OF SUBSTANCE-RELATED EMERGENCIES

Physicians must be familiar with the possible clinical presentations of substance abuse emergencies and know which chemicals are capable of producing particular symptoms. The DSM-IV lists dependence, abuse, intoxication and withdrawal as conditions relevant to all substances. Substance-induced delirium, persisting dementia, persisting amnestic disorder, psychotic disorder, mood disorder, anxiety disorder, sexual dysfunction, sleep disorder, and hallucinogen persisting perception disorder (flashbacks) are other organic mental syndromes with varying applicability to children and adolescents.

Drug withdrawal emergencies can be precipitated by cessation or relative dosage decreases of stimulants, opiates, and central nervous system depressants. Psychosis can be induced by phencyclidine, hallucinogens, central nervous system depressants, stimulants, and alcohol, and must be differentiated from acute mania, schizophrenia, depression with psychotic features, and organic brain syndromes. Cannabis, stimulants, and hallucinogens can induce panic reactions, which must be distinguished from panic produced by cardiac or thyroid disorders, obsessive compulsive disorder, and true panic and phobic disorders. Flashbacks are very frightening and often related to hallucinogens and cannabis, but are also present in posttraumatic stress disorders, affective disorders, schizophrenia, and organic brain syndromes. Although organic brain syndromes are most likely to occur with stimulants, phencyclidine (PCP), hydrocarbons, central nervous system depressants, and atropinelike drugs, any substance can cause organic brain syndrome in susceptible individuals in certain settings. Trauma, electrolyte and metabolic abnormalities, vitamin deficiencies, and brain injury also may masquerade as drug abuse emergencies if not suspected in a complete differential diagnosis. Schuckit (1989) has suggested emergency treatment guidelines and a decision-making process for adults that can be applied to children and adolescents as well. Anyone who has ingested enough of any substance to compromise vital signs must be assumed to have a toxic reaction. The reaction may consist of confusion, hallucinations, or delusions that remit after proper treatment. Patients with stable vital signs manifesting withdrawal symptoms must be assumed to be in an actual withdrawal state, even if psychotic symptoms or confusion is part of the picture, for these problems may be subsumed as part of withdrawal. An individual with stable vital signs, no obvious withdrawal symptoms, but significant confusion should be regarded as having an organic brain syndrome. Any transient psychotic symptoms can be expected to resolve after the organic brain syndrome has been sufficiently treated. Last, a patient with stable vital signs, no confusion or withdrawal symptoms, but with hallucinations, delusions, and/or paranoia without adequate insight should be treated for a nonsubstance abuse psychosis. This decision-making process may be especially helpful in conceptualizing the assessment and management of patients with multidrug overdoses, in which absolute identities and quantities of ingested substances cannot be determined.

With these diagnostic and treatment principles in mind, let us consider specific substances abused, their likely emergency presentations, differential diagnoses, and treatments.

Alcohol

Alcohol is the psychoactive substance most often abused by adolescents. The most common emergency problems are due to toxic reactions or overdose and resultant impairments. Adolescents frequently are involved in drunken driving accidents, and one-third to one-half of all accidents involve intoxicated drivers. Although teens are statistically less susceptible than adults to alcohol-related fractures, subdural hematomas, gastric hemorrhaging, and industrial accidents, they may be more likely to abuse alcohol with other unspecified substances. Hypoglycemia, acidosis, and electrolyte imbalances are occasionally dangers in younger drinkers.

Alcohol is a central nervous system depressant. It is rapidly absorbed from the gastrointestinal tract, and the degree of intoxication and impairment is directly related to the blood alcohol level, the rate of increase of the blood alcohol level, and the duration of time the level is maintained. The most common indications of alcohol intoxication in adolescents include ataxia; slurred speech; diminished reflexes; aggressive or belligerent behavior; impaired memory, concentration, and judgment; nausea; vomiting; and tremors. Teens often ingest large quantities in short periods, a combination that can lead to stupor and coma. Coma is virtually assured at levels of 400 to 500 mg per deciliter (dl), but small, inexperienced drinkers may become comatose at 200 mg per dl. Features of alcohol coma include hypothermia, respiratory depression, weakened pulses, and urinary retention or incontinence. Serum levels of 600 mg% are typically fatal.

Treatment consists of maintaining adequate airway and ventilation, correcting electrolyte and metabolic abnormalities, and general supportive care and observation until the alcohol has been sufficiently metabolized. When recent ingestion of a large volume of ethanol has occurred, gastric lavage may minimize later toxicity. Some advocate administering fructose *per os* or intravenously to facilitate ethanol metabolism, but this is seldom done due to the high incidence of abdominal pain and lactic acidosis that ensue after this therapy. If opiates are suspected as part of a multidrug overdose, naloxone should be given. In extreme cases, dialysis may be required to lower blood alcohol concentration. If the adolescent has a drinking problem of a few to several years' duration, he or she should receive thiamine 50 to 100 mg intramuscularly and be discharged with the recommendation for multivitamin supplementation.

Alcohol withdrawal symptoms are uncommon in adolescents because most alcohol-abusing teenagers are episodic binge drinkers. More frequent chronic alcohol drinking may occur yielding dependency and withdrawal symptoms. Such symptoms arise 4 to 6 hours after the last drink and may persist for 72 hours before remitting. Agitation, restlessness, tremors, hyperreflexia, and autonomic excitation are the principle features, although seizures are a rare occurrence. Benzodiazepines are the treatment of choice, especially chlordiazepoxide (Librium) 25 to 100 mg per day in divided doses or diazepam (Valium) 5 to 20 mg every 6 hours. These medications have relatively long half-lives, active metabolites, and produce stable serum concentrations over time. The dosages will vary, depending on the patient's size, but should be tapered and discontinued over 5 to 7 days after symptoms begin. Carbamazepine (Tegretol) also has been given at doses and serum levels similar to those used for seizure treatment. Carbamazepine may be continued longer than benzodiazepines, especially in patients with significant symptoms of affective or anxiety disorders. Alcohol-idiosyncratic intoxication, or pathological intoxication, is an uncommon disorder in which individuals have extreme behavioral changes after consuming very small amounts of ethanol. Age of onset may be in adolescence, and this diagnosis should be considered when alcohol intake is accompanied by sudden onset of confusion, disorientation, hyperactivity, amnesia, and disinhibited, assaultive behaviors uncharacteristic of the patient. Alcohol-idiosyncratic intoxication may last from a few minutes to 24 hours. Treatment must consist of prevention of harm to the patient and others. Chlordiazepoxide and diazepam in doses identical to those used to treat alcohol withdrawal also may be helpful.

Delirium tremens is not seen in childhood and adolescence as many years of drinking are required to be at risk for this condition. Alcoholic amnestic disorder is very rare before the age of 35, as is alcohol hallucinosis. Regardless of the alcohol problem encountered, emergency treatment is not complete without referral to appropriate, longer-term outpatient substance abuse treatment.

Amphetamines/Sympathomimetics

Amphetamine or similarly acting sympathomimetic agents include stimulants that may be taken orally, intravenously, or by intranasal administration. Street forms are rarely pure and often contain caffeine or other contaminants. Onset of action varies from a few seconds to a few hours, depending on route of administration and drug strength. Intoxication is characterized by central nervous system hyperactivity, including tachycardia, hypertension, restlessness, nausea, vomiting, hyperthermia, hyperventilation, insomnia, and mood changes ranging from euphoria to irritability. Aggressivity, anxiety, panic, anorexia, abdominal pain, chest pain, pressured speech, and impaired judgment are also common. Toxicology screens may be helpful in retrospect, but clinical decisions usually are required before results are known. Fatal overdoses range from the equivalent of 100 to 200 mg dextroamphetamine in the novice user to 1 gram or more in tolerant individuals. Death is caused by cardiac arrhythmias, hyperthermia, stroke, or cardiovascular collapse. Treatment of amphetamine intoxication or overdose includes airway maintenance and prevention of shock and circulatory collapse. Gastric lavage for oral ingestion should be accomplished by nasogastric tube if the patient is conscious or after intubation if he or she is unconscious. Hyperthermia should be managed by ice packs or cooling blankets. Seizures should be treated by intravenous diazepam, although intubation should be attempted in the event of diazepam-induced apnea or laryngospasm. Hypertension should be addressed with appropriate doses of antihypertensive medication. Amphetamine excretion may be facilitated by acidifying the urine with 250 to 500 mg ammonium chloride every 3 to 4 hours. If agitation is extremely severe, a low dose of a high-potency neuroleptic such as haloperidol may be helpful, but in order to avoid anticholinergic crises, low-potency medications should not be used.

The DSM-IV recognizes amphetamine (or amphetamine like)-related disorders, including dependence, abuse, intoxication, withdrawal, intoxication delirium, psychotic disorder with delusions or hallucinations, mood, anxiety, and sleep disorders, sexual dysfunction, and disorder not otherwise specified. Most of these conditions also may present as psychiatric emergencies. Signs and symptoms of amphetamine withdrawal include fatigue, dysphoria, intense drug craving, agitation, irritability, insomnia but increased dreaming when sleep does occur, apathy, and suicidality. Physical and psychiatric withdrawal symptoms usually begin insidiously but within 72 hours of stopping or significantly decreasing usage. Acute problems peak by day 4 or 5, but several weeks of depression may follow. Patients in withdrawal are at high suicide risk, and appropriate precautions should be taken. A quiet environment should be provided, and sleep should be permitted. Some clinicians prescribe the dopamine agonist bromocriptine (Parlodel), 0.625 to 2.5 mg per day in divided doses, for treatment of sleep disturbance, anergia, and depressive symptoms. Patients who develop delirium or psychosis usually do so within 24 hours of prolonged moderate- to high-dose usage. Delirium is characterized by fluctuating levels of consciousness, confusion, inattention, and loss of goal-directed behavior. Unlike delirious patients, those who are toxic or delusional remain oriented. Paranoia, mood lability, auditory or tactile hallucinations, and repetitious behaviors are common. Psychotic disorders with delusions usually indicate chronic use, although they can occur after large single doses. The clinical presentation is determined by the combination of premorbid personality traits, physical condition, dose and duration of ingestion, and other drugs used. Differentiation of amphetamine psychotic disorders with delusions or hallucinations from paranoid schizophrenia may be difficult to impossible. Psychotic disorder with delusions is more common than delirium and may last for several months. Treatment of delirium and psychotic disorders include measures already discussed for intoxication and appropriate measures to ensure the patient's safety, up to and including hospitalization. Low-dose, high-potency neuroleptics, such as haloperidol 2 mg to 5 mg intramuscularly or *per os,* may target the acute psychotic symptoms. Again, after the acute emergency patients should be referred for longer-term drug rehabilitation services. (Tani 1991)

Caffeine

Caffeine is a ubiquitous ingredient in legal beverages, over-the-counter medications, and food products. A single cup of coffee contains 100 to 150 mg caffeine. Toxic reactions are rarely severe enough to reach emergency status, but the equivalent of 1 gram caffeine (7–10 cups of coffee) can induce muscle twitching, arrhythmias, and psychomotor agitation. Many drugs of abuse are contaminated with large amounts of caffeine, and adolescents may unknowingly accumulate high doses in short time spans. Death has occurred with the consumption of 8 to 10 grams, primarily due to arrhythmias, grand mal seizures, and respiratory failure. If caffeine intoxication is suspected, beta blockers should be given for tachyarrhythmias and benzodiazepines for seizures. Central nervous system symptoms resolve as the serum caffeine level falls. Other DSM-IV caffeine-related disorders, usually nonemergent, include anxiety disorder, sleep disorder, and disorder not otherwise specified.

Cannabis

"Cannabis" refers to marijuana, hashish, and varying strengths of delta-9-tetrahydrocannabinol. It is generally smoked, occasionally eaten, and most users have mild to moderate reactions that never come to medical attention. Signs and symptoms of cannabis intoxication include sedation, euphoria, sensory enhancement, hunger, the sensation of slowed time, depersonalization, derealization, tremor, tachycardia, ataxia, nystagmus, increased perspiration, and conjunctival injection. Intoxication occurs almost immediately after inhalation, lasts 30 to 45 minutes, and resolves within 3 to 4 hours. Users are at high risk for automobile and other accidents during this time. New users may have symptoms resembling panic attacks. Treatment of cannabis intoxication and intoxication delirium includes management of suicidal and violent behaviors. Generally, excited patients can be talked down in a calm, supportive fashion. If necessary, panic and anxiety may be treated with benzodiazepines. It must always be remembered that marijuana may be contaminated by other substances, such as phencyclidine. Cannabis-induced psychotic disorder, with delusions, and cannabis-induced psychotic disorder, with hallucinations, occur after substance use. Manifestations of these disorders may include panic, flashbacks, confusion, visual hallucinations, paranoia, aggression, disorientation, and delusions. Differential diagnosis includes schizophrenia, bipolar disorder, and alcohol and hallucinogen intoxication. Treatment is similar to that of cannabis intoxication, with a time-limited use of low-dose, high-potency neuroleptic medications to treat psychotic symptoms, if necessary. (Schwartz 1987)

Cocaine

Cocaine emergencies are similar to amphetamine intoxication, withdrawal, delirium, and delusional disorders. Cocaine is smoked or snorted, has a half-life of 1 hour, and is the most self-reinforcing drug of abuse. Unchanged cocaine is detectable in blood and urine for only 12 hours after use, so the most reliable screen will detect cocaine's major metabolite, benzolecgonine; however, treatment cannot wait for the return of toxicology screens. Early signs of cocaine overdose include tachycardia, hyperthermia, hypertension, and acute psychosis. If present, seizures should be treated with intravenous diazepam. Dysrhythmias should be treated with appropriate doses of beta blockers, lidocaine, or phenytoin, and hyperthermia should be treated with cooling blankets. Cocaine is highly tissue-bound, rendering dialysis ineffective. Urinary acidification increases the possibility of renal toxicity and is likewise unhelpful. Intubation and artificial respiration may be required. Myocardial infarction may result from arrhythmias and coronary vasospasm. Benzodiazepines for sedation in the presence of psychotic symptoms may be more helpful than neuroleptic medications. (Tani 1991, Woodward and Selbst 1987)

Drug-dealing adolescents are susceptible to the "body packer syndrome," in which small packages of cocaine are ingested with a constipating drug for the purpose of smuggling. A single package contains 3 to 7 grams of cocaine, and rupture or leakage of even 1 to 3 grams can be fatal. When this situation is suspected, packages should be located radiographically. If successful evacuation cannot be accomplished within 48 hours by mild laxatives under extensive medical monitoring, surgical removal should be performed.

Hallucinogens

Hallucinogens include lysergic acid diethylamide (LSD), 2,5 dimethoxy-4 ethyl-amphetamine (STP), diethylhyptamine (DET), dimethyltryptamine (DMT), mescaline, psilocybin, and jimson weed. Hallucinogens have structural similarities to catecholamines and serotonin. LSD is the prototype hallucinogen and frequently is combined with phencyclidine, cocaine, caffeine, or strychnine. This class of substances has resurged in popularity on the streets and with teenagers in recent years. Emergency problems related to abuse may be due to extreme anxiety, "bad trips," intentional or accidental overdose, toxicity from accompanying substances ingested with LSD, or intercurrent trauma. The DSM-IV recognizes 10 hallucinogen-related disorders, including: abuse, dependence, intoxication, persisting perception disorder (flashbacks), intoxication delirium, psychotic disorder with delusions, psychotic disorder with hallucinations, mood disorder, anxiety disorder, and disorder not otherwise specified.

The clinical presentation of acute intoxication is influenced by the particular hallucinogenic agent, the dosage, other drugs used, half-life, the setting, and the patient's premorbid personality, physical and emotional health, and expectation of the drug's effects. Clinical findings include hypertension, tachycardia, hyperthermia, body image distortion, colorful geometric images and visual hallucinations, illusions, confusion, heightened sensory awareness, mood lability, euphoria, depersonalization, and derealization. The user may exhibit paranoia, severe anxiety or panic, impaired judgment, time distortion, and rarely aggression against self or others. Synthesia, giving the name of one sense to the function of another, is characteristic of hallucinogens. Flashbacks may occur after one or more experiences with a drug, usually last a few minutes, and may recur long after cessation of use. LSD trips can mimic schizophrenic agitation or unmask latent psychosis in predisposed individuals. The substance is usually ingested orally, often in sugar cubes, and doses of LSD as small as 35 micrograms can induce visual hallucinations. Death is extremely rare, although seizures are not uncommon.

The LSD user, unlike those abusing amphetamines, cocaine, or alcohol, typically is fully oriented and frequently will give a reliable drug use history while simultaneously hallucinating and experiencing other hallucinogenic effects. Low doses produce symptoms that may be confused with cannabis intoxication. LSD effects begin within 1 hour after ingestion, typically last 4 to 16 hours, but may continue for a few days. Treatment is primarily supportive. Oral ingestion of LSD may be treated by gastric lavage, charcoal, and a cathartic, but these measures are not used unless massive amounts have been taken. Some serum toxicology screens are helpful if they can detect and confirm the presence of hallucinogens in the blood. Most overdose patients respond favorably to reassuring caregivers "talking them down" and providing orienting information in a quiet, well-lighted room. Benzodiazepines are advised if the user is anxious or needs sedation. Chlorpromazine should be avoided to prevent serious hypotensive episodes and because low-potency neuroleptics lower the seizure threshold. High-potency neuroleptics, such as haloperidol, are used with success by some physicians in place of benzodiazepines. Flashbacks are usually time-limited and require no specific treatment. LSD use has been known to precipitate the first manic episode of a bipolar disorder. LSD psychotic disorders and amphetamine psychotic disorders are sometimes difficult to distinguish. Amphetamine psychotic disorders are usually paranoid in tone and occur after chronic abuse, whereas LSD intoxication is characterized by greater pupillary dilatation, non-frightening hallucinations, and a clearer sensorium. Hospitalization is indicated if the patient is harmful to self or if psychotic symptoms have not remitted in 24 hours. (Kulig 1990)

Inhalants

Inhalant intoxication is also known as glue sniffing or solvent or hydrocarbon intoxication. Hydrocarbon abuse is prevalent in grade-school populations, peaking in 11- to 12-year-olds. Duration of abuse is 1 to 2 years, and glue sniffing is second only to alcohol in substances used by adolescent and children. The list of volatile hydrocarbons that can produce the desired altered but pleasurable mental status is limitless. Aliphatic petroleum products, such as diesel and fuel oils, kerosene, gasoline, and petroleum ether are abused. Turpentine and other natural oils, benzine, toluene and other aromatic hydrocarbons, and halogenated hydrocarbons are choice agents of abuse. Fumes may be inhaled directly from the container or from a plastic bag into which the hydrocarbon has been poured. The most dangerous route of administration is spraying aerosols directly into the nose or mouth. Hydrocarbons are lipophilic, readily absorbed from the pulmonary circulation, and transported to the central nervous system where they act as depressants, and then are eliminated by an hour after inhalation. Severe overdose can produce central nervous system depression, seizures, and coma. Clinicians have been debating the role of emesis and gastric lavage for solvent overdose; probably it should not be attempted for amounts less than 1 milliliter of solvent per kilogram of body weight. Gastrointestinal evacuation should be pursued for oral ingestions if the substance is known to have significant renal, hepatic, or cardiac toxicities or if an additive in the solution is known to be toxic. Under no circumstances should emesis or gastric lavage be undertaken without a cuffed endotracheal tube in place. Assisted ventilation and oxygenation are indicated for abnormal blood gases. Deaths are chiefly due to dysrhythmias or from accidents during intoxication. Psychiatric manifestations include mild euphoria or depression, delusions, paranoia, and aggression that may manifest as violence toward self or others. Chronic use may lead to cerebellar degeneration and delayed thought processing. When recognized, youths abusing solvents should be referred to appropriate outpatient treatment facilities. (Gay 1987, Wasson 1991)

DSM-IV has recognized the different chronological and clinical manifestations of inhalant-related problems by specifying the diagnostic categories of abuse, dependence, intoxication, intoxication delirium, persisting dementia, psychotic disorder with delusions, psychotic disorder with hallucinations, mood disorder, anxiety disorder, and disorder not otherwise specified.

Nicotine

Nicotine is generally considered harmful medically after years of chronic use, but overdoses occasionally are seen in children and teenagers. Nicotine transiently increases heart rate and blood pressure, which can induce panic attacks in predisposed individuals. Ingestion of 60 mg is fatal in adults, and smaller quantities are potentially fatal in children. Overdose symptoms include nausea, vomiting, diarrhea, abdominal pain, dizziness, bradycardia, hypotension, respiratory depression, and convulsions. Death usually is due to severe respiratory compromise. Treatment consists of supporting respirations and blood pressure and gastric lavage or activated charcoal for oral ingestions. Renal excretion may be facilitated by urinary acidification with 500 mg oral ammonium chloride every 3 to 4 hours. Hospitalization is required in only the most severe cases.

Heroin and Other Opiates

Opiates include the naturally occurring substances codeine, opium, and morphine, the semisynthetics, heroin, hydromorphone (Dilaudid), and oxycodone (Percodan), and the synthetic compounds meperidine (Demerol) and propoxyphene (Darvon). Opiates are prescribed legitimately for analgesia but are abused for the side effects of sedation, mood alteration, and clouding of consciousness. Opiates are frequently part of a polysubstance abuse picture, used with other central nervous system depressants. This class of compounds is associated with multiple medical problems, especially abscesses, tuberculosis, pneumonia, hepatitis, bacterial endocarditis, HIV infections, septic emboli, and mycotic aneurysms.

While children and adolescents present occasionally after overdose on prescription narcotics they find available in the homes of friends and relatives, the 1990's have seen a resurgence in the popularity and availability of heroin and closely-related derivatives and imitations. Therefore, discussion will focus on heroin as the prototypic opiate emergency.

Signs and symptoms of heroin intoxication include apathy, drowsiness, dulled pain sensation, mood variability, nausea, constipation, flushing, bradycardia, hypothermia, hypertension, slurred speech, psychomotor retardation, and impairments in memory and judgment. At higher doses, seizures, coma, and death are possible. The classic triad of opiate toxicity is comprised of respiratory depression, constricted or pinpoint pupils, and decreased levels of consciousness. Heroin overdose is an acute medical and psychiatric emergency, and must be distinguished, if possible, from ethanol or barbiturate intoxication and hallucinogen hallucinosis. Any comatose adolescent suspected of heroin abuse or without clues for medical etiology should receive airway and respiratory

support and intravenous naloxone 0.01 mg per kilogram up to 0.4 to 2.0 mg in an adult-size person. If impaired consciousness is due to narcotic overdose, the response to naloxone or the similarly acting narcotic antagonist nalorphine or levallorphan is rapid. However, agonist half-lives are much shorter than opiate half-lives, and naloxone must be repeated relatively frequently to prevent resurgence of opiate toxicity.

Heroin withdrawal is extremely frightening and incapacitating but does not pose the life-threatening dangers of other substance abuse emergencies. Signs and symptoms include increased perspiration, lacrimation, rhinorrhea, tachypnea, tachycardia, pupillary dilation, and piloerection. Diarrhea, fever, hypertension, vomiting, insomnia, and orgasmic sensations are common. The patient is typically anxious or panicked, depressed, irritable, craves more heroin for symptom alleviation, and may become combative or aggressive. These problems should be differentiated from barbiturate or other hypnotic withdrawal or flu-like syndromes. Opiate withdrawal is precipitated by cessation or reduction of dosages. Withdrawal from most opiates including heroin, manifests within 6 to 8 hours, peaks in 2 to 4 days, and resolves in 4 to 5 days. Methadone has a much longer half-life, and symptoms may not appear for 3-days or disappear until after 14 days. Cross-tolerance exists among opiates, and medically supervised withdrawal is accomplished by substituting methadone or another oral long-acting opiate and gradually weaning over 1 to 2 weeks. Methadone dosages of 20 to 40 mg per day are begun, then gradually tapered. Children and adolescents usually do not require the long-term methadone maintenance therapy used for older addicts.

Phencyclidine

Phencyclidine is a white crystalline substance that may be taken intravenously, nasally, or by smoking. Oral ingestion may be indicative of a suicide attempt. PCP may be contaminated by or be a contaminant of LSD, marijuana or hashish, cocaine, or psilocybin. Onset of signs and symptoms is quite rapid, and may include confusion, hypertension, fever, tachycardia, increased salivation, hyperactive reflexes, ataxia, myoclonus, psychomotor agitation, decreased pain sensitivity, stereotypies, and vomiting. Pupils may be constricted but often are of normal size. Hiccoughs, spasticity, increased auditory sensitivity, and tachypnea are not infrequent. PCP has the characteristic pattern of eliciting a horizontal followed by a vertical nystagmus. Psychiatric manifestations may mimic paranoid schizophrenia or schizophreniform disorder, with thought disorder, ideas of reference, hallucinations, paranoia, agitation, tangentiality, negativism, and mood lability. Behavior becomes increasingly bizarre, aggressive, and potentially harmful to self or others as the dose increases. A severe overdose can produce comas in which the eyes remain open, or status epilepticus, respiratory failure, or arrhythmias, all of which may lead to death. PCP intoxication also must be differentiated from a mania, encephalitis or other organic brain syndrome, and hallucinogen or amphetamine intoxication.

PCP intoxication is divided into 3 stages for evaluation and management. PCP can be measured in blood, urine, and gastric contents, but turnaround time is too long to be clinically useful in the emergency setting. In Stage I, the patient is disoriented, potentially harmful to self or others, but still conscious. He or she should be kept in a calm, quiet environment where vital signs can be monitored and someone can reassure and orient the patient. Oral secretions may be increased, and the suctioning should be done from the external corners of the mouth to avoid laryngospasm. Ipecac should never be given for PCP ingestions as it increases the risk of seizures. If vital signs indicate the beginnings of an adrenergic crisis, propranolol 40 to 80 mg 3 times a day may be administered. Agitation is best treated by diazepam 10 to 30 mg in divided doses. Stage II patients are unconscious but without medical complications. Responses may be elicited to noxious stimuli. In addition to Stage I interventions, catheterization may be needed for PCP-induced urinary retention. Furosemide may increase excretion. Again, deep suctioning and intubation should be avoided. When the patient becomes conscious, Stage I management should be resumed.

Stage III PCP intoxication means the patient is unconscious, possibly seizing, and in adrenergic crisis. At this stage, airway and respiratory support and maintenance of vital signs are crucial to prevent death. Furosemide and ascorbic acid should be given to enhance excretion, and diazepam or other anticonvulsants may be required for seizures. Cooling blankets or sponge baths are used to treat hyperthermia, and beta blockers are needed to treat acute hypertension. Hospitalization in an appropriate medical setting is required. As the patient improves, Stage II then Stage I care is implemented then gradually weaned.

Although mild PCP intoxication may clear rapidly, a psychosis can appear that may last indefinitely and require low doses of high-potency neuroleptics. All cases of PCP overdose must be assumed to be life-threatening until proven otherwise.

Sedatives, Hypnotics, and Anxiolytics

The grouping of sedatives, hypnotics, and anxiolytics in the fourth edition of the *Diagnostic and Statistical Manual of Mental Disorders* includes barbiturates, benzodiazepines, methaqualone, diphenhydramine, and various other "sleeping pills" used by adolescents. These drugs frequently are used in suicide attempts and are even more dangerous when combined with other central nervous system depressants, such as alcohol or opiates. The pharmacokinetics of the individual chemicals may vary, but the signs and symptoms of intoxication and withdrawal are quite generalizable. Sedation, somnolence, irritability, derealization, depersonalization, disinhibition of aggressive and sexual impulses, mood lability, slurred speech, motor incoordination, ataxia, and impairment of memory and judgment are common. In more serious overdoses, hypothermia, hypotension, respiratory depression, shock, and coma are possible. Death results from central nervous system depression. Sedative hypnotic intoxication can be distinguished from opiate intoxication by the administration of intravenous naloxone. Opiate antagonists do not reverse sedative hypnotic drug effects.

Acute treatment of sedative hypnotic intoxication must be guided by the history and neurological examination. Toxicology screens will confirm the diagnosis but are not helpful emergently. Pupillary reflexes are slow to react, corneal reflexes are initially absent, and pain and deep tendon reflexes are diminished. These neurological findings indicate the level of coma and improve over time. The airway should be maintained, even if intubation and artificial respiration are required. Blood gases should be monitored and oxygen administered. Intravenous access should be established, urine output monitored, and fluids replaced. If the substances were ingested orally in the preceding 4 to 6 hours, gastric lavage is indicated, and repeated use of activated charcoal may hasten elimination. Medically induced diuresis is occasionally helpful, but not if vital signs are stable, reflexes intact, or the overdose consists only of diazepam or chlordiazepoxide. Cardiac arrhythmias are especially common with short-acting barbiturates and must be treated with appropriate antiarrhythmic medications. Peritoneal or hemodialysis are final treatment options when the preceding measures are insufficient to treat the acute overdose.

Sedative hypnotic withdrawal is typically undertaken in an inpatient setting due to the possible medical complications. Withdrawal from a short-acting substance may begin in less than 6 hours after the last dose and peak in 2 to 4 days, whereas days to weeks may pass after the last dose of a long-acting sedative hypnotic before withdrawal begins. Withdrawal signs and symptoms can be separated into four stages. Stage I includes orthostatic hypotension, tremor, nausea, vomiting, diaphoresis, difficulty sleeping, poor appetite, abdominal cramping, hyperreflexia, and anxiety. Stage II consists of hallucinations in addition to Stage I symptoms. Generalized seizures mark Stage III. Stage IV is a life-threatening constellation of problems, with the added findings of delirium, hypertension, tachycardia, hyperpyrexia, confusion, and disorientation. Vital signs must be monitored at least every 4 hours during the first few days of treatment and every half hour if blood pressure and pulse are abnormal. Thiamine 100 mg *per os* twice a day, pyridoxine 100 mg *per os* every day and multivitamin and zinc supplementation are advisable.

Detoxification begins when the withdrawal syndrome is stabilized; hence stabilization must be established with a detoxification process foremost in mind. Most adolescents who have been dependent on sedative hypnotics long enough to go into withdrawal can be treated with adult protocols, but doses of some cross-dependent drugs used for detoxification may need to be lowered. Phenobarbital is the most frequently used agent because its long half-life of 80 to 120 hours produces more stable blood levels, it is relatively safe medically, and toxic doses are much lower than fatal doses. Phenobarbital usually does not disinhibit patients, leading to fewer behavior problems in the treatment setting. Tables exist that convert the doses of several central nervous system depressant drugs to phenobarbital equivalents (Smith, 1984). When the total daily phenobarbital equivalent dose is figured, it should be given in divided doses every 6 hours to a daily maximum of 500 mg. After 2 days of stable vital signs, the daily dose should be decreased by 30 mg, or 10% per day. If doubt exists about the amount of sedative hypnotic being abused, a pentobarbital challenge can establish the dose of phenobarbital necessary to start detoxification. Pentobarbital 100 mg *per os* is given every hour until the patient becomes intoxicated, then the amount of pentobarbital is converted to phenobarbital equivalents.

When the sedative hypnotics of abuse are solely or primarily benzodiazepines, the longer-acting benzodiazepines clonazepam (Klonopin), clorazepate (Tranxene), or diazepam may be used for detoxification. Benzodiazepine challenge tests exist to obtain the stabilization dose used as the starting point for detoxification. Oxazepam (Serax) 30 mg *per os* every half hour is given until the patient is sleepy. The total dose of oxazepam is halved to convert to the 24-hour dose of chlorazepate. Clorazepate is given in divided doses every 6 hours then tapered by 10% per day if vital signs remain stable. Another option is to convert oxazepam dosage into clonazepam equivalence, then taper by 10% per day.

Sedative hypnotic withdrawal includes anxiety and drug-seeking behaviors. Around 10% of patients develop hallucinations, deliria, or organic brain syndromes. These complications require inpatient hospitalization. Confusion clears relatively sooner for younger than older patients. In addition, central nervous system depressants may elicit an acute-onset psychosis with auditory hallucinations and paranoid delusions. This normally clears within a few days to 2 weeks and rarely requires intervention with neuroleptic medications. Barbiturate and sedative abuse also may produce an amnestic syndrome similar to alcohol abuse, with onset typically in the late 20s or early 30s.

Steroids

The fourth edition of the *Diagnostic and Statistical Manual of Mental Disorders* has no specific category for steroids, but steroid-induced disorders may be classified under Other (or Unknown) Substance-Induced Disorders Clinicians should be familiar with steroid effects due to increased popularity in recent years.

Patients may come to a psychiatrist's attention with side effects of steroids prescribed for medical purposes or problems from illicit steroid abuse. No predictable relationship exists among type, onset, and severity of symptoms with the duration or dosage of steroids used. Most frequently seen psychiatric manifestations include mania or euphoria, depression, and psychosis. Psychotic symptoms may include auditory hallucinations and paranoid and grandiose delusions. A long history of abuse may lead to dementia.

The first step in treating steroid-induced psychiatric symptoms is to determine the advisability of discontinuing the steroids. The answer may be quite obvious in the case of athletes receiving injections to enhance physical abilities but not as clear-cut in patients receiving steroids for severe medical illnesses. In such cases, the steroid must be decreased to the lowest effective dose and the patient kept safe if alternative medical treatment is not possible. Fortunately, symptoms of steroid psychosis and mood disorders normally subside when the substance is discontinued. If symptoms are severe, a time-limited treatment with low-dose haloperidol may be helpful in keeping the patient safe and more comfortable.

Over-the-counter Products

Another category of frequently abused substances are over-the-counter preparations. Teenagers are at high risk to abuse these substances, for they are readily available, at low cost, difficult to monitor, and too infrequently suspected. Diet substances, consisting primarily of phenylpropanolamine, are abused on a regular basis. Phenylpropanolamine is a sympathomimetic drug, and its effects and treatment are discussed in the section on amphetamines and similarly acting drugs. Ephedrine and pseudoephedrine are found in nasal decongestants and bronchodilators and act analogously to phenylpropanolamine. Many over-the-counter medications contain caffeine and ethanol. Antihistamines are possible substances of abuse. Diuretics and laxatives are not traditionally considered to be addicting, but patients with eating disorders use great quantities and may become psychologically and physically dependent (Pentel 1984).

Conclusion

Despite the attention to substance abuse by law enforcement, government, education, and other institutions in contemporary society, illicit and abusable drugs continue to threaten the health and lives of children and adolescents. In addition to the emergency situations described in this chapter, substance abuse has serious comorbidity which further increases the critical aspects of numerous other acute and chronic psychiatric conditions (Jaffe 1996). Psychiatric and medical emergencies are among the most frequently encountered in clinical practice, necessitating recognition and understanding by psychiatrists and all professionals caring for children and adolescents.

REFERENCES

Bailey, G. W. (1989). Current perspectives on substance abuse in youth. *Journal of the American Academy of Child and Adolescent Psychiatry, 28,* 151–162.

Boehnert, M. T., Lewander, W. J., Gaudreault, P., & Lovejoy, F. H. (1985). Advances in clinical toxicology. *Pediatric Clinics of North America, 32,* 193–211.

Feltner, R., Izsak, E., & Lawrence, H. S. (1987). Emergency department management of the intoxicated adolescent. *Pediatric Clinics of North America, 34,* 399–421.

Ferry, F. T., & Yeager, A. M. (1987). Poisonings and ingestions. In F. E. Ehrlich, F. J. Heldrich, & J. J. Tepas III, *Pediatric emergency medicine* (pp. 239–268). Rockville, MD: Aspen Publishers.

Gay, M. (1987). Abuse of solvents and other volatile substances. In J. A. Black II, *Pediatric emergencies* (pp. 529–532). London: Butterworth's.

Hoffman, R. S., & Goldfrank, L. R. (1990). The impact of drug abuse and addiction on society. *Emergency Medicine Clinics of North America, 8,* 467–480.

Jaffe, S. L., ed. (1996). Adolescent substance abuse and dual disorders. *Child and Adolescent Psychiatric Clinics of North America, 5,* 1–256.

Kaminer, Y. (1991). Adolescent substance abuse. In R. J. Frances & S. I. Miller, *Clinical textbook of addictive disorders* (pp. 320–346). New York: Guilford Press.

Kulig, K. (1990). LSD. *Emergency Medicine Clinics of North America, 8,* 551–558.

Pentel, P. (1984). Toxicity of over-the-counter stimulants. *Journal of the American Medical Association, 252,* 1898–1903.

Rich, C. L., Young, D., & Fowler, R. C. (1986). San Diego Suicide study: I. Young vs. old subjects. *Archives of General Psychiatry, 43,* 739–745.

Saechetti, A. D., Ramoska, E. A., Montone, H., & Carraccio, C. (1987). Initial management of adolescent overdoses. *Pediatric Emergency Care, 3,* 5–9.

Schuckit, M. A. (1989). *Drug and alcohol abuse* (3rd ed.). New York: Plenum Medical Book Company.

Schwartz, R. H. (1987). Marijuana: An overview. *Pediatric Clinics of North America, 34,* 305–317.

Slaby, A. E., & Martin, S. D. (1991). Drug and alcohol emergencies. In N. S. Miller, *Comprehensive handbook of drug and alcohol addiction* (pp. 1003–1030). New York: Marcel Dekker.

Smith, D. (1984). Benzodiazepine dependence potential: Current studies and trends. *Journal of Substance Abuse Treatment, 1,* 163–167.

Tani, S. A. (1991). Cocaine and amphetamines. In M. Grossman & R. A. Dieckmann, *Pediatric emergency medicine: A clinician's reference* (pp. 363–364). Philadelphia: J. B. Lippincott.

Thorpe, F. G. (1987). Acute psychiatric conditions. In J. A. Black II, *Paediatric Emergencies* (pp. 519–528). London: Butterworth's.

Verabey, K., & Turner, C. E. (1991). Laboratory testing. In R. J. Frances & S. I. Miller, *Clinical textbook of addictive disorders* (pp. 221–236). New York: Guilford Press.

Wason, S. (1991). Hydrocarbons. In M. Grossman & R. A. Dieckmann, *Pediatric emergency medicine: A clinician's reference* (pp. 371–372). Philadelphia: J. B. Lippincott.

Woodward, G. A., & Selbst, S. M. (1987). Chest pain secondary to cocaine use. *Pediatric Emergency Care, 3,* 153–154.

SECTION VI
Forensic Child and Adolescent Psychiatry

31 / The Rights of Children and Adolescents

Judith R. Milner

Children's and adolescents' rights have aroused much interest among scholars of psychiatry and the law in recent years. Early on, Adams, Berg, Berger, Ducene, Neill, and Ollendorff addressed this area in their book, *Children's Rights* (1971). It is important to make one distinction from the outset of this discussion. There are two groups of children's rights advocates: One group (sometimes derisively called "kiddie savers") advocates increasing children's protection under the law, and the other group advocates increasing children's civil or political liberties (so-called kiddie libbers). These forms of child advocacy are not mutually exclusive, but they do lead to different priorities. A historical review of contributions to the rights of young people helps to explain the present state of their rights (Adams and Fras, 1988).

The 16th Century

Both protection under the law and the granting of certain civil liberties to children have evolved over the centuries against the backdrop of prevailing societal views of children (Cleverly and Phillips, 1986). Let us look at how children have been viewed historically. According to Philippe Ariès (1962) in *Centuries of Childhood*, before the 16th century childhood was not considered a separate and distinct phase from adulthood. Children were considered merely to be miniature adults without unique features or unique needs. This view of childhood is illustrated in the works of Brueghel the Elder, who depicted his subjects as small adults. Children were portrayed with the same facial features and bodily proportions as adults, but diminutively. As small adults, children obviously were less able to perform as much work as adults, less able to protect themselves, and certainly more of a liability. It is no wonder that Lloyd de Mause reports that the farther one looks back in history, the bleaker the life of children becomes. For centuries, children were beaten and some-times killed, starved, tortured, sexually abused, and sold into slavery.

Only in the 16th and 17th centuries did mothers and nannies—a group without much political clout themselves—begin to advocate for childhood as being a distinctly separate stage with specific features and needs. They spoke as well for the right of children to be protected from the abuses that had been so prevalent in preceding generations. This plea also was taken up by the clergy, which helped, and by philosophers. As early as 1524 Martin Luther urged the education of German children in public schools and advocated literacy for all German people. In 1580 Michel de Montaigne in his *Essais* called attention to the right of the child to be a child and not a miniature adult. A new era began to dawn, accompanied by the introduction of children's clothes, children's games, and institutions designed for the education of children—at least male children. Children's rights to medical treatment also began to be considered. In 1545 Thomas Phayre wrote *Boke on Children,* the first pediatric text in English.

The 17th Century

Although ideological trends in the 17th century may have favored children's rights, young people still had no protection under the law. If anything, the law seemed to work to their disfavor. In 1601 the English Poor Law, passed during Elizabeth I's reign, established the virtue of child labor in law for the next three centuries. Advocates of childhood education, however, continued to press forward. In 1618 Johann Amos Comenius, a Moravian leader, published *School of Infancy,* in which he described types of education suitable for the child's first 6 years. In 1654 Comenius published the first picture book for children in Nuremberg.

Of major import during the 17th century were the writings of John Locke (1632–1714), noted British academic, doctor, philosopher, and political theorist. According to Locke, the child comes into the world with a mind like a blank tablet, a *tabula rasa*. For the most part, Locke believed that a person's subsequent formation of values and ideas, as well as major accomplishments, were a product of the education received. Since all children start life with the same potentialities, later inequalities between adults are a result of environmental influences, both enhancements and deficiencies. Locke's views gave impetus to early American revolutionaries and laid the groundwork for future avid environmentalists, such as Claude Adrien Helvetius (1715–1771). Helvetius blamed all of humanity's defects on poor education, suggesting that this task be taken out of the hands of the church and be made the responsibility of an enlightened government. Locke also influenced future educators, such as Maria Montessori (1870–1952).

The 18th Century

The declarations of Helvetius can be appreciated when examining contemporary views of the 18th-century child. By then children often were regarded as unique entities who were entitled to an education, but the right to an education was not yet guaranteed under the law. Also, the responsibility for education lay solely in the hands of the church. Educators in the Puritan evangelical tradition of the seventeenth and eighteenth centuries in Britain and the United States held that in any educational program man's inherent sinfulness must be taken into account. John Wesley, the founder of the Methodist movement, contended that the first task of education was the restraint of self-will in the child. The child was viewed as being inherently defective and sinful; hence all extremes of physical and psychological coercion and repression of young children were justified as a means to the end of purification. So, although they had the theoretical right to an education, so to speak, children had no presumed right to protection from the educators.

Certainly the erratic Swiss genius Jean-Jacques Rousseau was a ray of bright light for 18th-century children. In direct opposition to the evangelists, and as a student of John Locke's, he regarded the child as being inherently good, only to be ultimately corrupted by society. In his revolutionary novel *Èmile* (1762), he advocated freedom in education. Another 18th-century intellectual and educational reformer, Johann Heinrich Pestalozzi, in 1774 described how adjustment integrates physical, intellectual, and moral factors. He also observed and kept a diary of his own child, and emphasized direct observation of children as the best means for knowing the child. Dietrich Tiedemann followed suit by keeping the first careful journal record of a child's growth in 1787.

Even blind and deaf children were thought to have the right to education in the eighteenth century. In 1784 Valentin Haüy established the first school for the blind in Paris and Jacob Rodriguez Périère taught deaf mutes to communicate. And in 1798 Jean Itard treated Victor, the "wild boy of Aveyron," at Paris's Institution for the Deaf and Dumb.

During the 18th century strides were made in the field of pediatrics, reflecting and reinforcing the attitudes of then-current social reformers. In 1800 Johann Peter Frank (1745–1821) first urged attention to social pediatrics—school hygiene, the state's responsibility for child health, and the need of medical care for "bastards," orphans, and fostered infants.

The 19th Century

By the 19th century abuses of children under the English Poor Law seemed to reach a pinnacle in Britain. From the age of 3 or 4, armies of young children were marshaled to work in the factories or the mines, with no regard being given to their well-being. Not only were they deprived of education, they also were deprived of sleep, food, and humane or even safe working conditions. Children were sold as slaves, and many were permanently maimed or even killed on the job. Women and children were considered to be cheap labor, and they certainly experienced the least protection and the most violation during the early years of the Industrial Revolution.

The works of Karl Marx and Friedrich Engels drew extensively on British government reports of the florid and horrendous abuse of working-class children in the British factory system. They advocated not only an end to the abuses but a reinstatement of childhood education for all children. They pushed for a socialist education that was not under the control of the church or the bourgeoisie. In 1848 they wrote *The Communist Manifesto.*

Interestingly, there was great opposition in Britain to the passing of laws that would protect working-class youth on the grounds that no one had the right to interfere with the liberties of the industrial managers. Nevertheless, by the second half of the 19th century, the Factory Acts began curbing the most blatant abuses. And later British Factory Acts required some schooling for child workers—poor in quality though it was. Unfortunately, widespread passage of similar child labor laws did not occur in the United States until the twentieth century. In 1900, 1.7 million U.S. children under the age of 16 were employed in paying occupations.

Elsewhere in 19th-century Europe other children who were born to working-class parents may have been more fortunate. They had the opportunity to be considered by Sigmund Freud—probably an opportunity more advantageous for boys than for girls. In 1909 Freud published his paper on the treatment of "Little Hans," who was Herbert Graf, the son of Max Graf. Although most of Freud's theory of childhood is based on his work with and observations of adults, his contributions did significantly change the way that children were viewed by the larger society. With Freud children became both more human and more wicked. Certainly children began to be viewed as sexual beings with rich unconscious lives. James Scully, a British physician, in 1895, stated that access to the unconscious lives of children might be gained by observing their play. Most important, Freud emphasized the later impact of traumatic events, including mishaps and downright abuses in child rearing.

During this time there was increasing interest in the field of child development, and much effort was being placed onto clearly delineating stages in the growth of the normal child. In 1830 Bronson Alcott published behavioral observations of his daughters. In 1868 Jean Heroard published a journal of the early life of Louis XIII of France. In 1875 Francis W. Parker, called the father of progressive education by John Dewey, began education for child development in the curriculum of Quincy, Massachusetts, schools. Recognition of children's distinctiveness grew in the 19th century, as did concerns about their rights.

In 1881 Wilhelm Preyer published The *Mind of the Child,* an account of his son's development during his first 3 years of life, using a crude approximation of time sampling techniques. Charles Darwin also was a major contributor to the field of child study, publishing a series of observations on his own children, "A Biographical Sketch of an Infant," in *Mind* in 1877. Both Preyer and Darwin, however, espousing the theory of recapitulation, were less interested in childhood as a unique stage of development than they were in deriving the correct time at which adult capabilities are achieved. Hence, as their predecessors had done, they tended to view children merely as miniature adults or adults with imperfect capacities.

In the latter part of the century, John Dewey, a major educational reformer, attempted to discredit these views by reintroducing the concept of the importance of experience in the education of children; he proposed a progressive experiential model of education incorporating the principles of communal learning. A fuller appreciation of child development would be gained in the following century with Jean Piaget, but certainly these were important forerunners.

In 1891 G. Stanley Hall published a journal called *Pedagogical Seminary,* the first journal in child psychology, emphasizing studying normal child development. Some academic trends also helped to articulate the rights of children. In 1893 Millicent W. Shinn's *Notes on the Development of a Child* was published—a pre-Gesell study of early childhood behavior. In 1894 the Illinois Society of Child Study was founded.

In the field of medicine major strides were made in the study of children, with beginning legitimization of the field of child psychiatry. Pervasive developmental disorder was described in the literature. Some highlights included: 1809: John Haslam's textbook described an autistic 5-year-old admitted to Bethlem Asylum ("bedlam") in 1799. Thought disorders were discussed.

- 1812: Benjamin Rush made perhaps the first reference to insanity in children in his book; he himself had a psychotic son.
- 1838: Jean Étienne Dominique Esquirol differentiated the mentally defective from the psychotic child, attempted to classify insanity into age groups, and saw insanity as having an emotional basis. The groundwork was laid for later diagnosis and treatment of affective disorders.
- 1845: Wilhelm Griesinger, the first "psychiatrist of the self," advised educational treatment of disordered children and described both mania and melancholia in children. The possibility of the occur-

rence of obsessive compulsive disorder in children was considered.

- 1868: W. W. Gull described anorexia nervosa as a picture similar to tuberculous consumption.
- 1871: Ewald Hecker described pubertal psychosis, *Hebrephrenie.*
- 1874: Karl Ludwig Kahlbaum described *catatonia.*
- 1887: Hermann Emminghaus wrote on psychic disturbances of childhood, dividing psychoses into those due to physical causes and those due to psychosocial conditions. He called for separate diagnostic schemes for adults and children.
- 1894: J. Jules Séglas at Salpêtrière said obsessions might occur before puberty. Eating disorders were diagnosed.

Children's rights to receive proper psychiatric treatment and to achieve mental health were promulgated.

Scholarly works in the field of child psychiatry began to appear in the literature. In 1844 the *American Journal of Insanity* (forerunner of *the American Journal of Psychiatry*) began, but only in 1890 did it begin to print articles dealing with children.

- 1848: Édouard Seguin wrote the first textbook on mental retardation.
- 1854: Charles West, in London, wrote on the higher incidence of moral insanity in children and urged pediatricians to be aware of childhood mental disorders.
- 1856: Louis-Pierre Paulmier wrote a thesis on nervous afflictions in childhood.
- 1890: John M. Keating's *Cyclopedia* had 4 chapters on childhood psychopathology, including hysteria and insanity.
- 1890: Nils wrote on hysteria in children.
- 1899: Marcel Manheimer wrote *Mental Difficulties of Childhood.*

The 1800s also saw the establishment of more facilities for the education of children, both normal and those with special needs, touting the basic right of all children to an education.

- 1817: The Reverend Thomas Gallaudet set up a program to educate the deaf in his Connecticut parish.
- 1825: The first "day nursery" was established in the United States by Robert Owen in New Harmony, Indiana.
- 1829: The Perkins Institution for the Blind was founded in Boston.
- 1837: Friedrich Froebel opened the first kindergarten in the village of Blankenburg, Thuringia.
- 1837: Édouard Seguin, a Christian socialist, established a school for "idiots" in Paris; he wrote a treatise on the treatment of idiots in 1846.

- 1840: J. Guggenbühl, C. M. Seagert, and J. Conolly opened schools for the retarded in Switzerland, Germany, and England, respectively.
- About 1848: Samuel Ridley Howe established the first state school (Massachusetts) for the retarded in the United States under Seguin's influence.
- 1860: Elizabeth Peabody established the first U.S., English-speaking kindergarten in Boston.
- 1887: Annie Sullivan, a teacher from the Perkins Institution, began teaching Helen Keller to communicate.
- 1898: The National Federation of Day Nurseries first met.
- 1899: John Dewey published *The School and Society.*

Most remarkably, in the 19th century, children's rights first began to be protected by law were enacted. Other laws in the interest of children besides the British Factory Acts. Children's rights advocates became more vocal, and poor and homeless children began to be viewed as among those in need of special services. In 1852 Paul Siogvolk called for "The Rights of Children" in *Knickerbocker,* an American periodical. In 1853 the Children's Aid Society was founded to aid New York's homeless and destitute children. In 1870 a case of child abuse was resolved by a landmark decision to include children under a cruelty-to-animals law in New York State. This was the first law in the United States to "interfere" with parental ownership of children and a step to protect children and adolescents, long exempted from the full range of rights accorded to adults and bound by law to obey their parents, even under penalty of death if they had not reached the age of 16. In 1892 Kate Douglas Wiggin (author of *Rebecca of Sunnybrook Farm*) published *Children's Rights,* admonishing parents to make sacrifices and serve their children's changing needs, thereby allowing a child to have his or her own world.

Interestingly, many of the laws passed regarding children in the United States in the second half of the 19th century were designed to regulate the daily behavior of juveniles, ensuring social propriety—especially if they were the children of immigrant or poor parents. The passage of bills that circumscribed activities open to children provided the segue into and the justification for subsequent juvenile court practice. In 1899 Illinois and Colorado passed laws that provided for the establishment of juvenile courts.

Ideally, the juvenile courts would have reclaimed wayward youths and provided them with informed guidance and protection from parents who historically, had near omnipotence under the law. In practice, the courts often served merely to bolster parental power and failed to grant due process and basic constitutional guarantees to the juveniles whom they were designed to serve. They did, however, help initiate a body of law pertaining to juveniles that was separate from that applying to adults, which indicated that juveniles were considered to be in some way in need of special considerations.

Early laws regulating behavior certainly reflected the puritanical bent of their authors and no doubt would have been readily endorsed by John Wesley. New York State, for example, passed numerous laws circumscribing children's behavior during the last two decades of the 19th century. Children under 16 years of age were prohibited from entering dance halls, saloons, theaters, museums, skating rinks, or any place serving alcohol, unless accompanied by an adult. Reformers felt that theaters and even ice-skating rinks could predispose youths to lives of corruption and crime. Minors also were prohibited from carrying guns, entering gambling halls, or patronizing pawnbrokers without adult accompaniment. Although perhaps somewhat overzealous in issuing their moral imperatives, these same reformers helped to raise public consciousness about the impact of child labor on the next generation and pioneered legislation in Connecticut and in Massachusetts that mandated education for working youths and limited the workday to 10 hours for children. No doubt they would have been considered to be "kiddie savers" today.

The move to pass child labor laws in the United States did not begin in earnest until the American Federation of Labor (AFL) made the abolition of child labor their top priority in their first meeting, held in 1881. Although they couched their demands in the language of social justice, their primary concern seemed to be the devastating effects on adult wages of having such a large workforce of children getting low wages. By taking up the cause of ending child labor, the union movement also gained the political support of middle-class reformers who shared this interest.

The 20th Century

Only in the 20th century have major changes concerning the rights of young people been reflected in societal laws, values, and policies. In this century consistent social change regarding the progressive growth of children and adolescents has occurred in educational, medical, and legal realms. Some of the major thinkers of the 20th century whose contributions helped to form the backdrop against which major changes have taken place are Jean Piaget, Benjamin Spock, John B. Watson, B. F. Skinner, Jerome Kagan, and Carl Rogers.

Jean Piaget was a Swiss psychologist who viewed himself in many ways as the intellectual successor to his countryman Jean-Jacques Rosseau. Piaget regarded children as functioning beings in their own right, who passed through stages of cognitive development that were singular and different from adult cognitive functioning. He devoted his life to identifying and describing these stages. Like Locke, Piaget saw the infant as merely a bundle of reflexes. All that was learned was learned through interaction with or exploration of the environment. All children formed their own set of mental structures that would enable them to "assimilate" the environment. As children passed through the various stages of development, they could master more and more difficult tasks, and the mental apparatus became more complex. Development was thought to be continuous but nonetheless occurred in demarcated stages.

Another figure of major import is Dr. Benjamin Spock, of the United States whose popular child-care handbook sold over 30 million copies. Dr. Spock, later accused of fostering permissiveness in parents and hence spoiling a generation of children, was heavily influenced in his writings by evolutionary theory, by psychoanalytic theory, by medical studies in pediatrics in such areas as childhood diseases and infant nutrition, and by his own passionate political commitments. He championed the rights of children as well as parents as human beings and stressed that all members of the family had vital needs and responsibilities. His own political activities included resistance to the Vietnam War during the 1960s and subsequent trial in 1967 for conspiracy to violate the Selective Service Act.

John B. Watson and B. F. Skinner were deterministic in their approach to child development. Following Locke, they believed that children come into the world like blank slates and are formed by their experiences. Since the world seems to reward, punish, and shape behavior randomly, these psychologists were proponents of uniformly shaping children's behavior in desirable ways. Opponents of determinism argued that to do this would deprive the individual of his or her autonomy—of the basic human right to freedom. Jerome Kagan, in *The Nature of the Child,* argued that there were several forces at work shaping the growing child—social, biological, and familial—and that the child's response to these various factors could not be absolutely determined before the fact. Carl Rogers, too, celebrated the human being's basic right to freedom and emphasized the importance of choice and personal creativity in determining what the individual becomes. Humanists have consistently advocated for increasing children's civil liberties.

Against this lively and variable philosophical framework, the 20th century has seen many changes regarding the legal rights and civil liberties of children and adolescents—too many to elaborate here. But it will highlight some of the major changes that have occurred in this century that affect children's educational, medical, and legal rights.

EDUCATIONAL RIGHTS

School attendance became mandated by laws passed in the late 19th and early 20th century. Thanks to the efforts of the American Federation of Labor (AFL), in 1900 a fact-finding and lobbying campaign was mounted that led to the establishment of local child labor committees in several of the states with the worst records on child labor. Ultimately the National Child Labor Committee (NCLC) was founded in 1904 for the purpose of pressing for protective legislation requiring schooling of all children, in part to take them out of mills, mines, and fields. In 1916 the Owen-Keating Act was passed, forbidding interstate shipment of goods manufactured by children under 14 (or under 16 if children worked more than 8 hours per day in producing them). In Britain, the 1918 Education Act made school attendance compulsory and forbade children to be employed for wages during school hours. Certainly there was much resistance to the passage of these laws, in both Britain and in the United States. Universal public education in the United States was not guaranteed until 1926, when Mississippi, the last holdout, finally passed a law requiring such education. In fact, in 1922, a constitutional amendment that forbade child labor was invalidated by the U.S. Supreme Court. In 1936 Congress passed the Fair Labor Standards Act, restricting labor of

youths under age 16 years. This law was upheld by the Supreme Court in 1941.

Facilities for the education of children, including children with special needs, continued to increase in number and in sophistication. In 1907 Maria Montessori, the first female physician to be graduated from the University of Rome (1894), set up her Casa dei Bambini in Rome's San Lorenzo slums, applying educational strategies used earlier only with retarded children to a wider range of children. In 1921 A. S. Neil founded Summerhill in Leiston, Suffolk, a free and self-governing school. In 1924 Susan Isaacs founded Malting House School, in England, for preschoolers. Her book, *Intellectual Growth in Young Children,* published in 1930, began a running debate with Jean Piaget.

Major Supreme Court decisions in the 20th century also have had a significant impact on the enactment and enforcement of children's and adolescents' right to an education. These decisions have been reviewed by Ruetter (1982). These cases have been largely decided after World War II, an era that has seen an expansion of civil rights and liberties for all people. In recent years this trend appears to have reversed, and the tendency to limit rights may well continue.

In many states there existed statutes that may have infringed on the rights of youths, parents, and teachers by virtue of their undue rigidity. Early Court decisions seemed to reverse this trend. For example, in *Meyer v. Nebraska,* in 1923, the Supreme Court upheld the teacher Meyer's right to teach the German language in a public school. This overturned a Nebraska statute that forbade the teaching of subjects in any language other than English because it was somehow unpatriotic and threatened not only the public safety but also the general welfare of the American people.

The cornerstone case for parental rights was *Pierce v. Society of Sisters of the Holy Names of Jesus and Mary,* decided in 1925. The Supreme Court essentially overturned an Oregon statute that required all "normal" children between the ages of 8 and 16 who had not completed the eighth grade to attend a public school, thereby precluding their right to attend a private school. After this ruling, parents were allowed to send their children and adolescents to private schools. The most extensive Supreme Court discussion of parent rights vs. state rights regarding the education of children occurred during the 1972 case,

Wisconsin v. Yoder. In *Yoder,* the Supreme Court exempted the offspring of Wisconsin's Old Order Amish community from the last 2 years of the state's compulsory educational requirements.

Children's rights advocates have faulted these Supreme Court decisions, particularly the latter two, on the grounds that the assumption that parents and children have coextensive interests is sometimes erroneous (Melton, 1982). Recent research indicates that young persons do have interests that are appreciably different from those of their adult caregivers. Nevertheless, Supreme Court justices have rarely considered young people's opinions and preferences while making major decisions that would affect their lives. Traditionally, the courts have operated on the premise that the interests of offspring and parents are coextensive because of the former's need for protection, which the family is assumed to provide. This premise may be sugar coating, however, for historically, parental rights are derived from the "property interest" reflected in the economic benefits of their children's labor.

Looking individually at the above-mentioned cases, this misassumption becomes more obvious. In the *Meyer* case, for example, it is not clear whether the children's rights are being addressed. It looks more as if the rights of the teacher, Meyer, are being upheld. No one asked children whether they wanted to be taught a foreign language in school.

Religious Freedom: Mueller (1986) has provided a review of judicial cases affecting children's religious rights. In both the *Pierce* and *Yoder* cases, the issue of children's religious freedom is paramount. In *Pierce,* the Court upheld the parent's rights to send children to private religious schools, where the youngsters would receive proper religious indoctrination. Again, no one asked the children whether they preferred attending public or parochial school.

Some people assume that the religious identity of young people derives from their family and heritage. Others believe that religious identity is acquired through religious training and indoctrination. More progressive thinkers believe that a child's cumulative interaction with a whole spectrum of environmental influences leads him or her to choose a religious faith. And a truly enlightened view is that the source of religious identity is inspiration—that religion springs from the individual heart. Proponents of the latter two views are children's rights advocates who wish to increase children's religious as well as other liberties and who consequently view the *Pierce* decision as against the rights of the child.

In the *Yoder* case, the chief dissenter and strongest advocate of children's rights was Justice William O. Douglas. The majority held that Amish parents' religious freedom was violated by state law compelling school attendance of their children beyond eighth grade. Douglas argued that the key interests were those of the youths, who were not consulted in this case. He stated eloquently:

It is the future of the student, not the future of the parents, that is imperilled in today's decision. If a parent keeps his child out of school beyond the grade school, then the child will be forever barred from entry into the new and amazing world of diversity that we have today. The child may decide that this is the preferred course, or he may rebel. It is the student's judgment, not his parents', that is essential if we are to give full meaning to what we have said about the Bill of Rights and of the right to be masters of their own destiny. If he is harnessed to the Amish way of life by those in authority over him and if his education is truncated, his entire life may be stunted and deformed. The child, therefore, should be given an opportunity to be heard before the State gives the exemption we honor today. (quoted in Melton, 1982, pp. 245–246)

The Court does seem to have considered the freedom of children and adolescents to choose their own religion in *Grand Rapids School District v. Ball* (1985). Here the Court struck down a state-sponsored program providing secular instruction in private schools. The Court feared that were the program to continue, children would infer a symbolic link between religion and government. This inference could affect later religious choices.

Freedom of Expression: The Supreme Court also has addressed students' rights to the freedom of expression of their unique views. In February 1969 the Court upheld their right to freedom of speech in the case of *Tinker v. Des Moines Independent Community School District.* The principals of the Des Moines, Iowa, schools, having learned that a group of students was planning to wear black armbands as a protest against U.S. involvement in Vietnam, decided to require the students to remove the armbands, with a penalty of suspension for noncompliance. The Supreme Court ruled that the school authorities' position was unconstitutional.

Due Process: Students' rights to due process

also have been addressed. In 1975 several students in the Columbus, Ohio, school district received suspensions of 10 days or less for their participation in student demonstrations. The Supreme Court, in *Gross v. Lopez.* ruled that the right to public education was in fact a property right. Accordingly, students could not be deprived of it without receiving both some sort of a notice and a hearing, thus ensuring the students due process.

Corporal Punishment: The Supreme Court ruled in 1977, in *Ingraham v. Wright,* that these same procedural safeguards need not apply regarding the infliction of corporal punishment on school children. The discussion surrounding this case clearly indicates that the continued use of "paddling" as a means of disciplining school children was viewed as laudable, harking back to John Wesley.

Freedom from Discrimination: Laws have been passed aimed at protecting children from discrimination in education. On May 17, 1954, in *Brown v. Topeka Board of Education.* the Supreme Court found the laws of 21 states requiring or permitting racial segregation in public schools to be in violation of the equal protection clause of the 14th amendment.

On May 31, 1955, in *Brown II*, the implementation decree, the Court established a structure for moving to dismantle dual school systems. The 1972 Emergency School Aid Act provided funds to school districts for eliminating "minority group isolation." In 1976 Title VI of the Civil Rights Act of 1964 barred discrimination based on "race, color, or national origin" in educational activities receiving federal financial assistance. Also in that year, Title IX of the Education Amendments of 1972 prohibited discrimination on the basis of sex in education programs or activities receiving federal financial assistance.

Currently, children infected with HIV comprise a growing minority that suffers from discrimation in education. The death rate for AIDS continued to rise to 15.1 per 1,000 in 1994. At this time there are about 8.5 million HIV-positive women and about 1 million HIV-infected children in the world. Many of these children live in homes with mothers who are dying or who have died. Some are homeless; some are cared for by social services. The normalizing process of attending school and becoming socialized could improve the quality of these children's lives (Oletto et al., 1994).

Unfortunately, although the equal protection clause of the United States Constitution prevents a governmental unit from improperly depriving an individual or a class of individuals of a right, admission to school for HIV-positive children seems to be more difficult than expected. Even in nursery schools there are problems of acceptance. Sometimes the parents of fellow pupils refuse to allow their children to go to school because of the presence of an HIV-positive child. Often parents of the HIV-positive child are forced to withdraw him or her from school. The process of exclusion is particularly traumatic for these children who already have suffered multiple losses (Blackman & Appel 1987). When litigation has arisen, the courts have consistently overturned exclusions and reinstated children to the school system. Under the Americans with Disabilities Act, all HIV children have the right to an education. Even the threat of an HIV positive child biting another child does not pose a significant enough risks to the health, safety, or welfare of others to deny that child the right to an education.

Children with Special Needs: Laws attempting to ensure the educational rights of children with special needs also have been passed by Congress and modified by the Supreme Court. In 1976 Title I of the Elementary and Secondary Education Act of 1965 made federal funds available to local public education agencies for the purpose of better serving the educational needs of "educationally deprived children" in both public and nonpublic schools. In 1975 the Education for All Handicapped Children Act (PL 94–142) provided public funds to states for assuring all handicapped children the right to a "free appropriate public education." Children's rights' advocates have faulted Congress in the passage of this act by because the law did not seek to provide handicapped children with an education that was equal to that afforded to children without special needs or to maximize their potential. It sought rather to identify and evaluate handicapped children and to provide them with access to a free public education.

Minors do have minimal rights when it comes to psychoeducational assessment. The implementing regulations for PL 94–142 require that written parental consent be secured for all procedures involved in psychoeducational assessment, including testing, interviewing, and observation (although the Department of Education is now proposing to eliminate this requirement). Clearly, minor children do not have the right to participate in the consent process at all. The only time when they may participate is at the Individual Education Plan (IEP) meeting, where the law states that the child may participate "where appropriate." This is rather nebulous, but "appropriate" circumstances for children's participation are not described in greater detail.

RIGHT TO MEDICAL TREATMENT

The rights of children—at least middle- and upper-class children—to receive quality medical care have been given increasing emphasis in the 20th century. In 1906 Massachusetts was the first state to require medical examinations for all school pupils. A series of such laws helped to pave the way for young people's rights to medical care. So did some developments within pediatrics.

- 1908: Archibald Garrod described alcaptonuria, the first known inborn error of metabolism.
- 1946: John Caffey, a pediatric radiologist, reported an interesting radiological syndrome of multiple long-bone fractures along with subdural hematomas in children—there was no mention that it was parent-induced.
- 1952: Jonas Salk's hypodermic vaccine against poliomyelitis was tested.
- 1953: James and Joyce Robertson produced a landmark film. A Two-Year-Old Goes to Hospital.
- 1960: C. H. Kempe spelled out the battered child syndrome as parent-induced.

In the 1990s, pediatricians have advocated for legislative reform. Harvey (1991) describes the need for a National Child Health Policy. He cites in his argument the increasing numbers of children with no health insurance and living in poverty, the increasing incidence of chronic and handicapping conditions in children, and the decreasing numbers of children who currently are eligible for Medicaid. Landrigan and Carlson (1995) appeal to policy makers to implement environmental health policies that address children's unique vulnerabilities to toxins. Christoffel (1991) argues for the passage of legislation to restrict children's access to firearms and to reduce corporal punishment in schools (Dolins & Christoffel, 1994).

Child Psychiatry: The 20th century witnessed the growth of child psychology and the birth of child psychiatry; these in turn provided an ever-increasing rationale for young people's rights. The following notable events have contributed to the growth of child psychiatry in the century.

- 1905: Benjamin Knox Rachford, head of pediatrics at Cincinnati General Hospital, wrote *The Neurotic Disorders of Childhood.*

- 1912: Ernest E. Southard established a children's clinic in Boston's Psychopathic Hospital; he was one of the first to use the multidisciplinary approach and later coined the term "*social psychiatry.*"
- 1913: The Louisville, Kentucky, Child Guidance Clinic was founded and the Phipps Clinic in Baltimore began accepting children as patients.
- 1916: Bernard Glueck set up the first orthopsychiatry team (three disciplines) in the Westchester County Welfare Department, New York.
- 1917: The Judge Baker Guidance Clinic was established in Boston by William Healy, M.D., and Augusta Bronner, Ph.D., his wife.
- 1919: Hermine Hug-Hellmuth treated a child using play therapy and Melanie Klein started treating children.
- 1920: Lightner Witmer at Penn State described Don, a 3-year-old with a "fear psychosis."
- 1922: Alfred Adler established the first child guidance clinic in Vienna, and several U.S. child guidance clinics were established on a pilot or demonstration basis by the Commonwealth Fund.
- 1923: A children's psychiatric service was started at Bellevue Hospital, New York, and the Children's Clinic was started at the Allentown, Pennsylvania, State Hospital.
- 1924: Otto Rank's book, *The Trauma of Human Birth,* was published, giving primacy to the mother in the child's mental life, and so was attacked by more patriarchal analysts.
- 1932: Howard Potter defined infantile schizophrenia at meeting of the Psychiatric Association.
- 1933: Jesse Taft, a Rankian psychologist who taught in the Pennsylvania School of Social Welfare, published *Dynamics of Therapy in a Controlled Relationship,* the first book on child therapy. Also the term "child psychiatry" was first used.
- 1935: Leo Kanner published the first U.S. textbook on child psychiatry. Also, E. D. Bond and L. H. Smith described attention deficit disorder with hyperkinesis in American postencephalitic patients. This phenomenon had earlier been described in Europe.
- 1941: Adelaide Johnson and coworkers coined the term "school phobia."
- 1943: Leo Kanner described infantile autism in 11 children—8 boys, 3 girls.
- 1952: The second edition of the *Diagnostic and Statistical Manual of Mental Disorders* was published; it included a few categories of children's disorders.
- 1958–61: Nathan Ackerman explicated family therapy.
- 1963: The Community Mental Health Centers Act was passed.
- 1966: The Group for the Advancement of Psychiatry, Committee on Child Psychiatry, published *Psychopathological Disorders in Childhood.*

During the 20th century, professional and governmental organizations and agencies were founded specifically for the purpose of advocating for children in the fields of medicine and child mental health.

- 1909: The first White House Conference on Children was held under the auspices of Theodore Roosevelt.
- 1912: The Children's Bureau was established in the U.S. Government.
- 1920: The Child Welfare League of America was formed.
- 1931: The Third White House Conference on Children was held.
- 1937: The first congress on child psychiatry was held in Paris.
- 1946: The National Institute of Mental Health was established by the Mental Health Act.
- 1948: The World Health Organization was established in Geneva under the auspices of the United Nations.
- 1958: The American Academy of Child Psychiatry was formed, with membership by invitation.
- 1959: The American Board of Psychiatry and Neurology, Inc., established a subspecialty Committee on Certification in Child Psychiatry.
- 1963: The U.S. Children's Bureau first took a stand that day care benefited both children and "families." Also, the American Psychological Association formed a section on clinical child psychology.

Joint Commission on Mental Health of Children: In 1965 the Joint Commission on Mental Health of Children was established in the U.S., supporting child advocacy. In 1969 an effort was made by the commission to gain a consensus on children's rights, so that legislators could be held accountable. To that end the Joint Commission enumerated the following rights of children:

- to be wanted
- to be born healthy
- to live in a healthy environment
- to obtain satisfaction of basic needs
- to receive continuous loving care
- to acquire the intellectual and emotional skills necessary to achieve individual aspirations and to cope effectively in our society
- to receive care and treatment through facilities that are appropriate to children's needs and that keep them as closely as possible within their normal social setting

Right to Consent: With increased availability of both medical and mental health services for children and increased monies available for research, a whole new realm of young people's rights has emerged. This domain includes children's rights to consent to or refuse medical—including psychiatric—treatment and participation in research protocols as well as the right to obtain treatment without parental consent (Gaylin, 1982). An entire book by Melton, Koocher, and Saks (1983) called *Children's Competence to Consent* has been devoted to this subject. A more specific recent work, entitled *Children's Consent to Surgery,* has been written by Anderson (1993).

Children's competence to consent to either medical treatment or research is influenced by their developmental level (Billich, 1986). Although this varies according to the individual, certain generalizations can be made. The capability to reason is an essential element of consent. Reasoning refers to the manner in which a decision is made. According to this element, children must be able not only to comprehend material information but also to weigh risks and benefits of various alternatives in a rational manner. Piaget (1932) described basic reasoning shifts that occur between preoperational, concrete-operational, and formal-operational stages. These are summarized by Koocher and DeMaso (1990). Children aged 2 to 6 years, in the preoperational stage, are limited to their own experiences as a primary data base for decision making. Fantasy and magical thinking are powerful operants and may carry equal weight with reality-based data in decision making, thus impairing competence. Children of this age tend to have a self-centered perspective and do have difficulty objectifying. Thus, most young children below the age of 6 or 7 years often do not think logically and have limited capacity to give consent.

The older child, age 7 to 11 years, in the concrete-operational period, for the first time becomes capable of taking the perspective of another person and using that in decision making. The children are able to observe, ask questions, and integrate the data they obtain in a more logical and effective manner than at earlier ages. At this age, children are able to explore their motivation from the perspective of another person. They think in concrete terms, so they may not be able to consider all the ramifications of a decision; on the other hand, they often tend to reach the same decisions as older groups who use more abstract reasoning (Weithorn, 1980). Thus, the National Commission for Protection of Human Subjects of Biomedical and Behavioral Research has recommended that all children whose mental age is 7 and older must give their assent before they may participate in research, and, if they do not, that their dissent be honored. Of course, this is not legally binding. Parents still have the final say.

Theoretically, the adolescent years herald the arrival of formal-operational thinking, although in reality, only approximately one-third of the population acquires this. During the state of formal operations, adolescents become able to use hypothetical reasoning in such a manner that permits them to extrapolate and theorize about future events and outcomes. The ability to understand contingencies and consider probabilities is important in being competent to give informed consent. Weithorn (1980) found that 14-year-olds reasoned as maturely as adults about hypothetical medical and mental health treatment decisions. Similar findings have been made about adolescents' decision making on abortions (Lewis, 1980) and participation in research (Keith-Speigel & Mass, 1983). Thus, above age 14, all potential research subjects must give their informed consent separate from their parents.

Thus, from a cognitive perspective, and speaking generally, it would seem that adolescents have more cognitive capability for giving informed consent. Preadolescents ideally would become progressively involved in decision making in preparation for adolescence. Although 12-year-old children may have a greater capacity for abstract thought, voluntariness appears to be limited before the age of 14 years by an unwillingness to resist authority figures such as parents. Thus, although understanding and reasoning abilities seem to be present earlier, adolescent's reluctance to express personal preference may limit competence prior to age 14 years old (Erlen, 1987). Again, this would depend on the individual youngster and the nature of the medical decision. Some youngsters seem to be precocious in the development of autonomous thinking, and some seem to be delayed. Cognitively impaired youths may have impeded capacity for giving informed consent. Cognitive development may be impaired by many conditions—mental retardation, psychiatric disturbance (Axis I or II or both), drug or alcohol abuse, medical problems, socioeconomic deprivation, and child abuse or neglect, just to name a few.

Concerning minors' consent to medical treatment, the Juvenile Justice Standards Relating to the Rights of Minors, approved by the House of Delegates of the American Bar Association in 1979, affirm that with certain exceptions, parental consent should be required for the treatment of unemancipated minors. Some of the exceptions are as follows. Emergency medical care inter-

preted liberally may be rendered to a child or adolescent without consent from the parent or guardian. Although, generally speaking, an emergency situation is one in which endangerment of life or limb occurs, it can simply mean that "health" or "mental health" might be endangered in the absence of immediate treatment (Sigman & O'Connor, 1991). In 22 states and the District of Columbia, competent minors may arrange for all necessary medical care, according to the "mature minor doctrine." In the remaining jurisdictions, competent minors often may arrange for medical care involving contraceptives, pregnancy, abortion, veneral disease, drug and alcohol abuse, and psychiatric disorders without parental consent, although parental notification sometimes is required (Treloar, Peterson, Randall, & Lucid, 1991).

According to Greydanus and Patel (1991), especially in cases of rape, incest, and sexual abuse, adolescents may consent to treatment on their own. In acute cases, construed as emergencies, they may be treated without their consent. Some states now have statutes authorizing examination and treatment of minors alleged to be victims of sexual assault, on their own consent. There may be parental notification requirements, unless, of course, the parents are suspected of being the perpetrators. Adolescents may consent to examination and treatment of the abuse and its sequelae, including sexually transmitted diseases, pregnancy, and psychiatric problems.

The issue of adolescent abortion has been particularly controversial. In 1976, in *Planned Parenthood of Central Missouri v. Danforth*, the Supreme Court held that a Missouri statute requiring parental consent before minors could obtain an abortion was unconstitutional. In *Bellotti v. Baird*, a 1979 case, the Supreme Court held that if a state did choose to require parental consent prior to an adolescent female's obtaining an abortion, she must have other alternatives. Other alternatives consisted of her being allowed to appeal to the court directly for consent. The court would be required to authorize the abortion if she established either "that she is mature and well-informed enough to make intelligently the abortion decision on her own" or that "the desired abortion would be in her best interests." In 1981 in *H.L. v. Matheson*, the Supreme Court upheld a Utah statute requiring physicians to "notify, if possible," parents of a minor seeking an abortion. The Court made it clear that in this case, they considered themselves to be dealing with an unemancipated minor living at home with her parents.

The Supreme Court has not yet provided a clear, specific definition of what constitutes a "mature" minor.

In July, 1989, The Supreme Court made a decision upholding state regulation of abortion. Since this time, most states have enacted legislation calling for some form of mandatory parental involvement prior to a minor securing an abortion. These laws generally require parental consent or notification before a minor's pregnancy is aborted. Major medical and mental health professional organizations generally are opposed to mandatory parental notification. Not only does it violate the privacy rights of the adolescent, but it is a major concern that when parental notification is mandated, anticipated parental anger or possible rejection decreases the likelihood that an adolescent will come forward about her pregnancy until it is too late to abort safely (Committee on Adolescence, 1996; Worthington et al., 1991).

Regarding sterilization, individuals can be sterilized only after giving their fully informed and voluntary consent. There has been considerable ethical controversy in recent years regarding sterilization of minors and of persons with mental retardation. Currently court orders are required for the sterilization of young adults and mentally retarded minors, males and females. Parental consent is not sufficient.

Right to Refuse Treatment: According to Greydanus and Patel (1991), at times the emergency room physicians confront minors who refuse to consent to care. Generally, in the case of an emergency, a nonemancipated minor does not have the right to refuse reasonable care. According to Rice (1991), when a minor refuses recommended emergency medical treatment and the parents cannot be contacted, the treatment should begin. Rice goes on to say that physicians in emergency situations should provide whatever life-saving care is necessary for minors, even when it is against parental consent and/or religious beliefs. Child protective services should be contacted if parents refuse to consent to necessary emergency medical treatment for their minor child.

The Group for the Advancement of Psychiatry (1989) addresses the difficult question of when children in their own right can refuse life-sustaining treatment. Schowalter, Ferholt, and Mann (1973) cite the case of a 16-year-old girl suffering from glomerulonephritis who, with the consent of her parents, was allowed to stop dialysis and die from her disease. The authors comment that the following safeguards must be in place in

any such situation: (1) it must be determined that the minor's decision has been made in a rational and informed manner; (2) the minor's cognitive capacity to understand death must be assessed; and (3) the amount of suffering and the quality of the child's life must be taken into account. Certainly there continues to be much controversy regarding this topic.

What about the rights of newborns to die? According to the 1984 amendments to the Child Abuse Prevention and Treatment Act known as the Baby Doe regulations, all newborns are required to receive maximal life-prolonging treatment, except under certain specified conditions. Neonatologists take issue with the application of these regulations to severely damaged newborns, expressing concern that compliance with the law often causes unnecessary severe pain to infants and merely prolongs the process of dying (Kopelman, Irons, & Kopelman, 1988).

Laws vary widely among states in permitting minors to refuse mental health services, particularly inpatient services. In most cases, a parent may voluntarily commit a minor without his or her consent, if the treatment is considered to be necessary and beneficial. A competent minor does have the right to refuse treatment, except when the minor is considered to be of sufficient danger to self or others to be involuntarily commitable. Medication is administered to "voluntarily" committed adolescents against their wills, and little seems to come of it, as long as clear documentation is provided. Another legally and ethically unclear area concerns the right of an adolescent to leave the hospital after being "voluntarily" committed by his or her parents.

These areas are still not clearly legally delineated. Supreme Court decisions in these areas traditionally have reflected neither what we know to be developmentally correct nor what research has told us. A key case regarding minors' rights to refuse medical treatment was *Parham v. J.R.* (1979). In this instance, under the tender ministrations of Chief Justice Warren Burger, the Court decided that a formal due process hearing was not constitutionally required before minors were "voluntarily" committed to mental hospitals by their parents or guardian. Minors seem to have been afforded greater due process rights in Canada, where the Child and Family Services Act makes provisions for court review of admissions of children to all locked treatment facilities. For children ages 12 or older admitted to open wards or long-term residential placement, the act provides for an initial review only if the minor objects to the placement. Recent legislation enacted in the United States does seem to give minors more legal clout. For example, amendments to the law governing admission of minors to psychiatric units passed during the 1991 Florida Legislature theoretically would allow minors who felt their privacy rights had been violated by unwanted psychiatric hospitalizations to sue the admitting physician, the facility, and their parents (Mutch & Myers, 1994).

Organ Donation/Research: According to Lewis (1985), organ donation for transplantation in children is becoming increasingly common. For children under the age of 14 years, assent is required. For adolescents, informed consent must be obtained. For children under the age of 14, the custodial parent traditionally is the decision maker. Recently there has been discussion of the potential need to include another relatively more independent decision maker in the process.

It has even been proposed that a panel be established for the purpose of sanctioning the parent, who must in the final analysis make decisions for children who are not capable of giving informed consent. The panel would be analogous to the Institutional Review Board (IRB) for biomedical research. Its purpose would be to ensure that the parents are competent, informed, and have a more or less conflict-free, benign relationship with the child; and that the child has been reasonably informed and heard. Only if the parents are found to be incompetent would it be necessary to invoke a guardian ad litem and judicial review.

In research, the review board serves to protect the rights of research subjects and to ensure the ethical conduct of research involving human subjects. The board reviews and prescribes procedures for obtaining the assent of the child as well as the permission of the parent or guardian for the child's participation in research. Children who are capable of meaningful assent must be provided with a fair explanation of what their participation will involve. If a child objects and stands no chance of benefiting from the procedure, the procedure should not be done.

The Institutional Review Board also determines under which circumstances adolescents may consent to participate in research without parental consent. These are usually minimal risk studies that spell out justification for dispensing with parental consent in the protocol.

AIDS-related research with youths presents a unique legal and ethical conundrum. Questions regarding adolescents' competence to consent to HIV-antibody tests, sex research, and AIDS education arise. Should adolescents be allowed to participate in AIDS-related research, or should they be prohibited? Is the threat of AIDS sufficient to intrude upon the privacy rights of adolescents, imposing upon them greater surveillance and perhaps segregation, ostensibly to protect them from their own behavior or from exploitation by others? (Melton, 1989).

These are questions that remain to be answered. In fact, the entire area of minors' competency to consent to or refuse established or experimental treatments is one in which there is huge disagreement among the two groups of child advocates described earlier. Those child advocates who seek to protect young people tend to be in favor of more restrictive laws regarding minors' consent. Those who seek to liberate children feel that they should be given more autonomy in making decisions that will ultimately affect their lives. Melton (1983) states that the primary benefit of increasing children's autonomy is the growth of moral development. Moreover, in the long run, according to this view, experiencing true democracy will tend to make one more tolerant and egalitarian.

RIGHTS IN THE JUVENILE COURTS

Two groups of children are likely to fall under the jurisdiction of the juvenile court system—those children whose parents demonstrate abuse, neglect, or unavailability, and those children who have committed offenses, including status offenses. Let us look at how the juvenile justice system historically has dealt with these two groups.

Juvenile Offenders: The law to establish the first U.S. Juvenile Court was enacted in 1899, and the court was established in 1900. After this, William Healy M.D. was recruited to study the nature of delinquency. To do this, he established, in 1909, the Chicago Psychopathic Institute to serve the juvenile court. Other notable dates include:

- 1914: Homer Lane, an American, founded Little Commonwealth, a self-governing community for 40 to 50 delinquent children in Dorset, England.
- 1915: Healy published the book The *Individual Delinquent.*
- 1918: August Aichorn established his home for wayward boys in Vienna.
- 1920: Shortly after the Soviet revolution, Anton S. Makarenko organized the Gorky Colony (Besp-

rizornije) for the rehabilitation of homeless and delinquent children.
- 1921: The Commonwealth Fund held a conference on juvenile delinquency.
- 1925: Aichorn published *Wayward Youth*.
- 1934: Joseph Stalin decreed that children in the Soviet Union over 12 years of age would be punished as adults—for example, they would be sentenced to 8 years in a labor camp for stealing potatoes or grain.

In the United States, the juvenile justice system was derived from an old principle of Anglo-American law, the *parens patriae* doctrine of English law, which articulates that the state has a duty to protect those who are not able to protect themselves, including youths. Thus the aim of this system was to rehabilitate and reform troubled youths. But after years of improper funding and failure to accomplish its stated goal, the juvenile justice system has undergone dramatic changes in recent years, partially as a result of Supreme Court findings. In 1967 *In re Gault* the Supreme Court extended to juveniles accused of crimes the same procedural due process rights that were afforded to adults.

Implicit in the *Gault* decision was the understanding that the juvenile justice system had failed youths and, in fact, in some cases, doled out harsher sentences to juveniles on weaker evidentiary standards than to adults. In 1970 *In re Winship* held that the standard of proof in juvenile delinquency proceedings must be as stringent as that for adult defendants. However, in a later decision, *McKeiver v. Pennsylvania* (1971), the Supreme Court upheld a state rule that denied juvenile defendants the right to a jury trial. Also, in 1979, in *Fare v. Michael C.*, the Supreme Court did not see a police officer's denial of Michael C.'s request to have his probation officer, whom he trusted, present during police interrogation, as a violation of his rights to due process. Thus we see that the Supreme Court is inconsistent in its adoption of either a pro *parens patriae* stance or a stance advocating increased due process rights for juveniles.

Two more recent cases seem, at least in spirit, to contradict the *Gault* decision. In 1984, in *Schall v. Martin*, the Supreme Court upheld a New York law allowing preventive detention of a juvenile accused of committing a crime because he was at risk for committing further crimes. The preventive detention, of course, occurred prior to his first hearing. Youth rights advocates and dissenters in the Supreme Court asserted that this entailed a violation of due process rights, because the juvenile was, in essence, being detained and punished for unadjudicated acts. This *Schall* holding relies on a *parens patriae* philosophy of child protection, but it also infringes on the juvenile's right to liberty. In 1985 the Supreme Court's finding in a second case, *New Jersey v. T.L.O.*, states that juveniles are not entitled to the protection from warrantless searches that currently is extended to adults.

One group of children's rights' advocates feel that since adolescents have achieved a minimal level of developmental competency, as juvenile offenders they should be afforded the same rights and responsibilities as adults. There is also a movement afoot to eliminate the Person in Need of Supervision (PINS) Petition on the grounds that it protects parents' rights but violates juveniles' rights. Once classified as a PINS, a teenager may be supervised by the court for years without ever having committed a crime. In this view, incorrigibility is viewed as a status offense, a category that has been eliminated for adult offenders.

Unfortunately, what we often see in practice is that juveniles are given increased responsibility for their actions and punished more severely, but not afforded greater rights to protect themselves. We know that, as a group, delinquents tend to have lower-than-average IQs and poor school performance (often with long-term placement in special education), and often come from impoverished backgrounds. According to Grisso (1983) it is not even clear that juveniles understand the nature of their *Miranda* rights when they are informed of them. In one study, over 90% of the juveniles waived rights to silence and counsel (Grisso & Pomicter, 1977).

Nevertheless, since the landmark decision in 1966 of *Kent v. United States*, which allowed waiver of juveniles to adult court, we have witnessed a growing trend to try youngsters as adults. Currently, in 8 jurisdictions, no minimum age is required for waiver. Thus in Alaska, Arizona, Florida, Maine, New Hampshire, Oklahoma, South Carolina, Washington, West Virginia, Wyoming, and federal districts, any child of any age can be prosecuted as an adult for any crime. In Delaware, Indiana, Nevada, and Pennsylvania, persons of any age charged with a capital offense are always prosecuted in adult courts. For states that do have minimum age requirements, the range extends from 10 years in South Dakota, to 13 or more in Georgia, Illinois, and Mississippi, to 16 years of age in most states. Thankfully, we have seen a small countertrend in recent years for states to move toward higher minimum ages for transfer. Once juveniles are transferred, they usually are found guilty (Benedek, 1985) and sometimes even sentenced to death. The United States is one of only 7 countries now legally permitting the death sentence for juveniles (Haggerty, 1994). Of those 7, the United States leads in the number of juveniles put to death in the last 6 years (6 since 1990).

The Abused Child: It is commonly held that there was no protection for abused children in this country until 1870, when a landmark decision was made in New York State to include children under a cruelty-to-animals law. By and large, states were reluctant to interfere with parental management of children, and, prior to 1963, a finding of child abuse required that the child had to die from the alleged abuse. Since 1962 standards have been increasingly more flexible and realistic, attempting to protect the young from potential lasting harm.

Finally, in 1973, the Child Abuse Prevention and Treatment Act and the establishment of the first federal agency to address child abuse, the National Center on Child Abuse and Neglect, stimulated increased research and treatment for abuse victims and their families. Despite apparent efforts of the Juvenile Justice Standards Project to limit the realm of allowable state intervention into child abuse cases, the numbers continue to escalate. In 1960, 749 battered children were identified in the United States. By 1994, this number had grown to an estimate of over 1 million cases, or an incidence of 2.5%, with close to half a million children in foster care (Krugman, 1995).

Child sexual abuse is another growing area of concern. Research indicates that approximately 1 in 3 girls and 1 in 6 boys will experience at least 1 sexually abusive episode by the time they reach adulthood. The sale and distribution of child pornography on the Internet adds a whole new dimension to the range of possibilities in which child sexual abuse may occur.

Children and adult children have the right to recover damages for child abuse and neglect, in some cases dating from in utero. We are seeing an increasing number of such cases in the courts, ranging from child sexual abuse to wrongful life actions and prenatal neglect. Defendants in these cases are parents, physicians, and other professionals entrusted with the care of children.

Children and Adolescents in Custody Disputes: Another group of youths who fall under the purview of the court, and who also need to have guaranteed and protected rights, are children who are the subject of custody litigation. Chapter 33 discusses this topic in greater detail. But here let us say that with 1 out of every 2 marriages ending in divorce today, a sizable number of children are affected.

In most U.S. jurisdictions today the standard for determining who shall have custody of the child is based on the child's best interests. This standard rejects the earlier "tender years doctrine," according to which the mother was regarded as the natural caregiver of young children and hence automatically awarded custody. The Uniform Marriage and Divorce Act gives judges discretionary powers to determine the best interests of the child in contested custody cases. These include interviewing children in their chambers, appointing guardians ad litem to represent the interests of the child, and calling on domestic relations investigators or other mental health professionals for assistance. Pearson, Munson, and Thoenes (1983) find that judges rarely use these discretionary powers and question whether the judicial system truly is serving the best interests of the child.

Twenty states now require by statute that consideration be given to children's wishes in custody cases. In most other states, case precedents suggest the importance of seeking children's views about their custody preference. Again, however, the degree of weight to be given to these opinions is a matter of judicial discretion.

In most jurisdictions today, joint custody tends automatically to be the preferred divorce adjudication. There is really very little research on the outcome of joint custody and certainly no assurance that this is necessarily in the best interest of the child. Indeed, some would argue that it addresses the best interests and needs of the parents but not necessarily those of the child (Tibbits-Kleber, Howell, & Kleber, 1987). According to Wallerstein and Johnston (1990) the benefit of joint custody to children seems to be proportional to the level of cooperation between the divorced parents. Where there is ongoing parental conflict, joint custody and forced visitation can be destructive to the children.

Conclusion

Major strides have been made in the 20th century to secure the rights of the child in the areas of education, medical and psychiatric treatment, and the law. Some of the decisions made by the Supreme Court regarding children's rights have been contradictory, and a conflict is being played out that has embroiled opposing groups of children's rights advocates. One group wants more protection for children under the law but strives to obtain this in a fashion that may, in fact, limit their autonomy or impinge on their civil liberties. The other group advocates for increasing the civil liberties of children, allowing them to be autonomous masters of their own fate to the limit that is developmentally appropriate. While there does not seem to be an easy resolution to this dialogue, it does not seem to be an either/or proposition. Certainly children need more autonomy and increased civil liberties when developmentally appropriate. Weithorn (1980) showed that many 14-year-olds are capable of making adult decisions. But all 14-year-olds are not functioning at the same level. A

14-year-old male who has borderline intellectual functioning, a visual perceptual learning disability, and a history of child abuse with possible neurological sequelae may not be as competent to make a decision regarding his fate in juvenile court as a 14-year-old from a middle-class family who has had top-notch pediatric care all of his life and has attended private schools. Certainly there is no question that children and adolescents still need protection under the law, some more than others. But perhaps it needs to be protection that also protects their civil liberties and ensures that they understand and are receiving their due process rights.

Laws are very important both to protect children and adolescents and to give them the freedom to exert their own competencies. But laws need to backed up by federal expenditure of funds to ensure that children are being afforded the rights to which they are entitled. Although conceived with good intentions, the juvenile justice system was doomed to failure because of inadequate funding. It is hoped that legislators and the electorate will learn from these lessons of the past before it is too late for the educational and medical systems that care for children.

REFERENCES

Adams, P. L., Berg, L., Berger, N., Duane, M., Neill, A. S., & Ollendorff, R. (1972). *Children's rights.* London: Panther Books.

Adams, P. L., & Fras, I. (1988). *Beginning child psychiatry.* New York: Brunner/Mazel.

Alderson, P. *Children's Consent to Surgery.* Buckingham: Open University Press, 1993.

Ariès, P. (1962). *Centuries of childhood.* London: Jonathan Cape.

Bellutti V. Bairel, 443 U.S. 622 (1979).

Benedek, E. P. (1985). Waiver of juveniles to adult court. In D. L. Schetky & E. P. Benedek (Eds.), *Emerging issues in child psychiatry and the law.* New York: Brunner/Mazel. 13,180–190.

Billick, S. B. (1986). Developmental competency. *Bulletin of the American Academy of Psychiatry and the Law, 14* (4), 301–309.

Blackman, J. A., & Appel, B. R. (1987). Epidemiologic and legal considerations in the exclusion of children with acquired immunodeficiency syndrome, cytomegalovirus or herpes simplex virus infection from group care. *Pediatric Infectious Disease Journal, 6,* 1011–1015.

Brown V. Board of Education, 347 U.S. 483, 74 S. Ct. 686, 691 (1954).

Brown V. Board of Education, 349 U.S. 294, 75 S. Ct. 753 (1955).

Cleverley, J., & Phillips, D. C. (1986). *Visions of childhood.* New York: Teachers College.

Christoffel, K. K. (1991). Toward reducing pediatric injuries from firearms: Charting a legislative and regulatory course. *Pediatrics, 88,* 294–305.

Committee on Adolescence. (1996). The adolescent's right to confidential care when considering abortion. *Pediatrics, 97,* 746–750.

de Mause, L. (1975). Our forebearers made childhood a nightmare. *Psychology Today, 85.*

Dollins, J. C., & Christoffel, K. K. (1994). Reducing violent injuries: Priorities for pediatrician advocacy. *Pediatrics, 94,* 638–651.

Erlen, J. A. (1987). The child's choice: An essential component in treatment decisions. *Children's Health Care, 15* (3), 156–160.

Fare V. Michael C. 442 U.S. 707, 995 S. ct. 2560 (1979). In re Gault, 387 U.S. 1, 1967.

Gaylin, W. (1982). The 'competence' of children: No longer all or none. *Journal of The American Academy of Child Psychiatry, 21,* 153–162.

Greydanus, D. E., & Patel, D. R. (1991). Consent and confidentiality in adolescent health care. *Pediatric Annals, 20,* 80–84.

Grisso, T. (1983). Juveniles' consent in delinquency proceedings. In G. B. Melton, G. P. Koocher, & M. J. Saks (Eds.), *Children's competence to consent.* New York: Plenum Press, 8, 131–148.

Grisso, T., & Pomicter, C. (1977). Interrogation of juveniles: An empirical study of procedures, safeguards, and rights waiver. *Law and Human Behavior, 1,* 321–342.

Grand Rapids School District v. Bull, 473 U.S. 3216 (1985). 373, 105 S. Ct.

Gross V. Lopez, 419 U.S. 565, 95 Ct. 729 (1975).

Group for the Advancement of Psychiatry. (1989). *How old is old enough? The ages of rights and responsibilities.* New York: Brunner/Mazel.

Haggerty, R. J. (1994). The convention on the rights of the child: It's time for the United States to ratify. *Pediatrics, 94,* 746–747.

Harvey, B. (1990). Presidential address—Why we need a national child health policy. *Pediatrics, 86,* 1–6.

H. L. U. Matheson, 450 U.S. 398 (1981).

Ingraham U. Wright, 430 U.S. 651 97 S. Ct 1401 (1977).

Joint Commission on the Mental Health of Children. (1969). *Crisis in child mental health: Challenge for the 70's.* New York: Harper & Row.

Keith-Speigel, P., & Maas, T. (1983). Children and consent to participate in research. In G. B. Melton, G. P. Koocher, & M. J. Saks (Eds.), *Children's competence to consent.* New York: Plenum Press.

Kent V. United States. 383 U.S. 541 86 S. Ct. 1045 (1966).

Koocher, G. P., & DeMaso, D. (1990). Children's competence to consent to medical procedures. *Pediatrician, 17,* 68–73.

Kopelman, L., Irons, T., & Kopelman, A. (1988). Neonatologists judge the "Baby Doe" regulations. *New England Journal of Medicine, 318,* 677–683.

Krugman, R. D. (1995). From battered children to family violence: What lessons should we learn?," *Academic Medicine, 70* (11), 964–967.

Lacey v. Laird, 139 N.E. 2d 25, 166 Ohio St. 12 (1956).

Landrigan, P. J., & Carlson, J. E. (1995). Environmental policy and children's health. *The Future of Children, 5,* (2), 34–52.

Lewis, M. (1985). Organ transplants, research, and children. In D. H. Schetky & E. P. Benedek (Eds.), *Emerging issues in child psychiatry and the law.* New York: Brunner/Mazel.

McKeiver V. Pennsylvania, 403 U.S. 528 (1971).

Melton, G. B. (1982). Children's rights: Where are the children? *American Journal of Orthopsychiatry, 52* (3), 530–538.

Melton, G. B. (1989). Ethical and legal issues in research and intervention. *Journal of Adolescent Health Care, 10,* 36S–44S.

Melton, G. B., Koocher, G. P., & Saks, M. J. (Eds.). (1983). *Children's competence to consent.* New York: Plenum Press.

Meyer V. Nebraska, 262 U.S. 390, 43 S. Ct 625 (1973).

Mueller, L. L. (1986). Religious rights of children: A gallery of judicial visions. *Review of Law and Social Change, 14* (2), 323–351.

Mutch, S. A., & Myers, W. C. (1994). Psychiatric hospitalization of children in Florida. *Journal of the Florida Medical Association, 81* (7), 470–474.

New Jersey V.T.L. O., 105 S. Ct. 733, 83 L. Ed. 2nd 207 (1984).

Oletto, S., Giaquinto, C., Seefried, M., Ruga, E., Cozzani, S., Mazza, A., De Manzini, A., D'Elia, R., & Zacchello, F. (1994). Paediatric AIDS: A new child abuse. Acta Paediatrics (Suppl.), *400,* 99–101.

Parham V. J. L. & J. R., 442 U.S. 584 (1979).

Pearson, J., Munson, P., & Thoenes, N. (1983). Children's rights and child custody proceedings. *Journal of Divorce, 7* (2), 1–21.

Piaget, J. *The Moral Judgment of the Child.* New York: Kegan, Paul, Trench, Trubner, 1932.

Pierce V. Society of Sisters of the Holy Name of Jesus and Mary, 268 U.S. 510, 455. Ct. 571 (1925).

Planned Parenthood of Central Missouri v. Danforth, 428 U.S. 52 (1976).

Rice, M. M. (1991). Medicolegal issues in pediatric and adolescent emergencies. *Emergency Medicine Clinics of North America, 9* (3), 677–695.

Ruetter, E. E. (1982). *The Supreme Court's impact on public education.* Phi Delta Kappa and National Organization on Legal Problems of Education, Bloomington, Indiana.

Schall V. Martin, 467 U.S. 253, 104 S. Ct. 2403 (1984).

Showalter, J. E., Ferholt, J. B., & Mann, N. M. (1973). The adolescent patient's decision to die. *Pediatrics, 51,* 97–103.

Sigman, G. S., & O'Connor, C. (1991). Exploration for physicians of the mature minor doctrine. *Journal of Pediatrics, 119* (4), 520–525.

Tibbits-Kleber, L., Howell, R. J., & Kleber, D. J. (1987). Joint custody: A comprehensive review. *Bulletin of the American Academy of Psychiatry and the Law, 15* (1), 27–43.

Tinter V. Des Moines Independent Community School District, 393 U.S. 503 (1969).

Treolar, D. J., Peterson, E., Randall, J., & Lucid, W. (1991). Use of emergency services by unaccompanied minors. *Annals of Emergency Medicine, 20,* 297–301.

Wallerstein, J. S., and Johnston, J. R. "Children of Divorce: Recent Findings Regarding Long-Term Effects and Recent Studies of Joint and Sole Custody", *Pediatrics in Review.* 11:197–204, 1990.

Weithorn, L. A. (1980). *Competency to render informed treatment decisions: A comparison of certain minors and adults.* Unpublished doctoral dissertation, University of Pittsburg.

In re Winship, 397 U.S. 358 (1970).

Wisconsin v. Yoder, 406 U.S. 205 (1972).

Worthington, E. L., Larson, D. B., Lyons, J. S., Brubaber, M. W., Colecchi, C. A., Berry, J. T., Morrow, D. (1991). Mandatory parental involvement prior to adolescent abortion. *Journal of Adolescent Health, 12* (2), 138–142.

32 / The Child and the Law

Daniel T. Goyette and Peter L. Schuler

Historical Evolution of the Juvenile Court Concept

Prior to the early 19th century, children who were accused of committing criminal offenses were tried and sentenced in the same manner as adults. Children who were convicted served their sentences along with adult criminals in jails. Little, if anything, was provided in terms of real correctional treatment or rehabilitation. To no one's surprise, the commingling of juvenile and adult prisoners proved to be abusive for the young offenders in many respects.

Various social pressures came to bear in the early 1800s concerning the inadequate attention given to the needs of children. The social reform movement that occurred was in part a response to the problems caused by the Industrial Revolution. This movement had its underpinnings in what was later recognized as a religious and moral awakening in the United States.

The first reform efforts were not, however, directed toward massive procedural change in the relationship between the child and the state. Rather, the reforms were initiated to temper the harshness of certain aspects of the existing system.

One element of the reform movement was the creation of houses of refuge in a number of cities. These institutions were developed to keep young delinquents separate from adult criminals. The House of Refuge in New York was created in 1824 and was designed to care for all types of children who were in need of state support and placement. It became a model for future juvenile institutions. However, despite the best intentions of the reformers and their opposition to the incarceration of juveniles, the houses of refuge themselves, in practice, became jails.

Many of the children held in the houses of refuge or other institutions had committed no crime. They were placed there solely because they had been abandoned, neglected, or otherwise abused by their parents. The early reformers believed that these children, as well as other troubled youths, could be rehabilitated if they were removed from their home environment for a period of time.

The law soon came to recognize the power of the state to remove children from their neglectful parents for placement in refuge houses and other institutions. In 1839 the doctrine of *parens patriae* emerged from the decision reached in *Ex Parte Crouse,* which justified this intrusion on the basis of acting for the welfare of the child and the state.

Toward the end of the 19th century, reformers became increasingly involved with children who had committed or who by their personality traits were likely to commit criminal offenses. The name "child-savers" was given to those who worked to change the behavior of delinquents and predelinquents. During this period, a medical model for delinquency flourished. Problems were considered to be "pathological." Children were considered to be "diseased" and in need of a "cure." Deviants from social norms were considered "unsocialized" or "maladjusted."

This new reform movement was not a true or complete break from the past. It emphasized the importance of traditional social values and institutions. "Child-savers" placed increasing importance on moral absolution. Children needed to be saved from the evils of movies, alcohol, tobacco, and the like. As more and more child welfare legislation was passed, the population of juvenile institutions increased to include children who were found to be begging, destitute, wandering, or associating with unsavory persons, such as thieves or prostitutes.

The culmination of the reform movement was the creation of the first juvenile court in Chicago in 1899. The establishment of the court marked the beginning of a separate and distinct judicial framework wherein the primary focus was the welfare of children. Here the humanitarian concerns of the reformers combined with the beliefs of social scientists to predict and correct human behavior under a benign legal process in which the judge acted as a father figure. Other states soon followed suit by creating their own juvenile court systems.

The 1940s saw the development and use of individual counseling in juvenile cases. Treatment providers in the juvenile justice system also showed greater interest in the application of psychoanalytic theory in response to delinquent behavior. Psychological testing, which was refined during World War II, was increasingly relied on as a diagnostic tool. The 1940s also began a trend that focused the juvenile court's attention on the individualized treatment needs of children under its jurisdiction.

During the 1950s and 1960s the individualized treatment model began to lose some support, and group models began to emerge as the preferred approach to the problems of juveniles. The idea developed that lower-class boys were creating their own deviant subculture due to their own inability to conform to middle-class norms. One such approach, the Guided Group Interaction approach, was based on such subculture theories as well as principles of psychotherapy. Variations of this modality were used a great deal in delinquency treatment programs, particularly in public institutions.

Recently emphasis in treatment has been focused on community-based services rather than institutional care. The provision of community-based services is more cost effective than institutional care, which may account for its recent popularity, at least in part. With community-based treatment, a child is allowed to remain in his or her own home or a group home while under the supervision of a probation officer or court monitor. The child's relationships with school, family, peers, and neighborhood are examined, and the child is afforded the opportunity to participate in specialized programs and counseling in the community designed to assist him or her in improving the quality of relationships with others in the community. The theory maintains that delinquent acts will diminish as the child's potential for growth is maximized.

Legal concepts such as "reasonable efforts" and the "least restrictive alternative" stem from the view that treatment is most effective when children receive it while living with their family or in a familylike setting in their community. Many communities currently run community-based programs. Some states, such as Massachu-setts, have replaced many of their institutions with community-based services.

As originally conceived, the juvenile court system was to serve as a social welfare agency. Young offenders were to be provided treatment for their wrongdoings rather than to be punished. Proceedings were to be informal, thus sparing children from the rigors of a full-blown criminal trial. In exchange for this special treatment, young offenders were denied the procedural safeguards that are guaranteed to adult criminal defendants. Statutes setting forth juvenile court jurisdiction were sparsely worded, and juvenile court judges were granted extensive discretionary powers. Little distinction was made between delinquency and neglect cases. Adjudication and disposition usually were done in a single hearing.

Landmark Supreme Court Cases Shaping Juvenile Law

Throughout the first half of this century, the courts did little to alter the juvenile court system. However, beginning in 1966, the United States Supreme Court rendered a series of decisions that extended a broad range of procedural rights to children that had previously been denied to them.

The decision in *Kent v. United States*, 383 U.S. 541 (1966), held that there must be a certain amount of fundamental fairness in the procedure whereby the juvenile court judge decides whether an alleged juvenile offender is tried in juvenile court or prosecuted as an adult in criminal court. Among other considerations, the Court held that such an accused juvenile is entitled to be represented by counsel and to be provided with all social service records and reports that the judge will consider in deciding whether to waive jurisdiction. If jurisdiction is waived, the juvenile court must give a written statement of reasons for the transfer decision that is sufficient to form the basis for review on appeal.

The case of *In re Gault*, 387 U.S. 1 (1967), dealt with the legal requirements necessary prior to finding a child to be delinquent and committing the child to a state facility. Realizing that states often fail to provide appropriate treatment for adjudicated delinquents, the Supreme Court set forth specific rights for alleged offenders in juvenile court delinquency proceedings. These rights include the right to counsel, the right to adequate and timely notice of charges, the right to confrontation and cross-examination of witnesses, and the privilege against self-incrimination. In the wake of *Gault,* most states enacted laws to provide these constitutionally mandated requirements. These rights form the procedural basis of the juvenile court system today. They serve to ensure that juvenile court judges use reliable information and that accused delinquents are treated fairly. Those children who cannot afford counsel are provided publicly furnished counsel. The *Gault* decision struck a fairer balance between the interests of the state and the liberty interests of children.

The decision in *In re Winship,* 397 U.S. 358 (1970), altered the standard of proof required in juvenile court delinquency adjudications. Many juvenile courts prior to *Winship* allowed findings of delinquency to be based on the lesser standards of "preponderance" or "clear and convincing" evidence. These courts reasoned that the civil nature of juvenile proceedings and the treatment orientation of juvenile dispositions permitted a lesser standard of proof than that of "beyond a reasonable doubt," which is required in adult criminal cases. In holding that due process of law requires that juveniles be afforded the same protections as adult defendants with respect to the state's burden of proof, the Court stated that the rehabilitative mission of the juvenile court would not be compromised by requiring more proof for adjudication.

However, one year later, the Supreme Court reversed the trend of affording juvenile offenders broader procedural rights. In *McKeiver v. Pennsylvania,* 403 U.S. 528 (1971), the Court held that a child does not have a constitutional right to a trial by jury in a delinquency proceeding.

But expansion of juvenile procedural rights was resumed four years later. In *Breed v. Jones,* 421 U.S. 519 (1975), the Court held that subjecting a child to a criminal trial as an adult, after the child has been adjudicated a delinquent in a juvenile court proceeding for the same offense, violates the double jeopardy clause of the fifth amendment to the U.S. Constitution.

In addition to the expansion of juvenile procedural rights just enumerated, the liberty interest of children was emphasized with the passage of the Juvenile Justice and Delinquency Prevention Act of 1974. This act, and its amendments, provided funding for states to assist them to provide for nonsecure placements and treatment programs for runaways and other status offenders.

However, in order for states to receive funds under the act, each state was required to develop a program to reduce on a yearly basis its population of status offenders confined in jails or secured detention facilities. The policy promoted in the Juvenile Justice and Delinquency Act of 1974 and its amendments recognized the dangers of mixing status offenders with other children who had delinquent tendencies, and recognized implicitly the unfairness of confining individuals in a lockup facility for conduct that would not be criminal if committed by an adult. While some states have worked diligently to reduce or eliminate their status offender population in locked facilities, other states have made use of technicalities or exceptions within the law to continue the practice of incarcerating runaways, truants, and children with other noncriminal behavior problems.

In the 1980s and the 1990s a more punitive approach to the treatment of young offenders developed, and limitations were placed on the expansion of juvenile rights. In *Schall v. Martin,* 467 U.S. 253 (1984), the Supreme Court held that the section of the New York Family Court Act that authorized pretrial detention of accused juvenile delinquents was constitutional. That statute provided that a juvenile's liberty interest may, in appropriate circumstances, be subordinated to the state's *parens patriae* interest in preserving and promoting the welfare of the child, which in this case was defined as incarcerating him or her based on a judge's finding that there was a serious risk that the juvenile may commit another crime in the community if released pending trial in the juvenile court. The legal presumption of innocence to the contrary, the Supreme Court ruled in the case that while children were entitled to due process in juvenile court proceedings, their rights were not violated if they were held without bail after a detention hearing wherein a judge made the legal finding that detention was necessary to protect the child and society from potential consequences of future criminal acts.

In *New Jersey v. T.L.O.,* 469 U.S. 325 (1985), the Supreme Court ruled that there were limits to children's expectation of privacy in school situations. In that case, the Court held that the fourth amendment's prohibition against unreasonable searches and seizures, while applying to searches conducted by school officials of students, need not require strict adherence to the requirement that searches be based on probable cause to believe that the subject of the search has violated or is violating the law; rather, legality of the search of the student depends simply on the reasonableness of the search, considering all the circumstances. Thus the Supreme Court denied expansion to children of privacy rights that are normally afforded to adults.

It was argued in *Stanford v. Kentucky,* 492 U.S. 361 (1989), that imposition of capital punishment on an individual who committed a capital crime while he or she was 16 or 17 years of age violated evolving standards of decency and thus constituted cruel and unusual punishment under the eighth amendment. In that case, the Court held the defendant failed to show that there existed a national consensus opposing the imposition of the death penalty as inhumane. The Court rejected defense arguments that 16- and 17-year-old offenders should be treated with leniency in capital cases because they have less developed cognitive skills than adults and were thus less likely to fear death as punishment for the offense of murder. The defense also unsuccessfully argued that society's interest in retribution in capital cases should be moderated in cases involving 16- and 17-year-old defendants because they are less blameworthy due to their immaturity and natural tendency to be irresponsible. Thus the decision in the *Standford* case upheld the right of states to execute 16- and 17-year-olds for capital crimes in states where such punishment is authorized by state statute.

Modern Structure of Juvenile Court

Present-day juvenile courts are structured to provide and promote the best interest of children that are brought before them. The concept of the juvenile court's jurisdiction is nothing more than judicial power that is afforded the juvenile court by the state legislature to intervene in the life of a child or a family assuming legal prerequisites are met. Many statutes setting forth juvenile court jurisdiction are loosely written, giving rise to a broad interpretation of what constitutes an appropriate exercise of the juvenile court's power. Actions are generally broken down to the following categories:

- Delinquency actions are actions where it is alleged that the child has committed a crime.
- Status actions are actions where it is alleged that the child is a runaway, beyond the control of parent or custodian, or a habitual truant from school.

- Dependency actions are actions where it is alleged that a child is neglected, abused, or is in the custody of a person who cannot provide for the child's proper needs.
- Mental health actions are actions that provide for the civil commitment and treatment of juveniles who are in need of psychiatric hospitalization due to mental illness.

State statutes generally outline the manner in which a case progresses through the juvenile court system. The initial appearance of a child before the court is generally referred to as an arraignment. At an arraignment, the child is generally made aware of the facts that are alleged in the petition, and advised of his or her statutory rights, and counsel is either provided for by the family or appointed by the court. In most jurisdictions, publicly furnished counsel is provided to the vast number of children involved in juvenile court actions. Either at arraignment or a few days thereafter, a hearing generally is conducted to determine the appropriate placement for a child while his or her case is pending final resolution. The case then is continued, usually to an adjudicatory hearing, where the court will make a finding of whether the allegations in the petition are true either by an admission on the part of the child or by the taking of evidence. If the child is accused in a delinquency action, he or she will have the benefit of the presumption of innocence, and the burden of proof is on the prosecutor to prove guilt beyond a reasonable doubt. Generally, children in delinquency actions have the same rights as adults in a criminal trials; the children have a right to testify in their own behalf and have witnesses subpoenaed to testify for them, if available. Children also are entitled to have experts provided to them for forensic analysis, and their right to cross-examine accusers face to face under oath is preserved. If the court finds that the allegations in the petition are true, then it generally orders a social worker employed by the country or the state to conduct an investigation and to make recommendations concerning how the case should be resolved. Usually the finding of a social worker's investigation is reduced to writing, and at the dispositional hearing the child's attorney generally has the right to present evidence and to make arguments on behalf of the child and to contradict and contest information that the child feels is not in his or her personal interest. The next section discusses dispositional options and the treatment of children whom the state seeks to prosecute as adults.

Most state statutes permit children at least one

appeal of their adjudication and disposition. Statutes also provide for the periodic review of dispositions, allowing courts to have continuing input concerning the treatment issues of children who appeared before the court.

Roles of Juvenile Court Personnel

It is important to the roles and functions of the various personnel involved in a juvenile court case. The prosecutorial function generally entails advocacy to promote the best interest of the child as defined by the state. More often than not, prosecutors define this to be what is most likely to protect the public; often that entails attempting to incarcerate or restrict the liberty of young offenders. The judicial function is distinguishable from the prosecutorial function primarily because the judge serves as a fact finder. For the system to work properly, juvenile judges must be impartial and weigh evidence fairly as it is presented to them. Often juvenile judges have a certain amount of expertise and experience in handling juvenile matters. Their familiarity with treatment resources and juvenile problems in general allows them to play a more active role in cases with young offenders. The defense function is that of an advocate for the child. With incompetent children or with those who otherwise are uncertain or uncommunicative about what legal position they want to take, the defense lawyer must advocate the position that represents the least restrictive alternative considering the children's liberty interest. Defense counsel's role is often referred to as advocating for the best interest of the child as defined by the child. This would stand in comparison to the role of the judge, who after listening to the exchange and testing of facts and ideas in the interplay between the defense and prosecution, makes the ultimate decision of what constitutes the child's best interest. Finally, guardian ad litem counsel generally is provided to children in dependency actions, setting up a guardianship only for the specific litigation.

Dependency actions are generally, civil in nature. While children may be ordered removed from their homes and placed in foster homes, the law does not view these actions in the same way as it does delinquency or status cases. Consequently, children in dependency actions are not guaranteed the full range of constitutional protections that normally are provided to delinquents and status offenders. In dependency actions, the parents of a child generally are represented by their attorneys, and the child is represented by the guardian ad litem. The guardian ad litem is to make an independent assessment of what he or she believes to be in the child's interest; that may differ from what the child defines as his or her interest. In certain cases, the child and the guardian ad litem may be at odds over an issue, such as placement with a particular parent. Oftentimes dependency actions deal with a situation wherein the prosecutor and the guardian ad litem favor one course of action, which attorneys for the parents opposed. The primary goal in dependency actions is protection of the child. If fault is determined in a dependency proceeding, it is the fault of the parent and not the child. In dependency proceedings children are viewed more as victims.

Generally speaking, court social workers are responsible for monitoring cases that are pending before the court. If problems arise while a case is pending, usually a court social worker brings it to the attention of the court, and court hearings deal with the problems. Theoretically, treatment issues are not to be addressed until the court adjudicates whether it has jurisdiction to order treatment; commonly, however, the parties consent to treatment in an attempt to prevent the need for a formal adjudication. Treatment may be provided by a number of resources, ranging from social workers and counselors hired by the state or county to provide residential treatment services, psychiatrists, psychologists, clinical social workers, counselors, educators, and other representatives of governmental agencies.

While juvenile court proceedings may be formal or informal at the option of the child, a common that the role players in juvenile court are consensus builders with respect to the handling of juvenile cases in treatment of the child. Quite the contrary, in most jurisdictions juvenile court proceedings are full-blown adversarial proceedings. In the adversarial system of justice, different sides of an issue are taken up, and representatives of each side will vigorously present their own position and attack the weakness of the opponent's position. Only in a vigorous adversarial system will the truth emerge and provide the opportunity to explore and identify the most appropriate ways to determine the best interests of troubled children.

Role of the Mental Health Professional

Juvenile court proceedings have come to rely increasingly on input from mental health professionals. These mental health professionals can provide judges with vital information concerning personalities, pathologies, and problems of children in need. In order for mental health specialists to be most effective in juvenile court proceedings, they must first ensure that they are provided with correct information concerning the history of the child and the facts in the particular case. If called upon by the court to give an opinion with respect to the child's legal competency or criminal responsibility, mental health professionals should ensure that proper forensic training has been provided and that the mental health examination is conducted in consideration of all legal parameters. If called upon to testify in a juvenile court proceeding, mental health practitioners should be able to answer challenging questions with respect to their observations and opinions and to understand and appreciate that aggressive questioning by an opposing attorney is a meaningful exercise in the juvenile court's continuing task of ensuring that accurate information is presented to the court and that all information is thoroughly tested through the adversarial system.

One of the most frequently misunderstood areas of juvenile court involves the legal requirement that a child must be competent to stand trial. Competency to stand trial is a legal concept that refers to a criminal defendant's present capacity to appreciate the nature and consequences of the proceedings against him or her and the ability to participate rationally in his or her own defense. Since the *Gault* decision mandates that juvenile offenders must be afforded due process and fairness, the law requires that the juvenile court make a legal determination of an accused child's competency when reasonable grounds exist to believe that a child may be incompetent. It is important to note that the standard for competency to stand trial requires a much higher showing of social maturity and more developed levels of psychological and cognitive functioning than does the standard of determining the competency of a child witness. Mental illness, mental retardation, age, immaturity, physical handicap, behavior disorders, dependency, and poor academic functioning are all factors that can bear upon the competency of a child to stand trial.

Once the issue of competency is raised in the juvenile court, the child will be required to undergo 1 or more psychological evaluations by a qualified mental health professional. The evaluation should be conducted under established forensic norms. After the completion of the evaluation, the mental health professional generally submits a report to the court concerning whether the child is incompetent, whether the child will become competent in the foreseeable future, and what type of treatment is required, if any is available, for the child to attain competency. Since the question of competency to stand trial is a legal one, the court decides the issue of competency after an adversarial hearing where counsel for the parties are allowed to present evidence and cross-examine witnesses. This requires the testimony of the mental health professional who performs the competency evaluation.

There is no special competency standard for children. A child, like an adult criminal defendant, must have the capacity to appreciate the nature and consequences of the legal proceedings against him or her and participate rationally in his or her defense. To allow a marginal range of competency that falls short of the adult standard would jeopardize due process and the fundamental right to be both physically and mentally present when important questions concerning personal liberty are decided.

Despite the legal provisions requiring a child to be competent to stand trial, various states have had difficulty in implementing programs for children whom the juvenile court has determined to be incompetent to stand trial.

Another frequently misunderstood area deals with what is commonly known as the insanity defense. Apart from the issue of competency, the law generally provides that criminal defendants may defend against a criminal charge if they, as a result of mental illness or retardation at the time of the offense, lacked substantial capacity either to appreciate the criminality of their conduct or to conform their conduct to the requirements of law. Juvenile offenders are entitled to use this defense in appropriate cases. After conducting a forensic evaluation in connection with this issue, 1 or more mental health professionals may be called upon to provide trial testimony. An acquittal by reason of insanity usually results in the initiation of civil commitment proceedings to determine whether the child may be released back into the community.

Currently, trials involving the insanity defense in cases of children accused of crimes are rare. Perhaps this is due to the fact that some states have enacted statutes which make acquittal by reason of insanity much more difficult, if not virtually impossible. Another consideration is the current social reluctance to find mental impairment as a defense to criminal behavior, especially when the trier of fact perceives a defendant to be dangerous.

Questions of competency, however, are far more common. As American society sees a greater role for the courts in resolving social problems, younger and younger children are being brought before the juvenile court. There is no arbitrary age or threshold point where legal competency can be assumed. Each case must be decided on its own merits, along with all factors that bear on the issue of competency. In any event, all children under the age of 14 should be screened by the juvenile court for competency to stand trial based on the age and maturity factors alone.

With respect to the issue of immaturity and criminal liability, particularly in the area of sex offenses, most state statutes set forth ages that prohibit consensual sexual contact between children and children and adults. Some states prohibit all sexual contact between children of certain ages; however, in practice, young girls rarely are charged for having consensual sex with young boys. The role of the mental health professional in these types of cases is more often to assess whether a young offender has the profile of a persistent sexual offender and to determine what type of treatment is appropriate, assuming there is an adjudication.

Most juvenile court statutes cloak juvenile court proceedings in a veil of confidentiality. Mental health professionals working with juveniles should remember this fact. Also, state law does govern the right of privilege with respect to certain types of information that is provided to mental health professionals. The mental health professional should take pains to ensure that he or she is not disclosing a confidential communication or other confidential information when disclosing information about a child patient to another person or authority. While some states have relaxed confidentiality standards in certain types of cases, the concept that young offenders' cases should be handled in anonymity is an integral part of the juvenile court system. The potential for effective treatment and rehabilitation is maximized when the criminal stigmatization of children is avoided.

Most public attention directed at the juvenile crime problem focuses on the serious offender, who in fact comprises only about 5% of juvenile delinquency adjudication in this country—a fact that is often overlooked. Nevertheless, the small percentage of delinquent youths presents the juvenile court and the community with a number of complex and challenging issues to resolve in a way that both recognizes the need to protect the public and yet does not lose sight of the individualized treatment and rehabilitation goals and principles that are the essence of the juvenile justice system. The issues involved are weighty and not easily joined. They involve, quite literally, the very future of our society and its willingness to provide the appropriate authority and resources to assure that the nation's courts can deal effectively with serious juvenile offenders.

States vary in the manner in which they treat serous offenders. A growing number of states allow for the automatic prosecution of juvenile offenders as adults at the discretion of the prosecutor. Accordingly, some states allow the direct filing of certain charges in adult court in cases of juvenile offenders. Other states permit the automatic transfer of jurisdiction to adult court of young offenders after it is shown in the juvenile court that there is probable cause that a felony offense has been committed and that the child committed the offense. A trend which emerged in the 1990s from a number of state legislatures reversed the long-held juvenile court philosophy that trial as an adult for juvenile offenders should be the exception rather than the rule. The emergence of crack cocaine, a proliferation in the use of handguns, an increase in gang activity, and increased focus of media attention upon the violent crimes of young offenders were significant factors which shaped public opinion on the juvenile crime issue. When the call to do something about the juvenile crime problem was heard by lawmakers, the result was harsher treatment for young offenders. This included legal provisions making it much easier to try juvenile offenders as adults.

Notwithstanding these new laws which make trial in adult court automatic or much easier for certain offenses, most states retain statutes which set forth the procedures where a waiver of jurisdiction is sought by the prosecutor. These statutes permit the exercise of discretion by the court with respect to whether the young offender should face trial as an adult. While state statutes may vary greatly with respect to the age limits and types of offenses that may subject a young offender to adult prosecution, most statutes mandate 2 specific types of adjudicatory hearings at the juvenile court level. Assuming that the prosecution seeks transfer to adult court, the state first must prove by competent evidence that there is probable cause to believe that a felony offense has been committed and that the child committed that offense. Essentially, this process requires the juvenile court judge to determine whether sufficient evidence exists to believe that a child more likely than not committed a serious offense. If the court makes such a finding, then generally a second type of proceeding is required to comply with the transfer statutes. This second type of proceeding generally is referred to as a "waiver" or "transfer" proceeding, wherein the child's life and personality are put under a microscope, and judicial determinations are made based on the evidence presented in the hearing and applied to specific criteria for transfer. Among the criteria that are mentioned in waiver statutes are:

1. Seriousness of the offense charged
2. Whether the offense was against persons or property
3. The maturity of the child as determined by the environment
4. The child's juvenile record
5. The best interest of the child and the community
6. Prospects of adequate protection of the public
7. The amenability of the child to treatment considering the resources that are available in the state's juvenile justice system

After considering all the evidence presented in the hearing, and after making findings of fact, the court decides whether the child shall be prosecuted as an adult after applying the facts and considering them along with the statutory waiver criteria. Generally, if the court decides to waive jurisdiction and allow the child to be prosecuted as an adult, he or she will be prosecuted as if he or she were 18 years of age or older; however, some states do permit a child convicted as an adult to be treated in a juvenile treatment facility until the child reaches 18. If the juvenile court decides that the child shall not be tried as an adult, then he or she is prosecuted in juvenile court, generally in the same fashion as other juveniles alleged to be delinquent offenders.

The mental health professional has a very important role to play in connection with waiver proceedings. Whether the child has suffered from mental illness is a vitally important issue in the waiver process. Psychiatrists and psychologists may be asked to give testimony concerning the child's mental illness, how the mental illness may have influenced the criminal behavior, and the type of mental health treatment required to heal the patient and to minimize the possibility of further criminal behavior in the future. Psychiatric testimony is particularly germane to the transfer decision. Information on whether a young offender is suffering from a personality disorder helps to assist the court in determining whether the child can be treated using available resources or whether confinement in a penitentiary is necessary to protect the public if the prognosis for rehabilitation is poor. The mental health expert may be called upon to speculate as to the likelihood of rehabilitation and to the probability of future dangerousness of the child as well as provide the court with information concerning how the impact of imprisonment in the adult system would affect the child and the community in the long run. In addition to giving information about personality, in the transfer proceeding the mental health specialist may be called upon to give information about how the child is functioning developmentally, the child's intellectual level, and what specific educational potentials exist for him or her. The mental health specialist also may be asked to testify about various dysfunctions that the child has suffered, such as child abuse or neglect during early life, the mental impact of a traumatic experience such as the loss of a loved one, the level to which drug or alcohol dependency exists in the child and the problems that are caused by chemical dependency, and the specifics of any treatment modalities reasonably calculated to bring an improvement in the child's condition and to diminish the possibility that he or she will become a repeat offender. Generally, the juvenile courts place great weight on the testimony of mental health professionals in waiver proceedings. Despite the fact that the trend exists in some states for children to be prosecuted as adults for serious offenses, some courts decline to transfer young offenders for prosecution as adults in serious cases where testimony concerning a child's mental condition can give a reasonable explanation for the criminal behavior and project a reasonable prognosis for improvement of behavioral problems with treatment.

As mentioned in an earlier chapter, children charged with offenses—serious and not so serious—may find themselves incarcerated without the right to bail upon the showing of probable cause and the potential for dangerousness. States vary in the types of facilities used to house young offenders pending final disposition of their legal charges. While federal law requires that all incarcerated juveniles be separated by sight and sound from adult offenders, in some states children are still held in jails and placed in positions where they do come into contact with adult offenders. In larger cities, children often are held in large detention facilities, where their basic needs are met on a daily basis but no real treatment is provided until the court makes a final determination on how their cases are to be dealt with. In many states repeated offenders spend more and more time in interim detention facilities because space is not available in treatment programs that should be in place at the end of the juvenile court pipeline.

There are 3 purposes of the juvenile court with respect to the delinquent:

First, the court must make a determination of facts to determine whether the allegations set forth in the petition are true—whether the state can prove that the child committed a delinquency offense beyond a reasonable doubt.

Second, if the court finds that the child did not commit a delinquency offense, it loses jurisdiction over the child and must release him or her, if the child is in custody. If the court finds that the child committed a public offense, then generally it orders an investigation to determine what is in the best interest of the child, specifically what treatment is necessary to make it less likely that the young person will commit another criminal offense, and to attempt to correct any problem areas or stress source in the child's life that may place him or her at risk to reoffend.

Third, once the investigation has been completed and a report is filed with the court, the court must then make an actual determination with respect to the facts presented in the investigation and must make specific recommendations concerning treatment to the treating authority, specifying the level of liberty restriction placed on the child while receiving treatment. Common examples of juvenile court dispositions are as follows:

- Symbolic or monetary restitution
- Participation in counseling
- Attendance in a special school program
- Participation in treatment with a psychologist or a psychiatrist

- Confinement in a juvenile detention center
- Placement on probation in the community
- Commitment as a ward of the state for residential placement in a treatment facility or a training school

Ideally, the dispositional order should identify all of the child's treatment needs and should specify how those needs are to be met. Ideally, the concept of individualized treatment means that the state should provide specialized attention and treatment to children that particularly address the problems that have been identified by the juvenile court. Given this age of scarce resources, especially when it comes to state funding of juvenile justice programs, most states are not equipped to provide for the individualized needs of children, especially those who are committed to the state for residential placement. Especially in states that place large populations of adjudicated delinquents closely together in large training schools, the lack of individualized attention and treatment continues to remain a problem. States such as Massachusetts, which treat even violent youthful offenders in small-group homelike settings, appear to have much better results as far as effecting long-term changes in behavior than other states that do not provide this type of small, close supervision.

For children who are committed wards of the state, residential treatment does provide a period of time for them to be placed under strict supervision. Group and individual attention often is provided as well as schooling and vocational education. It is hoped that juveniles going through structured residential treatment benefit from the constant attention and reinforcement of prosocial behavior and values. Treatment programs often are modeled on a level system, where behavior is shaped and good behavior is rewarded by an increase in privileges. As the young offenders progress through the program, treatment personnel plan to transfer the children back into the community for a successful return. Ideally, problems in the community are identified and the children are given skills to assist them in overcoming those problems when they return to their old environment. In reality, children who recidivate after leaving a structured treatment facility become overwhelmed by problems that exist in their old neighborhoods. Continued problems such as poverty, disease, drug and alcohol abuse, negative peers and poor role models, and absent or dysfunctional families all work against the child after his or her return home. Some researchers believe that the enormity of these social forces makes it likely that the child will relapse into the same behaviors that brought him or her initially before the juvenile court. Return to a negative neighborhood after a period of treatment is in fact, one of the major problems facing children who have been committed. For those children, a better course of treatment might be a slow transition back to the community, such as treatment in a group home and even preparation for an independent living situation, away from the old neighborhood and the various problems associated therewith.

The Child as a Victim

There is much confusion with respect to the number of crimes that are committed against children in the United States. No single source of information provides statistics with respect to the number of criminal offenses perpetrated on them. Existing sources of information are severely limited with respect to the types of crime for which data are collected pertaining to young victims. In the past, attempts to compile reliable statistics have been undermined by the variety of definitions and reporting practices involved. Given the sketchy nature of the data involved, however, it is widely assumed that children tend to become victims of crimes more often than is generally expected.

No one knows for certain what proportion of crimes against children are reported to child protection agencies or to law enforcement. In some cases, a child may lack the verbal skills necessary to complain properly about the incident. It is not uncommon for children to keep to themselves their complaints about various forms of abuse and neglect. Too, adults may not take the complaints of a child seriously, readily dismissing them as fantasies or untruths. Even when a child complains of abuse to an adult, in some instances no further action is taken. Adults may ignore reported problems, hoping they will work themselves out without the intervention of outside authorities. Studies also have shown that child-serving professionals, such as doctors, psychologists, teachers, and social workers, sometimes fail to report incidents of child abuse to officials, although in recent years the trend seems to be in favor of making a report through proper channels even in questionable cases.

When an investigation reveals that there is an indication that a child has been neglected or abused, social workers generally are called upon to take some immediate action. If the neglect or abuse is perpetrated upon the child by a family member, action generally is taken in the juvenile court for the primary purpose of protecting the child and serving his or her best interests. A petition generally is taken setting forth the specific facts giving the court jurisdiction to decide the case and requiring the court to give attention to the needs of child. If the child's safety appears in danger, the court addresses the issue of whether he or she should be placed outside the home soon after court action is initiated. The child's case is then scheduled for an adjudicatory hearing to determine whether the facts alleging the abuse or neglect are true. While the case is pending, social workers and law enforcement personnel may continue to investigate the facts. Since reunification of a child with the natural family is usually the statutory goal of most juvenile court proceedings, social workers generally develop strategies to correct the situation at home so the child may return as soon as possible. Treatment strategies may include a wide range of community resources, including counseling for family members, treatment for drug and alcohol problems, assisting family members in improving their living situation, intervention by various support groups, and monitoring by various social service agencies. The juvenile court may specifically order family members involved in the court process to participate in and cooperate with treatment as well as to refrain from certain acts. Sanctions imposed on family members for violations of court orders may include incarceration following an adjudication for contempt of court. If the juvenile court finds that the allegations in the petition are true, the court may exercise a wider scope of power to enter orders pertaining to the family and may even order removal of the child from the family permanently, with eventual termination of all parental rights.

Becoming involved with the court system and the various social service agencies often is a no-win situation for a neglected or an abused child. Children often suffer physically and mentally from the original abuse that brought them into the system; once involved in the system, however, victimization can continue due to the loss of stability the child suffers which may last for years, even until the child reaches adulthood. It is not uncommon for children who enter care to develop special needs, some of which have been created by the juvenile justice system's attempts to protect them from further neglect or abuse. It is widely known that children who have been deprived of growing up in their natural homes have difficulties in adjusting to foster care. While policy and law favors the return of children to their natural homes, far too many never break free of the foster care system. Many grow up in a number of homes, which causes them great adjustment difficulties and may even play a part in causing them to act out with wayward and delinquent behavior later on. No one can deny the importance of having loving and caring parents physically present in the home while children are growing up. Children who grow up in the foster care system undoubtedly are at a significant disadvantage compared to those who grow up in their natural homes with adequate parents.

The Child as a Witness

In order for children to be allowed to testify in a judicial proceeding, they must be determined by the court to be competent as a witness to testify. This concept differs significantly from the concept that a criminal defendant must be competent to stand trial. Legal competency as a witness is the subject of the law of evidence. It refers to the presence of characteristics, or the absence of disabilities, that render a witness legally fit and qualified to give testimony in a court of justice. The issue of competency differs from that of credibility. The issue of competency is determined before a witness is allowed to give testimony. Credibility refers to the amount of weight that a trier of fact gives to the testimony. Competency is a preliminary issue to be decided by the court. Credibility is an issue to be resolved by the jury or the trier of fact in the case.

The idea behind competency is that a certain threshold of reliability must be met before evidence can be admitted in a judicial proceeding to the fact finger. Historically, individuals could be considered incompetent to testify for various reasons, ranging from their age, their marital relation to a criminal defendant, to their religious beliefs. During the last decade, there has been an explosion in the reporting and the prosecution of child sex abuse cases. Due to the increase in these kinds of cases, the issue of child witness competency has been the subject of much discussion and judicial decision.

When judges are convinced that child witnesses can intelligently relay facts, distinguish between what is true and false, and understand the importance of the oath and the consequences of lying, courts traditionally have found child witnesses to be competent. The test of a child's competency derives from the landmark Supreme Court case *Wheeler v. United States*, 159 U.S. 523 (1895). In that case, the court found a 5 ½-year-old witness competent to testify because it believed that the child was "intelligent," that the child understood the difference between telling the truth and a falsehood, and that the child knew the consequences of lying. The court also believed that the child was able to understand the requirements of the oath that was taken at the time the child was sworn in as a witness. In the years that followed the *Wheeler* decision, American courts have set forth criteria that are utilized in determining whether the child is competent to testify:

1. A child must understand the difference between truth and fantasy and appreciate the obligation and responsibility to speak the truth.
2. A child must have sufficient mental capacity at the time of the occurrence in question in order to observe or receive and record accurate impressions of the occurrence.
3. The child must have sufficient memory to retain an independent recollection of the observations.
4. A child must have the capacity to communicate or translate truly into words the memory of such observation and be able to understand simple questions about the occurrence.

Since 1975 there has been a trend away from requiring specific competency criteria. The common law rule that originally provided that children under 14 years of age were incompetent to testify as witnesses essentially has been abandoned. More lenient federal and state rules generally make it easier for children to be qualified as witnesses. Under federal law, a legal presumption exists that children are presumed to testify as witnesses. Competency standards in the various states are found in state statutes, state court rules of evidence, and codified rules of evidence.

As stated earlier, the competency hearing takes place immediately before a child is about to be sworn in as a witness. Traditionally, mental health experts were not called upon to give their opinion as to whether a child witness was competent to testify, even though such professionals have the knowledge and are in the position of shedding light on the legal criteria involved in the competency assessment. A typical competency determination begins with the court asking several questions of the child witness concerning the criteria. Generally a court's criteria tend to be rather concrete and limited. After the court's questioning, generally the attorneys then are allowed to question the child further. Usually the attorney for the party who may be damaged by the child's testimony will question the child more deeply on the issue of competency and seek to have the child prevented from testifying due to incompetency. Judges tend to be protective of children in these types of proceedings. If a judge senses that a child is uncomfortable or otherwise intimidated by the courtroom setting, the competency determination may be conducted in chambers. As stated earlier, the current trend is for the courts to find most children, including very young children, competent to testify as witnesses. Once that determination is made, the party calling the child witness will begin with direct examination. During direct examination, the child witness will be asked questions of which he or she may have some firsthand knowledge. Unlike adult witnesses, the party calling the child witness is entitled to use leading questions; that is, the party may ask questions that suggest an answer. The problem of finding most children competent as witnesses presents very specific challenges to the criminal defense attorney who must cross-examine the child witness.

Given the recent dramatic increase in the number of child sexual abuse cases, more and more individuals in this country are finding themselves subjected to the possibility of substantial terms of penal incarceration. In many sex abuse cases, the only evidence of the abuse is the uncorroborated testimony of a child. Defense attorneys feel that a more critical approach to the witness competency standard should be taken due to the fact that a child's view of reality may have been altered substantially, to the extent that the child may not know the difference between truth and fantasy at the time of his testimony. It is generally conceded that children are more susceptible of being influenced by adults or other persons in positions of authority than are older witnesses. Young children love to imitate sounds that they hear and repeat words even when they do not know their meaning. Defense attorneys often contend that allegations of sexual abuse are sometimes no more than the result of suggestions made during suggestive inquiries and interviews by parents, social workers, and police officers. A defense attorney's challenge then on the basis of witness incompetency generally tries to emphasize the issue of fairness.

If there is a question concerning the child witness's ability to withstand suggestion, then the testimony should not be presented to the trier of fact due to the possibility that an innocent person may be convicted. Many people remember the McMartin Preschool case, which was the longest-running criminal trial in U.S. history. In the McMartin case, Raymond Buckey, his 63-year-old mother, and several other preschool teachers were accused of sexually abusing a number of children in the McMartin Preschool in Los Angeles, California. The sheer number and nature of the allegations involved in the case caused many observers to question the reliability of child witness testimony in criminal cases. For the attorney challenging child witness competency, the key to the incompetency argument is that children incorporate what they hear and say into what they remember. Once a postevent suggestion is made, children will incorporate that event or suggestion into their memory of the original event. If child witnesses are sufficiently tainted by postevent information, then they will not be able to recollect reliably and relate information about the event in question. Any psychologist or psychiatrist can testify to these basic concepts. Recently, however, in the wake of increased numbers of sexual abuse claims and the tendency of most therapists in the field to claim that children do not fabricate stories of abuse, some psychologists have begun to embark on a technique used for many years in Germany, known as the Statement Validity Assessment.

Statement Validity Assessment involves a psychological assessment based on analysis of the witness, his or her possible motives for making a false allegation, and the content of statements. After reviewing all of the statements the child has made, within the context in which they were made, to whom they were made, in response to what question or stimuli, and in light of that particular child's knowledge learned through television, older children, school sex abuse programs, and so on, the expert assesses the validity of the statements. If the information provided to the child through the interview process or other outside influences has tainted his or her ability to remember an event accurately, the expert may be able to testify in support of a motion to exclude the child's testimony as incompetent. The expert may never need to interview the child him- or herself. The expert is basing his or her testimony on the content of the statements, on the information available to the child witness, and on what the interviewer said to or showed the child.

Once the judicial determination is made that a child witness is competent to testify, the child is then subjected to direct examination in the presence of the trier of fact by the party calling the child as a witness. If the case being tried deals with allegations of abuse perpetrated by the defendant on the child, children's rights advocates have recently argued that child witnesses often suffer serious emotional distress if required to testify face to face with alleged abusers. Accordingly, several states have enacted statutes providing one-way shielding of the child from the person accused. Such statutes that prevent a criminal defendant from meeting face to face with accusers during the criminal trial process conflict directly with the confrontation clause of the sixth amendment of the U.S. Constitution. In 1990 the U.S. Supreme Court resolved the conflict in interests by upholding a Maryland statute that permitted the use of a one-way video camera to separate the defendant from a child testifying in a sex abuse case. Maryland v. Craig, 110 s.ct. 3157 (1990). Under the Maryland statute, once the child was determined to be competent to testify, expert testimony could be introduced to show that direct confrontation with the defendant will result in the child suffering serious emotional distress such that the child cannot reasonably communicate. When such a finding is made, the statute authorized the use of a one-way video camera enabling

the child to testify from a room outside the courtroom. Only the prosecutor, the defense attorney, and a therapist or other support person are allowed to be present in the room with the child when the child testifies. The defendant, the judge, and the jury viewed the televised testimony in the courtroom. The defendant and the judge were allowed to communicate with the attorneys by electronic means.

The finding in *Craig* is another example of how the law has evolved favoring the interest of accusers over the accused. Inherent in the *Craig* decision was the finding that the child's testimony was sufficiently reliable to justify exceptions to the traditional hearsay rule, which traditionally required actual face-to-face confrontations between a witness and an accuser.

In cases that involve children as criminal defendants, the law is clear: Such children have the absolute right to testify in their own defense. The fact that children have to be found competent to stand trial almost always guarantees that children will be competent to testify as witnesses for themselves. A fundamental right in all criminal prosecutions is that criminal defendants have a right to testify in their own behalf if they so choose. It should come as no surprise, however, that children who are accused of crimes are often at a disadvantage when their cases are brought to trial—especially when a case turns out to be a swearing contest between an adult and a child. Oftentimes children's inability to use language to the same extent as adults places children at a disadvantage at trial. A general lack of social maturity and life experience further often puts children at a disadvantage when testifying.

33 / The Child and Adolescent Psychiatrist and the Law

William Bernet

Overview of Forensic Child Psychiatry

Forensic psychiatry is the medical subspecialty in which psychiatric expertise is applied to legal issues. There are 4 parts to forensic psychiatry. Its

most colorful aspect is the assessment of criminal behavior, dealing with the evaluation and treatment of individuals who have been arrested. This includes the issues of competency to stand trial and criminal responsibility. The second broad division of forensic psychiatry covers the assessment of mental disability. It includes the evaluation of individuals who have been injured on the job; the assessment of plaintiffs who claim that they were injured and are now seeking compensation from a defendant; and the assessment of the competency of individuals to perform specific acts, such as making a will. The third broad division pertains to the legal aspects of general psychiatric practice, such as the civil commitment of involuntary patients, the doctrine of informed consent, the requirement to protect third parties from dangerous patients, and matters of privilege and confidentiality. The fourth broad division is forensic child psychiatry, which is an unusual medical subspecialty because it can be conceptualized as a subdivision of both forensic psychiatry and child psychiatry. The interface between child psychiatry and the law is a very young discipline. Schetky and Benedek (1985, 1991) and Nurcombe and Partlett (1994) have published books that focus on the subspecialty of forensic child psychiatry.

COMPONENTS OF FORENSIC CHILD PSYCHIATRY

Forensic child psychiatry concerns the following issues:

The Legal Rights of Children and Adolescents: Child and adolescent psychiatrists should participate in the way our society defines the legal rights and responsibilities of minors. For instance, whether our society gives adolescents the right to authorize their own medical and psychiatric care should be influenced by what is known about adolescent cognitive and social development. Another example is the competing rights of adolescents to confidentiality and of their parents to have access to certain medical information.

Delinquent Behavior and the Juvenile Justice System: The forensic child psychiatrist may evaluate juveniles who have been arrested, in order to determine their understanding of the charges against them and their competency to assist in the preparation of their defense. The psychiatrist may evaluate clients' mental states at the time of the alleged offense if an insanity defense is being considered. The court might request a psychiatric evaluation in order to determine if a juvenile who has been accused of committing an unusually serious offense should be tried as an adult. The forensic child psychiatrist might evaluate and treat youngsters who already have been adjudicated and who are now assigned to juvenile detention facilities. The evaluation and treatment of juvenile sexual offenders are sometimes done by programs specifically designed for that purpose.

Mental Disability: Child psychiatrists also may perform forensically oriented evaluations when they assess clients for some legal or administrative purpose. For instance, they may see patients who claim that they are mentally disabled and seek benefits from the Social Security system. The legal question may be whether a child has a particular disability that would qualify him or her for specific educational services. In the context of a civil lawsuit, the forensic child psychiatrist may see a child who claims to have been injured by another person and to have sustained a condition such as posttraumatic stress disorder.

Legal Aspects of Child Psychiatric Practice: The purview of forensic child psychiatry also includes issues such as the civil commitment of minors, the requirement to protect third parties, and medical malpractice.

Custody and Visitation Disputes: Many child psychiatrists, irrespective of their having a particular interest in forensic issues, may have to deal with custody and visitation disputes. This issue is discussed later in this chapter.

The Evaluation of Neglected and Abused Children: Psychiatrists in private practice as well as those employed by courts or other agencies see children who may have been physically, sexually, or psychologically abused. The reason may be to assist the court in determining what happened to the child, to make recommendations regarding placement or treatment, or to offer an opinion on the termination of parental rights. The evaluation of physically and sexually abused children is discussed later in this chapter.

Forensic psychiatry is complex because it has such a disparate constituency and because it overlaps with so many other areas of knowledge. Its scientific basis ranges from information on criminal behavior, to senile dementia, to child development. However, some general principles apply to all aspects of forensic psychiatry and are considered in this chapter: the importance of defining one's role accurately, the problem of bias, the misuse of psychiatric expertise, and the concept of levels of proof.

ROLE DEFINITION

Many times psychiatrists must keep straight in their own mind and clarify to others whom their client is and what their exact role is in the current situation. The client may be the person the psychiatrists are examining or it may be someone else. Psychiatrists may function as therapists or as evaluators. In the specific case under consideration, to whom is the psychiatrist professionally, financially, and ethically responsible?

This issue comes up in general psychiatric practice in many ways. Are psychiatrists who work for a student health service ethically responsible for the welfare of the student or the welfare of the university? Is the therapist of an adolescent obligated to meet the needs of the adolescent, who is the patient, or the needs of the parents, who pay the bill? Is the medical director of a for-profit hospital responsible to the patients in the hospital or the owners of the hospital? In clinical and administrative psychiatry, these ambiguities and potential conflicts usually are resolved by blending the requirements and demands of the competing entities, by seeking out common ground, by compromise, by good communication, and by role clarification.

In most aspects of forensic psychiatry, the psychiatrists' roles are quite distinct, and it is always important for them to keep straight what their mission is. Any confusion in this regard will be magnified and highlighted by the legal processes and will compromise the psychiatrists' work, whether they are intending to be therapists, evaluators, consultants, or administrators. However, psychiatrists should not leave clinical expertise at the door when they are consulted about a forensic issue. Barnum (1986) has described how it is sometimes possible to integrate these roles and to provide a solid clinical solution to what was initially a forensic problem.

First, forensic child psychiatrists need to know whether they are doing a forensic evaluation, which is intended to be read by attorneys and used at court, or whether they are performing a clinical evaluation and psychotherapy. This is an important issue in psychiatric custody evaluations and also in work with abused children. For instance, when a separated or divorced parent brings a child for a psychiatric evaluation, it is important at the very beginning to clarify whether the parent is seeking an evaluation that can be used in court for some legal purpose, such as seeking a change in custody or in the visitation arrangements. Usually parents know whether they are seeking an expert opinion to help in a court case or are simply concerned about the child's depression and want counseling. Sometimes parents are so upset and confused themselves that they do not know what they want, so psychiatrists should meet with the parents first to collect the basic facts of the situation and to explain what the

choices are. Sometimes parents want both jobs done—want the psychiatrist to treat the child's depression and also to be ready to testify in court that the parent who brought the child for evaluation and treatment is certainly the preferable custodial parent. If that is the case, psychiatrists can explain that they can do either a psychiatric custody evaluation or a clinical evaluation and therapy, but not both. It is also useful to explain this distinction to the attorney involved.

Second, forensic child psychiatrists need to know and to keep straight who hired them and to whom they owe professional and ethical responsibility. For instance, suppose that a psychiatrist has been appointed by the court to perform a custody evaluation. She has thoroughly evaluated the family and has concluded that it will be in the child's interests for the father to have sole and permanent custody. However, the psychiatrist also has found that the father has a significant flaw that has not previously been known to the mother or to the court. Specifically, he smokes marijuana once or twice a month with his friends after work. Despite his substance abuse, the psychiatrist still feels that the father is the preferred parent. The question is, should the psychiatrist include that information in her report to the court? This question creates a conflict because it is in the child's interests for the psychiatrist to suppress the information about the father's drug use (because the mother's attorney might be able to use that information to attack the psychiatrist's opinion), but it is in the court's interests for the psychiatrist to include this new information (so that the court will have as large a fund of data as possible on which to base a decision). In this relatively simple example, the psychiatrist has been appointed by the court and owes to the court a full report, including the strengths and weaknesses of both parents.

THE PROBLEM OF BIAS

Psychiatrists and other mental health professionals do not realize how easily and how often they become biased in their work with patients and families. Despite all that is known about unconscious processes (such as countertransference) and conscious motivations (such as greed and desire for popularity and fame), it is common for therapists to base conclusions on their own preconceived assumptions rather than on the data that have been presented. Bias seems more prevalent in forensic cases, because the person doing the evaluation is immersed in and buffeted by anger, threats, deceit, tragedy, innuendo, and various forms of hypocrisy, flattery, and bribery. It is extremely important for psychiatrists to be aware of their own motivations as well as the agendas of the other professionals involved in the case. Bias is important in forensic cases in two ways.

First, it is easy to understand that bias creates a distorted filter through which evaluators view the situation. A mental health professional who has very definite opinions about family relationships is likely to apply those rules in a way that distorts all the other facts in a case. Consider this situation.

A psychiatrist was asked to conduct a custody evaluation on a 6-year-old girl. He recommended that the mother should have permanent custody of the child. On cross examination at trial, the psychiatrist acknowledged that it was his opinion that mothers should *always* have custody of 6-year-old girls, unless the mother was clearly an unfit parent. Because the psychiatrist obviously was biased regarding the point at issue, the court disregarded his entire evaluation.

The second reason that bias is a problem in forensic child psychiatry is more subtle. That is, psychiatrists who enter a case with a particular bias are likely to change the situation that they believe they are studying objectively. This distortion may occur most commonly in the investigation of child sexual abuse, as in the next case.

A girl's therapist had reason to believe that the child had been sexually abused by her father. The therapist asked the girl if the father had ever done any "bad touching," which the girl disclaimed. The therapist asked if the father had ever touched her peepee when he put her to bed or gave her a bath, which the girl denied. The therapist asked if the father might have done those things and instructed the girl not to tell anybody, which the girl denied. The girl wanted to go to the bathroom. The therapist said that she could not go to the bathroom until she told what the father had done. So the girl said that her father had touched her peepee many times during her bath and that it hurt her. Then the therapist let her go to the bathroom and praised her for being a good girl, and a brave one for telling what the father had done.

Forensic psychiatrists may be biased in many ways, ranging from benign or downright malicious. Psychiatrists might be collecting data for a research project or a book, so they tend to elicit information that is consistent with their thesis and ignore other aspects of the case. Evaluators might have countertransference effects, which could be derived from their past experiences with their own parents, children, or former spouses. Evaluators might be working with a particular mission in mind; for example, that it is their job to find as many child molesters as possible and put them in jail. Or it might be their mission to protect men who had been falsely accused of child molesting, by exposing the inadequate evaluations done by the local social service agency. In any case, evaluators with a mission are in danger of doing biased evaluations because they are predisposed to see the data in a particular way. The most extreme form of bias is being a hired gun, when mental health professionals develop an opinion that simply reflects the agenda of the attorney who hired them. Not only do hired guns corrupt the particular case being worked on, but such practitioners also lower the credibility of the ethical professionals in their community.

With all these dangers of bias, is there any hope of conducting a neutral, competent forensic evaluation? What should be the mind-set of professionals who endeavor to accomplish an unbiased evaluation? There are several safeguards. Psychiatrists should try to be aware of their own conscious and unconscious motivations. They should be saying something like this to themselves: "It really doesn't matter to me whether the mother or the father ends up with custody of this child. It really doesn't matter who will end up winning this case. All that really matters to me is to collect accurate and meaningful data and to organize it in a way that is scientifically and medically valid." Another safeguard against bias is for psychiatrists to explain comprehensively the reasons for their conclusions in the written report, so that the court will fully understand the bases for the opinions.

MISUSE OF PSYCHIATRIC EXPERTISE

Some forensic psychiatrists misuse their expertise by manipulating the court into believing something that may not be true. A common method used by unscrupulous psychiatrists and other mental health professionals is to use jargon or complex psychological terminology to cloak their conclusions with a higher degree of certainty. In one case, for instance, a psychiatric expert witness attempted to explain why a sadistic pedophile had confessed his behavior to the police by attributing the confession to "identification with the aggressor." His use of the term was inconsistent with its meaning in the psychiatric literature, and he misused the concept to arrive at an erroneous conclusion, but it took another expert witness to explain the error to the court (Perr, 1990). In another case, a mental health professional expounded at length on the significance of "family secrets." He then applied his own idiosyncratic definition of the phrase to a custody dispute and concluded that custody should transfer from the father to the mother. In another case (cited in Herman, 1990a), a mental health professional testified that a little girl had the symptoms of the "child sexual abuse syndrome." He then asserted that the child must have been sexually abused because she had those symptoms, which goes beyond our current diagnostic abilities.

DEGREES OF CERTAINTY

An important aspect of legal decisions is the standard of proof or the level of certainty that must be established in order for a judicial decision to go a particular way. There are several levels of certainty: (1) probable cause; (2) preponderance of evidence; (3) clear and convincing proof; and (4) proof beyond a reasonable doubt.

The least exacting level of certainty to achieve is "probable cause." In the practice of criminal law, probable cause would be defined as cause sufficient to lead a reasonable person to suspect the person arrested had committed a crime. In psychiatric practice, that may be a sufficient level of certainty to report a suspected instance of child abuse.

In civil cases, the side prevails that establishes a "fair preponderance of the evidence." This can be expressed quantitatively as being 51% certain.

In some cases that involve psychiatric evidence, the level of certainty is "clear and convincing proof," which is proof necessary to persuade by a substantial margin, which is more than a bare preponderance. In most states civil commitment and paternity suits and the insanity defense must be proven to a degree that is clear and convincing. In most circumstances the proof that child abuse has occurred must be clear and convincing.

Finally, criminal cases require proof that is "beyond a reasonable doubt," which means proof that is beyond question. To convict a specific person of child abuse would require proof beyond a reasonable doubt.

One of the most puzzling terms in forensic psychiatry is "reasonable degree of medical certainty." When physicians testify in court, frequently they are asked if their opinions are given with a reasonable degree of medical certainty. The problem is that there is no specific meaning for that term. At one time or another, physicians have taken it to mean about the same as beyond a reasonable doubt, the same as clear and convincing, and even the same as the level of preponderance of the evidence. Rappeport (1985) has proposed that reasonable medical certainty is a level of certainty equivalent to what a physician uses when making a diagnosis and starting treatment. The implication is that the degree of certainty would depend on the clinical situation. The diagnosis of syphilis is accomplished with almost 100% certainty, since there is a reliable laboratory test for that purpose. The determination that a child has posttraumatic stress disorder as a result of a specific event is made with considerably less confidence, but may still be made with a reasonable degree of medical certainty.

KNOWLEDGE OF THE LAW

In performing a forensic evaluation, it is important to know the legal issue involved that is the basis for the dispute in the first place and the reason for the evaluation. The pertinent legal issue may be defined in an actual law that the federal or state legislature has passed, or it may be embodied in case law. For instance, in some states the legislature has passed a law that lists the factors that judges must consider in deciding a disputed custody case. Other states do not have any law at all that offers guidance in such a case, so attorneys and judges must look to how earlier cases in that state have been decided. The cases that become legal precedents usually have been heard by an appellate court or the highest court of that state. Such a court publishes its decisions and usually explains its reasoning so that those principles can be followed in subsequent cases. Occasionally a forensic psychiatrist needs to study the regulations that a state agency has published regarding a particular issue. For instance, a psychiatrist who has been asked to offer an expert opinion about the placement of an emotionally handicapped youngster would want to read the actual regulations that the local school boards are expected to follow in that state.

There are several ways for psychiatrists to obtain the laws or other documents that might be needed in order to be fully informed regarding a forensic issue.

1. Forensic cases almost always involve at least one attorney. Most clients who seek a forensic evaluation already have an attorney. Usually that attor-

ney is happy to send the psychiatrist a copy of the pertinent law or the precedential cases.

2. Most public libraries have carry a complete set of the laws of the state in the reference section. A well-organized index will help locate the law on any topic. Since many laws are changed every year, usually it is necessary to look up the text in a basic volume and also in the most recent supplement.

3. State medical societies sometimes publish a booklet with all of the laws that apply to the practice of medicine. However, medical societies are more likely to publish the laws that pertain to death certificates and communicable diseases; they might leave out the laws that relate to child custody, the involuntary hospitalization of minors, and the confidentiality of psychiatric records.

4. It would be a worthwhile project for local psychiatric societies to collect and publish the laws that relate to the practice of psychiatry. Forensic issues are becoming increasingly important in the practice of all psychiatrists.

5. In order to be informed of new issues as they evolve, psychiatrists could subscribe to a service such as the *Family Law Quarterly* or the *Mental and Physical Disability Law Reporter.*

TRAINING AND CERTIFICATION

Training programs in general psychiatry and fellowships in child psychiatry devote a small amount of time to forensic issues and even less time to child forensic psychiatry. One reason is that forensic child psychiatry must compete with so many other important subjects for "air time." The second reason is that there are so few forensic child psychiatrists available to do the teaching. Child psychiatrists who have been interested in focusing on this subspecialty have been tutored or mentored by more experienced clinicians; have found ways to share experiences with other psychiatrists, social workers, and psychologists with similar interests; and have worked independently to break new ground and to gain expertise. There are about 30 1-year fellowship programs in forensic psychiatry; some of them focus in part on the issues of forensic child psychiatry.

Since 1976 it has been possible to become board certified in forensic psychiatry. The examinations first were given by the American Board of Forensic Psychiatry. The examinations focused primarily on the adult aspects of forensic psychiatry, but the curriculum did include some topics of child forensic psychiatry, such as the juvenile justice system, child abuse, sexual abuse, child custody disputes, and adoption. In 1991 the American Psychiatric Association recognized forensic psychiatry as an official subspecialty and requested that the American Board of Psychiatry and Neurology prepare to examine individuals for "added qualifications in forensic psychiatry." Since the American Board of Psychiatry and Neurology started to examine and to certify psychiatrists in forensic psychiatry in 1994, the American Board of Forensic Psychiatry no longer gives its examination.

Custody and Visitation

BRIEF HISTORY OF DIVORCE AND CHILD CUSTODY

The history of child custody disputes was eloquently reviewed by Derdeyn (1976). Throughout most of recorded history, it was understood that the children of a marriage were the property of the father, and he routinely took custody of the children when divorce occurred. During the latter part of the 19th century, however, both the English and American legal systems started to act on behalf of the child and to consider the relative moral fitness of the competing parents. The "tender years" doctrine, which was introduced in the late 19th century, presumed that young children should be raised by the mother because she had a stronger attachment and would provide better care.

Since the 1920s lawmakers and courts have placed emphasis on "what is best for the interest of the child," as expressed by Justice Benjamin Cardozo (*Finlay v. Finlay,* 1925). That is a very broad concept, but it is important because it implies that the needs of the child are more powerful than the rights of either parent. In applying the best interests test, however, courts almost always gave custody to the mother. Since the 1970s, with the tremendous emphasis on equality between the sexes, many fathers have challenged the assumption that the mother should be the custodial parent and the father the noncustodial parent. A landmark case (*Ex parte Devine,* 1981) established that the tender years presumption violated the 14th amendment to the United States Constitution. Fathers now receive custody in about 10% of all divorces, but in a higher percentage of contested cases.

Many aspects of parental separation and divorce hurt the children. The long list of potential hurts include the sense of uncertainty and insecurity because the family will not be together the way it used to be; the embarrassment when the child's friends find out about the parents' divorce; the prospect of moving several times before the custodial parent settles down again; the daily and weekly disruptions to everyday life as one shuttles from one household to the other; the loss of the noncustodial parent, as he or she drifts farther out of one's life; and the inevitable financial hardships, because it costs more for a divorced family to live in 2 households than it did for the intact family to live together. The thing that hurts children most is the fighting between the divorcing parents, which is manifested largely through adversarial custody disputes. Wallerstein (1991; Wallerstein & Blakeslee 1996; Wallerstein & Kelly, 1980) has reviewed the short-term and long-term effects of divorce on children.

The practice of forensic child psychiatry is evolving, so there is no standard procedure for conducting custody and visitation evaluations. A number of psychiatrists and other mental health professionals have published the principles and procedures that they think are important in conducting these evaluations: Ackerman (1994), Ash and Guyer (1986), Benedek and Benedek (1980), Gardner (1982), Goldstein, Freud, and Solnit (1973), Goldzband (1988), Haller (1981), Herman (1991), and Weiner, Simons, and Cavanaugh (1985). In addition, guidelines for performing child custody evaluations have been adopted by the American Psychiatric Association (1988a) and the American Academy of Child and Adolescent Psychiatry (1997).

ROLE OF THE PSYCHIATRIST

Custody decisions and disputes involve psychiatrists in several ways. The most frequent way finds a child already in psychotherapy when his or her parents decide to separate or divorce, and a decision must be made regarding the child's custody (Bernet, 1983; Gardner, 1991). A court might order that a child receive therapy as part of its custody decree, so that is also a potential role for a child and adolescent psychiatrist. The psychiatrist might serve as a mediator for divorcing parents, offering an alternative to the adversarial process that usually characterizes custody disputes (Marlow & Sauber, 1990; Miller & Veltkamp, 1987). The psychiatrist may be a counselor for the divorced parents, with the intention of helping the mother and father learn to parent their child in a cooperative rather than a hostile manner (Barnum, 1987; Garrity & Baris, 1994). Finally, the psychiatrist may perform psychiatric custody and visitation evaluations. These evaluations usually consist of psychiatric evaluations of the child and of both parents and recommendations that are intended to be in the best interests of the child. In performing custody evaluations, the psychiatrist may be an employee or consultant to the court or may be an independent psychiatrist who has been invited to conduct the evaluation by one or both of the parties.

THE PSYCHIATRIC CUSTODY EVALUATION

In conducting the psychiatric custody evaluation, it is usually best to have access to all members of the family. That is, the evaluator would want to interview both parents, stepparents, all the children, and other significant individuals. The evaluator might want to interview grandparents, a baby-sitter, school personnel, or the therapist who has treated a member of the family. There are 3 ways in which the psychiatrist is able to interview both parents. Sometimes the mother's attorney and the father's attorney agree on having a particular psychiatric expert conduct the evaluation. A second route is that the judge who is hearing the case orders both parties to participate in the custody evaluation. Finally, a cumbersome process sometimes occurs in which the mother has already consulted a psychiatrist or other mental health professional and the father has already consulted a different individual. The parties agree to swap interviews, so that the mother's expert has a chance to evaluate the father and vice versa. A psychiatrist who has evaluated both parents usually can comment on the strengths and weaknesses of both describe the child's attachment to both, and make specific recommendations regarding custody and visitation.

In other circumstances the psychiatrist may not be able to do a full custody evaluation. That is, one-sided evaluation might be performed, interviewing only 1 parent and the child. For instance, the mother might consult the psychiatrist and bring the child for evaluation, but the father may refuse to come to any appointment. In such a case the psychiatrist could make limited observations and recommendations, such as commenting on the psychiatric condition of the mother and the child, describing the mother's parenting skills, and evaluating the attachment between the mother and the child. In such a case the psychiatrist would not be able to say anything about the psychiatric status of the father. Also, usually no recommendations regarding custody could be made because the psychiatrist had no way of comparing the mother with the father.

If the psychiatrist is embarking on a one-sided custody evaluation, it is important to determine whether the parent who is bringing the child actually has the authority to authorize it. Usually it is considered unethical to see a child for psychiatric evaluation without the permission of the custodial parent. An exception would occur if it were truly a psychiatric emergency.

FORMAT FOR THE EVALUATION

Although practitioners may vary in their approach, the following are common components of a child or adolescent psychiatrist's custody evaluation.

Initial Conference: Usually it is helpful to have an initial conference with both parents in order to make sure that they and the psychiatrist all have the same understanding regarding the purpose and the format of the psychiatric custody and visitation evaluation. This meeting is used to review and resolve all of the administrative aspects of the evaluation. The following is clarified: the basic chronology of the marriage, including the births of the children, the separation(s), and the divorce; the legal status of the case, such as the mandate of the court order, the schedule of pending legal action, and the names of the attorneys; and the current situation, including the current visitation schedule. The initial meeting is used to schedule all of the testing and interviews that constitute the evaluation. In the meeting with both parents the psychiatrist can obtain the written authorizations to obtain additional information from the pediatrician, teachers, therapists, and other pertinent individuals. It is also wise to obtain written permission from both parents to release clinical information to both attorneys and to the court at the end of the evaluation. That is, it should be made explicit that this is a forensic evaluation, that it is not therapy, and that it is not confidential. The payment of the fee for the evaluation should be determined—a typical arrangement is for the parents to divide the cost of the evaluation and to arrange for the payment prior to starting the evaluation or at the time of each appointment. Finally, the psychiatrist can use the initial meeting to see whether the parents really want to go ahead with a long and tedious evaluation or whether they are willing to negotiate with each other to arrive at some solution to the dispute, making the evaluation unnecessary.

Parent Meetings: The psychiatrist meets with each parent individually in order to complete a psychiatric evaluation and to assess that person's parenting attitudes and skills. It seems more efficient to have one long meeting of 2 or 3 hours rather than multiple short meetings. Although psychiatrists have different priorities as far as what information is collected from each parent, a typical agenda includes: a brief history of the marriage; a brief history of the period of separation and divorce; information about each child, such as that parent's view of the child's strengths, weaknesses, and reactions to the divorce; the parent's past history, including education, work history, and legal problems, such as arrests; the parent's psychiatric history, including symptoms, episodes of treatment, and how it might have affected his or her relationship with the child; the parent's medical history, including use of drugs and alcohol; and that parent's proposal for the child's custody and visitation. In order to assess parenting attitudes, the evaluator might present several hypothetical situations involving children for the parent to assess and resolve. It is useful to ask questions such as "If you are granted custody of the child, how would you help the child maintain a good relationship with the other parent?" and "If you lose custody, how would you maintain a good relationship with the child?" In any case, the evaluator should follow the same outline with both parents. As with any psychiatric interview, the evaluator is interested not only in the content of the answers but also in the way the parent approaches the task of the interview and the parent's style of relating to the interviewer.

Child Meetings: The purpose of meetings with the child is to complete a psychiatric evaluation and to assess the child's attachment to each parent and also, in some circumstances, to determine the child's preference about where to live and reasons for that preference. The child should be interviewed at least twice, because each parent should bring the child for the appointment at least once. The format and content of the interviews depend on the child's age.

With preschool children, the psychiatrist may want to start the interview with the parent and the child together. The evaluator could invite the parent and child to engage in some play activity together, such as drawing pictures or building with blocks, and could ask them to plan a weekend outing together. It should be possible to make observations about how both the child and the parent deal with such an assignment. After about half the meeting the parent can be excused from the room, having been informed about the procedure prior to the interview. At that point, the evaluator can collect data as to how the child and parent deal with separation. During the last part of the meeting, the psychiatrist can use play or other techniques to complete the evaluation.

With latency-age children, the evaluator can use a semistructured interview commonly used in psychiatric evaluations of children, introducing topics or tasks that pertain to family relationships. Simple projective questions can be helpful, such as the baby bird story, the deserted island story, going on a picnic, and the magician who can grant 3 wishes.

In using the baby bird story, the evaluator says that he wants the child to help him make up a story. The evaluator may say, "One time there was a baby bird that lived in a . . . [The child says, 'nest'.] The bird lived in the nest with its . . . ['mother bird'] and . . . ['father bird']. One day there was a very big storm and there was a lot of rain and . . . ['lightning'] and . . . ['thunder'] and ['wind']. There was so much wind that the mother bird was blown over in that direction and the father bird was blown over in the other direction. The baby bird was blown out of the nest. The baby bird, by the way, could fly, but only a little bit. Tell me what happens next in the story." At that point the evaluator prompts the child to finish the story with as much detail as possible.

In using the deserted island story, the evaluator says that he wants the child to help with a new story. The evaluator asks the child if he knows what an island is and then what a deserted island might be. If necessary, the evaluator "sets the scene" by providing a brief description of a deserted island. Then the evaluator proposes that the child might go on a trip to a deserted island and asks questions such as: "How would you get there?" "What provisions would you need to take?" "Who would you take with you?" The child might list several people. The evaluator can say: "Suppose you only have room to take one person with you to the deserted island. Who would you take? Why would you take that person?" The picnic story is similar, but a picnic might be more familiar to some children than a deserted island.

In using the magician story, the evaluator first asks the child if he knows what a magician is. He sets the scene with a description of what a typical magician looks like and what he does. Then the evaluator says, "Suppose you are walking down the street. You see a magician, who has on a black outfit and a cape. The magician comes up to you and says, 'Freddie, I am a magician. I can give you anything that you want. I can change anything in your life that has happened to you.

I can make anything happen in the future that you may want. Tell me something that you want me to do.'" After the child replies, the magician offers two more wishes.

The child might express himself through drawings, such as draw-a-person, drawing his family doing something exciting, or drawing a picture of something nice and something nasty. It is instructive to make a list of the parents and stepparents and ask the child what he or she likes and does not like about each person. The dislikes might include information about verbal and physical abusiveness and parental behavior such as alcohol and drug abuse. The child might be asked to describe the current custody and visitation arrangements and say whether he or she would want them changed in any way. If the evaluator chooses to elicit the child's preferences, it should be done in a way that minimizes the importance of the question. It is useful to mention that it is really the judge who is going to decide this issue, not the child or the interviewer. Because of the possibility of parental indoctrination, the interviewer can explore what each parent told the child to say to the psychiatrist and what the parents say about each other.

With adolescents, the psychiatrist may take the tack of asking the youngster to explain his or her view of the current situation: his or her perception of the relationship between the parents, what he or she knows about the reasons for the divorce, and the effects of the divorce on his or her own life. Most adolescents can discuss the pros and cons of life with each parent, the merits of particular visitation arrangements, and how to keep their own lives from becoming entangled with their parents' issues. Adolescents may have definite opinions about where they want to live and what they want to say to the judge. The evaluator should explore in detail the reasons for youngsters' preferences and also other aspects of the case, such as how adolescents intend to maintain a good relationship with both parents.

Outside Information: In conducting a custody evaluation, the psychiatrist should collect information from certain outside sources, having obtained permission from one or both parents. Usually it is helpful to interview other individuals who live in the household, such as stepparents, grandparents, nannies, and other siblings who are not directly involved in the custody dispute (as is the case with children over 18, stepsiblings, and half siblings). It might be helpful to speak with the family's pediatrician, who may provide relatively unbiased observations about both parents' skills and attitudes. School teachers and day care workers can be very insightful and observant, although at times they may be co-opted by a parent. Finally, it is important to speak to previous and current psychotherapists of the child and of the parents. Although it frequently is advisable for therapists to avoid making formal recommendations or testifying in court, it can be helpful for them to discuss their observations of the parties with the individual who is conducting the complete forensic evaluation.

Psychological Testing: In some custody evaluations, standardized psychological testing can be very informative. For instance, both parents can be asked to take a personality inventory, such as the Minnesota Multiphasic Personality Inventory or the Millon Clinical Inventory. Both parents can fill out questionnaires regarding the child, such as the Child Behavior Checklist. These tests may be utilized as screening devices and as adjunctive sources of information, to help evaluators ensure that they have not missed some important issue. In some circumstances it would be helpful to use formal intellectual testing (if there is a question about a parent's mental capacity) or a battery of projective tests (if there is a question about the diagnosis of a parent's mental illness). In any case, the same tests should be administered to both parents.

Bricklin (1984, 1995) introduced several standardized psychological tests that are specifically intended for custody evaluations. The Bricklin Perceptual Scale, for instance, consists of asking the child 32 questions about the mother and the same 32 questions about the father. For example, one of the questions is "If you had to memorize a long, boring poem for school, how well would Mom do at being patient enough to help you learn this?" The questions are mixed together in such a way that the interviewer is never asking the child to directly compare the merits of the parents. What is creative about this test is that the child answers the questions verbally and also nonverbally, by punching a hole in a card with a stylus. The child's nonverbal responses can be measured and the 64 cards scored to give a composite score that indicates which parent is the preferred parent for that child. The nonverbal responses are less susceptible to bribery and loyalty conflicts than are verbal responses. The theoretical basis for the test is the notion that both parents may seem to outside observers to be equally qualified to be the custodial parent, so what is really important is whether the child him- or herself perceives one of

the parents as being more nurturing or desirable.

Conference with Attorneys: At the end of the evaluation some psychiatrists schedule a conference with the 2 attorneys or, alternatively, with the attorneys and parents together. Other psychiatrists simply prepare the written report and send it to the attorneys and to the court. The advantage of the face-to-face conference is that it gives the psychiatrist an opportunity to explain to the parties his or her recommendations and reasons for arriving at them. The psychiatrist can explain why certain factors were considered more important and why other issues were less crucial. Such a meeting gives the parents and attorneys an opportunity to ask questions where both sides have access to the psychiatrist's answers. Parents and attorneys deal with these wrap-up conferences in many ways. Sometimes it leads to a constructive discussion of the details of custody and visitation arrangements.

THE WRITTEN REPORT

The written report should be done carefully because it will be seen by several people and readers will tend to attach undue significance to isolated sentences and phrases. Probably the best approach is to make the report detailed enough so that readers fully understand the procedure that was followed and the basis for the conclusions and recommendations, but not to include every piece of data that was collected. An outline for a typical report includes the following headings:

- Identifying Information: Names and birth dates.
- Background Information: A very brief chronology of the marriage and a statement of the current status of custody and visitation and a summary of the court order authorizing the evaluation. A statement about the circumstances of the referral and the specific purpose of the evaluation should be included.
- Procedure for This Evaluation: Including an explanation of the various meetings that were held, the psychological testing utilized, and the outside information that was collected.
- Observations: Includes a separate section for each family member. Each parent is discussed individually, with a summary of that person's strengths, weaknesses, personality traits, significant medical and psychiatric problems, and whether these factors have a bearing on the person's ability to be a good parent. Each child can be discussed individually, with a summary of his or her biopsychosocial strengths and weaknesses, identification of any psychiatric disorder, and a comment about how the

child is coping with the parents' divorce. In addition, the report should address the child's attachment to each parent and whether the child has a preference regarding custody and the reasons for the preference. The evaluator may comment on whether the child seemed unduly influenced by one of the parents.

- Conclusions: A list of specific statements that the psychiatrist believes are supported by the data. This could include, for instance, that one parent has had a major mental illness in the past that is likely to continue to be a problem in the future; or that a parent has personality characteristics that compromise his or her parenting abilities; or that the children are uniformly attached and bonded to one parent more than the other.
- Recommendations: Should follow logically from the conclusions. The psychiatrist can make recommendations regarding the custody of the child, the visitation schedule, whether the visitation should be supervised, whether any member of the family should be in psychotherapy, and whether the parents should attend parenting classes.

CRITICAL FACTORS

It is always understood that in contested cases, the decision regarding custody is guided by seeking the best interests of the child. In any specific case there is plenty of room for attorneys and parents to argue about exactly what constitutes the best interests of this particular child. In some cases all the choices look somewhat bleak and the court may be guided by the principle of the least detrimental alternative.

There is no standard set of guidelines for what factors should be taken into consideration and what weight should be given to each factor. Each state has its own laws and precedents that spell out the issues for judges to consider. The prototype for many state laws was Michigan's Child Custody Act of 1970. It is likely that psychiatrists and judges are influenced by their personal values when they make recommendations and hand down decisions in these cases. The factors that follow are the issues that many legislatures and courts and mental health professionals think are important in child custody determinations.

FACTORS ASSOCIATED WITH THE PARENTS

Critical issues here include the parental rights doctrine; the parents' morals, attitudes and parenting skills, history of caregiving; continuity of caregiving; the parents' physical and mental health;

religious beliefs; structure of the household; finances; and allegations of abuse.

Parental Rights Doctrine: When the dispute is between a biological parent and some other individual, such as a grandparent or an uncle or a foster parent, it is generally held that the biological parent has a greater right to the child as long as he or she is considered "fit." At times this seems to contradict the principle of pursuing the best interests of the child, since a child might be removed from a wonderful foster home and returned to biological parents who are marginal.

Parental Morals: Courts look with disfavor on parents who have a history of felony convictions, prostitution, substance abuse, and adultery. Attitudes about morals are influenced by time and by geography. It used to be thought that parental dating after the separation but before the divorce was considered immoral, but such conduct is now acceptable.

Parental Attitudes and Parenting Skills: The psychiatrist should be able to size up whether the parent truly tunes in to the child's emotional and physical needs *or* simply considers the child a narcissistic extension of him- or herself *or* is extremely anxious, passive, and helpless in common child care situations. Another issue is whether the parent truly appreciates that it will be in the child's interests to have a good relationship with both the mother and the father.

History of Caregiving: In some families one parent has been much more involved with day-to-day child-rearing activities. That is, that parent has fed and bathed the children, supervised their homework, organized their birthday parties, and taken them to the pediatrician, which may favor that person to be the custodial parent.

Continuity of Placement: Usually it is presumed preferable to maintain the status quo unless there is a good reason to change it. Usually a parent cannot file for a change in custody unless there has been a change in circumstance since the last time the court decided the issue.

Physical Health: As a physician, the psychiatrist is an appropriate person to assess whether the parent has a serious or a chronic illness that would compromise his or her ability to nurture the child.

Mental Health: The psychiatric evaluation should reveal any serious psychiatric condition or any significant drug or alcohol abuse. The psychiatrist should be able to comment on whether the psychiatric condition will impair parenting skills. A history of repeated hospitalizations for schizophrenia would be ominous, while a past history of a severe postpartum depression might have very little impact on current and future parenting abilities. The specific diagnosis may not be as important as an assessment of the person's parenting skills in the present and the future.

Religious Beliefs: Although this is not a psychiatric issue, courts seem to prefer a parent who is devout over one who is disinterested in religion. A psychiatrist might be asked to comment on whether a person's religious beliefs have reached the point of becoming fanatical or even delusional, which certainly could affect one's style of parenting. Also, the issue of religion might be a consideration if the child already has had an attachment to a particular faith and interrupting that attachment would be confusing or disruptive.

The Households: A parent who has remarried may be able to provide a more traditional family-oriented atmosphere. The psychiatrist should be aware of the type of household and the general neighborhood where each parent lives.

Financial Considerations: This generally is not a factor, since ideally payment of child support tends to equalize financial differences. However, a psychiatrist and a court might consider it meaningful if there is a great difference between the households, which would affect the child's opportunities to live in a safe neighborhood and attend a good school.

Allegations of Physical or Sexual Abuse: In recent years allegations of abuse have complicated the psychiatrist's evaluation of custody disputes. What typically happens is that one parent alleges that someone in the other household—the parent, stepparent, or perhaps a boyfriend—has sexually abused the child. The alleging parent usually wants contact with the other parent to be curtailed or discontinued.

FACTORS ASSOCIATED WITH THE CHILD

Critical issues in this regard include the child's attachment to the parents and his or her preference end genders.

The Child's Attachment to the Parents: This extremely important issue can best be assessed by a mental health professional who is experienced in interviewing and evaluating children. Indications of the child's attachment and bonding can be found in observations of the child and parent playing together; in the baby bird story, the picnic story, the family drawing, the lists of likes and dislikes, and other parts of the semistructured interview; and in testing such as the Bricklin Percep-

tual Scales. Many children have a solid, positive attachment to both the mother and the father, which is certainly desirable to see in a child of divorced parents. However, it is significant if the child's attachment is found to be much stronger to one parent than the other.

The Child's Preference: Many children understand exactly what the parents are disputing but do not care where they will be living, as long as they continue to see both parents. Other children are able to articulate a definite preference and can give reasons that seem valid. For instance, the child might convey that the father is warm and nurturing and the mother is cold and aloof—and the psychiatrist has made the same observations about the relatedness of the parents. The legal effect of the child's preference usually depends on the child's age and varies from state to state. In general, a court is likely to give more serious consideration to a definite preference expressed by an adolescent than that of a child.

The Child's Gender: Some courts and also some mental health professionals have felt that there is a slight preference for placing custody with the parent of the same gender as the child. This is a factor that might be contributory, but not decisive, to the final recommendation.

COMMON SCENARIOS

Two Competent Parents: It is a common scenario for 2 parents, who are both fully competent and nurturing in their own way, to dedicate a huge amount of energy, money, and self-esteem to the fight over custody. Either of the parents could do a perfectly good job raising the child. It does not help the court very much to do an evaluation and send a cursory report back to the judge saying that neither parent has a mental disorder and both are fit to have custody of the child, period. The judge already knows that. It is more helpful to go down the factors just mentioned and indicate which ones favor the mother and which ones favor the father. The significance or weight attached to each factor also could be roughly indicated. By presenting the data in this way, both the psychiatrist and the judge could tally up the list and determine that one parent is slightly preferred over the other parent.

Two Deficient Parents: In some disputes, the evaluator may find that neither parent has the skills, attitudes, and ego strength to be fully satisfactory. In such cases, the evaluator must be satisfied with the least detrimental alternative. Such cases also may be opportunities to be creative and offer additional suggestions that might benefit the children. For instance, supportive therapy or parenting classes or ongoing mediation between the parents might be helpful. The evaluator might recommend some continuing involvement by a capable relative or continuing supervision by a social service agency.

One Competent, One Deficient Parent: This kind of evaluation seems easier, since the psychiatrist can clearly recommend which parent should have permanent custody of the child. In addition, however, the evaluator can make specific suggestions that would help the noncustodial parent become more capable. The evaluator also would want to point out that it is important for the child to continue to have a good relationship with both parents.

LESS COMMON SCENARIOS

Parent vs. Stepparent: Consider the situation in which a girl was raised from infancy by a mother and a stepfather. The mother died when the girl was 10 and a custody dispute ensued between the biological father, who had not seen the child in years, and the stepfather. In one such case a compromise was achieved in which the girl made a gradual transition from living with the stepfather to living with the father and the girl was allowed to have some continuing contact with the stepfather.

Homosexuality: In California and New York, it is common for male homosexuals and lesbians to obtain legal custody of their children, but that is less common in other parts of the country. The custody evaluation involving a homosexual parent should be based on objective data and not on stereotypes. The professional literature (Bozett, 1987; Kleber, Howell, & Tibbits-Kleber, 1986; Patterson, 1992) on this issue indicates that homosexuals can provide healthy, nurturing homes, although the children may be affected by social stigmatization in the community.

Masked, Reverse Custody Dispute: Two parents, both successful professionals, divorced, agreed to joint custody, and arranged for the 2 adolescent children to alternate living in the 2 households on a week-to-week basis. The parents were pretending that they were doing this to ensure that the children had the opportunity to relate to both of them, but in fact neither parent was willing to compromise his or her career in order to be a more consistent parent. The teenage children said that they would be happy living with either

the mother or the father but hated going back and forth every week.

Dispute Over Frozen Embryos: In a Tennessee case (*Davis v. Davis,* 1990), a married couple arranged for in vitro fertilization of several of the wife's eggs by the husband's sperm. The fertilized eggs were frozen for later use. The couple divorced and each of them wanted control over the embryos. The Court of Appeals created a simple solution to this kind of case: the embryos should be considered joint property, and nothing at all can be done with them unless both parties agree.

Grandparent Visitation: In recent years courts have started to consider whether grandparents have the right to visit their grandchildren, even without the agreement of the children's parents. Some state legislatures have passed laws that provide for grandparent visitation under certain circumstances. Herman (1990b) has suggested that psychiatric experts will be asked to make recommendations regarding grandparent visitation after considering the potential benefits and the aggravation of family conflict that might occur.

Parental Kidnapping: A tragic outcome of child custody disputes is that one may kidnap the child (Herman, 1990b; Schetky & Haller, 1983). This may occur if a parent arrogantly concludes that his or her own circumstances are above the law or if he or she believes the child may be in danger if allowed to visit the other parent. An underground network may assist parents in abducting children; private commando units have been hired to bring them back. Federal laws (the Uniform Child Custody Jurisdiction Act and the Parental Kidnapping Prevention Act) and an international agreement (the International Child Abduction Remedies Act) provide procedures and sanctions to address some aspects of this issue.

POSSIBLE OUTCOMES OF CUSTODY DISPUTES

Joint Custody: In joint legal custody both parents have equal rights and responsibilities regarding major decisions—regarding issues such as the child's education, medical care, and religious upbringing—and neither parent's rights are superior. It is expected that both parents are able to communicate with each other and are willing to take each other's opinions into consideration. In some states it is assumed that the parents will have joint custody, unless it can be shown that some other arrangement would be preferable. Even when the parents do have joint legal custody, the child usually lives primarily in one household and has visitation at the other one. Courts regularly require that joint custody orders include language to the effect that if the parties cannot agree on any particular issue, one party (usually the parent with actual physical custody) will have the final and exclusive decision on that issue (Atwell, Moore, Nielsen, & Levite, 1984; Folberg, 1984; Tibbits-Kleber et al., 1987).

Sole Custody: With sole custody, the child usually lives primarily with the custodial parent and has visitation with the noncustodial parent. This is the most common arrangement, and it usually results in the mother having custody. It would be helpful if the parents, the courts, and society generally would define more clearly the rights of the noncustodial parent, since this is an area of confusion and contradiction (Bernet, 1993b). From the purely legal point of view, for example, only the custodial parent can authorize a pediatrician to examine and treat a child. But in actual practice pediatricians routinely treat children at the request of noncustodial parents, stepparents, grandparents, and even baby-sitters.

Shared Custody: This arrangement is used infrequently, but it deserves greater consideration. Under shared custody, one parent has authority and control over certain specific aspects of the child's life and the other parent has authority over other aspects. Although the parents are encouraged to communicate and consider each other's opinions, they are not required to do so.

For example, the child lives with Parent A from Sunday evening to Friday evening and that parent is completely in charge of the child's education. The child lives with Parent B from Friday evening to Sunday evening every weekend and that parent is completely in charge of the child's weekend activities, including religious upbringing and the soccer schedule.

Shared custody is a way to take advantage of the strengths of both parents. It also might be appropriate if one parent works primarily during the week and the other parent works on weekends.

Split Custody: In split custody, the children are divided between the parents. It is generally considered advantageous to keep the siblings together, mainly because children of divorce feel threatened, insecure, and wounded, and they need all the support and consistency they can find. If the brothers and sisters are living together, they have the sense that at least part of the family is still in one piece. In other circumstances it may be advantageous to separate the siblings. Consider the following example.

Divorced parents had 3 children, Tom (age 12), Dick (8), and Harry (6). Both parents worked full time, so it was sure to be a major task for either of them to be a single parent for 3 sons. Initially the mother had custody of all the children, but it did not work out well. Tom was an impulsive, difficult youngster with a severe learning disability, who required a great deal of structure and individualized attention. Dick and Harry excluded Tom from most of their activities. The father wanted to go back to court to obtain custody of all the boys. A mediator helped the parents work out a different solution, that the mother would continue as the custodial parent for Dick and Harry and the father would have custody of Tom.

When siblings are living in different households, visitation can be arranged so that they are actually together more than half their waking hours. For instance, the every-other-weekend visitation can be scheduled in such a way that the siblings are always together every weekend.

INDOCTRINATION AND ALIENATION

The participants in custody disputes frequently are concerned that the other parent is actively indoctrinating the child. It might be alleged that the indoctrinating parent is causing the child to favor that person (usually the custodial parent) and to reject the innocent parent (usually the noncustodial parent). Mental health professionals have noticed during forensic evaluations and also during the treatment of children of divorce that these youngsters may greatly favor one parent over the other (Clawar & Rivlin, 1991; Gardner, 1992a; Loeb, 1986).

The forensic psychiatrist and the judge should not jump to the conclusion that the child who prefers one parent very strongly is the victim of parental indoctrination. There are several possible explanations for this situation.

1. The child actually may have been abused, neglected, or disliked by one parent, so it is easy to understand why the child would favor the kinder parent.
2. The custodial parent may, in fact, systematically have induced the child to favor her (this allegation is usually made against the mother) by emphasizing her own relationship with the child and denigrating the father. If that is actually occurring, it could be driven by several possible mechanisms: by the mother's realistic appraisal of the situation, by her spitefulness, because of her own emotional needs, or because of paranoia or some other psychosis.

3. The custodial parent, usually the mother, may have contributed to the polarization of the child's feelings but not purposefully. For instance, the mother may be an anxious person who worries a great deal and communicates her anxiety to the child. She might start crying when the child leaves for visitation but insist that the child should go anyway.

4. A child may end up greatly favoring one parent over the other even though neither parent really did anything at all to cause it to happen. Perhaps the child does have a slightly better attachment to and a preference for one parent. The child has worried over the loss of the noncustodial parent and is afraid that he or she also is going to lose the remaining custodial parent. So the child experiences a greatly exaggerated attachment to the custodial parent.

5. Finally, there is a common psychological mechanism through with the child's affections could become extremely polarized. Specifically, intense like of one parent and dislike of the other could be his or her resolution to the tension created by cognitive dissonance, a concept introduced by a psychologist Leon Festinger (1957). Suppose that the mother and father have been fighting with each other very intensively. Because of cognitive dissonance, it would be impossible for the child to figure out a way to have affection for both of them. The child would try to reconcile 2 dissonant thoughts, "I love my mother" and "I love my father." The dissonance creates a tension in the child's mind that is resolved by believing that he or she loves one parent and hates the other.

Gardner (1992a) and Dunne and Hedrick (1994) have used the term "parental alienation syndrome" for these cases. Gardner offered suggestions as to how the custody in these cases should be decided. The ultimate goal would be for the child to have a reasonably good relationship with both parents. Gardner would assess whether the degree of parental alienation is mild (child expresses dislike for the father, but is willing to visit him), moderate (child expresses considerable dislike for father, professes reluctance to visit, but settle down and are comfortable with the father once the visit is underway), or severe (child is quite disturbed and fanatical in his dislike for the father). Gardner would also assess whether the mother (again, assuming she is doing the indoctrination) is changeable or treatable. In less severe cases and if the mother seems treatable, the child would stay with the mother and all parties would engage in counseling to help the child have a good relationship with the father. In more severe cases and if the mother lacks insight and does not seem

treatable, the child should live with the father. Once the child is comfortable with the father, it should be possible to allow phone calls and visitation with the mother.

Child Maltreatment

THE SCOPE OF CHILD ABUSE

It has been estimated that more than one million children in the United States are abused or neglected each year. Approximately 1,200 children die each year as a result of abuse. Mental health professionals and law enforcement personnel in different jurisdictions do not use exactly the same terminology and definitions for child abuse. For the purpose of this chapter, some generic definitions are offered.

Neglect is the failure to provide adequate care and protection for children. Physical neglect may involve failure to feed the child adequately, failure to provide medical care, or failure to protect the child from danger. The most extreme form of neglect leads to the syndrome of failure to thrive. Because it is difficult to define "adequate care," it is harder to recognize and identify less serious degrees of neglect.

Physical abuse is the parental infliction of injury by beating, punching, kicking, biting, or otherwise. The abuse can result in injuries such as broken bones, internal hemorrhages, bruises, burns, and poisoning.

Sexual abuse of children refers to sexual behavior between a child and an adult or between 2 children, when one of them is older or more dominant. The sexual behaviors include touching breasts, buttocks, and genitals, whether the victim is dressed or undressed; exhibitionism; fellatio; cunnilingus; and penetration of the vagina or anus with sexual organs or with objects. Pornographic photography usually is included.

Ritual abuse of children is a form of sexual abuse that occurs in conjunction with rituals that ceremonially invoke magical or supernatural powers. It usually involves multiple perpetrators and intimidation of the victims to prevent disclosure. Ritual abuse is a controversial phenomenon, and its prevalence is not clear. Other forms of abuse, such as child pronography and repetitive abuse by a psychotic parent, may be mistaken for ritual abuse (Bernet & Chang, 1997, Nurcombe & Unützer, 1991).

Mental or emotional abuse certainly occurs, but it is hard to sustain legally. Emotional abuse occurs when the parents or guardians cause serious emotional injury by repeatedly terrorizing or berating a child. When it is serious, it is usually accompanied by neglect or physical abuse or sexual abuse.

BRIEF HISTORY OF CHILD ABUSE

Nineteenth-century laws prohibited cruelty to animals. Some early cases of child abuse were tried under those laws, since state legislatures had not yet passed laws that prohibited cruelty to children. In the 1870s the Society for the Prevention of Cruelty to Children was founded, and New York was the first state to adopt a child protection law, which became the model for other states. Up until the 1960s it was thought that physical abuse of children was rare—partly because physical discipline of children was generally more acceptable and partly because of societal denial that horrible things were happening to children.

In the 1860s a French forensic pathologist described severe child abuse, after performing autopsies on children who had been beaten to death (Tardieu, 1868). In the 20th century the rediscovery and recognition of child abuse was not accomplished by a psychiatrist, social worker, pediatrician, or minister but by a radiologist in a hospital emergency room. Caffey (1946) noticed a syndrome of children with multiple skeletal injuries and chronic subdural hematomas. He published his discovery, and soon it was recognized that many children brought to emergency rooms had been physically abused by caregivers. Kempe, Silverman, Steele, Droegmueller, and Silver (1962) described the battered-child syndrome again, and in the following years every state passed laws requiring mandatory reporting of child abuse. The identification, evaluation, and treatment of abused children have been discussed by Besharov (1990), Helfer and Kempe (1968, 1976), Kempe and Kempe (1978), and Schmitt (1978).

It took a separate societal realization during the 1970s to acknowledge the extent of sexual abuse. It was known that incest occurred, but most people thought that it must be very unusual and that it happened among very deviant families. We now know that incest and other forms of sexual abuse are not rare. Abright (1986), Bulkley (1981), Corwin and Olavson (1993), Faller (1988), Finkelhor (1979, 1986), Friedrich (1990), Hunter (1990), Myers (1992), Schetky and Green (1988), Sgroi

(1982), and Yuille, Hunter, Joffe, and Zaparniuk (1993) have contributed to the legal and psychiatric literature regarding child sexual abuse. The American Academy of Child and Adolescent Psychiatry (1988, 1997) has published guidelines for the evaluation of children who may have been sexually abused.

ROLE OF THE PSYCHIATRIST

There are several forensic contexts in which a psychiatrist may evaluate children who may have been physically or sexually abused. The psychiatrist may evaluate children in a private psychiatric practice for a forensic purpose; may evaluate children and collaborate with other mental health professionals in a government agency, such as protective services; or may work with an interdisciplinary team at a pediatric medical center.

In a different role, psychiatrists may provide therapy for abused children and their families in both outpatient and inpatient settings. Many psychiatric hospitals and residential treatment centers have specialized programs for abused children and adolescents. There are also programs for adolescent sexual abuse perpetrators, many of whom were also victims of sexual abuse.

Psychiatrists may deal with these issues on the level of public policy by sharing information with and educating attorneys and judges regarding the psychiatric aspects of abuse and the developmental needs of children (Goldstein, Freud, & Solnit, 1973, 1979; Goldstein, Solnit, Goldstein, 1996). In some states, psychiatrists have helped shape the laws that control how the legal system deals with abused children—including the criteria for reporting abuse and the methods of evaluation and the procedures for hearing the child's testimony.

EVALUATING THE CHILD
WHO MAY HAVE BEEN ABUSED

Cases of abuse come to the attention of the authorities in many ways. Sometimes the abused child him- or herself initiates the referral by telling a relative, family friend, or teacher what has happened. Sometimes a teacher, friend, or physician suspects abuse, asks the child about it, and reports the concern to protective services. Sometimes a psychotherapist is seeing a child who has an emotional problem and learns about the abuse during the course of the evaluation or treatment. Finally, the abuse may be discovered accidentally, as when a child is brought to an emergency room and found to have gonorrhea or multiple old fractures. If a child psychiatrist (or any physician or mental health professional) has reason to believe that physical or sexual abuse has occurred, the federal government and all states require that the circumstances must be reported to the agency that is legally authorized to investigate the matter. This requirement was reinforced in the landmark case of *Landeros v. Flood* (1976).

The evaluation of a possible victim of abuse should adhere to the same basic principles as any thorough psychiatric evaluation. That is, the examiner should take a history and strive to collect data that are as complete and accurate as possible; the interview of the child should lead to observations about both conscious and unconscious processes and should address both form (the way the child communicates and how he or she relates to the interviewer) and content (what he or she actually says); and the examiner should keep an open mind regarding the differential diagnosis and the possible explanations for the data collected.

In addition to these basic principles, there are specific guidelines for the forensic evaluation of the child who may have been abused:

1. Make an audiotape or videotape of all the statements made by the interviewer and by the child, starting with the first meeting. This is important in order to reduce the number of times the child is interviewed and also to preserve the integrity of the evaluation. A child may give extremely convincing statements during the initial interviews but later retract the statements because of internal and external pressures. Also, the most convincing way to show in court that the child was not induced to make allegations of abuse is to have a recording and a transcript of the initial interviews.

2. Follow a consistent method to do a complete psychiatric evaluation, not just a history of the abuse incident. Build into the evaluation a way to test the child's ability to describe specific experiences. For instance, ask the child to describe 2 specific events, such as a holiday celebration or a shopping trip, that can be verified by an adult. Also, build into the evaluation an assessment of the child's understanding of telling the truth as opposed to pretending and make-believe. A full psychiatric evaluation might turn up a completely different explanation for why a child might have particular symptoms or behavior. It might turn up the underlying motivations of the adults involved.

3. Try to develop an accurate history of what happened by collecting information from involved adults and also the child. One scenario is that the possible perpetrator is the person who has brought the child for medical care. For instance, an abusive parent may bring the child to an emergency room. In that case, the evaluator would need to assess the parent's attitude and motivation and perhaps confront the parent with the fact that the bruises and other injuries were caused by beatings rather than by an accidental fall.

4. Another possibility is that the parent brings the child and accuses another person of the physical or sexual abuse. In that case, the parent who brings the child for evaluation usually can relate how the allegations of abuse first arose. For instance, did the child spontaneously make statements, or did someone ask the child questions before statements were forthcoming? If possible, interview the alleged perpetrator. He or she may give a frank description of abuse or may be able to offer some other legitimate explanation for what has happened.

5. Determine if the child has manifested symptoms that are more likely to occur in an abused child. Children who have been physically or sexually abused may manifest a wide variety of nonspecific emotional symptoms, such as fearfulness, hostility, depression, academic underachievement, somatic complaints, sleep disturbance, eating disorders, and running away. In general, children who have been physically abused are more likely to act out aggressively, while children who have been sexually abused are more likely to manifest inappropriate sexual behaviors.

6. Develop rapport with the child, which means being friendly without being pushy. It might be necessary to see the child two or more times before there is sufficient trust for the child to relate difficult material. It is important for the child to feel safe, believed, and supported during the interview. Sometimes it is helpful to let the child know that other children have had similar experiences and that they benefited from talking about what happened to them.

7. Try to determine if coaching has occurred. Coaching may have been either positive (the accusing parent encouraging the child to falsify or exaggerate) or negative (the perpetrator intimidating the child to keep the abuse a secret). One way is simply to ask in a natural manner at the onset of the interview something like "What did your mom tell you to tell me today?" Or at the end: "Is there anything we forgot to talk about that

your mom wanted you to say?" Or ask the child if the alleged perpetrator ever asked him or her to keep any secrets or threatened to hurt the child if he or she disclosed the abuse.

8. Have a strong stomach. Psychiatrists who evaluate or treat abused children have to be willing to hear material that may be extremely sad, grisly, and repugnant. They must accept the fact that physical and sexual abuse really occurs. Otherwise, the interviewers will communicate to the child to keep the information to him- or herself.

9. Try to use indirection in the interview, so that the child provides information spontaneously. If the alleged perpetrator is one of the parent, for instance, the interviewer might tell the child to make a list of things that he or she likes and does not like about both parents. The child might spontaneously describe instances of abuse when listing a few things he or she does not like about one parent. Engaging the child in a general discussion or introducing play materials also may lead to spontaneous statements. It works better to proceed from more general statements ("Sometimes children think that their parents are too strict.") to more specific questions ("Did your father ever hit you?"). Yuille et al. (1993) described the "stepwise interview" that consists of moving from free narrative, to general questions, to specific questions, to the use of interview aids, such as drawings and anatomically detailed dolls.

10. Try very hard to avoid contaminating the interview or inducing the child to make a specific statement or support a suspected allegation. The most common way to contaminate the interview is to ask leading questions (such as "Your daddy touched your bottom, didn't he?") and suggestive questions ("Did your daddy touch your bottom?"). Inexperienced interviewers make the error of repeatedly asking the child the same suggestive question. After several denials, the child eventually will endorse the suggestion. Children are suggestible in some circumstances and may create a story for the first interviewer and repeat it as a fact to the second interviewer (Ceci & Bruck, 1995). Quinn, White, and Santilli (1989) described several subtle ways in which the interviewer's behaviors affect the data that is collected in child abuse investigations.

11. Use restatement as an interview technique. This communicates to the child that the interviewer is trying hard to understand what is being said. The interviewer must be careful, of course, not to use restatement as a way to reinforce the child to say what the interviewer wants to hear. A

good way to use restatement is to play somewhat dumb and vague in the restatement, so that the child is more in control by correcting the interviewer's version. For instance, "I don't think I'm understanding this right. You seem to be saying that you thought that a man touched you somewhere on your bottom." Or the interviewer could purposefully say a crucial point the wrong way, to see if the child really sticks to the story: "Let me make sure I have this right. What you said was that at your family reunion your Uncle Bob took you in the bathroom and touched your private." Actually, the child had already said that it was Uncle Joe who did it.

12. Consider using anatomical dolls in evaluating children who may have been sexually abused. No specific or definitive test can be done with these dolls to determine if sexual abuse has occurred, although children who have been sexually abused are more likely to engage in sexualized doll play. Some children find these dolls useful to describe and to show what they experienced when they were abused. Also, anatomical dolls may help the clinician to determine the extent of the child's sexual knowledge, which may have been learned through either abusive or nonabusive experiences. Use of anatomical dolls should be only one part of a complete psychiatric evaluation. These dolls should not be forced on a reluctant child, who might perceive them as one more form of provocative overstimulation. This issue was reviewed by Everson and Boat (1990).

13. Use children's drawings and other projective methods. The interviewer can ask the child to draw a person—after seeing which gender is done first, the interviewer then can ask for the opposite gender. Or the instruction could be to draw the child's family doing something exciting or to draw something scary. The evaluator could draw or provide a picture of a nude person and ask the child to name body parts. The child might be able to draw what happened during the abusive incident. Drawing pictures is a good way to document the child's version of the incident and also to help the child recover further memories.

14. Ask the child if cameras were involved in the sexual activities and whether the child was shown sexually oriented photographs or videos.

15. Use different techniques to evaluate very young children. It may be helpful to have the nonoffending parent in the interview. Careful observations of the child's behaviors might be more useful than directly questioning him or her. The therapist might choose to stage activities that trig-

ger the child's associations, such as diapering or introducing specific toys and books.

16. Employing hypnosis or amytal is usually contraindicated in a forensic evaluation. These techniques may elicit false memories. Also, after use of hypnosis or amytal, the child probably would be disqualified as a witness at any trial related to the allegations.

17. Consider interviewing the child and the alleged perpetrator together, after first discussing the plan with the child and considering the possible risks. The purpose of the joint interview is not to assess the validity of the allegation. A joint interview may be helpful in cases where the evaluator has concluded that the allegations are false and is assessing the possibility of the child visiting the accused parent.

18. Collect and organize information about the abuse in addition to completing a general psychiatric assessment. Who was the perpetrator? What did the perpetrator do? Where did it happen? When did it start and when did it end? How many times? What was the method of initially engaging the child, and how did the abuse progress over time? How did the perpetrator induce the child to maintain secrecy? Was the child aware of specific injuries or physical symptoms associated with the abuse?

SYMPTOMS, SYNDROMES, AND PATTERNS

Child abuse has been associated with several clinical patterns. In conducting the evaluation, it is helpful to see if the case fits into a typical pattern or syndrome.

Cicchetti and Toth (1995) reviewed the literature regarding the psychological effects of physical abuse and neglect. They noted a wide range of effects, including affect dysregulation, disruptive and aggressive behaviors, and insecure and atypical attachment patterns. These children manifested impaired peer relationships, such as increased aggression or social withdrawal, and academic underachievement.

Sgroi (1982) described a pattern that is typical of intrafamilial sexual abuse and other sexual abuse that occurs over a period of time. The process evolves through 5 phases: the engagement phase, when the perpetrator induces the child into a special relationship; the sexual interaction phase, in which the sexual behaviors progress from less intimate to more intimate forms of abuse; the secrecy phase; the disclosure phase, when the abuse is discovered; and the suppression phase, when the family pressures the child to retract his or her statements.

Summit (1983) described the child sexual abuse accommodation syndrome. He characterized the sexual abuse of girls by men as having 5 characteristics: secrecy; helplessness; entrapment and accommodation; delayed, conflicted, and unconvincing disclosure; and retraction. The process of accommodation occurs because the child learns that she "must be available without complaint to the parent's sexual demands." The child may find various ways to accommodate—by maintaining secrecy in order to keep the family together, turning to imaginary companions, or employing altered states of consciousness. Other abused children become aggressive, demanding, and hyperactive. Perhaps they have identified with and learned these behaviors from chaotic households in which most communication is through angry outbursts.

Beitchman, Zucker, Hood, da Costa, and Akman (1991) reviewed the effects of child sexual abuse. They found that victims of child sexual abuse are more likely than nonvictims to develop a preoccupation with sexuality and some type of inappropriate sexual behavior. The abused children manifested excessive sexual play, masturbation, seductive or sexually aggressive behavior, and age-inappropriate sexual knowledge. In adolescents, there was evidence of promiscuity.

Friedrich, Beilke, and Urquiza (1987) and Friedrich and Grambsch (1992) found that children who have been sexually abused are more likely than normal children to manifest inappropriate sexual behaviors, such as trying to undress other people, talking excessively about sexual acts, masturbating with an object, imitating intercourse, inserting objects into the vagina or anus, and rubbing the body against other people. It is possible for a normal child who has never been abused to exhibit these behaviors. In order for the behaviors to be indicative of sexual abuse, they would need to be numerous and persistent.

Terr (1991) described the psychological sequelae of children who have experienced acute and chronic trauma. She listed 4 characteristics that occur after both types of trauma: visualized or repeatedly perceived memories of the event; repetitive behaviors; fears specifically related to the trauma; and changed attitudes about people, life, and the future. Children who sustained single, acute traumas manifested full, detailed memories of the event; a sense for "omens," such as looking for reasons why the event occurred; and misperceptions, including visual hallucinations and peculiar time distortions. On the other hand, children who experienced severe, chronic trauma, such as repeated sexual abuse, manifested massive denial and psychic numbing; self-hypnosis and dissociation; and rage.

DIFFERENTIAL DIAGNOSIS OF AN ALLEGATION

The accusation that a person has physically or sexually abused a child is an extremely powerful statement. It can lead to a very elaborate investigation, which itself may be harmful to the child; disruption of family relationships; extensive and expensive legal processes; and incarceration. There was a time when statements made by children were pretty much taken at face value. In recent years, however, allegations of abuse, especially sexual abuse, have occurred quite frequently in many different circumstances: in the context of custody and visitation disputes, in day care centers, and in youth activities such as ballet class and scouts. In some of these cases, professional evaluators and courts have concluded that abuse did not occur. The problem is that sometimes children and parents make allegations that are not factual (Everson & Boat, 1989; Gardner, 1992b; Schuman, 1986). It has been estimated that about 5 to 10% of the allegations of child sexual abuse are false.

The decision about whether an allegation is truthful is made in court and not in a psychiatrist's office. However, the child and adolescent psychiatrist may be able to collect information in a careful manner that a judge or jury would find helpful in making the final decision. In order to be helpful, the psychiatrist needs to maintain an open mind and not jump to a conclusion. The psychiatrist should consider all the possibilities in the differential diagnosis (Bernet, 1993a).

It Really Happened: The child and the parent are accurately reporting events that occurred and the child was actually abused. This may be the case 90% of the time.

Parental Misinterpretation and Suggestion: The parent is an anxious, fearful, and histrionic individual. The parent has taken an innocent remark or neutral piece of behavior, made it into something worse, and accidentally induced the child to endorse his or her interpretation. As a re-

sult, the child is relating the truth as he or she understands it, even though it is not factual.

Misinterpreted Physical Condition: This may account for the allegation of abuse. For instance, a girl who said that her father hurt her bottom may have had a rash and the father was applying ointment to it. The child with "cigarette burns" may have had infected mosquito bites.

Parental Delusion: The parent is a severely disturbed, paranoid person. He or she has actively shared a distorted worldview with the child, and they now have the same delusion. The parent and child may share a *folie à deux,* or the child may simply give in and agree with the delusional parent who persistently insists that abuse occurred.

Parental Indoctrination: The parent fabricated the whole story. This type of parent would be more likely to teach the child a rote statement for presentation to the authorities.

Interviewer's Suggestion: Previous interviewers may have asked leading or suggestive questions.

In other words, there are several ways in which children can be influenced by outside people to believe or to state that they have been abused. Since 1980 there has been a great deal of research on the suggestibility of children. The research has shown that children are able to recall accurately large amounts of information, especially when it involves something that actually happened to them. On the other hand, research shows that adults can influence children of all ages to believe things that did not happen. This issue has been reviewed by Ceci and Bruck (1993, 1995) and by Goodman and Bottoms (1993).

Fantasy: The child has confused fantasy with reality, which is more likely to occur with younger children and those with certain mental disorders. For instance, a child in a nursery school might have heard the allegations of another child and then talked as if it had happened to himself. Some children relate accounts of abuse that have bizarre, improbable, or fantastic elements. There are many mental mechanisms by which these fantastic accounts come about (Everson, 1997). In some circumstances, a child who actually was abused may provide an accurate account that was later embellished with bizarre details derived from his or her fantasies. A true allegation may be embedded in a fantastic tale.

Delusion: Although apparently rare, delusions about sexual activities may occur in older children and adolescents in the context of a psychotic illness.

Misinterpretation: The child may have misunderstood what was observed, so he or she later reported in inaccurately. For instance, a child may have observed sexual intercourse but reported that she saw people fighting.

Miscommunication: A false allegation of abuse may arise out of a simple verbal misunderstanding. The child may misunderstand an adult's question; the adult may misinterpret or take the child's statement out of context.

Confabulation: If there are gaps in the child's memory, he or she may fill them in with whatever information seems to make sense to the child and others at the time. Confabulated statements usually are brief, inaccurate responses to questions posed by another person.

Pseudologia Phantastica (or fantasy lying and pathological lying): The concept was used by Anna Freud (1965) to describe how normal children who were able to understand the significance of lying regressed "to infantile forms of wishful thinking" because of some severe frustration or disappointment. A 5-year-old boy, for instance, exuberantly related how a friend's mother died and the friend put his penis in her blood, how he himself saw his teacher's airplane blow up, and how a person in a clown outfit was in the therapist's bathroom.

Innocent Lying: Young children, especially around age 4 to 5, frequently make false statements because that seems to be the best way to handle the situation they are in. Gesell and Ilg (1946) described how the normal 4-year-old "tells tall tales."

Deliberate Lying: Older children fully understand the moral issues involved but may choose to avoid or distort the truth for some personal advantage. For instance, an adolescent girl might accuse her stepfather of impregnating her in order to shield her boyfriend.

Overstimulation: Schetky and Green (1988) described how some parenting practices, such as genital touching and nudity, can result in chronic sexual overstimulation. The parent's seductive behavior, although not necessarily abusive in itself, becomes more problematic in the context of parental separation and divorce.

Group Contagion: Epidemic hysteria may have influenced the parents and the child. Social scientists have shown that rumors take on a life of their own. People tend to modify what they have heard in a way that meets their own emotional needs. The rumor may become even more convincing as it is retold.

Perpetrator Substitution: One of the vexing aspects of these evaluations is that the child actually may have been sexually abused (so is manifesting symptoms consistent with abuse) but is identifying the wrong person as the perpetrator (so is making a false allegation). The substitution may be result of one of the mechanisms already described. For instance, the substitution could be the result of the child's fantasy, an example of confabulation, or an instance of deliberate lying.

ASSESSING THE CHILD'S CREDIBILITY AND COMPETENCY

There is no simple, absolute test for knowing whether a child is describing accurately a real event that actually happened to him or her. In assessing the child's statements in detail, however, several factors seem to indicate that a child is more or less credible. Some of these factors have been described by Benedek and Schetky (1987a, 1987b), Clawar and Rivlin (1991), Green (1986), Nurcombe (1986), Nurcombe and Partlett (1994), Quinn (1988), and Raskin and Esplin (1991, 1992). None of these criteria is known to indicate definitively whether abuse has occurred.

Spontaneity: If a child spontaneously volunteers that something happened, it seems more likely that he or she is relating a real event. On the other hand, a child seems less credible if he or she relates a story that has been memorized or tells about the alleged abuse only when a parent repeatedly admonishes him or her to tell the story.

Age-Appropriate Terminology: The child is more credible if he or she gives a detailed description of an event and uses childish terminology. If the child happens to use an adult term, such as "cunnilingus," the examiner could play somewhat dumb and ask what is meant by that word or who had told that word.

Generally Consistent: Over a period of several weeks, one would expect a child's description of an incident to be basically consistent but to have slight variations with retelling. If the child is relating his or her own memory of an actual experience, the basic plot would remain the same but some details would vary. The child may relate the story in a piecemeal fashion, bit by bit, rather than all at once. However, a child who has been programmed would be more likely to give exactly the same account each time—a rote, stereotyped statement. The indoctrinated child also would relate many highly inconsistent stories over time.

Appropriate Affect: As the child describes the

abuse, the examiner would expect to see some evidence of discomfort, such as anxiety, fearfulness, and defensiveness. The discomfort occurs because the child is relating something that stirs up unpleasant memories and also because it is embarrassing to discuss it. Examiners would expect children to be defensive if they feel they are saying something bad about a person whom they love or is dependent on. If a child comes into the office and happily and eagerly relates an incident, the interviewer should wonder what is happening. For instance, has the child figured out that the interviewer is very interested in hearing about sexual activities and she has thought up a new story as a present? There are notable pitfalls in trying to assess "appropriate affect." A child might be anxious and uncomfortable because he or she is lying, not because he or she is relating an embarrassing experience. A child might be emotionally bland because he or she has repressed the traumatic experience.

Idiosyncratic Sensory Detail: A truthful child is more likely to relate a verbatim conversation. The child who is relating an actual trauma is more likely to recollect and relate specific memories that are peripheral to the main event. For instance, the child might have a memory of a particular aroma associated with the perpetrator or a specific physical characteristic. The child might have focused on some irrelevant detail, such as the flowers on the bedspread. The child might relate an interruption or an unexpected complication during the incident. It is unlikely that an indoctrinating adult would suggest that kind of detail.

Candid Style: A truthful child is more likely to make spontaneous corrections as he or she relates what happened or even take some of the blame. Such a child is also more likely to admit that there are some details that he or she can no longer remember.

Comparing the History with the Interview: Children are more likely to be credible if their symptoms (e.g., masturbating by putting objects in the vagina) are consistent with what they relate in the interview (that a man put his finger in her private area). It may be useful to compare the clinical data with the police report and other independent sources of information.

Interaction with Parents: When the allegation of abuse occurs in the context of a custody dispute, observe the child with the parents. If a mother has brainwashed a child to allege sexual abuse by the father, the child may frequently look to the mother for guidance and for approval. The child may be very hostile to the father when the mother is present but warm and affectionate when she leaves the room.

Evaluation of Parents: A psychiatric assessment of the alleging parent may reveal that he or she has a significant mental disorder that could be the basis for a false allegation.

Children's competency refers to their ability to testify in court in a reliable, meaningful manner. Young children may not understand the implications and significance of the legal proceedings but still be competent to relate their story. Children need to be intelligent enough to understand simple questions and verbal enough to give simple answers. They should be able to tell the difference between reality and make believe and to understand the difference between lying and telling the truth.

PHYSICAL FINDINGS

Physically abused children may have injuries commonly seen after physical punishment, such as bruises on the buttocks and lower back, perhaps at different stages of healing. Bruises with the configuration of hand marks, pinch marks, and strap marks usually indicate abuse. Certain types of burns are caused by abuse, such as multiple cigarette burns and scalding of the hands, feet, perineum, and buttocks. Subdural hematoma and abdominal trauma, leading to ruptured liver or spleen, may occur. There may be radiologic signs of multiple broken bones. A child who has been shaken may have intracranial bleeding or characteristic retinal hemorrhages (Ludwig & Kornberg, 1992; Monteleone & Brodeur, 1994; Reece, 1994).

In cases of sexual abuse, it is not necessary to have specific physical findings in order to be convinced that abuse occurred. Most sexually abused children do not have any corroborating physical findings. Some may have physical findings, such as trauma to the genital or rectal area; foreign bodies in the genital, rectal, or urethral openings; abnormal dilatation of the urethral, vaginal, or rectal openings; sperm in the vagina; trauma to the breasts, buttocks, lower abdomen, or thighs; sexually transmitted diseases; and pregnancy (Heger & Emans, 1992; Sgroi, 1982).

Muram (1989) introduced a system of classifying the medical findings of girls who may have been abused. He described 4 categories: girls who have normal-appearing genitalia; girls who have nonspecific findings (inflammation, scratching, purulent discharge, and small skin fissures or lacerations in the area of the posterior fourchette); girls who have specific findings that strongly suggest sexual abuse (recent or healed lacerations of the hymen and vaginal mucosa, enlarged hymenal opening, teeth marks, and laboratory reports of venereal disease); and girls who have definitive findings of sexual abuse (the presence of sperm).

COMMON DISPOSITIONS

Having completed the evaluation, psychiatrists should list their conclusions and recommendations, including the supporting data. They should remember that the basic purpose of the evaluation is to determine whether abuse occurred, whether the child needs protection, and if the child needs medical or psychiatric treatment. There are a number of possible outcomes to cases in which physical or sexual abuse has been alleged. Psychiatrists should keep these possibilities in mind when making recommendations. Protective services or the court usually makes the actual decision regarding placement.

In one outcome, the court determines that physical or sexual abuse has occurred and removes the perpetrator from the home. This has the advantage of protecting the child from further abuse and also making it clear that the adult was in the wrong. It is hoped that the nonabusing parent will provide a supportive atmosphere. The court may specify that the perpetrator undergo treatment and/or incarceration before returning to the home.

In another outcome, the court determines that physical or sexual abuse occurred and removes the child from the home. The child is placed in a foster home while the parents participate actively in an outpatient treatment program. When the court is convinced that rehabilitation is truly under way, it may allow the child to return home and continue supervision by a child protection agency.

In another scenario, the court determines that a child was sexually abused by the father and removes the child from the home. The father refuses treatment and goes to jail. Since the home is now safe, the child returns home and the mother is encouraged to support the child's treatment.

Another outcome may occurs when the court determines that neglect or abuse occurred and removes the child from the home. While the child is in a foster home, therapists attempt to rehabilitate the parents. After trying up to 2 years with no success, the therapists report to the court that the parents have not changed. The court then makes the decision to terminate parental rights of both the mother and the father. The children may continue in the foster home or may be adopted by another set of parents.

When clinically indicated, the psychiatrist should make recommendations regarding psychotherapy. Many of these children who have been severely traumatized and who have serious psychiatric symptoms will require intensive psychotherapy. Some may require inpatient treatment. Other children who were minimally abused may be handled by a crisis intervention approach, in which the child and the parents come for only 2 or 3 meetings. Such a brief intervention would be appropriate if the child has supportive parents, does not have any significant symptoms, and is able to discuss the abuse in an appropriate manner.

Confidentiality

Psychiatric patients have a right to be assured that information that they have related in therapy will not be revealed to other individuals. Psychiatrists and other mental health professionals have an obligation to protect their clients' privacy. Because of their legal obligations and also their ethical requirements, psychiatrists have endorsed the importance of confidentiality for patients and their therapy. The concept of confidentiality is not absolute, and there are many exceptions to confidentiality in clinical and forensic practice. The legal and clinical aspects of confidentiality for child and adolescents psychiatrists have been addressed by Holder (1985), Slovenko and Usdin (1966), and Wilson (1978).

ETHICAL AND LEGAL FOUNDATIONS

An awareness of the importance of confidentiality was present at the beginning of the history of medicine. Although not every statement in the Oath of Hippocrates should be taken literally, the section on confidentiality is pertinent: "Whatsoever things I see or hear concerning the life of men, in my attendance on the sick or even apart therefrom, which ought not to be noised abroad, I will keep silence thereon, counting such things to be sacred secrets."

The American Medical Association has promulgated ethical principles for many years, principles that include the importance of confidentiality. The American Psychiatric Association (1988b, 1993) has published both general principles and detailed guidelines regarding patient confidentiality.

Federal law and federal regulations protect the confidentiality of patients who are treated by alcohol and substance abuse programs. In some states either the medical licensing act or separate statutes define the physician's obligation to maintain patient confidentiality. Various state agencies, local medical societies, and hospitals have promulgated lists of the rights of patients. The statement of patient rights usually includes a reference to confidentiality, such as "Your communication to the staff and any information recorded about you and your illness will not be released without your written consent."

CONFIDENTIALITY IN CLINICAL PRACTICE

The issue of confidentiality in clinical child and adolescent psychiatry is complex, because its importance will depend on the age and developmental level of the patients, their psychopathology, their relationship with their parents, and the specific topic in question.

Therapists working with adolescents may disagree on whether it is advisable to discuss dangerous sexual behaviors, pregnancy, and serious drug use with parents. Most therapists would maintain confidentiality regarding sexual activities and occasional drug usage that might be considered normal adolescent experimentation. However, most therapists would want parents to become aware of their child's extreme sexual promiscuity, pregnancy, serious delinquent behavior, and serious substance abuse. In such cases therapists would tell the adolescent patient that he or she must be honest with the parents about these behaviors and that the next family meeting would be a good time to discuss the issue.

Psychotherapy with adolescents does not ordinarily degenerate into legalistic haggling over the adolescent's right to privacy vs. the therapist's obligation to discuss certain information with the parents. If a teenager has a proper alliance with the therapist, both understand that they want the youngster to achieve a legitimate sense of psychological independence, which means that he or she will have thoughts, opinions, feelings, and behaviors that he or she may choose not to share with the parents. Second, the teenager and the therapist both will understand that it may be important for the parents to have certain kinds of information regarding what happens in therapy. Third, both the teenager and the therapist will expect that the therapist will use basic common sense in whatever communications he or she may have with the parents.

In every jurisdiction in the United States, child protection laws require physicians and other professionals who deal with children to report physical abuse of children and sexual abuse to proper authorities, which usually means the social service agency such as child protective services. Usually physicians are obligated to report the abuse even they have never seen the child. For instance, they must report the abuse if they have heard of it from the child's parent or from the perpetrator. This obligation does not mean that physicians should take every allegation at face value. It is possible, for instance, that a parent who wonders if her child has been abused consults the pediatrician. The pediatrician may listen to the concern, examine the child, and conclude that there is no "reasonable suspicion" that abuse occurred; therefore, it would not be reported.

An interesting related question is whether the laws that require the reporting of child physical abuse and sexual abuse mean that a therapist should report long-past child abuse, even when no current child is in danger. The issue comes up when adult patients describe abuse that occurred when they were children. There is enough ambiguity in the way the laws were written so that patients, a therapists, and child protective agencies may interpret them quite differently. Most therapists seem to feel that reporting abuse that occurred many years previously is neither legally nor ethically required (Weinstock & Weinstock, 1988).

Child protection laws give immunity to individuals who report abuse, so that they cannot be sued by angry parents. However, the laws do not protect practitioners who engage in or suggest illegal activities. For instance, a therapist determined that a child may have been sexually abused by her father, a noncustodial parent. The therapist reported her suspicion to protective services and also advised the mother to withhold visitation.

Upon investigation, the sexual abuse allegation was never substantiated, so the father sued the therapist. The therapist's reporting her suspicions to protective services was protected from the civil lawsuit; however, her advising the mother to withhold visitation was not protected.

CONFIDENTIALITY IN FORENSIC EVALUATIONS

Forensic evaluations are frequently done on behalf of some person or agency other than the client. It is important for the client to know that the evaluation will not be confidential.

In juvenile court, for instance, an adolescent may be evaluated in order to determine whether he or she is mentally competent to go to trial and whether an insanity defense might be appropriate. First of all, the evaluation should not occur without the knowledge and the permission of the defendant's attorney or parents. If the evaluation has been ordered by the court, the adolescent should be informed that the evaluation is not confidential. The youngster should be told that the results of the evaluation will be sent to the defense attorney, to the prosecuting attorney, and to the judge.

Confidentiality does not apply in many forensic situations, such as in civil cases in which a child is evaluated to determine degree of disability or the extent of a psychiatric injury. In such evaluations the youngster and the parents should be fully informed that the information collected will be sent to the attorney who requested the evaluation. The information eventually may be revealed in a public court. Often it is useful to remind these clients of the difference between an evaluation for some legal purpose and a therapeutic relationship.

Confidentiality also is waived when an individual institutes a personal injury or a medical malpractice lawsuit. That is, the defendant has the right to know about and to obtain the records of other related medical care. For instance, a child who had previously been in psychotherapy was severely bitten by a dog and sustained both physical and psychological injuries. The child sued the dog's owner, who was able to obtain the earlier treatment records in order to show that the child had emotional problems even before being bitten. In cases like this, the therapist should have either the client's permission or a court order before releasing any records.

The lack of confidentiality in psychiatric custody evaluations sometimes creates confusion for both children and parents. A child might tell the psychiatrist that there is something important he wants to say about a parent, but he is afraid that the parent will find out and punish him. Of course, that piece of information may be exactly what the psychiatrist wants to know. The psychiatrist might be able to reach some kind of compromise by telling the child that she will try to keep the information in her head but will not write it in the notes and will not put it in a formal report. Also, the psychiatrist might need to educate the young client that there are some things, such as information about abuse, that must be told to the judge. Another kind of situation occurs in a custody evaluation when a parent brings in a lengthy written diary and asks the psychiatrist to read it. Before accepting it, the psychiatrist should clearly explain to the parent that any material that he or she reads in conducting the evaluation may be requested by the opposing parent and attorney in the future.

Although the content of a psychiatric custody evaluation usually is revealed in court, the content of psychotherapy meetings is not necessarily revealed to anybody. Frequently a child or a parent already has been involved in psychotherapy and then becomes a party in a custody dispute (Bernet, 1983). In such a situation, psychotherapists may feel that it is in the interests of the client and of that person's therapy for them to remain out of the custody dispute as much as possible. Therapists may refuse to submit a written report or to testify in court, although they might be willing to give information informally to the person who is conducting the full psychiatric custody evaluation. Therapists may explain to the parent and to the attorney that it is not in the child's interests to violate the child's confidentiality by testifying. If therapists are subpoenaed, they could respond by showing up at court and explaining to the judge their reluctance to testify. If they felt very strongly about the matter, they might attempt to quash the subpoena. The court may hear a psychiatrist's objections and still order him or her to testify. In that case, most psychiatrists would agree that it is time to give in and go ahead and testify.

PRACTICAL CONSIDERATIONS

Although the concept of confidentiality is always given the highest respect, it is very hard for most clinicians to maintain complete secrecy.

Therapists seem to have an extremely strong urge to discuss case material with colleagues, although they are prone to perceive the threat to patient confidentiality to be from external agencies rather than from within themselves (Goldstein, 1989). These conversations sometimes occur in elevators, cafeterias, and other public places where they can be overheard by total strangers. This urge to discuss cases probably derives from the fact that clinical material is both extremely interesting (so the therapist wants to tell about it in order to show off in some way) and extremely anxiety-provoking (so the therapist wants to find reassurance by sharing the case with a colleague). Psychiatrists who feel they must talk about a case can find a way to do it an appropriate manner. If they are puzzled about a clinical issue, they can confer in a formal setting with a consultant or a supervisor. If they feel a particular case has instructive potential, they can disguise the material and present it to a professional group. If a colleague asks about a case in a crowded elevator, it can be suggested that they talk about it later.

Since there are so many exceptions to the doctrine of confidentiality, clinicians should be aware that any written record may be read by the patient or by many other people. Wise psychiatrists will protect themselves from future chagrin by always keeping this in mind when they dictate an evaluation or write a progress note. That is, they will word their observations carefully so that at some future point they will not embarrass the patient, the therapist, or some other party.

It seems only fair that prospective patients should know the limits of confidentiality. There is a way to inform patients in an efficient manner without drawing undue attention to the issue. That is, clinicians can have an office brochure with the most important administrative information in it, such as office hours, billing procedures, and how to use the answering service. The brochure also could explain that the therapist values confidentiality very highly but that there are several specific exceptions that clients should be aware of.

RELATED ISSUES

The concept of privilege is an aspect of confidentiality that may arise in a judicial setting. A person has the right of testimonial privilege when he or she has the right to refuse to testify or to prevent another person from testifying about specific information. For instance, a man may claim privilege and refuse to testify about conversations he had with his attorney, because such discussions are considered private under the concept of attorney-client privilege. Likewise, a man may claim that his therapy is covered by physician-patient privilege and prevent the psychiatrist from testifying about him. The man may waive the right to physician-patient privilege and allow his psychiatrist to testify. In fact, the psychiatrist needs to realize that it is up to the patient to make that decision, not the psychiatrist. In other words, the psychiatrist ordinarily should go ahead and testify if the patient has waived his right to privilege.

In general, adults have a right to know what is in their own hospital and outpatient psychiatric records. Many adolescents would have that right also if they were to assert it through legal channels. However, the most therapeutic way to honor that right is hardly to photocopy the entire file and send it to the patient in the mail. Usually the therapist would want to discuss the reasons for the patient's curiosity and perhaps reveal certain parts of the file in a way that has a constructive effect on the patient. An inpatient psychiatrist might tell an adolescent patient what she is writing in the chart that day and even show him the note. It might be useful to share certain parts of a psychiatric evaluation with an adolescent and to ask the patient to correct any statements that might be inaccurate. In other words, an attitude of open communication with an adolescent usually defuses the possible battle over the youngster's wish to read the entire record. Of course, the psychiatrist should not reveal opinions and information to the patient if it would harm the patient mentally.

Does confidentiality continue after a patient's death? The right to confidentiality does continue after death, but sometimes it must be balanced with the family's right to certain information. For instance, suppose a child or adolescent patient were to commit suicide. It would seem to be appropriate for the patient's therapist to meet with immediate family members and for all of them to try to make sense of what had happened. That meeting might involve the therapist's sharing certain kinds of information with the family, but it would not need to include extensive, detailed revelations regarding the patient's fantasy life as it unfolded during therapy. But suppose the adolescent's death was newsworthy for some reason and a local reporter requested clinical information from the therapist. Unless the circumstances were unusual, it would not be ethical for the therapist to release information to the media, even if he or she had the parents' permission.

Current Trends, Future Directions

Forensic child psychiatry is a young, emerging subspecialty of psychiatry. There is a good deal of clinical experience and expertise in the field, but we need more research in many areas to guide the future practitioners of this subspecialty. There is a wide and sometimes contradictory range of opinion regarding issues in forensic child psychiatry: whether there is a sound basis for distinguishing true from false allegations of child sexual abuse; whether satanic ritual abuse is a serious national problem or simply a contemporary urban legend; whether children can be easily led to make false allegations; whether very young children may be damaged by moving between the households of divorced parents; whether it is risky for a child to be raised by a homosexual parent; and so on. There are many other issues in forensic child psychiatry that should be studied in a systematic way.

Increased interdisciplinary dialogue can enrich the field of forensic child psychiatry. Social workers, psychiatric nurses, psychologists, and psychiatrists assess children for forensic purposes—there should be more collaboration among these professionals. The annual meetings of professional organizations provide opportunities for interdisciplinary panels and workshops. The child abuse review committees in larger hospitals and teaching programs lend themselves to interdisciplinary dialogue as specific cases are presented and discussed. In local communities it is possible to organize "forensic interest groups," which meet periodically to discuss topics of mutual concern. On a national level, the American Professional Society on the Abuse of Children (APSAC) was founded in 1987. APSAC brings together mental professionals, law enforcement officials, medical personnel, attorneys, protective service personnel, and researchers, who share an interest in the assessment and prevention of child abuse. In

some aspects of child forensic psychiatry, the field is divided between the "believers" and the "skeptics" regarding a particular issue. If both sides are open-minded and sincere, these divisions should be resolved by dialogue, collaboration, and mutual study.

It is intriguing to predict how evolving social factors will impact the issues of forensic child psychiatry. It is likely that divorce will continue to increase in this country and that increasing numbers of children will grow up in multiple households. Since we are a litigious society, our children will continue to be the victims of child custody disputes: parental alienation phenomena will become better known and easier to recognize, so attempts will be made to make divorce less adversarial. One step in that direction is the introduction of "parenting plans," that a few states already require before a divorce is granted. The divorcing parents are expected to put together an agreement, perhaps with the help of a mediator, regarding their child's custody, visitation, and other arrangements. It is hoped that the use of negotiated parenting plans will reduce the adversarial nature of divorce. At some distant future time, perhaps we will no longer use the words "custody" and "visitation."

The forensic child psychiatrist of the future will no doubt rely on a broader base of research in many areas—child development, psychopathology, psychology, sociology, even neurophysiology—than we have had in the past. The steps by which children process abuse experiences will be clarified, as will the steps by which they create false memories. Perhaps a specific part of the brain will be identified that "lights up" when the child recollects memories of abuse, but does not react when the child simply thinks fantasies that resemble abuse. We will have a better understanding of the strengths and weaknesses of various forms of family life: intact families; divorced families; blended families; children raised by single parents, homosexual parents, disabled parents, and grandparents. As the scientific basis for forensic child psychiatry gradually expands, the future offers much promise in understanding the psychiatric aspects of legal issues involving children.

REFERENCES

Abright, A. R. (1986). Psychiatric aspects of sexual abuse. *Bulletin of the American Academy of Psychiatry and the Law, 14,* 331–343.

Ackerman, M. (1994). *Clinician's guide to child custody evaluations.* New York: John Wiley & Sons.

American Academy of Child and Adolescent Psychiatry. (1988). Guidelines for the clinical evaluation of child and adolescent sexual abuse. *Journal of the American Academy of Child and Adolescent Psychiatry, 27,* 655–657.

American Academy of Child and Adolescent Psychiatry. (1997). Practice parameters for the forensic evaluation of children and adolescents who may have been physically or sexually abused. *Journal of the American Academy of Child and Adolescent Psychiatry, 36,* 423–442.

American Academy of Child and Adolescent Psychiatry. (In press). Practice parameters for child custody evaluations. *Journal of the American Academy of Child and Adolescent Psychiatry, 36.*

American Psychiatric Association. (1988a). *Child custody consultation: A report of the Task Force on Clinical Assessment in Child Custody.* Washington, DC: Author.

American Psychiatric Association. (1988b). *Guidelines on confidentiality.* Washington, DC: Author.

American Psychiatric Association. (1993). *The principles of medical ethics with annotations especially applicable to psychiatry.* Washington, DC: Author.

Ash, P., & Guyer, M. (1986). The functions of psychiatric evaluation in contested child custody and visitation cases. *Journal of the American Academy of Child Psychiatry, 25,* 554–561.

Atwell, A. E., Moore, U. S., Nielsen, E., & Levite, Z. (1984). Effects of joint custody on children. *Bulletin of the American Academy of Psychiatry and the Law, 12,* 149–157.

Barnum, R. (1986). Integrating multiple perspectives in forensic child psychiatry consultation. *Journal of the American Academy of Child Psychiatry, 25,* 718–723.

Barnum, R. (1987). Understanding controversies in visitation. *Journal of the American Academy of Child and Adolescent Psychiatry, 26,* 788–792.

Beitchman, J. H., Zucker, K. J., Hood, J. E., daCosta, G. A., & Akman, D. (1991). A review of the short-term effects of child sexual abuse. *Child Abuse & Neglect, 15,* 537–556.

Benedek, E. P. (1986). Forensic child psychiatry: An emerging subspecialty. *Bulletin of the American Academy of Psychiatry and the Law, 14,* 295–300.

Benedek, R. S., & Benedek, E. P. (1980). Participating in child custody cases. In D. H. Schetky & E. P. Benedek (Eds.), *Child psychiatry and the law.* New York: Brunner/Mazel. pp 59–70.

Benedek, E. P., & Schetky, D. H. (1987a). Problems in validating allegations of sexual abuse. Part I: factors affecting perception and recall of events. *Journal of the American Academy of Child and Adolescent Psychiatry, 26,* 912–915.

Benedek, E. P., & Schetky, D. H. (1987b). Problems in validating allegations of sexual abuse. Part 2: clinical evaluation. *Journal of the American Academy of Child and Adolescent Psychiatry, 26,* 916–921.

Bernet, W. (1983). The therapist's role in child custody disputes. *Journal of the American Academy of Child Psychiatry, 22,* 180–183.

Bernet, W. (1993a). False statements and the differential diagnosis of abuse allegations. *Journal of the American Academy of Child and Adolescent Psychiatry, 32,* 903–910.

Bernet, W. (1993b). The noncustodial parent and medical treatment. *Bulletin of the American Academy of Psychiatry and the Law, 21,* 357–364.

Bernet, W., & Chang, D. K. (1997). The differential diagnosis of ritual abuse allegations. *Journal of Forensic Science, 42,* 32–38.

Besharov, D. J. (1990). *Recognizing child abuse.* New York: Free Press.

Bozett, F. W. (Ed.). (1987). *Gay and lesbian parents.* New York: Praeger.

Bricklin, B. (1984). *Bricklin Perceptual Scales: Children's-Perception-of-Parents Series.* Doyleston, PA: Village Publishing.

Bricklin, B. (1995). *The custody evaluation handbook: Research-Based solutions and applications.* New York: Brunner/Mazel.

Bulkley, J. (Ed.). (1981). *Child sexual abuse and the law.* Washington, DC: American Bar Association.

Caffey, J. (1946). Multiple fractures in long bones of infants suffering from chronic subdural hematoma. *American Journal of Roentgenology, 56,* 163–173.

Ceci, S., & Bruck, M. (1993). Suggestibility of the child witness: A historical review and synthesis. *Psychological Bulletin, 113,* 403–409.

Ceci, S., & Bruck, M. (1995). *Jeopardy in the courtroom: A scientific analysis of children's testimony.* Washington, DC: American Psychological Association.

Cicchetti, D., & Toth, S. L. (1995). A developmental psychopathology perspective on child abuse and neglect. *Journal of the American Academy of Child and Adolescent Psychiatry, 34,* 541–565.

Clawar, S. S., & Rivlin, B. V. (1991). *Children held hostage: Dealing with programmed and brainwashed children.* Chicago: American Bar Association.

Corwin, D. L., & Olavson, E. (Eds.). (1993). Clinical recognition of sexually abused children. *Child Abuse & Neglect* [special issue], *17,* 1–185.

Davis v. Davis, 15 TAM 39–4, Tenn. Ap., E.S., September 13, 1990, Franks.

Derdeyn, A. P. (1976). Child custody contests in historical perspective. *American Journal of Psychiatry, 133,* 1369–1376.

Devine, Ex parte, 398 So. 2d 686, Supreme Court of Alabama, 1981, Maddox.

Dunne, J., & Hedrick, M. (1994). The parental alienation syndrome: An analysis of sixteen selected cases. *Journal of Divorce & Remarriage, 21,* 21–38.

Everson, M. (1997). Understanding bizarre, improbable, and fantastic elements in children's accounts of abuse. *Child Maltreatment, 2,* 134–149.

Everson, M. D., & Boat, B. W. (1989). False allegations of sexual abuse by children and adolescents. *Journal of the American Academy of Child and Adolescent Psychiatry, 28,* 230–235.

Everson, M. D., & Boat, B. W. (1990). Sexualized doll play among young children: Implications for the use of anatomical dolls in sexual abuse evaluations. *Journal of the American Academy of Child and Adolescent Psychiatry, 29,* 736–742.

Faller, K. C. (1988). *Child sexual abuse:* An interdisciplinary manual for diagnosis, case management, and treatment. New York: Columbia University Press.

Festinger, L. (1957). *A theory of cognitive dissonance.* Evanston, IL: Row, Peterson.

Finkelhor, D. (1979). *Sexually victimized children.* New York: Free Press.

Finkelhor, D. (Ed.). (1986). *A sourcebook on child sexual abuse.* Beverly Hills, CA: Sage.

Finlay v. Finlay, 240 N.Y. 429, Court of Appeals of New York, July 15, 1925, Cardozo.

Folberg, J. (Ed.). (1984). *Joint custody and shared parenting.* Washington, DC: Bureau of National Affairs.

Freud, A. (1965). *Normality and pathology in childhood: Assessments of development.* New York: International Universities Press.

Friedrich, W. N. (1990). *Psychotherapy of sexually abused children and their families.* New York: W. W. Norton, 1990.

Friedrich, W. N., Beilke, R. L., & Urquiza, A. J. (1987). Children from sexually abusive families: A behavioral comparison. *Journal of Interpersonal Violence, 2,* 391–402.

Friedrich, W. N., & Grambsch, P. (1992). Child Sexual Behavior Inventory: Normative and clinical comparisons. *Psychological Assessment, 4,* 303–311.

Gardner, R. A. (1982). *Family evaluation in child custody litigation.* Cresskill, NJ: Creative Therapeutics.

Gardner, R. A. (1991). *Psychotherapy with children of divorce.* Northvale, NJ: Jason Aronson.

Gardner, R. A. (1992a). *The parental alienation syndrome:* A guide for mental health & legal professionals Cresskill, NJ: Creative Therapeutics.

Gardner, R. A. (1992b). *True and false accusations of child sex abuse.* Cresskill, NJ: Creative Therapeutics.

Garrity, C. B., & Baris, M. A. (1994). *Caught in the middle: Protecting the children of high-conflict divorce.* New York: Lexington Books.

Gesell, A., & Ilg, F. L. (1946). *The child from five to ten.* New York: Harper.

Goldstein, J., Freud, A., & Solnit, A. (1973). *Beyond the best interests of the child.* New York: Free Press.

Goldstein, J., Freud, A., & Solnit, A. (1979). *Before the best interests of the child.* New York: Free Press.

Goldstein, J., Solnit, A., & Goldstein, S. (1996). In the best interests of the child: The least detrimental alternative. New York: Simon & Schuster.

Goldstein, R. L. (1989). When doctors divulge: Is there a "threat from within" to psychiatric confidentiality? *Journal of Forensic Sciences, 34,* 433–438.

Goldzband, M. G. (1988). *Custody cases and expert witnesses: A manual for attorneys,* second edition. Englewood Cliffs, NJ: Prentice-Hall.

Goodman, G. S., & Bottoms, B. L. (1993). *Child victims, child witnesses: Understanding and improving testimony.* New York: Guilford Press.

Green, A. H. (1986). True and false allegations of sexual abuse in child custody disputes. *Journal of the American Academy of Child and Adolescent Psychiatry, 25,* 449–456.

Haller, L. (1981). Before the judge: The child-custody evaluation. *Adolescent Psychiatry, 9,* 142–164.

Helfer, R. E., & Kempe, C. H. (Eds.). (1968). *The battered child.* Chicago: University of Chicago Press.

Helfer, R. E., & Kempe, C. H. (Eds.). (1976). *Child abuse and neglect: The family and the community.* Cambridge, MA: Ballinger Publishing.

Herman, S. P. (1990a). Forensic child psychiatry. *Journal of the American Academy of Child and Adolescent Psychiatry, 29,* 955–957.

Herman, S. P. (1990b). Special issues in child custody evaluations. *Journal of the American Academy of Child and Adolescent Psychiatry, 29,* 969–974.

Herman, S. (1992). Child custody evaluations. In D. H. Schetky & E. P. Benedek (Eds.), *Clinical handbook of child psychiatry and the law.* Baltimore, MD: Williams & Wilkins. pp. 91–103.

Holder, A. R. (1985). *Legal issues in pediatrics and adolescent medicine.* New Haven, CT: Yale University Press.

Hunter, M. (1990). *The sexually abused male.* Lexington, MA: Lexington Books.

Kempe, C. H., & Helfer, R. E. (Eds.). (1972). *Helping the battered child and his family.* Philadelphia: J. B. Lippincott.

Kempe, R. S., & Kempe, C. H. (1978). *Child abuse.* Cambridge, MA: Harvard University Press.

Kempe, C. H., Silverman, F. N., Steele, B. F., Droegmueller, W., & Silver, H. K. (1962). The battered child syndrome. *Journal of the American Medical Association, 181,* 17–24.

Kleber, D. J., Howell, R. J., & Tibbits-Kleber, A. L. (1986). The impact of parental homosexuality in child custody cases: A review of the literature. *Bulletin of the American Academy of Psychiatry and the Law, 14,* 81–87.

Landeros v. Flood, 17 Cal.3d 399, Supreme Court of California, 1976, Mosk.

Loeb, L. (1986). Fathers and sons: Some effects of prolonged custody litigation. *Bulletin of the American Academy of Psychiatry and the Law, 14,* 177–183.

Ludwig, S., & Kornberg, A. E. (1992). Child abuse: A medical reference. New York: Churchill Livingstone.

Marlow, L., & Sauber S. R. (1990). *The handbook of divorce mediation.* New York: Plenum Press.

Michigan Compiled Laws Annotated. Child Custody Act of 1970, Section 722.23.

Miller, T. W., & Veltkamp, L. J. (1987). Disputed child custody: strategies and issues in mediation. *Bulletin of the American Academy of Psychiatry and the Law, 15,* 45–56.

Monteleone, J. A., & Brodeur, A. E. (1994). *Child maltreatment: A clinical guide and reference.* St. Louis, MO: G. W. Publishing.

Muram, D. (1989). Child sexual abuse—Genital tract findings in prepubertal girls. *American Journal of Obstetrics and Gynecology, 160,* 328–333.

Myers, J. E. B. (1992). *Legal issues in child abuse and neglect.* Newbury Park, CA: Sage Publications.

Nurcombe, B. (1986). The child as witness: Competency and credibility. *Journal of the American Academy of Child Psychiatry, 25,* 473–480.

Nurcombe, B., & Partlett, D. J. (1994). *Child mental health and the law.* New York: Free Press.

Nurcombe, B., & Unützer, J. (1991). The ritual abuse of children: Clinical features and diagnostic reasoning. *Journal of the American Academy of Child and Adolescent Psychiatry, 30,* 272–276.

Patterson, C. J. (1992). Children of lesbian and gay parents. *Child Development, 63,* 1025–1042.

Perr, I. N. (1990). "False confessions" and identification with the aggressor: Another forensic misuse of a psychiatric concept. *Bulletin of the American Academy of Psychiatry and the Law 18,* 143–151.

Quinn, K. M., (1988). The credibility of children's allegations of sexual abuse. *Behavioral Sciences and Law, 6,* 181–199.

Quinn, K. M., White, S., & Santilli, G. (1989). Influences of an interviewer's behavior in child sexual abuse investigations. *Bulletin of the American Academy of Psychiatry and the Law, 17,* 45–52.

Rappeport, J. R. (1985). Reasonable medical certainty. *Bulletin of the American Academy of Psychiatry and the Law, 13:* 5–15.

Raskin, D. C., & Esplin, P. W. (1991). Assessment of children's statements of sexual abuse. In J. Doris (Ed.), *The suggestibility of children's recollections.* Washington, DC: American Psychological Association. pp. 153–164.

Raskin, D. C., & Esplin, P. W. (1992). Statement validity assessment: Interview procedures and content analysis of children's statements of sexual abuse. *Behavioral Assessment, 13,* 265–291.

Reece, R. M. (1994). *Child abuse: Medical diagnosis and management.* Philadelphia: Lea & Febiger.

Schetky, D. H., & Benedek, E. P. (Eds.). (1985). *Emerging issues in child psychiatry and the law.* New York: Brunner/Mazel.

Schetky, D. H., & Benedek, E. P. (Eds.). (1992). *Clinical handbook of child psychiatry and the law.* Baltimore, MD: Williams & Wilkins.

Schetky, D. H., & Green, A. H. (1988). *Child sexual abuse: A handbook for health care and legal professionals.* New York: Brunner/Mazel.

Schetky, D. H., & Haller, L. H. (1983). Parental kidnapping. *Journal of the American Academy of Child Psychiatry, 22,* 279–285.

Schmitt, B. (Ed.). (1978). *The child protection team handbook:* A multidisciplinary approach to managing child abuse & neglect. New York: Garland STPM Press.

Schuman, D. C. (1986). False accusations of physical and sexual abuse. *Bulletin of the American Academy of Psychiatry and the Law, 14,* 5–21.

Sgroi, S. M. (Ed.). (1982). *Handbook of clinical intervention in child sexual abuse.* Lexington, MA: Lexington Books.

Slovenko, R., & Usdin, G. (1966). *Psychotherapy, confidentiality, and privileged communication.* Springfield, IL: Charles C Thomas.

Summit, R. C. (1983). The child sexual abuse accommodation syndrome. *Child Abuse & Neglect, 7,* 177–193.

Tardieu, A. (1868). *Etude Medico-Legale sur L'infanticide.* Paris: J. B. Baillière

Terr, L. C. (1991). Childhood traumas: An outline and overview. *American Journal of Psychiatry, 148,* 10–20.

Tibbits-Kleber, A. L., Howell, R. J., & Kleber, D. J. (1987). Joint custody: A comprehensive review. *Bulletin of the American Academy of Psychiatry and the Law, 15,* 27–43.

Wallerstein, J. S. (1991). The long-term effects of divorce on children: A review. *Journal of the American Academy of Child and Adolescent Psychiatry, 30,* 349–360.

Wallerstein, J. S., & Kelly, J. B. (1980). *Surviving the break-up: How children and parents cope with divorce.* New York: Basic Books.

Wallerstein, J. S., & Blakeslee, S. (1996). *Second changes: Men, women, and children a decade after the divorce.* New York: Houghton Mifflin Co.

Weiner, B. A., Simons, V. A., & Cavanaugh, J. L. (1985). The child custody dispute. In D. H. Schetky & E. P. Benedek (Eds.), *Emerging issues in child psychiatry and the law.* New York: Brunner/Mazel. pp. 59–75.

Weinstock, R., & Weinstock, D. (1988). Child abuse reporting trends: An unprecedented threat to confidentiality. *Journal of Forensic Science, 33,* 418–431.

Wilson, J. P. (1978). *The rights of adolescents in the mental health system.* Lexington, MA: Lexington Books.

Yuille, J. C., Hunter, R., Joffe, R., & Zaparniuk, J. (1993). Interviewing children in sexual abuse cases. In G. S. Goodman & B. L. Bottoms (Eds.), *Child victims, child witnesses: Understanding and improving testimony.* New York: Guilford Press. pp. 95–115.

34 / Ethics in Child Psychiatry

Sarah Robinson Flick and William J. Winslade

Ethical aspects of child psychiatry are far more pervasive and important than most psychiatrists realize and than many are willing to admit. A few who do appreciate the significance of ethical issues recently have begun to call attention to the need to address them. However, academic training and patterns of practice lag far behind the vital need for child psychiatrists to become informed about, sensitive to, and responsive to ethical issues in their work. In this chapter we offer a practical approach to ethics in child psychiatry. Our primary emphasis is on ethics in the context of the individual case, but we also mention broader policy implications that have serious ethical dimensions. We concentrate on a discussion of cases because clinicians typically are confronted with problematic cases before they become aware of their policy implications.

Typical discussions of ethics in child psychiatry begin with codes of ethics, principles, guidelines, or rules. We do not deny that abstractions and generalizations can be useful and should be consulted when appropriate. Our view, however, is that the vitality of ethics is found in the complex, subtle, ambiguous, and unique facts and factors influencing particular cases. Thus we stress the importance of beginning where the action is, namely, in the midst of the real human dramas in which child patients involuntarily find themselves to be players, often central figures.

The approach to ethics in child psychiatry that we recommend begins with rather full case descriptions rather than brief vignettes. The latter are effective to illustrate single issues, but the former bring out the inherently contextual and irreducibly complex features of ethics in child psychiatry practice. Furthermore, ethics is inextricably linked to developmental, social, economic, legal, and other dimensions of the child's world. Although we cannot present all aspects at once, we stress that they must be taken as a whole in order to address effectively the ethical issues.

Having identified the individual clinical case as the heart of ethics, we realize that to get to the heart we must have some sort of approach in mind. Our approach is to provide a heuristic framework for thinking about ethics. The framework is neither a set of principles or codes nor a rich architecture of theory, but a minimal scaffolding designed to provide perspective on and paths to ethical aspects of child psychiatry. The following discussion brings out some of the key ideas that provide a way of thinking about ethics that may be helpful to practitioners.

Although an identified patient is generally the focus of attention in a given clinical situation, it is important to realize that any evaluative or prescriptive intervention involves and affects other individuals and entities, such as family members, peers, schools, and social agencies. In addition, the individual child or adolescent, considered from a developmental perspective, does not remain static but changes and matures over time. Ethical conduct and practice in child psychiatry thus calls for an awareness of and respect for an individual's community of caregivers as well as the individual's present and future developmental status.

An appreciation of typical patterns of development is essential for formulating an ethical approach to the practice of child psychiatry. A child psychiatrist's patient population may range from infants to adolescents; during no other phases of the life cycle do such dramatic changes in identity and capabilities appear. From infancy throughout the preschool years, children are highly dependent on their caregivers. Latency-age children remain dependent on adults but can begin to understand the implications of psychiatric intervention and can participate in their evaluation and treatment, including rendering assent. Adolescents assume a progressive degree of independence and can become involved to a greater degree in their own mental health care. The child psychiatrist must be able to assess the child's degree of maturation in such areas as cognition, abstraction, attitudes toward authority, and moral development. It is important to recognize the interplay between the concepts of a child's right to receive psychiatric care and his or her privilege of participating in and assenting to such care. The child psychiatrist must maintain an appreciation of the child's developmental vulnerabilities as well as his or her strengths.

Recent dramatic advances in child and adolescent psychiatry result from progress in neurobiology and related changes in pediatric psychopharmacology. The 1990s, designated as the "Decade of the Brain," has focused attention on scientific investigations and clinical uses of various medications. Many more pharmacological options are available to clinical practitioners. The ethical practice of child psychiatry requires that the individual physician stay informed about the current literature and practice standards. A related issue is the need to maintain a clinically appropriate balance between pharmacological treatment and other modalities, such as psychotherapy. As more sophisticated approaches to pharmacological intervention become available, it is important to strive for equally sophisticated assessment and treatment protocols in the emotional, social, behavioral, and cognitive domains.

It is generally accepted that a "biopsychosocial" approach to the evaluation and treatment of psychiatric disorders in children and adolescents represents the state of the art in the field. We believe, however, that prioritization of the individual child's development requires the practitioner to move beyond the biopsychosocial model. The truly ethical child psychiatrist must be aware of and appreciate moral and cognitive development. Children and adolescents have differing emotional and behavioral vulnerabilities depending on their age, gender, and other developmental factors. The child psychiatrist should maintain an interest in and respect for the emerging body of knowledge in this area.

Historically, the child psychiatrist has faced a need to balance participation, responsibility, and authority among the patient, his or her parents or primary caregivers, and the state. The ethical principle of respect for persons generally implies the primacy of the child and his or her right to grow and develop in order to attain an optimal quality of life. Thus the ethical practice of child psychiatry requires a knowledge of development, an appreciation of systemic interactions, and the flexibility to address situational variations.

The capacity to appreciate the distinctive world of the child is a necessary prerequisite in the ethical practice of child psychiatry. The legal and ethical status of children has been in question throughout modern history. Over the years, the rights of children as persons have become an increasing focus of interest and concern. The very nature of childhood implies ongoing change; treatment considerations differ from child to child as well as with the same child across time. This dynamic of development and change implies that any intervention, although effective in the present, may become untenable later. The child psychiatrist must be prepared to reassess each individual situation continually. If the child psychiatrist is to assume the role of facilitator of the growth and development of children, he or she will need to attain a level of comfort and competence in balancing value variables and value conflicts.

The traditional principles of medical ethics must be informed by the unique dynamics relevant to children. Respect for persons may be defined as the primacy of the individual child or adolescent. The principle of autonomy requires the development of competence. A potentially dangerous imbalance is inherent even in the practice of adult psychiatry; in child psychiatry the "power differential" between clinician and patient is magnified by the child's developmental vulnerabilities. Issues of informed consent and privacy suggest a need for increased sensitivity to children as persons. The risk that well-intentioned paternalism can deteriorate into authoritarianism applies not only to the child's physician but also to his or her parents and to the state. The principle of beneficence finds practical application in child psychiatry. For example, the rare need for restraints, whether physical or chemical, must be examined in the light of their potential to harm the child. In addition, the child psychiatrist has ample opportunity to remove potentially harmful impediments to the child's development, such as intervening in abusive situations and serving as a child advocate in the legal and political arenas. The principle of justice prompts child psychiatrists to advocate for fair distribution of resources for children and to avoid undue compensation for themselves. One of the more distressing occurrences in child psychiatry involved the late 1980s trend of proprietary psychiatric hospitals encouraging elective admissions without adequate evaluation or attempts to pursue the less expensive alternative of outpatient intervention. This practice was confronted in the legal arena and has receded to some extent. With the advent of managed care, questions of the availability of resources of services for children with emotional of behavioral difficulties will continue to arise.

Not infrequently, child psychiatrists are asked to interact with the legal system. They may be asked to perform "court-ordered" evaluations based on their knowledge of development, of interpersonal processes in families, and of parental pathology. They may encounter communication problems in the legal arena and be faced with integrating a "therapeutic" style into an often adversarial situation. In custody determinations, the child psychiatrist may be asked to evaluate the quality of parenting and a child's developmental needs and preferences. It is important in such a situation to evaluate all family members and to maintain an evaluative stance, refraining from assuming a posture of treatment. The same caveats apply to involvement in situations of termination of parental rights or evaluations of juvenile offenders. When asked to address situations involving physical or sexual abuse, the child psychiatrist ideally is involved in the evaluation process from the outset. Other possible opportunities for the involvement of child psychiatrists include the preparation of and advice to counsel regarding child witnesses.

Questions of confidentiality also draw on the concept of "developmental ethics." At what age, or developmental level, does the child or adolescent become entitled to confidentiality, and where are the limits set? The physician-patient privilege must be evaluated in light of the youth's developmental status. As the child ages and matures, decisional autonomy and authority become more critical from a pragmatic as well as an ethical standpoint. The individual patient should be informed of the limits of privacy, recognizing the need to balance the parents' responsibility and authority with the child's ability to trust his or her psychiatrist. The boundaries between individual and family therapy often become blurred in treatment unless clearly defined from the outset.

The child psychiatrist who prioritizes the optimal development of children will face the reality that the mental health and development of children are low priorities in public and political arenas. A scarcity of resources renders children who are poor, and perhaps homeless, a particularly vulnerable population. There is a great need for a continuum of psychiatric care for all children, and the poor, who are at special risk, have the least access to such care. The child psychiatrist may consider pro bono work or advocacy in the public and/or political setting. The traditional bias of "preservation of the family" must be defined and reinterpreted in the light of psychosocial circumstances. The child psychiatrist has the responsibility of understanding and remaining sensitive to cultural conditions in evaluation and treatment. The question of the need for psychiatric diagnoses (and any resultant risk of "labeling" a child in the future) to obtain reimbursement from third-party payors must be considered in the light of ethical practice. Finally, there is a tremendous need to improve efforts at prevention in child psychiatry at the primary, secondary, and tertiary levels. White House conferences in 1909, 1930, 1969, 1975, 1978, and 1981 all specified the mental and emotional health of children as a national priority; however, the reality remains far behind the vision. There is a shortage of professionals specializing in the mental and emotional care of children. Perhaps an "ethics of optimism" would focus on protective factors, resilience, and the child psychiatrist's role in facilitating the optimal growth and development of all children.

Selected Cases Illustrating Ethical Issues

In this section we describe several cases that pose complex clinical issues intertwined with ethical problems. We provide detailed case descriptions in order to bring out contextual complexities of the cases more fully than would be done by presenting vignettes. Even so, we realize that nuances that arise in clinical interactions cannot be captured in our longer descriptions. However, sufficient detail can be given to enable the reader to explore with us some familiar but subtle questions of ethics in clinical practice. These cases address ethical issues inherent in and related to confidentiality, informed consent, the legal arena, and working with underserved populations such as the poor.

CONFIDENTIALITY

The problem of confidentiality in psychiatric treatment with regard to children is complicated when the psychiatrist stands in a special relationship with both the child patient and the parent(s) or guardian. The child may disclose information to the psychiatrist that he or she does not want the parents or guardian to know, such as that concerning sexual behavior. Also, the parents might provide information to the psychiatrist that they do not want the child to know. The psychiatrist must then determine who should have access to such information. Ideally, the psychiatrist may, as in the next case, be able to find an opportunity, with appropriate informed consent, to use otherwise confidential information to advance treatment. In other situations, no satisfactory solution may be found that does not subordinate the interests of one party or the other. For example, if a psychiatrist, against the child's wishes, discloses to the parents that a child patient has engaged in some proscribed behavior, such as sexual activity or drug use, the child may no longer trust or cooperate with the treatment. If the parents learn that the psychiatrist withheld information that they believed they had a right to know, then they may terminate the therapy. The psychiatrist may have to walk a narrow path to protect the interests and preferences of his patients.

Many complex views concerning confidentiality can arise in treatment contexts. We have selected a case that illustrates aspects of confidentiality bound up with other ethical issues.

CASE EXAMPLE: TYLER

Tyler is a 14-year-old boy whose parents brought him to an outpatient child psychiatry clinic for evaluation of "behavior problems." During the evaluation, Tyler revealed that he had had suicidal thoughts of several months' duration with a concrete plan in place. It was recommended that the patient be hospitalized, and he was admitted to an adolescent inpatient unit the following day.

Tyler lived with his adoptive father, his biological mother, and his two younger half brothers. He stated that his problems began approximately 3 years prior to admission when he witnessed the death of a favorite adult friend in an accident. Following this episode, Tyler complained of initial and middle insomnia as well as "flashbacks" of the accident. He stated that he would actually see the accident and that it was very real to him, and from time to time he would hear male and female voices yelling and screaming but was unable to distinguish any specific words that they were saying. Tyler slept about 5 hours a night and complained of feeling tired all the time. He acknowledged difficulty with concentration and often being distracted by thoughts of death. These symptoms progressively worsened and were particularly exacerbated about 6 weeks prior to admission following the patient's breakup with his girlfriend. Tyler admitted to decreased self-esteem and frequent thoughts of suicide. He visualized hanging himself and had bought a rope for this purpose.

His parents reported that the had been a "problem"

since he failed the third grade. He was sent to a residential treatment facility for 1 year at age 10 because of reported discipline problems. He had been suspended from school several times during the preceding year. During the summer prior to his admission, Tyler attended a military academy for 4 weeks, and his parents noted some subsequent improvement in his behavior. However, upon his return from the military academy, he continued to complain of depressive symptoms and to experience recurrent thoughts of death.

Tyler had a history of recurrent problems with school. He was in the principal's office on one occasion, having been repeatedly oppositional with a teacher. His adoptive father was called and he went to the principal's office. The patient and his adoptive father scuffled in the office, and the local children's protective agency was notified. Tyler was suspended from school for 2 weeks and psychiatric evaluation was recommended.

The patient's family history was significant for alcohol abuse by the patient's adoptive paternal grandmother. Also of significance was his parents' disclosure early in his hospitalization that the patient had never been told that he was not the biological son of the man he believed to be his father. The patient's mother had not married Tyler's biological father; the boy was an infant at the time of his mother's marriage to his adoptive father. Although Tyler's parents' concern for him seemed evident, they were puzzled regarding the etiology of his problems and felt that perhaps he needed more discipline. They stated that they were not aware that he had felt depressed or suicidal. They expressed interest in learning better ways to communicate with the patient. However, they were very reluctant to discuss the issue of Tyler's biological father and stated that they would prefer to keep that issue a "secret," because they felt that if Tyler learned that he had been adopted, he might not want to "obey" his adoptive father any longer.

Tyler stated that he was very angry with his parents because he had not been told that he was being taken to the hospital. He felt that he had always been treated differently from his brothers and knew of no reasons why this should be true. He said he was tired of getting hit by his father and that no one really understood or cared about him. He felt very discouraged by the recent breakup with his girlfriend and said he saw no reason to keep on living. He reported that he did enjoy the military academy and that he usually felt less depressed while away from home. Although quite despondent, Tyler was able to voice some of his concerns. He agreed to stay in the hospital and hoped that he would eventually feel better. He wanted to go to college someday and become an attorney to "put criminals in jail."

In summary, the patient was an adolescent young man who had never felt equal to his peers or his siblings and who struggled with chronically low self-esteem. He had suffered at least 2 major losses—the death of his adult friend and the breakup with his girlfriend. In addition, it was likely that he perceived on some level that he differed from his brothers because of his biological father's absence. Although he had never been formally told that he was adopted, he had clear concerns about being "different" from his brothers. He found it very difficult to trust his parents and other adults and felt rejected by having been "sent away" from home to live elsewhere. He felt more comfortable with female peers and adults and found them to be less threatening than males. However, this preference was problematic for the patient because he perceived that his parents expected him to be "manly and tough." He was a sensitive young man who was overwhelmed by his feelings at times and was confused about "appropriate" emotional expressiveness. His anger was chronically directed interiorly, leading to a clinical picture of depression. Although frequently attempting to defend against symptoms of depression with oppositional behavior, his despair was evidenced by frequent and sudden episodes of tearfulness when discussing his losses.

Upon admission to the hospital, Tyler was placed on suicide precautions, which were maintained for 5 days. He gradually began to respond to the milieu and his mood improved somewhat, although he continued to experience moderate dysphoria and some difficulty with sleeping and concentration. He was treated with an antidepressant medication to which his depressive symptoms responded partially. It became apparent that the patient had serious difficulty relating to family members, most specifically his father. He could not join with and participate in family therapy and, in fact, was absent from the first several family sessions.

The psychiatrist felt that the "secret" of the patient's adoption probably continued to affect the relationship between the patient and his parents. After much deliberation, Tyler's parents decided to disclose the fact of the boy's adoption during a family therapy session. At this point, Tyler agreed to join the family therapy sessions, and although initially saddened by the discovery of his adoption, he subsequently began to communicate much more freely with his parents and particularly with his adoptive father. The patient's adoptive father also experienced great relief in being able to discuss the adoption freely and openly with his son. In general, family communication patterns improved following the disclosure; and Tyler and his family were able to process the implications of the patient's adoption at some length and with beneficial effect. The patient participated actively in all unit activities and was able to go home for several weekend passes. These seemed to help him begin to reintegrate with his family and his community at home. At the time of discharge, he was essentially free of any depressive symptomatology. The patient and his family were followed in outpatient therapy for approximately 1 year after his discharge. At the end of this period, the antidepressant was tapered and discontinued without adverse sequelae. The patient continued to do well and treatment was terminated.

This case raised several ethical questions. The issue of the family "secret" of Tyler's adoption highlights the common dilemma of balancing the adolescent's developmental identity issues and their clinical importance with working with the parents' expressed need to retain control (and fear of losing control) by keeping the secret. Maintaining rapport with the family and supporting their continued involvement in the patient's treatment maximized the patient's opportunity to engage in treatment and continue to grow and develop. However, a point was reached where the parental desire to keep the secret was strongly challenged and confronted as maintaining secrecy became countertherapeutic and impeded the patient's age-appropriate growth in the arena of identity and autonomy. Although parental needs and desires are of great importance, the child psychiatrist must remain aware of their impact on the child's or adolescent's growth and development.

CONSENT TO TREATMENT

The following case illustrates how complex family relationships can obstruct the treatment of individual children. Children's needs are sometimes sacrificed and overridden by the interests of other family members. The psychiatrist may be unable to find a satisfactory way to serve the individual child if the parents are uncooperative. We present this unusual and challenging case in detail to illustrate such difficulties and frustrations.

CASE EXAMPLE: LAURIE

Laurie is a 15-year-old young woman who was brought to an outpatient crisis clinic for psychiatric evaluation. She was accompanied by her father and stepmother, who stated that they had become increasingly concerned about changes in Laurie's behavior over the past several weeks. They felt that she was becoming more oppositional as well as more seclusive and withdrawn. During a recent argument, Laurie had stated several times that she wished that she were dead. She also had serious school problems with failing grades in several courses. The patient's father had a history of alcohol abuse and affective disorder. It was felt that hospitalization was indicated for further evaluation, and the patient was subsequently admitted to an adolescent inpatient unit.

Laurie stated that her difficulties began about 2 years prior to her admission. At that time, she was living with her biological mother, brother, and several cousins in another state. She reported several episodes of sexual abuse occurring during this time. She reported being raped by a male relative as well as by her mother's boyfriend. She also reported some sexual abuse perpetrated by a female relative over a period of some months during this time. One year prior to Laurie's admission, her father and his wife visited the patient and her family. Following this visit, the patient decided to live with her father, in part because she began to feel unwelcome in her mother's home after the incident with the mother's boyfriend.

Laurie reported difficulties getting along with her stepmother, beginning with her arrival in her father's home. The patient's father and stepmother had been married for about 6 years. The patient felt that her stepmother was jealous of her father's closeness to her and that she was also jealous of a developing friendship between the patient and her stepmother's female relative. The patient felt that her stepmother was too strict with her and was unhappy because her father generally acceded to his wife's wishes rather than to Laurie's. She also had problems adjusting to her new school and stated that she had made no real friends her own age. During the preceding summer, her stepmother was out of town for a couple of months on business. During this time, Laurie "ran the household" and cared for her father, who had several medical problems. When the patient's stepmother returned, the conflict between her and Laurie escalated. At the same time, Laurie's older brother moved into her father's home. Laurie identified his presence in the home as a significant stressor for her; she perceived parental favoritism toward him. In addition, the family moved out of a duplex house they had been sharing with the stepmother's female relative, limiting Laurie's access to a person whom she identified as a primary source of support. She subsequently "ran away" to this individual's house, which further distressed her parents. Laurie became confused and upset because her father preferred that she "act like a child," while her stepmother expected her to "act like an adult." She also reported that she could not trust people and felt that intimacy was very threatening, stating "everyone I get close to leaves me." Upon admission to the hospital, Laurie admitted to fatigue, initial and middle insomnia, an erratic appetite, crying spells, sadness, feelings of worthlessness, and thoughts of death without specific suicidal plans.

Laurie remembered feeling very close to her father as a small child. He had left the family on the patient's birthday when she was a preschooler. She reported having no further contact with him except for occasional phone calls until she entered adolescence. At that time, they began to reestablish a relationship. The patient stated that she had been very worried about her father. He had been diagnosed as having an affective disorder and also as being dependent on alcohol. His relationship with his second wife (the patient's stepmother) had been turbulent and involved physical abuse of her, leading to several separations. He also had a cancerous skin lesion removed the year prior to Laurie's admission. Although there had been no apparent recurrence or metastasis, both the patient and her father seemed very concerned that this illness would ultimately be fatal for him. The patient's father had not kept follow-up appointments for this problem, feeling that such care would be futile. He had been treated for his psychiatric problems as both an inpatient and an outpatient. He did not attend Alcoholics Anonymous and felt that his alcoholism was "under control."

Laurie's parents expressed concerns about her apparent interpersonal difficulties. They stated that it was difficult to trust her and felt that she often lied to them. They acknowledged that the patient's stepmother made most parental decisions about the patient and that the patient's father acceded to her even when he was in disagreement. The patient's father was very quiet. He appeared to be anxious and stated only that he wanted the patient to come home. He expressed general dissatisfaction with and distrust of the mental health system. The patient's stepmother also seemed anxious and somewhat angry about her dissatisfaction with psychiatry, particularly with respect to her husband's history. She and her female relative acknowledged that they felt that the patient had "come between them," creating distance and conflict in a previously harmonious relationship. The patient had been seen in outpatient therapy for several months earlier in the year of her admission to the hospital. This psychotherapy had been stopped because the patient's parents felt that the "problems were solved." They were unable to articulate their treatment goals for Laurie's hospitalization. The patient's father found this task particularly difficult, stating that he viewed the patient as an "angel" and that he was the one who was "sick." While the stepmother seemed committed to supporting the patient's treatment in the hospital, her father was much more ambivalent, repeatedly stating that he really wanted his daughter to be at home. He acknowledged that his own need for her presence at home seemed greater than her need for treatment, but tentatively agreed to try to participate in and support the patient's therapy.

During the mental status examination, the patient was noted to be a casually dressed and groomed young woman who was alert and cooperative. She made good eye contact but was somewhat restless, occasionally walking around the room. She became tearful several times, usually when speaking of her father. Laurie's speech was normal in all respects. Her mood was depressed and slightly anxious. Her thought processes were clear and coherent. There were no apparent delusions. She admitted to hearing a deceased relative's voice reprimand her; she was unable to localize this voice but stated that it was always derogatory and punitive. She stated that she knew that the voice was not real. Although she denied specific suicidal ideation, she admitted to recurrent thoughts of death and feeling that life was not worth living. She seemed preoccupied with thoughts of her stepmother's female relative as her only source of emotional support, and admitted to harboring prominent concerns about her father's health. She described herself as superstitious. Her memory was grossly intact, sensorium was clear, and abstraction capacity was age-appropriate. In general, the patient seemed eager to talk and to engage with her therapist. However, she demonstrated much lability of affect and marked ambivalence about her commitment to treatment. She stated that her problems were all her stepmother's fault and that she did not need to work on them. These statements were interspersed with self-deprecating comments. Laurie appeared quite concerned about her relationships with her father, stepmother, and stepmother's female relative but was unable to come up with any expectations for change on her part or theirs.

In summary, the patient was an adolescent young woman who reported difficulty relating to her parents and a history of repeated experiences of sexual abuse. Her interpersonal relationships appeared to be troubled—she experienced much alienation from her peers and described herself as having no friends. While generally feeling isolated, the patient reported feeling an intense closeness with some adults, most notably her father and her stepmother's female relative. She seemed to have diffuse boundaries in these relationships and had much difficulty separating from these individuals. She described her father as extremely dependent on her and herself as extremely dependent on her stepmother's female relative. In both of these relationships, she attempted to displace her stepmother. This was particularly problematic, as the stepmother functioned as the patient's primary parental figure. The patient's sense of identity appeared vague and unformed; she was also troubled by chronic feelings of low self-esteem. In addition to these characterological problems, the patient sustained psychosocial stressors. Her father's history of substance abuse and affective disorder placed her at risk for the development of an affective illness. It was felt that her symptoms represented a response to a combination of long-standing difficulties and more recent stressors.

Laurie was admitted to an adolescent inpatient unit and placed on suicide precautions that were discontinued in the second week of her hospitalization. Following her admission, Laurie experienced some improvement of her mood, although depressive symptomatology remained prominent throughout her hospitalization. She engaged easily and eagerly in individual psychotherapy and expressed multiple concerns about relationships within her family. In the course of family therapy, it became apparent that relationships were conflictual on numerous levels; attempts were made to clarify some of the roles of various family members. Laurie's dysphoria and other symptoms of major depression persisted, and it was felt that a trial of antidepressant pharmacotherapy was indicated. Although repeated attempts were made to clarify the intent and rationale of this treatment approach with the patient's parents, they adamantly refused permission for a trial of antidepressant treatment. Although the patient was willing and desired to assent to such treatment, her parents continued to refuse. The risk involved in discontinuing treatment, including worsening of the patient's depression, were explained at length to her parents, and they demanded her release from the hospital.

At the time of discharge, Laurie did not meet criteria for involuntary commitment, and she denied suicidal ideation; however, the treatment team remained quite concerned about her prognosis. The parents were notified that the local children's protective authority would be made aware of their refusal to comply with recommended medical treatment for the patient. Although Laurie continued to complain of symptoms of major depression, no further treatment could be undertaken without parental consent, and the patient subsequently was discharged against medical advice. Laurie agreed to contact emergency resources (for which she was given telephone numbers) should her suicidal thoughts recur. The appropriate children's protective agency was notified of the treatment team's concerns about this patient and agreed to investigate further.

Several years following Laurie's discharge, her biological mother contacted the psychiatrist, stating that Laurie was living with her in a distant state and was very depressed. She was advised to seek further evaluation with a child and adolescent psychiatrist in her locale.

This patient presented as someone who, although initially ambivalent about psychiatric intervention, emerged from an inpatient evaluation with a clear clinical picture and clear indications for specific treatment. She had been able to engage with her caregivers in the hospital and had witnessed her peers benefiting from the same antidepressant medication that had been recommended for her. Although her condition of major depression could not be accurately described as "life-threatening" at the time of her discharge from the hospital, the consensus of the treatment team was that she was experiencing ongoing dysphoria that interfered with the quality of her life and threatened, over the long term, to compromise her emotional, social, and intellectual development. The patient was aware of these complications of her unhappiness and wanted to benefit from all available treatment modalities. She invested what energy she was able to gather in psychotherapy, and after psychotherapy alone had not helped her feel much better, she stated that she wanted to take medication.

The limiting factor in this case, restricting the patients' access to recommended treatment, was her parents' refusal to consent to a trial of antidepressant medication. In the patient's state of residence, parental consent must be obtained before treating a patient under 16 years of age in the absence of a life-threatening condition. There appeared to be complicating issues, such as Laurie's father's own psychiatric condition and desire to have her at home and "well," which may have impacted his capacity to provide truly informed consent. In the face of his refusal to consent to his daughter's treatment, the option remained for the treatment team to seek legal sanction for treating the patient against her father's will. It could be argued that, given the patient's age and her desire to engage in treatment, her wishes should prevail over her father's objections, particularly when his "objectivity" may have been compromised. However, the patient was very opposed to any legal intervention, stating that although she wanted treatment, she was more concerned about alienating her father and that if such intervention were pursued, she would refuse to cooperate.

The overall sense of the treatment team was that, although concerns were present about the patient's prognosis and about her father's refusal to consent to treatment, further attempts to "force" treatment would become counterproductive in the long run. The patient's family, and indeed the patient herself, would likely become more alienated from the treatment team in the process of adversarial interaction in the legal arena. It was felt that such action probably would not result in Laurie obtaining treatment, as local legal authorities typically did not overrule parental wishes in non–life-threatening situations, and even if this were to happen, that the patient would become more demoralized and less likely to participate in treatment in a productive manner. It also was felt that all attempts should be made to increase the likelihood that Laurie and her family would seek psychiatric treatment again if and when her depression should worsen. The decision to discharge the patient against medical advice was thought to reflect most clearly the clinical impression of the patient's caregivers in the hospital while, it was hoped, preserving the patient's perception of psychiatric care as helpful and in fact "caring," increasing the likelihood of her seeking assistance when needed in the future.

Another question involves developmental issues—at what age should an adolescent be empowered to consent to psychiatric treatment in the face of parental opposition? Often legal provisions sanction treatment in life-threatening situations, such as the presence of acute suicidality, regardless of the patient's age or parental consent; however, the clinician may be faced with dilemmas in which the patient is not in a life-threatening situation but is experiencing discomfort, or even pain, as well as threats to ongoing development. Traditionally, specific chronological ages have been used as "cut-offs" for determining who (the patient or his or her parent) may consent to treatment. Certainly guidelines are necessary; nevertheless, an ethical perspective that emanates from the optimized development of the individual child or adolescent as a priority may challenge the absolutism of using chronological ages as criteria for seeking and consenting to medical treatment.

A related question involves the economics of such a situation. If an adolescent, even one who legally is of age to provide informed consent to treatment, is unable to pay for such services and his or her parent refuses to pay based on refusal to consent to treatment, who should bear the cost of the treatment? Mental health services for young people are typically not a priority in public funding, and resources are scarce at best. Clini-

cians may be challenged to search for creative solutions in order to provide access to treatment for such youngsters, including the consideration of pro bono work with such individuals.

THE LEGAL ARENA

The next case exemplifies a difficulty psychiatrists may face in providing court-ordered evaluation and treatment. Not only may the family present obstacles to treatment, but the court may not provide assistance or guidance even when requested. Lack of financial support for children's services also hampers the practice of psychiatry in a public arena.

CASE EXAMPLE: ANNA

Anna is a 4-year-old girl who presented for psychiatric evaluation and treatment at the request of the court system. She was accompanied by her biological mother and her paternal grandmother. At the same time of the evaluation, the patient was living with her paternal grandmother. The court had requested evaluation and treatment to explore the renewal of a relationship between the child and her mother, with the long-term goal of possible return of the child to her mother.

The patient's parents were divorced when she was an infant. Prior to the divorce, her parents engaged in numerous physical fights. After the divorce, Anna was placed in the custody of her paternal grandmother by the court because of the reportedly unsafe environment in both parent's homes. Both parents were given visitation privileges. However, when the patient was almost 3 years old, her grandmother stopped allowing her mother to visit. The grandmother alleged that the patient had returned from a visit with her mother with injuries that the child reportedly stated her mother had inflicted on her. Following this incident, the patient was evaluated at a community mental health center with complaints of nightmares, stuttering, and fears about "monsters." At this time, the grandmother stated that she would like further information from the treatment team to "help" her obtain full legal custody of Anna. The patient's mother had attempted to obtain the legal system's assistance in enforcing her visitation rights; however, although the court did not deny her visitation rights, it also did not enforce them. The child was seen for a few sessions at the community health center and was felt to be adjusting adequately and no longer in need of psychiatric treatment.

Although an investigation by the local children's protective agency failed to substantiate the grandmother's allegations of maternal abuse, considerable animosity remained between the grandmother and mother. When the patient was 4 years old, both of her parents had remarried. Her mother again sought to obtain full legal custody of the child, and it was at this point that the court requested psychiatric evaluation and treatment of the child.

With respect to the mental status examination, the patient appeared to be an attractively dressed and groomed young girl who was alert and cooperative. Her level of activity appeared to be appropriate for her age. Her speech was normal in rate, rhythm, tone, volume, and latency. The patient's mood appeared to be basically euthymic, although her affect was slightly anxious at the outset of the interview. She denied hallucinations, and there were no apparent delusions. No thoughts were expressed of harming herself or others. She eagerly engaged in appropriate play with puppets, puzzles, blocks, and a dollhouse. The patient was observed to seem happy to see her mother and was very affectionate with both her and her grandmother. She was friendly to the staff at the clinic.

Both the patient's mother and grandmother were rather guarded in the initial evaluation session. When interviewed separately, each spoke at length of her concerns about the child, particularly with respect to being in the care of the other woman. The patient's mother felt that her separation from Anna was harmful for the child and that her grandmother was actively attempting to interfere in a negative fashion with the relationship between the patient and her mother. The patient's grandmother expressed her continued concerns that Anna's physical safety would be jeopardized if she were returned to her mother's care. When interviewed together, in the presence of the child, both women remained relatively quiet and seemed reluctant to engage in conversation.

In summary, the patient was a 4-year-old girl who presented for evaluation and treatment at the request of the court. Her grandmother reported symptoms of anxiety and oppositional behavior in the patient, which she felt were exacerbated by any contact between the patient and her mother. Little evidence of these symptoms were noted in the clinical setting, although it appeared that the enforced and lengthy separation from her mother had been difficult for the patient. It was agreed that "treatment" (or rather an extended evaluation) would be undertaken at the request of the court. The treatment team requested that the patient, her grandmother, and her mother be seen in weekly sessions where the patient and her mother could be observed together. It was further agreed that the cost of the sessions would be shared by the patient's mother and grandmother and that feedback would be provided to both the mother's and grandmother's attorneys and the court.

The patient, her mother, and her grandmother were seen concurrently by a child psychiatrist and a social worker for a total of 10 sessions. The first 2 sessions were devoted to clarifying goals and objectives of the treatment. It was decided that the patient and her mother would be observed by the child psychiatrist while the grandmother would be seen by the social worker. The child was observed to express affection to both her mother and grandmother at each session. She appeared to be relaxed at play with her mother, who was observed to interact appropriately with her daughter. After 4 more sessions, it was recommended to the court that the patient spend a greater amount of time visiting her mother, under the neutral supervision of a third party. The sessions had produced no evidence indicating that the patient should not spend more time with her mother. It was also recommended that a guardian ad litem be appointed for the patient.

Subsequently, a month's hiatus of treatment occurred because of the job termination of both therapists and the need for selection of a new child psychiatrist and social worker. When the new treatment team met with the patient, her mother, and grandmother, similar procedures were followed. Anna remained relaxed in her mother's company and her mother supportively and effectively interacted with her. Again it was recommended that visitation between Anna and her mother be increased. Attempts to help Anna's mother and grandmother negotiate such visits met with significant resistance. The patient's mother stated repeatedly that she was unable to afford to pay a "professional" observer, and the patient's grandmother was unwilling to allow Anna to visit with her mother unless the observer was a paid supervisor with a clinical and/or legal background. Suggestions that the visitation occur at the patient's school were unacceptable to the grandmother on the basis of her feelings that such visitation would disrupt the patient's curriculum and education. As the mother and grandmother argued about the visitation in a progressively more conflictual manner, Anna became visibly upset and agitated. It was finally agreed that the patient and her mother would visit at a local restaurant (supervised by the grandmother) prior to the next appointment; however, at the appointed time, the mother failed to appear. At that point, the grandmother was unwilling to cooperate with any further visitation. It was the opinion of the treatment team that the most potentially damaging circumstance for the patient was the ongoing conflict between and hostility expressed by her mother and grandmother. Essentially each woman was unwilling to cooperate with the other. It was felt that no further therapeutic progress could be made without increased contact between the patient and her mother to afford the opportunity of further assessment of this relationship. The court was advised of this opinion, and the treatment team requested further direction. No further direction was provided by the court.

Some weeks after the final session, the therapists received a telephone call from the grandmother's neighbor. She expressed concern about the patient's safety while in the grandmother's care, reporting that the patient was sometimes given over-the-counter medication so that she would "calm down." She also alleged that the grandmother told the child that her mother was a bad person and wanted to hurt her. The neighbor reported that upon hearing such statements, the patient would become upset and behave aggressively and defiantly. The local children's protective agency was notified of these concerns, as was the court. Again, the court provided no further direction.

Approximately 1 year following the final session, the child psychiatrist was subpoenaed. The patient had been removed from her grandmother's custody and was living in a foster home. Her mother again was petitioning for custody. In court, the child psychiatrist was asked to comment on the patient's clinical condition, on the assessment of a second psychiatrist, and on the suitability of both the patient's mother and grandmother as caregivers for the patient.

In this case, the child psychiatrist was faced with a number of complicated ethical questions. Initially there were questions about Anna's clinical "need" for treatment. Much of the clinical work that was in the therapeutic realm actually was directed to the patient's mother and grandmother; however, it was Anna who received a diagnosis and established a record of psychiatric treatment. All clinical work was done at the request (in fact, at the order) of the court; however, the court provided little or no response when the treatment team made repeated requests for further direction.

The decision to discontinue treatment reflected the treatment team's sense of futility. Recommendations regarding visitation were not carried out, and the persistent hostility between Anna's mother and grandmother was clearly upsetting to and painful for the patient. It was felt that no further intervention could take place without some sense of cooperation between the two women; no such sense was forthcoming.

Payment for "clinical services" was another issue. The agreement was made that the patient's mother and grandmother would share the cost of the sessions. Although the clinic used a sliding scale to assess patient fees, the legal nature of the services provided to the patient dictated the assessment of a full fee.

The child psychiatrist was summoned to appear in court approximately 1 year following the final session. It was agreed that the time required for this appearance would be billed to the summoning attorney, who represented the patient's mother. It was explained that little, if anything, could be said regarding the patient's current clinical status. In court, the child psychiatrist was, in fact, asked to "speculate" about Anna's current clinical condition. Nothing, of course, could be said in this regard since the child psychiatrist had not seen the patient for a year. The child psychiatrist was also asked to comment on a second psychiatrist's evaluation of Anna, which had occurred some months after the final session. Again, little could be said about this report as there was no data available upon which to base an opinion. Finally, the child psychiatrist was asked to assess the parenting potential of both the mother and the grandmother. Although little of substance could be said in this regard, the question did afford the child psychiatrist the opportunity to state that continued confusion regarding the ultimate location of the patient's residence was potentially harmful to her. The patient was aware of the roles of both her mother and grandmother and was affectionately attached to both women. The expressed conflict between them was distressing to the patient and had the potential for impeding her further growth and development as well as limiting her potential to obtain emotional security. It was stated that, unless the patient's mother and grandmother were able to engage in a concerted and mutual attempt to direct their efforts cooperatively in the direction of Anna's benefit and to obtain some expertise in negotiating with each other, Anna would continue to be torn and confused by the conflict demonstrated between these two women, both of whom were very important to her.

In this case, although initiated and maintained at the behest of the court, the child psychiatrist took a stance most congruent with optimizing the patient's opportunity for developing as an individual. This position was certainly more complicated and cumbersome than a more straightforward but simplistic approach of rendering an opinion to the court regarding the most suitable guardian for the patient. However, prioritizing the patient's individual social and emotional development called for the clinically honest approach of "not having all the answers." Recommendations could be, and were, made regarding factors likely to optimize the child's chances for growth. It was again suggested that increased opportunity for visitation between the patient and her mother be provided in order to continue assessing the viability of the girl's eventual permanent return to her mother's care. It was also recommended that any family members permitted to have contact with the child be required to interact with each other in a spirit of cooperation and to consistently place her interests above their own.

THE POOR

The next two cases show how the lack of resources affects and may undermine therapeutic efforts. Psychiatrists who provide services to children who lack resources are constrained by many factors, including economic considerations. In the face of such limitations, as much as possible must be done to give children an opportunity to maximize their potential. We present these cases to illustrate a variety of ethical issues bound up with the problems of lack of resources.

CASE EXAMPLE: SARAH

Sarah is an 11-year-old girl who presented to an outpatient crisis clinic for psychiatric evaluation accompanied by her mother. The director of a local social service agency had requested that she be seen and evaluated for "supportive therapy." The patient was residing at a local youth shelter with her adolescent brother because their mother was preparing to go to a state hospital in a distant city for substance abuse treatment. The patient was a fifth-grade student. Referring complaints were the patient's anxiety relating to her impending separation from her mother as well as her caregivers' concern that the patient was "in denial" regarding her mother's alcoholism. Upon presentation to the clinic, the patient's chief complaint was "My mom's an alcoholic and I guess we need to talk about that."

The patient's mother acknowledged that she had abused alcohol and other drugs for most of the patient's life. She stated that she felt guilty because her daughter had had to assume inappropriate levels of responsibility. She was concerned about what she perceived as the patient's chronic anger toward her and was fearful that the patient might impulsively start living on the streets, as the family had often been homeless and the patient considered herself "streetwise." She stated that the patient "lied and exaggerated" to cover up her family's problems and that she and the patient argued frequently.

Sarah was the product of a full-term pregnancy complicated by maternal use of alcohol and amphetamines. Her birthweight was within normal limits. Her mother had no recollection of any perinatal difficulties. The patient's mother described her as shy, well-behaved, impulsive, and stubborn. She began school at age 4, repeating two grades because of frequent moves. The patient was an A student. She had had no prior psychiatric evaluation or treatment.

With respect to the mental status examination, the patient was neatly and appropriately dressed and groomed. She was alert and cooperative, articulately describing her situation. Eye contact was sparse at the outset of the interview but increased as the interview progressed. There was no psychomotor agitation or retardation. Speech was normal in rate, rhythm, volume, tone, and latency. The patient's mood was basically euthymic with an anxious affect. Her thought processes were clear and coherent. She denied hallucinations and there were no apparent delusions. The patient expressed anger and her perception of injustice with respect to her mother's alcoholism. She described her own dreams and plans to be a "doctor and a good mother." She denied thoughts of harming herself or others. Her sensorium was clear. Immediate and recent memory were intact. Abstraction capacity was adequate for her age. Sarah appeared to have good insight, stating that she had done very well for someone in her situation and that she wanted "help and counseling" so that she would be all right at the shelter while her mother was gone. Her judgment did not appear to be significantly impaired.

In summary, the patient was an 11-year-old girl who had sustained both the chronic stressor of her mother's alcoholism and resultant chaotic lifestyle and the recent stressor of an impending separation from her mother. She was able to express her anger about her situation while maintaining that she loved and needed her mother. Despite these chronic and acute stressors, the patient seemed to be functioning remarkably well. Some of her caregivers had become concerned about whether her apparent good adjustment was genuine and adaptive or driven by denial and "pseudomaturity" that would later cause problems for her. The patient was in the habit of publicly minimizing her problems, particularly with her peers, to the extent that her caregivers felt that she was "lying" about her situation. When questioned carefully about this behavior, the patient reported that her problems were private and that she preferred to discuss them in "private" situations— with trusted adults or in Alateen meetings. She stated that she did better in school if she did not think or talk about her problems. It was felt that although Sarah did experience anxiety and anger about her situation and felt confined by her need to maintain an optimistic attitude, in general, she exhibited a picture of remarkable resilience.

The patient was seen for 4 sessions of individual supportive psychotherapy. She was brought to the sessions by a staff worker at the shelter and returned to the shelter in a taxicab following her appointments. She interacted eagerly with her therapist. During the sessions, she said she felt homesick for her mother. She described her goals for the future and expressed frustration about having had to "grow up too soon." The shelter staff reported that she was very well behaved and helpful with the other children.

During the course of her therapy, Sarah contracted a viral illness. She stated that she felt sad that her mother was not there to take care of her; however, Sarah appropriately sought and received nurturing attention from her therapist and caregivers at the shelter.

Toward the end of their mother's treatment at the state hospital, the patient became anxious about the prospects of her mother's maintenance of sobriety. Her final appointment was scheduled following her mother's return from the state hospital; however, this appointment was not kept. The therapist was contacted by the social service agency director who was concerned because the patient's mother had reportedly relapsed following treatment. The local children's protective agency was contracted, and they visited the patient at school, where they found her to be doing well. Sarah's mother had made and kept follow-up appointments with the girl's pediatrician but reportedly did not wish for her daughter to continue in psychotherapy, either on an individual or a family basis.

As members of the medical and mental health communities, child psychiatrists are trained to detect and treat disorders. Complaints of subjective distress or impairment in function are categorized into syndromes and diagnoses by clinicians who are alert to the identification of psychopathology. Traditionally, much effort has been devoted to delineating "risk factors," and as a result, the child psychiatric community is more knowledgeable about risk factors than the prediction of competence and health. However, the identification of protective factors is an important task for clinicians striving to direct efforts in caring for children at risk toward maximum efficiency and efficacy. Economic deprivation, social disorganization, and accumulation of unfortunate life changes can lead to impaired adjustment, which may be heightened or exacerbated by such factors as a genetic vulnerability to psychiatric illness. Resilience often is viewed as the absence of pathology; it may, in fact, be more the result of successful coping and mastery. If child psychiatrists truly prioritize the optimal development of the individual child, protective factors become very important.

Ethical intervention with children at risk involves not only decreased exposure to risk factors but increased exposure to protective factors. Studies suggest that a positive balance between risk factors, stressful events, and protective factors modulates outcome in children at risk. Further study is needed more clearly delineate and define specific protective factors.

Another ethical issue raised by this case involves the question of diagnosis and the related issue of reimbursement. It would seem speculative at best to assign a definitive psychiatric diagnosis to a child who, despite multiple stressors, maintained a high level of functioning and denied any cardinal psychiatric symptoms. The "labeling" of such a child as a psychiatric patient might have important implications for her future. However, it appeared that regular contact with a supportive and interested adult, in the context of psychotherapy, was very helpful in facilitating the patient's immediate adjustment to a stressful situation. In general, reimbursement is not provided for services without definitive diagnoses, and public resources allocated for such interventions are rare as well. The question remains as to how to optimize such a child's development and the role of the child psychiatrist in providing or perhaps facilitating such services in response to felt (or chosen) ethical obligations.

EXAMPLE: BRYAN

Bryan is a 7-year-old boy who came for psychiatric evaluation and treatment at an outpatient clinic, accompanied by his mother and preadolescent sister. He was brought to the clinic because of his mother's sense that she "couldn't take it any longer." She complained that he constantly fought with his sister and was inattentive, disobedient, overactive, and noisy. Although Bryan generally calmed down when separated from his sister, his mother continued to feel anxious and unable to cope with his behavior. Bryan spent the daytime hours at a baby-sitter's house where he reportedly experienced few problems. He reportedly was respectful of his maternal grandfather, who used firm limit-setting to manage the patient's behavior.

Bryan's biological father was never married to his mother. He reportedly committed suicide shortly before the patient's birth.

The patient's mother reported that he sustained sex-

ual and physical abuse as a preschooler perpetrated by his sister's biological father (his stepfather). The sister was also a victim of this abuse and reported it approximately 1 year after it began. The patient's mother subsequently separated from her husband (the alleged perpetrator of the abuse) and began a relationship with her current boyfriend. He, however, had difficulty keeping a job, and the patient, his mother, and his sister moved in with his maternal grandparents. The grandparents did not allow Bryan's mother's boyfriend to come onto their property because they did not approve of him.

The patient had first begun to experience significant problems following the disclosure of the abuse he and his sister had suffered. He was hospitalized for disruptive behavior problems. His mother was told that he had attention deficit disorder and he was treated with an antidepressant, which resulted in some behavioral improvement, according to his mother. The family moved several times over the next couple of years because of financial problems, and the patient received no consistent medical or psychiatric care. Bryan's mother attributed his current difficulties to his lack of medication. She expressed concern about the patient running into the street and displaying physical aggression toward his sister. She also expressed frustration regarding her current situation, stating that she very much disliked being dependent on her parents but she realized that she had no other resources at present.

On examination, the patient was a 7-year-old boy who appeared somewhat small for his age and was rather disheveled. He was alert, active, and restless in the examination setting. He initiated frequent arguments with his sister. He maintained minimal eye contact with the examiner. Speech was normal in tone, volume, rate, rhythm, and latency; however, the patient had significant difficulties with articulation. His mood was basically euthymic, but his affect was irritable. He denied any hallucinations and there were no apparent delusions. The patient denied any thoughts of harming himself or others, although his play indicated aggressive themes. The patient was friendly and pleasant when seen individually in the playroom; when in the company of his mother and sister, he was constantly moving around the room and interrupting the conversation.

The patient had sustained severe physical, emotional, and sexual abuse; he subsequently began to exhibit significant behavior problems and was admitted to a psychiatric hospital. Although he reportedly improved with the use of an antidepressant, his follow-up care was inconsistent. The family had moved repeatedly, which was disruptive for the patient and his sister. At the time of the evaluation, they were living with their maternal grandparents but were not allowed to have visitors. This situation was particularly stressful for the patient's mother, who reported an escalating sense of frustration and hopelessness. Hence, the patient was subjected to environmental stressors, both in the psychosocial and emotional arenas, in addition to his attentional problems and history of abuse.

It was decided that a team approach would be most helpful in the treatment of Bryan and his family. The patient's mother was asked to make a commitment to remain in the local geographical area in order to protect the patient from further interruption of his treatment and she agreed. Following medical workup, Bryan was started on an antidepressant because of his reported prior response. Attempts were made to see the boy in individual psychotherapy and his family in family therapy; however, such an approach proved futile because the patient did not remain still in the presence of his mother and sister but intruded constantly in physical and verbal ways. Furthermore, the patient's mother was persistent in wanting to discuss her own concerns and her own feelings, leaving no time or motivation to discuss parenting issues. She did not respond to redirection, nor did the patient.

The decision was made to adopt a new format in the hopes of maintaining the patient and his family in treatment. At the beginning of each appointment, the family was seen together for a brief period by the child psychiatrist and therapist. During this time attempts were made to improve the family's ability to communicate with each other. The children were seen sequentially in individual play therapy by the therapist, while the patient's mother was seen individually by the child psychiatrist, who allowed her to focus on her own needs and issues in a psychodynamic context. Finally, Bryan was seen briefly by the child psychiatrist for a medication check. The patient's mother was asked to keep daily records of Bryan's behavior and to keep a diary of her own thoughts and feelings.

Following the implementation of this approach, the patient's behavior began to improve. Both children were noted to behave in a progressively more appropriate manner during the family portion of the sessions. Bryan and his sister engaged eagerly in play therapy, and both were able to function adequately in school.

The patient's mother disclosed a complex and chaotic history during her individual sessions. She had had numerous stormy interpersonal relationships throughout her life and was continually struggling with poverty. She formed a rather intense attachment to the child psychiatrist and was very compliant with treatment in terms of keeping appointments and performing the "homework" of the patient's behavioral charts and her own diary. Although environmental stressors continued (loss of several jobs and interactional difficulties with her parents), the patient's mother was able to make use of her individual sessions to explore her own identity and to formulate goals for the future.

After nearly a year of treatment, Bryan was doing much better. The departure of the child psychiatrist from the clinic afforded the opportunity for the patient's mother to process her experience of separation. Treatment was continued for several months after the child psychiatrist departed; however, the family elected to move to a neighboring area and treatment was again interrupted. Some months later Bryan was admitted to another psychiatric hospital with recurrence of behavior problems and increasing symptoms of conduct disorder. Again the patient's mother had difficulty attending to parenting issues in treatment but managed to comply superficially with the treatment team's expectations. At the time of discharge, the patient had again improved. The family was subsequently lost to follow-up.

Ethical questions raised by this case brings into play again the perspective of prioritizing the child's optimal individual development. Bryan and his family were not a "good fit" for traditional models of intervention. It quickly became apparent that psychopharmacotherapy, family therapy, play therapy, or psychodynamic psychotherapy for the patient's mother would not be of much benefit to Bryan or his family if employed in isolation or in a fragmented fashion. It was felt that the concurrent use of all these modalities in one setting would maximize the patient's chances of remaining in treatment and of continuing to grow and develop. In order to offset the course of this family's crisis-oriented life, attempts were made to introduce structure in the form of "homework"; these assignments were complied with, perhaps in response to the mother's perception of being respected and cared about by the treatment team. Although the chosen approach was expensive for the treatment team in terms of time and energy expenditure, it appeared to produce beneficial results, at least in the short term.

The basic dynamic in treatment involved a process of trying to perceive the family's needs, recognizing that they would be unable to attend to specific treatment issues when basic emotional survival needs were unmet. The goal of the team was to instill hope in Bryan and his family and to provide a positive experience of the mental health system. The patient's prognosis was guarded in the face of ongoing financial and emotional stress. It was felt that attempts to provide the family with respect rather than judgment would maximize the patient's continuing access to assistance from the mental health community.

This family had had multiple experiences of the community mental health system on both an inpatient and outpatient basis. They were witnesses to the inadequacy of this system. Public funding for mental health is scarce and not a national priority. Public funding for the mental health needs of children and their families is even more scarce and nonexistent in many places. The psychosocial stressor of poverty places children at risk for emotional and behavioral disorders, and the pattern often is perpetuated generationally. The ethical practice of child and adolescent psychiatry mandates an awareness of these difficulties regardless of one's own patient population and confers an obligation to serve as a political and economic advocate for the mental and emotional health and development of children and adolescents. Creative solutions will be needed to address the problems of intergenerational poverty and their impact on the mental health of children.

Conclusion

In this chapter we addressed ethical issues in child psychiatry from a clinical perspective. We stressed the importance of balanced choices of treatment modalities, the optimization of the individual child's growth and development, and the need for an appreciation of the perspectives of children and adolescents as individuals engaged in processes of continual change. An orientation to and appreciation of ethics in the training of child psychiatrists is also essential. A commitment to ethical practice will serve to anchor the child psychiatrist of the future, who will certainly face numerous challenges in the face of ongoing changes in the fields of medicine, social service, and economics.

The case of Tyler raised a number of concerns about confidentiality and the limits of privacy. His parents' "secret" about his adoption was an important impediment to his successful resolution of typical adolescent issues of identity. Helping both the patient and his parents decrease their hidden agendas allowed the family to facilitate of Tyler's progress. Child psychiatrists must take care to define their capacity to both honor and clarify the limits of confidentiality among patients and family members as well as other individuals involved with patients.

The case of Laurie illustrated the importance of issues related to informed consent. Her treatment was viewed as partial because of her parents' refusal to consent on her behalf to a trial of antidepressant medication. The child psychiatrist must maintain a current awareness of local legal options regarding informed consent to treatment. Each clinician will be faced with the need to facilitate and document informed consent and, in its absence, make reasonable decisions regarding disposition of patient care. Again, the individual child's developmental level frequently affects such decisions, which should be informed by the primacy of the child.

Reviewing the case of Anna provides several opportunities to consider the work of the child psychiatrist in the legal arena. These considerations are not simply classical forensic issues but relate to the importance of advocacy for the individual child. While trying to assist the court, the treatment team faced the reality of constraints inherent in conflicts among Anna's family members. A child psychiatrist in court may encounter requests or even demands from any or all parties present, including the judge. It is important to present material and formulate responses that are consistent with sound clinical practice and respect the needs of children.

Finally, the cases of Sarah and Bryan demonstrate the need for ethical perspectives when treating underserved populations. Sarah was a child with a remarkable capacity for resilience, which the child psychiatrist was challenged to reinforce. The clinician must be careful to identify and strengthen protective factors while striving to address and minimize risk factors. A commitment to prevention in child psychiatry will advance the development of all children at risk. Bryan was a child limited as much by his psychosocial constraints as by his psychiatric syndrome. Careful attention to the patient's mother and sister (in addition to medication management and individual therapy) improved his outcome in the short term; however, discontinuation of treatment led to further difficulties for Bryan. As health care reform raises questions regarding optimal length of treatment and use of resources in mental health systems, the child psychiatrist (as an individual and often as a team leader in a public system) will face critical decisions relating to treatment planning for children with inadequate resources. These decisions will inevitably include ethical components and will continue to challenge the field in the next century.

The cases presented by no means exhaust all pertinent ethical issues in child psychiatry. They do represent an attempt to explicate ethical factors commonly present in clinical practice. It is likely that these factors, and certainly others, will become more complex in the years ahead. Child psychiatrists, whether seasoned or newly trained, will do well to use the lens of a sound knowledge base of child development and of primacy of the child to focus their process of ethical decision making. It is important to remember that the ethical conduct of child psychiatrists in the future may well remain a sign of hope as the field itself strives to optimize its own growth and development in the service of all children.

SUGGESTED READINGS

Adler, R. (1995). To Tell or Not to Tell: The Psychiatrist and Child Abuse, *Australian & New Zealand Journal of Psychiatry, 29* (2), 190–198.

American Academy of Child Psychiatry. (1982). *Principles of practice of child and adolescent psychiatry.* Washington, DC: Author.

Arnold, L. E., Stoff, D. M., Cook, E., Jr., Cohen, D. J., Kruesi, M., Wright, C., Hattab, J., Graham, P., Zametkin, A., Castellanos, F. X., McMahon, W., & Leckman, J. F. (1995). Ethical issues in biological psychiatric research with children and adolescents. *Journal of the American Academy of Child and Adolescent Psychiatry, 34* (7), 929–939.

Battle, C. U., Kreisberg, R. V., O'Mahoney, K., Chitwood, D. L. (1989). Ethical and developmental considerations in caring for hospitalized adolescents. *Journal of Adolescent Health Care, 10,* 479–489.

Conoley, J. C., Larson, P. (1995). *Ethical Decision Making in Therapy: Feminist Perspectives.* New York: Guilford Press.

Dulmus, C. N., Wodarski, J. S. (1996). Assessment and Effective Treatments of Childhood Psychopathology: Responsibilities and Implications for Practice, *Journal of Child & Adolescent Group Therapy, 6* (2), 75–99.

Ehrenreich, N. S., & Melton, G. B. (1983). Ethical and legal issues in the treatment of children. In I. B. Weiner (Ed.), *Handbook of clinical child psychology.* New York: John Wiley & Sons.

Fassler, M. D. (1992). Ethical issues in Child and Adolescent Psychiatry, *Journal of the American Academy of Child and Adolescent Psychiatry, 31,* 3.

Geraty, R. D., Hendren, R. L., Flaa, C. J. (1992). Ethical perspectives on managed care as it relates to child and adolescent psychiatry. *Journal of the American Academy of Child Adolescent Psychiatry, 31,* 3.

Green, J., & Stewart, A. (1987). Ethical issues in child and adolescent psychiatry. *Journal of Medical Ethics, 13,* 5–11.

Hesson, K., Bakal, D., Dobson, K. S. (1993). Legal and Ethical Issues Concerning Children's Rights of Consent. *Canadian Psychology, 34* (3), 317–328.

Johnson, H. C., Cournoyer, D. E., Bond, B. M. (1995). Professional Ethics and Parents as Consumers. *Families in Society, 76* (7), 408–420.

Jones, D., Dickenson, D., Devereux, J. (1994). The Favoured Child? *Journal of Medical Ethics, 20* (2), 108–111.

Koocher, G., Keith-Spiegel, P. (1990). *Children, ethics and the law.* Lincoln: University of Nebraska Press.

Levine, M., Anderson, E., Ferretti, L., Steinberg, K. (1993). Legal and Ethical Issues Affecting Clinical Child Psychology. *Advances in Clinical Child Psychology, 15:* 81–120.

Macklin, R. (1992). *Social Research on Children and Adolescents: Ethical Issues.* Newbury Park: Sage Publications.

Melton, G. B., Stanley, B. H. (1996). *Research Ethics: A Psychological Approach.* Lincoln: University of Nebraska Press.

Michels, R. Training in psychiatric ethics. *Psychiatric Ethics,* 295–305.

Munir, K., & Earls, F. (1992). Ethical principles governing research in child and adolescent psychiatry. *Journal of the American Academy of Child and Adolescent Psychiatry, 31,* 3. pp. 408–14.

Parker, J. G. (1995). Chemical Restraints and Children: Autonomy or Veracity? *Perspectives in Psychiatric Care, 31* (2), 25–29.

Racusin, R. J., & Felsman, J. K. (1986). Reporting child abuse: The ethical obligation to inform parents. *Journal of the American Academy of Child Psychiatry, 25* (4), 485–489.

Schetky, D. H. (1992). Ethical issues in forensic child and adolescent psychiatry. *Journal of the American Academy of Child and Adolescent Psychiatry, 31,* 3. pp. 403–407.

Schneider, S. (1986). The adoptee: Interface between psychiatry, law and ethics." *Med Law, 5,* 441–444.

Schoeman, F. Childhood competence and autonomy. *Journal of Legal Studies,* pp. 267–287.

Schoeman, F. (1985). Parental discretion and children's rights: Background and implications for medical decision-making. *Journal of Medicine and Philosophy, 10,* 45–61.

Schwartz, I. M. (1989). Hospitalization of adolescents for psychiatric and substance abuse treatment. *Journal of Adolescent Health Care, 10,* 473–478.

Scott-Jones, D. (1994). Ethical Issues in Reporting and Referring in Research with Low-Income Minority Children, *Ethics & Behavior, 4* (2), 97–108.

Sondheimer, A., & Martucci, L. C. (1992). An approach to teaching ethics in child and adolescent psychiatry. *Journal of the American Academy of Child and Adolescent Psychiatry, 31,* 3. pp. 415–22.

Sondheimier, A. (1996). Ethics and Child and Adolescent Psychiatry: Curricular Design and Clinical Teaching, *Academic Psychiatry, 20* (3), 150–157.

SECTION VII

Professional Issues in Child and Adolescent Psychiatry

35 / Health Insurance and Child/Adolescent Psychiatry

David B. Pruitt and Laurel J. Kiser

What Does Mental Health Care for Children and Adolescents Cost?

According to prevalence estimates, 20% for children and adolescents in the United States have a diagnosable mental disorder; of those, 19 to 13% display substantial functional impairment due to a serious emotional disturbance (Friedman, Katz-Leavy, Manderscheid, & Sondheimer, 1996). Thus the costs associated with providing treatment are substantial. In 1990 cost estimates for mental health treatment of children and adolescents reached 4.8 billion, a figure representing about 7.1% of the total yearly expenditures for mental health care. If the costs of mental health care for adolescents are split into service components, it is estimated that 46% of the costs for care were spent on inpatient care, 28% on residential treatment, and 26% on ambulatory and outpatient services (Hoagwood & Rupp, 1994). Not only are the costs of mental health care for children and youths substantial, as with other types of health care, they have been increasing rapidly. For illustration, the cost of treatment in residential treatment centers rose from $978 million in 1986 to $1.305 billion in 1988 (Sunshine, Witkin, Atay, & Mandertscheid, 1991).

Clearly the cost estimates listed here cover only the delivery of direct services. As with all other parts of our health care system, the focus is on the treatment of mental illness versus the promotion of mental health. Thus this chapter focuses primarily on the funding of treatment for mental illness in children and adolescents.

Who Pays for Mental Health Care for Children and Adolescents?

Who pays for the promotion of mental health and the treatment of mental illnesses for children and adolescents? Norman V. Lourie (1979) lists the following programs and funding sources that concern children with mental health needs:

- Medicaid and early and periodic screening
- Maternal and child health
- Women, infants, and children initiatives
- School health programs
- Education for the handicapped
- Vocational rehabilitation
- Child welfare
- Nutrition programs
- Youth and delinquency
- Social services: Title XX of the Social Security Act covers a wide range of services to children, including day care, foster home care, community care, and so forth

Lourie stresses the overlapping roles and responsibilities of the different social/health programs and funding sources. Certainly responsibility for the funding of mental health services to children and adolescents with mental disorders is shared by "multiple key service systems, including agencies for mental health, general health, education, child welfare, juvenile justice, and substance abuse" (Hoagwood & Rupp, 1994, p. 53). For purposes of this chapter, we view mental health and mental illnesses as generally perceived broader terms funded through more diversified sources. Psychiatric care, when allied with medical care, is funded by health care insurers, private and public, and incorporates the underlying concept of medical necessity. "Simply stated, it [medical necessity] means that health insurance should pay only for medical procedures performed in the treatment of a specific medical diagnosis" (Lourie Howe, & Roebuck, 1996, p. 42).

Following a brief description of the historical foundations of health insurance, this chapter presents overviews of the major funding sources for psychiatric treatment for children and adolescents, including indemnity insurance, managed care, and Medicaid. In each section a brief historical background is presented, followed by current trends and issues specific to child and adolescent populations. Estimates of mental health care expenditures suggest that 44% are paid by private insurance companies, 28% by the federal government, and the remaining 28% by state and local government (Geraty et al., 1994).

HISTORICAL FOUNDATIONS OF HEALTH INSURANCE

Insurance coverage for child/adolescent psychiatric treatment is interwoven with past, present, and future relationships to general medical health insurance. Kevin Anderson (1991) traced health insurance in the United States to 1798, when Congress established a prepaid health care plan funded through reductions in wages, the Marine Hospital Service for Merchant Sailors. Geraty traced the history to the "horse and buggy days [when] only individuals with funds to pay for private care were able to receive care. Charitable organizations and physicians with a generous spirit began to provide care for patients without funds. The concept of insuring healthcare as a method of payment initially began in the early 20th century" (Geraty, Hendren, & Flaa, 1992, p. 398).

Indemnity health insurance (protection or security against future damage or loss) developed in the late 1800s (Anderson, 1991) and grew in popularity during and after World War II, when there existed stiff competition for workers and restraints on wage increases. Health insurance took on fringe benefit meaning to the worker and became an employer bargaining chip pushed by union negotiators in wage and benefit discussions. Private-sector insurance companies multiplied, including Blue Cross/Blue Shield.

Blue Cross/Blue Shield: The development of Blue Cross/Blue Shield is an example of the fortuitous and whimsical developmental history of the private health insurance industry in the United States. "During the Depression, hospitals' desire for a secure source of payment and patients' desire for insurance against large medical expenses combined to set the stage for the birth and growth of Blue Cross Hospital Insurance" (McGuire, 1986). Initially these plans funded only hospital care, which was equated with catastrophic care. As the attractiveness of these insurance benefits escalated, so did the number of commercial health insurance plans, and competition drove the evolution of outpatient insurance coverage with physician services being covered specifically under the Blue Shield plan. Blue Cross/Blue Shield plans developed in various states with little or no competition between the individual plans (Muszynski et al., 1984).

Working men and women sought this expanding insurance coverage, and, in the mid-1960s, a component of Lyndon B. Johnson's Great Society provided expanded health insurance to the elderly through Medicare and to the poor through Medicaid. The goal of these programs was universal health care access; the remaining population of uninsured or underinsured were to be provided health care through tax-supported city and county hospital and clinic systems. The public quickly became accustomed to the very best, or at least the highest technological aspects of health care. Yet out of the Vietnam War and the Great Society, there came general economic and health care inflation with a vengeance. President Richard Nixon assessed the political forces (the public demanded free care, quality care, and free choice of their individual physician) and decided that competition in the health care marketplace was the answer; this competition stimulated development of prepaid health maintenance organizations.

Inflation continued in all public and private insurance programs; the political sacred cow of Medicare dealt with this inflation through a prospective payment system, paying hospitals a fixed dollar amount based on diagnosis (diagnostic-related groups, or DRGs). Medicaid dealt with the inflation through cutting benefits and tightening income-qualifying eligibility standards. Psychiatry was viewed as different from the rest of health care in that benefits for mental disorders were separate and unequal. And as Medicare and Medicaid constricted and restricted their payments, hospitals and medical educators attempted to pass along their costs to the private insurance patient population. The private insurance sector responded with managed care programs, which developed and evolved rapidly.

Separate and Unequal: While physical illness traditionally has been well insured, mental illness receives lesser insurance coverage. Recently there has occurred a major erosion of psychiatric benefits. The historical, traditional focus of inpatient coverage and the insurers' reluctance to expand outpatient mental disorder coverage on a par with physical-illness coverage has had perplexing effects. The outpatient psychiatric insurance coverage has generally had significant dollar deductibles, patient copayment, and limited yearly and lifetime maximum benefits that are significantly lower than that offered for physical illnesses. Insurers have resisted giving parity in the coverage of mental illness ostensibly due to moral hazards and adverse selection. "Moral hazard" relates to the prospect that recipients who have insurance coverage will utilize more of that type of health service. "Adverse selection" relates to the fact that insurance companies that offer more attractive insurance coverage in a given health area will attract a sicker patient population in that particular area (McGuire, 1986). The issue of parity for mental health will remain a major focus within the health care reform debate.

INDEMNITY HEALTH INSURANCE

Employers purchase indemnity insurance plans to cover the costs of health care for their employees. These plans are based on premiums that are calculated based on population risk assessments done by the insurer. Typically the premiums are a shared expense between the employer and employee. Under indemnity plans, approximately 7% of the total health care dollar is allocated for mental health care (Freeman & Trabin, 1994).

The insurance industry has viewed indemnity plans as a claims payment business versus a care management business (Geraty et. al., 1994), with utilization of medical and mental health services dictated solely by benefit design. Under these plans, providers are reimbursed on a fee-for-service basis; the potential underlying fiscal incentive is to provide more services.

Traditionally, indemnity insurance plans established separate benefit packages for general health and for mental health/substance abuse. Under the mental health benefit package, plans created 2 funding buckets, 1 for inpatient and 1 for outpatient treatment. In addition, often these plans were structured to favor inpatient psychiatric treatment through better reimbursement or through severely limiting benefits for outpatient care. Typical plans limited outpatient visits to 30 per year with significant copayments-and set 30- to 60-day limits on inpatient treatment with little or no copayment (Lourie et al., 1996).

Another mechanism indemnity plans use to limit their risk exposure is to impose yearly and lifetime maximums on mental health care. These plan limitations often place the burden of long—term care for children with serious emotional disturbances on families or, in many instances, on publicly funded programs. Parents of such children often are placed in the difficult position of turning to public assistance when they have exhausted the limited private resources available to them; frequently they are required to relinquish custody of their child to the state to procure appropriate treatment resources.

MANAGED CARE

Just as the nonpsychiatric medical health care system was forced to deal with the issue of cost through a prospective payment system and diagnostic-related groups, psychiatry became the special recipient (victim?) of managed behavioral health care. "Managed care companies typically do not own hospitals or operate medical facilities, but rather sell a variety of services to insurers, corporations, and third-party administrators to help them determine when, where, and how patients should receive health care services. These services include case management, utilization review, quality assurance, preferred provider arrangements, creative pricing, the goal being reduction in healthcare costs" ("Wall Street's Darlings," 1987, p. 1). The American Managed Behavioral Healthcare Association (AMBHA) has determined that managed care companies can achieve cost savings of up to 40 to 50% by reducing unnecessary utilization and by decreasing unit costs (discounted fee-for-service arrangements, volume discounts, etc.). These cost savings are offset by 10 to 15% added administrative costs for net savings of between 25 and 40% (Melek, 1994).

Geraty et al. (1992) traced the evolution of managed care through peer and utilization review committees in hospitals (first generation); through external utilization managed care companies with precertification, concurrent review, and discharge planning (second generation); through service delivery systems such as health maintenance organizations that negotiate regarding cost and quality of care based on certain criteria (third generation); to organized systems of care consisting of providers with similar treatment practice philosophies and styles (fourth generation).

Managed care contracts often are based on prepaid capitation agreements. In other words, the management company is paid a set amount for each enrollee covered by the contract. Capitation arrangements usually are figured using a single capitation rate for the entire population of covered lives versus risk-adjusted rates that take into account the varying treatment needs of different populations, such as children, adolescents, or the serious and persistently mentally ill. Under capitation only about 3% of the total health care dollar is allocated for mental health and substance abuse treatment (Freeman & Trabin, 1994). Due to the nature of capitation, the potential fiscal incentives under this system of service delivery favor underidentification and treatment.

The forces that created managed care, specifically those within child and adolescent psychiatry, produced overutilization of the most expensive, inpatient forms of treatment. Theoretically and ideally, mental health managed care encourages flexibility in the development of various treatment settings and funding for all components of the psychiatric continuum of care, balancing access to service with cost of those services and the quality of the overall treatment process. In reality, too many of the managed behavioral health care companies are predominately driven to reduce costs, obstruct access to care, and ignore a population in need of treatment. For many child and adolescent psychiatrists, managed care has resulted in (1) restrictions on reimbursable services, (2) strict adherence to medical necessity/level-of-care placement criteria, (3) discounted rates, and (4) increased administrative time and costs.

MEDICAID

Medicaid is the primary, federally regulated, health insurance program for low-income persons. It is financed by federal and state government and administered by the states (Muszynski, Brady, & Sharstein, 1984). The federal guidelines allow states flexibility on what services they provide, who provides those services, income eligibility criteria of the served population, the treatment setting for delivering the services, and the funding formulas set between state and federal government. Historically, Medicaid has been a major financier of mental health care.

In traditional Medicaid programs, consumers have the freedom to choose their own providers, who are reimbursed on a fee-for-service basis. Physician/provider compensation, under this fee-for-service agreement, is often low compared with the usual and customary rates paid by private insurers. As with indemnity insurance, benefit packages available under traditional Medicaid programs favor inpatient over outpatient treatment.

Escalating health care costs have jeopardized the ability of many states and the federal government to maintain the Medicaid mandate. Between 1983 and 1993 the Medicaid costs rose $100 million, and 10 million more recipients were enrolled in the program. In order to contain costs, states have moved aggressively to reform their Medicaid programs. Armed with waivers from the Health Care Financing Administration (HCFA), a majority of states have begun to implement managed Medicaid programs, many of which include

provisions for the delivery of mental health and substance abuse services. Shifts in the delivery of care under managed Medicaid have resulted in a tightening of "medical necessity criteria," establishment of gatekeepers or utilization review procedures to control access to services, use of expanded services including community-based, inpatient alternatives, and movement away from fee-for-service payment mechanisms to capitation arrangements.

Issues Specific to the Funding of Child and Adolescent Psychiatry

How does the funding of mental health care impact children and adolescents? Funding mechanisms and insurance reform have numerous effects on the treatment of children and adolescents with psychiatric disorders.

MULTIPLE FUNDING SOURCES

The fact that there are multiple players and stakeholders involved in the delivery and payment of mental health services to children and adolescents is of major significance. The inability of the various social/health/educational/legal programs to coordinate service delivery and pool resources severely hampers the current system of care. Problems with the current system include lack of coordination in service planning and implementation, duplication of services, underidentification of treatable problems, failure of a large proportion of children with mental health needs to receive any services, and significant cost-shifting between service systems.

ECONOMIC CONSIDERATIONS DRIVING CARE DECISIONS

Economic considerations frequently influence the decisions made regarding mental health care provided for children and adolescents. Rather than the medical needs and interests of the child, level-of-care placement decisions for mentally ill children are too often driven by financial factors. Inpatient psychiatric treatment of adolescents provides perhaps the most striking example of utilization driven by economic policy. The insurance industry, in addressing concerns regarding cover-

488

age for mental illness, designed policies favoring the use of in-hospital treatment. Thus the lucrative nature of inpatient psychiatric care for children and adolescents led to overutilization of the modality and proliferation of for-profit, institutional programs. This traditional emphasis on costly institutionalization was maintained at the expense of viable alternatives, such as community-based programs, family preservation programs, case management, and coordination services (Inouye, 1988).

Recent changes in benefit structures limiting the inpatient benefit have resulted in decreases in both admissions and length of stays, highlighting the effect of benefit design on utilization (Patrick et al., 1993). Policy redesign must include safeguards designed to prevent clinical decision making from being overly influenced by marketplace considerations (Craig, 1988).

NEED FOR COMPREHENSIVE CARE

We in child and adolescent psychiatry interface with patients who have a significant number of chronic illnesses many of them can be placed in the moderate to severe range of disability. Comorbid and concurrent psychiatric, social, educational, and medical troubles often are found. The nature and definition of child/adolescent psychiatric illness and the treatment setting that can best deal with a specific illness at a specific severity level can vary. The overlaps and boundaries between systems providing services in mental health, education, juvenile justice, housing, and social services add complexity. Due to these ambiguities and complexities, which McGuire (1986) described as a lack of understanding of the technology of mental health treatment, children and adolescents require a comprehensive approach to treatment.

Continuum of Care: This specific patient population needs a coordinated continuum of services for effective treatment. As mentioned earlier, economic influences have profoundly affected the delivery of mental health care to children and adolescents. During the 1970s and 1980s, there was a significant increase in the number of inpatient hospital beds for children and adolescents and a dearth of alternatives to inpatient programs. The need to treat children and adolescents in the least-restrictive, yet therapeutically appropriate, setting through a coordinated, continuum of care was thwarted, and even professional standards and ethics were compromised.

As child psychiatric professionals, we should be able to determine the appropriate formula of outpatient, intensive outpatient, day treatment, partial hospital, inpatient and residential treatment slots necessary to serve a given population adequately. Treatment outcome studies should allow us to determine which treatment setting best serves a particular child. Treatment protocols, along with appropriate internal and external utilization review monitoring, should allow a balancing of cost, treatment effectiveness, access to care, and appropriate treatment intensity. Spending too much money or too little money, overutilization or underutilization of mental health services, all have significant ethical, moral, and political fallout. The desire to match a child's or adolescent's treatment needs with the appropriate level of service along the continuum should drive patient placement decisions.

THE NEED FOR COVERAGE OF SERVICES TO PARENTS AND FAMILY MEMBERS

The vast majority of children and adolescents live as dependents within some form of family. As such, much of their existence, health, and wellness is integrally related to the functioning of their caregivers and other family members. Treatment of children and adolescents in isolation of this reality provides only partial and temporary cures and solutions. In order to obtain the desired treatment outcomes, insurance companies need to fund therapeutic services for parents and families adequately.

THE NEED FOR LONGER LENGTHS OF STAY

Child and adolescents typically require longer lengths of stay than do adults to address their treatment needs adequately. Longer stays in treatment are necessary due to the complexities in diagnostic assessments often encountered, the number of comorbid conditions treated within this population, and the dependency and interrelated issues of parental and family functioning. Banchik (1993) estimates that adults require an average of 12 to 16 visits to intensive partial hospital programs; adolescents often require 20 or more. Similar differences in length-of-stay requirements among various age groups are noted throughout the other modalities along the continuum of care.

THE NEED FOR HIGHER COSTS
PER UNIT OF SERVICE

In addition to requiring longer lengths of stay, the costs to providers of caring for children and adolescents are greater. Increased unit costs are associated with the need for higher staff–patient ratios and the need for staff members with additional and specific training and experience in the assessment and treatment of child and adolescent disorders (Pruitt et al., 1987). Thus at each level of care, the unit costs on child and adolescent services should be higher than on adult services; reimbursement rates should correspond.

THE NEED FOR EARLY INTERVENTION
AND PREVENTION

Due to the developmental and dependency issues specific to child and adolescent psychiatry, early identification of and intervention with mental illness provides special treatment opportunities. The earlier problems and risk factors are identified and ameliorated, the easier is the task of stopping the progression of illness (Pruitt et al., 1987). Health insurance funding of prevention and wellness programs and also early identification screenings are of critical importance. Additionally, long-term contracts for provision of care are necessary to provide the appropriate incentives for improving population health.

Conclusion

The question of how we fund mental health and treatment for mental illness will be a major challenge in the next year, decade, and century. There will be no simple solution. We are products of our history and should learn from that history. Attempts at national health care reform have been numerous, from a variety of separate measures to sweeping overall reform. Some of those bills attempted to modify the present system through mechanisms to provide coverage to the underinsured and uninsured. The pivotal issues were cost, quality, and access to health care. Shorter-term stopgap solutions involve different funding formulas, different managed care concepts, and different insurance benefits design strategies. For the longer term, a reorganization of the method and source of payment and modification of the system of delivery of services will dominate.

The basic inherently inflationary problems of the present system are forcing reform of our major health care systems. The resultant reform will most likely contain provisions for basic health care with more extensive rationing of specialty services ("Caring for the Uninsured and Underinsured," 1991). It is essential that psychiatry and child psychiatry be included in the basic packages and not be considered elective.

Much of health care reform will be carried out in the political arena. Child/adolescent psychiatry must be able to carry out a convincing political dialogue. To do so, it must view itself within the context of psychiatry, pediatrics, and medicine in general. Our allies, the coalition that will be formed, may consist of very strange bedfellows—organized medicine, academic medical centers, consumer patient groups such as the National Alliance for the Mentally Ill (NAMI), pediatricians, psychologists, and social workers. Forming coalitions to advocate for children will be essential. We must advocate for children and, at times, for psychiatry even in a self-serving fashion if we are sure that the survival of child and adolescent psychiatry is important to the well-being of children. We must persuade the politicians who represent the public that by serving children and practicing prevention, we foster the making of adults who will display a lifelong increase in their work, health, and social productivity.

REFERENCES

Anderson, K. (1991, March 11). How the cost spiral started: Indemnity plans "doomed to fail." *USA Today,* Section 2B.

Banchik, D. (1993). The psychiatric services industry: The next generation. Irvine, CA, L.H. Friend, Weinress & Frankson.

Caring for the uninsured and underinsured. (1991).

Journal of the American Medical Association, 265 (19), 2437–2624.

Freeman, M. A., & Trabin, T. (1994). Managed behavioral healthcare: History, models, key issues, and future course. Behavioral Health Alliance.

Friedman, R. M., Katz-Leavy, J. W., Manderscheid, R. W., & Sondheimer, D. L. (1996). Prevalence of serious emotional disturbance in children and adolescents. In R. W. Manderscheid, & M. A. Sonnenschein (Eds.), *Mental health, United States, 1996*. Washington DC. U. S. Department of Health and Human Services. pp. 71–88.

Geraty, R., Bartlett, J., Hill, E., Lee, F., Shusterman, A., & Waxman, A. (March/April 1994). The impact of managed behavioral healthcare on the costs of psychiatric and chemical dependency treatment. *Behavioral Healthcare Tomorrow, 3* (2), 18–30.

Geraty, R., Hendren, R. L., Flaa, C. (1992). Ethical perspectives on managed care. *Journal of the American Academy of Child and Adolescent Psychiatry, 31* (3), 398–402.

Hoagwood, K., & Rupp, A. (1994). Mental health service needs, use, and costs for children and adolescents with mental disorders and their families: Preliminary evidence. In R. W. Manderscheid & M. A. Sonnenschein, (Eds.), *Mental health, United States, 1994*. Washington, DC. U. S. Department of Health and Human Services. pp. 52–61.

Lourie, I. S., Howe, S. W., & Roebuck, L. L. (1996). Lessons learned from two behavioral managed care approaches with special implication for children, adolescents, and families. In R. W. Manderscheid, & M. A. Sonnenschein (Eds.), *Mental health, United States, 1996*. Washington, D.C. U. S. Department of Health and Human Services. pp. 27–44.

Lourie, N. V. (1979). The impact of multisource funding. In I. N. Berlin and L. A. Stone (Eds.), *Basic handbook of child psychiatry*, (vol. 4, p. 508). New York: Basic Books.

McGuire, T. G. (1986). Economics of mental health: Financing and service usage. In R. Michels & J. O. Cavenar, Jr. (Eds.), *Psychiatry* Greenwich, Connecticut, Jai Press, Inc. (vol. 5, p. 3637).

Melek, S. P. (1994). *Managed behavioral healthcare cost report*. Washington, DC: American Behavioral Managed Healthcare Association.

Muszynski, S., Brady, J., & Sharstein, S. S. (1984). Paying for psychiatric care: Private health insurance coverage. *Psychiatric Annals, 14* (12), 866–867.

Pruitt, D. B., Enzer, C., Geraty, R., Gillman, A., Graffagnino, P., Hartmann, L., Sendi, I., & Axelson, A. (1987). *Child and adolescent psychiatry: Treatment and insurance issues*. Washington, DC: American Academy of Child and Adolescent Psychiatry.

Sunshine, J. H., Witkin, M. J., Atay, J. E., & Manderscheid, R. W. (1991). *Residential treatment centers and other organized mental health care for children and youth: United States, 1988*. Rockville, MD National Institute of Mental Health Statistical Note No. 198.

Wall Street's darlings: Managed care companies carving insurance niche. (1987, February 6) *American Medical News*. pp. 16–20.

36 / Managed Care as Viewed from the Managed Behavioral Health Care Organization Perspective

Ian A. Shaffer and Marsha H. Nelson

This chapter looks at how managed behavioral health care organizations (MBHOs) emerged and how they attempt to achieve optimal balance in meeting the needs of patients, providers, and payors.

Managed care for behavioral health evolved out of a desire by third-party payors to address 2 issues: cost containment and a concern about the value received for dollars spent within their benefit plans. Many plans had already attained some measure of cost control by implementing benefit limits (i.e., by "capping" the maximum number of days or visits available to patients within a benefit year or cycle). Increasingly, however, concerns arose about the adequacy, appropriateness, and quality of the care being delivered. Was it really helping people? There seemed to be little concrete evidence that it was. That lack of evidence coupled with rising costs contributed to a credibility gap between payors and providers of care. This, in turn, led payors to look for another entity that could attend to both the cost and the qualitative aspects of care. In the late 1980s, this fact was highlighted in a private conversation with executives of one of the largest insurance companies in the country. They were seeking the services of a managed behavioral health care organization because they knew that their capped behavioral health benefit was not sufficient to cover treatment for extremely ill individuals. They wanted to feel assured that that those who were very sick would get the coverage they needed and that the benefit would not otherwise be "exploited." Under those conditions, they stated that they would consider lifting their benefit maximums and going with a virtually unlimited benefit.

Similarly, any organizations that wanted to avoid significantly limiting their benefits felt compelled to take steps to stabilize sharply rising costs. However, they too wanted demonstrated value for the dollars they were willing to spend. One such organization was a multinational Fortune 500 company known for the generous benefits it made available to employees. Concerned about escalating costs, it surveyed its employees, asking, among other things, how they chose practitioners when seeking treatment for mental illness and substance abuse. The survey showed that a majority of its employees and their dependents selected behavioral health care providers from the Yellow Pages. Once the company discovered this, concern arose over whether benefit plan beneficiaries were connecting with the level of care and practitioner that represented the optimal, most cost-effective match for their needs. The company decided to bring managed care to its behavioral health benefits to achieve cost containment while preserving the existing benefit level. The decision also reflected a desire to help assure the quality of treatment services, which was achieved by supporting linkage to appropriate providers of care at the point of referral, by monitoring care to assess ongoing quality, and by facilitating the provision of all medically necessary services.

The foregoing examples are typical of the path taken by increasing numbers of behavioral health care payors who moved into managed care. Currently the ranks of such payors are being increased by public sector payors (states, countries, and cities) that are seeking federal Medicaid waivers to permit them to utilize managed care. Their story is the same—on the one hand, costs spiraling out of control putting benefits at risk, and, on the other, a desire to measure and, where indicated, to improve the quality of the care being received. The challenge for MBHOs in achieving these objectives is to find an effective way to balance the interests of all the affected constituencies—the patients, the providers, and the payors. All share the goal of wanting the patient to get well (or attain the maximum improvement possible), but sometimes disagreement arises about the best way to achieve that goal. Balancing these competing interests successfully is essential to retaining access to treatment for those in need.

How an MBHO Works

To maintain consistency in clinical decision making, MBHOs establish clinical criteria for admission to and continuing treatment within the various levels of care. Increasingly, they are also developing diagnosis-based treatment guidelines and protocols. Early on, MBHOs believed that if they made public their criteria, they would lose their competitive edge in the marketplace. They also believed that if providers were in possession of the criteria, some might use this knowledge to try to mislead reviewers. Failure to share their criteria sets openly undermined cooperation between practitioners and MBHOs. It heightened distrust and reinforced the suspicion that MBHOs were purely after cost control and would try to achieve lower costs by creating hidden obstacles to care. MBHOs recognized the need to enhance the working relationship and to improve provider satisfaction with managed care, so they began releasing their clinical criteria. Today most MBHOs share their criteria for care. (For more details on this subject, see the discussion by Rodriguez, 1994.)

In developing their clinical criteria, MBHOs seek to match treatment resources to patient needs in the context of a managed care philosophy. To do this they strive to incorporate national consensus standards of appropriateness. What is the philosophy of managed care? The American Psychiatric Association was an early provider of peer review and utilization review services. It took the position that if appropriate treatment were provided at the least restrictive level at which the patient could be cared for safely, cost containment logically would follow. (The distinction between peer review and utilization review is articulated by Shueman and Penner, 1988, who also provide a good history of the pioneering role of the American Psychiatric and American Psychological associations in the early development of behavioral health managed care practices.) One example of the managed care philosophy is the definition of medical necessity utilized by Value Behavioral Health, the MBHO at which both authors are employed. It defines medically necessary treatment as being a service or supply that it has determined is:

1. An adequate and essential therapeutic response provided for evaluation or treatment consistent with the symptoms, proper diagnosis, and treat-

ment appropriate for the specific participant's illness, disease, or condition as defined by standard diagnostic nomenclatures the fourth edition of the *Diagnostic and Statistical Manual of Mental Disorders* or its equivalent in the current edition of the *International Classification of Diseases*

2. Reasonably expected to improve the participant's illness, condition, or level of functioning

3. Safe and effective according to nationally accepted standard clinical evidence generally recognized by mental health or substance abuse care professionals or publications

4. The appropriate and cost-effective level of care that can safely be provided for the specific participant's diagnosed condition in accordance with the professional and technical standards adopted by Value Behavioral Health

The process used by Value Behavioral Health to develop clinical criteria and policies reflects practices common among MBHOs. Initially, these criteria were developed through a joint study project with the quality assurance committee of a major Washington, D.C., area hospital. Subsequently, Value Behavioral Health's clinical criteria, as well as its clinical policies, continue to be regularly revised and updated; as new needs are identified, ongoing development and revision occur. Typically, such new policy development originates in the course of interaction with providers; specifically, this occurs when requests are received for certification of new modalities or programmatic approaches to care. A need to develop and/or revise clinical criteria also may be triggered as new data enter the field—as when findings are published by clinical organizations or academic institutions. To cope with this continuous influx of information, the Corporate Medical Affairs Department acts to coordinate clinical policy/procedure/criteria development. Input may be obtained from internal and external experts in the subject area as well as from current literature, clinical organizations, and treatment providers. Any proposed criteria revisions and additions that arise from this input are then reviewed by a body of senior clinicians who comprise Value Behavioral Health's Clinical Policy Committee. Once the material and revisions have received their final critique, the company will approve the criteria. At this point, the approved policies are incorporated into the corporate Clinical Policy and Procedure Manual. Then, these clinical criteria are shared with the providers of care through a provider manual.

Implementation of clinical policies must take into account the requirements of the third-party payors that purchase the MBHO's services. For example, in order to have the maximum flexibility to manage care, MBHOs typically advocate for more extensive, rather than limited, benefits. Payors, however, sometimes present benefit programs with limited coverage. This means that clinical "certification" decisions involve a balance between the available coverage, on the one hand, and a recognition of the patient's current as well as potential future needs, on the other. Providers sometimes fail to distinguish the MBHO from the benefit plan that it is administering and erroneously conclude that the MBHO is once again trying to limit access to care in an effort to save money.

Payors hold the MBHO accountable for both the level of expenditure and for such qualitative aspects of care as access and appropriateness of clinical decision making. Accordingly, payors impose varying levels of oversight on the MBHO's activities. Thus many payors bring in outside consulting firms periodically to review the MBHO's policies and procedures as well as to audit their implementation. One company, with three-quarters of a million employees and enrolled dependents covered by its benefit plan, utilized a Mental Health Advisory Board to oversee its managed behavioral health care program (Astrachan et al., 1995) The Advisory Board, composed of prominent clinicians representing psychiatry, psychology, and social work, participated in policy development for the client's benefit plan and went to the MBHO several times a year to review records, assess policies and procedures, and observe performance. The Board also received quarterly quality assurance reports to ensure that the MBHO was not sacrificing quality while fulfilling its mandate to justify expenditures under the plan. The Board examined quality of care along such dimensions as provider credentialing and network maintenance (appropriate density and mix), management of referral calls at the requisite level of urgency, appropriate use of the client's Employee Assistance Program, adequacy of MBHO staffing in needed specialty areas for peer review (e.g., child and adolescent psychiatry, addictions), and the effectiveness with which the MBHO worked with treatment providers to assure use of a broad spectrum of services under this client's almost unlimited benefit plan.

In short, MBHOs must implement their care

management programs in the context of the payors benefit plan and program objectives. Among these objectives is the monitoring of the levels of satisfaction with the program on the part of both patients and providers for the purpose of improving it. Surveys generally are used to track this. Therefore, MBHOs continuously seek ways to become more user friendly both for patients and for treatment providers. Periodically, new or revised clinical policies, procedures, or criteria are debated internally. When this happens, the changes are always considered in light of several factors, including their likely impact on patients and providers as well as their contribution to meeting client (payor) objectives and to supporting sound clinical practice.

Managed Care Successes

While the question of the overall impact of managed care on health care delivery is still unanswered, there have been some measurable successes. Mary Jane England and Veronica A. Vaccaro have reviewed the managed care strategies that were emerging from the debate over how to balance quality and cost. Writing in *Health Affairs* in 1991, they observed: "Major U.S. companies are beginning to show that these new systems enhance early detection of mental health problems, offer a broad scope of services, provide continuity of care, reduce cost shifting to individuals, grant generous and protective benefits, and improve the overall quality of care" (p. 129). In a publication funded by the Child, Adolescent, and Family Branch of the Center for Mental Health Services, Lourie, Howe, and Roebuck (1996) noted: "Discussions with parents of children and adolescents with severe emotional disturbances who were served within managed care plans also indicated that extremely positive results have occurred" (p. 18).

What are these positive developments? First, access to care has been improved. Over and over, as MBHOs implement programs for their clients, the data show that more people obtained behavioral health services than did so prior to the initiation of managed care. Typically, the increase is 15% or more. We believe the number of people coming to treatment rises consistently under managed care. There are several possible reasons for this:

1. MBHOs collaborate with employers and other payors to diminish stigmatization of behavioral health care. Rather than being demeaned, people are encouraged to call the MBHO when they think they might need treatment.
2. A 24-hour access line is created through which people can seek information about services and be referred to an appropriate, convenient treatment provider. This offers a simple, confidential way that individuals can come to care.
3. Follow-up by MBHOs, particularly in urgent and emergency situations, helps assure that those who most need care will get it.
4. As Lourie, Howe and Roebuck (1996) note, the current trend toward integration of managed care and employee assistance programs has created a gateway to treatment. The first few outpatient visits being provided without copayment strongly recommends itself to people in earlier stages of a disorder.

Managed care has had a positive impact on the range of services covered by health plans. Generally, before managed behavioral health care, benefit plans typically covered traditional inpatient and outpatient services with a strong financial incentive to use inpatient services. Now benefits are also commonly available for a variety of alternative levels of care, such as residential treatment, partial hospitalization, halfway houses, 23-hour beds, and home care. With a greater range of services available, treatment plans can be more creative and flexible, allowing the intervention to be matched more specifically to an individual's needs. Availability of the MBHO's care manager as a consistent presence across levels of care enhances the opportunity, particularly in complex cases, for continuity of care and linkage from one level to the next.

In addition to expanding the range of services covered, advocacy by MBHOs has resulted in expanding the types of clinicians whose services now eligible for payment. In some ways, this may appear to be a mixed blessing (Ritvo, 1994). Psychiatrists, in particular, have felt pressure from some MBHOs to alter the focus of their practice away from psychotherapy to the biological aspects of care and to complex patients. Some MBHOs (and payors) continue to recognize the advantage of comprehensive care provided by a psychiatrist for individuals with biological and psychosocial issues. Concerns over this issue point up the need for practitioners to look closely at the policies and cultures of MBHOs and to evaluate carefully their compatibility with a particular MBHO before joining its provider panel.

Some of our colleagues who perform peer review for MBHOs report an additional advantage of managed care in behavioral health. They note that the consultation they are able to provide through the peer review process is often appreciated, particularly in isolated areas where practitioners may not always have an opportunity for case discussion with peers. Currently health maintenance organizations are increasingly turning over their mental health and substance abuse care for specialized management by managed behavioral health care organizations. As a result, MBHO staff psychiatric peer reviewers have the opportunity to provide consultation to primary care physicians, enhancing the possibility of early identification and effective response to behavioral health problems.

Last, to once again quote England and Vaccaro (1991), "Of no small consequence, these systems also contain costs" (p. 129).

Managed Behavioral Health Challenges

When practitioners discuss their concerns in dealing with MBHOs, certain issues come up repeatedly. These reflect areas in which MBHOs continue to struggle to find ways to be more user friendly while meeting the objectives of the clients who purchase their services.

One of the most commonly mentioned problems for practitioners in managed care is the paperwork. It is an issue which the MBHOs continually ponder, looking for ways to streamline the mutual workload. At Value Behavioral Health, for instance, over the years the Outpatient Treatment Report has undergone many transformations. The quest is always to make it more mutually efficient and supportive of our mandate from payors to ensure high-quality, appropriate care. Most MBHOs are actively exploring whether computer technology can meet their mandate and minimize the paper requirements. The solution, however, will not be simple; among others, issues that must be resolved include, cost issues (for providers and MBHOs), learning curve issues, and confidentiality issues.

Continuity of care is another area of considerable concern to most practitioners (Ritvo, 1994; Sabin, 1994b). Many practitioners, along with

their patients, have faced the prospect of having to terminate treatment because the patient's employer switched managed care companies or implemented managed care for the first time, and the practitioner was not a member of the MBHO's provider network. Economic realities have dictated the use of provider networks, but MBHOs and payors alike are concerned about disruptions of care. As we all share the goal of wanting the patient to get well (or to maximize improvement), disruptions that could result in setbacks are of common concern. MBHOs typically work with the payor to develop a transition plan, allowing a period of time for patients and their care providers to consider the situation and, if necessary, plan for the patient's shift to another provider. MBHOs recognize, however, that in some clinical conditions such a transition would not be appropriate, as in the case of a bipolar patient who has been seeing a psychiatrist for a number of years and remained well stabilized.

As they work to keep the interests of all constituencies in balance, MBHOs strive to keep their primary focus on the patient. This, at times, puts MBHOs at odds with providers. As an example, the MBHO will support comprehensive evaluations for children and adolescents before extended treatment in specialized settings such as a residential treatment center begins. It also will insist on family involvement in the treatment of children and adolescents, unless contraindicated.

MBHOs must continually seek more effective ways to communicate with their provider networks. Given the size of these networks, this is a major challenge, but an important one to resolve. An article by Wickizer, Lessler, and Travis (1996) looked at how the use of utilization management affected the lengths of stay of hospital inpatients. It turned out that almost all patients were initially approved by an MBHO for the same brief length of stay. Therefore, the authors concluded that MBHOs must be adhering to strict treatment protocols that fail to distinguish among varying clinical conditions. More variability was found in the total lengths of stay approved, but the authors were not sure why. They speculated that it could reflect more individualization of patients in the continued stay review process. But they found it equally plausible that the variation could derive from differences in benefit coverage or from other factors. In fact, it is precisely because MBHOs are trying to assure a focused, individualized treatment plan that, barring unusual circumstances, they generally certify a brief stay at the initial review. The intent is to allow a comprehensive evaluation to take place and a patient-specific treatment plan to be developed. Once this has occurred and the patient's needs and initial response to treatment are known, the lengths of stay certified can be more aligned with the specific patient's condition. Continuing misunderstandings such as this demonstrate the need for an ongoing dialogue between the professional associations and managed care.

Individual MBHOs strive to communicate effectively with their network providers about policies and processes. Practitioners who belong to multiple networks receive material from each MBHO and must understand the variations. Standardization would resolve much of the associated stress. Complete standardization is unlikely, however, given the competitive nature of the industry.

Another frequently raised issue is the level of expertise of the care managers. In response to this concern, the American Managed Behavioral Healthcare Association recently surveyed its members regarding the professional qualifications and experience of their care managers. Fifteen of 18 members responded. While there was some variation among companies, results showed that the typical care manager was a registered nurse or licensed masters' level clinician with 5 or more years of experience. Twelve of the 15 responding companies indicated that care managers are either supervised by a physician or have physicians as their clinical consultants and trainers.

Last, but certainly not least, is the universal concern about confidentiality. Patients, providers, payors, and MBHOs share this concern, although interpretations of what and where the boundaries lie may vary. Some providers have expressed the belief that any information expressed in the context of the therapeutic relationship must never be shared, because to do so may threaten the patient's ability to use the relationship effectively. This position sidesteps the issue of accountability to the payor. Another point of view was expressed by Carol Shaw Austad and Michael F. Hoyt (1992) writing in *Psychotherapy:*

Because the psychotherapist collects a fee and the fee is paid by a government, employer, or insurance plan, a third party has entered the therapeutic relationship. . . . The act of asking the supplier of services to explain the treatment that he or she renders is a reasonable request and implies that the asker (consumer or payer) is becoming more knowledgeable. . . . Economic accountability and good-quality care are mutually inclusive if

motivated by a desire to give all people high quality healthcare. (p. 116)

MBHOs do not need (or want) to know everything about the patient. They do need information that will make clear the rationale for the level of care and interventions being utilized. Discussing "Ethical Issues in Managed Mental Health," Stephen R. Blum (1992) offers helpful advice. "Given the prevalence of third-party payment arrangements, patients should be told as part of the informed consent process, as proximate to the start of therapy as possible, that there is information that the clinician must tell others in order to assure coverage of the care provided. The patient should be told what that information consists of, to whom it will be given and should give explicit consent for it to be communicated" (pp. 261–262). It is important to recognize that the way the need to share information is communicated to patients has a great deal to do with their ability to accept this reality of their third-party coverage.

What the Provider Can Do

Providers of care can do a number of things to ease the burden of dealing with MBHOs:

• Those who choose to work with patients whose coverage contains managed care components should be willing to work within the philosophy of managed care. "Managed care asks psychiatrists to redefine their professional responsibility and to consider optimal treatment for the individual patient in the context of the needs of a larger population" (p. 2) (Sabin 1994c). Sabin refers to this as a "stewardship responsibility for societal resources," (p. 2) which must now be integrated with the traditional emphasis on improving the welfare of individual patients without consideration of societal impact. This means choosing appropriate, cost-effective treatment options that are conducted in the least restrictive environment in which the patient can be safely managed. Again quoting Sabin: "Managed care treatment is not synonymous with short-term treatment. . . ." (p. 5). The emphasis is, instead, on cost-effective care.

• When making their health plan selection, individuals may not have fully investigated or completely understood their chosen plan (La Puma &

Schiedermayer, 1996). It is important, however, that they come to understand what to expect under managed care, so they may fully and actively participate in the treatment process (Sabin, 1994a). This means discussing candidly with the patient the nature of benefit limits as well as the need to share some clinical information with the MBHO.

• Providers should not leap to the assumption that any questioning by a care manager of a proposed treatment plan means the MBHO does not care about quality and is just trying to save money at the expense of the patient (Sabin, 1994b). While cost savings is a concern, a well beneficiary still saves the most money.

• When communicating with an MBHO about a patient, providers should describe the patient's condition and the goals of treatment in terms of functional impairments. Albeit important, diagnosis does not by itself convey the medical necessity for treatment. "The major advantage of using the impairment language is having the capacity to describe in behavioral terms the patient's visible, quantifiable manifestations of the diagnosis" (Goodman, Brown, & Deitz, p. 41 1992). MBHOs avoid subscribing to any particular theoretical orientation. They strive instead to understand the clinical rationale for a proposed treatment by noting the severity of the patient's functional impairments and evaluating the likely impact of the proposed care on those impairments. Similarly, clearly articulated dysfunctions and goals, stated in behavioral terms, enable the provider and the care manager to discern progress in treatment more readily.

• All managed care plans have appeal mechanisms. They exist as MBHOs recognize the potential for peers to disagree. As an advocate for the patient, ". . . physicians should assist patients with medical or financial issues that are unreasonable or discriminatory, or that would injure a patient's medical interests" (La Puma & Schiedermayer, p. 168 1996). It is important for practitioners to be familiar with the appeal process and what time limits, if any, apply so they can be most effective in their patient advocacy role.

Future Trends

The managed care environment is evolving rapidly. Expansion of managed care into the public sector is accelerating. Currently an increasing number of states are applying to the federal government for waivers that would enable them to place their behavioral health benefits under managed care.

The entry of government into the managed care marketplace is occurring in conjunction with increasing sophistication of private-sector payors. All this increases the importance of showing value for treatment dollars spent, which requires collaboration between providers and MBHOs. They must determine appropriate outcome measures and produce useful data sets demonstrating the effectiveness of whatever treatment is being provided. Failure to generate meaningful outcomes data, by making only anecdotal information available, raises the level of skepticism about the value of behavioral health care and its need to be included in benefit plans.

Pressure for cost efficiency is also increasing. As a result, MBHOs are evolving their provider networks toward smaller core groups of practitioners who provide a significant proportion of care in areas with large concentrations of covered individuals. Such groups comprise a range of disciplines and specialty practice areas. They have access to a spectrum of levels of care and can respond on an emergency basis. Accordingly, they enable MBHOs to provide efficient access to care. In addition, by working closely with these practitioner groups, MBHOs are able to support them in developing programs for oversight of their own care. Ultimately, this will return care decisions to providers.

REFERENCES

American Managed Behavioral Healthcare Association. (1996, April 15). Case manager qualifications in AMBHA member companies. *Executive director's report* #96–39.

Astrachan, B. M., Essock, S., Kahn, R., Masi, D., McLean, A., & Visotsky, H. (1995, July). The role of a payor advisory board in managed mental health care: The IBM approach. *Administration and Policy in Mental Health, 22* (6). pp. 581–595.

Austad, C. S., & Hoyt, M. F. (1992, Spring). The managed care movement and the future of psychotherapy. *Psychotherapy, 29* (1). pp. 109–118.

Blum, S. R. (1992). Ethical issues in managed mental health. In S. Feldman (Ed.), *Managed mental health services.* Springfield, IL: Charles C Thomas. pp. 245–265.

England, M. J., & Vaccaro, V. A. (1991, Winter). Commentary: New systems to manage mental health care. *Health Affairs.* pp. 129–137.

Goodman, M., Brown, J., & Deitz, P. (1992). *Managing managed care: A mental health practitioner's survival guide.* Washington, DC: American Psychiatric Press.

La Puma, J., & Schiedermayer, D. (1996 February). Ethical issues in managed care. *American Journal of Managed Care, 2* (2). pp. 167–171.

Lourie, I. S., Howe, S. W., & Roebuck, L. L. (1996). Systematic approaches to mental health care in the private sector for children, adolescents, and their families: Managed care organizations and service providers. Washington, DC: Georgetown University Child Development Center, National Technical Assistance Center for Child Mental Health.

Ritvo, J. H. (1994). The role of the psychiatrist: The clinician's view. In R. K. Schreter, S. S. Sharfstein, & C. A. Schreter, (Eds.), *Allies and adversaries: The impact of managed care on mental health services.* Washington, DC: American Psychiatric Press. pp. 108–116.

Rodriguez, A. R. (1994). Quality-of-care guidelines: The managed care view. In R. K. Schreter, S. S. Sharfstein, C. A. Schreter (Eds.), *Allies and adversaries: The impact of managed care on mental health services.* Washington, DC: American Psychiatric Press. pp. 169–178.

Sabin, J. E. (1994a). A credo for ethical managed care in mental health practice. *Hospital and Community Psychiatry, 45* (9). pp. 859–860.

Sabin, J. E. (1994b). Ethical issues under managed care: The managed care view. In R. K. Schreter, S. S. Sharfstein, & C. A. Schreter (Eds.), *Allies and adversaries: The impact of managed care on mental health services.* Washington, DC: American Psychiatric Press. pp. 187–194.

Sabin, J. E. (1994c). The impact of managed care on psychiatric practice. *Directions in Psychiatry, 14* (9). pp. 1–7.

Shueman, S. A., & Penner, N. R. (1988). Administering a national program of mental health peer review. In *Handbook of quality assurance in mental health.* Ed. by George Stricker & Alex R. Rodriguez New York: Plenum Press. pp. 441–453.

Wickizer, T. M., Lessler, D., & Travis, K. M. (1996). Controlling inpatient psychiatric utilization through managed Care. *American Journal of Psychiatry, 153* (3). pp. 339–345.

37 / The Practice of Child and Adolescent Psychiatry in the Era of Managed Care (Practitioner Perspective)

Susan Villani

In the field of child and adolescent psychiatry, the decade of the 1990s is notable for the remarkable changes that have occurred in the day-to-day practice of delivering care to emotionally disturbed children and adolescents. The swiftness of change has been all-encompassing, creating a new lexicon for clinicians to learn whether they were just finishing training or had been practicing for 20 years. The paradigm shift heralding the change superimposed business language and management theory onto health care with the goal of curtailing rising costs. While corporations voiced major concerns about the escalation of the cost of care, the federal budget careened out of control, and health care professionals as a group were unable to mobilize to contain costs on their own, business entrepreneurs who understood what corporations wanted and how health care economics worked entered the marketplace. According to Geraty, Hendren, and Flaa (1992), "Managed care represents more than a new approach to health; it represents a new shift in societal values. Society is declaring that there are limits to health care spending and that employers, the government, and individuals are reaching the extent of their resources."

These entrepreneurs were farsighted individuals, many of them physicians by training, who understood the excesses and lack of solid outcome data prevalent in medicine, psychiatry in general, and even more in child and adolescent psychiatry. With corporations eager to hear of ways to stop rising costs, managed care companies were created to reduce costs for their owners and supporters and to make a profit as a result of the reduced costs.

While the stated goal of managed care companies has been to control price, service, and quality, the implementation has been quite different; it has focused on 2 rather simplistic ways of curtailing costs: controlling access to services and continuing to curb the demand for ongoing services. With this, the concepts of preauthorization of services and utilization review were born. The delivery of services to emotionally disturbed children and adolescents changed from practice rooted in developmental theory, with quality-of-life goals for the long term, to managed care with a focus on symptom relief.

This chapter considers the practice of child and adolescent psychiatry across the spectrum of care from inpatient, to outpatient, to community-based public sector settings. It expands on the concepts of access control and utilization review as applied to outpatient and inpatient settings. The resultant emergence of the continuum of care is described along with the necessary trend for clinicians to think more of alternative settings for the evaluation and treatment of severely disturbed youths. I discuss how this has created a new challenge for clinicians to expand from thinking only of diagnosis and needed service, to thinking of triaging patients into the least costly, most effective interventions and level of care. Finally, I describe how these changes, and the further emergence of a highly competitive health care marketplace, have influenced the fiscal base of private practices, mental health care delivery systems, and academic institutions.

Being a Provider

The term "provider" is new and distinct to the era of managed care. Managed care companies typically process applications submitted by professionals seeking to become providers of services through managed care. The applications usually are quite lengthy, and ask questions about preferred modes of practice, availability, typical number of sessions for various ages of patients served, as well as the standard demographic questions and training history and professional certification. Once an application to be a provider is submitted to a managed care company, it is reviewed, a process that may take weeks to months, and is either accepted or rejected. Each managed care company has designed itself in a specific way and seeks to have certain numbers and types of practitioners. Many companies choose to have a small number of providers whom they rely on heavily, often referred to as preferred providers. It is not

uncommon for a managed care company to close off new applications whenever it has enough providers to deliver the care that it has contracted to provide. Regardless of a physician's professional training or expertise, and national reputation in a specified area, if he or she has not applied for and been accepted by the managed care company, services he or she renders to the company's patients will not be reimbursed. In general, managed care companies any place a high value on child and adolescent psychiatrists who are: comfortable with treating a wide range of diagnoses; in favor of short, symptom-focused treatment; comfortable with prescribing medications for patients receiving psychotherapy from others; and easily accessible and friendly to patients, families, and their reviewers. Once accepted to be a provider for a managed care company, the child and adolescent psychiatrist agrees to participate in the company's preauthorization and review practices and to accept its rates of payment (often remarkably reduced) for specific services. In exchange, the psychiatrist accepts patients whose care is monitored by the managed care company.

Outpatient Care

The single most important change since the introduction of managed care has been the rapid increase of child and adolescent psychopharmacology and the subsequent financially driven decision by managed care companies to reimburse child and adolescent psychiatrists almost exclusively for the purpose of prescribing and monitoring medication. Individual psychotherapy, family therapy, and group therapy (unless the group is for the purpose of monitoring medication), under the company's cost-containment perspective, are time-consuming endeavors now to be done by mental health professionals who are less costly per hour, such as social workers and psychologists. The circumstances that might lead to authorization of payment for a child and adolescent psychiatrist to see a patient in psychotherapy are medical-legal complications, failed treatment with other professionals, or cases that have been high utilizers of services in the past. Such cases are extraordinary and usually come to the child and adolescent psychiatrist after extensive review within the managed care company, often by the company's medical director.

What has become the usual and customary practice of outpatient child and adolescent psychiatrists is to see many new evaluations per week and a plethora of brief medication checkup appointments. Patients are referred through 3 routes: a primary care physician who wants consultation to guide treatment of a patient; an individual therapist who has been seeing the patient and now wants him or her evaluated for medication; or the managed care company itself who may have chosen to have new patients seen initially by a child and adolescent psychiatrist for the purpose of diagnostic screening and treatment planning. Companies that utilize child and adolescent psychiatrists at the youth's point of entry into their system a diagnostic evaluation to assess the need for medication. If there is no need for medication, the patient is to be referred on immediately to a social worker or psychologist for whatever follow-up is indicated.

With any of these routes of referral, if medication is indicated, the expectation is for it to be prescribed quickly, within the first session or two. Most managed care companies agree to reimburse 1 to 2 evaluative sessions, their reviewer is to be contacted thereafter. The purpose of the psychiatrist's call to the reviewer is to submit to a review of the diagnosis, the proposed treatment plan with specific goals, and clarification of what professional discipline will deliver the care. If the reviewer agrees to the plan, he or she authorizes payment for a specified number and type of sessions over a clearly defined period, to accomplish the stated goals. These decisions usually are guided by protocols that have been developed within a particular managed care company based on its experience with a specific age and patient diagnosis. For example, the expectation for the uncomplicated treatment of an adolescent with major depression may, under a particular company's protocol, be: initial evaluation, 6 medication follow-up appointments over the next 6 months, and brief focused individual therapy for 2 to 3 months with a social worker. How the psychiatrist spaces the visits over time is generally not of concern to the company. When the 6 months has ended or the number of visits has been used up, it is the responsibility of the psychiatrist to call the company, review the case's progress toward stated goals, and get authorization for more treatment as necessary. Almost all managed care companies also require the submission of an initial written treatment plan and modified plans as indicated with clearly defined behavioral goals and objectives. If the plan is not submitted in a timely fashion or if the review calls are not made, there is no payment for the service.

In addition to communicating with the company, the child and adolescent psychiatrist also must communicate with the referrer. When the referrer is the primary care physician, the goal may have been to have the psychiatrist assume the treatment of the patient or merely to receive consultation about the primary care doctor's prescriptions. If the primary care physician is part of a contract that assumes financial risk, he or she may want to resume prescribing with the child and adolescent psychiatrist providing consultation. In a financial risk contract, a group of physicians has agreed to a set amount of money to provide all care to a defined group of patients. If those patients need to be seen by specialists, payment to those specialists comes from the pool of money that has been contracted to be given to the primary care physicians. Such contracts carry clear financial incentives for primary care physicians to assume the total care of patients, within the degree of comfort of their own expertise and training.

When the referrer has been a social worker or psychologist who is seeing the patient, it is important for the child and adolescent psychiatrist to clarify that the treater has discussed the referral with the managed care company and that it agrees with the need for referral. Preauthorization for the evaluation is essential for payment to occur. Developing good working relationships with social workers and psychologists who are providing therapy, knowing their skill level and how they work with patients and families, are important aspects of any child and adolescent psychiatrist's outpatient practice under a managed care company. Outpatient group practices have become more the norm than solo private practice child and adolescent psychiatry for exactly this reason. Child and adolescent psychiatrists often find it much easier, more efficient, and more cost effective to work within a multidisciplinary group than to try to establish trusting, working relationships with many providers in different sites.

Besides expecting psychiatrists to provide initial assessment and medication management of patients, managed care companies expect that patients will be seen quickly. Being able to provide an appointment within 24 hours of receiving a call, and in some cases within 8 hours, often is a requirement for being considered to be a company provider. This kind of urgent assessment capability has moved the outpatient practice of child and adolescent psychiatry more into the mainstream of medical subspecialities. It also requires the child and adolescent psychiatrist to think in terms of *triage*, a topic to be discussed more fully later.

Inpatient Care

To managed care companies, inpatient hospitalization is a last resort for patients who are at risk of harming themselves or others or who have been rendered unable to care for themselves due to severe psychotic or depressive symptomatology. In order to admit the patient to the hospital, preauthorization of the managed care company's payment must occur. This is done by the evaluating clinician calling the company and reviewing the findings of the evaluation; the company reviewer who then decides whether the patient needs 24-hour physician and nursing monitoring. Meeting these criteria has given rise to the term *medical necessity*. Usually the initial authorization for inpatient care is given for only 1 to 2 days, with planned telephone review follow-up by the company case manager or reviewer (terms that are used interchangeably) to occur with either the hospital utilization review staff or directly with the treating physician.

The purpose of the hospital stay is to stabilize the dangerous or life-threatening behaviors quickly; the patient is to be moved to a less restrictive and less costly setting as soon as this can be accomplished safely. Under this paradigm, the average length of stay for adolescents is 4 to 6 days and for younger children 10 to 12 days. Hospital staff and the managed care companies confer frequently either daily or every 2 to 3 days. Reviews occur by telephone and focus on whether the patient still meets medical necessity criteria. If the company feels that the patient no longer meets these criteria, then payment for services will be denied. The first step after a denial, if the physician feels continued stay is indicated, is to appeal the decision. Usually this involves reviewing the case with another reviewer higher up in the company reviewer hierarchy. Appeal also may involve sending a letter documenting the reason(s) for appeal or sending part or all of the medical record. At the point when the denial is issued, the managed care company is no longer responsible for paying the hospital or the physician for services. Most hospitals have families sign a financial responsibility statement upon entry into the hospital. This in effect is a contract that says the parent(s) agree to pay whatever is not covered by insurance. When the company denies payment, the hospital must inform the parent(s) that their family's insurance is no longer paying and that the parents are responsible for payment for services rendered from that time forward if the appeal is not granted.

The physician's assessment during hospitalization is no longer centered on comprehensive diagnostic and treatment issues. While observation of the patient in the inpatient milieu usually brings to the attention of the clinician many questions and issues that warrant addressing, the inpatient physician must push those matters aside and stay focused on getting the patient out of the hospital promptly. As stated by Harper (1989) in his seminal work, "The purpose of the inpatient hospitalization is to get the patient out of the hospital." Identified diagnostic and treatment issues need to be documented carefully with clear recommendations about how they should be followed up after discharge. This information is passed on to the next level of care, whether that means back to the outpatient referrer or step-down to a less restrictive level within a continuum of care, such as day hospital or respite care with day hospital.

This transformation of inpatient units to short stay has required a total reeducation of the staff members who work on them and a retooling of the hospital support systems surrounding inpatient units. The decline in the average length of stay has led to a rising number of admissions, yet a net decrease in total bed days. A specific unit that less than a decade ago admitted and discharged between 60 and 100 long-stay patients in the course of a year will now serve 500 to 600 patients. Often this requires multiple admissions and discharges in a given day, all of which are oriented toward crisis intervention. Scheduled admissions do not occur using this paradigm, because by definition if patients are stable enough to wait until a scheduled time, then they do not meet medical necessity criteria. Admissions thus occur predominantly in the evenings and at night, with very few patients entering the hospital during the day. Even if the process of identifying the need for hospitalization begins in the daytime, patients often do not make it through the preauthorization process in less than 4 to 6 hours. The managed care company may even request a second opinion about the need for hospitalization by one of its preferred providers.

Likewise, milieu treatment and family therapy on inpatient units have undergone dramatic changes in order to meet the needs of patients and families quickly and narrowly. By necessity, families are seen immediately and required to come for family therapy almost daily. Behavioral symptoms are identified and rapidly addressed. Groups that are educative in focus, such as substance abuse groups and sex education groups, are held frequently throughout the week. Medications are started within the first few days of the stay, and both patients and families have to be educated quickly, yet thoroughly, as to the risks and benefits of the recommended medication(s). Parents have to join with the treatment team almost immediately to focus not only on what led to the hospitalization but also on discharge planning.

Similarly, diagnostic tests are limited to ones clearly necessary to stabilize the patient's behavior. Comprehensive diagnosis is no longer the goal of the hospital stay. Neurological tests such as computed tomography scans and magnetic resonance imaging often are deferred until the patient has left the hospital. When an electroencephalogram magnetic resonance imaging is necessary prior to initiating mood-stabilizing medications, it must be ordered and completed within a day or two. Psychological testing, particularly complete projective testing, is now rarely accomplished during the course of a hospital stay. Instead, behavioral checklists, depression rating scales, and other easily administered and scored instruments are utilized to begin tracking the response to medication. Clarification of complex diagnostic issues using complete psychological testing requires special authorization from the managed care company in order for them to agree to pay for the costly battery of tests. The physician always must justify why these tests must be done in the hospital.

Utilizing the Continuum of Care

The dichotomous clinical decision tree of "outpatient or inpatient" has been replaced by the challenge to think "in a *triage* way" about many levels of care organized as a continuum of care. The continuum of care allows the patient to be treated in the least restrictive and least costly setting, with the goal of movement to a more or less restrictive

setting based on undisputed clinical need. In the managed care world, movement of the patient from one level of care to another requires review with the company and authorization of payment for the next level of care, unless the managed care company and the provider have negotiated a case rate or episode-of-care rate, terms that will be explained more fully later.

Ideally, programs with a continuum are fully integrated, clinically flexible, and comprehensive with respect to intensity and duration of treatment. A typical continuum of services may include the following:

- Outpatient
- Intensive Outpatient
- Home-Based Services
- Mobile Emergency Service
- Crisis Stabilization
- Observation Bed Capacity
- Respite Care
- Acute Residential Treatment
- Partial or Day Hospital Program
- Therapeutic Group Home
- Therapeutic Foster Care
- Acute Inpatient Program
- Residential Treatment

The challenges to the child and adolescent psychiatrist to understand and use the continuum effectively are multifold. First of all, he or she must know all the services available in the area. Since new services are developing rapidly as a response to cost containment measures, often it is hard to keep abreast of what has happened in the geographic locale. Second, the child and adolescent psychiatrist needs to think actively about when outpatient treatment is not working and then look for low-cost alternatives along the continuum that might be helpful to the patient and family. The decisive, judicious use of day hospital, intensive outpatient services, or home-based services can prevent many patients from needing a costly locked door inpatient unit. Also, with young children who have never slept away from home, day hospital or in-home treatment offers the distinct advantage of not contaminating the evaluation with the possible overlay of separation anxiety. Third, the child and adolescent psychiatrist must work with the managed care company's case manager to discuss what available services are covered by the patient's particular plan. While many companies now pay for day hospital, only a few have agreed to cover crisis beds, respite beds, therapeutic foster homes, and home-based services. Many have, however, shifted toward reimbursing intensive outpatient treatment in favor of reimbursing full-day treatment programs. These alternatives are becoming more commonly reimbursable services, but this is very specific to certain managed care companies that have chosen to manage care in this fashion.

Patients and families often do not know what services are covered and are inclined to read their inpatient coverage maximum as an entitlement, not as a maximum. For example, a 30-day calendar year inpatient coverage means that this is the maximum number of days that will be covered. Each inpatient stay will be managed to utilize the fewest number of days possible. Some companies also "convert" inpatient days to day hospital days. This means that instead of 1 inpatient day, the company will pay for 2 days in a day hospital.

A very recent development has been to diminish even the use of full days in day hospital. The company will question why a full day is necessary and whether the patient could be served equally well by attending the program for half days or perhaps even intensive outpatient services—for example, 1 group and 1 individual psychotherapy Monday, Wednesday, and Friday, designed specifically for the patient. The child and adolescent psychiatrist is constantly challenged to think very clearly about exactly what his or her patient needs in order to be treated adequately. Today's outpatient practices are comprised of patients who are less stable than in the past, this fact requires child and adolescent psychiatrists to be more readily available to their patients and families.

Flexibility and clinical continuity are central to the success of any system of care. Regardless of where a patient enters the system, the primary therapist and the child's psychiatrist (if different) should be able to move flexibly with the child from 1 level of care to another. This continuity is obviously essential for psychotherapy, medication trials, and effective family intervention.

Fiscal Impact

SYSTEMS OF CARE AND DEPARTMENTS

Prior to managed care cost containment efforts, large profits were garnered from inpatient child and adolescent psychiatric beds. The profits accrued for several reasons. First, because access was not determined by strict use of medical necessity criteria and continued stay was similarly not monitored by utilization review, inpatient beds were virtually almost always full. Insurance paid only for inpatient and outpatient services, so by default those patients who needed more than outpatient therapy were admitted to inpatient units. Second, the charges for hospital stay were determined by expenses submitted to government rate-setting agencies. States, through state regulatory agencies, set a daily rate for the bed, and insurers agreed to pay separately for individual professional charges. The hospital would resubmit to the rate-setting agency for new rates based on their new expenses, and the cost was merely passed on to the payors. When the hospital found its expenses increased, daily rates then were adjusted by resubmission to the rate-setting agency for an increase. A large private psychiatric hospital or an inpatient unit in a general hospital could easily plan its child and adolescent budget simply by taking the number of beds it had licensed, consider them 98% occupied, and multiply this by the bed rate plus the average daily billed professional and ancillary medical charges. It was accepted that the outpatient clinic services would not make money because of the necessary nonreimbursed time to deliver quality services to children and families. This was not a problem, however, because the inpatient profits could subsidize the outpatient loss. Issues such as rates of collection, clinician productivity, and payor mix were not considered because the inpatient profits so far exceeded the possible profit that could be garnered from prudent outpatient care that it simply was not worth the managerial effort and hassle. Particularly for academic departments, outpatient clinics were viewed as training sites where residents and fellows obtained experience in treating children and adolescents. Trainees were allowed and encouraged to treat patients in long-term therapy, and with medication, receiving supervision from senior staff on their cases in detailed fashion.

From the fiscal standpoint, the current situation is very different and alarming for both inpatient and outpatient work. For inpatient, the ratcheting down on both the access and continued stay has transformed inpatient units into high-volume (many admissions and discharges) settings whose census is extremely variable and wildly unpredictable. The triaging of patients to alternative settings along the continuum diverts them from the need for costly and restrictive inpatient care. In this era, it has become very difficult to predict inpatient occupancy over the course of a year and thus very difficult to plan adequate staffing. The acute stabilization, medical necessity model also has caused extreme variability in daily census secondary to rapid patient turnover. Units that operate using this paradigm can easily discharge 4 patients and admit 3 during the course of a day. Staffing the unit for an average daily census has limited relevance to the actual workload.

Simultaneous to expansion of the continuum and of access and utilization review, market forces have became prominent. As the payors began to question the need for and costs of services, rate-setting agencies in many states have become defunct. The payors virtually transformed the psychiatric hospital industry by deciding they wanted less expensive services. Through their power of controlling access, many managed care companies limited their referrals to hospitals with lower costs. The companies also began to review whether individual services provided to patients were necessary and soon instituted ways to deny payment unless reviewed and allowed by their reviewers. These disallowances rapidly became large budgetary and management problems. Almost all institutions experienced a rapid increase in bad debt secondary to managed care denial of inpatient days and of individual services. Since no outcome data are available to dispute that the more costly hospitals and services were indeed more clinically effective for patients, the payors' decision to use less costly hospitals and to deny payment of charges has gone virtually unchallenged.

In addition, new methods of reimbursing services emerged as ways to shift the responsibility for containing cost from the managed care company to the providers of care. Case rates, episode-of-care rates, and capitation rates are ways of reimbursing physicians, practices, or systems to care for patients regardless of diagnosis or severity of illness. Case rate and episode-of-care payment methods basically pay a set rate for an entire episode of illness, regardless of the level of care or time needed to treat the patient. The rates are said to be determined based on average lengths of stay and charges examined over a large population for a given period. Once an episode of care rate is established, there is no utilization review process. The physician is essentially managing the care within the given dollars at his or her discretion and risk. Capitation is similar in that a specified rate per month per enrolled "life" is paid into a pool of money that is then used to pay for all the care given to the "covered lives." The incentives are to provide only what is necessary, using the least costly providers and the least costly level of care. Most practicing child and adolescent psychiatrists have not received training in how to change their mode of practice to work within the confines of these new reimbursement techniques. Increasingly, professional meetings have focused on ways for clinicians to adapt to these changes.

The loss of inpatient bed days combined with the loss of the profit margin on each bed has transformed many departments of child and adolescent psychiatry that were profit centers into money-losing entities. The ability to respond quickly and decisively to the changes has literally meant the difference between survival and extinction. For example, a large private psychiatric hospital operating 98 inpatient beds in 1989 by 1996 was downsized to operating 57 beds, yet a multitude of other services were simultaneously developed. (See Table 37.1.) In order to work within the new managed care paradigm, 2 day hospitals were opened and operated, a residential treatment bed was added, and a respite service also was designed. The patients did not go away, but they were treated in less costly and less restrictive settings, and the services that were utilized provided less profit to the bottom line. The expansion of the continuum of care made both financial and clinical sense, but clearly it took a readiness to move quickly and decisively or risk being eliminated from the marketplace. In addition, without the inpatient profit, the efficient and profitable operation of all services needed to be carefully managed. The problem of start-up costs for new services also had to be addressed in new ways. The solutions are not easy and may come from grant money, corporate and/or community fund raising, or endowment. It is clear that mental health care systems that survive during this era will have been creative and resourceful.

OUTPATIENT CLINICS AND PRACTICES

The fiscal transformation of outpatient treatment has been equally dramatic as that described for departments and systems. For clinics, the emphasis for child and adolescent psychiatrists has been heavily shifted to being primarily medication management. While this can be viewed as a re-medicalization of the profession, it is clearly dollar-driven, with productivity—defined as the number of patients who can be seen in an hour—being key to the survival of outpatient settings. Individual therapy and family therapy are no longer the exclusive purview of the child and adolescent

TABLE 37.1

Example of a Developing Continuum of Care

1992	1994	1995–96	1996–97
Inpatient Beds 84 Adolescent 12 Child	*Inpatient Beds* 18 Adolescent Short 24 Adolescent Long 24 Child	*Inpatient Beds* 16 Adolescent 24 Child 17 Adolescent	*Inpatient Beds* 16 Adolescent 24 Child 17 Adolescent
	Residential Treatment Services Group Home for Boys	*Residential Treatment Services* Group Home for Boys Residential Treatment Center	*Residential Treatment Services* Group Home for Boys Residential Treatment Center Additional 24 beds
	Day Programs Adolescent Day Hospital Camp Care (2 weeks)	*Day Programs* Adolescent Day Hospital Child Day Hospital Camp Care (10 weeks)	*Day Programs* Adolescent Day Hospital Child Day Hospital Camp Care (10 weeks) Respite Service Saturday Program Mentor Program
Special Education School Elementary Middle High School	*Special Education School* Elementary Middle High School	*Special Education School* Elementary Middle High School Vocational Program	*Special Education School* Elementary Middle High School Vocational Program Therapeutic Preschool
Outpatient Services	*Outpatient Services*	*Outpatient Services*	*Outpatient Services* Child Psychopharmacelogy Clinic Home Health Care

psychiatrist and are done by social workers or psychologists. Self-pay patients are rapidly becoming the only ones who receive all of their treatment solely by the psychiatrist. In order to survive fiscally, the mix of professionals, the payor mix, the productivity of individual clinicians, and the ability to find ways to cover nonreimbursed telephone and case conferencing time are factors needing close managerial monitoring.

The same factors are essential for the child and adolescent psychiatrist in private solo practice. As these professionals have seen their practices transformed from delivering primarily individual and family psychotherapy services into predominantly medication management, they too have looked for ways to become more efficient and to augment their practice income in more stable ways. This has resulted in many child and adolescent psychiatrist having diverse practices that include a combination of jobs in several settings, such as school consultation, residential treatment consultation, or part-time employment with either private or public inpatient services. The number of child and adolescent psychiatrists who are successful at solo practice has become increasingly small and will likely further diminish to a small number who reside in urban areas and serve predominantly self-pay patients who can afford professional services.

Resulting Relevant Issues

The rapid changes brought about by managed care have created a number of knotty issues for clinical practice, training, and administration. For clinical practice, the fiscal imperatives have changed the mode of practice to medication management and brief psychotherapy. As both inpatient and outpatient treatment have shifted to brief intermittent treatment, often with the patient returning many times over the course of years, clinicians describe treating more and more patients whom they know in much less detail. There has also been a serious erosion of patient and family confidentiality secondary to the review process required by most managed care companies. Some state medical associations have sought to fight this through educating the public about what information the companies ask for and then working with educated consumers to draft local legislation to protect patient privacy.

The risk management issues that are now a part of clinical practice are also changing, consistent with the mode of practice changes. With clinicians managing more and more patients who are started on medications with less information than in the past, there is greater chance of side effects, poor outcome, and noncompliance problems. Similarly, in some geographic areas, the growing problem of violence, whether perpetrated by adults upon children and adolescents or by the children and adolescents on others, has further increased the risks inherent in both inpatient and outpatient practices. In effect, this has led to patients who were formerly treated in secure inpatient settings now being discharged quickly on multiple medications and then managed as outpatients.

Brief intermittent treatments in childhood for severely emotionally disturbed children and adolescents is unlikely to produce gains that will translate into better adult functioning. The risk of poor outcome over time takes a variety of forms, ranging from young severely emotionally disturbed adults who have no way of supporting themselves and will join the growing homeless population, to more patients entering the penal system, adding to the growing jail population of youths. Unfortunately, the literature available on outcomes prior to managed care is scant. And although many of the managed care companies describe being committed to quality care and good outcomes, few data have been published. This is partly due to the fact that the population of patients managed by any one company constantly changes as workers choose a different option for their health care coverage. The managed care company does little long-term planning for patients or families; since that patient or family may change insurance soon, long-term planning is not in the company's financial best interest. Immediate access control and utilization review have provided quick financial profit; longer-term outcome issues have been inconsistent with the quarterly profit incentives that are the guiding principle of most American businesses. As pointed out by Jellinek and Nurcombe (1993), "Data on utilization and outcome will take years to gather, validate and analyze."

For child and adolescent psychiatrists who work in the public sector or with indigent populations, managed care also has begun to have an impact on their practices. Prior to the late 1990s, few states had instituted managed care for the severely and persistently mentally ill. As states, however, became increasingly concerned about rising Medicaid costs, they too looked to contract with managed care companies to help manage the costs. As a somewhat interesting side note, prior to this, the severely and persistently mentally ill had been essentially managed out to the public sector on the premise that the managed care companies were contracting with employers to manage acute medical benefits. Companies initially were not designed to manage chronic, debilitating disease. The chronically disabled population had remained the responsibility of public monies through Medicaid and Medicare. As states have begun contracting with managed care companies to manage these dollars, the experiment of short-term profit versus longer-term gain is now being extended to larger numbers of severely disturbed children and adolescents. It is well known that children and adolescents with severe psychiatric illnesses are a complex group composed of children from extreme poverty; victims of abuse, often including sexual abuse; children of drug-addicted parents; as well as those with severe biologically based psychiatric disorders such as schizophrenia, severe obsessive compulsive disorder, and bipolar disorder. By definition, the severely disturbed child's or adolescent's problems extend into all areas of life, including school (Villani, 1992). This necessitates comprehensive treatment coordinated across the boundaries of social welfare agencies, the public school system, and the mental health system. The costs of caring for severely disturbed individuals always has been high and often is complicated by underfunded, overwhelmed social service agencies. It remains to be seen whether financially incentivized companies will be able to change for the better the overburdened social agencies that are the current safety net for severely disturbed children and adolescents.

The crisis for training programs during this era will primarily be felt as the next generation of child and adolescent psychiatrists begin their practices. Clearly, less training is available for learning the art of being a child and adolescent therapist. Clinicians who choose to be therapists likely will have to pay for supervision outside the residency training to gain expertise and to accept lower rates of reimbursement in exchange for adding variety to their practice. Similarly, the ability to consult to therapeutic milieus will be limited by training experience, especially if a clinician has been trained with only short-term inpatient models of care. On the reverse side, however, those who train where there is a full continuum of care available will be better suited to make triage decisions about the level of intervention that will be effective while less costly.

Child and adolescent psychiatrists who work in administrative roles face the daunting tasks of balancing unpredictable budgets with decreasing profit, managing increasing clinical risk in less restrictive settings, while simultaneously developing new services. Whether the child and adolescent psychiatrist has been hired as a part-time medical director at an outpatient clinic or is administering a large system of care, the rapid changes brought on by the managed care paradigm have made these tasks an integral part of the work. It has therefore become even more important for child and adolescent psychiatrists doing administrative work to become familiar with business management practices and comfortable with examining new modes of practice that are potentially more cost effective. Providing leadership through administrative roles during this era has become increasingly important to prevent the complex art and science of treating children from becoming reduced to shortsighted, bottom-line–oriented, profit-based incentives.

The rapidity of change in the last decade also has created the perplexing problem of how to keep abreast of changes. The standard ways in which physicians have learned new material, through journal articles and textbooks, do not provide information about changing modes of practice quickly enough. The professional literature has lagged behind the changing practices for several noteworthy reasons (Lazarus, 19). The first and primary reason is that the changes have originated from the cost management perspective of corporations and insurers whose value system is to improve the bottom line, not to contribute to the literature to advance knowledge relevant to the professional goals of providing treatment to emotionally disturbed children and adolescents. While managed care companies presumably have

a significant amount of data about what works and what does not available to them through their computerized systems, in the marketplace of competitive bidding against other managed care companies for business, the information generally is considered proprietary. The shared value system inherent in the professional ethics of medicine to tell colleagues about new treatments that work for patients and to publish the data quickly is not the same in the business world of medicine. While managed care companies will make publicly available their criteria for meeting medical necessity, their protocols for treatment of psychiatric disorders and their outcome data remain proprietary and are not released.

The second factor contributing to literature lag is how much time health care professionals must now spend adapting to the changes incurred by the managed care paradigm. Academicians who have traditionally written about such topics as inpatient outcomes are now overwhelmed with redesigning their systems with little time to write and reflect on the changes. And the time necessary to see the results of the changes is foreshortened by the next round of changes, causing even further confusion about cause and effect. Very few articles submitted to and accepted by refereed journals examine the outcomes of the new modes of practice and the variety of new treatment settings.

What has replaced standard refereed articles is a plethora of information from professional, local, and national newsletters and newspapers. Practicing child and adolescent psychiatrists read the expanded *American Academy of Child and Adolescent Psychiatry Newsletter,* which often approaches 30 pages, to keep abreast of topics ranging from how to understand one's salary (Fassler, 1996) to understanding systems of care, (Villani & Fassler, 1995). The short turn-around time from submission to publication gives these formats the advantage of getting information to their readership in timely fashion.

The Future

The future practice of child and adolescent psychiatry will likely be shaped by the national debate about health care insurance. Whether consumers of services will become motivated to move away from the managed care paradigm is unclear. They may become disenchanted with the quality of care they receive or angry about the profits returned to health care executives and seek, through local or national legislation, to regulate more tightly the managed care industry. This could lead to changes that would bring back into focus the longer-term goals of increased functioning in adult life that have always been the main, albeit hard to measure, goal sought by child and adolescent psychiatrists.

Whether national health insurance or a single-payor system replaces the current managed care system, some future changes are highly probable. Child and adolescent psychiatrists can likely look forward to an even wider array of services available for patients and families. More in-home services, flexible outpatient systems, and alternative health-oriented modalities used in preventive fashion will follow the dollars to keep patients out of the high-cost settings. For the most severely disturbed, wraparound services, "complex packages of service wrapped around the child" (England & Cole, 1992) will replace standard outpatient care, and brief stays of months in residential treatment centers will replace inpatient treatment. Psychiatric treatment also will likely be integrated into juvenile justice settings as more and more conduct-disordered youth are managed out of mental health care systems and into penal systems.

The trend toward diversified practices as described by Mao (1994), consisting of jobs at several sites, will likely continue. The providers, both practicing psychiatrists and managed care companies, actually will share some common characteristics. They will be knowledgeable about complex systems of care, flexible about how to use them, and able to demonstrate clinical outcomes as well as patient and family satisfaction. While the present era is fraught with tumultuous, often unsettling change, the future actually may bring improved and cost-effective care.

REFERENCES

Barglow, P., Chandler, S., Molitor, N., & Offer, D. Managed psychiatric care for adolescents: Problems and possibilities. *Managed Mental Health Care*, 261–271.

England, M. J., & Cole, R. F (1992). Building systems of care for youth with serious mental illness. *Hospital and Community Psychiatry*, 43 (6), 630–633.

Fassler, D. (1996, September–October). What's it worth?: Analyzing your salary. *AACAP News*,

Geraty, R. D., Hendren, R. L., & Flaa, C. J. (1992). Ethical perspectives on managed care as it relates to child and adolescent psychiatry. *Journal of the American Academy of Child and Adolescent Psychiatry*, 31, 398–402.

Harper, G. (1989). Focal inpatient treatment planning. *Journal of the American Academy of Child and Adolescent Psychiatry*, 28, 31–37.

Jellinek, M. S., & Nurcombe, B. (1993). Two wrongs don't make a right. *Journal of the American Medical Association*, 270, 1737–1739.

Kenkel, P. J. (1993, September). Filling up beds no longer the name of the system game. *Modern Healthcare*, 39–41, 44, 46, 48.

Lazarus, A. (1995). An annotated bibliography in managed care for psychiatric residents and faculty. *Academic Psychiatry*, 19, (2), 65–73.

Mao, A. R. (1994). How a young psychiatrist can make a living in the nineties. *AACAP News*.

Villani, S. (1992). Treatment of severely disturbed children and adolescents. *Manual of Clinical Child and Adolescent Psychiatry*, 187–199.

Villani, S., & Fassler, D. (1995, January–February). Systems of care, *AACAP News*, 30.

38 / Training in Child and Adolescent Psychiatry

Eugene V. Beresin

Current State of Training

The training of child and adolescent psychiatry residents commands a unique force in the growth and development of the specialty as a whole. For the university-affiliated medical and mental health center, residents are the lifeblood of the department of child and adolescent psychiatry: They constitute a focus for a system that provides clinical service, educational programs, and research. A residency is the glue that holds a clinical and academic division together. It requires the faculty to keep abreast of current advances in theory and practice, provides a forum for their collegiality and generativity in mentoring future specialists, and demands their upholding and transmitting the highest standards of ethical, humane patient care, critical thinking, and ongoing pursuit of knowledge and skills. Training programs are thus highly instrumental in stimulating and directing the field.

For the child and adolescent psychiatry specialty at large, residents indeed are our future. They will be the caregivers of and advocates for our youth and families. They will constitute a new generation of teachers, academicians, researchers, and administrators. While there is often great joy and inspiration in participating in their education and training, it is simultaneously an awesome task and tremendous responsibility for the faculty. For residents, it is yet another transition in their professional development, one that occurs after many exhausting years of training, when they are excited about finally obtaining expertise in their area of interest but often arriving at a time when they are most vulnerable—intolerant of yet another period of uncertainty, forced to develop a new sense of professional identity, and more conflicted about balancing career with personal life issues such as building families and paying off large debts. It takes a well-constructed and administered training program to create an atmosphere in which residents and faculty work with

and learn from each other; where everyone feels a strong sense of commitment to preventing and treating psychiatric disorders at the highest possible level; where residents and faculty feel safe enough to evaluate each other's performance openly and mutually; and, finally, where happiness, enthusiasm, and morale are high despite long hours, hard work, personal insecurities, external demands, and economic and social pressures negatively influencing clinical practice and education. The thrust of this chapter is devoted to understanding the essential ingredients in developing such a training program.

THE NEED FOR CHILD AND ADOLESCENT PSYCHIATRISTS

Workforce Shortages: Currently there is a severe nationwide shortage of child and adolescent psychiatrists. The most recent study of the Council on Graduate Medical Education (COGME), sponsored by the federal government, revealed that, in 1990, there were 3,199, child and adolescent psychiatrists, while 33,052 were needed (Council on Graduate Medical Education, 1990). Based on current trends in recruitment, COGME estimated that, in 2010, the supply will increase only 2.3%, yielding a need 8.2 times greater than the supply. It should be noted that the COGME study is "need-based," using epidemiological data of incidence and prevalence of major psychiatric illness and workload of the average psychiatrist. In contrast, "demand-based" determinations have been advocated by managed care companies, looking at what they believe the demand is for "medically necessary treatment." Some managed care vendors argue that the nation is actually four-fold in oversupply now and that our current general and child and adolescent psychiatry graduates should be cut in half in order to prepare for the future market demands (Scully, 1996). There is, to be sure, great controversy as to what the actual "market demands" are now and what they will be in the future. Regardless of how the numbers are massaged, most clinical service systems would now concur that child and adolescent psychiatrists are in undersupply. Moreover, training programs are obliged to recruit and train the best possible clinicians, educators, researchers, and administrators for the future.

In 1986 the Child Caucus of the American Association of Directors of Psychiatric Residency Training (AADPRT) conducted a national survey of 104 of the 126 training programs. The results indicated that 35% of programs were having trouble filling their classes and 53% of programs were having difficulty recruiting highly qualified residents (Beresin & Borus, 1989). Moreover, the same study noted that 45% of programs were having difficulty recruiting faculty child and adolescent psychiatrists. Beresin and Borus found that 75% of programs had 6 or fewer full-time equivalent child and adolescent psychiatrists; 33% had only 2 to 4 such faculty. In 1987 Enzer, in an unpublished survey sponsored by the Society of Professors of Child and Adolescent Psychiatry (SPCAP) and the American Association of Chairmen of Departments of Psychiatry (AACDP), reported 100 vacant, funded faculty positions at 115 teaching institutions. Clearly, the shortage of faculty and the difficulty attracting highly qualified residents pose major challenges for the training of a needed cadre of child and adolescent psychiatrists, both as clinicians and academic leaders.

Problems and Potential Solutions in Recruitment: Obviously, we need a greater number of high-quality residents in child and adolescent psychiatry. The trend between 1979 and 1994 is worrisome since the data indicate that, during these years, there has been a 10% decrease in the number of programs approved by the Accreditation Council of Graduate Medical Education (ACGME) with only a 13% increase in the number of positions offered. Despite the increase in the total number of child and adolescent residents in training, this would only allow for 36 new graduates yearly if the trend were to continue. The good news is that in the past few years, all child and adolescent residency training slots have been filled.

However, other forces are cause for greater alarm. First, as a result of the 1996 Health Care Financing Administration ruling, there will be decreased federal subsidies for second certificate training, including child and adolescent psychiatry. Moreover, current diminished reimbursement for clinical services from managed care companies have caused many institutions to downsize residencies and fellowships. Even if the ACGME permits a greater supply of child and adolescent residency positions than in previous years, it is doubtful that most institutions will be able to support the current numbers. Second, many congressional leaders have endorsed a new report (Institute of Medicine, 1996) that proposes severe limitations on training international medical graduates. This report argues that there is an oversupply of specialists and strongly urges bringing the total number of first-year residency slots closer to the current number of graduates of U.S. medical schools. In 1995–96, 44% of all first-year psychiatry residents were international medical graduates. Eliminating them from the training pool would effectively decrease the number of psychiatry residents by nearly one-half, cause closure of a large number of psychiatric residencies, and threaten regions of the nation that rely heavily on international graduates to treat indigent inner city populations. It is not clear what the impact on child and adolescent residency recruitment would be, but there would likely be a strong reduction in general residents moving into our specialty, based on current interest and trends among medical students and general psychiatry residents.

The picture is even more worrisome from another viewpoint. Between 1988 and 1996 U.S. medical students entering psychiatry through the National Residency Matching Plan (NRMP) dropped by 40%. The total number of residency positions remained filled, however, through the large numbers of international graduates entering psychiatry. Five percent of U.S. medical students entered psychiatry in 1988 and in 1996 that figure had dropped to only 3.1% through the NRMP (Weissman, 1996). The constraints in financing of graduate medical education are putting great pressure on all psychiatric training programs to recruit U.S. medical graduates and for child and adolescent psychiatry training programs to recruit general residents as early as possible. This effort, however, should not preclude advocacy for maintaining a good pool of foreign graduates. However, even greater effort should be extended to recruit U.S. minority students. In 1995 only 11.5% of all psychiatric residents were African American and Hispanic. There is cause for concern for the future of child and adolescent psychiatry training if we consider that we are progressively losing general residents who initially expressed interest in the field when they entered general psychiatry training.

Weissman and Bashook (1986, 1987) found in

the mid-1980s that 30% of graduating senior medical students entering general psychiatry residencies were interested in child and adolescent training. However, by the postgraduate fourth year of training, interest dropped to 18%. In an informal poll of the AADPRT Regional Caucuses in 1992, most general psychiatry training directors noted similar percentages of initial interest in child and adolescent psychiatry among their new residents. However, over the past decade, only 12% of general residents entered child and adolescent training programs.

The biggest question in recruitment for child and adolescent residencies now is why there continues to be diminishing interest in the field during general residency training. There are many possible reasons for the decline in interest. There is little exposure to child and adolescent psychiatry during medical school training. Medical students are graduating with huge burdens of debt, currently averaging $80,000 to $100,000, and are less willing to add even one extra year to their training. The burgeoning areas of subspecialization within psychiatry may be drawing candidates away from child and adolescent psychiatry and enticing them toward other areas, such as forensic, geriatric, addiction, and consultation psychiatry. Child and adolescent psychiatry is often not a prominent part of early training experiences in general psychiatry. Many residents do not see youths and families until their third and fourth postgraduate year; meanwhile they have connected with faculty mentors in other areas of psychiatry.

Another major problem lies in the fact that, historically, child and adolescent psychiatry, in many medical centers, has been removed from the mainstream of general psychiatry training both physically and administratively. Often general residents have little or no contact with child and adolescent faculty for 2 or more years. Moreover, in many training centers the image of child and adolescent psychiatry unfortunately remains antiquated at best and negative at worst. Many general psychiatrists still perceive the field as having a soft clinical and research base dominated by vague models of play therapy and ill-formed theoretical and practice parameters. Finally, many general residents and faculty view child and adolescent psychiatrists as overworked, as they deal single handedly with children, families, social service agencies, pediatricians, other health care providers, schools, and probation officers. Often, they are straddled with excessive paperwork and

grossly underpaid. Residents are also witness to a current profound demoralization of child and adolescent psychiatry faculty as a result of changes in health care delivery, medical economics, and a lack of funding for teaching and research.

To help redirect the negative trend, several national organizations have begun major efforts aimed at increasing recruitment and interest in child and adolescent psychiatry. The American Academy of Child and Adolescent Psychiatry (AACAP) led a National Recruitment Conference on Child and Adolescent Psychiatry in 1989 involving all organizations invested in residency training; the AACAP, in conjunction with the National Institute of Mental Health (NIMH), coordinated a national conference in 1991 entitled "Interface between Child and General Psychiatry: Training and Research Opportunities"; the AADPRT formed a task force on the Collaboration between General and Child and Adolescent Training Programs; the AADPRT, in conjunction with NIMH, brought together leaders from all national organizations for 2-day task-oriented Recruitment Conference in 1992; finally, the AACAP initiated a recruitment task force following the latter meeting to implement some of its primary suggestions. The task force was then made a permanent standing AACAP Recruitment Committee in 1995.

The major actions recommended by these conferences to increase recruitment in child and adolescent psychiatry may be summarized as follows:

- Identify and track any early interest in child and adolescent psychiatry among medical students, general psychiatry, and pediatric residents.
- Provide faculty mentors for all those identified early in order to nurture their interest in the field. Organize high-quality clinical rotations and creative extracurricular activities (e.g., summer programs) to foster experiences with children and adolescents for those students. Select the most charismatic faculty to teach in core curricula at all levels of the educational process. Finally, sponsor forums for students and residents to better understand new developments, opportunities, and challenges in the field (e.g., career days, symposia, child and adolescent psychiatry clubs and retreats).
- Develop stronger ties between child and adolescent and general psychiatry training programs to provide early exposure to children, adolescents, and families in general residency training; integrate the child and adolescent faculty into the early phases of general residency training both as clinical supervisors of adult and child cases (both inpatient and outpatient) and teachers in the didactic curric-

ulum. This will enable residents to appreciate the value of developmental thinking at work.

- Dispel the negative image of child and adolescent psychiatry by demonstrating to medical students and residents what top-quality child and adolescent psychiatrists do in terms of clinical practice, teaching, and research.

- Bring the divisions of child and adolescent psychiatry closer into the mainstream of general residency training by placing child and adolescent faculty in visible administrative positions, such as departmental leaders and members of general psychiatry training, steering, and selection committees. Also, encourage child and adolescent faculty to present their work in public forums, such as case conferences and grand rounds.

- Foster collaboration in research projects. Currently there exist far more well-established research projects in adult than in child and adolescent psychiatry. Many adult studies can easily include a child and adolescent and/or family component. Increased research productivity will be a critical, if not the most important element, in stimulating bright young residents to enter the field and, at the same time, to advance our scientific knowledge base and credibility as a first-rate medical specialty.

The AACAP Recruitment Committee has initiated a national plan to further these goals. Each training program and medical school in the United States has a local recruiter, usually the director of child and adolescent residency training, whose mandate is to implement these objectives by working closely with the general training director, the director of medical student education in psychiatry, the division chief of child and adolescent psychiatry, and the department chairperson. At the national level, committee members have regular contact with the local recruiters and conduct annual surveys regarding helpful and harmful aspects of recruitment activities. A major tenet of the mission is that recruitment into child and adolescent psychiatry is an integral part of recruitment into general psychiatry. Hence the effort extends to all medical students and residents from all specialties with interests in youth and families. The 1997 the Workforce Committee of AADPRT will coordinate a similar effort with local recruiters in general psychiatry to work closely with child and adolescent recruiters. These projects will help the fields collaborate not only in recruitment but in many clinical, academic, and administrative areas.

TRAINING PROGRAMS: CERTIFICATION REQUIREMENTS AND STRUCTURE

Accreditation Council of Graduate Medical Education (ACGME) and Residency Review Committee: The ACGME is responsible for delineating training requirements for all medical specialty training programs. It maintains representatives from the American Board of Medical Specialties, the American Hospital Association, the Association of American Medical Colleges, the American Medical Association, and the Council of Medical Specialty Societies. The training requirements are divided into 2 broad categories: General Requirements and Special Requirements.

The General Requirements are broad in scope and apply to all medical specialties. They are concerned primarily with institutional (hospital and medical school) support for educational programs and generic training philosophy. As such, they govern issues such as institutional provision of the highest quality of health services, training, and education. They ensure that service or research requirements do not outweigh the program's educational mission, that there is ongoing supervision of residents, and that there is an administrative structure devoted to the management of resources dedicated to education. The program administration must be organized to involve the teaching staff in the selection of residents, program planning, program review, and evaluation of resident participation. The General Requirements also require a process for evaluation feedback, adequate compensation and benefits for trainees, mechanisms for grievance reporting and due process, acculturation assistance, availability of counseling services, and adequate physical facilities. ACGME site visitors survey each program every 3 to 5 years to verify that the requirements are met.

The Special Requirements are specific to each medical specialty or subspecialty. Each specialty has a Residency Review Committee (RRC), responsible for revising the Special Requirements every 5 to 10 years and conducting the ACGME program surveys. The Residency Review Committees Committee report to the ACGME. The Residency Review Committees members for psychiatry are nominated by the American Psychiatric Association (APA), the American Board of Psychiatry and Neurology (ABPN) committee, and the American Medical Association (AMA). There are 4 members of the RRC in child and adolescent psychiatry and 8 in general psychiatry.

The most recent revision of the Special Requirements for Child and Adolescent Psychiatry became effective in July 1995. When a revision is proposed, a draft is sent to all the child and adolescent programs directors (now approximately 120) and to most national organizations for review and feedback. A final revision is made by the ACGME Board.

The Child and Adolescent Special Requirements broadly include the following components. (For more details, see the Directory of Graduate Medical Education Programs, 1990–1991.)

1. Each program must provide a well-supervised, balanced experience with inpatients, outpatients, and consultees.
2. There must be a combination of didactic and clinical work that ensures knowledge of normal and abnormal development; developmental psychopathology; and biological, sociocultural, psychodynamic, behavioral, and familial aspects of childhood and adolescence and their problems. Residents must have training to treat patients competently when they come from various cultural backgrounds.
3. Opportunities must be available for developing conceptual understanding and clinical skills to treat infants, preschool, grade school, and adolescent children and families in a variety of modalities including short- and long-term psychodynamic, psychopharmacologic, behavioral, and family therapies. Residents must be exposed to a broad population of infants, children, adolescents, and families from all socioeconomic levels.
4. Work with outpatients must include diagnostic evaluations and an adequate experience with continuous care, including following some cases for at least 1 year.
5. Residents must understand the appropriate uses and limitations of psychological tests and should have the opportunity to observe some of their patients being tested.
6. There must be teaching in pediatric neurology, mental retardation, learning disabilities, and other neurodevelopmental disorders. Acquiring skill in working with severely disturbed children or young adolescents is an essential part of the training experience and must be achieved by having 24-hour responsibility for patients in settings with an organized treatment program, such as inpatient units, residential treatment facilities, partial hospitalization programs, and/or day treatment programs. This rotation must not be less than 4 full-time equivalent (FTE) months or more than 10 FTE months. Case loads must be assigned to offer in-depth training and not overload residents with service obligations.
7. A well-supervised consultation experience dealing with normal children and adolescents is essential in each of 3 areas:
   a. medical (pediatric inpatient and/or outpatient)
   b. schools
   c. forensic (e.g., courts, social service agencies)
   As part of the consultation experience, multidisciplinary clinical conferences and didactic seminars are essential.
8. Opportunities for clinical research projects and teaching community groups, medical students, and other residents must be available.
9. Graduate medical education must take place in an environment of inquiry and scholarship in which residents participate in the development of new knowledge, learn to evaluate research findings, and develop habits of inquiry as a continuing professional responsibility. The teaching staff is responsible for establishing and maintaining an environment of inquiry and scholarship.
10. Residents should have experience in the management of psychiatric emergencies and acute disturbances in children and adolescents.
11. Training must include supervised, active collaboration with other professional mental health personnel (psychologists, social workers, psychiatric nurses) in the evaluation and treatment of patients.
12. The didactic curriculum must be well organized, thoughtfully integrated, based on sound educational principles, and carried out on a regularly scheduled basis. Systemic formal instruction (prepared lectures, seminars, assigned readings, case conferences, etc.) must be integral to the residency. The didactic curriculum must cover normal and abnormal development; generally accepted theories and schools of thought; major diagnostic, therapeutic, and preventive procedures in the field of child and adolescent psychiatry; systematic instruction in basic biological, psychological, and clinical sciences relevant to psychiatry; psychodynamic theory; application of developmental psychological theories relevant to the understanding of psychopathology in children and adolescents, including the etiologies, epidemiology, diagnosis, treatment, and prevention of all psychiatric conditions that affect children and adolescents; and ethical aspects of psychiatric practice.
13. Each resident must have a postgraduate internship year with at least 4 months in internal medicine, pediatrics, or primary care medicine and 2 months of neurology, and a minimum of 2 years of accredited training in general psychiatry. The child and adolescent residency must encompass 2 full years of training.
14. Each training program must have a formal affiliation with or be an integral part of an accredited general psychiatry residency program.

15. The residency program in child and adolescent psychiatry must be under the leadership of a board-certified child and adolescent psychiatrist or one who possesses equivalent qualifications as determined by the Residency Review Committee. This person must devote at least half-time to the administration of the program and maintain responsibility for the quality and organization of the clinical and teaching activities. He or she must have at least 3 full-time equivalent fully trained child and adolescent psychiatrists in the program.

16. Each program must have at least 2 residents in each year of training.

17. A formal didactic and clinical training curriculum must be outlined and available to residents and faculty, including the stated goals and objectives of all educational experiences.

18. The training director is responsible for selection of residents, planning the curriculum, and evaluating individual residents.

19. The evaluation process must include an annual knowledge-based and clinical examination in addition to periodic assessments. Programmatic changes should be made on the basis of the evaluation process.

20. The program must provide opportunity for and document regularly scheduled meetings between the resident and the program director or designated faculty members. Mutual evaluations between residents and faculty are essential aspects of residency training and need to be reviewed on a regular basis between resident and training director. Residents must be advanced to positions of higher responsibility only on the basis of evidence of their satisfactory progressive scholarship and professional growth.

21. The training director is responsible to affirm that, upon graduation, the resident has exhibited no unethical behavior or unprofessional behavior and is unquestionably competent clinically.

22. There must be adequate physical facilities for learning, including offices, play materials, examination rooms, one-way mirrors, audiovisual equipment, and library resources.

The Special Requirements are, for the most part, a global list of criteria and do not specify how the guidelines are to be administered at each training site. The execution of the requirements is left to the discretion of the program director and his or her hospital facility. Obviously, clinical and didactic programs and faculty expertise along with institutional and fiscal constraints will vary from site to site. It takes great creativity and stamina on the part of the training director to mobilize resources effectively to produce a well-organized program. Models for the construction of a training program that meet the requirements are discussed later.

The ACGME has approved combined general psychiatry and child and adolescent psychiatry programs, which may be completed over 4 or 5 years after the first postgraduate year. These programs offer perhaps the greatest flexibility in program planning and integration of resources. At the same time, they necessitate either a single general and child and adolescent training director or a close partnership between 2 directors for an effective, well-coordinated residency. Programs in the same institution may offer multiple options for training, including both separate and combined tracks.

Since 1985 an innovative training sequence has been established, the Pediatric-Psychiatry-Child Psychiatry Program, otherwise known as the Triple Board Program. This training sequence allows graduating medical students 5 years of integrated training in pediatrics, psychiatry, and child and adolescent psychiatry. The program began with 6 centers. It was approved by the ABPN as a permanent track, permitting board eligibility for graduates in all 3 specialties. Now that it has been approved, the pediatric and psychiatry Residency Review Committees will have to construct a set of Special Requirements for the new program. All qualified institutions nationwide can apply for ACGME certification in Triple Board Training Programs.

American Board of Psychiatry and Neurology: While the ACGME and its Residency Review Committees accredit training programs, the ABPN certifies individuals as competent to practice. There are 2 formally acknowledged specialties for board certification, psychiatry and child and adolescent psychiatry. In order to be qualified to sit for the Child and Adolescent Psychiatry Board certifying exam, a candidate must have completed an internship year, at least 2 years of an ACGME-approved general psychiatry residency, and a 2-year ACGME-approved child and adolescent residency. The candidate must have passed the written and oral ABPN examinations in general psychiatry. The Child and Adolescent Board examination includes a written examination and oral examinations with clinical components in the preschool-age child, school-age child, consultation-liaison, and a live observed interview with an adolescent.

Many child and adolescent training programs

use their oral examinations as "mock board" examinations, both to assess clinical competence and to prepare for the ABPN examination. This is a highly controversial issue, for passing oral examinations may be extremely variable depending on the applicant's level of anxiety, the case material available, and particular individual traits and/or biases of the examiners. A number of medical specialty boards have eliminated oral examinations because of problems with reliability and validity. Standards for reliability and validity are easier to establish for written examinations.

As of October 1, 1994, all ABPN certificates in psychiatry and child and adolescent psychiatry have become time limited. Recertification is necessary every 10 years. Although the recertification examination format has not been established, most likely it will be in modular, written format. A modular examination is constructed in specified areas of expertise that are preselected by the applicants. While diplomats of the ABPN prior to 1994 will have lifelong certificates, many states appear to be moving toward using recertification as a primary means of relicensure.

RESIDENCY ADMISSION PROCESS

The admission process for child and adolescent residencies varies from program to program. Ideally, the training director should receive an application including:

1. A personal statement, which indicates origins, goals, and objectives for entering child and adolescent psychiatry. Additional biographical information, including both personal and professional experience, is highly useful.
2. A transcript from the candidate's medical school, including the dean's letter.
3. Letters of recommendation from the director of internship and general psychiatry training program, including summary evaluations of performance and personal qualities, and documentation of core ACGME requirements completed and/or incomplete rotations. This information is necessary, since the child and adolescent training director would need to supplement incomplete rotations for the candidate to graduate successfully from residency training and be eligible for ABPN certification.
4. Usually 2 or 3 letters of recommendation from service chiefs, the General Residency Department chairperson and/or individual supervisors.
5. A curriculum vitae.
6. Hospital and/or medical school application form,

which may be necessary for obtaining hospital appointments and/or state licensure.

The outset of the admission process on paper is, of necessity, a two-way street. Training programs should send applicants detailed brochures including an overview of the structure of the program and the goals and objectives of all clinical rotations and didactic seminars; a description of the clinical and academic facilities, faculty, research, and elective opportunities; and information regarding stipends and benefit packages.

While programs and applicants may look good (or bad) on paper, the applicant and members of the program must have a well-organized interview day in order really to get to know each other. Even the most seasoned training directors often have trouble deciphering the wealth of glowing dean's letters and stellar faculty recommendations, unless they are from well-known colleagues. It is essential for applicants to meet with the training director and division chief, if possible, and at least 1 or 2 other faculty members and residents. For optimal recruitment, it is desirable to request specific faculty members to meet with an applicant if they share mutual clinical and/or research interests.

A final reason for emphasizing an interview day is to reveal the true nature of a program's clinical experience, facilities, and philosophy. Many programs persistently carry myths that may have been true years ago but are no longer valid. The only way to dispel such myths (which tend to linger interminably) is to invite applicants to meet members of the program and encourage them to ask questions freely, in order to help them capture a glimpse of the program's current essence. The interactive process not only disseminates data but helps applicants and program personnel mutually evaluate personal styles and interests crucial for facilitating the finest matches.

Interviews with the residents are probably the most important part of the admission process from the standpoint of both the applicants and the training program. Applicants are more likely to "let their hair down" and openly reveal their strengths and weaknesses to residents (which they often conceal from faculty) and simultaneously ask questions about the program they often would not raise with the faculty. Each applicant comes with different desires about a training program and is most likely to believe what the residents say, with good reason. The residents are the acid test as to the nature and quality of the department and training experience. Residents, not training directors, sell programs. It is unwise for training directors or faculty to tell residents what to say in interviews. All interviewers should be as candid as possible about the strengths and weaknesses, the idiosyncrasies and the personalities that constitute a program. If an applicant accepts a program and gets what he or she saw, the new resident is more likely to be happy and fit in. If an applicant is sold a false package, there will be inevitable discontent, if not outright distrust. Satisfied, well-informed residents make solid programs. The admission process is akin to joining a team or a family. For the reasons just noted, residents' interviews and assessments of candidates are crucial in the mutual decision making between applicants and programs.

Once the interviews are completed, each interviewer should complete written evaluations and a simple rating scale. Regular meetings of the selection committee should review each applicant's written record and interview evaluations. Most important in this process is the discussion about the candidates. Obviously, superior academic achievements, clinical acumen, and leadership potential are important criteria for admission. However, equally important are the candidate's personal qualities and interests and his or her "goodness of fit" with the training program. The training director and selection committee need to have a clear understanding of what they are looking for in a good match, and they should openly discuss this. It is of great importance to hear what the resident members of the selection committee have to say, since they will be the front-line colleagues and teachers of their junior residents. A happy, well-balanced, cohesive peer group is necessary for the health and vitality of a training program. Therefore, the selection committee should have at least 1 resident from each class as voting members, in addition to the training director, division chairperson, and key service chiefs and supervisors.

Admission to a program also should be considered to be admission to the field. The selection committee should aim to choose diverse applicants who will fit in well in the program. High on the list of priorities should be a preference for minority and ethnic diversity, a balance of men and women, and applicants with special training, such as fluency in foreign languages, ability to use sign language for working with persons with deafness, and special expertise in other disciplines, such as

prior training in other medical and health care disciplines, teaching experience, or other clinically relevant training. As a field, perhaps more than in any area of psychiatry, we need researchers. Applicants with a firm grounding in research, such as M.D.-Ph.D.'s, those experienced in working on research teams, or those who show strong academic potential are all highly desirable. A model resident is perhaps the clinician-researcher.

We also should not underestimate the rigorous nature of our field and qualities valuable for working well clinically with youths and families in a multidisciplinary team. A good candidate is able to tolerate intense transference and countertransference brought out by working with severely disturbed children and families. He or she should be willing to put in long hours but be able to replenish energy expended. A good resident in child and adolescent psychiatry works hard and plays hard and is able to discuss feelings openly in supervision, to integrate complex psychosocial, cultural, and biological systems in the formulation and treatment of patients, to maintain intellectual integrity and curiosity, and, at the same time, to have a good sense of humor. Residents and faculty alike should all be able to step back and relish the fun they can have in their work.

THE CHILD AND ADOLESCENT PSYCHIATRY NATIONAL RESIDENCY MATCHING PLAN

Prior to 1992, there was no uniformity to the entry process nationally in child and adolescent psychiatry. In 1991, after the AACAP Training Committee conducted a national survey of 95 training directors and 534 residents regarding the entry process, a proposal was drafted for a National Uniform Entry Plan into Child and Adolescent Psychiatry. This proposal was refined by the AADPRT Child Psychiatry Caucus and won the approval of the AACAP, AADPRT, Association for Academic Psychiatry (AAP), APA, SPCAP, and AACDP. In 1992, 89% of programs joined the plan, which set the second Monday in November as the acceptance date for all applicants planning to enter training programs the following July (1993). Standards for expression of mutual interest between applicants and programs prior to making formal offers were set according to the guidelines for the National Residency Matching Program (NRMP). The APA Office of Education agreed to serve as a clearing house for unfilled positions. The National Child and Adolescent Training Consortium, with a representative from the

AADPRT, AACAP, AAP, APA, and SPCAP, was designated as an Oversight Committee to collect any reported problems, unethical behavior, or violations of the agreement. The plan was designated as a 3-year experiment, to be concluded with a thorough review by all major national organizations.

The National Uniform Entry Plan continued for 2 years. In 1993, following the second year of the plan, there was considerable interest in moving toward participation in the NRMP. Following thorough discussions at AADPRT and AACAP, a national vote of training directors was taken, and 96% of the field agreed to participate in the NRMP. Guidelines are as follows:

1. Applicants qualified to enter child and adolescent psychiatry may sign on for the match after their first postgraduate year.
2. The matching period begins in July of one year for acceptance the following July.
3. The standard rules of the NRMP apply. No program or applicant may make a prematch contingent agreement before match lists are due. However, nonbinding expressions of interest are acceptable.
4. Match lists in rank order are due at NRMP in mid-December, and results are distributed in mid-January.
5. The number of positions filled and remaining open are distributed to all participants and training programs when the match results are delivered.
6. Any problems with the match will be handled by the Psychiatry Match Review Board, the same board that handles the adult psychiatry match.

A major advantage of the child psychiatry NRMP is that it is only a 1-year match. Programs may select applicants any time before the match period for the following year. For example, programs may recruit first- or second-year postgraduates in general psychiatry programs for coming after their third and fourth postgraduate years. As long as recruitment takes place before 1 year prior to entry, acceptances are possible outside the formal NRMP. This flexibility allows for a range of recruiting plans. In the 3 years the child psychiatry NRMP has taken place, the general consensus is that it is highly successful.

CLINICAL AND DIDACTIC EXPERIENCE

Clinical Experience: The cornerstone of training in child and adolescent psychiatry is working with patients. The most common reason our residents enter specialty training is because they enjoy the engagement with youths and families. Often many are torn in medical school about choosing between pediatrics and child and adolescent psychiatry. The clinical arena is where residents can learn the most and acquire the basic skills and attitudes necessary for their careers. In many ways, the clinical experience has a much greater impact on their professional development and identity than any other part of the training program. Thus, when planning clinical rotations, the program director and faculty must be acutely aware of the physical plan, clinical population, clinical duties, duration of the rotation, and availability of faculty supervision. Clinical rotations should be organized over 2 years in a logical, educationally sound training sequence, in which the case load is carefully monitored for size and diversity in range of patients for evaluation and treatment. The resident should have progressively greater autonomous functioning. Despite managed care's emphasis on short-term treatment of psychiatric disorders, every effort should be made for residents to have longitudinal experiences with a number of children, adolescents, and families. Such experiences are essential for learning the intricacies of the growth and development of individuals and families.

Residents should have clinical experiences that teach them how to conduct effective diagnostic evaluations and develop biopsychosocial formulations of cases. They should be able to make accurate diagnoses based on the fourth edition of the *Diagnostic and Statistical Manual of Mental Disorders;* be familiar with a variety of interview techniques, including open-ended and structured interviews; and be competent in developing, initiating, and carrying out a comprehensive treatment plan that may include ancillary laboratory, pediatric, and psychosocial examinations and multimodal treatment techniques. They should have experience in conducting psychodynamic psychotherapy, family and group therapy, behavior and cognitive therapy, and pharmacotherapy. Residents should be training for cultural competence and be familiar with providing treatment to children and families of diverse racial and ethnic backgrounds. They should be able to provide consultation to pediatric teams, schools, courts, and social welfare agencies. They should have the opportunity to write special reports for schools and courts. In the clinical settings, residents should learn the administrative skills to lead and participate in multidisciplinary team structures. The fact that child and adolescent psychiatrists need to be trained as advocates for the welfare of children should be emphasized. Finally, residents need clinical and/or academic elective time to pursue areas of personal interest in some depth.

Providing such comprehensive experiences is one of the most difficult tasks of the training director. Naturally, one must work within the constraints of available hospital and affiliated resources and in the climate of current medical economics. The clinical goals and objectives, in terms of desired knowledge, attitudes, and skill acquisition, should be delineated for each rotation. I would like to propose a model rarely used in the tradition of child and adolescent training programs although it has worked well within my program, is in concert with contemporary available clinical service systems, and has, I believe, powerful pedagogic value.

Year 1 focuses on normal development, ambulatory diagnostic and treatment cases, and consultation psychiatry, with substantial clinical supervision and didactic seminars. Year 2 provides for inpatient, acute residential, and partial hospital experience and continuity of long-term cases, with a smaller degree of supervision. The rationale for this model is the changing nature of clinical child and adolescent psychiatry, in which inpatient, acute residential, and partial hospital stays are quite short and the lion's share of evaluation and treatment is in the outpatient sector. Long gone are the days of lengthy hospitalizations in which the resident could leisurely evaluate and treat children and families in the hospital milieu. Since inpatient work now primarily involves crisis intervention, rapid diagnostic assessment, clinical stabilization and protection, disposition planning, and triage and since inpatient diagnostic evaluations and interventions must be carried out in such short periods of time, residents need to arrive on their inpatient units well prepared. Inpatient work is more akin to intensive care unit rotations on medical and pediatric services, with a high degree of acute pathology. Having a full year of outpatient diagnosis and treatment under their belts, residents are best equipped to manage the short-term stays and limited goals effectively by serving as "junior attendings" on inpatient services. Traditionally residents begin on inpatient units in the first year. The rapid turnover of patients, massive amounts of administrative work, and need for intensely acute intervention significantly decreases their learning curve, even with the best supervision. This decrement in learning is clearly mitigated by moving inpatient work to year 2, when residents can utilize their accumulated knowledge base and skills in the ward setting. In the second year, residents ideally should be able to follow their patients from acute inpatient through residential and day programs that, it is hoped, are attached to the inpatient facility. Such a continuum allows for greater longitudinal contact with youths and families, even though the stays in such hospital programs are still quite brief. The following model of clinical rotations has proven successful. (Note how the model choosen is highly dependent on clinical and staffing resources.)

YEAR 1

Outpatient General Diagnostic Evaluations every other week, preferably with a faculty member present in the room. Six months can be devoted to "general diagnostics," including a variety of common outpatient clinic cases, carefully monitored for a range of ages and diagnostic categories. Six months should be devoted to "special diagnostics," including cases requiring a high technical level: infants; sexual and physical abuse cases; mental retardation, pervasive developmental disorders, learning disorders, and specific developmental disorders; adoption and custody; and care and protection and delinquency cases. From these diagnostics under close faculty supervision, residents should pick up some of the psychotherapy cases they would carry for 2 years.

Outpatient Family Diagnostic Evaluations every other week. These are often best conducted by a resident or faculty member behind a one-way mirror and/or using videotape, with a group of trainees and a faculty supervisor observing. Residents should pick up at least 1 family to treat over 2 years.

Outpatient Psychopharmacology Diagnostic Evaluations every other week. These require extensive supervision. Residents should pick up a reasonable number and variety of cases, which they will follow in their supervised psychopharmacology practice over 2 years.

Individual Psychotherapy Cases under supervision: minimum of 6 cases, including both long and short-term cases.

Family Therapy Case under supervision: minimum of 1 case.

Parent Guidance Case under supervision: minimum of 1 case.

Psychopharmacology Cases under supervision: Average case load could be 10 to 15 cases. The resident should treat, in *Behavior and Cognitive Therapy* under weekly supervision. Group supervision of an attending providing behavior and cognitive therapy is an essential part of this experience.

Consultation to Pediatrics: Six-month rotation, including supervision and walk rounds (10 hours/week).

Consultation to school: Three-to 6-month supervised rotation (4 hours/week).

Consultation to Court: Three-month supervised rotation (4 hours/week).

Pediatric Neurology: Three-month supervised rotation in which residents perform and observe neurologic examinations. It is also desirable to view the neuroradiological studies of the children examined (4 hours/week).

Normal Child and Adolescent Observation: Two- to 3-month rotation (4 hours/week).

Emergency Ward Coverage: On-call rotation with extensive supervision.

Clinical and/or Research Elective

Diagnostics should be *observed* as often as possible. I have found that the process of performing *brief* diagnostics with rapid triage in the presence of faculty is very helpful to residents, although it demands much faculty time. This model provides on-the-spot supervision and allows the faculty member to assist in the evaluation process and demonstrate clinical techniques. The model of residents performing diagnostics and psychiatric treatment unobserved is antiquated and far less effective than an interactive observational model. In this vein, regarding psychotherapy, it is extraordinarily useful for faculty to observe a number of resident sessions yearly, either directly or via videotape.

The number of psychotherapy, family therapy, parent, and psychopharmacology diagnostic evaluations and cases depends on the frequency of visits, severity of psychopathology, and general level of complexity. The numbers just listed seem reasonable for a basic training experience, but they should not be fixed in stone. It is useful for each resident to keep an accurate log of all his or her patient evaluations and treatment cases and review them regularly with the training director. Doing so will ensure adequate exposure to the full range of ages, gender, diagnostic categories, ethnic backgrounds, socioeconomic levels, and therapeutic modalities experienced. If deficits occur, the program director can talk with appropriate service chiefs to vary resident assignments.

A word should be mentioned about nontraditional, play experiences with children. While the essence of the residency is to learn clinical psychiatry, residents also need to understand how normal and abnormal children think and feel in a variety of contexts. Residents who are already

parents have an advantage over residents without children. Especially for the latter group, it is often useful (if the residents have time in their schedule) to provide nontherapy experiences with children early in training. The summer months are ideal for experiences such as attending a normal or therapeutic day camp, where residents act as counselors, not as doctors. Other summer experiences with children can be creatively designed and are truly inspirational for residents beginning a child and adolescent residency.

After this type of first clinical year, the resident is clearly equipped to become a team leader on an acute inpatient unit, while maintaining an outpatient practice under supervision and attending advanced seminars. The second year would be made up as follows.

YEAR 2

Latency and Preschool Inpatient, Acute Residential and Partial Hospital Rotation: Two-thirds time for 4 months.

Adolescent Inpatient, Acute Residential, and Partial Hospital Rotation: Two-thirds time for 4 months.

Clinical and/or Research Elective: Two-thirds for 4 months.

Ongoing Psychotherapy, Parent Guidance, Behavior and Cognitive, and Family Therapy: Cases under supervision.

Ongoing Psychopharmacology Clinic: Under supervision.

Group Psychotherapy: Cases in hospital and/or outpatient under supervision.

All inpatient rotations are intense and stressful, especially today, when the level of psychopathology in both youths and families is high and lengths of stay are short. Increasingly, there is less time for therapeutic interventions and a greater emphasis on rapid diagnosis, psychiatric stabilization, and disposition planning. Ideally rotations should, include experience with both younger children and adolescents. On-call is obviously a necessity but, given the rapid turnover and large number of late-night emergency admissions, frequency should not cause undue strain on residents and "service" should not outweigh the educational experience of reviewing cases. On-call duties, of course, must be tailored to the needs of the service system, but probably should not be more frequent than every 7 days, preferably less frequent.

Since the current trend is rapid discharge to stepdown units and partial hospital programs (i.e., day treatment, halfway and quarter-way houses, therapeutic residential or day schools, etc.), residents ideally should learn about the continuity in treatment systems. One model for this exposure is to assign residents 2 to 3 acute inpatient cases and, upon discharging a patient to partial hospital programs, allow the resident to follow the child and family "through the system." This model addresses the need for learning skills in partial hospital settings, while exposing the resident to the child's and family's experience of movement through a network providing continuity of care. Of course, this model is practical only if the training institution either contains partial hospital programs on site or is in close proximity to such centers.

As indicated earlier, it is important for residents to carry some outpatient cases under supervision, for up to 2 years. Inpatient, didactic, and elective time should not interfere with their outpatient practice. In this model, outpatient diagnostic evaluations are limited to year 1, so year 2 can focus on multimodal treatment at an advanced level. Elective opportunities will be described later.

Didactic Experiences: The structure, sequence, and function of seminars should be closely coordinated with the clinical experience. While teachers have different styles of presenting material, a few general guidelines should be considered in constructing seminars:

- Syllabi and educational objectives should be handed out in advance of each seminar, including a table of contents and all readings. Required weekly readings should not exceed 10 pages per seminar. Additional optional readings could be provided for future reference.
- Seminars should encourage active problem solving and interaction among residents and faculty.
- Audiovisual materials and modern educational technology such as videotape or computer simulations and one-way mirrors should be utilized liberally.
- Residents should be encouraged to make frequent presentations and lead discussions.
- At least a few conferences should be multidisciplinary.

Not all programs have sufficient faculty expertise to teach every area of child and adolescent psychiatry. This is understandable given the small numbers of faculty in many departments. Josephson and Drell (1992) have designed an innovative teaching method in which topics are presented in "modular format." Modules are user-friendly curricula designed to be implemented from 2 to 10

weeks or more, depending on the time allotted by the training program. Each module is designed for a specific number of weeks and consists of goals and objectives, along with annotated critical readings for that period. The model, advocated by AAP, AADPRT, AACAP, and SPCAP, currently is being utilized for curricula in many areas of child and adolescent psychiatry. The AADPRT and AACAP have discussed putting modular curricula on home pages on the World Wide Web, so training directors can have rapid access to a range of modules. This versatile system promises to be a great asset to the field. It is hoped that modules could be produced in all areas of child and adolescent psychiatry and updated regularly by experts in each topic area. Certain topics are in need of development and dissemination, including infant psychiatry, developmental neurobiology, psychopharmacology, behavior therapy (Beresin & Borus, 1989), substance abuse, forensic psychiatry, transcultural psychiatry, ethics, administrative psychiatry, and psychiatric aspects of AIDS.

Another way of increasing residents' exposure to excellent teachers is to consolidate a number of seminars between different training programs. For example, at Harvard Medical School, there are 3 training programs in child and adolescent psychiatry: the Massachusetts General and Mclean Hospital program, the Cambridge Hospital program, and the Children's Hospital program. In 1993 the 3 programs began sending all the residents to 2 first-year seminars (Child and Adolescent Development and Psychopathology) and second-year residents to 3 seminars (Quantitative Methods, Developmental Neuroscience, and Integrating Clinical Perspectives). All the residents reviewed this experience favorably. Not only does it broaden their academic experience, but it brings residents from different training programs together, providing them with an opportunity for sharing ideas about training experiences and developing collegial relationships.

In concert with the model of clinical experiences described earlier, Table 38.1 presents one sample scheme of seminars for year 1.

The sequence of seminars should be planned carefully. For example, emergency psychiatry, psychopharmacology, forensic psychiatry and trauma, and psychological testing should be offered early in the year, since they are vital for initial and emergency evaluations. It should be noted that these didactic seminars are distinct from first-year clinical rotations, where additional scholarly material is presented. For example, in court and

TABLE 38.1

Year 1 *Seminar Scheme*

Seminar	Time	Frequency	Length
Child & Adolescent Development	1 1/2 hrs	weekly	all year
Developmental Psychopathology	1 1/2 hrs	weekly	all year
Diagnostic Interviewing	1 1/2 hrs	weekly	all year
Psychotherapy	1 hour	weekly	all year
Family Therapy	1 hour	weekly	September–June
Psychopharmacology	1 hour	weekly	all year
Clinical Multidisciplinary Case Conference	1 hour	weekly	all year
Child and Adolescent Neurology and Neuropsychiatry	3 hours	weekly	8 weeks
Forensic Psychiatry and Trauma	1 hour	weekly	12 weeks
Behavior and Cognitive Therapy	1 hour	weekly	8 weeks
Primary Supervision (development of professional identity, ethics of practice, and clinical administration)	1 hour	weekly	all year
Pediatric Consultation Rounds	1 hour	weekly	6 months
Neurodevelopmental Psychiatry: Mental Retardation, Pervasive Developmental Disorders, and Developmental Disabilities	2 hours	weekly	4 weeks
Emergency Psychiatry	1 hour	weekly	4 weeks
Neuropsychological Testing	1 hour	weekly	2 weeks
Psychological Testing	1 hour	weekly	4 weeks
Infant Psychiatry	1 hour	weekly	9 weeks
Sexual and Physical Abuse	1 hour	weekly	4 weeks
Substance Abuse	1 hour	weekly	8 weeks
Adoption and Custody	1 hour	weekly	6 weeks
Bereavement	1 hour	weekly	2 weeks
Social and Community Psychiatry	1 hour	weekly	5 weeks
Cultural Competence	1 hour	weekly	4 weeks
Short-term Psychotherapy	2 hours	weekly	4 weeks
Group Psychotherapy	1 hour	weekly	September–June

school consultation rotations, seminars on pertinent clinical and research material are presented. Within the ambulatory rotations, additional conferences are offered as needed, for example in behavior and cognitive therapy, psychological testing, and so on. This is an extensive number of first-year seminars. While it is difficult to provide all of them, for purposes of this model of training, it is crucial to give the residents an intensive educational exposure to child and adolescent psychiatry in year 1. Year 2 can then focus on a greater degree of advanced clinical cases and serve to integrate models of psychopathology and its treatment.

Commonly, several very important topics are covered in multiple seminars; for example, ethics may be taught in "primary supervision," psychotherapy, forensic psychiatry, consultation rounds, and clinical case conferences. Transcultural issues, an often neglected topic, may be covered extensively in the family therapy seminar and be presented in clinical case conference, social and community psychiatry, and consultation rounds. Obviously, there is always inevitable redundancy

TABLE 38.2

Year 2 *Seminar Scheme*

Seminar	Time	Frequency	Length
Integrating Clinical Perspectives (advanced seminar building on year 1 topics; complex cases presented and discussed from multiple diagnostic and therapeutic perspectives)	1 1/2 hrs	weekly	40 weeks

Brief Intermittent Therapies
    Psychoanalysis/Psychodynamic
    Psychotherapy
    Psychopharmacology
    Behavior & Cognitive Therapy
    Family Therapy
    Cultural Diversity
    Psychological Testing and
    Psychoeducational Intervention
    Psychopathology
    Forensics and Trauma			

Quantitative Methods (research seminar)	1 1/2 hrs	weekly	22 weeks
Developmental Neuroscience	1 1/2 hrs	weekly	16 weeks
Inpatient and Residential Case Conference	1 hour	weekly	all year
Observed Preschool Treatment Case	1 1/2 hrs	weekly	all year
Advanced Child Development: Theory and Practice	1 hour	weekly	6 months
Integration of Theory and Practice	1 hour	weekly	6 months
Transition to Practice	1 hour	weekly	all year
Group Psychotherapy	1 hour	weekly	all year
Short-term Psychotherapy	2 hours	weekly	4 months

in many seminars. However, while some redundancy is essential to pedagogy (J.T. Coyle, 1995 personal communication), if the program director has all the syllabi and readings, he or she and the training committee can make periodic reviews and revisions of the curriculum. Table 38.2 presents a sample scheme of seminars for year 2.

The second-year seminars are designed to amplify and expand on the first-year seminars. Some innovative techniques may be used. For example, in quantitative methods, an effort can be made to demystify research methodology, an area often intimidating to residents. In one model (L. Baer & D. Norman, unpublished curriculum 1995), a basic text and articles are used as reading materials. The seminar itself is divided into two 45-minute sections: In the first section, the leaders use a laptop computer, hooked up to an overhead projector, and demonstrate how statistical methods are applied to simple, clinical hypotheses; in the second section, a local researcher speaks

about his or her work and how it developed. The residents have an opportunity to hear from a variety of researchers, full and part time, who have integrated scientific inquiry into their busy lives. In another model (M. Murphy, unpublished curriculum 1996), residents learn primarily how to read the scientific literature and hear about research ideas developed by a number of the faculty. We have used both models successfully in our training program.

A seminal feature of both clinical supervision and didactic teaching is to help residents learn to think clearly and scientifically. The application of intellectual curiosity and hypotheses testing is necessary and appropriate not only for traditional scientific inquiry and the acquisition of basic knowledge but also for everyday clinical practice. The excitement and stimulation of creative thinking should permeate all aspects of a well-crafted training program.

Elective Opportunities: It is essential to provide

residents with clinical and research elective time in both years of training. Child and adolescent psychiatry has grown tremendously over the past 2 decades, with increasing subspecialization. Residents need time and guidance to experiment in areas of potential future postgraduate training. Electives should be offered in didactic seminars, clinical subspecialties, and research training. While electives are important in developing special interests and skills, they should not compromise clinical training, which is the primary goal of residency training.

Elective time in year 1 and year 2 should be highly structured and approved by the training director. If at all possible, research projects should be encouraged. Moreover, residents should present a talk to the division on how they spent their elective blocks and/or produce a written manuscript or research proposal. These tasks not only help them prepare formal presentations but encourage research and writing, since most lectures should be scholarly in nature, even if the elective is clinical.

The role of the mentor is of particular importance in the elective experience. A useful structure is the development of a mentor system in which residents choose specific faculty members to help them on their career path. A mentor serves many functions: role model, advisor on career strategies, facilitator in helping the resident make local and national contacts, and, often, collaborator in research or clinical efforts. The available pool of faculty mentors should be chosen by the training director on the basis of their experience, wisdom, and charisma. Special efforts should be made to help residents develop full- or part-time research careers utilizing experienced mentors.

Examinations: Training programs are required to administer 2 formal examinations annually to residents: a written "knowledge-based" assessment and a clinical examination. The ACGME does not stipulate the form or content of the examinations. Many training programs utilize the Psychiatry Residency in Training Examination (PRITE) for its cognitive examination. The PRITE is a multiple-choice test, written by an Editorial Board under the auspices of the American College of Psychiatrists (ACP). The board consists of representatives from the college and other national organizations interested in training, resident representatives, and a board-certified neurologist. The PRITE has been utilized by virtually all general psychiatry training programs as the

standard knowledge-based examination. The test covers the entire field of general psychiatry, including sections on growth and development and child and adolescent psychiatry. Trainees take the examination under standardized conditions and receive not only their raw scores in each specialty area but an analysis of how they compare with general residents at their level of training, in their institution, and nationally, and how they stand among residents at all levels of training in the United States. An answer booklet is sent to them 6 weeks after the examination, including not only the questions and correct answers but references corroborating the answers. Hence, it is intended to serve a self-assessment function with remedial value. Many child and adolescent programs utilize the PRITE in some fashion for their residents, particularly as a preparation for their written ABPN examination. In 1994 a Child PRITE was established with its own Editorial Board, although a number of members overlap with the General Psychiatry PRITE. In its first year there were 50 questions. In subsequent years, the number will be increased to 100, to match the ABPN written child and adolescent psychiatry examination. Moreover, since the child psychiatry ABPN examination emphasizes the last 5 years of the literature, greater consideration is being given to making the Child PRITE similar in content.

The Editorial Board and the ACP currently are addressing some problems with the PRITE. While the PRITE has been used as the "gold standard" for an in-training examination, most residents and training directors have hoped it also would serve to assist residents in preparing for the ABPN written examination. Until recently, no effort was made to correlate PRITE scores with ABPN written sources. In the 1992 General Psychiatry PRITE examination, a correlation study was begun, cosponsored by the ACP and the ABPN. Residents taking the examination were asked for permission to compare their scores over 3 years of training with their ABPN scores. The investigators hoped to see evidence of increased knowledge accumulation over consecutive PRITE tests and a correlation between PRITE scores and ABPN written examination pass/fail rates. The results will be instrumental in establishing a closer relationship between the PRITE and ABPN examinations.

A number of educators wonder about the value of multiple-choice examinations as a means of assessing knowledge. They contend that scores may be skewed by test-taking ability, moreover, they question the role of such examinations in residency training. Some argue that, if examinations such as the ABPN and PRITE are testing knowledge base in the interests of assessing clinical competence, multiple-choice examinations may not adequately serve this function—may not be valid. Other formats are being used and/or considered, for example, essay examinations posing a series of clinical vignettes and asking a small number of relevant questions that demand the application of knowledge. The advantage of this format is that it reveals the utilization of knowledge and clarity of clinical thinking, perhaps better indicators of competence than knowing answers to fact-based questions. Others have advocated interactive-style tests, either on paper or via computer, which currently are used in a number of medical schools and by other postgraduate specialty boards.

The clinical examination, similarly, has been implemented by most programs in "mock oral board" format. Arguments against such a method were discussed earlier. Many programs in the same city or region have worked together to simulate the oral board experience. Many training directors contend that clinical evaluation should be built into the daily fabric of training programs, and formal testing, while a useful preparation for the boards, is superfluous in the assessment of clinical competence.

Evaluations: An ongoing process of mutual evaluation between residents and faculty is perhaps one of the most important components of the training program. It also is probably the most difficult system to operationalize, for many reasons. First and foremost, neither residents nor faculty find giving and taking criticism to easy. A constant thorn in the side of many training directors is actually getting residents and faculty to turn in their written evaluations in a timely fashion (if at all). Moreover, few residents and staff are able to be candid in delivering negative comments. Far too often, written evaluations are similar to letters of recommendation: They emphasize strengths and minimize or, at worst, omit weaknesses. The training director is ultimately responsible for the quality of the program and competence of its graduates. Defects in individuals and educational systems can be corrected only if problems are revealed. How then can one create a functional, healthy evaluative process and instill in all the motivation and sense of obligation to participate in it? The following suggestions may prove helpful:

Above all, in the words and spirit of D.W. Winnicott, the program director must help create a facilitating environment with sufficient "holding" and safety to stimulate a healthy maturational process for individuals and the program. Residents and faculty must feel safe enough to talk openly with each other about each other. This security emanates from the words and deeds of the program director. He or she should have individual meetings with residents and faculty at least twice yearly in which open, honest reciprocal feedback takes place. The director must listen, be heard, and, on the basis of feedback, initiate action to help fix what is impaired, both in the program and in individual residents and faculty. If everyone feels confident that critique will always be viewed as constructive, that retaliation or unwarranted punitive action is forbidden, and that corrective efforts will be initiated, a healthy process of evaluation can be established.

Hold group meetings of key faculty members at least twice yearly to discuss the program and, most important, to evaluate the progress of each resident. Written evaluations are far inferior to these meetings. Occasionally, faculty will disagree about a resident's performance. In an open discussion, oftentimes the disparity will be clarified by information known by one and not another. A frank discussion usually is more candid than what faculty are willing to put in writing. Finally, since many faculty only get to see a resident in one setting, each person working with the resident can develop a greater multidimensional understanding of the person and his or her strengths and weaknesses. This will clearly help all faculty in training the resident. Moreover, a broader perspective on the means toward growth may be achieved when faculty members put their minds together. Finally, meeting as a group gives all a sense of responsibility and staff cohesion in the process of training and educating the residents. This helps not only the residents but also the training director, when he or she must ask faculty to do things for the program.

Regular meetings with the residents, ideally with both classes together, should be held at least every other week or weekly to discuss the strengths and problems in the program. Resident group meetings provide ongoing feedback that helps the training director explore solutions to problems as they arise. It is far easier to iron out wrinkles in the system in this way than let them build to become monumental difficulties. Obviously, not all complaints can be resolved to everyone's satisfaction. However, the availability of the training director and the residents' sense of being heard is extremely important in maintaining morale. When possible, the director should offer the residents the opportunity to propose solutions to programmatic problems, such as call and seminar schedules. In my experience, some if not all of the best solutions to residency difficulties come from the residents themselves. The process of giving the residents a major role in the design and implementation of training goals and objectives helps them feel somewhat responsible for their own professional development. Moreover, when residents and faculty collaborate in many aspects of the program, all feel a greater sense of unity in the training mission.

Directors should make written evaluation forms as simple and easy to complete as possible (1 side of 1 page, if possible). Residents should complete evaluation forms regarding all clinical rotations, didactic seminars, and individual supervisors. Ratings on a 3- to 5-point scale are helpful for most variables assessed.

Residents should evaluate their clinical services in terms of variety of patients seen, quality of supervision in relevant areas of necessary knowledge and theory, application of therapeutic modalities, amount of administrative duties, and amount and quality of on-call duty. Didactic seminars should be rated for each instructor and/or module in terms of the quality of presentation and content, relevance to practice, and utility of the readings. Supervisors should be evaluated according to their contributions in specific clinical areas of training (e.g. psychotherapy, pharmacotherapy), availability to the resident, professionalism, helpfulness in applying theory and knowledge to practice, quality of teaching and ability to form a useful teacher-resident relationship. These are simply the bare bones of variables to be evaluated. Many more may be helpful to particular programs. It is valuable to have room on the form for brief open-ended comments concerning strengths and weaknesses of the training experience. Finally, a statement should be included that the resident and instructor have discussed their mutual evaluations and a place provided for both to sign.

Faculty should evaluate resident performance on clinical services, in didactic seminars, and in individual and/or group supervision. In each area, variables to be rated should include, at minimum, clinical skills (specify modalities), knowledge base,

professionalism, ethical behavior, ability to form a therapeutic alliance with patients, and ability to apply supervision provided. It is also helpful to include when and how often the faculty member observed the resident with patients and if he or she would feel comfortable referring patients to the resident. This is a fine way of gleaning the degree of confidence the faculty has in a particular resident's overall clinical skills. As in resident evaluations, there should be space on the form for comments regarding strengths, weaknesses, and degree of professional growth. A process of discussing the evaluations with the resident should be mandated. Both resident and faculty member should sign the form following their discussion.

A training director's resident summary evaluation form is a useful aid in consolidating all the verbal and written evaluations. These forms should be completed every 6 months and reviewed in the biannual meetings with residents. Such forms may be quite simple. They should indicate the month in the training program when the summary was made. Variables rated need only include clinical skill, knowledge base, professional attitudes and behavior, and ethical conduct. Open written sections on comments from the training director and comments from the resident, followed by both signatures, permits documentation of the mutual evaluation and feedback process.

Yearly off-campus resident and faculty retreats, with groups together, separate, or in some combination of each, may establish a forum for reflection on the overall training program. Occasionally they may be used to tackle systemic training problems, unhampered by the routine distractions of daily activities in the clinical training center.

The training program schedule should guarantee residents time to meet by themselves. The goals and objectives of a residency association go far beyond evaluation, particularly in forming group cohesion, but independent evaluation of the program is an essential feature of these meetings.

Residents and faculty should be encouraged to attend national meetings as a means of evaluating their programs. At annual meetings of organizations such as the AACAP, AAP, APA, and AADPRT, program members have an opportunity to attend committees and symposia on training or in specific areas of subspecialization, and see what is being done in other training institutions. Moreover, residents and faculty can meet with colleagues from other programs and discuss how training problems are handled. The more national involvement members of the program have, the more one can draw from a range of potentially helpful modifications to one's program.

THE RESIDENT PEER GROUP

It was mentioned earlier that satisfied residents make solid programs. The inevitable stress and inherent obligations in training can clearly work against their happiness quotient. Despite thoughtful interventions by the training director, division chairperson, and faculty, a certain degree of resident Sturm und Drang is intrinsic to the training enterprise. The formation of a close resident peer group can greatly diminish stress and enhance contentment in a number of ways. As described earlier, through a residency association and retreats, residents can bond together as active participants in modifying the training program. The training director should amplify their voice in any process of change.

Resident groups vary from year to year in their mix of personalities, "class character," and ability to form lasting individual personal and professional relationships. However, every opportunity should be made available for them to develop friendships and/or professional collegial ties both within and outside the training program. Process-oriented training groups, parties, regular meetings, group educational experiences, sharing cases, and collaborating in research projects are all helpful in fostering these relationships. In my experience, a close-knit residency is a key to success. Residents then are motivated to work well with each other, to share duties and responsibilities, to come freely to a peer's aid when need arises, to learn from and teach each other (a process that cannot be overemphasized), and to understand the value and necessity of sound, trusting relationships in professional life. All of these experiences will hold residents in good stead for their careers in child and adolescent psychiatry.

THE RESIDENT AS TEACHER AND LEADER

One of the defining features of clinical child and adolescent psychiatry is the multidisciplinary team approach. Residents must learn to work within team structure and, if appropriate, learn to be proficient as team leaders. Opportunities for this training experience should occur in inpatient, partial hospitalization, residential, outpatient, and consultation settings. Leadership and administrative training necessitates observation of faculty

expertise in this role, supervised individual clinical experiences, and didactic seminars. While it is true that some people are "born leaders," administrative skills can and should be taught.

Whether residents choose to work in academia or in clinical practice, as professionals in child and adolescent psychiatry, they must view themselves as teachers. The skills needed for teaching also require formal instruction and practice. Ideally, residents should understand the fundamental principles of pedagogy and be able to apply them in different formats (e.g., lecture, seminar, case conferences, clinical interviewing) and for a wide range of audiences, including psychiatric colleagues, other health care professionals, teachers, probation officers, and parents, among others.

DIFFICULTIES IN PROFESSIONAL TRANSITIONS

The Transition from General to Child and Adolescent Psychiatrist—Identity Formation: While the primary focus of child and adolescent psychiatry residency training is acquiring knowledge and clinical skill, equally important, and often sadly neglected, is attention paid to the development of a professional identity as a child and adolescent psychiatrist. Innumerable stressors in the transition from general psychiatry residency to the child and adolescent residency may impede the learning process. The most common transition problems include the following:

- The narcissistic injury of starting over and returning to "beginner status" yet again in the epic of medical training, after having achieved a sense of confidence and competence with adults.
- The loss of one's general residency peer group, particularly for those who change institutions.
- Loss of well-established adult patients and threatened weakening of skills in treating adults learned in general residency.
- The discomfort of working with children and adolescents for the first time. Residents must manage primitive defenses, often at a nonverbal level, without being able to use concepts and more advanced cognitive skills that they could use with adult patients. There are also greater problems with countertransference (e.g., acting out rescue fantasies, siding against and trying to undo actions of "bad" parents; overidentification with child patients, etc.).
- The stress inherent in working with dying and disabled children and grieving parents.
- The need to serve as judge and authority for physicians, parents, teachers, and courts in decision

making (e.g., mandated placement, care and protection, incarceration, court-ordered removal of parental custody, etc.) that will have a major, lifelong impact on the child and family at a time of limited knowledge and experience.
- The difficulty in embracing a developmental, conceptual approach, which requires greater integration of clinical models.
- The increasing problems of dealing with limited resources for children, such as hospital, residential, outpatient, educational, and community services.
- Coping with greater stress in one's personal life: Single residents have increased pressure to establish love relationships. Residents with significant others, particularly those with children, have increasing difficulty balancing work and family time. Residents with large student loans especially often envy peers who did not continue training and are out making a good living.
- The excessive time demands of child and adolescent psychiatry compared with adult psychiatry (e.g., meetings, phone calls, paperwork).
- The difficulty involved in professional identity formation for the child and adolescent psychiatry resident. It is greater than for the general psychiatry resident because:
  a. Residents must learn to cope with the generally negative image of child and adolescent psychiatry in medicine.
  b. Child and adolescent psychiatry is, perhaps, more general than adult (AKA "general") psychiatry. A tremendous amount of learning and integration must be accomplished in 2 short years, considering the intense demands of understanding the multifaceted developmental perspective. Moreover, there are multiple treatment modalities to learn, and each requires variations in technique when working with different age groups, disorders, families, ethnic backgrounds, and so on.
  c. There is a paucity of teachers and mentors in child and adolescent psychiatry nationwide. Most faculty are part-time clinicians, and there are few academic and research mentors. This is particularly true for many smaller programs.

Training directors, department and division chiefs, and faculty should be made aware of these problems in transition. Solutions to these pressures require attention and support from administration, faculty, and peers. Many of these issues can be addressed in the clinical and didactic rotations noted previously. Particularly important activities include:

1. Screening for the most adaptive and resilient residents in the admissions process.
2. Developing a "transition to child and adolescent psychiatry" module in one or more seminars, in

which many of the preceding issues can be discussed. Moreover, residents should be formally introduced to the specific characteristics of the field and work. Residents who make the independent, untutored discovery of the nature of our specialty and its particular stresses often feel resentful and disappointed.
3. Providing ample forums for residents to meet with the training director and faculty to discuss and strategize coping mechanisms for managing difficulties in transition and identity formation.
4. Enabling residents to observe the faculty in action and understand their identity and behavior in a variety of clinical settings.
5. Devoting ample time in the program for residents to learn how to integrate and apply models of development.
6. Promoting identity formation as a child and adolescent psychiatrist by supervising residents in consulting to physicians, nurses, and other health specialists, and facilitating the role of teacher of adult psychiatry residents, medical students, and parents. It must be emphasized that faculty support and advice always must be accessible.
7. Using all possible means to integrate child and adolescent psychiatry into the department and establishing visibly its special value to the department and medical school.
8. Helping residents maintain contact with general residency peers as much as possible socially, clinically, and academically.
9. Providing supervision for the continued treatment of some adult patients to maintain previously acquired skills (e.g., carrying those patients into child/adolescent training, private practice, moonlighting, etc.).

THE TRANSITION TO PRACTICE

Borus has described a neglected area of training, namely, the transition from residency to professional career (Borus, 1982). Residents universally experience great anxiety, even as early as at the end of training year 1, when considering career choices and struggling with the inevitable tradeoffs of choosing one path versus another. This often involves making compromises among professional interests, financial rewards, and personal values. The Transition to Practice seminar (Borus, 1982) can help residents in this period of turmoil. The seminar is particularly useful when it brings in child and adolescent psychiatrists working in diverse settings (e.g., general hospital, public sector, private practice, inpatient and outpatient practices of various kinds) and conducting a range and often patchwork of professional activities (clinical, administrative, academic, research, etc.). Faculty members should describe the evolution of their individual careers, including the details of personal decision making, job negotiations, running a private practice, working for community agencies, developing academic and research endeavors, becoming an administrator, and so on. The pros and cons of each career path should be candidly discussed with ample time for residents to ask specific questions. Another component of the seminar should include common problem areas in the transition to practice, such as the dual-career couple and the female professional. For this seminar to be useful, faculty members should focus on the nuts and bolts of their transition and practice. This is not a place for lofty, theoretical explications; rather, it is most appropriate to answer basic, concrete questions about beginning careers and their daily maintenance, along with integrating career with personal life.

ADMINISTRATION: THE ROLE OF THE TRAINING DIRECTOR

The Experience of Middle Management in Academic Medicine: The training director in academic residencies is in a unique position: He or she maintains authority without power. Without hiring or firing ability or control of a budget, the training director is in the uncomfortable position of asking faculty members to do many things for little material reward. The most effective residencies, with hardworking, cooperative faculty members, necessitate a cohesive, dedicated faculty that takes great pride, responsibility, and joy in residency training. The training director must lead this team and create the necessary value structure and ambiance for a responsive faculty group. A number of guiding principles may be posited in order to achieve such a system.

Above all, the training director needs the unconditional support of his or her department and division chiefs. If the chairpersons make it clear that child and adolescent residency training is a major priority, the work of the training director is, in effect, the word of the chief. It is hard for faculty members to refuse requests in this situation. Moreover, it places the training director in a wonderful position to help his or her faculty play a valued role in the department, by joining the team and mission of training.

The training director should always attempt to be an advocate for faculty promotion and professional advancement. He or she must be viewed as a direct line to the chairperson. The training director should make available including presentations at departmental and regional grand rounds, participation on important departmental committees, opportunities to join research teams, and creation of leadership positions within the department in subspecialty areas so that faculty members can be viewed as experts in clinical or academic areas. Every effort should be made to acknowledge faculty achievements (e.g., teacher of the year award, etc.). Part-time faculty and those in affiliated institutions should never be viewed as second-class citizens. They should be involved in as many training and departmental activities as possible.

Individual meetings with individual faculty members on a regular basis, biannual faculty meetings to review the residency, and retreats should be organized to maintain cohesion of the group and the mission of the training program. The training director should always be available for calls from the faculty and respond promptly. In short, each faculty member should feel valued and part of the training process.

A parallel, though slightly different, process is needed in working with the residents. While the training director does not have power, in the strict sense of the word, over faculty members, he or she does have power over the residents. Residents work hard and learn best when they are generally happy. Obviously "happiness" must be taken with a grain of salt, since residency is so stressful in many ways. The following are some suggestions for enhancing resident satisfaction and learning.

The training director always should be viewed as an advocate for the highest ideals of training. This requires being heard by the residents and standing up for their interests to ensure quality of the educational experience. While certain resident requests may be reasonable, if not ideal, for their training, they may not be feasible in a particular. However, discussing the issues with the residents and promoting their ideas with the administration goes a long way in maintaining morale. Residents need ongoing active discourse with the training director. When they are disheartened, he or she can provide support and also educate them about the realities of the medical system. The training director should embrace and transmit the motto that although: "You can't always get what you want, if you try, somehow you get what you need." What residents need most is a high-quality education. If they feel they are getting the best possible training, they tolerate the long hours of work much more readily.

An important role of the training director is nurturing career development. Residents should be directed to appropriate local and national mentors. Efforts should be made to send them to national meetings to understand the spectrum of available career opportunities and the most recent advances in the field. Residents should be encouraged to apply for national awards and prizes. A training director skilled in writing effective letters of recommendation is instrumental in their winning.

The quality of the resident's daily work life and education is helped immeasurably by the training director's attention to detail. Seemingly little amenities, such as attending to scheduling problems (e.g., preventing time conflicts between supervisors, service demands, conferences, etc.); delivering syllabi for seminars in a timely fashion; sending out announcements of special meetings and conferences; and managing the needs for office space and play materials, consistently scheduled seminar rooms, accessibility to audiovisual equipment, allowances for travel time in their schedule, and provision of a detailed orientation package are deeply appreciated by residents. In order to accommodate residents' many needs, an efficient, dedicated secretary or administrative assistant is critical. He or she becomes the central nurturing, parental figure for the program, and often is considered as valuable as the training director (if not more so).

It is imperative for residents' sense of well-being, learning experience, and professional development for the training director to create a facilitating environment that nurtures critical and creative thinking, unites the hearts and minds of trainees, instills a sense of excitement and enthusiasm toward learning requisite knowledge and skills, and, most important, embodies the fun that can be had in our field. The creation and perpetuation of this environment emanates from the training director and his or her implementing many of the principles noted already.

be underestimated. We desperately need to attract more high-quality physicians into child and adolescent psychiatry, particularly in research.

From the vantage point of academic child and adolescent psychiatry, there are a wealth of opportunities in blazing new trials. Increasingly, research in adult psychiatric disorders has uncovered the necessity of understanding disease from a familial and developmental perspective, including biological as well as social and environmental variables. The new neurodevelopmental paradigm for studying and teaching normal human development and psychopathology is a clear embodiment of this movement. Recent advances in our understanding of molecular genetics and neuronal development have definitively acknowledged both the incredible plasticity of the central nervous system and its complex interaction with other physiological systems as well as the importance of the interdependent relationship between the brain and the symbolic environment on an individual's development. Researchers of the future will, it is hoped, be able to explain the observations of astute clinicians and epidemiologists on the behavioral effects of the sociocultural environment, individual experiences, and relationships by pointing to the development of the child's neurophysiological system. This monumental enterprise will radically affect our understanding of health and disease, and perhaps guide new forms of clinical intervention. The curriculum of the future will be far more sophisticated in conveying the complex developmental interaction of genetics, temperament, neurophysiological systems, life experiences, and environmental forces.

It will be a remarkable time for child and adolescent psychiatry as a field, since the future direction of research has its primary focus on development and brain-environment interaction, and these areas have long resided within the purview of our field. With adequate resources and training, child and adolescent psychiatrists will have the opportunity to help lead the way in the acquisition of new knowledge.

Curriculum for the Future

FUTURE DIRECTIONS IN ACADEMIC TRAINING

In considering the future of academic training, the problems discussed regarding our present and projected shortage in residents and faculty cannot

FUTURE DIRECTIONS IN CLINICAL TRAINING

The clinical curriculum in the coming decades also will derive from advances in research. With the understanding that most psychiatric disorders have their origins, both biologically and psychosocially, in childhood and adolescence, the National Institute of Mental Health is gradually emphasizing the value of funding clinical and basic research in the developmental study of mental disorders, even as funds become increasingly difficult to appropriate. Advances in epidemiological and naturalistic longitudinal studies of large samples of the population (with and without treatment) will disclose a deeper appreciation of the etiology, course, and prognosis of child, adolescent, and adult mental disorders. Areas of particular interest now include research in attachment disorders; pervasive developmental disorders and other neuropsychiatric illnesses; attention deficit hyperactivity disorder; mood, anxiety, and psychotic disorders; conduct disorders; eating, obsessive compulsive, and addictive disorders; posttraumatic stress disorders; and the origins of personality disorders. These clinical research interests will enhance greater subspecialization within child and adolescent psychiatry and create a need for postresidency research fellowships, a process already well under way, although currently in only a handful of programs. The outcome of new research and fellowships will expand the current knowledge base and necessitate revision of our current curriculum regarding many of these disorders.

In concert with new findings in psychopathology, investigations into the efficacy of treatments will become necessary. While emphasis has been given to biological therapies, resulting in significant advances over the last decade, new research in the various psychotherapies may receive needed attention and funding. The utility of long- and short-term dynamic psychotherapies; family therapy; and behavior, cognitive, and group therapies must be established for specific psychiatric disorders. Moreover, with the advent of short-term inpatient treatment and the surge in partial hospitalization and outpatient programs, outcome studies are increasingly needed. The federal Center for Mental Health Services, among other national organizations, has acknowledged a great interest in studies of innovative systems of health care delivery and prevention services. Although the impetus for studying new treatment options is driven economically, it behooves the field to establish the credibility and efficacy of treatment procedures. As new studies inform us more about efficacious treatments, the clinical curriculum will change. Sadly, clinical rotations have been modified quite dramatically now, not on the basis of sound empirical studies but, rather, on the basis of medical economics and, in large part, the strength of the managed care movement.

THE IMPACT OF ECONOMIC CHANGES AND THE HEALTH CARE DELIVERY SYSTEM

The advent of managed care has had a profound impact on the delivery of health care services and, hence, the training environment of the residents. Currently, many programs are forced to train residents in short-term focal inpatient treatment, partial hospitalization management, short-term individual and family psychotherapies, and outpatient psychopharmacology. Behavioral, cognitive, and interpersonal psychotherapy models are increasingly emerging as alternatives to psychodynamic psychotherapies, which, except for a small number of short-term models, have largely had a long-term orientation. There is economic pressure to curtail long-term psychotherapies, since they are rarely reimbursed by managed care companies. As noted earlier, sound clinical training and high-quality patient care should not be driven by economics but rather by efficacy studies and clinical experiences that are educationally important for training. However, educators will need to provide instruction in a broader range of therapies than previously and to find creative ways to maintain long-term contact with children and families. Regardless of current market demands, residents must have the ability to learn psychodynamics as well as growth and development. This necessity mandates a longitudinal relationship with patients and families and contact frequent enough to provide an in-depth understanding of human psychological development, both normal and abnormal. The maintenance of this type of close doctor-patient relationship within psychiatry in the era of managed care will require great creativity on the part of training directors and chairpersons.

There are clear indications that the managed care industry is unwilling to participate in the funding of residency training programs. To make matters worse, a number of vendors have excluded resident treatment as a reimbursable service for its members. If this becomes a national standard, it threatens the fiscal underpinnings and availability of patient care experience of training programs in every medical specialty. Unfortunately, the primary care specialties, and subspecialties such as child and adolescent psychiatry, will be the most adversely affected, since specialties that do not perform many technical procedures are reimbursed the least. We have seen an ominous trend over the past 2 decades in the funding of residency training. Direct federal grants have been eliminated, there have been cutbacks in Medicare and Medicaid subsidies for training, most recently, caps on patient care reimbursements have been instituted by the insurance industry, which previously included overhead costs for residency training in teaching institutions. The final blow is the exclusion of anyone other than a board-certified physician for receiving payment for services.

Who then will pay for the next generation of residents? This seemingly simple question reaches deeply into the structure and economic substrate of the future health care delivery system. At this time, teaching institutions are devising creative financial planning for their residencies. Many are downsizing both their clinical services and their residencies dramatically. For example, Massachusetts General Hospital is cutting its residency and fellowship positions by 20%, based on projections of future federal funds for training and reimbursements for clinical services. Many institutions are being forced to merge into large corporate networks. All clinicians, both staff and trainees, are facing tighter controls on clinical productivity and accountability for authorization for patient services. Clearly medical practice is changing. Despite profound demoralization in all of medicine, residents and faculty must learn to-

gether the new principles of medical economics underlying managed care. It is not clear whether managed care will survive in the next decade. But, as clinical educators, we must both train our residents and faculty to understand the current principles and also maintain the basic skills of clinical practice regardless of the system of care.

In the face of such financial hard times, will we be able to maintain the values and ideals of residency education, including training for the highest quality of patient care, in spite of or, better yet, in concert with economic foundations of health care delivery? This is currently an unanswered question, but one that will determine the viability of residency training in the future. Its answer will, no doubt, require a collaborative effort including representatives of the ACGME, residency training programs, health care delivery institutions, national specialty organizations, the insurance industry, consumer groups, and state and federal governments. Regardless of the system of health care delivery, training directors, with the assistance of their chairpersons, must advocate maintenance of the highest standards of residency training, in order to graduate the finest quality of future clinicians, researchers, teachers, and administrators to further progress in our field.

REFERENCES

American Psychiatric Association. (1996). The 1995–96 Census of Residents. Washington, DC, American Psychiatric Association.

Council on Graduate Medical Education (1990). (Reexamination of the Academy of Physician Supply made in 1980.) Cambridge, MA: ABT Associates.

SUGGESTED READINGS

Accreditation Council for Graduate Medical Education. (1996). *Essentials and information items, 1996–1997.* American Medical Association, pp. 258–262.

Adams, P. L. (1975). The ideal training program in child psychiatry. *Journal of the American Academy of Child Psychiatry, 14,* 228–248.

Beresin, E. V., & Borus, J. F. (1989). Child psychiatry fellowship training: A crisis in recruitment and manpower. *American Journal of Psychiatry, 146,* 759–763.

Borus, J. F. (1982). The transition to practice. *Journal of Education, 57,* 593–601.

Cohen, R. L., & Dulcan, M. K. (Eds.). (1987). *Basic handbook of training in child and adolescent psychiatry.* Springfield, IL: Charles C Thomas.

The 1990–1991 *Directory of Graduate Medical Education Programs.* (1990–1991). Chicago, IL. 1990 American Medical Association.

Institute of Medicine Report. (1996). The nation's physician workforce: Options for balancing supply and requirements. Committee on the U.S. Physician Supply. Washington, DC: National Academy Press.

Josephson, A. M., & Drell, M. J. (1992). Didactic modules for curricular development in child and adolescent psychiatry education. *Academic Psychiatry, 16,* 44–51.

Kay, J. (1991). *Handbook of psychiatry residency training.* Washington, DC: American Psychiatric Press.

Re-examination of the Academy of Physician Supply made in 1980 by the Graduate Medical Education National Advisory Committee (GMENAC) for Selected Specialties Bureau of Health Profession in support of activities of the Council on Graduate Medical Education (1990). Cambridge, MA: ABT Associates.

Rowley, B. D., Baldwin, D. C., & McGuire, M. B. (1991). Selected characteristics of graduate medical education in the United States. *Journal of the American Medical Association, 266,* 933–943.

Schowalter, J. E. (1991). Recruitment, training and certification in child and adolescent psychiatry in the United States. In M. Lewis (Ed.), *Child and adolescent psychiatry: A comprehensive textbook* (pp. 1197–1201). Baltimore: Williams & Williams.

Scully, J. H. (1996) American Psychiatric Association Census Data, 1983–1994. W. Washington, D.C. American Psychiatric Association.

Weissman, S. (1996) Data from the National Resident Matching Plan (NRMP), 1988–1996. Loyola University, IL.

Yager, J., & Borus, J. F. (1990). A survival guide for psychiatric residency training directors. *Academic Psychiatry, 14,* 180–187.

39 / Administration in Child Psychiatry

David B. Pruitt

> Rather than like the hoop-skirt that covers the subject without touching it, this is more like the G-string that touches the subject without covering it.
>
> —WILBERT CORNELL DAVISON,
> FORMER DEAN AND CHAIRMAN OF
> PEDIATRICS, DUKE UNIVERSITY

This chapter attempts to define, clarify, and highlight some of the major areas related to administration in child and adolescent psychiatry. The knowledge base of administration is found in both academic and experiential resources. Some of the base resides in the textbooks and journals of schools of business administration, some within the pages of *U.S.A. Today, The Wall Street Journal* and *Barrons,* and much within the caverns of master administrators' minds, a source every successful administrator has tapped. Too often, administration is viewed as the hassles of daily life, yet for many in the field of child and adolescent psychiatry, the skill and need for mastery of this substantial and diverse knowledge base are becoming ever more important. This chapter attempts to pay attention to the scholarly substance as well as the tricks of the administrative trade.

Organizational Culture

Webster's New Collegiate Dictionary defines culture as "the integrated pattern of human behavior that includes thought, speech, action and artifact and depends on man's [*sic*] capacity for learning and transmitting knowledge to successive generations."

In Deal and Kennedy's (1982) outline of the development of corporate culture, they included the 5 elements: the business environment, values, heroes, rites and rituals, and cultural environment.

Regarding the business environment; they state: "each company faces a different reality in the market place depending on its products, competitors, customers, technologies, government influences, and so on . . . The environment in which a company operates determines what it must do to be a success. The business environment is the single greatest influence in shaping a corporate culture" (p. 13). In recent years the psychiatric business environment has become hotly competitive with inter- and intraprofessional competition plus severe economic constraints and pressures exerted by managed care. It is essential to identify the particulars of the business environment in which one competes.

Deal and Kennedy (1984) define values as: "the basic concepts and beliefs of an organization; as such, they form the heart of the corporate culture". In psychiatric organizations, the value element translates into the ideologies of one's culture, including such concepts as, in the clinical setting, treating the child in the least restrictive environment, or, in the academic setting, the differing importance of how to balance and allocate teaching, clinical care, and research (p. 14).

Heroes are the individuals whom one hopes others will emulate. "These achievers are known to virtually every employee with more than a few months' tenure in the company" (Deal & Kennedy, 1982, p.14). In the child psychiatric organization, this translates not only into local heroes but also into the theories and mentors that permeate the profession as a whole. Is one's hero Sigmund Freud or Salvador Minuchin? Biology or psychotherapy?

Rites and rituals "are systematic and programmed routines of day-to-day life in the company. In their mundane manifestation, which we call rituals, they show employees the kind of behavior that is expected of them. In their extravaganzas—which we call ceremonies—they provide visible and potent examples of what the company stands for" (Deal & Kennedy, 1982, pp. 14–15). Official and unofficial institutional dress codes, graduation ceremonies and banquets, or lack thereof, how one celebrates, how one grieves, are all important in this cultural regard.

"As the primary (but informal) means of communication within an organization, the cultural network is the 'carrier' of the corporate values and heroic mythology," according to Deal and Kennedy (1982, p. 15). This communication network is the vehicle for transmitting information within the institution. Whether one uses memos, meetings, or one-on-one personal encounters will influence this cultural network.

The administrative culture is determined by and determines the sort of decision-making, negotiation, and administrative style a person develops and lives by. Whether the administrator and organization are viewed as authoritarian or permissive, dictatorial or consensus building, hierarchical or team building, will be determined by and will determine the corporate culture.

Much has been written regarding the need for an increase in quality and productivity in American business. The need to model after the successes of the Japanese is well known to the auto industry and taught extensively in MBA programs. W. Edward Deming (1986) has written and taught about management and how quality and productivity can be improved. He outlined 14 points that are necessary for successful management to transform itself from the older traditional hierarchical management style to a new system based on teamwork. Inherent in Deming's method is a concern for the individuals involved in the team process, with the team members developing a long-term organizational relationship of loyalty and trust. Also inherent in the model is a leadership and negotiation style based on nonhierarchical principles. Certain systems are more or less conducive to the Deming method. The hospital system is less adaptable to the concept of mutual decision making. The care of children who have chronic mental illness necessitates an interdisciplinary team approach akin to Deming's method of management style.

How a person makes decisions will have multiple influences on the organizational culture. A person's philosophy regarding negotiation strategy will influence the specifics of his or her decision-making process. A Cold War U.S./Soviet strategy of negotiation is much different from and produces a different organizational culture from the negotiation strategy of Fisher & Ury (1983) called "Getting to Yes—Negotiating Agreement Without Giving In", which decides issues on merit rather than force. Negotiation styles and decision-making strategies affect how an administrator manages internal and external conflict.

A specific example of corporate culture so important in a psychiatric organization is staff growth and development. In an intensive clinical program, psychiatric aides are essential for a quality care program. Yet often these individuals cannot be paid what they are worth to the organization. If the organizational culture is able to provide growth and development, mentorship, and the message that the organization supports the psychiatric aide so that one day the aide may become the medical director, thereby encouraging further education, this may help offset the negative pay variables. Greenblatt (1972) personalized this administrative satisfaction with the description being "his reward is at the level of "father" who enjoys providing the affection and resources necessary for this 'children' to make their contribution to society" (p. 384).

Leadership

"When I became dean, my patients developed tenure," stated Dean Douglas Bond when he moved from the chairmanship of the Department of Psychiatry to the deanship of the College of Medicine at Case Western University, Cleveland, Ohio.

Definitions of leadership skills are many and often ambiguous. Greenblatt (1972) has summed up the leadership requirement as being "high energy and drive, physical endurance, high maturity, robust health, great intellectual ability, high capacity for concentration, the ability to appraise people without sentiment, the capacity to encourage and tolerate change, great resiliency, flexibility, creativity, steadfastness, determination, toughmindedness" (p. 379).

Some writers have differentiated between the manager and the leader to indicate that the former is more the technician and the latter more of the visionary. The leadership style that is more effective in a particular organizational structure and phase of organizational development, as well as the need for a person's particular leadership style to change and adapt to the maturation of the organization, are important requirements.

Organizational Structure

It is vital to identify and understand the organizational structure that is being administered. Organizational structure can be classified based on different defining characteristics and categories. Organizational size, function, funding source, position in the health care delivery system, and mission are a few of these definers. (Henry 1957) defined 4 types of organizational structures (Greenblatt, 1972):

1. Simple undifferentiated subordination: "One head is responsible for all and directs the operation of subordinates, all of whom perform a total complex operation (p. 382)." Example: An elementary school with a principal who functions as the boss and supervisor of the teachers.
2. Simple differentiated subordination: "One head is responsible for subordinates, each of whom carries out a different task (p. 382)". Example: "Modern supermarket with its division of workers into checkers, stockboys, butchers."
3. Multiple undifferentiated subordination: "The task is the 'package' but the worker has several supervisors, each of whom tells him how to do that part of the work which is the supervisor's responsibility" (p. 382).
4. Multiple differentiated subordination: "The task is split into small parts, each carried out by a separate group of workers, with each group having its own supervisor (p. 382)."

This classification system is based on the varying authority and responsibility of the members of the organization and on the established lines of communication and accountability within the organization.

A major interface between organizational structure and administrative styles exists. Administrative styles are defined by Kotin and Sharaf (Greenblatt, 1972) as being *tight*—meaning clearcut delegation of responsibility and authority with a hierarchical chain of command—or *loose*—meaning lacking clear hierarchy, role diffusion, and an informal set of communications. Others have defined this style as being hierarchical versus democratic.

The size of the organization affects the administrative style. Some administrators are people-oriented, wanting a hands-on management style, whereas others desire and function more efficiently with a larger chain-of-command style of organization and administration.

The organizational structure of hospitals varies among these: a federal veteran's administration hospital, local private nonprofit hospital, national-chain for-profit hospital, university hospital, and public hospital. Each has a different mission, each has a different hierarchical structure.

A smaller organization with fewer people allows easier consensus building. The larger the organization, the more the opportunity for development of a bureaucracy and a hierarchical approach. (Large need not translate into ridigity.) If culture, structure, and communication patterns mandate a democratic, egalitarian organizational setting, given the appropriate administrative resources dedicated to infrastructure design and implementation, consensus can be sought and maintained. For instance, the Mayo Clinic is a large system with recently developed remote geographical satellite sites, yet it continues to base decision making on a concensus-building committee structure and process.

Support Staff

CEOs are notorious for having desks you could land a Harrier jump jet on. But they have secretaries to sweep away the debris.
—LAWLOR, 1991.

Good organization of information is dependent on an effective support staff with the secretary playing a key role. Effective administrators often seriously joke that most of their good administrative points are due to their secretaries; their secretaries are working on the administrators' bad ones. Administrators often spend more time interviewing for less important organizational jobs than that of the secretary. It is essential to identify realistic and unrealistic expectations. Too often an administrator hopes that a personification of Radar (of *M*A*S*H* movie and television fame), who can read minds, know in advance what is needed, and effectively organize the administrator's life, will apply for the position. Although the pay is near-poverty wages, this individual is expected to have the same sort of ambition, dedication, and commitment that higher-paid, organizationally driven individuals might display. In many ways, there is no one professionally closer, no one who knows the administrator better, no person sharing a greater professional intimacy with him or her than a secretary. Administrators must utilize their creativity to overcome the weaknesses of the job description and recruit someone with the skills, dedication, and selflessness necessary to accept such a lopsided arrangement. When these individuals are recruited, the administrator must provide a culture that supports and encourages them. The understanding of child care issues, elderly care issues, supporting upgrading of "fringe benefits" such as family leave, health insurance, retirement support, and educational advancement opportunities are vital.

Communication Systems

As child and adolescent psychiatrists, we know well the importance of effective communication in therapy, education, and our own personal lives. Too often, however, we forget the importance of a communication system within our own administrative organization. Organizations vary in the ranking of communication on their priority list. Companies such as IBM and Fed Ex have viewed effective communication as essential with the belief that it will bring their companies a competitive edge.

Effective communication can be expensive. The practicalities of each communication system for child and adolescent psychiatry will vary depending on organizational philosophy. With a hierarchical, autocratic, military type of organizational philosophy, memoranda and chain-of-command communication is in order; a democratic, egalitarian, Deming organization utilizes committee meetings and open-door communication strategies.

An important part of communication assessment is a knowledge and expertise regarding the strategic utilization of developed and developing informational technology (Venkatraman with Akbhar, 1990). Use of computers and computer systems, word processors, dictaphones, daytime/nighttime telephone answering procedures, incoming-outgoing correspondence management, and development of an effective filing system are all important aspects of one's communication system.

Present and future computer capabilities, including word processing, deserve special interest and attention. The child psychiatric administrator may lack a sophisticated knowledge base in the computer sciences. The administrator need not know the specifics of computer operations in order to manage effectively the information operations, yet an appreciation for certain principles and guidelines related to computer technology is essential. The administrator must not be too far ahead of the computer technology. Spending thousands of dollars on a dysfunctional computer system that no organizational staff member will utilize causes distress to the administrator's mind, heart, and pocketbook. Best advice would be: Identify organizational needs before computerizing the organization and give special attention to functional areas where the computer application is best utilized—research, patient care, or education. (Greist, 1988). More and more, the computer can provide access to information much as the library has done in the past. Pollack and Bigelow (1991) have listed specific primary and secondary questions to ask before computerizing an organizational system. Computers will not bring organization to a disorganized system, or order where chaos exists. When appropriately utilized, computers can bring more order and structure.

How does the administrator handle paper? Incoming and outgoing correspondence? Some administrative experts believe that the appearance of a person's desk can tell a lot about the personality of that person. The average office worker has 36 hours of work piled up on his or her desk (Lawlor, 1991). Books have been written on the paper problem. A professional organizer costs $1,000 a day. Catchy rules exist, such as: the *four Ds:* Do it, Date it, Delegate it, Discard it; *always* leave your desk at the end of the day clear and clean; *only* have materials you are working with on your desktop; *keep* lists and *develop* a filing system related to due date and priority of the particular project. Some administrators have a "pending file" with the hope that if they wait long enough, the problem, project, or proposal in this file will go away. All of these procedures, strategies, and gimmicks have their administrative place and significance with the core communication theme being organization and infrastructure design.

Two often-overlooked administrative aspects of a communication system are the appointment book and when and how one answers and returns incoming telephone calls. While it is not good business to talk about business with an associate while playing golf, a lot can be learned about that individual's business practices by how he or she plays. A lot also can be learned about a given organizational communication system by the design and specifics of its telephone system. The busy clinician must determine whether to return telephone calls on the hour, for example, or when and if to be interrupted by a telephone call during a meeting versus a clinical hour, whether to permit a secretary to make appointments, or whether both administrator and secretary can give out appointments. All of these have significance and should be clearly spelled out.

Time allocation to practice administration is essential. Master administrators have developed different time allocation tricks and strategies. The ability to make administration look easy, the reality of being a busy person, yet having an empty appointment book schedule so as to be able to react and be available for administrative decisions are methods utilized. Ineffective administrators take a month to get someone an appointment; competent administrators, running larger, more complex systems, will be able to schedule an immediate emergency appointment within a busy schedule, when necessary. Administrators must be able to set priorities and rely on a support structure to help manage priorities while covering the necessary details, are essential. Travel mania must be avoided. If part of the administrator's role is to be out of town or out of the office, a system of in-house decision making must be developed and maintained.

Policy, Procedure, and Paperwork

New organizations are formed with the belief and hope that they can function without needless bureaucracy. The administrator soon learns that development of policies and procedures, with effective record keeping, is necessary for multiple internal and external reasons. External agencies audit the new administrator's hiring and firing practices, the Joint Commission on Accreditation of Health Care Organization (JCAHO) accredits according to certain guidelines, funding agencies will reimburse only if certain standards are met and documented. Much of the time, the bureaucracy is in place when the administrator is hired, yet opportunities exist to influence and change this infrastructure. The importance of striking a balance between overly cumbersome rules and the need for accountability, documentation, and due process is difficult and challenging. The necessity for formulating vacation and leave policies, after-hours and weekend call schedules, standing committees, and functional task forces will all vary depending on the size, function, and culture of the organization.

Hospital systems traditionally had a profit margin that allowed administrative departments including medical records, human resources, utilization review, and quality assurance. Movement to a more exclusively outpatient clinical care organization, which has a lower profit margin, often requires that these administrative responsibilities be shared more dramatically among clinical staff. Therefore, the need for internal acceptance by the rank-and-file staff members of the administrative policies, procedures, and paperwork becomes even more essential.

A specific example of the importance of a set procedure is the evaluation process. All employees need and deserve a regular, periodic evaluation. Whether this evaluation is tied to financial reimbursement or is mainly an information-gathering and sharing process, the importance should not be underestimated. Many child/adolescent psychiatrists like to give good news and hate to discuss problems. An effective evaluation process can prevent the development of longer-term major problems and can reinforce and reward successful employees.

The need to set a protocol and procedure for hiring and firing is essential. Due process is vital. Determining good hiring techniques will minimize the firings. The cowardly administrator does the hiring and delegates the firing. When hiring a new employee, a protocol should be followed with a set number of letters of reference that are checked, checked, checked. A carefully determined format for personal interviews should be established. Private businesses and psychiatry programs have learned how expensive and problematical a lack of discipline with appropriate hiring policies can be.

Strategic Financial Planning: Space and Resources

> If you torture the numbers long enough, they'll say anything.
>
> — ANONYMOUS

The financial ability to initiate, develop, and maintain a program is a key aspect of administration. The precise amount of detailed financial expertise that administrators need in financial planning and accounting skills varies. As with the need to understand the specifics of computer science or the intricacies and absolutes of statistics and research methodology, differences exist between equally effective administrators. The essential quality is for administrators to know their own expertise, to appreciate what they know and don't know, and to attract competent, knowledgeable advisors in certain areas. A grounding in finance can be accomplished, as with other core information of administration, in multiple fashions. Courses are available through graduate schools that will provide various levels of expertise. Most administrators will attempt to understand basic financial principles and attract competent fiscal officers who can handle the details (Livingston, 1990; Walter, 1990).

The physical space that an organization controls and maintains is vital infrastructure for its development. Many a chief executive officer has reflected that, given space, money can be raised. Efficiently built space with appropriate design for function and purpose is a key factor (Harper & Geraty, 1985). The cost of maintaining space is significant in the overall life of that space; conservative estimates claim that 75% of the total cost of the space is attributable to postconstruction utilization. Space that is effective and efficiently designed for the needs of child and adolescent psychiatry must be allocated differentially to outpatient, day treatment, and in-patient clinical space and to basic and clinical research. Strategic planning for short-term and longer-term fiscal and space requirements is essential. Predicting space needs into the several-year future, and coupling that projection with fiscal realities, allows for a more orderly, morale-boosting growth and transition phase. Employee income level is important, as is academic rank, and the administrator will quickly learn the importance of the amount and quality of space allocated.

Marketing and Administration

> Image is everything.
>
> QUOTE FROM ANDRÉ AGASSI,
> CANON CAMERA COMMERCIAL

The difference between marketing (education) and advertising (selling) is substantial and important. Marketing based on education of patients, their employers, the insurance executives, and the public in general is essential in a field as filled with stigma as child and adolescent psychiatry. The importance of the psychiatric administrator's having an understanding and commitment to marketing is vital. Turning marketing over to others often leads to a quick deterioration as the effort moves into advertising. Some may view the importance of educating others regarding what he or she is doing with disgust, yet it is a reality every administrator needs to face. It is essential to identify constituents, whether they are they legislators in a public state institution shareholders in a for-profit institution, or medical students in a university environment. Next, a strategy for marketing the importance of the program to the constituent group is necessary—whether the marketing takes place in a weekly meeting with the chair of the department to fully explain strategies, tactics, and efficiencies of the division of child and adolescent psychiatry or the marketing strategy is a public informational campaign that includes print, television, and radio public service announcements about the general importance of child and adolescent psychiatric services. Results of such ongoing marketing activities become fully evident at budget time. Not all administrators need to love marketing or, for that matter, like it, but they should respect or at least appreciate the importance of the process and develop a cadre of individuals through whom vital organizational accomplishments can be maintained.

Training in Administrative Child Psychiatry

How does a person learn the core, basic information, the basic science of administration? How does a person get experience? Which should come first? Related questions include: What is a person's professional identity and how does administration fit into that identity? Does such people consider themselves first and foremost a clinical child and adolescent psychiatrists? Academics? Administrators? Most of us do not answer or even formulate these questions in a premeditated fashion. Administrative training has a place in the child and adolescent fellowship training program. Presentation of the administrative material through seminars and journal clubs (talking about administration) or allowing trainees to obtain administrative experience under effective supervision (learning administration through doing) have different impacts. Many child and adolescent psychiatry fellows will not know that they are destined for some administration during their career. Therefore, 5 years out of training, many will discover the need to become more efficient in administrative subject matters. The local bookstore, workshops at the annual meeting of the American Academy of Child and Adolescent Psychiatry, lay press and nonpsychiatric publications such as *U.S.A. Today, Modern Health Care,* the *Journal of Health Economics,* the *Journal of the American Medical Association,* and courses offered by the American College of Physician Executives are useful possible resources. A few child and adolescent psychiatrists will discover that instead of administration being a component of their professional identity, it becomes the overriding substance. Six-week courses at Wharton or the Harvard School of Business or in the administrator's home academic institution are available to help. Certification in psychiatric administration is quickly proceeding toward subspecialty status. A very few psychiatric administrators will pursue a master's in business administration (MBA) degree.

The role of the senior mentor in administrative training is vital. There is a generic quality to administration; hence the senior mentor need not be specifically in child and adolescent psychiatry, possibly only in medicine or health care, but even that is not mandatory. Finding an individual who has accomplished many of his or her own goals, who needs not compete or tell the young administrator what to do but who can listen and respond with concern, direction, and support, allows the young administrator a sounding-board essential for administrative growth and development. Schowalter (1991) defined the mentor role as one who displays wisdom—"the possession of a broad view, a willingness and ability to be life as well as goal focused" (p. 873). As it is next to impossible to assign a mentor to a "mentee," the search and dance that goes on in this identification and matching process is complex.

Ethics in Administration

Some would find this section an oxymoron. Yet, if ethics is defined as "dealing with the right and wrong of certain actions, and the good and bad of such actions," administrators, surely have their share of such decisions. Child and adolescent psychiatry has a formidable scientific knowledge base, yet the profession still rests to a greater extent on the art of clinical practice and the moral integrity of the psychiatrist. The topic of ethics in administration is vital if one takes into account the pressures on the individual's decision making regarding diagnosis and where treatment should take place, the changing reimbursement systems, the intrusion into the physician/patient relationship by third and fourth parties, the pressures that the administrator faces in resource allocation and the resultant need to ration. Greenblatt (1972) identified this mixture of administrative/ethical motives with his statement, "the psychiatrist with his training should understand the motive that impels a politician and as an administrator, he must learn to do business with the politician and yet preserve his identity and integrity" (p. 382).

REFERENCES

Deal, T. E., & Kennedy, A. A. (1982). *Corporate cultures: The rites and rituals of corporate life.* Addison-Wesley.

Deming, W. E. (1986). *Out of the crisis.* Indianapolis, Indiana Massachusetts Institute of Technology, Center for Advanced Engineering Study (Publishers). Cambridge, Mass.

Fisher, R., & Ury, W. (1983). *Getting to yes: Negotiating without giving in.* Penguin Books, New York, NY.

Greenblatt, M. (1972). Administrative psychiatry. *American Journal of Psychiatry, 129* (4), 33–44.

Greist, J. H. (Guest Editor). (1988). 373–86 *Psychiatric Annals, 18* (4), 207–208. Computers in Clinical & Psychiatry.

Harper, G., & Geraty, R. (1985). Hospital and residential treatment. In R. Michels & Cavenar, J. O. Jr. (Eds.), *Psychiatry,* Vol. 2, 2nd Edition, pp. 1–20, Lippincott Basic Books, Philadelphia, Pa.

Henry, J: Types of institutional structure, in The Patient and the Mental Hospital. Edited by Greenblatt, M., Levinson, D. J., Williams, R. H. Glencoe, IL, Free Press, 1957, pp 73–90.

Lawlor, J. (1991). June 18 *U.S.A. Today,* p. 1A-2A. 36 hours of work piled on average desk.

Lawlor, J., U.S.A. Today, June 18, 1991, p. 7B. Expert imposes sanity on a reporter's system.

Livingstone, J. L. (1990). Accounting and management decision making. In E. G. C. Collins and M. A. Devanna (Eds.), *The portable MBA,* pp. 109–137. John Wiley & Sons, New York, NY.

Pollack, D. & Bigelow, D. (1991). Questions and factors to consider before computerizing system. *Psychiatric Times, 8* (7), 29–30.

Schowalter, J. E. (1991). Editor's note: What is wisdom? What is it worth? *Journal of the American Academy of Child and Adolescent Psychiatry, 30* (6), 873.

Venkatraman, N., with Zaheer, A. (1990). The strategic use of information technology. In E. G. C. Collins & M. A. Devanna, (Eds.), *The portable MBA,* pp. 238–266. John Wiley & Sons, New York, NY.

Walter, J. E. (1990). Financial management. In E. G. C. Collins & M. A. Devanna (Eds.), *The portable MBA,* pp. 138–173. John Wiley & Sons, New York, NY.

40 / **The Private Practice of Child Psychiatry**

Ivan Fras

It is difficult to draw the boundaries of the private practice of child and adolescent Psychiatry (hereinafter referred to as child psychiatry for brevity). To avoid being drawn into semantics, the teaching model of private practice will be the solo private practitioner who is largely and primarily office based, with hospital privileges as an optional extension of this model. This model provides for historical continuity all the way back to Hippocrates and Sigmund Freud, and offers not only the didactic advantage of clarity and definitive boundaries but also puts the entire focus on the practitioner. I shall discuss the entire field of private practice from the perspective of the practitioner as sole and complete agent—he or she is completely involved in the patient's care and does not delegate any part thereof to anyone else. I am doing this in spite of a radically changing scene where managed care has increasing control over the practitioner's choices of number of sessions allowed and even their length and frequency. The reason for adhering to the model presented herein is that it represents the very core of independent practice that will survive, even though modified, while managed care may or may not.

In order to bring some arbitrary order into a large body of materials, I shall divide it into two parameters: the necessary personal characteristics of the practitioner and the specific demands of the private practice or tasks to be accomplished, which is the successful care of the patient.

The Personal Attributes of the Private Practitioner

THE BASICS

The basics of all private practice apply in child psychiatry as well: Work hard, be available, look after referral sources. Hard work has universal applicability. The two other factors, availability and attending to referral sources, depend on the type of practice and location. In cases where many referrals come from schools and agencies, the child psychiatrist needs to be available for consultation with the consultees on a scheduled basis during working or school hours and on school days. These referrals rarely need off-hour (nighttime and weekend) availability. However, the practitioner has to organize his or her time with the educators so that their needs are met both factually and emotionally, the latter referring to the need of being accepted and supported by the practitioner. If the child psychiatrist expects to work with pediatricians and other health and mental health providers, he or she needs to adapt to their needs and work style. Finally, if the child psychiatrist's practice extends to hospitalized children, the private practitioner must be available at odd and unpredictable hours; this requirement may be somewhat scaled down in office practice.

As a general rule, looking after children will call for good daytime organization but will offer mostly uninterrupted nights and weekends. Caring for adolescents, on the other had, will require the opposite. A close affiliation with a hospital emergency room, is likely to generate a number of relatively acute and urgent referrals because of the increasing frequency of child abuse on the one hand and the sharply rising incidence of aggressive acts threatened or committed by children on the other.

Private practice offers *choices*. Child psychiatrists can limit their practice to well-organized referrals from schools, agencies, other mental health professionals, and pediatricians and family practitioners, and accept patients for thorough evaluations, consultations, and child psychiatric treatments that only child psychiatrists can provide. Put differently, practitioners can choose to offer only the highest-quality service, which will require patience on the part of the referrers and the families but will be warranted in terms of ultimate patient and referrer satisfaction. It takes time to develop such a practice, and practitioners probably have to survive an initial economic waiting period. Moreover, such a consultative practice depends on the ability and willingness of schools and other agencies to budget for the consultations, since third-party payors will not reimburse for such services. An alternative choice is to secure a much larger initial number of referrals by being available for child psychiatric emergencies. A similar choice is to combine children and ado-

lescents and, again, be available for emergencies of both age groups. The personal characteristics of child psychiatrists will partly determine their choices, but the main choice will be made on the basis of economic realities, which are likely to push practitioners into adapting to the demands of managed care. This means that the "high-volume" practice is likely to prevail.

THE REQUIREMENTS IN TERMS OF THE PRACTITIONER'S PERSONALITY

Private practitioners are more independent and free in what they choose to do and how their tasks will be accomplished. At the same time, they need to have a greater sense of responsibility. The public expects a greater degree of caring (and probably of demonstrativeness of caring) in solo private practice than in the less personal clinic or medical center or hospital setting. Solo private practitioners do not have the multilayered shield of colleagues and allied professionals to hide behind or fall back onto. The expected demonstrativeness will have to include visible response and responsiveness to the families and to the individual patient's overt and covert needs. Private practitioners must have a good grasp of psychodynamics, not only in the clinical sense of treating the child and the child's family but in a very practical sense of knowing how to respond to the public's need at the moment. The child's family will need a decisive leader at one point and a sensitive and circumspect listener or advisor at another. Successful private practitioners will have this ability to respond appropriately as a "natural." Furthermore, they must have greater patience and greater emotional flexibility and adaptability compared to the employed colleague.

There is no doubt that private practice teaches the psychodynamic skills of successful clinical leadership by the time-proven method of reward and punishment: Correct behavior toward the public will be financially and behaviorally rewarded—practitioners will be successful; incorrect behavior will be extinguished since practitioners will learn quickly what makes them lose patients.

Private practitioners must pay attention to the financial aspects of the practice for very cogent psychodynamic reasons. Although these are now largely regulated by third-party payors, or managed care organizations, there is sufficient variation and uncertainty about them that they continue to be a matter of leverage and control. As we shall see in other areas of control, such as scheduling and apportioning the length of the session, the question of the fee is of considerable emotional significance to both the family and the health care provider.

In private practice, this issue is closer to immediate reality than in any other way of practicing. Furthermore, the fee is also a pervasive, although not immediately visible, parameter of practitioners' skills. In the simplest terms, highly skilled and effective practitioners will have the feeling that they have earned their fee, and the same is likely to be true of the consumers. Even now the fee, or usually the "copay," is paid directly to practitioners in enough cases that they will have to justify the work done and the fee collected more directly than in a less personal practice. Another dimension is the presentation of the fee: The need to explain the fee remains in a number of cases in spite of the leveling of many of the fees by third-party payors, since the extent of coverage is highly variable. The technicality of structuring the fee for a particular intervention, including the extent and duration of the intervention, offers important dimensions to skilled and sensitive practitioners who have to make sure that the office staff is appropriately skilled and sensitive as well. Finally, there are long-term countertransference issues at work for child psychiatrists in private practice. Successful private practitioners are those who stay away from the extremes of financial sadism and masochism. It is easy to argue against the former: Greed has no place in medical practice. It is the other extreme that is more complicated. When practitioners take on a disproportionate number of patients who cannot contribute to their livelihood, the reasons may range from normal, healthy altruism to personal ineptness. The egodystonic result of such factors is likely to interfere with the therapeutic process. Staying away from the extremes reflects understanding of the role of private practice in American health care. It is not the way to exceptional financial gains nor is it a way to correcting social injustice on a large scale.

When fees are not already set by managed care, the interpersonal handling of negotiations about fees can contribute to a positive feeling between practitioner and the patient's family, or it may contribute to the opposite. Solo private practice teaches us that fees should not be discussed in the presence of children and that practitioners should make very sure never to commit themselves to a set fee since such a statement is likely to put them into a financial straitjacket: If more work is required, they may feel that there is no way out of the contract and someone is going to suffer—unfortunately, in the final analysis, it will be the patient. Fees need not be discussed with each and every family. To do so reflects rigidity and lack of recognition of the potential of the fee negotiating process. Most families may know what their insurance company's fee structure is; unfortunately, they tend to overestimate the extent of coverage. On the other hand, it is important that practitioners answer all inquiries about fees, especially whenever they sense that there are unspoken questions and the family's attitude is one of great insecurity.

OTHER ISSUES OF CONTROL

Successful private practitioners are in charge of the proceedings. One of the reasons that families select the private sector is a complex interplay between their wish to retain sufficient control over the care of their child and, at the same time, to put themselves into the hands of a health provider who is simultaneously under their control and is in charge. There will be significant variations in these components, depending on the family. A balance has to be achieved between the family's wish to be in control and their needs to be dependent. Ultimately, the practitioners have to assume leadership and be in charge.

In the simplest terms, private practitioners should be competent, caring, and personable clinicians showing respect for the family's unique needs and problems and a commitment to hard work. They should have a good grasp of psychodynamics, from the training in general psychiatry, supplemented by knowledge and experience with psychodynamics as they apply specifically to parenting. The clinicians are expected to shape and guide the flow of psychodynamics so that one of the basic premises of child psychiatry may be fulfilled: understanding the parental and family psychodynamics without interpreting them overtly because child psychiatrists do not treat the parents.

Instead, child psychiatrists deal with parental psychodynamics sufficiently to gain access to the child and be allowed to help the child. This is of practical importance in solo private practice, when treatment of the child often depends on the goodwill of the parents.

One of the tools that child psychiatrists possess to establish and maintain control is the length of the session. No matter who appears to be formally in charge, it is the person managing the time span and the intervals between sessions who is in actual control of a considerable portion of the proceedings. Dosing time and interval is nearly equivalent to the dosing of medicine, and private practitioners can make exceptionally astute use of these parameters. The old rule of influencing issues of transference and countertransference by varying the length and frequency of the session applies to child psychiatry as well.

It is best to apportion diagnostic time according to the clinical needs, and it is here that practitioners have to exert self-discipline and self-observation to prevent being led into areas that are fascinating but not sufficiently pertinent to the child's problem.

It follows that, in the last analysis, the most important issue of control is clinician self-control and self-discipline. In private practice more than anywhere else, child psychiatrists must constantly remind themselves that the family has brought the *child* to be diagnosed and treated and that the child psychiatrists must adhere to the mandate— that is, the implied or specifically articulated contract with the child's parents. If the child turns out to be indeed only the "ticket of admission," this needs to be so stated and appropriate changes in goals and mandates recommended. Unless this is the case, however, getting lost in the family dynamics will turn child psychiatrists into family therapists. While in itself this is not necessarily unhelpful, it does leave us to ask: If it were to happen too frequently, who would then practice child psychiatry?

The Therapeutic Alliance

Any consideration of private practice must keep in mind one fundamental factor: It must be successful or the practice will not survive. Child psychiatrists in private practice works for the benefit of the child but are employed by a responsible adult. Practitioners will be judged primarily by that adult or set of adults, and only secondarily by the child or adolescent. Beginners in private practice—whether recently graduated residents whose training is usually in a highly academic set-ting, or experienced clinicians who leave a faculty or other salaried position and are used to gauging success by the response of peers, supervisors, or administrators—may not simple fact that they are judged by the child's parents.

THE THERAPEUTIC ALLIANCE WITH THE PARENTS

The building of a solid therapeutic alliance with the parents comes first, not only in chronological sequence, but because it ensures treatment; conversely, the absence of such a therapeutic alliance may often prematurely end the child's treatment.

Private practitioners have an immediate initial advantage if they take the history from the parents. If they employ other mental health professionals—for instance, a social worker—this important function will be left to someone else. If child psychiatrists do employ a social worker, it behooves the physicians to select and train that mental health professional very carefully. Incentives and morale among such employed professionals must be high because the task is a demanding and important one, since it is likely to set the tone for subsequent work.

History taking in private practice is an important process of introduction and laying the groundwork for treatment. Child psychiatrists start the process of tuning in on the parents' overt and hidden agenda. Weaving it into the fabric of scientific inquiry, clinicians set the tone of how they will deal with the parents and let them know they are in charge as well as responsible for the entire diagnostic and treatment process. One thing that the history taking reveals is whether family members are bringing the child against their own wishes. This is less commonly seen in private practice, but when it occurs, it should be addressed at the very outset. Private practitioners have the professional and political freedom to discontinue any further work, depending on the expressed wishes of the parents. The most common example is that of a child who has been referred by the school, with the school insisting that professional help is sought, while the parents find nothing wrong with the child and blame the school or a particular teacher for whatever happens in school. Private practitioners are not in employed by the school or anyone else, and should emphasize that they work for the child and are employed by the family, whose members are held responsible for following the clinician's advice and thus looking after their child's well-being. The family is also responsible for paying the agreed-upon fees and/or taking care of their part of the insurance paperwork. The child and his or her family must be spared clinical intervention that may be doomed to failure; in this way practitioners will maintain their reputation.

COMMUNICATIONS WITH THE FAMILY AND THE ISSUE OF CONFIDENTIALITY

For child psychiatrists, intergenerational communication is a must. Child psychiatrists in private practice must be the hub of all communications. The lines of communication have to be set up early and serviced throughout the course of diagnosis and treatment.

The system of communications cannot be set up without clarifying confidentiality first. With the important exceptions of parental abuse or neglect, legal competence, or lack of custodial rights on the part of the parents, private practitioners must adhere strictly to confidentiality to the world outside the parents and their offspring. Strict adherence to this principle makes this part of confidentiality simple. However, intrafamily confidentiality is more complex. Most practitioners will find it useful to establish its dimensions early on. From the point of view of most preschool and early grade school children, it is no problem, as they expect doctors to share nearly everything with the parents. Depending on the age of the child, either no statement about confidentiality, when the child is young, or a limited statement, when the child is in grade school, need be made; an increasing amount of confidentiality is expected as the child's age advances. The parents should be similarly informed.

As concerns confidentiality and communication with significant other agents in the child's life, there exists considerable variation in each private practitioner's style, and, even more important, there exists and must exist considerable flexibility and variation as to how confidentiality and communication with schools and similar agencies is handled in each case. Some families simply will not allow disclosure of psychiatric work to the schools; others will allow only limited interaction between the practitioner and the school; and yet others will expect an inordinate amount of work to be done between the schools and the clinician. Either too much or too little communication will be both clinically and economically counterpro-

ductive; here too private practitioners have the freedom to decline cases where they are unreasonably restrained in communicating outside of the family on the one hand or where excessive demands are made in this direction on the other. Most private practitioners ultimately will find that the child's parents, provided they are competent and not abusive, are the ultimate authority to go by.

When it comes to adolescents, intrafamily confidentiality becomes more complex, but confidentiality vis-à-vis the school may become simpler: Adolescents sometimes reveal problems and the treatment to the school and, thereby, often force the parents to give consent.

Some skilled practitioners establish excellent rapport with adolescents in treatment, especially when the disorder is an intrapsychic conflict, well internalized. Often they establish this rapport at the cost, and perhaps risk, of decreasing parental involvement. Few physicians are likely to be so lucky, especially in the future, to have adolescents with internalized conflicts. The rest will see adolescents with various degrees of acting-out behavior. Under those circumstances, a judicious relationship with the parents is necessary. This hard-line approach not only sets up predictable structure, but it helps to screen out those acting-out adolescent patients who are inappropriate for the freestanding private psychiatric practice.

Once again, private practice offers child and adolescent psychiatrists the freedom and the independence to express their clinical findings and recommendations in a tactful, supportive way, but, in the last analysis, with the freedom for both psychiatrists and families not to engage in work, as with parents who, in their dealings with their adolescent, lack understanding of adolescent developmental needs. Private practitioners should not agree to do any work merely to satisfy the parental demands; they must work for the child's or adolescent's well-being. This can be accomplished by making the initial session or sessions consultations, so that the parting of ways does not occur when therapy is well underway.

When child/adolescent psychiatrists work with, or employ, a social worker, the psychiatrists may have the opportunity to work with the child or adolescent primarily and leave the intrafamily communication to the social worker. This gives the social worker an important part to play in the private practice; the proper selection and training of social workers in a collaborative private practice is imperative.

MAKING A CREDIBLE DIAGNOSIS

Sometimes families that bring a child to a private practitioner expect a clearly defined product. This product is a state-of-the-art diagnosis, which then has to be communicated to the parents in an intelligible and credible way.

Child psychiatrists can make use of their general psychiatric skills to tune in to the parents without becoming *their* psychiatrists. Beginning private practitioners need not worry whether they have the talent to be outgoing or charismatic; families with a child in distress ultimately look for professional competence, which includes engaging the parents.

As part of getting parental acceptance of the diagnosis, child psychiatrists need to offer tolerance and patience: The parents may not accept all of the doctor's views and recommendations, and the last thing that should happen is a test of wills. Doctors should never go along with unacceptable parental views, but there should be room for diplomacy. Clinicians need to work within the family's sociocultural and philosophic belief system, and their presentation of the diagnosis should be within that system and within the parents' specific abilities to understand.

ESTABLISHING GOALS

Having taken a comprehensive history and established a clear diagnosis, and at the same time having established communication with the parents, the next step, that of agreeing on goals, will follow naturally. The initial goals will be the parents' since without them the child would never be seen by the clinician. It is important for private practitioners to take careful and comprehensive notes of those goals and record them. Much of this will be done during history taking, but following the diagnostic evaluation, the goals will be discussed in a formal way. Defining goals is of particular importance in private practice, since the relationship is clearly one of contracting for a particular product (state of the art diagnosis) and expecting to get it. Having evaluated the child and family, clinicians must decide whether these goals are appropriate and whether they need to be modified or supplemented by their own suggested goals for this child's benefit. Blind adherence to parental goals is tantamount to abrogating ethical responsibility. By contrast, ignoring parental goals may doom any hope for fulfillment of comprehensive and clinically sound goals.

Fortunately, most parental goals are reasonable and in the best interests of the child. The postevaluation conference with the parents will clarify and in a way codify and formalize these goals. Clinicians should make written note of these goals, since rather frequently, as treatment progresses, the parents' perceptions of the goals, especially those arrived at jointly by them and the child psychiatrist, undergo changes. Clinicians must be able to remind the parents of what they had initially agreed on. Under the best of circumstances, these goals are used to determine when treatment can be stopped. Under more difficult circumstances, reassessment and reaffirmation of goals, sometimes on a periodic basis, are necessary to keep the treatment going and to support the parents as well as the patient.

I do not want to create the impression that the child is a passive recipient of goals that are handed down by the consortium of parents and child psychiatrist; the child needs to be progressively engaged in the formulation of goals, although initially probably children will have little to offer in this regard; even adolescents will have input relatively rarely. The coordination of the parents' and the child's goals of treatment is part of the treatment and will reflect in the buildup and maintenance of the therapeutic alliance with the child. Thus the initial goals will help begin the therapeutic alliance and the amalgamated goals will maintain it.

RECOMMENDATION FROM THE SOURCE OF REFERRAL

The referral source's role in the therapeutic alliance is self-evident. Private practitioners also must realize that they can benefit specifically from a good relationship with the source of referral.

When child psychiatrists encounter resistances, either from a parent or from the child, they can turn to the source of referral for clarification and support. This can happen especially when the referring agent has had a relationship of trust with the family; examples are a trusted pediatrician, family practitioner, social worker, or even member of the judiciary. The child psychiatrists then can use their working alliance with the source of referral to bolster the therapeutic alliance. A word of reassurance or encouragement from the kindly family doctor who has looked after the child since birth can make the difference between success and failure. If the referring source him or herself is an individual practitioner, that source can be more supportive to an individual private practitioner than to a larger group of people such as an agency.

An even more basic contribution from the source of referral is the understanding of the child and of the family who was referred. Private practitioners who do all of the work themselves again have the significant advantage if they can obtain firsthand information from the family about the referrer's opinions and suggestions as well as from the referring person. The family in turn will sense the rapport between the specialist and the source of referral. This results in a three-way dialogue: between the practitioner and family, practitioner and referrer, and referrer and family.

A great deal has been written about what psychiatry has to do to maintain a rapport with the referral sources. There is no universally applicable rule except to state that communication with the source of referral is, of course, essential. However, how this is done depends on the type of practice and personalities involved. What really counts is meeting the referrer's needs: These may be the personal needs of the health provider who referred the patient; more important, they are more likely to be the clinical needs of the referring provider toward that family. The referring professional should not have to tell the family he or she does not know what the specialist is doing. Maintaining communication is especially difficult when several professionals work together, such as in school systems. One practical way of looking after those sources is to set up a schedule of consultations to the schools or agencies and be appropriately compensated.

TIME AND SCHEDULING

The aggregate of scheduling, including the intervals between sessions and the length of the sessions, becomes an art when it unites clinical, especially psychodynamic, factors and economic realities. Clinical considerations should always supersede all other factors. Taking into account the parents' psychodynamic and sociocultural factors, child psychiatrists try to optimize transference. Simultaneously, they also must keep track of their own countertransference issues. Parents who are trying to blur the lines between their child's problems and their own problems, especially if they are suffering from personality disorders, present special clinical challenges. It is here that realities of financial reimbursement can play a positive role. Most third-party payors now limit payments

for interventions with parents; this, plus good clinical sense, should keep practitioners' focus where it belongs—on the child. Experienced private practitioners can apportion time and frequency of sessions not only in a negative sense (i.e., to prevent the emergence of excessive transference from the parents themselves) but also in a positive sense in that urgent clinical situations are given more frequent and, when necessary, longer sessions.

OTHER CONSIDERATIONS

It is useful to bear in mind the fact that the relationship between the parents and private practitioners is a more personal one than in other types of medical practice. Seemingly insignificant courtesies extended to the parents are very valuable. These include flexibility in scheduling, accommodating parents' work schedules, and paying attention to seemingly small details, most of which are observed outside the formal session. One of the most important of these is the pratitioner's insistence that a parent must always wait for the child in the waiting room. To insist that the child never be left in the practitioner's office alone builds the therapeutic alliance with the parents and is, moreover, excellent legal prevention in today's climate of high levels of suspiciousness for child abuse.

Extending an invitation to the less involved parent, usually the father, is another proof of wisdom on the part of practitioners. Even well-functioning, intact families have hidden difficulties that child psychiatrists may not have time to ascertain, and they may get a one-sided picture if only one parent is heard all of the time.

When and how much and for how long practitioners spend time with the parents depends on the individual case and the practitioners' styles. Again, psychodynamic and sociocultural factors in the parents together with the clinical needs will dictate how times and sessions are apportioned. In general, private practitioners must be more flexible and less dogmatic in this respect than are institutional practitioners. The economic reality that the parents choose practitioners and, to a great extent, pay for the private treatment of their child may produce some sense of ownership of the practitioners in the parents' minds. Practitioners should and can resist these pressures by strict adherence to professional and ethical standards in order to maintain professional independence. However, courteous behavior and attentiveness to reasonable parental needs implies recognition of the reality of parental economic power.

Finally, some parents need the reassurance of seeing the physical surroundings in which their child will be interviewed. Some parents need a guided tour of the play area and a few words of explanation as to how the session is likely to be conducted. If child psychiatrists happen to have an interest in children's art or collect antique toys, displaying some of these items in the waiting room or corridors serves to reassure parents and children that they have entered a friendly world not devoid of personal interest.

The Therapeutic Alliance with the Child/Adolescent

While the initial therapeutic alliance must be with the parents, as treatment goes on, the therapeutic alliance with the child or adolescent assumes increasing importance. Whereas the therapeutic alliance with the parents ensures the initiation and setting up of the diagnostic and treatment process, a minimum therapeutic alliance with the child needs to develop if treatment is to last. Success will result from a therapeutic alliance with the parents combined with a working therapeutic alliance with the child or adolescent. In most instances, when difficulties arise in the therapist-child relationship, the alliance with the parents is what enables treatment to continue. Occasionally the realization that the child likes to work with a therapist sways ambivalent parents to continue treatment. For beginning practitioners, the main pitfall here is trying too hard to please the parents, thereby preventing the establishment of the therapeutic alliance with the child.

When difficulties arise in either component of the therapeutic alliance, it may be useful for practitioners to review with the parents, and possibly with the child as well, the reasons why treatment was undertaken in the first place. In such cases the usefulness of the private practitioner's involve-

ment from the very beginning, his or her own history taking, and the clearly spelled out diagnosis and agreement on goals are obvious.

The Therapeutic Alliance with Third-Party Payors

It is a fact of life especially pertinent to modern private practitioners that the greatest part of the cost of medical services are paid by third parties and not by the patient's family. It is another urgent fact of life that these third parties must make every attempt to contain costs. Fortunately, the third fact of life is that insurance companies and managed care agencies are run by people, and these people can and also should be related to since they too are human.

Many basic structures in today's managed care are practically immutable, such as the structure of fees, deductions, copayments, and number of visits authorized. However, special and exceptional circumstances do arise; here practitioners' rapport with people administering the benefits may make a difference. Courtesy, patience, and a conscious effort by private practitioners to explain the clinical demands of a particular situation to the insurance company educates the personnel at the office of the third party payor. Practitioners should not be discouraged by the fact that they may speak to different people at different times; persistence will result in a more personal relationship between the third party and practitioners. Certainly the office staff can handle this part of the negotiations, provided they have been properly inspired by the practitioners and their goodwill and morale persist.

The demands of the private practice are no different in a hospital environment, except that independent private practitioners probably are held to higher standards of responsibility by all concerned. The advantage of private practice is that in most setting, private practitioners can provide continuity of care from hospital to office practice.

REFERENCES

Practice Parameters for the Psychiatric Assessment of Children and Adolescents. (October, 1995) AACAP

Official Action. *Journal American Academy of Child & Adolescent Psychiatry*, 34:1386–1402.

41 / Child Psychiatry and Behavioral-Developmental Pediatrics

Jerry Heston

Child and adolescent psychiatry and pediatrics have been associated ever since child psychiatry has existed as a distinct medical specialty. (Herein I sometimes use the term "child psychiatry" to refer to child and adolescent psychiatry.) Indeed, pediatric consultation-liaison is a major aspect of contemporary child psychiatry. While the association is long-standing, it has not always been an easy relationship. Despite having the interests of children and adolescents as common goals, differences in orientation, training, and practice patterns have sometimes resulted in significant conflicts between the two professions. In the best of situations, they are mutually supportive; more often the relationship includes varying degrees of tension; in some cases the two are competitive.

The tension between both areas is amplified in areas where the professions meet and sometimes overlap. The historical conflicts in pediatric consultation-liaison child psychiatry are examples of stress generated when the fields interact closely. While the differences between the fields are a reality and are unavoidable, the potential for achieving common goals continually brings them together. Enlightened pediatricians and child/adolescent psychiatrists realize the importance of their efforts to build a sturdy bridge between their camps.

Behavioral or developmental pediatrics (referred to here as behavioral-developmental pediatrics) is the subspecialty of pediatrics devoted to developmental and behavioral aspects of young persons' health care. Behavioral-developmental pediatrics and child/adolescent psychiatry share many areas of interest. Because of overlap in these areas of specialization, the conflicts between pediatrics and child psychiatry are acted out. It is also an area where common ground may be found.

This chapter focuses on the relationship between child psychiatry and pediatrics, especially behavioral-developmental pediatrics. While they share many interests, there is a great deal of reciprocal misunderstanding regarding the characteristics of each of the professions. After exploring some of these differences, the child psychiatrist's knowledge of behavioral-developmental pediatrics will be increased. Herein the development and history of this pediatric subspecialty are reviewed. Theoretical orientations and training experiences are discussed in order to appreciate similarities and differences between the professions. Areas of practice and spheres of influence are explored to identify potential conflicts and liaisons. By understanding more about behavioral-developmental pediatrics, child psychiatrists may be more prepared and more successful in negotiating the conflicts between the specialties.

This chapter may need a disclaimer. The pattern is to emphasize and identify differences or conflicts. The orientation may seem negativistic and the reader may wonder why anyone should negotiate mine-filled territories, that it all seems hopeless. (Even the titles and references in past literature seem hopeless: *liaisons dangereuses* and "The Burned-Out Missionary"—(Rothenberg, 1968, Work, 1978.) The overall goal—the one toward which both professions are working—is, however, very hopeful and optimistic. When professionals from both areas are able to work together, children and adolescents will benefit. The physical, mental, behavioral, and social needs of our common patients can be met better through cooperation and understanding.

History

The history of child psychiatry with its roots in adult psychoanalysis and the American juvenile delinquency/child guidance movement has been recorded and presented completely in other chapters. Suffice it to say here that child psychiatry developed out of a need to have fuller understanding of psychopathology both in terms of etiology and treatment. Behavioral-developmental pediatrics, on the other hand, was developed to understand more fully normal growth and development in young people and thereby increase knowledge of variations in development. This difference is not only historical, it is also theoretical and presents itself over and over in the relationship between the two disciplines. This divergence in orientation between psychopathology and normal development is profound and cannot be underestimated. These differences can be seen as the "unconscious themes" at the basis of many conflicts between the two fields. This reason alone is enough to look at how behavioral-developmental pediatrics grew out of general pediatrics, a developing field in its own right.

Pediatric literature addressed behavioral and developmental issues early in its history. L. Emmett Holt, for example, wrote about nail-biting, thumb-sucking, and masturbation in his 1897 textbook, *The Diseases of Infancy and Childhood*. Contents included advice regarding feeding, toilet training (it was recommended that training begin as early as 6 months of age), and parenting (it was reported that playing with babies less than 6 months old could cause mental problems). This text and similar others had a profound influence on the development of pediatrics in the United States (Minde & Minde, 1986).

In the late 1920s and on into the 1940s, several institutes were developed to study child development largely from a medical orientation. During this period Dr. Arnold Gesell, a pediatrician, was studying human development at the Yale Child Study Center. While the basic research done at these programs was extremely valuable to the development of both child psychiatry and pediatrics, it was thought to be secondary to mainstream pediatric research. In pediatrics primary emphasis was given to the study of the causes and prevention of major childhood diseases, such as infectious disease and nutritional disorders.

The middle of this century from the 1940s through the 1960s was a period of tremendous growth in the field of pediatrics. The basic research of earlier periods resulted in astounding therapeutic advances. Many diseases that had been previously untreatable, and even fatal, were able to be treated successfully treated for the first time. During this golden age of pediatrics, growth and development continued to be a secondary priority.

The field of pediatrics continued to grow during the 1960s. As the major childhood diseases were controlled, pediatricians began to look at the importance of growth and development in the health care of their patients. The federal government supported widespread study into mental retardation and other handicapping conditions. Multidisciplinary child development centers were established in many cities. Pediatricians played major roles in the leadership of these programs. The American Academy of Pediatrics stressed the development of well-child care and anticipatory guidance by pediatricians (Richmond & Janis, 1983). The 1970s saw continued growth in this aspect of pediatrics as the pediatric research literature reported on various aspects of health care and behavior. Major contributions in this area included Brazelton's work on early mother-infant interactions (Brazelton, 1963) and Kempe's recognition of child abuse (Kempe et al., 1962).

It was out of this environment that the field of behavioral-developmental pediatrics was established. The discipline is still in its infancy, and debates about its relative merit continue both within pediatrics and outside in related specialties such as child and adolescent psychiatry (Friedman, 1985). Regardless of the future of the field, its own development has served to focus pediatrics, as well as child/adolescent psychiatry and other related fields, on the importance of normal growth and development in the overall health care and understanding of children.

Training

Further differences between child psychiatry and behavioral-developmental pediatrics can be seen in the differences in training in the fields. Recognition of the differences might allow for increased appreciation for each field's individual characteristics and be conducive to insight leading to better relations between the professions.

Fellowship training in child and adolescent psychiatry follows a residency in general psychiatry. Residency training stresses evaluation and treatment of mental disorders and includes education in differentiating primary psychiatric problems from those secondary to medical illness. Postresidency training continues that orientation, refocusing it on issues pertinent to child psychiatry. Most fellowship curricula include pediatric neurology but usually do not focus on general pediatric medicine. Thus, from a pediatric point of view, child and adolescent psychiatry is sometimes criticized as being "nonmedical."

Training in behavioral-developmental pediatrics begins with a pediatric residency that focuses on children's health care and includes ambulatory care as well as tertiary care in specialized units such as neonatal and pediatric intensive care units. Although there is a general policy in pediatric training to strengthen education in ambulatory medicine, including behavioral and developmental issues, most programs still emphasize tertiary and subspecialty care. Clinical rotations in behavioral-developmental pediatrics usually are offered depending on availability of interested faculty members. Rotations in child psychiatry are rare and, when available, usually are offered only on an elective basis. While psychiatry training is censured as "nonmedical," pediatric training is criticized for neglecting the psychological and social aspects of health care.

After completion of a 3-year postdoctoral residency in pediatrics, interested pediatricians can enter a fellowship in behavioral-developmental pediatrics, most of which are of 2 years' duration. In addition to behavioral-developmental pediatrics, programs in adolescent medicine have been developed for pediatricians, internists, and family practitioners who are interested in the behavioral aspects of medicine. Fellowship curricula cover a wide variety of topics pertinent to the field, including normal growth and development, mental retardation, physical handicaps, attention deficit hyperactivity disorder, learning disabilities, enuresis, eating disorders, teenage pregnancy, and child abuse. There is some variation across training programs; some fellowships emphasize "behavioral" pediatrics (mother-infant attachment, adjustment to chronic disease, etc.) while others stress "developmental" pediatrics (mental retardation, children with multiple handicaps, etc.). From child psychiatry's point of view, behavioral-developmental pediatrics can be criticized as focusing on mild problems and having limited treatment options. Indeed, there is concern among some pediatricians that a focus on development and behavior does not constitute a subspecialty but should be included in every general pediatrician's fund of knowledge.

In addition to training, medical specialty board certification is an aspect of a professional identity. Physicians who have completed fellowship training in child and adolescent psychiatry (and also have been certified in general psychiatry by the American Board of Psychiatry and Neurology) may apply for special certification in child and adolescent psychiatry. Following the completion of a pediatric residency, physicians may apply for certification by the American Board of Pediatrics. The certification exam includes all aspects of general pediatrics, a small portion of which is devoted to development and behavior. While there is currently no subspecialty board certification in behavioral-developmental pediatrics, there are proposals that developmentally oriented fellowships might be recognized through a joint pediatric-neurology board.

The different emphasis in training between child psychiatry and behavioral-developmental pediatrics is clear. Also apparent is the fact that training in child and adolescent psychiatry is associated with a sense of identity as a general psychiatrist with expertise in the area of child and adolescent mental disorders. Following training in behavioral-developmental pediatrics, such a sense of identity is not always seen. This uncertain identity or lack of consensus regarding specific area of expertise is a major contributor to the conflicts between child/adolescent psychiatry and behavioral-developmental pediatrics as well as its parent specialty, pediatrics.

Occasionally these conflicts and differences are personified when a pediatrician or pediatric resident seeks training in child psychiatry. (The reverse, a psychiatrist becoming a pediatrician, is rare.) Such physicians frequently address issues of identity and allegiance to both fields. This can be expanded to a systemic level, when departments of psychiatry and pediatrics compete for patients, funding, areas of expertise, and even trainees.

Professional Practice

Added to differences in training background and board certification, the professions of behavioral-developmental pediatrics and child psychiatry are practiced in fairly different circumstances, which also often promotes conflict. While the disciplines share some common ground, frequently their approaches to that common ground are different.

Child and adolescent psychiatrists practice medicine in many settings and from a variety of theoretical approaches. Nonetheless, there is general acceptance as to the range of psychiatric practice. Psychiatrists work in outpatient private practices, on inpatient units, in partial hospital programs, in community mental health centers, in universities, on pediatric wards, and in a variety of other settings. There they are seen as experts on the mental health of children, including disturbances of behavior, emotions, and thinking as well as reactions to stress, family functioning, and psychological aspects of physical illness. In general, child psychiatrists organize their diagnostic communication around the fourth edition of the *Diagnostic and Statistical Manual of Mental Disorders*. While there are individual and regional differences in psychiatric practice, an overall picture of a child psychiatrist's practice is fairly easily reached.

The practice of a behavioral-developmental pediatrician is not so easily described. The lack of a sense of identity, the ongoing debate about the existence of the subspecialty or the need for specialization in behavior or development, contribute to the difficulty in describing what these pediatricians do. Pediatricians with training in this field are somewhat limited in areas of practice. Some work in academic pediatrics promoting research in the area and teaching pediatric residents the importance of behavior and development in the general practice of pediatrics. Despite recommendations by many organizations, including the American Academy of Pediatrics and Graduate Medical Education National Advisory Committee, that growth and development receive emphasis during residency training, the number of academic positions in the area is limited to large medical universities, especially those with multidisciplinary child developmental centers. Another practice site for behavioral-developmental pediatricians is in general pediatric ambulatory care. Practitioners in these areas use their specialized training to deal with the multiple behavioral or developmental problems that present in primary care (Christophersen, 1982). Estimates are that 25 to 30% of pediatrician visits are prompted by behavioral and developmental concerns. This practice style complements the argument that behavioral-developmental pediatrics is one aspect of pediatrics and not a subspecialty.

While the field of child psychiatry is very wide and there are occasional debates about its limits and breadth of expertise, a consensus regarding the domain of the specialty usually can be reached. There are, however, uncertainties about which specific areas of children's growth, behavior, and development should concern behavioral-developmental pediatricians. Some physicians limit the scope of practice to normal development and parental education. Areas emphasized in this model include infant development, feeding practices, toilet training, bedtime patterns, and other aspects of anticipatory guidance. Other models for the practice of behavioral-developmental pediatrics are more far-ranging and include diagnosis and treatment of eating disorders, depression, and other syndromes traditionally associated with psychiatry. Moderate models outline a scope of interest between these poles (Haggerty, 1982), including psychological and educational aspects of chronic physical disease, hyperactivity and learning disorders, enuresis and encopresis, and various psychosomatic disorders. Other behavioral-developmental pediatricians have a more "neurologic" approach and address mental retardation, cerebral palsy, and other disabling conditions. The areas of competence in the field of behavioral-developmental pediatrics are extremely variable. It is impossible to make a general statement about the limits of practice in the area; each individual practitioner must be evaluated separately.

Just as there is extreme variation in specific areas of expertise, there is discrepancy in therapeutic interventions undertaken by behavioral-developmental pediatricians. While some advocate using skills of psychiatrists such as family therapy or long-term psychotherapy, most pediatricians feel that they are untrained and avoid these therapeutic approaches. Behavioral-developmental pediatricians are more likely to be more directive in their plans. Behavior therapy, environmental manipulation, and direct advice are common interventions in pediatric practice (Haggerty, 1982). Also, just as child psychiatrists are using behavior-changing pharmacotherapy more often, so are behaviorally oriented pediatricians. These pediatricians may, however, use pharmacotherapy as a single treatment modality. For instance, treatment of attention deficit hyperactivity disorder by a pediatrician might be focused on stimulants without family therapy or school liaison. As research into the effectiveness of psychopharmacology increases, behavioral-developmental pediatricians may increase their use of such interventions.

The practice of behavioral or developmental pediatrics is very broad, broad to the point of being poorly defined. Potential conflicts with child psychiatry are seen as pediatrics comes close to and sometimes overlaps psychiatry's areas of competence and therapeutic strategies. At the same time, behavioral-developmental pediatrics struggles for a sense of identity within the medical profession.

Conclusion

While behavioral-developmental pediatrics and child and adolescent psychiatry have a great deal in common, they have significant differences, differences that sometimes result in conflicts where resolution is difficult to find. It is as if the professions look at the same object and because of their divergent backgrounds are unable to meet on any common ground. The meeting ground is contested in spite of general acceptance of common interests and attempts by individuals from both fields to negotiate some sort of coexistence.

These negotiations have resulted in several suggestions regarding models for interaction. No specific model has achieved widespread acceptance, but child psychiatrists should be aware of a proposal by some pediatricians that they, given their primary care relationship with patients and their relatively greater numbers, should serve to provide the initial evaluation and care for children's behavioral, emotional, and developmental problems. Problems that are severe or beyond the scope of pediatricians (as expected, there is no agreement as to what such problems would be) or that are refractory to their interventions would be referred to psychiatrists. This assignment of a tertiary role to the child psychiatrist is based on the more specialized training and the relative sparsity of practitioners in the field.

Another model of cooperation between pediat-rics and child psychiatry is based on training. In response to a growing field of candidates interested in receiving postdoctorate training in both pediatrics and child psychiatry, a new fellowship was designed in the late 1980s. These programs, referred to as triple board programs, were designed as joint efforts among departments of pediatrics, general psychiatry, and child and adolescent psychiatry. Residents who complete training are eligible to sit for board certification examinations in all three specialties. In addition to educating physicians in both pediatrics and psychiatry, an added benefit has been improved collaboration between the two disciplines beyond the training program (Showalter, 1993).

The proposed models have defenders and attackers from both psychiatry and pediatrics, and the debate on merits of the different models is beyond the scope of this chapter. It is important, however, for psychiatrists to know about their pediatric colleagues and how pediatricians view child psychiatrists. A more functional pattern of interaction will follow when all involved are aware of differences and expectations of they share.

This chapter has attempted to highlight some of those differences by describing the developing field of behavioral-developmental pediatrics in contrast to that of child and adolescent psychiatry, to emphasize that conflicts come out of differences in orientation.

The historic conflicts between the two fields are well known. Certainly, resolutions of those frictions is not the purpose here. Our goal is increased understanding. As psychiatrists more fully understand and appreciate their colleagues from different orientations, solutions to the conflicts will be found. Both pediatrics and child psychiatry have similar goals for the children they serve. These goals will be easier to meet when all are steadfast in their efforts to work together for the common end.

REFERENCES

Brazelton, T. B. (1963). The early mother-infant adjustment. *Pediatrics, 32,* 391.

Christophersen, E. R. (1982, April). Incorporating behavioral pediatrics into primary care. *Pediatric Clinics of North America, 29,* 261–296.

Friedman, S. B. (1985, August). Behavioral pediatrics: Interaction with other disciplines. *Developmental and Behavioral Pediatrics, 6,* 202–214.

Greene, C. M. (1984, December). Mutual collaboration between child psychiatry and pediatrics: Resistances and facilitation. *Developmental and Behavioral Pediatrics, 5,* 315–318.

Haggerty, R. J. (1982, April). Behavioral pediatrics: Can it be taught? Can it be practiced? *Pediatric Clinics of North America, 29,* 391–398.

Kempe, C. H., Silverman, E. N., Steele, B. F., Dragmueller, W., & Silver HK. (1962). The battered child syndrome. *Journal of the American Medical Association, 181*, 17.

Minde, K., & Minde, R. (1986). *Infant psychiatry*. Beverly Hills, CA: Sage Publications.

Richmond, J. B., & Janis, J. M. (1983). Ripeness is all: The coming of age of behavioral pediatrics. In M. D. Levine, et al., (Eds.), *Developmental-behavioral pediatrics*. Philadelphia: W.B. Saunders.

Rothberg, M. B. (1968). Child psychiatry-pediatrics liaison. *Journal of the American Academy of Child Psychiatry, 7*, 492–509. pp. 15–25.

Showalter, J. E. (1993). Tinker to Evers to Chance: Triple board update. *Journal of the American Academy of Child and Adolescent Psychiatry, 32*, 243.

Work, H. H. (1978, September). The burned-out missionary. *Pediatrics, 62*, 425–427.

42 / Research in Child Psychiatry

Alan Apter

Mental disorders in children have been the subject of serious study for the past century beginning with the pioneering work of the early giants of the field such as Henry Maudsley, Sigmund Freud, and William Healy. Child and adolescent psychiatry remains a young and largely uncharted field. Only in the past few decades has systematic empirical research taken a central role in placing our field in the mainstream of medical and psychological science.

Psychodynamically Oriented Research

Initially, most research in childhood mental disorders came from the psychoanalytic tradition. With the rise of empirical methods of research, this dynamic tradition has come under attack. Polarization has occurred between this tradition and that which sees child psychiatry as an empirical science in the tradition of logical positivism. Although in North America empirical (and especially biological) research often is viewed as the only worthwhile approach to research in child psychiatry, it is important to realize that other methods of inquiry and other sources of epistemology are important for our profession.

Although some attempts have been made at doing empirical research in child psychoanalysis, such as that of Fonegay from the Anna Freud Center in London, it is probably most useful to adopt the position of Merton Gill, who is firmly in favor of defining psychoanalysis as a hermeneutic discipline. The hermeneutic position is that psychoanalysis deals with meanings. Hermeneutics is the discipline of interpretation that lies at the heart of psychoanalysis. Interpretation, devoted to discovering hidden meanings, is the preoccupation of the dynamic psychotherapist.

Researchers in the hermeneutic tradition devote most of their attention to psychoanalytic theories of technique, such as types of communication by patients and types of interventions by therapists, and higher-level concepts such as countertransference, resistance to the awareness of transference here and now, resistance to the resolution of transference, and propositions about the interrelationships among all these.

Donald Spence drew attention to the notion of narrative truth as opposed to historical truth. He believes that both free association on the part of the patient and evenly hovering attention on the part of the therapist are highly active processes whereby both the rambling talker and the attentive listener are trying to make coherent sense out of what is being said by self and other. Hence both talking and listening can be seen as attempts to enrich the narrative truth of the utterance. When we listen to a patient talking, we supplement the patient's associations with our own in order to give the text a narrative form so as to better understand. Thus the therapist's listening can be viewed as active constructive listening in the service of understanding. The therapist often gives unwitting interpretations that lead the patient to make more coherent statements, which then enable the therapist to make all formal interpretation of the material that he or she has, in fact, helped actively to create. Associations and interpretations are continuously inserted into the developing narrative and become true as they become familiar and lend meaning to otherwise disconnected pieces of the patient's life story. This activity is a form of research that gives meaning to the work done by therapists with both adults and children.

The narrative or story is jointly developed by both participants in therapy. Each partner makes contributions of different sorts, at different times, and with different degrees of awareness, reflectiveness, and conflictednes. It is clear that the story is not simply uncovered. Multiple narratives can be constructed, and several different models can account for the same pieces of clinical material. Good analysts seem to work within a hermeneutic circle, using a provisional formulation to build a scaffolding in support of the early data, taking subsequent data to reframe, to extend, or to dismantle the scaffolding, and using the revised framework to see further into the patient's story.

Freud saw psychoanalysis as an empirical natural science and tried to formulate this in his famous "Project," but as Roy Schafer has also pointed out, a "native realism" always underlaid Freud's models. Schafer also has addressed the problem of "alternative meanings" at length. Each therapy can develop using a number of metaphors/models with each one having its own intrinsic value. Analysis as a journey is one example; another is analysis as a wartime prison or a happy and safe closed place.

The kind of research described as hermeneutical is done within the context of therapy; it takes place either during a session or afterward, possibly in discussion with other colleagues or by immersion in the relevant literature. Empirical research by contrast, in child and adolescent psychiatry provides us with a general set of facts about our patients; a collective set of patients or subjects provides us with an epidemiological snapshot. This kind of research is written "with a nomothetic pen" and not an idiographic one. Although these statistical profiles are important and valuable, they may mislead clinicians. As Berman (1992) pointed out, checklists, scales, and profiles describe the modal patient; however, they may obscure the discriminations necessary to translate these statistically significant scores into clinically relevant information. Therefore, intensive clinical observations always must supplement empirical research. This "idiographic" approach to research is also in the Freudian tradition of psychiatric and psychological research.

The case method of research and teaching has long been used in other academic professions, such as law and business. Even in general medicine, case studies often are used in grand rounds. A noteworthy example of the integration of case studies and empirical research is Pfeffer's book *The Suicidal Child* (1986). In a study derived primarily from empirical research, she uses 86 case vignettes to illustrate her text. "Cases, well described, bring a concrete reality to our teaching . . . they provide an anchor on academic flights of speculation". Theory and research come to life in the presentation of case material, each being given the opportunity to be tested against clinical practice. A case simply presents a factual outline, posing issues requiring judgement and the application of clinical principles" (Berman, 1992).

Empirical Clinical Research in Child Psychiatry

Although hermeneutic and idiographic research are still of paramount importance to child and adolescent psychiatry, clinical empirical research is vital to the survival of our field if we wish to remain a part of modern medicine. The methodology of such research has been refined continuously, and definite sets of rules determine the "anatomy and physiology" of this kind of research (Hulley, Newman, & Cummings, 1988).

The first step of any research endeavor is the articulation of a *research question*. Ideally this question involves a controversy or uncertainty about an issue in child and adolescent psychiatry that the investigator would like to resolve. Research questions are initially vague and reflect a general concern. An example would be "Does adolescent suicide have a genetic etiology?" This interesting question must be translated into an operational and researchable issue. Often this can be done by breaking the question down into more concrete parts and singling them out as the focus for the research project. So in our example, a more specific research question would be: (1) What proportion of adolescent suicides have a family history of suicide? (2) What are the different characteristics of adolescent suicides with and without a family history of suicide? (3) Do adolescent suicides have a higher proportion of specific polymorphisms of the tryptophan hydroxylase gene than do persons in the general population?

According to Hulley *et al.* (1988), a good research question should pass the "so-what" test. The answer to the question should make a useful contribution to our body of knowledge. The question also must be researchable or feasible to study. A good research question is significant in that it is based on relevant research on the subject; the researcher should recognize how the findings of the study will help resolve uncertainties and influence policy and clinical practice.

An investigator may have many different reasons for taking up a particular research question; some may be related to the need for financial support or for building a career. The most relevant reason for pursuing a research question, however, is that it is interesting. This motivation grows as the research endeavor proceeds, and it "provides the intensity of effort needed for overcoming the many hurdles and frustrations of the research process" (Hulley et al., 1988).

Cummings, Browner, and Hulley (1988) have summarized the characteristics of a good research question as follows:

1. The study must be feasible—the investigator must be able to recruit an adequate number of subjects; he or she should have enough technical expertise to carry out the study; he or she should be able to afford the study in terms of time and money, and the idea should be manageable in scope.
2. The idea must be interesting and novel in that it confirms or refutes previous studies, extends previous findings, and provides new findings.
3. The research must meet ethical standards.
4. The idea should be relevant to scientific knowledge, to clinical and health policy, and to future research directions.

Scholarship and experience are two important prerequisites for developing a research question. Good research questions often arise from journal articles and scientific meetings but also from thinking about clinical practice and problems. One of the important but problematic developments of academic child and adolescent psychiatry over the last 10 years, especially in the United States, has been the rise of professional researchers without clinical responsibilities. The danger exists that research questions may be divorced from real clinical practice. Cummings et al. (1988) also emphasized 2 general kinds of solutions when researchers find difficulty in working out research question. The first is to get good advice. "The single most important decision for an investigator who is not yet experienced is his choice of a senior scientist to serve as his mentor." If possible, it is best to work in a team that includes investigators each of whom has particular experience in the different areas of the study. New investigators are encouraged to find good mentors who can help them articulate important research questions. This experience and collaboration can be one of the most rewarding aspects of doing research in child and adolescent psychiatry. The development of the Internet and electronic mail have facilitated this kind of endeavor enormously; now it is comparatively easy to make contact with even foremost experts in a particular field of research.

The second piece of advice is that, early on, the research question should be transformed into a written 1 to 2 page study protocol that relates to subject selection and methods of measurement. The study plan develops gradually from an iterative process of designing, reviewing, pretesting, and revising. The written study plan forms the basis for receiving advice and comments from colleagues.

Several kinds of study designs are appropriate for research in child and adolescent psychiatry. Researchers can stand away from the events they (and a panel) wish to study and observe them in objectively, or they can test the effects of an intervention and perform an experiment. If investigators choose an observational design, their next decision is whether to make the measurements on a single occasion (in a cross-sectional study) or over a period of time (in a longitudinal study). The question then arises of whether to deal exclusively with past and present events in a retrospective study or to follow study subjects prospectively for events that have not yet occurred (Hulley et al., 1988).

In a cross-sectional study, the child and adolescent subject is examined at a certain point of time in development—for example, as a baby or at age 10 years. Many cross-sectional studies in series may give us an idea of how a certain line of development occurs, for example, language or play. In a longitudinal study, youngsters are studied over a long period, perhaps even from infancy to adulthood. Longitudinal studies are difficult to carry out since they span long periods of time and may have to involve generations of researchers. However, since child and adolescent psychiatry is essentially a developmental discipline, the longitudinal prospective approach often is held up as the ultimate standard, especially when combined with a randomized experiment. This kind of study enables us to understand continuity in the life of the young person and to develop a cohort of young people. This cohort can be followed over time and the life story of each individual child can be charted. From a number of such stories, a coherent collective story can be woven. Following up of a cohort of children at high risk for schizophrenia in Israel revealed the importance of distortions of cognitive development for adult-onset schizophrenia. Longitudinal developmental research can uncover continuities and discontinuities in a child's functioning over time and can describe behavioral stabilities. It is reasonable to assume that some symptoms that appear in early childhood will remain constant or will lead to the development of yet other kinds of subsequent difficulties. For example, children with delays in language development may still have communication difficulties later in life, and these communication problems may presage the later development of anxiety and depression. Yet other symptoms or phenomena may show discontinuities. Some children may show short periods of anxiety and depression that pass and have no implications for difficulties in later life.

However, no one approach is always superior to all others. The research question should determine which research design is most efficient for getting a satisfactory answer. For example, the relatively low cost of retrospective case control studies makes them particularly attractive for certain kinds of questions.

Descriptive, open-ended studies are often a useful and easy way to begin studying a topic (Hulley et al., 1988); these studies explore the lay of the land, describing distribution of diseases and the characteristics of the population. An example of such a research query is: What is the prevalence of suicidal behavior in the families of adolescent suicide attempters? Descriptive studies usually are followed by analytic studies that try to discover cause-and-effect relationships by analyzing associations, for example: What risk factors in the family favor transmission of the suicidal behavior to the adolescent children? The final step should be an experiment to establish the effects of an intervention. Here a question might be: Does early intervention in families showing suicidal behavior prevent suicide in their offspring? Or, more fancifully, can the protein product of the polymorphism be identified and neutralized so as to prevent suicidal behavior in adolescents? An analytic approach combined with a longitudinal one is particularly useful in child and adolescent psychiatric

research and can be used to study why some developmental phenomena are continuous and others are not. For instance, such a study could try to detect what influence temperament has on the continuity and discontinuity of symptoms.

Clinical research methodology places great emphasis on careful selection of subjects who will be participating in the study. After specifying the selection criteria, considerations of how to find the subjects and recruit them must be made. The methods of sampling must take into account factors such as Berkson's bias, which states that clinic samples are nonrepresentative of what the disease looks like in the community since they are more likely to be affected by comorbidity. This is especially important in child and adolescent psychiatry, since dysfunctional families may be more likely to bring their children for treatment than highly functional families, thus giving rise to misleading conclusions about the role of family function in a given psychopathology, such as adolescent suicide (Peterson, 1996). On the other hand, community sampling is far more difficult and expensive than using a clinic sample; its generalizability is obtained at a greater cost.

Another important issue in clinical research is the choice of variables to be controlled and assessed. In other words, which characteristics of the subjects studied should be measured? In descriptive studies, individual characteristics are measured one at a time; in analytic studies, the interrelationships between 2 or more variables are analyzed in order to predict outcomes and to draw inferences about cause and effect. In considering the association between 2 variables, the one that is presumed to precede the other is called the predictor variable and the one that comes after is the outcome variable. Thus child abuse would be a predictor variable and suicidal behavior in adolescence would be an outcome variable. Most observational studies have many predictor variables, such as child abuse, loss of a parent, and difficult temperament, and many outcome variables, such as suicidal behavior, violent behavior, and substance abuse.

Clinical investigators have to have a plan for data management and data analysis. For all but the most simple observational studies, this always includes a hypothesis-testing component specifying in advance at least one main hypothesis. This hypothesis is a rephrasing of the research question so as to make it suitable for statistical analysis. For example, adolescent suicide attempters will have a higher incidence of family violence than adolescents who do not attempt suicide. Descriptive inductive studies do not require a hypothesis because their purpose is to describe how the variables are distributed (e.g., the prevalence of suicide in a certain catchment area) rather than how the variables are associated with one another (Hulley et al., 1988).

At the end of the research project, investigators should be able to draw conclusions and inferences from the study. One set of inferences regards the internal validity of the study, or the degree to which the conclusions correctly describe what went on in the study; the second set of conclusions relates to the study's external validity, or how generalizable the study's findings are for the rest of the world. These questions relate to the reliability of the methods used; will the same methods in the hands of another investigator give the same results (interrater reliability) and will the same method give the same results over time (test-retest reliability)? They also relate to the validity of the method: does the instrument used in the research actually measure what it is supposed to measure?

Cohen (1997) regarded the following areas of empirical research as most relevant for child and adolescent psychiatry: developmental psychopathology, epidemiology, genetics, brain structure and function, basic neurochemistry and neuropharmacology, clinical pediatric psychopharmacology, psychosocial treatment research, and social science research.

Developmental Psychopathology

To a large extent, work done in adult psychiatry has had a major influence on research done in child and adolescent psychiatry. Nevertheless, child and adolescent psychiatric research is a unique endeavor and should not constitute a simple downward extension of research on adult mental disorders. Research into the causes and determinants of the disorders of children requires a developmental perspective, taking into account a wide variety of developmental disciplines including cognitive and language functions, social and emotional processes, behavior and learning, and changes occurring in the anatomical structures and physiological processes of the brain over the course of childhood. The developmental approach to the study of psychopathology requires researchers to be aware of a very complex balance among biological, psychological, and social factors that constantly interact in different ways over time. In addition, there are balances and interactions of risk and protective factors in the youngster and in his or her environment. Emergent functions and competencies interact with the tasks of the different developmental stages and thus influence the expression of the various disorders, leading to new symptoms and difficulties. At different times and in different contexts, particular stresses or underlying psychopathological mechanisms may give rise to completely different clinical phenomena.

The complexity of the developmental approach to the study of child and adolescent psychiatric disorders means that these studies are the province of many diverse disciplines. Some focus on directly studying and helping young people and their families, others on the social systems that influence child and adolescent mental health and supply the needed services—such as schools, municipal, state and national agencies, and the various caregivers. Still others center around normal development, providing an essential context for understanding what can go wrong.

Important advances in empirical research in the psychological sciences have occurred during the past century. This has led to vastly increased understanding of areas such as behavior, motivation, and the acquisition of cognitive and language skills. Developmental psychology has begun to give us insights into how psychological processes evolve over the course of development. Most of this research has focused on normal development; the field of developmental psychopathology has only just begun to emerge as a discipline in its own right. However, many areas of normal development have major relevance for the understanding of psychopathology in childhood and adolescence. Studies on maternal-infant bonding, separation-individuation, attachment, attentional mechanisms, and learning have enriched our approaches to maladjusted children. Important research also has been conducted on the formation of self-image and the acquisition of defense mechanisms and coping styles.

The relationship between childhood disorders and the abnormalities of adult life have been attracting considerable attention. Although these studies necessarily have a long gestation, findings on the continuities and discontinuities between childhood and adult life are already having an impact on the way we think about childhood disorders.

Research is not simply the accumulation of an array of isolated and unconnected facts. Rather it should be a continuity of programmatic, hypothesis-driven investigations. It is important that we have a theory that generates hypotheses that can be tested. Although the place of theory is not what it once was, and the "grand developmental theories of Freud, Piaget and social learning no longer generate the clinical and scientific hypotheses that they once did" (Rutter et al., 1995), the new and exciting field of developmental psychopathology has become a recognized discipline in itself (Cichetti & Cohen, 1995). The theories of developmental psychopathology are now the source of many research questions in child and adolescent psychiatry. Over the last 2 decades this orientation has had a tremendous impact on child and adolescent psychiatric research. This approach originated in a number of developmental theories such as organismic developmental theory, psychoanalysis, and Piaget's structural-developmental theory. All these theories have now been applied to the study of young children with psychopathology, and confirmation or modification of these theories has resulted. The major thrust of this line of investigation has been into the relationship between normal and pathological development. The field of developmental psychopathology considers studies of normal and abnormal development to be mutually enriching. What constitutes a case? The reason for the relatively recent crystallization of a number of subdisciplines into a line of inquiry subsumed under developmental psychopathology can be attributed to the maturation of the related disciplines. Only after a sufficient corpus of research knowledge on normal biological and psychological development across the life span had been accumulated could researchers interpret the findings of their investigations of psychopathological processes and atypical development. (Cichetti & Cohen, 1995)

Formerly, it was thought that childhood was a time of happiness and carefree bliss. In fact, however, research has shown that even in the earliest years of life, emotional and behavioral difficulties are common and become increasingly so as the child grows up. Nowadays is as hard to imagine that a child can go through life without encountering times of hardship, suffering, and emotional and behavioral upheaval as it is to conceive of a child going through life without having any of the common childhood infections or an accident.

Systematic community studies in preschoolers have found rates of moderate mental disorders in 7.5 to 11% of children of preschool age; 25% of mothers of kindergarten children rate their children as being overactive and lacking in concentration (Verhulst & Koot, 1995). Epidemiologists have a rule of thumb that 15% is the cutoff before pathology gives way to a developmental phase. Many of these children suffer from sleep disturbances; by age 8, about 10% of children will have had transient tics. These are not always clinical illnesses and may, for some children, represent "growing pains." A major conceptual problem for child and adolescent psychiatrists is to decide on what is due to normal developmental phase and what to a clinical case. Should this be decided by the degree of objective impairment of functioning or by the degree of subjective suffering? It seems that only prospective longitudinal studies conducted within the context of a developmental psychopathological approach can resolve this critical issue. In some cases there is an obvious discontinuity between normal and abnormal functioning. The social withdrawal of an autistic child is not merely severe shyness, and the thought disorder or hallucinations of a schizophrenic child are not simply reflective of an overactive imagination.

Developmental psychopathology views childhood disorders as they are related to normal development. For example, attention deficit disorder with hyperactivity is not seen as a discrete medical syndrome but rather as related to malfunction of physiological development on the road to the attaining of attentional skills and goal-directed motor behavior. The theory is that in order for attentional skills to develop normally, integrity of the central nervous system, including cortical and subcortical areas, is required. At the same time, of course, the child must develop appropriate cognitive and social skills from stable and consistent interactions with parents. Both the biological and the psychological processes basic to attentional skills as well as their interactions can be studied over the developmental life span.

Sometimes the complexity of developmental research requires the use of techniques from different disciplines in a single project. This enables researchers to investigate the problem on many different levels. For example, a study may include a video recording of a child's behavior along with a direct interview with the child or his or her parents and blood sampling for metabolite or hormonal concentrations in order to characterize the child's difficulties.

Epidemiology

Psychiatric disorders in childhood occur in all countries of the world, in all socioeconomic strata of society, and in all ethnic and cultural groups. Epidemiological research examines the nature, prevalence, and etiology of these disorders in large populations. This is the main distinction between epidemiological and clinical research. The latter often includes just a limited number of subjects. Child psychiatric epidemiology has made extensive progress since the early work of Rutter and his colleagues in the late 1960s. Today methodologies for developmental epidemiology are quite sophisticated. The subject has recently been extensively reviewed by Costello and Angold (1995). Child psychiatric epidemiology involves the use of a number of varied methods, such as structured interviews from many informants, teacher evaluations, and data obtained from all kinds of agencies to determine the incidence (number of new cases every year) and the prevalence (number of cases in the community at a given point in time) of childhood psychopathology.

Although most psychiatric disorders of childhood and adolescence are seen throughout the world, the incidence and prevalence of the various disorders may vary from country to country. There is extensive underutilization of services by children; in some places fewer than 10% of children in need will be seen by child and psychiatrists (Cohen, 1997). In developing countries, only the most severely disturbed children ever see a psychiatrist. Epidemiology has shown that psychotic children and children with disruptive and destructive tendencies are most likely to be referred; quiet children who are anxious and depressed and suffer from the so-called internalizing disorders are likely to be neglected until a crisis situation, such as a suicide attempt, occurs. Then "caseness" will be detected.

Child and adolescent psychiatrists working in a clinical setting often see a biased picture of what the disorder is really like because of ascertainment bias, since referred children are more likely to have more severe forms of the disorders. Furthermore, very often the signs and symptoms are complicated by comorbidity with other problems, and the children more often come from families that are unable to cope with the children's difficulties. For example, a clinician may recognize Tourette's disorder as a severe illness with aggressive behavior, learning problems, obsessions, and compulsions, while the epidemiologist in the community may see that most children with Tourette's disorder have mild motor and vocal tics but are generally well-adjusted youngsters.

One of the most important tasks of epidemiology in child and adolescent psychiatry is the comprehensive assessment of the risk factors associated with specific disorders. Parental mental disorder is a vitally important risk best displayed by community studies evaluating both parents and children; such studies are important in advancing our field. Furthermore, attempts to identify high-risk segments of the population for further study are valuable (e.g., children whose parents are on welfare and children who are in foster care); etiological factors such as marital discord, harsh and inconsistent discipline, head injury or drug abuse can be discerned to good effect (Institute of Medicine, 1989). Community studies delineate such protective factors as specific talents, high intelligence, physical activity, and supportive families, and their role in certain disorders. Sometimes genetic studies in conjunction with epidemiological studies can determine the role played by genetic vulnerability in conjunction with social-environmental factors in producing an illness. Hence, a patient with a genetic vulnerability for anorexia nervosa will not develop the illness if she does not live in a society that emphasizes thinness. Nor will a child with a genetic vulnerability to Tourette's disorder develop the illness if not subject to birth traumata.

A frequently employed technique in developmental epidemiology is the use of the case control design, whereby subjects with the condition are identified and compared with subjects who do not have the disorder. The control subjects are matched for variables that may confound the study (confounder variables). Examples are age, sex, ethnic group, schooling, and socioeconomic status. The case control study has the disadvantage (shared with any design that relies on people's recollections or records such as medical charts) of being vulnerable to biases in recollection or availability of past data (Verhulst & Koot, 1995).

Traditionally, psychiatric epidemiology has studied the frequency of psychopathology in the community, but in truth it has much broader implications. Clinical researchers with a special knowledge of epidemiology have been able to contribute to knowledge about the classification, course, and outcome of the mental disorders that afflict the young. More important, epidemiology has raised research questions for child and adolescent psychiatry, such as how to conceptualize and assess juvenile psychopathology (Verhulst & Koot, 1995). Many symptoms associated with psychopathology are common in children in the community; these include fears and worries, depression and unhappiness, intrusive thoughts and rituals. These epidemiological facts have forced child and adolescent psychiatrists to rethink notions about the continuity and/or discontinuity between normality and psychopathology. Yet another early finding in epidemiological studies was of the discrepancies in information gathered from teachers, parents, and children. This finding highlighted an issue that is still unresolved in childhood psychopathology. Other research questions that have arisen from epidemiological research with children include the role of comorbidity and concern the design of longitudinal studies.

Epidemiology is first and foremost an empirical science. Although it can be used to test hypotheses derived from theories and epidemiology itself can be derived from theory, basically it rests on the systematic collection of observations of the pathological phenomena in a defined population. In addition, epidemiology requires collection of data—including clinical data—in a manner that renders data quantifiable. According to Verhulst and Koot (1995), the most important recent developments in the epidemiology of youth psychopathology include

the systematic co-ordination of information derived from standardized assessments of different informants (e.g., parent, teacher, clinician and child). Standardized assessments of problem behaviors in large epidemiological samples of clinically referred and non-referred children have provided the data needed to develop strategies for coordinating information from multiple sources.

The idea that data concerning clinical phenomena can be collected in a standardized, quantifiable manner has had a tremendous influence (both good and bad) in areas of child and adolescent psychiatry very far afield from epidemiology and represents one of the most radical departures from the clinical case or theoretical method of research that is the hallmark of hermeneutic studies.

Genetics

A major influence on research in child and adolescent psychiatry has been the explosion in neuroscience over the past 3 decades. Both the number of neuroscientists and the range of their investigations have increased dramatically. Indeed by presidential proclamation, 1990 to 1999 was declared to be the decade of the brain. Many studies regarding the human brain are being conducted at the National Institutes of Health, particularly the National Institute of Mental Health. The neurosciences include neuroanatomy, neurochemistry, electrophysiology, and neuropharmacology, along with the key elements of molecular genetics, molecular biology, and cell biology. Geneticists and cell biologists study the genes that control the development and maturation of the brain, the mechanisms that regulate the functions of the neurons, and the communication between them as well as the interactions among brain, behavior, emotion, and thought. Not only the classic Mendelian disorders but also diseases of complex and multifactorial etiology (such as those treated by child and adolescent psychiatrists) are now susceptible to investigation at the DNA level.

The development of the human brain is under genetic control from the first moments of conception to the final stages of maturation in the late stages of adolescence. Genes also seem to be involved in neuronal decay in old age. Genetic mutations and variations in genetic expression may be responsible for minor or major alterations in brain functioning. Genetic research has discovered the basis of over 2,000 causes of mental retardation. Interestingly, over 70 diagnostic categories in which mental retardation is an associated feature are linked to the X chromosome. Examples of disorders of interest to child and adolescent psychiatrists with known human genetic bases are Down syndrome, Lesch-Nyan syndrome, phenylketonuria, and fragile X syndrome. Other disorders that are now subject to an intensive search for a genetic basis include autism, Tourette's disorder, eating disorders, adolescent suicide, obsessive compulsive disorder, schizophrenia, and affective disorders.

Genetic disorders may be classified as follows (Brock, 1993):

1. Mendelian or single-gene disorders show a mutant allele or a pair of mutant alleles at a single genetic locus. They may be inherited or be the re-

sult of new mutations. When inherited, the transmission patterns are simple and classified as autosomal dominant or recessive or X-linked dominant or recessive. Their major importance in child and adolescent psychiatry has been in the field of mental retardation.

2. Chromosome disorders are caused by the loss or gain of 1 or more of the 46 chromosomes of the diploid cell. A majority of the chromosome disorders are de novo events arising from major mutations in the parents' germ cells. Of particular interest to child and adolescent psychiatrists are Turner's syndrome (XO) and Kleinfelter's syndrome (XXY), from which much has been learned about the development of gender schema and identity.

3. Multifactorial disorders are thought to involve interactions between genes and environmental factors, although the number and nature of both genes and environmental factors are poorly understood. Occurrence and recurrence rates are estimated empirically. Probably several common child psychiatric disorders, such as neuroses, phobias, and maladjustive personality traits, fall into this category.

4. Somatic genetic disorders are mutations that arise in the genetic material of specific somatic cells, including neurons, and often give rise to tumors. The somatic event is not inherited, although there is a complex interaction between inherited and somatic mutations.

5. Mitochondrial disorders arise from mutations in the mitochondrial genome, which is quite distinct from the bulk of DNA carried by chromosomes in the cell nucleus. Mitochondrial DNA is transmitted only through the maternal line, and patterns of inheritance are different from those seen in the Mendelian disorders.

The first step in genetic research is to show that the disorder being investigated is likely heritable. This involves showing that the disorder is more common in the families of individuals with the disorder than in the families of a control group of subjects without the disorder. Increased incidence of a disorder in a family does not necessarily mean that the disorder is inherited, however, since many other influences may be at play, including learning and cultural, and other environmental conditions. These circumstances can be teased out by comparing concordance rates between monozygotic and dizygotic twins, especially if the twins were separated at birth and then reared apart.

Once the heritability of a disorder is suspected to be highly likely, then the mode of inheritance can be investigated. One method of doing this is

by sorting on high-density families. Many such families have been identified for the study of psychiatric disorders in early life, such as affective disorders, attention deficit disorders, Asperger's syndrome, autism, tics, and obsessive compulsive disorder. Once such a family has been identified, a family tree or pedigree can be drawn to demonstrate graphically the relationships between the various family members. An ideal family for study is one in which there are many family members coming from many different generations and all still living.

Ideally, only 1 parent in each generation should have the disorder. It must be possible to describe the phenotype definitely, preferably using structured psychiatric interviews and reliable diagnostic criteria. The next step is to obtain genetic material (DNA) from the blood or other tissues of all the family members. After the DNA is analyzed using the methods of molecular biology, and the sequences of amino acids of the various genes can be determined for each family member. The investigators then try to find a statistical link between certain genes on the DNA and the presence or absence of the disorder. Doing this requires the use of mathematical models, which in turn depend on a hypothesis regarding the mode of inheritance, the degree of penetrance of the gene, and the prevalence of the disorder within the population.

Linkage analysis is the statistical method most commonly used to determine the connection between a gene (or amino acid sequence) and a disorder. Linkage analysis is essentially a statistical analysis of a set of reproductive events in which the probability of alleles at one genetic locus cosegregating with alleles at another locus because the alleles are close together on the same chromosome is compared to the statistical probability that this could have happened by chance. Usually one of the loci is chosen because it shows a suitable DNA polymorphism (the allele may have more than one form of amino acid sequence) called the marker locus, while the other is a disease locus that may or may not be occupied by a disease-causing allele (Brock, 1993). Unfortunately, this method has not as yet proven successful in child and adolescent psychiatry, probably because many child psychiatric disorders are complex disorders in which there is seldom any clear pattern of inheritance; there are uncertainties about diagnosis (e.g., when do normal obsessions fade into true obsessive compulsive disorder); there is disease heterogeneity (e.g., schizophrenia is probably a group of different disorders); and the childhood psychiatric disorders have a variable age of onset and most probably involve many genes, rather than one gene or reflect both genetic and environmental circumstances.

Mathematical models attempting to handle the segregation of several causative gene loci are very complex and must make untestable assumptions about the interactive effects between different genes. In order to handle these difficulties, linkage analysis has had to employ simplifying procedures such as sibling-pair analysis, candidate gene linkage analysis, and haplotype relative risk measures. Nonetheless, we may have to wait for a reasonable map of the human genome before we see results that are telling for child and adolescent psychiatry.

If a gene can be found, it can then be cloned and the protein products produced by the action of the gene can be analyzed and tested for. This, theoretically, should lead to major advances in the treatment of the disorders under discussion.

An important caveat of genetic research is the study of genetic-environmental interactions. This is not a simple matter. It appears that certain genetic influences tend to expose an individual to specific environmental stresses. Hence, the hypothesized gene for "novelty seeking" will lead one adolescent to take dangerous risks while another will live in a more restrictive or quieter mode and 2 children living and growing up in the same family may have very different experiences. Psychotic children, for instance, will confuse their parents who will then behave in an inconsistent manner toward the children. Children with a low threshold for dealing with life events (thought to be related to low serotonin metabolic turnover) may cause parents to overprotect them. Such microenvironments are easiest to identify when studying monozygotic twins. Although such twins share 100% of their genetic material, they are rarely completely concordant, even for Mendelian traits; even in utero, different environments, such as different levels of blood supply, will influence the expression of their separate but equal genetic material ("genotype").

Brain Structure and Function

The past decade has brought an explosion of new methods for studying brain structure and func-

tion, many of which are now being used to study mental illness in children and adolescents. It is well known that children with brain lesions show aberrations of behavior with a wide range of psychiatric disturbances, including mental retardation and attention deficit disorder. However, in general very little is known about the structure and function of the brain in young persons with psychiatric disorders.

Electrophysiological research into brain function using such methods as the classic electroencephalograph and evoked and event-related potentials enables us to understand how the brain responds to stimuli. These methods enable us to explore how the brain deals with visual and auditory information, starting with the sensory organ (ear and eye) and passing through the ascending neural tracts until they excite the cerebral cortex. These methods also are used to investigate higher cortical functions such as anticipation, planning, and decision making.

Child and adolescent psychiatrists now can use some of the new methods of brain imaging, since the methods are noninvasive and do not use radioactive materials. Consequently they are especially suited for use in children. Early studies used computerized tomography scanning to illustrate large brain lesions such as tumors, enlargement of the brain ventricles, and congenital malformations. Today, however, the most common method used to study early-onset neuropsychiatric developmental disorders is magnetic resonance imaging (MRI). This method produces high-resolution, good-quality pictures of the brain, enabling three-dimensional images and volumetric analysis of brain regions of specific interest (such as the basal ganglia in tic disorders like Tourette's).

An important advance has been the adoption of magnetic resonance imaging for the study of the brain while the subject is performing specific tasks requiring brain activity. This method, called functional MRI (FMRI), is able to study brain activity in relation to brain structure. Thus we can image the brain while the child is reading, hearing, or thinking about a word or performing specific neuropsychological tests. An important use of this tool is to compare children who have specific disorders with normal children on cognitive test paradigms. For example, we can test the brain activity of an autistic child who is trying to differentiate between a picture of a sad face from a one of a happy face or a child with Tourette's disorder who is trying to inhibit an impulse, such as the urge to blink. We also can examine areas of the brain that are activated when a dyslexic child tries to comprehend the meaning of a word. Functional magnetic resonance imaging can be used for longitudinal studies of development as well as for cross-sectional studies of current functioning or psychopathology. Magnetic resonance spectroscopy (MRS) uses a magnetic field to determine the biochemical composition of neural tissues without requiring invasive procedures, such as biopsy of the brain. Until now neurochemical research in children has been restricted to the examination of peripheral markers, but this new technique holds the promise of examining the biochemical functioning of the brain centrally.

Other methods of investigating brain function are related to the brain characteristic metabolism and biochemical functioning. Radioactive ligands are injected into the body and are bound by receptors in the brain. The specific distribution of the emitted radioactive activity gives an idea of the structural functioning of the brain under different physiological conditions (such as during an anxiety attack) or while the subject is performing a cognitive task. With these procedures, the pattern of radioactivity is converted into an anatomical picture by a computer program. The most widely used method is positron emission tomography (PET) and the single-photon emission computed tomography (SPECT). The use of these methods in children is limited by their potential hazards of excessive radiation.

The most direct method of examining the brain is by brain autopsy after the death of a child who has suffered from a psychiatric disorder. For this purpose brain banks have been set up to collect the brains of children whose parents give consent for postmortem study. Samples of this brain tissue then can be distributed to researchers doing work in this area. This kind of research has been fruitful in adult psychiatry and in neurology and is just beginning to make an impact in child and adolescent psychiatry. It should be of special importance in the study of autism, childhood schizophrenia, adolescent suicide, and other severe developmental neuropsychiatric disorders. An example is the finding of low levels of glutamate and normal levels of dopamine and serotonin in the brains of children with Tourette's disorder, a finding that forced many early theories about the pathophysiology of the disorder to be revised.

A major conceptual advance in developmental psychopathological research derived from these studies of brain function and structure is the realization of the importance of the cortico-striato-thalamic circuits (CSTCs) in child psychiatric disorders. These circuits consist of parallel series of connections that include feedback mechanisms to connect the cortex to the thalamus and basal ganglia. Areas of the brain responsible for functions such as thought, speech, and abstraction are connected in these circuits with areas responsible for automatic behavior and integration. Special circuits are activated during motor activity, perception, thinking, and arousal. When these circuits are functioning properly, they allow for the integration of cognition, affect, perception, and planning. A wide variety of research techniques has been employed to investigate these circuits, including imaging, neurochemistry of postmortem brains, and behavioral studies, especially for Tourette's disorder and attention deficit hyperactivity disorder.

Because it is important to investigate the relationship of childhood experiences and brain structure and function, some research on this correlation has suggested that amblyopia may result in degeneration of the optic nerve and there has been some evidence that early child abuse leads to diminished hippocampal volume. This will be a future challenge for new research.

Neurochemistry and Neuropharmacology

Just as the whole brain or a single area of it can be seen as integrating many different psychological and physiological processes at a macroscopic level, the single neuron can be seen as doing so at the microscopic level. An individual neuron receives diversified incoming information from hundreds and thousands of neurons. At the same time, it is influenced by other factors such as hormones, immune reactions, and biological rhythms. Also, significant integrating mechanisms within the neuron include the regulation of protein function and of gene expression. Much of the research into the biochemistry of childhood and adolescent psychiatric disorders involves the synaptic junctions between neurons. Most synapses involve the termination of a presynaptic neuronal axon on a postsynaptic cell body, axon, or dendrite. In those synapses the dendrites release neurotransmitters and the postsynaptic receptors are either on the dendrites or on the axons.

Neurotransmitter receptors are the sites of action for virtually all of the psychotherapeutic and psychoactive drugs used today. The techniques of molecular biology have led to the identification of many subtypes of receptors and to the sequencing of the specific protein receptors. Basic neurochemical research has contributed much to the understanding of many psychiatric disorders of youth.

The dopamine hypothesis of schizophrenia grew from the observation that certain drugs that block dopamine receptors will reduce psychotic symptoms, and dopaminergic drugs such as amphetamines and levodopa can induce psychosis. While dopamine agonists improve attentional processes, dopamine antagonists are also useful for treating tics. Dopamine activity also may be low in depression. The bioamine hypothesis of mood disorders was derived from the observation that drugs that prevent the reuptake or catabolism of norepinephrine are effective in alleviating the symptoms of depression. In youths, as already indicated, drugs that affect the dopimanergic systems may alleviate attention deficit and tics, which implicates dopamine pathways in the pathogenesis of the corresponding disorders.

Diminished serotonin levels have been linked mainly with depression. Increased serotonin plasma levels, on the other hand, have been found in autism and other severe neuropsychiatric conditions. The introduction of a variety of new drugs has inaugurated new and exciting areas of speculation about the relationship between serotonin and anxiety disorders (such as obsessive compulsive disorder) as well as between serotonin and schizophrenia. There is also evidence that serotonin may play a role in such behaviors of interest to child psychiatrists as suicidal behavior, aggression and violence, and emotional lability.

Clinical Psychopharmacology

The clinical psychopharmacology of adults and immature youths differs in many respects but, unfortunately, in practice, child and adolescent psychiatrists have tended to rely on research done in adults. Researchers and the pharmaceutical industry have shied away from the ethical issues involved in medication research with children. As a result, medications are used widely in children without the solid base of specific supportive knowledge that exists in adult psychopharmacology.

The pharmacodynamic differences between adults and children may account for the reduced efficacy of anti-depressant medications in children. Lack of central nervous system maturation also may be an important factor to investigate in children's reactions to pharmacologic agents. Furthermore, the fact that neurotransmitter activity undergoes many changes as development occurs may exert a potential influence on treatment response.

Systematic research in this area is required to evaluate the efficacy of the drugs (Do they statistically improve clinical measurements of psychopathology?), the effectiveness of drugs (Do they improve the lot of child psychiatric patients in regular clinical practice as opposed to a research setting?), and the safety of these medications.

Clinical psychopharmacological research requires meticulous attention to detail since subjective biases can introduce confounding variables at every stage of the investigation. Trials should occur with randomized subjects where inclusion and exclusion criteria are clearly articulated. Double-blind and placebo controls yield surer results. Some studies use control groups; others use crossover designs by which the same child receives placebo at one time and active drug at another, usually under double-blind conditions.

This kind of research has led to the production of a number of rating scales that try to measure signs and symptoms of child psychiatric illness in a reliable manner. These scales have had a great influence on modern psychiatric thinking and have enabled us to measure objective changes in our patients' conditions. They are used with almost all kinds of child and adolescent psychopathology.

While these kinds of studies represent the "gold standard" of research endeavor for biological psychiatry in practice they are very difficult to perform. Therefore, child and adolescent psychiatrists often perform open studies—not double-blind and often not placebo-controlled. Since so few research studies occur in child and adolescent psychopharmacology, there may still be a place for open trials done directly on children and adolescents. Yet the ethical implications of this dearth of psychopharmacological research done directly with children and adolescents should mandate increases in definitive drug studies with this age group.

Psychosocial Treatment Research

An immense variety of treatment methods are used to help children with emotional and behavioral difficulties; empirically testing the efficacy of these therapies in the same way as has been done for psychopharmacological research is a current necessity. Although this is an extremely difficult task, very valuable work is being done in the area. As for any empirical research, the target population must be described in detail. The goals of therapy must be clearly articulated, and the measuring instruments must be reliable and valid. The study should be capable of being replicated. In order to be certain that the therapeutic method used is the same as that intended, detailed manuals containing explicit instructions must be written before the study can be carried out. Quality control is maintained by strict supervision that often uses video and/or audio recording methods. Control groups can be given alternative therapies, or sometimes a waiting-list control can be used.

Improvement with and without treatment should be assessed by raters who are blind to the therapeutic method being used, and efforts should be made to keep the caliber and quality of the therapists as constant as possible. The finding that behavioral conditioning of simple organisms can change the organization of the neuronal synapse has made behavioral research even more exciting, but because it is so difficult and time-consuming, progress will necessarily be slow. Unfortunately, mainly behavior therapy and cognitive therapy have been studied empirically in child and adolescent psychiatry until now, and not the dynamic (or expressive) types of therapy. At present, it is also necessary to determine whether the efficacy of the best single treatment can be enhanced by combining it with another therapy, as is seen when pharmacotherapy combined with psychosocial treatment may be more promising than either one alone.

Social Science Research

The systematic investigation of the disorders themselves remains the central focus of child and adolescent psychiatric research. Clinical investigators may come from various clinically oriented disciplines other than psychiatry, notably including clinical psychology, pediatrics, psychiatric nursing, and social work. In addition, the allied professions of child and adolescent psychiatry include education, speech and language pathology, occupational and physical therapy, and juvenile justice. The clinical disciplines under our umbrella have sometimes not viewed research as integral to their mission of providing care to children. "Fortunately, this attitude is changing, and the systematic study of mental disorders is increasingly being coupled with ongoing efforts to treat them" (Institute of Medicine, 1989).

The contributions of the social sciences to child psychiatric research add yet another dimension. These include such varying disciplines as epidemiology, biostatistics, ethology, sociology, anthropology, ethology, and economics. These disciplines study areas that range from the nuclear family, through schools and school systems, to the delivery of health care services.

Conclusion

There is an "ethical imperative" to conduct research in child and adolescent psychiatry and an "immorality of not knowing" (Klin & Cohen, 1994). For obvious reasons, the prejudice against doing research on youths derives from the need to counter thoughtless studies that may harm individuals and distort the scientific pursuit of truth. In a field as young and uncharted as child and adolescent psychiatry, far more is unknown than is known. The objections to research with this population have left whole areas of behavior, psychopathology, and possible treatments barred to systematic examination. "An acknowledgement of the extent of the unknown carries with it a responsibility, indeed a moral mandate, to conduct research. The moral dictum first do no harm goes hand in hand with strive to prevent or minimize harm be it the result of congenital anomaly, disease process or societal inequities" (Klin & Cohen, 1994). This imperative applies to both the hermeneutic and the empirical lines of research into child and adolescent mental health and mental disorder.

REFERENCES

Berman, A. L. (1992) Five potential suicide cases. In R. W. Maris, A. L. Berman, J. T. Maltsberger, & R. I. Yuffit (Eds.), *Assessment and prediction of suicide* New York: Guilford Press.

Brock, D. J. H. (1993). *Molecular genetics for the clinicians.* Cambridge University Press.

Cichetti D., & Cohen, D. J. (1995). *Developmental psychopathology.* New Haven, CT: Yale University Press.

Cohen, D. J. (1997). Research in child psychiatry. In A. Apter, A. Weizman, Y. Hatab, & S. Tyano (Eds.), *An introduction to child psychiatry.* Tel Aviv: Dionon Press.

Cummings, S. R., Browner, W. S., & Hulley, S. B. (1988) Conceiving the research question. In S. B. Hulley & S. R. Cummings (Eds.), *Designing clinical research.* Baltimore, MD: Williams & Wilkins.

Hulley, S. B., Newman, T. B., & Cummings, S. R. (1988). Getting started: The anatomy and physiology of research. In S. B. Hulley & S. R. Cummings (Eds.), *Designing clinical research.* Baltimore, MD: Williams & Wilkins.

Institute of Medicine. (1989). *Research on children and adolescents with mental, behavioral and developmental disorders.* Washington, DC: National Academic Press.

Klin, A., & Cohen, D. J. (1994). The immorality of not knowing. In J. Y. Hatab (Ed.), *Ethics and child mental health* Jerusalem: Gefen Press.

Pfeffer, C. (1986). *The suicidal child.* New York: Basic Books.

Verhulst, F. C., & Koot, H. M. (1995). *The epidemiology of child and adolescent psychopathology.* Oxford Medical Publications

NAME INDEX

Name Index

SUBJECT INDEX